Freedom in the World

The findings of the *Comparative Survey of Freedom* and the Map of Freedom include events up to 1 January 1994.

Freedom in the World
The Annual Survey of Political Rights & Civil Liberties
1993-1994

Freedom House Survey Team

Adrian Karatnycky
Survey Coordinator

Kathleen Cavanaugh
Charles Graybow
Douglas W. Payne
Joseph E. Ryan
Leonard R. Sussman
George Zarycky

James Finn
General Editor

Freedom House

First published in 1994

Cover design and maps by Emerson Wajdowicz Studios, N.Y.C.

The Library of Congress has catalogued this serial title as follows:

Freedom in the world / —1978-
New York : Freedom House, 1978-
v. : map; 25 cm.—(Freedom House Book)
Annual.
ISSN 0732-6610=Freedom in the World.
1. Civil rights—Periodicals. I. R. Adrian Karatnycky, et al.   I. Series.
JC571.F66 323.4'05-dc 19   82-642048
AACR 2   MARC-S
Library of Congress   [84101]
ISBN   0-932088-81-3 (pbk.)
          0-932088-82-1 (cloth)

Distributed by arrangement with:

University Press of America, Inc.
4720 Boston Way
Lanham, MD 20706

3 Henrietta Street
London WC2E 8LU England

Contents

Foreword

Freedom in the World is an evaluation of political rights and civil liberties in the world's nations and related territories, now numbering 190 and 63 respectively, that Freedom House provides on an annual basis.

Freedom House is a non-profit organization based in New York that monitors political rights and civil liberties around the world. Established in 1941, Freedom House believes the effective advocacy of human rights at home and abroad must be grounded in fundamental democratic values and principles.

Freedom House first began to evaluate political rights and civil liberties during the 50s, when racial violence broke out in the United States. The first year-end review of freedom was completed in 1955. During those early years, the project was called the Balance Sheet of Freedom, and later the Annual Survey of the Progress of Freedom. By the late 1960s, the Freedom House Board of Trustees felt there was a need to create a single standard by which to measure and record the development of freedom around the world.

When Freedom House's *Comparative Survey of Freedom* was finally established in the early 1970s, democracy was in a perilous condition in many states and on every continent: Spain, Portugal and Greece were under military rule; the world's largest democracy, India, was sliding toward martial law; an American president faced the possibility of impeachment; Africa was torn by both factional strife and racial conflict; and the prospects for liberalization—not to say democratization—in Eastern Europe, Latin America and Asia were dim. By the 1980s this dispiriting picture had changed and we witnessed a decade of unprecedented gains in democratization and freedom in much of the world. The year of 1993, however, dissipated much of the euphoria produced by these gains. In the last year there has been a sad and severe diminution of freedom in many countries.

The *Survey* project has continued to develop over the years, being incorporated in the late 1970s into *Freedom in the World*, where it is now complemented by regional essays and country-by-country reports. In 1989 it became a year-long effort produced by our regional experts, consultants, and human rights specialists. As the resources listed at the back of this book attest, the *Survey* acquires its information from a wide range of diverse sources.

Especially valued among these are the many human rights activists, journalists, editors and political figures around the world who constantly inform us of the human rights situation in their own countries. Sometimes the mere act of objectively reporting government crackdowns, repression and extra-judicial killings puts these courageous individuals and their families at great risk. At other times, these personalities are cast into the midst of political change and, as prime actors in their nation's life, pay the ultimate price.

Western journalists play an increasingly important role in the movement for human rights by their ability to penetrate nearly inaccessible places where local human rights advocates are either nonexistent or are unable to project their urgent message to the world. For example, Freedom House has been privileged to receive extensive reporting from

American journalists covering the conflicts and practice of "ethnic cleansing," in Bosnia and Croatia. Faced with the usual pressures of covering a war situation, these men and women took the time to provide us and others with specific cases of horrendous human rights abuses, including the creation of detention camps. European and Latin American journalists offered moral and sometimes personal support to the courageous community of human rights activists on the island of Cuba; without their concern, many of the deteriorating conditions in that society would not have come to light.

Of special note in 1993 was the World Conference on Human Rights sponsored by the United Nations in Vienna (14-25 June), the first under the U.N. auspices in twenty-five years. A delegation from Freedom House participated very actively at the conference; reported both individually and collectively on the successes and failures of the meeting; and have continued to monitor the threats to human rights that were and are sharply posed by a number of the participating countries, many of which receive low ratings in this year's *Freedom in the World*. It is also worth noting that among the more than 2,000 non-governmental organizations (NGOs) attending the conference were a number of burgeoning NGOs from Asia. Operating under conditions of both political and financial stress, the staff and members of these organizations provide detailed, hard information that was, and sometimes still is, difficult for them to disseminate and for outside organizations to procure. At great personal risk they defy the vigorous attempts of their own governments to relativize, and therefore trivialize, human rights.

Throughout the year Freedom House personnel regularly conduct fact-finding missions to gain more in-depth knowledge of the vast political transformations affecting our world. During these week-to-month long investigations, we make every effort to meet a cross-section of political parties and associations, human rights monitors, religious figures, representatives of both the private sector and trade union movement, academics and the appropriate security forces and insurgent movements where they exist. The *Survey* project team also consults a vast array of published source materials, ranging from the reports of other human rights organizations to newspapers and magazines, large and small, from around the world.

During the past year, Freedom House traveled to Angola, Austria, Belgium, Cambodia, Canada, Croatia, Cuba, the Czech Republic, the Dominican Republic, El Salvador, Ethiopia, France, Germany, Hungary, Ireland, Guyana, Poland, Portugal, Russia, Serbia, Spain, Switzerland, Thailand, Ukraine and the U.K.

The coordinator of this year's *Survey* team is Adrian Karatnycky, executive director of Freedom House. Other members include Dr. Joseph E. Ryan, *Survey* methodologist, Kathleen Cavanaugh, Charles Graybow, Douglas W. Payne, Leonard R. Sussman and George Zarycky. The general editor of *Freedom in the World* is James Finn; the managing editor and editorial assistant are Mark Wolkenfeld and Pei C. Koay, respectively. This year's research assistants were Art Boguslaw Artman, who made a major contribution to both the research and preparation of many country reports, Shahrazad Elghanayan, John Glass, Adam Handler, Christina Pendzola, Dmitri Starostin and Elizabeth Szonyi.

Substantial support for *Freedom in the World, 1993-1994* has been generously provided by The Pew Charitable Trusts and the Lynde & Harry Bradley Foundation, Inc. ■

Ed.

The Comparative Survey of Freedom 1993-1994: Freedom in Retreat

Adrian Karatnycky

As 1993 drew to a close, freedom around the world was in retreat while violence, repression and state control were on the increase in a growing number of countries. The trend marked the first increase in five years of states characterized by the absence of basic human rights and struck a dramatic blow to the democratic renaissance that began in 1989.

In all, the number of people living in "Free"[1] societies, or those enjoying a good range of political rights and civil liberties, fell by 300 million, while the number denied basic freedoms rose by 531 million. The proportion of people who are Free, today, stands at 19 percent—the lowest since 1976.

Nevertheless, the number of countries, especially in Central and Eastern Europe, that have made successful, if still fragile, transitions to democracy is impressive. And a number of emerging democracies and free societies has achieved further stability in the last year. However, other democracies are denying their citizens fundamental rights.

The collapse of Soviet bloc communism raised the hope that greater political opportunities worldwide would lead to successful democratic transitions to freedom. Over the last few years tremendous gains were recorded, but this year's results reveal that the progress of freedom around the world has been thwarted by increased ethnic, religious, economic, cultural and historical tensions. The year saw increasing cooperation between states that deny their citizens a full range of basic rights, or "Not Free" countries. And a number of stable democracies registered an erosion of freedom as a result of widespread political corruption and clandestine influence peddling by powerful economic interests.

Much of the decline in freedom is attributable to the disintegration of multi-ethnic states, often amid mounting economic difficulties and growing Islamic fundamentalism.

The decline in freedom can also be attributed in part to the failure of the democratic nations to promote a new, compelling international structure to create stability, economic growth and respect for human rights. Part of the shift away from freedom is the result of an awareness among tyrants that they can flout international law and the democratic community, which has proved incapable of exerting its influence in behalf of freedom in Bosnia, Somalia and Haiti.

While the West searches for means to promote a new international system based on markets and democratic rights, tyrants are creating new networks of mutual aid and cooperation to strengthen each other. In the absence of strong leadership by democracies, the growing economic resources of a number of the most repressive states—China and Iran among them—also permit these tyrannies to exert greater influence in the global affairs.

The growth of freedom in the world has also been stunted by the lack of support from the West. The collapse of the West's main rival has led the industrial democracies to turn inward. Foreign aid spending by the U.S., Japan, and West European states is under pressure as a result of domestic economic difficulties. One major international donor, Germany, is focus-

Freedom in the World—1994

The population of the world this year is estimated at 5.505 billion residing in 190 sovereign states and 63 related territories, a total of 253 places. The level of political rights and civil liberties as shown comparatively by the Freedom House *Survey* is:

Free: 1,046.2 billion (19.00 percent of the world's population) live in 72 of the states and in 45 of the related territories.

Partly Free: 2,224.4 billion (40.41 percent of the world's population) live in 63 of the states and 5 of the related territories.

Not Free: 2,234.6 billion (40.59) percent of the world's population live in 55 of the states and 13 of the related territories.

A Record of the Survey
(population in millions)

SURVEY DATE	FREE		PARTLY FREE		NOT FREE		WORLD POPULATION
January '81	1,613.0	(35.90%)	970.9	(21.60%)	1,911.9	(42.50%)	4,495.8
January '82	1,631.9	(35.86%)	916.5	(20.14%)	2,002.7	(44.00%)	4,551.1
January '83	1,665.1	(36.32%)	918.8	(20.04%)	2,000.2	(43.64%)	4,584.1
January '84	1,670.7	(36.00%)	1,074.8	(23.00%)	1,917.5	(41.00%)	4,663.0
January '85	1,671.4	(34.85%)	1,117.4	(23.30%)	2,007.0	(41.85%)	4,795.8
January '86	1,747.2	(36.27%)	1,121.9	(23.29%)	1,947.6	(40.43%)	4,816.7
January '87	1,842.5	(37.10%)	1,171.5	(23.60%)	1,949.9	(39.30%)	4,963.9
January '88	1,924.6	(38.30%)	1,205.4	(24.00%)	1,896.0	(37.70%)	5,026.0
January '89	1,992.8	(38.86%)	1,027.9	(20.05%)	2,107.3	(41.09%)	5,128.0
January '90	2,034.4	(38.87%)	1,143.7	(21.85%)	2,055.9	(39.28%)	5,234.0
January '91	2,088.2	(39.23%)	1,485.7	(27.91%)	1,748.7	(32.86%)	5,322.6
January '92	1,359.3	(25.29%)	2,306.6	(42.92%)	1,708.2	(31.79%)	5,374.2
January '93	1,352.2	(24.83%)	2,403.3	(44.11%)	1,690.4	(31.06%)	5,446.0
January '94	1,046.2	(19.00%)	2,224.4	(40.41%)	2,234.6	(40.59%)	5,505.2

ing much of its resources on reabsorbing East Germany, and is devoting more of its aid resources to Central and Eastern Europe in a justifiable effort to promote regional stability in its backyard. As a consequence, many of the poorer countries of the world—including those making efforts to promote democracy and freedom—are increasingly neglected.

The results of the *Survey*

The world continued rapid political change in 1993, with nearly one-third of countries registering significant changes in status. However, it became clear that the changes of 1993 were unlike those of 1989-92, when the collapse of totalitarianism had first widened the ranks of Partly Free transitional states, many of them eventually joining the ranks of the Free. In 1993, ratings changes tended to mark the erosion of freedom, 43 countries registering a decline in their level of freedom and 18 recording gains. This year, 72 countries are rated as Free, 63 Partly Free, and 55 Not Free. The last category jumped dramatically, up from 38 Not Free last year.

The new entrants into the ranks of the countries rated Not Free by Freedom House are: Azerbaijan, Bahrain, Burundi, Egypt, Eritrea, Ethiopia, Guinea, Indonesia, Ivory Coast, Kenya, Mozambique, Nigeria, Oman, Swaziland, Tanzania, Tunisia, United Arab Emirates, and Yugoslavia. While they represent most regions of the world, they are affected by at least one of two critical factors. With the exception of Swaziland, each of the new Not Free countries is either: 1) a multi-ethnic state in which there is no dominant majority ethnic group (defined as representing more than two-thirds of the population), or the dominant ethnic group is denied power, or 2) a Muslim state, usually confronting a serious challenge by fundamentalist Islamic groups. In the case of Indonesia both ethnic and religious factors are at work.

Within the Not Free category, there is a special class of the worst rated countries. This group of nations grew in 1993 by two-thirds from 12 to 20. Such Not Free countries are typified by pervasive government control over the daily lives of citizens and the banning of independent organizations. A country may also join this category when extreme violence and warlordism dominate the people in the absence of an authoritative, functioning central government. Afghanistan, for instance, is now in this category because it has most of the factors that make it nearly impossible to maintain political rights and civil liberties: widespread chaos and civil war, ethnic and religious tensions, poor economic conditions, and little or no cultural and historical links to the principles of democracy. Somalia, also in this category, shares these ills, not because of ethnic and religious strife but because of inter-clan rivalries.

Most of this year's decline in freedom occurred as a result of deteriorations in Partly Free countries. With the exception of some erosion of freedom in Latin America, Free societies, as a rule, managed to maintain their freedoms largely intact and to escape the kind of volatility that affected Partly Free societies in transition.

The major regional trend registered in the *Survey* was the upheaval and dramatic change

The 20 Worst Rated Countries*
Afghanistan
Angola
Bhutan
Burma (Myanmar)
Burundi
China
Cuba
Equatorial Guinea
Haiti
Iraq
Korea, North
Libya
Saudi Arabia
Somalia
Sudan
Syria
Tajikistan
Turkmenistan
Uzbekistan
Vietnam

The 6 Worst Rated Related Territories

East Timor (Indonesia)
Irian Jaya (Indonesia)
Kashmir (India)
Kosovo (Yugoslavia)
Nagorno-Karabakh (Armenia/Azerbaijan)
Tibet (China)

* For explanation of Survey Methodology see p. 671.

in Sub-Saharan Africa. Some of these regimes opened up the political process to multiparty competition. Other states, while initially giving lip-service to the need for democratization, increasingly diverged from this path, tightening control or resorting to mass repression and carnage. The result was a growing divergence in the degree of freedom Africa's inhabitants enjoy, states such as Cape Verde, Sao Tome and Principe, Madagascar, Mali, and Niger making notable, if fragile, progress toward free expression, a multiparty system, democratic elections, and reduced state intrusion into economic and civil life.

In total, 27 African countries registered measurable changes in their level of freedom. In all, 8 countries showed improvement while 19 registered a decline. Of the world's eight new democracies in 1993, five were established in Subsaharan Africa. At the same time, most of Africa's setbacks were the result of transitions to democracy that were reversed or crushed.

Freedom vs. democracy?

Ironically, while the state of freedom deteriorated worldwide, the number of democracies continued to grow, increasing from 99 at the end of 1992 to 108 as 1993 drew to a close. Part of this trend may well have been influenced by a greater emphasis on democratic processes in the foreign policy and foreign aid priorities of the U.S. and several other industrial democracies.

The apparent contradiction between the growth of new democracies and the decline in freedom requires some explanation.

Are democracies no longer to be identified with freedom? Clearly, democracy is a prerequisite for freedom. Indeed, all Free countries are democracies.[2] The balance of democracies are rated Partly Free and represent societies under ethnic, economic and political stress. The sole exception is war-ravaged Bosnia, which, because of violent circumstances far beyond the control of its democratically oriented government and authorities, is rated Not Free.

Typical of democracies in which there are significant constraints on freedom are India, Pakistan and Turkey. In each polity, power has usually transferred from one political party to another as a result of competitive and open elections. But in the case of India, regional, ethnically and religiously motivated insurgencies and high levels of political violence linked to electioneering undermine the level of freedom enjoyed by India's citizens. In Pakistan and Turkey democratic electoral processes resulted in changes of government. Still, the persistent and overarching influence of the military limits the powers of democratically elected leaders. As in India, Turkey's increasingly brutal and heavy-handed efforts to suppress separatist sentiments and movements among its Kurdish population contribute to its Partly Free rating.

In these examples, we can see that while democracies expand the range of freedoms enjoyed by citizens, they do not effectively protect all basic human rights, political rights, and civil liberties characteristic of fully free societies. Thus, in recent years, while democracy has made progress around the world and while many states have successfully built cohesion and consensus on the basis of democratic choice, democracy does not always achieve or guarantee the kind of social, economic, ethnic and political stability that secures a state's Free status. Such a status requires far more than a democratic process. It requires a democratic society of informed and engaged citizens. Nevertheless, the correlation between democracy and freedom remains: two-thirds of democracies are Free and all Free societies are democracies.

A new polarization

With most Free states in 1993 preserving their status, and with several, particularly in Central and Eastern Europe, consolidating their freedom, the world appears on the road to a new post- Cold War bi-polarity—with a community of Free nations on the one hand and an increasingly repressive group of Not Free states on the other. While the Not Free states hold power in the name of different ideologies or belief systems, there are growing signs of their cooperation. This trend, while still in its early stages, has the potential to replace the traditional East-West or North-South divides as a significant factor in international life.

Increasingly, Freedom House has monitored a web of growing inter-relationships among the most repressive states. In part, this includes trading in military armaments and materiel, collaborating to help break sanctions imposed by the international community in international terrorism, and to erode human rights standards at the U.N. and in regional multilateral bodies. However, it is still premature to speak of an "international of the not free" because many of the alliances are ill-formed and brittle.

The polarization of the world into democratic/free and dictatorial/unfree camps is occurring at a rapid pace. Nowhere is this trend better observed than in the former Soviet empire. Just five short years ago, countries like Czechoslovakia and administrative entities like the Uzbek SSR broadly exhibited common economic and political features; today the gap in freedom between the Czech Republic and Uzbekistan is greater than the gap between the U.S. and *perestroika*- and *glasnost*-driven USSR. The diversification in these states is profound and multi-dimensional. Once part of a single economic and political space, their diverging economies and value systems make long-term cooperation highly questionable.

In Poland, the Czech Republic and Hungary, the difficult transition to freedom appears stable, but in some ex-Soviet and ex-Soviet bloc states gains for freedom remain fragile. The enormous difficulties—including economic decline, rising unemployment, potential inter-ethnic disputes, problems of coping with the power of the old economic and political networks of the ex-Communist nomenklatura, as well as the psychological and social legacies of decades of totalitarianism—are proving greater than anticipated.

The trend toward electing ex-Communist parties of the Left, manifested in the last eighteen months in such states as Lithuania, Poland and Romania, is emblematic of the rocky transition to free markets and democracy.

Profound changes were registered in a number of states of the former USSR. Growing political repression and violence characterized Tajikistan, where a brutal, Russia-backed Communist government inaugurated a wave of terror after displacing a coalition government in December 1992. In Turkmenistan, President Saparmurat Niyazov tightened already near total control by extending the official adulation of his person. And in Uzbekistan repressions against moderate and secular opposition groups exacted a growing toll, forcing more opposition groups out of the country or into the underground.

Freedom was severely restricted in Kazakhstan, where free trade unions were intimidated and the free press harassed. In Ukraine, an ex-Communist nomenklatura stymied all efforts at economic reform and blocked privatization, while using its considerable power to control nationwide television as national elections approached. As the year drew to an end, Ukraine's authorities tightened the lid on private entrepreneurs and voted for an electoral system that eliminated the importance of political parties and strengthened the hand of local nomenklatura-linked industrialists, collective farm directors, and local government officials.

Georgia registered a decline in freedom attributable, in part, to civil war and external aggression. Armenia's active prosecution of a war against Azerbaijan contributed to freedom's decline in the latter country, as ex-Communist boss Gaidar Aliyev skillfully orchestrated a *coup d'état* against Azerbaijan's democratically elected president and ushered in a wave of repression against political opponents, including parliamentarians from the Mejlis.

Among the ex-Soviet states, only Estonia registered gains by regularizing citizenship laws to give voice and vote to Russians and other non-indigenous nationalities in local elections. And while Russia's 12 December election holds out the promise of a more rapid transition to a free market and political pluralism, the country's involvement in a number of ethnic conflicts on its periphery and substantial sentiment among the Russian people for a Great Russian state sent ominous signals about the future path of that giant Eurasian state.

Amid freedom's global retreat this year, where are the next arenas for potential democratic transitions? The biggest question mark surrounds the countries of South and East Asia. There, with the exception of South Korea and the Philippines, gains for freedom have been scant. While a number of the Asian tigers have certainly attained the level of economic freedom and prosperity to make transitions to democracy and, while many of them have a high degree of ethno-national cohesiveness, longstanding cultural impediments continue to stand in the way of fully fledged transitions to freedom.

The Indian sub-continent, too, has made little progress. Indeed, recent years have seen setbacks for freedom in Pakistan, India, and Bangladesh. Even more bleak are the prospects for gains for freedom in most of the Arab and many of the Islamic states.

If the collapse of the Soviet threat led many to conclude that the tyrannies and dictatorships would increasingly be isolated pockets of economic misery, crisis and decline, reality has proved far more complex.

When one looks at trends in Asia and the Middle East, traditional ideas about the inter-relationship between economic prosperity and democratic change have to be re-examined. For although democracy has traditionally been an engine of prosperity, and free markets have helped to propel demcoratic transformations, a number of Not Free states now have increasing economic, industrial and military resources. These states are able to make skillfull use of their natural and labor resources to propel economic growth while holding a tight grip on political change. Emblematic of this trend is China's rapid economic expansion. But such countries as Iran and Iraq, too, possess important financial resources that can be used to bol-ster anti-democratic allies.

The Third Wave breaks?

Have the democratic freedom revolutions that originated in Latin America in the early 1980s, moved on to the Philippines, through to Eastern Europe and the ex-USSR, and later to Sub-Saharan Africa, run out of steam?

The full answer to this question cannot

The Global Trend			
	Free Countries	Partly Free Countries	Not Free Countries
1984	52	54	58
1992	76	65	42
1993	75	73	38
1994	72	63	55

be given on the basis of a single year's trans-formations and trends. Indeed, 1993 demonstrated the stabilization and durability of demo-cratic changes in a number of former dictatorships.

Still, with a deep reduction in the roster of Partly Free and transitional countries, the period of rapid democratic expansion and democratic prospect appears to have ended.

One important effect of this new trend will be to reduce the effectiveness of consen-sus-based international organizations, especially the U.N., which is suffering from its fail-ure to achieve stabilization in Somalia and Bosnia.

The intransigence of the anti-democratic and Not Free states was evident at the U.N. Vienna Human Rights Conference held in June 1993. There a bloc of Asian tyrannies, with China playing a leading role, worked in alliance with such states as Cuba and Syria to water down long standing international human rights instruments.

Certainly, the collapse of the USSR held out the promise of a more flexible and effec-tive United Nations system. The year's trends put this promise into question. With an in-creasing number of U.N. states hostile to democracy and the values of a free society, China playing an increasingly important role as a new global actor, Russia rapidly reshaping its own assertive foreign policy, and the U.S. shying away from a stronger role in interna-tional affairs, the consensus that was built around the military action against Iraq is un-likely to be repeated in coming years.

Another effect of these recent events is that dictatorial states, whose leaders were un-certain about the emerging post-Cold War new world order, are beginning to test the new post-Cold War order. Now, in the face of U.S., Western, and international inaction, they believe they have few constraints on how they maintain power. The failure of the West and of the international community to act in Bosnia, the feckless U.N. intervention in Somalia, and the failure to punish the Haitian generals constitute a green light for those who are willing to use brute force in a bid to consolidate absolute power.

Nor is international development aid as potent an instrument as it was before. Leaders in the Third World have already borne the brunt of declining funds. With Western Europe and Japan mired in low growth, and the U.S. budget deficit re-inforced by a growing mood of isolationism, the industrial democracies should pay heed to the trends monitored by Freedom House in allocating aid. With a number of democracies on shaky ground, and the number of countries in which freedom is likely to make progress in the coming years diminishing, the U.S. government and its democratic allies should pool their resources to strengthen transitions for freedom and democracy in settings where there is an opportunity to make a difference.

The American response

What do Freedom House's findings suggest for the administration's foreign policy?

In response to the main trends in this year's *Survey,* the U.S. administration should:

a) lead the way in developing a consensus among international foreign aid donor countries to target assistance to those countries that adhere to democratic principles and basic freedoms.

b) recognize that the hardening of dictatorships and the increase in the number of unfree regimes will place severe limitations on efforts to summon up an effective consensus at the United Nations and regional multilateral bodies.

Efforts to develop coherent multilateral approaches should, therefore, focus on strengthening multilateral institutions—like NATO and the OECD—which are composed of democracies. Other formal and informal multilateral democratic structures should be developed at the regional level.

c) revisit plans to drastically scale back U.S. radio broadcasting services, including Radio Free Europe/Radio Liberty and the Voice of America. The administration should find substantial resources to fund an Asia Democracy Radio and should work to significantly increase the resources of the bi-partisan National Endowment for Democracy.

d) place greater emphasis on finding mechanisms to address the needs of ethnic and national minorities in societies in transition to democracy. Democracy-building assistance should focus on this factor.

e) encourage the academic and public policy community to take a closer look at the failure of democracy to find roots in most of the Islamic world. It should develop a long-term strategy that promotes democratic values and basic freedoms in the Islamic world, without opening the door to fundamentalism and greater repression.

Above all, there is a great need for leadership at home. The administration should make a greater effort to build support for the idea that the promotion of democracy is central to U.S. foreign policy goals. In recent months, the democracy message has become attenuated.

With the world increasingly unfree and conflict-ridden, the growing public mood supporting withdrawal from foreign affairs is out of synch with the more ominous global setting and should be reversed. ▬

Notes

1 - See "Survey Methodology," p. 671. Freedom House ranks countries as Free, Partly Free, and Not Free.

2 - The nominal exceptions are the principality of Monaco and Liechtenstein.

Adrian Karatnycky, executive director of Freedom House, is coordinator of the Comparative Survey of Freedom.

The United States: A Changing World, Uncertain Responses

James Finn

During the past year the United States has shown what a country with vast resources can do when it turns its attention to large issues—without a governing vision. A roll call of important foreign policy matters faced by the new administration and a vigorous and ambitious president would include those invoked by place names: Somalia, Haiti, North Korea, Bosnia, China and Russia, or by label: NAFTA, nuclear proliferation, multilateralism, GATT, foreign aid, intervention, environmental concerns, human rights and democracy. Americans were divided on many of these issues in 1993 as they were on domestic matters as varied as the national deficit and the budget; health care reform, race and ethnicity; crime in the streets and in the schools; censorship, immigration, speech codes and constitutional rights.

When the barbarians were at the gate

Each year since the fall of communism has made it increasingly clear how useful it was, in many ways, to have the barbarians at the gate. They were unwelcome and worrisome, but their presence focused our national political attention and provided a compass for U.S. policies. Now they are gone, the compass is absent, and we have yet to find a replacement. As Anthony Lake, national security adviser, observed, the present administration is the first since that of Harry Truman that "has not had a single defining issue against which it could define itself." And, he added, the administration that took over foreign policy guidance in 1993 "is being asked both to define the questions and to provide the answers."

In apparent response to expressed skepticism that it had done so adequately, the administration initiated a foreign policy blitz. In addition to Mr. Lake, the U.S. ambassador to the U.N., the secretary of state, and finally, President Clinton himself spoke on the foreign policies of the U.S. Alas, their comments were overrun by the events.

No single foreign policy issue can illustrate all of the undeniably real difficulties to which these speakers referred, but Somalia presents many of them. When Mohammed Siad Barre was toppled by one of Somalia's resistance movements in 1991, he left as his legacy a poor, strife-torn country racked by disease and famine whose competing warlords obstructed food relief being provided by the West. The United Nations Security Council and the Bush administration decided in December 1992 to commit armed forces that would ensure safe delivery of humanitarian and food relief. The initial period of what was dubbed Operation Restore Hope achieved encouraging results. Food relief flowed to the millions of Somalis whose bloated bellies and shrunken limbs had been a feature of Western media for months prior to the Operation, tons of weapons used by the Somali warlords were destroyed, and formerly conflict-torn areas were restored to a semblance of peace and order.

Those who had supported this venture said their rationale for the intervention had proved to be sound. The lives of millions of people were salvaged without exposing American forces to an unacceptable risk. The United States had enhanced its moral authority by showing that it could act selflessly; it had no strong national interest in Somalia. The intervention also served as a warning, a deterrence, to similar violations there or elsewhere. At a time when human life seemed to be treated lightly in other ongoing conflicts, it countered that devaluation.

But the end was not yet. Somalia and its continuing problems were to be turned over to the care of the U.N., which was to have in place approximately 20,000 troops, some thousands of which were to be Americans. This was to be not merely a peace-keeping but a peace-making force. But before that transfer took place and most American troops had departed, U.N. Secretary General Boutros Boutros-Gali wanted to have the country pacified and the warlords disarmed, including most particularly General Muhammed Farah Aidid, who had been charged with killing Pakistani peacekeepers in the middle of the year. ("The American troops will leave when I say they can come out," Boutros-Gali asserted at one point.) American policy joined with that of the secretary general on some points, a high government official charging that those who questioned the militant pursuit of Aidid were "advocates of appeasement."

But an unsuccessful attempt by American rangers to capture Aidid and break his control resulted in the death of hundreds of Somalis and—more important to the American public—eighteen American soldiers. (Secretary of Defense Les Aspin had earlier turned down a military request for armored reinforcements that would have prevented this loss.) Public dismay in the United States intensified when television exhibited the body of a dead American being dragged through dusty streets by jubilant Somalis. The official American response was to engage in acrimonious and unseemly exchanges with Boutros-Gali, to settle for the status quo—although Clinton also dispatched additional American troops to Somalia—and to make plans to withdraw American forces from Somalia as soon as decency permitted.

As the year drew to a close, the president of Ethiopia opened a U.N.-sponsored conference on Somalia during which he told the Somalis that the international community was prepared to assist their country "but make no mistake, there is a limit to what the community is prepared to do to help you and for how long." Back in Somalia, General Aidid called for the departure of all U.N. relief forces and peacekeeping troops, their place to be taken by an independent, neutral group. Days later, the United States, which had earlier placed a bounty of $25,000 on Aidid's head, provided air transportation for him so that he could attend a conference intended to reconcile disputing Somali factions. Thus ended Operation Restore Hope.

Critics of Restore Hope judged the venture to have been flawed from the beginning. If the acknowledged need of others and the lack of a defined national interest of our own are to be the combined criteria for intervention, as they were in this case, there is no end to the number of troubled areas that vie for our moral consideration. Even a superpower cannot engage all of them. National interest must be invoked as a limiting principle. Second, the use of U.S. troops under other than U.S. command had not been adequately considered. Powered by a belief that multilateralism is a good in itself, the U.S. initially seemed ready to place U.S. troops under U.N. command in Somalia. But when Boutros-Gali formulated a policy for their use that ran counter to that of the United States, the putative multilateralism collapsed. Third, there appeared to have been little awareness that the initial humanitarian aid might take on a military and then a political dimension. There was, thus, no *terminum ad quem* to the program, nothing that would designate the point at which policy makers could judge their policy to have been fulfilled. According to these critics the entire policy was improvised. Nothing demonstrated this better than the extreme degree to which the initial engagement and the effective withdrawal of U.S. troops from Somalia were influenced by public response to the video images. Sound U.S. policies cannot derive from or rely on such undeniably powerful but essentially transient mood swings induced by television.

Haiti's dismal chapter

The debacle in Somalia was closely followed by another dismal chapter in U.S. involvement in Haiti, when, on 11 October, the *Harlan County*, an American naval vessel, approached Port-au-Prince but, on being greeted by a howling group of armed Haitians, simply turned and sailed back home. The ship, part of a U.N. operation, was bringing army engineers to help rebuild some of Haiti's roads. The project was based on the assumption that Fr. Jean-Bertrand Aristide, duly elected president in 1990 and overthrown the following year, would be restored to office before the end of the month. But the military leaders who had carried out the coup and had dominated the country since reneged on an agreement, brokered by the U.S., that they would step down. Sanctions that were lifted on the basis of the agreement have been restored and may have enough bite to affect change, but the sight of the mighty U.S. being rebuffed by thuggish elements of a small island nation remained a discouraging picture.

As to the war in Yugoslavia, the only thing clear was the West Europeans' lack of will or ability to stop a war, complete with crimes against humanity, taking place in their own backyard. The U.S. tried, and failed, to fill the leadership vacuum, offering and withdrawing proposals for intervention in baffling succession.

The great concern is not that in these three quite different situations—Bosnia, Haiti and Somalia—U.S. policies have failed or, in Secretary of State Warren Christopher's bland phrase, "things have not worked exactly as we had planned." Some failures are inevitable. The deeper worry is that there was no overall policy to shape and guide strategic and tactical questions, certainly not one that has been communicated to the American people. Several people within the foreign policy establishment have rejected or countered such analyses and have pointed to areas where the U.S. has registered positive gains: In Russia, the Middle East, in limiting the proliferation of nuclear and other dangerous weapons, and in advancing democracy and market economies in Asia. As legitimate as these claims may be, critics respond that they do not add up to or fill the need for a foreign policy that can be described, defended and deployed. No member of the administration has yet enunciated, they point out, what could accurately be termed the Clinton policy of intervention.

Of budgets, health care and NAFTA

It was anticipated, which is not to say welcomed, that foreign policy would be on-the-job training for Bill Clinton to a greater degree than it is for most presidents. It was also anticipated that he would devote much of his redoubtable energy to domestic questions, where his true interests lie. He did not disappoint. Of the many items on the domestic menu, three tower over most of the others: the federal budget, health care reform and NAFTA, a combined domestic/foreign policy issue.

According to the administration's numbers, Clinton's initial economic plan would reduce the deficit by almost 500 billion over a period of five years. After serious haggling over what taxes should be levied or increased and what expenditures should be cut or capped, the vote on the budget proposal seemed a tossup. As it turned out, the Clinton forces needed every vote they received, including the tie-breaker cast by Vice-President Albert Gore. And, as it also turned out, it passed without a single Republican vote in its favor. The political debts the president incurred to win the squeaky-close vote are only partly visible. This was both a real and a symbolic victory for the president. Defeat in the budget fight would have raised serious questions about his ability to govern, even with a Congress controlled by his own party.

The North American Free Trade Agreement, which is intended to gradually do away with trade barriers in North America over a fifteen-year period, scrambled the usual party alignments. Its proponents argue that it will improve productivity, create jobs, lower costs and raise income—in Canada, Mexico and the U.S. Its U.S. detractors say it will lose U.S. jobs to the underpaid workers in Mexico, prolong the recession and reduce the general standard of living in the U.S. They also asked if we could countenance the appalling working conditions under which poor Mexicans labor. These economic arguments pitted the president against some of his most active supporters, including the leadership and the grassroots in the labor movement. They also enlisted in the president's cause many not always found there—business leaders and many influential Republicans.

But these economic reasons were only part of the debate. The president said it would be difficult for him to argue for freer world trade if he failed to extend it to his neighboring countries. Further, the liberating economic effect of the agreement would advance modernization, and therefore processes that would further democratization in our neighbor to the South. But, referring to the political system that has been Mexico's for over sixty years, Senator Daniel Patrick Moynihan pointedly asked, "Can we have free trade with a country that does not have free elections?"

The debate was notable for the range of people it energized, from the hierarchy of business, labor and government to assembly line workers and out-of-work job seekers. President Clinton, who had seemed almost somnolent over NAFTA for months, once again came from behind to wrest a solid if not overwhelming victory. The club he wielded was composed largely of pork, but it accomplished his purpose and no one in Washington discounted his success. He emerged from the bruising struggle notably strengthened.

One sidelight of the overall debate was that waged by Vice-President Gore with Ross Perot on television. Revered by his followers as an iconoclastic truth-teller and dismissed by his critics as an ill-informed demagogue, Ross Perot was generally judged to have fared badly and emerged as a much diminished figure.

It remains to be seen if the administration can muster as much support and as much bipartisan support for the health reform bill. The purpose of the bill, according to Hillary Rodham Clinton, its principal architect and proponent, is to provide good universal medical care at an acceptable cost. Because the intended reach of the program is so extensive, because it touches so many sectors of our society, and because it gives so much control and responsibility to the government, it has aroused passionate support and equally passionate resistance. Some supporters translate the project into the language of rights, saying it is the right of every citizen to have adequate health care. Critics express deep skepticism that the government will be able to deliver on this promise, or that it should attempt to do so. Whatever the final shape of the package that will be voted on, the outcome will extend far beyond the end of this century. If the bill is approved, it will change remarkably the delivery of health care for almost everyone in the United States; if rejected, it will be long before such a bold program is again attempted.

The crisis of the spirit

Although many Americans followed the debates over these large issues closely, polls indicated that they were more interested in what touches them closer to home: violence and crime, the failures and flaws in the educational system, the spread of drugs, the breakdown in family life, the persistent problems of the urban underclass, the welfare system and the need to reform it.

Many of these are problems that cannot be resolved in Washington. The president can, however, use his "bully pulpit" for guidance and leadership. President Clinton took on that role when, from the very pulpit that Martin Luther King, Jr. used to deliver his last sermon, he gave a remarkable address to a group of black ministers. Speaking to what he termed "a great crisis of the spirit that is gripping America today," he cited statistics— 37,000 Americans killed by gunshot wounds yearly, 160,000 children staying home from school each day for fear of violence. And he conjectured that if King saw the country today he would acknowledge the advances made by black Americans, but he would also say, "I fought for freedom but not for the freedom of children to have children and the fathers of the children to walk away from them....I did not fight for the right of black people to murder other black people with reckless abandonment."

"Unless we deal with the ravages of crime and drugs and violence," the president added, "and unless we recognize that it's due to the breakdown of the family, the community, and the disappearance of jobs, and unless we say some of this cannot be done by government because we have to reach deep inside to the values, the spirit, the soul, and the truth of human nature, none of the other things we seek to do will ever take us where we need to go."

In stressing that black citizens have to shoulder more responsibility for what is happening in their own communities the president was striking some notes that black speakers, including Jesse Jackson, have sounded recently. It was notable, however, that a white person, even the president, could get the respectful attention he was accorded by the black ministers. This could not have happened, one participant said, ten years ago. This marks a shift in social attitudes that has potential long-term effects.

Other indications of changing attitudes on contested social questions include the passage, after years of effort, of the Brady bill, which imposes a waiting period on the purchase of handguns. Of more symbolic than practical importance, it is a break in the deep resistance to gun control in this country and has prompted the Clinton administration to explore other anti-crime measures. There are similar indications of changes in how to regard teenage pregnancy, out of wedlock children, and welfare benefits. New Jersey, for example, has decided not to give additional cash benefits to mothers who have children while on welfare.

Many social analysts who differ on how to cope with these issues agree that they are related to work, and to the need for increased employment. This is what links these essentially local problems with economic growth in the U.S., NAFTA, GATT and the entire global economy. It is also what links these social issues with advances in high-tech development, and the decisions of both government and private entrepreneurs to invest, or not, in future-oriented large scale ventures.

During his first year in the White House, President Clinton worked hard to persuade the American people of the importance of these links. He stressed the growing reality of global economic interdependence, of the relation between democracy and international stability, and of the need to enhance human rights in the U.S. if we are to promote human rights abroad.

Even as he coped with the myriad problems that land on the president's desk, Clinton managed to keep observers off balance. For example, in the waning weeks of the year he met with Salman Rushdie, the writer who is under a death sentence from Muslim fundamentalists. Clinton was excoriated by many Muslims, but he received high praise from many, including human rights advocates, for his principled stand. The praise was soon undercut when his aides announced that the meeting hardly deserved the name because it was so brief, more a passing in the hallway than an actual meeting. And months after he provided the White House as a venue for the agreement, sealed with a handshake, between Prime Minister Rabin of Israel and PLO leader Yasir Arafat, Clinton's administration publicly distanced itself from the agreement.

With all the vast, unresolved problems on its own doorstep and its struggle to find its appropriate role in the changed international order, it is evident that the United States, even at this stage in its history, still deserves to be called the American experiment.

Canada

In Canada, which is the foremost trading partner of the United States (Mexico being third), NAFTA is also an item for debate, but the odds for its adoption were rated good both before and after Canada's national election in late October. Of more importance to the Canadians is the government that will make the final decision. The fortunes of the ruling Progessive Conservative (Tory) party had been transferred from the highly unpopular Brian Mulroney to Kim Campbell in the hope that a younger person promising change would allow the Tories to retain political control. But the weak economy and what was generally agreed to be an inept campaign by Campbell doomed those hopes. (A campaign, she said at one point, is not the place to debate serious issues.)

The Tories were swept away in decisive fashion—even Campbell lost her seat in Vancouver—in favor of the Liberal Party led by Jean Chretien. The final tally of seats won (or lost) and the total number of parliamentary seats for each party were: Liberal Party +99,178; Progressive Conservative Party (-151), 2; *Bloc Quebecois* +46, 54; Reform Party +51, 52; New Democratic party (-35) 8; Independent Conservative 1.

With this vote, the Bloc Quebecois, which favors separating the province of Quebec from the rest of Canada, becomes the leading voice of the opposition. Mr. Chretien, himself a Quebecker who does not favor separatism, has taken on with his new office the task of keeping Canada intact. He has also, if he is to fulfill his campaign pledges, to reduce the national deficit, now greater than that of the United States in per capita terms, and to create many new jobs in the next couple of years. ▬

James Finn is senior editor of Freedom Review.

Latin America: Giving Democracy a Bad Name

Douglas W. Payne

In much of Latin America the poor performance of politicians and elected governments and the shameless behavior of socioeconomic elites are slowly but inexorably eroding people's confidence in the democratic process. Certainly, authoritarian traditions rooted in Spanish and Portuguese colonialism weigh heavily against the modernization of Latin American political culture. And, yes, the need to adapt to a demanding and unforgiving global economy is a daunting challenge for every Latin American government. But all that rings hollow for most Latin Americans, disgusted by the entrenched corruption of political elites who claim to represent them, and hard pressed to survive in a region where the income gap between rich and poor is the biggest in the world and growing every year.

Corruption exists and will continue to exist in the world's established democracies, but most are firmly rooted in a rule of law through which it can be curbed. In Latin America rule is still based more on power than law, the exceptions being Costa Rica and Chile, and to a lesser extent Uruguay. In a majority of countries the traditionally dominant sectors of society—armies, oligarchies and the political classes—continue to enrich themselves at public expense with relative impunity. Judicial systems are less about justice than providing protection for those who can pay for it and punishing those who cannot. Voters can chase presidents and legislators at election time, but government remains a racket dominated by the powerful and the well-connected.

"Politicians are all corrupt"

On the eve of the June 1993 Bolivian elections the *Financial Times* (London) interviewed a market vendor and a carpenter whose differing opinions reflect the shifting popular sentiment in Latin America. Vladimir Benita, the vendor, said: "It's important that we vote so that we get a good government. We're proud to be a democracy after so many years of dictatorship." During the 1980s probably a majority of Latin Americans shared Mr. Benita's optimism as country after country graduated to elected civilian government after years of military rule.

But high expectations are fading in the 1990s amid widespread anger and frustration. Zairo Villasuelo, the Bolivian carpenter, said: "I wouldn't vote if it wasn't compulsory. Politicians are all corrupt." Most Latin Americans now hold similar views, as reflected in declining voter participation and dozens of opinion polls conducted throughout the region.

One survey, carried out by the Spanish publication *Cambio 16* (19 July 1993) in eleven countries spanning each subregion of Latin America, showed that almost 80 percent of those polled had no faith in politicians or political parties. It was particularly ominous that nearly half had little trust in their electoral systems, since for most Latin Americans the ballot box is the only way to have a say in how they are being ruled.

In much of the world there is a mounting popular backlash against insider politics and the abuse of power. Mature democracies feature institutions and independent civil societies that are essential to the self-correcting process through which democracy preserves itself. In Latin America, however, democratic institutions are weak and an emergent civil society, where it is not suppressed, has still to achieve the strength or coherence to act as an effective channel of influence for average people seeking to improve their lives. Aside from periodic trips to the ballot box, most Latin Americans remain inhabitants rather than citizens of their countries.

The failure of Latin America's political classes to change their traditional ways is not only giving democracy a bad name. It is undermining the market reform process needed to transform failed statist economies so they are fit for global competition. Market economies will not succeed in Latin America unless there are clearly established rules and effective governments to enforce them.

At the same time, the idea of economic reform is becoming discredited in the popular view. Restructuring has generally been imposed from above and privatization has mostly been a sweepstakes for the rich and politically connected. That has left the rest of society to bear the brunt of harsh austerity measures and reinforced the stratification of grossly inequitable societies. As scandals involving bribery, drug-trafficking and influence-peddling grab headlines, workers, peasants, small business and the shrinking middle class increasingly see economic reform as just another scheme by traditional elites to preserve economic power and privilege.

Disaffection appears to be greatest among Latin American youth. A majority of Latin Americans is under the age of thirty, and almost half is under fifteen. It is the coming generation that ultimately will determine whether democracy survives. Yet studies by the U.N. Children's Fund (UNICEF) indicate that nearly 80 percent of the poor, who constitute at least half the population in Latin America, are children. They have little access to basic education, let alone institutions that provide an appreciation of democratic values, and are easily lured into the ranks of extremist groups—nationalists, millenialists and dogmatists of the left and right.

Among them are 40 million street children, 7 million in Brazil alone. In Colombia they are called *chinches*, or bed bugs, in Bolivia, *polillas*, or moths, and in Peru, piranhas. Spawned in wretched urban shantytowns, they line the streets of burgeoning cities in every country, prone to delinquency and prey to vigilante groups paid by merchants to eradicate them. Those that survive graduate to drug-trafficking and other criminal enterprises like extortion rackets and kidnapping rings.

With families disintegrating women have emerged as stalwarts among the marginalized. The informal sector, or black market, accounts for up to half of all economic activity in a number of Latin American countries. Poor women, forced to organize in order to survive and save their children, have demonstrated an ability to form social and economic units more democratic and efficient than the governments that shun them.

Women are also making greater contributions within the region's struggling civil society—neighborhood associations, peasant federations, worker movements, journalism, and small business, professional, legal service and rights groups. By asserting themselves in such roles, however, women are breaking the bonds of Latin America's rigidly male-dominated society and the result has been escalating domestic violence and discrimination.

Despite the dire circumstances that afflict most of the region, Latin Americans continue to be exposed to democratic ideas and models of civil society spread through advanced communications and modern transportation. Breaking down commercial barriers, as governments have done to lure trade and foreign investment, has meant the erosion of psychological barriers to modernity that have sustained the region's authoritarian traditions since independence from Spain and Portugal. But without a change in the nature of Latin American politics, cynicism and disillusionment will set in, providing fertile ground for a new generation of aspiring autocrats and enhancing the likelihood that Latin America's historical pendulum will swing back toward instability and repression.

Rhetoric and reality

Although democracy is in the balance in Latin America, you would hardly know it from listening to most of the region's political leaders. The divergence between their rhetoric and reality is nearly as wide as the income gap between Latin America's rich and poor. That was particularly evident during the seventh meeting of the Rio Group held in October 1993.

Latin American presidents now gather at three different annual meetings. Spain and Portugal join in the Ibero-American summits. The Organization of American States (OAS) includes the United States, Canada and the English-speaking Caribbean. But at the Rio Group meetings the Latin American leaders are on their own. The members of the Rio Group are Argentina, Bolivia, Brazil, Chile, Colombia, Ecuador, Mexico, Paraguay, Peru, Uruguay, and Venezuela. At Rio Group meetings, Central America and the Caribbean each send one head of state to represent their respective regions.

The 1993 Rio Group meeting was hosted by Chilean President Patricio Aylwin. Aylwin is one of the many heroes in the fight against dictatorship in Latin America, but he is one of the few in the struggle to strengthen democracy. He played a key role in assembling the center-left coalition that overcame great odds to oust Gen. Augusto Pinochet in the 1988 plebiscite in Chile. Since his election in 1989 President Aylwin has led a broadly representative, remarkably clean government that has been responsive to a wide social base.

The Aylwin government is the only one in Latin America that has combined market economics with social policies that have made substantial reductions in poverty. It is also stands out because it recognizes labor rights and is sympathetic to the plight of workers hurt by economic restructuring. Moreover, Aylwin has deftly kept at bay the unrepentant Pinochet, who left behind a set of laws that allows him to remain head of the army until 1997.

Aylwin, in his inaugural address to the Rio Group in Santiago, encouraged his fellow Latin American leaders to address realistically the negative trends in the region. He stated that the high social costs of economic reform could not be blamed solely on global conditions, and suggested that governments in the region be more mature in assuming their responsibilities. He characterized Latin American democracies as "incomplete," and stated, "Political power sometimes seems too distant from the concerns and interests of common citizens."

But Aylwin's fellow heads of state were having none of it. Following two days of meetings the group issued the "Declaration of Santiago," a self-congratulatory, ultimately cynical document that stated: "The values and principles of representative democracy are gaining status throughout the region...We are pleased to see that the strengthening of democracy is walking hand in hand with significant progress toward economic liberalization... We are dealing maturely with our difficulties."

That must have come as news to the people who live in the countries represented by the signers of the declaration. Mexicans, for instance, would have been intrigued by President Carlos Salinas de Gortari's endorsement of representative democracy. Salinas has moved Mexico's economy into the first world—but by wielding the enormous power of a 64-year-old state-party system. Economic modernization put Mexico first in line for a trade agreement with the U.S., making it the envy of Latin Americans who believe free trade alone will cure what ails their countries.

In 1993 the Clinton administration was backing Mexico's effort to become the twenty-fifth member of the first-world club, the Organization for Economic Cooperation and Development. Mexico would be the first new O.E.C.D. member in thirty years, the first from Latin America—and the first that does not allow its citizens to choose their government through free and fair elections.

Two of the leaders present in Santiago were not elected at all. Brazilian President Itamar Franco, the former vice-president, landed in office in 1992 when the Brazilian congress, compelled by mass demonstrations and the media, impeached his predecessor, Fernando Collor de Mello, on charges of gross corruption. Franco seemed overwhelmed even before coming to Santiago, as four-digit inflation and criminal violence threatened to spiral out of control in Latin America's most populous nation. After he returned, a massive corruption scandal involving congressman, cabinet ministers, state governors and assorted captains of industry brought the government to a virtual halt. Amid rumors of a military coup, many Brazilians wondered how the nation could be steadied in time for the October 1994 election.

Venezuelan President Ramon J. Velasquez was selected by the Venezuelan congress to hold the nation together following two bloody coup attempts by nationalist military officers and the impeachment of former President Carlos Andres Perez after he was charged with corruption. When Velasquez returned from Santiago, someone put a pardon for a prominent drug trafficker on his desk and Velasquez duly signed it.

Initial investigations cleared Velasquez, a respected former senator, of wrongdoing. But his private secretary, legal advisors to his cabinet and a justice ministry official were implicated. Coming on top of assorted other official corruption scandals, the incident damaged the Velasquez government's tenuous credibility only a month before it was to oversee national elections in December. Amid a string of mysterious urban bomb attacks, and with former President Rafael Caldera leading in the polls with the support of leftist parties, the media were filled with rumors of a plan by sectors of the military to abort the election.

Do the "Fujimori"

Peruvian President Alberto Fujimori, backed by the military, dissolved Peru's congress and suspended the constitution in April 1992. Eighteen months later he came to the Rio Group meeting in Santiago, where the Chilean press dubbed him "El Perdonado," the pardoned one. Fujimori had danced around OAS protests by holding a state-engineered election for a new congress. The congress produced a new constitution that, in essence, ratified Fujimori's *autogolpe*, or self-coup, by codifying nearly paramount executive authority and allowing for reelection.

That was good enough for the OAS, which gave its approval to Fujimori's acrobatics and, in effect, overturned its own declaration of June 1991 to defend representative democracy against all threats. The international financial community, enamored of Fujimori's market economic policies, expressed its approval too by lifting the economic sanctions imposed on Peru in 1992. No matter that Fujimori, with the help of Vladimir Montesinos, a Latin American Rasputin who unofficially runs Peruvian state intelligence, controls the military, the police, the judiciary and all policy-making sectors of the state.

Fujimori, having broken the law and gotten away with it, has stretched the definition of democracy well beyond acceptable limits. His apologists counter that a strong hand was necessary because of the threat posed by the Maoist Shining Path guerrillas. They also praise the results—the capture of Shining Path leader Abimael Guzman, and note that Fujimori is popular.

But Fujimori's appeal is primarily a function of the general disdain for Peru's feck-less, self-serving political class that practically ran the country into the ground after the return to civilian rule in 1980. Aside from cutting inflation, Fujimori has yet to deliver economically. His popularity appeared to be waning in late 1993 as voters only narrowly approved his new constitution, despite the government's advertising blitz and spending spree. The Fujimori-Montesinos team may yet need to apply more blatantly repressive measures to maintain power. As it is, Peru remains a world leader in the number of people "disappeared." How much more credibility is the OAS willing to lose by looking the other way?

By coddling Fujimori the OAS has also risked giving a green light to other aspiring autocrats poised to take advantage of the scorn for politics-as-usual in the region. In coun-tries like Brazil and Venezuela, where the wheels of government are threatening to fly off the axle, "Fujimorization" has become part of the daily political discourse in the media and on the streets. It reached the point in Brazil where amid the coup rumors in late 1993 a leading cabinet official felt compelled to state, "We don't want any 'Fujimoris' and we will not have them."

When Guatemalan President Jorge Serrano dissolved the congress in May 1993, head-lines throughout Latin America blared "Serrano does a Fujimori." Serrano's *autogolpe* lasted less than a week, however. Serrano had no Montesinos to secure the deal with the military, who flinched in the face of pro-democracy demonstrations and the threat of inter-national economic sanctions. Serrano was sent packing, replaced by Latin America's third caretaker president, Ramiro de Leon Carpio, a respected human rights activist. Within months, de Leon found himself handcuffed by the same corrupt congress Serrano had tried to eliminate, while in the background lurked the military, prepared as always to veto what-ever policies it did not like.

Argentine President Carlos Menem appeared more intent upon doing a "Peron" than a "Fujimori." Gen. Juan Peron, the founder of Menem's Justicialist Party, is the only Ar-gentine president to secure reelection. Menem, emboldened by the international financial community's embrace of his economic reforms and the popular relief at the ending of hyperinflation, has maneuvered since 1992 to overturn the constitutional ban against re-election. But in the 1993 congressional elections his party fell short of winning the neces-sary two-thirds majority.

Undeterred, Menem went over everybody's head to cut a deal with Raul Alfonsin, his predecessor and leader of the opposition Radical party. Alfonsin, hoping to salvage a de-clining political career, agreed to back a reelection amendment in exchange for reducing the presidential term from six to four years and some reforms to limit the powers of the executive. That proved easy for Menem to swallow since he has not been inclined to re-spect the limits on presidential authority that already exist. His economic program has been implemented mostly by decree, while legal challenges to his policies have been blocked by the Supreme Court which Menem expanded and packed with loyalists in 1990.

Menem's autocratic impulse has been especially evident in his antagonism toward the Argentine media, which have been instrumental in exposing the rampant corruption in his government. In 1991 he initiated a campaign to entangle journalists and writers in a web of lawsuits, while his aides leveled a barrage of verbal attacks. In 1993 the attacks became violent, including beatings of journalists by thugs linked to Menem's Justicialist party.

Journalists continue to be killed in Latin America at an alarming rate, particularly in Colombia and Mexico. But the assault on the media in Argentina reflects a newer pattern of more sophisticated, selective intimidation by elected governments caught up in scandal.

Hybrids and narcocracies

Since the end of World War II Latin America has swung between dictatorship and elected government in approximately ten-year cycles. With politicians again making a mess of things, many Latin Americans are bracing for a new cycle of military rule. The region's military commanders, however, appear reluctant to step in this time. They do not want to deal with complicated economic problems, and they also fear that full-scale military coups would mean economic isolation.

Nonetheless, there are pockets of officers in many of the region's militaries who are imbued with an atavistic nationalism and emboldened by the popular outrage at rampant official corruption. Such is the profile of the soldiers who nearly overthrew the government in Venezuela in 1992. Like-minded officers from around the region sent them messages of support, and they are heroes among many of Venezuela's poor. It was by appropriating much of their populist rhetoric that candidate Caldera pushed to the top of the polls in the months before the December presidential elections.

One model of failed democracy is already on display in Fujimori's Peru, a civilian-led authoritarian regime that retains the trappings of democracy, with the military on board as the palace guard. Another scenario is evident in Central America, where in every country but Costa Rica, militaries tolerate elected civilian governments in exchange for the freedom to conduct themselves as armed corporations, feasting on national economies and above the law. That now seems to be the case as well in Paraguay following the election of President Juan Carlos Wasmosy in May 1993. Gen. Lino Oviedo, not Wasmosy, is the man to watch in Paraguay.

However, such hybrid forms are inherently unstable. A number of officers shunted aside by the Fujimori-Montesinos regime in Peru attempted a coup in late 1992. If Fujimori's popularity continues to fade, and if the Shining Path is able to stage even a partial comeback as it looked to be in late 1993, Peru might be in for a new round of tumult.

In Nicaragua the unofficial power-sharing arrangement between the Sandinistas and the Chamorro government has brought the country to the verge of political anarchy and economic ruin. As in Guatemala, the final word will probably come from the military. That means Gen. Humberto Ortega, who is in the process of becoming, like the dictator Somoza he fought to overthrow, the only man to see in Nicaragua.

Meanwhile, many left-wing organizations have dispensed with armed revolution and opted for the electoral road to power. They are looking to take advantage of the popular backlash against traditional political elites in the numerous elections scheduled throughout the region in 1994. The question is how their old adversaries in the military would react if they were to win. Would the Brazilian military tolerate Luis Inácio "Lula" da Silva of the Workers Party in the presidency? Is the Salvadoran military ready to accept a president elected with the backing of the former FMLN guerrillas?

Overall, the erosion of democracy in Latin America has been uneven and further instability could still manifest itself in unforeseen ways. However, what all the countries of Latin America share is the inability to resist the proliferating hemispheric drug and money-laundering trade. The networks of patronage, payoffs, graft and illegal transactions that define Latin American political culture make governments, banking systems, judiciaries and electoral campaigns highly susceptible to penetration and compromise. The spectacle of Venezuelan President Velasquez signing the pardon for a notorious trafficker is only the tip of the iceberg. At the same time, the principal effect of the U.S. hinging its anti-drug assistance on the involvement of the region's militaries has been to increase drug-related corruption within the militaries themselves.

The so-called "drug war" initiated by Washington in the 1980s has been won by the traffickers. Billions of dollars spent on interdiction have hardly made a dent in the northward flow of drugs. But the war really was over once the traffickers realized they did not have to fight it. They learned that what alarms Latin American governments most is not drug-trafficking per se, but the violence associated with it. Medellín cartel leader Pablo Escobar took on the Colombian state with all guns blazing, and was finally hunted down and killed by Colombian security forces.

The Cali cartel, however, has studiously avoided direct confrontation and now operates the largest cocaine and heroin operation in the region with relative impunity. The children of cartel leaders are trained in the world's finest business schools and take up executive positions in what is one of the smoothest run corporations in Latin America. The Cali cartel, having diversified its investments throughout Colombia's economy, has become virtually indistinguishable from that country's traditional socioeconmic elites.

Hundreds of other drug operations, including a new generation in Medellín, have adopted the Cali approach. All are benefiting from the lowering of trade barriers and expanding drug markets in Europe, and all are finding that Latin America's corrupt political systems and law enforcement provide an accommodating environment for their enterprise. Venezuela now rivals Panama as a money-laundering center, and Mexico has become a trampoline for up to 70 percent of the cocaine coming into the U.S. from the source countries of the Andes. In Latin America today there is not one country where drug traffickers cannot operate with relative ease.

Caribbean flashpoints

There was no mention of the Caribbean in the Santiago declaration. Maybe that was because Jamaican Prime Minister P.J. Patterson, who was to represent the region at the Rio Group meeting, was unable to attend for health reasons. For whatever reason it was a stunning omission, given the ongoing tragedy in Haiti and Fidel Castro's apparent determination to make the final chapter of the Cold War in Latin America an ugly episode.

The nations of the English-speaking Caribbean are relatively solid democracies. But they are buffeted by global economic changes and afraid they will be left out in the cold, whipsawed between large trading blocs in Europe and North America. More immediately, they are concerned that events in Haiti and possible upheaval in Cuba will disrupt the entire region and cause a drop in the all-important tourist trade.

It is difficult to envision a lasting solution to the Haitian crisis. The problem is foremost a political culture that is rooted in a history of constant all-or-nothing struggle for power, and practically immune to outside influence since Haitian independence nearly two hundred years ago. The continued intransigence of the Haitian military in the face of diplomatic and economic pressure in 1993 reconfirmed that intervention in Haiti must be done forcefully or not at all.

But Washington and the United Nations remained reluctant to reinstate Jean-Bertrand Aristide, the country's first freely elected president, by force. The military, aware of the international community's waning resolve, seemed determined to ride out economic sanctions, even if it meant the total devastation of the country.

Across the Windward Passage from Haiti, the Cuban people continued to endure a diet of deprivation and repression. There appeared little likelihood that Fidel Castro's limited, China-style economic reforms could save the economy from complete collapse. In 1993 European and Latin American governments implored Castro to open the political system to avert a violent end to his rule. But he rebuffed their counsel, evidently unwilling to go down without a fight. ▬

Douglas W. Payne is director of hemispheric studies for Freedom House.

Africa: Terra Incognita   Stephen Smith

By 1993, four years after the fall of the Berlin Wall, the "wind of democracy" that swept over Africa appears to be exhausted in several countries, in particular those of the Sahel, which have been all but forgotten by the international community. With meager resources, these countries are left with virtually no future. In other countries, such as Sudan, Zaire and Somalia, factional struggles too easily "explained" as flareups of "tribalism" have attained levels of self-destruction verging on national suicide.

Only South Africa, engaged in a process of negotiated dismantling of apartheid, could nourish the continent's hopes of political and economic renaissance. And even here, persistent violence has made the hope seem fragile, all the more so as South Africa's evolution also depends on the peaceful resolution of the proxy wars between the U.S. and the Soviet Union which have ravaged southern Africa. The rise of a "fertile crescent" at the tip of the continent is therefore, for the time being, no less hypothetical than the success of other attempts at regional settlements designed to overcome African "balkanization." In 1993, the global economic slump underscored the fact that "pan-Africanism" was only rhetorical. Overall, only 6 percent of the continent's international trade is based on inter-African commerce, even if the expanding informal economy, largely based on transnational trade, does not appear in the official statistics.

"Authoritarian restorations"

Increasingly on the margins of international affairs, Africa saw new examples of "authoritarian restorations:" in Zaire, Cameroon, Togo, Djibouti, Kenya, and in Nigeria, too, where it took the classic form of a military dictatorship. Dividing the continent between a few countries, for the most part oil-rich, still viewed as useful, and other, vaster zones fated to become *terrae incognitae*, the outside world did not exert much real pressure for democratization, either because it felt no interest in committing itself or because its commercial interests were more important. When the gap between rhetoric and action (or rather inaction) became intolerable, particularly in the face of the Somalian tragedy, the West responded with humanitarian interventions. In this regard, 1993 was definitely a watershed year for Africa: instead of political involvement, which implies a long-term commitment, the outside world substituted occasional rescue operations. Born a quarter century ago on African soil, in Nigeria's secessionist province of Biafra, modern humanitarianism seems to have become the last rites delivered to a dying continent, balm accompanying its descent into the hell of abandonment.

Somalia: from intervention to "humanitarian war"

There were no television cameras in Somalia on 9 December 1993, nor were photographers clicking away, nor was there an army of journalists with pens drawn. Yet a year earlier to the day such a media army had waited on the beach of Mogadishu for the landing of the humanitarian armada that the U.S. had decided to send to the Somalian coast in order—according to George Bush—"to do God's work." Following its veto of the U.N. Security Council decision, in April 1992, to send 3,500 Pakistani blue helmets, the U.S. had decided, on Thanksgiving Day and against the backdrop of a presidential election year, to send 29,000 American soldiers to the Horn of Africa to put an end to a famine of biblical proportions that threatened to take 300,000 lives. Bringing the whole world along, the American initiative put Somalia in the world's headlines. The Somalian tragedy, the only Africa story to have overcome the wall of indifference in 1993, with the exception of the end-of-apartheid story in South Africa, came to represent Africa in the eyes of the world: an archaic continent, with a violent, chaotic, deadly, stone age environment of killing and hate directed even against foreigners come to the rescue, with neither reason nor restraint. This was, in 1993, the message of Mogadishu.

On 4 May the U.S. transferred the authority for their "military-humanitarian" mission to the U.N., although they had still not disarmed the rival factions. However, it kept for itself all the key command positions, thus maintaining control, in effect, on the international "salvation army." Thus, a purely American strike force became the arm of an intervention which, far from engaging in the supply of food and other assistance promised to the NGOs on the scene, became mired in the traps of Somali politics. Due to the delays, and according to what reliable medical statistics there were, those who "had" to die were already dead by November 1992. This is why the stakes in 1993 became essentially political, and the key objective was something called "national reconciliation." With large numbers of well-supplied troops that were, however, almost perfectly ignorant of the terrain and with no help from experts who might know something about Somalia's history and society, the U.N. nonetheless wanted to dictate the political agenda for Somalia's "reconstruction." It soon ran up against the strong man of south Mogadishu, Gen. Mohamed Farah Aidid. Unlike other chieftains, Aidid, who had been the most determined opponent of the dictator Siad Barre (overthrown in January 1991), did not care to rely on the "dividends" of a peace imposed from the outside and paid for by the international community. Authoritarian and ferociously nationalist, tempted to erect his own regime on the shambles of the defeated dictatorship, Aidid insisted on unifying under his wing the war ravaged and famine wracked country. In May 1993, Gen. Aidid refused to take part in the "reconciliation conferences" called by the U.N., organizing instead, on his own authority, the "estates general of the Somali nation," in open defiance of the U.N. In this context of challenge and tension occurred the deadly ambush of 5 June, which took the lives of twenty-four blue helmets. Thus began five months of "humanitarian war."

Without making an independent inquiry, the U.N. determined that Gen. Aidid was politically and legally responsible. Although it is true that strong evidence against him was subsequently assembled, the fact remains that the U.N. Security Council condemned Aidid within forty-eight hours of the attack and demanded that those responsible be arrested and punished. This Security Council resolution justified the military escalation in the weeks ahead whose supposed purpose was to "capture" Gen. Aidid, who was placed on a "wanted" list, complete with a $25,000 reward. In effect, in the context of a society structured along clan lines, this manhunt immediately took on a collective dimension. The U.N. transformed itself into a clan that was engaged in a vendetta against Aidid's Habr Guedir clan. In July 1993, without warning, a private home serving as a meeting place for elders of the Habr Guedir clan was destroyed by American airpower, with seventy-three dead as a result. Four foreign journalists who arrived at the scene were, in turn, massacred by an angry crowd.

Paying no heed to criticism from within, let alone from the NGOs and the media, the U.N. dug in deeper, all the more obstinately as the Americans, who occupied all the command posts, hoped for a military solution. If Aidid could be neutralized, south Mogadishu would be pacified, just as the rest of the country was, U.S. authorities said over and over. This continued until 3 October, when elite American troops, sent into the heart of a pro-Aidid neighborhood to arrest a score of his closest aides, walked into a trap and were cut to pieces. Out of a hundred-strong task force, twenty-six were killed and fifty wounded in night-long street fighting. Mike Durant, the pilot of one of three helicopters that was shot down, was captured. The nude crucified body of one of his compatriots was dragged through the streets of Mogadishu. America was traumatized by this act of barbarism projected on a continent which always had been regarded as savage and dangerous. Carried away by its own emotional reaction, the American public forgot that the fighting on 3-4 October also claimed at least 300 Somali victims, as well as the International Red Cross could determine. On 8 December, the eve of the first anniversary of the American landing in Somalia, officials in Washington gave to the *New York Times* the results of five months of "humanitarian war": 10,000 dead, caught in the crossfire between clan fighters and blue helmets or between rival clans. Ten thousand dead in five months is more than sixty killed each day.

Somalia set the tone for African news coverage in 1993, written in blood and finally in defeat. After their military debacle of October, the Americans turned 180 degrees: the warrant for Aidid was rescinded, the "warlord" turned into a statesman—here again, before the results of the inquest into the May trap were in. Twisting the U.N.'s arm and announcing the pullout of the 9,000 remaining American soldiers by April 1994, the Clinton administration was looking only for a discreet way out, since honor was not possible. At year's end the idea was to enlist the help of Ethiopian president Meles Zenawi to put together a regime of national reconciliation. Under American protection, Aidid travelled to Addis Ababa in December 1993, but he was unable to find a satisfactory compromise with the other Somali factions. Should a deal be made before the final U.S. pullout, which probably will be followed by that of the U.N., it is entirely probable that it will be "revised" later on the ground: by force of arms, just as in the days before the world's ephemeral intervention in the affairs of Somalia.

Southern Africa: Polarized hope

On 10 December, the receipt of the Nobel Peace Prize by ANC President Nelson Mandela and South African President F.W. de Klerk made official the promise of a "new South Africa, free and democratic." Indeed, all year long, in the context of a negotiating forum that brought together the principal political forces in the country, the "country of apartheid" fashioned the outline of a future free of discrimination. A provisional constitution, to be based on a federal state composed of nine largely autonomous provinces, was drafted; a Transitional Executive Council (TEC), including blacks at the highest level of government for the first time in 341 years of colonial history, was put in place. Its function will be to watch over the fairness of the first multiracial vote, based on the "one man one vote" principle, which is scheduled for 27 April 1994. Overall, the South African transformation, without doubt the most fascinating political experience on the continent, thus was kept on track.

Nonetheless, important problems developed. The Mandela-de Klerk "couple," heart and motor of the transformation, showed clear signs of exhaustion under the stress of cohabitation. It was, surely, unable to stop the daily violence which has taken more than

7,000 lives since the end of 1990. In addition to the appalling growth of crime, the Goldstone Commission investigation showed that elements of the army and the secret services engaged in clandestine operations against the ANC. Several generals were retired by executive order, but President de Klerk's ability to control rogue elements, particularly in the security services, was called into question. As was, for that matter, the ability of Nelson Mandela and of the Zulu leader Mangosuthu Buthelezi to stop the outright war that has raged among their followers in the black townships. According to the Goldstone Commission, this inter-ethnic conflict is the main source of political violence in the country.

In this context, the assassination by a white extremist, on 10 April, of the general secretary of the South Africa Communist Party (SACP), Chris Hani, who also was a charismatic leader of the ANC, could have blown the lid off. All the more so as the slow pace of the constitutional negotiations was a source of frustration to the young radicals in the black ghettos, who identified with Hani. Moreover, the police investigation revealed that there were strings linking the assassin, a forty-year old Polish immigrant named Janusz Walus, to the parliamentary far-right. It was thus an encouraging sign that instead of an explosion, the opposite occurred, as the negotiators, conscious of the dangers, quickened the pace of their work over the summer. In the end, nineteen of the original twenty-six negotiating partners signed off on the transitional constitution and the TEC. The others—the Inkatha Freedom Party, the white extreme right, and the leaders of some of the homelands that had been proclaimed "independent" in the time of "grand apartheid," which aimed to exclude blacks from their own country—shut themselves off in a "refusal front." Yet Mandela and de Klerk, each in his own way and in the framework of the new legal system, persisted in their avowed aim of bringing them back into the transformation process.

In the short run, the choices are radically clear: South Africa might go through a "decolonization" that will fail just as much as it did elsewhere on the continent, if not more so in view of the accumulated hate due to years of discrimination. In this perspective, the history of the southern cone of Africa will reach a summary point with the departure of the whites from the Cape—the very place where, in 1652, the first Dutch settlers landed. "White" Africa will have been nothing but an accident of history, coinciding with a landward expansion tied to the discovery of gold and other subterranean wealth in southern Africa. On the other hand, if the "white tribe" is able to negotiate a lasting integration in the midst of a new South Africa, proof will have been given that on the basis of negotiated equity, multiracial cohabitation is possible, even in a context heavily weighed by the past. In this case, the South African experience, which evolved significantly in 1993, would seem to be an anthropological laboratory rich in findings for the entire world, from ex-Yugoslavia to the U.S.

The Cold War heritage

The future of South Africa will be influenced by the fate of its neighbors, particularly Mozambique and Angola. In these two former Portuguese colonies, wracked by civil wars that were kept going during the Cold War, as confrontational theaters between the "Free World" and the "Revolutionary Internationalist Forces" supported by Moscow, the U.N. was given responsibility for pacification. In Mozambique, the U.N. got involved in 1993, attempting to separate and disarm the belligerents and to organize elections that at the earliest would take place in 1994. The infrastructure and the care taken in this operation reflect the failure of an similar attempt in Angola: in this country, which has been at war without interruption since the first anti-Portuguese attacks in the mid-60s, there was a flareup of fraticidal violence in 1993, more deadly than any previous one. Following September 1992 elections that it lost but whose fairness it questioned, the rebel movement of Jonas Savimbi, National Union for the Total Independence of Angola (UNITA), took up arms again against the government, previously "Marxist," of President Eduardo Dos Santos and his Popular Movement for the Liberation of Angola (MPLA). In merciless battles, in particular in the town of Cuito, 1,000 civilians a day died, according to the reports by the rare aid workers still on the scene. Moreover, the civil war provoked a famine of a dimension previously unknown in this country. Prevented from working in their fields, peasant farmers and their families starved to death while the capital of Luanda found itself without essential food-stuffs. In its poorer neighborhoods, which resemble the worst favelas of South America, death and disease stalk the inhabitants, with no hope of rescue.

At the initiative of the U.N. special representative in Angola, the Malien Alioune Blondin Baye, the UNITA-MPLA dialogue resumed in December 1993 in the Zambian capital of Lusaka. UNITA and MPLA agreed to a new ceasefire and the transport of humanitarian aid. However, a formula for power-sharing, with Savimbi's men getting some of the min-istries, remained beyond reach. Thus it is difficult to imagine how Savimbi and Dos Santos will find it possible to "cohabit." The level of anarchy has reached such a point that even when a military truce is proclaimed, uncontrollable violence will continue in the form of organized banditry. In the final analysis, the international community did not provide itself with the means necessary to execute its own stated goals of pacification, nor did it take responsibility for the burdensome Cold War heritage and the "regional conflicts" that came with it. Less tragically—for the moment—this problem of the Great Powers' African sur-rogates also exists in Ethiopia. Though war has been avoided since the independence proc-lamation of the secessionist northern province of Eritrea in May 1993, the ancient Abyssinia nonetheless is on the way to disintegration. The Oromo majority, in the south, feels alien-ated in a state that has little effective authority but that is dominated by the northern Tigreans.

Another poorly managed Cold War heritage is the issue of democratizing this conti-nent which went directly from colonial status to alignment in either of the two camps, Soviet or American. To be sure, there were elections in 1993 in several countries: Congo, Togo, Burundi, Central African Republic, Gabon, Guinea. But these votes led either to coups, for example in Burundi, where the democratically elected president was assassi-nated in the course of a military putsch on 21 October, which provoked horrendous inter-ethnic massacres leavings tens of thousands of dead in this small central African country, or to massive frauds which gave these elections the appearance of being staged for the outside world, the better to maintain dictatorships. The army and money remained under the control of the "dinosaurs" in power, such as Zaire's Marshal Mobutu or General Eyadema in Togo. The end result of "democratization," in its 1993 African vintage, often was noth-ing but the restoration of authoritarianism.

Gabon's presidential election, on 6 December 1993, was marked by massive fraud followed by the announced re-election with an absolute majority of the incumbent, Omar Bongo, who has been in power for twenty-six years. Gabon is an oil eldorado in the equa-torial forest, producing 15 million tons of oil for a population of scarcely a million. Along with Nigeria, Congo and Angola, Gabon is one of the rare countries that constitutes a real stake for the outside world, since the collapse of prices for such resources as minerals and agricultural products like coffee and cocoa limited the importance of countries such as Zaire and Ivory Coast. In fact, the U.S. has an $880 million trading deficit with Gabon, which is to say approximately the amount of aid Washington gives the entire continent.

For the U.S., but also, especially, for France, which is very active on the continent large regions of which it colonized, Gabon is part of "useful" Africa—as opposed to the vast "useless" zones that are without wealth, notably the Sahel, where even the dramatic rebellion of the Tuaregs, the "blue men" of the desert, is not considered newsworthy. Soon there will be, as on the first maps of Africa in the sixteenth and seventeenth centuries, written over large blank spaces the word *Nigritie*, the "lands of the blacks," or *hic sunt leones*, "lions dwell here."

In Gabon, by contrast, oil brings with it foreign interest which, unfortunately, expresses itself, as it does in the rest of "useful'" Africa, in the form of support for dictatorship and "stability," which in 1993 was the catch-all word in a continent adrift and desperate. France, as the most active foreign power on the continent during the Cold War, was the continental policeman, with the approval of the U.S. which had "subcontracted" the job, and it immediately approved Bongo's re-election. But without a Soviet threat to justify its privileged access to African markets in return for a constabulary role, will France be able to maintain its position? In 1993, the "oil war" between the French Elf-Acquitaine and American companies in the Congo and Gabon may have foreshadowed a politico-commercial rivalry that is sure to grow worse. Where it is still "useful," Africa is no longer France's private preserve. And this implies, tragically, that where Africa is "useless," even France, without "superprofits" in other, "useful" parts of the continent, could definitively pull out. ▬

Stephen Smith is the Africa correspondent for the Paris daily Liberation.

The Middle East: Moment of Illusion, or Hope?

David A. Korn

The Government of Israel and the PLO team, representing the Palestinian people, agree that it is time to put an end to decades of conflict and confrontation, recognize their mutual legitimate and political rights, and strive to live in peaceful coexistence and mutual dignity and security...."

With these startling words in preamble unimaginable even a few weeks earlier, Yitzhak Rabin and Yasir Arafat put their signatures, on 13 September 1993, to a plan to achieve an "historic reconciliation through the agreed political processes." A plan to end more than a quarter of a century of Israeli occupation of the West Bank and Gaza and cede those territories to Palestinian administration and eventually (as the Palestinians insist and as Rabin's supporters do not deny) statehood. And not just a plan, but a timetable for its implementation:

• 13 December 1993: Agreement to be reached on "an accelerated schedule" for Israeli military withdrawal from Gaza and Jericho. A five year "interim period" to begin.

• 13 April 1994: Israeli withdrawal from Gaza and Jericho to be completed and agreement to be reached on "the structure, numbers of members, powers and responsibilities of an elected Palestinian authority."

• 13 July 1994: Election of a Palestinian Interim Self-Government Authority to administer the West Bank and Gaza with power over education and culture, health, social welfare, taxation, tourism and internal security.

And so on until 13 December 1998, when the interim period ends and agreement is to be reached on the "final status" of the West Bank and Gaza.

Historical inevitability?

It all came with such dizzying suddenness. At first it seemed a dream, not daytime fact but middle of the night hallucination: that handshake between Rabin and Arafat, the meeting in Cairo a little later between Arafat and American Jewish leaders. Yet hardly had the pundits recovered from their own astonishment before they began explaining that it had been all but inevitable. There had been ten rounds of talks between Israel and a delegation of West Bank and Gaza notables. They had produced virtually nothing; by the summer of 1993 the two sides were hardly closer to agreement than when the peace conference convened in Madrid in October 1991. Time was running out for everyone. Prime Minister Yitzhak Rabin had come to office in June of 1992 promising peace and prosperity. If he could not deliver peace, there would be no prosperity either, for the continuation of Israel's economic boom was dependent on foreign investment which would take flight at the breakdown of diplomacy. So if Rabin wanted to leave his mark on history or, of more immediate concern, to win reelection for the Labor Party in 1996, he had to have an agreement.

The circumstances were perhaps even more compelling for the PLO. Since the Gulf War, it had lost the financial backing of Saudi Arabia and the oil rich Persian Gulf states.

Its resources were fast running dry. Its followers were defecting to the Islamic fundamentalist Hamas in droves. Yasir Arafat and the men around him in Tunis stood in danger of becoming anachronisms, as ineffectual and pitiable as exiled royalty, and they knew it. Israel stood in danger of having to face a Palestinian movement taken over by fanatics who made the PLO seem tame. What, then, could have been more natural than that the two sides should come to terms? Had they not, after all, been carrying on furtive talks for quite some long time?

For Arafat and his associates it came down to accepting a compromise that fell far short of their long stated demands, one that would leave them open to accusations of betrayal and to vicious attack by their large array of Palestinian rivals. For Israeli leaders, it meant agreeing to concessions that would almost without fail—whether or not one wished to acknowledge it—open the way toward the Palestinian state on the West Bank and Gaza that they had vowed never to accept.

Credit must go in the first instance to Rabin and to Arafat. But the hero of the piece has to be Israel's Foreign Minister Shimon Peres who seized the initiative to hammer out an agreement in months of secret talks with senior PLO officials. Rabin, whose relationship with Peres has often been that of rival, graciously acknowledged Peres' achievement in the statement he made after signing his letter to Arafat on 10 September. "I want to thank you, Shimon," Rabin said turning toward Peres, "for your efforts to bring about a success."

A trusted intermediary was also necessary for success. It appeared in the persons of Norway's able Foreign Minister, Jorgen Holst, and of its energetic young State Secretary, Jan Egeland. Holst and Egeland provided the secret channel, and the meeting place, for talks between Peres and Mahmoud Abbas, Arafat's foreign affairs advisor. The channel was established by Egeland and Peres' deputy, Yossi Beilin, in a meeting in Jerusalem on 10 September 1992. It bore fruit exactly one year later.

American diplomacy, which prided itself not a little arrogantly on being the indispensable go-between in Arab-Israeli negotiations, this time found itself stuck in the role of red-faced cuckold. The Israeli-Palestinian talks were carried on behind the back and, until very near the end, without the knowledge of even the most senior American officials. The U.S. contribution, if such it may be called, consisted principally in the dogged pursuit of a negotiating strategy that excluded the PLO and that Peres had the acuity to understand could only be doomed to failure.

And yet it was American diplomacy, not of 1993, but of the late 1970s, that made it all possible. The "Framework for the Interim Period" signed by Rabin and Arafat is lifted straight from the document hammered out in two grueling weeks of negotiations at Camp David in September 1978 by President Jimmy Carter. Only two elements were missing from the Camp David text: mutual recognition by Israel and the Palestinian Liberation Organization, and the PLO's agreement to accept a gradual and peaceful evolution toward statehood. They came fifteen years later to crown Carter's labor with success.

Not yet the beginning of the end

But anyone who thought the 13 September agreement had essentially resolved the Arab-Israeli dispute was dreaming. As one Israeli observer put it, "this may be the beginning of the end, but it is not yet the end of the beginning." Indeed, by the close of 1993 there were grounds for wondering if it was even that. December 13, the deadline for agreement to be reached on the withdrawal of Israeli troops from Gaza and Jericho, passed with no agreement. What happened was typical of Arab-Israeli negotiations. To reach agreement in September, Israeli and Palestinian negotiators had to leave unresolved a number of key issues: how big would the autonomous Jericho district be? How much of Gaza would Israel continue to occupy to protect its settlements there? Who would control the border between the territories and Jordan and Egypt? How would the Israeli army operate to protect Israeli settlers inside the territories? How many Palestinian prisoners would be freed by Israel, and when?

It was assumed or at least hoped that the good will and the momentum generated by the 13 September agreement would propel the parties over these remaining obstacles. And yet, no sooner was the agreement signed than a counter-momentum began to develop, put into play by opponents on both sides—Palestinian extremists who vehemently rejected any compromise with Israel, and Israeli settlers and right-wingers who just as vehemently rejected any concessions to the Palestinians. Hamas and other Palestinian rejectionists began killing Israelis, and Israeli settlers and other right-wingers began attacking Palestinians; and overly zealous Israeli security forces added to the mayhem by pursuing their campaign against leaders of the Palestinian intifada as though nothing at all had changed. As a result, public support for the 13 September agreement was soon undermined on both sides. At the negotiating table Palestinians and Israelis sought to shore up their domestic positions by standing tough on the critical issues. And doubts began to emerge about the ability of Arafat and the PLO, after all these years in exile, actually to set themselves to the task of governing the West Bank and Gaza.

Even more daunting obstacles lie ahead. The agenda that Israeli and Palestinian negotiators will ultimately be charged with settling is a kind of diplomatic mission impossible. What powers will the Palestinian Authority have during the interim period? Who will control water resources? How will the return of Palestinian refugees from the 1967 war be accomplished? How will the security of Israelis in the West Bank and Gaza and of Israeli settlements be assured during the five year interim period? And what in particular of Jerusalem? Any one of these or a dozen other issues could bring the entire process to the point of collapse.

For a moment it seemed that peace might break out in the Middle East in 1993 every bit as fast as communism fell in Eastern Europe two years earlier. Syria and Jordan would join the Palestinians in settling their disputes with Israel, and the rejectionist camp would be reduced to those two international outlaws, Saddam Hussein's Iraq and Muammar Qadhafi's Libya.

Jordan is an obvious candidate for a peace treaty with Israel, if only because there are no territorial issues to be settled (King Hussein gave up his claim to the West Bank and Gaza in favor of the PLO in 1988). Shortly after the Israeli-PLO signing ceremony, Israeli and Jordanian officials released to the press the text of an agenda for peace treaty negotiations. Foreign Minister Peres sped off to Amman at the beginning of November for talks with Hussein. Peres returned with an economic agreement but no peace treaty. Senior PLO officials say they want a Jordanian-Israeli treaty, to back up their own agreement with Israel, but not too soon, not until they are assured that theirs is working.

King Hussein's hand for peace was strengthened in November when Islamic fundamentalists suffered a setback in Jordan's parliamentary elections. Still, for Hussein to go to the signing table with Israel independently of Syria and in advance of a green light from the PLO would be a risky business. One out of two Jordanians is Palestinian or of Palestinian origin, and in Hafez al Assad Hussein has a mean and dangerous neighbor. At the same time, however, Hussein doesn't want to be left empty handed while the Palestinians scurry off with a cornucopia of international aid. So he keeps a wary eye out in all directions. He wants the economic benefits of peace with Israel but, as always, fears the political consequences of moving too fast. At year's end he seemed more interested in giving the impression he was on the verge of peace than in actually getting there.

The Syrian factor

And what will Syria do? For over two years, rumors promoted by American and Israeli diplomatic insiders have been rife that Syria and Israel are on the point of the big break-through. Yet so far nothing has come of it. Hafez al Assad was outraged that the PLO struck a deal with Israel without first asking and getting his approval (which he very likely would have withheld). He sulked after the 13 September celebration and balked at returning to the negotiating table. He continues to harbor in Damascus some of the fiercest Palestinian opponents of the Israeli-PLO agreement.

American diplomacy has nonetheless rightly recognized peace between Israel and Syria to be the key to a broader Middle East peace settlement. That is why at year's end Secretary of State Warren Christopher made yet another push to bring the governments in Damascus and Jerusalem together. The problem is to reconcile Syria's demand for return of the Golan Heights with Israel's requirement for security. It is not insurmountable, and Christopher is said to have dangled before the Israelis the incentive of stationing U.S. forces on the Golan Heights during an interim withdrawal period. But the prevailing sentiment in Israel favors caution. Both the Israeli public and many in the Israeli government are reluctant to commit the country to a second territorial pullback before knowing whether and how the first will work out. At the moment Rabin can hardly afford more political daring. His government's existence hangs on the narrowest of majorities. And it is still unclear whether Assad, a crafty tactician, is truly ready to make peace with Israel or is merely scheming to get back the Golan Heights. Those who know his history may be excused for suspecting the latter.

High risk, potential reward

It is quite possible that the September 1993 agreement could turn to disaster. Differences in interpretation could stall implementation of the agreement and bring it to collapse. Or Israeli military withdrawal from Gaza and the West Bank could be followed by raging civil war, with an irredentist Palestinian regime emerging from the ruins.

Yet even in the worst of circumstances, stepping back from the agreement is likely to be more dangerous than moving forward with it. The enterprise is fraught with risk, but it also holds enormous potential for the advancement of freedom and democracy. For the first time in their history, the Arabs of the West Bank and Gaza *could* enjoy democratic self government. Israel *could* be freed from the debilitating burden of maintaining military occupation over a people of a different language and culture, and from the opprobrium that attaches thereto and that has steadily sapped its international standing. An Israeli-Palestinian reconciliation would inevitably entrain peace treaties between Israel and Syria and Jordan, no matter how reluctant their leaders, and very likely with other Arab states of the Near East and North Africa as well. The reduction of tensions and the opening of borders that would follow could launch the Middle East into an era of unprecedented prosperity, giving hope to millions and expanding the frontiers of freedom throughout the region. It could even circumscribe the appeal of militant political Islam, now clearly the major threat to freedom and democracy in the Middle East.

The fundamentalist wave

Militant political Islamic fundamentalism is not a single movement but it does have a single purpose: to gain power, dismantle the secular state and annul its laws and install a state based on religious dogma—as interpreted by whoever does the installing. To put it plainly, militant political Islamic fundamentalism is totalitarianism disguised in the garb of religion. Like other totalitarianisms before it, it is as ready to use the ballot box as the gun in its quest for power.

This absence of scruple in exploiting the processes of democracy to destroy democracy poses a fundamental dilemma for all those who value—or aspire to—the democratic state. It is an unspoken assumption of democracy that a people that has gained the right freely to elect its own government will never knowingly give its vote to a party or an individual who would deprive it of that right. But what if this assumption should prove untrue? Must the verdict of the ballot box be respected at all cost? To what extent might a government be entitled to annul the popular verdict and curtail basic liberties in the face of a challenge from a group whose intentions are clearly inimical to democracy and to secular government? In short, is it justifiable to subvert democracy in the name of saving it?

Neither the government of Egypt nor that of Algeria had attained the condition of democracy at the moment it had to face these questions, but both seemed headed in that direction. Algeria put itself in transition from one party rule to democracy in 1988. Municipal elections were to be the first step down that road. They were held in June 1990, and they were swept by the Front Islamique du Salut (FIS), a militant Islamic fundamentalist group whose proclaimed aim is to do away with the secular state and its freedoms and install in Algeria a theocratic Islamic state. When the FIS repeated its sweep in the first round of parliamentary elections in December 1991, the Algerian army, a secularist bastion, took over, declared martial law, arrested and tried the FIS leaders and banned the party. The arrests and the ban set off a carnage that has brought Algeria to the brink of civil war. The security forces hunt down and kill, or arrest and torture, members of the FIS, while FIS squads murder government officials, police and army officers, western trained intellectuals and anyone else who happens to get in their way. The killings have become daily events and have reached lows of cruelty rarely attained even in Algeria's war of independence. One of the most shocking took place on 22 June 1993 when an FIS squad seized Muhammad Boukhobza, the director of Algeria's National Institute for Global Strategy, a foreign policy think tank, and cut his throat in his home under the eyes of his wife and children. In the fall of 1993 FIS militants began targeting the foreign—mainly French—community, kidnapping and killing several foreigners and warning all to leave or face death. A mass exodus ensued. This is sure to compound Algeria's economic difficulties, and that obviously is the fundamentalists' goal. Algeria has little tourism but its important oil and gas industries employ many foreign technicians, and French citizens also play an important role in the business community.

A new government headed by Rehda Malek, former Algerian ambassador to the United States and former foreign minister, is said to be pursuing contacts with the opposition to find a way out of the impasse. Even in the best of circumstances, however, Algeria's road back toward democracy will not be an easy one; and an eventual takeover by Islamic militants is not to be excluded. The issue in Algeria is not solely secularism versus theocracy.

It is massive unemployment and poverty, and a record of corruption and ineptitude on the part of the secular Front de Liberation National that governed Algeria from 1962, when the country became independent, until the January 1992 military takeover. The advocates of secular democracy face the difficult challenge of showing that they have more to offer the Algerian people than do those of theocratic totalitarianism.

Between militant Islam and secular government

Egypt emerged in 1993 as the other major battleground between militant political Islam and secular government. Until the Islamist terror campaign began in late 1990, Egypt had seemed safely headed toward gradual democratization. The single party system installed under Nasser in 1953 was dismantled in 1976. By the late 1980s thirteen political parties had been authorized and had competed more or less freely in parliamentary elections. Opposition parties were exercising their right to criticize the government, and the press enjoyed greater freedom than at any time in decades. To be sure, power remained concentrated in the hands of President Husni Mubarak, and Mubarak's National Democratic Party kept a comfortable parliamentary majority through means that were not always in the best traditions of democracy. Mubarak, however, was under pressure from the United States, his major ally, to loosen his grip, and he seemed to understand the need to do so. His government's major failing was its inability to make more than a small dent in the poverty in which the great majority of Egyptians live. Steps to relieve the government of crushing subsidies and to dismantle the Egyptian economy's sclerotic state sector have brought higher prices for bread and other staples, and the threat of greater unemployment—all without significant compensating benefit for the average Egyptian. The rise concurrently with economic liberalization of a new moneyed class that flaunts its affluence without offering any redeeming social merit also has not helped. And as if all this were not enough, the Egyptian government's ponderous bureaucracy has proven itself incapable of attending speedily to the needs of the people.

It was a setting ripe for exploitation. Islamic fundamentalists deftly seized the opportunity, bringing in their own neighborhood clinics, schools and charitable organizations. When an earthquake struck Cairo this past July, the "Islamists" were on the scene providing food, shelter and medical care to the survivors long before government services arrived. Nothing could more effectively have dramatized the government's ineptitude and the Islamic fundamentalists' claim to be the true friend of the people. Barred from running candidates in public elections, the fundamentalists have targeted trade unions and professional associations. By taking advantage of the dispersion of secular votes and of low membership turnout, they have won control of a great many, even the scientific and legal ones. They even boast of having a "liberated district" of half a million people in Cairo.

The program of fundamentalists

The dark side of the fundamentalist program is its harsh intolerance, and its vicious attacks on Egypt's Coptic Christian minority and on secular Muslim intellectuals. In its effort to bring down the Egyptian state, the militant fundamentalist Islamic Group has targeted not only police and high government officials but secular intellectuals, and the country's most lucrative foreign exchange earner, the tourism trade, killing and wounding tourists in Cairo and at antiquity sites around the country. President Mubarak has responded by invoking emergency powers, curtailing press and private freedoms, giving his security forces free rein to hunt down members and sympathizers of the Islamic Group and turning those arrested over to military courts for trial. The military courts have issued what for Egypt is an unprecedented number of death sentences—thirty-nine in all since December 1992 when terrorism cases were first referred to them. An unprecedented number of executions—eighteen since the summer of 1993—has been carried out, and allegations of widespread torture of suspects held in Egyptian prisons appear to have ample foundation.

Egyptian officials claim that Mubarak's iron fist policy is working. Periodically the government has announced that it has broken the back of Islamic fundamentalist opposition. But each announcement has been followed by more attacks on police, high government officials and tourists, and by more government raids on Islamic group strongholds. A booming Egyptian birth rate and a low economic growth rate have combined, it appears, to produce for the fundamentalists an almost unlimited supply of young men ready to risk their lives to kill a policeman, a government minister, a secular intellectual or a foreign tourist.

Without question, the fundamentalist cause draws its main strength from Egypt's domestic ills. This does not mean, in Egypt's case at least, that foreign subversion is of no consequence. The Islamic fundamentalist regimes in Iran and Sudan have provided substantial aid to Islamic Group terrorists in Egypt, in money, in training and in arms. Egypt is a prime target for takeover by militant Islamic fundamentalism, first of all because it is the key country in the Arab Middle East but also because of its government's close ties with the United States, its peace treaty with Israel and its efforts to promote peace between Israel and the Arabs. Egypt is the cornerstone of the network of relationships that underpin U.S. interests in the Middle East and of the Arab-Israeli peace effort. If an Islamic fundamentalist regime were to come to power there, the reverberations would bring both tumbling down in very short order.

Few who know the Egyptian scene think a fundamentalist takeover likely anytime soon. Still, the standoff between the government and the fundamentalists basically favors the latter. It deprives the government of badly needed revenues from tourism, frightens off foreign investment and dims prospects for a return to democratization and for remedying the social ills from which the fundamentalists draw their strength. In much the same way as Yeltsin in Russia, Mubarak's struggle with the fundamentalists has forced him into ever greater reliance on the army. So long as he enjoys its backing, there is no force in Egypt that can oust him. Should he be assassinated or lose the army's favor, he would very likely be replaced by a military regime. Western analysts believe—or is it merely a hope?—that a military regime would not differ greatly in orientation from Mubarak's government; for where would Egypt get its arms, not to speak of its food, if it turned against the U.S.? Still, no one contends that a military regime would not be a serious step backward for Egypt.

The bright spots for freedom...

The retrogression in Algeria and Egypt notwithstanding, there were bright spots for freedom in the Arab and Islamic Middle East during 1993.

In Morocco important advances were made already in 1992 when, on the proposal of King Hassan, a new constitution was adopted that enlarged the powers of the parliament and placed limits on those of the monarch. Parliamentary elections were held in June 1993. The government coalition won 116 of the 222 seats in contest. The four major opposition parties claimed that the rules prejudiced them, but overall the elections were deemed to have been free and fair. Apparently owing largely to King Hassan's traditional—and carefully cultivated—role as national spiritual leader, political Islamic fundmentalism has not been able to gain a significant foothold in Morocco.

Although Hassan retains broad powers, he deserves recognition for impelling his country along the path toward freedom and democracy. He continues, however, to stall on holding the U.N. mandated referendum (to which he has agreed in principle) to determine the future status of the Western Sahara.

No less credit should go to King Hussein of Jordan where major progress was registered in 1993. If Hussein has been cautious when it comes to concluding a formal peace treaty with Israel, he has moved decisively to liberalize government within Jordan. The liberalization movement was launched in 1989 with parliamentary elections—the first since 1956—and has continued ever since. In January and February 1993 the Jordanian government licensed seven additional political parties and authorized the establishment in Amman of a center for the study of human rights. In May the parliament passed a law that rescinded the government's unlimited authority to penalize newspapers and that gave journalists the right to due process.

The liberalization appears to be working. Islamic fundamentalists and their sympathizers, who seemed set possibly to catapult to power in Jordan through the ballot box after the 1989 parliamentary elections, suffered a major setback in elections held in November 1993. The fundamentalists and their allies fell from thirty-two seats to eighteen in the eighty member Jordanian legislature. Even before that, in May, secular members of Jordan's parliament blocked a bill introduced by fundamentalists that would have required segregation of the sexes in high schools and colleges.

Perhaps the major threat today to the democratic process in Jordan, and to the country's stability, is the declining health of the monarch. Hussein was operated on for cancer last year. His physicians have since reportedly declared him free of the disease but in his public appearances he has not looked well. It is unclear whether his brother and designated successor Hassan, long waiting in the wings, has the stature to hold the country together in the face of pressures that could be exerted by the rise of a Palestinian state on the West Bank and in Gaza.

Freedom and democracy also advanced, during 1993, in Yemen, in the southwestern corner of the Arabian peninsula. Unification of the north and south was followed, in April, by parliamentary elections for which some 95 percent of eligible voters are said to have turned out. For the first time, women took part in the balloting. The campaign was marred by minor violence and international observers noted some irregularities at the polls but did not judge these serious enough to affect the overall results. Considering the turbulent history of the two Yemens over the past three decades, and the still rather chaotic nature of the newly unified country, this is quite remarkable.

But the brightest spot of all for freedom and democracy in the Islamic Middle East, this past year as during the previous one, was the Kurdish region of Iraq. Saddam Hussein's war on the Kurds, in the spring of 1991, left their northeastern highland territory in ruins. After a time of uncertainty following the Iraqi army's withdrawal, the Kurds decided that their best hope for survival lay in building the full gamut of institutions of democracy. The process was put in motion by the election of a parliament in May 1992. These were the first free and fair elections—certified as such by observers from the U.S., Western Europe and Latin America—in the entire history of the Kurdish people. They produced a 100 member legislature which in its turn selected an executive. Freedom of speech and the press flourished right from the start, even before laws were passed to protect them, with dozens of newspapers springing up and several competing television channels coming on the air. By the spring of 1993 civil administration was fully functioning, an independent albeit still fledgling judiciary was in place, and civil and political rights were being protected to an extent unknown in earlier times.

This Kurdish foray into democratic self government has disconcerted Arabists in the State Department's Middle East bureau whose concern for the unity of the Iraqi state matches their earlier notion that Saddam Hussein was an asset for peace and progress. No matter that the promotion of democracy is a key plank in the Clinton administration foreign policy, officials at State responsible for the Middle East have done as little as possible to advance the Kurdish effort. They have listened gravely to the Kurds urgent pleas for lifting U.N. economic sanctions against their region (the sanctions, voted in 1990 to punish Saddam Hussein's government for its seizure of Kuwait, paradoxically have ended up punishing not only Saddam but his victims) but the sanctions have continued unabated.

There is a real danger of failure. Not because of any lack of enthusiasm for democracy on the part of Iraqi Kurds or effort to make it work. The threat comes from the severe economic hardship imposed by the Baghdad and Tehran governments' blockade of the Kurdish region and by the continuing U.N. economic sanctions. It comes perhaps even more from the repeated border attacks on the Kurds by the Iraqi and Iranian armies, designed to instill fear and disrupt normal life; and from Turkey's ambivalent attitude toward the Kurdish experiment and uncertainty over whether Ankara will continue to allow on its soil bases of the allied air umbrella that protects the Kurds from all-out assault by Saddam Hussein's army.

The Iraqi Kurdish experiment in democracy stands as a beacon, indeed as an inspiration, to the other peoples of Iraq and neighboring countries where despotism reigns. Should the great Western democracies, misled by a false *realpolitik*, allow it to be crushed, the message will reverberate throughout the region.

...and the grim ones

Until the untimely death of President Turgut Ozal in May of last year, Turkey seemed on the road to bringing its large Kurdish minority to full citizenship and participation in the country's democratic processes. With Ozal's demise, however, the partisans of repression again got the upper hand. Well before the end of the year, the entire southeastern region of Turkey had become a war zone, with martial law imposed, arbitrary arrest, torture and execution common, and the Turkish army burning entire Kurdish villages in a repeat of its scorched earth policies against the Kurds of the 1920s and 1930s. American diplomats, fearful of alienating an ally in the struggle for influence in Muslim republics of the former Soviet Union, have done little to influence the Turkish government toward a more enlightened policy. But Turkey will not survive as a democracy—and may ultimately not even be able to maintain the integrity of its borders—if it fails to offer equal cultural, linguistic and political rights to its Kurdish citizens. Kurds currently comprise between 15 and 20 percent of the Turkish population and their numbers proportionate to ethnic Turks are projected to rise substantially in the next century.

Western visitors to Iran report that the government has been attentive to the needs of the urban poor, who in general appear better off now than before the revolution. That is almost certainly the best that can be said for the Tehran regime, which may be a democracy for the mullahs but remains a dictatorship for everyone else, and a threat to freedom of religion and free expression everywhere. The Islamic regime's shameful repression of Iran's small Bahai minority—solely on grounds of religion—continues unabated. Over the past decade more than 200 Iranian Bahais have been executed, several thousand imprisoned and the remaining hundreds of thousands denied education and employment. As for free expression, this past year the Islamic regime doubled its bounty on Salman Rushdie to over 2 million dollars while its clerics renewed their fatwah calling for Rushdie's murder. Iranian security services have been found to be responsible for a series of political murders in Europe during recent years. The U.S. government this past year branded Iran "the world's most dangerous state sponsor of terrorism."

Iran has also become the major foreign friend and collaborator of the outlaw Saddam Hussein regime. The Iranian government openly flouts the U.N. prohibition on trade with Iraq. It serves as a channel for the procurement of spare parts, machinery and chemicals that the Baghdad regime would otherwise be unable to obtain. And it helps Saddam Hussein keep himself in foreign currency by allowing use of its ports for the transshipment and export of Iraqi oil, in violation of the U.N. embargo. Evidently the totalitarian affinities of the Tehran and Baghdad regimes have now come to outweigh the antagonisms of eight years of savage warfare.

The situation in Iraq remains unrelievedly grim. Three years after his resounding defeat in the Gulf War, Saddam Hussein is still firmly entrenched in Baghdad. His survival—when almost everyone thought him finished—is a lesson in the power of an efficient police state that enjoys the loyalty (bought, it is true) of a substantial minority of the population, i.e. Iraq's Sunni Muslims. Owing to the U.N.'s persistence, Saddam has had to sacrifice those elements of his nuclear weapons and chemical warfare industries that he could not hide. Conventional weapons manufacturing capacity, however, is said to have been restored to 80 percent of its pre-war level. Saddam has carefully eschewed major challenge to the Kurds and their allied protectors in the north but he has proceeded brutally to suppress Shiite dissidence in the south. Over the past year, the Iraqi army has pursued a savage campaign against Shiite dissidents who took refuge in the vast marshes of southeastern Iraq, using artillery, tanks and, allegedly, even chemical weapons. Concurrently, Iraqi military engineers have drained large areas of the southern marshes, making a desert where there was once a thriving Marsh Arabs culture, under pretext of development. In draining the Iraqi marshes, Saddam Hussein adds ecological crime to his many other crimes against humanity.

Next door to Iraq, Syria is a somewhat less grimly purposeful police state. There is absolutely no sign that Hafez al Assad's regime is prepared to take steps toward democratization, but with the collapse of its Soviet patron it has recently sought to make certain cosmetic improvements on the human rights side. It has released some political prisoners and, for the first time, has allowed entry of representatives of Amnesty International. Still, the record is far from good. A report issued by the United States National Academy of Sciences in 1993 named Syria the world's largest jailer of scientific personnel. This unsavory distinction arises from mass arrests in 1980 and 1981 of members of the Syrian engineering and medical associations, many of whom were kept in prison for over a decade without trial and some of whom were tortured and died there. These and similarly objectionable Syrian government practices have drawn almost no U.S. government expressions of opprobrium, apparently owing to State Department hopes that Syria will at last join in earnest in peace negotiations with Israel.

In Kuwait, opposition efforts to curb the powers of the ruling Sabah family and introduce a greater measure of democracy appear stalled for the time being. In Saudi Arabia, the "reforms" enacted by decree in 1992—providing for a system of local governance and the appointment of a "consultative council"—have brought no discernible liberalization.

Paradoxically, the Saudi state, ruled by the strict precepts of Islam, finds itself locked in a struggle with militant political Islam. Thus far the Saudi "Islamists" have not resorted to violence; their tactic, which they have pursued with only partial success, has been to try to insinuate themselves into key positions in Saudi institutions.

Domestic peace is kept in Saudi Arabia by vast distributions of money to the major segments of society. However, these handouts, together with mammoth arms purchases and payoffs to foreign governments, have depleted the once seemingly inexhaustible Saudi treasury. Some experts worry that a prospective cutback in domestic subsidies could undermine stability in Saudi Arabia. With or without such a development, liberalization is clearly not in the offing.

The year ahead

Nineteen-ninety-four will be the decisive year in the Middle East. It will tell whether the agreement between Israel and the PLO can be made to work. It will tell whether the end of Israel's occupation, assuming it in fact occurs, will bring democratic self government, or dictatorship, or simply chaos, to the West Bank and Gaza. And whether greater harmony or greater strife will be the lot of Israelis, Palestinians and other Arabs. The test will be the elections that are planned for July 1994. Arafat has promised the people of the West Bank and Gaza "democracy, democracy and more democracy." If Israeli and Palestinian negotiators manage to surmount the obstacles in their path, and if Arafat can deliver on his promise of democracy and reconciliation, a broader peace will inevitably ensue and a new era will truly open for the Middle East. ■

David A. Korn is a writer and former diplomat. He is the author of Stalemate: The War of Attrition and Great Power Diplomacy in the Middle East, 1967-1970 *(Westview Press, 1992) and, most recently,* Assassination in Khartoum *(University of Indiana Press, 1993).*

Asia: The Authoritarian Challenge

Charles Graybow

When United States President Bill Clinton hosted a dozen other Asia-Pacific heads of state in Seattle in mid-November, the remarkable diversity among the leaders underscored two powerful regional trends. The two largest blocs of leaders were a core of democrats and three authoritarian rulers: President Suharto of Indonesia, China's Jiang Jemin and Singapore's Goh Chok Tong.

The dynamic economies in East Asia have given Suharto, Jiang, Goh and others the confidence and clout to reject political pluralism in favor of home-grown authoritarian systems. And one of the most vocal proponents of this authoritarian approach, Malaysia's Mahathir Mohamad, audaciously skipped the summit, claiming it reeked of economic neo-colonialism.

In Asia today, authoritarian Indonesia, Malaysia and Singapore are the models that nominally socialist China, Laos and Vietnam are copying. Led by China, these six countries collectively represent some 1.45 billion people, or roughly one-fourth of the world's population. The challenge posed to liberal countries is neither expansionistic or hegemonistic; rather, it is to the very notion of democracy as a good in itself. As Singapore's venerable Lee Kuan Yew has put it, they will prosper while Australia becomes "the poor white trash of Asia."

This challenge to democracy is especially acute because in post-War East Asia, authoritarian governments have presided over a phenomenal increase in their citizens' material welfare. In Indonesia, for example, Suharto's programs have reduced poverty from 60 percent of the population in the early 1970s to about 15 percent today, lowered infant mortality, and provided roads, schools and hospitals to once-destitute rural areas. A younger generation of Indonesians has not known, for the most part, the daily hunger pains common to children in the 1960s.

Fundamental freedoms attacked

Paradoxically, in a year in which South Koreans and Japanese saw sweeping political reforms strengthen their democratic systems, authoritarian countries openly attacked the universality of fundamental liberties enshrined in the 1948 Universal Declaration of Human Rights. In late March and early April forty-nine Asian countries met for five days in Bangkok to craft a regional agenda for the June United Nations World Conference on Human Rights in Vienna. What emerged, the Bangkok Declaration, argued that fundamental freedoms such as speech, press and the right to democratically change one's government are not inalienable, but must instead be considered "in the context of... national and regional particularities and various historical, religious and cultural backgrounds." The Declaration defined a nation's right to economic development as inalienable, and declared Western attempts to link development assistance to human rights records as an infringement on national sovereignty.

On one level the Bangkok Declaration reflects the premium many Asian leaders, and ordinary citizens, put on internal stability as a vital prerequisite for economic growth. South Korea metamorphisized from a poor, politically unstable country into an industrial power under General Park Chung Hee's often-brutal 1961-79 authoritarian rule. Perhaps not surprisingly, 83.5 percent of the respondents in a March 1993 survey by *Chosun Ilbo,* the South Korean daily, rated Park "the best president" since the country regained independence after World War II.

For Indonesians who lived through the aborted leftist uprising in the mid-1960s, during which hundreds of thousands of suspected Communists and sympathizers were slaughtered, or Malaysians who recall the destructive 1969 anti-Chinese riots, the last two decades have for the most part brought tranquility and prosperity. Today, many authoritarian countries cite India, the Philippines and other countries beset by ethnic conflicts and insurgencies as examples of how instability can stunt economic growth.

Development with power

But while most authoritarian leaders are clearly committed to development, the underlying agenda for many is to maintain power, when necessary through coercion and force. China, Laos and Vietnam ban all political opposition, while in "softer" authoritarian countries opposition groups do participate in the political process but face significant barriers to coming to power. In Malaysia and Singapore, regular parliamentary elections merely provide the government with a superficial cloak of democracy. Beneath this, power is maintained via harsh Internal Security Acts that are frequently used against political dissidents, highly restrictive speech and press laws that stifle free debate, election laws that deny opposition candidates fair campaigning opportunities, and state-run media that promote the ruling party.

The Bangkok Declaration's thesis that Asian cultural norms relativize individual rights and political pluralism is taken to its most absurd extreme by the Burmese military junta, which justifies its brutal repression on the grounds that its citizens are simply unfit for democracy. But Aung San Suu Kyi, the Nobel Laureate whom the junta has kept under house arrest since 1989, has pointed out that the Burmese peoples' indigenous Buddhist beliefs favor limits and checks on authority and an egalitarian, participatory form of government. For the leaders of these authoritarian countries, talk of cultural and developmental rights is generally a smokescreen for suppressing political rights and civil liberties.

Further, several Asian governments are outwardly hostile towards investigations of human rights abuses. In 1992 Indonesia banned NGOs from receiving any economic assistance from the country's former colonial ruler, the Netherlands, due to the Dutch government's insistence on linking development aid and human rights. Indonesian NGOs such as the Legal Aid Institute and the Institute for the Defense of Human Rights, which are frequently the only outspoken opposition to the government's policies, had received over four-fifths of their funding through Dutch NGOs and have had to limit their activities in recent months for lack of funds.

Asian responses

There is, however, an Asian response to Asian authoritarianism. Today some 2,000 NGOs in the region are tapping into a solid grassroots support for political pluralism and individual rights. The continuing democratic evolutions in formerly authoritarian Taiwan, South Korea and Thailand obliterate the myth that democracy is an alien, Western concept. The impetus for change comes not from Western pressure or from some infatuation with Western ideas, but from ordinary citizens fed up with regimes that deny them the dignity of free choice in voicing opinions and choosing their leaders.

In many countries economic growth has created a self-confident middle class with the means to challenge their rulers' authority. In Thailand, the May 1992 demonstrations against a military-backed government were coordinated via cellular telephones and fax machines. Although in India, Papua New Guinea and several other democracies official corruption has soured popular attitudes towards the political process, elsewhere the onset of multipartyism allows citizens to express their aspirations. In May, Cambodians who had never been asked their opinions about anything by previous governments turned out in overwheming numbers to participate in U.N.-supervised elections, despite a high risk of violence from Khmer Rouge guerrillas.

Although authoritarian regimes come in many forms, all are finding it difficult to satisfy diverse segments of society. This is so even in Singapore, the "prototypical" East Asian authoritarian country. Beginning in 1965 under the brilliant leadership of founding Prime Minister Lee Kuan Yew, the government encouraged high savings rates, placed the most talented students in the bureaucracy, established generous social programs and encouraged foreign investment. The government's emphasis on meritocracy, and a near-total absence of corruption, gave it a certain legitimacy authoritarian governments in other parts of the world lacked.

But the ruling People's Action Party's (PAP) popularity is slipping. The country held elections in August for an expanded presidency, but the government purposely drew narrow qualifications, allowing it to reject two would-be opposition candidates for not having the proper "integrity, good character and reputation." Instead, the government put up a token challenger to run against the PAP's candidate, Ong Teng Cheong.

The challenger, a retired nonpartisan civil servant, didn't bother campaigning and rated Ong "a far superior candidate." Yet Ong won with only 58.7 percent of the vote, a clear rebuff to the PAP, which has seen its share of the vote drop in parliamentary elections from 75 percent in 1980 to 63 percent in 1988 and 61 percent in 1991. For many of the working-class Chinese who form the PAP's traditional base, the highly elitist party, with its feverish emphasis on savings over consumption, has lost touch with their needs.

China's paramount leader Deng Xiaoping openly admires Singapore's authoritarianism, and since December 1978 has gradually allowed capitalism to flourish in the hopes that a well-fed, well-clothed population will forget about democracy and accept the Communist party's monopoly on power. Former *New York Times* Beijing Bureau Chief Nicholas Kristof neatly describes this as "Market-Leninism."

On the surface at least, Deng's economic approach has been highly successful. In 1993 economic growth is expected to be around 13 percent for the second year running. It's worth noting that since the violent 1989 crackdown on pro-democracy demonstrators in Tiananmen Square, the only significant protests in the country have involved money, not politics. In August 1992 thousands rioted outside the Shenzen stock exchange after applications for new shares ran out. This year, thousands of peasants beat up local Party officials and ransacked government offices in Sichuan Province and elsewhere in more than 200 incidents across the country to protest crushing ad hoc taxes and random land seizures by provincial governments.

These protests are no doubt worrisome to a leadership that launched its revolution in the name of the peasants, and serve as a stark reminder that while China has some similarities with Singapore—a Confucian tradition that respects legitimate authority, for example—its huge size makes maintaining tight control over an increasingly affluent society far more difficult. Other dramatic, if subtle, changes are occurring. Millions of Chinese have been liberated from the stifling control of the *danwei*, or state work unit. For years the Communist party has used the danwei to micromanage nearly every important aspect of citizens' lives, from housing to childbearing to choice of residence. Now, the spread of satellite dishes, shortwave radios and fax machines makes it harder for the government to limit access to foreign news and ideas.

The wildcard in China's immediate future is the likely seccession crisis after the death of the eighty-nine-year-old Deng, who is reportedly in failing health. Most experts agree that Deng's handpicked successor, President and Party General Secretary Jiang Zemin, lacks the power base to survive politically after the patriarch dies.

China may simply go through a power struggle similar to the one after Mao died in 1976, when several top figures were purged but stability was maintained. But an emerging middle class, as well as growing income disparities between the flourishing coastal areas and the still-struggling countryside, makes China a vastly different country than the one Mao left behind. Given China's size, the potential for instability is staggering. Some dire predictions foresee entire provinces seceding, perhaps led by predominantly Muslim Xinxiang Autonomous Region.

Indonesia also faces a potential succession crisis. The lack of democratic structures has concentrated power at the top and created a vacuum at lower levels. The seventy-two-year-old Suharto remains widely popular, and in March had himself re-elected to a sixth five-year presidential term by his largely hand-picked parliament. But when Suharto finally decides to stand down, divisions within the military and among the archipelago's 350 ethnic groups could lead to chaos.

In a startlingly candid statement, in October Suharto accused his ruling Golkar party of having "failed to meet the public demands for greater democracy, better respect for human rights, social justice and protection of the environment." Suharto has also begun a process of "civilianization," giving numerous top government positions to civilians rather than military figures.

Malaysia has allowed somewhat greater political freedom than Indonesia—two of the thirteen state governments are in opposition hands—but like Suharto, Prime Minister Mahathir has used the cover of consensual politics to stifle opposition. In recent years the government has cut back sharply on development funds to the two-opposition controlled states, Sabah and Kelantan, and has taken measures to limit debate in parliament, including reducing speaking time on the floor. The government's economic and educational policies continue to favor ethnic Malays over the Chinese minority.

At the ruling United Malay National Organization's November party poll, delegates elected Finance Minister Anwar Ibrahim as deputy president, putting him nominally in line to eventually succeed Mahathir, who has been in office since 1981. Anwar represents a younger, urban-oriented, ethnic Malay elite that should increasingly assume leadership positions in the next several years, easing out the conservative, rural-based old-guard.

Sweeping changes: South Korea...

The two strongest Asian democracies favoring universal human rights at the Bangkok Conference, South Korea and Japan, experienced potentially far-reaching changes in 1993. Although the fall of Japan's ruling Liberal Democratic Party after thirty-eight years in power has received the most attention, South Korean President Kim Young Sam's first year in office was no less dramatic. A former dissident, Kim joined the ruling Democratic Liberal Party in 1990 after receiving assurances he would be its 1992 presidential candidate. Although many reform-minded Koreans branded him an opportunistic turncoat, Kim nevertheless beat his rival, former dissident Kim Dae Jung, at the December 1992 election.

Considering his "defection" to the government, few expected he would shake things up the way the feisty, liberal-minded Kim Dae Jung perhaps might have. But Kim's newfound stature as an establishment politician in fact gave him greater leeway with the military and other conservative elements of society than Kim Dae Jung would have had.

In February 1993, Kim took office as South Korea's first civilian president in thirty-two years he pledged to eliminate the last vestiges of authoritarian rule, as well as the graft that permeated every level of the puissant bureaucracy. By year's end thousands of bureaucrats had been removed either for corruption or for suspicion of impropriety. Kim also fired at least a dozen right-wing generals loyal to former hardline President Chun Doo Hwan, and weakened the surveillance powers of the internal security units.

...and Japan

In Japan, the post-War political order that had presided over perhaps the most spectacular industrial expansion in world history was shunted aside in favor of a potentially more egalitarian, honest and responsive arrangement. In the past five years, a series of corruption scandals had confirmed what everyone had known for decades: that the conservative, staunchly anti-Communist Liberal Democratic Party (LDP), which had ruled continuously since being formed with American backing in 1955, maintained illicit connections with big businesses and the *yakuza*, or mafia. For years citizens accepted these links because the government continuously provided a strong economy. The main opposition, the left-wing, pro-North Korea Japan Socialist Party (JSP), hardly provided a credible alternative. Moreover, in rural areas a farmer could always count on his LDP MP to have the road into town repaved, or to brighten his daughter's wedding with a surreptitious envelop of cash.

However, many were shocked at the enormity of the recent scandals. Moreover, after the Cold War ended the LDP could no longer win votes by warning that the country faced a Communist threat. Suddenly, the government's protectionism, bid-rigging and lavish public works spending in the countryside, all favoring its rural stronghold at the expense of urban consumers, came under harsher scrutiny. A younger generation of politicians in the ruling party also favored a more engaged international role abroad, but as with other changes, this could only be accomplished through greater public debate rather than the backroom politics favored by the party elders.

The most powerful of these elders, Shin Kanemaru, resigned from parliament in October 1992 after admitting he had accepted an illegal $4 million contribution from the Sagawa parcel delivery company. As head of the ruling party's largest faction, Kanemaru had used his influence to install the previous four prime ministers. Police arrested Kanemaru on tax evasion charges in March 1993, and found in his house a $50 million hoard of cash, gold bars and securities, the spoils of his connections with the construction industry.

Growing public unrest forced Prime Minister Kiichi Miyazawa to promise an electoral reform package by June. However, his plan to replace the Diet's multiple-seat constituencies, which had fostered lavish spending and corruption by forcing candidates of the same party to compete against each other in the same district, with single-seat constituencies, would have sharply cut the opposition's representation. Miyazawa and his allies hoped to trap the opposition into either accepting the "reforms" or being tainted as anti-reform if they rejected them. The plan backfired spectacularly as fifty-five pro-reform LDP MPs joined the opposition in an historic no-confidence motion in June, bringing Miyazawa's government down and forcing fresh elections.

In pre-election scare tactics, LDP elders warned that Japanese that bringing a fractious multiparty government to power would jeopardize the country's economic and social stability. At the 18 July elections the LDP took a 223-seat plurality in the 501-seat Diet, reflecting its sheer size relative to the new reform parties and the loyalty of its rural voters. However, on 4 August a seven-party coalition of the JSP and several conservative and centrist parties, three of which LDP dissidents formed prior to the election, united to elect Morihiro Hosokawa as prime minister, breaking the LDP's streak of naming nineteen straight prime ministers and smashing its hopes of forming a minority government.

In November the lower house of parliament passed a landmark reform package that scrapped the multiple-seat system and outlawed campaign contributions to individual candidates. However, in the upper house the LDP and several JSP dissidents combined to block the legislation, fearing a loss of seats under the new system, forcing Hosokawa to extend the parliamentary session until late January 1994.

The events in Japan have not been lost on Taiwan's Koumintang (KMT), which has been in power since the Communist takeover on the mainland in 1949. There is a real possibility that the democratic reforms President Lee Teng-hui has initiated since 1988 will allow for the party's ouster in the 1995 parliamentary elections. In August the KMT suffered its first serious fissure in four decades when six reform-oriented MPs quit to form the New Party. KMT stalwarts undoubtedly know that Japan's Hosokawa had pulled a similar move in forming the Japan New Party in May 1992, slightly more than a year before the LDP's downfall.

Among democracies, the Philippines is "The Sick Man of Asia," with some 70 percent of its citizens impoverished. The euphoria following the February 1986 "People's Power" revolution that ousted longtime strongman Ferdinand Marcos in favor of Corazon Aquino has long given way to the gloomy reality that, even without Marcos, the Philippines is still a semi-feudal country dominated by a political elite that protects its oligarchical business interests with private armies, and wracked by three separate insurgencies as well as endemic corruption.

In 1993 President Fidel Ramos, who succeeded Aquino in June 1992 in the country's first peaceful transition of power in twenty-seven years, continued tentative peace negotiations with the Communist New People's Army (NPA), the separatist Muslim Moro National Liberation Front on southern Mindanao Island, and the right-wing elements in the military that had launched seven coup attempts against Aquino.

U.N. experiment: Cambodia

Cambodia has taken a sharply different path towards democracy than other Asian nations. Rather than a slow evolution, the country became a laboratory experiment for the United Nations' ability to stabilize a country and hold free elections. An October 1991 accord ended the civil war between the Communist government and three guerrilla groups. But the Khmer Rouge, responsible for more than one million deaths during its 1975-78 rule, reneged and repeatedly attacked government troops, ethnic Vietnamese, and U.N. soldiers and civilians. Meanwhile, in early 1993 government agents killed dozens of workers and candidates of Prince Norodom Ranariddh's FUNCINPEC party.

The country braced for a major Khmer Rouge offensive during the May election, but none came. In the event, FUNCINPEC won a narrow majority of the seats, and in September formed a unity government with the former Communists. A new constitution guaranteed basic rights and returned revered "father figure" Norodom Sihanouk to the throne, thirty-eight years after he had abdicated to play a greater role in politics.

The U.N. completed its withdrawal in November, leaving the country free of foreign influences for the first time since the early 1960s. Significant problems remain. The Khmer Rouge still controls 15 percent of the country and is negotiating for a role in the new government. Moreover, the country lacks the structures of civil society, including established trade unions; vibrant, independent newspapers; and religious and voluntary organizations that are needed for expanding and preserving democracy.

The British colony of Hong Kong is also taking a unique route to democracy, one that puts it on the front line in the authoritarian vs. democracy issue. Hong Kong is an anomaly— a free but largely undemocratic place. The British appoint the governor, and only twenty of the sixty seats in the Legislative Council (Legco) are directly elected, yet citizens enjoy all fundamental freedoms. In 1992 new governor Christopher Patten attempted to give the colony a firmer democratic grounding before China reasserts control in 1997 by modestly expanding the franchise for Legco's forty indirectly elected seats, but Beijing immediately rejected Patten's proposals.

In 1993 Britain and China failed to reach a compromise over the proposals, and by year's end London appeared ready to give Patten a formal go-ahead to introduce the reforms unilaterally. But Patten will first need Legco's approval, which is no certainty given the powerful, conservative business community's overwhelming opposition to anything that would rankle China.

India, Pakistan and Bangladesh: Selfishness and greed

On the Asian subcontinent, the welfare of the billion-plus citizens of India, Pakistan and Bangladesh has been subjugated to the selfishness, greed and shortsightedness of their leaders. In India, several years of rising fundamentalism climaxed in December 1992 in the northern town of Ayodhya when 200,000 Hindu fundamentalists demolished a sixteenth century mosque built on a holy Hindu site.

In January 1993 the frenzy came to Bombay, a city long-admired for its avant-garde cultural scene and ethnic tolerance. Nine days of anti-Muslim pogroms left 600 people dead and 2,000 injured. The killings, and the accompanying arson and looting of Muslim homes and businesses, were organized by Hindu gangs and sanctioned by the Bombay police. A wave of bombings hit the city in March, possibly organized by underworld Muslim gangs.

How did the secularism championed at independence in 1947, and enshrined in the 1950 constitution, erode so drastically? In part because the Congress Party, which has ruled almost continuously since independence, has lost its moral legitimacy and sense of national purpose. The successors of Mohandas Ghandi and Jawaharlal Nehru have been unable or unwilling to articulate a vision of a religiously tolerant, multiethnic nation, and the party is hopelessly plagued by corruption. Hindu fundamentalist leaders meanwhile attract converts by citing a "threat" from Sikh extremists in Punjab and Muslim separatists in Kashmir.

New fault lines appeared at elections in November for the four northern state assemblies that the federal government had dissolved following the Ayodhya demolition. All four had been held by the Hindu-fundamentalist Bharatiya Janata Party (BJP), and the voting shaped up as a critical test of the funadmentalist group's appeal. Many expected a BJP sweep, but in the event the party took control of just one state, while the Congress Party took two. But in Uttar Pradesh, India's most populous state, two small regional parties hold the balance of power, a clear setback to both the Congress Party and the BJP. These two smaller parties attracted a new alliance of poor lower-class Hindus and Muslims who feel neglected and alienated by the major parties.

Bhutto's return

Benazir Bhutto returned to power in Pakistan in October, capping a wild political year. The country's political instability since the repeal of martial law in 1985 stems from excessive powers the Eighth Amendment grants to the indirectly elected president, including the right to dismiss the prime minister. In April President Ghulam Ishaq Khan sacked Prime Minister Nawaz Sharif, the third time in five years a president has done so. In May, in a encouraging show of judicial independence, the Supreme Court invalidated the dismissal and allowed Sharif to returned to office. In July, Army chief Abdul Waheed Kakar brokered a compromise under which both Sharif and Khan resigned, paving the way for fresh elections.

Few Pakistanis had heard of Moeen Qureshi, a former World Bank official, when he was appointed as caretaker prime minister until the elections. In less than three months, he had singlehandedly demonstrated that the main obstacle to Pakistan's economic development came from a lack of political resolve. Beholden to no one, Qureshi introduced an agricultural tax, published a list of 5,000 prominent citizens, including Bhutto, who had defaulted on major bank loans, canceled several of Sharif's pork-barrel development projects, devalued the currency, and ordered a crackdown on druglords operating in remote areas. In October the army supervised clean elections in which Bhutto's Pakistan People's Party and its smaller allies took 121 seats in the 217-seat National Assembly, against 72 seats for Sharif's Pakistan Muslim League.

The most far-reaching poverty-eradication, literacy and public health programs in South Asia have been in Sri Lanka, where the government continues to struggle against Tamil separatists fighting for independence in the north and east of the country. The wave of assassinations in recent years peaked on 1 May when a Tamil suicide bomber killed President Ranasinghe Premadasa. As evidence of the country's growing political maturity, Premier D.B. Wijetunge succeeded Premadasa as president, and voters calmly elected provincial councils in late May.

Burma and North Korea: repression rules

Burma and North Korea continue to be the most repressive regimes in Asia. The ruling State Law and Order Restoration Council (SLORC) military junta in Burma held an off-again, on-again "National Convention" throughout 1993 to approve principles for a new constitution. In reality, the junta expected the hand-picked delegates to meekly sign-off on guidelines establishing a permanent leading presence for the military after power is eventually transferred to a civilian government. However, the delegates boldly refused, forcing the junta in September to suspend the convention until early 1994.

North Korea's citizens live in the most tightly controlled country in the world. In 1993 the country refused to allow the International Atomic Energy Agency full access to its secret Yongbyon nuclear complex, the site of its suspected nuclear weapons program, raising fears that the country is indeed pursuing an atomic bomb. In March, North Korea became the first nation to pull out of the Nuclear Non-Proliferation Treaty. By the fall the U.S. hinted it might offer North Korea incentives, such as an end to the annual Team Spirit military exercises with South Korea, in return for cooperation on the inspections.

Future U.S. responses

It is appropriate to note that democracy was not on the agenda at Seattle. Authoritarian countries know that their value to the West is no longer measured by the abstract, theoretical balance-of-power calculations of the Cold War, but by the highly tangible size of their growing markets. Even Australia, long a champion of human rights and egalitarianism, is cautioning the U.S. to be flexible as it faces a February 1994 deadline on whether to revoke Indonesia's preferential tariffs due to the country's poor record on labor rights.

The U.S. has already postponed an investigation into Malaysia's refusal to allow its electronics workers, many of whom work for American-owned companies, to form a national union. And the Clinton administration faces a June 1994 deadline for renewing China's Most Favored Nation trade status, which it has conditioned on improvements in the country's human rights situation. In Seattle, however, Chinese spokesman Wu Jianmin opined that "East and West have different conceptions of human rights," underscoring the lack of common ground between the countries.

In the coming years, the Pacific Rim's increasing private sector integration will make decisions regarding Asian trade more numerous, requiring the U.S. and other democracies to articulate a sensible, realistic strategy balancing economic needs and moral imperatives. ▬

Charles Graybow is a consultant at Freedom House.

European Union—
Now What?

Roger Kaplan

On New Year's Day 1993 the European Single Market went into effect, achieving the promise of economic union among the twelve-nation Economic Community. Thus ended a chapter in European history, one that began in 1950 when Frenchmen Robert Schuman and Jean Monnet declared that cooperation must exist on the ground before it could be achieved politically.

And on 1 November, All Saints' Day, the European Community, still referred to by many as the "European Economic Community" or the "Common Market," officially became the European Union (EU). Thus began, on a Christian holiday founded in sorrow but touched by hope, a new chapter in European history.

Many were too hardup to notice. The looming failure of EuroDisney, a two-year old theme and amusement park that had been launched on a wave of optimism about the internationalization of business and culture, the collapse of the Renault-Volvo merger, and the continuing layoffs in such basic industries as steel and textiles, seemed an apt symbol of the times, and if the point needed stressing, it was done by German Chancellor Helmut Kohl, who rebuked his countrymen for abandoning their characteristic work ethic: "Germany is not an amusement park," he said. But attempts at forging new deals among the "social partners," usually stressing more work and fewer benefits, were angrily rejected by workers in Belgium, Spain and France, and had mixed success in Italy and Germany. The Swiss, Norwegians, Swedes, Finns, and even the Austrians (striving for respectability) doubted whether their governments, all of which had applications pending or under review to join the EU, had the right idea. In the southern countries, Italy and Spain in particular but France as well and Greece more ambiguously, voters disgusted with the corruption rotting away their democratic polities threw the rascals out. Looming over this odd mix of unity and rancor was the biggest issue of all: the Yugoslav war—and the failure of Europe, of the European Union, to do anything about it.

The new Union, as a political concept, was not under strain, partly because the British and the Danes—along with currency speculators—convinced the Europeanists that Europe, institutionally, politically and economically is not an all-or-nothing proposition: it can advance at different speeds, with individual states deciding when to participate fully in joint economic or security institutions. The EU's difficulties were inherent in the member states themselves, problems stemming from the exhaustion of the welfare state in recessionary times, the weakening of civic and family values, and the frustrations of being—to simplify only slightly—the world's most prosperous region and politically weakest entity. Throughout the fall European governments dealt with strikes that were motivated more by insecurity about existing employment and benefits than by demands for better deals. These, as well as the continuing political violence in Northern Ireland, Spain and Italy, horrifying but limited, reminded Europeans that the good society was still in the making. The wars in the Balkans and the Caucassus, and massacres, mayhem and armed subversion in former African possessions were like a bitter reproach to the European wish, expressed in everything from protectionist stances in successfully completed GATT negotiations (a victory for EU cohesiveness) to recurrences of anti-Americanism and Japanophobia, to be left alone in the little corner from which they once ruled the world.

Thus, even as the Single Market gave Europeans the unified economic space promised since the 1957 Treaty of Rome, they sought protection from Japanese cars, American movies, and Polish produce. Interestingly enough, they were unable, or unwilling, to protect their currencies from market fluctuations, which battered the French, Swedish, Spanish, Italian, Portuguese and British currencies to the point where the SME (or ERM, the mechanism for keeping currencies, inflation rates, and interest rates closely in line) was several times pronounced dead (it lives, just). They revised their constitutions to restrict asylum seekers and ordinary migrants from points east and south, in keeping with the EU Treaty's single border.

Trade union members have been waiting, and waiting some more, for tangible benefits of the "social chapter" which the moderate Left, notably French President François Mitterrand and European Commission President Jacques Delors, have been describing, since they proposed it ten years ago, as the indispensable counterweight to the liberalized market which they, men of the Left, put in place in the late 80s.

Criticism of neo-laissez-fairism, which European leaders felt they had no choice but to embrace in order to keep up with the U.S. and Japan, is by no means confined to the labor movement and its allies on the social democratic and socialist Left. There is a deep conservative tradition in Europe which, also, denounces the individualistic ethic, which they delight in referring to by such epithets as "casino" or "savage" capitalism or (still) "Reagano-Thatcherite ultraliberalism," or more simply, the "jungle." Without the Soviet threat, this conservative tradition is more readily able to break with its erstwhile classical liberal allies. This explains (in part) the strains in the conservative-liberal coalition (CDU-FDP) in Germany, or the angry call by the conservative president of the French National Assembly, Philippe Seguin, to resist the "social Munich" caused by liberal monetary policies (meaning tight money and a strong currency) designed to keep European currencies on track toward convergence.

Ironically indeed, "ultraliberalism" did not make good politics in the year of the Single Market. France's new conservative prime minister, Edouard Balladur, extolled the role of the (albeit leaner) state. John Major's difficulties stem in part from his need to balance the claims of the Thatcherite legacy and those of the Tory state-interventionists like Michael Heseltine (who led the revolt against Thatcher in 1992).

The Europeans' sense of their countries and their new Union as morally hollow stems in part from being out of sorts, out of purpose, and out of cash. But no one doubted, either, that in the one large moral enterprise that was available for the immediate taking, namely to intervene in the Yugoslav wars, Europe failed: not for lack of knowledge, and probably not for lack of public indignation and will, but for lack of political will.

Toward Union

There had been some close calls on the way to Union, with the French approving the Maastricht Treaty in a September 1992 referendum by the narrowest of margins, and the Danes approving it, in a May referendum, only after rejecting it in 1992. In Great Britain's House of Commons the Treaty was approved 292-112 in May, but only after the "Eurosceptics" nearly undercut John Major's government. And it was not until October that the German constitutional court decided the Treaty did not contradict that country's Basic Law.

Winning is what counts, but most Europeanists, not to mention their more enlightened detractors, knew that in many ways Maastricht was already behind the curve. The unreadable Treaty of Union is not a document to which anyone would spontaneously swear allegiance. "It is a bad treaty," said former German Chancellor—and unimpeachable Europeanist—Helmut Schmidt, "in which the fundamental issues are mixed up with less important ones." For Europeanism to remain credible, its champions know they need to look good, and fast. But the mud of political and economic stagnation was thick in Europe in 1993, and despite acts of heroism—notably in Italy, where a brave band led a popular revolt against political-gangster corruption—it was not the most inspiring year on record.

The Maastricht Treaty confers "European citizenship" on citizens of member states, which should, by and by, allow Italian residents of London, for example, to stand in local, and eventually national, elections. This pleased the Left but displeased the Right. Actually, in many countries the cleavage was less between Left and Right than between "nationals" and "Europeanists." But both of these schools included unnatural allies united only in their dislike of liberal centrists like German Chancellor Helmut Kohl and Spanish Prime Minister Felipe Gonzalez, who best represent the European project in its Maastricht Treaty phase. Both on the extreme-liberal Right (what American calls libertarianism) and on the radical Left (which today has little foothold in the mainstream socialist parties, including Italy's ex-Communist Democratic Party of the Left, PDS), the new EU is viewed favoring big business and labor. Yet this is in line with the social democratic civilization, based on private enterprise and statist redistribution, which produced nearly fifty years of peace and prosperity. The question is whether the model is spent and the union without a fresh purpose.

To be sure, there is the matter of personalities. Men like Kohl, *a fortiori* François Mitterrand and Jacques Delors, are haunted by memories of Europe's wars. A younger leadership was emerging in 1993, represented by many members of the shadow cabinet of British Labour Party leader John Smith, or by the young (born 1947) leader of the German SPD, Rudolph Scharping. A former leader of the Jusos (young Socialists) and the minister-president of Rhine-Palatinate (Kohl's job in the 70s), Scharping takes Europe for granted, but by the same token cannot be expected to expend great enthusiasms on it. On the other hand, Gro Harlem Brundtland, whose Labor party won (again) in Norway, wants her country to join, as does her liberal-conservative neighbor in Sweden, Carl Bildt. The Danish referendum, in which all the parties, trade unions, media, and business associations urged a "yes," reflected the difference between elites and public opinion in Scandanavia. The Swiss are generally pro-Europe at this point in opinion surveys, but they rejected membership in the EEE[1] in a referendum. Some of this lessening of the Eurosteam is doubtless sensible, reflecting a pragmatic approach to a still uncertain future. Thus even as German Chancellor Helmut Kohl used "new chapter" rhetoric to greet the day, British Prime Minister John Major—who belongs to Scharping's generation—warned against the "politics of illusion" that the Euro-enthusiasts fostered.

Power to whom?

The Treaty of Union goes beyond free trade zonism to prepare the way for full monetary union and a single defense and foreign policy. Countries, notably Great Britain and Denmark, that do not like this do not have to participate. The principle of a Europe moving at several gears is accepted, though it remains to be seen how this will work out in the growing body of European law, which takes precedence over national law, so long as it does not contradict national constitutions: an ambiguity that will take years to work out, and much lawyering. Josef Joffe of the *Süddeutsche Zeitung* says the Court maintained the primacy of national parliaments over the European Parliament.

This institution, located at Strasbourg and directly elected since 1979, saw its powers enhanced under the Treaty, notably in that it can veto decisions of the Council of Ministers (the Union's executive, of which the Commission is the arm). But, absent some precedents, it is unclear how this is going to work out, or whether this will result in more democratic governance, as its partisans claim. There is a left-wing current of anti-Maastrichism which says the Treaty is technocratic and anti-democratic and favors reinforcing the Parliament even more. But there is also a current which dislikes the idea of one more level of government, and a remote one at that.

Although Europe, the project, and the much-maligned Eurocrats in Brussels, got a good pounding between the signing of the Treaty in February 1992 and its final ratification in the fall of 1993, politicians in power took most of the heat for the unemployment crisis. Liberal economists blame the high costs of labor, including the high costs of laying off workers. Voters blame it on incumbents.

Shocks at the polls

The first shock at the polls came in France in March. The governing Socialists knew they were in trouble. They had called for a yes on the Maastricht Treaty, which President Mitterrand had submitted to referendum, the previous September, and they very nearly lost it. The party split on the issue, with the "republicans" breaking ranks. Though of course all socialists consider themselves to be in the republican tradition, the term increasingly is appropriated by the heirs of the Jacobin line, centralizing and statist, who oppose the more liberal approach of new party-leader Michel Rocard. The Left's ostensible constituency, salaried workers, voted against Maastricht. But the Socialists were unprepared for the tidal wave that hit them in March. The new Assembly contained 57 Socialists, 12 independent Lefts, 24 Communists, and 460 liberal-conservatives.

Neither British Prime Minister John Major nor German Chancellor Helmut Kohl had to face the voters. Major, despite a surge in the British economy after a prolonged recession, had more than enough trouble with the "Thatcherites" in his Tory party, and had to keep an eye on the rising stars of the new Labour party leadership, such as John Smith, John Prescott and Gordon Brown.

Helmut Kohl often appeared to be in trouble, with the CDU losing local elections steadily to the SPD and facing the very real, if still improbable, possibility of national defeat in 1994. Kohl, who had made himself the champion of rapid reunification after the fall of the Berlin Wall, was rebuffed in the eastern Land of Brandenburg, which was carried by the ex-Communist candidate in December. Kohl also had to contend with a right-wing, led by the Bavarian CSU leader Edward Steubel, who called for less Europe and more Germany. The chancellor supported a Saxon, Steffen Heitmann, for the presidency, a post that in Germany is important for the moral authority that it represents. Outgoing president Richard von Weizsaecker is one of the most respected men in Germany and has spoken out forcefully against the neo-Nazi violence.

But Heitmann, chosen by Kohl as a symbol of reconciliation between eastern and western Lander, gave the impression that he believes Germans should stop apologizing for their past, a sentiment Germans do not expect of the president of the Bundesrepublik. Heitmann's supporters said it was a typical case of national hypocrisy, but the Saxon leader withdrew. Kohl is likely to nominate another easterner, Richard Schroder, but he will have to contend with the Social Democrat candidate, Johannes Rau (minister-president of North Rhine-Westphalia), as well as the Free Democrat spoiler, Hildegard Hamm-Bruchher.

In Spain, Prime Minister Felipe Gonzalez had a close call in June elections, and his PSOE found itself without an absolute majority in the Cortes for the first time since 1982. The Socialists have been hurt by kickback scandals, and Gonzalez played his personal popularity to the hilt to carry the elections. He also placed the top anti-corruption prosecutor, Jose Garzon, high on his party list, to show that bad apples did not reflect institutional rot. His new government, formed with Catalan and Basque votes but not ministerial participation, was dominated by Socialist "renovators" (liberals).

Europe, however, was not an issue, since there is a broad pro-European consensus in Spain. This is partly because Europe represents the opening to the world—and to freedom—that was not possible during the Francoist decades, but it is also because Spain, like Portugal (and Ireland, southern Italy, and Greece), benefits handsomely from the EU's development programs, known as the structural funds and the new (since Maastricht) cohesion funds. Whether these work better than the schemes to "develop" Third World countries on which they are modeled has not yet been proven, but they are appreciated in the places for which they are designed, such as Andalusia, Greece, Ireland, and the eastern German Lander.[2]

European welfare and subsidies are easily criticized. As much as 15 percent of the EC budget may be embezzled. No one is sure. Over half of the EC budget goes to agriculture (5 percent of west Europe's population), and it is simply impossible to get at the bottom of agricultural fraud, let alone do anything about it.

To these criticisms the Europeanists reply that what is needed is more Europe, not less. A bureaucracy responsible to a strengthened executive and a stronger Parliament, with help from an effective Europolice organization, can attack fraud and drug trafficking. Raymond Barre, the former French prime minister, believes that Poland and other central European countries should be brought in without delay, and the countries of the EFTA (Norway, Sweden, Finland, Austria, Switzerland) as soon as they want to. Barre argues that even the countries of eastern Europe should be brought in as soon as possible, that is to say as soon as they demonstrate their active (not rhetorical) commitment to democracy, human rights, free circulation of people, money and goods.

Europe, superficially, does not look depressed. Cities are clean, high-speed trains run on time, crime is low by American standards, free health care is available. But when you get beyond the spic-and-span downtowns you find enough misery to understand that comparisons with the 30s are not out of line. The crucial difference is the social safety net. But this is straining under the impact of prolonged unemployment combined with tears in the social fabric due to weaker family structures, less disciplined educational system, drugs and, according to some, diminished church attendance.

There are about 18 million unemployed in the EU and there may be 20 million by the end of 1994.[3] Carlos Ferrer Salat, chairman of UNICE (the European employers' federation), says: "Europe has the most costly and rigid labour market in the world, and Spain"—he is from Barcelona—"has the most costly and rigid market in Europe."

Spain has an official unemployment level of 20 percent (triple the official U.S. rate and ten times the official Pacific rim rate) but more people seem to be working there than in France, which has about 12 percent. In less mature welfare states, people learn to make do with mixes of official benefits and unofficial jobs. At any rate, the debate on "managing work" spread across Europe in 1993. Its outcome may influence European competitiveness (and thereby its ability to sustain acceptable levels of prosperity) in the years ahead.

The work debate, though it focuses for rhetorical convenience on working time is, more deeply, a debate about the relationship between productivity and society. In France, Michel Rocard says you must work less to produce more jobs, but with less income, at least until productivity increases. The liberals say there is no need to have national, let alone European, working-time regulations; what is needed is more flexibility. The Germans are beginning large-scale experiments in working-time modifications, notably at Volkswagen, where a four-day week was instituted in October, with 10 percent pay-cuts (management had asked for 20 percent) and a day for job retraining.

VW represented the strength of the German social pact, but Kohl warned that the country is living beyond its means. Construction workers demonstrated against reductions in their "bad weather" benefits. They are compensated when the weather keeps them off the job, but under new proposed rules this benefit would apply only to the winter months.

Concerned about the viability of their social democracies, the Europeans knew they had to maintain some sort of global credibility. The EU calls for a single foreign and security policy, and one of the first things it did was to offer Serbia a relaxation of the U.N.-imposed sanctions if it eased up (or persuaded the Bosnian Serbs to ease up) on territorial claims in Bosnia. Many observers felt this was a fitting way to end a year in which the putative new superpower had let a slaughter take place under its figurative nose, but here again, the Europeanists could plead that something could have been done had there been "more" Europe. Until the EU came into being, they say, Europe, as a political entity, had no competence in the matter. And did the "unilateralists" offer anything better? The champions of "NATO's new missions"? The globalists of the U.N.?

Keeping it safe for natives

The EU is also supposed to organize a common internal security policy. In practice this means, in the short term, getting control of Europe's borders. As in other matters, this produced a cleavage between the "little Europe" protectionists and the "new superpower" visionaries. The best way to keep out waves of huddled masses, the latter say, is to help them help themselves. But the needs are great and the demands never-ending. In North Africa, half the population is under thirty and unemployed, and fanatics are bidding for power. Across much of eastern Europe, misery and war stalk the lands.

However, the immigration debate also touches upon the issue of what it means to be a Frenchman, a German, a Dane—or a European. To many little-Europe men, particularly on the Left and among the Green parties, nationalism is old hat when not mischievous. Multicultural, multiethnic societies are better. In Germany, the mainstreams of the CDU and the SPD put together legislation both to restrict immigration and facilitate the acquisition of citizenship. The idea now is to make it possible for those who do get in to become integrated, rather than create non-German communities living apart from the rest of society.

Indeed, integration is very much on the agenda in France as well, after several years during which multiculturalism ("the right to be different") was fashionable. The French also have tightened immigration rules and have made the acquisition of citizenship more difficult, in order to distinguish between applicants who want to be French and those who need a place to stay.

On the surface, this stiffening of the national idea, and of notions of civic responsibility that accompany it, runs counter to the pan-Europeanism of the pro-Maastricht Euroenthusiasts. In the past several years, and particularly this past year as European nations had to get their laws in harmony with the European directives that render the Single Act operational, there was a great deal of "We are Europeans" rhetoric, complete with the Ode to Joy as anthem. A reaction was inevitable.

Italy's citizen revolt

One positive aspect of the inward turn has been to take a fresh look at the corrupt practices that to some degree could be tolerated in expansive years but that became intolerable in lean ones. Particularly in the Latin countries, judges (state prosecutors) went after politicians, businessmen and gangsters engaged in countless variations of the basic kickback. In Italy the process has been close to revolutionary. The Christian Democratic and Socialist Parties have been all but wiped out, as leaders up to and including Christian Democrat Giulio Andreotti (DC), seven times prime minister, under investigation for links with the mafia, and the country's longest-serving prime minister, socialist Bettino Craxi (PSI), investigated for municipal corruption in Milan, lost their credibility. President Oscar Luigi Scalfaro attacked politicians' attempts to vote themselves an amnesty, and Pope John Paul II went to Sicily to attack the mafia. At least 3,000 people were in jail or under arrest by mid-1993, with even great names of Italian business like Carlo de Benedetti and Raul Gardini—who committed suicide—implicated in the *mani puli* (clean hands) investigations.

The citizens' revolt in Italy, with the prosecutors in the vanguard, demonstrated that "republican virtue" and "responsibilities of citizenship" at some point have to go from talk to action. *Arrestateli tutti* (arrest them all) was the slogan, showing the citizens getting in step behind the marshals in a country supposedly too blasé for virtue. But it was not just a matter of confounding the cliches. Getting behind the marshals could mean getting killed, and the marshals themselves, notably the courageous anti-mafia judges, often paid with their lives, as did Giovanni Falcone and Paolo Borsalino, both murdered in 1992. Leoluca Orlando, the successful anti-mafia, anti corruption mayoral candidate in Palermo, Sicily, was frequently in hiding.

Thoughtful observers doubt the war against the mafia can be won in a decisive sense. But "the octopus" can be weakened by repeated blows at its leadership, its markets, and at the political-business elites with which it does business. In this regard the capture of Salvatore "Toto" Riina, the boss of all bosses, in Palermo, in January, was of great symbolic, as well as substantial, importance. Riina is suspected of having ordered the Falcone assassination as well as the murder, ten years ago, of the *carabinierri* general Carlo Alberto Dalla Chiesa (who had dismantled the terrorist Red Brigades). Both men's wives were murdered at their sides, lending some bitter piquancy to Riina's family-values poses in the courtroom.

Already in 1992, the state had sent 7,000 soldiers to Sicily, passed tough anti-Mafia laws and intensified the *pentiti* (informer-protection) program, often in cooperation with U.S. law-enforcement. The most famous informer, Tommaso Buscetta, claims Craxi took

$29 million in bribes in Milan and says Andreotti himself was the mafia's top inside fixer in Rome. It is difficult to overemphasize the heroism of Italian law-enforcement in this deadly game because, as terrorist bombings showed, there is absolutely no safety from the mafia, no matter how high you are. When Andreotti said he feared for his life (implicitly suggesting that he did indeed know certain things about the mafia-state links), no one laughed.

Italian voters, in a stunning April referendum, signaled they had enough of a system in which the spoils and patronage had come to eclipse governance almost entirely. The vote, with a 77 percent turnout, represented "a shocking indictment of the political class and the political system that have controlled Italy for almost half a century," observed the *Economist*'s John Andrews.

In the November municipal elections, one of the biggest landslides in western Europe in living memory, the traditional parties were beaten, with the important exception of the ex-Communists, now called the Democratic Party of the Left, which openly proclaimed its allegiance to the north-European social-democratic values. (At Strasbourg they sit on the democratic left benches, unlike the French comrades.) The ex-PCI had not been implicated in municipal corruption as much as the other parties (though they ran many cities and some observors claim they played the system just like the others), and of course they had never belonged to the ruling coalitions at the national level, the *partitocracia*. Moreover, the DC could no longer wave the anti-Communist, anti-Soviet flag, as they had done for fifty years. Indeed, evidence that the Cold War was no longer a factor in Italian politics was evident in the strong showing of the MSI (neo-fascists) in Naples and their photogenic standard bearer, Alessandra Mussolini. (She lost the runoff to the PDS candidate.)

The *partitocracia* remains in power at the national level, but with the government of Carlo Azeglio Ciampi (who left the Bank of Italy in May) essentially in a caretaker role. The old-order parties, overwhelmed by revelations about past abuses both venal and political, are doing their best to limit the scope of political and financial reform. However, Ciampi has exploited Italy's precarious position, and the repeated attacks on the lira, to rally a consensus for a tough budget package based on a tax hike and spending cuts that would keep the public sector deficit below 9 percent of gross domestic product. The bets were that he would get the budget passed by the end of the year (as required by law) and keep to the political calendar which calls for a new parliament to be elected, with new rules and new constituency boundaries, in March 1994.

Whether this means Italy will become politically polarized remains to be seen; but neither the MSI, which has never disowned its Mussolinian heritage, nor the PDS, which has broken with the Stalinist past, appears to be be tempted by anti-democratic solutions. Arguably more troublesome for the country's political future is the fact that Italy remains two distinct countries, economically and otherwise. This may not be enough reason to break up this newcomer among European nation-states, as the Northern League's Umberto Bossi would like, but it underscores the political challenge faced by Italy's reforming patriots. These socio-economic gaps underscore the limits of integration-via-economics. There seems to come a point where a rising tide does not carry all boats, it leaves some boats stranded. At this point, politics must take over.

The politics of leadership or the politics of self-interest? In the last days of the year, the French government showed its regard for European laws and treaties by releasing Iranian terrorists over the protests of Swiss prosecutors who wanted to try them for murder. Then

France got in the way of President Clinton's offer to send NATO to the rescue in Bosnia. Thus Europe, in 1994, had a big agenda. ▄▄

Notes

1 - The EEE, or EEA, for European Economic Area, is the coordinating body of the EC and the EFTA.

2 - The cohesion funds are supposed to go to regions where income is less than 75 percent of the EU average, but no government can resist this sort of pork so they make deals whereby "poor" areas that are in fact very close to average get pieces of the action as well.

3 - Eurostat, the EC's (now EU's) raw research arm, said the unemployment level in June was 11.5 percent, about 17 million, and rising, compared to "only" 8.4 percent in 1990.

Roger Kaplan is editor of Freedom Review.

Former Soviet Union: Ballots, Bullets and Barricades

Paige Sullivan

In 1993, democratic institution-building took some hard knocks in the former Soviet Union (FSU). Presidents assumed extraordinary powers and adopted emergency anti-crisis plans in almost every former republic. Nationalist and leftist extremist groups (inside and outside of parliaments) called for marches, rallies and even armed opposition to the Yeltsin government. The Caucasus remained mired in civil war. Moldova remained preoccupied with its clash with Russia over the Transdniester. The mafia, underpaid policemen and rogue armies all inflicted damage on the delicate democratic structures trying to take root in the second year of post-Communist evolution in Soviet successor states.

The one bright spot to emerge in a year of much chaos and bloodshed was the recognition that things could not keep going as they were and that early parliamentary elections would be necessary in a number of the new states. There seemed to be a recognition that younger, more professional politicians needed a chance to show what they could do. So, by year's end, three of the former republics—Russia, Ukraine and Kazakhstan—were making frantic and hasty preparations for elections to the Parliament and local governing bodies between December and the spring of 1994, almost two years in advance of legislated terms.

However, in the fragile states of the FSU, most people are too busy eking out a meager existence and too resentful of the poverty and chaos they see around them every day to think about democratic ideals, civic responsibilities, the fine points of market economics, or local politics. The average Russian today spends about 75 percent of his subsistence wages on food. Many factories on the brink of bankruptcy pay far below the minimum subsistence level ($10), which is just enough for one person to eat for a month. Rents in state-owned apartments are almost nothing, but the plumbing smells and buildings are crumbling.

These societies are bereft of the historical experience and civic traditions necessary to make a smooth and relatively harmonious transition to democratic norms. There will be little substance to democracy until living standards and opportunities are raised, mafia rings and crime brought under control, education at grass-roots levels expanded and overhauled.

Russia: authoritarianism shows its hand

Although the price in terms of human rights and civil liberties was dear, President Boris Yeltsin took Russia out of the hands of the parliament and into his own control in the second half of the year. On 21 September 1993, in direct violation of the Constitution of the Russian Federation and the Law on the Presidency passed in summer 1991, Yeltsin introduced direct presidential rule in Russia by dissolving both the Russian Congress of People's

Deputies and the Russian Parliament (Supreme Soviet). In the aftermath of Yeltsin's action, on 3-4 October, a small parliamentary group led by former Vice President Aleksander Rutskoi and Chairman of the Supreme Soviet, Ruslan Khosbulatov, with their neo-Bolshevik supporters waving the hammer and sickle in the streets, kindled an armed rebellion which ended in the deaths of over 100 innocent people.

Following this tragedy, which might have ended in civil war had it not been for the Russian Army's belated intervention on Yeltsin's side with an attack on the parliament building, the president issued a long list of what he called "emergency" authoritarian limitations on democratic freedoms in Russia: 1) he closed and banned several opposition publications (some Communist, some nationalist); 2) reinstituted government censorship; 3) restricted by decree what candidates for the 12 December parliamentary elections could say on government-subsidized air time about the government-drafted constitution that was to be subjected to referendum on the same day; 4) decreed the government's right to amend the new draft constitution at any time prior to the referendum; 5) banned several political parties that had taken part in the October upheaval from contesting seats in the new parliament; 6) put local soviets (governing councils) in disloyal power centers under control of his personally appointed administrators.

In Yeltsin's mind these illegal and undemocratic actions were justified and necessary to bring order to the Russian state and to facilitate new parliamentary and presidential elections and the adoption of a constitution to replace the Soviet-era constitution (1978) which has been in force since Russia declared independence in 1991. Part of Yeltsin's reaction was consistent with a Russian tradition of strong, cruel figures assuming an almost parental authoritarian control over the people. Yeltsin was also probably expressing his own insecurities after a long and humiliating clash with conservatives in parliament. The harsh measures he adopted may even have been influenced by the increased clout of the police and the Army following the October upheaval. Whatever the complex reasons, Yeltsin's authoritarian measures had two consequences. First, they paved the way for the emergence of a liberal opposition to the current government, which may become an alternative to the extreme nationalist and leftist oppositionist tradition set so far. Second, they showed Russian citizens and politicians alike how much they have to lose if they slip back into the past.

Leftist-Nationalists: gains and mischief

Riding on a wave of popular discontent and disillusionment, Russian leftist and extremist parties added muscle to their numbers and influence in February by holding a "revival-unification congress" that aimed to combine the forces of the various small Communist parties active since the Constitutional Court's ban on forming Communist party cells in Russia. The draft political statement envisaged the eventual creation of a "federation" of Communist parties of the FSU. The new party's aims were consummately anti-democratic. It rejected the "capitalization" of the economy, called for numerous social "protections," opposed a market in land resources, and favored reintroducing state planning.

The resultant Communist Party of the Russian Federation (CPRF) became Russia's largest party in 1993 (boasting 600,000) and submitted a list of 182 candidates for the 12 December elections. Heading the list were Gennadiy Zyuganov, (Party Chairman, and a founder of the National Salvation Front); Valentin Chikin, (editor of *Sovetskaya Rossiya*); Gennadiy Seleznev, (who was dismissed by Yeltsin in October when *Pravda* was ordered to change its name); and Anatoly Lukyanov, currently standing trial for his role in the 1991 August coup attempt against former Soviet President Mikhail Gorbachev. The CPRF claims that Boris Yeltsin's policies reflect the geopolitical interests of the USA. The CPRF and other Communist parties in Russia also believe that ties between former republics of the USSR must be restored and a great state re-created.

The Communists and their sympathizers were encouraged by an apparent surge in their popularity. Living up to their anti-democratic reputations, five smaller Communist parties of Russia issued a statement on 29 October calling for a campaign of civil disobedience to disrupt the "initiation of elections" on 12 December. However, the elections were held smoothly.

The Russian constitutional contest

In rather simple terms, constitutional issues lay at the root of the inordinately vicious series of clashes between Boris Yeltsin and Ruslan Khosbulatov in 1993. The main issue was how much relative power the constitution should give to the executive and legislative branches. The 12 December elections also included a referendum in which the electorate was asked to accept or reject a constitution drafted by Yeltsin and approved by the leaders of the 88 administrative regions of the Russian Federation (thereby by-passing the congress).

A constitutional assembly (appointed by Yeltsin) was convened following a significant victory for Yeltsin in a 25 April referendum containing four questions covering the President's economic reform policies and early parliamentary and presidential elections. The referendum supported his policies, which he took as a mandate to resolve the constitutional impasse between himself and the Russian parliament.

Several leading members of the parliament, including one of Khasbulatov's deputies, Nikolai Ryabov, as well as the Chairmen of the Council of the Republics and the Council of the Nationalities, supported Yeltsin's proposal to draft a new constitution with a constitutional assembly and wanted to enter into a constructive dialog. But Khasbulatov, surprised and outraged at Yeltsin's victory, ignored the parliamentary support for Yeltsin and chose to continue the confrontation. He convened selected members of almost 2,000 local soviets and drafted a parliamentary version of a new constitution. Ironically, neither the presidential nor the parliamentary version foresaw a single, powerful parliamentary speaker like Khasbulatov.

Yeltsin's proposed constitution provided for such a powerful president that it became a major election issue, creating rifts among the democrats and provoking opposition by several center-right and moderate parties and organizations. Yeltsin's team rushed out 20 million copies of the 100-page document and threatened to ban any candidate who dared to criticize it, calling such criticism "mud-slinging."

The new electoral process

For many, the 12 December Russian parliamentary elections offered the last hope of deliverance from the authoritarianism of Russia's past. Surveys showed that more than a third of the people felt that the elections would determine Russia's fate. People apparently concluded that the new parliament would be more important than the president or the government (although for the president and his supporters the referendum on the draft constitution was even more important than parliamentary elections). The Russian people knew they were getting not only a new cast of characters to make and amend their laws, but new political institutions with a new constitution, a bill of rights, and an entirely new electoral process.

New institutions, defined in a series of presidential decrees issued after Yeltsin's dissolution of Parliament in September, created a new federal structure of power to replace the former Communist system of soviets (councils). This structure consists of a two-house parliamentary body—the Federal Assembly. The upper house, the Council of Federation, has 176 members, two from each of the 88 administrative regions of the Russian Federation. The eighty-ninth region, Chechnya, claimed independence in 1993 and refused to participate in the elections. These deputies represent the interests of their regions, much like the U.S. Senate.

The lower house, the State Duma, has 450 members, half elected from single-candidate districts and half elected through a system of proportional representation in which deputies are chosen from lists provided by participating political parties, in accordance with the proportion of the popular vote won by each party.

The draft constitution stipulated a term of four years for legislators in both houses. An addendum to the constitution however, reduced the terms of those elected in 1993 to two years. Furthermore, deputies to the Council of the Federation will, in future, be appointed by regional governments rather than elected directly.

The electoral process was democratic, but confusing. It involved three ballots, one for the Council of Federation and two separate ballots for the State Duma—one for the federal party lists and one for candidates in certain regional districts. Confusion arose over the ambiguity of the initial legislation, daily clarifications, and the fact that all previous Soviet elections had been of the simple, majoritarian type.

The party line-up

The most popular parties and blocs going into the elections were those led by Gaidar, Yavlinskiy, Zyuganov and Shakrai. Zyuganov and Vladimir Zhirinovsky, leader of the extreme nationalist Liberal Democratic Party (LDP), who gained increased popular recognition during the campaign, represented the intransigent opposition, attracting the votes of Communists and nationalists.

The Russia's Choice bloc (*Vybor Rossii*), led by deputy Prime Minister Yegor Gaidar, represented by far the best known electoral bloc and ideological orientation in Russia today. Although Yeltsin did not personally endorse any one party, his close affinity to the members of his cabinet who helped form the bloc during the election campaign was obvious and the bloc itself nurtured the image of being "the president's party." Russia's Choice united seven movements and organizations, most important of which were Democratic Russia and Russia's Choice movement. Since its creation in October, 1990 Democratic Russia has been the leading liberal democratic force in Russia. This was the movement of the anti-Communist democrats who were swept into power in local and national parliaments in the March 1990 elections and coordinated Yeltsin's campaign for first president of independent Russia.

Unlike most of the other parties and blocs that were formed mainly out of electoral convenience, with little or no grass roots organizations, Russia's Choice had an organization and a well-known program. It strongly supported the president and his constitution. As for Russia's federal structure, the bloc endorsed the president's decision to remove all references of sovereignty for the republics from the new constitution. It regards the separation of autonomous republics as a dangerous threat to the future of the Russian Federation. In foreign policy, Russia's Choice emphasizes the importance of forging neutral alliances with democratic, industrial countries. It also advocates an assertive Russian policy toward the "near abroad," as demonstrated by the U.N. statements of Andrei Kozyrev,

Yeltsin's Foreign Minister and a member of Russia's Choice, in which he has appealed for international recognition of Russia's "sphere of interest" in the other former Soviet republics, with a mandate to intervene whenever there are ethnic conflicts to be quelled.

The Yavlinskiy-Boldyrev-Lukin bloc is led by Grigorii Yavlinskiy, well known for his leading role in drafting the 500-day economic plan in 1990, which was rejected by Mikhail Gorbachev. During the fall of 1991, Yavlinskiy supported the preservation of the Soviet Union, one economic union within the USSR and one currency. He advocated a gradual approach to economic reform and, since 1991, a "regional" approach to economic reform based on his experiences in Nizhniy Novgorod. Yavlinskiy tended to position himself during the electoral campaign as the loyal opposition to Yeltsin's government.

The shocking Russian election results

In spite of the democrats' lead, Westerners and Russians alike were dismayed when the LDP finished with 24 percent of the vote, followed by Russia's Choice (15 percent); the Communist Party (11 percent); Women of Russia (8.7 percent);the Agrarian Party (8 percent) (a conservative ally of the CPRF), the Yavlinsky-Boldyrev-Lukin bloc (7 percent); the Party of Russian Unity and Accord (5.7 percent).

The reformers failed to form a solid bloc with a clear message. Their squabbling confused the voters who were swayed by the siren-songs and promises of the extremists, whose messages—nostalgia for a romanticized past or dreams of a unrealistic future—essentially played on the same escapist chord.

Russia's Choice did better by its individual candidates than by its party lists. As the tally of independent candidates came in on 15 December, Gaidar's bloc emerged as the largest in the new parliament, with 94 seats against 78 for the LDP. Nevertheless, the election results jolted the reformers, and Gaidar called for a broad "anti-fascist" parliamentary coalition.

Several prominent conservatives were elected to the parliament, including one of the leaders of the attempted coup of August 1991, Vasilii Starodubtsev, and one of the coup instigators, the former speaker of the USSR parliament, Anatoly Lukyanov. Aleksandr Nevzorov, anchor man of the ultra-right TV show, "600 Seconds," which had been closed down by the authorities in the aftermath of Yeltsin's showdown with parliament, won a seat in St. Petersburg.

The Communists expected to receive up to 80 seats in the new state Duma. Sidestepping the question of a "red-brown" coalition with the LDP, Zyuganov said on 15 December that his party would cooperate with those who shared its views. As the year ended, such a coalition, and the regression that was likely to follow, was a distinct possibility.

Mitigating the ominous results of the elections was the success for Boris Yeltsin's new constitution, narrowly approved by referendum. Fifty percent of all eligible voters had to vote for the constitution for it to pass. According to Russian journalists, 51 percent of eligible voters went to the polls and 52 percent of those voted for the constitution. (Yeltsin changed the Referendum Law to require only a simple majority of those voting in future referenda.)

The constitution gives the president strong powers, including the dissolution of parliament if it repeatedly rejects his choice for prime minister. Many reformers and Western observers who had criticized the "presidentialism" of the proposed constitution before the referendum remarked on the danger of a very strong executive at a time when ultra-nationalist forces are on the rise. The constitution also contains a fully democratic bill of rights (on the U.S. model), whose effectiveness remains to be tested.

Ukraine: cracks in its democratic underpinnings

Two-and-a-half-years have passed since the proclamation of Ukraine's independence, which was confirmed by over 90 percent of the voters in a nationwide referendum. During that period, the nomenklatura of the former Ukrainian Communist Party, which forms the bulk of the Supreme Council (or parliament) and commands local level governing bodies, has continued to stymie democratization, privatization and the introduction of a free market system on the territory of Ukraine, contributing greatly to the general atmosphere of crisis in 1993.

Two crisis situations swelled to major proportions in Ukraine in 1993—one internal and one external, threatening to erode the country's fragile democratization and state-building process. The first crisis accompanied a devastating economic collapse, which by year's end included 70 percent hyper-inflation per month, massive fuel, medicine and food shortages and high unemployment. Meanwhile, Russia stepped up policies meant to pressure Ukraine and draw it back into its sphere of influence.

Economic woes and political repercussions

Ukraine's economic woes fanned the flames of popular resentment and disillusionment, which fed directly into the goals of the Communist Party of Ukraine (CPU). Adding to the already numerous forces against liberal economic and political reform the CPU held two congresses (one in March and one in June) in the eastern oblast of Donetsk. These attracted the support of 529 delegates from every oblast of Ukraine and Crimea. At the congresses, the Party Secretariat stated its goal to become the legal successor to the former CPU and to register all former CPSU and CPU members in Ukraine before 1 January 1994. As a recruitment device, the CPU added Russophone slogans to its economic populism, benefiting from a strident clash between Ukrainian nationalists who oppose economic integration with Russia and easterners who are calling for such integration. (Economic integration with Russia, however, is unlikely to be the salvation of the Ukrainian economy, as Leonid Kravchuk reminded the leftist deputies in September.)

Most Russians do not consider Ukraine a legal entity, much less a sovereign state. Essentially, it was this unrelenting refusal by Russia to grant Ukraine political legitimacy which stymied the resolution of a long list of political, social and military issues between the two countries in 1993 and even exacerbated tensions. Ukrainian nationalists, pointing to provocative Russian actions such as the congressional resolution claiming ownership of Crimea, stiffened their stance against any compromise with their giant neighbor.

Russia stepped up its pressure on Ukraine after its government announced that it would retain its nuclear status. In late November, Russia cut Ukraine from its electricity grid, forcing Ukraine to cancel exports to Central and Eastern Europe. Russia also announced and instituted a planned increase in the price paid by Ukraine for oil, from $90 per ton to the world price of $100 per ton by the first quarter of 1994. The Russian government also issued statements refusing to further assist in the maintenance of Ukraine's nuclear weapons. Although all of these Russian policies can be justified financially, they come at the worst possible time.

Highlighting the Ukrainian political year were three interrelated events, which also indirectly involved Ukrainian-Russian relations: 1) the resignation of Prime Minister Leonid Kuchma on 21 September following his second unsuccessful attempt to gain extraordinary powers from the Parliament in order to implement an economic stabilization and reform plan; 2) the cancellation of a referendum vote on confidence in the Parliament and the president on 23-24 September; and 3) discussion of the "Treaty on the Formation of Economic Union" (with the CIS, Commonwealth of Independent States).

During the discussion of the treaty, parliamentarians from the left praised it as the only salvation to Ukraine's economic troubles, while those in the center questioned the Treaty's vagueness, and those on the right called it a renewal of the USSR. Parliament Chairman Ivan Pliushch questioned the wisdom of integrating with a country that held territorial claims against Ukraine. Pessimists on the question of CIS unification are reminded of the Stalinist policy of "autonomization" instituted in the year following Lenin's death. Optimists call it an organization which is evolving into something similar to the European Community.

President Leonid Kravchuk, who attended the entire Treaty debate, announced at the end that he would attend the 24 September CIS Meeting in Moscow and sign the Treaty as an associate member in order to avoid isolation from the CIS market. The agreement still had to be ratified by Parliament, however, before it could go into effect.

The divisive issue of relations with Russia followed regional lines. Western Ukraine is dominated by nationalists who jealously guard Ukrainian sovereignty while Ukraine's eastern and southern regions contain large Russian populations, besieged miners and heavy industrialists. Both sides in the dispute had legitimate concerns. But these concerns have led to dangerous emotions. In November, Nikolai Azarov, chief of the Labor Party of Ukraine, whose political clout was boosted when President Kravchuk appointed one of its leaders, Viktor Landyk, deputy Prime Minister, warned: "The concern of western Ukraine to avoid economic union with Russia may lead to civil war." Such an outcome could result in the permanent stationing of Russian troops in Ukraine, as in Georgia and Tajikistan.

Despite the gloom, the democratic process was in full evidence as parties and civic organizations prepared for parliamentary and presidential elections in March and June 1994, respectively. As the political focus shifted to the future, the democratic opposition met several times to build an election alliance. At a major meeting on 11 November, attended by Rukh and more than thirteen other reformist parties and organizations, Lev Lukyanenko came forward with a detailed program for political coordination. At the meeting, the democrats stated their aim to create a reform-minded government which would transfer property to private ownership, key to Ukraine's development as a democratic nation.

The Baltics: election pains

Although the Baltic states escaped the humiliation of being forced to join the Commonwealth of Independent States out of economic necessity, thereby ceding their economic sovereignty as several former Soviet republics did in 1993, they could do little to halt their economic decline or internal political quarreling. Furthermore, the Lithuanian government did sign an "Agreement on Trade and Economic Relations Between the Russian Federation Government and the Lithuanian Republic Government" on 18 November, which made Lithuania the first to break ranks on remaining free from Russian entanglements. The election laws of the three countries changeed to a system of proportional representation, in which a threshold of 4 percent of the total ballots cast had to be met for a party to seat candidates in parliament. The barrier was instituted to prevent groups from paralyzing parliamentary debate. Despite the barriers, however, in Estonia nine groups were represented; in Lithuania, eleven; and in Latvia, eight. In each case, two or three parties held greater relative power, but the result was still partial legislative paralysis and confusion as alliances kept changing and new political entities were formed.

In June, Latvia held its fifth parliamentary elections since the Republic of Latvia was first proclaimed in 1918. Latvians who fled the country in World War II and their descendants were allowed to vote. Nevertheless, the number of eligible voters in the 1993 election was smaller than in the 1990 elections held in Latvian SSR. At that time, the electorate included Soviet soldiers and all other Soviet citizens living in the republic. Latvia struggled all year with the international community over its Citizenship and Immigration Law. The Latvian population is made up of 52 percent Latvians, 34 percent Russians, 4.5 percent Belarussian, 3.4 percent Ukrainians, 2.3 percent Poles and small percentages of other minorities. Latvia's Supreme Council has denied citizenship to those people settled there after the Soviet Union annexed the republic in 1940. This has excluded most of the Russians, Belarussians, and Ukrainians. No provision has yet been made for their naturalization and thousands have been denied residency permits because the draft naturalization law is still being debated in the Council. One reason for the delay is that some Latvians believe that Russians in Latvia are a fifth column, bent on restoring the Russian empire.

In March, the Lithuanian Democratic Labor Party (LDLP), successor to the former Lithuanian Communist Party, won seventy-five of the 140 seats in the Seimas, firmly entrenching its power. The balance of power shifted against Sajudis, now the democratic opposition, which gained only 30 seats. The LDLP's popularity substantially waned, however, as it began to dismantle the economic reform program of the previous governments but failed to offer a coherent new program of its own. As a result, the LDLP and its Sajudis opposition failed to resolve their differences, and even intensified their suspicions of one another.

Increasing its political hold over the country, the LDLP placed loyal party members in key positions at all levels of government, which gave it the image of a monolithic political force and led to accusations that it was trying to reinstitute one-party rule in Lithuania. The disparate groups that make up the LDLP's political base thrived during the year on the hostility many of them continued to feel toward Sajudis's efforts to restructure society in 1991-92. The agricultural sectors tended to harbor the most intense grudge against Sajudis for its land ownership reform program. The LDLP appealed successfully for support to the small businessman as well as the large factory manager by promising not to close factories and assuring former Communist party members-turned-entrepreneurs that their profits were safe. Many former Communists have become wealthy through the process known in post-Communist countries as "nomenklatura privatization." The LDLP's tactic of cautiously steering clear of sensitive economic issues also worked to their favor. Sajudis, in the meantime, formed itself into a registered conservative political party (Homeland Union), led by former President Landsbergis, but failed to resolve many of the internal disputes and problems that led to its fall from power in 1992.

Of the three fledgling Baltic democracies, Estonia earned the greatest adulation from international observers for its efforts to reconcile its voting laws with human rights principles. A new Estonian law made it possible in 1993 for foreign non-citizens, including many of the 500,000 Russians living in Estonia, to cast ballots in local elections. As a result, the new 64-member city council of Tallinn includes an ethnic Russian deputy chairman who was a former editor of the *Estonian Communist*. Twenty-five other new local officials are also alleged to owe their positions to the voting of Russian minorities. (About one-third of the Estonian population of 1.5 million consist of native Russian speakers, of whom one in ten are currently citizens.) A moderate, centrist coalition that favors accommodation with the Russians shut out the nationalists to gain passage of the new voting law, a political move which caused President Lennart Meri's party, the Propatria Coalition of five market-oriented parties and hard-line nationalists to call the 1993 local elections a "dark day for Estonian democracy." One Fatherland Party member was quoted saying that the Estonian government was "crazy." As an important political aside, the Estonian People's Front ceased its activity in November by an overwhelming majority vote of the delegates, marking the end of the "Soviet opposition" era in Estonia.

Central Asia: glimmers of democratic hope for a few

In the Central Asian Republics civil liberties remained significantly curtailed, but a glimmer of progress was noticeable at the very end of the year.

In Kazakhstan, on 30 November, a group of people's deputies proposed spring elections to the parliament and local governing bodies. Carrying out what many local soviets in Russia had refused to do, about one hundred Kazakh soviets had already "self-dissolved" by November. In addition, the parliament called for an end to the Supreme Soviet (parliament) and the election of a new "professional parliament." How politically liberal the new parliament and local soviets will be is questionable insofar as the traditionalists are still very strong in Kazakhstan. Nevertheless, if elections are held next year, they will be one small, welcome step forward in helping Kazakhstan break out of the shackles of a former era.

In Kyrgyzstan, President Askar Akayaev, recognizing the grave economic and political situation in his small country, decreed a 30 January referendum on confidence in himself.

Turkmenistan's President Saparmurad Niyazov received nomination from the "Democratic Party of Turkmenistan" (the republic's former Communist party) for an additional fiv- year term. Under the republic's constitution, no president may serve more than two consecutive terms of five years. The Turkmen "democrats," however, proposed making Niyazov the republic's president for life. Niyazov, who has declared himself Turkmenbashi—leader of Turkmen the world over—has all but destroyed the glimmer of democracy in his country replacing it with a personality cult worthy of Stalin. Turkmenistan was the only former Soviet republic to stay out of the CIS.

Tajikistan was wracked by civil war on its Afghan border throughout the year, causing some observer to call it "the war without end." Tens of thousands of Tajik refugees remained in Afghanistan and the Tajik government grew more dependent on Russian and Uzbek troops to maintain a semblance of stability. Observers compared the situation to that in Afghanistan following the 1979 invasion, albeit in a different world context. Tajikistan's Communist government took power in November 1992 following a failed attempt to form a coalition government of prodemocratic parties. The Supreme Soviet, elected in 1990, was still 94 percent Communist, and political practices in 1993 were still reminiscent of Stalinist times. Candidates for parliament ran unopposed and received 98 percent of the vote. The defense minister, deputy prime minister and deputy NSC (former KGB chief) ruled with iron fists. Political opponents were tried in absentia or forced to admit their "guilt". All opposition parties were banned—in a republic that in 1990 and

1991 was the first Central Asian republic to have introduced a modestly functional multiparty system.

Transcaucasus: strongmen leading war-torn states

Prospects of Lebanization in the Transcaucasus loomed large as 1993 drew to a close with no end in sight to the tragic wars engulfing the region.

Azerbaijan: A series of battlefield reverses in the beginning of the year in the war against Armenian forces gradually undermined popular suppor tfor the democratic government of Abulfaz El'chibey. Taking advantage of El'chibey's diminished standing, traditional Azeri strongmen and Russian ally, Geydar Aliyev, fought his way back into power. Aliyev had been stripped of his authority many years before by Mikhail Gorbachev, who distrusted Aliyev's ties to the Brezhnev nomenklatura.

Aliyev deftly maneuvered to consolidated his hold on Azerbaijan and to convince Russia to come in on Azerbaijan's side in the conflict with Armenia. One of Aliyev's first presidential actions was to make Azerbaijan a member of the Commonwealth of Independent States (CIS). Aliyev also reached out to Iran. In a speech in Baku, Iranian President Hashemi Rafsanjani expressed "joy at the return of the Muslim of Azerbaijan to the embrace of the Islamic *ummah* and the victory over communism." Despite the lip-service to democracy and the free market, the new state was basically governed under a Stalinist model.

As was true with all the southern periphery states, Azerbaijan's involvement with Moscow and the CIS increased dramatically, with Moscow virtually dictating aspects of Baku's economic and political policies. In the critical energy sector, for example, in November Russia forwarded a proposal on the route of an oil/gas export line from Afghanistan, which would be built through the joint efforts of the two countries. The line may join up with the Druzhba or run through the Caucasus to Novorosiysk. Total cost of the line would be in the range of $4 million. Russian Minister of Energy, Yuriy Shafrankik, stressed that the energy agreement was political as well as economic, which seemed confirmed by the fact that it coincided with a week-long secret meeting on Nagorno-Karabakh in Baku. The proposal also coincided with President Aliyev's meeting with U.S. Energy Secretary, William White, having been hastily drafted and transmitted by an urgent phone call to Aliyev from Boris Yeltsin. The proposal provides for Russia's share in Azerbaijan's energy consortium with the West for developing the Caspian oil field to increase to 20 percent, though it was not clear whether the 20 referred to investigation participation or to benefits. The fuel bank which will finance the oil cooperation will be created within the framework of the CIS. Ukraine, Uzbekistan and Kazakhstan have already agreed to this proposal. These negotiations, therefore, effectively created a united organization of former USSR oil-producing republics under Russia's umbrella.

Armenia: Democratic governance survived in Armenia through 1993, mainly because President Levon Ter-Petrosvan was successful in helping the Armenians in Nagorno-Karabakh prosecute their war against Azerbaijan. By the end of 1993, Armenian backed forces had launched attacks from Nagorno-Karabakh that extended the province's reach to the border of Iran. Meanwhile, Karabakh adopted Armenia's currency, the dram, and by November had introduced enough drams into the economy to replace the Russian ruble.

However, there were disturbing signs that Azeri and Armenian terrorists and extremists in Nagorno-Karabakh were defying the CSCE-arranged cease-fire in October and the United Nation's Security Resolution 884, creating serious problems for the Armenian government. In late November, the Armenian Foreign Minister condemned the blowing up of the railway link between Armenia and Georgia by what he alleged were Azeri "militaristic circles," who were trying to force the Armenian people to their knees." Such events could threaten democracy in Armenia whose economy is racked by hyperinflation and the collapse of its currency due to Russia's recall of pre-1993 rubles, in violation of its own agreement for a "single ruble zone" with Russia. When Russia later enacted the recall, all of the ruble zone signatories experienced the collapse of their financial systems, which made them all more dependent on their huge neighbor to the north. Each one revised its policy and adopted its own currency, but as Ter-Petrosyan announced with some bitterness in an address to the nation in November, "it was Russia itself that stood outside the ruble zone." Still the president said he would "search for more productive and mutually advantageous ways for further development of cooperation with Russia and the former Soviet republics." He did not want to be seen as pursuing an "anti-Russian policy" and was acting in concert with Uzbekistan and Kazakhstan.

Shevardnadze and Georgia

The evolution of events in 1993 was arguably the most tragic for the Georgian Republic. The country became the unhappy victim of a dual-sided civil war: on one side Abkhazian separatists, with the apparent backing of the Russian military, inflicted a series of military defeats on the government of Head of State and Chairman of the Supreme Council, Eduard Shevardnadze. One the other side, forces loyal to ex-President Zviad Gamsakhurdia (Zviadists) also attacked Shevardnadze and his Georgian government forces. In their view, Shevardnadze had to be removed because he had failed to protect Georgian independence and had seized power undemocratically in 1992. Faced with this civil strife on two fronts, which has already caused the deaths of thousands and the dislocation of tens of thousands of Georgian people, Shevardnadze was forced into the humiliating position of having to call upon Russian troops for salvation. This was especially difficult given Shevardnadze's own belief, expressed frequently in 1993, that Russia had incited the recalcitrance in Abkhazia, destabilizing the country and forcing it ultimately to relinquish part of its sovereignty to Russian influence. The price Russia asked for aiding Shevardnadze with its internal wars was Georgia's entry into the CIS—a price which Shevardnadze (and his compliant congress) paid in October.

Shevardnadze was for all essential purposes the sole decision-maker in Georgia in 1993. Despite the fact that he established democratic law-making structures last year, he invited all twenty-six parliamentary parties into the government and executive structures alongside former Communist party executives. He said he envisaged the future parliament "not as a democracy of the majority, but as a compromise of all political forces." As a consequence of the political paralysis brought about by such a policy, the government of Prime Minister Tengiz Sigua collapsed in August and was replaced by Otar Patsatsia. Even under the new government, however, the parliament was unproductive. The most active of the reformist parties in parliament are the National Democrats, the Greens, the Republicans and the Democrats. Apart from the National Democrats, there is little discipline in the parties, and membership outside the parliament is insignificant. Definitions of party programs as "liberal" or "radical" depends almost entirely on their agreement or non-agreement with Shevardnadze, with "radicals" usually opposed.

Shevardnadze combines the positions of Parliamentary Chairman and Head of State under the Law on State Power, which gives him power to call regular or extraordinary parliamentary sessions, propose constitutional changes, issue orders and decrees, introduce legislation and return bills (once,) chair parliamentary debates and the parliamentary collegium. With parliamentary approval, he has the right to appoint and dismiss the prime minister, his ministers, the general procurator, chairman of the Intelligence and Information Committee, and president of the National Bank. In October, parliament granted him some exclusive powers, such as conducting inter-state relations and appointing all senior military personnel and state representatives in the provinces (prefects and mayors) without parliamentary approval. Most importantly, he has the power to create his own policy-advisory apparatus, outside the parliament, and to supervise the state administration. His control of the government obviously represents a significant centralization of power, augmented last July by additional power to issue normative acts having the force of law in the sphere of economics and to chair the cabinet and dismiss any senior official from his position and appoint a new candidate without parliamentary approval.

In the economy, the overly large Cabinet of Ministers, still tied to the old Communist model, had no power to control the National Bank's excessively liberal credit policies or to push through reform against resistant central and provincial structures. The weakness of the government and frequent confrontations among them permitted Shevardnadze to acquire the powers he ultimately wielded. But Shevardnzadze's lack of leadership in institution-building and reform has only contributed to Georgia's governing crisis. ▬

Paige Sullivan is a research associate at the Center for Strategic and International Studies, Washington, DC.

East-Central Europe:
And Now the Hard Part   George Zarycky

During Poland's 1989 round-table negotiations between Solidarity and the ideologically bankrupt Jaruzelski junta, a farmer atop his wagon was asked by a Western news crew what should be done with the Communists. Without hesitating, he silently pointed to a line of trees along the road and made a gesture suggesting a noose. Just four years later, the Communists had staged a dramatic comeback. In September's national elections, the "post-Communist" Democratic Left Alliance (SLD) swept 171 of 460 seats in the Sejm (the parliament). At its nucleus are the Social Democracy of the Republic (SdRP), the direct successor of the Communist-era Polish United Workers Party (PUWP), and the former official OPZZ trade union federation. Its coalition partner, the Polish Peasant Party (PSL)—a descendent of the PUWP's long-time satellite, the United Peasant Party—gained 132 seats. The new government of Prime Minister Waldemar Pawlak, the thirty-four-year-old PSL leader who served briefly as prime minister from June-July 1992, included sixteen of twenty-one cabinet ministers who are former members of the PUWP or the old Peasant Party. The SDL-PSL coalition enjoys a comfortable 66 percent majority, almost enough to pass a constitution and overrule a presidential veto.

How did the Communists go from the gallows to governing in a country whose post-war history was so thoroughly anti-Communist and anti-Russian? Though widely anticipated, Poland's turn to the Left at a time when so-called "shock therapy" reforms gave it the fastest growing economy in Europe has raised serious questions. Would the new government roll back key market programs? What of ambitious plans to privatize or close money-losing state enterprises? Did the election signal a popular nostalgia for paternalistic centralism that eliminated class and income disparities through a bogus egalitarianism based on shared hardships? After five prime ministers, four governments, three national elections and two parliaments did Poland's election results presage a tropistic regional orientation toward a more familiar authoritarianism and order?

Politics: the Polish paradox and beyond

Poland's nod to self-styled "post-Communist" Communists was part of a marked regional resurgence or continued popularity of left-socialist, "reform- neo- ex-Communist" national hybrids. A recent poll showed that over 70 percent of the population in East-Central Europe believed the state should provide a place to work, as well as a national health service, housing, education, and other services. But in the four years since the collapse of the East bloc, the countries of East-Central Europe—while facing the same broad challenges of dismantling a forty-year-old, Soviet-imposed totalitarian and centralized system—have diverged along differing historical, cultural and geographic paths into states where democracy is relatively strong and those where democracy has yet to take firm root.

In Poland, Hungary, Slovenia, the Czech Republic, and to some extent Slovakia, post-

Communist Communists have emerged as pro-market, pro-competition and pro-reform socialists, not unlike left-wing parties in Western Europe. Poland's SDL seems part of a long socialist tradition and, unlike the rural-based PSL, appears committed to privatization and market reforms, albeit at a slower pace. In Hungary, where the centrist ruling Hungarian Democratic Forum (MDF) has purged its ultra-nationalist component but continues to slip in the polls, the death of Prime Minister Jozef Antall can only boost the prospects of the reform-Communists who oversaw the 1988 palace coup that ousted the hard-line Kadar regime and are viewed by many as capable, pro-market technocrats. Czech Communists, badly splintered between ultra-hardliners and moderates, still make up the second-largest parliamentary block.

What most of these countries have in common—and what attenuates but does not completely eliminate an authoritarian backlash—is a vibrant and entrenched civil society, functioning (though often chaotic) multi-party parliaments and other democratic institutions, several free-and-fair elections under their belts, and other indices of genuine pluralism. So while the Czechs, for example, still grapple with the composition of a constitutionally mandated upper house, laws get passed and signed. (With the exception of impoverished Albania's Democratic Party, nowhere does one-party have over half the seats and can rule alone). What's more, these countries, despite weak party structures, often obstructionist political-social elements, and constitutional gray areas have thus far steadfastly and rather successfully stuck to an incremental path of democratic change and market transition, much of it on the fly. This in itself is rather remarkable just four years after the disintegration of orthodox regimes, the collapse of the Warsaw Pact military alliance and the Council for Mutual Economic Assistance (CMEA) trading bloc, and with war raging in the Balkans. In much of East-Central Europe, the forty-plus year interregnum of Soviet rule could not completely destroy pre-Communist infrastructures as well as literal and psychological avenues to the West.

On the other side of the Communist constellation are states where members of the *ancien regime* and *nomenklatura* have retained prominent positions in government and where important democratic political institutions, for various historic-social-cultural reasons are stunted or non-existent. In Romania, the ruling Party of Social Democracy of Romania (PSDR), led by President and former Ceausescu ideologue Ion Iliescu, is essentially opposed to loosening the government's grip on the economy and is tethered to its ultranationalist and leftist coalition allies. Opposition movements and parties are fragmented into scores of organizations. The Bulgarian Socialist Party (BSP) has, with 106 seats, only eleven less than the badly fractious Union of Democratic Forces (UDF) which was ousted from power after losing a non-confidence motion in 1992. Like Romania, Bulgaria has been sluggish in implementing market reforms, and this year's draft budget was criticized by reformers for offering too much aid to a wide range of inefficient state enterprises and for giving continued control of the economic sector to the former nomenklatura, including members and former members of the BSP.

The ongoing conflagration in the Balkans continues to define politics in Croatia, Macedonia, Bosnia-Herzegovina and the rump-Yugoslavia (Serbia and Montenegro). The regime of former Communist Gen. Franjo Tudjman in Croatia has used the war as a pretext to purge moderate elements from the ruling Croatian Democratic Union (HDZ), tighten its grip on the media, and arrest political opponents. Major economic reforms are on virtual hold. Serbia's strongman Slobodan Milosevic has used television and truncheons to cow democratic opponents and his erstwhile allies of the fascist-nationalist Serbian Radical Party led by Seselj. Rump-Yugoslavia's economy is a basket case, the banking system has all but collapsed, inflation hovers at triple digits, and reform in any sense of the word is nowhere on the horizon. Bosnia lies plundered and helpless, victimized by Serbian and more recently Croatian aggression. Macedonia, with its substantial Albanian minority and a troubled history of Bulgarian, Greek and Serbian machinations, remains a tinderbox, though the presence of some 300 U.S. troops along its border with Serbia has helped keep things calm for now.

Is communism back?

Is communism back to stay in East-Central Europe and what are the regional ramifications? Poland's political crisis grew out of parliamentary gridlock exacerbated by the fact that twenty-nine parties were represented under a 1991 electoral system that wasn't modified until 1993. As a result, the moderate government of Prime Minister Hanna Suchocka never enjoyed the support of a stable majority. Paradoxically, President Lech Walesa's decision to dissolve parliament and call for new elections came amid sustained economic progress. GDP rose by over 4 percent in 1993. Industrial production was 7.6 percent higher in the first six months of 1993 than in the comparable period the year before. While unemployment was about 15 percent and climbing by mid-year, private sector employment accounted for 60 percent of the workforce. There were 1.7 million private firms and figures showed that in 1992 private sector jobs compensated for the 500,000 that vanished in the state sector.

While privatization of giant state enterprises had yet to be implemented, the economy was definitely on the upswing. Yet 56 percent of citizens polled felt the country was moving in the wrong direction. Why?

For one thing, while nearly half of Poles are employed in the private sector, there is a persistent perception—a legacy of communism—that new wealth and rich businesses are inherently corrupt or in the hands of the old *nomenklatura*. Moreover, as RFE/RL's Louisa Vinton has pointed out, another holdover of the Communist's gigantism mindset is that wealth and value are determined by the size of an enterprise and the number of employees, and that the huge though inefficient state firms are a cornerstone of Poland's national economy, long providing job security and other benefits regardless of the output of work. Throw in an innate fear of domination by foreign interests, and privatization looks less attractive to many. These debilitating factors are also present in varying degrees in Hungary, the Czech Republic, Slovakia, Slovenia, indeed everywhere in the region where governments have had trouble with or been reluctant to dismantle giant, money-losing enterprises.

The continued appeal of socialist-left solutions has marginalized not only the center, but right-wing nationalists as well. In Poland, the big losers were parties closely linked to the conservative, socially intrusive policies of the Catholic Church on abortion and other issues. In Hungary, the MDF purged the right-wing, anti-Semitic clique led by Istvan Csurka, whose 1992 essay blamed the country's ills on Jews, international bankers and liberals and suggested a resurgence of a Greater Hungary. However, similar rantings continue to have appeal in Romania, where ex-Communists fine tuned their message with populist-nationalist demagogy, appealing to anti-Hungarian and anti-Semitic passions and xenophobia.

The post-Communist trend has been accompanied over the last few years by the weakening of the broad-based coalitions that toppled Communist regimes and launched market reforms. Bulgaria's UDF is badly factionalized and Romania's Civic Alliance has splintered. In the Czech Republic, voters abandoned the Civic Forum. In Slovakia, the Public Against Violence commands no support. In Poland, Solidarity—which initiated the no-confidence vote—was shut out of the Sejm, capturing seven seats in the 100-member Senate. President Walesa's moderate Non-Party Block to Support reform barely cleared the 5 percent hurdle, capturing just twenty seats.

These movements, which opened their societies to the prospects of democracy, now find themselves far from power. The diminished popularity of many liberal-intellectual groups, while unfortunate, is understandable and may actually signal maturation rather than regression. The dissidents symbolize an older era that many people would rather forget. They reminded non-dissidents of their own quiescence during the Communist era. For others, they represent warriors from a struggle already won. Some of the internecine conflicts within the democratic movement were part of an evolutionary process of political differentiation. Nevertheless they did dissipate the strength of post-Cold War political groupings. Simultaneously, Communists regrouped, using existing structures and networks, discipline and shared ideology. The Communist political and industrial order—once derided as ossified and out-of-touch—has proven much more resilient and adaptable than predicted.

Lustration loses its luster

A controversial factor in the political resiliency of former Communists has been the reluctance of governments to pursue aggressive de-Communization. The Czech Republic's much-debated "lustration laws," aimed at excluding senior Communists officials from holding certain political or public offices, were vehemently attacked in the press and by international human rights groups on civil liberties and constitutional grounds. Over the last two years, Bulgaria has proposed several measures to exclude ex-Communist leaders from political, security, business and educational institutions, but the drafts met stiff resistance from Socialists and democrats alike. This February, the Constitutional Court did uphold the so-called Panev Act that bars persons connected with "the supreme structures of the former Bulgarian Communist Party and security services" from holding "managerial offices at scientific establishments, such as chiefs of departments, deans, rectors, and chief editors of serials." The law, which caused an outcry among some human rights groups in the West, did lead to the removal of several thousand formerly Communist-affiliated academic staff from managerial positions. Meanwhile, several prominent Bulgarian Communists were prosecuted and convicted for criminal offenses, including former Communist leader Teodor Zhivkov, and former prime ministers Andrei Lukanov and Georgi Atanasov.

Poland resisted an across-the-board housecleaning, some democrats even acknowledging the Party's role in keeping Soviet tanks at bay. Many Hungarians still appear to view the ex-Communists as early advocates of economic and political reform. In Romania, the government and other institutions continue to be permeated by ex-Communists, partly because few capable figures in the country are entirely untainted by the Ceausescu years.

The issue of de-communization and the rule of law remains nettlesome throughout the region, creating legal and moral contretempts. While witch-hunts and revenge-motivated purges would ultimately exacerbate social tensions and undermine democracy, it is clear that civic education, a greater sensitivity to the social repercussions of rapid economic transformation, and restrictions on high-level former Communists who engaged in clearly illegal activities are integral to any meaningful transition.

Bumps on freedom's road

The possible ascent of the Left and its effect on the consolidation of democratic gains in much of East-Central Europe is an open question. While Poland's SDL has assured that their aim is not retrenchment but reform with a "more social face," and that they are committed to foreign investment, the conclusion by some Western analysts that they represent "social democracy" may be overly sanguine. Future economic progress—in Poland and elsewhere—is contingent upon privatizing the state sector, the pace and scope of which now seem less certain. And while there are definite independent institutional constraints that can prevent Poland's new government from too radically altering the country's economic course, the pervasive differentiation between rich and poor and growing social discontent could lead to conflicts over the rate of reform that whet the authoritarian appetite.

More immediate threats to the stability and security of further democratization were such issues as failure to draft and adopt post-1989 constitutions, deteriorating economic conditions, corruption, ethnic tensions—both domestic and regional—and control and character of the broadcast media. Future political developments in Russia were a critical factor in efforts by most East-Central European countries to formulate military policy, seek greater regional security cooperation and/or strive for full integration in the North Atlantic Treaty Alliance (NATO), the European Community (EC) and other European institutions.

A less tangible challenge facing the region's governments was overcoming growing cynicism, voter apathy and gloom among citizens who appear to have lost faith in the political process, probably because they expected democracy and freedom to translate into instant economic improvement. A disturbing trend throughout much of the region was the percentage of unrepresented voters in national parliaments. In Hungary, Poland, the Czech Republic and Slovakia, relatively unfragmented parliaments were achieved by inadvertently disenfranchising large numbers of voters. In Bulgaria, the Czech Republic and Slovakia, a quarter of the voters chose parties that failed to clear electoral thresholds. While these figures would not be overly alarming in established democracies, the inherent potential for parliamentary instability and voter alienation is worrisome where democracy is so new. An eventual shake-out of marginal, "paper" parties and unwieldy coalitions should improve stability, particularly when and if voters and leaders realize how many parties essentially share the same basic beliefs.

Another destabilizing factor was ongoing corruption in government, particularly relationships between the *nomenklatura* and private business interests. In Romania, the infamous Caritas pyramid scheme was launched in collusion with right-wing politicians from ethnically tense Transylvania, including rabid nationalist Gheorghe Funar of the Party of Romanian National Unity (PRNU). Much of what's left of rump-Yugoslavia's economy is in the hands of the government-criminal mafia. So-called *nomenklatura* privatization has also caused popular resentment at the exploitation of power and privilege by the new elite in Poland, Hungary, the Czech Republic, Slovenia and elsewhere. As mentioned, some of this frustration has awakened nostalgia for more authoritarian methods to restore order and stamp out graft.

This year also saw the intensification of the struggle for media reform. From Hungary and the Czech Republic to Croatia and Romania opposition groups claimed government control of television and radio denied them equal access. In Hungary, a year-long "media war" over control of radio and television resulted in several dismissals, including the suspension by state television of a liberal editor of a late-nights news program and his replacement by a pro-government journalist. In Slovakia and Romania, the broadcast media, while nominally independent, are in effect controlled by people loyal to the government and the ruling party. In October, MPs of the ruling Movement for a Democratic Slovakia moved to dismiss the head of Slovak Television, complaining that it was too critical of the government. In March, the director of Czech Radio resigned, citing as a reason interference by the Board of Radio Broadcasting. In Serbia and Croatia, television is used by the government as an instrument of propaganda and misinformation, with air time virtually denied anti-government voices.

Finally, democracy and human rights were undermined by discrimination and ethnic violence around the region. Gypsies were favorite targets of attack and bias in housing, employment and education from Hungary to Romania to the Czech Republic. Serbia continued its repression of 2 million ethnic Albanians in Kosovo. Romanian-Hungarian relations remained tense over the substantial Hungarian minority in Transylvania, which has pressed for greater autonomy and self-administration. For its part, Hungary has expressed concern about the 600,000-strong Hungarian minority after the Czechoslovak breakup. While full-blown ethnic violence was limited to the former Yugoslavia, ethnic and minority issues were a potential flashpoint throughout the region.

Economies: engines of democracy?

An important signpost of future social and democratic development was the state of national economies. Throughout East-Central Europe, the symbiosis between democratization and market reforms remained a key dynamic in charting the area's present and future course. And the overall picture offered a mixed bag.

In the three years following the overthrow of old-line Communist regimes, the countries of the region experienced a prolonged and precipitous fall in output. With the collapse of COMECON, most export markets disappeared virtually overnight. Living standards dropped dramatically, though not as sharply as is usually assumed. Inflation and unemployment sailed up as price liberalizations and dislocations took hold. Public resentment toward "shock therapy" reforms or market mechanisms led to political squeamishness or indecision, as did the persistence of the old-guard *nomenklatura* protecting its turf.

By year's end, Poland, Hungary, the Czech Republic, Slovakia, and Slovenia had the largest private sectors and the most readily convertible currencies in the region and relatively low rates of inflation. Between them, they attracted some $13 billion in foreign investment 1992-93. Throughout the region, governments, through voucher schemes and other plans, managed to oversee the privatization of mostly small businesses and enterprises. In Poland, the private sector's share of GDP in 1992 was 45 percent and 60 percent of total employment; in the Czech Republic, it was 20 and 23 percent; in Hungary, 40 and 16.7 percent. In Romania, it was 25 percent of GDP, and 20 percent in Bulgaria.

And while all East-Central states generally had problems with macroeconomic stabilization, budgetary issues, the slow pace of privatization of state property and enterprises, dysfunctional post-Communist banking and financial systems, as well as unresolved issues dealing with regional economic integration and trade, progress was recorded in varying degrees. Poland, Hungary, the Czech Republic, Slovenia, and, to some extent, Slovakia, have come closest to institutionalizing a viable market system. Bulgaria and Romania continue to be plagued by political gridlock, hyperinflation, plummeting output, and continued dominance of state ownership. Political elites in Serbia, Croatia and the other Yugoslav successor states have placed national security and nation-building above economic transition. Some economists predict that the worst of the economic transition has yet to come. The European Bank for Reconstruction and Development reported that it might take East-Central Europe thirty-five-years to catch up with per capital levels in the OECD.

Important questions remain: will citizens of East-Central Europe accept the fact that there are no overnight economic miracles, that the road to capitalism will be long and painful, and that austerity and social dislocation will continue in the foreseeable future? If the economic engines sputter and die, can democracy survive? The answers are yes and probably not. A determining factor in the economic outcome is the role of the West. Thus far, the West's role has been muddled. Hundreds of millions of assistance dollars have been wasted on high-paid western consultants and trainers, instead of empowering local groups. The economic recession in Europe and Germany's costly absorption of East Germany have stymied substantial investment and closed EC markets to goods and products from the former East Bloc. As Josef Olesky of Poland's victorious SLD told the Western press: "Poland's economy depends on fast export growth. How can the West expect us to grow and not buy our goods? This situation naturally contributed to estrangement of the workers and more votes for us."

All this and NATO too?

Looming over these crucial processes is the shadow of a dangerous nemesis. Toward the end of the year, there were diplomatic flurries throughout the region as leaders and foreign ministers petitioned Euro-statesmen and U.S. secretaries of state and defense, Warren Christopher and Les Aspin, to quit talking about new partnerships for peace and enlargement doctrines and admit Europe's former Warsaw Pact nations as full members into NATO. In making the Czech Republic's case, President Vaclav Havel in October spoke of the country's precarious security situation due, not to the ongoing war in the Balkans, but to the unstable situation in Russia. Throughout much of East-Central Europe, there was a wary focus on Russia, with officials expressing real fear of a resurgence in Moscow of empire-restoring, Communists-nationalists. Ironically, one sure way lingering nostalgia for a Communist past would vanish overnight is if hardline Communist-nationalists ousted Boris Yeltsin.

By year's end, prospects for expanding NATO to include any former East Bloc countries, including the oft-vaunted Visegrad Four (Poland, Hungary, the Czech Republic and Slovakia) had receded. Yet, in barring membership, the U.S. and its allies continued to resist East-Central Europeans forging their own collective security alliances to fill the vacuum. Any possible threat from Russia aside, Romania, Bulgaria, Hungary, among others, continued to express deep concerns about the threat of an expanded Balkan War.

And then there's Bosnia

As the year ended, so too did any real hope for resolute action by Europe or the U.S. to end Bosnia's agony. The bankruptcy of ideas and groveling before Serbia reached unexplored lows when European negotiators suggested that they would lift the sanctions against Serbia—which had driven the Serbian economy to its knees and were the only punitive steps against Belgrade's aggression—if Milosevic could use his good offices to bring Bosnia's murderous Serbs into line and get them to agree to give up a little more of the land taken by force and genocide. The new administration in Washington seemed all too willing to wash its hands of the whole affair, blaming the Europeans, recalcitrant Bosnian Muslims, and lack of consensus for its own lack of leadership.

On the ground, the Bosnian position grew more untenable, as the Muslim's erstwhile Croatian allies turned their guns around and made their own rapacious land grab. Diplomatically, Muslims were being painted as the heavies, obstructionist and difficult when they refused to give away sovereignty rights that no one but themselves had the courage and moral fortitude to defend. They were being chastened for not buying into Lord Owen's vision of what was fair and proper.

As for the East-Central Europeans, virtually shut out of the peace-process, the peril of civil and territorial strife related to Bosnia was real enough. War spreading to Macedonia could ultimately involve Bulgaria, Greece, and Serbia. Bulgaria has its own tensions with the large Turkish minority. An explosion in Kosovo would draw in Albania and possibly Turkey. A new Croatian-Serbian conflict is by no means far-fetched. Meanwhile, millions of civilian refugees from Hungary to Croatia are taxing humanitarian and relief systems as yet another winter settles in.

Equally as menacing, the Bosnia conflict has, to many, legitimized the use of force without fear of international reprisal to settle ancient ethnic and territorial scores. Hungarians are concerned about their minorities in Slovakia and Romania. Romanian pretensions to Moldova could lead to conflict with Russia and Ukraine. The fate of Polish minorities in western Ukraine, Lithuania and Russia could further complicate relations with these states. And then, of course, there are the simmering conflicts in the former Soviet Union.

For all of its many problems, there is reason for guarded optimism about the ability of this region to overcome the formidable obstacles to democratization and market reforms left over after the collapse of four decades of Communist rule. What seems clear is that forces of regression and reaction, though weakened, should not be counted out just yet. Poland's post-Communist Communists may yet prove to be benign caretakers of a smooth transition. Citizens from Budapest to Bucharest may be sagacious enough to understand that what seems like anarchy or chaos is part of a prolonged process to fine-tuning democracy, that gangsterism and corruption are as much by-products of the old system as the new, and that whatever illusions they may have had about living almost as well as the West under communism were just that—chimerical—and that in many ways they are closer to the developing world than to Europe. ▬

George Zarycky is Central European specialist for Freedom House.

The Survey of Press Freedom: Governments Would Dictate Press "Responsibility" Leonard R. Sussman

Widespread proposals to restrict journalists reflect post-Cold-War tensions. The frustrations of greater political freedom in the absence of economic progress lead to problem-prone lawmaking affecting the news media. In 1993, only totalitarian states still defended censorship. Yet nowhere in Eastern Europe, the former Soviet Union or Africa is the press free of threats to enforce "responsibility," defined by government. And this year European democracies joined that bandwagon.

The end of harsh central controls in former totalitarian countries has not yet produced viable democracies, free-market economies or news media independent of the new ruling parties. Public frustration over unfulfilled promises and unsatisfying news media feeds official efforts to restrict journalists. The ethics of journalism, though often inadequately practiced, is overwhelmed when lawmakers dictate journalistic performance.

Harshest censorship accompanied bloody fighting in the Balkans, the dictatorial stand-off in Haiti, and the aborted October coup in Russia. There, despite a new constitutional draft forbidding censorship, President Boris Yeltsin briefly censored even friendly papers, temporarily banned a dozen others, and closed several anti-Semitic and neo-fascist publications.

Paying the highest price for journalistic integrity, at least 74 newspersons were killed in 27 countries in 1993. Seven journalists died during the October insurgency in Moscow, 11 fell during military action in Croatia and Bosnia-Herzegovina, 5 in Somalia, and 2 in a helicopter crash in Afghanistan. Another 49 newspersons were murdered in 22 countries because of opposition to their work.

In Algeria, 9 journalists' deaths are attributed to religious terrorists. Five died in Colombia. In Turkey, official action to repress Kurdish demands for autonomy left 4 journalists and 2 support staffers dead.

Killing of a journalist sometimes cannot be readily listed as the murder of a news messenger, as such. When a journalist is killed, however, we consider his profession first. For, where the rule of law or democratic processes are weak or do not exist, the benefit of the doubt should go to the journalist, rather than to governments or law enforcement who may not want to pursue or reveal the perpetrator, or admit that a journalist was targeted for professional reasons.

Some 1,178 cases of press-freedom violations were reported last year in 107 countries, including the most free nations. Forty-seven journalists were kidnapped in 17 countries. Some 368 were arrested in 48 nations. Attackers wounded 50 newspersons in 13 countries. Another 46 were beaten and 74 otherwise assaulted. Death threats were received by 92 journalists in 28 countries. Other harassment was reported by 128 journalists in 37 countries. Since 1988, an average of 68 journalists have been killed each year, and an average 997 cases of press-freedom violations reported.

In 1993, despite continuing instability, press freedom expanded in nine countries. Benin,

Press Freedom: Struggle and Toll —1993

These statistics are inclusive through 31 December. Additional cases for 1993 are likely to be reported throughout January 1994. These record only the physical and psychological harassment of journalists and the media. The figures do not reflect other forms of official and unofficial editorial censorship, and diverse methods of economic and political pressuring of the mass media. The statistics are a clue, however, to those visible attacks which generate self-censorship by journalists.

This year, as before, the figures inevitably underestimate both the number of cases and the individuals involved. Some single cases here involving the closing of media facilities affect scores of journalists. Many cases are not reported, though journalists are increasingly aware that maltreatment of the messenger by governments and others is aimed primarily at all citizens. The fate of journalists, therefore, should be considered of interest and importance to everyone, everywhere. *Sources: Freedom House correspondents, Committee to Protect Journalists, Reporters Sans Frontieres, and IFEX (International Freedom of Expression network).*

	1993 [ ]—countries	1992	1991	1990	1989	1988	1987	1986	1985	1984	1983	1982
Journalists killed	74[a] [27]	107[b] [27]	62 [19]	45 [19]	73 [24]	46	32	19	31	21	14	9
Kidnapped, Disappeared	47 [17]	34 [9]	20 [7]	16 [8]	38 [8]	14	10	13	13	5	4	11
Arrested, Detained	368 [48]	225 [52]	298 [42]	168 [45]	354 [33]	225	188	178	109	72	80	145
Expelled	12 [9]	24 [13]	22 [12]	31 [14]	75 [14]	24	51	40	9	22	19	23

Other Statistics

	1988	1989	1990	1991	1992	1993
Journalists wounded:	28 in 7 countries	23 (8)	42 (9)	43 (6)	66 (22)	50 (13)
Journalists beaten:	40 in 6 countries	16 (3)	16 (9)	51 (14)	64 (25)	46 (13)
Journalists otherwise assaulted:	50 in 12 countries	91 (18)	83 (25)	57 (18)	190 (32)	74 (19)
Death threats and other threats to journalists:	43 in 9 countries	51 (13)	50 (22)	69 (18)	95 (36)	92 (28)
Journalists' homes raided or destroyed:	12 in 8 countries	12 (8)	3 (1)	6 (4)	7 (6)	2 (2)
Charges filed against journalists:	48 in 6 countries	23 (7)	31(10)	65 (15)	55 (20)	33 (7)
Films or manuscripts confiscated:	82 in 13 countries	41 (15)	43 (23)	62 (18)	98 (27)	41 (19)
Press credentials withdrawn or refused or expulsion threatened:	16 in 8 countries	32 (9)	44 (17)	36 (9)	17 (9)	38 (11)
Journalists harassed:	46 in 10 countries	189 (23)	171 (60)	126 (21)	117 (43)	128 (37)
Closed publications or radio stations:	40 in 12 countries	38 (11)	50 (16)	28 (14)	18 (14)	53 (16)
Banned publications or radio programs:	31 in 10 countries	88 (23)	43 (12)	91 (13)	90 (42)	56 (16)
Bombed or burned publications or radios:	9 in 9 countries	22 (5)	13 (11)	19 (13)	30 (15)	33 (21)
Occupied publications or radios:	7 in 4 countries	10 (7)	30 (20)	29 (14)	34 (17)	21 (15)

Total cases of all forms of attack, harassments: 1993: 1,178 in 107 countries

1992: 1,264 in 123 countries

1991: 1,022 in 72 countries

1990: 889 in 92 countries

1989: 1,164 in 84 countries

1988: 465 in 70 countries

1987: 436 in 57 countries

a. Afghanistan, 2; Algeria, 9; Angola, 3; Argentina, 1; Bosnia, 9; Colombia, 5; Congo, 1; Croatia, 1; El Salvador, 1; Georgia, 4; Guatemala, 2; Honduras, 1; India, 2; Italy, 1; Lebanon, 1; Lithuania, 1; Mexico, 3; Peru, 1; Philippines, 1; Russia, 8; Rwanda, 1; Somalia, 5; South Africa, 1; Tajikistan, 3; Turkey, 4; United States, 1; Venezuela, 1.

b. Angola, 2; Azerbaijan, 2; Bosnia, 25,; Chad, 3; Colombia, 5; Croatia, 4; Egypt, 1; Ethiopia, 1; Georgia, 1; Guatemala, 2; Haiti, 1; Hong Kong, 1; India, 5; Lebanon, 2; Liberia, 1; Mexico, 1; Papua New Guinea, 1; Peru, 10; Philippines, 5; Russia, 1; Rwanda, 2; South Africa, 1; Sudan, 1; Tajikistan, 7; Turkey, 15; Ukraine, 1; U.S., 1; Venezuela, 5.

Data compiled by Jessie Miller and Leonard R. Sussman

Estonia, Guyana, Lithuania and Taiwan entered the free-press group. Moving from not free to partly free were Cambodia, Croatia, Kuwait and Yemen.

In eighteen countries news media lost significant freedom. Dropping from free to partly free were Honduras, Hungary, India, Mongolia, Nepal, Papua New Guinea, Romania, Thailand and Zambia. Going from partly free to not free were Egypt, Ghana, Guinea, Indonesia, Kenya, Mozambique, Nigeria, Swaziland and Tanzania. The number of countries without press freedom increased by 10 percent.

At year-end, of 184 countries surveyed for press practices, 68 have free news media (37 percent), 61 are partly free (33 percent) and 55 are not free (30 percent). This represents a one-percent decline in the free group over 1992. The drop would be a significant 3 percent, however, if the survey had not examined for the first time five small Pacific states which appear in the free-press category.

Left unresolved, even in otherwise free-media countries, was the relationship of the press to the new ruling parties, and particularly the role permitted independent media when political strains develop. Year-long debates over proposed media laws, therefore, alarmed press-freedom advocates.

"European media ombudsman"

The best model for a free press was not promoted by democracies. While their governments and journalist and publisher associations offered substantial capital support and training for fledgling news media in Eastern Europe and the former Soviet Union, the Western European governments set dangerous legalistic models for the developing democracies.

The Council of Europe considered adopting a code on journalist ethics and a mechanism to regulate press fairness. The Parliamentary Assembly of the Council defends the action as supporting truth and integrity in reporting. The International Federation of Newspaper Publishes (FIEJ) calls it "one of the most profound attacks on the freedom and independence of the press in recent years."

Indeed, the Council's call for a "European media ombudsman" was reminiscent of similar demands at UNESCO forums, over the past twenty years. There, developing countries supported by the Soviet Union favored government action to assure balanced reporting. The United Nations Educational, Scientific and Cultural Organization formally ended such discussions in 1989, and since then has been actively promoting press freedom in Africa, Eastern Europe and Central Asia. The United States, which withdrew from UNESCO in 1985, has completed reappraisals and is likely to return to UNESCO in 1995.

The World Conference on Human Rights at Vienna in June provided another showdown for press freedom. In advance meetings in Asia and Africa, the developing countries signaled they would reject as Western hangups the longstanding definitions of human rights in international covenants. They indicated, too, they would rewrite Article 19 of the Universal Declaration of Human rights. It defines press freedom without restrictions.

The final Vienna document equivocates. It offers the media "freedom and protection"— but "guaranteed within the framework of national law." That leaves news media hostage to domestic politics without the influence of internationally accepted freedom codes such as Article 19.

The October meeting of the Commission on Security and Cooperation in Europe (CSCE) heard the British spokesman on behalf of the Europeans back the European convention's restrictions. He said the right to freedom of expression "cannot be absolute, regardless of the consequences." In the United Kingdom itself, after sensational violations of privacy by the tabloids, parliamentarians considered but still held off applying legislative "cures."

No freedom, indeed, is absolute. There are obvious clashes of rights even in a free society. Free-press advocates argue, however, that it is potentially dangerous for governments or intergovernmental agencies to catalogue possible restrictions beforehand, and monitor violations of a governmental code.

This may limit some sensationalism, but also impose socially undesirable self-censorship by journalists. Whether press responsibility is left to free journalists or government officials depends largely on whether one regards government or the public itself as the ultimate overseer. If it is the public, then neither government nor journalism should be controlled by the other, libertarians argue. And, as the FIEJ president declared, by taking such steps themselves democratic states set a bad model for the nascent democracies of Eastern Europe.

These countries, says Mico Gjikhima, Albania's director of Radio Tirana, "are restructuring their organs to adapt to pluralism but they are still handicapped by the deeply rooted traditions of four decades of totalitarian rule." In Hungary, journalists and 4,000 supporters in the streets protested the government's cancellation of radio and television programs which criticized official policy. A new press-law draft would "suffocate Albanian journalism," editors there declare. The new director-general of Bulgarian television, acting like the new regime in Romania, sacked moderate TV programmers and restored Communist-faction producers. Poland's broadcast law stipulates that programs "may not advocate activities contrary to the law or to the interests of the Polish state" or "contrary to morality and the general interest." Such broad reservations typically sustain censors or self-censors on many public issues.

In the Balkans, where journalists' lives as well as their freedoms are daily at risk, some eighty regional newspersons met in November to plead for help in sustaining independent journalism. They concluded that warring Balkan communities cannot be reconciled without independent electronic media, especially local community radio and TV networks. As a sign of reality, the meeting condemned the takeover in May by Serbian authorities of Albanian press and broadcast facilities in Kosovo.

Dangerous Turkey

Turkey remains one of the most dangerous countries in the world for journalists critical of government policies. Four journalists and two support staffers were murdered; dozens were beaten, threatened with death, arrested, sentenced, fined, or had their publications banned or confiscated—mainly because they support the appeal of Turkish Kurds for autonomy. The PKK, the Kurdish militants, increasingly gains broad support among Kurds in Turkey. Their call for negotiation with Turkish authorities is reported by Kurdish journalists, but rejected by Ankara officials. Violence increases, along with ever-stronger bans on Kurdish journalists and publications. In mid-December, the leading newspaper sympathetic to the Kurds, *Ozgur Gundem,* was banned for ten days and its entire staff detained.

In the wake of the press crackdown during the October putsch in Moscow, publishers and editors of sixty Russian newspapers formed an association to remove the obstacles preventing the development of a free and independent press in their country. The members, representing many shades of political opinion, discussed practical policies to enlarge press freedom, rather than Russian politics. The focus was on ending press bids for government favors, and developing solidarity when one or another publication is persecuted.

Yet several messages emerged from the Yeltsin victory in October. The first, transmitted by reinstituted censors, was use of the media to support Yeltsin's choice for parliamentarians. The second, and more hopeful, was Yelstin's creation of a special "arbitration court" to "protect mass media against unlawful interference in their activities during the electoral campaign and unhindered propaganda for or against candidates." Yet during the campaign the president warned the parties they would lose the vital boon of free television time if they criticized the Yeltsin-sponsored draft constitution. The constitution's paragraph on press freedom, however, is the best of several press laws written in the Soviet Union and Russia. The new version does not provide voluminous details fraught with loopholes for potential press-controllers. Which press policy prevails in 1994 may determine whether the new association of Russian editors and publishers can expect substantial freedom for an independent press, or whether self-censorship will rise again.

African journalism

That syndrome remains the hallmark of most African journalism. In 1993, nowhere was it better demonstrated than in Nigeria. The latest military crackdown in November sent new chills through the news media. The commanding general lifted bans on outlawed news organizations but warned them to be careful what they report: a classic invitation to self-censorship in a country of sometimes vibrant, diverse journalism.

At mid-year, leading African journalists met in Zimbabwe to push for greater press freedom in Africa. Two years earlier, UNESCO had called them together for the same purpose. Afterward, there were some temporary improvements and more official promises of liberation. They were followed, however, by distinct retrogression in many African countries. In Tanzania, for example, where officials had been promising greater press freedom, the broadcast services were now formally declared the mouthpiece of the ruling party. Radio Tanzania, moreover, concluded an agreement with Radio China International to provide the major source of technical, administrative and training assistance for Tanzania.

In Kenya, where rulers boast of improvement in human rights policies, police impound newspapers, reporters are threatened, attacked and jailed, and—says Blamuel Njururi, editor of the *Nairobi Weekly Observer*—"police informers are in every aspect of Kenyan life. You've got them in almost every newspaper." After years of harassment and imprisonment, Njehu Gatabaki, courageous editor of *Finance* magazine, announced he could no longer publish. "The government will not give me a chance," said the most persecuted journalist of East Africa.

Ghana, which proclaims itself a democracy, still has state control of all radio and television, and the country's most influential newspapers are also owned by the government.

At the Zimbabwe conference, Richard Steyn, editor-in-chief of *The Star,* the leading South African newspaper, said moves toward democracy in most African countries have been largely cosmetic. Top posts at African broadcast services are controlled by the state, based on political rather than professional merit, Steyn said. Back home, SABC, the South African national broadcast service, was slowly opening its leadership and programs to blacks. Most notable, Ivy Matsepe-Casseburi, a black woman who has long fought for liberation, is the new chairperson of South Africa's broadcast services. Though the anti-apartheid revolution may not materialize until the elections of April 1994, the revolution at SABC is proceeding. Black political leaders appear on talk shows, though some news bias remains. Higher standards of professionalism in journalism are developing.

Asia...

Notable media professionalism has developed in parts of Asia—Japan, South Korea, Taiwan, Thailand, Hong Kong (though press freedom is diminishing in advance of China's takeover in 1997), and India. India's press freedom is marred, however, by the growing violence that spawns self-censorship, complete control by the Delhi center over radio and television, and enactment of a new cable law that provides licensing and implies content-control as well.

"The most striking aspect of the media in India today is the overwhelming extent of state control in which they operate" states K.S. Venkateswaran, an Indian lawyer researching press controls worldwide. In Venkateswaran's 1993 book on Indian media law, Nani Palkhivala declares in the foreword that "our radio and television are boneless, spineless and gutless."

China moved on two tracks as President Jiang Zemin flew to discuss trade and human rights with President Clinton in November. On one course, China opened a 4,700-kilometer domestic fiber optic telecommunications link, said to be the longest in the world. The cable will carry simultaneously tens of thousands of messages—probably commercial calls and not mainly politically risky, personal ones. At the same moment, however, the government restricted foreign television programming, tightened the unauthorized publication of newspapers and magazines, cracked down on independent filmmakers, and threatened satellite-dish owners.

...and Latin America

The record in Latin American last year mirrored the global story: "Democracy alone is no guarantee of free expression for either the press or individuals," said the Inter American Press Association in November. Chile is attempting to impose new educational requirements for journalists that can prove restrictive as well as educative. Canada prohibits certain forms of news during election campaigns. That country, Costa Rica, El Salvador and Bolivia use electoral codes to "unreasonably limit political advertising in periods leading up to voting," IAPA noted. Numerous lower-court actions in Canada bar the press from reporting important cases, including those focusing on freedom of expression itself.

Latin America's record of press murders remains high. Five were killed in Colombia last year, 3 in Mexico, 2 in Guatemala, and one each in Argentina, El Salvador, Honduras and Venezuela. A pro-Aristide broadcaster of Haitian descent was murdered in Miami.

There are some heartwarming signs. Hernan Lopez Echague, an ardent Argentine reporter for *Pagina 12,* was badly beaten twice in a month for writing that the government, facing an election, was using thugs to attack journalists. After the second attack, Lopez's colleagues put his name as the only byline on all manner of stories in the newspaper.

Journalists on the courageous Guatemalan paper *Siglo XXI* ("21st Century") have been beaten, threatened with death and their papers burned. Yet when President Jorge Serrano tried to impose a dictatorship in May, *Siglo XXI* appeared overnight with a special edition warning of the coup. The paper was roundly attacked. It appeared next with blank pages, and only sports and foreign news. Domestic news pages appeared in black under the heading *Siglo XIV* ("14th Century"). The opposition rallied, and Serrano was forced to step down. Guatemala's newspaper returned to the twenty-first century. ■

Leonard R. Sussman is senior scholar in communications of Freedom House, and adjunct professor of journalism and mass communication at New York University.

The Survey 1994— The Year in Review   Joseph E. Ryan

The complexities of evaluating the state of freedom in today's shifting political scene are caught in a single paradox: the number of democracies increased in 1993 but the number of people denied most political rights and civil liberties also increased. In absolute numbers—although not in terms of percentage—there are more people living in societies that are Not Free than at any time since 1972, when Freedom House began monitoring political rights and civil liberties around the world.

Another measure of the deplorable decline in freedom during 1993 is that of the twenty-seven countries that changed categories—moving from Free to Partly Free or Partly Free to Not Free, or the reverse—only three were positive changes. And of thirty-nine countries in which there were changes in the observance of political rights and civil liberties without a category change, only sixteen marked improvements and twenty-three a decline. As the accompanying boxes show at a glance this latter group includes major countries such as Greece and Italy, Japan and Mexico. The number of worst rated countries increased from the previous year's "dirty dozen" to twenty. Measured in these terms, 1993 could well be termed the year of freedom's great retreat.

The following comments offer, very briefly, the reasons for the ratings of countries that changed from one category to another and those that changed only within the categories. (They do not include the changes that were made for purely methodological reasons to achieve greater discrimination, but only those that were made for actual changes within the countries. Additional information about the methodology immediately precedes the tables and ratings on page 671.) More extended explanations for the changes will be found in the following individual reports on each country and related territory.

Free Countries

Andorra, which joined the United Nations in 1993 and has changed classification from a territory to a Free country, has adopted a constitution that provides the country's first written guarantee of rights. The **Czech Republic** appears for the first time in this *Survey*. It has maintained the former Czecho-Slovakia's Free rating. **Estonia** allowed non-citizens to participate in local elections. Ethnic Russians and other long-time residents had excellent showings in several cities and regions. **Greece** placed restrictions on discussion of the Macedonia issue. The government put citizens on trial for wrongthink and wrongspeak on the Greek claim to the former Yugoslav Republic of Macedonia. Problems continued with corruption and restrictions on ethnic and religious minorities.

Guyana joined the Free category in 1993-94 for having made a successful transition to liberal democracy. **Italy** faced an ever-growing, multi-layered government corruption scandal. Mafia violence against anti-crime crusaders undermined efforts to clean up the state. On a positive note, the country approved a new electoral system that is designed to reduce the number and influence of traditional parties in future parliaments. **Jamaica** lost ground on the civil liberties side, due to an increase in violence and brutality by the security forces. **Japan** suffered from a spreading government corruption scandal. Elections forced out the long-ruling Liberal Democratic Party and brought in a multiparty coalition committed to political and economic reform. Some members of the new coalition had profited handsomely from the corruption, but had escaped just in time to new parties. As happened in Italy, the coalition voted in a new electoral system that is designed to produce cleaner elections in the future. New districts will be more equal in population. The system combines elements of Anglo-Saxon and list-voting.

South Korea's new administration lifted some Cold War restrictions on civil liberties and brought some new, liberal faces into government. The country's tensions with North Korea escalated as the North developed materiel for nuclear weapons and massed troops along the border with the South. **Monaco** joined the United Nations in 1993, and has changed classification from a territory to a Free country. **Nauru**'s government cracked down on media criticism of the country. Government agents threatened reporters to give favorable reports about Nauru. Some critical publications were confiscated. The government became a subject of international ridicule for wasting public trust funds on a musical about Da Vinci and the Mona Lisa that flopped on London's West End.

St. Lucia declined in civil liberties in 1993, the result of police killings during a banana farm strike. **Sao Tome and Principe** continued to consolidate the gains of its democratic transition, begun in 1989-90. The **Solomon Islands** experienced some spillover effect from the separatist conflict in Bougainville, Papua New Guinea. Papuan troops made some incursions into the Solomons in pursuit of alleged separatists and their supporters. **Vanuatu** experienced some improvements in political rights and civil liberties. The government moved away from earlier policies that attempted to restrict religion and political opposition.

Partly Free countries

Bangladesh has lost some of the promise it showed in democratic transition in 1991. Political violence has increased, and Islamic fundamentalists made some attacks on more moderate activists. **Brazil** fell from Free during 1993. Security force violence against homeless children, civil unrest and political corruption drove the country down. Voters rejected a monarchy and a parliamentary system in a referendum, but their existing presidential-legislative democracy is increasingly dysfunctional. Some politicians made headway calling for a restoration of military rule. **Cambodia** held transitional elections for a constituent assembly. Voting was generally free and fair. Royalists and the ruling Communists became the two leading parties. The former monarch, Prince Sihanouk, became King again, with a great deal of popular support. The Khmer Rouge continue to occupy significant parts of the country, and did not run in the election.

The **Central African Republic** held democratic transitional elections in 1993. This marked a formal end to military rule. The **Comoros** experienced politically tinged riots in February 1993. President Djohar's government attempted to limit the opposition through apparent gerrymandering. His son-in-law spent the year intriguing successfully to remove a series of revolving door governments from office. In December elections, the government won twenty-one seats and the opposition eighteen. The opposition said they would boycott the legislature. The **Dominican Republic** declined to Partly Free, owing to a general deterioration of democratic institutions. In **Gabon**, there was some small improvement in political rights and civil liberties as the government and opposition prepared for the country's first competitive presidential election in December 1993. Since President Omar Bongo put his daughter on the election commission, its fairness may be dubious.

Georgia fell within Partly Free, because the country endured both a bloody separatist conflict within the Abkhazian region and a violent comeback attempt by deposed President Zviad Gamsakhurdia. The parliament granted head of state Eduard Shevardnadze emergency powers to deal with this extraordinary situation.

Lesotho held multiparty transitional elections. The voters swept the opposition Basotho Congress Party into office. However, the elected government, the royal family and the military competed for power in the postelection period. **Madagascar** completed the democratic transitional elections it had started in 1992. Opposition leader Albert Zafy replaced longtime ruler Admiral Didier Ratsiraka. **Mexico** slipped within Partly Free. The Mexican government tightened its control over politics and civic activity. Security forces used tear

27 Countries that Changed Categories		
Countries	**1993**	**1994**
Azerbaijan	Partly Free	Not Free
Bahrain*	Partly Free	Not Free
Bangladesh	Free	Partly Free
Brazil	Free	Partly Free
Burundi	Partly Free	Not Free
Cambodia	Not Free	Partly Free
Dominican Republic	Free	Partly Free
Egypt	Partly Free	Not Free
Estonia	Partly Free	Free
Ethiopia	Partly Free	Not Free
Guinea	Partly Free	Not Free
Guyana	Partly Free	Free
Honduras*	Free	Partly Free
Indonesia*	Partly Free	Not Free
Ivory Coast (Cote D'Ivoire)	Partly Free	Not Free
Kenya	Partly Free	Not Free
Mozambique	Partly Free	Not Free
Nepal	Free	Partly Free
Nigeria	Partly Free	Not Free
Oman*	Partly Free	Not Free
Papua New Guinea	Free	Partly Free
Swaziland	Partly Free	Not Free
Tanzania	Partly Free	Not Free
Tunisia	Partly Free	Not Free
United Arab Emirates*	Partly Free	Not Free
Yugoslavia (Serbia & Montenegro)	Partly Free	Not Free
Zambia	Free	Partly Free
New countries rated previously as part of a country		
Czech Republic	—	Free
Slovakia	—	Partly Free
New countries rated previously as territories		
Andorra	Free	Free
Eritrea	Partly Free	Not Free
Monaco	Free	Free
New territories rated previously as part of a country		
Nagorno-Karabakh	—	Not Free

*Methodological adjustment.

16 Gains in Freedom Without Changing Category	23 Declines in Freedom Without Changing Category
Central African Republic	Afghanistan
Gabon	Angola
Korea, South	Bhutan
Lesotho	Comoros
Liberia	Congo
Madagascar	Equatorial Guinea
Malawi	Georgia
Morocco	Greece
Niger	Italy
Pakistan	Jamaica
Panama	Japan
Peru	Mexico
Sao Tome & Principe	Nauru
Seychelles	Nicaragua
Vanuatu	Senegal
Yemen	Solomon Islands
	Tajikistan
	Togo
	Turkey
	Turkmenistan
	Ukraine
	Uzbekistan
	Zaire

gas, mass arrests, beatings and torture during several state elections. The state also sought to intimidate opponents through warnings, anonymous death threats, unwarranted detention and jailings on dubious charges. **Morocco** finally held parliamentary elections that the King had postponed several times over a period of years. On paper, parliamentarians have increased power. In reality, King Hassan remains in charge.

Nepal's fragile democracy lost some ground due to civil unrest and some government restrictions on civil liberties. **Nicaragua** slipped within Partly Free as no viable rule of law put the country on the verge of political anarchy. **Niger** held successful democratic transitional elections. In **Pakistan**, Benazir Bhutto returned as a prime minister following several months of political instability and a fairly orderly election. The military and the presidency remain the arbiters of power, having evicted Nawaz Sharif from the premiership and installed an interim, technocratic government. **Panama** improved slightly in political rights with reasonably well-organized preparations for next year's elections. **Papua New Guinea** suffered from growing violent crime and the secessionist conflict in Bougainville. **Peru** moved up slightly on the basis of a somewhat free constitutional referendum. **Senegal**'s civil liberties declined, due to a secessionist conflict in Casamance and various restrictions on the opposition.

In the **Seychelles**, multiparty elections took place. However, the vote confirmed President Rene in office and gave his party the overwhelming number of seats in the legislature. **Slovakia** appears for the first time as an independent country in this *Survey*. The government's mistreatment of ethnic minorities and its crackdown on the independence of the media have placed the new state in Partly Free. In **Turkey**, the government's war against the Kurds intensified. The state restricted the Kurdish MP's freedom of movement and political activities. The military has increased its influence on government policy. In **Ukraine**, a new law restricts the electoral activities of parties, thereby weakening the democratic opposition and strengthening the dominant ex- (and not so ex) Communists. The government restricted civil liberties by imprisoning a reporter for "slandering" President Leonid (Lenny the Hetman) Kravchuk.

Yemen held its first election since the unification of the two Yemeni states in 1990. The legislative vote was marred by irregularities, but several parties participated and won seats. **Zambia** returned to a state of emergency in 1993 for the first time since the democratic transition in 1991. Citing an alleged coup plot backed by Iran and Iraq, President Frederick Chiluba restricted civil liberties and opposition political activities.

Not Free countries

Afghanistan's descent into violence intensified as Islamic fundamentalist factions battled for control. More than 10,000 have been killed in Kabul alone. **Angola** has returned to civil war since late 1992 when Jonas Savimbi's UNITA forces refused to accept the results of the first round of elections, which the governing MPLA won. More than 100,000 people have been killed during the past year. That is one-quarter of the more than 400,000 deaths since the first cycle of civil war began in 1975. In **Azerbaijan**, old-line Communist and military elements replaced President Elchibey as war dragged on with Armenians in Nagorno-Karabakh.

The feudal Kingdom of **Bhutan** has evicted more than 100,000 ethnic Nepalese over the last two years. Bhutan's laws strip people of their citizenship retroactively, and force them to document their right to live in a land that has little documentation of anything. During 1993 **Burundi** underwent two dramatic changes. First, it had an initially successful transition to democracy. After years of military rule under the Tutsi minority, the country finally had a head of state from the Hutu majority but the Tutsi military elite overthrew and assassinated President Ndadaye. Thousands died in renewed ethnic strife and hundreds of thousands became refugees. **Chad** had a marginal improvement in freedom as nascent political parties and some rudimentary expression developed. **Egypt's** freedom declined in 1993 as Islamic fundamentalist violence and government crackdowns eroded the countries' already weak rights and liberties. **Equatorial Guinea**'s alleged transition to democracy proved bogus. Severe restrictions on the development of opposition groups and the continuation of existing human rights abuses forced the country back down to the bottom of Not Free. Most voters and parties boycotted the tainted general election on 22 November 1993.

Eritrea and **Ethiopia** both put off transitions to democracy. The former remains a one-party state, while the latter allows opposition groups to exist, but within limits. Eritrea appears for the first time as a country in this *Survey*. In theory, **Guinea** is having a transition to democracy. In practice, the government has attacked the opposition violently. In October, 63 people died in an anti-government demonstration after security forces attacked them. The demonstrators had demanded a neutral interim government and impartial administration of the December elections. **Ivory Coast (Cote D'Ivoire)** fell from Partly Free to Not Free. In September, the Liberian civil war spilled over into Ivory Coast. Several armed men from Liberia slipped across the border and attacked a refugee camp. There were at least two casualties. In November, Ivorian mobs rampaged through the streets attacking Ghanaians after a soccer match. They burned alive or beat to death scores of people from the neighboring country. In December, President Felix Houphouet-Boigny died after thirty-three years in power. His death will change the politics of the country, allowing a successor generation to come to power. It is too soon to tell whether the new leadership will be able to maintain the late leader's dominant party system.

Kenya fell from Partly Free to Not Free, dragged down by rising violence and President Daniel arap Moi's disregard for the legitimacy of opposition parties and parliamentary power. Mired in chaos and civil war, **Liberia** made tentative plans for a political transition in 1994, but at press time, negotiations among the warring parties were not successful. Opposition forces in **Malawi** pushed for and won a referendum on multipartyism. This was a major blow against the kleptocratic, one-party regime of President Hastings Banda. However, the elections the democrats hoped for had not taken place by year's end. **Mozambique** postponed transitional elections until 1994. Although the governing FRELIMO and the opposition RENAMO negotiated, the country remained divided into competing armed camps. **Nigeria**'s military staged a coup in November, ending the facade of joint civilian-military control. Earlier in the year, then-ruling General Babangida had the results of the presidential election nullified, thereby preventing the inauguration of Moshood Abiola. By year's end, the military abolished all political parties and levels of civilian government. **Swaziland** held fairly meaningless, partyless parliamentary elections. Scarcely 15 percent of the voters bothered to turn out. The royal family retained most power. Private armies also appeared, causing fear among human rights activists.

   Tajikistan's hardline neo-Communist government continued a bloody struggle with Islamic fundamentalists for control of the country. **Tanzania** underwent severe regional tensions. Pressures rose for splitting the country into its component parts, Tanganyika and Zanzibar. **Togo** continued its downward slide. The military continued to dominate the government which it tried to legitimize through unfree, unfair elections. **Tunisia**'s freedom declined in 1993 as Islamic fundamentalist violence and government crackdowns eroded the country's already weak rights and liberties. **Turkmenistan** remained in the grip of hardline President Niyazov. **Uzbekistan**'s President Karimov has crushed all opposition forces, consolidating power in his hands. Rump **Yugoslavia** (Serbia and Montenegro) experienced a severe government crackdown on democratic opposition groups in the run-up to December's Serbian elections. **Zaire**'s corrupt dictator, Mobutu Sese Seko, clung to power as his country lost almost all sense of order. Oppositionists negotiated the appointment of one of their own as prime minister. It was not clear how much this meant, especially since Western powers unsuccessfully demanded Mobutu's departure. Unpaid soldiers looted civilian areas as the government became increasingly unable to provide for them or anybody else.

Related Territories

Following the peace agreement between Israel and the Palestine Liberation Organization, the **Israeli-Occupied Territories** changed status to include **Palestinian Autonomous Areas** in the Gaza Strip and the city of Jericho. Freedom of Palestinian nationalist expression increased in 1993, and local autonomy is expected to begin in December 1993. Muslim separatists and the Indian army continued intense fighting for control of **Kashmir**. The Portuguese colony of **Macao** fell ever more under Chinese influence as the date of its 1999 accession to China approaches.

   In **Nagorno-Karabakh**, which appears for the first time as a Not Free related territory in this *Survey*, Armenians continued their war with Azerbaijan. In **Northern Ireland**, the level of violence escalated in the second half of the year. Both IRA and Loyalist terrorists attacked innocent civilians, as usual. Loyalist attacks on Nationalist politicians increased as a punishment for the peace plan proposed by the leading Nationalist and Republican politicians. The **Northern Marianas** registered a decline in civil liberties following reports of severe exploitation of Asian immigrants. **Rapanui (Easter Island)** natives gained protected status under new Chilean law. **Vojvodina**'s limited freedoms declined along with the rest of rump Yugoslavia. ■

Joseph E. Ryan is resident scholar at Freedom House.

The Map of Freedom—1994

(Numbers refer to the map, pages 92-93)

FREE STATES

6 Andorra
10 Argentina
13 Australia
14 Austria
17 Bahamas
20 Barbados
22 Belgium
23 Belize
24 Benin
27 Bolivia
30 Botswana
34 Bulgaria
40 Canada
42 Cape Verde

48 Chile
57 Costa Rica
60 Cyprus (G)
62 Czech Republic
63 Denmark
65 Dominica
68 Ecuador
73 Estonia
78 Finland
79 France
83 The Gambia
85 Germany
88 Greece
90 Grenada
96 Guyana

100 Hungary
101 Iceland
106 Ireland
109 Israel
110 Italy
112 Jamaica
113 Japan
118 Kiribati
120 Korea (S)
131 Liechtenstein
132 Lithuania
133 Luxembourg
142 Mali
143 Malta
144 Marshall Islands

147 Mauritius
150 Micronesia
152 Monaco
153 Mongolia
158 Namibia
159 Nauru
161 Netherlands
164 New Zealand
172 Norway
183 Poland
184 Portugal
193 St. Kitts-Nevis
194 St. Lucia
196 St. Vincent and
    the Grenadines

197 San Marino
198 Sao Tome & Principe
205 Slovenia
206 Solomon Isls.
209 Spain
215 Sweden
216 Switzerland
227 Trinidad & Tobago
232 Tuvalu
236 United Kingdom
237 United States
238 Uruguay
240 Vanuatu
248 Western Samoa

FREE RELATED TERRITORIES

2 Aland Isls. (Fin.)
5 Amer. Samoa (US)
8 Anguilla (UK)
12 Aruba (Ne)
16 Azores (Port)
25 Bermuda (UK)
32 Br. Vir. Is. (UK)
41 Canary Isls. (Sp)
43 Cayman Isls. (UK)

45 Ceuta (Sp)
47 Channel Isls. (UK)
50 Christmas Is.
    (Austral.)
52 Cocos (Keeling Isls.)
    (Austral.)
56 Cook Isls. (NZ)
75 Faeroe Isls. (Den)
76 Falkland Is. (UK)
80 French Guiana (Fr)
81 French Polynesia (Fr)

87 Gibraltar (UK)
89 Greenland (Den)
91 Guadeloupe (Fr)
92 Guam (US)
108 Isle of Man (UK)
137 Madeira (Port)
138 Mahore (Mayotte) (Fr)
145 Martinique (Fr)
148 Melilla (Sp)
154 Montserrat (UK)
162 Ne. Antilles (Ne)

163 New Caledonia (Fr)
168 Niue (NZ)
169 Norfolk Is. (Austral.)
171 No. Marianas (US)
176 Palau (US)
182 Pitcairn Islands (UK)
185 Puerto Rico (US)
187 Rapanui (Easter Is.)
    (Chile)
188 Reunion (Fr)
192 St. Helena and

    Dependencies (UK)
192a   Ascension
192b   Tristan da Cunha
195 St. Pierre-Mq. (Fr)
213 Svalbard (Norway)
224 Tokelau (NZ)
231 Turks & Caicos Isls. (UK)
244 Virgin Isls. (US)
246 Wallis & Futuna Isls. (Fr)

PARTLY FREE STATES

3 Albania
9 Antigua & Barbuda
11 Armenia
19 Bangladesh
21 Belarus
31 Brazil
35 Burkina Faso
38 Cambodia
44 Central African
    Republic
53 Colombia
54 Comoros
55 Congo

58 Croatia
66 Dominican Republic
70 El Salvador
77 Fiji
82 Gabon
84 Georgia
86 Ghana
93 Guatemala
95 Guinea-Bissau
98 Honduras
102 India
114 Jordan
116 Kazakhstan
123 Kuwait
124 Kyrgyz Republic

126 Latvia
127 Lebanon
128 Lesotho
135 Macedonia
136 Madagascar
140 Malaysia
149 Mexico
151 Moldova
155 Morocco
160 Nepal
165 Nicaragua
166 Niger
175 Pakistan
177 Panama
178 Papua New Guinea

179 Paraguay
180 Peru
181 Philippines
189 Romania
190 Russia
200 Senegal
201 Seychelles
203 Singapore
204 Slovakia
208 South Africa
210 Sri Lanka
212 Suriname
218 Taiwan (China)
221 Thailand
225 Tonga

229 Turkey
234 Ukraine
242 Venezuela
249 Yemen
252 Zambia
253 Zimbabwe

PARTLY FREE RELATED TERRITORIES

61 Cyprus (T)
99 Hong Kong (UK)
122 Kurdistan (Iraq)
134 Macao (Port)
170 Northern Ireland (UK)

NOT FREE STATES

1 Afghanistan
4 Algeria
7 Angola
15 Azerbaijan
18 Bahrain
26 Bhutan
29 Bosnia-Herzegovina
33 Brunei
36 Burma (Myanmar)
37 Burundi
39 Cameroon
46 Chad
49 China (PRC)
59 Cuba

64 Djibouti
69 Egypt
71 Equatorial Guinea
72 Eritrea
74 Ethiopia
94 Guinea
97 Haiti
103 Indonesia
104 Iran
105 Iraq
111 Ivory Coast
117 Kenya
119 Korea (N)
125 Laos
129 Liberia
130 Libya

139 Malawi
141 Maldives
146 Mauritania
156 Mozambique
167 Nigeria
174 Oman
186 Qatar
191 Rwanda
199 Saudi Arabia
202 Sierra Leone
207 Somalia
211 Sudan
214 Swaziland
217 Syria
219 Tajikistan
220 Tanzania

223 Togo
228 Tunisia
230 Turkmenistan
233 Uganda
235 United Arab
    Emirates
239 Uzbekistan
243 Vietnam
250 Yugoslavia
251 Zaire

NOT FREE RELATED TERRITORIES

28 Bophuthatswana
    (SA)

51 Ciskei (SA)
67 East Timor (Indo.)
107 Irian Jaya (Indo.)
115 Kashmir (India)
121 Kosovo (Yugo.)
157 Nagorno-Karabakh
    (Armenia-Azerbaijan)
173 Occupied Territories
    (Isr.)
222 Tibet (China)
226 Transkei (SA)
241 Venda (SA)
245 Vojvodina (Yugo.)
247 Western Sahara

This Map of Freedom is based on data developed by Freedom House's Comparative Survey of Freedom. The Survey analyzes factors such as the degree to which fair and competitive elections occur, individual and group freedoms are guaranteed in practice, and press freedom exists. More detailed and up-to-date Survey information may be obtained from Freedom House.

89

237

101

75

40

108
170
106
236
47

195

16

184   209
87   45
137   155

25

PACIFIC OCEAN   ATLANTIC OCEAN

41
247

237   146   142

17   185
59   244 32   42
149   231   8   9
23 97 193 154   83 200   95
43   91   95   94   111 86
112 162 66 65   202
93 70 57 12 227 90 145   129
177   165   96 194
242 20 196   192a
53   212 80
68
180   31

27

48   179

238

10

5
168   81
56   182 187

76

FREEDOM

HOUSE

FREE ☐   PARTLY FREE ▨   NOT FREE ■

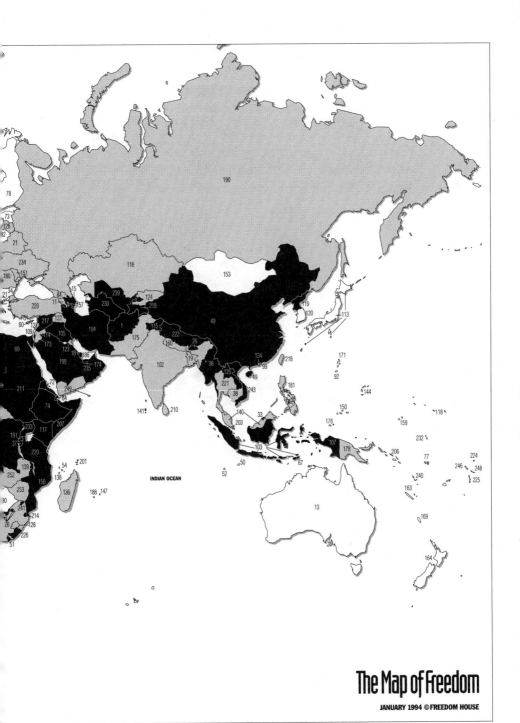

INDIAN OCEAN

The Map of Freedom

JANUARY 1994 ©FREEDOM HOUSE

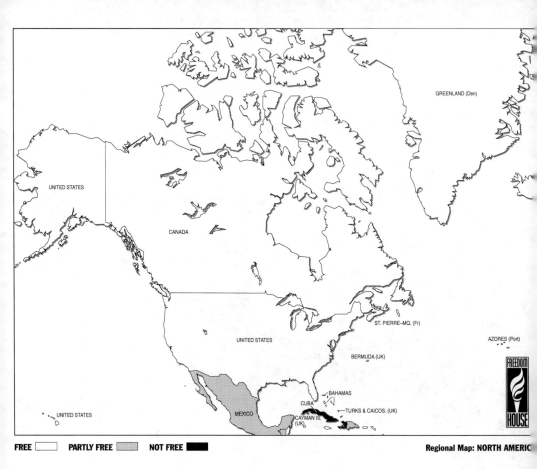

GREENLAND (Den)

UNITED STATES

CANADA

UNITED STATES

ST. PIERRE–MQ. (Fr)

AZORES (Port)

BERMUDA (UK)

UNITED STATES

MEXICO

BAHAMAS

CUBA

TURKS & CAICOS. (UK)

CAYMAN IS. (UK)

FREEDOM HOUSE

FREE   **PARTLY FREE**   **NOT FREE**   **Regional Map: NORTH AMERIC**

MEXICO

GUATEMALA

BELIZE

HONDURAS

NICARAGUA

EL SALVADOR

COSTA RICA

PANAMA

CUBA

CAYMAN IS. (UK)

HAITI

JAMAICA

DOMINICAN REP.

NE. ANTILLES (Ne)

ARUBA (Ne)

TURKS & CAICOS. (UK)

PUERTO RICO (US)

VIRGIN IS. (US)

ST. KITTS–NEVIS

BR. VIRGIN IS. (UK)

ANGUILLA (UK)

ANTIGUA & BARBUDA

MONTSERRAT (UK)

DOMINICA

GUADELOUPE (Fr)

MARTINIQUE (Fr)

ST. LUCIA

ST. VINCENT AND
THE GRENADINES

BARBADOS

GRENADA

TRINIDAD
& TOBAGO

VENEZUELA

COLOMBIA

GUYANA

SURINAME

FRENCH GUIANA (Fr)

ECUADOR

PERU

BRAZIL

BOLIVIA

RAPANUI/EASTER IS. (Chile)

CAIRN IS. (UK)

CHILE

PARAGUAY

URUGUAY

ARGENTINA

FALKLAND IS. (UK)

PARTLY FREE   NOT FREE

Regional Map: SOUTH AMERICA

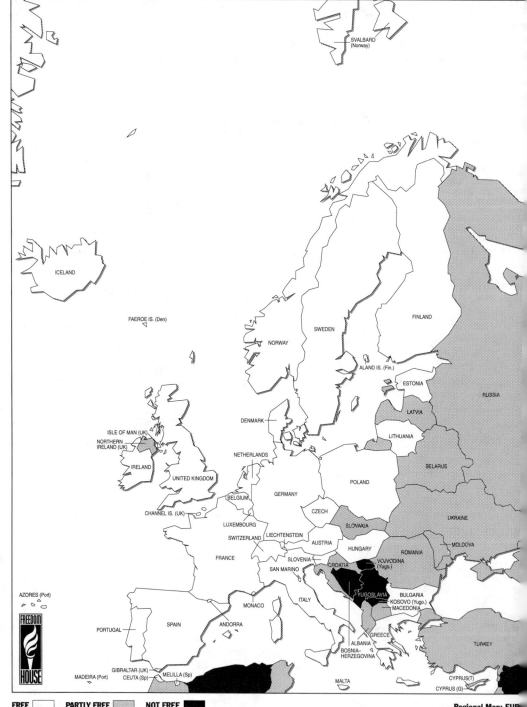

FREE ☐   PARTLY FREE ▨   NOT FREE ■

Regional Map: EUR

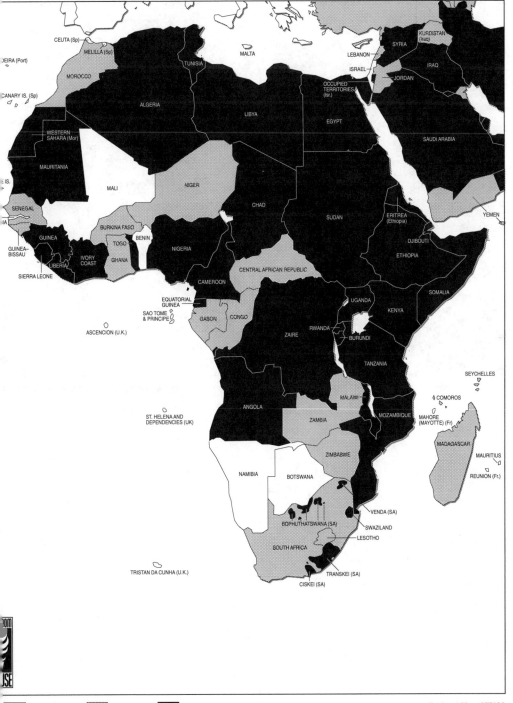

CEUTA (Sp)
MELILLA (Sp)
DEIRA (Port)
TUNISIA
MALTA
MOROCCO
CANARY IS. (Sp)
ALGERIA
LIBYA
EGYPT
WESTERN
SAHARA (Mor)
MAURITANIA
E IS.
MALI
NIGER
SENEGAL
IA
CHAD
SUDAN
GUINEA
BURKINA FASO
TOGO
BENIN
GUINEA-
BISSAU
NIGERIA
SIERRA LEONE
LIBERIA
IVORY
COAST
GHANA
CAMEROON
CENTRAL AFRICAN REPUBLIC
EQUATORIAL
GUINEA
SAO TOME
& PRINCIPE
ASCENCION (U.K.)
GABON
CONGO
UGANDA
ZAIRE
RWANDA
BURUNDI
KENYA
TANZANIA
SOMALIA
KURDISTAN
(Iraq)
SYRIA
LEBANON
ISRAEL
JORDAN
IRAQ
OCCUPIED
TERRITORIES
(Isr.)
SAUDI ARABIA
YEMEN
ERITREA
(Ethiopia)
DJIBOUTI
ETHIOPIA
SEYCHELLES
COMOROS
MALAWI
MOZAMBIQUE
MAHORE
(MAYOTTE) (Fr)
MADAGASCAR
MAURITIUS
REUNION (Fr.)
ST. HELENA AND
DEPENDENCIES (UK)
ANGOLA
ZAMBIA
ZIMBABWE
NAMIBIA
BOTSWANA
VENDA (SA)
BOPHUTHATSWANA (SA)
SWAZILAND
LESOTHO
SOUTH AFRICA
TRISTAN DA CUNHA (U.K.)
TRANSKEI (SA)
CISKEI (SA)

PARTLY FREE   NOT FREE   Regional Map: AFRICA

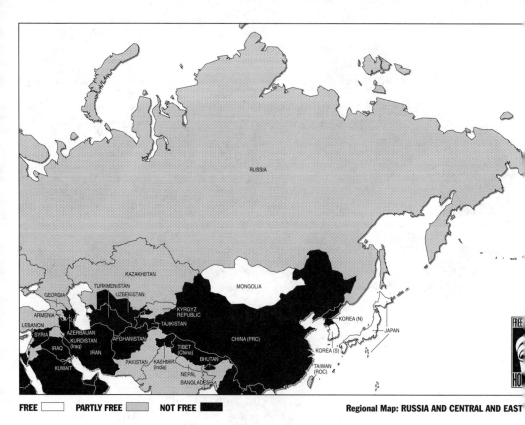

FREE ☐ PARTLY FREE ▨ NOT FREE ■   Regional Map: RUSSIA AND CENTRAL AND EAST

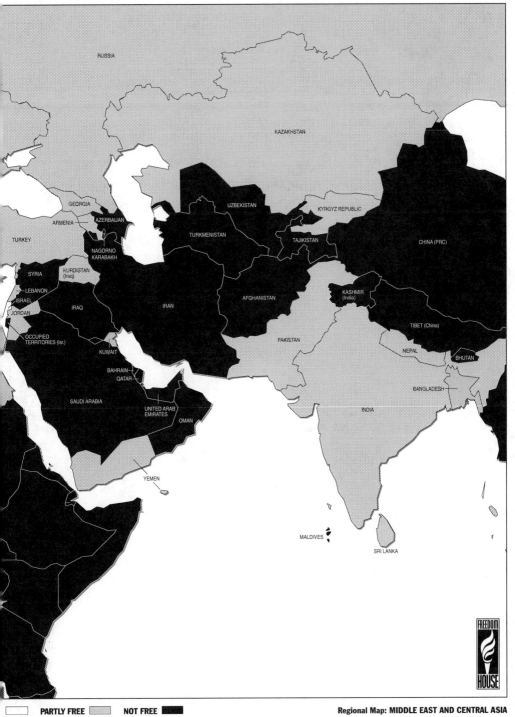

RUSSIA

KAZAKHSTAN

GEORGIA

ARMENIA

AZERBAIJAN

UZBEKISTAN

KYRGYZ REPUBLIC

TURKEY

TURKMENISTAN

TAJIKISTAN

CHINA (PRC)

NAGORNO
KARABAKH

SYRIA

KURDISTAN
(Iraq)

LEBANON

ISRAEL

JORDAN

IRAQ

IRAN

AFGHANISTAN

KASHMIR
(India)

TIBET (China)

OCCUPIED
TERRITORIES (Isr.)

KUWAIT

PAKISTAN

NEPAL

BHUTAN

BAHRAIN

QATAR

BANGLADESH

SAUDI ARABIA

UNITED ARAB
EMIRATES

OMAN

INDIA

YEMEN

MALDIVES

SRI LANKA

FREEDOM
HOUSE

PARTLY FREE   NOT FREE

Regional Map: **MIDDLE EAST AND CENTRAL ASIA**

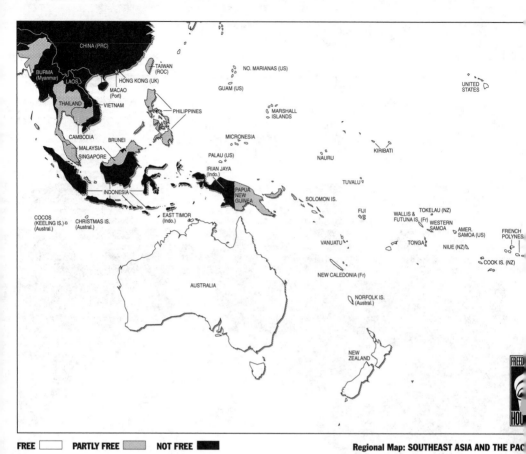

CHINA (PRC)

BURMA
(Myanmar)

TAIWAN
(ROC)

NO. MARIANAS (US)

HONG KONG (UK)

LAOS

MACAO
(Port)

GUAM (US)

THAILAND

VIETNAM

PHILIPPINES

MARSHALL
ISLANDS

UNITED
STATES

CAMBODIA

BRUNEI

MICRONESIA

MALAYSIA

SINGAPORE

PALAU (US)

NAURU

KIRIBATI

IRIAN JAYA
(Indo.)

INDONESIA

PAPUA
NEW
GUINEA

TUVALU

SOLOMON IS.

COCOS
(KEELING IS.)
(Austral.)

CHRISTMAS IS.
(Austral.)

EAST TIMOR
(Indo.)

FIJI

WALLIS &
FUTUNA IS. (Fr)

TOKELAU (NZ)

WESTERN
SAMOA

AMER.
SAMOA (US)

FRENCH
POLYNES

VANUATU

TONGA

NIUE (NZ)

COOK IS. (NZ)

NEW CALEDONIA (Fr)

AUSTRALIA

NORFOLK IS.
(Austral.)

NEW
ZEALAND

FREED

HOU

FREE   **PARTLY FREE**   **NOT FREE**

Regional Map: SOUTHEAST ASIA AND THE PAC

Introduction to Country and Related Territory Reports

The *Survey* team at Freedom House wrote reports on 190 countries and 63 related territories.

Andorra, the Czech Republic, Eritrea and Slovakia join the country reports section in this edition. Nagorno-Karabakh, a territory disputed by Armenia and Azerbaijan, appears as a territory for the first time.

Each report begins with brief political, economic, and social data. This information is arranged under the following headings: **polity, economy, political rights, civil liberties, status, population, purchasing power parities (PPP), population, life expectancy, and ethnic groups.** There is also a brief explanation of **ratings changes** since the last yearbook. When actual events or trends changed the rating, a succinct explanation follows. When modifications in methodology caused a ratings change, the heading notes that. Readers interested in understanding the derivation of the ratings and the methodological modifications in this *Survey* should consult the chapter on methodology.

More detailed information follows in an **overview** and in an essay on the political rights and civil liberties of each country.

Under **polity**, there is an encapsulated description of the dominant centers of freely chosen or unelected political power in each country. Most of the descriptions are self-explanatory, such as Communist one-party for China or parliamentary democracy for Ireland. Such non-parliamentary democracies as the United States of America are designated presidential-legislative democracies. European democratic countries with constitutional monarchs are designated parliamentary democracies, because the elected body is the locus of most real political power. Only countries with powerful monarchs (e.g. the Sultan of Brunei) warrant a reference to the monarchy in the brief description of the polity. Dominant party polities are systems in which the ruling party (or front) dominates government, but allows other parties to organize or compete short of taking control of government. There are other types of polities listed as well. Among them are various military and military-influenced or -dominated regimes, transitional systems, and several unique polities, such as Iran's clergy-dominated parliamentary system. Countries with genuine federalism have the word "federal" in the polity description.

The reports label the **economy** of each country. Non-industrial economies are called traditional or pre-industrial. Developed market economies and Third World economies with a modern market sector have the designation capitalist. Mixed capitalist countries combine private enterprise with substantial government involvement in the economy for social welfare purposes. Capitalist-statist economies have both large market sectors and government-owned productive enterprises, due either to elitist economic policies or state dependence on key natural resource industries. Mixed capitalist-statist economies have the characteristics of capitalist-statist economies plus major social welfare programs. Statist systems have the goal of placing the entire economy under direct or indirect government control. Mixed statist economies are primarily government-controlled, but also have significant private enterprise. Developing Third World economies with a government-directed modern sector belong in the statist category. Economies in transition between statist and capitalist forms may have the word "transitional" in the economy description.

Each country report mentions the category of **political rights** and **civil liberties** in which Freedom House classified the country. Category 1 is the most free and category 7 is the least free in each case. **Status** refers to the designations "free," "partly free," and "not free," which Freedom House uses as an overall summary of the general state of freedom in the country.

The ratings of countries and territories that are different from those of the previous year are marked with an asterisk (*). The reasons for the change precede the "Overview" of the country or territory.

Each entry includes a **population** figure which is sometimes the best approximation that is available. For all cases in which the information is available, the *Survey* provides **life expectancy** statistics.

Freedom House obtained the **Purchasing Power Parities (PPP)** from the U.N. Development Program. These figures show per capita gross domestic product (GDP) in terms of international dollars. The PPP statistic adjusts GDP to account for real buying power. For some countries, especially for newly independent countries, tiny island states, and those with statist economies, these statistics were unavailable.

The *Survey* provides a listing of countries' **ethnic groups**, because this information may help the reader understand such questions as minority rights which the Survey takes into account.

Each country summary has an **overview** which describes such matters as the most important events of 1993 and current political issues. Finally, the country reports contain a section on **political rights** and **civil liberties**. This section summarizes each country's degree of respect for the rights and liberties that Freedom House uses to evaluate freedom in the world. These summaries include instances of human rights violations by both governmental and non-governmental entities.

Reports on related territories follow the country summaries. In most cases, these reports are comparatively brief and contain fewer categories of information than one finds in the country summaries. ▬

Afghanistan

Polity: Competing war-
lords, traditional rulers,
and local councils
Economy: Statist
Population: 17,362,000
PPP: $714
Life Expectancy: 42.5

Political Rights: 7*
Civil Liberties: 7*
Status: Not Free

Ethnic Groups: Pashtun, Tajik, Uzbek, Hazara
Ratings Change: *Afghanistan's political rights and civil liberties ratings
changed from 6,6 to 7, 7 because of increased violence.

Overview: **A** year after Islamic *mujahideen* resistance groups overthrew a
Soviet-backed regime in April 1992, factional fighting
continued to kill thousands of civilians in the capital, Kabul.
An accord in March 1993 extended President Burhanuddin
Rabbani's term and installed his chief rival, Gulbuddin Hekmatyar, as prime minister of
an interim government, but throughout the year armed militias remained in control of
the country, jeopardizing plans to hold elections in mid-1994.

Decades of Russian and British influence over Afghanistan ended in 1919 when the
British relinquished control over the country's foreign affairs. A series of coups and
assassinations brought instability until King Mohamed Zahir Shah came to power in
1933. In 1973 his cousin deposed him in a coup and established a republic. In April
1978 the Khalq faction of the Communist People's Democratic Party of Afghanistan
(PDPA) came to power in another coup.

Under President Hafizollah Amin, this government unleashed a wave of repression
and instituted a highly unpopular agrarian reform program. On 24 December 1979 the
Soviets began airlifting tens of thousands of troops into Kabul, and three days later
installed Amin's rival Babrak Karmal of the PDPA's Parcham faction as president.

The Soviets soon had 115,000 troops in Afghanistan but were unable to overcome
fierce resistance from rebel mujahideen fighters supported directly by Iran and Pakistan
and covertly by China, the United States and others. In May 1986 the Soviets replaced
Karmal with secret service head Mohammad Najibullah, who proved no more effective
against the mujahideen. Faced with a stalemate, the Soviet Union withdrew its last
troops in February 1989.

The collapse of the Soviet Union in late 1991 hastened the fall of the Afghan government. By early 1992 most of the provinces were in mujahideen control. In January
President Najibullah, a member of the majority Pashtun ethnic group, tried to remove many
non-Pashtun commanders from the military. This provoked powerful General Abdul
Rashid Dostam, an Uzbek, to defect to the mujahideen and establish his own militia.

By April several local government militias in the north had defected and formed
alliances with non-Pashtun mujahideen units headed by Ahmed Shah Masoud, the
ethnic Tajik military commander of the moderate fundamentalist Jamiat-i-Islami
(Islamic Society). In addition, rifts between ethnic groups that had largely been
subsumed during the civil war now came to the fore, as these northern units split from

southern Pashtun mujahideen fighters headed by Gulbuddin Hekmatyar, leader of the anti-Western, militant fundamentalist Hizb-i-Islami (Islamic Party).

On 16 April 1992 Najibullah fled to the U.N. compound in Kabul, where he remains. On 24 April the rebel groups agreed to a two-year, three-phase power sharing plan. The first stage established an emergency fifty-one-member Islamic Jihad Council headed by a Pashtun cleric, Sigbatullah Mojaddidi. Later, a Pan-Afghan Grand Council would select an eighteen-month interim government to draft a constitution, create government institutions, and prepare for nationwide elections.

On 25 April Kabul finally fell to the mujahideen. Three days later the rebels proclaimed the Islamic Republic of Afghanistan, with Mojaddidi as head of state. Despite an arrangement which gave the premiership to a member of the Hizb-i-Islami, Hekmatyar had his militia attack Masoud's troops, which controlled Kabul. Hekmatyar claimed the new government was not Islamic enough, in part because it had allied itself with Dostam, a former Communist. Despite the fighting all parties remained in the government. The second transitional phase began on 28 June as Jamiat-i-Islami leader Burhanuddin Rabbani, an ethnic Tajik who had headed the Pakistani-based Afghan Interim Government-in-exile for several years, took over as president of a Leadership Council for a planned four-month term.

By late August fighting between the mujahideen militias had killed several thousand civilians and driven 600,000 others out of the capital. Throughout the summer and fall, clashes also occurred between the Sunni Muslim Ittehad-i-Islami group backed by Saudi Arabia and the Iranian-backed, Shiite Hezb-i-Wahadat group, which demanded greater representation in the interim government.

On 30 December a Grand Council, consisting of tribal elders, religious leaders and militia commanders, elected Rabbani to a two-year presidential term. Five of the nine factions represented on the council, including Hekmatyar's Hezb-i-Islami, boycotted it over claims that Rabbani had bribed several delegates. By this point four major groups controlled most of the country. In the north, Dostam's Uzbek-dominated militia, the most powerful armed group, ruled six provinces from a base in Mazar-i-Sharif. Masoud's Jamiat-i-Islami controlled most of Kabul as well as several other regions. The Hizb-i-Wahadat controlled six provinces in central Afghanistan. The largest area, south and east of Kabul, was dominated by Pashtuns loyal to Hekmatyar.

On 1 January 1993 the Grand Council formed a parliament from among 20 percent of its 1,355 members. The Council also decreed that only Muslims could work for the government, banned all non-Muslim organizations and ordered radio and television to conform to Islamic principles. Two days later the Council swore in Rabbani as president of the country.

On 19 January government forces began attacking positions held by Hekmatyar's Hezb-i-Islami on the southern and eastern flanks around the capital. Hezb-i-Islami countered with renewed attacks on the capital aimed at forcing Rabbani to step down and hold national elections. In early February, Hekmatyar and the Hezb-i-Wahadat, which controlled parts of western Kabul, formed an anti-government alliance. By the middle of the month, rocket attacks in this latest round of fighting had killed at least 1,000 civilians and wounded 4,000 others.

An accord brokered by Pakistani premier Nawaz Sharif in early March called for Rabbani to remain as president until mid-1994 and for Hekmatyar to be named prime minister, with the two choosing government ministers together. It created a sixteen-member defense council, consisting of two members of each of the eight parties to the accord, to establish a national army. The plan also stipulated elections would be held within eight months for a constituent assembly, which would draft a new constitution. To appease the fundamentalists, the agreement excluded a role for Dostam.

However Hekmatyar demanded Masoud's removal as defense minister so that the Jamiat-i-Islami would not control both the presidency and the top defense post. By early May troops loyal to Masoud were again battling Hekmatyar's troops in the capital. On 20 May, following two weeks of fighting that killed more than 500 civilians and wounded another 5,000, Masoud agreed to step down under a plan in which the defense and interior ministries would be headed by commissions for two months. After that, new ministers would be elected for each post by commanders from each of the country's twenty-nine provinces. The agreement also gave cabinet posts to the country's ten major rebel groups. On 17 June Hekmatyar and the new cabinet were finally sworn in.

On 27 September the government announced that rebel leaders had approved an interim constitution to carry the country through general elections in mid-1994. Although the most contentious issue had been protection for Shiite Muslims in this predominantly Sunni country, the government provided few details of the draft, leaving it unclear whether the Shiites received the assurances they had sought. Factional fighting broke out again in Kabul in October. By year's end more than 10,000 people had been killed in the capital since the Communist government fell in April 1992.

In another key development, in mid-July Russian troops guarding Tajikistan's border launched rocket and artillery attacks against Tajik opposition fighters based in northern Afghanistan. By mid-August Afghanistan claimed that Russian and Tajik attacks had killed some 750 civilians and displaced several thousand others. Talks between the Tajik and Afghan foreign ministers during the month failed to end the skirmishes.

The continued turmoil has hampered the country's efforts to recover from the civil war, during which an estimated 1.2 million people were killed, many of them civilians, while 5 million fled to other countries and 1 million were internally displaced. Some 3.8 million refugees remain in camps in Pakistan and Iran. Complicating matters, at least 10 million uncleared mines lie scattered throughout the country. More than 70 percent of the workforce is unemployed and few public services exist. Only the northern region controlled by Dostam has reasonably efficient services and administration. In October President Rabbani said the civil war and subsequent fighting had destroyed 80 percent of the country's infrastructure, requiring $4 billion to repair.

Political Rights and Civil Liberties: Afghans cannot change their government democratically. The unelected nominal national government in Kabul lacks authority over much of the countryside, which is controlled by rival militias. Tens of thousands of people, mostly civilians, have been killed in clashes between rival Islamic groups since the Communist regime fell in April 1992. There are credible reports of torture and extrajudicial killings carried out by the rival groups against their opponents. Members of the Sikh and Hindu minorities are often targeted for crime and random violence and thousands have fled the country.

The new government has attempted to establish Islamic law throughout the country. In January 1993 a Grand Council of religious and tribal leaders declared that only Muslims could work for the government. It also banned all non-Muslim organizations and ordered all television and print media to conform with Islamic principles. Freedoms of speech, press and assembly are sharply restricted by these decrees. There are few independent publications in the country, and the government strictly controls radio and television content. By law females must wear traditional body coverings. Girls cannot attend co-ed schools, severely limiting their educational opportunities in a country where few schools operate for either sex.

Justice is administered according to Islamic law by the government, and by Islamic law or tribal customs by the factions controlling the countryside, in either case without regard to any due process rights. Freedom of movement within the country is hampered by continued factional fighting, as well as by the millions of uncleared landmines strewn across the country. Afghanistan had no independent labor movements during the Communist regime, and it is doubtful any such groups would be allowed to operate under the new regime.

Albania

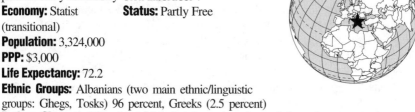

Polity: Presidential-parliamentary democracy
Political Rights: 2*
Civil Liberties: 4*
Economy: Statist (transitional)
Status: Partly Free
Population: 3,324,000
PPP: $3,000
Life Expectancy: 72.2
Ethnic Groups: Albanians (two main ethnic/linguistic groups: Ghegs, Tosks) 96 percent, Greeks (2.5 percent)
Ratings Change: *Albania's political rights rating changed from 4 to 2 and its civil liberties rating changed from 3 to 4 as a result of modifications in methodology. See "Survey Methodology," page 671.

Overview:
In 1993, the Albanian government of President Sali Berisha faced continued political polarization amid measured economic gains and charges that, in the absence of a new constitution, the ruling Democratic Party was showing authoritarian tendencies. The year also saw the arrests and sentencing of former Communist party leaders.

Situated between Greece and Serbia on the southern Adriatic coast of the Balkan Peninsula, this tiny, predominantly Muslim nation gained independence in 1912 after 450 years as a Turkish suzerainty. It was annexed by Italy in 1939. A one-party Communist regime was established in 1946 under World War II partisan leader Enver Hoxha until his death in 1985. During his repressive reign, religion was outlawed, mosques and churches were razed, and autarkic economic policies left Albania the poorest, most primitive country in Europe.

In 1990, following the collapse of Communist regimes throughout East-Central Europe, Ramiz Alia, who had succeeded Hoxha as first secretary of the Albanian Party of Labor (Communist), was elected president as head of the Socialist (former Communist) Party (SP) in elections marred by irregularities.

In March 1992 elections, preceded by months of intense social unrest and a mass exodus of Albanians to Greece, Italy and elsewhere, the Democratic Party won 92 seats and the Socialists 38. The Social Democratic Party (SDP) picked up 7 seats, the Union for Human Rights of the Greek Minority, 2, and the right-wing Republican Party, 1. President Alia resigned, and less than a week later lawmakers elected Sali Berisha president by a margin of 96 votes to 35. He became Albania's first non-Communist ruler since World War II. Alexander Meksi was named prime minister.

In January, the government's campaign against former Communists was high-lighted when Nexhmije Hoxha, the seventy-two-year-old widow of the late Communist leader, was sentenced to nine years' imprisonment for misuse of government funds between 1985 and 1990. Subsequent arrests, however, were at least partly politically motivated, including the jailing of SP leader Fatos Nano, who had served as prime minister from 25 March to 4 June 1991 and led the SP's walkout of parliament in June. On 20 August, former President Alia was jailed along with seven other top Communists charged with pilfering Italian humanitarian aid. Former Prime Minister Vilson Ahmeti was sentenced to two years' imprisonment for misusing aid funds.

The failure of the government and political parties to agree on a draft constitution spurred a 16 June walkout from parliament by the SDP (which had supported the government), the SP and the two members of the Human Rights Party of the Greek Minority. The crucial disagreement was over presidential powers, with the DP backing a strong executive and the opposition parties calling for a parliamentary republic.

The walkout by the SP, which consistently obstructed government initiatives, was aimed at fostering political instability. On 1 April the Socialists had voted against approving a section of the draft constitution devoted to fundamental human rights and freedoms that had been inserted in response to a personal legislative initiative by President Berisha. The Greek Minority party saw the crisis as an opportunity to gain concessions from the government for Albania's Greeks (estimated at 60,000 by Albania and at 250,000 by Greece) in southern Albania. For its part, the SDP, led by Skender Gjinushi, blamed the government for the "drastic" economic methods dictated by the International Monetary Fund and the World Bank. Although SDP deputies returned to parliament just prior to the summer recess, the political gridlock continued when parliament reconvened in September.

Following the arrest of Nano, the SP denounced the government as "Ballist-fascist," a reference to the wartime opposition party, Balli Kombetar. Actions by the Berisha government did raise questions about increased authoritarianism. In July, Idajet Beqeri, leader of the tiny Albanian Unity Party, was imprisoned for slander because of an article describing President Berisha as the "murderer" of Albania and charging him with setting up a fascist state. The SP was not alone in criticizing the sentence. Gramoz Pashko, a founding member of the DP and a member of the Democratic Alliance (which ultimately split off from the DP), said the imprisonment was undemocratic.

Meanwhile, rifts continued in the DP, which in 1992 had purged several moderates. Extremist elements in the DP gained momentum with the government taking a hardline against "former Communists" and their allies. The DP's newspaper, *Rilindja Demo-kratike*, frequently published personal and inflammatory attacks on opposition figures.

The government continued economic reforms launched in 1992, including a cut in unemployment benefits, reduction of wage subsidies, price liberalization, complete land privatization, and gradual privatization of most state enterprises as well as of trade, transportation and the fishing and mining industries. Clashes over economic policies emerged between the SP and nationalists, many of them former landowners and merchants whose wealth was confiscated by the former regime. The conflict had intensified after the SP won a majority of seats in local elections in July 1992. In response, local DP officials refused to distribute international food aid to towns where former Communists won. The DP was also accused of using food aid and bribes to win two local elections in 1993.

The government did manage to restore public order, which had been lacking when it took over in April 1992. Prices in June 1993 fell after strident budget-deficit cuts. The currency was stabilized early in the year, as did industrial output, which had fallen over 60 percent, the most precipitous economic collapse in Eastern Europe. The 1993 harvest was projected to be larger than the year before following the privatization of 80 percent of farm land.

President Berisha did give into the nationalists over the question of property restitution. In April, a highly controversial Law on the Return of Properties to Former Owners was passed allowing former owners to reclaim their land, even if it had been built over. The Association of Free Traders of Albania protested the measure, which made former proprietors co-owners with current traders. Other provisions called for current owners who bought their shops to pay rent to former owners. By year's end the law seemed unworkable, partly because the country still lacked a justice system to sort out property claims. The law also discouraged foreign investment. Western countries had handed over more than $1 billion in aid, mainly as food, which was sold by the government as its main source of revenue. Only $20 million in foreign investment had arrived in the country.

The IMF praised Tirana for its adherence to "shock" prescriptions for revitalizing the economy and there were signs of a working macroeconomy. Still, at least 230,000 Albanians were jobless, with the number expected to rise.

There were continuing problems with neighboring Greece. Albania's June expulsion of an orthodox cleric from southern Albania led the Greek government to begin deporting 30,000 of an estimated 200,000 Albanian migrant workers, who had sent back an estimated $400 million to their homeland. Tensions also escalated with neighboring Macedonia, which has a sizable Albanian minority. Albania feared that the war in Bosnia would spill over into Kosovo, the Albanian enclave inside Serbia.

Political Rights and Civil Liberties:

Albanians can change their government through democratic means. The 1992 election to the 150-member National Assembly was generally regarded as free and fair, although there were some reports of irregularities.

The country is slowly restructuring its judicial system and implementing the rule of law. However, police have wide-ranging authority with little institutional oversight. There is a shortage of legal experts and lawyers. The executive branch has interfered with the judiciary and procuracy by dismissing judges and prosecutors on political grounds. A new constitution has yet to be implemented.

Political parties, civic organizations, independent trade unions, and student groups are allowed to organize, but there have been restrictions on the rights of expression and association. In June, police beat back six busloads of people in Gjirokaster at a rally supporting expelled Greek Orthodox Archimandrite Chrysostomos Maidonis. Authorities had earlier denied Greeks permission for the rally. In July, Idajet Beqeri of the Albanian Unity Party was imprisoned for "slandering" the president.

The independent press is, in large part, controlled by political parties. *Rilindja*

Demokratike has stridently attacked opposition figures, often with no pretense of objectivity. In March, Tirana's Prosecutor's Office charged Aleksander Frangaj, editor of *Koha Jone*, with "spreading false information" after a story that the defense ministry was concentrating tanks in southeastern Albania, home to the Greek minority. In September, the Albanian Helsinki Committee protested what it called "crimes committed by unknown persons against Albanian journalists." In June, ATA press service journalist Fatmir Elezi was beaten to death by unknown assailants. An Italian journalist was detained by police in violation of legal procedure. The Committee also reported attacks against journalists from *Drita* and *Zeri I Rinise*, and demanded "concrete measures against individual policemen who transgress the legal principles guaranteeing the right to a free press."

Radio and television are state monopolies. In September, the Socialist paper, *Zeri i Popullit*, charged that government-run television and radio are biased toward the regime and refuse to cover their position on issues, an allegation backed by other groups.

Freedom of movement and foreign and domestic travel are guaranteed and met in practice.

Restrictions on religious activity have been officially lifted in this predominantly Muslim country. There are Orthodox and Roman Catholic minorities. Greeks, Macedonians, Gypsies, Vlachs, and Gabels have been pressing various cultural demands. Omonia, a Greek cultural association, pressed for classes in the Greek language through eighth grade.

The Law on Major Constitutional Provisions does not address women's rights. The majority of Albanians are non-practicing Muslims but Islamic traditions do not accord women equal treatment with men. Women do have equal access to higher education and some professions.

Under Article 1 of Law No. 7516, trade unions are independent social organizations free from employer, state and party interference. The Independent Confederation of Trade Unions of Albania (BSPSh) is an umbrella organization for several unions. There are several independent unions, such as the miners', and a relic of the former "official" trade union with ties to the SP.

Algeria

Polity: Civilian-military
Economy: Statist
Population: 27,256,000
PPP: $3,011
Life Expectancy: 65.1
Ethnic Groups: Arabs (75 percent), Berbers (25 percent)

Political Rights: 7
Civil Liberties: 6
Status: Not Free

Overview: In 1993 Algeria experienced an escalation of violence in a tug of war between the ruling military-dominated Higher State Council (HCE) and the radical Islamic opposition. The violence began with the cancellation of election results in January 1992.

President Chadli Benjedid's democratization process came to an abrupt end following the first round of parliamentary elections in December 1991 in which the radical Islamic National Front (FIS) captured 188 out of the 230 seats. The military cancelled the second round of elections, scheduled for January 1992, because it was clear the FIS was going to win.

The FIS had vowed to establish a theocratic state and impose *Sharia,* the Islamic law, as the supreme law of the country. The widespread support for the fundamentalist FIS was a protest against the National Liberation Front (FLN), which had ruled Algeria since its independence in 1961 after a bloody liberation war against France, its former colonial ruler. The majority of Algerians viewed the FLN as corrupt and blamed it for high unemployment, inflation and an acute housing shortage for the rapidly growing population, 70 percent of whom are under the age of fifteen.

In addition to stopping the elections, the army forced President Benjedid to resign, instituting a collective presidency, later known as the Higher State Council (HCE), with Mohammad Boudiaf, a veteran of the war of independence, as its chairman. Shortly thereafter, amid increasing violence, the HCE imposed a year-long state of emergency, arresting the FIS leaders and activists and banning the party. Despite the ban the violence escalated with shootouts between the militants and the security forces, and assassinations became more common. One of the victims was HCE Chairman Boudiaf, killed in June 1992 by an apparently fundamentalist soldier.

On 14 January 1993, the new HCE chairman, Ali Kafi, promised to hold a referendum on a new constitution and invited political parties, with the exception of "those who practiced or supported violence," to participate in planning policies for the future. Shortly after the start of the dialogue, the talks with the opposition collapsed due to the resistance of the secular parties, such as the Front of Socialist Forces (FFS), Movement for a Democratic Algeria (MDA), and the Berber-based Rally for Culture and Democracy (RCD), which opposed the participation of the moderate Islamic parties, Hamas and Ennahda.

In February, in a move to clamp down on corruption, an Algiers court began proceedings against a former chief of staff, General Mustafa Benloucif, who had allegedly diverted more than $6 million from government funds for his private use.

In May, Kafi repeated the HCE's intention to hold a constitutional referendum and pledged to review the electoral law so as to exclude religious or ethnic-based political parties from participating in the election. He also pledged to keep the transitional period between the referendum and the planned new elections as short as possible. On 21 June, after a series of discussions, the government sent out the drafts of a "democratic management of the transition" to political parties and social organizations, providing a blueprint for constitutional changes that promised a modern Muslim state with a free-market economy. On 21 August, the HCE dismissed Prime Minister Belaid Abdesselam, replacing him with Redha Malek, who promised more bold economic reform. One of the most urgent economic issues facing the new government was the rescheduling of its $26 billion external debt, whose servicing absorbed three-quarters of export revenues.

In the face of the rising violence, on 5 December 1992 the HCE imposed a curfew in and around the capital, Algiers, and 300 local councils, almost all elected on the FIS ticket, were dissolved and replaced with government appointees. In 1993 the circle of violence continued to escalate, with gun battles between the militants and security forces occurring regularly in the cities and spreading to the countryside. Increasingly, violent groups attacked the political and intellectual elites, journalists, and foreigners working in Algeria. Besides the fundamentalist groups there were rumors of the "financial-military mafia" within the HCE fomenting and even participating in the violence in order to justify the repressive measures imposed under the state of emergency, and cling to power. The tide of terrorism sweeping the country was often compared to the violence during Algeria's struggle for independence in the 1950s.

On 11 January the government executed two soldiers convicted of attacking a naval facility in 1992. They were the first to be executed since the start of the violence. Several days later, the FIS published a communiqué, for the first time publicly condoning the anti-government violence. On 9 February the HCE extended indefinitely the state of emergency imposed a year earlier. On 13 February, Defense Minister General Khaled Nezzar escaped unharmed when a bomb exploded as his motorcade passed through an Algiers suburb.

On 22 March, in the first protest march sanctioned by the HCE, at least 50,000 protesters denounced the fundamentalists for the wave of terrorist attacks, which in the previous week claimed the lives of three high-ranking government officials. Before the march began signs appearing on a number of mosques vowed its disruption, and some protesters shouted anti-government slogans. There was no violence during the protest march, but on the same day, a group of militants attacked the Ksar el-Boukhari military barracks in central Algeria, killing eighteen soldiers and capturing a quantity of weapons. Twenty-three militants died in the ensuing battle. Following the attack the army ordered a large military operation to track down the group responsible for its execution, killing twenty-three militants by the end of the month.

By the end of March, the HCE broke off diplomatic relations with Iran and Sudan, accusing them of aiding the militants. In early April, a secret group calling itself the Safeguard of the Algerian Republic threatened to destroy the fundamentalists and their accomplices in and out of the country, and the official security forces killed Omar El Eulumi, a major militant leader.

In mid-June a surprise attack killed 50 soldiers near Algiers. On 22 June terrorists assassinated professor Muhammad Boukhobza, a noted sociologist. Shortly thereafter the writer Tahar Djaout and Mahfoud Boussebsi, a hospital director, became the next victims. On 21 August, a group of assailants killed Kasdi Merbah, a former prime minister, after he had urged the militants to lay down their arms. In September and October seven foreigners working for the government were kidnapped and executed. By late 1993, more than 2,000 people had died in violence since the imposition of the state of emergency.

Political Rights and Civil Liberties:

Algerians lost their nascent right to change their government democratically in January 1992, when the army canceled the second round of the national elections and placed the military-led Higher State Council in control of the country. The elected members of the local councils were replaced with government appointees.

The state of emergency reinforced the power of the security forces to set up detention centers, order house searches, ban marches, dismiss local authorities, and order trials by military courts. The security forces conducted an extensive crackdown on citizens, especially suspected militants and their sympathizers. In October 1992, the HCE established special secret courts to issue sentences to suspected terrorists, by-passing regular judicial safeguards. Proceedings are kept secret, as are the names of judges, and the rights of suspects to defense attorneys are often violated. In January, five attorneys withdrew from a case of suspected arms traffickers as a protest against the violation of the suspects' rights. They were replaced by five unnamed military attorneys. Nineteen of the seventy-nine suspects in the case received death sentences. In March 1993, Amnesty International published a report accusing the authorities of widespread torture to extract confessions. Some 9,000 people have been detained without formal charges since the imposition of the state of emergency and, as of March, more than 1,000 were still held without charge.

Article 96 of the Penal Code provides a maximum three-year sentence for possessing, distributing or displaying materials "harmful to the national interest." In February, Maitre Brahim Taouti, a lawyer for the imprisoned deputy FIS leader Ali Belhadj, was sentenced for carrying Belhadj's statement out of prison and distributing it to his followers.

In January 1993, the HCE introduced a tighter press law limiting journalists' access to information on political violence, and required them to obtain police permission before publication of such information. The introduction of the law followed the suspension of the independent daily *El Watan* for writing "prematurely" about the killing of five police officers, that is before the official news agency released the information. In March, a reporter from the Reuters news agency was arrested after writing an inaccurate news story about a cabinet member's assassination. In April, a court charged and jailed a newspaper publisher for criticizing the sweeping powers of the special courts. Increasingly since May 1993, the terrorists have targeted journalists for assassination. On 17 May, the editor of *El Watan* escaped unscathed from an ambush by unidentified assailants. In August, two journalists from the state television and news agency were shot and killed. On 20 October, journalists staged a day of protest after several more colleagues were killed, including an assistant television news director. During that day, no daily newspapers were published and several hundred journalists held a "No to genocide" banner, demanding state protection.

Women have fewer rights than men and are legally under the guardianship of their fathers, brothers or husbands. In March, Prime Minister Belaid Abdesslam promised to give women a more prominent position in public life, within the framework of the sharia, and urged them to persuade men committed to violence "to return to the right path" and give up their arms.

Although the law prohibits discrimination against the Berbers, who comprise a quarter of the population, there have been many restrictions placed on the Berber language, schools and culture. With independence, the authorities conducted an Arabization program aiming at fostering a common Algerian identity. In April, some 10,000 protesters, defying a government ban, marched in the capital of the Kabyle region to commemorate a 1980 Berber uprising at the University of Tizi Ouzou.

Although Islam is the official religion, other faiths are legal but may not proselytize. Following the imposition of the state of emergency, the government replaced most of the pro-FIS clergy in the country's 10,000 mosques. Roadblocks, nightly curfews and frequent random searches of travelers limit the Algerians' right to travel freely within their own country. Men may travel and emigrate rather freely, but women must obtain travel permits from their male guardians.

In November 1992, the authorities imposed new laws allowing them to close down associations, labor unions, private companies and local councils deemed to support the fundamentalist organizations. The main trade union is the General Union of the Algerian Workers (UGTA). The UGTA has openly opposed the idea of a theocratic Algeria, and has joined the HCE in organizing rallies condemning the fundamentalist violence.

Andorra

Polity: Parliamentary democracy
Economy: Capitalist
Population: 54,000
PPP: na
Life Expectancy: na
Ethnic Groups: Andorran (Catalan), Spanish, Portuguese, French, other European

Political Rights: 2
Civil Liberties: 1
Status: Free

Overview:

In 1993 Andorra became a sovereign nation with a new constitution and U.N. membership. From 1278 through early 1993, Andorra was a territory under the joint control of France and the Bishop of Urgel, Spain. The country's new constitution and independence resulted from an internal power struggle and outside pressure from France and Spain.

Andorra began 1992 in political deadlock. Oscar Ribas Reig, the head of government, had been unable to pass a budget for eleven months. Although the General Council (parliament) had decided to draft the first constitution, conservatives blocked Ribas's attempt to codify rights in a written constitution. Ribas had only 12 supporters in the 28-member General Council. After a technically illegal demonstration, the parliament voted to dissolve itself. In a two-round election in April 1992, reformist Ribas backers won 17 of the 28 seats. On 2 February 1993, the pro-Ribas majority adopted a constitution with entrenched human rights, parliamentary democracy, and a highly limited role for a combined constitutional monarchy for the French president and the bishop of Urgel. Andorran voters approved the constitution overwhelmingly in a referendum on 14 March 1993. This vote affirmed the country's sovereign status and paved the way for its admission to the U.N. on 28 July 1993.

In the general election on 12 December, Riba's National Democratic Group won 8 of the 28 parliamentary seats. He expected to form a ruling coalition with other parties. The Liberals and New Democracy won 5 seats each. Independents won 10 seats in Andorra's first openly multiparty elections.

Although for centuries the French president and the Spanish Bishop had representatives there, Andorra had no locally chosen head of government until 1981. In 1991 Andorra joined the European Community customs union. Its neighbors are forcing the principality to modernize and liberalize its economy. Andorra is feeling inflationary pressure from prices in Spain and France, whose currencies circulate there.

The number of Spanish and Portuguese immigrants is growing faster than the native population. The government has proposed easing citizenship requirements.

Political Rights and Civil Liberties:

Andorrans have the right to change their government by democratic means. Women have had the franchise since 1970. There are some limitations on voting rights for young, first-generation Andorrans. Otherwise, there is universal suffrage for Andorran citizens at age eighteen. Only a minority of the population is Andorran, so only about 10,000 may vote. Before the adoption of the constitution, there were technically no political parties, but there were factions and associations that had effective party functions. Article 26 of the constitution accords Andorrans the right to create political parties, which must be democratic and conduct lawful activities. The judiciary has the responsibility to dissolve parties not meeting these standards. Andorra has democratically elected local (parish) governments.

There are two competing, private weekly newspapers. There is a local public radio and television service. French and Spanish media are easily available. The constitution guarantees freedom of expression, communication and information, but it also allows for laws regulating rights of reply, correction and professional confidentiality. There is freedom of assembly, but organizers of demonstrations must give authorities advance notice and take care not to "prevent the free movement of goods and people."

In 1990, the co-princes issued the first Andorran penal code which eliminated the death penalty. The constitution confirms this prohibition. Convicts go to French and Spanish prisons. The country is building its own independent judicial system. By tradition, when a corpse is found, judges ask it three times, "Who killed you?"

Trade unions and other economic groupings have freedom of association. The constitution outlines social and economic rights including employment, housing and social security. Andorrans have a largely tax-free private enterprise economy. There is religious freedom, subject to limitations "in the interests of public safety, order, health or morals, or for the protection of the fundamental rights and freedoms of others." The constitution guarantees the Roman Catholic Church "the preservation of the relations of special co-operation with the State in accordance with the Andorran tradition."

Angola

Polity: Dominant party (insurgency)
Economy: Statist
Population: 9,545,000
PPP: $1,225
Life Expectancy: 45.5
Ethnic Groups: Ovimbundu (38 percent), Kimbundu (25 percent), Bakongo (17 percent), other
Ratings Change: *Angola's political rights and civil liberties ratings changed from 6,6 to 7,7 because of an aborted democratic transition and a return to civil war.

Political Rights: 7*
Civil Liberties: 7*
Status: Not Free

Overview: Angola's first multi-party national election, held in September 1992 under U.N. supervision, was to mark the beginning of Angola's road to democracy. Shortly after the elections, however, fighting again broke out between the government forces of The Popular Movement for the Liberation of Angola (MPLA) and those of the National Union for the Total Independence of Angola (UNITA), amid reports of gross human rights violations by both sides. In the wake of the renewed fighting and in a departure from recent U.S. foreign policy, President Bill Clinton formally recognized the Government of the Republic of Angola in May of 1993 and urged longtime U.S. ally Jonas Savimbi to end military hostilities.

The September elections were part of an agreement reached in the Bicesse Peace Accord that was signed in May of 1991 as part of a permanent ceasefire agreement between the MPLA government headed by Jose Eduardo dos Santos and the rival UNITA party led by Jonas Savimbi. In the parliamentary vote, the MPLA emerged with 53.74 percent (securing 129 seats) compared to 34.10 percent for UNITA (securing 70 seats). In a close presidential race, Dos Santos gained 49.57 percent of the vote (just short of the absolute majority needed to win outright), compared to 40.07 percent for Savimbi. UNITA quickly discounted the elections as fraudulent and refused to take part in a second presidential ballot. UNITA maintained that the government unduly influenced election results, although U.N. officials and most other international observers monitoring the results claimed that the elections were "generally free and fair."

Angola has four primary political movements: In addition to the MPLA and UNITA are two smaller groups, the National Front for the Liberation of Angola (FNLA) and the Front for the Liberation of the Enclave of Cabinda (FLEC).

Founded in 1956, the MPLA was successful in winning the 1975-76 civil war and now forms the government led by President Jose Eduardo dos Santos. Long believed to be guided by Marxist ideology, and previously supported by the former USSR and Cuba, the party is based on the Kimbundu tribe of north-central Angola. The MPLA's main rival party is UNITA. Founded in 1966 by a former deputy of FNLA, Jonas Savimbi, it is based on the Ovimbundu tribe (the largest in Angola) of central and southern Angola. Since his defeat in the 1975/76 civil war, Savimbi has continued to lead a rebellion based on his tribal homeland, with substantial support from, among others, the United States, South Africa and Zaire. Militarily moribund since the mid-1970's, the FNLA was established in 1960 by Holden Roberto and is based on the Bakongo tribe of northern Angola and Zaire. The FLEC was founded in 1963, and is dedicated to securing independence for the oil rich province of Cabinda in Southeast Angola.

Angola emerged from a fifteen-year war for independence from Portugal (1961-1975) only to find itself embroiled in an internal power struggle. Angola became a bloody battleground spurred on by Cold War rivalries. UNITA, led by Jonas Savimbi, success-fully campaigned for support from the West (and, in particular, from the Reagan adminis-tration), with Savimbi portraying himself as a "freedom fighter" leading a pro-democratic party against the then-Marxist regime of the MPLA. As the Cold War came to a close, so too did much of the financial and military support from the U.S. and USSR.

Although the United Nations made a number of attempts to negotiate an end to the conflict, the first success came in 1991 with the signing of the Bicesse Accord. The ceasefire that followed held for nearly a year throughout most of Angola, but fighting again erupted as the election neared. One provision of the accord called for the establishment of a National Electoral Commission (CNE) which would oversee the parliamentary and presidential elections that were to be held in the last quarter of 1992. The commission did not convene until May 1992 and UNITA subsequently charged the Dos Santos government with using the delay for pre-election politicking. In the month prior to the elections, forty people were reported killed in politically related violence.

The elections themselves were remarkably quiet and approximately 90 percent of the population voted. Just prior to the elections, the MPLA and UNITA agreed to form a coalition government regardless of the election results. However, UNITA subse-quently rejected its defeat at the polls and fighting resumed. Despite a number of promises by Savimbi to return to the negotiating table, UNITA rebels continued to seize control of territory within Angola. With each new position claimed, Savimbi's bargaining power increases. By mid-January of 1993 UNITA forces had seized military control of more than half the country and by September, that figure had increased to almost 70 percent.

In September of 1993 the U.N. Security Council passed a resolution which called for an embargo on the sale of arms and arms-related materials as well as petroleum and petroleum-related products to the UNITA rebels if a ceasefire was not respected. No ceasefire agreement was reached and the measure took effect on 25 September. The resolution further stated that as of 1 November, the secretary general reserved the right to impose further sanctions.

Political Rights and Civil Liberties: The resumption of civil war nullified the possibility for Angolans to change their government by democratic means. Despite the U.N.'s continued efforts to negotiate an end to Angola's bloody civil war, the fighting continues. Since the end of colonial rule in 1975, an estimated 450,000 people have been killed and over two million people (one-fifth of the population) have been displaced as a result of the ongoing power struggle between the MPLA and UNITA. War and famine claim an additional 1,000 casualties each day. In 1993, the United Nations World Food Programme (WFP) estimated that 2 million Angolans would face starvation unless emergency food airlifts, which had been blocked by both sides, were allowed to resume.

For the children of Angola, the war has been particularly cruel. The death toll among children is higher now than at any time during the previous sixteen years of war. In September 1993, hospital officials in Angola's capital of Luanda reported that one child died every hour. UNICEF reported that 10 percent of all Angolan children were severely malnourished and countless numbers had been orphaned.

While politically related violence between the ceasefire agreement of 1991 and the 1992 elections was minimal, there were a number of killings attributed to tensions between MPLA and UNITA. Shortly after the elections, however, human rights groups reported gross human rights violations by MPLA supporters as well as UNITA forces. To date, these human rights violations continue unabated. Aid workers claim that ideological cleansing, known as *limbeza,* has become a standard feature of the civil war. While both sides deny the allegations, aid workers maintain that thousands of politically motivated killings have been systematically carried out by special police loyal to the MPLA and by UNITA rebels.

UNITA soldiers have allegedly killed a number of civilians suspected of being MPLA sympathizers as well as government soldiers and members of provincial electoral councils in a number of provinces including Benguela, Bie, and Malanje. In the coastal town of Catombela and in Huambo, reports indicate that UNITA has targeted those it feels symbolize the cultural elite of Angola (predominantly whites and mixed-race Angolans). Prisoners of UNITA forces have alleged that they were subjected to numerous beatings and torture while in custody.

For its part, the government has been accused of summarily executing UNITA military and civilian sympathizers. Reports indicate that the government has illegally detained UNITA members. UNITA members have charged that during their detention they were subjected to cruel and inhumane treatment by government forces.

The Peace Accords had called on UNITA and MPLA forces to release all prisoners of war under the supervision of the International Committee of the Red Cross. Despite this agreement, both sides allege that a number of detainees were not released and additional prisoners of war continue to be taken by both sides.

Angolans are not free from undue government and rival party interference into personal and family life. Both the MPLA and UNITA have exchanged accusations of arbitrary search and seizure of personal and business property. The judiciary system within Angola is not free from government interference. While the 1991 Angolan Constitution provides detainees with the right to both legal counsel and habeus corpus, these provisions are reportedly ignored as a result of the ongoing struggle between the MPLA and UNITA.

Angola's press is, on the whole, not free. The government controls the only daily newspaper, television station and national radio. The sole Angolan news agency is also under government control. However, just prior to the elections, the media began to show signs of some degree of independence. Some editorial comment was tolerated and UNITA was able to circulate a daily newspaper and transmit programs on its radio station without interference. As the fighting resumed, however, the intimidation, arbitrary detention, and execution of journalists by both UNITA and the MPLA increased dramatically.

While the Peace Accords provide for freedom of movement for both people and goods within Angola, respect for the stipulation varies. Reports indicate that UNITA forces have made a number of areas virtually inaccessible.

Antigua and Barbuda

Polity: Dominant party
Economy: Capitalist-statist
Population: 64,000
PPP: $4,000
Life Expectancy: 72.0
Ethnic Groups: Black (89 percent), other (11 percent)
Ratings Change: *Antigua and Barbuda's political rights rating changed from 3 to 4 as a result of methodological modifications. See "Survey Methodology," page 671.

Political Rights: 4*
Civil Liberties: 3
Status: Partly Free

Overview: After a drawn out internal dispute, the long ruling Antigua Labour Party (ALP) selected Lester Bird to succeed his father, Vere Bird, as party leader. The eighty-two-year-old prime minister had said he would step down prior to the elections due by March 1994. The opposition feared the ALP would again resort to election fraud to perpetuate the Bird dynasty.

Antigua and Barbuda is a member of the British Commonwealth. The British monarchy is represented by a governor-general. The islands became self-governing in 1969 and gained independence in 1981. Formally a parliamentary democracy, Antigua and Barbuda has been dominated by the Birds and the ALP for over two decades.

In the 1989 elections, marred by irregularities and fraud, the ALP maintained control of the House of Representatives, retaining fifteen of seventeen seats. The United National Democratic Party (UNDP) won one seat and the Barbuda People's Movement (BPM) won the Barbuda seat. Also competing was the leftist Antigua Caribbean Liberation Movement (ACLM) and a number of smaller parties. In separate elections two weeks later, the BPM took all five Barbuda Council seats.

As in previous elections, the opposition made credible charges that the ALP exerted undue influence over the nominally independent electoral supervisor and used bribery and intimidation at polling time. In response to a petition filed by UNDP, a high court annulled the results in one constituency. Before it could rule on six other contested constituencies, ALP members holding the contested seats resigned and the government announced by-elections. The UNDP boycotted the by-elections and demanded electoral reform.

Since 1989 the ALP has contended with a succession crisis as Vere Bird Jr. and Lester Bird competed for the party mantle held by their father. Papa Bird favored Bird Jr., at least until the 1990 Israeli arms scandal.

In April 1990 the government of Colombia protested that Israeli arms had been sold to the Antiguan government and shipped to the Medellin drug cartel with the knowledge of Bird Jr., the minister of public works and national security advisor. Bird Jr. denied the allegation, but international pressure forced his father to permit an independent inquiry.

A commission headed by prominent British jurist Louis Blom-Cooper implicated Bird Jr. and the chief of the ninety-member Antiguan Defense Force. The report concluded that the country faced being "engulfed in corruption" and had fallen victim to "persons who use political power as a passport to private profit." To defuse opposition calls for his resignation, Bird banned Bird Jr. from politics for life.

In 1992 the exposure of a scheme in which Bird had siphoned public funds into his personal account led to a new round of opposition protests and demands that he step down. In February, the UNDP, the ACLM and the Progressive Labour Movement (PLM) united to form the United Progressive Party (UPP). Baldwin Spencer, holder of the UNDP seat in the parliament, became the UPP leader. On the eve of a widely successful general strike called by the UPP, Bird announced he would not run in the general election due by 1994.

The bitter succession battle lasted until September 1993 when Lester Bird was elected to lead the ALP upon the retirement of his father in 1994. The other top party post, ALP chairman, went to his brother Vere Jr., whose ban from politics turned out to be not so permanent.

The UPP held its first national convention in April 1993 to prepare its campaign to unseat the Bird dynasty in 1994. Spencer was re-elected UPP leader. Tim Hector, ACLM activist and outspoken journalist, was named UPP deputy leader. The UPP vowed to fight against corruption and electoral fraud.

Political Rights and Civil Liberties: Constitutionally, citizens are able to change their government by democratic means. But elections are tainted by serious irregularities and undue influence exerted by the ruling party over the electoral authorities.

The political system is a parliamentary democracy with a bicameral parliament consisting of a seventeen-member House of Representatives elected for five years and an appointed Senate. In the House, there are sixteen seats for Antigua and one for Barbuda. Eleven Senators are appointed by the prime minister, four by the parliamentary opposition leader, one by the Barbuda Council and one by the governor-general. Barbuda has limited self-government through the separately elected Barbuda Council.

Political parties, labor unions and civic organizations are free to organize and an independent Industrial Court mediates labor disputes between unions and the government. The free exercise of religion is respected. Opposition demonstrations are occasionally subject to police harassment.

The judiciary is relatively independent but weak. It has been nearly powerless to address the entrenched corruption in the executive branch. There is an inter-island court of appeals for Antigua and five other former British colonies in the Lesser Antilles. There are no political prisoners.

Most newspapers are associated with political parties and include *Outlook*, the outspoken leftist weakly edited by Tim Hector. *Outlook* and other papers that probe government corruption are subject to systematic legal harassment by members of the ruling ALP and gag orders. Radio and television are either owned by the state or members of the Bird family and news coverage is biased. In 1990 the Antigua Broadcasting Service declined to provide coverage of the arms scandal inquiry, despite the approval of the jurist heading the investigation.

Argentina

Polity: Federal presidential-legislative democracy
Economy: Capitalist
Population: 33,533,000
PPP: $4,295
Life Expectancy: 71.0
Ethnic Groups: Europeans (mostly Spanish and Italian), mestizos, Indians, Arabs

Political Rights: 2
Civil Liberties: 3
Status: Free

Overview:

In congressional elections President Carlos Menem's Peronist party fell short of the two-thirds majority needed to amend the constitution and thereby overturn the one-term limitation on the presidency. Menem then cut a back-room deal with Raul Alfonsin, his predecessor and one-time nemesis, to get support for constitutional reform that would allow Menem to run for reelection.

The Argentine Republic was established after achieving independence from Spain in 1816. A federal constitution was drafted in 1853. Democratic governance has frequently been interrupted by military takeovers. The end of authoritarian rule under Juan Peron (1946-55) led to a period of instability marked by left-wing violence and repressive military regimes. After the military's defeat in the 1982 Falkland/Malvinas war, Argentina returned to elected civilian rule in 1983.

Most of the constitutional structure of 1853 was restored in 1983. The president and vice-president are designated for six-year terms by a 600-member electoral college. The electoral college is chosen on the basis of proportional representation, with each of the 23 provinces and the federal district of Buenos Aires having twice as many electors as the combined number of senators and deputies. The legislature consists of a 257-member Chamber of Deputies directly elected for six years, with half the seats renewable every three years, and a 48-member Senate nominated by provincial legislatures for nine-year terms, with one-third of the seats renewable every three years. Two senators are directly elected in the Buenos Aires federal district. Provincial and municipal governments are elected.

President Alfonsin (1983-89) oversaw the prosecution of former military leaders for gross human rights violations during the "dirty war" against leftist guerrillas, and weathered three military rebellions led by the nationalist *carapintada* (painted face) faction of the army.

Menem won the presidency in 1989, defeating Eduardo Angeloz of the incumbent, moderate-left Radical Civic Union (UCR). Menem campaigned as a populist in the traditional Peronist manner. But after taking office amid a severe economic crisis, he stunned many followers by initiating a market-based economic reform program. By 1991 Menem was besieged by corruption scandals involving government officials and members of his family. But inflation had been reduced to two percent a month and voters showed their approval as the Peronists retained a working congressional majority during legislative elections in 1991.

However, with even some Peronists opposing his program to dismantle Argentina's statist economy, Menem implemented policy mostly by decree. As of September 1993 he had invoked emergency laws to issue 244 "decrees of necessity and urgency," 91 percent of all such decrees issued since 1853. Attempts by legislators to challenge Menem in court have been blocked since 1990, when Menem pushed a bill increasing the number of Supreme Court justices from five to nine through the Peronist-controlled Senate and stacked the court with politically loyal judges.

Menem also has used the Supreme Court to uphold decrees removing the comptroller general, whose main function is to investigate executive wrongdoing, and other officials mandated to probe government corruption. A number of top prosecutors have been removed and replaced with officials who had been targets of their investigations.

By 1992 Menem's self-assurance, rooted in the favorable response to his economic policies from international financial institutions and popular relief over the cutting of inflation, had evolved into a quest for reelection. In an interview in June 1993, Menem stated, "I'll be here until 2001. And in 2001, we'll see."

Throughout 1993 Menem conducted an all-out campaign to win a two-thirds Peronist majority in the Chamber of Deputies in the October midterm elections. Political tension rose when Peronists were implicated in a series of death threats and physical attacks against prominent journalists critical of Menem. In August Interior Minister Gustavo Beliz resigned after publicly charging that Peronists were seeking Menem's reelection "at any price," including buying congressional votes. Beliz, with a reputation for honesty, had been appointed to improve the image of Menem's scandal-ridden government.

On 5 October, with Menem's approval rating in opinion polls falling to about 40 percent, the Peronists failed to win two-thirds of the seats in the Chamber. Menem then called for a referendum on constitutional reform. Radical party leader Alfonsin, fearing a loss would leave him with nothing, agreed to secret talks with Menem.

In March Alfonsin had said Menem's reelection "would be a tragedy because this is an unscrupulous government." Earlier he had likened Menem to Adolf Hitler and former Paraguayan dictator Alfredo Stroessner. But six weeks after the October election, and without consulting other Radical leaders, Alfonsin agreed to support presidential reelection. In exchange Menem accepted a modified form of parliamentary government, new Supreme Court appointments and a mandated spoils system that gives the Radicals new Senate seats and control of certain federal agencies. Alfonsin was expected to use the spoils to bring the Radicals in line on reelection. The next step would be elections in April 1994 for a constituent assembly.

Political Rights and Civil Liberties: Citizens are able to change their government through elections. Constitutional guarantees regarding freedom of religion and the right to organize political parties, civic organizations and labor unions are generally respected. The political landscape is dominated by two parties, but there are more than a dozen other parties, from Communist to fascist, many of them represented in the Congress and in municipal governments.

However, the constitutional separation of powers and the rule of law have been undermined by President Menem's propensity to rule by decree and his manipulation of the judiciary (See "Overview"). Menem's autocratic impulse has also been evident in his antagonism toward the media, which has created a climate in which journalists have come under increasing attack, and in the government's use of internal political spying, which was exposed in 1993.

The judiciary is nominally independent, but under Menem it has been made into a political instrument of the executive. Menem stacked the Supreme Court in 1990 in order to block attempts by the Congress to curb his authoritarian style of rule. Then in 1993 he forced a number of the same judges he appointed in 1990 to resign as part of the deal with Alfonsin to secure presidential reelection.

Overall, the judicial system is politicized and riddled with the corruption endemic to all branches of the government, creating what Argentines call "juridical insecurity." In late 1992 the justice minister resigned in protest after Menem announced he personally would appoint the members of what was to be an independent penal appeals court. Menem replaced the minister with his legal affairs secretary.

Despite twenty major corruption scandals and the resignations of nearly two dozen senior government officials since 1989, no investigation has ended in a trial. Polls in 1993 showed that more than 80 percent of Argentines do not trust the judicial system, and that corruption ranked second—behind low salaries—among issues that most concern them.

The human rights community was influential in the prosecution of military officers during the Alfonsin administration. Since condemning Menem's 1990 pardon of military officers convicted for human rights violations, rights groups have received anonymous threats and been subject to various forms of intimidation. In 1993 the Inter-American Commission on Human Rights of the Organization of American States determined that the 1990 pardons were incompatible with Argentina's treaty obligations under the American Convention on Human Rights.

Newspapers and magazines are privately owned, vocal, and reflect a wide variety of viewpoints. Television and radio are both private and public. Since 1989 there have been an increasing number of incidents of media intimidation, including fifty cases of physical attacks, by security forces and shadowy groups apparently linked to the ruling Peronist party. Journalists and publications investigating official corruption are the principal targets.

Following the lead of Menem, who regularly excoriates the media, the interior ministry initiated an ongoing libel-suit campaign against investigative journalists. The government also has cut advertising to critical media and enacted restrictive media laws. During the 1993 congressional election campaign journalists received hundreds of death threats, Hernan Lopez Echague of *Pagina 12* was twice severely beaten, and a radio station was bombed. No arrests were ever made. On 16 September Menem stated that such attacks were "occupational hazards" and that he could do nothing to stop them.

After the urban food riots in 1989-90, Menem issued a decree giving responsibility for internal security to the military for the first time since the return to civilian rule. Amid a sharp increase in street crime in recent years, there have been frequent reports of arbitary arrests and ill-treatment by police during confinement. Police brutality cases rarely go anywhere in civil courts due to intimidation of witnesses and judges.

Labor is well organized and dominated by Peronist unions. But union influence has diminished because of corruption scandals, internal divisions, and restrictions on public sector strikes decreed by Menem to pave the way for his privatization program.

The nation's Catholic majority enjoys freedom of religious expression. The Jewish community, numbering up to 250,000, is occasionally the target of anti-Semitic vandalism.

Armenia

Polity: Presidential-par-liamentary (transitional)
Economy: Statist transitional
Population: 3,583,000
PPP: $4,741
Life Expectancy: 69.0
Ethnic Groups: Armenians (93 percent), others

Political Rights: 3*
Civil Liberties: 4*
Status: Partly Free

Ratings Change: *Armenia's political rights rating changed from 4 to 3 and its civil liberties rating changed from 3 to 4 as a result of modifications in methodology. See "Survey Methodology," page 671.

Overview:
War in the predominantly Armenian Nagorno-Karabakh enclave in Azerbaijan and its political and economic ramifications were central issues for President Levon Ter-Petrossian. With the Karabakh war spilling over into Azerbaijan proper, Armenia came under international pressure to settle the five-year conflict. Azerbaijan's railroad blockade and the intermittent cut-off of supply routes in Georgia exacerbated severe economic problems, leaving much of the country without fuel and electricity during the winter months.

This land-locked, predominately Christian Transcaucus republic was ruled at various times by Macedonians, Romans, Persians, Mongols and others; it was obtained by Russia from Persia in 1828. Prior to their defeat in World War I, the Ottoman Turks controlled a western region, and between 1894 and 1915, engaged in a systematic campaign of genocide. The Russian component came under Communist control and was designated a Soviet Socialist Republic in 1922, western Armenia having been returned to Turkey.

Armenia officially declared independence from the Soviet Union on 23 September 1991. A unicameral, 249-member parliament had been created following multiparty elections in May 1990. Ter-Petrossian's umbrella Armenian National Movement (ANM) won 56 seats. Opposition parties included the Armenian Revolutionary Party (ARF-Dashnak) with eleven members and the Armenian Democratic Party of Armenia (Ramgavar) with fourteen. On 16 October 1991, Ter-Petrossian was overwhelmingly elected president. Armenia became a member of the Commonwealth of Independent Nations (CIS) in December 1991, and joined the United Nations in March 1992.

Nineteen-ninety-three opened with a political crisis. On 2 February, President Ter-Petrossian fired Prime Minister Khosrov Arutunyan, a former Communist appartchik, and his entire cabinet over the course of economic reforms. The prime minister had sought more government regulation over the economy and was opposed by those favoring a free-market approach. Hrant Bagratyan was appointed prime minister by presidential decree.

The crisis triggered a series of anti-government demonstrations in Yerevan, the capital, with over 100,000 people on 5 February demanding the resignation of the president, the dissolution of parliament, and the creation of a constituent assembly empowered to draft a new constitution. Meanwhile, the ARF-Dashnak rejected the president's call for participation in a new government. The party, popular among Armenia's widespread and influential diaspora, identified the lack of a constitution and the concentration of power in the presidency as the root causes of the country's political and economic problems. Nationalists opposed the president's continued refusal to officially recognize the independence of Nagorno-Karabakh. By year's end, Karabakh's Armenian fighters had gained control of most of the disputed region, and had seized Azeri territory outside the enclave to expand a corridor linking it to Armenia. The seizure of Azeri territory led to warnings from Iran and Turkey. On 8 February, the president decreed a state of emergency for the Armavir district "in response to danger-ous incidents in Armenia's border district with Turkey." Attempts to mediate the crisis under the auspices of the Conference on Security and Cooperation in Europe (CSCE) produced few results. The conflict had claimed some 3,000 lives and forced an estimated 400,000 Karabakh Armenians to flee, straining an already badly crippled economy.

In April Karabakh Armenians launched an offensive against Fizuli and Kelbajar, southeast of Nagorno-Karabakh, sparking a wave of Azeri refugees and further straining relations with Turkey and Iran, home to 1.5 million Azeris. The Azeris and Turkey accused the Russian Seventh Army, based in Armenia, of siding with Karabakh Armenians.

At 19-30 April meetings in Moscow, the U.S., Turkey and Russia drew up a plan to restart the stalled CSCE-sponsored negotiations. It called for an immediate ceasefire followed by the withdrawal between 9-14 May of Armenian forces from Kelbajar and a two-month moratorium on all military activity. On 25 May, over 20,000 demonstrators in Yerevan protested the government's endorsement of the U.S.-Turkish-Russian plan.

On 26 May, Armenia and Azerbaijan agreed to the tripartite peace initiative, but the Armenian defense chief of the enclave cast doubt on the plan's viability by rejecting the agreement on the grounds that it did "not guarantee the safety of Karabakh's civilians."

On 7 June, a newly revised CSCE plan on Karabakh was submitted to the Arme-nian, Azerbaijani and Nagorno-Karabakh governments. The plan, based on United Nations Resolution 822, called for an immediate ceasefire and a phased withdrawal of military forces from Kelbajar. The plan effectively replaced the earlier tripartite U.S.-Turkish-Russian initiative. President Ter-Petrossian made his first official visit to Karabakh, seeking to persuade Karabakh parliamentarians to accept the CSCE plan. However, Karabakh Armenian forces looted and burned the western city of Agdam in Azerbaijan. The Karabakh parliament on 14 June agreed to accept the CSCE plan but asked for a one-month delay.

In more domestic issues, on 24 June the Constitutional Commission completed drafting a constitution featuring clear division of powers. The commission planned to submit the document to parliament and for a national referendum. The constitution would have created a 100-member legislature, the National Council, to replace the Supreme Soviet.

By mid-month, five opposition parties—the Democratic Party, the Republicans, the Liberal-Democratic Party, the ARF-Dashnak, and the Union of Constitutional Law—joined forces to create a constitutional council of civil consent. The parties dismissed the constitution draft as an attempt to "place [the] springs of democracy under threat."

On 18 August, the U.N. Security Council demanded an immediate, complete and unconditional withdrawal of Armenian forces from Azerbaijan. The foreign ministry notified the CSCE that the government consented to implementation of U.N. Security Council Resolution 822, but demanded modifications to keep a strategic highway out of the conflict zone. On 23 August, Armenian forces captured Fizuli, and continued forcibly depopulating areas of Azerbaijan to the north, east and south of Karabakh. The Karabakh leadership in Stepanakert ignored urgent requests by Armenia that it abide by internationally brokered ceasefires.

Tensions escalated as Turkey on 3 September moved troops to the Armenian border and demanded that Armenia "immediately and unconditionally" withdraw from occupied parts of Azerbaijan. The warning came amid reports that Iran was sending troops to its 230-mile border with Azerbaijan to block refugees from flowing into Iran. Azerbaijan claimed Karabakh Armenian forces had captured Goradiz, a key town on the Iranian border. On 7 September, the Iranian foreign minister warned that Teheran "would not remain silent vis-a-vis growing unrest across Iranian borders." Turkey's new prime minister, Tansu Ciller, made an urgent visit to Moscow as part of a flurry of diplomatic efforts to avoid a widening of the five-year-old conflict. Azerbaijan's President Gaidar Aliyev and President Ter-Petrossian also made hurried trips to Moscow.

By the end of the month warring Karabakh Armenians and their Azeri foes held their first direct talks, under Russian auspices in Moscow. The two sides agreed to extend a ceasefire to 5 October.

With the situation somewhat stable, the Armenian parliament on 27 September rejected a proposal for early parliamentary elections in 1994 (elections are due in 1995). While support for the ruling ANM had plummeted, none of the 30 rival parties presented a real challenge to the government with the possible exception of Dashnak and the newly registered Armenian Communist Party, which sought to capitalize on nostalgia for an era of stability and comparative economic well-being.

Meanwhile, fighting resumed in late October. In response to an Azeri attack, spearhead by Afghan *mujahideen* fighters, Karabakh Armenians captured the entire southeast corner of Azerbaijan, sending tens of thousands of refugees into Iran.

The war and subsequent blockade by Azerbaijan crippled Armenia's economy. Over 450 factories were almost completely shut down for lack of fuel. Homes, schools and hospitals went unheated. While some natural gas shipments resumed from Georgia, the energy crisis was severe. By mid-year, the economy had shrunk by 50 percent from the year before. Industrial output was down 40 percent.

In mid-November, the government introduced its own currency, the dram. President Ter-Petrossian said Armenia was forced to leave the so-called ruble zone because of unreasonable demands by Russia and the Russian Central Bank.

Political Rights and Civil Liberties: Armenians can change their government democratically and a multiparty system is in place despite the absence of a new constitution. There are over 30 political parties. The Young Communist League was restored in 1993. Laws prohibiting funding from abroad were aimed primarily at the ARF-Dashnak, which enjoys the support of wealthy Armenians in Europe and the U.S.

Legislative reforms of the judicial system have yet to be initiated, and there is no presumption of innocence. Defendants do have the right to attend their trials, confront witnesses and present evidence. The court appoints an attorney for any defendant who needs one.

While freedom of expression is generally recognized, the press faced several restrictions in 1993 besides the lack of supplies and paper. In July, the government announced that 278 news media were registered, and that twenty that were unregistered would be closed. On 20 November, reporters from three opposition newspapers, *Erkir*, *Azatamart*, *Voice of Armenia*, and the *Ailur* news agency were deprived of accreditation by the foreign ministry. The ministry maintained that the newspapers' theoretical and political analyses tended to end in unethical personal insults. Television and radio are state-owned and access to certain political groups has been limited.

Freedoms of movement, association and assembly are guaranteed and respected. There are generally no significant restrictions on religion. Deeply ingrained, traditional attitudes discriminate against women. Only a handful of cases of sexual abuse, rape or domestic violence against women have gone to trial.

The lack of a constitution hinders the advancement of legal guarantees for workers. Some small independent trade unions are allowed to exist, but most are holdovers from the Soviet era.

Australia

Polity: Federal parliamentary democracy
Economy: Capitalist
Population: 17,753,000
PPP: $16,051
Life Expectancy: 76.5
Ethnic Groups: European (95 percent), Asian (4 percent), aborigines (1 percent)

Political Rights: 1
Civil Liberties: 1
Status: Free

Overview: Prime Minister Paul Keating led the ruling Australian Labor Party (ALP) to the country's biggest postwar upset in the March 1993 parliamentary elections. With Australia in the midst of its worst recession since the 1930s, Keating staved off near-certain defeat by exploiting fears over the opposition's proposed Goods and Services Tax (GST). In December the parliament approved guidelines for resolving aboriginal land claims, which have skyrocketed since a landmark 1992 High Court decision recognized the existence of native land titles.

The British claimed Australia in 1770 and initially used the Botany Bay area as a penal colony. In January 1901 six states formed the Commonwealth of Australia, adding the Northern Territory and the capital city of Canberra as territorial units in 1911. The Queen of England is the nominal head of state in this parliamentary democracy. The country's directly elected bicameral parliament consists of a 76-member Senate, drawing 12 members from each state plus two each from the capital and the Northern Territory, and a 147-member House of Representatives.

Since World War II political power has alternated between the center-left ALP and the conservative coalition of the Liberal Party and the smaller National Party. Prime Minister Bob Hawke led the ALP to four consecutive national election victories between 1983 and March 1990 and took steps to sharpen the resource-rich country's economic competitiveness, including floating the currency, deregulating the financial system and reducing tariffs. In 1990 the country slid into a recession, which many Australians blamed on then-Treasurer Paul Keating's tight monetary policy. However, in December 1991 Keating beat Hawke in a no-confidence vote among Labor MPs to become prime minister, largely by deriding Hawke's defense of aboriginal and environmental causes over business interests in a time of economic hardship.

Unemployment hit a postwar high of 11.4 percent in November 1992 and held at over 11 percent in early 1993, augering poorly for the ALP going into the 13 March 1993 national election. During the campaign, opposition Liberal Party leader Dr. John Hewson pitched his *Fightback Mark II* program, which called for greater privatization and economic decentralization, further tariff reductions, extensive changes that would diminish union power, and a controversial 15 percent GST. The ALP offered a continuation of its more gradual liberalization program, which aims at increasing competitiveness while largely maintaining the country's generous social services.

Keating skillfully made the GST the focal point of the election, playing to voters' fears of price increases and higher taxes while ignoring Hewson's proposal to cut personal taxes and abolish seven indirect taxes. On election day, the ALP took 80 seats; the Liberal Party, 49; the National Party, 16; and independents, 2. Elections for 40 of the 76 Senate seats left the ALP with 32 seats; the Liberal Party, 29; the center-left Democrats, 8; the National Party, 5; and the Greens, 2. In achieving the upset the ALP positioned itself towards the political center to attract support beyond its traditional working-class base.

Throughout much of the year the government grappled with ways to handle an explosion in aboriginal land claims, filed in the wake of a June 1992 High Court ruling that granted the Meriam people ownership of a few square miles on the Torres Straight off the northern coast. The Court overturned the doctrine of *terra nullius* (no man's land), which had considered Australia to have been empty when the British settlers came. It recognized instead that native titles to the land predated the British arrival and were still valid in government-owned areas providing the indigenous peoples had maintained a close connection to the land. However the ruling, based on a claim filed by Eddie Mabo in 1982, awarded actual title only for the area under review. Almost immediately, aboriginal groups around the country announced several major land claims, in some cases for entire parts of the continent. Farmers and mining companies feared the Mabo decision would threaten the long-term leases they held on government land.

A compromise package approved by parliament in December drew broad support from aboriginal groups and farming interests. Pastoral leases held by non-aborigines will be exempt from native title claims, but in return the government will compensate aborigines on pastoral lands where native title has been extinguished. In addition, aborigines will be allowed to convert their own pastoral leases into native title, thus giving them a permanant claim to such land. The more controversial aspect involves mining leases, which will be validated until they expire, after which aboriginal groups will have an opportunity to prove a claim to the land. Where these claims are upheld, the indigenous holders will not have an outright veto on development, but they will have a "right to negotiate" over future use.

During the year, Keating continued to call for the country to sever its formal link to the British monarchy in favor of a federal republic by the year 2000. The prime minister said the move would help Australia establish an independent, multicultural identity and further orient the country economically towards Asia, where 60 percent of its trade is already directed. Keating hopes to have an Australian head of state open the 2000 Summer Olympic Games, which were awarded to Sydney in September.

Political Rights and Civil Liberties: Australians have the democratic means to change their government. Although there is no written constitution, fundamental freedoms are respected in practice, and the judiciary is fully independent of the government.

The country's major human rights issue is the treatment of its indigenous population of 229,000 Aborigines and 28,000 Torres Strait islanders. Life expectancy for Aborigines is fifteen to twenty years lower than for non-Aborigines and unemployment six times higher. A 1991 government study found Aborigines are incarcerated at a rate 29 times higher, often after having been unable to afford a fine or denied bail for minor offenses. Most arrests are alchohol-related. Once in jail, they are far more likely to commit suicide or be abused by guards than non-Aborigines. The government now provides "bail hostels" for Aborigines denied bail for lack of a fixed address. The Aboriginal and Torres Straight Islander Commission has been set up to give these groups greater control over governmental programs established for them.

The country's labor relations system is being restructured. Currently, the Industrial Relations Committee (IRC) sets central wages and standards after considering input from the government, unions and employers. Some company-level bargaining is allowed, but the IRC retains the right to veto agreements. Conservatives want workers and employers to negotiate directly with each other, with or without union intermediaries. However, the Australian Center for Trade Unions says individual employment contracts would essentially pit workers against each other, and eliminate many benefits. The government too wants a more flexible system, but would retain national awards as a safety net.

Austria

Polity: Federal par-
liamentary democracy
Economy: Mixed
capitalist
Population: 7,938,000
PPP: $16,504
Life Expectancy: 74.8

Political Rights: 1
Civil Liberties: 1
Status: Free

Ethnic Groups: Austro-German majority, Slovene minority, and
Eastern European immigrant and refugee groups

Overview: Controversies over immigration policy and right-wing politics
were major news stories in 1993.

The small Republic of Austria was formed in 1918 after
the defeat of the Austro-Hungarian Empire in World War I. Austrian independence ended
in 1938 when Nazi Germany annexed its territory. After Germany's defeat in World
War II, the Republic of Austria was reborn in 1945, but the Western Allies and the
Soviet Union occupied the country until 1955 when they signed the Austrian State Treaty.
This agreement guaranteed Austrian neutrality and restored its national sovereignty.

The Austrian system of government features a largely ceremonial president, chosen
directly for a six-year term. Thomas Klestil, a member of the Christian Democratic
Austrian People's Party (OVP), replaced fellow conservative Kurt Waldheim as
president in a two-round election in 1992. He appoints the chancellor, the government's
chief executive, whose party or coalition commands majority support in the National
Council, the 183-member lower house of parliament. Its members are elected directly
for four-year terms. The upper house is the 63-member Federal Council, which the
provincial assemblies choose by proportional representation. Federal Council members
have four- to six-year terms, depending on the term of their respective provincial
assemblies. The chancellor is Social Democrat Franz Vranitzky, who took office in 1986.
Following inconclusive National Council elections in 1986, the Social Democratic Party
(SPO) began a grand coalition government with the OVP. In the general election in
1990, the senior partner in the ruling coalition, the SPO, won 43 percent of the vote and
81 seats in the lower house, a gain of one seat. Its junior partner, the more conservative
OVP, garnered only 32 percent and 60 seats, a 17-seat decline. Picking up conservative
votes, the right-wing populist Freedom Party took 17 percent and 33 seats, a gain of 15
seats. The environmentalist Greens attracted 4.5 percent and won 9 seats, a gain of one.

Following the People's Party's disappointing performance in the 1990 election, the
Socialists renewed the coalition with the OVP, in order to exclude the Freedom Party
from government. Led by Joerg Haider, the Freedom Party has made significant gains
in local and regional elections in recent years. The trend continued in 1993, when the
Freedom Party more than doubled its vote to 20 percent in Graz's municipal elections.
Voters responded favorably to the party's anti-immigrant stance. In January 1993, the
Freedom Party sponsored a twelve-point anti-immigrant, anti-refugee petition. The
party intended the petition to force parliament to deal with its issues. Haider had
predicted that more than 700,000 people would sign, but only 417,000 did so. A broad

anti-Haider coalition, including the major parties, religious leaders, intellectuals and artists, opposed his campaign with large rallies in Vienna and other cities. Disturbed by Haider's campaign, former presidential candidate Heide Schmidt and four other Freedom Party parliamentary dissidents set up the Liberal Forum, a new, more moderate party. In their first electoral contest, the Liberals won three seats in Lower Austria's provincial legislature in May 1993. The Liberals' success threatened the Freedom Party nationally by providing a less extreme alternative to SPO-OVP domination. However, Haider's group still gained ground in Lower Austria.

Alarmed by the activities of neo-Nazis, the Austrian police arrested several right-wing extremists, including would-be Fuehrer Gottfried Kuessel, and uncovered a neo-Nazi organization in January 1992. Neo-Nazis had made plans to try to topple the government. In September 1993, a jury convicted Kuessel on nine of eleven counts, including violating a law banning Nazi activities. He was sentenced to ten years in prison In 1992, Parliament passed legislation placing new restrictions on neo-Nazi activities.

Since the collapse of communism in Eastern Europe in 1989, Austria has sought to redefine its international role. It used to present itself as a bridge between the two camps in Europe, but is now seeking to join the European Union (EU). The EU is positive towards Austrian membership on political and economic grounds, but is concerned that Austrian neutrality could cause problems if the Union gets involved in defense policy. Austria is moving away from its reluctance to join a Western security structure. The country hopes to join the Union by 1995, and began negotiating for membership in February 1993.

In March 1993, former Chancellor Fred Sinowatz and two other ex-ministers went on trial for illegal weapons sales to Iran. The jury cleared them of charges that they had covered up the sales, but it convicted former Interior Minister Karl Blecha of falsifying documents and suppressing evidence.

Political Rights and Civil Liberties:

Austrians have the right to change their government demo-cratically. Voting is compulsory in some provinces. Four parties won seats in the 1990 National Council elections.

Nazi organizations are illegal, and the 1955 State Treaty prohibits Nazis from enjoying freedoms of assembly and association. However, for many years old Nazis found a home in the Freedom Party, which still seems sympathetic to certain Nazi ideas. In 1992, the parliament made the following offenses criminal: belittling the Holocaust and publicly denying, approving or justifying Nazi crimes against humanity. These limits on expression apply to print, broadcast and other media. The same legislation also lightened jail sentences for Nazi activities, because juries often acquitted people in cases for which they felt the sentences were too harsh. The Austrian police enforce anti-Nazi statutes unevenly, tending to act more when extremist activities get international attention.

The country's provinces have significant local power and can check federal power by choosing the members of the upper house of parliament. A Slovene minority has had some disputes with the Austro-Germans over bilingual education.

The media are generally very free. There are a few, rarely used restrictions on press freedom which allow the removal of publications from circulation if they violate laws on public morality or security. Broadcast media belong to an autonomous public corporation. There is freedom of religion for faiths judged consistent with public order and morality. Recognized denominations must register with the government.

The judiciary is independent. Refugees have long used Austria as the first point of asylum when they have left Eastern Europe and the former Soviet Union. Until 1990, Austria had an open door policy for people fleeing Eastern Europe. Since 1990, Austria has required that all prospective newcomers apply for a visa first. The country had concluded that it needed to draw a distinction between economic refugees and politically persecuted arrivals. By March 1993, Austria decided to close its doors to Bosnian refugees. In September 1993, Austrian police broke up a Chinese-Vietnamese gang that had earned more than $2 million smuggling people across the Austrian borders.

Business and labor groups are strong and play a major role in formulating national economic policy. Most Austrian workers must belong to Chambers of Labor, which represent workers' interests to the government. Trade unions, on the other hand, negotiate for workers with management.

Austria has generous welfare provisions and several state enterprises. However, the current government is trimming the size of the public sector.

Azerbaijan

Polity: Presidential-military
Economy: Statist transitional
Population: 7,152,000
PPP: $3,977
Life Expectancy: 70.0
Ethnic Groups: Azeris, other Turkic, Russians

Political Rights: 6*
Civil Liberties: 6*
Status: Not Free

Ratings Change: *Azerbaijan's political rights and civil liberties ratings changed from 5, 5 to 6, 6 because old-line Communist and military elements replaced President Elchibey and war dragged on with Armenia over Nagorno-Karabakh.

Overview:

Military losses to Armenian forces in the predominantly Armenian enclave of Nagorno-Karabakh and surrounding Azeri territory, economic stagnation, and the increased authoritarianism of the Azerbaijan Popular Front (AzPF) regime under President Abulfaz Elchibey led to a June coup by a renegade army commander and the subsequent restoration to power of former Azeri Communist Party leader Gaidar Aliyev.

The events marked the culmination of two years of political instability in this former Soviet republic bordering Russia, Georgia, Armenia and Iran. Persia and the Ottoman Empire competed for Azeri territory in the sixteenth century, with the former gaining control in 1603. The northern sector, ceded to Russia in the early nineteenth century, joined Armenia and Georgia in a short-lived Transcaucasian Federation after the 1917 Bolshevik Revolution. It proclaimed its independence the following year, but was subdued by Red Army forces in 1920. In 1922, it entered the Soviet Union as part of the Transcaucasian Soviet Federal Republic, becoming a separate Soviet Socialist Republic in 1936.

After the collapse of the Soviet Union in 1991, the Azeri electorate voted for independence in a 29 December referendum. Three months earlier, Ayaz Mutalibov, a hard-line Communist, was elected president. The AzPF under Elchibey held only 40 of 360 seats in the Communist-dominated Supreme Soviet elected in a fraud-marred vote in 1990. Amid anti-government rallies in October, the Supreme Soviet created a National Council, a permanent fifty-seat legislature half of whose members would be picked by the president, half by the opposition.

On 7 June 1992, after months of instability, AzPF leader Elchibey was elected president with 59 percent of the vote. He had campaigned on a promise to withdraw the country from the Commonwealth of Independent States (CIS) and keep Nagorno-Karabakh in the country.

Nineteen-ninety-three opened amid an intensification of fighting in Nagorno-Karabakh and political instability. On 26 January, Prime Minister Rakhim Guseinov resigned after a disagreement with President Elchibey over a proposed executive reorganization that would have significantly reduced the premier's power. He was replaced by Elchibey ally Ali Masimov. Military gains by Armenian forces led Defense Minister Rahmin Gaziev to step down on 19 February. The president dismissed Suret Guseinov, in charge of Azeri forces in the Karabakh war, who was accused of retreating as a provocation to launch a coup in conjunction with the Russian Army in Gyandzha.

In March, the opposition turned up the pressure on the regime. The radical Azerbaijan National Independence Party (NIP) headed by Etibar Mamedov called for a series of demonstrations to demand that the government resign for mishandling both the economy and the five-year-old Karabakh war.

In early April, Karabakh Armenians launched a new offensive against the Azeri towns of Fizuli and Kelbajar southeast of Nagorno-Karabakh, sparking a wave of Azeri refugees. It also sparked warnings from Iran, home of 1.5 million Azeris living in the north, with Teheran threatening intervention to staunch the flow of refugees across its border.

At 19-30 April meetings in Moscow, the U.S., Turkey and Russia drew up a new peace plan intended to restart stalled negotiations sponsored by the Conference on Security and Cooperation in Europe (CSCE). Meanwhile, Panakh Guseinov, a founding member of the AzPF, was appointed prime minister by the National Council.

The government continued its repression of dissident activities. In early May, NIP members were among twenty people arrested in Geydzhali for holding an unsanctioned meeting.

On 26 May, Azerbaijan and Armenia agreed to the tripartite peace initiative, but the Armenian defense chief of the enclave cast doubt on the plan's viability by rejecting the agreement on the grounds that it did not guarantee the safety of Karabakh's civilians.

Military setbacks and growing political uncertainty had a impact on the morale of Azeri forces. On 27 May, the Azeri parliament extended for two months the national state of emergency that had been decreed in April after the occupation of Kelbajar. The government also reported the arrest of 500 Azeri army deserters. Military patrols and heightened security were evident in Baku on 3 June.

Clashes between government forces and rebel military units intensified in June. On 7 June, Prime Minister Guseinov offered to resign after forces loyal to thirty-five-year-old renegade commander Col. Suret Guseinov, in control of the several-thousand-strong 709th Division, seized Gyandzha, Azerbaijan's second-largest city. The fighting, which left over sixty dead, was spurred by government forces' attempts to confiscate weapons left behind by the last units of the Russian Army that left Gyandzha at the end of May. The fighting and instability led President Elchibey to ask former Communist Party boss Aliyev to become premier, but he refused. On 15 June, with rebel forces in control of over half the country and moving on Baku to oust Elchibey, the National Council elected Aliyev chairman of the Azerbaijani parliament. Aliyev immediately began negotiations with Col. Guseinov. On 18 June, President Elchibey fled to his home town in Nakhichevan.

With Elchibey's departure, Aliyev in a television address claimed to have assumed presidential powers in accordance with the constitution. The National Council initially declined to transfer power to Aliyev. Speaking from Nakhichevan, Elchibey affirmed that he would remain president. On 21 June, the National Council appealed to President Elchibey to return to the capital. Col. Guseinov declared at a televised press conference that he was assuming supreme power in order to fill "a power vacuum." On 23 June, the president announced he would agree to a national referendum on confidence in his government. The next day, the National Council voted 33 to 3 with one abstention to transfer presidential power to Aliyev. Three days later, rebel leader Guseinov met with Aliyev and agreed to withdraw his forces from Baku. After further negotiations, the National Council voted on 30 June by 38 votes to one to appoint Col. Guseinov prime minister with supreme responsibilities for the ministries of defense, security and interior.

By July, Armenian Karabakh forces had captured Agdam, leading new Prime Minister Guseinov to issue an urgent appeal for all men with military training to report for duty or face punishment. Meanwhile political unrest was reported in several Azeri regions, some still loyal to the deposed president. On 17 July, police clashed with hundreds of Elchibey supporters in Baku and raided AzPF headquarters. Several activists were beaten and detained, and phones and faxes were destroyed. The crackdown included the arrests of Elchibey's cabinet ministers and former officials, among them former speaker Isa Gambarov.

On 26 July, Azerbaijan and Armenians in Nagorno-Karabakh agreed to a three-day ceasefire along the borders of the disputed enclave. Days later, the U.N. Security Council unanimously condemned the seizure of Agdam and other captured areas in Azerbaijan. As the month drew to a close, parliament voted to hold a referendum on 28 August on confidence in the Elchibey government. The state of emergency, first declared in April, was extended another two months. Presidential elections were scheduled for the fall.

August saw a new Karabakh Armenian offensive. On 23 August, Fizuli fell to Armenian forces, who continued forcibly depopulating areas of Azerbaijan to the north, east and south of Karabakh. The Karabakh leadership in Stepanakert ignored Armenian government requests that it abide by internationally brokered ceasefires.

On 31 August, the government announced the official results of a referendum on public confidence in ousted President Elchibey, claiming that 97.5 percent of nearly 4 million voters had voted no confidence in the former dissident nationalist. The non-binding referendum cleared the way for Aliyev, the former KGB general, to assume executive authority.

By the end of September, for the first time in the conflict, warring Karabakh Armenians and their Azeri foes held direct talks under Russian auspices in Moscow. The two sides agreed to extend a ceasefire until 5 October. On 22 September, parliament lifted the nationwide state of emergency in an apparent effort to appease the CIS. The law had included curfews, checkpoints and banned demonstrations. Two days later, it became part of the CIS.

Presidential elections were held on 3 October. Aliyev won an overwhelming victory, allegedly getting 98.8 percent of the vote. Two other candidates got less than 1 percent each. The AzPF boycotted the vote, charging that Elchibey was the country's only legitimate leader. Western observers declared the vote "undemocratic" given that major political parties did not field candidates and the mass media provided biased coverage favoring Aliyev, who was sworn in on 10 October. By the end of the month, fighting had resumed between Azeri forces and Karabakh Armenians near the Iranian border.

On 23 November, a Russian radio station reported that Prime Minister Guseinov had resigned.

Besides the Karabakh war, the other major issue was the economy in this oil-rich country. In January, the National Council adopted a law on privatization phased in over two years, stipulating that no more than 49 percent of an enterprise can be foreign-owned. On 26 May, parliament adopted a national currency law that said the local manat would be determined by market mechanisms. Despite the ongoing political and military crisis, negotiations continued with eight major western oil companies over development of offshore oil reserves in the Caspian Sea estimated at 4 billion barrels or more.

In July, responding to Russia's drastic monetary reforms, Azerbaijan began withdrawing pre-1993 rubles from circulation in order to "secure stability on the internal market." The government gave the Azeri national bank two days to work out ways to exchange the obsolete rubles for the manat. Nevertheless, there were outbreaks of panic, with crowds besieging banks. The country abandoned the ruble completely on 1 September when the manat became sole legal tender in the country. The same month, Western oil companies were told that the government expected to receive at least 80 percent of the revenue from any deal it signed.

The war and the slow pace of reform left the economy in sad shape, with a monthly inflation rate of 1,300 percent in the spring.

Political Rights and Civil Liberties:

The current government of Azerbaijan wrested control of the country by force, ousting democratically elected President Elchibey in June. Presidential elections in October were won by acting President Aliyev, a former KGB general and Communist party leader, in a vote that was deemed "undemocratic" because it excluded most major parties.

The so-called National Council continues to act as an interim legislature pending parliamentary elections as yet unscheduled. The judiciary is not independent and is structured like the old Soviet system. After the June takeover by pro-Aliyev forces, the rights of assembly, association, and free expression—already curtailed under a nationwide state of emergency—were further compromised with the arrests and detention of opposition AzPF activists and former government officials. Opposition forces were also persecuted under the Elchibey regime, particularly activists associated with the National Independence Party. In February, activist Mekmat Mamedov was killed by police who shot him at point-blank range in a Baku hotel. In March, a journalist with the Social Democratic Party publication *Istigal* was kidnapped by interior ministry forces.

The Aliyev regime has censored opposition newspapers. In a 30 July statement, a group of journalists accused the government of a "violation of democratic principles, human rights and freedom of expression." Earlier, copies of the biggest opposition newspaper, *Azadlyg,* and *Mukhalifat* were confiscated because they published statements by the U.S. State Department and the Helsinki Watch human rights group. Members of such parties as the AzPF, the NIP and the Musavat party have been arrested and detained.

The war in Nagorno-Karabakh and surrounding areas revived several abusive traditions, including hostage-taking of military personel and trading of human beings. Aid workers reported in September that a buyback of a young officer is five female hostages, forty-four gallons of gasoline and a million rubles. Hostage-taking has a time-honored place in the history of the Caucus mountain regions. The war has also killed thousands of civilians and displaced hundreds of thousands of refugees.

There is no state religion, though most Azeris are Shiite Muslims. There are significant Russian and Jewish populations that can worship freely. Christian Armenian Churches have been vandalized or closed and the few Armenians left in Azerbaijan would certainly not feel secure enough to attend services. The war has limited freedom of movement.

There have been reports of continued persecution of the small Kurdish minority. On 25 March, over 10,000 Lezgins staged a demonstration on the frontier between Daghestan and Azerbaijan to demand "unification" of the Lezgin people.

Cultural norms and the Karabakh war have resulted in discrimination and violence against women, who are frequently exchanged for hostages and forced into sexual slavery. Young men in some areas still kidnap their brides.

In late December 1992, police used violence to break up two unsanctioned demonstrations organized by the Turan independent trade union. Workers nominally have the right to strike.

Bahamas

Polity: Parliamentary democracy
Economy: Capitalist-statist
Population: 268,000
PPP: $11,235
Life Expectancy: 71.5
Ethnic Groups: Black (85 percent), white (15 percent)

Political Rights: 1
Civil Liberties: 2
Status: Free

Overview: During his first year in office Prime Minister Hubert A. Ingraham of the ruling Free National Movement (FNM) made some headway in reducing a gaping budget deficit and turning around an economy that had contracted by 20 percent between 1987-91. However, he was criticized for extensive police round-ups and deportations of Haitian immigrants.

The Commonwealth of the Bahamas, a 700-island nation in the Caribbean, is a member of the British Commonwealth. It became internally self-governing in 1967 and was granted independence in 1973. The British monarchy is represented by a governor-general.

Under the 1973 constitution, there is a bicameral parliament consisting of a forty-nine-member House of Assembly directly elected for five years, and a sixteen-member Senate with nine members appointed by the prime minister, four by the leader of the parliamentary opposition, and three by the governor-general. The prime minister is the leader of the party that commands a majority in the House. Islands other than New Providence and Grand Bahama are administered by centrally appointed commissioners.

After twenty-five years in office, the Progressive Liberal Party (PLP) led by Lynden O. Pindling was swept from power by Ingraham and the FNM in the parliamentary elections held on 19 August 1992. The PLP, dogged by allegations of corruption and high official involvement in narcotics trafficking, had lost ground to the FNM in the two previous elections. Ingraham, a lawyer and former cabinet official expelled by the PLP in 1986 for his outspoken criticism regarding drug and corruption allegations, had become the FNM leader in 1990.

The main issues in the 1992 campaign were corruption and economic recession. The forty-five-year-old Ingraham vowed to bring honesty, efficiency and accountability to government. Pindling, at the time the Western hemisphere's longest-serving, freely elected head of government, relied on his image as the father of the nation's independence.

But many voters were born since independence and many workers had been left unemployed as a result of a five-year economic downturn. The PLP and the FNM are both centrist parties, but the FNM is more oriented to free enterprise and a "less government is better" philosophy. What appeared to move most voters toward the FNM was the perception that the Pindling government had become ineffectual and unresponsive.

With 90 percent of the electorate voting, the FNM won thirty-two seats in the House of Assembly to the PLP's seventeen. Pindling held on to his own seat and became the official opposition leader. He and other members of the former PLP government became targets of a wide-ranging corruption probe initiated by the Ingraham government in 1993.

Political Rights and Civil Liberties:

Citizens are able to change their government through democratic elections. Unlike previous balloting, the 1992 vote was relatively free of irregularities and allegations of fraud. In 1992, indelible ink to identify people who had voted was used for the first time.

Constitutional guarantees regarding the right to organize political parties, civic organizations and labor unions are generally respected, as is the free exercise of religion. Labor, business and professional organizations are generally free, and unions have the right to strike. Nearly 30 percent of the work force is organized and collective bargaining is prevalent.

There is an independent Grand Bahama Human Rights Association, as well as at least two other independent rights groups. In recent years, there has been an increase in violent crime and continuing reports of police brutality during the course of arrests and interrogations. Human rights groups have also criticized the harsh conditions and overcrowding in the nation's prisons.

A major concern is the condition of the illegal Haitian immigrant population, which is estimated at 50,000, nearly 20 percent of the Bahamian population. The influx has created tension because of the strain on government services. Human rights groups charge that Haitians are treated inhumanely by the police and the public and are deported illegally. Following through on a campaign pledge, the Ingraham government began taking a tougher stand on illegal Haitian immigrants in the fall of 1992, rapatriating many to Haiti and starting the construction of a detention center.

In the summer of 1993, the government was criticized by rights organizations for systematic police round-ups and deportations of hundreds of Haitians. The government said that in accordance with the law Haitians who had been in the Bahamas since before 1980 would be given favorable consideration in establishing their status.

Full freedom of expression is constrained by strict libel laws. These laws were used by the former Pindling government against independent newspapers, but the Ingraham government has refrained from the practice. Under Pindling, radio and television were controlled by the government and often failed to air pluralistic points of view. At the end of 1992 the Ingraham government amended media laws to allow for private ownership of broadcasting outlets. In 1993 two newspaper companies were awarded the first-ever licenses to operate private radio stations and dozens of applications were received from investors wanting to set up cable television stations.

The judicial system is headed by a Supreme Court and a Court of Appeal, with the right of appeal under certain circumstances to the Privy Council in London. There are local courts, and on the outer islands the local commissioners have magisterial powers. Despite anti-drug legislation and a formal agreement with the United States in 1987 to suppress the drug trade, there was lingering evidence that under Pindling drug-related corruption continued to compromise the judicial system and Bahamian Defense Force.

Bahrain

Polity: Traditional monarchy
Economy: Capitalist-statist
Population: 548,000
PPP: $10,706
Life Expectancy: 71.0

Political Rights: 6
Civil Liberties: 6*
Status: Not Free

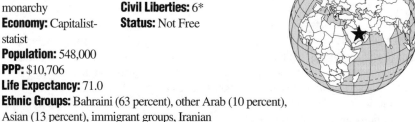

Ethnic Groups: Bahraini (63 percent), other Arab (10 percent), Asian (13 percent), immigrant groups, Iranian
Ratings Change: *Bahrain's civil liberties ratings changed from 5 to 6 as a result of modifications in methodology. See "Survey Methodology," page 671.

Overview:
This Persian Gulf archipelago off Saudi Arabia achieved full independence from the British on 14 August 1971. The Al Khalifa family has held the throne since 1782. The current Emir, Sheik 'Isa ibn Salman Al Khalifa, assumed power in 1961, and rules along with his brother, Prime Minister Khalifa ibn Salman Al Khalifa, and his son, crown prince Hamad ibn 'isa Al Khalifa. The December 1973 constitution provided for a National Assembly consisting of the cabinet and thirty popularly elected members. However, the

Emir dissolved the National Assembly in August 1975, ostensibly for debating "alien ideas," and has not reconvened it since then.

On 16 December 1992 the government created a thirty-member, appointed *majlis al-shura*, a consultative council consisting of business and religious leaders. This body convened for the first time on 16 January 1993, but is unlikely to have much practical impact. In foreign affairs, in July the International Court of Justice scheduled exploratory hearings for February 1994 on an ongoing territorial dispute with Qatar over several small islands.

Political Rights and Civil Liberties:

Citizens of Bahrain lack the democractic means to change their government. Political parties and opposition movements are not permitted. The Emir rules by decree and appoints all government officials, including the fifteen-member cabinet, the municipal councils in urban areas, and the *mukhtars* (local councils) which govern in rural areas. The only political recourse for citizens is to submit written petitions to the government, and to appeal to the Emir and other officials at *majlises*, regularly scheduled audiences. The ruling family is from the Sunni Muslim minority, which dominates top government positions and often receives preferential treatment in social services.

The Interior Ministry handles internal security through the police and its Security Service, and maintains informal control over most activities through pervasive informer networks. The Ministry can enter homes without a warrant, although this is done infrequently. The 1974 State Security Act allows the government to detain people accused of anti-government activity for up to three years without trial. Detainees can appeal after three months, and thereafter every six months from the original date of detention.

Ordinary civil and criminal trials feature the right to counsel, open proceedings, and the right of appeal, but cases tried in Security courts are exempted from these guarantees, and defendants do not receive fair trials. Nevertheless, defendants are acquitted reasonably often in Security cases, indicating a fair degree of judicial independence. According to the U.S State Department, credible sources indicate that of the estimated 220-270 prisoners in the country, forty to seventy may be political prisoners.

Despite constitutional guarantees of free speech, citizens do not publicly criticize the regime for fear of being detained. The privately owned newspapers also refrain from criticizing the government. Public political meetings and political organizations are not permitted, and the few private associations allowed to operate are closely monitored by the government.

Women face fewer cultural and legal retrictions than in other Islamic countries, but are still discriminated against in the workplace through unequal wages and opportunities. Islam is the state religion, but Christians, Hindus, Jews and others are generally permitted to worship freely. Citizens can move freely within the small country, but passports for foreign travel are occasionally denied for political reasons. The government discourages the formation of labor unions, and none exist. Workers do not have the right to bargain collectively or strike. The government has instead encouraged the formation of closely controlled, elected "workers committees" and, since 1982, joint labor-management consultative committees (JCC), although these hold little independent power. Thirteen JCC's have been set up, representing approximately 70 percent of the industrial workforce.

Bangladesh

Polity: Parliamentary democracy
Economy: Capitalist-statist
Population: 113,882,000
PPP: $872
Life Expectancy: 51.8
Ethnic Groups: Bengali (98 percent), Bihari (1 percent), various tribal groups (1 percent)
Ratings Change: *Bangladesh's civil liberties rating declined from 3 to 4 because of increased violations by police and security forces.

Political Rights: 2
Civil Liberties: 4*
Status: Partly Free

Overview:

Two years after Khaleda Zia's Bangladesh National Party (BNP) came to power in the country's freest elections ever in February 1991, efforts to alleviate widespread poverty have been sidetracked by political rivalries between Zia and opposition leader Sheik Hasina, a bloated bureaucracy, a hugely inefficient state sector, natural disasters and pervasive violence.

Bangladesh won independence in December 1971 after India invaded then-East Pakistan and defeated the occupying West Pakistani troops. In 1981 army rivals assassinated President Ziaur Rahman in an unsuccessful coup attempt. In March 1982 Army Chief of Staff Gen. H.M. Ershad came to power after ousting Rahman's short-lived successor. The country's democratic transition began with Ershad's resignation on 6 December 1990 following weeks of intense pro-democracy demonstrations.

Bangladesh's freest elections were held on 27 February 1991 for the 300 directly elected seats in the 330-member National Assembly (30 seats are reserved for women). The contest centered on two dominant personalities: the BNP's Khaleda Zia, widow of assassinated president Rahman, and the secular, pro-India Awami League's Sheik Hasina, daughter of assassinated independence Prime Minister Sheik Mujibar Rahman. On election day, the BNP took 138 seats; the Awami League, 89; Ershad's National Party, 35; the fundamentalist Islamic Assembly, 19; with the remainder split among smaller parties and independents. The Islamic Assembly threw its support behind the BNP, allowing it to name 28 of the 30 women's seats and secure a parliamentary majority. In March BNP-leader Zia became the first female prime minister of this primarily Muslim country.

In a 15 September 1991 referendum, 84 percent of the electorate approved plans to scrap the country's presidential system in favor of a Westminster-style parliamentary democracy. On 19 September parliament reappointed Zia as head of government with executive powers, and six days later it approved the BNP-nominated Abdur Rahman Biswas for the new, essentially ceremonial presidency.

Since the 1991 election, the opposition Awami League has exploited the government's tacit alliance with the Islamic Assembly and its controversial leader, Golam Azam. Many Bangladeshis consider Azam a traitor for having supported Pakistan during the 1971 war. Azam fled to Pakistan after the war, was stripped of his Bangladeshi citizenship for treason in 1973, and returned to the country in 1981 with a Pakistani passport.

Facing intense pressure from the opposition Awami League as well as at the grassroots level, in March 1992 the government arrested Azam for violating the Foreigners Act by heading a political party without being a citizen. The arrest touched off rounds of rioting between his supporters and opponents seeking his trial and execution. In April 1993 the High Court rejected the 1973 decision and ordered the government to restore Azam's citizenship, and in July ordered his release from jail for lack of cause.

In another divisive political issue, Sheik Hasina has called for the government to lift the immunity protecting the leaders of a 1974 coup that killed her father, Sheik Mujibar Rahman. Prime Minister Zia set up a parlimentary panel in 1991 to review the immunity but, perhaps to protect coup leaders now active in politics, no action has yet been taken. The Awami League called a massive protest on 20 August to protest the government's intransigence, drawing 100,000 people in the capital, Dhaka.

During the year a series of peace talks failed to make significant progress in ending the twenty-year-old Shanti Bahini (Peace Force) insurgency in the southeastern Chittagong Hill Tracts (CHT), waged by the Chakma and other Buddhist tribes. For years the government tacitly encouraged an influx of Muslim Bengalis into the 5,300-square-mile CHT in order to avoid overcrowding in other parts of the country. The Buddhist tribes now make up 60 percent of the CHT's population, down from 90 percent four decades ago, and want greater autonomy from the national government. Some 50,000 Chakmas who have fled to India since 1986 refuse to return to Bangladesh, fearing army reprisals, despite a repatriation accord signed in May 1993.

Campus battles between militant student wings of political parties have also plagued the country in recent years. In early February the worst violence in several years left one student dead and more than 200 wounded at the northern Rajshahi University after rival groups tried to hold a meeting at the same location. Several other campuses reported violence throughout the year, often involving the governing BNP's Nationalist Student Party.

In 1993 natural disasters continued to devastate Bangladesh. Six days of monsoon rains placed half the country under water in July, leaving some 7 million homeless or marooned. In addition, a cholera epidemic killed several thousand people in the spring. Despite these difficulties, the country is self-sufficient in rice for the first time since independence. Under prime minister Zia the government has met demanding World Bank macroeconomic targets by restricting state spending and promoting foreign investment. But economic growth remains below the 5.5 percent annual rate needed to improve conditions for the 50 million people living in absolute poverty, and privatization plans have been strongly attacked by unions and civil servants.

Political Rights and Civil Liberties: Citizens changed their government in generally free and fair parliamentary elections in February 1991. Twenty people died and more than 100 were injured in the January and February 1992 village council elections, yet they were far less violent than similiar elections in 1988. Partisan violence during the January 1993 municipal elections killed at least two people and wounded dozens, forcing polling to be suspended at six centers.

Key human rights problems involve the police, army and paramilitary units. Police frequently torture suspects during interrogations, leading to several deaths each year, and abuse prisoners in the lowly Class "C" cells. In the Chittagong Hill Tract (CHT) area, Shanti Bahini insurgents accuse security forces of rape, torture and illegal detention of Buddhist villagers. In addition, cycles of attacks by the Buddhist insurgents and reprisals by Muslims living in the area are common.

The 1974 Special Powers Act (SPA) allows police to detain suspects for an interim period of thirty days to prevent any "prejudicial act," although suspects are frequently held longer before being charged. If formally charged, they can be held while being investigated, subject to a judicial review after six months. Opposition leaders charge that political detentions under the SPA often amount to little more than personal revenge. In November 1992 parliament passed The Supression of Terroristic Offenses Bill for an initial two-year period. The Bill authorizes special tribunals for offenses including extortion and hijacking.

The judiciary is independent of the government. The system as a whole, though, is undermined by a severe backlog of some 500,000 cases and rampant corruption, particularly in the criminal courts. On 27 June three judges were suspended for corruption, although such punishment is rare.

Freedom of speech is generally respected. Most of the country's 120 daily newspapers, 440 weeklies and more than 300 magazines were launched after Ershad's ouster and freely criticize the government. Publications are heavily dependent on the government or state-owned enterprises for advertising revenues, and in 1992 the Minister of Information suggested that the government would apportion advertising to newspapers based on their "objectivity," rather than their circulation. While this has not been formally done, in practice advertising apportionment is often politically slanted. News coverage in the state-owned broadcast media favors the government.

In July the government banned author Taslima Nasreen's book, "Lajja" (Shame), saying it could provoke communal tensions. The book criticizes Muslim revenge attacks on Hindus following the December 1992 demolition of a mosque in India. In mid-October police placed Nasreen under twenty-four-hour protection after she received threats from a little-known group, the Council of Soldiers of Islam.

Freedom of peaceful assembly is generally respected, but political protests frequently turn into violent battles between activists and police. Although Islam is the official religion, the government allows the Buddhist, Christian and Hindu minorities to worship freely.

In January resettlement to Pakistan finally began for the first of some 270,000 Bihari Muslims, who opted for Pakistani citizenship after independence. In the southeast some 265,000 Rohingya Muslims who have fled Burma since 1991 are living in refugee camps, where they are often abused by Bangladeshi troops. However, most have refused repatriation, fearing new attacks by the Burmese army. Internal travel is unrestricted, except in parts of the CHT. Civil servants must get government permission to travel abroad, and citizens considered to be security risks are barred from traveling abroad.

Most unions are linked to political parties, and clashes between unions are frequent. Civil servants and workers in the Chittagong Export Processing Zone are barred from unionizing, and all unions face restrictions on who can hold office. The 1958 Essential Services Ordinance permits the government to bar strikes for three months in any sector it considers essential, and this is occasionally done in industries that are only marginally essential. Strikes are frequent and are often accompanied by violence.

Barbados

Polity: Parliamentary
democracy
Economy: Capitalist
Population: 260,000
PPP: $8,304
Life Expectancy: 75.1
Ethnic Groups: Black (80 percent), white (4 percent),
mixed (16 percent)

Political Rights: 1
Civil Liberties: 1
Status: Free

Overview:

Midway through a five-year term Prime Minister Erskine Sandiford and the governing Democratic Labour Party (DLP) appeared to have turned the economy around after a deep three-year slump. However, popular discontent still ran high, with at least a quarter of the work force unemployed.

Barbados, a member of the British Commonwealth, became internally self-governing in 1961 and achieved independence in 1966. The British monarchy is represented by a governor-general.

The system of government is a parliamentary democracy. The bicameral parliament consists of a 28-member House of Assembly elected for five years by direct popular vote, and a 21-member Senate, with twelve senators appointed by the prime minister, two by the leader of the parliamentary opposition, and seven by various civic interests. Executive authority is invested in the prime minister, who is the leader of the political party commanding a majority in the House.

Since independence, power has alternated between two centrist parties, the DLP under Errol Barrow, and the Barbados Labour Party (BLP) under Tom Adams from 1976 until Adams' death in 1985. Adams was succeeded by his deputy, Bernard St. John, but the BLP was soundly defeated in the 1986 elections. The DLP took 24 seats and Barrow returned as prime minister. Barrow died in June 1987 and was succeeded by Erskine Sandiford.

The DLP's majority was reduced in 1989 when four parliamentarians, led by Richie Haynes, broke away to form the National Democratic Party (NDP). Haynes became the leader of the opposition on the strength of the NDP's four-three seat advantage over the BLP.

Economic issues dominated the campaign for the 1991 election. The gross domestic product declined in 1990 for the first time in seven years, primarily because of decreased revenues from tourism, manufacturing, and the sugar industry. Higher oil prices, a result of the Persian Gulf crisis, cut into already dwindling hard currency reserves. The opposition parties ran against rising unemployment and increasing drug abuse and crime, particularly among youth. Nonetheless, the DLP won an eighteen-seat majority in the January 1991 election. The BLP, led by former foreign minister Henry Forde, bounced back from its dismal 1986 showing to take ten seats. The NDP failed to break the two-party system, winning no seats. Voter participation dipped to 62 percent, down from 76 percent in 1986.

As the economy continued to decline, the Sandiford government pushed austerity legislation, including a public sector pay cut which passed in the House by one vote. Near the end of 1991, the country was crippled by a two-day general labor strike backed by the BLP and mass demonstrations, a level of turbulence not seen in Barbados in decades.

In 1992 Sandiford ignored threats of a no-confidence motion in parliament and pressed forward with an IMF-prescribed stabilization program and a revision of the tax system. Economic growth appeared to have been restored in 1993, but unemployment remained high. Sandiford appeared to be making a political comeback in August when he managed to secure an agreement on wage and price controls with organized labor and the private sector.

Earlier in the year the DLP saw its majority slip to seventeen seats when Leroy Trotman, a powerful labor leader, quit the party. He retained his seat as an independent. Meanwhile, Forde resigned as BLP leader for health reasons. Owen Arthur, the forty-three-year-old BLP "shadow" finance minister, was elected to replace him. Under Arthur, and with an eye toward the next elections due in 1995, the BLP began developing proposals for integrity legislation and reform of the political system.

Political Rights and Civil Liberties:

Citizens are able to change their government through democratic elections. Constitutional guarantees regarding freedom of religion and the right to organize political parties, labor unions and civic organization are respected.

Apart from the parties holding parliamentary seats and the NDP, there are other political organizations including the small left-wing Workers' Party of Barbados. There are two major labor unions and various smaller ones, which are politically active and free to strike. Human rights organizations operate freely.

Freedom of expression is fully respected. Public opinion expressed through the news media, which are free of censorship and government control, has a powerful influence on policy. Newspapers are privately owned, and there are two major dailies. There are both private and government radio stations. The single television station, operated by the government-owned Caribbean Broadcasting Corporation (CBC), presents a wide range of political viewpoints.

The judicial system is independent and includes a Supreme Court that encompasses a High Court and a Court of Appeal. Lower court officials are appointed on the advice of the Judicial and Legal Service Commission. The government provides free legal aid to the indigent.

In 1993 human rights concerns continued to center on the rising crime rate, occasional allegations of police brutality, and the government's decision to propose constitutional changes to resume public flogging of criminals. In 1992 human rights groups protested that flogging violated a constitutional ban on torture or inhuman and degrading punishment, and in September 1992 the Court of Appeal formally outlawed the practice.

Belarus (Byelorussia)

Polity: Presidential-
parliamentary
Economy: Statist
transitional
Population: 10,263,000
PPP: $5,727
Life Expectancy: 72.0

Political Rights: 5*
Civil Liberties: 4*
Status: Partly Free

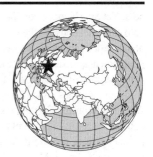

Ethnic Groups: Belarussians, Russian, Ukrainians, Poles
Ratings Change: *Belarus's political rights rating changed from 4 to 5
and its civil liberties rating from 3 to 4 as a result of modifications in
methodology. See "Survey Methodology," page 671.

Overview:

In its second full year of independence, Belarus (formerly the
Byelorussian Soviet Socialist Republic) was in the grip of
political paralysis pitting the Soviet-era Belarussian Supreme
Council (parliament), its chairman, Stanislau Shushkevich, and the conservative prime
minister, Vyachislav Kebich all against each other. Key issues included a new constitution, the pace and scope of economic reforms, and economic and security relationships
with the Commonwealth of Independent States (CIS), which Belarus and the other
Slavic former republics, Russia and Ukraine, founded in 1991.

The territory that is now Belarus was a part of the tenth century Kievan realm. After
a lengthy period of Lithuanian rule, it merged with Poland in the sixteenth century. It
came under the Russian Empire after Poland was partitioned three times in the eighteenth century. It became a constituent republic of the USSR in 1922.

In 1993, Belarus had yet to hold post-Soviet parliamentary elections. In March
1990, multi-candidate elections were held for republican-level and local legislatures
throughout the USSR. The democratic Belarusian Popular Front (BPF) gained 37 of
360 seats in the Belarus parliament, with the Communists winning most of the rest. On
17 March 1991 Belarus participated in Soviet President Mikhail Gorbachev's Union-
wide referendum on the preservation of the Soviet Union. Since then, Belarus has been
the only former Soviet republic that has not introduced the post of president and,
therefore, has never held a presidential election. The head of state is Council Chairman
Shushkevich, a nationalist-minded centrist. The cabinet of conservative Prime Minister
Kebich is made up largely of former Communists.

Nineteen-ninety-three saw political maneuvering by the hard-line parliament, the
centrist-liberal Shushkevich, an obstructionist prime minister and the democratic opposition, which continued to back the dissolution of parliament and elections even before the
adoption of a new constitution. In February, parliament lifted the ban on the Belarus Communist Party (BCP). The conflicts came to a head in July, when parliament moved to pass a
no-confidence vote to remove Shushkevich, partly because of his opposition to a year-old
CIS collective security pact. The move was thwarted by the democratic opposition, which
boycotted the vote, thus ensuring there was no quorum. The BPF joined extra-parliamen-
tary parties like the Belarusian Farmer's Party and the Belarusian United Democratic Party
in calling the vote a "Communist coup," adding that parliament had exhausted its useful-

ness. Yet Shushkevich continued to resist opposition calls that he dissolve parliament and hold early elections. At the close of the year, Shushkevich continued to press for adoption of a new draft constitution envisioning a presidential republic and clearly delineating government structures and the balance of power, and suggested that at the very least the old constitution be used as a basis for drafting a new electoral law.

A contentious issue throughout the year was Belarus's relations with the CIS. In April the Supreme Council instructed Chairman Shushkevich to agree to sign a CIS collective security agreement with the proviso that Belarusian troops be barred from military actions outside Belarus and from relocating in other countries. Parliament was supported by Prime Minister Kebich, strongly pro-Russian, who openly spoke out against Belarus neutrality and tied the pact to the need to form an economic union of CIS states. For his part, Shushkevich postponed holding a referendum to determine Belarus neutrality. At the end of the month, leaders of the Social Democratic Gromada, the Belarusian Democratic Party, the Belarusian Peasant Party, and a number of other parties and movements supported Shushkevich's stand that Belarus become part of a belt of neutral countries that were formerly part of the Warsaw Pact.

In May Prime Minister Kebich praised a parliamentary resolution on economic integration with the CIS, as well as parliament's support for the collective security treaty. Both actions were opposed by the Independent Trade Union (ITU), which noted that a military union with the CIS would not provide extra jobs for Belarusian workers but help Russian workers. The union reiterated its support for Shushkevich's opposition to the security pact. On 14 May, after a one-day summit in Moscow, nine of ten CIS leaders (Turkmenistan abstained) agreed to a declaration of intent to form an "economic union" of the former Soviet Republics.

On the weekend of 11 July, the prime ministers of Belarus, Russia and Ukraine signed a "declaration on economic integration" that committed them to an economic treaty by 1 September. Prime Minister Kebich denied that the non-Slavic CIS members were left "out in the cold" by the declaration, but there would be certain conditions for them to join the new "union within a union."

In August, with its economy floundering, Belarus sought a new currency union with Russia. The move followed the Russian central bank's withdrawal of pre-1993 bank notes, which caused the Belarus coupon (the hare) to plummet. Shushkevich said: "We are ready to establish common credit and bank policies, a common tax policy and to set aside all customs duties."

Because 70 percent of all imports, including 90 percent of energy supplies, come from Russia, some Belarus democrats complained that Russia was using economic blackmail to undermine the country's sovereignty. As a whole, Belarus's economy continued to suffer from the government's reluctance to scrap a command economy and implement market reforms and privatization. Despite rationing of certain goods, Belarusian officials insisted the country had maintained the highest standard of living in the former Soviet Union. It held its decline in production to 10 percent—half the collapse in Russia—and claimed a 1992 budget deficit of only 4.6 percent of gross domestic product. Nevertheless, the economy limped along. In late October, the chairman of the State Committee for Property reported that the rate of privatization in Belarus was extremely slow. He named the negative attitude of many local soviets of people's deputies and the unwillingness of individual ministries and departments to actively pursue privatization as key obstacles to change.

In other issues, Belarus—one of four nuclear powers in the former Soviet Union—ratified the Strategic Arms Reduction Treaty (START 1) on 4 February. The lawmakers voted 218 to 1, with 60 abstentions, to approve the treaty, which was signed by the United States and the Soviet Union in 1991.

Political Rights and Civil Liberties:

Without a post-Soviet constitution, or clearly defined new electoral laws, and with elections tentatively scheduled for March 1994, Belarusians have limited ability to change their government. Wrangling between the hard-line Supreme Council and Chairman Shushkevich over whether the country ought to ultimately be a presidential or a parliamentary republic continued in 1993. As yet, Belarusians, unlike their counterparts in other former Soviet republics, have not voted for a president.

Political parties and organizations are allowed to exist and function openly. The government lifted the ban on the Communist party in February. There are approximately ten political parties and several political organizations, though their membership tends to be small and concentrated in the larger urban areas.

The judicial system is essentially the same three-tiered structure from the Soviet era, and lacking a clear understanding of an independent judiciary, judges continue to be influenced by the political leadership. Attendance at public trials may be arbitrarily restricted. In the spring of 1993, parliament dealt with the issue of the KGB. Much to the alarm of the independent Belarus League for Human Rights, the security agency retained broad intrusive powers. The KGB can set up structures such as political parties, trade unions, civil movements and other organizations.

There are limitations on freedoms of the press and speech. All major newspapers are heavily subsidized by the government. The Council of Ministers continues to own and control nine major publications with a total daily press-run of 1.5 million. When a parliamentary organ, *Narodnaya hazeta,* refused to publish an interview with a goverment official it received an ultimatum: either the editors leave their offices in the House of the Government and move to other facilities or electricity and other utilities would be cut off. On 1 January a popular non-state television channel, Channel 8, and several other local radio and television stations were shut down by Prime Minister Kebich. The prime minister also ordered "a careful check" of all organizations operating with cable networks and satellite television in order to determine their "compliance with technical requirements and legal standards." As a result, commercial television companies have been denied broadcasting rights as of 1 January. Shows critical of the government have been canceled.

Although the constitutional draft (which has been criticized by international experts as containing undemocratic elements) guarantees freedom of speech, the right is restricted by the wide applicability of slander laws and secrecy clauses. In March well-known writer Svetlana Aleksievich faced charges brought by pro-Communist forces in connection with the stage adaptation of her book *The Zinc Guys,* which contained testimonies from mothers of soldiers killed in the Afghan war.

Freedom of movement and travel are respected. Nevertheless, there is an internal passport system and the "propiska" (pass) system requires Belarusians to register their place of residence; they may not move without official permission. A draft law was proposed to abolish the system.

Freedom of religion is guaranteed by law and usually respected in practice.

Catholics (with strong links to Poland) and Jews have complained about the reluctance of authorities to return churches and synagogues.

Fledgling women's organizations have sprung up to document discrimination and abuses, such as domestic violence. There are no legal restrictions on the participation of women in politics and government, though social barriers to women in the public arena exist.

There are several independent trade unions, such as the Independent Trade Union of Belarus. Union organizers often face various forms of harassment from management, public officials, and leaders of the Federation of Trade Unions of Belarus, a direct descendent of the former Soviet trade union council. The federation enjoys unofficial government support, and retains the administration of various social functions and pension funds.

Belgium

Polity: Federal parliamentary democracy
Economy: Capitalist
Population: 10,074,000
PPP: $16,381
Life Expectancy: 75.2
Ethnic Groups: Fleming (55 percent), Walloon (33 percent), mixed and others (12 percent), including Moroccan, Turkish and other immigrant groups

Political Rights: 1
Civil Liberties: 1
Status: Free

Overview:
The death of King Baudouin and the implementation of federalism were the most important events in Belgium in 1993.

Modern Belgium dates from 1830 when the territory broke away from the Netherlands. A constitutional monarchy, Belgium has a largely ceremonial king who symbolizes the unity of this ethnically divided state. The death of King Baudouin on 31 July shook the country emotionally, because he was a popular, stabilizing figure during thirty-two years of often bitter linguistic strife. In order to send the nation a message of continuity, the government decided that Baudouin's brother, Albert, should be King, not Albert's son, Philippe, who had been the presumptive heir.

The Dutch-speaking Flemings make up about 55 percent of the population and the Francophone Walloons about 33 percent. The rest of the population is of bilingual, mixed, or other background, including a small German minority near the German border. Belgium is divided into separate linguistic zones for the Flemings, Walloons, Germans, and multicultural Brussels, the headquarters of the European Commission. Since summer 1993, Flanders and Wallonia, the Flemish and Walloon zones, have been operating their own powerful regional parliaments. Brussels and the German area also have elected legislatures. This new federal system may or may not prevent Belgium from splitting into two independent states. On 25 April 1993, thousands of Belgians demonstrated in Brussels against splitting the country. The disastrous ethnic conflict in Bosnia-Herzegovina has tempered somewhat the demands for separatism. However, there are frequent disputes between the two dominant language groups. For much of Belgian history, the Walloons dominated the culture and the economy, while the Flemish had no legal status. To inspire Flemish enlistment in World War I, the king promised "equality in right and in fact."

Due to ethnic divisions, Belgian political parties are split along linguistic lines. Both Walloons and Flemings have parties ranging across the political spectrum. Governments come and go rapidly. There have been more than thirty cabinets since World War II. However, many of the same politicians and political parties reappear frequently in coalition governments. The bicameral parliament has a Senate, which combines directly and indirectly elected members, and a Chamber of Representatives, which the people elect directly on the basis of proportional representation. Each house has a term of up to four years. The heir to the throne has the right to a Senate seat. The current Senate has 181 members, and the Chamber of Representatives 212.

After forming a governing coalition of four Socialist and Christian Democratic parties, Jean-Luc Dehaene became Belgium's new premier in February 1992. Dehaene, a Flemish Christian Democrat, formed the four-party coalition after two other politicians had failed to do so following the inconclusive general election of November 1991.

That election produced losses for the Christian Democrats, Socialists, Francophone Liberals, and Volksunie, a moderate Flemish party. The right-wing Flemish Vlams Blok, the Greens, Flemish right-wing Liberals, Flemish Libertarians, and the Francophone National Front made gains. The small Francophone Federalists held their ground. Because the voters increased the standing of environmentalist and anti-immigrant parties, the government is under pressure to address their concerns. For example, Vlams Blok has demanded the repatriation of foreigners.

The Dehaene government has a deficit-reduction program aimed at meeting the standards for European currency union. Public debt is 130 percent of gross national product. Austerity measures include stricter welfare policies, higher social security taxes, and closing tax loopholes. The government nearly collapsed in March 1993 because the governing parties failed to agree on deficit reduction. After King Baudouin rejected the cabinet's offer to resign, the coalition agreed on an austerity budget. Communal tensions arise over this issue, because the more prosperous Flemings subsidize the Walloons heavily through taxes. Trade unions staged a general strike against austerity in November.

Political Rights and Civil Liberties: Belgians have the right to change their government democratically. Nonvoters are subject to fines. Political parties organize freely, usually along ethnic lines. Each language group has autonomy within its own region. However, tensions and constitutional disputes arise when members of one group get elected to office in the other's territory and refuse to take competency tests in the regionally dominant language.

In general, there is freedom of speech and of the press. However, Belgian law prohibits some forms of pornography and incitements to violence. Libel laws may have some minor restraining effects on the press and restrictions on civil servants' criticism of the government may constitute a small reduction of freedom of speech. The four-way zoning of the country has provoked numerous disputes over the rights of outsiders and local linguistic minorities to move across internal cultural borders and to use their preferred languages. The municipalities around Brussels have the right to refuse to register new residents from countries outside the European Union.

Autonomous public boards govern the state television and radio networks, and ensure that public broadcasting is linguistically pluralistic. The state has permitted and licensed private radio stations since 1985. There is freedom of association. Most workers belong to trade union federations. The largest labor group is Catholic and another major federation is social democratic.

Freedom of religion is respected. The state recognizes and subsidizes Christian, Jewish, and Muslim institutions. Other faiths are unrestricted. The monarch and his consort have a religious role. According to Belgian tradition, the seventh son or seventh daughter born to any Belgian family has the king or queen as godparent.

The judiciary is independent. The government appoints judges for life tenure. Belgium has a generally good record on the rights of the accused, but there have been some problems with extended pretrial detentions. A central government commission handles political asylum cases. Linguistic zoning and racism against immigrants limit opportunity. However, Belgium has taken important steps toward sexual equality, including prohibition of sexual harassment.

Belize

Polity: Parliamentary democracy
Economy: Capitalist
Population: 199,000
PPP: $3,000
Life Expectancy: 69.5
Ethnic Groups: Majority of mixed ancestry, including black, Carib, Creole and mestizo

Political Rights: 1
Civil Liberties: 1
Status: Free

Overview: Former Prime Minister Manuel Esquivel returned to power after his United Democratic Party (UDP) won a narrow victory in early elections held on 30 June 1993. There was speculation that George Price, the leader of the losing People's United Party (PUP) and the dominant figure in Belizean politics for decades, might retire.

Belize is a member of the British Commonwealth. The British monarchy is represented by a governor-general. Formerly British Honduras, the name was changed to Belize in 1973. Internal self-government was granted in 1964 and independence in 1981.

Because neighboring Guatemala refused to recognize the new state, Britain agreed to provide for Belize's defense. In 1991 Guatemala recognized Belize and diplomatic relations were established. However, by the end of 1993 a final accord on Guatemala's 134-year-old claim to an undefined part of Belizean land had still not been achieved.

Belize is a parliamentary democracy with a bicameral National Assembly. The 28-seat House of Representatives is elected for a five-year term. Members of the Senate are appointed, five by the governor-general on the advice of the prime minister, two by the leader of the parliamentary opposition, and one by the Belize Advisory Council. In the first post-independence election in 1984 the center-right UDP won twenty-one seats in the House, overturning thirty years of rule by George Price and the PUP. Businessman Manuel A. Esquivel became prime minister.

In the 1989 elections Price returned to power as the PUP won 15 seats in the House to the UDP's 13. A UDP defection to the PUP later increased the margin to 16-12. The Belize Popular Party (BPP) failed to win a seat. In municipal elections held in 1991, the PUP won majorities in five out of the country's seven Town Boards.

In May 1993 Price called snap elections for 30 June 1993, fifteen months before they were due. Price felt compelled to renew his mandate in the wake of political instability in Guatemala and the announcement that Great Britain would be withdrawing most of its 1,600 troops. He was confident of winning as the PUP only months earlier had easily won a by-election that increased its parliamentary advantage to seventeen-eleven and swept all nine seats in the Belize City Council elections.

In a tumultuous campaign the UDP assailed Price for being too soft on the Guatemala threat and the British withdrawal. It accused the PUP government of corruption, including being involved in a $30-million passport scam in which wealthy Asians were allowed to purchase citizenship. The UDP also charged the PUP with awarding citizenship to Central American immigrants to bolster the PUP vote.

The UDP won the election, taking sixteen seats to the PUP's thirteen (prior to the vote the number of seats had been increased to twenty-nine to prevent a tie). Five seats were won by margins of five votes or less and the PUP actually won the popular vote with 51.2 percent. The determining factor in the election may have been the return of the National Alliance for Belizean Rights (NABR) to the UDP fold after splitting off in 1992. The NABR takes a hard-line position on the Guatemala issue.

London later confirmed that Belize would be responsible for its own defense starting in 1994. But the issue was overshadowed by charges that PUP officials had tried to bribe two UDP legislators to switch parties and bring down the government.

Political Rights and Civil Liberties:

Citizens are able to change their government through free and fair elections. There are no restrictions on the right to organize political parties. Civic society is well established, with a large number of non-governmental organizations working in the social, economic and environmental areas.

Labor unions are independent and free to strike. There are about half a dozen trade unions, but the percentage of the work force that is organized has declined in recent years to less than 20 percent. Disputes are adjudicated by official boards of inquiry, and businesses are penalized for failing to abide by the labor code. There is freedom of religion.

The judiciary is independent and nondiscriminatory and the rule of law is guaranteed. The Belize Human Rights Commission is independent and effective.

In recent years, human rights concerns have focused on the plight of migrant workers and refugees from neighboring Central American countries—primarily El Salvador and Guatemala—and charges of labor abuses by Belizean employers. Among an estimated 30,000 aliens in Belize (nearly 15 percent of total population), at least 6,000 have registered under an amnesty program implemented in cooperation with the United Nations High Commissioner for Refugees. After a peace accord was reached in El Salvador in December 1991, the UNCHR began a repatriation process for Salvadoran refugees in Belize.

There also has been concern about the increase in violent crime, much of it related to drug trafficking and gang conflict. Because most of the 600-member police force goes unarmed, the former PUP government in 1992 instituted a policy of joint patrols between the police and the 600-member Belize Defense Force.

There are five independent newspapers representing various political viewpoints. Belize has a literacy rate of over 90 percent. Radio and television have played an increasingly prominent role in recent years, especially in the last two elections when they were saturated with political ads. There are fourteen privately owned television stations including four cable systems. There is an independent board to oversee operations of government-owned outlets.

Benin

Polity: Presidential-parliamentary democracy
Economy: Statist-transitional
Population: 5,075,000
PPP: $1,043
Life Expectancy: 47.0
Ethnic Groups: Aja, Barriba, Fon, Yoruba

Political Rights: 2
Civil Liberties: 3
Status: Free

Overview:

In 1993, the government of President Nicephore Soglo continued to grapple with Benin's chronic economic problems and incidents of religious violence between animists and Muslims.

The republic of Dahomey, a former center for the black African slave trade, achieved its independence from France on 1 August 1960. Gen. Ahmed Kerekou seized power in a 1972 coup. He renamed the country "Benin" in 1975 and established a Marxist-Leninist state under the banner of the Benin People's Revolutionary Party (PRPB). By 1988, Benin was effectively bankrupt, plagued by official corruption and incompetence, and besieged by widespread work stoppages and student-led strikes. In December 1989, after a series of moves to consolidate its hold on power, the regime entered into negotiations with the exiled political opposition in an effort to fend off economic and political disaster. The resulting Paris agreement laid the foundation for the country's transition to a multiparty democracy.

A national conference assumed sovereign control of the country in early 1990, appointing an interim government to prepare for democracy. Stripping Kerekou of his effective power as president, though not his formal position as head of state, the conference selected an interim prime minister, Nicephore Soglo, a former World Bank official, to lead the country through a year-long transition to competitive elections. Local multiparty elections in late 1990 were followed by legislative and parliamentary elections during the first quarter of 1991. In addition, a new democratic constitution was ratified by popular referendum. In March 1991, two rounds of balloting for president resulted in a conclusive victory for Prime Minister Soglo over Gen. Kerekou.

The Soglo administration set out to address the acute economic problems facing this largely agricultural society. Farmers raise karite, nuts, cocoa, coffee, cotton and palm oil. Only 10 percent of the country's 2 million workers are skilled. Soglo implemented an unpopular austerity program that included budget cuts made under International Monetary Fund (IMF) restructuring guidelines. The government scaled back a public sector swollen with university graduates, which led to protests in 1992.

On 8 February 1993, civil servants began a three-day strike against the 1993 budget they said had contained "no substantial measures...to alleviate the suffering of workers, the youth and the people;" the strikers demanded the cancellation of the IMF's Structural Adjustment Program (SAP) launched in 1989. The same month, Pope John Paul II visited Cotonou on the Gulf of Guinea.

In mid-February, the national forum of political parties of Benin met to mark the third anniversary of the national conference which began the democratization process. Some twenty-three opposition parties and three organizations reviewed progress since the national conference. The conference focused on five points: access to state media and information; the role of political parties; economic and social developments; the constitutional institutions and party charters; organization of elections; and the political situation in neighboring Togo. The forum decided to create a platform for consultations, dialogue and exchanges called the National Convention of Forces of Change, consisting of parties committed to the full implementation of the 11 December 1990 constitution.

Religion was behind a series of social disturbances in the spring. In April, clashes between Yoruba Muslims and Goun animists left several dead or injured in Porto Novo. The events capped month-long confrontations that included burning and looting after animists charged Muslims with desecrating a sacred idol.

In September, the prime minister announced a cabinet reshuffling, although the composition of the government changed very little.

Political Rights and Civil Liberties:

Benin's citizens can change their government democratically. Twenty-five parties are represented in the National Assembly. Professional and non-governmental organizations are permitted, among them the Human Rights Commission, the Study and Research Group on Democracy and Economic and Social Development, the Association of Christians Against Torture, and the League for the Defense of Human Rights in Benin.

Although government control of radio and television has raised the issue of opposition access to broadcast media, there is a lively and often irreverent free press. Over the last few years, there have been instances when the government has threatened legal action against "irresponsible journalism." Prime Minister Soglo singled out three publications for practicing what he called "rotten journalism," and urged journalists to receive some training abroad to improve their skills and judgments. Two papers, *Le Soleil* and *Tam Tam Express* had called the president's wife "an ugly witch," alleging she had an inordinate influence in national politics. In the past, the editor of *L'Observatuer* has been fined and imprisoned for six months.

The Soglo government has made a special effort to professionalize law enforcement personnel in order to eliminate arbitrary behavior such as levying on-the-spot "fines" on innocent passers-by. The judiciary is independent; the constitution provides that judges and other appointed officials are answerable only to the law in carrying out their duties and may not be removed. In March, Soglo pardoned twenty-three people serving sentences of from one to ten years for their part in violence during the 1991 elections.

There are no major restrictions on religion, though the year saw clashes between Muslims and animists. Of Benin's 5 million people, about one-fifth are Catholics, about one-eighth are Muslim and most of the rest follow vodun, the form of spiritual worship that gave voodoo its name after African slaves carried the practice to Haiti and elsewhere across the Atlantic centuries ago.

Both domestic and international travel are generally unrestricted for political reasons, though roadblocks and checkpoints have been set up to exact bribes from travelers.

Women continue to face discrimination and violence, particularly in traditional rural areas. They do not enjoy the same educational opportunities as men. Female circumcision is carried out; one reliable non-Beninese source has estimated that up to 50 percent of Beninese women have undergone the procedure.

Labor unions are allowed to organize and strike.

Bhutan

Polity: Traditional monarchy
Economy: Pre-industrial
Population: 785,000
PPP: $800
Life Expectancy: 48.9
Ethnic Groups: Bhotia (60 percent), Nepalese (25 percent), indigenous (15 percent), Tibetan refugees
Ratings Change: *Bhutan's civil liberties rating changed from 6 to 7 because of increased repression against ethnic Nepalese.

Political Rights: 7
Civil Liberties: 7*
Status: Not Free

Overview:

In 1993 the major human rights issue in this isolated Buddhist Himalayan Kingdom continued to be the treatment of ethnic Nepalese in the south. Many have been stripped of their citizenship and claim abuse by security forces, and some 85,000 have already fled the country. The government claims those who left were mostly illegal immigrants, and accuses pro-Nepali groups of trying to foment unrest to overthrow the monarchy.

The British began guiding Bhutan's affairs in 1865; India took over this role in 1949, agreeing not to interfere in domestic matters. In 1972 nineteen-year-old Jigme Singye Wangchuk succeeded his father to the throne. The King governs the country with the assistance of a Council of Ministers and a Royal Advisory Council. A 150-member National Assembly meets briefly twice a year to enact laws and approve senior appointments. Although the King cannot veto legislation, in practice his influence is always enough to ensure passage of legislation he considers important. Every three years 105 National Assembly members are elected by village headmen in Buddhist areas and family heads in Hindu regions. Twelve more Assembly seats go to religious groups and thirty-three are appointed by the King. Political parties are discouraged and none exist.

In the late 1980s the government began marginalizing the Nepali-speaking minority (known as *Lhotshampas*, or southerners), who first moved into southern Bhutan in large numbers in the late nineteenth-century. The ruling Buddhist majority feared being swamped by the Nepalese in the long-run, mindful that a similiar process had led neighboring Sikkim to be annexed by India in 1974. The country's sixth five-year plan (1987-92) introduced a program of Driglam Namzha (national customs and etiquette) to reinvigorate Buddhist culture. The government banned the teaching of the Nepalese language in schools, and required citizens to adopt the national dress of the ruling Drupka class. Candidates for the civil service were required to speak Dzongkha, the indigenous language spoken by only about one-fifth of the population.

The program took more extreme measures after the 1988 census showed Nepalese to be in the majority in five southern districts. In 1989 the King declared nearly all the Nepalese in the country illegal immigrants under a 1985 Citizenship Act. The Act had made 1958 the cutoff year for automatic citizenship. Anyone born in the country after 1958 had their citizenship stripped if both parents were not citizens. Those who did not qualify had to apply for citizenship, prove proficiency in written and spoken Dzongkha, and present evidence of having lived fifteen years in the country.

Such evidence is impossible for most in a society that is highly illiterate and lacks basic administrative systems, notwithstanding the government's claim that the word of a village leader is considered acceptable proof. Thousands were forcibly expelled, while others fled from conditions reportedly including arbitrary arrests, rape and beatings by the army and police forces. The government claimed that those expelled were simply Nepali citizens who had come to Bhutan to work since 1958 and had been exposed by the 1988 census.

In the summer of 1990 the newly formed Bhutan People's Party (BPP) organized several protests in the south against the measures, frequently attacking government offices and schools. Several were killed after security forces violently dispersed demonstrators in September 1990, although initial claims of up to 300 deaths later appeared to be hugely exaggerated. The government outlawed the BPP shortly thereafter, accusing it of engaging in terrorist attacks on officials. By the end of 1992 some 85,000 Lhotshampas had fled to refugee camps in Nepal and India.

In an interview in *The Nation* (Bangkok) in May 1993, Foreign Minister Lyonpo Dawa Tsering repeated the government's claim that "the majority of the people who are leaving the country are illegal residents," although he conceded that "a big chunk of genuine Bhutanese nationals has left the country." In October Bhutan began ministerial-level talks with Nepal on ending the refugee issue.

Political Rights and Civil Liberties:

Bhutanese citizens lack the democratic means to change their government. The King wields sovereign power, and policymaking is centered around the King and a small number of Buddhist aristocratic elites. Political parties are discouraged, and none exists. The Bhutan People's Party, which now operates out of Nepal, and the People's Forum for Human Rights are both outlawed. The government and dissidents accuse each other of human rights abuses, although lack of access to the kingdom makes such charges difficult to confirm. In the absence of a need for warrants, police frequently enter houses in the south to search for dissidents. The police and army are accused of arbitrary arrests, beatings, rape and robbery, as well as torture of prisoners and detainees.

The 1989 decree requiring Bhutanese to wear the national dress is enforced infrequently in the north, but fairly strongly in the south. In late 1990 the government banned the use of the Nepalese language in schools, ostensibly because of a UNICEF finding that students were being overwhelmed by having to study Nepali, English and Dzongkha.

Judges are appointed by and can be dismissed by the King, and handle all aspects of cases, including investigation and prosecution. There are no jury trials or lawyers, although a defendant has the right to the services of a *jambi*, a person familiar with the law. Only 12 percent of the population is literate, so the print media has little impact. The state-owned weekly, *Kuensel*, is the country's only regular publication and reflects government views, although foreign papers circulate freely. Criticism of the King is not permitted in the media. The country has no television, and since 1989 the kingdom has banned antennas to prevent people from catching foreign broadcasts. The government must approve all assemblies and associations, and there are no civil sector institutions such as communal, economic or professional groups.

The Druk Kargue sect of Mahayana Buddhism is the official state religion, monasteries and shrines are subsidized by the government, and some 6,000 Buddhist lamas (priests) wield fairly strong political influence. Hindus and others are allowed to worship freely, although proselytizing is illegal. Citizens can move freely within the country and travel abroad, although only 3,000 visitors are allowed into the kingdom each year. Unions and collective bargaining are not permitted.

Bolivia

Polity: Presidential-legislative democracy
Economy: Capitalist-statist
Population: 8,035,000
PPP: $1,572
Life Expectancy: 54.5
Ethnic Groups: Quechua Indian (30 percent), Aymara Indian (25 percent), other Indian (15 percent), Mixed (10-15 percent), European (10-15 percent)

Political Rights: 2
Civil Liberties: 3
Status: Free

Overview:

President Gonzalo "Goni" Sanchez de Losada was inaugurated on 6 August 1993. After leading a field of fourteen candidates in the 6 June election, he took office at the head of a three-party coalition. Vice President Victor Hugo Cardenas, an Aymara Indian, became the first indigenous leader in Latin America to hold such a high national office.

Since achieving independence from Spain in 1825, the Republic of Bolivia has endured recurrent instability and extended periods of military rule. The armed forces, responsible for over 180 coups in 157 years, returned to the barracks in 1982. The 1967 constitution was restored with the election of President Hernan Siles Suazo. The 1985 election of President Victor Paz Estenssoro of the Nationalist Revolutionary Movement (MNR) marked the first transfer of power between two elected presidents in twenty-five years.

The constitution provides for the election every four years of a president and a Congress consisting of a 130-member House of Representatives and a 27-member Senate. (Following reforms made in 1993, the terms will be extended to five years beginning in 1997.) If no presidential candidate receives an absolute majority of votes, Congress makes the selection from among the three leading contenders. Municipal elections are held every two years.

Sanchez, the former planning minister under Paz Estenssoro and architect of an austerity program that had ended hyperinflation, won a slim plurality in the 1989 election. Retired Gen. Hugo Banzer, head of the conservative National Democratic Action (ADN) and former military dictator (1971-78), came second. Jaime Paz Zamora of the social democratic Movement of the Revolutionary Left (MIR) came third. Sanchez's MNR won 49 seats in the Congress, the ADN 46 and the MIR 41. Banzer agreed to back Paz Zamora for president in exchange for half the cabinet positions. Paz Zamora was elected president by Congress in August 1989.

The MIR-ADN coalition's term in office was marked by factionalism and corruption scandals. Student protests and paralyzing labor strikes against the government's privatization plan were frequent. Widespread discontent with traditional politics led to the emergence of populist, anti-establishment alternatives. Both the Civic and Solidarity Union (UCS) led by beer magnate Max Fernandez and the Conscience of the Fatherland party (CONDEPA) led by former talk show host Carlos Palenque scored well in the 1991 municipal elections.

The 1993 election campaign came down to a duel between the MNR's Sanchez and Banzer of the incumbent ADN-MIR "Patriotic Accord." Fernandez, a mestizo with humble origins, appealed to the country's ethnic and cultural underclass, but his candidacy was undercut by unconfirmed allegations that he was involved in cocaine trafficking. Sanchez's selection of Cardenas, one of Bolivia's foremost Indian leaders, as his running mate, and his reputation for honesty despite his wealth, appeared to give him an edge over Banzer.

On 6 June Sanchez took 33.8 percent of the vote, Banzer 20 percent, Palenque 13.6, Fernandez 13.1 and Antonio Aranibar of the leftist Free Bolivia Movement (MBL) 5.1. With no candidate winning a majority, the horse-trading began in the newly elected Congress. Sanchez's MNR had won 69 seats in the bicameral legislature, 9 less than the total for a working majority. Sanchez secured the backing of Fernandez, whose UCS took 21 seats, and Aranibar, whose MBL took 7. The three-party coalition, with 97 out of 157 seats, elected Sanchez president. Both the UCS and the MBL were rewarded with cabinet positions.

Sanchez had campaigned for more efficient government, but his initial efforts to cut the bureaucracy led to a series of labor strikes in the fall. The first challenges to his anti-corruption platform were a scandal involving the Supreme Court and mounting evidence of pervasive graft and influence-peddling under the Paz Zamora government. Evidence of illegal arms trafficking involving former government and military officials prompted Sanchez to replace all the armed forces commanders in October. The new commanders denied that the sudden overhaul had caused unrest within the officer corps.

Possibly the greatest test for the new government was making good on its commitment to incorporate the marginalized Indian majority into the political and economic life of what is the poorest country in South America. Vice-President Cardenas was expected to lead on political reform. Sanchez's promise to distribute widely the proceeds from privatizing state companies through "popular" shares hinged on attracting the necessary foreign investment.

Political Rights and Civil Liberties: Citizens are able to change their government through democratic means. In 1991 a new electoral court consisting of five relatively independent magistrates was created, and a new voter registration was carried out. But there remains disenchantment with a system in which the president is ultimately chosen by the Congress. Opinion polls show overwhelming support for directly electing the president by a simple majority.

Constitutional guarantees regarding free expression, freedom of religion, and the right to organize political parties, civic groups and labor unions are generally respected. But political expression is restricted by recurring violence associated with labor strife and the billion-dollar-per-year cocaine trade. Also, the emergence of small indigenous-based guerrilla groups has caused an overreaction by security forces against legitimate government opponents. The languages of the indigenous population are officially recognized, but the 40 percent Spanish-speaking minority still dominates the political process.

The political landscape features political parties ranging from fascist to radical left. There are also a number of indigenous-based peasant movements, including the Tupac Katari Revolutionary Liberation Movement headed by Victor Hugo Cardenas, the nation's new vice-president.

There is strong evidence that drug money has penetrated the political process through the corruption of government officials and the military, and through electoral campaign financing. The drug trade has also spawned private security forces that operate with relative impunity in the coca-growing regions. Bolivia is the world's second largest producer of cocaine. A U.S.-sponsored eradication program has drawn political fire from peasant unions representing Bolivia's 50,000 coca farmers, the Bolivian Workers Confederation, the nation's largest labor confederation, and nationalist sectors of the military.

Unions are permitted to strike and have done so repeatedly against the economic restructuring programs of three successive governments that have left more than a quarter of the work force idle. Strikes, however, are often broken up by force, frequently with the use of the military.

The judiciary, headed by a Supreme Court, is the weakest branch of government. Despite judicial reforms implemented in 1993, it remains riddled with corruption, overpoliticized and subject to the compromising power of drug traffickers. A revamped Supreme Court won accolades in early 1993 for convicting fugitive former dictator Gen. Lucas Garcia Mesa (1980-81) and a number of his cronies on murder and corruption charges. But in October, seven of the twelve justices faced impeachment charges in the Congress for soliciting bribes in an extradition case.

Human rights organizations are both government-sponsored and independent. Their reports indicate an increase in police brutality, torture during confinement and harsh prison conditions since 1991. There has been occasional intimidation against independent rights activists.

The press, radio and television are mostly privately owned and free of censorship. Journalists covering corruption stories are occasionally subject to verbal intimidation by government officials and violent attacks. There are a number of daily newspapers including one sponsored by the influential Catholic church. Opinion polling is a growth industry. Seven years ago there was no television, but now there are more than sixty channels. The impact has been most evident in the media-based campaigns of the prominent political parties.

Bosnia-Herzegovina

Polity: Presidential-par-
liamentary democracy
(mostly foreign-occupied)
Economy: Mixed-statist
(severely war-damaged)
Population: 4,010,000
PPP: na
Life Expectancy: 70.0
Ethnic Groups: Pre-war—Slavic Muslim (44 percent),
Serb (33 percent), Croat (17 percent)

Political Rights: 6
Civil Liberties: 6
Status: Not Free

Overview: In 1993 Serb-backed militias continued their twenty-one-
month war against Bosnian Muslims and the government of
President Alija Izetbegovic. By mid-year, Croatian Defense
Units (HVO) and Croat army regulars turned their guns on erstwhile Muslim allies.
Muslim unity unraveled as one local leader sought a separate peace with the Serbs.
Internationally brokered ceasefires and peace plans were routinely ignored. NATO
threats to enforce "no-fly" zones and U.S. and European saber-rattling about retaliatory
strikes against Serb positions proved hollow. By year's end, casualties were estimated at
250,000 and the capital, Sarajevo, remained besieged. Residents faced intense shelling
and another winter of fuel shortages, power outages and dwindling food and medicine.

Bosnia-Herzegovina became one of six constituent republics of Yugoslavia in
November 1945. During World War II, internecine conflict killed 700,000, mainly Serbs.
As Yugoslavia broke apart, the republic held multiparty elections in September 1990, with
the three nationalist parties representing Muslim, Serb, and Croat constituencies winning
most of the 240-member Assembly seats. In a February 1992 referendum boycotted by
Serbs, 99 percent favored secession from Yugoslavia. The same month, the three main
national groups, meeting in European Community (EC) (now European Union)-brokered
talks in Lisbon, agreed to recognize existing borders. Participants included Radovan
Karadzic, leader of the Bosnian Serbs, and Mate Boban, head of the Croatian Democratic
Union, who would later head the self-styled Croatian republic within Bosnia. President
Izetbegovic issued a declaration of independence 3 March 1992. Within weeks, Muslim,
Croat and Serb leaders agreed to divide Bosnia into three autonomous units based on the
"national absolute or relative majority" in each area. The agreement was never enforced.

The United States recognized Bosnia on 7 April. Not wanting to be part of a
Bosnian state, 100,000 Serbs supplied by the Serbian government of Slobodan
Milosevic attacked outgunned Muslims and their Croat allies. By year's end, Serbs
controlled over 70 percent of the country and a systematic policy of "ethnic cleansing"
had killed or displaced hundreds of thousands of Muslim, Croat and Serb civilians. The
Vance-Owen plan—named for former U.S. Secretary of State and U.N. mediator Cyrus
Vance and EC negotiator Lord David Owen—which called for the partition of Bosnia
into ten autonomous ethnic provinces, was widely criticized. Over 20,000 U.N.
peacekeepers did not deter Serbian aggression.

Nineteen-ninety-three opened with some hopes of a settlement, as the parliament of the Serb republic in Bosnia voted on 19-20 January to accept the principles of Vance-Owen. All three sides called for changes in the map dividing the country into ten cantons. Peace talks moved from Geneva to the U.N. at the end of the month.

By February, Serbs intensified "ethnic cleansing," expelling Muslims from what would be Serb- or Croat-controlled areas under the agreement. The U.S., which first rejected Vance-Owen for legitimizing Serb military gains, said it would "do its share to enforce a settlement." The U.S. was not prepared to lift the embargo on arms to the Muslims. In mid-month, the U.N. High Commissioner on Refugees unexpectedly suspended most relief operations in the country, endangering 1.6 million people dependent on aid. Earlier, the Bosnian government threatened to stop convoys to Sarajevo until supplies were delivered to some 200,000 Muslims in besieged towns in eastern Bosnia.

In March, as Karadzic, Boban and President Izetbegovic met with U.N. mediators in New York, Serb forces were close to seizing several Muslim enclaves in eastern Bosnia. On 3 March, Serbs massacred 500 civilians in Cerska, target of the first U.S. airdrop.

On 9 March, after a ten-day assault by Serb forces on Srebrenica and Konjevic Polje in eastern Bosnia, Bosnia's military commander ordered a counter-offensive against Bosnian Serb troops in the east "to prevent the massacre of innocent people" in Muslim enclaves. Fearing thousands more would die, President Izetbegovic demanded that any peace plan include a strict timetable and provisions that U.N. or NATO peacekeeping troops have enforcement power. The Bosnians also demanded there be one constitution for the country, not a series of documents, one for each autonomous provinces.

By month's end, President Izetbegovic refused formal talks until Serbs lifted the siege of Srebrenica and stopped shelling Sarajevo. Attempts to airlift sick and wounded from Srebrenica were interrupted when Serbs bombarded landing zones.

On 2 April, shunning appeals from Karadzic and Serbia, the Bosnian Serb parliament rejected even a conditional acceptance of the Vance-Owen version already approved by Muslims and Croats. Meanwhile, the Croatian Defense Council told the Bosnian army it had until 15 April to withdraw from areas included in the three Croat-dominated provinces envisioned under Vance-Owen. Fighting between HVO and Muslim forces included "ethnic cleansing."

With Vance-Owen near collapse, the U.N. attempted to establish "safe areas" and "safe havens" to protect civilians. Bowing to pressure from Serbia and possible U.S. air strikes, Karadzic on 2 May signed the plan. Yet, Serbian offensives continued throughout Bosnia. Heavy shelling, infantry attacks and high casualties were reported in Goradze, one of three eastern Muslim towns not in Serb hands. Bosnian Serbs rejected the Vance-Owen plan in a 17 May referendum as Muslim-Croat battles intensified in Mostar.

On 22 May, the U.S., Russia and three European allies agreed on a joint strategy to contain fighting and protect safe havens. The plan, immediately denounced by the Muslims, paid only lip service to Vance-Owen. Serb leaders told Russian mediators they would not accept international monitors on their border with Bosnia, a provision of the plan. The U.N. Secretariat criticized the "safe havens" proposal as unworkable and validating "ethnic cleansing," adding that humanitarian conditions in Sarajevo, Bihac, Goradze, Srebrenica, Tuzla and Zepa were "appalling."

By June, Serb forces had overrun several Muslim villages around Goradze, a "safe area." The Serbs barred U.N. observers from the area. Serbs shelled Srebrenica, openly defying the U.N. Security Council resolution.

Attempts to revive negotiations by Lord Owen and Thorvald Stoltenberg, the new

U.N. negotiator, proved difficult. Croatia and Serbia proposed a plan to divide Bosnia into three ethnic states with a federal or confederal constitution. In an abrupt reversal, Lord Owen advised the Bosnian government to accept the plan and recognize that it could not retake land lost to Serbs and Croats. His statement effectively doomed Vance-Owen and European- and American-sponsored efforts to persuade Serbs to relinquish territory. President Clinton signaled the U.S. might accept a partition allowing Serbs to keep land seized by force.

Subsequently, the EC urged President Izetbegovic to accept the Serbian-Croatian plan and rejected his appeal to lift the arms embargo. President Izetbegovic was pressured by the collective presidency to be less hostile toward the proposal. A majority of the collective presidency revolted on 23 June, voting to participate in partition talks. The 7-2 decision threw the beleaguered Bosnian government into crisis. The seven, including Fikret Abdic, the only Muslim, went to Geneva to discuss the Serb-Croat plan.

After weeks of wrangling, the government rejected the partition proposal and appealed for U.S. political and military support to maintain Bosnia's integrity. The collective presidency also adopted a plan to establish Bosnia as a federal state. By mid-July, Serb forces seized strategic villages west of Goradze and increased pressure on Sarajevo. Muslim-Croat fighting escalated around Mostar and Travnik.

When talks resumed in Geneva on 27 July, the Bosnian government initially insisted on a centralized state of three "federal units" with boundaries not drawn strictly along ethnic lines. Three days later, President Izetbegovic gave way to mediators' pressure, agreeing to demands for the country's partition despite opposition by some military and political leaders. But Izetbegovic refused to negotiate further until Serbs pulled back from two strategic mountains outside Sarajevo.

Serb intransigence and the imminent fall of Sarajevo again led NATO to threaten air strikes. On 6 August, mediators suspended the Geneva talks for three days, apparently to step up pressure on President Izetbegovic and his divided delegation. Serb leader Karadzic had agreed to withdraw Serb forces from heights overlooking Sarajevo.

When talks resumed, all sides agreed "in principle" to demilitarize and place Sarajevo under temporary U.N. control. A sticking point continued to be a post-war map defining future borders. The map required Serbs and Croats to return conquered territories, and asked Muslims to give up land where they had been a pre-war majority.

On 28 August, Bosnia's parliament rejected the partition proposal. The Geneva talks collapsed after Bosnian Muslims refused to accept an accord unless Serbs and Croats agreed to cede more land, giving Bosnia access to the sea. In late September, secret negotiations on a British warship failed over territory issues. On 29 September, Bosnia's parliament demanded the plan be renegotiated to include "international guarantees" that NATO peacekeepers would be stationed immediately.

In October, Fikret Abdic proclaimed the Bihac region's autonomy from the Sarajevo government. He subsequently made a peace pact with President Milosevic in Belgrade. A similar deal with Bosnian Croats gave Bihac free access to the Croatian port of Rijeka.

With Muslim-Croat tensions mounting, the Bosnian army on 6 November moved to disband the Croatian militia that had helped defend Sarajevo. Attempts to restart the Geneva process collapsed over territorial concessions. On 3 December, Bosnian leaders vowed their besieged capital would not be divided. Serbs blocked delivery of clothes and winter supplies to millions of Bosnians despite an agreement to allow convoys free passage. A meeting of the three factions and EC foreign ministers in Brussels did lead to a short-lived Christmas truce. Sarajevo came under fierce artillery attack at year's end.

Political Rights and Civil Liberties: War and the self-proclaimed Serbian and Croat "republics" within Bosnia-Herzegovina seriously undermine the political and human rights of Bosnian citizens. The country is run by a ten-member, multi-ethnic collective presidency chaired by President Alija Izetbegovic and a sixty-five-member parliament. The Sarajevo-based government has no control over some 75 percent of the country, and the rule of law has broken down in most areas.

Human rights violations were rampant throughout 1993. Civilians, including non-Muslims, faced deportation, execution, sexual abuse, torture, and unlawful imprisonment. The war has displaced over one million people. In March, a military court imposed the death penalty by firing squad on two Serbs found guilty of murders and rapes while serving with Serb forces. Violations of war crime conventions were endemic, as "ethnic cleansing" continued in much of the country. Bosnian Croats admitted inhumane conditions in prison camps holding thousands of Muslims. U.N. officials concluded the camps were part of a Croat drive to clear Muslim Slavs from western Herzegovina. In late October, the U.N. documented a massacre site in central Bosnia where Croat forces had murdered and raped defenseless civilians. Muslim forces also engaged in summary executions, forced displacement of civilians, torture and rape. All sides used food as a weapon, blocking U.N. relief convoys.

Most newspapers stopped printing by 1993. The Sarajevo daily, *Oslobodjenje*, came out sporadically because of power outages, material shortages, and shelling. Radio transmission was sporadic. War made domestic and international travel difficult and risky. Refugees and relief convoys were frequently attacked. Freedom of association and assembly were circumscribed by war. Muslims, Catholic Croats and Orthodox Serbs practiced their religions in areas they controlled. Mosques, churches and cemeteries were intentionally targeted in war zones. Trade unions were made moot by economic and social dislocation.

Botswana

Polity: Parliamentary
democracy and
traditional chiefs
Economy: Capitalist
Population: 1,403,000
PPP: $3,419
Life Expectancy: 59.8

Political Rights: 2*
Civil Liberties: 3*
Status: Free

Ethnic Groups: Tswana, Baswara, Kalanga, Kgagaladi and European
Ratings Change: *Botswana's political rights rating changed from 1 to 2 and its
civil liberties rating from 2 to 3 as a result of modifications in methodology. See
"Survey Methodology," page 671.

Overview: Major news stories in Botswana in 1993, one of the few
working African democracies, included the failure of the
opposition to form a united bloc, corruption scandals, and
the persistence of drought.

Botswana, a land-locked country located in Southern Africa, has one of the world's
lowest population densities. Formerly a British colony, it gained independence in 1966.
Since independence, the Botswana Democratic Party (BDP) has won all the elections
and has ruled the country uninterrupted, with some members of the opposition accusing
it of electoral rigging. The opposition parties include the Botswana People's Party (BPP),
the Botswana Independence Party (BIP), the Botswana Progressive Union (BPU), and the
Botswana National Front (BNF). The country's president is Sir Ketumile Masire who is
also the leader of the BDP.

On 20 January 1993, the BPP called for the government to resign, citing its failure
to improve the living standards of the majority of *Batswana*, high unemployment and a
growing gap between the affluent and the poor, and high levels of corruption. Despite
high economic growth rates, the majority of Batswana continue to earn their living
through subsistence farming, receiving only about 20 percent of the country's income,
while two-thirds of the income goes to the richest 20 percent. In order to create a viable
alternative to the BDP, the opposition leaders continued their attempts to form a
coalition capable of unseating the ruling party. Former attempts to establish a united
opposition coalition floundered in 1990 when the BIP rejected the BNF's threats of
violence if the BDP continued to win the elections. In February, the secretary general of
the BPP, Matlhomola Modise, blamed the failure of new coalition talks between the
BPP and the BNF on a northern group of BNF whom he accused of being more interested
in gaining positions of power than in removing the BDF government from office.

Amid allegations of widespread curruption among public officials, not excluding
the president, Masire lashed out at the practice, promising better control and
enforcement, and repeatedly urging the population to "sharpen the perception of
moral values."

During the year, the country was crippled by drought which began the previous
year. As a result, farmers' incomes fell sharply and the number of malnourished
children increased. The country became more dependent on foreign aid donors.

The construction of the largest airbase in sub-Saharan Africa continued to generate speculation and controversy. Despite the government's statements that the base, whose cost amounted to 20 percent of the country's Gross Domestic Product, was built solely with public funds and was to serve the defense needs of Botswana, domestic and foreign media continued to speculate about the alleged U.S. financing of the project and its future use for the American armed forces.

Despite its small population, Botswana played an important role in peacekeeping activities abroad. More than 300 members of the Botswana Defense Forces (BDF) distinguished themselves in U.N. peacekeeping activities in Somalia, and in April, a contingent of 1,000 more soldiers arrived for similar purposes in Mozambique.

Political Rights and Civil Liberties: Citizens of Botswana can change their government democratically, but the same party has governed the country since independence. Independent political parties and various other associations exist. The judiciary is independent. Citizens are protected from arbitrary arrests, and in most cases suspects must be charged before a magistrate within forty-eight hours of detention. Suspects charged under the National Security Act (NSA) may be detained indefinitely. The NSA has rarely been invoked, however.

The right to assemble is usually respected, but permits for gatherings may be denied if there is a risk of violence. The *Kgotla*, or village meetings, are a traditional forum of discussion concerning local and national issues.

The constitution prohibits discrimination based on ethnicity, but in 1992 the Botswana Christian Group, a religious consortium, charged that the Bushmen (Baswara or San) are subjected to pervasive discrimination, widespread torture, and forced relocation from their ancestral land. The government charged that the report had been prepared under the influence of "foreign agitators" and refused to answer the charges. Of the 39,000 Bushmen, only about 3,000 continue to lead a nomadic life, while the majority has been forced to settle in government approved areas and rely on public assistance.

Although the government-owned media such as Radio Botswana, the Botswana Press Agency (BOPA), and the *Daily News* newspaper tend to present government views, the four independent weeklies favor the opposition. The independent press has become increasingly aggressive in recent years in criticizing public officials. In early 1993, five cabinet ministers filed a joint law suit against the *Botswana Guardian* and its sister publication the *Midweek Sun* following the publication of a series of articles alleging that a group identified as "Big Five" was preparing to oust the president from office.

Free trade unions in the private sector exist, but the right to strike is severely circumscribed. Public servants may form professional associations but are not allowed to enter into wage bargaining.

Freedom to travel in and out of the country is guaranteed in law and unhindered in practice.

Brazil

Polity: Federal presidential-legislative democracy
Economy: Capitalist-statist
Population: 151,989,000
PPP: $4,718
Life Expectancy: 65.6
Ethnic Groups: Caucasian (53 percent), black mixed (46 percent), pure Indian (less than 1 percent)

Political Rights: 3*
Civil Liberties: 4*
Status: Partly Free

Ratings Change: *Brazil's political rights rating changed from 2 to 3, principally the result of the advancing deterioration of political institutions and increasing military influence in politics.

Brazil's civil liberties rating changed from 3 to 4, principally the result of a growing climate of lawlessness and insecurity related to escalating criminal violence and a national breakdown of police discipline. See "Political Rights and Civil Liberties" below.

Overview: With a weak caretaker president, the economy in shambles, the congress paralyzed by corruption scandals and confidence in civilian rule waning, many Brazilians wondered how the country was going to make it to the next presidential election in October 1994.

After gaining independence from Portugal in 1822, Brazil retained a monarchical system until a republic was established in 1889. Democratic rule has been interrupted by long periods of authoritarian rule, most recently under military governments from 1964 to 1985.

The return to civilian rule in 1985, the result of a controlled transition transacted by the military with opposition political parties, led to the presidency of Jose Sarney, the first civilian leader in twenty-one years. A bicameral Congress, elected in 1986, produced a new constitution.

The 1988 constitution provided for a president to be directly elected on 15 November 1989 for a five-year term. The Congress was retained, with an eighty-one-member Senate directly elected for eight years and a 503-member Chamber of Deputies directly elected for four years. Brazil is divided into twenty-six states and the Federal District of Brasilia. State governors and legislatures are elected, as are municipal governments.

Fernando Collor de Mello, a forty-two-year-old political newcomer, came first among twenty-two candidates in the first round of the 1989 presidential election. In the second round he took 53 percent of the vote to defeat Luis Inacio "Lula" da Silva of the leftist Workers' Party (PT) and become the first directly elected president in nearly three decades.

Collor vowed to end official corruption and modernize the economy. But two shock programs failed to control inflation and left the economy in deep recession. Plans to overhaul the statist economy were undermined by a hostile Congress wielding the 1988 constitution, a populist document that mandates spending on behalf of a vast array of special interests and makes structural reform virtually impossible.

In 1992 Collor was directly tied to a $55-million graft and influence-peddling scheme. Under pressure from the media and a wave of popular protests, the Congress—a diverse and generally feckless group of nineteen parties tied to labor, big business and regional interests—impeached him. Facing a corruption trial in the Senate, Collor resigned in December 1992.

Itamar Franco, the vice president, took over. He appeared overwhelmed and his performance was inept. By fall 1993, with monthly inflation having risen from 26 to 35 percent, violent crime spinning out of control, and the social fabric crumbling, his poll ratings were barely above single digits.

In accordance with the constitution a plebiscite was held on 21 April to decide whether to keep the presidential system, change to a parliamentary system, or reestablish a monarchy. Although voting is obligatory, the referendum was marked by apathy and high abstention. Those who went to the polls voted overwhelmingly to retaining the presidential system. Opinion polls indicate that Brazilians trust congress the least of the nation's institutions, a sentiment apparently confirmed by their rejection of a parliamentary system.

The constitution also mandated that it be reviewed in 1993. The process did not get underway until the fall, and was then derailed by a massive corruption scandal involving dozens of legislators, cabinet ministers, state governors and assorted captains of industry, especially in the construction business.

The 300,000-member military stayed out of the impeachment of Collor. But with political and economic chaos increasing in 1993, with right-wing voices demanding a restoration of "order," and with opinion polls indicating a nostalgia for military rule, the armed forces leaned on Franco for more money and a greater say in government. Franco, adrift and fumbling, embraced what local analysts called the "military anchor," appointing generals to traditionally civilian cabinet posts and a retired colonel to head a federal security force. By fall 1993 Franco's public appearances were mostly at military ceremonies. The growing influence of the military become more evident in December when Franco exempted the armed forces from budget cuts in 1994.

The military did not appear interested in a coup, although a number of analysts raised the specter of a "Fujimori" solution— the dissolution of congress in favor of presidential-military rule as in Peru. Lula da Silva announced he was running again for president and led in the polls throughout 1993. Da Silva, a fiery leftist and traditonally an arch-nemesis of the armed forces, seemed to assuage the fears of some officers in 1993. But the question remained how the military would react if da Silva were to win in October 1994.

Political Rights and Civil Liberties: Citizens are able to change their rulers through elections at the national and local levels. However, the government was nearly paralyzed in 1993 by corruption scandals and the steady decomposition of state institutions. The congress, with nineteen parties represented, has become a labyrinthian racket for the self-aggrandizement of its members, who in 1993 reformed the electoral law to keep secret the source of campaign financing. Civil rule was further undermined in 1993 as the military took advantage of a weak caretaker president to exert excessive influence on government policy. Constitutional guarantees regarding freedom of religion and expression and the right to organize political and civic organizations are generally respected. However, escalating criminal violence, much of it fueled by the burgeoning drug trade, and a national breakdown of police discipline have created a climate of lawlessness and generalized insecurity in which human rights are violated on a massive scale with impunity.

Brazil's national police are among the most violent and corrupt in the world. Going back to military rule, police in each state receive military-style training. Although nominally commanded by elected officials, military police throughout the country are under the jurisdiction of military courts in which they are rarely held accountable. Beneath the military police are the local civil police whose inefficiency and corruption are used by the military police to justify their tactics of simply eliminating criminals and suspected criminals.

Brazils's numerous independent human rights organizations have documented the steady increase in killings by the military police and the systematic abuse in police detention centers. Killings during actions by the Sao Paulo military police alone jumped from about 300 in 1987 to nearly 1,500 in 1992. In October 1992 over a hundred inmates were summarily executed by military police during a riot at a Sao Paulo prison. Conditions in Brazil's overflowing, violence-plagued penal system are wretched and the military police are responsible for quelling disorders.

Vigilante "extermination" groups linked to the police and financed by local merchants are responsible for hundreds, possibly thousands, of extra-judicial killings a year. Violence, including disappearances, against the 35 million children living in poverty, at least a fifth of them living in the streets of burgeoning urban centers, is systematic, with more than four "street kids" murdered daily, either by vigilantes or drug-traffickers.

The climate of lawlessness is reinforced by a weak judiciary. It is headed by an eleven-member Supreme Court whose members must be approved by the Senate and which is granted substantial autonomy by the constitution. However, the judicial system is overwhelmed (with only 7,000 judges for a population of more than 150 million) and vulnerable to the chronic corruption which undermines the entire political system. It has been virtually powerless in the face of organized crime, much of it drug-related.

There is little public confidence in the judicial system and poorer citizens, beset by inflation and unemployment, have resorted to lynchings, with hundreds of mob executions reported in the last two years. The middle class, unable to afford costly private security measures, is targeted by kidnappers-for-ransom who often operate in league with police.

Violence associated with land disputes continues unabated. Brazil's landowners control nearly 60 percent of arable land, while the poorest 30 percent share less than two percent. The income gap between rich and poor in Brazil is wider than in any other country in the world. Every year, hundreds of activists, Catholic church workers and rural unionists are killed by paramilitary groups in the pay of large landowners, with very few cases brought to court. The military police in rural areas act as the instruments of local landowner elites.

There are continued reports of forced labor of thousands of landless workers by ranchers, often with the complicity of local police, in the Amazon and other rural regions. Workers are held in virtual slavery by large landowners through debt bondage and coercion. Although forced labor is against Brazilian and international law, the judicial response to forced labor can most generously be described as indifferent and the practice continues with impunity.

Rubber tappers and Indians continue to be targets of violence, including assassination, associated with Amazon development projects initiated under military rule and the gold rush in the far north. The constitution gives Brazil's quarter-million Indians legal sanction, but the government has been unwilling to stop invasions by settlers and miners into Indian reserves. In August 1993 dozens of Yanomami Indians were massacred by miners.

Domestic violence is prevalent, particularly against women and children. Protective laws are rarely enforced. In 1991 the Supreme Court ruled that a man could no longer kill his wife and win acquittal on the ground of "legitimate defense of honor," but juries have generally ignored the ruling. Forced prostitution of children is widespread.

Industrial labor unions are well organized, politically connected and prone to corruption. The right to strike is recognized and there are special labor courts. The constitution makes it virtually impossible to fire public sector workers and there have been hundreds of strikes in recent years against attempts to privatize state industries. Child labor is prevalent and laws against it are rarely enforced.

The press is privately owned, vigorous and uncensored. There are daily newspapers in most major cities and many other publications throughout the country. The print media have played a central role in exposing official corruption. Radio is mostly commercial. Although overseen by a government agency, television is independent and a powerful political instrument. Roughly two-thirds of the population is illiterate, but 85 percent of households have television sets. The huge TV Globo dominates, but there are three other networks, plus educational channels.

Brunei

Polity: Traditional monarchy
Economy: Capitalist-statist
Population: 277,000
PPP: $14,000
Life Expectancy: 73.5
Ethnic Groups: Malay (65 percent), Chinese (20 percent), other (15 percent)

Political Rights: 7
Civil Liberties: 6
Status: Not Free

Overview:

Located on the northern coast of the Southeast Asian island of Borneo, Brunei became a British protectorate in 1888. The 1959 constitution provided for five advisory councils: the Privy Council, the Religious Council, the Council of Succession, the Council of Ministers, and a Legislative Council. In 1962 the leftist Brunei People's Party (PRB) took all ten of the elected seats in the twenty-one-member Legislative Council, and late in the year British troops crushed a PRB-backed rebellion. The Sultan then assumed constitutionally-authorized emergency powers for a stipulated two-year period. These powers have been renewed every two years since then, and elections have not been held since 1965. Sultan Haji Hasanal Bolkiah Mu'izzadin Waddaulah ascended the throne in October 1967.

Following a gradual period of decreased British participation in internal affairs, full independence came on 1 January 1984. The Sultan serves as prime minister and has nearly complete authority over the country. Currently only the Council of Ministers, composed largely of the Sultan's relatives, and the Legislative Council, with all members appointed by the Sultan, are convened. In 1985 the government recognized the moderate Islamic Brunei National Democratic Party (PKDB), followed a year later by the offshoot Brunei National United Party (PPKB). However, in 1988 the government dissolved the PKDB and detained two of its leaders for two years, reportedly after the party called upon the Sultan to hold elections. The PPKB currently has fewer than 100 members and wields no influence.

Although the country's oil reserves have provided one of the highest per capita incomes in the world, in recent years the government has been concerned with rising unemployment. The government's Sixth Development Plan, released in June 1993, calls for greater technical and business training for the indigenous workforce.

Political Rights and Civil Liberties:

Citizens of Brunei lack the democratic means to change their government. There are no elections at any level. The only means of popular participation is through appointed village headmen and district officials, and occasional petitions to the Sultan. The constitution does not protect freedoms of speech, press, assembly or association, and these rights are restricted in practice.

A 1988 law makes forty-two criminal offenses, including drug-related crimes, subject to corporal punishment, although given the low crime rate this rarely occurs. Police have broad powers of arrest without warrants, and the Internal Security Act (ISA) allows the government to detain suspects without trial for renewable two-year periods. There have been no detentions under the ISA since several dissidents were released in 1990.

The judiciary is independent of the government. Hong Kong provides judges for the High Court and Court of Appeals. Defendents receive adequate procedural safeguards with the notable exception of the right to trial by jury. The one independent newspaper frequently practices self-censorship by avoiding issues of religion and the Sultan's role in society, and the government owns the only television station.

Although the constitution guarantees the right of non-Muslims to practice their religion freely, since 1991 the government has been asserting the primacy of Islam through a national ideology of Malay Muslim Monarchy, which allegedly dates back more than 500 years. The government frequently refuses non-Muslims permission to build new places of worship, and has closed some existing ones. Women face discrimination in the right to obtain a divorce and in earning equal pay and benefits. Muslim women must wear the *tudong*, a traditional head covering.

Citizens can travel freely within the country. Some expatriate workers are limited in traveling abroad during their first year under contract. The government must approve all trade unions, but does not interfere in their affairs. Four exist, covering just 5 percent of the workforce. The constitution neither recognizes nor prohibits strikes, and in practice none occurs.

Bulgaria

Polity: Parliamentary democracy
Economy: Statist-transitional
Population: 8,954,000
PPP: $4,700
Life Expectancy: 72.6

Political Rights: 2
Civil Liberties: 2*
Status: Free

Ethnic Groups: Bulgarian (85 percent), Turkish (9 percent), Gypsy (3 percent), Macedonian (3 percent)
Ratings Change: *Bulgaria's civil liberties rating changed from 3 to 2 as a result of modifications in methodology. See "Survey Methodology," page 671.

Overview:

In 1993, the government of Prime Minister Lyuben Berov survived several no-confidence votes, as the increasingly fragmented Union of Democratic Forces (UDF) sought to oust what it considered a government that was sluggish in implementing market reforms, privatization and de-communization. By year's end, the political stalemate continued to the detriment of an already hard-pressed economy and long-term political stability.

Bordered by the Black Sea on the east, Bulgaria is nestled between Romania, Turkey and Greece to the north and south, and the former Yugoslavia to the west. It was occupied by Ottoman Turks from 1396 to 1878, and did not achieve complete independence until 1908. It was on the losing side in both World Wars, and Communists seized power in conjunction with the "liberation" of Bulgaria by the Soviet Army in 1944. From 1954-1989, the country was in the grip of Communist Party strongman Todor Zhivkov, who was forced to resign one day after the fall of the Berlin Wall.

The current government—the third in five years since the fall of the Zhivkov regime—was formed in December 1992 after the collapse of the UDF government under reformist Filip Dimitrov. Prime Minister Berov, a non-party technocrat and former economic advisor to President Zhelyu Zhelyev (who had been elected president in January) was backed by the Turkish-based Movement for Rights and Freedoms (MRF) and the (formerly Communist) Bulgarian Socialist Party (BSP). The UDF, which had won 111 of 240 seats to the unicameral parliament in 1991, with the BSP winning 106 seats and the MRF 23, had split with its former leader, President Zhelyev.

Early in 1993, the UDF accused the Berov government of systematically purging several pro-reform, UDF-appointed officials. In February and March, a number of the country's top administrators were removed, including the heads of government committees on energy and tourism. The government also dismissed an entire commission investigating arms trafficking charges against the Kintex company. A number of non-elected district governors were also removed. The UDF also charged the government was interfering with the independent judiciary and with national television, particularly after the February dismissal of journalist Asen Agov, a well-known UDF supporter, as the new director-general of Bulgarian National Television (BNT).

By mid-April, the government came under pressure from the UDF for its failure to implement privatization laws passed in 1992, and to fulfill a 1993 budget draft which included an indirect offer of economic aid to a wide range of of state enterprises, and the continued control of much of the economic sector by the nomenklatura, including members and former members of the BSP.

In May, amid increased calls for Berov to resign, the UDF launched demonstrations and protests in Sofia, the capital, urging early elections. Few heeded the UDF's call for mass action, and public reaction outside Sofia, the capital, was largely indifferent. On 13 May, however, police and security forces moved in to disperse a small rally in front of the parliament building, injuring the UDF's parliamentary leader. After the incident, Berov said on national television that his government would not be forced to resign by "street pressure." Within days, the UDF tabled a motion of no-confidence, which was supported by a small faction of the BSP dissatisfied with the cabinet's failure to change agricultural policy. On 27 May the no-confidence motion was rejected.

The summer saw increased tensions between President Zhelyev and the UDF, which he helped organize as an umbrella democratic opposition in 1989. UDF supporters erected a tent city in front of President Zhelyev's offices, and Vice President Blaga Dimitrova, a former Zhelyev ally and running mate, went on national television to call for early elections. She resigned on 30 June, claiming that Berov's so-called "nonpartisan" cabinet had many current or former BSP members.

In mid-June, the government survived yet another no-confidence motion. The vote was 126-84 for a reshuffled cabinet. The vote marked a significant setback for the UDF. The centrist New Union for Democracy (NUD) cooperated with the BSP and the MRF in supporting the government. Earlier in the month, the NUD, made up of deputies who left or were expelled from the UDF, helped push through the 1993 budget with a two-thirds majority. The vote ratified the government's efforts to keep the budget deficit to a ceiling of 7.9 percent of GDP to meet IMF requirements for a new standby agreement in the face of demands for higher spending on social security and subsidies. The government still lacked firm support from any of the major political groups, making it difficult to move ahead on laws needed for economic reform. Privatization remained slow and there was clearly a lack of consensus on how best to speed the process.

In July, President Zhelyev rejected a UDF proposal to hold elections in mid-November, noting that early elections would favor the BSP. At the end of the month, the government survived yet another UDF-sponsored no-confidence motion. The UDF based its motion on a May decree on local taxes, charging that the government had exceeded its constitutional authority.

Continued political gridlock and the government's lack of a solid political base undermined efforts to address the country's economic problems. Inflation was expected to remain around 80 percent, exacerbated by the reduction of energy subsidies in May and the introduction of a Value Added Tax late last year. Since reneging on its debts in 1990, Bulgaria—the country most dependent on trade with its COMECON partners—was deprived of access to normal bank finance and unable to attract more than a minuscule amount of foreign investment. Unofficial estimates put total foreign investment over the last three years at around $100 million, compared to $5 billion for Hungary during the same period. The foreign debt stood at $11 billion and unemployment was expected to top 17 percent by year's end. The 50 percent decline in industrial output exposed the nature of the old centrally planned economy with its enforced dependence on Soviet raw materials and markets. The private sector, although unable to fill the gap left by the collapse of state industry, saw its share of a shrinking GDP rise to an estimated 20-25 percent.

Bulgaria continued to lag behind other former East Bloc countries in terms of privatization. While widescale restitution did return thousands of shops and other forms of property to former owners in towns and villages and was accompanied by a partial and controversial restitution of land in the countryside, formal privatization was usurped by widespread hidden or nomenklatura privatization, which meant illegal asset stripping and theft of state or municipal property by enterprising bureaucrats.

Privatization and reform legislation remained incomplete. Bankruptcy legislation, which would allow for the closing of chronic money-losing enterprises, had yet to be finalized, as were specifics of compensation laws.

In October, President Zhelyev urged the West to help his country make up the huge trade losses it suffered because of the United Nations embargo against Yugoslavia. At a Council of Europe summit, he claimed that Bulgaria lost the equivalent of $1 billion last year because of sanctions, and requested credit facilities, the opening of Western markets to Bulgarian products, Balkan bridge and freeway construction projects and the reconstruction of the country's telephone and communications network.

Political Rights and Civil Liberties:

Bulgarians have the right to change their government democratically under a multiparty system enshrined in the 1991 constitution. Parliamentary elections that year and the presidential election in January 1992 were judged free and fair by international observers.

Under the constitution, the judiciary is guaranteed independence and equal status with the legislature and executive branch. In January, amendments to the Penal Code were passed. In addition to specifically protecting property rights, the amendments criminalized the disclosure and circulation of information and documents concerning the Security Services' recruitment of full-time and part-time collaborators and the activity of those collaborators. The standard was intended to protect national security.

Controversy continued to surround so-called lustration laws aimed at preventing former high-ranking Communist party members from government and public posts. In 1992, the Constitutional Court had struck down several UDF-backed laws to ban members of Communist organizations from public positions, including lustration provisions in the Banking Law and the Pension Law. On 11 February, however, the Constitutional Court upheld a very similar law, the so-called Panev Act that bars persons connected with "supreme structures of the former Bulgarian Communist Party and security services" from holding "managerial offices at scientific establishments, such as chiefs of departments, deans, rectors, and chief editors of serials." President Zhelyev signed the bill into law, despite efforts by the NUD parliamentary faction to include amendments. The law led to the removal of several thousand formerly Communist-affiliated academic staff from managerial positions. The law was condemned not only by Bulgarian politicians, but by several international human rights organizations.

Meanwhile, several prominent Communist officials were prosecuted for criminal offenses. In January, parliament stripped immunity given to Aleksandr Livov, former head of the Bulgarian Communist Party and aide to Zhivkov, who was charged with unlawfully granting money to foreign Communist parties and movements. On 12 March Zhivkov—already convicted and sentenced to seven years' imprisonment for embezzlement in 1992—faced new charges of corruption and inciting ethnic hatred. In

June, a former government official and three others went on trial for their part in the violent death of 14 inmates of prison camps run by the former ruling Communists. In August, Andrei Lukanov, the last Communist prime minister, was charged with diverting the equivalent of $60 million in state funds to leftist governments and Communist parties abroad in the late 1980s. The following month, former Premier Georgi Atanasov reported to prison in Sofia, becoming the first former Politburo member to start serving time after being convicted of Communist-era crimes.

Bulgarians can express themselves freely, and there are lively independent media, including over 600 newspapers (135 of which are privately owned, and 125 of which are owned by various political organizations). Political or trade-union publications rarely publish "self-critical" articles. There are no private television stations in Bulgaria, but more than half a dozen independent radio stations are operating in Sofia. The public media organizations—Bulgarian National Television (BNT) and the Bulgarian Telegraph Agency (BTA)—continue to be the most influential institutions on the domestic media scene. In February, parliament dismissed Asen Agov as BNT director-general, partly for his pro-UDF views.

Freedoms of association and assembly are generally respected. Political parties can organize freely although there are restrictions on parties being formed along ethnic, religious or racial lines.

While ethnic tensions have lessened in the last few years, there were reported cases of discrimination against Turks, Pomaks (ethnic Bulgarian Muslims), and especially Gypsies (Roma). On 21 June the leadership of the Gypsy Union held a news conference and charged that Gypsies are routinely subject to job discrimination, police violence and human rights violations, a view supported by Bulgarian and international human rights groups.

Freedom of worship is respected, although the government regulates churches and religious institutions through the Directorate on Religious Beliefs. There are few restrictions on international and domestic travel, and special residence permits are no longer required for major urban areas.

There are several women's organizations in Bulgaria. However, women often face de facto discrimination at work, rape laws are relatively lax (the maximum sentence is eight years), and the labor codes offer limited protection for pregnant women or those with small children.

Bulgaria has two large labor union confederations, the Confederation of Independent Trade Unions of Bulgaria (KNSB), a successor to the Communist party's trade union, and Podkrepa, a union formed in 1989 and active in the democratization movement. Unions have the right to strike, except for political reasons, and have exercised that right. While the constitution prohibits unions from engaging in political activities, both confederations have been active in parliamentary politics. Independent human rights groups reported a few cases of Podkrepa members being dismissed from their jobs.

Burkina Faso

Polity: Dominant party (military dominated)
Economy: Mixed statist
Population: 9,962,000
PPP: $618
Life Expectancy: 48.2
Ethnic Groups: Bobo, Mossi, Samo, other

Political Rights: 5
Civil Liberties: 4*
Status: Partly Free

Ratings Change: *Burkina Faso's civil liberties rating changed from 5 to 4 as a result of modifications in methodology. See "Survey Methodology," page 671.

Overview:

Nineteen-ninety-three brought about little change in the political landscape in Burkina Faso. During 1992, under the leadership of President Blaise Compaore, Burkina Faso instituted a series of controlled democratic reforms and a government reconstruction which, although limited, was cautiously viewed as promising.

Since gaining independence from France in 1960, Burkina Faso has been governed by successive military dictatorships. Burkina Faso's current head of state, President Blaise Compaore, seized power in a military coup in 1987. Originally opposed to a multi-party system, in 1991 Compaore allowed several independent political parties to legally join the ruling Organization for Popular Democracy/Labor Movement (ODP/MT) and its allies. As the number of opposition forces continued to grow, the Coordination of Democratic Forces (CDF) was formed. While opposition parties were able to organize, they were not able to exercise any control over the rate and substance of political change. The opposition parties called on the government to convene a sovereign national conference of all Burkinabe political forces to take interim control of state affairs pending multiparty elections scheduled for December 1991 and January 1993. President Compaore denied this request.

Following President Blaise Compaore's refusal to convene a sovereign national conference, opposition candidates refused to participate in the presidential election. Amid violent protests, the election was held. Only 25 percent of those registered to vote took part and the low voter turnout denied Compaore the mandate he sought. The government subsequently condemned the violence and indefinitely postponed multiparty legislative elections that were to be held on 9 January. He did agree to convene a "national reconciliation forum" to begin political dialogue between the government and opposition party members. The forum was quickly suspended when the government would not comply with opposition parties' demand that the proceedings be televised.

The CDF coalition proved tenuous, however, as one key coalition member joined Compaore's administration as minister of state. Other members soon decided to contest rather than boycott the rescheduled multiparty legislative elections. In May 1992, the legislative elections were held. Voter turnout was only 35 percent, and Compaore's Organization for Popular Democracy (ODP/MT) claimed 78 out of a possible 107 seats.

Political Rights and Civil Liberties: **B**urkinabes continue to have limited ability to change their government. The first multiparty presidential elections in 1991 were plagued with accusations of irregularities and were held against a background of violence and intimidation. Compaore's victory was secured with a low voter turnout and without opposition party candidates. Despite the low voter turnout, international monitors indicated that the legislative elections were mostly free and fair. As Compaore's ODP-MT party continues to dominate political life in Burkina Faso, it is too early to tell whether opposition party members will have any substantive influence on government policy.

After flagrant human rights abuses were documented following the presidential elections of 1991, the Burkinabe Movement for Human Rights (MBDHP) reported improvement in the governments human rights record for 1992. While the MBDHP has been allowed to operate without overt intimidation, several members of the group, including the group's president, were ousted in 1992. The move was believed to be a result of the then-president's high-profile human rights activities. No political prisoners were reported in 1993.

Civil and criminal court cases are adjudicated fairly by a regular court system. However excessive use of force by security forces continues to be a problem. Those detained for suspected criminal offenses allege that they were beaten and tortured in order to obtain convictions.

The 1991 constitution guarantees freedom of speech and press. Burkina Faso has both independent print and broadcast media and the media does have some degree of freedom and independence from government interference. However, scattered attempts at intimidation of the press have occurred and although the government has tolerated some degree of critical reporting, all papers practice some degree of self-censorship.

Student demonstrations against education cuts in January of 1993 tested the government's commitment to allow freedom of peaceful assembly. While the demonstrations were peaceful, the students were dispersed by security forces with tear gas, sword belts and truncheons. There is limited freedom of association. Foreign travel appears to be unrestricted. Trade unions are allowed to form, strike and bargain collectively.

Women do not share equal rights with men. Women continue to occupy subordinate positions in education, employment, property and family rights. Women constitute only one-third of the total student population in the primary, secondary and higher education systems. In rural areas, women fair considerably worse. There are disproportionately fewer women in schools, the practice of female genital mutilation continues, and there exists a high rate of domestic violence against women. The government has made some attempts to educate people through the media on issues of domestic violence and genital mutilation.

Burma (Myanmar)

Polity: Military   **Political Rights:** 7
Economy: Mixed statist   **Civil Liberties:** 7
Population: 43,456,000   **Status:** Not Free
PPP: $659
Life Expectancy: 61.3
Ethnic Groups: Burman (68 percent), Karen (7 percent),
Shan (6 percent), Rakhine (4 percent), Chin, Kachin,
Mon and Arkanese totaling 1 million

Overview:

Burma's ruling military junta opened a National Convention in January 1993, expecting the hand-picked delegates to rubber-stamp guidelines for a new constitution granting the army a permanant leading role in politics. In a bold rebuff, the delegates repeatedly refused to approve the army's proposals, forcing the junta to adjourn this convention several times throughout the year. However, given the army's near-total emasculation of the political opposition, and its cease-fire deals with most of the ethnic-based guerrilla armies in the countryside, eventual approval of the guidelines and a new constitution is all but guaranteed.

Occupied by the Japanese in World War II, Burma achieved independence from the British in 1948. Prime Minister U Nu led a parliamentary democracy for a decade before resigning when his Anti-Fascist People's Freedom League (AFPFL) splintered. A caretaker government under army commander General Ne Win organized elections in 1960 which briefly brought U Nu back to power. The army overthrew the civilian government in 1962 amidst an economic crisis, political turmoil and threats from ethnic rebel groups.

During the next twenty-six years, Ne Win's Burmese Socialist Program Party (BSPP) turned one of Southeast Asia's richest countries into an impoverished backwater. In September 1988 approximately 3,000 people were killed when the army cracked down on massive, peaceful pro-democracy demonstrations. Army leaders General Saw Maung and Brigadier General Khin Nyunt placed the country under the military rule of a new State Law and Order Restoration Council (SLORC). The junta said it would hold elections and transfer power to a civilian government.

The first competitive elections in three decades were held on 27 May 1990. The National League for Democracy (NLD) attracted widespread support, mostly due to its dynamic secretary general Aung San Suu Kyi, who had been placed under house arrest in July 1989 for her pro-democracy activities. The party won 392 of the 485 parliamentary seats, while the SLORC-sponsored National Unity Party, the successor to the BSPP, won just 10.

The SLORC refused to recognize the results and jailed hundreds of NLD members, including several elected MPs. In December 1990, a core of NLD MPs set up a government-in-exile in rebel-held territory near the Thai border, but no country has recognized it. In December 1991, following a ceremony in London granting Aung San Suu Kyi the Nobel Peace prize in absentia, several hundred student demonstrators were arrested at Rangoon University and all schools were closed.

In 1992 the junta began a curious process of superficial liberalizations but continued to maintain tight control. Observers credited the moves to eighty-two-year-old former leader Ne Win, who remains the country's ultimate arbiter. On 23 April General Than Shwe replaced hardliner Saw Maung as prime minister and junta leader. On 23 June, the SLORC opened the first of three rounds of "coordination meetings" with twenty-eight representatives of seven parties, including the NLD, and announced it would hold a constitutional convention in early 1993.

The regime reopened the universities on 24 August, and in September lifted the nationwide overnight curfew and removed two martial law decrees that had allowed military judges to try civilians in Mandalay and Rangoon. The junta also released more than 1,000 "political prisoners" by year's end, although outside groups claimed many were simply common criminals.

The SLORC convened a National Convention on 9 January 1993, ostensibly to adopt guidelines for a constitution to be drafted later by a constituent assembly. In reality, the 699 hand-picked delegates, representing the NLD and nine other parties, as well as ethnic minorities, peasants and professional groups, were expected to quietly approve a set of principles drawn up by the junta that included granting the military a permanant leading role in society. From the outset the delegates were sequestered and warned against any disruptive activities, including speeches that might "damage loyalty to the state." The junta abruptly adjourned the Convention after two days.

The Convention met again for brief sessions in February, March and April, but adjourned each time because the delegates refused to approve the guidelines regarding the military. Despite a ban on walkouts, by early April dissidents reported that 97 of the hand-picked delegates had already left in frustration. Following a two-month recess, on 7 June Chief Justice Aung Toe reconvened the delegates and asked them to approve specific elements of a military-dominated polity patterned after the Indonesian model. The Chief Justice said the constitution should give the armed forces a fixed number of seats in parliament and emergency powers in times of crisis. The president is to have a military background, be chosen by an unelected electoral college and hold full executive powers. In mid-September the junta adjourned the convention until January 1994, having achieved little. Two top generals severely reprimanded NLD chairman Aung Shwe and Khun Tun Oo, the leader of the Shan Nationalities League for Democracy, for dissenting from the army's guidelines.

The military junta has been able to stall on a political deal because it faces little internal opposition. In recent years the SLORC has made peace with most of the ethnic insurgency armies that have been fighting for greater autonomy for their people since independence. In 1989 the Communist Party of Burma's four Wa-dominated armies agreed to a ceasefire in return for being allowed to keep their weapons and maintain control over their respective areas. Similiar deals were subsequently made with the Shan State Army, the Pa-O National Army, and the Palaung State Liberation Army. Many of these former rebel armies are now involved in cross-border trade with China in timber, gems, jade and opium. In the fall, the government began talks with the 6,000-man Kachin Independence Army in the north. A ceasefire would leave the 4,000-man Karen National Union in the south as the largest of the three remaining militias fighting the SLORC.

During the year, the first of some 270,000 Muslim Rohingyas from Arakan Province who have been forced by the *Tatmadaw* (Burmese army) into Bangladesh since 1989 were repatriated. The Rohingyas accuse the army of murder, rape and torture. By early September 34,500 refugees had been repatriated, but many others were too scared to return.

The government is slowly liberalizing the economy and tolerates a thriving black market. The country is the world's largest opium producer and entire parts of the Shan State are controlled by druglords with private armies, including Khun Sa's 8,000-man Maung Tai militia. Although there is a substantial middle class and an abundance of teak, jade and other natural resources, much of Burma is impoverished. The U.N. Children's Fund says 10 percent of children suffer from severe malnutrition.

Political Rights and Civil Liberties: Burmese citizens cannot change their government democratically. The ruling military junta has all but decimated any political opposition. Since the 1990 election 107 opposition MPs have been imprisoned, forced to resign, or have left the country. Another MP died while imprisoned. Several dozen political parties have been banned, while the remaining ten are closely monitored and restricted.

The junta denies its citizens fundamental rights. Freedoms of speech, press and association are non-existent. In February 1993 the U.N.'s Special Rapporteur for Burma, Yozo Yokota, issued a report describing "serious repression and an atmosphere of pervasive fear" in the country. The army forces villagers to act as human minesweepers ahead of troops and frequently uses civilians as porters, often until they die of exhaustion or hunger. Young teenagers have been pressed into battle against rebel groups, often stiffened first with shots of liquor. Members of the rebel movement are subjected to torture and arbitrary executions.

In the eastern Kayah and Karen states the army has forcibly relocated thousands of villagers into government-controlled towns for fear they might provide support to the rebels. In recent years the government has also forcibly relocated 500,000 residents of the capital, Rangoon, to squalid satellite "new towns."

Diplomats and the U.S. State Department say there are at least 1,000 political detainees, who along with common criminals are beaten and mistreated. Prison conditions are especially harsh, and forced labor is common. Although the judiciary is wracked by corruption and influenced by the military, some basic due process rights are observed in ordinary civilian trials.

On 27 April a court sentenced retired seventy-four-year-old Brigadier General Aung Gyi, one of the few remaining outspoken critics of the regime, to a six-month prison term ostensibly for not paying for eggs he had ordered for his food business. In recent years the general had criticized the junta in interviews, and had written a series of critical open letters to Ne Win. Nobel Laureate Aung San Suu Kyi, who has never been charged, has been under house arrest since July 1989 under the Law to Safeguard the State From the Dangers of Subversive Elements, which allows arbitrary detention without trial for up to five years.

The Directorate of Defense Services Intelligence, headed by powerful hardline Brigadier General Khin Nyunt, maintains an elaborate network of spies and informants, routinely searches homes, intercepts mail and monitors telephones. Before the junta reopened universities in August 1992, professors were forced to attend re-education camps and were told to report on students. The schools continue to be tightly watched.

The army killed several monks and arrested hundreds in an October 1990 raid on monasteries suspected of supporting pro-democracy activities. At least 300 monks are believed to remain in prison, and religious practice is closely monitored. Trade unions, collective bargaining and strikes are illegal.

Burundi

Polity: Military dominated **Political Rights:** 7*
Economy: Mixed capitalist **Civil Liberties:** 7*
Population: 5,830,000 **Status:** Not Free
PPP: $625
Life Expectancy: 48.5
Ethnic Groups: Hutu (85 percent), Tutsi (14 percent),
Twa pygmy (1 percent)
Ratings Change: *Burundi's political rights rating changed from
6 to 7 and its civil liberties rating from 5 to 7 because of a military
coup that brought about renewed ethnic clashes, an end to civilian
rule, and allegations of gross human rights violations.

Overview: On 21 October 1993 President Melchior Ndadaye, Burundi's
first democratically elected head of state, and at least six top
aides were killed when the newly elected government was
overthrown in a military coup. The coup, orchestrated by senior military officers from
the minority Tutsi tribe, was an attempt to nullify the results of Burundi's first multiparty elections and abort Burundi's transition to democracy. While it appears that the
coup has collapsed, international observers report that anywhere from 10,000 to
150,000 people have died as a result of the ongoing ethnic clashes.

Burundi has four main political movements: the Party for the Liberation of the
Hutu People (Palipehutu); the Burundi Front for Democracy (Frodebu); the Unity for
National Progress (Uprona); and the People's Reconciliation Party (PRP).

Until April 1992, Uprona was the country's only legal political party (President
Jean Pierre Buyoya resigned his leadership of Uprona in March of 1992 in order to
make the office of the president non-partisan). Both Palipehutu and Frodebu were
initially established to oppose Tutsi dominance of society and government in Burundi.
While Palipehutu carried out a violent campaign of resistance, Frodebu sought to attain
independence through non-violent methods. Frodebu condemned Palipehutu's use of
violence while Palipehutu claimed that the Frodebu party was willing to compromise on
the Hutu right to rule. Despite similar goals, tension between the two groups preceding
the elections remained high.

In June 1993, Burundi held its first multi-party presidential elections. In an
unexpected victory, Ndadaye, a member of Frodebu, defeated incumbent President
Buyoya, gaining 60 percent of the popular vote. (Buyoya, a member of the minority
Tutsi tribe, had seized power during 1987 in a bloodless coup.) Legislative elections
were held in late June. The Frodebu party won 72.55 percent of the popular vote
(securing sixty-five seats), while Uprona captured only 21.86 percent of the votes
(sixteen seats). Independent observers designated both elections "free and fair"

The multi-party elections were to mark the beginning of Burundi's transition to
democracy. Since independence from Belgium in 1962, Burundi has been governed by
leaders who, like Buyoya, came to power as a result of a military coup. The country is
ethnically divided between the majority Hutu tribe which comprises about 85 percent of the
Burundi population and the minority Tutsi tribe which makes up about 14 percent, with the

remaining 1 percent comprised of the Batwa (pygmies). Despite the clear majority, the Hutu's were dominated by the ethnic Tutsi minority who commanded key, top military, judicial, educational and governmental posts since Burundi's independence from Belgium.

Prior to the reforms and subsequent elections, allegations of gross human right violations were lodged against security forces loyal to the government. During 1965, 1972 and again in 1988, Tutsi-dominated security forces systematically killed members of the Hutu tribe. The Carnegie Endowment for International Peace investigated the violence that occurred in April of 1972 and concluded that there was "...systematic killing of as many as a quarter of a million people [Hutu]...over a four month period men, women and children were savagely murdered at a rate of more than a thousand a day." The report went on to say, "They tried to skim off the cream of the Hutu tribe, to kill every possible Hutu male of distinction over the age of 14."

Again in 1988, ethnic violence against the Hutu's resulted in an estimated 5,000 deaths. Under increasing international donor pressure and amidst continuing ethnic strife, Buyoya introduced legislation to abolish ethnic discrimination and foster national unity. A draft National United Charter, approved in December of 1990, paved the way for a new constitution that would further the democratization process.

During 1992, Buyoya continued to institute controlled political reforms. In March, Burundians voted to adopt a new Constitution that instituted a multi-party system to replace the one-party state system that had long dominated Burundi's political life. The new Constitution mandated that all political parties must include both Hutu and Tutsi ethnic groups and disallowed any political organization which promoted "tribalism, divisionalism, or violence." The Constitution also stipulated that servicemen could not seek public office. In April, Buyoya passed a law that legalized opposition parties and cleared the way for multi-party presidential and legislative elections.

Political Rights and Civil Liberties: While negotiations continue to date, it is likely that the military will be unable to retain control in Burundi. Reports indicate that the army has agreed to return to their barracks and restore power to the remaining civilian government. The government has requested an international peacekeeping force be dispatched to Burundi and both the U.N. and OAU have agreed to consider this possibility. However, given the chaos which reigns in Burundi, it remain unclear when or if this transition will be successful. Reports indicate continuing widespread violent protest against the military, in particular, against those of the ethnic Tutsi minority.

As access to areas outside the capital is limited, it is not possible to assess the full impact of the fighting or to obtain an accurate count of those killed or displaced as a result of it. While some banks reopened in the capital during the week following the coup, most businesses and schools remained closed. Highways have been blocked and communications are poor, especially to outlying areas. Attempts by the inter-national press to reach areas outside the capital have been blocked by the military. The military has attempted to seal off the borders and seized control of the national airport.

As reports of widespread massacres continue, it is clear that Burundians are, once again, subject to political terror. Ethnic clashes were reported in a number of villages and the U.N. Human Rights Commission reports that approximately 342,000 refugees have fled Burundi to neighboring Rwanda since the coup and an estimated 235,000 have gone to Tanzania and Zaire. Although there were diplomatic efforts to return Burundi's ousted civilian leaders, the International Committee of the Red Cross (ICRC) reported that rival ethnic groups set their homes and farms on fire in battles across Burundi.

Burundi's media are not free and independent. In February 1992, the legislature passed a law that guaranteed freedom of speech and permitted privately owned periodicals and broadcasting facilities. Several privately owned newspapers emerged, but newspaper readership remained limited. Under this law, opposition parties were allowed access to state owned radio and television stations for campaigning purposes. However, very few Burundians own a television and most of those who do receive only the single government-controlled station. Despite some minor inroads in lifting government restrictions on the press during 1992, the media were still significantly restricted. The election of Melchior Ndadaye had been expected to further ease press restrictions, but national radio and television stations were placed under direct military control following the coup.

Cambodia

Polity: Monarchy, constituent assembly, and Khmer Rouge occupation
Economy: Statist
Population: 8,997,000
PPP: $1,100
Life Expectancy: 49.7
Ethnic Groups: Khmer (93 percent), Vietnamese (4 percent), Chinese (3 percent)

Political Rights: 4*
Civil Liberties: 5*
Status: Partly Free

Ratings Change: *Cambodia's political rights rating changed from 6 to 4 because of multiparty elections held in May. Its civil liberties changed from 6 to 5 because of an increase in freedom of association and expression.

Overview:

Cambodia held its freest election ever in May 1993, nineteen months after a U.N.-brokered peace accord nominally ended a civil war between a Vietnamese-installed Communist government and three guerrilla factions. However the last of the U.N.'s 22,000 peacekeeping troops withdrew in November, and doubts persist over the new coalition government's ability to sustain the democratic transition. The radical Khmer Rouge guerrillas remain a threat in the countryside, hardliners from the former Communist government dominate the army and provincial governments, and decades of violence have ruined the economy.

Cambodia achieved independence from France in 1953 under King Norodom Sihanouk. The King abdicated in 1955, becoming Prince Sihanouk, to serve as head of government. In 1970 army general and prime minister Lon Nol overthrew the Prince in a bloodless coup. Following several years of fighting Lon Nol's right-wing regime fell to the Communist Khmer Rouge in April 1975. Led by Pol Pot (Brother Number One), the Khmer Rouge ruthlessly emptied and destroyed cities in a genocidal attempt at creating a classless agricultural society. More than one million Cambodians died through torture or starvation. Vietnam invaded in December 1978 and installed the Communist Kampuchean People's Revolutionary Party, led largely by Khmer Rouge defectors.

In 1982, three anti-Vietnamese groups joined in an uneasy coalition to fight the government and the occupying Vietnamese army. Led by Prince Sihanouk, the three groups were: the Chinese-backed Khmer Rouge; the Prince's Sihanouk National Army; and the Khmer People's National Liberation Army, led by a former prime minister, Son Sann. By September 1989 Vietnam had removed all of its troops. The three resistance armies seized more territory but were unable to overthrow the government.

In 1991 several rounds of internationally supervised talks yielded a Paris peace accord on 23 October. It was signed by Prince Sihanouk, Son Sann, nominal Khmer Rouge leader Khieu Samphan, Cambodian Prime Minister Hun Sen and the representatives of eighteen countries. Although the Vietnamese-installed government was to remain largely intact, the Paris Accord called for a U.N. Transitional Authority in Cambodia (UNTAC) to run five key ministries in advance of national elections to be held in May 1993. The Accord placed Prince Sihanouk at the head of a largely symbolic Supreme National Council (SNC), composed of the leaders of the four factions. To reduce the threat of armed conflict, UNTAC would place troops in temporary cantonments and return 70 percent of the soldiers to civilian life.

In 1992 the process threatened to unravel as the Khmer Rouge refused to comply with the cantonment and demobilization phase of the peace process, claiming that Vietnamese soldiers and advisors remained in the country and controlled the government. Fighting continued between the government and the guerrillas throughout the year. On 30 November, the UN Security Council imposed trade sanctions on areas of the country under Khmer Rouge control, and agreed to hold the elections with or without the rebel group. By December UNTAC had 16,000 peacekeeping troops and 6,000 civilian police and administrators on the ground.

The Khmer Rouge ignored the 28 January 1993 deadline for party registration, essentially removing itself from the political process. Despite the presence of the U.N. troops, widespread violence on several fronts wracked the country in the runup to the May elections. The Khmer Rouge attempted to tap nationalist sentiments through a series of massacres of ethnic Vietnamese, mostly in March and April, that killed more than 100 civilians and caused 30,000 others to flee their homes along the central Tonle Sap lake. Government-backed terrorist attacks killed dozens of party workers, mostly from the royalist opposition United Front for an Independent, Neutral and Free Cambodia (FUNCINPEC) party headed by Prince Sihanouk's son, Prince Norodom Ranariddh.

Meanwhile, sporadic fighting continued between the government and the Khmer Rouge. On 13 April Khmer Rouge officials pulled out of the capital, Phnom Penh, raising fears that the group planned to violently disrupt the election. In the weeks prior to the vote the guerrillas stepped up their attacks on U.N. and civilian targets, and in early May briefly overtook the capital of Siem Reap province.

The 23-28 May election opened with UNTAC troops bracing for Khmer Rouge rocket and mortar attacks on polling stations. But throughout the vote, violence was minimal and random. In some areas, the Khmer Rouge, which had earlier warned peasants they would be killed if they voted, escorted villagers to polling areas with instructions to vote for FUNCINPEC. Some guerrillas even voted themselves. Ultimately, an astonishing 89 percent of the 4.7 million registered voters cast ballots. Final results for the 120 member National Assembly gave 58 seats to FUNCINPEC, which benefited from its ties to the still-revered Prince Sihanouk; the government's Cambodian People's Party (CPP), 51; Son Sann's Buddhist Liberal Democratic Party (BLDP), 10; and Moulinaka, a FUNCINPEC offshoot, one.

On 4 June an unelected Prince Sihanouk announced he would serve as prime minister in a coalition government of the CPP and FUNCINPEC. Prince Ranariddh immediately protested aligning with his former battlefield enemies, forcing an angry Sihanouk to scrap the plan the next day. On 12 June Prince Norodom Chakrapong, another Sihanouk son and a CPP official, unexpectedly led seven of the country's twenty-one provinces to form an "autonomous zone" to protest alleged voting irregularities, raising fears of a new civil war. The new National Assembly opened in crisis on 14 June and gave Sihanouk broad powers as head of state to "save the nation." The next day the seccessionist movement collapsed, apparently after prime minister Hun Sen had personally intervened. On 16 June Prince Ranariddh and Hun Sen finally agreed to serve as co-presidents of an interim government with Prince Sihanouk serving as head of state, clearing the way for a new constitution to be drafted by the National Assembly.

Throughout the summer Prince Ranariddh and Hun Sen maneuvered for leading roles in the new government. Although Prince Ranariddh claimed the presidency by virtue of FUNCINPEC's parliamentary plurality, the CCP still carried substantial clout in the country through the loyalty of thousands of soldiers and police, as well as all twenty-two of the provincial governors. A compromise announced on 17 September made Prince Norodom Ranariddh First President of the new government and Hun Sen Second President, without clearly defining their roles.

A new constitution adopted on 21 September created a constitutional monarchy in which the king "reigns but does not rule," has the power to make governmental appointments after consultation with ministers, and can declare a state of emergency if the prime minister and cabinet agree. Legal scholars expressed concern that many of the rights guaranteed in the constitution appeared to apply only to ethnic Cambodians, leaving the status of the Vietnamese in question. On 24 September Sihanouk formally returned to the throne after thirty-eight years and ratified the constitution at an elaborate Royal Palace ceremony. Many privately claimed the King's installation undermined the democratic process, as he had effectively gained power without standing in any election.

The apparent rapproachment between former battlefield rivals Prince Ranariddh and Hun Sen and the formation of a new national army has further isolated the Khmer Rouge. The rebel group continued intermittent attacks throughout the summer on civilian, U.N. and military targets, but by the fall more than 2,000 frontline Khmer Rouge guerrillas had defected to the national army. The government launched heavy attacks on Khmer Rouge strongholds in several central and northwestern provinces in August and October, but by years' end the situation had stalemated. The Khmer Rouge, which still has an estimated 12,000 regular soldiers, continues to press for 15 percent control of government ministries, while rejecting calls to surrender territory.

Foreign aid donors have pledged $900 million to rebuild the country's wrecked infrastructure. Years of indiscriminate logging by the warring factions to finance their activities have severely harmed the environment.

Political Rights and Civil Liberties: Cambodians elected a new government in May 1993 in the country's first multiparty voting since a 1972 presidential election. Despite some minor irregularities, including broken plastic security seals on ballot boxes and occasional shelling near some polling areas, the vote was easily the freest in the country's history. Prior to the election, the U.N. registered 95 percent of the eligible voters, and repatriated most of the 370,000 refugees who had fled to Thai border camps during the civil war.

However, the U.N. had been unable fully to provide the "neutral political environment" envisioned in the October 1991 peace accords. Dozens of party workers were killed, including some 200 from the beginning of March to the time of the election, along with 65 U.N. workers. Both the victorious FUNCINPEC and to a far greater extent the government's Cambodian People's Party (CCP) intimidated voters prior to the election. The government warned voters that their ballots would not be secret, and that they might lose jobs and homes if they voted against the CPP. Some CPP officials even told voters their ballots would be monitored via satellite. The government-controlled television channel regularly denigrated FUNCINPEC leader Prince Norodom Ranariddh, and no other party had access to state-controlled media. To help balance the situation, UNTAC opened its own radio facilities and offered all groups equal access.

In the run-up to the election UNTAC refused to set up an independent tribunal to try the few perpetrators of political violence it arrested; as a result none was prosecuted since the government courts refused to hear the cases. The country's legal system has been revamped by UNTAC, but there is a severe shortage of judges and lawyers and it will take time to determine how independent and impartial the new judiciary is. Previously, there had been no due process, and detainees and prisoners were routinely mistreated.

In the months preceding the election, the Khmer Rouge massacred dozens of ethnic Vietnamese citizens. None of the other political groups condemned the violence, for fear of being branded pro-Vietnamese. Many of the estimated 500,000 Vietnamese in Cambodia have roots in the country going back several generations, although others only entered in recent years to find work.

Civil liberties are in theory now guaranteed, and in practice Cambodians do enjoy many freedoms denied to them by the previous government. However, rival groups still have access to large amounts of weapons, and fear of reprisals often force self-censorship on free speech and restrictions on other activities. Soldiers from the former Communist government continue to commit random acts of violence against civilians in the countryside. It also remains to be seen how much freedom the country's nascent labor unions will have.

Cameroon

Polity: Dominant party (military-dominated)
Economy: Capitalist
Population: 12,756,000
PPP: $1,646
Life Expectancy: 53.7
Ethnic Groups: Adamawa, Bamiléké, Beti, Dzem, Fulani, Mandari, Shouwa, other—over 100 tribes and 24 languages

Political Rights: 6
Civil Liberties: 5
Status: Not Free

Overview:

In 1993, following the previous year's disputed presidential elections, the government and the opposition attempted to organize national conferences to address constitutional issues. After President Paul Biya moved to legalize opposition parties and adopt democratic reforms, he and his ruling Cameroon People's Democratic Movement (CPDM) and the main opposition parties agreed in 1991 to hold multiparty parliamentary elections in the fall of 1992. However, in a unilateral move the President hastened the elections to March, leaving the opposition little time to prepare. Subsequently, of the sixty registered parties only thirty-two participated; others, including the strongest opposition group, the Social Democratic Front (SDF), decided to boycott the elections. The SDF, under the charismatic leadership of John Fru Ndi, has its main base in the anglophone western part of the country. The election results gave the CPDM eighty-eight of the 180 legislative seats, which allowed it to form a coalition with the six elected members of the Democratic Movement for the Defense of the Republic (MDDR). The largely northern and Muslim National Union for Democracy and Progress (UNDP) won 68 seats and formed the backbone of parliamentary opposition.

Disregarding the wishes of the opposition and his own prior statements that he would not hold presidential elections until the spring of 1993, President Biya set the date as 11 October 1992, leaving less than thirty days for the electoral campaign.

According to official results, Biya received almost 40 percent of the vote, while Fru Ndi who represented a coalition of opposition groups called the Union of Forces for Change (UFC) received about 35 percent. According to the opposition, the international observers and even some members of the public administration the election was marred with fraud. In the ensuing dispute both Biya and Fru Ndi declared themselves to be the winners. Faced with widespread protests denouncing the election irregularities, Biya declared a state of emergency in the opposition stronghold of Western Cameroon, and Fru Ndi was placed under house arrest at his home in the city of Bamenda. One-hundred-and-thirty-five of Fru Ndi's supporters converged around his house in a gesture of solidarity and protection.

International criticism and suspension of foreign aid led the government to lift the state of emergency in December. The attempts by the Anglican archbishop of Cape Town, Desmond Tutu, to mediate between the government and the opposition proved futile.

Shortly after his election, Biya nominated Simon Achidi Achu to the recently restored post of the prime minister. Achu came from the same constituency as Fru Ndi, and became the first anglophone prime minister of the country. Because the powers of the prime minister were circumscribed, he was dismissed by the opposition as a window dressing aimed at pacifying the anglophone part of the population.

On 30 March 1993 the minister of information accused the UFC of producing a secret plan aimed at destabilizing the country. In his words, the plan called for assassinations, urban guerrilla warfare, and kidnapping of foreigners. The UFC rejected the accusations and countered with their own, saying that it was in reality the government's plan to destabilize the country and blame it on the opposition.

Following his release from house arrest in January 1993, Fru Ndi reiterated his demands to hold new presidential elections. He also distanced himself from separatist organizations calling for the independence of the two anglophone provinces. On 20 February he denounced the government for the appointment of foreigners, mainly French, to high civil service positions. In April, during a UFC meeting, Fru Ndi announced a proposal to convene a "sovereign national conference," to include opposition, government, and international observers for the purpose of rewriting the constitution.

In March, Biya put forth his own proposal for a constitutional conference. On 1 May, however, he claimed that he was misinterpreted and what he meant was that after the publication of the new constitutional draft Cameroonians would be allowed to express their opinions regarding the constitution to a technical committee appointed by Biya.

During the year, the government introduced unpopular measures to restructure the economy. Early in the year the government reduced the salaries of the bloated civil service by up to 20 percent, thus avoiding massive layoffs. Following the introduction of fees for university education and the delays in salary payments to university faculties, students and educators began an indefinite strike to present their demands. In April, following a murder of a student who allegedly paid the fees despite the boycott, the government expelled eighteen activists of a student organization called the Parliament from the University of Cameroon. The authorities accused the activists of having committed the murder, and later arrested them without bringing the case to court.

Parallel to the rise in popularity of the largely anglophone based SDF and its leader John Fru Ndi throughout Cameroon, another group, the Cameroon Anglophone Movement (CAM) expanded its activities. While the SDF did not espouse ethnic division, the CAM advocated the return to the principles of a two-state federation between the majority francophone and the minority anglophone population. In case the Cameroon government refused to reactivate the federative structure the CAM chairman Martin Ekwoge Epie warned of secession and establishment of an independent anglophone state of Southern Cameroon. Besides the CAM, the conferences of traditional chiefs from anglophone areas and other opposition groups addressed the need for creating a federal structure.

Political Rights and Civil Liberties:

The citizens of Cameroon do not have the right to change their government democratically. While the results in the 1992 spring parliamentary elections were deemed to mirror the wishes of the voters, despite boycott from some opposition parties, the fall presidential elections were marred by fraud and irregularities. The Constitution favors the president over the National Assembly (parliament) by vesting wide-ranging powers in the former without legislative or judicial oversight. The President has the right to dissolve the Assembly and convoke new elections at any time, and to rule by decree when the Assembly is not in session. In addition, various government agencies are directly responsible to the presidency. Although since 1990 multipartyism has been allowed and opposition parties occupy almost half of the National Assembly seats, Cameroon remains in effect a single party state, with the ruling CPDM having control over the state bureaucracy.

The judiciary is not independent but is a part of the civil service subordinate to the Ministry of Justice. Although the courts are usually free from government interference in civil and criminal cases, in political cases they usually render decisions favorable to the government. In a few cases where the courts asked the government to pay financial compansation to plaintiffs, the government refused.

There have been numerous cases of arrest and detention without warrant. Following the disputed presidential elections some 200 opposition supporters were detained and many of them were tortured. Although the law proscribes beating and torture of suspects, these occurrences are fairly common in both criminal and political cases.

By law the citizens are granted the right to assemble in public meetings. In practice, however, the police have often violently dispersed peaceful protesters or detained protest organizers prior to planned demonstrations.

The right to free speech and freedom of the press are severely restricted. The 1990 press law authorizes prepublication censorship, licensing of journalists and newspaper vendors, suspension of publications, and restrictions on foreign publications. Journalists in the government-controlled radio and television and in the government-owned newspapers are part of the civil service. In the aftermath of the last presidential election the government stepped up its harassment of the independent press. Following the banning of the newspaper *Le Massager*, its publisher and editor Pius Njawe began publishing under the name of *Le Massagere*, the feminine form of the former. Njawe and the publisher of the *Cameroon Post*, Paddy Mbawa, spent several months in hiding following indications that they were on a government hit list. The copies of the *Cameroon Post* were confiscated in January. In May, the Cameroonian Press Freedom Organization (OCALIP) denounced the prison sentences of six to eight months and heavy fines imposed on the journalists and publishers of *L'Expression Nouvelle* and *L'Opinion* for having published articles implicating high-ranking officials with corruption.

In domestic travel unrestricted by law, the police often use roadblocks and frequent document checks in order to control the movement of illegal aliens and political opposition. Permission to travel abroad is often denied and passports of critics of the government confiscated.

Freedom of religion is guaranteed by law and usually respected in practice although religious organizations are required to register with the government.

The new Labor Code passed in 1992 broke up the monopoly of the CPDM-controlled Confederation of Cameroonian Workers (CSTC) by allowing workers to form and join independent trade unions. The new Code provides for wage bargaining and recognizes strikes, but only after mandatory arbitration, and allows the unions to affiliate with international organizations.

Canada

Polity: Federal parliamentary democracy
Economy: Capitalist
Population: 28,138,000
PPP: $19,232
Life Expectancy: 77.0
Ethnic Groups: British, French, other European, Asian, Caribbean black, aboriginal or native (Indian and Inuit), others

Political Rights: 1
Civil Liberties: 1
Status: Free

Overview: In the general election held on 25 October 1993, Canadian voters threw out Prime Minister Kim Campbell and her Progressive Conservative Party (Tories). Jean Chretien became the new Prime Minister as his Liberals took 177 of the 295 seats in the House of Commons. The Liberals pledged to renegotiate the North American Free Trade Agreement (NAFTA) with the U.S. and Mexico (but reversed themselves) and to establish a major public works employment program. Hurt by 11 percent unemployment and an angry electorate, the Conservatives lost all but 2 seats. Regional parties wiped out the Tory bases in the western provinces and in the predominantly Francophone province of Quebec. Led by ex-Conservative Lucien Bouchard, Bloc Quebecois, a party favoring Quebec's independence, became the leading opposition party with 54 seats. The right-wing, Western-based Reform Party captured 52 seats under leader Preston Manning. Audrey McLaughlin's socialist New Democratic Party (NDP) lost more than 30 seats, retaining only 9. An independent ex-Conservative won the remaining seat.

The regional divisions in the election stem from Canada's history. The French and British colonized different parts of Canada in the seventeenth and eighteenth centuries. Following the Treaty of Paris in 1763, Britain governed both the Francophone and Anglophone areas until it granted home rule in 1867. The British monarch remains the titular head of state, acting through the largely ceremonial Canadian Governor-General. Britain retained a theoretical right to overrule the Canadian Parliament until 1982, when Canadians established complete control over their own constitution.

The Canadian Parliament is bicameral. The House of Commons has 295 members elected from single-member districts (ridings). The Senate has more than 100 members whom the government appoints to represent the country's provinces and territories. There is growing sentiment to abolish the Senate, which many Canadians view as a superfluous chamber of political patronage appointees. Mounting public disgust forced the senators to undo a $6,000 (Canadian) expense allowance senators had granted themselves in 1993. The provinces have some significant local powers including interprovincial trade restrictions.

At the federal and provincial levels, there is an increasingly fractious multiparty system. The governing Liberal Party is headed by Chretien, an anti-separatist Quebecker. It supports activist government economic policies. The Progressive Conservatives (Tories), who support free trade and business-oriented economic policies, held power under Prime Minister Brian Mulroney from 1984 until his resignation in 1993. Hampered by popularity ratings below 20 percent, Mulroney stepped down in order to give a new leader a chance to lead the Tories to electoral victory. Defense Minister Kim Campbell replaced Mulroney after she defeated Environment Minister Jean Charest for party leader at the Conservative convention in June. Campbell's general election campaign included an early gaffe about the long-term nature of high unemployment and a refusal to discuss cutting social programs until after the election.

Following the devastating defeat in 1993, Campbell resigned the Tory leadership. The NDP also has serious problems. It barely survived in the House of Commons. New Democrats control three provinces including Ontario, Canada's largest. However, the NDP's provincial governments have undermined its national support. Public sector austerity and other NDP provincial policies in Ontario have caused some trade unions to disaffiliate from the party. Since April 1991, Bloc Quebecois has been the federal affiliate of Parti Quebecois (PQ), the provincial independence party headed by Jacques Parizeau. The provincial Equality Party backs Anglophone rights in Quebec.

Preston Manning's fast-growing, anti-bilingual Reform Party swamped the Tories in the West at the 1993 general election. Manning emphasizes strict budget cuts and smaller government as alternatives to the federal budget deficit. Another anti-bilingual party, the Confederation of the Regions Party (CoR), has been the chief opposition in New Brunswick, the only officially bilingual province, since 1991. In the West, the

Social Credit Party has controlled some provincial governments. Founded as a movement to control the economy through currency manipulation, the "Socreds" are a populist conservative party, supported in Western agricultural areas. The left-wing National Party, led by Mel Hurtig, holds no parliamentary seats, but it competed with the NDP for leftist votes in 1993. The Natural Law Party won no seats at the last election, but it offered unusual policies such as yogic flying and transcendental meditization.

In 1982, Canada's constitution added a charter of rights and freedoms. One constitutional clause, known as the "notwithstanding clause," permits provincial governments to exempt themselves from applying the charter within their jurisdictions. After holding out against the new constitution, Quebec agreed to accept it in 1987 in return for a recognition by the federal government and the other provinces that Quebec constitutes a "distinct society" within Canada. This was the heart of the Meech Lake accord, named after the place where the constitutional negotiations took place. Quebec invoked the "notwithstanding clause" to keep its provincial language law which restricts the use of English in signs.

The Meech Lake deal, which required unanimous provincial approval, died in 1990, because two provinces failed to ratify it.

The pact's failure angered Quebec's Francophone majority and increased support for Quebec sovereignty. With the death of Meech Lake, the Quebec government decided to hold a referendum on sovereignty by 26 October 1992. Offering a plan for exclusive provincial control over twenty-two fields of government, Quebec's Liberal Premier Robert Bourassa demanded that Canada approve radically decentralized government or face such a plebiscite. Eventually, Mulroney countered with his own set of constitutional reforms. Then the federal and provincial governments negotiated over the constitution at Charlottetown, Prince Edward Island, and produced a package that included a recognition of Quebec as a distinct society within Canada. Consequently, Quebec put off the sovereignty issue, and voted on the same constitutional reforms as the rest of Canada on 26 October 1992.

With 56 percent of the voters disapproving, the package lost. With the defeat of the Charlottetown deal, federal politicians focused on the faltering economy, but Parti Quebecois persisted with a strategy for Quebec's independence. Since Premier Bourassa announced his retirement effective in early 1994, the Quebec Liberals will face a provincial election with a new leader against Parti Quebecois. If PQ wins, it has promised another vote on sovereignty by 1995. PQ leader Jacques Parizeau has set 24 June 1995 as the date for Quebec's independence. He is willing to lead Quebec's secession even if it is supported only by "Quebeckers of old stock."

The possible break-up of Canada has many serious implications. For example, a sovereign Quebec would have to negotiate its economic relationship with Canada and new trading arrangements with other countries, especially with the US and Mexico. Other possible costs of independence include severe economic stress and loss of territory for Quebec, especially if Indians were to attempt secession. The province's departure from Canada would leave Francophones in other Canadian provinces without Quebec's political and cultural protection.

Political Rights and Civil Liberties:

Canadians have the right to change their government by democratic means. Due to government canvassing, Canada has nearly 100 percent effective voter registration. Prisoners have the right to vote in federal elections. In the 1993 general election, the federal government extended voting rights to Canadians living abroad for less than five years. The federal voting service, Elections Canada, also encouraged turnout with three days of advance voting for people unable to vote on 25 October.

Canada prohibits the broadcasting of new, scientific public opinion polls within three days of the general election. Old or unscientific polls are exempt from this regulation. In April 1993, the House of Commons passed a "gag law," legislation limiting individuals and groups other than political parties to $1,000 (Canadian) spending on advocacy advertisements during election campaigns. The National Citizens Coalition, a conservative-libertarian group, filed and won a lawsuit to overturn this limit, on the grounds that the law restricted freedom of expression.

The provinces, especially Quebec, have significant powers. In recent years, Canada and the provinces have given more autonomy to the aboriginals. As power devolves to native groups, questions arise about the constitutionally guaranteed equal rights of native women under the traditionally patriarchal tribal governments. At the U.N. Human Rights Conference in Vienna in June 1993, the Canadian government allegedly objected to the letter "s" in a reference to rights of "indigenous peoples." Reportedly, the government feared that putting the plural form in a declaration might imply a right of aboriginals to secede from the country. However, in 1992-93 the Canadian government negotiated with the Inuit to create Nunavut, a largely Inuit homeland, out of the Northwest Territories. Once operational in 1999, the new jurisdiction will have one-fifth of Canada's territory.

In general, civil liberties are protected by the Charter of Rights and Freedoms. However, the "notwithstanding clause" allows liberties to be curtailed. There are also several limits on freedom of expression, ranging from unevenly enforced restrictions on hateful expression and pornography to rules on reporting. After human rights tribunal hearings in 1993, the government ordered the neo-Nazi Heritage Front to stop a phone line that promoted racial hatred. Willful promotion of racial hatred is against the criminal code, but there are increasing levels of harassment and vandalism against minorities. Toronto, the world's most multicultural city with 140 cultures, is also the home of several hate groups.

The media are generally free, but there are some restrictions. Canadian law prohibits "split runs" for foreign-based publications, meaning, for example, that an American magazine may not duplicate its U.S. edition with a mere change of advertisements for the Canadian market. The law also prohibits tax deductions for Canadian advertisements placed in magazines printed outside the country. There is an autonomous government broadcasting system, the CBC, which has both English and French channels. There are also private broadcasters, magazines, and newspapers. In 1991 the Canadian Radio Television and Telecommunications Commission (CRTTC) relaxed regulations dictating the precise mixtures of music radio stations could play, but there are still rules defining and encouraging "Canadian musical content." The CRTTC is expanding the number of specialty television channels and has eased rules for religious broadcasting. During the 1993 election, the courts sided with the CBC when it excluded National Party leader Mel Hurtig from televised debates. The judges found that forcing his inclusion would have been dictating program content. Bloc Quebecois also complained unsuccessfully when Radio Canada excluded it from a series of debates. In 1993, PEN Canada, the writers' group, condemned Customs Canada for seizing gay-oriented books at the border. The Inter-American Press Association (IAPA) attacked the Canadian judiciary in 1993 for barring the press from reporting on some court cases, including ones dealing with freedom of expression. The IAPA also reported that courts have banned the reporting of such restrictions, which is "the most striking new affront to freedom of the press in the last year."

A generous welfare system supplements a largely open, competitive economy. Rights for property owners are generally strong, but increasing Indian land claims have led to several rounds of litigation and negotiation.

Trade unions and business associations are free and well-organized. In 1993, the Canadian Auto Workers and Chysler negotiated an equity clause in a contract giving workers the right to strike if management cannot or will not resolve a complaint of harassment based on sex, race or religion.

Religious expression is free and diverse. However, there are some special rules about religious education. Since the founding of the Canadian government in 1867, in various provinces there have been state-supported religious (or "separate") school systems, but not all denominations have government-backed systems. Ontario's Education Act has a vague requirement that teachers must uphold Judeo-Christian virtues. The province used this regulation in 1993 against Paul Fromm, a white supremacist, whom the authorities were attempting to dismiss. British Columbia permitted Sikh policemen to wear turbans on duty in 1993.

The judiciary is independent, and the courts often overturn government policy. In 1993, the Ontario Court of Appeal overturned the conviction of a black drug dealer, and suggested screening future juries for racial bias.

Homosexuals won the right to serve in the armed forces in 1992 when the Supreme Court applied the equal rights provisions in the Charter to them. In 1993, a military tribunal examined the alleged racism of troops in Somalia. Some soldiers had apparent links with right-wing racist groups.

Quebec's language laws limit the cultural and educational rights of non-French Canadians, but the province reformed the laws in 1993. Immigrants may not send their children to Anglophone schools in Quebec, although Anglo-Canadians may do so under some circumstances. New rules will expand these circumstances for Anglophone children after 1993. The U.N. Human Rights Commission condemned Quebec's law bannning English on outdoor commercial signs in 1993. The U.N. called the law a violation of the International Covenant on Civil and Political Rights, which guarantees freedom of expression. The provincial Liberals moved to allow English on signs as long as the French lettering predominates. The Quebec ruling party also abolished the language police, who had fined La Brecque Auto Service $7,000 (Canadian) for not having its sign say "Service Auto La Brecque." Parti Quebecois has promised to relax the language laws in an independent Quebec.

In 1992, Canada accepted an Argentinian homosexual's application for asylum. By validating his argument that his sexual orientation had been the cause of his persecution, Canada set an international precedent for asylum cases. In 1993, Canada set another precedent by granting asylum to a Saudi woman who had refused to wear a veil.

Cape Verde

Polity: Presidential-par-
liamentary democracy
Economy: Mixed statist
Population: 395,000
PPP: $1,769
Life Expectancy: 67.0
Ethnic Groups: Mestico/Mulatto, Black African, European

Political Rights: 1
Civil Liberties: 2
Status: Free

Overview: **A** small archipelago off the coast of west-central Africa, Cape
Verde began its post-colonial existence in 1975 politically
linked to Guinea-Bissau, another former Portuguese depen-
dency. The relationship was severed in 1979 after the government in Guinea-Bissau was
overthrown in a coup. The 1980 constitution established a one-party state under the leftist
African Party for the Independence of Cape Verde (PAICV) led by President Aristides
Pereira. Legislative authority was vested in a unicameral National People's Assembly.

Cape Verde's move toward a multiparty system began officially at a PAICV party
congress in February 1990. The leadership advocated constitutional amendments to
pave the way for competitive elections and eliminated reference to the guiding role of
the PAICV in society. The Assembly later voted to permit alternative party slates in
parliamentary polling and direct elections for president.

Carlos Veiga, a former PAICV activist, led the eight-month-old opposition party,
Movement for Democracy (MPD), to a convincing win in January 1991 parliamentary
elections. In February's presidential election, MPD-supported independent candidate
and former Supreme Court justice Antonio Mascarenhas Monteiro beat incumbent
Pereira, who had ruled for fifteen years.

In August 1993, Nigerian radio reported a coup attempt, but Cape Verde officials in
the capital denied the story.

In January, Prime Minister Veiga rejected calls for a "government of national
coalition" on the second anniversary of the MPD's coming to power. He was responding to a question about his "call for social consultation." The prime minister said that a
government of national coalition "is not necessary anymore especially when the MPD
has a comfortable majority in parliament." In 1991, the MPD won 56 of 79 seats.

A key priority for the government was the privatization of certain industries. The
prime minister said in January that the program would be completed in four years. He
said that the civil service, estimated to be 12,000, would gradually be reduced by half.
The prime minister went on to say that the privatization plan was not part of an
International Monetary Fund (IMF) Structural Adjustment Program (SAP). He also
charged that his PAICV opponents were "damaging through its critics the image of the
country abroad."

The country's per capita income is among the highest in West Africa. Many
citizens survive on remittances sent by expatriates working abroad or Social Security
checks sent to retirees who spent their working lives in the U.S. Agricultural opportunities are limited on the arid islands and the fishing industry is still underdeveloped.

Political Rights and Civil Liberties: Citizens are able to change their government through free and fair elections. Criminal and civil cases are generally adjudicated fairly and expeditiously; there are no known political prisoners. Public criticism of the government is tolerated, but the regime has on occasion warned the press to avoid sensationalism. The most widely read newspaper, radio and television, are controlled by the government, but coverage is generally fair and balanced. National Assembly sessions are broadcast live in their entirety.

Freedoms of assembly, association and religion are guaranteed by law and respected in practice in this predominantly Catholic country. There are no restrictions on domestic or foreign travel.

The Constitution prohibits sex discrimination and guarantees full equality of men and women; in practice, however, male-oriented African and Portuguese values exclude women from certain jobs and women are often paid less then men. Domestic violence against women remains common in rural areas.

Workers are free to form and join independent unions; seven were created in 1992. The largest confederations are the Coordinated Council of Free Labor Unions (CCLS) and the National Union of Cape Verde Workers, formed and controlled by the former government.

Central African Republic

Polity: Presidential-legislative democracy (military influenced)
Economy: Capitalist-statist
Population: 3,109,000
PPP: $768
Life Expectancy: 49.5
Ethnic Groups: Baya (34 percent), Banda (27 percent), Mandja (21 percent), Sara (10 percent)

Political Rights: 3*
Civil Liberties: 4*
Status: Partly Free

Ratings Change: *The Central African Republic's political rights rating changed from 6 to 3 and its civil liberties rating from 5 to 4 because of democratic transitional elections marking a formal end to military rule.

Overview: In 1993, following the first democratic elections in more than a decade, the country's ruler, General Andre Kolingba, decided to step down, leaving the country to civilian rule.

This sparsely populated country received its independence from France in 1960, following decades of colonial rule, but continues to remain economically and politically dependent on its former metropolis. Following the overthrow of the self-styled emperor Bokassa I in 1979, who was accused of ordering massive human rights abuses and leading the country towards financial disaster, the country held its first presidential election in 1981, in which the country's first elected President David Dacko was re-elected. Dacko's reign ended after only six months, when General Andre Kolingba formed a military junta.

In order to legitimize his rule, Kolingba promulgated a new constitution in 1986 that re-established the presidency, with Kolingba guaranteed a six-year term as the country's head of state. The constitution also designated the Central African Democratic Assembly (RDC) as the country's sole legitimate political party.

Faced with mounting social tensions and pressured by international aid donors to launch political and economic reforms, Kolingba announced in 1991 the abandonment of the single party system in favor of multipartyism. His refusal to grant the national conference on the future constitutional arrangements the right to amend the existing laws led to the withdrawal of the opposition United Forces Coalition (CFD) from the debate. The Supreme Court annulled the results of the first round of presidential elections held in October 1992 after the government and the opposition accused each other of voting irregularities and incitement to violence. Although the president's formal term of office expired in late November, Kolingba extended it until after new elections, scheduled for February 1993.

In December 1992, Kolingba appointed General Thimotee Malendoma as prime minister. Malendoma's Civic Forum party had been suspended from the CFD in August for participating in the government-sponsored national debate, despite the Coalition's boycott.

On 28 December, shortly after his appointment as prime minister, Malendoma made a speech broadcast over the national radio and television in which he accused Kolingba of obstructing preparations for the election. In January 1993, a former presidential candidate and a leading member of the CFD, Abel Goumba, charged Kolingba with perpetrating a *coup d'etat* by prolonging his presidential mandate and expressed concern about the influence of the military in the interim government.

On 7 February Kolingba and three former presidential candidates agreed to set up a "National Provisional Council for the Republic" (CNPPR) to act as an interim legislature until the holding of new legislative election. The CNPPR was to be composed of the president of the Economic and Regional Council (second and largely advisory chamber of the parliament) and all the presidential candidates from the aborted October election, including President Kolingba. Immediately afterwards, Dacko, who became CNPPR chairman, announced that the elections slated for 14 and 28 February were rescheduled for 18 April and 2 May.

On 9 February the CFD and another opposition coalition, the Cooperation Council of the Moderate Parties (CEM), issued a joint statement that called for immediate elections and criticized the formation of the CNPPR. Both groups accused Kolingba and the opposition candidates who had joined the Council of attempting to monopolize the political life of the country.

On 25 February Kolingba dismissed Malendoma as prime minister, emphasizing the latter's public criticism of the slow process of democratization, and alleging that it was Malendoma's unwillingness to cooperate with Kolingba that caused the electoral delay.

Two days later, Kolingba nominated another former candidate, Enoch Lakou of the Social Democratic Party, to succeed Malendoma. In his first public address on 24 March Lakou announced another delay in the elections, blaming the Electoral Commission for not completing the necessary preparations.

In May, following Kolingba's announcement that the elections would be held in October, despite the Electoral Commission's date for late May, Goumba indicated that the army should take control of the electoral process. On 20 May several opposition groups and presidential candidates under the auspices of the Central African Human

Rights League formed the Union of Forces Devoted to Change (UFAC), an umbrella group whose main task was to act as a watchdog over the electoral preparations. UFAC also proposed that the elections be held in July. On 18 June, Kolingba bowed to the opposition and forwarded the first round of elections to 22 August.

By the election date eight candidates registered to run for president, and 496 candidates contested the 85 National Assembly seats. On 28 August, with almost all the votes counted, the Electoral Commission released the unofficial election results. Of the 1.2 million registered voters 62 percent cast their ballots. Thirty-seven percent of those voted for Ange-Félix Patassé, a former health minister under the Bokassa regime and leader the People's Liberation Movement. Dacko came in second with more than 21 percent of the vote, while Goumba, the only candidate who had consistently criticized all former dictators, received slightly less than 21 percent. Kolingba came in a distant fourth with 11 percent of voter support.

The next day, on the eve of the release of final election results, Kolingba decreed an alteration in the electoral code and the makeup of the Constitutional Court, purportedly for increasing their "credibility and efficiency." Immediately after the pronouncement, the seven opposition candidates denounced the move as Kolingba's attempt to cling to power. The French government responded quickly by suspending all cooperation and aid. Suprised by the stark internal and external response, Kolingba recanted the decrees by the end of the day and offered his resignation.

On 1 September, the day the final election results were announced, Kolingba decreed the release of all prisoners, including the former emperor Bokassa, who had been sentenced for having committed atrocities during his rule. During the second round of elections on 19 September, Patassé won with 52 percent of the vote, becoming the next president.

Political Rights and Civil Liberties: After twelve years of autocratic government by General Kolingba, the citizens of the Central African Republic were able to elect their head of state and legislature in August and September 1993, in the country's second democratic election. Despite some irregularities, such as the Electoral Commission's decision to allow unregistered voters who showed up with identification forms and two witnesses to vote in the election, and the detection of people carrying several voting cards on election day, international observers from seventeen countries viewed the vote as generally free and fair.

The independence of the judiciary is compromised by insufficient funding and corruption, and interference by the executive branch, especially in cases where the government's definition of national security is involved. Although legal counsel and public trials are prescribed for the accused, in many cases prisoners are held without a trial.

All media are government owned and controlled. Prior to Kolingba's resignation the media were heavily biased in his favor. Before the 1992 election the opposition parties were given some free access to radio and newspapers. Shortly thereafter, however, Kolingba again tightened his grip on the media. On 4 February, shortly before being dismissed by Kolingba, Prime Minister Melendoma fired the Minister of Information for refusing to give free access to the opposition.

The freedom for individual citizens and groups to express in public their points of view has in recent years become more common and accepted without the fear of reprisal. Although the opposition parties lacked access to the regular media throughout much of the year, they often published stenciled and photocopied pamphlets without government interference.

Since 1989, when a new Labor Code went into effect, workers have been free to organize and join the trade union of their choice. However, the law requires that only one trade union federation be registered, and that union officials be employed as full-time wage earners, thus restricting union activities to their spare time.

Throughout the year there were frequent protests and strikes by disgruntled students, civil servants, and army troops demanding the payment of scholarship and salary arrears. On 26 April the paramilitary troops fired on demonstrators, killing two, after university students protested in downtown Bangui demanding Kolingba's resignation. Following their return to work in February after a four month strike, the civil servants resumed their strike in April. In May, soldiers of the Presidential Guard and other units surrounded government buildings demanding the payment of their salaries.

Although the constitution stipulates equality of all citizens, there is a wide gap in economic and educational opportunities and political influence among the eighty ethnic groups. The indigenous forest dwellers, Ba'aka (pygmies), are subject to various forms of exploitation which the government fails to address. Despite a 1966 law against female genital mutiliation, it is still widely praticed, especially in rural areas.

Chad

Polity: Military
Economy: Capitalist
Population: 5,351,000
PPP: $559
Life Expectancy: 46.5
Political Rights: 6
Civil Liberties: 5*
Status: Not Free

Ethnic Groups: Arab, Bagirmi, Sara,Wadai, Zaghawa, Bideyat Gorane, other
Ratings Change: *Chad's civil liberties rating changed from 6 to 5 as a result of modifications in methodology. See "Survey Methodology," page 671.

Overview:
Despite President Idriss Deby's pledge to make human rights and democratization the primary objective of his government, Chad remains plagued with an appalling human rights record and a government that appears reluctant to move forward on its reform agenda.

Deby, a member of the Patriotic Salvation Movement (MPS), seized control of Chad's government from Hissein Habre in December of 1990. In March 1991 the MPS enacted a National Charter which annulled the 1989 constitution, convened a thirty-month transitional government and concentrated power in the office of the presidency. The Charter also outlined the government's commitment to protect fundamental rights and freedoms including the freedom of speech and association, freedom of the press, freedom of movement, property rights and the rights of trade unions to organize. In 1992, the charter was amended to designate the prime minister as chief of government and to allow twenty-six political parties to operate.

In October 1992, the government announced that it would convene a National Conference comprised of members of government as well as independent organizations and opposition groups. The purpose of the conference was to review Chad's political and social problems and to discuss ways to achieve both stability and democracy and to protect human rights. The conference took place during January-April of 1993. The conference elected Education Minister Fidele Moungar to serve as interim prime minister during a twelve month transition period. General and presidential elections were promised at the end of that one-year period.

In October 1993 Moungar was removed from office in a "no-confidence" vote by the Deby-controlled transitional legislature. Increasingly, Moungar and Deby were locked in a power struggle as Moungar pushed for reforms that would increase the pace of adopting a multiparty system.

Since gaining independence from France in 1960, Chad has endured an intermittent civil war spurred on by tribal and factional rivalry. Chad is roughly divided between the Saharan and Arab Muslims living in the northern, central and eastern regions, and the Sudanian zone ethnic groups (predominately Christian farmers), in the south. Despite the fact that there are over 200 ethnic groups in Chad, substantive power remains in the hands of only a few minority ethnic groups from northern and eastern Chad.

Political Rights and Civil Liberties:

Chadians do not have the right to change their government democratically. While multiparty elections are scheduled for 1994, increasingly Deby's commitment to following his reform agenda has been called into question. Ethnic clashes continue and Amnesty International has reported gross human rights violations by security forces loyal to Deby. No attempt has been made by Deby's government to investigate allegations of human rights violations or to restrict the use of lethal force against noncombatants or detainees.

Political power remains concentrated in the hands of a small number of minority groups, and persecution solely on the grounds of ethnic origin continues unabated. Chadians are not protected from political terror and are subject to torture. Amnesty International reports that at least 500 unarmed civilians have been extrajudicially executed since October 1991. These executions were said to have occurred mainly during counter-insurgency operations or in reprisal attacks on those believed to be associated with rebel groups because of their ethnic origin or residency. Chad continues to hold political prisoners.

Chadians do not have equal access to an independent, nondiscriminatory judicial system. Ordinary courts have been partially replaced by the Military Court and Special Court of Justice where defendants, who are usually held on politically motivated crimes, are often presumed guilty. Sentences are commonly subject to manipulation by the regime.

While the National Charter provides for freedom of speech and assembly, open political activity continues to be curtailed by the security forces. Restrictions have been eased on journalists since Deby came to power. However, journalists regarded as critical of the government were subject to intimidation and assault during 1992 and three journalists were killed during 1993. No independent judicial investigation has been conducted regarding these deaths.

The Chadian Human Rights League (LTDH), which was set up to investigate and publicize human rights violations by security forces, operates under precarious conditions. In February 1992, the vice president of LTDH, Joseph Behidi, was killed. A six month government investigation concluded that Behidi had been killed by an armed gang. The results of the investigation were called into question when the victim's car was found near the headquarters of a security force. Human rights groups assert that Behidi was killed by off-duty soldiers. In October 1993 opposition leader Abbas Koty was killed by security forces. Amnesty International charges that Koty was executied extrajudicially.

The rights of trade unions to operate is established in the National Charter. In practice, however, trade union members are subject to intimidation and detention. During 1992 trade unions organized a series of strikes to protest unpaid salaries and redundancies. In response to the strike, the government arrested union leaders.

Chad is a secular state and freedom of religion is respected. International travel is not guaranteed. While internal travel is allowed (except in military zones), the U.S. State Department reports that many travelers have complained of roadblocks set up by security forces and criminals who demand money before allowing passage.

Women do not have status equal to men. Women's rights are not protected by traditional law or through the Penal Code. The UNDP reports that the literacy rate for women is significantly lower than for men and that, on average, females receive one-third the education of males. Domestic violence against women is common and women have only limited legal recourse against the batterer. Female genital mutilation (circumcision) is widespread. The percentage of Chadian women who have been subject to this procedure may be as high as 60 percent. The Deby government has made no effort to stop this practice.

Chile

Polity: Presidential-
legislative democracy
Economy: Capitalist
Population: 13,492,000
PPP: $5,099
Life Expectancy: 71.8
Ethnic Groups: Mestizo, Spanish, other European, Indian

Political Rights: 2
Civil Liberties: 2
Status: Free

Overview:
Eduardo Frei, son of former President Eduardo Frei (1964-1970) of the incumbent Coalition for Democracy swept to victory in the 11 December 1993 presidential elections. The Coalition, however, did not secure the two-thirds majority in the Congress needed to amend the constitution that dates back to military rule and limits civilian authority over the armed forces.

The Republic of Chile was founded after gaining independence from Spain in 1818. Democratic governance predominated in this century until the overthrow of the socialist government of Salvador Allende in 1973. Gen. Augusto Pinochet became head of state, dissolved Congress, banned independent political activity and repressed dissent severely.

The 1980 constitution provided for a plebiscite in which voters could reject another presidential term for Pinochet. In October 1988, 55 percent of Chilean voters said "no" to Pinochet, which meant the government had to hold competitive presidential and legislative elections in 1989.

The campaign of the sixteen-party "Command for the No" was based on reforming the constitution. After the plebiscite, the Command and the government negotiated an agreement on fifty-four constitutional changes. The number of elected senators in the Congress was raised from twenty-six to thirty-eight (with nine still to be appointed by the Pinochet government) and the ban on Marxist parties was lifted.

The center-left Coalition for Democracy (formerly the Command for the No) nominated Christian Democrat Patricio Aylwin for president. Right-wing parties backed either Hernan Buchi, Pinochet's former finance minister, or businessman Francisco Errazuriz. Because Aylwin vowed not to make major changes in the free-market, free-trade thrust of the economy, civil-military relations ware the main issue. The 1980 constitution allows Pinochet to remain commander of the army, the largest branch of the 57,000-man armed forces, until 1997.

In December 1989 Aylwin won the presidency with 55.2 percent of the vote. The Coalition won a 72-48 majority in the 120-member Chamber of Deputies, and 22 of 38 elected Senate seats. But with 9 senators appointed by the outgoing government, it fell short of a majority in the 47-seat Senate.

President Aylwin oversaw a broadly representative, remarkably clean government that was responsive to a wide social base. His approval ratings remained high as his administration successfully combined market economics with social policies that made substantial reductions in poverty. That provided a strong base for Frei, who was nominated in the Coalition primary in May 1993.

But attempts to reform the non-democratic elements of the constitution fell short. In early 1993 right-wing senators blocked bills that would have given the president power to remove military commanders and eliminate the nine designated seats in the Senate.

Aylwin was deft at handling a number of incidents with the unrepentant seventy-eight-year-old Pinochet. The most serious occurred in May 1993. Pinochet in 1978 passed an amnesty for all political crimes. But that did not stop the government from investigating thousands of human rights cases brought to light by a goverment commission in 1991. Although the military was immune from prison terms, by May 1993 hundreds of cases were being heard in civilian courts. That and allegations of corruption against Pinochet's son prompted Pinochet to make a one-day show of force by the army in the streets of Santiago.

Aylwin, backed by popular outrage at the display, publicly upbraided Pinochet. Pinochet, to his chagrin, received no support from right-wing parties or the other armed services. In subsequent negotiations Aylwin got the military to agree to cooperate in the ongoing rights cases in exchange for secrecy in the proceedings. The government hoped fresh evidence would help to locate bodies of people "disappeared" under military rule. But the agreement was blocked by the left wing of the Coalition which objected to secret hearings. That guaranteed that the human rights issue would carry over into the Frei administraton.

Frei, a fifty-two-year-old businessman and Christian Democrat, maintained an overwhelming lead in the polls in the run up to the election. Running a distant second was the right-wing opposition candidate, lawyer Arturo Alessandri. On 11 December Frei won with 58 percent of the vote against 24 percent for Alessandri. A handful of leftist and right-wing candidates split the remainder. Prior to the election the main political parties agreed to amend the constitution to make the presidential term six years.

During his campaign Frei vowed to maintain the fight against poverty, strengthen the educational system and continue pursuing greater civilian authority over the armed forces. However, the Coalition lost a seat in the Senate and two seats in the Chamber of Deputies, leaving it still short of the two-thirds majority needed to reform the constitution.

Political Rights and Civil Liberties: Citizens are able to change their government through free and fair elections at the national, regional and municipal levels, and democratic institutions are better established than in any other Latin American country outside of Costa Rica.

However, the 1980 constitution installed under military rule, while substantially reformed, still limits civilian authority over the armed forces. The president cannot remove armed force commanders or reduce the military budget. The constitution also allowed the outgoing regime in 1990 to appoint nine out of forty-seven senators. The Aylwin government was able to whittle away at the military's autonomy. The armed forces sent top brass to the Congress to explain military expenditures and the navy and air force invited senators and deputies on inspections and military maneuvers.

In 1990 a Truth and Reconciliation Commission was formed to investigate human rights violations committed under military rule. Pinochet tried to block it, but with a number of his own officers apparently in favor of an apolitical role for the military, he backed down.

The Commission's report implicated the military and the secret police at the highest levels in the death or disappearance of 2,279 people between September 1973 and March 1990. However, in 1978 the Pinochet regime issued an amnesty for all political crimes, and the Supreme Court, packed by Pinochet before leaving office, has blocked the government's efforts to lift it. Investigations of hundreds of cases nonetheless took place in civilian courts (see "Overview").

The Supreme Court, however, after persistent coaxing by Aylwin, made a dramatic turnaround on a related issue—the 1976 murder in Washington of former Chilean ambassador to the U.S., Orlando Letelier, and his assistant, Ronni Moffit. In late 1991, the Court ruled that the alleged authors of the crime—retired Gen. Juan Manuel Contreras and Col. Pedro Espinosa—be tried in civilian courts. Under Pinochet the power of military courts was greatly expanded at the expense of the civil court system. Contreras and Espinosa were convicted in November 1993, the first time a civil court had convicted ranking officers for crimes committed during the Pinochet era. They were sentenced to seven and six years in prison, respectively, pending appeal.

The successful persecution of the Letelier case breached the wall of impunity around the military and renewed the possibility of lifting the 1978 amnesty. Meanwhile, advances were made in a number of cases not covered by the 1978 amnesty, as several civilian judges showed determination despite legal and political pressures on their jurisdiction.

In January 1993 three right-wing opposition senators voted with pro-government senators to impeach a Supreme Court justice charged with dereliction of duty in handling human rights cases. The vote was an important step in strengthening congressional oversight of national institutions, and enhanced the chances for the Coalition's proposal to expand the number of Court justices and dilute the power of Pinochet appointees.

Most of the laws limiting political expression were eliminated by the 1989 constitutional reforms and the political spectrum runs from Marxist to fascist. Religious expression is unrestricted, although Mormon temples are occasionally the targets of attacks by left-wing radicals.

The Aylwin government restored nearly complete media freedom. There are scores of publications representing all points of view. Radio is both private and public. The national television network is operated by the state, but open to all political voices.

There are three noncommercial television stations run by universities. However, a number of restrictive laws remain on the books, including one that grants power to military courts to convict journalists for sedition or libeling members of the armed forces. A journalist licensing law also remains in place.

Negotiations between the Aylwin government, labor unions and the private sector have resulted in significant reforms of the draconian labor code inherited from the Pinochet regime. Strikes are legal, collective bargaining has been expanded beyond the level of the firm and worker benefits increased. Still, some provisions that violate international labor standards remain on the books.

There were nearly 400 political prisoners when the Aylwin government took office. By the end of 1993, all but eleven had been pardoned. The remaining prisoners, convicted of violent actions by military courts, were expected to have their cases retried in civil courts.

There continue to be sporadic terrorist actions by remnants of the Manuel Rodriguez Patriotic Front (FPMR), the former armed wing of the Communist party, and the anarcho-hedonist Lautero Front. Human rights groups have expressed concern about anti-terrorist legislation which broadened police powers. There are frequent reports of abuses including torture, although there is no evidence of a systematic policy.

In 1990 Chile ratified the Inter-American Convention on Human Rights and formally recognized the jurisdiction of the Inter-American Human Rights Court for the interpretation and enforcement of the provisions contained in the convention.

China

Polity: Communist one-party
Economy: Statist
Population: 1,178,526,000
PPP: $1,990
Life Expectancy: 70.1
Ethnic Groups: Han Chinese (93 percent), Azhuang, Hui, Uygur, Yi, Miao, Manchu, Tibetan, Mongolian, others

Political Rights: 7
Civil Liberties: 7
Status: Not Free

Overview:

In 1992 Chinese paramount leader Deng Xiaoping outmanuevered hardliners and won wide support for speeding the country's transition to a market-based economy. A year later evidence suggested that the frenzy of freewheeling business activity is undermining the nominally Communist regime's once tight central control over society. Political dissent and basic rights are still stifled, but new affluence in the cities is freeing millions from dependence on state work units. In the countryside provincial administrators are usurping power from the center and have fomented peasant riots through ad hoc levies and land seizures. In the short-term, however, the regime's most pressing concern is controlling soaring prices, mindful that inflation was the catalyst in the 1986 and 1989 pro-democracy protests.

Chinese Communist Party (CCP) Chairman Mao Zedong proclaimed the People's

Republic of China on 1 October 1949 following victory over the Nationalist Kuomintang. In 1966 Mao began the Cultural Revolution in an attempt to regain control over a fractious CCP. The national campaign terrorized intellectuals and anyone remotely suspected of foreign influences. By its end in 1976, up to a million had died, and millions more had been disgraced, including party secretary Deng Xiaoping. Following Mao's death in September 1976, Deng assumed several top level posts, and in 1978 he introduced a cautious program of economic reforms under the guise of socialism.

By the mid-1980s, calls for democracy began to increase. In December 1986 students protested in several cities demanding political liberalization and improved living standards. In 1987 CCP hardliners sacked Party Secretary General Hu Yaobang, whom they blamed for allowing the protests, and replaced him with Zhao Ziyang.

In April 1989 several thousand students gathered in Beijing's Tiananmen Square to mourn Hu's death, later boycotting classes to demand economic reforms and to protest rising prices. By mid-May the protests had spread to other cities, and several thousand students had begun hunger strikes. The Beijing demonstrations ended in a bloody army assault on Tiananmen Square on 3-4 June, in which hundreds, perhaps thousands, were killed. The hardliners in the party seized the opportunity to sack liberal officials and arrest some 10,000 people involved, many of them students. Jiang Zemin, a conservative, replaced the relatively moderate Zhao Ziyang as party chief.

In the ensuing years, the government has concentrated improving living standards through free-market reforms in order to keep the people from protesting the CCP's political hegemony. Policies are ultimately shaped by a core of aging revolutionary veterans, foremost among them the eighty-nine-year-old Deng, who no longer holds any official posts. These leaders, whose ranks dropped to six in March 1993 with the death of hardliner Wang Zhen, are themselves divided, with the strongest opposition to the reforms coming from eighty-eight-year-old conservative Chen Yun.

In 1992 Deng made his strongest push to advance the reforms so they would be irreversible after his death. In January he made a highly symbolic surprise visit to the booming Shenzen and Zhuhai Special Economic Zones in southern Guangdong Province, where he urged factory mangers speed up investment plans. At the CCP's 14th Party Congress in October 1992, the party adopted the vague concept of a "socialist market economy" and elevated economic reformer Zhu Rongji to the seven-man Politburo standing committee, the party's highest formal power structure.

With Deng reportedly in failing health, much of the political manuevering in 1993 involved the related issues of the economy and efforts to ensure a smooth succession after his death. When the rubber-stamp National People's Congress opened its annual two-week session on 15 March, several aging veterans were formally retired from official positions, allowing a younger set of leaders to be promoted. Both President Yang Shankun and NPC Chairman Wan Li stood down, marking the first time since the 1949 revolution that no cadres from the fabled 1934 Long March held official top posts. The NPC named party secretary Jiang to succeed Yang as president of the country, and re-elected him as chairman of the Central Military Commission.

On 28 March the NPC re-elected premier Li Peng to a second five-year term. Although Li ran unopposed, 330 of the 2,977 delegates either voted no or voided their ballots, an unusually high number considering they were chosen specifically for their obediance. Many Chinese abhor Li for his supposed leading role in the Tiananmen Square crackdown. The next day the Congress amended the constitution to adopt Deng's free-market policies. The NPC also named Qiao Shi, the CCP's former internal security chief, as its chairman, and named Zhu Rongji first vice-premier in charge of the economy.

By mid-year the country's astounding 13.9 percent economic growth rate had driven inflation to 21.6 percent in the larger cities. Zhu was appointed to head the Central Bank with a mandate to curb reckless lending and property speculation by local banks. In mid-November the CCP Central Committee announced plans to gradually subject coddled state enterprises to market forces. Bowing to pressure from Deng, the Committee ignored an austerity program instituted by Zhu and called for accelerated growth.

The economic reforms of recent years have created a growing income disparity between the flourishing coastal and urban areas and the 900 million peasants in the still-struggling countryside. In February, peasants rioted at post offices in several provinces when they were unable to cash IOUs for government grain purchases.

Peasants have also been squeezed by illegal taxes levied by local officials for everything from education to water and land use. In December 1991 the government limited taxes to 5 percent of the peasants' income, but this is frequently exceeded; in extreme cases legal and illegal taxes, along with mandatory grain assessments, consume up to one-third of the peasants' incomes.

In some areas the peasants have fought back. The most serious disturbance occurred on 3-6 June in Renshou county, Sichuan Province, when more than 10,000 peasants, angered over levies charged for building a highway, attacked local officials and government offices. The Agriculture Ministry quickly banned over forty fees on peasants. During the year, there were also peasant protests in Guangdong and central Henan provinces over state land seizures. Meanwhile, powerful bureaucrats have used their connections to reap fortunes in business, and have also created the country's worst corruption problem since the Koumintang era. In August the government responded with a major anti-graft campaign.

Abroad, the government faced criticism from the United States over its political repression, arms sales, and a 5 October underground nuclear test. In June, the U.S. extended China's Most Favored Nation trade status for another year, but made subsequent extentions dependent on human rights improvements. The U.S. is particularly concerned with the export of prison-made goods.

Political Rights and Civil Liberties: Chinese citizens cannot change their government democratically. The Chinese Communist Party (CCP), controlled by a handful of aging revolutionaries, holds ultimate authority. While ordinary Chinese now face less intrusion by the government than in the past, the regime does not tolerate dissent, lacks effective judicial safeguards, and has one of the worst human rights records in the world. China admits to holding some 3,500 "counterrevolutionaries," while outside observers estimate the number of political prisoners at 20,000 or more.

Immediately after the 1989 Tiananmen Square crackdown, the government tightened social restrictions and curbed some economic reforms. In the past two years, though, private economic activity has been allowed to flourish. In addition to the spectacularly successful Special Economic Zones in the south, the small-scale township and village enterprises, where management is generally independent from the government, have slowly improved living standards for many in the countryside. These successes have removed millions of Chinese from dependence on the *danwei*, or state work unit, eroding the once-pervasive influence of the CCP. Officially, only 25 million Chinese work in private firms, although the informal sector has swollen to perhaps 100 million people. For some 100 million others in state enterprises, however, the *danwei* still controls everything from the right to change residence to permission to have a child.

In 1993 the government released several prominent dissidents imprisoned for their role in the 1979 Democracy Wall movement and the 1989 pro-democracy protests, including the country's most famous dissident, Wei Jingsheng. These high-profile releases were undoubtably meant to curry favor with the U.S. and other Western trading partners, and to boost Beijing's chances of landing the prestigious 2000 Summer Olympic Games, which were ultimately awarded to Sydney.

Torture of prisoners and detainees is widespread, and ordinary workers generally receive the worst treatment. Suspects are frequently abused to extract confessions. Two special types of punishment exist: the laojiao, or "re-education through labor" camps, and the laogai, or "reform through labor" camps. The laogai is a criminal punishment requiring a court order. The laojiao provides for administrative detention for up to four years without a hearing. The latter is used to detain some 100,000 people each year, including dissidents.

The judiciary is subservient to the CCP and due process rights are generally ignored. The accused are presumed guilty and over 99 percent are convicted. Defense lawyers generally appeal for leniency rather than truly defend the accused.

China's harsh one-child family planning policy is applied inconsistently from region to region. Because local officials are personally responsible for the birth rates in their areas, the policy is often zealously enforced through sanctions and in some cases through forced contraception and sterilization. Couples adhering to the policy receive education, food and medical benefits, while those failing to comply face a loss of benefits and are fined. Failure to pay the fine often results in seizure of livestock or other goods and destruction of homes.

As male children are economically valuable because of their labor and ability to care for aging parents, expecting mothers frequently use ultrasound machines to determine a baby's sex. Female fetuses are frequently aborted, and infanticide is practiced in a small percentage of births. According to an official study obtained by the *New York Times* in July, the ratio of male to female births in 1992 reached 118.5:100; a normal ratio is roughly 105.5:100. In December the government aroused international concern by proposing legislation aimed at preventing "births of inferior quality" through sterilazation of women considered likely to pass defects to their children.

In the past few years social and cultural restrictions have been eased, and sexual morality is no longer rigidly enforced. More than 1,600 newspapers and 6,400 magazines are published, often featuring gossipy articles and discussion of previously taboo subjects such as homosexuality. Freedoms of press, political expression and association are nonexistent. However the spread of satellite dishes and shortwave radios has made it harder for the government to control access to information.

Religious practice is generally restricted to government-sanctioned "Patriotic" churches. Small, unofficial Catholic and Protestant churches are often tolerated provided they maintain a low profile, although scores of such churches have been closed in some provinces, and hundreds of bishops and priests remain in detention. Muslims face restrictions in building mosques and in providing religious education to youths under eighteen.

All unions must belong to the CCP-controlled All-China Federation of Trade Unions, and independent trade unions are illegal. Strikes are officially permitted only to protest dangerous working conditions, although workers have staged strikes over low wages and inadequate living conditions at several foreign-owned factories.

Colombia

Polity: Presidential-
legislative democracy
Economy: Capitalist-
statist
Population: 34,943,000
PPP: $4,237
Life Expectancy: 68.8

Political Rights: 2
Civil Liberties: 4
Status: Partly Free

Ethnic Groups: Mestizo (58 percent), Caucasian (20 percent),
Mulatto (14 percent), Black, (4 percent), Indian (1 percent)

Overview: The government of President Cesar Gaviria, dogged by
scandal, began its last year as the nation braced for the 1994
elections amid mounting political violence.

Colombia won independence from Spain in 1819. The Republic of Colombia was
established under the 1886 constitution. Politics has been dominated by the Liberal and
Conservative parties that in 1957 formed the National Front in which they ruled
together. After 1974 the two parties competed in direct presidential and congressional
elections. Municipal elections were held for the first time in 1988.

Gaviria, the Liberal candidate, was elected president in May 1990 and initiated a
process of political reform. In December 1990 voters elected a constituent assembly that
included politicians from left to right, former left-wing guerrillas and labor, religious
and native Indian leaders.

The new constitution was promulgated in 1991. It provided for the dissolution of
the Congress elected in 1990 and new elections for an expanded bicameral Congress. It
abolished the system of discretionary funds that allowed members of Congress to pay
for patronage and re-election campaigns at public expense, prohibited legislators from
holding second jobs, and barred their relatives from running for office.

The constitution lifted the president's authority to appoint the governors of the
nation's twenty-seven departments, who are now elected. It also limited presidents to
single four-year terms, gave Congress veto powers over the Cabinet and restricted state-
of-emergency powers to ninety days. However, because it regulates so many areas of
the nation's political, social and economic life, it increased the likelihood of juridical
gridlock.

The October 1991 congressional elections indicated that Colombian society would
only slowly absorb the political reforms. Despite a new voter system that gives all
parties equal billing on the ballots and the participation of more than a dozen highly
diverse political groups, only three of every ten eligible voters turned out. The abstention rate, high even by Colombian standards, was similar in the 1992 municipal
elections.

The Liberal and Conservative machines, with the capability to get supporters to the
polls, continued to dominate the political system. In 1991 the Liberals won 56 of 102
seats in the Senate and 86 of the 161 seats in the Chamber of Representatives. Three
Conservatives factions took 24 seats in the Senate and 44 in the Chamber. The Democratic Alliance M-19, a former guerrilla group, won 10 percent of the vote.

Gaviria sought to reduce drug-related violence and corruption, which have seriously weakened the authority of the state. Medellin cartel leader Pablo Escobar surrendered in 1991 in exchange for a promise of lenient court treatment, and after it was clear the new constitution would ban extradition to the U.S. He ran his operation from a cushy compound until mid-1992, then bribed his way out during a botched attempt to transfer him to a real prison.

Gaviria hoped the new constitution would entice still active guerrilla groups to join the political system. But talks with the Revolutionary Armed Forces of Colombia (FARC) and the National Liberation Army (ELN), the country's two oldest insurgent groups, broke down in 1992. The guerrillas, having raised substantial funds through kidnapping and drug trafficking, unleashed a major offensive. The government, whose approval rating had dropped to less than 20 perecent, installed a state of emergency in December 1992 and unleashed the military against both Escobar and the guerrillas.

By fall 1993 most of Escobar's lieutenants had been captured or killed and the Medellin cartel had fractured into dozens of independent operations headed by a new generation of traffickers. Escobar himself was killed in a shootout with security forces on 2 December. The Cali cartel, in turn, having avoided a direct confrontation with the state, had cemented its status as the largest cocaine and heroin trafficking operation in the hemisphere.

The ELN and the FARC struck back in August 1993 with a terrorist offensive that targeted police, government officials and economic infrastructure, especially oil pipelines. In October, with the campaign for the 1994 elections getting underway, the guerrillas bombed the offices of a dozen congressional and presidential candidates.

When the congress began considering tougher anti-terrorist measures, the ELN declared the body a "military target." In November Senate Vice-President Dario Londono, who was shepherding anti-terrorist laws toward a legislative vote, was murdered. Numerous other prominent political figures received death threats, raising the specter of the 1990 campaign in which hundreds of people—including three presidential candidates—were killed by drug traffickers, left-wing guerrillas, and the military.

Despite heavy security, the campaigns for the 13 March 1994 legislative elections and the 8 May 1994 presidential vote were in full swing by the end of the year. Many candidates were running on anti-corruption platforms as opinion polls showed wide-spread diseffection with politics-as-usual. In 1993 more than a hundred current and former legislators, dozens of municipal officials, and members of the Gaviria government including Gaviria himself had to answer corruption charges.

The presidential frontrunners were Ernesto Samper of the Liberals, who was trying to distance himself from Gaviria, and Conservative Andres Pastrana, the youthful former mayor of Bogota.

Political Rights and Civil Liberties: Citizens are able to change their government through elections. The 1991 constitution provides for much broader participation in the political system, including two reserved seats in the Congress for the country's small Indian minority. It also expands religious freedom by ending the privileges of the Catholic church, which has long enjoyed the advantages of an official religion.

However, constitutional rights regarding free expression and the freedom to organize political parties, civic groups and labor unions are severely restricted by political and drug-related violence and the government's inability to guarantee the security of citizens, institutions and the media. Elections are marked by a high rate of voter abstention because of increased political violence during campaigns and a widespread belief that politics is too corrupt for elections to matter.

Political violence in Colombia continues to take more lives than in any other country in the hemisphere, with nearly twelve killings and disappearances per day. The military and security forces are the most responsible, followed by right-wing paramilitary groups, left-wing guerrillas, drug-traffickers, and hundreds, possibly thousands, of assassins-for-hire. All perpetrators of political violence operate with a high degree of impunity.

Another category of killings is the "social clean-up"—the elimination of drug addicts, street children and other marginal citizens by vigilante groups often linked with the police. Overall, criminal violence results in more than sixty-five murders per day. Despite a new anti-kidnapping law, kidnappings occurred in 1993 at a rate of nearly two per day, about half by left-wing guerrillas.

There are a number of independent human rights organizations, but rights activists, as well as labor, peasant and student organizations, are consistently the targets of violence and intimidation. Dozens of trade unionists were killed in 1993 as Colombia retained its status as the most dangerous country in the world for organized labor.

Over the last decade the entire judicial system has been severely weakened by the onslaught of the drug cartels and generalized political violence. Much of the system has been compromised through corruption and extortion. In the last eight years, more then 300 judges and court personnel as well as a justice minister and an attorney general have been killed.

Under the new constitution, the judiciary, headed by a Supreme Court, was revamped. A U.S.-like adversarial system was adopted and government prosecutors are able to use government security services to investigate crimes. Previously, judges investigated crimes without the help of major law enforcement agencies.

The new measures have brought some success in dealing with common crime, but the judiciary remains overloaded and ill-equipped to handle high-profile drug cases. To protect the judiciary from drug traffickers, the Gaviria government instituted a system of eighty-four "faceless judges." But traffickers are able to penetrate the veil of anonymity and judges remain under threat. Colombia has yet to successfully prosecute a major trafficker. In 1993 it was discovered that the Cali cartel had infiltrated the Attorney General's office.

Upon enactment of the 1991 constitution, the government lifted a state of siege imposed in 1984 in response to drug-related violence. It was hoped that removing the measures would diminish the sense of impunity within the army and security forces. The military, however, was untouched by constitutional reform. No demands were made on spending accountability and mandatory military service was left intact. Moreover, the constitution guarantees that cases involving police and military personnel accused of human rights violations be tried in military rather than civilian courts. In effect, the military and police remain accountable only to themselves. The state of exception in effect through most of 1993, as allowed by the constitution, only reinforced the sense of impunity.

Radio is both public and private. Television remains mostly a government monopoly and news programs tend to be slanted. Moreover, the "right to reply" provision of the new constitution has resulted in harsh judicial tutelage over all media.

The press, including dozens of daily newspapers and weekly magazines, is privately owned. Although no sector of Colombian society has been left untouched, the press has been hit especially hard by the drug-related and political violence. Dozens of journalists have been murdered in the last decade, five in 1993. Numerous others have been kidnapped and nearly every newspaper, radio station and broadcast news program is under constant threat. A number of newspapers have been forced to close their regional offices and a few radio stations have been forced off the air.

Comoros

Polity: Dominant party
Economy: Capitalist
Population: 512,000
PPP: $721
Life Expectancy: 55.0
Ethnic Groups: Majority of mixed African-Arab descent, and East Indian minority
Ratings Change: *Comoros's civil liberties rating changed from 2 to 4 because of elite intrigue, civil unrest and political violence.

Political Rights: 4
Civil Liberties: 4*
Status: Partly Free

Overview:

Political instability and civil unrest dominated the Comoros in 1993, as they have for years. The country experienced a series of revolving door governments as the executive and legislature struggled for power. In February 1993, the streets of Moroni, the capital, exploded. A land dispute escalated into major rioting. Security forces clashed with civilians, but were unable to stop crowds from burning and stoning property. The mobs believed that President Said Mohamed Djohar was taking sides in the land dispute that began the disturbances.

The Comoros, a tiny state consisting of islands in the Indian Ocean off Madagascar, declared independence from France in 1975. The first President, Ahmed Abdallah Abderrahman, served briefly before being ousted in a coup. Abdallah resumed leadership in 1978 after seizing power with the assistance of Colonel Bob Denard, a French mercenary. Abdallah stood for election unopposed in 1978 and 1984, consolidating the power of his one-party regime. He fought off several coup attempts, but was assassinated in 1989, allegedly on Denard's orders. Supreme Court Justice Djohar became interim president and, under French pressure, Denard's mercenaries left the country.

Djohar became President in his own right after winning a two-round presidential election in 1990. Irregularities and allegations of fraud marred that election. First-round winner Mohamed Taki challenged the results, but the Supreme Court validated them. Subsequently, the state charged Taki with complicity in an alleged coup attempt. Under French influence, Taki formed a coalition with Djohar. A national reconciliation conference followed. In December 1991, all Comoran parties acknowledged the legitimacy of Djohar's presidency.

In 1992, there was a series of interim governments, coup attempts, riots and scandals. Djohar sacked Taki as prime minister after the latter hired a French mercenary as an advisor. Oposition demonstrators clashed with security forces in the streets of Moroni in September 1992. Then army mutineers and two sons of former President Abdallah attempted a coup. The government put down the uprising and accused Taki of backing the coup. The court convicted the coup plotters in 1993 and sentenced them to death. After pressure from Amnesty International, President Djohar cancelled the prisoners' executions.

Disturbances and irregularities undermined the two-round legislative election in November 1992. After some rescheduled voting in December, the regime seemed to have a majority. However, on 2 May 1993 parliament voted no confidence in Prime Minister Halidi, by a margin of 23 to 2 with 16 abstentions. On 26 May Djohar appointed Said Ali Mohamed to be Halidi's successor. In June, Djohar dissolved the legislature after a majority introduced a censure motion against the government. Djohar considered this action unconstitutional, but they demanded elections within the constitutionally required forty days. However, the government did not schedule elections until November. Djohar dismissed the premier, and replaced him with Ahmed Ben Cheikh. The president's son-in-law, Mohamed M'Changama, was behind the various rounds of appointments and dismissals throughout 1993.

Disturbed by the number of opposition groups, Djohar made it clear he wanted to reduce the number of parties from twenty-four to three. Reflecting on the Comoran instability, he said to French radio in July, "If the government is dissolved every month or twenty days, it means something is not working." He also declared, "I think that the country is not well-prepared to set up a real democracy."

After the government allegedly gerrymandered legislative districts for the general election, sixteen opposition parties threatened to boycott the vote. They also complained about government stacking of the election commission. Even some pro-Djohar parties complained. Djohar set up his own party, the Movement for Democracy and Renewal, the successor to the Movement for the Triumph of Democracy.

A two-round election, postponed four times and punctuated by fraud and violence, became at least a four-round election 12-29 December. The government won 21 seats to 18 for opposition parties. Three seats remained vacant. Two people died and several were wounded. The opposition pledged to boycott the legislature.

Political Rights and Civil Liberties:

Comorans have a theoretical right to change their government by democratic means, but electoral fraud and irregularities, constant coup attempts and elite intrigues are the factors that really change their governments. Numerous political parties exist, but President Djohar attempts to limit them through political imprisonments and alleged gerrymandering.

There is generally free expression. Foreign media are available. However, security measures taken around coup attempts reduce these freedoms intermittently. The government also bans assemblies sporadically. The frequent civilian riots and army mutinies leave the country with poor civilian-military relations and only spasmodic protection from political terror. Prison conditions are grim. Cells are overcrowded and unsanitary.

Women are somewhat better off in the Comoros than in other Muslim countries. They have both political and property rights. Islam is the state religion. Other faiths may function, but may not proselytize.

The population has only limited economic opportunities. The goods produced by private farms fetch low prices in the world market, and public sector workers are at the mercy of the government's poor finances. Trade unions may exist and workers may strike, but collective bargaining is weak.

Congo

Polity: Presidential-parliamentary democracy (Military-influenced)
Economy: Mixed statist
Population: 2,422,000
PPP: $2,362
Life Expectancy: 53.7
Ethnic Groups: Bakango, Lari, Bembe, M'bochi, Vlli, pygmy, other
Ratings Change: *Congo's political rights rating changed from 3 to 4 and its civil liberties rating from 3 to 4 because of political and ethnic violence.

Political Rights: 4*
Civil Liberties: 4*
Status: Partly Free

Overview:
Disputed legislative elections led to outbreaks of political and ethnic violence that severely tested the democratization process under President Pascal Lissouba of the Pan-African Union for Social Democracy (UPADS).

Ten years after winning independence from France in 1960, the African Republic of the Congo was established as a one-party, Marxist-Leninist state ruled by the Congolese Workers' Party (PCT). Gen. Denis Sassou-Nguesso seized power in a 1979 coup and ruled as both president and PCT chairman until early 1991, when a national conference limited the president's functions. The PCT's rubber-stamp legislature was disbanded and a High Council of the Republic oversaw a one-year transition to multiparty democracy. In 1992, a 125-seat National Assembly was elected. The UPADS won 39 seats; the Congolese Movement for Democracy and Integral Development (MCDDI), 29; the PCT, 19; and two smaller parties split the rest. Then-Prime Minister Andre Milango finished fourth in the first round behind Sassou-Nguesso, who threw his support to Lissouba, allegedly in exchange for immunity from persecution on corruption charges. In the second-round presidential elections, Lissouba received 61 percent, with the MCDDI's Bernard Kolelas garnering 39 percent.

By fall, the PCT joined with a new seven-party coalition, the Union of Democratic Renewal (UDR), to bring down the government of Prime Minister Stephane Maurice Bongho-Nouarra of the pro-Lissouba, 43-party National Alliance for Democracy (AND). With a parliamentary majority of 66, the PCT-UDR bloc demanded that President Lissouba choose a prime minister from its ranks; instead he dissolved the Assembly and called for new elections. After violent protests, a compromise was reached: legislative elections were put off until 1993 and Claude Antoine da Costa was selected to head a government consisting of 60 percent PCT-UDR ministers and 40 percent from the AND.

In early 1993, the PCT-URD accused Prime Minister da Costa of running a parallel government by appointing special advisors to circumvent the opposition-dominated cabinet. The government was angered when the pro-opposition communication minister appointed politicians close to the opposition as directors of official radio and television. Meanwhile, a third political force, the Democratic Center, was created by the merger of six smaller parties.

The first round of voting for the new National Assembly began on 2 May with charges by the opposition of fraud and irregularities that included improper voter registration, incomplete voter lists, and instances of persons voting more than once in the capital, Brazzaville, and in many of the over 2,000 polling stations. There were also charges during the campaign that the members of the presidential guard had broken into a television station to prevent a news broadcast from showing huge PCT-UDR rallies.

On 17 May, the Congolese election commission asked a military and police panel to rule on some disputed results from the first-round election. Four days later, the interior minister announced that 60 pro-Lissouba parties had gained 62 seats, 49 going to the opposition, and that 11 seats required a second round of voting, which was postponed from 23 May to 6 June because of delays in announcing first-round results. The PCT-UDR said it would boycott the second round because of irregularities in round one.

Violence erupted shortly after the second round; a gun-battle near the home of the commerce minister left several dead. There were reports that polling stations and ballot boxes had been destroyed by armed forces belonging to the opposition. Reporters were banned from visiting several polling places. Demonstrations in Brazzaville led to clashes with police.

On 9 June, Gen. Joachim Yhombi-Opango, who led the country from 1977-79 and was head of the pro-Lissouba forces, accused opposition leader Kolelas of instigating violence by calling for "civil disobedience." Three days later, armed opposition supporters in Brazzaville's Bacongo, Makelekele and Talangai areas set up barricades in the streets, ostensibly to protect the homes of Kolelas and former military ruler Sassou-Nguesso. The protests were fueled by a government announcement that the second round of voting had given Lissouba's supporters an overall majority in the Assembly. By mid-June, civil unrest and violence had increased, spreading to the interior of the country. Attempts to set up meetings between the president and opposition failed, and Kolelas said he preferred a "military solution" to the political crisis.

On 23 June, former head of state Gen. Yhombi-Opango was appointed prime minister by the president. In response, the PCT-URD opposition established a parallel government and legislature. Some 50 opposition members boycotted the new National Assembly. The next day, the government barred state radio and television from broadcasting statements by political groups.

In July, the Supreme Court denounced the proclamation of the results of the legislative elections and irregularities in the second round, but made no recommendations. On 7 July, renewed violence led the government to impose a curfew in Brazzaville. By mid-July, the clashes began to take on an ethnic dimension since the country's political parties were divided on ethnic, tribal and regional lines. The fighting pitted Bembe supporters of the president against the Lari people of opposition leader Kolelas. The army also seemed divided, with officers supporting Sassou-Nguesso and other elements supporting the president. Fighting spread to Pointe Noire, an economic center. Each side accused the other of atrocities after badly mutilated corpses were discovered. Meanwhile, the ethnic dimension led 800-1,200 Bembe refugees to flee neighborhood strongholds of the opposition in Brazzaville.

On 16 July the government imposed a fifteen-day state of emergency to put down armed rebellion by opposition forces. The move came after the death toll had left thirty dead, mostly at the hands of armed opposition gangs, and forced 40,000 people to flee their homes.

On 23 July the Organization of African Unity (OAU) appointed a special envoy to the strife-torn country. Three days later, presidential and opposition forces, in an attempt to end the violence, issued a "joint statement" which called for the release of kidnap victims, the disarming of private militias and gangs, and the removal of barricades in Brazzaville. At the same time, Gabon President Omar Bongo sent special representatives to the Congolese capital to mediate the conflict. Negotiations were to take place in Libreville, Gabon's capital. Violence escalated in early August after the government extended the state of emergency for an additional fifteen days.

After five days of meetings in Libreville, all sides agreed to an accord announced 4 August that, among other provisions, confirmed the first round of elections but called for a new round of elections for eleven disputed seats. Sporadic gunfire erupted in Brazzaville as some opposition militants protested their leaders' acceptance of the Libreville Accords. On 17 August the state of emergency was lifted, though the curfew remained in effect in the capital.

On 17 September new elections for the eleven seats were scheduled for 3 October and the curfew was lifted in Brazzaville. Nevertheless, an estimated 15,000 armed opposition militiamen remained in the capital.

The opposition gained seats in the October vote. On 10 October, it was announced that of the eleven seats contested, the Kolelas opposition coalition won eight compared to three by the presidential group.

Tensions erupted again in November when government security forces moved against opposition militia in the Bacango section of the capital. The government maintained that under conditions of the Libreville Accords, opposition militias should have disbanded. The action came after opposition militia kidnapped two top government officials. By 4 November about thirty people had been killed in clashes between militiamen and the army, among them a journalist kidnapped by opposition forces. President Lissouba said that as the democratically elected head of state he was under no obligation to "negotiate" with armed gangs even as opposition forces asked for a dialogue.

By December, fighting had intensified as the death toll climbed to over fifty. On 13 December opposition leader Kolelas, a representative of presidential forces, and the Army chief of staff issued a joint statement appealing for calm. Nevertheless, the French media reported that "ethnic cleansing" operations had begun in Brazzaville as Bembe and Lari people continued to kill each other. In Brazzaville's Mfilou suburbs, journalists reported mounds of decomposing bodies with limbs hacked off. Refugees reported that opposition militiamen painted signs on the homes of Bembe telling them to get out or prepare to die. By the end of the year, government and opposition efforts to restore order were ignored as revenge-killings escalated along ethnic lines.

Political Rights and Civil Liberties: Congolese have the means to change their government democratically, but the second round of legislative elections in 1993 was boycotted by the main opposition coalition and marred by charges of irregularities and violence that left at least thirty dead in June-July. After a new second-round election in October was held without major incidents, a government crackdown on armed opposition militia led to new fighting that quickly degenerated into tribal violence.

The 1991 national conference that launched the democratic transition led to a constitution that called for an independent judiciary, but the judiciary is not wholly free from government interference. The year's violence also brought charges of Army brutality and extrajudicial executions. In August, several members of the opposition were arrested for suspected possession of arms, but all were subsequently released for lack of evidence. In March, police arrested scores of Tuareg tribesmen for "loitering" as part of a campaign to expel illegal immigrants.

The year's violence inhibited freedom of expression. While over sixty political parties and groupings exist, ethnic and tribal tensions made it dangerous for some citizens to proclaim their political affiliation. The presence of armed opposition militia responsible for killings, looting and mayhem also circumscribed the rights of free expression and association in many areas of Brazzaville.

State-run radio and television were run by pro-opposition directors until political tensions increased following the 2 May elections. Service was suspended for several days in May, and the opposition subsequently claimed that it was being denied access. In June, the director of the official Congolese Information Agency was suspended after publishing the names of the opposition's "shadow" government set up after the 6 June voting. During the year, the official media were prevented from publishing party programs or statements. Independent print media faced government and opposition pressure, but there were few reports of official tampering with private publications.

The political and ethnic violence encumbered freedom of movement; tens of thousands were reportedly displaced. There are no serious restrictions of freedom to worship, and many denominations are represented in government and other social institutions.

Tribal violence impinged on ethnic and minority rights. Lari-Bembe conflicts caused scores of deaths, mutilations, kidnappings, and expulsions. Northern Pygmies face discrimination, particularly in employment, where they are often exploited and underpaid. International organizations have characterized some as living in virtual slavery. Pygmies are excluded from government positions.

While sex discrimination is officially banned, discrimination against women in terms of employment and education is endemic. Adultery is considered illegal for women, but not for men, and male polygamy is accepted. Wife-beating is an accepted practice. Nonetheless, there are some positive developments, including pay equity and job opportunities, particularly in the white-collar and government sectors.

The Congolese Trade Union Confederation remains a powerful force, and there are small, competing unions as well.

Costa Rica

Polity: Presidential-
legislative democracy
Economy: Capitalist-
statist
Population: 3,270,000
PPP: $4,542
Life Expectancy: 74.9
Ethnic Groups: Spanish with mestizo minority

Political Rights: 1
Civil Liberties: 2*
Status: Free

Ratings Change: *Costa Rica's civil liberties rating changed from 1 to
2 as a result of modifications in methodology. See "Survey Methodology," page 671.

Overview:

Opinion polls in fall 1993 showed Jose Maria Figueres of the
opposition National Liberation Party (PLN) with an edge over
Miguel Angel Rodriguez of the incumbent Social Christian
Unity Party (PUSC) in the campaign for the 6 February 1994 presidential election. Both
candidates were running against controversial pasts as much as each other.

Costa Rica achieved independence from Spain in 1821 and became a republic in
1848. Democratic constitutional government was instituted in 1899 and briefly
interrupted in 1917 and 1948. The 1949 constitution, which bans the formation of a
national army, has been the framework for democratic governance ever since.

The constitution provides for three independent branches of government—
executive, legislative and judicial. The president and the fifty-seven-member Legislative Assembly are elected for four years and are prohibited from succeeding themselves. The Assembly has co-equal power, including the ability to override presidential
vetoes.

President Rafael A. Calderon Jr. of the conservative PUSC defeated Carlos Manuel
Castillo of the social democratic PLN in the 1990 election following primary elections
in both parties. The PLN was tainted by charges of drug trade connections among party
officials. A number of PLN officials resigned from party positions following reports of
involvement issued by a special Assembly commission. The campaign was marked by
mutual accusations of corruption and illegal campaign funding.

Nearly 80 percent of the electorate went to the polls in 1990. Calderon took 51.4
percent of the vote against 47.3 percent for Castillo. Exit polls showed many voters had
turned away from the PLN because they feared an excessive concentration of power in
one party. The PLN had held the presidency for two straight terms, and sixteen out of
the previous twenty years.

In the Assembly the PUSC won 29 seats, the PLN 25. The three remaining
seats were won by the left-wing Pueblo Unido party, the Cartagines Agricultural
Union, and the Generalena Union. The PUSC won a majority of the 81 municipal
district races.

Calderon implemented a structural adjustment program to reduce a widening public
sector deficit and a mounting foreign debt. The program received high marks from
international creditors and private economists, but provoked a widespread backlash,

including a series of public-sector labor strikes, from a population used to some of the best social services in Latin America.

In the 1993 PUSC primary election, businessman and legislator Miguel Angel Rodriguez defeated Juan Jose Trejos for the presidential nomination. In the fierce six-person PLN primary, Jose Maria Figueres prevailed with 57 percent of the vote. The thirty-eight-year-old Figueres is the son of former President Jose "Pepe" Figueres, a national hero for leading the fight to preserve democracy in the 1948 civil war.

Throughout 1993 young Figueres contended with charges that as a policeman in 1973 he was involved in the murder of a drug dealer. He dismissed the allegations, but his attempts to block further investigation created intense friction within the PLN during the primary. Figueres also was implicated in a scandal dating back a decade in which foreign investors lost their money. By fall 1993 it was unclear whether his candidacy would get full party backing.

Rodriguez, in turn, was dogged by corruption charges—that he sold unsafe meat to the U.S., illegally imported cattle, and used his influence as a legislator to further the interests of his brewery. Rodriguez denied the allegations and countered that he too was being smeared.

Figueres, despite the taint of scandal, was leading Rodriguez in the opinion polls in fall 1993 by as much as seven percentage points. Rodriguez was trying to respond to fears of economic insecurity with a promise to launch a "social adjustment program" if elected. But Figueres, as the PLN leader in the legislature, was heading the opposition to the Calderon government's unpopular economic policies. His high profile and the mystique of his late father appeared to have won him strong support among the poor and middle classes.

Political Rights and Civil Liberties:

Citizens are able to change their government, at both the national and local levels, through free and fair elections. In fall 1993, and for the eleventh time since 1949, the executive branch turned control of the police over to the independent electoral commission for the duration of the election period. Although the political landscape is dominated by the PLN and the PUSC, more than a dozen other parties run candidates in presidential, legislative and local races.

Numerous allegations implicating both major parties in drug-tainted campaign contributions were made during the 1990 election. New campaign laws have since been instituted to make party financing more transparent. Nonetheless, Costa Rica remains an easy target for drug traffickers because it has no army, navy or air force.

Constitutional guarantees regarding freedom of religion and the right to organize political parties and civic organizations are respected. However, in recent years there has been a reluctance to address restrictions on labor rights and mounting threats to press and media freedom.

The Calderon government has supported Solidarity, a forty-year-old employer-employee organization that private business has used as an instrument to prevent independent unions from organizing in the private sector. Private business has virtually made Solidarity membership a requirement for employment, while it has fired hundreds of workers who tried to form independent unions. The government, under pressure from the International Labor Organization and the International Confederation of Free Trade Unions, promised in 1991 to change labor laws to conform to international standards regarding the freedom to organize and bargain collectively. A new and greatly improved labor code was passed finally at the end of 1993 after the U.S. threatened to remove Costa Rica's trading privileges.

Labor abuses by multinational corporations operating in the *maquilas*, or free trade zones, are prevalent. Minimum wage and social security laws are frequently ignored and the fines for non-compliance are minuscule. Women maquila workers frequently suffer sexual harassment, are often worked overtime without pay, and fired when they become pregnant.

The press, radio and television are generally free. There are a number of independent dailies and weeklies serving a society that is 90 percent literate. Television and radio stations are both public and commercial, with at least six private television stations providing an influential forum for public debate. However, freedom of expression is marred by a twenty-two-year-old licensing requirement for journalists. A 1985 Inter-American Human Rights Court ruling determined that licensing of journalists is incompatible with the American Convention on Human Rights.

Moreover, there have been a number of alarming incidents in recent years involving censorship. Humberto Arce, editor of the daily *La Republica*, alleges he was fired in June 1993 because of political pressure exerted by supporters of PLN presidential candidate Jose Maria Figueres. The paper denied the charge. Arce, backed by most of the nation's journalists, a number of whom reported incidents of intimidation by Figueres backers, initiated a lawsuit. In another incident the Supreme Court ordered a state-run television channel to reinstate a talk-show host who had been summarily fired for trying to air a program on the government's solid-waste disposal program.

The judicial branch is independent. Its members are elected by the legislature. However, because of criticism that the judiciary was becoming over-politicized, the legislature passed new laws in 1993 to guarantee selection of judges based more on experience and ability. There is a Supreme Court with power to rule on the constitutionality of legislation, as well as four courts of appeal and a network of district courts. The members of the national election commission are elected by the Supreme Court.

The judicial system has been marked by delays in the hearing of cases, creating a volatile situation in overcrowded prisons and increased inmate violence. The root of the problem appears to be budget cutbacks affecting the judiciary and the nation's economic slump, which has led to a rise in violent crime and clashes in the countryside between squatters and landowners.

In recent years the judiciary has been called upon to address unprecedented charges of human rights violations made by the independent Costa Rican Human Rights Commission and other rights activists. A number of cases, including allegations of arbitrary arrests and accusations of brutality and torture in secret jails, have been made against police units, leading to the formation of a special legislative commission to investigate rights violations. In 1993 the government established an official ombudsman as a recourse for citizens or foreigners with human rights complaints. The ombudsman has the authority to issue recommendations for rectification, including sanctions against government bodies, for failure to respect rights.

The murder of two suspected drug traffickers by police in February 1992 added to an ongoing controversy over the large amounts of military training the nation's various police branches have received in the last decade. In 1993 a legislative commission was working on a proposal to reorganize the police under one ministry, with minimum standards for hiring police within a civil service structure that allows for "eminently civilian training."

Croatia

Polity: Presidential-par- **Political Rights:** 4
liamentary democracy **Civil Liberties:** 4
(partly foreign occupied) **Status:** Partly Free
Economy: Mixed-
statist
Population: 4,427,000
PPP: na
Life Expectancy: 70.0
Ethnic Groups: Croats (77 percent), Serbs (12.2 percent),
Muslims (1 percent), Hungarians, Slovenes, Czechs, Albanians,
Montenegrins, Ukrainians, others

Overview: **R**enewed outbreaks of fighting in Serb-controlled areas,
polarization in the ruling Croatian Democratic Union (HDZ),
charges of increased authoritarianism, economic stagnation
and hostilities between Bosnian Croats and their erstwhile Muslim allies were among
key issues facing President Franjo Tudjman in 1993.

From the twelfth century until after World War I, most of what is Croatia was ruled
by Hungary. In 1918, it became part of the Kingdom of Serbs, Croats and Slovenes,
renamed Yugoslavia in 1929. Following the Nazi invasion in 1941, a short-lived
independent state was proclaimed by the *Ustasa* movement, an indigenous fascist group
that oversaw the massacre of thousands of Serbs. In 1945, Croatia became one of the
six constituent republics of the Federal People's Republic of Yugoslavia under former
Communist partisan leader Josip Broz (Tito).

On 25 June 1991, Croatia and Slovenia declared independence from an unraveling
Yugoslav federation. Within a month, forces of the Serb-dominated Yugoslav People's
Army (YPA) backed by armed Serb militias seized large parts of Croatia. By year's
end, Serbs controlled about one-third of the country and declared an autonomous
region, the Krajina Serbian Republic (RSK). The fighting killed over 10,000 and left
700,000 displaced. In December, all sides agreed to the deployment of U.N. peacekeeping troops (UNPROFOR) in three regions with predominantly Serb populations. In
1992, Croatia accused the 16,000-strong U.N. forces of maintaining the status quo of
Serb dominance by failing to disarm as many as 16,000 Serb paramilitary forces,
confiscate heavy weapons and repatriate refugees. Meanwhile, Serb forces continued
"ethnic cleansing" in areas under their control. In 2 August presidential elections,
President Tudjman won 56.73 percent of the vote, followed by Drazen Budisa of the
Croatian Social-Liberal Party (HSLS), 21.87 percent; and Slava Dabcevic-Kucar of the
Croatian People's Party (HNS), 6.02 percent. Finishing fourth with 5.4 percent of the
vote was Dobroslav Paraga of the neo-fascist Croatian Party of Rights (HSP), named
for the far-right party that produced the *Ustasa*.

On 22 January 1993, one month before the UNPROFOR mandate was due to
expire, Croatian forces penetrated U.N. peacekeeping lines and launched an offensive in
Krajina. The objective was to establish a new ceasefire line 20 km southeast of the
existing line, threaten the Serb's Krajina "capital" of Knin, secure and eventually

rebuild the Maslenica bridge connecting Zagreb, the capital, and inland Croatia with Split, Dubrovnik and the rest of the Dalmatian coast.

Three days later, U.N. Security Council Resolution 802 called on Zagreb to withdraw its forces behind the original ceasefire line. President Tudjman announced Croatian troops would withdraw only after Croatian police had taken over the areas and when Serb militias had returned the heavy artillery looted from U.N.-supervised stores. After six days, the Serbs launched a counter-offensive and detained U.N. officials, leading France and Britain to dispatch naval vessels in the Adriatic in case U.N. forces had to be protected or evacuated. Russia, Germany and others threatened Croatia with sanctions.

President Tudjman's strategy helped the HDZ in 7 February regional elections for a new Upper House of Districts, a largely rubber-stamp body, and over 8,000 county and town councils. Despite declining popularity due to deteriorating economic conditions, the HDZ took nearly two-thirds of the seats in the upper house and did well in local and municipal elections in areas of Dalmatia and elsewhere most directly affected by the war.

By late February, when it became clear that Serbia was not prepared to aid the Krajina Serbs militarily and after Krajina Serb leader Milan Babic was temporarily ousted by the RSK Assembly, Babic accepted U.N. peacekeeping forces to monitor parts of Croatia that were home to about 600,000 Serbs until refugees fled the civil war. Croatia agreed to extend the UNPROFOR mandate with some conditions.

On 29 March, President Tudjman accepted the resignation of the seven-month-old government of Prime Minister Hrvoje Sarinic. The resignations appeared designed to placate popular anger over a series of financial scandals that many felt underscored the broader problem of the emergence of a new corrupt HDZ-based nomenklatura. The government was also unpopular because of a 2,300 percent annual inflation rate that had reduced much of the population to near-poverty levels, massive power cuts in Dalmatia that crippled industry and the once lucrative tourist trade, and what was often perceived as a high-handed style of ruling that had left unions without a voice in some key social programs and led to the muzzling of the press.

In early April, new Prime Minister Nikcia Valentic vowed to reinvigorate the economy by launching a massive public works program to repair infrastructure. He also seemed to suggest that regional districts would be effectively subordinated to the federal government.

On 6 April, Croatia and rebel Serbs from the self-styled RSK signed a ceasefire in Geneva ending two months of conflict in the disputed enclave. Under the accord, Croatian forces agreed to withdraw behind the 1992 ceasefire line, while the Serbs would return heavy weapons to U.N. control, and ethnically mixed "pink zones" previously policed by the Serbs would also be placed under U.N. control. Nevertheless, sporadic, and at times intense fighting and shelling continued through much of the year.

Meanwhile, rifts were threatening the HDZ, with the nationalist, right-wing faction led by Deputy Prime Minister Vladimir Seks squaring off against the "liberal" wing led by former Yugoslav president and Parliament Speaker Stipe Mesic. An independent poll indicated that the "liberal" faction would attract three times more voters than the conservative wing.

In May, the uneasy alliance between Bosnian Muslims and Croats collapsed with fierce fighting in the Bosnian city of Mostar. Appalled by the carnage and images of thousands of Muslims being herded into detention camps, the European Community

(EC) and the U.N. threatened sanctions against Croatia despite President Tudjman's improbable assertions that his government had little control over Bosnian Croats. The fighting rekindled long-held speculation that Serbia and Croatia planned to carve up Bosnia-Herzegovina. Croatians hoped to "cleanse" Mostar of Muslims as part of a drive to consolidate a mini-republic of Herzeg-Bosna in south-central Bosnia. In June, President Tudjman announced in Geneva after meetings with Serbian President Slobodan Milosevic and Bosnia-Herzegovina President Alija Izetbegovic that Croatia and Serbia agreed to make a joint Bosnian peace proposal which would divide the country into three ethnic states with a federal or confederal constitution. The proposal, a departure from the Vance-Owen peace plan, was ultimately rejected, and by June Bosnian Muslims regained some territory won earlier by Croats.

Back in Croatia, Serbs planned an internationally condemned referendum on joining the RSK with a Bosnian Serb "state." The two-day vote on 19-20 June was held in Croatia's four U.N. peacekeeping zones and was meant partly to put pressure on Milosevic not to deal away Krajina in any negotiations. As expected, a majority voted for the measure, but Bosnian Serb leaders said any plans for unification were "premature."

The Croat-Muslim fighting in Bosnia led to repression of Muslims in Croatia. Bosnian Muslims were evicted from refugee centers, the Croatian police harassed Muslims, while others were forcibly conscripted into the Croatian Army.

In July, escalation was avoided in Krajina when Croats abandoned plans to rebuild the Maslenica bridge and both sides agreed to let U.N. troops move into the area and take control of the bridge and airport. However, by the end of the month, the Croats reneged on the 16 July agreement and refused to withdraw troops until Serbs placed their heavy weapons under U.N. control, a condition not in the original accord. The Croats maintained that the condition was part of U.N. Security Resolution 802. On 1 August, Serb artillery resumed firing shells near the Maslenica bridge.

Political opposition to President Tudjman's authoritarian ruling style continued to grow. On 27 July, fifteen leaders of all major parties met to discuss the need to reverse some key policies, particularly regarding the partition of Bosnia. In a subsequent declaration, the leaders protested the HDZ's total domination of the government and the policy of cooperating with the Serbs in Bosnia. The opposition demanded a greater say "in all strategic decisions," and threatened to walk out of parliament if the government continued its "autocratic fashion."

On 9-10 September, Croatian forces crossed a U.N. demarcation line and captured three villages in some of the fiercest fighting in two years. Serb fighters banned U.N. peacekeepers from entering the combat area in Krajina and shelled Kalovac, thirty miles south of Zagreb. On 12 September, rebel Serbs launched rocket attacks just outside the Croatian capital and listed fifty possible military targets. President Tudjman ordered his forces to halt the offensive for twenty-four hours during which he proposed that the two sides work out a ceasefire. On 15 September, under a U.N.-sponsored truce, 500 Canadian and French U.N. troops were deployed in dangerously exposed buffer zones along the confrontation lines around Gospic. The offensive, which included atrocities against Serb civilians, was seen by many as President Tudjman's response to increased pressure from tens of thousands of refugees because of lack of progress in regaining Serb-held territories. It also put pressure on the U.N. to change the UNPROFOR mandate that expired at the end of the month.

On 4 October, the U.N. Security Council approved Resolution 871 extending the mandate of more than 20,000 peacekeepers in the former Yugoslavia, including 12,600 in Croatia. The convoluted wording of the resolution warned Serbia to stop its interference in the internal affairs of Croatia, though it stopped short of Croatian demands for a tougher measure.

On 6 October, three opposition parties, including the HSLS, walked out of Parliament because of what they said was the HDZ's refusal to deal with proposed legislation to promote freedom in the media by liberalizing television and radio laws. The HSLS was joined by autonomist parties from Istria and Dalmatia (DA). The DA recalled President Tudjman's 24 September speech in which he effectively called the regional parties enemies of the state, and a mysterious explosion at the DA's Split headquarters.

President Tudjman responded on 12 October by reshuffling the cabinet on the recommendation of Prime Minister Valentic. The changes effected primarily the economics, health and social fields, which were the focus of increased public discontent amid rising inflation, a declining standard of living, and a new government austerity package. Four days later, the second HDZ convention overwhelmingly re-elected Tudjman as party president. He reaffirmed his role as the premier political force by leaning on right-wing hardliners to withdraw their candidacies for the HDZ executive body in favor of moderates.

In December, Croatian and international human rights groups reported the government had forced thousands of its enemies from their homes and from the country. The actions were directed mostly against Serbs, who once constituted a sizable minority, but also against Croats opposed to President Tudjman's rule. Over 10,000 homes were reportedly blown up or razed, and about 280,000 Croatian Serbs fled the country as a result of the campaign.

The end of the year also saw disputed "presidential" elections in the RSK. After Milan Babic announced victory, challenger Milan Martic, the RSK interior minister, complained of irregularities and vote-rigging. The elections were eventually nullified.

Political Rights and Civil Liberties: The citizens of Croatia have the means to change their government democratically, but a constitutionally strong presidency and repressive measures have left President Franjo Tudjman as absolute leader. While there is a prime minister heading a cabinet, critical decisions are made in the name of the National Security Council, a sixteen-member body packed with the president's supporters, including his son. The HDZ-dominated parliament is largely a rubber stamp. With the absence of a coordinated opposition, the HDZ—though factionalized—remains the principle political organization in the country.

The fact that one-third of the country remains in the control of rebel Serbs has also placed limits on free political expression and such things as the right to vote.

Opposition parties are allowed to organize, but the government repressed dissent in several cases in 1993. In June, four leaders of the right-wing Croatian Party of Rights (HSP) went before a military court charged with "inciting forceful change of the constitutional order of Croatia." In July, police raided HSP headquarters maintaining that the party did not have a proper deed for the property. In October, several members of a separatist party in Dalmatia (DA) were detained by police.

The judiciary is not wholly free from government interference. The power of judicial appointments and dismissals is firmly in the hands of an influential parliamentary committee dominated by the right-wing of the HDZ. Paradoxically, the 1990 constitution provides guarantees for judicial independence, including a Judicial Council of Judges (yet to be appointed) responsible for disciplining, removing and appointing judges.

The government remains in strict control of radio and television, effectively denying access to the opposition. Newspapers have also faced repressive measures. On 8 March, journalists at *Slobodna Dalmacija* went on strike to protest a government decision to impose a new editorial board on the newspaper. Three days later, the new government-imposed board dismissed a number of leading editors and writers. The formerly independent magazine *Danas* was similarly taken over in 1992. The system of state-owned newsstands has also kept independent journals from the public. In April, UNPROFOR charged the government with censoring U.N. broadcasts.

The record of guaranteeing the rights of Serbs and other minorities has been spotty. Croatian and international human rights organization alleged that thousands of Serbian homes were burned or razed. Serb parties are allowed to exist and are represented in parliament. However, some Serbs have been denied citizenship, without which they cannot own property. Another ethnic issue concerned autonomy demands by Istria, the small peninsula at the top of the Adriatic just east of Trieste that went from Italian to Yugoslav control in 1945. Some 30,000 ethnic Italians and 250,000 Croatians, Slovenes and some Serbs live there. In February's regional and local elections, the Istrian Democratic Party (DDI) achieved a 73 percent landslide victory over the HDZ, which charged the DDI with being a secessionist movement. New laws from Zagreb threaten Italian schools and cultural institutions, leading Istrians to seek greater regional autonomy.

The disintegration of the Croat-Muslim alliance in Bosnia led to actions against 350,000 Muslim refugees and other Muslims in Croatia. The U.N. High Commissioner for Refugees (UNHCR) reported expulsions, forcible conscription and harassment, some of it fueled by one-sided Croatian television coverage of the Croat-Muslim fighting in Bosnia.

The resurgence of fighting along the border of Krajina led to atrocities against civilians by both Serb and Croat forces. The realities of war have also restricted freedom of movement in the country. While freedom of religion is nominally assured, Roman Catholic Croats were persecuted or expelled from Serb-controlled areas, and Orthodox Serbs suffered at the hands of Croats.

In July there was a split in the trade union movement. One side was the Croatian Unified Trade Union (HUS) and the Coordinating Committee of Croatian White-Collar Trade Unions, and on the other a coalition patched together from the Federation of the Independent Trade Unions of Croatia, the Confederation of the Independent Trade Unions of Croatia and the Union of Trade Unions of Public Employees (MSJD). The conflict emerged around negotiations with the government on wages and salaries.

Cuba

Polity: Communist
one-party
Economy: Statist
Population: 10,957,000
PPP: $2,200
Life Expectancy: 75.4

Political Rights: 7
Civil Liberties: 7
Status: Not Free

Ethnic Groups: Caucasian (estimated 40-45 percent), and black
and mulatto (estimated 55-60 percent)

Overview: It appeared unlikely that Fidel Castro's limited, China-style
economic reforms could save a dying economy that had con-
tracted by nearly 50 percent since 1989. With Cubans enduring
a diet of deprivation and repression, European and Latin American governments implored
Castro to open the political system to avert violent upheaval. He rebuffed their counsel.

Cuba achieved independence from Spain in 1898 as a result of the Spanish-
American War. The Republic of Cuba was established in 1902, remaining subject to
U.S. tutelage under the Platt Amendment until 1934. On 1 January 1959 Castro's
guerrillas overthrew the dictatorship of Fulgencio Batista, who had ruled for eighteen of
the preceding twenty-five years.

Since 1959 Castro has dominated the Cuban political system, transforming it into a
one-party Communist state. Communist structures were institutionalized by the 1975
constitution installed at the first congress of the Cuban Communist Party (PCC). The
constitution provides for a National Assembly which, in theory, designates a Council of
State which, in turn, appoints a Council of Ministers in consultation with its president
who serves as head of state and chief of government. In reality, Castro is responsible for
every appointment. As president of the Council of Ministers, chairman of the Council
of State, commander-in-chief of the Revolutionary Armed Forces (FAR) and the first
secretary of the PCC, Castro controls every lever of power in Cuba. The PCC is the
only authorized political party and it controls all governmental entities from the national
to the municipal level. All political activity outside the PCC is outlawed.

After the collapse of the Eastern bloc, Castro reaffirmed Cuba's adherence to
Marxism-Leninism and made "Socialism or death" the official slogan. In 1990 he
announced that Cuba was entering a "special period in peacetime," meaning a drastic
austerity program involving severe cutbacks in energy consumption and tighter
rationing of food and consumer items.

The dissolution of the Soviet Union ended Castro's last hope that he would not be
cast adrift. In deals with former Soviet republics Cuba has been able to reconstitute only
about one quarter of its lost trade. International credits have dried up because Cuba
cannot service it $6 billion debt with Western lenders. At the fourth PCC congress in
1991 Castro rejected pluralist democracy as "complete rubbish" and Communist rule
was reconfirmed. The PCC Politburo was expanded to include younger members, but
the result was a further concentration of people loyal to Castro. The congress gave
priority to wooing foreign investment and development of the tourist trade.

In 1992 Castro oversaw a series of constitutional revisions. Castro now heads a newly created National Defense Council, whose mission is to "direct the nation in conditions of a state of war, during the war, or general mobilization or a state of emergency." That freed Castro from having to make time-consuming explanations to the PCC apparatus and gave him greater ability to foil any possible concentration of discontented officers in the military.

The establishment, in principle, of direct elections to the National Assembly was designed mostly to convince Spain and Latin America that Cuba was open to political reform and therefore deserving of greater economic cooperation. But little aid was forthcoming in 1993. Rather, European and Latin governments, led by Spain and Colombia, pressed Castro to open the political system to avoid a violent breakdown of his regime. But Castro was having none of it, apparently believing he could maintain his grip through the Single Vigilance and Protection System installed in 1992. The system coordinates the military, the police and the neighborhood Committees for the Defense of the Revolution.

In mid-1993, with Cuba on the verge of devolving into a pre-industrial society, Castro announced a series of economic reforms—legalization of the U.S. dollar and an increase in the number of Cuban exiles allowed to visit the island. The aim was to increase hard currency flows, but the measures appeared to heighten social tensions as those with access to dollars from abroad began emerging as a new monied class. Moreover, there were indications of mounting resentment in the 150,000-member armed forces who were left out of the dollar reforms.

In late summer a number of protests, including riots and looting, took place during the nightly electricity blackouts. These incidents prompted a state security crackdown. According to military defectors, armed forces chief of staff Gen. Ulises Rosales del Toro issued a statement to all military bases in September, saying that if necessary the military would "move on to rifles and tanks" against those opposing the regime.

In October the government announced reforms emphasizing foreign investment in state enterprises and allowing limited private and cooperative farming. A month later Castro denied that such measures meant Cuba was resorting to capitalism, stating that "Cuba will never renounce Marxist principles." The question remained whether limited reforms amid widespread deprivation would unleash forces in Cuban society beyond Castro's control.

Political Rights and Civil Liberties:

Cubans are unable to change their government through democratic means. All political and civic organization outside the PCC is illegal. Political dissent, spoken or written, is a punishable offense. The elections for the National Assembly held in 1993 were totally controlled by the state, with only candidates that supported the regime allowed to participate.

With the possible exception of South Africa, Indonesia and China, Cuba under Castro has had more political prisoners per capita for longer periods than any other country. In 1993 there were an estimated 500 to 2,000 political prisoners, most of them locked in with common criminals. Numbers could not be confirmed because no international human rights monitors have been allowed on the island since 1988. Since 1991 the U.N. has voted annually to assign a special investigator on human rights in Cuba, but the Cuban government has refused to cooperate.

The educational system, the judicial system, labor unions, professional organizations, cultural groups and all media are tightly controlled by the state. Outside of the Catholic church, whose scope remains limited by the government, there is no semblance of independent civil society. Members of four small labor groups that have tried to organize independently were subject to repression and torture during detention in 1993.

Since December 1992 Cuba's community of human rights activists and dissidents has been subject to particularly severe crackdowns. Hundreds of human rights activists and dissidents have been jailed or placed under house arrest. The more prominent are occasionally released when Castro, hunting for foreign economic aid, wants to deflect international criticism. Activists are frequently assaulted in the streets and in their homes by plainclothes police and the "rapid action brigades," mobs organized by state security, often through the Committees for the Defense of the Revolution (CDRs). Workers who attempt to organize independent unions are subject to firings, beatings and arrest. Nonetheless, rights and opposition groups continue to mushroom, with possibly as many as one hundred existing in 1993.

There is continued evidence of torture and killings in prisons and in psychiatric institutions, where a number of the dissidents arrested in recent years have been incarcerated. Since 1990 the International Committee of the Red Cross has been denied access to prisoners. According to Cuban rights activists, more than one hundred prisons and prison camps hold between 60,000 to 100,000 prisoners of all categories. In 1993 vandalism was decreed to be a form of sabotage, punishable by eight years in prison. Men and women infected with the HIV virus are subject to compulsory medical quarantine, making Cuba's AIDS policy the most repressive in the world.

Freedom of movement and freedom to choose one's residence, education or job are restricted. Attempting to leave the island without permission is a punishable offense and crackdowns were severe in 1993. Noted Cuban writer Norberto Fuentes was jailed after trying to leave clandestinely, then released after twenty days pending trial. There were a number of incidents in which Cuban marine patrols threw grenades and shot at swimmers trying to reach the U.S. naval base at Guantanamo Bay. At least three people were killed in July when security forces opened fire on people trying to swim to a U.S. registered speedboat that had come for them.

Official discrimination against religious believers was lifted by constitutional revision in mid-1992. The measure was welcomed by the Catholic church, which has seen an increase in membership in recent years. However, it was not clear that discrimination had actually ended in practice. In September 1993 the Catholic Bishops Conferences issued its most critical pastoral in three decades. Publicly backed by the Pope, the letter called for an end to one-party rule and the state security system. The government's response: blistering attacks in the state-controlled media.

As has been evident during the trials of human rights activists and other dissidents, due process is alien to the Cuban judicial system. The job of defense attorneys registered by the courts is to guide defendants in their confessions.

The government has continued restricting the ability of foreign media to operate in Cuba. Journalist visas are required and reporters whom the government considers hostile are not allowed entry. Foreign journalists interviewing dissidents risk being detained, expelled or beaten up. In 1993 *Miami Herald* reporter Mary Speck was expelled and her notebooks confiscated after she entered Cuba on a tourist visa.

Cyprus (Greek)

Polity: Presidential-
legislative democ-
racy
Economy: Capitalist
Population: Entire island: 717,000, Greeks: 574,000
PPP: $9,953 (sector not specified)
Life Expectancy: 76.2
Ethnic Groups: Greek majority, Turkish minority, and
small Maronite, Armenian, and Latin communities

Political Rights: 1
Civil Liberties: 1
Status: Free

Overview:
In February 1993, voters elected Glafkos Clerides of the
Democratic Rally (DISY) as Cypriot president. Clerides
defeated the incumbent president George Vassilliou, an
independent. In other developments, the U.N.-sponsored talks with the representatives
of the Turkish Republic of Northern Cyprus (TRNC) were suspended after the two
groups failed to make any progress toward the reunification of the two communities.

Cyprus gained independence from British colonial rule in 1960. Since independence, the country has been plagued by tensions and sporadic violence between the
Greeks and Turkish Cypriots. The U.N. established a 2,000-member peacekeeping
force in 1964. Responding to an unsuccessful coup attempt aimed at unifying Cyprus
with Greece, Turkey invaded in 1974 and occupied the northern portion of the island,
installing 35,000 troops. As a consequence of the invasion, approximately 200,000
Greek Cypriots were forced to flee their homes and settle in the south of the island. In
1983, the Turkish Cypriots declared independence, a move condemned by the U.N.

No candidate won outright in the first round of presidential elections on 7 February
1993, the incumbent President Vassiliou receiving slightly more than 44 percent of the
vote. Vassiliou, running as an independent, was supported by the Communist Progressive Party of the Working People (AKEL) and by the small leftist Democratic Socialist
Renewal Movement (ADISOK). Glafkos Clerides of the conservative Democratic
Rally (DISY) placed second in round one with almost 37 percent of the vote. The third
candidate, Paschalis Pascalides with support from the centrist Democratic Party (DIKO)
and the leftist Fighting Front, received 19 percent of the vote. In the second round
Clerides received slightly more than half the votes, defeating Vassiliou. The president is
elected for a five-year term and appoints his own cabinet.

With the economy booming, the central issue during the campaign was the
candidates' attitude toward the U.N. secretary general's "set of ideas" for peaceful
reunification of the Greek and Turkish parts of the island. The proposal, presented in
1992, sought to unite both communities on a federal basis which would guarantee each
of them wide-ranging autonomy in conducting their communal affairs. The proposal
advocated the return of an extended territory under the Turkish control to Greek Cypriot
administration. Vassiliou accepted the proposal but the TRNC president Rauf Denktash
countered with new demands to safeguard the Turkish Cypriot interests.

The organizations representing the Greek Cypriot refugees from the north, accused
Vassiliou of betraying their interests by not addressing the issues of their return to their

homes. In his electoral campaign, Clerides promised to insist on radical changes to key clauses of the "set of ideas."

The U.N.-sponsored talks reconvened in New York on 24 May, but were soon dogged by accusations that Denktash was unprepared to discuss on the basis of the "set of ideas." Following a recess in mid-June, Denktash described the proposal as biased in favor of Greek-Cypriots and said that basic changes were necessary before the talks could continue.

Political Rights and Civil Liberties: Greek Cypriots can change their government democratically. Suffrage is universal and compulsory, and elections are free and fair.

The judiciary is independent and continues to operate under the tradition of the British legal system, including the presumption of innocence and the right to due process. Cases are usually tried before a judge, although a request for trial by jury is usually granted.

Freedom of speech and press is respected. There is a proliferation of independent and party-affiliated newspapers and periodicals. Since 1990, in addition to government-owned radio stations, several independent ones are allowed to operate. In 1992, the first independent television station began to broadcast. In addition, cable services from around the world are available throughout the island.

Freedom of assembly and association is respected. Workers have the right to strike, and most of the labor force belongs to independent trade unions. Due to the high economic growth rates in recent years and the concomitant labor shortage, the government relaxed the issuance of work permits to foreign workers, who often work below the level of Greek Cypriot wages.

Freedom of movement for the residents is respected, with the exception of traveling to the north, which is discouraged if it involves filling out entry cards issued with the TRNC inscription.

The Greek Orthodox Church has the character of a state institution; all its property and activities are exempt from taxation, and the Church wields a considerable influence on the direction of public policy. However, freedom of worship is respected, and other religious groups are allowed to operate.

Czech Republic

Polity: Presidential parliamentary democracy
Economy: Statist (transitional)
Population: 10,302,000
PPP: na
Life Expectancy: na
Ethnic Groups: Czechs (94 percent), Slovaks (4 percent), Roma (2 percent)

Political Rights: 1
Civil Liberties: 2
Status: Free

Overview: After the "velvet divorce" officially dissolved the seventy-four-year-old Czech-Slovak union on 1 January, Prime Minister Vaclav Klaus and the ruling Civic Democratic Party

(ODS)-led, four-party coalition government faced a nagging economic recession, relations with the newly independent Slovak Republic, and integration into European economic and military structures.

Czechoslovakia was created in 1918 with the collapse of the Austro-Hungarian empires. Until then, Czechs and Slovaks existed separately for a millennium. The Czechs had their own state—the Kingdom of Bohemia—which experienced periods of independence and subjugation by Austria and Germany. The Slovaks endured a long history of Hungarian rule. Soviet troops helped establish the Communist People's Republic of Czechoslovakia in 1948, a one-party dictatorship renamed the Czechoslovak Socialist Republic in 1960. In 1968, after Soviet tanks crushed the so-called "Prague Spring" led by reformist leader Alexander Dubcek, it became one of the East Bloc's most repressive regimes. In November 1989, however, the government was forced to negotiate with the grass-roots oppositionist Civic Forum led by playwright and former political prisoner Vaclav Havel. The so-called "velvet revolution" peacefully ended forty-one years of Communist rule.

By 1992, strains between the country's two constituent republics worsened over such issues as the pace and scope of reform, disproportionate Western investment in the Czech republic, and increased Slovakian nationalism. On 25 November, the federal Assembly voted to dissolve the federation, and thus itself and other federal institutions, on 1 January 1993.

Nineteen-ninety-three opened with a key constitutional question: the composition of the eighty-one-member Senate (upper chamber) in the bicameral parliament. The 200-member House (lower chamber) was formed from the republican body elected in 1992. But politicians could not agree on how to constitute the Senate, a new body which, under the constitution, has a role in electing the president, takes on some legislative power should the House be dissolved, and has the right to return legislation to the lower chamber if a majority of the senators vote against it. Draft proposals to fill the provisional Senate with former members of the old federal Assembly were rejected as unconstitutional and unfair, since several parties represented in the old National Council had no member in the federal Assembly. Some lawmakers advocated holding Senate elections in 1994. By year's end, the issue had yet to be resolved and, under the constitution, the House continued to perform the functions of the Senate.

Among parliament's first duties was the election of the president. The Klaus government supported Havel, who won handily on 26 January, but not before being excoriated before a national television audience by speakers from the right-wing Republican Party and three Moravian parties.

The coalition government of Prime Minister Klaus, a staunch pro-market reformer, faced little concerted resistance in parliament, mainly because of a badly fragmented opposition. With 105 of 200 seats, the ruling coalition, consisting of the ODS, the Civic Democratic Alliance, the Christian Democratic Union-People's Party, and the Christian Democratic Party, proceeded to implement market reforms and a second phase of privatization amid signs of an economic slowdown. Meanwhile, the Communist Party of Bohemia and Moravia, which in 1992 captured slightly more than 14 percent of the vote and thirty-five seats, had split into several warring factions, including hard-line former officials who called "for a return to the conditions before November 1989." The Social Democratic Party was also riven by factionalism, while the right-wing Republican Party hovered at a popularity rate of around 6 percent.

The key issue facing the government was the economy. In the spring, the government announced the second phase of privatization, earmarking 2,100 firms; the first wave was completed before the break-up of the former Czechoslovakia and some 1,500 companies were privatized by vouchers alone. On 22 April, a new bankruptcy law, which effected an estimated one-third of the 1,500 privatized firms, established a protective period of three to six months during which debtors and creditors would attempt to reach a settlement. Its long-term impact was not immediately clear because the distribution of vouchers was far from complete. On 5 May the government started distributing shares of 987 state enterprises, and by the end of June about 2 million people and 400 investment funds were expected to have bought in.

The Czechs had managed initially to stave off high unemployment, budget deficits, high inflation and other by-products of market reforms that afflicted other countries in East-Central Europe. There were signs in 1993, however, that the government was aware of the inevitable social shocks once unprofitable enterprises were closed . It scrapped plans announced by President Havel in 1990 to abandon the lucrative arms manufacturing business, maintaining that domestic pressure had increased to retain industries in which the country could compete internationally. The finance ministry downgraded economic growth projections for 1993 to 1 percent and announced that inflation, aggravated by a value added tax in January, would be around 17 percent. But while the Czech National Bank reported that public and private demand rose 12 percent and 16 percent respectively in the first half of the year (compared to 1992), industrial production dropped 4 percent (the fourth decline in four years) and gross domestic product fell 1 percent in the first six months compared to 1992, when output had already declined sharply. Efforts to build a market economy were hampered by recession in West Europe, the collapse of trade in the east (including Slovakia), and rising protectionism in Western markets.

In August, the Industry Ministry warned that the lower quality and rising costs of Czech products were causing a decline in local demand. Meanwhile, the government rejected calls for devaluation to make Czech products more competitive, noting companies must become more efficient. The government was concerned that inflation and rapidly rising wages would undermine prospects of recovery and frighten foreign investors, who invested more than $1 billion in the Czech territory in the three years before the Czechoslovakia split. It also remained to be seen how long Czech workers would endure wage controls that forced their paychecks down about 15 percent in inflation-adjusted terms since 1990.

Another key issue during the year was the souring of relations with Slovakia. On 8 February the two states cancelled the treaty maintaining the Czechoslovak koruna as their common currency, trade plummeted by 50 percent, and throughout the year both governments accused each other of stalling on dividing assets of the former Czechoslovakia. In mid-March, the Czech government announced that it would seize those shares that Slovaks had purchased in Czech companies under the voucher privatization scheme in 1992, unless Slovakia agreed to pay what the Czech government claimed were Slovakia's debts. By May, the Czech government decided to allow the transfer of privatized shares to Czech investors, partly since the earlier decision disturbed domestic and foreign investors because it held up voucher distribution and suggested that investment in the Czech Republic might be subject to political attacks. In July the two countries agreed to set up joint patrols along their common border to reduce the flow of illegal immigrants from Eastern Europe. On 4 November the Czech interior minister announced that the division of the former Interior Ministry, involving property worth $340 million, had been completed.

In international affairs, the government continued to press for the country's inclusion in the North Atlantic Treaty Organization (NATO). In a November article published in a German paper, President Havel said that his country's "geopolitical situation is precarious," referring to the possible emergence of a hard-line, imperial Russia.

Political Rights and Civil Liberties: Czechs can change their government democratically under a December 1992 constitution that enshrined a multiparty democratic state. Besides electing representatives, citizens are able to exercise power through direct means (referendums) in accordance with a special constitutional law.

The definition of judicial power in the constitution corresponds to the European concept of a state based on the rule of law. The four-tiered judicial system (the Supreme Court and the chief, regional and district courts) also includes a Constitutional Court composed of fifteen members appointed by the president for ten years. So-called lustration laws, passed in 1991 to bar top level Communists, security officials and collaborators from public life, continued to be controversial. At the time he signed the measures, then president of Czechoslovakia Havel objected to what he considered collective guilt and the presumption of guilt. In 1992, ninety-nine parliamentary deputies brought the lustration law before the Constitutional Court, which ruled most of the laws were constitutional. On 9 July 1993 the Czech parliament passed a law that lifted the statute of limitation for some crimes committed in the Communist era back to 1948. Opposition leaders contended that the measure was unconstitutional because it retroactively turned into crimes certain acts that were legal or would not have been punished by the old regime.

Political parties, professional organizations, cultural groups and other non-governmental associations can organize freely. Czech radio and television are no longer state-owned; they have been transformed into public broadcasting corporations with their own property and are supervised by independent committees elected by the parliament. Independent associations protecting the freedom and working conditions of journalists have been established. The relationship between Czech Radio and Television and the independent boards supervising these institutions has been problematic. On 24 March the director of Czech Radio, Ivan Mejstrik, resigned, citing interference in the radio's work by the Board of Radio Broadcasting. On 16 July the minister for economic competition said that the government should restrict the share of foreign capital in mass media, as is done in France, Italy and Portugal. Independent newspapers and periodicals are flourishing, though they vary in quality and objectivity. Some Czechs have complained about the proliferation of pornography and periodicals subscribing to ethnic hatred and anti-Semitism.

Although ethnic and minority rights are protected under law, there have been problems, particularly for the Gypsy (Roma) population numbering anywhere from the official estimate of 150,000 to 350,000, many of them recent arrivals from Slovakia. Romanies are officially recognized as a national minority and allowed to use the Romany language, form political parties and establish cultural organizations, but they have often been denied equal access to housing, employment and public services. In the last three years, violence against Gypsies has left twenty-six dead in the former Czechoslovakia. Several municipal and federal draft laws have tried to restrict the rights of Gypsies or evict them outright, though most have been ruled unconstitutional. Skinhead attacks have also been reported against Vietnamese, who came to the region as laborers. In November a leader of the Sudeten Germans said that Prague was not abiding by agreements it had signed with Germany regarding the German minority, but other Czech-German leaders disavowed his remarks.

Freedom of religion is guaranteed and respected, and there is no official church. A key issue in 1993 was the restitution of Roman Catholic Church property nationalized by the Communists after 1948. There was parliamentary disagreement on the issue, particularly since it can conceivably effect fully 1 percent of all Czech lands. At year's end, negotiations were continuing.

There are no major restrictions on domestic or foreign travel. There are several women's associations, and there are no legal obstacles based on gender. Women have held key government and public posts.

Workers enjoy and exercise the right to freely organize into unions, the major one being the CKOS (the Czech Confederation of Trade Unions.)

Denmark

Polity: Parliamentary democracy
Economy: Mixed capitalist
Population: 5,178,000
PPP: $16,781
Life Expectancy: 75.8
Ethnic Groups: Overwhelmingly Danish, a small German minority, various small immigrant groups

Political Rights: 1
Civil Liberties: 1
Status: Free

Overview:

In 1993 Denmark adopted with qualification the Maastricht treaty on European union and installed a new center-left government.

On 18 May 1993 Danes voted by 56.8 percent for European integration. This vote reversed a 1992 referendum in which Danes rejected Maastricht. Polls showed that voters wanted to keep their Danishness and not be overwhelmed by larger European countries, especially Germany. Before the 1992 vote, the government had known that anti-German sentiment could be an obstacle to the treaty, so it negotiated for a treaty protocol giving the country the right to prohibit Germans from purchasing summer homes in Denmark. Before the 1993 referendum, Denmark and the European Community (now European Union) reached a set of agreements allowing the country to opt out of common European defense, justice and economic policies, and out of a common European citizenship. These changes made the treaty acceptable enough to pass on the second attempt.

Denmark's center-right government resigned in January 1993 after an official inquiry found Conservative Prime Minister Poul Schlueter guilty of covering up a visa scandal in 1987. Social Democrat Poul Nyrup Rasmussen replaced Schlueter after assembling a four-party, center-left government, the first coalition with a parliamentary majority since 1972. The other government parties are the centrist Radicals, the Center Democrats and the Christian People's Party.

Denmark is the oldest monarchy in Europe and the only Scandinavian country presently a member of the European Union. Today the role of royalty in state functions is largely ceremonial. Since 1972, Denmark's ceremonial head of state has been Queen Margrethe II. Real political power rests with the parliament, the *Folketing*, a unicameral chamber consisting of 179 members, 135 of whom are elected in seventeen districts. As autonomous regions, Greenland and the Faroe Islands each send two representatives to the Folketing. The remaining forty Danish seats are allocated on a proportional basis to representatives chosen from parties that receive more than two percent of the popular vote. Because of the large number of parties and the low 2 percent hurdle needed to enter the Folketing, Danish parliamentary politics are marked by shifting and collapsing coalitions.

The center-left government is trying to overcome 12 percent unemployment with expansive fiscal policies. It raised interest rates in February 1993 in order to fend off speculation against the krone, the Danish currency. In April, Danish fishermen staged strikes and demonstrations against fish imports and for more subsidies for their industry. After the passage of the European referendum, the government proposed major income tax cuts spread over five years. However, the government also offered higher gas and environmental taxes.

The coalition parties suffered setbacks in local elections in November 1993. The opposition Liberals made significant gains, and hope to translate that success into votes in the parliamentary elections due in 1994.

Political Rights and Civil Liberties:

Danes have the right to change their government by democratic means. There is a wide range of political parties, including various Communists, a radical right-wing party, a green party and a party advocating the philosophy of the nineteenth-century economist Henry George. There is free assembly and free association. There is no death penalty and no reports of extrajudicial killings, disappearances or torture performed by an arm of the state. However, in May 1993, police in Copenhagen shot and wounded ten leftist, anarchist demonstrators who rioted after the European referendum. The rioters had hurled cobblestones, rocks and metal bars at the police. In their defense, police argued that they did fire warning shots and were in a life-threatening situation before shooting at the crowd. In another outbreak of violence, Kurdish separatists attacked Turkish offices in Copenhagen with rocks and firebombs in November 1993.

There is a free press and a selection of publications which reflect a variety of political and religious opinions. Forty-five newspapers are printed on a daily basis in Denmark. The state finances radio and television broadcasting. However, the state-owned television companies have editorial boards that operate independently of the state. One television channel is one-third owned by the state. The state permits independent radio stations, but regulates them tightly. The media as a whole reflect a wide variety of political opinion and are frequently critical of the government.

The Lutheran Church is the established church of Denmark, receiving its finances from the Danish state. Over ninety percent of the Danish populace is affiliated with the state church. There is freedom of worship for all. Religions function openly and there is no official discrimination against people for their religious beliefs.

Discrimination against people based on race, sex, and language is illegal in Denmark. However, there have been reports of attacks by civilians on recent non-Nordic immigrants and refugees. During 1993, 2,000 asylum-seekers arrived each month, especially from Bosnia, and the country strained to provide for them. The state has not made any major attempts to combat the rise of racism inside Denmark, but the Danish state has pioneered equality for homosexuals. In 1989, Denmark became the first country ever officially to sanction marriages between people of the same gender.

Workers have the right to organize and strike. Ninety percent of the wage earners in Denmark are affiliated with free trade unions. The umbrella organization in the labor movement is the Danish Federation of Trade Unions, which is linked with the Social Democratic Party. Labor organizations not affiliated with the Danish Federation of Trade Unions have organized, but not without meeting fierce resistance from the more established unions and their federation.

Djibouti

Polity: Dominant party
Economy: Capitalist
Population: 481,000
PPP: $1,000
Life Expectancy: 48.0
Ethnic Groups: Issas, Afars, Arabs

Political Rights: 6
Civil Liberties: 6
Status: Not Free

Overview:
In May of 1993, Djibouti held its first contested presidential election. President Hassan Gouled Aptidon defeated four other candidates and gained 60 percent of the popular vote, securing his fourth term in office. The four opposition candidates, all from the Issa ethnic group, represented the Party for Democratic Renewal (PRD), the National Democratic Party (PND), United Movement for Democracy (MUD) along with one independent candidate. The election was boycotted by the Revolutionary Front for Unity and Democracy (FRUD).

International observers to the elections declared that the voting was plagued with irregularities and, in a joint communique, the four opposing candidates claimed that the elections were " the object of massive fraud and riddled with serious incidents" and further stated that the election was "neither free nor democratic."

Djibouti is a small country covering only 9,000 square miles. Its 500,000 inhabitants are ethnically divided between the Afar ethnic group, which comprises about 35 percent of the population and occupy the northern and western regions of Djibouti, and the southern Issa ethnic group which comprises about 50 percent of the population. Since 1991, armed insurgents representing the Afar people (FRUD) have been waging a violent campaign to secure greater rights for the Afars, claiming that political power is concentrated in the hands of Issa people. Amnesty International (AI) alleges that Djibouti's security forces have committed "gross human rights violations including rape, torture and extrajudicial executions...in reprisal for losses inflicted" by FRUD.

Since gaining independence from France, Djibouti has been governed by Aptidon, an Issa, from the Popular Rally for Progress party (RPP). Largely as a result of the armed insurgency, Aptidon announced a series of measures intended to institute "reasonable multipartyism" and a new democratic constitution to protect a number of political and civil rights. A national referendum in September of 1992 adopted the proposed constitutional changes.

Political Rights and Civil Liberties:

Djiboutians are not able to change their government democratically. During the presidential elections in May of 1993 and the legislative elections in December 1992, international monitors reported widespread fraud. In both cases, voter turn-out was below 50 percent and the elections took place against a background of fear and intimidation. Although some opposition parties were allowed to contest the elections, stringent regulations prevented additional parties from competing.

As a result of the FRUD guerrilla campaign, security forces targeted those from the Afar ethnic group for reprisals. Amnesty International reports that Afars have been the victims of gross human rights violations. Extrajudicial executions were reported in late August and early September of 1993 in the districts of Tadjourah. In September, army troops reportedly detained hundreds of Afar men. Those who attempted to resist arrest were killed, and others were held in military camps where they were subjected to torture, beatings and denied food.

The new constitution protects the freedom of assembly and association. However, the government has effectively banned political protest. While the constitution also permits opposition parties to form, in effect, the ruling party determines which can be legalized. Supporters of those parties legalized during 1992/1993 were subject to intimidation and arrest.

Djiboutians do not have access to an independent judicial system. It is common for the government to interfere with the judicial process. The constitution states that imprisonment cannot occur unless an arrest decree is presented by a judicial magistrate. In practice, however, security forces frequently arrest demonstrators and others involved in political activity without proper authorization.

Article 15 of the new constitution protects freedom of speech, but pending its implementation, freedom of speech is severely curtailed. During 1992, those who criticized the government or the RPP were routinely arrested and detained for substantial periods before facing defamation charges. A prominent human rights activist and former member of parliament, Mohamed Houmed Soulleh, president of the *Association pour la defense des droits de l'homme et des libertes* (ADDHL) was arrested in September 1993, criticizing the government for committing gross human rights violations. Despite pressure from international human rights groups, Soulleh continues to be held. The television, radio stations and one newspaper (*La Nation*) in Djibouti are state owned and operated.

Although workers have the right to join unions and strike, the government does not allow the unions to operate freely.

As a result of the civil war, internal travel between north and south is not possible. International travel is generally not restricted. Although Djibouti is predominately Sunni Muslim, there is no state religion and the freedom to worship is respected.

Dominica

Polity: Parliamentary democracy
Economy: Capitalist
Population: 71,000
PPP: $3,901
Life Expectancy: 76.0
Ethnic Groups: Black and mulatto with a minority Carib enclave

Political Rights: 2
Civil Liberties: 1
Status: Free

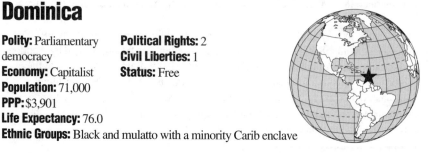

Overview:

Prime Minister Eugenia Charles, the first woman to head a government in the English-speaking Caribbean, gave up the leadership of the ruling Dominica Freedom Party (DFP) in August 1993, but said she would continue to lead the government until the next elections due by May 1995.

Dominica has been an independent republic within the British Commonwealth since 1978. Internally self-governing since 1967, Dominica is a parliamentary democracy headed by a prime minister and a House of Assembly with twenty-one members elected to five-year terms. Nine senators are appointed, five by the prime minister and four by the opposition leader. Over half the island's population depends directly or indirectly on banana production.

Charles narrowly won a third term in the 1990 elections as the ruling DFP won in just eleven of twenty-one constituencies. The newly formed United Workers Party (UWP) led by Eddison James, former head of the Banana Growers Association, took second with six seats and displaced the leftist Dominica Labor Party (DLP), with four seats, as the official opposition.

The death of DLP leader Michael Douglas led to a by-election in the northern constituency of Portsmouth in July 1992. The election was won by Douglas's brother, Rosie, who in January 1993 was elected DLP party leader.

In August, after the seventy-four-year-old Charles said she would relinquish the DFP leadership, External Affairs Minister Brian Alleyne defeated three other candidates in a vote of DFP delegates to become the new party leader. In September the DLP won all eight seats in the Portsmouth town council elections.

Political Rights and Civil Liberties:

Citizens have the right to change their government democratically. There are no restrictions on political or civic organizations. In 1992 primary school teachers boycotted the first day of classes to protest the government's refusal to recognize the Dominica Association of Teachers as their bargaining agent. The government contended that the right to conduct salary negotiations belongs, by law, solely to the civil service union.

Since the last elections, the approximately 3,000 Carib Indians, many of whom live on a 3,700-acre reserve on the northeast coast, have been represented in the House of Assembly by Carib parliamentarian Worrell Sanford. In October 1993 Sanford resigned his seat. A by-election was expected to be held in early 1994.

Freedom of religion is generally recognized. However, the small Rastafarian community charges that their religious rights are violated by a policy of cutting off the "dread locks" of those who are imprisoned. It also charges that non-Dominican Rastafarians, especially women, are harrassed by immigration officials who single them out for drug searches.

The press is generally free, varied and critical. Television and radio, both public and private, are open to pluralistic views. Opposition parties have charged that the board appointed to oversee state-run media is manipulated by the government. Nonetheless, in 1990 television was used for the first time as an effective campaign tool by all parties.

There is an independent judiciary and the rule of law is enhanced by the court system's embrace of the inter-island Eastern Caribbean Supreme Court. The government has criticized travel by citizens to Cuba and Libya, but does not restrict travel to those countries.

The Dominica Defense Force (DDF) was disbanded in 1981 after it was implicated in attempts to overthrow the government by supporters of former Prime Minister Patrick John. John was convicted in 1986 for his involvement and given a twelve-year prison sentence. He was released by executive order in May 1990 and now heads the National Workers Union.

Dominican Republic

Polity: Presidential-legislative democracy
Economy: Capitalist-statist
Population: 7,621,000
PPP: $2,404
Life Expectancy: 66.7

Political Rights: 3*
Civil Liberties: 3
Status: Partly Free

Ethnic Groups: Complex, mestizo and mulatto (70 percent), Caucasian (15 percent), and black (15 percent)
Ratings Change: *The Dominican Republic's political rights rating changed from 2 to 3 because of the continuing erosion of public and political institutions and unchecked official corruption.

Overview: With the approach of the 16 May 1994 elections, eighty-seven-year-old President Joaquin Balaguer appeared to be angling yet again to run for reelection. Leading in the polls was Jose Francisco Pena Gomez, a black social democrat and former mayor of Santo Domingo. With Balaguer supporters already playing the race card in 1993, the campaign looked to be volatile.

Since achieving independence from Spain in 1821 and Haiti in 1844, the Dominican Republic has endured recurrent domestic conflict. The assassination of Gen. Rafael Trujillo in 1961 ended thirty years of dictatorial rule but led to renewed turmoil. The military overthrow of the elected government of leftist Juan Bosch in 1963 led to civil war and U.S. military intervention in 1965. In 1966, under a new constitution, civilian rule was restored with the election of Balaguer of the right-wing Social Christian Reformist Party (PRSC).

The constitution provides for a president directly elected for four years, a Congress consisting of a 120-member Chamber of Deputies and a thirty-member Senate also directly elected for four years. The governors of the twenty-six provinces are appointed by the president. Municipalities are governed by elected mayors and municipal councils.

Balaguer was reelected in 1970 and 1974 but defeated in 1978 by Silvestre Antonio Guzman of the social democratic Dominican Revolutionary Party (PRD). Guzman's inauguration marked the first time that an elected president had transferred power to an elected successor. The PRD repeated in 1982 with the election of President Salvador Jorge Blanco, but Balaguer was elected again in 1986.

The main rivals in the May 1990 election were Balaguer and fellow octogenarian Bosch of the leftist Dominican Liberation Party (PLD). Other contenders were the PRD's Pena Gomez, and Jacobo Majluta, who had split from the PRD to form the Independent Revolutionary Party (PRI).

Campaign issues included rising unemployment, poverty, and official corruption. Although marred by sporadic violence resulting in a number of deaths and injuries, the campaign was one of the most wide-open in the nation's history. In addition to daily rallies, voters were inundated by political advertisements, media talk shows, and campaign coverage by nearly a dozen newspapers.

Monitored by former U.S. President Jimmy Carter and other international observers, Dominicans voted for president and legislative and municipal candidates. The abstention rate of 40 percent was the highest since the establishment of democratic rule. The initial count gave Balaguer the edge over Bosch, with Pena Gomez coming in a strong third. Both leaders claimed victory, with Bosch making credible claims of fraud. Carter intervened and the front-runners agreed to a recount by the Central Electoral Council.

The recount gave Balaguer 35.1 percent of the vote against 33.8 percent for Bosch, but the PRSC lost its legislative majority. In the Chamber of Deputies, Bosch's PLD took 44 seats, the PRSC took 42, the PRD 32, the PRI two. In the Senate, the PRSC obtained 16 seats, the PLD took 12, and the PRD 2.

During the September 1992 official celebration of the 500th anniversary of Columbus's arrival in the New World there were widespread protests and violent police crackdowns. Many people, especially blacks, were outraged at Balaguer's spending spree, including the construction of the colossal "Columbus Lighthouse" costing an estimated $70 million. The country is the fourth poorest in the Western hemisphere. Balaguer, blind and in ill-health, seemed dejected and some local analysts predicted he would bow out in 1994.

But in 1993, after Pena Gomez jumped ahead in the polls, Balaguer started acting like a candidate. He reshuffled his cabinet and, as he had in previous campaigns, began redirecting government resources into populist spending programs. By the fall he no longer ruled out running, health permitting.

The fifty-seven-year-old Pena Gomez, son of a Dominican mother and a Haitian father, led in the polls throughout the year with around 40 percent. Balaguer trailed by 5-10 percent. Pena Gomez promised greater social spending and electoral reform to end consecutive presidential terms. Bosch looked to be less of a factor, as the PLD suffered from deep internal divisions.

By mid-1993 Balaguer supporters, taking advantage of the turmoil in nextdoor Haiti, were questioning Pena Gomez's citizenship and patriotism. Dominican elites are predominantly white or light-colored, while the poor and lower classes are mostly black or mulatto. Balaguer distanced himself from these attacks. But elections have been marked by violence in the past, and the race issue threatened to make the 1994 campaign explosive.

Political Rights and Civil Liberties: Citizens are able to change their government through elections, but electoral fraud has undermined the integrity of the system. An opinion poll in 1992 showed that 68 percent of Dominicans believed Balaguer rigged the 1990 vote. Polls also show a high rate of political indifference among younger people. In 1993 a new registration system using voter indentification cards was devised, but numerous procedural errors prompted widespread criticism of electoral authorities.

Constitutional guarantees regarding free expression, freedom of religion and the right to organize political parties and civic groups are generally respected. There are over a dozen political parties from left to right that run candidates in elections. But political expression is often restricted by the climate of violence associated with political campaigns and government-labor clashes, and by the repressive measures taken by security forces and the military.

Human rights groups are independent and active. In 1993 they reported that prison conditions remained poor, and that nearly nine out of ten prisoners had yet to be tried. There also were continuing allegations of police brutality, including torture, and arbitrary arrests by the security forces. Criminal violence, much of it drug-related, and police corruption threatens the security of citizens. Poor women are vulnerable to criminal rings who promise jobs in Europe for a fee, then press the indebted women into prostitution in Spain and Germany.

Labor unions are well organized. Although legally permitted to strike, they are often subject to government crackdowns. Peasant unions are occasionally targeted by armed groups in the hire of large landowners. A new labor code in 1992 established standards for workplace conditions and strengthened the right to bargain collectively. But companies in the twenty-seven industrial free zones, employing almost 10 percent of the nations's workforce, have refused to comply. More than 200 free-zone workers have been fired for union organizing since the code went into effect. Worker conditions in the zones remain below international standards and discriminatory practices against women workers are prevalent.

The government has been criticized for the slave-like conditions of Haitians, including children, forcibly recruited to work on state-run sugar plantations. The government has responded by forcibly repatriating tens of thousands of the estimated 500,000 Haitians living illegally in the Dominican Republic. A large number of black Dominicans have also been expelled. Repatriation was discontinued in 1993 after international criticism. The new labor code recognizes the right of sugar workers to organize, but reports of abuses continued in 1993 as the influx of refugees fleeing repression in Haiti heightened anti-Haitian sentiment.

The media are mostly private. Newspapers are independent and diverse but subject to government pressure through denial of advertising revenues and taxes on imported newsprint. There are dozens of radio stations and at least six commercial television stations, but broadcasts are subject to government review. In 1992 the government banned Creole radio broadcasts to Haiti.

Supreme Court judges are elected by the Senate. The Court appoints lower court judges and is also empowered to participate in the legislative process by introducing bills in the congress. But the judicial system is over-politicized, and like most other government institutions, riddled with corruption. The courts offer little recourse to those without money or influence.

Ecuador

Polity: Presidential-
legislative democracy
Economy: Capitalist-
statist
Population: 10,286,000
PPP: $3,074
Life Expectancy: 66.0

Political Rights: 2
Civil Liberties: 3
Status: Free

Ethnic Groups: Complex, Indian (approximately 35 percent),
mestizo (45 percent), Caucasian (10 percent), and black (10 percent)

Overview:

President Sixto Duran Ballen's economic modernization plan
was delayed as he entered his second year in office still
hamstrung by an opposition-dominated legislature. Amid
labor strikes and political gridlock, his ratings in opinion polls plummeted.

The Republic of Ecuador was established in 1830 after achieving independence
from Spain in 1822. Its history has been marked by interrupted presidencies and periods
of military rule. The last military government paved the way for a return to civilian rule
with a new constitution approved by referendum in 1978.

The 1978 constitution provides for a president elected for a four-year term by
universal adult suffrage, with a second round of voting between the two front-runners if
no candidate wins a majority in the first round. There is a 77-member unicameral National
Chamber of Deputies with 65 members elected on a provincial basis every two years,
and 12 elected on a national basis every four years. Municipal governments are elected.

In the 1988 election Duran of the ruling right-wing Social Christian Party (PSC) ran
third against Rodrigo Borja of the social democratic Democratic Left (ID) and Abdala
Bucaram of the populist Ecuadorian Roldosist Party (PRE). Borja defeated Bucaram in
the run-off and succeeded President Leon Febres Cordero of the PSC. Borja's term was
marked by confrontations between the executive and the legislature as opposition
parties ganged up to block government initiatives by using a legislative majority to
impeach six cabinet ministers. Impeaching government officials, allowed by the
constitution, has been a staple of the country's fragmented politics since the return to
civilian rule. Borja also contended with labor strikes, Indian groups demanding
autonomy and land, and a failure to alleviate the 60 percent poverty rate.

More than a dozen political parties registered for the 1992 election. The leader in
the opinion polls was Duran, who had split from the PSC to form the Republican Union
party (PUR), followed by PSC's Jaime Nebot and Bucaram. Raul Baca of the ruling ID
trailed badly. On 17 May 1992 Duran came first with 31.9 percent of the vote. Nebot,
with 25 percent, edged out Bucaram, 21.5 percent, to make it into the second round.

With both Duran and Nebot advocating market economic policies, the run-off
campaign was a clash of personalities. Duran, an architect with considerable experience
in public office, offered the patrician style associated with the elite of Quito, the nation's
highland capital where he was once mayor. The forty-five-year-old Nebot, a lawyer and
businessman, displayed the fiery demeanor characteristic of coastal Guayaquil, the
nation's largest city and business hub.

On 5 July 1992 Duran won the run-off with 57 percent of the vote, but he took office with a weak hand. In May his PUR had won only 13 of 77 legislative seats. The PSC had won 21, Bucaram's PRE 13, with the remaining 26 divided among ten other parties. Nebot opted to stake out opposition turf, underscoring the fact that personal rivalries count more than ideology in Ecuadoran politics.

Duran had promised a program of gradual economic reform. But when he unveiled a series of shock measures after taking office, the response was a series of labor strikes and civil disturbances that prompted him to mobilize the military. Protests continued on and off through 1993, led by the United Workers Front (FUT), representing close to a quarter of the work force.

By early 1993 opposition parties had initiated impeachment proceedings against a number of cabinet ministers. Duran's first anniversary address to the legislature in August was marked by uproar and violent scuffles in the chamber. By October twenty legislators had changed parties, many siding with Duran amid widespread allegations of bribery. Opinion polls showed that the legislature remained the least respected institution in the country. With the government gridlocked, and amid a protracted teachers strike, Duran saw his approval ratings drop to less than 20 percent.

Sol Rojo (Red Sun), a small guerrilla organization that sympathizes with the Maoist Shining Path guerrillas in Peru, emerged in late 1992. In 1993 it claimed responsibility for a number of dynamite attacks against public buildings and media installations.

Political Rights and Civil Liberties:

Citizens are able to change their government democratically. Constitutional guarantees regarding freedom of expression, religion, and the right to organize political parties, labor unions and civic organizations are generally respected. There are more than a dozen political parties ranging from right to left. Competition is fierce and election campaigns are marked by sporadic violence.

Opinion polls and increased voter abstention in recent years indicate that the credibility of political institutions is declining. There is also evidence that drug traffickers have penetrated the political system through campaign funding and sectors of the military through bribery. Ecuador has become a transshipment point for cocaine passing from neighboring Colombia to the U.S.

Labor unions are well organized and permitted to strike. Hundreds of national and local work stoppages have taken place in recent years in response to government efforts to restructure the statist economy. In 1991 unions protested amendments to the sixty-year-old labor code, which reduced statutory severance pay and put limits on public sector strikes.

Newspapers, including at least six dailies, are privately owned or sponsored by political parties. They are free of censorship and outspoken. Radio and television stations are privately owned, although the government controls radio frequencies. Broadcast media are supervised by two independent associations. There are nearly a dozen television stations, mostly commercial, that play a major role during political campaigns.

The judiciary is headed by a Supreme Court appointed by the legislature. Reforms passed in 1992 were designed to decentralize the system and make it more efficient. The Supreme Court was also given authority to act as a court of appeals. The Court, however, is frequently caught in political tugs-of-war between the executive and the legislature, and its impartiality is often in doubt. The judiciary, in general, is undermined by the corruption that afflicts the political system.

Independent human rights organizations operate freely. They report on frequent allegations of police brutality, torture and rape of female detainees by security forces, particularly during rural land disputes. In 1991 the government dissolved a police investigative unit implicated in many abuses and announced a human-rights training program for police. But rights activists have since charged that abuses are still committed with impunity because police personnel are tried in police rather than civil courts. In 1993 the military announced that officers and soldiers would undergo human rights training.

The National Confederation of Indigenous Nationalities of Ecuador (Conaie) stunned Ecuador's establishment in June 1990 by mobilizing more than a million people across the country in what is referred to as "the uprising." Since then indigenous groups have continued to mobilize to demand land grants, sovereignty for the indigenous population including oil and mineral rights, and the disbanding of paramilitary units used in the countryside by large landowners.

In 1993 government officials charged indigenous groups with wanting to "establish a state within a state." The government and the military have generally sided with landowners and multinational oil companies as they continue to infringe upon land rights granted to Indians in the eastern Amazon region by the former Borja government. In May Indians attempting to present an alternative agrarian reform bill to the legislature were forcibly kept away from the building by police.

Egypt

Polity: Dominant party (military-dominated)
Economy: Mixed statist
Population: 58,292,000
PPP: $1,988
Life Expectancy: 60.3
Ethnic Groups: Eastern Hamitic (90 percent), Greek, Syro-Lebanese, other
Ratings Change: *Egypt's political rights rating changed from 5 to 6 because of increasing terrorist violence and corresponding government crackdowns.

Political Rights: 6*
Civil Liberties: 6
Status: Not Free

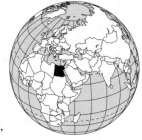

Overview: In 1993 the Egyptian authorities continued a massive crackdown on militant fundamentalists seeking to overthrow the government and set up an Islamic state. However, President Hosni Mubarak's government has done little to alleviate the country's widespread impoverishment, unemployment and chronic official corruption, the root problems that have driven thousands of youths to join the radicals in recent years.

The British granted Egypt independence in 1922. In July 1952 military leaders overthrew the monarchy, establishing a republic a year later. The 1971 constitution adopted under President Anwar al-Sadat granted executive power to the president, who is nominated by the People's Assembly and elected for a six-year term by a national referendum. The president names the cabinet and appoints military leaders, provincial governors and other officials. In 1979 Sadat signed an unprecedented peace treaty with Israel providing for the return of the Sinai Peninsula, captured by Israel in 1967. Islamic militants angered over this peace accord assassinated him in October 1981.

His successor, Hosni Mubarak, has gradually eased some speech and press restrictions, but despite the outward trappings of a multiparty system, politics is still dominated by the President's military-backed National Democratic Party (NDP). Most policies are implemented through presidential decrees, which have the power of law, and the 454-member People's Assembly primarily approves rather than initiates policy.

At the November 1990 parliamentary elections the NDP took 383 seats; the leftist National Progressive Unionist Party, 6; independents, 55. Ten seats were set aside for presidential appointees. The sixty-five-year-old Mubarak won a third presidential term on 4 October 1993, winning 96.3 percent approval as the sole candidate in a national referendum. Privately, however, many Egyptians express extreme disillusion with an ossified political system, endemic bureaucratic corruption, and widespread poverty and overcrowding. More than 20 percent of the workforce is unemployed, another 20 percent are underemployed. Seventy percent of the population is illiterate.

This disillusion has been tapped by the fundamentalists, primarily the non-violent Muslim Brotherhood and the radical Islamic Group, itself composed of some forty-five factions. In response, Mubarak has promoted the government as a staunch supporter of Islam in an effort to co-opt orthodox Muslims who might otherwise side with the fundamentalists. To bolster its pro-Islam credentials, the government promotes religion through the media, and frequently bans or censors anything considered offensive to Islam, including books, films and plays.

In spring 1992 the Islamic Group sharply escalated what had for years been routine attacks against members of the Coptic Christian minority. The fundamentalists also began targeting tourists in an effort to cripple an industry that normally brings in $2.2 billion per year in revenues and is the largest source of earnings for the government. In late October, the government began trying fundamentalists accused of terrorism in military courts in an effort to expedite the trials. In December, thousands of police raided the Cairo slum of Imbaba as well as militant strongholds in southern Egypt, detaining some 1,700 suspected radicals. By years end, however, terrorist attacks and shootouts had killed some eighty Coptic Christians and police.

The cycle of terrorist attacks and police raids continued unabated in 1993. In March, one of the bloodiest months, at least fifty police and militants were killed. The fundamentalists also expended their attacks to official targets, making assassination attempts on Information Minister Mohammed Safwat el-Sharif; Maj. Gen. Osman Shahin, the commander of Cairo's central military area; and Interior Minister Hussein Mohammed al-Alfi. In addition, several top security officials were killed throughout the year.

The military courts trying terrorism cases came to quick verdicts and had high conviction rates. For example, a military court hearing the first case involving attacks on tourists convicted thirty-two extremists of terrorism on 22 April, sentencing seven to death. Overall, it took the court just forty-four days to try a group of forty-nine suspects. Over the summer the government began carrying out death sentences for convicted terrorists. Fifteen militants were executed in June and July alone, an unprecedented figure in Egypt this century. By years' end the government had hanged twenty-nine extremists.

A related issue involves the fate of the fundamentalists' spritual leader, Sheik Omar

Abdul Rahman, who has resided in the United States since May 1990. On 4 July Egypt asked the U.S. to extradite the Sheik to retry him on charges of fomenting antigovernment riots in Fayoum, south of Cairo, in 1989. Egyptian courts have acquitted the Sheik three times, once on charges of having ordered Sadat's assassination in 1981. However, in August U.S. prosecutors indicted the Sheik on charges of orchestrating the February 1993 bombing at New York's World Trade Center, leaving the Egyptian request in limbo. Many question the Mubarak government's true desire to try the Sheik, knowing that a guilty verdict, and perhaps a death sentence, could set off an unheard of wave of terrorist attacks.

Political Rights and Civil Liberties: The ruling National Democratic Party's control over the People's Assembly, the media, the large public sector, labor unions and political parties effectively prevents Egyptians from having the democratic means to change their government.

In May 1991 parliament voted to extend the state of emergency, in effect since the 1981 assassination of President Anwar al-Sadat, until June 1994. Since the terrorism upsurge began in May 1992, police have arrested more than 5,000 suspects. Under the Emergency law, suspects can be detained without charge for ninety days, and for an additional six months without a court order. The Interior Ministry's General Directorate for State Security Investigations has been accused of repeated human rights violations, including detaining women and children as young as eight to persuade suspects who are relatives to turn themselves in, and torturing suspects to extract information and coerce confessions. The Emergency Law also gives police broad powers to place suspects under surveillance and to conduct searches without warrants. This is frequently used not only against fundamentalists, but also activists, journalists and writers.

The President appoints judges according to nominations from the Higher Judicial Council, a constitutional body composed of senior judges, attorneys, and law professors. Although there is still considerable government influence on the judiciary, in recent years the courts have shown greater independence. For example, on 14 August 1993 a civilian court aquitted twenty-four fundamentalists charged with murder on the grounds that their confessions had been obtained through torture. When a suspect is convicted under the Emergency Law, the only appeal is to the president.

Egyptian citizens and private publications freely criticize government policies, but the government has broad control over the media. A press law prevents direct criticism of the president or foreign heads of state. Although journalists can generally criticize the president mildly without receiving sanction, in October three members of the opposition Socialist Labor Party were detained for three days for publishing articles in their party paper urging President Mubarak to provide information on an unspecified arms deal. The Prosecutor General can ban media coverage of sensitive issues, and in 1993 he occasionally limited coverage of the fundamentalist terrorism trials.

Most major newspapers are state-owned and are uncritically supportive of the government. In the runup to Mubarak's October reelection these newspapers featured constant endorsements of the president. The ruling party also influences the Higher Press Council, which must approve applications for new publications. In this country with high illiteracy, radio and television are the primary sources of information. The government uses its control of the electronic media to promote its policies, and opposition candidates and issues are denied coverage.

Under the Emergency Law the Interior Ministry must grant approval for public meetings and demonstrations, and few are held. The Private Organizations Law requires the Ministry of Social Affairs to license "private organizations," and allows it to dissolve private or nongovernmental organizations (NGO) for engaging in political or religious activities. The Ministry can also merge two or more NGOs, which has been done to shut down undesirable groups. The government refuses to license the Egyptian Organization for Human Rights on the grounds it enagages in political activities.

Islam is the state religion. In November 1992 the government placed all of the country's mosques under the control of the Ministry of Religious Affairs, and police have closed many unlicensed mosques. The Ministry of Interior frequently confiscates books and pamphlets by fundamentalists, as well as materials considered offensive to Islam.

The small Jewish minority is generally not bothered, but Coptic Christians, who comprise 17 percent of the population, face significant difficulties. Many Copts have been murdered, and Copt houses, shops and churches have been burned and vandalized. Copts are underrepresented in top government and army positions, and in public schools teachers often embarass Coptic students. An archaic 1856 law from the Ottoman empire requires non-Muslims to obtain a presidential decree to build or repair places of worship; Copts say they frequently have difficulty obtaining this. Egyptians are free to travel within the country. Unmarried women under twenty-one must obtain permission from their fathers to travel abroad, and married women must get permission from their husbands.

In February parliament passed a law designed to limit the influence of Muslim extremists in the twenty-one professional unions. In the past, the fundamentalists had taken advantage of low turnout to win control of union offices. The new law makes voting compulsory and requires 33 percent participation to validate a union election. All trade unions must belong to the government-influenced Egyptian Trade Union Federation (ETUF). Strikes are illegal but do occur.

El Salvador

Polity: Presidential-legislative democracy (military influenced)
Economy: Capitalist-statist
Population: 5,151,000
PPP: $1,950
Life Expectancy: 64.4
Ethnic Groups: Mestizo (89 percent), with small Indian and Caucasian minorities

Political Rights: 3
Civil Liberties: 3
Status: Partly Free

Overview: The peace process appeared to bog down as the country prepared for the 20 March 1994 elections. Death squad-style killings and delays in creating an impartial police force threatened to compromise the vote, the first in which former left-wing guerrillas would be participating.

El Salvador declared independence from the Captaincy General of Guatemala in 1841. The Republic of El Salvador was established in 1859. More than a century of civil strife and military rule followed.

A 1979 coup by reformist officers was the first breach in the historical alliance between the military and the landed oligarchy. But the reform attempt was undermined by civil war as the Farabundo Marti National Liberation Front (FMLN) squared off against the military and right-wing forces.

Salvadorans elected a constituent assembly in 1982 and a new constitution was drafted in 1983. It provides for a president and vice-president elected for a five-year term, and a unicameral National Assembly elected for a three-year term. Municipal elections are held every three years. Jose Napoleon Duarte of the Christian Democratic Party (PDC) was elected president in 1984. He defeated Roberto d'Aubuisson, a cashiered army officer linked to right-wing death squads who founded the National Republican Alliance (ARENA) in 1981.

In 1987 exiled politicians allied with the FMLN returned to form the Democratic Convergence (CD). ARENA took a moderate turn as businessman Alfredo Cristiani replaced d'Aubuisson as ARENA chief and led the party to victories in the 1988 legislative and municipal elections. Cristiani won a first-round victory in the 1989 presidential election, taking 54 percent of the vote against the PDC's Fidel Chavez Mena and the CD's Guillermo Ungo.

In 1990 the government and the FMLN agreed to U.N.-mediated negotiations. The talks resulted in a complicated peace pact signed in January 1992. The FMLN agreed to disarm within ten months and the government agreed to cut the 60,000-member military by half and eliminate counterinsurgency units. A U.N. peacekeeping force would monitor the process and assist in the formation of a civilian-led national police force that would include former guerrillas and replace the old security forces.

The accord also called for investigations and removal of military officers responsible for rights abuses, a program to provide land for former FMLN combatants and peasant sympathizers, reorganization of the judicial and electoral systems, and FMLN participation in economic reconstruction programs.

The accord nearly broke down in late 1992 as the military refused to consider purging any officers. The FMLN finally demobilized in December 1992 after Cristiani agreed to remove over 100 officers accused of rights violations by early 1993. The military remained intransigent until the March release of the report by the U.N.-sponsored Truth Commission. Although the commission documented FMLN abuses too, it found the military to be the worst rights violator during the war and implicated most of the high command including Gen. Emilio Ponce, the defense minister. The report turned up the pressure on the military, in El Salvador and Washington, and by mid-1993 more than 100 officers had been purged and Ponce had resigned.

The FMLN, after gaining legal recognition, opted to back Ruben Zamora, a former ally and the candidate of the CD, for president. Chavez Mena was again nominated by PDC. The social democratic National Revolutionary Movement (MNR) was expected to support Zamora. ARENA nominated Armando Calderon Sol, the mayor of San Salvador with roots in the conservative wing of the party. Calderon Sol led in the polls, but with considerably less than the 50 percent needed for a first-round victory.

The government's reluctance to carry out the police and land reform components of the peace accords angered the FMLN. Tensions rose further when three former FMLN commanders and an activist were murdered in the fall, all but one evidently by reactivated death squads. It appeared that Cristiani was losing power within ARENA and that the right-wing of the party, in league with recently retired military officers, was angling to eviscerate the accords. There was concern about how far they might go to stop a potential FMLN-PDC-CD-MNR coalition from winning a second round of voting if Calderon Sol failed to reach 50 percent in the March vote.

In December Cristiani agreed to form a joint U.N.-government commission to investigate the killings, and to discuss with the FMLN a specific timetable for completing land transfers and the establishment of a civil police. But with the far-right apparently trying to provoke the FMLN into returning to violence, the postwar transition remained uncertain.

Political Rights and Civil Liberties:

Citizens are able to change their governments through elections, but the military exerts inordinate influence in the political process. The constitution guarantees free expression, freedom of religion and the right to organize political parties, civic groups and labor unions. Although the 1992 peace accords led to a significant reduction in human rights violations, political expression and civil liberties continue to be restricted by right-wing death squads and military security forces that operate with impunity.

The FMLN achieved legal recognition in 1993 and prepared to run candidates in 1994 for the eighty-four-member National Assembly and municipal offices. In 1993 a new five-member electoral commission was formed. For the first time it included a representative from the Left, but the staff belonged mostly to the ruling ARENA. The commission was criticized for delays and errors in registering voters.

A U.N. observer mission to monitor human rights has been in place since mid-1991 and issues regular reports. Under the peace accord the government established a human rights ombudsman office in 1992. There are also a number of independent rights groups, including the highly professional Tutela Legal.

Killings of former FMLN guerrillas rose from three in 1992 to twenty-three in the first ten months of 1993. But with a sharp increase in criminal violence in recent years it is difficult to discern motive in many murder cases, for example the killing in June of the Catholic bishop assigned to the military. The U.N. mission reported nearly a hundred death squad-style killings in the first eight months of the year. In the fall three former FMLN commanders were killed. There were also reports of dozens of death threats, hundreds of arbitrary detentions, incidents of torture, and renewed public threats by death squads like the Secret Anti-Communist Army. Also in the fall, at least four members of ARENA were killed in unclear circumstances. In December 1993 the Cristiani government agreed to the formation of a joint U.N.-government panel to investigate the rise in apparently political killings.

Underlying all rights abuses is the absence of an effective system of justice. The judiciary, understaffed and riddled with corruption, often functions as an enforcement arm of the military and the ARENA party. The conviction of two officers in the 1989 murder of six Jesuit priests is the only time military officers have been held accountable for human rights violations, despite overwhelming evidence of military involvement in the deaths of thousands of civilians.

The 1992 peace accord called for an overhaul of the judiciary. The 1993 Truth Commission recommended that all fourteen Supreme Court judges be fired. But

President Cristiani and the president of the court flatly refused and reforms have been minimal. Most judges do not cooperate with the U.N. mission monitoring human rights and judicial reform.

Two amnesty laws have added to the sense of impunity. The FMLN and the government agreed to the first in 1992, which covered most rights violations by both sides during the war. In March 1993 the Cristiani government pushed a blanket amnesty through the congress which immunized the military from charges recommended by the Truth Commission in its report published a week earlier.

The accord also called for a new National Civilian Police incorporating former FMLN guerrillas. But training has been slow and underfunded, and up to 500 former members of disbanded security forces have been integrated into the new force. The paramilitary National Police, which it was supposed to replace, was actually augmented by up to 1,000 former soldiers from disbanded army units. The National Intelligence Directorate was only nominally disbanded and continued to function within the military.

Most media are privately owned. Election campaigns feature televised interviews and debates between candidates from across the political spectrum. In 1992 the FMLN's formerly clandestine Radio Venceremos was newly installed in San Salvador and began competing with nearly seventy other stations. The media are still occasionally targeted by political violence. The offices of the right-wing *El Diario de Hoy* were attacked in November 1993 by masked men apparently linked to the FMLN. A number of left-leaning journalists reported death threats.

Labor, peasant and university organizations are well organized after being nearly decimated in 1980-82. Strikes are not permitted in the public sector. The government and the private sector have stalled union efforts to reform an archaic labor code. Unions that strike are subject to intimidation and crackdowns by police. Nearly a dozen trade unionists were killed in the first ten months of 1993, apparently by death squads, while dozens more were detained. Unions are denied the right to organize in the newly created export processing zones.

Organizers of the sixth Latin American and Caribbean Feminist conference held in Costa del Sol in November received anonymous death threats. Owners of hotels renting space to the conference were also threatened but no incidents were reported.

Equatorial Guinea

Polity: Dominant party (military-dominated)
Economy: Capitalist-statist
Population: 379,000
PPP: $700
Life Expectancy: 47.0

Political Rights: 7
Civil Liberties: 7*
Status: Not Free

Ethnic Groups: Fang (75-80 percent), Bubi (15 percent), Puku, Seke and others (5-10 percent)
Ratings Change: *Equitorial Guinea's civil liberties rating changed from 6 to 7 because of severe restrictions on the development of opposition groups and continuing human rights abuses.

Overview:

In the legislative election of 21 November 1993, the ruling Democratic Party of Equatorial Guinea scored a lopsided victory. Most opposition parties and the majority of voters, including the Bubis, the largest ethnic minority, abstained from the vote. Opposition parties won only a fragment of the eighty-seat legislature. Before the election, a group of Bubis demanded autonomy. After the election, security forces arrested a Bubi village council president and beat two men for carrying pro-Bubi independence literature. The U.S., Spain and other Western powers rejected the election as illegitimate. The government accused the American ambassador of witchcraft and "taking traditional medicine given to him by election-boycotting parties so the vote would come out badly." The so-called basis for this charge was the diplomat's election-day visit to British war graves. The country's long record of human rights abuses and its persecution of opponents made free and fair elections impossible. An allegedly competitive presidential election is set for 1996.

Since gaining independence in 1968, Equatorial Guinea has been governed ruthlessly by its two presidents, Macie Nguema Biyogo and his nephew, Teodoro Obiang Nguema Mbasogo. Obiang overthrew Macie in 1979, and had him executed for his genocidal policies against the population. Soon after gaining power, however, Obiang continued the repressive policies, albeit on a smaller scale. Pressured by donor countries to institute democratic reforms, since 1991 he has presented himself as a moderate leader willing to accept political opposition.

After Obiang's announcement of an "era of pluralism" in January 1992, the political opposition and exile groups demanded the unconditional legalization of political parties other than Obiang's Democratic Party of Equatorial Guinea (PDGE). In addition, the opposition called for the release of political prisoners and abolition of torture, access to media and financial assistance to political parties, and an electoral timetable.

President Obiang agreed to the legalization of the political parties, and by late January 1993 ten opposition groups were formally registered. A joint consultative conference to discuss the process of democratization was held from 10 February to 18 March. Chaired by the Prime Minister Sylvester Siale Bileka, the conference discussed the preparation of a voter register based on a new census, to be used in the next legislative election, and the participants issued a joint statement stating their determination to "pursue the path of reconciliation and pardon." At the end of the conference the government and the opposition agreed to form a monitoring commission to supervise the implementation of the adopted measures.

During the conference the government continued repressing dissent outside the capital. On 12 February the police in Nsok-Nsomo arrested and tortured forty activists of the legalized Popular Union (UP). According to a local government representative, the UP acted "against the principles of the ruling Democratic Party."

In May, the opposition accused the president of reneging on the promise to establish the joint monitoring commission, and refused to participate further in discussions with the government. The opposition denounced the increased military presence in the capital.

Despite the opposition's announcement that it would boycott the legislative elections if a new voter register were not compiled, President Obiang dissolved the single-party sixty-seat National Assembly on 2 July, and called for the new election to be held on 14 September. However, after a steadfast rejection by the opposition to participate, in early August Obiang announced the postponement of the election until December. At the same time, he renewed a crackdown against the opposition. In late August, the police and military forces arrested at least fifty people, twenty of whom were said to be soldiers. Five of those arrested were tortured to death. Following the arrests, the government accused the opposition of planning to recruit the soldiers to "physically eliminate" the president and members of the government.

Political Rights and Civil Liberties:

Citizens of Equatorial Guinea lack the means to change their government democratically. The single-handed rule of the self-appointed President Obiang and his party prevents most citizens from influencing public policy in any meaningful way. The opposition parties, registered by a presidential decree, face harassment and intimidation, especially outside of the capital. All of these factors caused the 1993 legislative election to have little meaning.

In a 1990 report, Amnesty International reported that a "culture of terror" had developed in the Equaguinean society. This culture remained in 1993. There were reports of police torture to extract confessions in criminal cases, and occasional torture of political opponents, often resulting in death. In December 1992, American Ambassador John Bennett asked the police to return the finger nails they had extracted from student demonstrators during interrogations. Unnamed sources responded with a note to the embassy in early 1993, threatening Bennett with death for his "arrogance, imperialism and stupidity." The State Department withdrew Bennett temporarily for safety. Frequently, the regime claimed that those who died in custody committed "suicide." In August 1993, Morocco withdrew 500 troops who had acted as presidential bodyguards since 1979. The judiciary is controlled by the regime. Freedom of association, with the partial exception of members of the legalized political parties, is illegal and repressed.

There is only one opposition newspaper. In June, the opposition reported that the government placed a ban on foreign radio broadcasts.

The Catholic Church, representing a large majority of the population, has been persecuted in a move to rid the country of a "foreign influence." In August, Jose Louis Engono, a priest and a critic of the government, went into hiding in order to avoid arrest.

No free trade unions exist. Citizens and residents of the country have to obtain permission for travels within the country and abroad.

Eritrea

Polity: One-party **Political Rights:** 6
Economy: Mixed statist **Civil Liberties:** 5*
Population: 3,000,000 **Status:** Not Free
PPP: na
Life Expectancy: na
Ethnic Groups: Afar, Arab, Beja, Bilin, Jabarti,
Kunama, Saho, Tigrawi

Ratings Change: *Eritrea's civil liberties rating changed from 4 to 5 because the government delayed steps toward democratic transition.

Overview: In 1993 Eritrea became an internationally recognized country, following a referendum in which the overwhelming majority of voters opted for independence.

With the eviction of the Ethiopian army from Eritrea's capital Asmara in 1991, the three-decade old insurgence, the Eritrean People's Liberation Front (EPLF), achieved its objectives: the removal of Ethiopian control over territory adjacent to the Red Sea. The coincident overthrow of the Marxist-Leninist regime of Mengistu Haile Mariam in Ethiopia by their comrades-in-arms allowed the new Ethiopian rulers to confirm the right of Eritreans to national self-determination. The EPLF leadership transformed itself into the Provisional Government of Eritrea (PGE), headed by EPLF's secretary-general Issaias Aferworki.

In order to gain international recognition, the PGE announced a 1993 referendum to settle the question of independence. Of primary importance for the new government, however, was the rebuilding of the infrastructure devastated by the decades-long conflict. By the time of independence Eritrea, which under Italian colonial rule was one of the most industrialized regions in Africa, had one of the lowest incomes per capita in the world, and two thirds of its inhabitants relied on outside food assistance. Shortly after its establishment, the PGE implemented a program of reconstruction in which thousands of former rebels agreed to work in development projects without pay for two years. The program consisted of clearing landmines, planting trees, and constructing dams, terraces, and ponds to boost agricultural production. Prior to the official declaration of independence, the country was unable to obtain funds from international lending institutions, relying instead on the contributions of its vast exile community, comprising almost one third of all Eritreans.

Following the victory over Ethiopian forces and the expulsion of the Ethiopian government officials, the EPLF became the de facto new state administration. The PGE, the provincial and local councils, and the military, were all EPLF dominated. Other rebel groups, primarily the Islamic oriented factions of the Eritrean Liberation Front, felt excluded from the decision making and threatened the resumption of guerrilla warfare should their demands for inclusion in the government be ignored. In November 1992, after declaring 23-25 April 1993 as the date for the referendum, the PGE rejected the registration of political parties prior to the referendum, declaring that achieving independence had priority over ideological differences.

The referendum devised by the PGE required a "yes" or "no" for independence, the latter being a vote for Eritrea's status quo as an Ethiopian province. The limitation to only two options, with no opportunity to vote for the renewal of a federal status with Ethiopia, which existed prior to 1961, was criticized by members of the dominant Amharic nationality within Ethiopia. The choice of the color of ballots in the referendum in which the majority of the voters are illiterate underscored the preferences of the PGE: blue, connoting courage, for independence; and red, in the local tradition connoting death, for Eritrea remaining an Ethiopian province.

In February, the referendum commission began issuing identity and voter registration cards to people over the age of 18 who were eligible for Eritrean citizenship. Of the almost 1.2 million registered voters, some 860,000 were residing within Eritrea, and the remainder in refugee camps in Sudan, Saudi Arabia, Western Europe, and North America. In February, the United Nations special envoy arrived in Asmara to supervise the conduct of the referendum, and organizations and individual voters were allowed to publicize their views for or against the independence.

The April referendum gave astounding support for independence. The results showed a 98.5 percent turnout with 99.8 percent favoring independence. No major irregularities were reported, and the U.N. delegation declared the vote to be free and fair.

Even before the formal declaration of independence on 24 May, the country was internationally recognized by a host of countries, including Ethiopia. On 21 May the PGE issued a decree delineating the functions and duties of the government. The National Assembly, consisting of members of EPLF Central Committee in addition to others drawn from the ranks of provincial administrators and other activists, was to perform legislative functions. Its duration was not to exceed four years during which a special National Assembly-appointed commission was to prepare the country's first constitution. The State Council was to become the new executive, replacing the PGE. The next day, the Assembly elected Aferworki to be the new president.

On 7 June Aferworki appointed the State Council with twenty-five cabinet members, most of whom were members of the EPLF. Despite his pre-referendum pledges that the EPLF would dissolve and political parties would be allowed to compete after Eritrea was formally independent, Aferworki asserted after his election that developing state institutions had priority over political pluralism.

On 28 May, in a ceremony marking Eritrea's admission to the Organization of African Unity (OAU), Aferworki blasted the organization and African leaders for their neglect of Eritrea's struggle for independence, and charged them with political and economic ineptitude in managing their countries.

Political Rights and Civil Liberties: Although the citizens of Eritrea have achieved formal independence, at present they lack the possibility to change their government by democratic means. The present government, consisting almost entirely of members of EPLF, came to power in May 1991 after a prolonged guerrilla war. The EPLF, claiming to represent the interest of the entire population, has monopolized the political life of the country starting from the village councils to the interim legislature, the National Assembly. Despite Eritrea's ethnic and cultural differences, the opposition to the EPLF rule within the country has been almost nonexistent, due primarily to the still lingering post-independence euphoria. Most of the opposition leaders remain in exile, however, and the EPLF refused to allow them to take part in the government. The work on the new constitution that, according to President Aferworki, will guarantee the full spectrum of political and civil rights, has begun only recently and is scheduled to be completed by 1997.

In May the decree on establishing the interim government called for the appointment of a Supreme Court to be chosen by the National Assembly. Lower courts had already been established. The decree granted the judiciary formal independence from the legislature and the executive. However, all the formerly existing Ethiopian laws had been nullified, and the National Assembly has yet to adopt a new constitution and a set of civil and criminal law.

Following the victory over the Ethiopian forces, the EPLF rounded up about 12,000 suspected collaborators accused of human rights abuses. Although most of them were released prior to the declaration of independence, 275 of them still remained in custody without being formally charged. According to government officials, the detainees are former collaborators with the worst record of abuses and with "ossified" attitudes towards the new government.

Freedom of the press is severely limited. There is only one newspaper convening political and social issues, the government-owned *Hadas Eritra (*New Eritrea*)* which appears twice a week in a Tigrinya and Arabic version. The circulation is 25,000 and 5,000 respectively. Three other newspapers are owned by the Catholic and Orthodox Churches and publish mostly on church activities and religious and theological issues. People in ethnic groups that lack a written alphabet rely primarily on the government-owned *Dimtsi Hafash* (Voice of the Masses) radio station. The station broadcasts in the six major languages of the country. The emigre opposition groups have criticized government control over the media and have argued that as long as there is no multipartyism there can be no independent media.

In its attempt to monopolize the political and social life of the new state, the government discourages the creation of independent associations. In March, it dissolved the Regional Center for Human Rights and Development in Asmara for its criticism of the treatment of political prisoners. With its victory in 1991, the EPLF disbanded the Ethiopian-controlled trade and peasants' unions. Shortly thereafter, the PGE promulgated a new Labor Code allowing workers to establish and join a trade union of their choice. The Code also set into law the right to bargain collectively and to strike as a final resort. In practice, however, the EPLF dissolved its associate workers', women's, and youth organizations, and has refused to revive them.

Freedom of religion is generally respected and, in a society equally divided between Christians and Muslims, the government strives to maintain a balance in the appointments to public office.

Estonia

Polity: Presidential-
parliamentary democracy
(ethnic limits)
Economy: Statist
(transitional)
Population: 1,550,000
PPP: 6,438
Life Expectancy: 71.0
Ethnic Groups: Estonian (61 percent), Russian, Ukrainians,
Germans, others (39 percent)

Political Rights: 3
Civil Liberties: 2*
Status: Free

Ratings Change: *Estonia's civil liberties rating changed from 3 to 2
because it allowed non-citizens to participate in local elections.

Overview:
Among the key issues facing the coalition government of
Prime Minister Mart Laar in 1993 were a controversial law on
aliens, October's local elections, a militant Russian minority,
the pace of Russian troop withdrawal, and the economy.

Dominated by Sweden in the sixteenth and seventeenth centuries and annexed by
Russia in 1704, Estonia became independent with the collapse of the Russian Empire in
1918. Two decades of independence ended when Soviet troops occupied Estonia during
World War II as a result of the 1939 Hitler-Stalin pact, which incorporated Estonia,
Latvia and Lithuania into the Soviet Union. Under Soviet rule, over 100,000 Estonians
were deported or died in labor camps. Government-sponsored Russian immigration
substantially changed the ethnic composition of Estonia's population during the Soviet
period; ethnic Estonians constituted 88 percent of the population before Soviet rule and
just over 61 percent in 1989.

Estonia's road to independence from the USSR started in 1988 when the Estonian
Supreme Soviet (later Supreme Council) proclaimed that its laws superseded those of
the Soviet Union. In 1989, Estonian was restored as the official language. On 18 March
1990, the pro-independence Popular Front won the republic's first free elections since
1940. Before the elections, a vote was held for an alternative, 499-member "Congress
of Estonia," composed of independence groups which acted as a nationalist lobby and
"shadow"parliament with no legislative power. On 3 March 1991, 78 percent of voters
approved a plebiscite on independence. One day after the attempted coup against Soviet
President Mikhail Gorbachev, the Supreme Council declared Estonia's independence,
which was subsequently recognized by most countries, including the crumbling USSR.

In 1992, Estonian's ratified a new constitution. The Pro Patria coalition of five free-
market-oriented parties gained one-third of the parliamentary seats. Pro Patria formed a
narrow majority with the Estonian National Independence Party and with the Moderates.
Subsequently, parliament elected Lennart Meri president, even though he polled less
popular votes than the Supreme Council Chairman and head-of-state Arnold Ruutel, whose
Communist past and ties to industrial managers undermined his candidacy. By year's end
the Supreme Council was replaced by a new 101-member State Assembly (Riigikogu).

An emotionally charged issue was a Citizenship Law which required a two-year residence period beginning 30 March 1990, a one-year waiting period from the day of applying for citizenship; and a basic proficiency in Estonian. The law's adoption disenfranchised a large majority of the 600,000 Russians living in Estonia, preventing them from voting in the constitutional referendum and national elections. The law on national elections stipulated that only citizens could vote or run in national elections. The one-year waiting period for citizenship made it impossible for applicants to acquire citizenship in time for the 1992 parliamentary elections, the result being that there are no ethnic Russians in parliament. Proponents of the citizenship law claimed that up to 50,000 Russians were eligible for automatic citizenship but never bothered to apply for it.

In 1993, the issue of citizenship and alien rights soured relations with Russia. Russia's foreign minister alleged in February that the Estonian government was backing the nationalist, anti-Russian Estonian Decolonization Fund, a charge denied by the government. In February, the Riigikogu approved a law that made passage of a language test a requirement for citizenship. On 23 March, parliament overwhelmingly approved amendments to the citizenship law so that citizenship would be acquired equally through paternal and maternal lineage.

On 19 May, parliament, after much discussion, passed a law on local elections that allowed resident non-citizens to vote but barred them from running as candidates. A month later, parliament passed a law decreeing the phasing out of education in Russian in grades 10 to 12 at state schools by the year 2000.

On 21 June, parliament adopted a Law on Aliens that officially designated all non-citizens—about 600,000, mainly Russian-speaking people—as aliens. Under the terms of the law all aliens had to obtain residence and work permits within two years if they wished to remain in Estonia. They had to decide whether they wished to apply for Estonian citizenship, take out Russian or other non-Estonian citizenship, or apply for an alien's passport. The law led to immediate charges of discrimination and "ethnic cleansing" from the predominantly Russian-populated northeast part of Estonia and from Moscow. President Meri responded by submitting the law to the high commissioner on national minorities of the Conference on Security and Cooperation in Europe (CSCE) and to the Council of Europe for evaluation. In response to CSCE recommendations, parliament voted to include a new article in the law guaranteeing residence and work permits to any alien who had settled in Estonia prior to 1 July 1990 and had been registered as a permanent resident in the former Estonian SSR. As a result, on 8 July the Estonian parliament amended the law, taking note of most of the specific criticisms by the international experts but leaving the basic thrust unaltered. Parliament continued to demand that resident permits would still be denied to anyone who served in a career position in the armed forces of a foreign state, which meant that the many thousands of former Soviet Army officers who retired to Estonia faced expulsion.

The amended law did not dissuade the overwhelmingly Russian-speaking cities of Narva and Sillamae from going ahead on 16 and 17 July with referenda on national-territorial autonomy within Estonia for the two cities. Although both referenda were pronounced unconstitutional by the chancellor of justice and the Supreme Court, the government allowed the votes to go ahead. Both cities voted overwhelmingly for autonomy, but the turnout in Narva was much lower than organizers had hoped, and the Estonian authorities claimed in fact less than the required 50 percent had voted there. On 15 August, the Supreme Court formally annulled the results of the referendum in Narva.

While amendments to the law on aliens made it more in conformity with international and European standards, the government failed to take full note of CSCE recommendations regarding the acquisition of citizenship by long-standing residents. The citizenship law which placed so many into the alien category remained the real issue.

Non-citizens, who nationally made up about 20 percent of potential voters, were a factor in 17 October's local and municipal elections, particularly in cities with large Russian populations. (Non-citizens made up 33 percent in Tallinn, 79 percent in Narva, 54.5 percent in Kohtla-Jarve, and 94 percent in Sillamae.) Election results showed the depth of Russian-speaking discontent. While turnout was low in most of the country, it was high in Russian-speaking areas. So-called Russian lists did well in Russian-speaking areas.

Russian response to the fate of Estonia's Russian minority included cutting off natural gas supplies to Estonia on 25 June, a day after Russia's President Boris Yeltsin accused Estonia of creating a system of "apartheid." Estonia was entirely dependent on Russia for gas, and had only three to four days supply in reserve. Some officials in Moscow claimed the cut-off was for non-payment. While the flow of gas was resumed five days later, Russia had signaled its displeasure with Estonia's citizenship and alien laws.

In foreign policy, a key issue continued to be the withdrawal of Soviet troops from its territory. In May, the Russians continued to insist that they would pull out all the estimated 25,000 troops from the Baltics by 1999. Russia's suspension of the withdrawal was sharply criticized by NATO and the CSCE for linking troop withdrawal with Russian-speakers' rights.

Despite uncertainties about energy brought on by Russia's five-day cut-off of natural gas in June, Estonia was considered the most advanced former Soviet republic in its transition to a market system. In February, parliament overwhelmingly passed a 1993 budget. Despite Russian protests, Estonia became part of the Council of Europe. While large-scale privatization still lacked comprehensive legislation, a disciplined austerity program did show results. Subsidies to industry were cut-off, prices were allowed to rise freely while wages were kept down, the central bank was prohibited from printing new money, and the budget was balanced. As a result, inflation dropped dramatically. Small private businesses were about 20 percent of the economy. The Estonian krone has been stable since its introduction in 1992. Exports boomed and foreign investment flooded in. Estonia also broke its dependence on the former Soviet economy, with most of its trade oriented north toward Finland and Scandinavia rather than east toward Russia.

Political Rights and Civil Liberties: Estonians have the rights and means to change their government democratically, although restrictive citizenship and alien laws have effectively disenfranchised a high percentage of non-Estonians from the political process.

The constitution has enshrined a multiparty system, and several parties function freely and without interference, including several organizations representing the Russian minority. On 13 November, the Estonian Popular Front, which had spearheaded independence efforts, voted to dissolve itself. On 20 November, the Estonian National Progressive Party held its founding meeting.

The judiciary is independent and free from government pressures. Estonians can freely express their views and there is a lively independent press, including English-language and Russian-language publications. In August, the Privatization Agency announced the sale of *Ravha Haal*, the largest daily, to a joint-stock company. Once owned and operated by the state, Estonian radio and television networks have been converted to joint-stock operations. Estonian radio launched a commercial channel in May 1993. It competes with fifteen local FM-band commercial stations. A new commercial television company, EVTV, began broadcasting on 1 August. Two others were scheduled to open before the end of the year.

Freedom of conscience and religion is guaranteed by law and honored in practice. There are no significant restrictions on emigration or domestic and international travel. The citizenship, language and alien laws have been called discriminatory against Russians and other non-Estonians. Amendments have accommodated some concerns, but elements of these laws continue to cause concern among international rights organizations.

Women possess the same legal rights as men and are legally entitled to equal pay for equal work.

The Central Organization of Estonian Trade Unions (EAKL) was created in 1990 to replace the Soviet confederation. There are some thirty unions in the country and the right to strike is legal and has been used without government interference.

Ethiopia

Polity: Dominant party (transitional)
Economy: Statist
Population: 53,746,000
PPP: $369
Life Expectancy: 45.5
Ethnic Groups: Afar, Amhara, Harari, Oromo, Somali, Tigrean, others
Ratings Change: *Ethiopia's civil liberties rating changed from 4 to 5 because it put off a transition to democracy.

Political Rights: 6
Civil Liberties: 5*
Status: Not Free

Overview: In 1993, following a referendum in which the Eritreans overwhelmingly opted for independence, the Transitional Government of Ethiopia (TGE) recognized the independence of Eritrea, Ethiopia's former northeastern province adjacent to the Red Sea. The consolidation of power in the hands of the Ethiopian People's Revolutionary Democratic Front (EPRDF) and the regional organizations it controlled, led to continued ethnic conflicts and suppression of dissent prior to general elections scheduled for 1994.

The dominant movement within the EPRDF was the Tigrean People's Liberation Front (TPLF) of the northern Tigre province. It was started in 1975 as a Marxist-Leninist student group to oppose the policies of the Ethiopian dictator Mengistu Haile Mariam. Within the multimember EPRDF coalition, the TPLF, which characterized itself as "revolutionary democratic," launched other ethnically based movements committed to its political program, including the Oromo People's Democratic Organization (OPDO) and the Amhara-based Ethiopian People's Democratic Movement (EPDM).

Following the defeat of the Mengistu regime in May 1991, the EPRDF won control of the country. Shortly thereafter, it convened a conference of twenty-six political groups that had opposed Mengistu's rule. The political groups assembled in the conference agreed to set up a Transitional Government of Ethiopia (TGE) which was to serve for two years and elected the TPLF/EPRDF leader, Meles Zenawi, as the country's interim president and head of government. The conference adopted a National Charter empowering a multi-party, eighty-seven-member Council of Representatives to act as a legislature until national elections scheduled for early 1994. The EPRDF held 32 seats, including 10 held by the TPLF, and 26 seats were allocated to the Oromo groups. The Council replaced the former 835-member National Assembly, previously dominated by the Workers' Party of Ethiopia (WPE), which collapsed with the fall of Mengistu. The new government rejected the Marxist-Leninist ideology of the Mengistu regime and the former platforms of its constituent members, such as the TPLF, and promised to institute democracy and to respect human rights.

The June 1992 regional elections, viewed as the "beginning of opening up of the political system" by international observers, were marred by EPRDF's heavy-handedness in assuring its own and its allies' electoral victory. According to official results, more than 96 percent of the voters cast their votes for EPRDF-favored candidates.

In preparation for the 1994 national elections, the TGE pushed for a new constitution to replace the interim charter in effect since 1991. The Constitutional Commission, appointed by the TGE and the Council of Representatives from among its constituent members, began its work on 1 March. On 13-15 March, representatives from emigre groups and several political organizations in Ethiopia met in Paris at the Peace and Reconciliation Conference. The Conference stated that the transitional period had failed to advance the cause of peace and democracy in Ethiopia, and accused the EPRDF of reverting to old-style tactics reminiscent of the Mengistu era to maintain its hold on power. The Conference called for an all-inclusive Conference on Peace and Reconciliation to be held in Ethiopia in the shortest time possible. In the aftermath of the Paris meeting, the Council of Representatives expelled the Southern Ethiopian People's Democratic Organization (SEDPC) from the TGE. The SEDPC, composed of ten ethnic organizations, was one of the signers of the Paris Conference statement criticizing the government.

In 1991, the Eritrean People's Liberation Front (EPLF), a guerrilla group fighting for the territory's independence, defeated Ethiopia's Mengistu forces. With the overthrow of the Mengistu regime by the TPLF-led forces, an EPLF ally, the new Ethiopian government acknowledged Eritrea's right to hold a referendum on independence and recognize the subsequent results. The decision was criticized by opposition groups, most notably the All Amhara People's Organization (AAPO) which strove to maintain the country's unity. The government justified the decision on the grounds that a military solution to the thirty-year-old conflict was impossible, and that separation, in case of affirmative referendum results, was the only option. On 4 January 1993 the TGE security forces killed at least one Addis Ababa University student and injured more than fifty, during a demonstration protesting the U.N. involvement in the planned referendum. During the 23-25 April U.N. supervised referendum more than 99 percent of Eritrean voters opted for independence, which was subsequently recognized by Ethiopia's government.

Since the TGE's 1991 decision to divide the country into fourteen semi-autonomus regions (*kilel*), the AAPO has accused the government of fostering ethnic policies reminiscent of South Africa's apartheid, and attempting to dismantle Ethiopia as a country. In June the AAPO's president, Asrat Woldeyes, presented a large number of violations committed by parties and groups forming the TGE against members of the Amharic ethnic group. These included stigmatizing Amharic-speakers as *neftegna* (settlers) in the ethnically designated regions where they and their ancestors have lived for centuries; imprisoning AAPO officials without charge for hoisting Ethiopian flags; prohibiting entrepreneurial activities; and discriminating in allotting public assistance.

Armed opposition groups continued to attack the EPRDF forces acting as the de facto national army. In February the government released 16,000 Oromo prisoners-of-war from detention camps in an attempt to restart negotiations with the Oromo Liberation Front (OLF), which quit the government just prior to the 1992 regional elections, accusing the EPRDF of prefabricating the results in the Oromo region in OPDO's favor. The OLF responded to the prisoner release by stating that it will continue to fight EPRDF militarily as long as it attempts to dominate political life in Ethiopia. Another guerrilla group, the Kefagn ("dissatisfied") Patriotic Front fought against the annexation of a fertile part of the Gondar region to the Tigrai province.

Following the January Addis Abbaba University protests, the government warned the students against "unlawful activities" and ordered a temporary suspension of its operations. In addition, the authorities arrested the university's president, Alemayehu Tefarra, and his two vice-presidents, all of whom were dismissed from their posts. In March, the government agreed to re-open the university by appointing Duri Mohammed, the minister of planning, as the new president. In April, Duri ordered the dismissal of forty-one faculty members, many of whom were internationally recognized in their academic fields, on the grounds of "poor performance" of the students. According to the remaining faculty members, who responded by publishing a statement critical of the dismissal, the real reason was that those dismissed had criticized the government. Shortly after the dismissal, President Meles remarked in an interview that as the university's employer he was free to "hire and fire" all of the faculty members at his pleasure.

Political Rights and Civil Liberties:

Ethiopians are not able to choose their government in free and fair democratic elections. The June 1992 regional elections, the first attempt at multiparty elections in Ethiopia's history, were marred by various irregularities, including fraud and intimidation, media bias in favor of the ruling EPRDF coalition, and political assassination by the ruling parties and their opponents. The scheduled 1994 national elections do not promise a significant improvement in the ability of the opposition groups to contest the elections on an equal basis with the TGE-represented parties.

The judiciary is formally free, although most of the judicial appointees have been EPRDF nominees. In February, the Addis Ababa High Court ordered the release of three government officials of the previous regime, after they submitted complaints stating that they had been detained without charge. The lack of trained police in many localities led to frequent complaints about police harassment and unlawful use of force against ordinary citizens. On 25 February, 1,100 former police officers dismissed by the TGE protested in the capital for the return to their jobs.

Although press censorship has been abolished and private media have been allowed to publish, a new law prohibits the publication of information " leading to great harm," such as inciting ethnic groups against each other. Most of the media remain state-owned and self-censorship is prevalent.

The stated intention of the TGE to institute a market economy has been only partially achieved, as the question of property rights has not yet been solved. All of the farmland and most of the industry remain in state hands, although the farmers are free to sell their produce at market prices, and the retail trading and other services are in private hands. According to the EPRDF, the government wants to retain the title to the farmland for the time being in order to prevent it from being purchased by the affluent Amhara elite, from whom it had been confiscated under the Mengistu regime. One of the tasks of the Constitutional Commission is to provide a legal solution to the question of land ownership.

Although the National Charter guarantees freedom of movement outside and inside of the country, the latter was made difficult in practice due to the continued armed clashes in various parts of the country, and due the policies of certain local and regional governments discouraging some groups of people from moving out of the area of their jurisdiction or preventing others from moving in.

The population is almost equally divided between Christians and Muslims and freedom of religion is guaranteed. There were sporadic acts of violence between the two major groups. There was also a conflict within the Ethiopian Orthodox Church regarding the appointment of the new Patriarch Paulos, who belongs to the Tigrean ethnic group and who replaced the ousted Patriarch Makarios, an Amhara appointed during the Mengistu era.

The right of workers to organize in trade unions is guaranteed in the interim charter, and some 300 trade unions have been organized on a local level, although no new nation-wide labor confederation to replace the Mengistu Ethiopian Trade Union (ETU) confederation has been established.

Fiji

Polity: Parliamentary democracy and native chieftains (ethnic limits)
Economy: Capitalist
Population: 757,000
PPP: $4,427
Life Expectancy: 64.8
Ethnic Groups: Indians (49 percent), Fijian (46 percent), other Pacific islanders, Chinese (6 percent)

Political Rights: 4
Civil Liberties: 3
Status: Partly Free

Overview:
On 29 November 1993 Prime Minister Sitiveni Rabuka called snap elections for February 1994, after five ethnic Fijian MPs defected to join the opposition in defeating a budget motion.

Earlier in the year opposition from militant ethnic Fijians forced Rabuka to scrap plans for including Indo Fijians in a unity government.

Fiji's paramount chiefs ceded sovereignty over these South Pacific islands to the British in 1874 to end frequent territorial conquests among rival kingdoms. The country achieved independence in 1970. The current population is roughly evenly split between ethnic Fijians and the descendants of Indian agricultural workers who migrated to the islands in the early 1900s. After the April 1987 elections the Indian-backed National Federation Party (NFP) was able to form a government with the trade union-supported Fiji Labor Party (FLP), breaking the seventeen-year rule of the predominantly ethnic-Fijian Alliance Party.

Alarmed by the emerging political influence of the Indian community, (then) Lieutenant Colonel Sitiveni Rabuka led a pair of bloodless coups in 1987 that over-threw Bavadra and a subsequent provisional government. With 84 percent of the land held by ethnic Fijians, the coups were supported by many who feared the Indians would confiscate their property. Ratu Sir Kamisese Mara took over as prime minister of an interim government.

In January 1990 the country returned to full civilian rule. In July the interim government promulgated a new constitution guaranteeing ethnic Fijians a perpetual majority in parliament. It set aside for them 37 of the 70 seats in the House, and 24 of the 34 seats in the unelected Senate. The Indians received 27 of the remaining House seats, with 5 going to "other races," mostly Chinese and European, and one to the island dependency of Rotuma. The unelected Great Council of Chiefs, a group of traditional rulers, secured the right to select the president and appoint the ethnic Fijian Senate seats.

The first elections since the coups, and under the new constitution, were held over eight days in May 1992. In balloting for the ethnic Fijian seats, the Fijian Political Party (FPP) took 30 seats; the extremist Fijian Nationalist United Front, which called for the expulsion of all Indians, 5; and independents, 2. The Indian seats were split between the NFP with 14 and the FLP with 13. The General Voters Party (GVP) took the 5 seats reserved for other groups. On 2 June President Sir Penaia Ganilau named Rabuka prime minister of a coalition government consisting of the FPP, the GVP and several independents. The NFP and the FLP agreed to support the government outside the coalition after Rabuka agreed to review the 1990 constitution. On 4 December the prime minister startled the parliament by announcing he would invite the opposition into a national unity government, pending approval by the Great Council of Chiefs.

In 1993 Rabuka faced a backlash from nationalist ethnic Fijians who considered the proposed unity government a sellout to the Indians. The organized opposition came from the militant right-wing Taukei (indigenous) Movement, which had planned the 1987 coups. On 7 April Taukei leader Josaia Diani publicly called on fellow Taukei member Rabuka to step down as premier rather than cede some power to the Indians.

Although the Great Council of Chiefs held a two-day meeting on the unity government proposal in late May, full discussions could last up to two years. The Council appointed a fifteen-man committee to coordinate district and provincial meetings throughout the islands to gauge popular opinion on both the unity plan and the constitution itself. In June the FLP withdrew its support of the government over Rabuka's failure to review the 1990 constitution. Meanwhile, on 25 August the Taukei further heightened tensions by warning of another coup if the FLP continued to seek changes to the constitution.

A related issue is the future of the 1966 Agricultural Landlord and Tenants Act, set to expire in 1996. Under the Act Indian farmers hold some 20,000 leases on ethnic Fijian-owned land, and operate many successful sugar plantations. Prime Minister Rabuka has committed the government in principle to extend the Act, but in practice the future of both the national unity government and the Act could ultimately rest on Indian acceptance of the 1990 constitution.

President Ganilau died on 16 December. A successor will be named in January 1994.

Political Rights and Civil Liberties:

Fijians elected a government in May 1992 under a constitution that ensures ethnic Fijians a majority in parliament and requires the prime minister to be an ethnic Fijian. An unelected interim government promulgated the constitution in 1990 without a referendum, casting serious doubt on its legitimacy. In addition to rejecting the concept of "one-man, one vote," it allows parliament to suspend constitutionally protected civil liberties in emergency situations, theoretically allowing ethnic Fijians to do so unilaterally through their guaranteed majority. To perpetuate politics along traditional lines, the ethnic Fijian seats are heavily weighted towards the rural areas, where voters tend to support ethnic Fijian parties and traditional leaders in greater numbers.

Occasional police abuse of detainees is a continuing problem; further, police convicted of abuse generally receive light punishments. The judiciary is modeled on the British system and is independent of the government. Defendents receive adequate due process rights.

Freedom of speech is largely unabridged, although the Public Order Act prohibits speech or actions likely to incite racial antagonism. The government-produced *Nightly News Focus* television report has been criticized for its limited coverage of opposition views. In a related matter, the government is in the process of setting up the country's first permanant television service. Under current plans provincial councils will have a 51 percent stake in a joint venture that will include local and foreign investors, the latter most likely being an Australian or New Zealand company.

Some legal restrictions on press rights remain. The Press Correction Act (PCA) allows the Minister of Information to order a paper to print a "correcting statement" to an article. If a paper refuses and a court finds it guilty, individuals involved can face a fine and/or imprisonment for up to six months. Under the PCA the government can also arrest anyone who publishes "malicious" material, including false news that can cause public disorder. Although the government rarely exercises these restrictions, their existence leads newpapers and private radio stations to practice self-censorship regarding sensitive political matters.

Freedom of religion is respected. Freedom of movement at home and abroad is unrestricted. Workers have the right to join independent unions and strike. The government has promised a review of laws passed in November 1991 placing restrictions on union activity, including making them liable for damages during strikes, and preventing individuals from holding more than one union leadership position.

Finland

Polity: Presidential-
parliamentary democracy
Economy: Mixed
capitalist
Population: 5,050,000
PPP: $16,446
Life Expectancy: 75.5
Ethnic Groups: Finns, Swedes, Lapps (Samil)

Political Rights: 1
Civil Liberties: 1
Status: Free

Overview: In 1993 Finland suffered from a sluggish economy and negotiated for entry into the European Union (EU). The country also made a major decision about energy policy.

Since 1990, Finnish economic output has fallen by 10 percent. Unemployment has grown from less than 5 percent to 20 percent. The collapse of the Soviet Union in 1991 eliminated a large market for Finnish goods. The Finnish government hopes to reorient the country to the West by joining Europe. Prime Minister Esko Aho's center-right government applied for EC membership in March 1992. The country belongs to the European Economic Area (EEA). The EEA countries have an open market agreement with the EU.

The Conservatives and the opposition Social Democrats are pro-EU, but Aho's agricultural Center Party is divided on the issue. On the one hand, the Center's supporters worry about European farm policy. On the other hand, the party's conservative voters may not want to break the coalition government over Europe, thereby risking that the Left might return to power. In an apparent effort to win agricultural support for Europe, Aho named farm lobbyist Heikki Haavisto foreign minister in May 1993. Haavisto is the main Finnish negotiator with the EU, which the government hopes Finland will join in 1995.

The present constitution of Finland dates from 1919. It provides for a 200-seat parliament elected by universal suffrage, based upon proportional representation, for a four-year term. The head of state is the president, who serves a six-year term, and has some significant powers. The president appoints the prime minister from the party or coalition which commands the majority of the parliament. The president can initiate and veto legislation, is directly responsible for foreign affairs and has the responsibility for some domestic affairs. In addition, the president may dissolve the parliament at any time and call for elections. The term of President Mauno Koivisto, a Social Democrat, expires in 1994. As of late 1993, the leading candidate to succeed him was Martii Ahtisaari, a U.N. diplomat who has the Social Democrats' nomination. Ahtisaari's candidacy began after he received high ratings in a public opinion poll. His popularity stems from his having been away from the country and outside domestic politics. There will be a two-round presidential election by popular vote in January 1994. Previously, an electoral college made the final presidential choice.

Aho's government has been in office since 1991. The previous government had been a coalition dominated by Social Democrats and Conservatives. Due to economic decline, the Social Democrats and Conservatives lost ground in the 1991 election.

Aho's Center Party increased its representation in the parliament and formed a coalition with the Conservatives, the Finnish Christian Union, and the Swedish People's Party, which represents the Swedish ethnic minority.

The center-right coalition has had to struggle simultaneously against rising deficits and joblessness. The government has made cutbacks in spending, but the labor movement has resisted Aho's proposals for lower wages. Finns believe increasingly that the economic downturn will undermine their strong social welfare system.

In September 1993 the parliament rejected building a fifth nuclear energy plant, by a vote of 107-90. The government had decided to suspend party discipline and allow members a free vote. Consequently, Finland will turn to other sources of energy. Business interests fear that the economy will stall without more nuclear power.

Political Rights and Civil Liberties: Finns have the right to change their government by democratic means. The indigenous Swedish and Lappic (Sami) have full political and cultural rights.

There is a wide selection of publications available to the Finnish public. Newspapers are private. Traditionally, many parties have owned or controlled newspapers, but several dailies have folded in the 1990s. For years, the press restrained itself in dealing with issues sensitive to the Soviet Union, but this self-censorship died with the Soviet Union, if not before. The Finnish Broadcasting Corporation controls most of the radio and television programming in Finland. There are programs for both Finnish and Swedish speakers. Limited private broadcasting is also available.

There are two established churches in Finland, one Lutheran and the other Orthodox. The state finances both of the established churches through a special tax, from which citizens may exempt themselves. There is freedom of worship for other faiths.

It is illegal to discriminate on the basis of race, religion, sex, language or social status in Finland. There have been cases of civilian attacks on non-Nordic immigrants. The government has condemned this violence and has taken action to fight racism. In addition, the Finnish state investigates cases of sex discrimination.

Workers have the right to organize, bargain and strike. An overwhelming majority of Finns belong to free trade unions. The Central Organization of Finnish Trade Unions (SAK) dominates the labor movement in Finland.

France

Polity: Presidential-par-
liamentary democracy
Economy: Mixed
capitalist
Population: 57,678,000
PPP: $17,405
Life Expectancy: 76.4

Political Rights: 1
Civil Liberties: 2
Status: Free

Ethnic Groups: French, regional minorities (Corsican, Alsatian, Basque, Breton), and various Arab and African immigrant groups

Overview:

In the major political development of 1993, French voters installed an overwhelming center-right majority in the National Assembly. Voting in a two-round ballot in March and April, the electorate overturned the previous Socialist-Communist majority, in place since 1988. The new Assembly is composed overwhelmingly of members from the neo-Gaullist Rally for the Republic (RPR), led by Paris Mayor Jacques Chirac, and the center-right Union for French Democracy (UDF), led by Charles Million and whose best known figure is former President Valery Giscard d'Estaing.

The current system of government, the Fifth Republic, dates from 1958. As designed by Charles De Gaulle, the presidency is the dominant institution in this mixed presidential-parliamentary system. The people elect the president directly through a two-round system. In the first round, candidates of all parties appear on the ballot. If no candidate reaches a majority, then a runoff takes place between the two top contestants. Socialist Francois Mitterrand became president in 1981, and won reelection in 1988. The parliamentary bodies are the 577-member National Assembly, which the people elect directly in two rounds, and the 318-member Senate, which is chosen by an electoral college of local elected officials. The Assembly is elected for five years and can be dissolved by the president.

As the 1993 Assembly election neared, the Socialists faced the possibility of defeat as voters blamed them for mounting unemployment, labor unrest, an AIDS-tainted blood supply, a tough agricultural trade deal, and violent racial tensions between the French and immigrant populations. An additional factor was voter fatigue with Mitterrand after his twelve years in office. Despite the expectation of defeat, the scale of the rout surprised most observers. The center-right took 80 percent of the Assembly seats. Prior to Mitterrand's election to the presidency, his closest constitutional advisor, Robert Badinter (now on the constitutional court) had expressed the view that the president should resign when rebuffed in a national poll. However, Mitterrand insisted on "cohabiting" with the new majority, as he had after a similar Socialist reversal in 1986.

In the vote, the Communists maintained their parliamentary representation with twenty-seven seats, but the far-right National Front and the environmentalist parties, the Greens and the Generation Ecology, won no seats. The election commission looked into several allegations of illegally excessive campaign spending, but no election results were overturned.

Mitterrand's ostensible reason for staying in his post was to protect the social insurance programs which he claimed, during the campaign, the conservatives wanted to roll back. However, Chirac stated that the French welfare state (much of which is of Gaullist origin) was inviolable. A former prime minister, Chirac declined that post in 1993, preferring to concentrate on his Paris mayoralty and his probable 1995 run for the presidency. The new government, headed by Edouard Balladur, ordered an audit that showed the public deficits to be far greater than acknowledged by the retiring Prime Minister Pierre Beregovoy. Depressed by the defeat and tainted by an interest free loan from Roger-Patrice Pelat (a businessman involved in an insider trading scandal), Beregovoy committed suicide on 1 May 1993. Mitterrand blamed the media and in this was seconded by his last square of loyalists, notably the retiring Culture Minister, Jack Lang. By late December, a judge concluded that Pelat had also made substantial payments to Francois Mitterrand during 1972-80 and to Gilbert Mitterrand, the president's son, during 1981-89.

Without calling into question the French social security system, Balladur raised taxes and tightened benefits, and emitted a major bond to be paid in part by the sale of privatized companies. The privatization program ran into trouble in the fall, however, when workers at not-yet-privatized, and financially bleeding, Air France successfully defied management and government and prevented layoffs called for in the pre-privatization restructuring plan. Balladur maintained a high approval rating (over 60 percent) despite a gloomy economic scene marked by growing unemployment (12 percent) and negative GNP growth.

In other social unrest, French crews in fishing fleets rioted (on shore) over softening markets which they blamed on European Union (EU) policies, and went so far as to kidnap British fisheries officials on the high seas. The government mediated this difficulty with its European partners.

French troops participated in peacekeeping operations under the U.N. flag in Bosnia, Croatia, and Somalia. They made brief "jumps" into Zaire and Burundi to evacuate French nationals and protect civilians during periods of disorder. Less dramatically, French diplomats went to the mat successfully against the U.S. in the final stages of the GATT negotiations, seeking to impose their views on trade policy in agriculture and feature and television film.

Political Rights and Civil Liberties: The French have the right to change their government by democratic means. Political parties receive public financing. The government may place up to five years of restrictions on the political rights of anyone convicted of committing racist, anti-Semitic or xenophobic acts. Under the Fifth Republic constitution, the president has significant emergency powers and the right to rule by decree under certain circumstances. These represent potential threats to democracy. France has democratically elected local governments, but there is a strong tradition of centralized government.

The press is largely free, but there are some restrictions on expression, and the government is involved in subsidizing journalism and registering journalists. The state is secretive, and limits criticism of the president. The broadcast media became increasingly free and competitive in the 1980's. There is no government monopoly; private radio stations are growing.

France's anti-terrorist policy includes the expulsion of suspected Basque terrorists, a procedure that is also applied to foreigners believed to be assisting Middle Eastern terrorist organizations. The laws contain "urgency" procedures that allow the government to expel foreigners without any possibility to appeal the decision. There is no right to *habeas corpus*. Among the indigenous cultural minorities, the Corsicans have a separatist movement that engages in sporadic terrorist acts on the island of Corsica and the French mainland.

In view of the continuing probes of illegal political fundraising activities, mainly on the Socialist side, it appeared the judiciary was developing a tradition of independence that is not institutionalized in the Constitution. Leading newspapers revealed the existence of a presidential snoop patrol which specialized in spying on journalists.

In 1993, the constitutional right to asylum was amended to bring it in conformity with the new rules set out under the Treaty of European Union, which went into effect in November. Critics charged that the amendment rendered granting asylum arbitrary rather than obligatory, but some constitutional experts did not believe the change curtailed asylum rights.

There is freedom of religion. In 1993, the Balladur government made it easier for private (including religious) schools to receive financial assistance from the national government. There were conflicts between some Muslim girls and school administrators in public schools over the students' right to wear *hijebs* (Muslim veils) in class. French law prohibits wearing religious garb and symbols in state schools.

The French maintained the lowest rate of female elected officials in western Europe, but at their fall congress the Socialists called for candidate lists with equal numbers of males and females, at least for the European elections scheduled for the spring of 1994. Despite having strong female electoral bases, neither the RPR nor the UDF made such significant gestures to women. However, one of Balladur's three Ministers of State is Simone Veil, arguably the most popular politician in France after the prime minister himself. The sports and youth minister and the head of the National Democratic Confederation of Labor (CNDT) are women. Trade unions are free. There are competing Communist and non-Communist labor federations.

On the racial front, a consensus in all parties seemed to be emerging in 1993 to resist all calls for multiculturalism, quotas in hiring or anything else, and to encourage anti-segregationist housing policies. France has strict anti-racist legislation but "ghettos" have developed in areas where immigrants from black Africa, the Maghreb, and Asia are concentrated.

Gabon

Polity: Dominant party
Economy: Capitalist
Population: 1,123,000
PPP: $4,147
Life Expectancy: 52.5

Political Rights: 5*
Civil Liberties: 4
Status: Partly Free

Ethnic Groups: Duma, Fang, Mpongwe, Shogo, others
Ratings Change: *Gabon's political rights rating changed from 4 to 5 because they held a dubious presidential election accompanied by political violence.

Overview: In 1993 President Omar Bongo won a renewed term in office in an election marred by confusion and irregularities.

Situated on the west coast of central Africa, Gabon gained independence from France in 1960. Its first president, Leon M'Ba, created a one-party state under his Gabon Democratic Bloc (BDG). M'Ba died in 1967 and was succeeded by Bongo, who outlawed all opposition groups and maintained a one-party rule of the BDG, renamed the Democratic Party of Gabon (PDG). He was elected president in 1986 to a seven-year term, running unopposed as the sole PDG candidate.

Economically, the Gabonese have long enjoyed the highest standard of living in sub-Saharan Africa. The country's economic backbone were the oil reserves, controlled mostly by the French. The Bongo regime has promoted a free-market system, but at the same time neglected to develop an economic infrastructure necessary to attract foreign investment. Due to corruption and mismanagement—Bongo's personal wealth is estimated to amount to several billion dollars—by the early 1990s Gabon had the highest capital flight rate in the developing world, double its GDP, according to the World Bank. In August 1993, the government announced the introduction of austerity measures to control a swelling budget deficit.

Widespread political unrest prompted Bongo to take steps toward multipartyism in 1990. Competitive legislative elections were held in October 1990. The PDG retained more than half of the seats in the 120-member National Assembly with the remainder won by the opposition. The largest opposition groups are the National Rally of Lumberjacks (RNB), the Gabonese Progress Party (PGP), and the African Forum for Reconstruction (FAR).

In the subsequent two years, the opposition parties continued to pressure the government for political concessions, including equal access to the media, opposition participation on the national electoral commission, and an accurate census of the population.

On 15 June 1993 the government announced the date of the presidential election to be 5 December and, in case none of the candidates received the absolute majority of the votes required for election, a run-off date of 19 December. By October, the official number of candidates, including Bongo, rose to thirteen.

In the run-up to the elections, Bongo withdrew from his stated commitment to allow international observers to train local civic action groups and to participate in monitoring the elections. On 12 October Bongo instituted new requirements in order to discourage the opposition, stipulating that all candidates report by 15 October to a government physician for a series of physical exams testing for AIDS, diabetes and cholesterol. The new requirements were announced when Bourdés-Ogouliguendé was on a visit to France but he interrupted his visit and immediately returned to Gabon, qualifying to maintain his candidacy. Eventually, only two candidates were disqualified because of administrative hurdles.

Following the 5 December election the electoral commission announced that Bongo had won with 51 percent of the vote, thus eliminating the need for a run-off. The second candidate, RNB's Paul Mba Abessole, received 27 percent of the vote. The opposition immediately denounced the results as fraudulent and Abessole declared himself the winner. Subsequently, several people were killed and property destroyed during clashes between opposition supporters and government troops.

Political Rights and Civil Liberties:

The right of citizens to change their government democratically, prescribed in the new constitution, has been circumscribed by electoral manipulation in favor of President Bongo. On 10 November the opposition listed a number of irregularities attributed to the government, including the discovery of 200,000 proxy ballots, constituting almost half of the total number of voters, and an excess of ballot boxes. Bongo excluded the opposition from participating in the electoral commission, except as observers, and on 10 September he appointed his daughter, Pascaline, to be the commission's co-chairman. During the first multi-party legislative election in 1990, there were credible charges of ballot rigging by the government and the PDG, as well as by the opposition.

Since 1992, when the legislature granted greater autonomy to the courts and improved the career paths of the judges, the judiciary has strengthened its independence from executive interference. Nevertheless, the pressure on the courts from the executive remains strong, particularly in opposition and security related cases. Bongo's wife continues to head the Constitutional Court.

Torture remains an accepted practice to extract confessions from suspects, and the physical conditions of prisons are poor, with insufficient food, inadequate medical facilities, and crumbling buildings.

Freedom of speech and expression by opposition leaders and ordinary citizens remains relatively open, although the opposition alleged that its members and supporters in the civil service faced harassment and sometimes dismissals because of their convictions.

Since 1991, the state and private press has become more critical of the government. The state media, including the main daily *L'Union,* expanded their coverage of opposition activities. In 1993, however, the government attempted to curb the private media. On 5 April the government began jamming the broadcasts of Radio Liberté, Gabon's only independent radio station. The Minister of Communication, Patrice Nziengui, accused the station, authorized to operate by the National Council of Communication, of operating illegally and violating public order. On 9 September Nziengui ordered the indefinite closure of all independent newspapers, citing as reasons their "irresponsible" criticism of the government.

Government authorization is required for all public meetings, although in practice, protests and rallies often take place without permits. The largest single demonstration in 1993 occurred on 24 May, when RNB supporters protested in the capital against the jamming of Radio Liberté.

Freedom to form and join political parties and professional associations is generally respected, although, as noted earlier, civil servants may face harassment because of their activities. Freedom of religion is respected and there is no state religion. Catholic and Protestant Christians constitute the majority of the population. President Bongo, however, is a member of the Muslim minority. The Gabonese have the right to travel and migrate internally and externally. Exit permits for foreign travel were abolished in 1991. Since 1992, when the monopoly of the PDG, affiliated Gabonese Labor Confederation (COSYGA) was lifted, workers have had the right to form and join trade unions of their choice.

The Gambia

Polity: Presidential-legislative democracy
Economy: Capitalist
Population: 930,000
PPP: $913
Life Expectancy: 44.0
Ethnic Groups: Mandingo, Fulani, Wolof, Jola, Serahuli
Ratings Change: *The Gambia's political rights rating changed from 1 to 2 as a result of modifications in methodology. See "Survey Methodology," page 671.

Political Rights: 2*
Civil Liberties: 2
Status: Free

Overview:
Located in West Africa, the tiny Republic of the Gambia is a narrow country surrounded on three sides by Senegal. Under British rule since 1588, it became a separate colony in 1888, achieved internal self-government in 1963, and became fully independent in February 1965.

President Dawda Jawara and his People's Progressive Party (PPP) have led the country since independence. Jawara has been directly elected under a multiparty system since 1982. On 29 April 1992, Jawara won re-election with 58.4 percent of the vote. His main political rival, Sherif Mustapha Dibba, leader of the National Convention Party (NCP), got 22 percent. Candidates from three minor parties divided the rest.

The unicameral, directly elected House of Representatives has fifty-one members who serve for five-year terms. In 1992 legislative elections, thirty-six seats were contested, with the PPP winning twenty-five, a loss of six. Apart from the NCP, other legal political parties include the Gambian People's Party, the United Party, the leftist People's Democratic Organization for Independence and Socialism, and the right-of-center People's Democratic Party.

A key concern in 1993 was that of refugees from Senegal's Casamance region, site of renewed outbreaks of rebel insurgency. Red Cross officials confirmed in March that over 600 refugees were registered at the society's branch office in Brikama.

On 22 April, police disclosed that two armed men believed to be members of the separatist Democratic Forces of Casamance were arrested in Sinabor on the Senegalese border after they attacked and killed a Gambian shopkeeper before looting his store.

Gambia's economic revival continued in 1993 under the government's program for "sustained development." Reflecting continued economic confidence, the 1991-92 budget included civil service salary increases and suspended scheduled tax increases.

Political Rights and Civil Liberties: Citizens of the Gambia have the means to change their government under a multiparty system. Political parties operate freely and openly.

The judiciary is independent of government interference, and the judicial system is based on the English model. Islamic *shari'a* law governs marriage, divorce, and inheritance for Muslims, and tribal customary law covers these areas for non-Muslims. Parliament abolished the death penalty on 7 April.

The principal newspaper and national radio station are government-owned, but all news media operate freely. *The Gambia Times* is published fortnightly by the PPP; *The Nation* fortnightly; and *The Worker*, thrice-weekly by the Gambia Labor Congress. There is no television service, but transmissions can be received from Senegal. Opposition politicals were given equal air time on the state-owned radio station during the 1992 campaign. There are generally no restrictions of association, assembly and movement. Several internal human rights organizations operate freely in the Gambia. Religious freedom is guaranteed and respected in practice.

Women's rights are circumscribed, particularly in rural areas which make up most of the country. Marriages are often "arranged," domestic violence occurs, and circumcision of women is common. Gambian women who have undergone this procedure could run as high as 60 percent. In 1993, a migrant worker from Gambia was charged in Paris with genital mutilation because she had both daughters circumcised, a crime in France since 1984.

All workers except civil servants are allowed to form unions and strike. The Gambian Workers' Confederation (GWC) and the Gambian Workers' Union (GWU) are competing labor federations.

Georgia

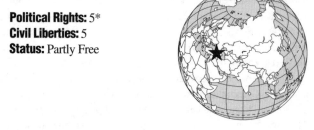

Polity: Parliamentary democracy (foreign military influenced)
Economy: Statist transitional
Population: 5,484,000
PPP: $4,572
Life Expectancy: 72.0

Political Rights: 5*
Civil Liberties: 5
Status: Partly Free

Ethnic Groups: Georgians (70 percent), Russians, Abkhazians, Armenians, Azeris, Ossetians, others (30 percent)
Ratings Change: *Georgia's political rights rating changed from 4 to 5 because of a Russian-backed separatist conflict within the Abkhazian region and a violent comeback attempt by deposed President Gamsakhurdia.

Overview: In 1993, the government of Eduard Shevardnadze faced the violent secession of the Abkhazia region, armed insurrection by supporters of ousted former President Zviad Gamsakhurdia, Russian machinations, a moribund economy and Georgia on the verge of fragmentation.

Absorbed by Russia in the early nineteenth century, Georgia proclaimed independence in 1918, gaining Soviet recognition two years later. In 1921, it was overrun by the Red

Army and became a Soviet republic. In 1922 it entered the USSR as a component of the Transcaucasian Federated Soviet Republic, becoming a separate union republic in 1936.

Georgia declared independence from the Soviet Union after a referendum in April 1991. Nationalist leader and former dissident Gamsakhurdia was overwhelmingly elected president in May. But by year's end, his erratic, often authoritarian behavior led to his violent ouster by opposition units led by former Prime Minister Tengiz Sigua and Jaba Ioseliani, head of the 2,000-man *Mkhedrioni* (Knights of Georgia) militia. After fierce battles in the capital, Tbilisi, Gamsakhurdia fled in early 1992 to the Chechen region in Russia. Former Soviet Foreign Minister Shevardnadze was asked by the State Council, which had temporarily assumed legislative and executive powers, to head a new government. On 24 August, Shevardnadze announced he would run for the office of Speaker of Parliament, and he was elected in October. Sigua was named prime minister.

In early 1993, separatists launched an assault on government forces in the Abkhazian capital, the Black Sea port of Sukhumi, leading President Shevardnadze to ask the United Nations to send peacekeepers to the region. Georgian-Abkhazian tensions first escalated in August 1992 when Tbilisi responded to local demands for greater sovereignty by sending in troops. With fighting increasing in February, Shevardnadze blamed rogue Russia Army units for supplying the mostly Muslim Abkhazians, who constituted only 18 percent of the region's 538,000 people, with troops, heavy weapons and aircraft, though he insisted Russian President Boris Yeltsin was not personally responsible.

Fighting intensified in March after Abkhazian forces launched an all-out offensive on Sukhumi. Allegations of Russian involvement were bolstered when a fighter plane piloted by a Russian was shot down. Meanwhile, on several occasions in April, thousands of Gamsakhudria supporters held unsanctioned rallies in Tbilisi.

In May, Shevardnadze moved to consolidate his power by easing out two military commanders who led the anti-Gamsakhurdia revolt and challenged his authority. Ioseliani was asked to step down from the National Security Council, National Guard commander Tengiz Kitovani was replaced and the guard's most decorated hero, Capt. Gia Karkarashvili, was named defense minister. On 14 May, a ceasefire between Georgian and Abkhazian forces was agreed in Moscow by Shevardnadze and President Yeltsin. The two pledged to ensure the withdrawal of all heavy weapons and aircraft from the conflict zone. On 23 May, pro-Gamsakhurdia loyalists rallied in the west Georgian town of Abasha calling for the government to resign. In another sign of internal discord, over 100 faculty members of the Tbilisi State University published an open letter to Shevardnadze condemning "the rise of flagrant human rights violations" and calling on the government to step down.

As severe shelling of Sukhumi continued in June, Shevardnadze warned of a Georgian military offensive response. There was strong evidence that the Abkhazians were supported by Russian troops from the self-styled Trans-Dniester Republic in Moldova. By early July, Georgia had lost control of more than half of Abkhazia. The government declared martial law in Abkhazia on 6 July as rebel troops advanced on Sukhumi. On 27 July, the Abkhazian parliament approved a Georgian-Russian compromise ceasefire that called for the withdrawal of all forces from Sukhumi. The same day, armed Gamsakhurdia supporters joined with units under the command of former Defense Minister Kitovani in western Georgia, presenting a fresh challenge to the beleaguered central government.

The country's growing political and economic problems led to the resignation of Prime Minister Sigua in early August and parliament named Shevardnadze temporary prime minister. On 6 August, Georgian government troops and Abkhazian forces began to withdraw from the war zone near Sukhumi as part of the Russian-brokered peace agreement. At the end of the month, Shevardnadze called for a referendum on confidence in the ousted Gamsakhudria, who had announced he was returning to Georgia to join his forces which controlled much of the western part of the country.

On 15 September, parliament granted emergency powers to Shevardnadze who had threatened to resign as head of state. The next day, Abkhazian forces launched a ferocious attack near Sukhumi, from which the government had withdrawn its heavy weapons. Shevardnadze, feeling betrayed by the Russians, went to the besieged regional capital. Pro-Gamsakhurdia rebels suspended their drive against the government to join the defense of Sukhumi. As Russian fighter planes bombed Georgian positions, Shevardnadze accused Russia of failing to stand by the 27 July peace agreement, as it had with two earlier Russian-mediated ceasefires. With the city on the verge of collapse, Shevardnadze refused a Russian proposal to send 30,000 troops to separate the warring sides, fearing what amounted to a Russian invasion force.

Despite last-minute reinforcements, Sukhumi fell to Abkhazian separatists on 27 September. The day before, Shevardnadze had agreed to accept the Russian troops, and to join the Commonwealth of Independent States (CIS). It was too late. In an emotional statement from a haven nine miles from the city, Shevardnadze attributed the defeat partly to Russia and partly to the pro-Gamsakhurdia insurrection. At least 500 Georgian soldiers were killed during the two-week siege and more than 2,000 wounded. Scores of Georgian officials, policemen and citizens were executed, thousands more were evacuated by Russian ships, while tens of thousands fled toward Tbilisi through rugged, snow-covered mountains. By 1 October, all of Abkhazia was in secessionist hands.

The government turned its attention to the pro-Gamsakhurdia rebellion. In early October, government forces recaptured the town of Khobi, within seventeen miles of the a strategic rail line linking Tbilisi to the Black Sea. Gamsakhurdia insurgents announced control of Poti, the country's main port. With political turmoil and intensifying lawlessness in Tbilisi, the government imposed an 11 P.M. curfew. Rebel guns were turned on Samtredia, 30 kms., west of the country's second-biggest city, Kutaisi.

On 18 October, Shevardnadze announced his army was near collapse and that the country needed Russian help to regain territory lost to ethnic and political warfare. Russian officials responded that they would consider joint action with other countries in the Caucasus region but would take no unilateral steps. Meanwhile, pleas for assistance from the West went unheeded. On 19-20 October, Russian military leaders deployed troops to guard rail and sea links in Georgia as pro-Gamsakhurdia forces advanced on Kutaisi. The move was part of an agreement between Russia and a desperate Shevardnadze that legalized the presence of 20,000 Russian troops in five bases in Georgia, with no date set for their withdrawal. Within days, government troops moved into a rebel stronghold near Kutaisi and recaptured Poti. By month's end, government forces advanced to within ten miles of the last opposition stronghold, Zugdidi, and issued an ultimatum to surrender.

The government announced on 3 November that it had seized Khobi as hundreds of Russian soldiers came ashore in Poti to help bolster the regime's efforts to control strategic sites. Two days later, the government announced that, with the help of Russian troops, its forces had taken Zugdidi and Gamsakhurdia had fled with 1,000 followers to Abkhazia. In mid-month, the government announced that the state of emergency would be extended indefinitely. Shevardnadze ordered parliament to take a two-month recess, and promised that the nation would get a new constitution and a new parliament.

In other ethnic issues, South Ossetia remained relatively quiet under de facto Russian protection. Ajaria, a small enclave bordering Turkey, was peaceful, but its pro-Moscow leadership remained at odds with the national government.

Civil war, violent and clannish politics inextricably mixed with criminal gangs pre-dating independence, left a once vibrant economy in tatters. From 1989 to 1992, the national economy shrank by 60 percent. The rate of inflation for 1992 was 1,339 percent. The number of officially registered unemployed increased by 22 percent in the first six months of 1993 compared with the last half of 1992. The country faced shortages of gas, oil and other key products because the Armenia-Azerbaijan war disrupted rail traffic. Virtually all the economy remains in government hands. In August, after Russia's decision to withdraw from circulation its old monetary denomi-nations left Georgia on the verge of financial collapse, government-issued coupons became sole legal tender.

Political Rights and Civil Liberties: Georgians have the right to change their government demo-cratically, but emergency powers, curfews and other factors have led to charges that the government, amid secessionist violence and insurrection, has grown more authoritarian.

Forty-six political parties and blocs participated in the October 1992 parliamentary elections. Organizations loyal to ex-President Gamsakhurdia faced repression and harassment. In October, press accounts and Georgian human rights organizations reported arbitrary arrests of academics and political activists suspected of being pro-Gamsakhurdia. The dragnet also caught members of the Green Party and others with no connection to the ex-president. Shevardnadze and other officials insisted that they carried out arrests only under state of emergency regulations. There were eyewitness reports of beatings and torture by police interrogators.

The political and secessionist crises also put pressure on the independent press. In June, a correspondent from the paper *Rezonans* was severely beaten by a government official in the Cabinet of Ministers building. The beating drew a sharp protest from the non-governmental Georgian Committee for Human Rights and Interethnic Relations. In July, the government issued a decree censoring news from Abkhazia.

Ethnic and minority rights also came under stress. In October, Georgian refugees from Abkhazia reported a brutal ethnic-cleansing campaign and other atrocities, including rapes, decapitation and mutilation of women. In November, sources reported kidnappings of ethnic Azerbaijanis, many held for ransom. Azerbaijanis organized several protests demanding that the government guarantee the constitutional rights of the Azeri national minority. South Ossetians continued to demand greater autonomy and unification with North Ossetia in Russia.

Freedom of religion is respected in this predominantly Christian Orthodox country. There are some restrictions on domestic and foreign travel, and the two-front war through-out most of the year made travel hazardous or impossible in certain areas. Government concern about the status of and discrimination against women is minimal. Access to edu-cation is unimpeded, but women are found mostly in traditional, low-paying occupations.

The 2 million-member federation of Georgian Trade Unions—successor to the official Communist structure—agreed not to strike or distribute leaflets during the state of emergency. Union leaders cited low wages and sus-picions about plans to privatize many state-owned businesses as issues of urgent concern.

Germany

Polity: Federal par-
liamentary democracy
Economy: Mixed
capitalist
Population: 81,064,000
PPP: $18,213
Life Expectancy: 75.2
Ethnic Groups: German and numerous immigrant groups

Political Rights: 1
Civil Liberties: 2
Status: Free

Overview:

In 1993, Germany continued to bear the burden of unification and economic recession. The parliament passed a restrictive asylum law to stem the tide of would-be immigrants. Although right-wing violence receded, attacks on foreigners killed eight people, and police reported a growing cooperation among extremist groups.

Following the defeat of the Third Reich by the Allies in 1945, Germany was divided into Soviet, U.S., British, and French occupation zones. In 1949, the Western Allies established the Federal Republic of Germany (FRG) under a democratic parliamentary system; the Soviets formed the German Democratic Republic (GDR), under Communist party control. With the collapse of the East German regime in November 1989, the citizens voted in that country's first and only democratic parliamentary election in March 1990, backing parties supporting a speedy reunification with the Federal Republic.

The West's absorption of the East was complete on 3 October 1990, the formerly centralized East Germany being divided into five states (*Laender*). On 2 December 1990,the first post-unification parliamentary election brought a victory to the conservative-liberal coalition, in power since 1982, led by Chancellor Helmut Kohl. In the election to the 662-member *Bundestag* (federal parliament) the Christian Democratic Union (CDU) and its Bavarian partner, the Christian Social Union (CSU), polled 43.8 percent of the vote, the liberal Free Democrats (FDP) received 11 percent, and the opposition Social Democrats (SPD), scored 33.5 percent. The ex-Communist Party of Democratic Socialism (PDS) and the Greens/Alternatives also won seats in the parliament.

The European recession has delayed the prosperity that Easterners hoped for after unification. Influenced by the poor economy, many voters turned to fringe parties in the the state and local elections in 1993. In the state election in Hessen on 7 March, the Greens, the junior partners in the governing coalition with the SPD, increased their support from 9.1 to 11 percent. The ultra-right-wing *Republikaner* party got 8.3 percent of the vote. In the Hamburg election on 19 September the Greens/ Alternatives almost doubled their share of the vote, ending up with 13.5 percent. Two ultra-right parties received a combined 7.6 percent.

Kohl's ministers of economics and transport resigned after allegations of financial improprieties. A similar scandal led to the resignation of the SPD leader Bjoern Engholm. He was replaced in June by Rudolf Scharping, the prime minister of Rhineland-Palatinate.

In preparation for another election in 1994—that of the Federal President, who is elected by an electoral college—Chancellor Kohl was criticized for his selection of

Steffen Heitmann to succeed the popular Richard von Weizsaecker. Although the CDU/ CSU nominated the largely unknown Heitmann in October, he was forced to withdraw a month later, after making controversial, right-wing statements about World War II, Jews, women, and aliens. By late 1993, Roman Herzog, President of the Constitutional Court, became the likely replacement candidate. The SPD nominated the prime minister of North Rhine-Westphalia, Johannes Rau, as its presidential candidate.

In August, faced with the continuing economic recession, the government unveiled plans to cut social spending, including reductions in welfare payments and unemployment benefits.

In foreign policy, for the first time since World War II, Germany sent troops outside the NATO operating area, despite a constitutional challenge brought by the SPD and the FDP. Following the Constitutional Court's decision allowing German troops to participate in non-combative roles in U.N. approved missions, German troops participated in the U.N. peace-making efforts in Somalia, and enforcing sanctions against Yugoslavia.

On 12 October 1993 the Constitutional Court ruled that the Maastricht treaty on European Union, approved by Bundestag in 1992, was constitutional, paving the way for its implementation. On 1 November 1993 the Union accord went into effect, binding Germany to the European Union (EU), formerly known as the European Community (EC).

Political Rights and Civil Liberties: Germans have the right to change their government democratically. The federal system allows for considerable amount of self-government among the sixteen states. Resident aliens holding citizenship of a European Union country are able to vote and stand for local elections. The difficulties in obtaining German citizenship through naturalization exclude many second- and third-generation resident aliens of non-EU origin from voting at all levels of government.

As a consequence of the Nazi era, German Basic Law (constitution) requires all parties to be democratic. In 1993, the government asked the Constitutional Court to ban the neo-Nazi Free German Workers' Party. The government has banned several other extremist associations. In December 1992 the federal and state authorities agreed to determine whether Republikaner activities could be classified as anti-democratic.

The press and human rights groups have accused the German justice system of "being blind in the right eye"—a reference to the contrast in the promptness of the police and the court system to prosecute leftist law-breakers, with the often sluggish pace of prosecution against rightists. Reports by the police and defectors indicated that right-wing and neo-Nazi groups were increasingly better organized and interconnected in 1993. Several human rights organizations expressed concern about the connections between the violent far-right groups and parts of the police and military. In the worst attack against foreign residents to date, on 29 May 1993 intoxicated youths hurled firebombs against a Turkish-occupied apartment house in the town of Sollingen, leading to the deaths of five people, including three children. On 30 December 1993, a court charged four of the alleged attackers with murder and arson. According to a government report, in the first eleven months of 1993, the number of violent crimes attributed to rightist groups fell to 1,699 from the 2,366 registered in the same period in 1992. Eight people died in racially motivated attacks, down from seventeen the previous year.

At the same time, leftist terrorists resumed their activities on 28 March 1993, with the bombing of a soon-to-be opened model prison, inflicting a $60 million damage. The attack, claimed by the Red Army Faction (RAF) urban guerrillas, followed a two-year lull during which the government offered to reduce prison sentences of RAF's incarcerated members in exchange for cessation of terrorist activities. On 27 June 1993, special anti-terrorist units made a botched attempt to arrest two leading RAF terrorists, during which one security agent and one suspected terrorist were killed. After the shootout, witnesses accused members of the anti-terrorist squad of deliberately killing the suspected terrorist following his capture. The allegations led to the resignation of the federal Minister of Interior, Rudolf Seiters, the chief prosecutor, Alexander von Stahl, and to the formation of a special investigative commission.

In September, responding to international and domestic criticism, the government proposed a package of tougher anti-violence laws aimed specifically at the rightist groups, including raising the maximum penalty for non-life-threatening injuries from three to five years. Earlier in June, the parliament passed a law retroactive to 1991, improving compensation for foreign victims of violence.

The legal issues connected to the East German past continued to engage the German court system. On 13 January 1993, a Berlin court ended the manslaughter prosecution against the former East German Communist leader, Erich Honecker, accused of having issued orders to shoot at refugees fleeing to West Germany. The court excused Honecker because of his advanced liver cancer, and he left for Chile. In September and October, four top Honecker aides were sentenced in connection with the border shootings. On 6 December, the former East German chief of intelligence, Markus Wolf, was sentenced for treason and bribery. The court rejected Wolf's claim that as a citizen of the East he could not have committed treason against West Germany. The government dismissed thousands of judges and civil servants in the East, accusing them of having acted as informants to the Communist secret police.

Rights of association, speech and protest are guaranteed in the constitution, except for anti-constitutional groups. Members of extremist organizations have long been barred from employment in the civil service. On 30 November 1993, the government threatened to fire civil servants belonging to the Republikaner party. A few days earlier, the government banned the Kurdistan Workers' Party (PKK) for attacking Turkish-owned businesses and diplomatic missions. The constitution prohibits the display of Nazi paraphernalia and quotations from Nazi speeches, except for academic purposes. In August and September, four states banned the display of Germany's World War I imperial flag, used during marches by extremist right-wing groups. In the course of 1993, the government clamped down on neo-Nazi rock groups, outlawing the production and distribution of songs advocating violence and racism.

German press and broadcast media are free and independent, and offer pluralistic points of view. Citizens and foreign residents are free to travel and live within and outside the country. To counteract the growing influx of asylum-seekers, the Bundestag passed an amendment to the constitution on 26 May, restricting asylum. The amendment and a new, more restrictive asylum law, provide for the immediate expulsion of asylees from "safe countries of origin," and for persons entering Germany from third countries deemed as "secure." Prior to the passage of the amendment, Germany and Poland reached an agreement on 7 May on the transfer of third-country asylum seekers entering Germany from Poland. Germany made similar agreements with other neighbors. As a result of the new measures, which went into effect as of 1 July, the number of asylum seekers declined by 26 percent in comparison with the year before.

Freedom of religion is respected, although members of some fringe religious and occult groups, including Scientology, may be barred from employment in the civil service.

Labor, business and farming groups are free, highly organized and influential. Management and labor have equal representation on major corporate boards. In April and May, metal workers in the East struck against employers' reneging on an accord to equalize Eastern and Western pay scales by 1994.

Ghana

Polity: Dominant party
Economy: Capitalist-statist
Population: 16,446,000
PPP: $1,016
Life Expectancy: 55.0
Ethnic Groups: Some fifty in number, the majority being Akan (including the Fanti), followed by the Ashanti, Ga, Ewe, and the Mossi-Dagomba

Political Rights: 5
Civil Liberties: 4*
Status: Partly Free

Ratings Change: *Ghana's civil liberties rating changed from 5 to 4 as a result of modifications in methodology. See "Survey Methodology," page 671.

Overview:

In 1993, a new constitution was put into effect marking the beginning of the Fourth Ghanaian Republic. Following the controversial presidential and parliamentary elections in the previous year, President Jerry Rawlings and his National Democratic Congress (NDC) continued to dominate the political life of the country.

Ghana, formerly known as the Gold Coast became, in 1957, the first African country to gain its independence from Britain. Since independence Ghana's political developments have oscillated between civilian and military rule. The last military coup d'etat, against the elected government of President Hilla Limann, occurred in 1981 and was led by Flight Lieutenant Jerry Rawlings.

In 1991, Rawlings proposed convening a Consultative Assembly to draft a new constitution. Despite criticism from independent professional and social groups for its lack of representation and its circumscribed agenda, closely controlled by Rawlings and the Provisional National Defense Council (PNDC), the Assembly began its work in the fall of the year. It completed its work with a referendum in April 1992 in which the overwhelming majority of the voters approved the new constitution, the alternative being continued rule by the PNDC.

Following their legalization in May 1992, political parties formed on the basis of traditional Ghanaian ideological bipolarity stemming from the struggle for, and early years of, independence. The populist platform derives from the socialist ideology espoused and implemented by the country's first president, Kwame Nkrumah. Its main tenets were collective (state) ownership of the means of production, economic and cultural self-sufficiency, and African solidarity. The other major ideology, is based on ideas promoted by J.B. Danquah, one of the leading pro-independence activists, and the former President K.A. Busia. The Danquah/Busia legacy emphasize the responsibility of the individual for one's own and social welfare, and favor a free-market economy.

Due to disagreements, the populist politicians were unable to form a united party, splitting into several factions, including the National Independence Party (NIP), the People's National Convention (PNC), the National Convention Party (NCP), and the People's Heritage Party (PHP). The pro-market forces were able to unite, establishing the National Patriotic Party (NPP). Rawlings established the National Democratic Congress (NDC) to act as the continuation of the PNDC.

In the November presidential election Rawlings won with 58 percent of the vote, followed by Albert Adu-Boahen of the NPP, who received 30 percent of the vote. Alleging widespread irregularities, the opposition parties boycotted the 29 December parliamentary elections, allowing the NDC to gain 189 out of the 200 legislative seats. The two parties allied with NDC gained nine seats while two independents also entered the parliament. In the aftermath of the November election, the NPP, PNC, PHP, and the NIP formed the Inter-Party Coordinating Committee (ICC) to express the common position of the opposition toward the government.

In January 1993 the new Constitution became effective and Rawlings and the new parliament were sworn in, marking the beginning of the Fourth Republic. At the time, the ICC stated the willingness of its members to abide by the new laws and accept the new institutional arrangements. As a gesture of its intention to follow a democratic path, the ICC statement called on the government to grant an unconditional amnesty to all exiles, and to commence the compilation of a new national voter register and the issuance of identification cards to all adults. According to the International Foundation for Electoral Systems (IFES), the previous register was flawed by listing more voters than was statistically possible, while many voters were unable to register.

On 7 April the NPP launched *The Stolen Verdict,* a compilation of the irregularities that occurred during the presidential election. In the aftermath of the election there were disagreements between the party's chairman, Bernard Jao da Rocha and the presidential candidate, Albert Adu-Boahen. Da Rocha favored a conciliatory approach to Rawlings and the new parliament, while Adu-Boahen vowed to "never recognize Rawlings as a legitimate leader."

Since 1983 when Rawlings began to implement the economic stabilization plan prescribed by the International Monetary Fund, Ghana has experienced a considerable economic growth. Increased gold production has become a key objective of the recovery program; by 1993 Ghana had become the second largest gold producer in Africa. The increased gold production has also contaminated both water supply and the land. In Tontokrom, a village most affected by the pollution, *Buruli Ulcer* has crippled hundreds of its one thousand inhabitants. The government's promises to pass more stringent environmental laws have not been implemented.

The relations between Ghana and neighboring Togo remained tense, the Togo government accusing Rawlings of harboring Togolese opposition and aiding them militarily. In February the ICC asked Rawlings to revoke his decision, following disturbances in Togo, to put the military on alert. In July the leaders of both countries asked Egypt, the current chairman of the Organization of African Unity (OAU), to mediate the dispute.

Political Rights and Civil Liberties: **D**espite multiparty elections in 1992 and the introduction of a constitution guaranteeing the citizens the right to elect and be elected to public offices, Ghanaians still lack the means to change their government democratically. Although international observers declared the elections "free and fair," the opposition provided a long list of abuses before and during the election. The political parties were able to register only five months prior to the presidential election and had to rely on their own financing, while the political forces close to Rawlings used state finances and patronage to conduct the campaign. The PNDC refused to update the national voter register or to allow the opposition to seat their members on the Interim Electoral Commission (INEC). The ICC opposition recorded a number of specific cases of voter harassment and misinformation, stuffing of ballot boxes and inconsistencies in ballot counting. The government refused to begin work on a new register until 1996, when the next elections are scheduled to be held.

Two types of courts exist in Ghana: the traditional common law courts based on the British model and the people's tribunals set up by Rawlings in 1982. Both are subject to government control and interference. The common courts are composed of legal professionals and follow the lengthy practice of due process, but the tribunals restrict the procedural rights of defendants and are staffed with appointees with little or no experience in legal matters. There is no appeal from their verdicts which include the death penalty.

Freedom of speech and assembly remains circumscribed. In December 1992 the *People's Daily Graphic*, a government newspaper, reported that about fifty people were arrested in the city of Kumasi after they had booed Rawlings during a ceremony. On 16 February the police arrested six leaders of a peaceful opposition protest march in the capital, and on 28 February the police withdrew the permit for a memorial rally commemorating the death of J.B. Danquah, citing threats from the ruling party activists.

The government owns and controls radio and television and the major newspapers. In setting up a Media Commission—a constitution-stipulated agency to oversee journalistic accuracy and accountability—Rawlings appointed a former PNDC press official as press chairman, violating the provision that the chairman be elected by the Commission.

Despite government harassment and financial difficulties, an independent press exists and is the major voice of opposition. Early in the year the Minister of Information attacked the independent press for alleged inflammatory statements, in his view amounting to high treason. In March the authorities arrested Roland Adotei Addo, a leading journalist from the weekly *Ghanaian Chronicle,* charging him with having written an article inciting the murder of a pro-government priest. In January the Ghana Committee on Human and People's Rights (GCHPR) launched its own publication, *the Ghana Human Rights Quarterly.*

Freedom of religion is generally respected in this predominantly Christian country, which also has a sizable Muslim minority. As one of its final acts, the PNDC abolished the Religious Bodies Registration Law, which restricted the full exercise of religious practices by the Jehova's Witnesses and the Mormons.

Trade unions are still governed by a 1965 law which grants the government broad regulatory powers over their registration and activities. In recent years, however, the once PNDC affiliated Trade Union Congress (TUC) became more independent and active on behalf of its members. In August TUC's secretary-general announced that the Congress will vigorously oppose the government's privatization plan. In late 1992, the Civil Service Association of Ghana (CSAG) was able to negotiate a 60 percent salary rise in an attempt to bring it on a par with other public sector employees. Although Ghanaians are generally free to travel within and outside of the country, members of the opposition are often denied the right; in December 1992 the authorities impounded the passport of NPP's Adu-Boahen.

Greece

Polity: Parliamentary
democracy
Economy: Mixed
capitalist
Population: 10,470,000
PPP: $7,.366
Life Expectancy: 76.1

Political Rights: 1
Civil Liberties: 3*
Status: Free

Ethnic Groups: Overwhelmingly Greek with Macedonian
and Turkish minorities
Ratings Change: *Greece's civil liberties rating changed from 2 to 3 because the
government reduced freedom of expression by imprisoning people with politically
unacceptable views of Macedonia and Alexander the Great.

Overview: **F**ormer Prime Minister Andreas Papandreou returned to power
after Greek voters gave his Pan-Hellenic Socialist Movement
(PASOK) a majority of seats in the general election held on 10
October 1993. Campaigning against the austerity and privatization policies of Prime
Minister Constantine Mitsotakis of New Democracy, PASOK won 170 of the 300
parliamentary seats. New Democracy captured only 111 seats. Political Spring, a new
nationalist party led by Antonis Samaras, a former New Democracy foreign minister,
took 10 seats. The Communists snared the remaining 9 seats. Twenty-three other parties
failed to clear the 3 percent of the vote required for parliamentary representation.

Located on the southern tip of the Balkan peninsula, Greece fought for independence
from the Ottoman Empire in the 1820s and 1830s. After its victory, the country became a
monarchy in 1835. In a series of wars in the early twentieth century, Greece increased its
territory in Europe. After Axis occupation during World War II, civil war broke out
between Communist and royalist forces. With Western aid, the constitutional monarchy
prevailed. In 1967, a military junta took control and held power until 1974, when the
country returned to parliamentary democracy but without the monarchy.

The Greek parliamentarians serve for a maximum term of four years. The political
party or coalition that wins a majority of seats forms the government. The parliament
elects the president, who is a largely ceremonial figure.

Two MP's forced the dissolution of parliament and the 1993 general election when
they resigned from the New Democracy caucus in September, depriving Mitsotakis of a
majority. They left the party over two major issues of the year, the privatization of
telecommunications and Mitsotakis's conditional recognition of Greece's neighbor,
known diplomatically as the Former Yugoslav Republic of Macedonia. Earlier in the
year, both issues caused Mitsotakis problems. After Mitsotakis agreed in March to
Macedonia's admission to the U.N., he survived a censure motion in parliament, 152-145.
Most Greeks fear that allowing Macedonia to call itself by that name threatens the Greek
province of Macedonia. Opposing privatization, public sector unions staged a two-day
strike in July against public utilities. The strike produced brownouts in electric power and
the occupation of the economic minister's office.

The unproductive economy is the main domestic problem. Under Mitsotakis, Greek officials blamed high inflation, the overstaffed bureaucracy and large deficits on the previous Papandreou governments. Under the Socialists, the state controlled two-thirds of the economy and employed one out of every five workers. New Democracy tried to change this situation through budget cuts and privatization, in order to meet the budgetary targets of the European Community (now European Union), which gives Greece substantial economic aid for infrastructure and other projects.

Upon taking office, Papandreou scrapped privatization sales that would have yielded an anticipated $1.5 billion. In order to make up for the revenue loss, he cracked down on tax evaders. As much as 40 percent of the economy goes untaxed. However, the tax collectors are often corrupt, and Athenian shopkeepers resent being major targets of the new policy. Papandreou also renationalized public transportation, ended the privatization of telecommunications and overturned a property settlement with former King Constantine. Papandreou caused some resentment by appointing Papandreou family members and other close associates to high offices. For example, his wife is head of the prime minister's office, and his son and personal physician have cabinet seats. Papandreou has also taken strong, Greek nationalist positions. For example, he advocates a parliament that would include ethnic Greeks from outside the country in a "non-negotiable line of defense."

During 1993 there were an estimated 500,000 illegal aliens, mostly from Albania and the Middle East, in Greece. Throughout 1993, authorities rounded up thousands of Albanian illegal aliens for forcible repatriation. Greeks blame Albanians for criminal activities. After Albania expelled a Greek Orthodox priest for advocating the merger of southern Albania with Greece, the latter retaliated by expelling 25,000 Albanians. In June 1993, Greece claimed it would expel all Albanian illegals. However, Greece accepted Greek refugees fleeing war in Abkhazia in Georgia.

Greece and the U.S. were involved in espionage episodes that became public in 1993. In May, an employee of the U.S. embassy in Athens was arrested in Virginia on charges of selling classified information to Greek military officers. In November, Greek police detained two bewigged U.S. embassy employees in Athens for carrying out security operations that Greece did not authorize. The pair returned to America.

On 12 November, anarchists rioted in Athens in response to an alleged swastika-carving in a girl's head by a neo-Nazi.

Political Rights and Civil Liberties: The citizens of Greece have the right to change their government by democratic means. Voting is compulsory for people aged eighteen to seventy. The bureaucracy is so cumbersome that when people move they do not transfer their voting addresses. Consequently, about 650,000 people needed holidays around the 1993 general election to go back to vote in their old home towns and villages.

The media have substantial freedom, but there are several politically related restrictions. For instance, publications deemed offensive to the president or to religious beliefs may be seized by order of the public prosecutor. Greece also has a controversial law that bans "unwarranted" publicity for terrorists, including terrorists' proclamations after explosions. In 1993, the government cracked down on people with dissenting views on its Macedonia policy and Greek nationalism. For example, four who questioned the Macedonia policy received nineteen-month sentences for "disseminating false information." A student received a one-year sentence for calling Alexander the Great, the ancient

Greek Macedonian emperor, "a miserable slayer of people." The government owns and operates the television stations, but time is allocated to all the major political parties.

There is freedom of association and all workers, except the military and the police, have the right to form or join unions. Unions are linked to political parties, but are independent of party and government control. Strikes against the government are permitted.

Greek Orthodoxy is the state religion and claims 98 percent of the population, at least nominally. The Orthodox bishops have the privilege of granting or denying permission to other faiths to build houses of worship in their jurisdictions. The constitution prohibits proselytizing by all religious groups. Sometimes police arrest Jehovah's Witnesses for seeking converts. Despite objections from Catholics, Jews, Muslims and other religious minorities, national identity cards required since 1992 list each person's religion. Greece offers noncombatant military service but does not provide a nonmilitary alternative to the universal conscription of men for national service. Jehovah's Witnesses and other conscientious objectors can be tried and sentenced to three to five-year terms in military prisons.

The Turkish Muslim minority, whose religious rights were guaranteed under the 1923 Treaty of Lausanne, objects to the Greek government's choosing the *mufti*, the leader of the Muslim community. The state prevents Muslims from controlling their own charities. Human Rights Watch reported in 1992 that the Turkish minority had gained improvements in property rights, but were still subject to expropriation, deprivation of citizenship, and cultural and linguistic rights.

In 1992 Amnesty International charged Greece with torture in its prison system and with failure to punish the perpetrators. The Greek government denied the charge, and said that an outside investigation would be "a grave insult" to the nation.

The Greek government places severe restrictions on former King Constantine. When he returned to Greece on a family vacation in 1993, the trip created a political uproar. All major parties denounced the trip. Although Constantine may not visit populated areas, the government had two missile boats and a plane tail him during his journey.

Grenada

Polity: Parliamentary democracy
Economy: Capitalist-statist
Population: 93,000
PPP: $4,081
Life Expectancy: 71.5
Ethnic Groups: Mostly black

Political Rights: 1
Civil Liberties: 2
Status: Free

Overview: **P**rime Minister Nicholas Braithwaite of the ruling National Democratic Congress (NDC) became increasingly unpopular as a result of the economic hardship caused by a three-year, IMF-inspired structural adjustment program. His administration suffered from internal squabbles and confronted broad opposition to its privatization program.

Grenada, a member of the British Commonwealth, is a parliamentary democracy.

The British monarchy is represented by a governor-general. The Caribbean island state became self-governing in 1958 and gained independence in 1974. The nation includes the islands of Carriacou and Petit Martinique.

Prime Minister Eric Gairy was overthrown in a 1979 coup by Maurice Bishop's Marxist New Jewel Movement. In October 1983 Prime Minister Bishop was murdered by New Jewel hard-liners. Bernard Coard and General Hudson Austin took control of the country and declared martial law. Sir Paul Scoon, the governor-general and the only duly constituted executive authority in the country, formally asked for international assistance. A joint U.S.-Caribbean military intervention removed Coard and Austin, and Scoon formed an advisory council to act as an interim administration.

In the 1984 elections the New National Party (NNP) of Herbert Blaize defeated Gairy's rightist Grenada United Labour Party (GULP). The NNP, a coalition of three parties, took fourteen of fifteen seats in the House of Representatives. The bicameral parliament also consists of an appointed Senate, with ten members appointed by the prime minister and three by the leader of the parliamentary opposition.

In 1989 the NNP coalition unraveled, leaving Prime Minister Blaize with the support of only six representatives in the House. Blaize formed The National Party (TNP) from among his remaining supporters, but died in December 1989. He was replaced by his deputy, Ben Jones, and elections were called.

The five main contenders in the 1990 campaign were: the TNP headed by Jones; the centrist National Democratic Congress (NDC) led by Nicholas Braithwaite, former head of the 1983-84 interim government; the New National Party (NNP) headed by Keith Mitchell; the leftist Maurice Bishop Patriotic Movement (MBPM) led by Terry Marryshow; and the GULP.

On 13 March 1990 the NDC won seven seats, the GULP four, and the NNP and TNP two each. After the GULP, NNP and TNP failed to form a coalition government, Braithwaite was appointed prime minister by the governor-general. One of the GULP's winning candidates defected to the NDC, giving the new government a one-seat majority. Gairy failed to win in his own constituency.

Since coming to power the Braithwaite government has maintained a shaky 10-5 majority that in 1993 included two GULP defectors and one from the NP. Winnifred Strachan, expelled from the GULP by Gairy, remained the official opposition leader as an independent.

Since 1992 the Braithwaite government has been under increasing pressure from opposition parties and labor unions because of its adjustment and privatization effort. Opinion polls in 1993 indicated deepening popular discontent in the face of rising unemployment—possibly as high as 30 percent—and general economic hardship. Disputes within the NDC led to the third cabinet reshuffle in three years. Few Grenadians believed the Braithwaite government had a chance of winning another term in the next elections, due in 1995.

In fall 1993 opposition parties and unions temporarily united against the government's planned privatization of the state-run electricity company. But the political opposition remained weakened by personal disputes and a general inability to capitalize on popular antagonism toward the Braithwaite government.

Political Rights and Civil Liberties: Citizens are able to change their government through democratic elections. Constitutional guarantees regarding the right to organize political, labor or civic groups are generally respected.

There are numerous independent labor unions but labor rights came into question in 1993. To resolve a two-year impasse involving strikes by port workers, the government passed a law in June that gives the government the right to set up a tribunal empowered to make "binding and final" rulings when a labor dispute is considered of vital interest to the state. The national trade union federation claimed the law was an infringement of the right to strike. The government countered that the law was pro-worker because it guaranteed the reinstatement of persons fired for trade union activities. Some violent incidents were reported during a hotel workers strike in late 1993.

The exercise of religion and the right of free expression are generally respected. Newspapers, including a number of weekly political party organs, are independent. Radio is both public and private and open to independent voices. Television is independently operated. In 1992, the home of the publisher of the weekly *Grenada Voice* was the target of an arson attack, possibly by one of an increasing number of drug-dealing gangs.

There is an independent, nondiscriminatory judiciary whose authority is generally respected by the police. In 1991 Grenada rejoined the Organization of Eastern Caribbean States court system, with right of appeal to the Privy Council in London. In 1990 the Braithwaite government set up a five-member committee, including independent public figures, to monitor worsening prison conditions. Like many Caribbean island nations, Grenada has suffered from a rise in violent drug-related crime.

In 1986, after a two-year trial, thirteen men and one woman, including Bernard Coard and Hudson Austin, were found guilty of the 1983 murder of Maurice Bishop and sentenced to death. In July 1991 the Grenada Court of Appeals turned aside the last of the defendants' appeals, and reports circulated that Coard and four others would be hanged. However, the government decided to commute the death sentences to life imprisonment for all fourteen defendants after a series of appeals by international human rights organizations.

Guatemala

Polity: Presidential-legislative democracy (military-dominated) (insurgencies)
Economy: Capitalist-statist
Population: 10,029,000
PPP: $2,567
Life Expectancy: 63.4
Ethnic Groups: Ethnically complex, with more than 60 percent Mayan and other Indian

Political Rights: 4
Civil Liberties: 5
Status: Partly Free

Overview: **R**amiro de Leon Carpio became president after the failure of Jorge Serrano's *auto-golpe* (self-coup) in May 1993. But de Leon Carpio was soon handcuffed by the same congress and supreme court Serrano had tried to dissolve. Throughout the crisis, it was evident that the military remained the final arbiter in how the nation is run.

The Republic of Guatemala was established in 1839, eighteen years after independence from Spain and following the breakup of the United Provinces of Central America (1824-1838). The nation has endured a history of dictatorship, coups d'etat, and guerrilla insurgency, with only intermittent democratic government. After a thirty-year stretch of repressive military rule, Guatemala returned to civilian government in 1985 with the promulgation of a new constitution and the election of President Vinicio Cerezo of the Christian Democratic Party (PDC).

The constitution provides for a five-year presidential term and prohibits reelection. A 116-member unicameral National Congress is elected for five years. The governors of twenty-two departments and the capital, Guatemala City, are appointed by the president. Municipal governments are elected.

In the 1990 presidential campaign, the frontrunner was former dictator Gen. Efrain Rios Montt (1982-83), whose law-and-order rhetoric struck a chord amid a mounting wave of political and criminal violence. He was ruled ineligible because the constitution bars former dictators from returning to power.

Serrano, a right-wing businessman, inherited Rios Montt's following. In the November 1990 election Serrano ran second to newspaper publisher Jorge Carpio Nicolle of the National Center Union (UCN). In the January 1991 runoff Serrano portrayed himself as an anti-politican and defeated Carpio by a 2-to-1 margin in a vote marked by a 55 percent abstention rate.

Serrano promised to negotiate peace with the left-wing guerrillas of the Guatemalan National Revolutionary Unity (URNG). By early 1993 U.N.-monitored talks remained deadlocked because the Guatemalan military would not allow the government to make concessions on human rights accountability. The military also refused to reduce its 40,000-member forces or dismantle the 500,000-member Self-Defense Patrols (PACs), a vast paramilitary apparatus through which it controls the countryside.

Stepped up guerrilla actions by the 1,000-member URNG added to a climate of insecurity caused by escalating criminal and political violence and a series of labor strikes. Serrano became increasingly isolated as he failed in attempts to strongarm the media and manipulate the congress and the supreme court.

On 25 May Serrano, with the backing of the military, dissolved the congress and fired the supreme court. The military changed its mind amid mass protests and threats of economic isolation by the U.S. and the Organization of American States (OAS) that frightened conservative economic elites. On 1 June the military sent Serrano packing and backed Vice-President Gustavo Espina to replace him.

The congress, under pressure from an alliance of unions, business sector moderates and civic groups, blocked Espina from taking office and instead selected de Leon Carpio , the human rights ombudsman in the Serrano government, on 5 June.

De Leon Carpio took office with wide popular support and vowed to purge the congress and the judiciary of corruption. Military officers who had backed Serrano were replaced in the high command by officers who had gained the upper hand by moving to oust him.

De Leon Carpio's honeymoon lasted less than a month as a majority of congress, wanting a return to business as usual, worked to undermine his reform program. There was also a resurgence of military repression and generalized violence, most notably the murder by unknown attackers of Jorge Carpio Nicolle, de Leon Carpio's cousin and former presidential candidate, on 3 July.

In August de Leon Carpio, his popularity declining, demanded the resignation of congress and the supreme court, in accordance with a recommendation by the Constitutional Court, the highest court in the land.

The congress and the court refused, setting off an institutional crisis that paralyzed the government. De Leon Carpio called for a national referendum to decide the issue. But the Constitutional Court, amid military saber-rattling, daily coup rumors and renewed URNG actions, ruled against him.

De Leon Carpio, increasingly isolated, was forced to negotiate with those institutions he had declared to be totally unfit. In November he agreed to a package of constitutional reforms which, if passed in a referendum, would lead to new legislative elections by mid-1994, with the new congress appointing a new supreme court.

Many in the broad alliance that helped bring de Leon to office labeled the deal a sell-out. By December labor unions and civic organizations were campaigning to overturn it in the referendum which was set for 30 January 1994. The military, satisfied that its interests were not threatened by the traditonal horse-trading that led to the deal, went about its business of hunting the URNG and controlling the countryside, unaccountable and immune to popular demands that its power be curbed.

Political Rights and Civil Liberties:

Citizens are able to change their governments through elections at the national and muncipal levels, but the powers granted to civilian administrations by the constitution are greatly restricted by the armed forces, the dominant institution in the country. The rule of law is undermined further by the endemic corruption that afflicts public institutions, particularly the legislature and the courts.

The constitution guarantees religious freedom and the right to organize political parties, civic organizations and labor unions. There are nineteen political parties from social democratic to radical right, most representing small interest groups.

However, political and civic expression is severely restricted by a climate of violence, lawlessness and military repression. Since 1990 there has been a dramatic increase in political and criminal violence including murder, disappearances, bombings and death threats. Politicians, student organizations, street children, peasant groups, labor unions, Indian organizations, human rights groups, and the media have all been targeted.

According to Guatemalan rights activists, the numbers of disappearances and political killings diminished in 1992 and in early 1993, but only as a result of more selective repression and psychological terror by security forces as the military tried (and failed) to avert the redesignation of a U.N. special human rights rapporteur.

The principal human rights offenders are the military, particularly the G-2 intelligence unit and the Presidential Military Staff (EMP); the rural network of paramilitary Self-Defense Patrols (PACs) which are an extension of the army; the police (under military authority); and a network of death squads-for-hire linked to the armed forces and right-wing political groups. There is also evidence that the military runs a network of clandestine jails in which people suspected of ties to the URNG guerrillas are tortured during interrogation.

President de Leon Carpio announced in August that the EMP was being "restructured." But the initial indications were that the unit was actually absorbed into military intelligence. Moreover, after de Leon Carpio took office there was a sharp increase in rights violations and a reversion to the earlier trend of systematic brutality—killings, abductions, torture, bombings. The principal targets were members of rights organizations and civic groups calling for political reform, the reigning in of the army and the purging of corrupt public institutions. Guatemala remains one of the most dangerous places in Latin America for human rights activists.

In August 1992 de Leon Carpio, then the official human rights ombudsman, characterized the situation as "a government without the power to stop impunity." Unfortunately, that is an accurate description of his own government. The undermining of his reform effort (as described in the "Overview") meant that the judicial system remained dysfunctional, a virtual black hole for any legal or human rights complaints. Security forces retain a monopoly over criminal investigations. Civil courts are corrupted and politicized. Those few judges working to establish a rule of law are targets of intimidation or worse. Military personnel are tried in military courts, with the exception of a few high profile cases drawing international attention.

The Runejel Junam Council of Ethnic Communities (CERJ) advocates for the country's Indians, a majority of the population and probably the most segregated and oppressed indigenous community in the Western hemisphere. Although mass killings and aerial bombings of Indians during army anti-guerrilla sweeps have diminished since 1985, they have not stopped. CERJ is a principal advocate of dismantling the PACs, which are a violation of the constitutional article that states no individual can be forced to join any type of civil-defense organization.

Labor unions often exercise their right to strike. But they are frequently denied the right to organize and subjected to mass firings and black-listing, particularly in export-processing zones. Unions are also targets of physical attacks and death threats, particularly in rural areas. The International Confederation of Free Trade Unions classifies Guatemala as among the ten most dangerous countries in the world for trade unionists.

The press and most of the broadcast media are privately owned, with several independent newspapers and dozens of radio stations, most of them commercial. Five of six television stations are commercially operated. Under the Serrano government, the media were subject to bombing attacks, arbitrary detention and death threats. There was a brief period of relief after de Leon Carpio took office, which ended with the killing of newspaper publisher Jorge Carpio de Leon by unknown attackers in July. During the fall the print media were increasingly under attack— bombings, physical attacks and threats, including a "hit list" disseminated by a death squad with twenty names, half of them journalists.

Guinea

Polity: Military
(transitional)
Economy: Capitalist
Population: 6,237,000
PPP: $501
Life Expectancy: 43.5

Political Rights: 6
Civil Liberties: 5
Status: *Not Free

Ethnic Groups: Fulani (35 percent), Malinke (25 percent),
Susu (15 percent), others
Ratings Change: *Guinea's status changed from Partly Free to
Not Free because of a rigged election and political violence.

Overview: In 1993 Guinea held its first presidential election, won by the
country's military ruler, Gen. Lasana Conté. The opposition
refused to accept the results, claiming electoral rigging.

Under the leadership of Ahmed Sekou Touré, Guinea declared independence from
France in 1958. Touré ruled the country until his death in 1984. Three days after he died, a
group of army officers under the leadership of Lasana Conté took power in a coup.

In October 1989, Conté promised to bring multiparty democracy to Guinea. In
December 1990, Guineans approved a new constitution, which calls for a presidential
system and a unicameral legislature to be set up within five years.

In April 1992, when the new constitution went into effect, political parties were
legalized. Legislative elections were scheduled for 27 December 1992, but two weeks prior
to the election date, Conté bowed to the demands of the opposition for their postponement.

By the end of 1993, forty three political parties, mostly ethnically based, were
registered. Of the three largest parties, members of the pro-Conté Party of Unity and
Progress (PUP) are largely Susu, those of the Union for the New Republic (UNR) are
predominantly Fulani, and members of the Rally of the Guinean People (RPG), led by the
charismatic former exilee Alpha Condé, are almost entirely Malinké.

In early April 1993, Conté played with the idea of establishing a "consensus
committee," consisting of the leaders of the forty three parties, to prepare the guidelines
and conditions for transition, prior to the holding of elections. For this reason, he began
a series of meetings with the leaders of several parties, allowing them to freely broadcast their assessments of the meetings via the state radio and television. After a short
period of "consultations" with a selected number of opposition leaders, Conté unilaterally declared a change in the electoral schedule, reversing the order of parliamentary
and presidential elections by planning to hold the letter before the former. In his original
agreement with the opposition, it was the newly elected legislature that was supposed to
set the date for the presidential election.

On 19 April, the government press circulated rumors of a foiled coup attempt led
by two high-ranking officers of the Air Force. The two plotters, whose names were not
made public, were allegedly arrested before they could carry out their plans. The
opposition immediately denounced the reports, accusing Conté of prefabricating the
events in order to prolong the transition period.

On 23 May, thirty one opposition parties in the umbrella Democratic Change called for mass protests against Conté's single-handedness in determining the electoral process. In a rally attended by 10,000 people, the party leaders predicted ethnic strife if opposition demands for speedy elections based on the original schedule were not met.

On 3 September, Conté announced the presidential election to be held on 5 December, with legislative elections coming sixty days afterward. The opposition responded by renewing calls on its supporters to organize mass protests throughout the country. During the following two weeks marked by demonstrations, rioting and looting, the government reported that 18 people had been killed by the security forces, and 198 others injured. The disturbances ended on 30 September when the government announced a ban on all demonstrations prior to the election. On 6 October, the Democratic Change issued a comuniqué, raising the number of dead and injured to 63 and 405, respectively.

Prior to 19 December presidential vote expatriate Guineans in neighboring countries attacked and occupied Guinean embassies, accusing the diplomats of stuffing the ballot boxes. Following the vote the Interior Ministry declared Conté the winner with 50.93 percent of the vote. Condé finished second with 20.85 percent of the vote.

Political Rights and Civil Liberties:

Despite the December presidential election, the government's high-handedness in controlling the electoral process inpeded Guineans right to change their government democratically.

The judiciary lacks independence from executive government interference. The judges are employed as civil servants and have no guarantee of tenure. The courts often defer to government authorities in politically sensitive cases. In addition, the lower court judges are often poorly trained, and there is a shortage of practicing attorneys. Corruption and nepotism are extensive. Minor cases are often handled by customary courts presided by village or neighborhood chiefs or wise men.

The new press law restricts the unimpeded dissemination of information and the free flow of ideas. The law permits the arrest of journalists and editors in cases of vaguely defined defamation and slander, including anything offensive to the president, disturbance of peace, and incitement to violence or racial and ethnic hatred. On 25 February, a court sentenced the editor of an independent newspaper, Jean Soumaoro, to a three-month jail term for "lies and defamation" after he had published an article implicating a military official in the shooting of demonstrators in 1991. In June, the Human Rights Association expressed concern about physical threats against journalists by supporters of the ruling and opposition parties. During the pre-election period, however, the government allowed the political parties to express their views freely in campaigns conducted on the state-owned radio and television stations. The programs were often severely critical of the government.

Government authorization is required for public gatherings and, under Article 22 of the constitution, when there is a doubt about state security or when there is a threat of violence the central government or a local authority has the right to ban demonstrations. In attempting to disperse protesters the security forces often resort to the use of live ammunition, as they did during the May and October protests. In late September, however, the president deplored the rash use of weapons by the police; subsequently two officers were reportedly arrested for shooting two protesters.

The government encourages the formation of nonpolitical and non-ethnic based organizations. Freedom of movement is largely respected, although the government may withhold the passports of opposition activists. Women, except those financially independent, must obtain permission from a male family member. Freedom of religion is respected, and the constitution states that the country is a secular republic. Muslim and Christian holidays are observed by the state, however, and the state media provide Muslim and Christian religious broadcasts.

Since 1988, workers have the right to join and organize independent trade unions. The strongest trade union remains the formerly single official National Confederation of Guinean Workers (CNTG). An independent organization is the General Workers Union of Guinea (UGTG). On 13 February, thirty three associations formed the National Federation of Guinean Unions and Associations (FNUAG). Its founders specifically rejected the new union's involvement in politics and promised to concentrate on advocating communal welfare and economic development for its members.

Guinea-Bissau

Polity: Dominant party (military-dominated) (transitional)
Economy: Mixed statist transitional
Population: 1,028,000
PPP: $841
Life Expectancy: 42.5
Ethnic Groups: Balanta, Fulani, Malinke, Mandjague as well as mulatto, Moorish, Lebanese and Portugese minorities

Political Rights: 6
Civil Liberties: 5
Status: Partly Free

Overview:

In 1993 Guinea-Bissau continued its "pre-election" period, begun a year earlier, with the on again/off again announcements and postponements of election dates by the country's ruler General Jao Bernardo Vieira.

Guinea-Bissau won independence from Portugal in 1973. The current president Jao Bernardo Vieira came to power in 1980, in a coup that overthrew the country's first civilian president, Luis de Almeda Cabral. The 1984 constitution codified the supremacy of the PAIGC (African Party for the Independence of Guinea-Bissau and Cape Verde). In 1989, Veira won another five-year term in indirect election.

At a party congress in January 1991, the PAIGC formally ended its role as a single official party. The leadership concluded that it needed to accept pluralism to receive Western investment needed for its economic liberalization program. The congress voted to propose a new electoral law and a thorough constitutional revision.

In May 1991, the National Assembly passed a law legalizing political parties. The legalized parties included the Guinea-Bissau Resistance/ Bafata Movement (RGB/MB), the Front for the Struggle of Guinea-Bissau Independence (FLING), and several smaller parties. At first, the regime proposed a three-year transition to multi-partyism, with elections coming at the end of 1993. In March 1992 the timetable was moved forward;

the presidential election was slated for 15 November, and legislative elections for 13 December. The opposition's demands for June 1992 elections were ignored.

In May 1992, PAIGC dissidents from the "121 group" broke away from the party and formed the Party of Renovation and Development (PRD). A year earlier, the group had called for a quicker pace of internal party democratization and national political liberalization. The PRD leadership joined other opposition parties in calling for the creation of a transitional administration to govern until elections.

A month before the presidential election scheduled for November 1992, Vieira postponed all elections until March 1993 at the earliest. As the year came to a close, the government indicated that elections might be pushed to late 1993, prompting widespread protests.

Vieira named an election commission in March 1993; however, he failed to appropriate a headquarters and funds for its operations. From among the opposition, only the tiny Democratic Front (FD) agreed to join in the work of the commission, while other parties refused. On 3 June the RGB launched a "National Salvation Plan," which called for parliamentary elections to be held between 9 and 16 November, the presidential election postponed until 1995. Lacking support from the other political parties, Vieira ignored the plan, and on 12 July he set the election date for 27 March 1994.

On 17 March 1993, shortly after the naming of the electoral commission, the government reported an attempted military coup with the aim of killing Vieira. In a subsequent government scenario of events, disputed by the opposition, the rebels shot and killed the commander of the elite Rapid Deployment Force (FIR), Major Rabalo de Pina, before being repelled by forces loyal to the president. Following a manhunt, forces loyal to Vieira caught Sub-Lieutenant Mario Soares de Gama and Sergeant Alexander Djau, accusing them of being the leaders of the coup. The security forces also arrested fifty other military personnel, including Amadou Mane, the soldier who allegedly killed Rabalo de Pina. After his arrest, Mane appeared on the government-controlled television on 14 April, claiming that his drink had been laced with alcohol while having lunch with the PRD leader Jao da Costa, immediately prior to the start of the coup. In the immediate aftermath of the broadcast, the government arrested da Costa, accusing him of having been involved in the coup. In another televised broadcast on the same day, da Costa, confronted by Mane, denied the charges. Despite lack of evidence linking da Costa to the coup, he was held in jail until 15 June, when the military tribunal due to try him ordered his release on condition that he refrain from political activity. Da Costa's release followed a protest campaign organized by the PRD, which formally announced his candidacy for president, and a campaign by Amnesty International. In August, after criticizing the president and his economic politices, da Costa and the RGB/MB leader Tagme Na Waie were rearrested and shortly afterward released.

Political Rights and Civil Liberties: Despite preparations for holding presidential and parliamentary elections, the citizens of Guinea-Bissau are still unable to change their government by democratic means. The ruling party continues to maintain sole control over the nature and timing of the transition, denying any role for the opposition. Because of personal rivalries, the opposition parties remain splintered and are unable to form a common platform.

The judiciary remains a part of the executive branch, and the regime retains the power to arbitrarily detain individuals suspected of anti-government activities. Political trials are held in secret by military tribunals. Early in the year, the legislature amended the constitution, revoking the Military High Court's right to order executions for violating national security, such as treason and attempts to overthrow the government. Following the failed March coup attempt, the army arrested opposition politicians without warrant, and refused to allow them access to legal counsel. Arrests and the conduct of trials in civil and criminal cases are often arbitrary, due to executive interference and the lack of qualified judges. In rural areas, the customary law prevails.

Despite the establishment of two independent newspapers in recent years, freedom of speech and press remains curtailed; journalists rarely directly criticize the president or high government officials, unless the latter lose the former's favor. The broadcast media have become more bold in criticizing specific government policies and giving coverage to the opposition.

Although religious groups must be registered by the government, freedom of worship is respected. Proselytizing is permitted and no religious group has been denied registration since 1982. The major religions consist of Christian, Muslim and Animist worshipers.

Despite the existence of informal police checkpoints on major roads to monitor the movement of people and goods, Guinea-Bissauians enjoy the right to unhindered travel within the country. There are no restrictions on foreign travel or emigration.

Until 1992 the only labor union in existence was the National Trade Union Confederation (UNTG), with close ties to the ruling party. Since then, several branch unions have broken away from the UNTG and pressed the government to negotiate with them directly, forcing the Confederation leadership to pursue workers' interests more strongly.

Guyana

Polity: Parliamentary democracy
Political Rights: 2*
Civil Liberties: 2*
Economy: Mixed statist
Status: Free
Population: 816,000
PPP: $1,464
Life Expectancy: 64.2
Ethnic Groups: Complex, East Indian (52 percent), black (36 percent), mixed (5 percent), Amerindian (4 percent), and the remainder European
Ratings Change: *Guyana's political rights and civil liberties ratings both changed from 3 to 2, principally because of progress in consolidating democratic rule, improvement in racial tolerance and respect for freedom of expression and indigenous rights. See "Political Rights and Civil Liberties" below.

Overview: In the year following the October 1992 electoral victory of the People's Progressive Party (PPP) over the People's National Congress (PNC), Guyana made significant headway toward consolidating democratic governance after twenty-eight years of authoritarian rule.

A member of the British Commonwealth, Guyana was ruled from independence in 1966 until 1992 by the black-based PNC. Under President Forbes Burnham, Guyana was redesignated a socialist "cooperative republic" and the PNC retained power through fraudulent elections and repression. In 1980 Burnham installed a constitution that provides for a president with strong powers and a sixty-five-seat National Assembly elected every five years. Twelve seats are occupied by locally elected officials.

Desmond Hoyte became president after Burnham died in 1985 and was reelected to a full term in an election that was fraudulent in every respect. With the statist economy in shambles, Hoyte began restructuring and seeking Western assistance.

In 1990 key U.S legislators and international human rights organizations convinced Washington to tie economic assistance to political reform. As the Guyanese opposition stepped up demands for free elections, Canada and Great Britain also applied pressure.

Cheddi Jagan's East Indian-based, Marxist PPP, the social democratic Working People's Alliance (WPA), and three smaller parties joined in the Patriotic Coalition for Democracy (PCD). A civic movement, the Guyanese Action for Reform and Democracy (GUARD), was formed, backed by the Anglican and Catholic churches, the Guyanese Human Rights Association (GHRA), independent labor unions, and business and professional groups.

Hoyte gave ground in 1990 when he asked the Council of Freely Elected Heads of Government headed by former U.S. President Jimmy Carter to help with electoral reform. Carter brokered three major changes demanded by the opposition—a new voter registration list, a preliminary vote count at the polling stations, and a revamped election commission. Hoyte also agreed to have the election monitored by Carter's group and a Commonwealth team.

After two postponements, two special extensions to the life of the parliament, two election commissions, and two failed efforts to create a valid voter registration list, the vote was finally scheduled for 5 October 1992. During the campaign, Hoyte touted recent economic growth and promised improved living conditions. But the social costs of the PNC's austerity program in what was already one of the poorest countries in the Western hemisphere had been severe.

Jagan believed the PPP could win on its own and the PCD unraveled. Jagan had moderated his Marxist rhetoric since the collapse of communism and presented himself as a democrat. In the end, race was the determining factor. Since the first elections under internal self-rule in the 1950s, the PNC and the PPP leaned on *apan jhaat*, a Hindi expression meaning "vote your race." With Indo-Guyanese outnumbering Afro-Guyanese by nearly 20 percent, the PPP won every election until 1964, when Burnham won thanks to the covert assistance of London and Washington.

The WPA, the only mixed race party in the country, campaigned for multiracial cooperation. It was also the only party other than the PPP and PNC to run a full slate of candidates. As expected, the Indo-Guyanese majority turned out for Jagan. Some in the PNC orchestrated violent disturbances, apparently trying to establish a pretext for annulling the vote. But with Carter and the Commonwealth observers pressing Hoyte to call off the PNC cadres and urging the election commission to proceed with the count, the process was completed.

Jagan was elected president with 52 percent of the vote, as Hoyte took 41 percent, percentages that mirror the country's racial composition. The WPA candidate, economist Clive Thomas, won less than two percent of the vote. In the legislature, the PPP emerged with 36 of 65 seats, the PNC taking 26, the WPA two, and the centrist United Force (UF) one.

Jagan was inaugurated soon after the election and promised the PPP would not seek revenge against the former rulers. And indeed, despite charges of discrimination by the

PNC, Jagan governed during his first year in office in a generally evenhanded manner. Meanwhile, the electoral loss led to infighting within in PNC.

In 1993 Jagan kept his promise by not reversing Hoyte's economic reforms, although the business community was critical of the government for slowing the pace of privatization of state industries. On the political side, Jagan oversaw a set of electoral reforms, supported by the main political parties, which paved the way for municipal and local elections to be held in June 1994, the first since 1976.

Political Rights and Civil Liberties:

Despite racial violence, registration foul-ups and delays in the voting process, the Guyanese people were able to express their political will in the 1992 election. The 1980 constitution gives the president of the country inordinate powers. The incoming PPP promised to reform the constitution to make it more democratic. In 1993 it took a significant step by negotiating with opposition parties an amendment that allows for a broader and fully independent national electoral commission.

The rights of free expression, freedom of religion and the freedom to organize political parties, civic organizations and labor unions are generally respected. However, without more explicit constitutional guarantees, political rights and civil liberties rest more on government tolerance than institutional protection. The judicial system, while nominally independent, remains understaffed and institutionally weak. Nonetheless, the right of habeas corpus is respected to a greater degree than under the former PNC regime.

Former President Hoyte took some steps to professionalize the police, but the force remains ill-trained and vulnerable to corruption, particularly given the penetration of the hemispheric drug trade in Guyana. Prisons are overcrowded and the conditions deplorable. There have been reports of prisoners dying of AIDS and other illnesses.

The Guyana Human Rights Association (GHRA) is independent, effective and backed by independent civic and religious groups.

Racial clashes diminished in the aftermath of the 1992 election. In 1993 the Jagan government took steps to establish a permanent body aimed at promoting racial tolerance.

Labor unions are well organized. The public sector unions have become more independent under the Jagan government. Agricultural unions are mostly allied with the ruling PPP. There are other independent unions. The right to strike is generally respected. There are a number of independent newspapers that operate freely, including the *Stabroek News* and the *Catholic Standard*, an outspoken church weekly.

Television and radio are mostly controlled by the government. The Jagan administration had promised a more independently run system. However, after recommendations were made by an independent commission, the government was slow to proceed. Nonetheless, the broadcast media allow for more pluralism than under the former PNC regime. Aside from government-controlled television there are a number of stations that rely mostly on foreign programming via satellite.

The 40,000 Amerindians residing in the interior of the country were either shunned or repressed under the PNC. President Jagan kept his promise to create a cabinet ministry of indigenous affairs, and appointed a man of Amerindian ancestry to head it. But the Amerindian Peoples Association was not appeased and continued to demand the right to govern themselves.

Haiti

Polity: Military
Economy: Capitalist-
statist
Population: 6,537,000
PPP: $933
Life Expectancy: 55.7
Ethnic Groups: Black (majority) and mulatto

Political Rights: 7
Civil Liberties: 7
Status: Not Free

Overview:

In 1993 the military regime signed a U.N.-mediated accord for the reinstatement of overthrown President Jean-Bertrand Aristide, then unleashed a campaign of terror and refused to comply with its terms. Aware of the international community's waning resolve, the military seemed determined to ride out economic sanctions, even if it meant the total devastation of the country.

Since gaining independence following a slave revolt in 1804, the Republic of Haiti has endured a history of poverty, violence, instability and dictatorship. A February 1986 military coup ended twenty-nine years of rule by the Duvalier family. The army ruled directly or indirectly for the next five years, often in collusion with remnants of the Tontons Macoute, the sinister paramilitary organization of the Duvaliers.

Under international pressure, the military allowed for the election of a constituent assembly that drafted a democratic constitution which was approved in a 1987 referendum. However, national elections were aborted amid the mass killing of voters. In 1990 the military gave way to a provisional government headed by Supreme Court Justice Ertha Pascal-Trouillot, who reinstated the constitution and called for elections.

The 1987 constitution provides for a president directly elected for five years, a directly elected parliament composed of a twenty-seven-member Senate and an eighty-three-member House of Representatives, and a prime minister appointed by the president.

In the internationally monitored December 1990 elections Aristide, a charismatic left-wing priest, took 67 percent of the vote in a landslide over Marc Bazin, a former World Bank official.

President Aristide formed a government from among loyal but politically inexperienced associates, and initiated a program to strengthen the judicial system, establish civilian authority over the military and end official corruption. The result was a dramatic reduction in political violence and greater respect for political rights and civil liberties than at any other time in the nation's history.

Haiti's mostly mulatto elites were furious over Aristide's bid to end their control over the economy. The military, used to enriching itself through graft, contraband and drug-trafficking, opposed Aristide's effort to create a civilian-led police force, as required by the constitution.

Aware of the forces against him, Aristide on occasion overstepped his constitutional authority by calling on supporters to defend the government through violent means. When Aristide returned from a trip abroad in September 1991 he knew that the military, backed by civilian elites, was plotting to overthrow him. In a speech alerting his supporters to the threat, he suggested they resort to dispatching government opponents by burning tires around their necks.

Aristide was overthrown on 30 September 1991 and narrowly escaped the country. The coup apparently was engineered by Maj. Michel François, who afterward became Lt. Col. François, chief of the Port-au-Prince military district. Military chief Gen. Raul Cedras defended the coup and the military installed a puppet government.

The Organization of American States (OAS) imposed an economic embargo and in February 1992 brokered an agreement for Aristide's return. But the accord fell through after Aristide rejected amnesty for the military and François's soldiers occupied the parliament. In June 1993 the military dumped puppet prime minister Marc Bazin. After the U.N. and Washington installed a global trade and oil embargo, the military agreed to negotiate with Aristide in New York.

The result of the U.N.-mediated talks was the 3 July Governor's Island accord. It called for Aristide to select a prime minister and a cabinet. A U.N. technical force would help create an independent police force. Once an amnesty had been passed freeing the military of responsibility for the coup, military leaders would resign, paving the way for Aristide's return on 30 October.

However, within days of the signing of the accord, the military unleashed a wave of repression against Aristide supporters. The primary instrument was the *attaches*, a military-sponsored network of armed civilian thugs that, for Haitians, was the second coming of the Tontons Macoute.

The repression escalated into a full-scale campaign of terror after Prime Minister Robert Malval assumed office on 30 August and international economic sanctions were lifted. Prominent Aristide supporters were murdered in broad daylight and Malval and his cabinet were physically barred from government offices.

On 12 October the U.S. ship *Harlan County*, carrying U.S. troops forming part of the U.N. technical mission, was ordered away from Port-au-Prince after armed demonstrators under the control of François seized port facilities. On 14 October Guy Malary, the justice minister, was machine-gunned in the streets. The next day Cedras was scheduled to resign, but did not. Economic sanctions were reimposed. The military, emboldened by the international community's reluctance to use force, remained defiant. The deadline for Aristide's return passed.

The military, apparently never intending to honor the accord, was already establishing a political base to consolidate its rule. It used a network of newly formed front groups headed by avowed Duvalierists, many of whom had only recently returned to Haiti. The most prominent, the Front for the Advancement and Progress of Haiti (FRAPH), demanded that Malval resign. FRAPH is controlled by Gen. Philippe Biamby, often described as the military chief of staff. Cedras, François and Biamby all have familial and professional roots in the former Duvalier regime. A number of members of the ancien regime, like former Tontons Macoute commander Franck Romain, returned from exile in the fall.

Malval met with military leaders at the end of November and afterward stated he would step down. He formally resigned on 15 December but agreed to stay on until Aristide named a successor or until Washington or the U.N. devised a different policy.

Political Rights and Civil Liberties: Although the 1987 constitution and the parliament were not formerly suspended after the coup, political rights and civil liberties are virtually nonexistent under military rule. The repressive structures of the Duvalier dictatorship have been reestablished and the country has returned to the absolute lawlessness of the past.

The prime minister and cabinet appointed by President Aristide after the Governor's Island accord were forcibly denied access to government resources and facilities, including state-run television and radio. The judiciary, purged of Aristide appointees after the coup, functions as an arm of the military, if at all. The parliament is dominated by neo-Duvalierists following bogus elections held in January 1993.

The chiefs of Haiti's 500-plus rural sections, disbanded by Aristide, were reinstated after the coup. Many are former Tontons Macoute and all run their sections as private fiefdoms through extortion, repression, and torture. Each chief operates under military district commanders in a loose system of warlords that can be best described as franchised terrorism.

Lt. Col. Michel François, military head of the district that encompasses Port-au-Prince, controls the city through the police, an arm of the military, and thousands of attaches, armed civilian thugs that operate as present-day Tontons Macoute. The attache system has been duplicated in the country's eight other districts, as each section chief and local military officer controls up to 150 attaches. Haitians use the words attache and Macoute interchangeably.

In mid-1993 the Inter-American Human Rights Commission (IACHR) of the OAS reported that 1,500 people had been killed since the coup and 300,000 out of a population of 6.5 million driven into hiding. Local monitors, which operate underground at great risk, put the number of killings at more than 3,000, charging that the military disposes of bodies in order to mask the toll. The IACHR reported sixty-eight extra-judicial killings and at least ten disappearances alone in the two months after the signing of the Governor's Island accord.

Since the coup, estimates are that some 40,000 Haitians attempting to flee by boat have been intercepted by the U.S. Coast Guard and 30,000 of them returned to Haiti. Local rights organizations report that many have been arrested and tortured, and some later found dead.

The entire population remains in a permanent state of fear of arrest, torture, disappearance, murder and extortion. Churches are frequently invaded as police hunt down Aristide supporters. Conditions in detention centers are wretched and it appears the only way to avoid torture is to pay off the police. Doctors report that victims of attacks who are able to escape detention are often tracked down in hospitals and hauled away.

Since the coup, the independent media have been either physically destroyed, repressed or intimidated into operating under a high degree of self-censorship. Most of the Creole radio broadcasts, the main source of news for the predominantly illiterate and non-French-speaking population, are shut down. Dozens of station managers and journalists have been imprisoned, tortured or driven underground or into exile. At least five have disappeared or been killed since the coup. Still existing media outlets were targets of armed assaults and raids following the Governor's Island accord.

The civil society which had been emerging under Aristide—peasant groups, cooperatives and community organizations—has been decimated. Moreover, the network of religious and humanitarian organizations that traditionally have provided the only help to the poorest nation in the Western hemisphere has nearly been throttled. These organizations are conduits for foreign aid, particularly in rural areas where two-thirds of the population live in extreme poverty.

Labor unions have been able to maintain a semblance of their pre-coup structures, although not in the export-processing zones where unions have been destroyed by local and foreign businesses taking advantage of the climate of terror and military repression. Leaders of still existing unions are subject to arbitrary arrest and torture. Forced labor of women and children is prevalent.

Grassroots organizations connected to the Catholic church remain subject to repression, and a number of pro-Aristide priests and nuns have been threatened and forced underground. Most of the Catholic bishops, however, have adopted a neutral position which the military portrays as approval of its regime. Willy Romelus, the only bishop to speak out in favor of Aristide's return, has been the target of military intimidation. The Vatican representative was the only prominent diplomat to attend the installation in 1992 of the military's last puppet government headed by Marc Bazin.

Foreign journalists, international human rights monitors and foreign diplomats, are subject to intimidation and violent threats by the military and its supporters and by section chiefs in rural areas. In October 1993 the U.N. and the OAS were compelled to evacuate 230 monitors from Haiti as threats to them escalated.

Honduras

Polity: Presidential-legislative democracy (military-influenced)
Economy: Capitalist-statist
Population: 5,628,000
PPP: $1,470
Life Expectancy: 64.9
Ethnic Groups: Relatively homogeneous mestizo, approximately 7 percent Indian
Ratings Change: *Honduras's political rights rating changed from 2 to 3 as a result of modifications in methodology. See "Survey Methodology," page 671.

Political Rights: 3*
Civil Liberties: 3
Status: Partly Free

Overview:

Carlos Roberto Reina of the opposition Liberal Party (PL) was elected president on 28 November 1993. He promised to challenge the military and a system of entrenched corruption that allows officials and business elites to remain above the law. The main obstacle: Gen. Luis Alonso Discua, widely viewed as the most powerful person in the country.

After achieving independence from Spain in 1821, and after the breakup of the United Provinces of Central America (1824-1838), the Republic of Honduras was established in 1839. Its history has been marked by military rule and intermittent elected government. A democratic trend began with the election of a constituent assembly in 1980, the election of President Roberto Suazo of the PL in 1981, and the promulgation of a democratic constitution in January 1982.

The constitution provides for a president and a 130-member, unicameral Congress elected for four years. Muncipal governments are elected. Governors of eighteen regional departments are appointed by the president.

The 1989 election was won by Rafael Callejas of the conservative National Party (PN), the other traditional party, ending eight years of PL rule and marking the first ballot-box transfer of power to an out-party in fifty-seven years. Callejas initiated a sweeping economic restructuring program, including massive layoffs, government spending cuts and an overhaul of the land reform system. The level of poverty grew to nearly 75 percent.

Since the return to civilian rule, the 24,000-member military has exerted great influence over civilian governments. It has used its clout to become a major player in the corruption-plagued economy. The constellation of military-owned businesses make the armed forces one of the ten largest corporations in the country.

By law, the Congress elects the armed forces commander for one three-year term from a list of nominees provided by the military. In reality, the military always gets its way. Gen. Discua, former head of military intelligence, became military chief in a barracks coup in 1990. In January 1993 he secured a second three-year term after he strong-armed his subordinates and cowed the congress by threatening to expose corrupt activities.

In February Discua ordered tanks into the streets of the nation's main cities, ostensibly to deter crime. The real reason was to make a show of force in response to mounting criticism of military corruption and human rights abuses. Pressed by the Catholic church and the U.S. embassy, Callejas formed a commission which recommended putting the military secret police under civilian control. But there was little follow-up in the congress as electoral politics took the spotlight.

In the primaries, the incumbent PN nominated Oswaldo Ramos Soto, a table-pounding right-winger and former Supreme Court president. The PL nominated Reina, a sixty-seven-year-old progressive and former president of the Inter-American Court of Human Rights. The vulgar and often inane campaign was marked by vicious personal attacks by both sides, and little attention to issues of concern to the electorate—poverty, the spread of AIDS, corruption and the status of the military.

On 28 November voters opted for change as Reina won with 52 percent of the vote. Ramos Soto took 41 percent. The PL won 70 seats in the congress, the PN 56, and two small left-wing parties the other four. The PL won a majority of the 290 municipal elections.

Reina promised to attack corruption through a "moral revolution," to add a "human face" to his predecessor's economic reforms, and to reign in the military. Standing in his way were Gen. Discua, who issued a pro forma statement of support for democracy after the election, and business and political kingpins, including some from Reina's own party, who have profited from the current system.

Political Rights and Civil Liberties: Citizens are able to change their governments through elections. The 1993 vote, however, was marred by administrative errors that left up to 100,000 registered voters incorrectly listed and unable to vote. Also, the head of the electoral commission overstepped the bounds of impartiality by publicly exhorting voters to "punish" the two traditional parties.

The military exerts inordinate influence over elected governments. It controls its own budget and the police, and has the final say in all matters that affect it. It is the principal violator of human rights in the country and generally operates above the law. It controls vast business, banking and agricultural interests, as well as all seaports, borders, airports, and customs. Through its control of the state telephone company, the military conducts illegal surveillance of all sectors of society. Although military service is compulsory under the constitution, the wealthy are usually let off the hook while the poor are gang-pressed into uniform during sweeps of public places.

Constitutional guarantees regarding free expression, freedom of religion and the right to form political parties and civic organizations are generally respected. There are numerous parties ranging from left to right. A handful of tiny left-wing guerrilla groups remain active, but since an amnesty in 1991 a number of radical-left groups have disarmed and formed political parties.

In January 1993 a government human rights office was established. In the summer, as a result of pressure from the public and the U.S. embassy, a colonel was convicted of the rape-murder of a young girl, the first time an officer had been convicted of a crime against a civilian. Three other officers were detained in another case pending trial.

But while the military appeared to be no longer untouchable, in 1993 it continued to violate rights with impunity and refused to cooperate with the government rights office. Independent rights monitors reported a number of extra-judicial killings, and alleged that Battalion 3-16—a virtual army death squad in the 1980s—still existed in some form despite the military's claim to have disbanded it. In one unresolved case, a once exiled Communist party member was murdered on 24 November.

Rights groups say most assassinations or violent attacks now stem from greed rather than politics, as economic interests, including the military and drug-traffickers, compete for profit and leverage. Targets include businessmen, trade unionists and peasant group leaders, who are also subject to arbitrary detention by police and, in some case, torture. Human rights activists and critics of military corruption report receiving death threats.

The judicial system, headed by a Supreme Court, is weak and rife with corruption. A few judges have asserted themselves in rights violation cases, but most are ambitious political appointees with no desire to confront the military or powerful elites. Despite the landmark case recounted above, most cases against the armed forces remain in the purview of military courts, away from the public eye, and usually result in dismissal of charges.

Labor unions are well organized and have the right to strike. However, the Callejas government employed the military and hired scab workers to break strikes in the banana and mining sectors. Labor leaders, religious groups and indigenous-based peasant unions pressing for land rights have been subject to repression and violent attacks. Unions have achieved collective bargaining agreements in some export processing zones, but are illegally barred from Korean-owned plants, where women workers are subject to sexual harassment, forced overtime without pay and physical abuse.

The press and broadcast media are mostly private. There are several newspapers representing various political points of view, but the practice of journalism is restricted by a licensing law. Some media have become targets of intimidation as they have become bolder in covering human rights cases and official corruption. Some journalists accept bribes, while others are threatened with losing their license. The military and the business sector issue veiled public threats. In January 1993 the home of the editor of the daily *Tiempo* was bombed. A reporter who said he could link former Battalion 3-16 members with the murder of a businessman left the country in February after receiving death threats.

Hungary

Polity: Parliamentary democracy
Economy: Mixed statist (transitional)
Population: 10,294,000
PPP: $6,116
Life Expectancy: 70.9

Political Rights: 1*
Civil Liberties: 2
Status: Free

Ethnic Groups: Hungarians (95 percent), Slovak, German, Romanian minorities, Croat and Bosnian Muslim refugees
Ratings Change: *Hungary's poltical rights rating changed from 2 to 1 as a result of methodological modifications. See "Survey Methodology," page 671.

Overview:

In 1993, Hungary's fourth year of post-Communist democracy, the government of Prime Minister József Antall confronted a split in the ruling Hungarian Democratic Forum (MDF), the difficulty of maintaining the momentum of market reforms in the face of economic uncertainty, and such regional issues as the condition of substantial Hungarian minorities in Romania, Slovakia and Serbia. Antall's death in December further undermined the MDF. Other key issues involved control of the media and the country's integration into European economic and security organizations.

With the collapse of the Austro-Hungarian empire after World War I, Hungary lost two-thirds of its territory under the 1920 Trianon Treaty that left 3.5 million Hungarians as minorities in neighboring Romania, Slovakia, Serbia and Croatia. Hope of regaining lost territory was at least partly responsible for Hungary's alliance with Hitler's Germany during World War II. After the war, Soviet forces helped install and uphold a Communist regime. In 1956, an armed uprising by Hungarians was brutally quashed by the Soviets and Hungarian Stalinists. Under Janos Kadar, Hungary, while politically repressive, enjoyed comparative economic well-being under so-called "goulash communism" which had aspects of a market economy. By the late 1980s, with the economy deteriorating, the ruling Hungarian Socialist Workers Party (HSWP) lost its sense of legitimacy. The ouster of Kadar in 1988 led the way to political reform and the eventual introduction of a multiparty system in 1989.

Hungary has a unicameral, 386-member parliament. After free elections in May 1990 the conservative MDF held 165 seats; the liberal Alliance of Free Democrats, 92; the Independent Smallholders, 43; the Christian Democrats 21; the Hungarian Socialist Party (formerly the HSWP), 33; and FIDESZ, a former student group, 22. Subsequent by-elections changed the composition somewhat. The ruling coalition includes the MDF, the Smallholders and the Christian Democrats. The head of state is President Arpad Goncz of the Alliance of Free Democrats.

The year opened with the MDF in the middle of an internal challenge from right-wing nationalists and deteriorating popularity just one year before scheduled national elections. In August 1992 a controversial article by MDF Vice President István Csurka had blamed Hungary's problems on a conspiracy of Jews, Communists, liberals and the

International Monetary Fund and even called into question the Trianon Treaty. During January, it appeared that Prime Minister Antall, trying to avoid a split in the MDF, avoided outright attacks on the extreme nationalists. At an MDF congress, Csurka and five of his followers were elected to the twenty-member party presidium, its highest policymaking body.

By spring, the prime minister had stepped up attacks on Csurka and his followers. In a March newspaper interview, he referred to Csurka's Hungarian Way Foundation as "a parasitic vine on the Hungarian Democratic Forum." In May, after a bilateral territorial agreement with Ukraine was passed by parliament, nationalist MPs refused to renounce Hungarian territorial demands against the Carpathian basin in Ukraine. Later that month, mounting tensions within the MDF led to the resignation of Lajos Fur, a party leader who helped hold the conservative and nationalist factions together. The Csurka faction, known as Hungarian Justice, the party-within-a party set up by Csurka and claiming the support of twenty-nine MPs, threatened to leave the MDF.

On 3 June the MDF voted to expel Csurka and three other right-wing nationalists from the parliamentary party. Five days later, rightist MPs began to turn Hungarian Justice into a parliamentary party, and Csurka claimed seventeen MPs had signed on. The split came amid strains within the ruling coalition over the government's harsh austerity budget to meet conditions for loans from the IMF and the World Bank. Meanwhile, opinion polls showed the MDF dipping below 10 percent, and the opposition FIDESZ showing strong gains. FIDESZ, which began as a student movement that refused membership to anyone over thirty-five, held a congress on 17 April and changed the rules to admit older activists. In 1990, it had captured 5.4 percent of the vote and twenty-two parliamentary seats.

The economy remained the most crucial concern. In March, the government set in motion plans to draw most of the population into the country's privatization program. It planned to offer millions of small investors concessions, including cheap credit, to buy assets remaining in state control. The conservative government was anxious to draw in popular support for privatization because of a widespread belief that foreigners and state company managers, many of them former Communists, had monopolized privatization (some 50-60 percent of privatized property was owned by foreigners). Hungary led the the way in telecommunications, basic utilities, labor quality and trade regulations. It had attracted $4.8 billion in accumulated foreign direct investment since reforms began. In May, opposition parties had called for privatization to be brought under direct supervision of parliament to insure that foreign companies not buy Hungarian firms just to take over the markets. The Christian Democrats, part of the three-party governing coalition, called for a halt in privatization in the food-processing sector.

In May Hungary reached a "gentlemen's agreement" with the IMF that cleared the way for a new credit facility. Under the accord, Hungary promised to bring the country's wayward public-sector deficit down from more than 7 percent of GDP in 1992 to 5.5 percent next year. Most government tax increases and spending cuts were slated for 1994, but a value added tax was passed by parliament in July by thirteen votes. In exchange, the IMF promised a credit of $700 million for 1993-94.

Given the MDF's declining popularity and next year's national elections, the government's austerity budget package was politically risky. There were some promising signs. In mid-August, the government announced that, after four years of recession and stagnation, Hungarian industry showed the first signs of recovery.

Through June, industrial production grew 5.5 percent. Yet, industrial production remained more than 30 percent down from the late 1980s and export statistics remained disappointing, dropping 27-28 percent over last year. In September, the government devalued the forint for the fifth time in 1993, offering some relief to exporters.

Another pressing issue was the so-called "media wars" over control of radio and television. In January, after parliament failed to pass a new law protecting the independence of the media and the government's December 1992 decision to bring control of state television finances directly under the prime minister's office, the heads of state radio and television tendered their resignations.

The crux of the conflict was the government's claim that journalists, including former Communists, consistently maintained an anti-government posture. In 1992, Prime Minister Antall ordered both media heads fired three times, but President Goncz vetoed each attempt. The issue continued to be contentious throughout the year. In October, state television suspended the liberal editor of a late-night news program and replaced him with a pro-government journalist. In early November, about 15,000 people held a silent vigil outside state television headquarters in Budapest to protest what they considered government assaults on press freedom.

In foreign affairs, Hungary showed concern for Hungarian ethnic minorities in neighboring countries and ultra-nationalist MPs continued to raise the issue of reuniting former Hungarian lands. In early October, foreign ministers from Hungary and Slovakia, which has an estimated 600,000 ethnic Hungarians, met in Vienna; Slovakia's Jozef Moravcik said his country would fulfill its commitment to the Council of Europe and allow the use of Hungarian family names and locality signs. Relations with Romania remained tense over the treatment of Hungarians in Transylvania.

In October the government expressed disappointment in a decision by the North Atlantic Treaty Organization (NATO) to put on hold the issue of allowing East-Central European countries to become members. During a visit to Budapest, U.S. Secretary of State Warren Christopher called for an "evolutionary process" toward membership called "Partners for Peace," which was unveiled in Germany by U.S. Secretary of Defense Les Aspin. It provided for joint exercises between NATO members and any European country that wished to apply, but would extend no security guarantees.

Political Rights and Civil Liberties: Hungarians can change their government democratically. The constitution and statutes guarantee an independent, impartial judiciary and a Constitutional Court.

On 12 October the Constitutional Court ruled that the first paragraph of February's Law on the Rendering of Justice, a statute dealing with the prosecution of certain war crimes and crimes against humanity during Hungary's 1956 October Revolution, was unconstitutional. But by lifting a statute of limitations, the court opened the way for bringing officials from the former Communist regime to justice for torture, mass shootings and other "inhuman" means used to suppress the 1956 revolution.

Citizens are free to express their views, with some minor restrictions. In May President Goncz signed a law banning the use of extremist symbols. Under the law, distributing symbols of totalitarianism, such as the swastika, the SS-badge, the arrow-cross, the hammer-and-sickle, and the five-pointed red star or using them in public are acts punishable by up to one year in prison or fine. The law exempts use of the symbols for educational, artistic or historical information purposes and does not apply to official symbols of states.

While Hungary has a broad range of independent newspapers and magazines, the government and opposition remain at odds over control of television and radio. Dismissals and resignations of several media officials and journalists for what they claimed were "political" reasons outraged democrats; for its part, the government argued that too often radio and television had shown an anti-government bias.

Freedom of assembly and association is guaranteed and respected. There are some 20,000 civic associations concerned with cultural, religious, social, human rights and political issues. Political parties can organize freely under a multiparty, pluralistic system enshrined in the constitution. On 3 October three social democratic parties united and adopted the name Social Democratic Party of Hungary (SDPH).

On 7 July parliament passed the Bill on National and Ethnic Minority Rights, banning discrimination against minorities and regarding their rights to national and ethnic self-identity as part of universal human rights and basic freedoms. The law recognizes all ethnic groups that have lived in Hungary for at least a century and who are Hungarian citizens but have their own language, culture and traditions. These groups include Bulgarians, Gypsies, Greeks, Croats, Poles, Germans, Armenians, Romanians, Ruthenians, Serbs, Slovaks, Slovenes and Ukrainians. Nevertheless, the country's estimated 500,000 Gypsies continued to suffer de facto discrimination in employment and housing. They have also been the victims of skinhead violence; in August, Gypsies staged a protest in the city of Eger after a Gypsy youth was beaten into a coma by skinheads. It was the city's twenty-fifth assault on Gypsies since 1991.

Freedom of conscience and religion is viewed as a fundamental liberty not granted by the state or other authority. There are no serious restrictions on domestic or foreign travel.

An estimated 2.5 million Hungarian workers are members of independent trade unions. The largest is the Confederation of Hungarian Trade Unions. There are also the Democratic League of Independent Trade Unions, the National Coordination of Autonomous Trade Unions, the Workers' Council, and the Trade Union Rally of Professionals.

Iceland

Polity: Parliamentary
democracy
Economy: Capitalist
Population: 266,000
PPP: $16,496
Life Expectancy: 77.8
Ethnic Groups: Icelander

Political Rights: 1
Civil Liberties: 1
Status: Free

Overview:

Economic recession and fishing disputes with Norway were the major events in Iceland in 1993.

Declining prices for fish and sluggish demand for Iceland's other big exports, aluminum and ferro-silicon, have caused economic distress in the country for two years. The Organization for Economic Cooperation and Development predicted in 1993 that unemployment could reach 6.1 percent by 1994. The government attempted to assist exports through devaluations of the krona. Iceland sparked disagreements with Norway by allowing Icelandic fishermen to fish in disputed waters.

The Prime Minister is David Oddsson of the conservative, pro-Europe Independence Party. In the 1991 parliamentary elections, his party obtained twenty-six seats in the legislature to become the strongest caucus. It formed a new coalition government with the Social Democrats, who hold ten seats. After nearly twenty years in government the Progressive Party went into opposition with thirteen seats. The left-wing People's Alliance and the Women's List hold the remaining fourteen opposition seats.

Iceland's parliament, the *Althing*, is a bicameral legislature subject to dissolution composed of sixty-three members elected to four year terms. Forty-nine members of the Althing are selected on the basis of proportional representation from eight districts with the remaining members chosen on the basis of the parties' percentage of the national vote. The Althing divides itself into two houses after elections, an upper house composed of twenty-one members selected by and from the Althing's representatives, and a lower chamber. Every four years, voters elect a president, the ceremonial head of state, who chooses the prime minister from the party or coalition able to command a parliamentary majority. Iceland has a parliamentary tradition dating from the tenth century. After disaffected Norsemen settled the country in the tenth century, Iceland flourished as an independent republic until the thirteenth century, when it came under Norwegian rule. In the fourteenth century, Iceland came under Danish control and remained under rigid colonial control until 1874, when it received limited autonomy within the Kingdom of Denmark. However, it was not until 1944, when British and American forces occupied Denmark, that Iceland achieved full independence.

A major political issue is Iceland's relationship with the European Community, an obstacle to its entrance into the European Community hinging on Iceland's fishing industry. Iceland fears competition with the heavily-subsidized fishing industries in the European Union and therefore seeks a compromise with the rest of the European states before possible entrance into the Union. The Independence Party supports tax reform to make the economy more competitive, and the Social Democrats back more market-oriented policies to advance the economy.

Political Rights and Civil Liberties: Icelanders have the right to change their government by democratic means. There is freedom of association. There is freedom of assembly, but some restrictions apply when it appears a riot may develop.

There is complete freedom of expression. The newspapers are a combination of independent and party-affiliated publications. There is a public broadcasting service, which is run by an autonomous board. The US Navy also broadcasts from its NATO base in Iceland. The constitution forbids censorship.

Over ninety-five percent of the population belongs at least nominally to the state-supported Lutheran Church. There is freedom of worship for non-established churches.

It is illegal to discriminate on the basis of language, race, gender and social status in Iceland. However, the Women's List alleges that there are cases of unequal pay for women. The government maintains a generous welfare system. Workers have the right to organize and to strike. Over ninety percent of all workers who are eligible to join are members of free labor unions. Enterprises belong to the Federation of Business.

India

Polity: Parliamentary democracy (insurgencies)
Economy: Capitalist-statist
Population: 889,725,000
PPP: $1,072
Life Expectancy: 59.1

Political Rights: 4*
Civil Liberties: 4
Status: Partly Free

Ethnic Groups: Indo-Aryan (72 percent), Dravidian (25 percent), other
Ratings Change: *India's political rights rating changed from 3 to 4 as a result of methodological modifications. See "Survey Methodology," page 671.

Overview: Throughout most of 1993 Indian Prime Minister P.V. Narasimha Rao's far-reaching economic restructuring program continued to be overshadowed by a rising militant Hindu fundamentalism expressed in deadly anti-Muslim riots in Bombay and in the seemingly increasing political appeal of the Hindu fundamentalist Bharatiya Janata Party (BJP). However, in November the BJP won only one of four critical state elections, indicating that many Indians reject the party's militant stance.

India received independence from Britain in February 1947. Faced with escalating political and religious tension, in July 1947 the country was partitioned into largely Hindu India, under Prime Minister Jawaharlal Nehru, and Muslim Pakistan. Nehru's daughter, Indira Gandhi, led India from 1966-1977 and from 1980 until October 1984 when her Sikh bodyguards killed her. Her son, Rajiv Gandhi, immediately took over as prime minister, later receiving a popular mandate at the December 1984 elections.

In the November 1989 elections, V.P. Singh of the socialist Janata Dal Party led the centrist National Front Coalition to victory, forcing the Congress Party into opposition for only the second time since independence. Singh's short-lived government failed to achieve any notable reforms and provoked communal violence. An August 1990 proposal to increase the quota of government jobs for members of "backward classes" led to widespread rioting across northern India. In September a sixteenth century mosque allegedly sitting on a holy Hindu site in the northern town of Ayodhya became the focus of communalist tensions. The Hindu fundamentalist Bharatiya Janata Party (BJP) organized a major march to the town, and by year's end nearly 1,000 were killed in Hindu-Muslim violence related to the temple issue.

In November 1990 Singh's government lost a no-confidence vote. In March 1991 a subsequent minority government under Prime Minister Chandra Shekhar collapsed. On 21 May, with balloting underway for a new parliament, Tamil separatists assassinated Rajiv Gandhi in Madras, throwing the country into chaos. When the voting finally concluded on 15 June, the Congress party (223 seats) and its smaller allies took 239 out of the 511 seats, the National Front 128, and the BJP and its allies, 123. The continuing success of the BJP, which held just 2 seats after the 1984 election and 88 after the 1989 vote, chronicled the rise in Hindu fundamentalism sweeping northern India. On 20 June veteran Congress Party politician P.V. Narasimha Rao became prime minister of a minority government.

In July 1992 new Muslim-Hindu clashes broke out in and around Ayodhya. Tensions rose throughout the fall, and on 6 December a mob of 200,000 Hindu fundamentalists swarmed into Ayodyha, destroying the mosque and touching off a week of violence in which 1,200 were killed and 5,000 injured across the country. In the aftermath, Rao sacked the four BJP-controlled state governments and banned three Hindu fundamentalist groups.

On 6 January 1993 Hindu-Muslim violence flared in Bombay and the nearby city of Ahmedabad. A dozen days of clashes with rocks, meat cleavers, homemade bombs and guns left more than 600 dead and 2,000 injured, mostly Muslims. Thousands of Muslim businesses and homes were looted and burned. Police tapes obtained by the *New York Times* revealed that the Bombay police purposely avoided aiding Muslim victims and in some cases even participated in the violence.

The fundamentalist upsurge has been attributed to a search by Hindus for a stronger national identity, fueled by fundamentalist claims that the national government favors Muslims and other minorities. Since Nehru's death in 1964, successive leaders have been unable or unwilling to articulate an attractive, secular multicultural form of Indian nationalism. Following the Bombay riots, Rao adopted a weak middle ground, neither strongly condemning the Hindu militancy nor adopting a firm secular line.

Reeling from charges that its response to Bombay had been too passive, on 10 February the government banned a planned BJP demonstration scheduled fifteen days later in the capital, New Delhi. The BJP, hoping to draw more than one million supporters and force Rao into calling early federal elections, pledged to hold the rally anyway. In late February police arrested more than 75,000 fundamentalists across the country as they headed towards New Delhi. Some 100,000 police officers and paramilitary troops arrested another 25,000 BJP supporters in the capital. Although potential violence had been averted, BJP supporters accused the government of using police-state tactics to ban an ostensibly political demonstration. On 12 March a series of bomb blasts in Bombay killed more than 300 people in one of the largest acts of urban terrorism in history. Investigators blamed the bombings on Muslim-controlled organized crime families. With the government's attention focused on dealing with communalist tensions, a new political threat came on 16 June when stockbroker Harshad Mehta alleged he had given Rao a $325,000 bribe in November 1991. Mehta had been behind the artificial price boom on the Bombay exchange in April 1992 that bilked investors out of $1.6 billion. In July, with confidence in his government plunging, Rao narrowly won a no-confidence motion, 265-251, his third victory in two years. Rao had planned to introduce a constitutional amendment banning the use of religious symbols and issues from election campaigns, but the no-confidence vote showed he could not muster the needed two-thirds parliamentary majority, forcing him to drop the plan on 24 August.

In the fall attention shifted to the critical November elections in the four northern states placed under federal rule after the Ayodhya incident. A BJP sweep would increase pressure for an early federal election. On 8 September the government announced new plans to set aside 27 percent of federal jobs for the "backwards classes," apparently timed to curry lower-caste support. With 22.5 percent of jobs already reserved for "Untouchables," the lowest caste, nearly half of all government jobs are now reserved for disadvantaged castes.

The government staggered the voting in Uttar Pradesh, Madhya Pradesh, Rajasthan and Himachal Pradesh over separate dates throughout November. Final results showed the Congress Party winning two states and the BJP just one. On 30 December ten Janata Dal MPs defected to the Congress Party to give the government its first majority.

The government faces three significant insurgencies: in Punjab, in the six states carved out of the former Assam Province between 1963 and 1986, and in Kashmir. *(A separate report on Kashmir appears in the Related Territories Section)*. In Punjab, a peaceful Sikh separatist movement turned violent in the early 1980s, and sharply escalated after Indira Gandhi ordered an army assault on the sacred Sikh Golden Temple in 1984. Several thousand soldiers, guerrillas and civilians were killed each year until the government began a massive police crackdown in July 1992. Since then more than 800 militants have surrendered to the authorities.

In six northeastern states, the United Liberation Front of Assam (ULFA), composed of Assamese nationalists backed by Naga and Kachin guerrillas, has been waging a low-grade separatist insurgency since 1979. The government reached a peace settlement with the ULFA in January 1992, but sporadic violence continues. In addition, the largest tribe in Assam, the Bodo, is seeking to drive other tribes out of the their section of the state. In October, Bodo guerrillas set fire to more than a dozen villages, leaving more than 10,000 homeless. In another northeastern state, Manipur, separatist Naga guerrillas attacked Kuki tribesmen over the summer, leaving 300 dead by September. On 31 December the government dismissed the elected government in Manipur and imposed direct rule. The government also periodically faces armed unrest and terrorism in several other states, including attacks by the Maoist People's War Group in Andhra Pradesh.

Prime Minister Rao's greatest success has been in slowly reforming the statist, inward-looking economy. Since July 1991 the government has slashed public sector subsidies, initiated extensive banking reforms, cut import duties, and made the rupee partially convertible. However, Rao appears unwilling to back deeper restructuring that could cost him political support, including privatizing state industries, further eliminating protectionist policies, and cutting the highly overstaffed bureaucracy, .

Tragedy struck in the pre-dawn hours on 30 September as the country's strongest earthquake in fifty-eight years devastated Maharashtra and several other central states, killing 9,748 people by official count.

Political Rights and Civil Liberties: Indian citizens can democratically change their government, but elections, and daily life, are marked by communal, caste-based, tribal and separatist violence. Corruption is rampant at all levels of government, and during election campaigns outright cash bribes are common in rural areas. Politics in several states, particularly Bihar, is increasingly dominated by criminal gangs.

Police, army and paramilitary forces are accused of widespread rights abuses in crackdowns against separatist militants in Punjab, Assam and other northeastern states. The authorities have raided thousands of villages in Assam, and soldiers are accused of harrassing and raping villagers and torturing detainees and suspects. In both Assam and Punjab, police can enter homes without warrants and have wide latitude in using lethal force against suspects. Human rights groups charge police with "staged killings," killing suspects after they have been detained and claiming death came during the chase. On 28 September the government established a five-member National Human Rights Commission, headed by former Chief Justice Ranganath Mishra, to investigate alleged abuses by the army and paramilitary forces.

The police and security forces have broad powers against suspects. The 1980 National Security Act allows police to detain suspected security risks for up to one year (two in Punjab) without trial, subject to approval by a board of three high court judges. The Terrorist and Disruptive Activities Prevention Act (TADA) allows police to detain individuals for up to a year for "disruptive" acts, which can include non-violent offenses such as verbally supporting separatist movements. Police reportedly use TADA against political leaders to prevent rallies and demonstrations, or simply as a means of holding people without a trial. Under TADA, voluntary confessions made to a superior officer are admissible as evidence; in practice, police reportedly torture detainees to extract confessions or as a form of extrajudicial punishment. Under the Terrorist Affected Areas Act, people accused of "waging war" against the government are presumed guilty in court. The Indian Telegraph Act authorizes tapping telephones and intercepting mail "in the interest of public safety."

The judiciary is considered independent of the government. Trials are generally conducted with adequate procedural safeguards, although judges are frequently bribed and the system is severely backlogged. Poor people often lack fair reprieve to the courts.

Police frequently abuse prisoners, particulary members of lower castes. Female prisoners are often sexually abused by guards and male convicts. The system has three types of cells, and conditions in Class "C" cells are the most brutal. Prisoners are assigned to Class "C" cells if they cannot prove they are either taxpayers or college graduates.

The country's vigorous press is often strongly critical of the government and of the security forces' alleged human rights abuses. The Press Council of India is an independent body of journalists that investigates reported lapses in journalistic ethics. Although the Council's practice of censuring journalists and newspapers carries no sanction, journalists say the threat of censure often leads to self-censorship. The Official Secrets Act allows the government to restrict publication of articles dealing with sensitive security issues; journalists say in practice this is occasionally used to limit criticism of government actions, particularly in Punjab. In Punjab and other violence-prone areas, journalists are frequently harrassed by militants and local officials. For example, in

February police in Assam briefly arrested the editor, publisher and printer of the weekly *Budhbar* after the paper published articles about the army killing a police chief. Some fifty other journalists were arrested and roughed up during a demonstration calling for the arrested journalists' release.

The right to peaceful assembly is generally respected. However the government banned a massive rally by the opposition BJP in February 1993 (See Overview section). All religious groups have the right to worship freely in this secular country. In many areas tribal customs often supercede the law and sometimes defy accepted norms of decency. For example, in August 1993 hundreds of villagers in Khandrawali, only fifty-five miles north of the capital, turned out to watch the beheading of a newly married couple accused of eloping. Citizens can travel freely within the country, except in certain border areas, and are free to travel and emigrate.

Workers can join unions and strike, although public sector unions must give two weeks prior notice. Authorities can ban strikes in certain "essential" industries. In August, several states used this power to ban a planned nationwide strike by the All India Motor Transport Congress, and police in Orissa state arrested several strike leaders. During a subsequent thirteen-day transport strike in September, police fired on striking truckers who attacked a convoy of fuel tankers, killing a driver. Forced child labor is a serious problem. According to the ILO, up to 5 million Indian children are held as indentured laborers. Altogether, the ILO says up to 44 million children under the age of fifteen are working.

Indonesia

Polity: Dominant party (military-dominated)
Economy: Capitalist-statist
Population: 185,160,000
PPP: $2,181
Life Expectancy: 61.5
Ethnic Groups: A multi-ethnic state—Javanese (45 percent), Sundanese (14 percent), Madurese (7.5 percent), Coastal Malays (7.5 percent), other (26 percent)

Political Rights: 7*
Civil Liberties: 6*
Status: Not Free

Ratings Change: *Indonesia's political rights rating changed from 6 to 7 and its civil liberties ratings from 5 to 6 as a result of methodological modifications. See "Survey Methodology," page 671.

Overview: Indonesian President Suharto began a sixth five-year term in March 1993 amidst growing restlessness among military leaders over an increasing "civilianization" of politics. In the past two years Suharto, himself a former general, has placed numerous civilians in provincial governorships, top civil service positions, and key diplomatic posts, and in October backed a civilian to head the ruling Golkar Party, apparently in an attempt to strike a balance between military and civilian political influence.

The fourth most populous country in the world, Indonesia consists of 13,677 islands of the Malay archipelago containing 350 distinct ethnic groups, including the politically dominant Javanese. The Dutch began colonizing the islands in the late sixteenth century. In August 1945, following the surrender of the occupying Japanese, the fiercely nationalist President Sukarno unilaterally proclaimed independence from the Dutch. In October 1965 the Army Strategic Reserve, led by General Suharto, thwarted a coup attempt by the Indonesian Communist Party (PKI). In the ensuing turmoil, several hundred thousand leftists and suspected sympathizers were killed. In March 1966 Suharto assumed key political and military powers, and one year later became acting president. He formally became president in March 1968.

Suharto's "New Order" administration has stressed economic development and stability. The guiding *Pancasila* philosophy consists of five principles–monotheism, justice for all citizens, political unity, democracy through consensus, and social justice. In practice, the government cites *Pancasila* to limit discussion of political change or religious and ethnic matters. The country is 87 percent Muslim, and the government and army remain wary of fundamentalist influences. Gross Domestic Product growth has averaged six percent since the early 1970s, and the percentage living in absolute poverty has decreased from nearly 60 percent in 1970 to 15 percent in 1990.

Suharto's political organization, Golkar, is a coalition of social and advocacy groups rather than a true political party. Besides Golkar, two significant parties exist, but neither considers itself an opposition party in the traditional sense. The Indonesian Democratic Party (PDI) is a coalition of Christian and nationalist groups that appeals to urban blue-collar workers and younger voters. It favors a more open political system, a greater focus on individual rights, and a more equitable distribution of income. The United Development Party (PPP) is a coalition of Islamic groups.

The 1,000-member People's Consultative Assembly meets once every five years to elect the president and vice president. Suharto has never faced any opposition, and these "elections" simply confirm his decision to have another term. The Assembly consists of 500 delegates chosen by the president and provincial governors, as well as members of the PDI and the PPP in proportion to their representation in parliament. The Assembly also includes the entire 500-member parliament, which has 400 elected legislators and 100 seats set aside for the military. The parliament has never initiated nor blocked a single piece of legislation during Suharto's tenure. Members of Abri (the armed forces) are not allowed to vote for fear of compromising the military's neutrality in its constitutionally established *dwifungsi* (dual function) as the stabilizing force behind the country's development.

At the June 1992 parliamentary elections, Golkar's share of the vote fell from 73 percent in 1987 to 67.5 percent, but the party still took a commanding 282 of the 400 contested seats. The PPP won 62 seats and the PDI 56. The government claimed that its solid albeit reduced majority proved that it still had strong support and that the vote was fair.

As the political focus shifted to the 1993 presidential election, the PDI came under pressure from many of its student supporters to radically challenge the political orthodoxy by nominating its own candidate, perhaps Gurah Sukarno Putra, son of the country's first president, rather than back Suharto. In January 1993, however, the party backed Suharto to avoid alienating the military and the government. Riot police forcibly broke up a demonstration by student activists outside the PDI meeting hall in the town of Kopo. In February, the PPP and Abri also backed Suharto.

On 10 March the People's Consultative Assembly, without bothering to vote, formally gave the seventy-two-year-old Suharto a sixth term. The next day the Assembly elected fifty-seven-year-old former armed forces commander General Try Sutrisno, who also ran unopposed, as vice president. Although Suharto had never made it clear whom he supported for the number-two post, since the beginning of the year Abri had openly backed Sutrisno, in effect forcing the president to go along or risk an open rift with the military. Many generals feel Suharto's increasing practice of placing civilians in top government positions threatens the military's political role. By having Sutrisno elected as vice president, the army is trying to groom a favorable successor. To a lesser extent, many generals are also annoyed that the president has granted his children control of hundreds of businesses.

Suharto announced a new forty-one-member cabinet on 17 March that dropped three key Berkeley-educated "technocrat" economic ministers, including Coordinating Minister Radius Prawiro, who had favored a pragmatic program of continued deregulation, a balanced budget, and emphasis on low-wage manufacturing exports. The new economic team largely consists of "technologists," led by Research and Technology Minister B.J. Habibie, favoring a substantial state role in backing expensive high-tech industries. Notably, Habibie also heads the Indonesian Muslim Intellectuals Movement (ICMI), which had complained that the previous cabinet contained eight Christians, including the three sacked ministers. The new cabinet contained just three Christians.

Suharto's strongest committment yet to the civilianization process came during Golkar's 20-25 October congress, when the president openly backed Information Minister Harmoko's election as the party's first non-military chairman. Suharto clearly sought to prevent the military from naming its own candidate. In late December the PDI elected Megawati Sukarnoputri, daughter of the late president, as its party chairman, rejecting a government backed candidate.

Political Rights and Civil Liberties:

Institutional barriers and President Suharto's political dominance effectively prevent Indonesians from being able to democratically change their government. All civil servants and employees of state-run firms must vote for Golkar. Some 36,000 former Communists are denied the right to vote. Political parties must embrace the consensus-oriented *Pancasila* philosophy, restricting their ability to campaign on potentially divisive issues such as religion or the dominant role of the Chinese minority in business.

In the June 1992 parliamentary elections, Golkar repeatedly restricted the activities of the PPP and PDI. In the weeks prior to the vote, the government banned seminars on politics and political debates from private television and radio. Candidates were allowed fifteen minutes per day on state radio and television, but speeches were reviewed beforehand.

The government faces armed separatist movements in Aceh, East Timor and Irian Jaya *(Separate reports on East Timor and Irian Jaya appear in the Related Territories section)*. In Aceh Province, on the northern tip of Sumatra, the army has killed some 2,000 civilians and Aceh Merdeka (Free Aceh) guerrillas since 1989.

In January 1993 Indonesia's Legal Aid Institute released a report calling the government the country's major human rights violator. The same month, President Suharto called for the creation of a state-financed national human rights commission, and appointed former Supreme Court Chairman Ali Said as its first chairman. Its powers and mandate have yet to be fully defined.

The judiciary is not independent. Judges are appointed and can be dismissed by the executive branch, are frequently pressured by the government and the military, and can often be bribed. The safeguards outlined in the Indonesian Criminal Procedures Code (KUHAP) are often ignored. Torture of suspects and prisoners is common and confessions are often forced. Police frequently use excessive force in routine situations.

The broadly defined 1963 Antisubversion Law allows suspects to be detained outside of regular KUHAP protections. In part because the government does not have to prove actual harm, only two people have ever been acquitted of subversion. In 1992 the U.S. State Department estimated that 300 persons were serving sentences for subversion. The Agency for Coordination of Assistance for the Consolidation of National Security (BAKORSTANAS) has wide latitude in dealing with suspected national security threats. Forced entry and surveillance of citizens are common.

The government cites *Pancasila* to restrict freedoms of speech and press. The written press is largely private, but the government regulates the number of newspaper licenses and the amount of advertising. Editors are often pressured by the government not to run stories and frequently practice self-censorship. The government operates the national television and radio networks, and the private companies serving some regions are required to use government-produced news reports, although radio stations frequently supplement these.

Freedom of association is generally not abridged, although the government occasionally denies permits to political meetings. During the March meeting of the People's Consultative Assembly, soldiers broke up a peaceful student demonstration calling for Suharto to step down.

Indonesia is the largest Muslim country in the world. The five recognized religions—Islam, Christianity, Buddhism, Hinduism, and the traditional practices of Aliran Kepercayaan—are generally allowed to regulate their affairs and worship freely. Advocating a Muslim state is illegal. Chinese citizens are forbidden to operate all-Chinese schools, cultural groups and trade associations, or publicly display Chinese characters.

The government prevents several thousand citizens, including some human rights workers, from leaving the country. Under the government's controversial "transmigration" policy, approximately 2,500,000 people have been voluntarily relocated since 1969 from the densely packed island of Java to Sumatra and Kalimantan. Critics say the policy, which has slowed in recent years, is environmentally destructive and disrupts those already living in the outlying areas.

In June, more than fifty non-governmental organizations issued a joint statement calling for full freedom to form trade unions. The requirements for union recognition are stringent—offices in at least twenty of the country's twenty-seven provinces, branch offices in at least 100 districts, and representation in at least 1,000 plants. Only the government-influenced All Indonesian Workers Union has managed to satisfy the conditions. In July police prevented the unofficial Welfare Labor Union of Indonesia, the country's largest independent trade union, from holding a congress. Workers have the right to strike, although organizers often lose their jobs. The United States has given Indonesia a February 1994 deadline to improve labor conditions or lose trade privileges granted under the Generalized System of Preferences.

Iran

Polity: Presidential-
parliamentary
(clergy-dominated)
Economy: Capitalist-statist
Population: 62,847,000
PPP: $3,253
Life Expectancy: 66.2
Ethnic Groups: Persian, Turkic, Arab, other

Political Rights: 6
Civil Liberties: 7*
Status: Not Free

Ratings Change: *Iran's civil liberties rating declined from 6 to 7 as a result of methodological modifications. See "Survey Methodology," page 671.

Overview:

Iranian President Rafsanjani won re-election in June to a second term, but the low turnout and the weak majority he received reflected widespread disillusionment with the 1979 revolution that toppled Shah Mohammad Reza Pahlavi's pro-Western regime and established the world's only Islamic republic. Most Iranians, struggling economically and harrassed into obeying fundamentalist cultural norms, have simply lost faith in the promises of their religious leaders.

Formal power in Iran is held by the president and by the twelve-member Council of Guardians, which must certify that all bills passed by the 270-member *majlis* (parliament) are in accordance with Islamic law. The eighty-nine-member Assembly of Experts, a body of Islamic scholars, decides the succession of the nation's religious leaders. Rafsanjani took office in 1989 with 94.5 percent of the vote and introduced limited free-market reforms to rebuild the economy following the 1980-88 war with neighboring Iraq. In his first term Rafsanjani managed to overcome opposition to the reforms from anti-Western, radical supporters of the late religious leader Ayatollah Ruhollah Komeini, mostly clerics who favored continued state control over large industries, keeping medium-sized businesses in the hands of Islamic cooperatives, and maintaining subsidies and price controls. The clerics' power base is the five main Islamic charity foundations that provide social services to the poor and operate numerous industries, employing hundreds of thousands of workers. In contrast, the *Bazar*, the powerful, traditional merchant and money-lending class, supported Rafsanjani, himself a Bazari.

Prior to the December 1990 elections for the Assembly of Experts, Rafsanjani successfully got the Council of Guardians to change the eligibility for Assembly membership. Many leading radicals were purged, and Rafsanjani's influence over the Assembly increased. Further support for the economic reforms came in early 1992 as the Council of Guardians rejected some 1,100 hardline candidates for the upcoming majlis elections. Final results of the vote, held over two rounds in April and May, gave pro-Rafsanjani candidates roughly three-quarters of the seats. With control of the majlis, the Assembly of Scholars and the backing of the Council of Guardians, the president had a mandate for cautious economic reform.

In May and June unskilled laborers in several major cities demonstrated against municipal governments that were trying to destroy their squatter settlements. Many of the president's supporters in the Majlis blamed the agitation on the economic liberalizations, and shifted their allegiance to the country's supreme religious leader, Ayatollah Ali Khameni, who opposed the reforms. On 24 August the president said the government would avoid introducing widespread reforms, and would allow only limited foreign investment.

Heading into the June 1993 presidential election, unemployment remained at 20 percent and inflation ran at over 40 percent. The Council of Guardians approved only three of 128 potential candidates to run against Rafsanjani, all relative moderates who ran half-hearted campaigns. On 10 June 1993 the fifty-eight-year-old president won a second four-year term, but with only 63.2 percent of the vote. Ahmad Tavakkoli, an editor of the right-wing *Resalat* newspaper who had attacked the government's bureaucracy and slow implementation of economic reforms, won a substantial 23.8 percent share. Surprisingly, only 57.6 percent of those eligible bothered to vote, even though a poll stamp on identity cards grants preferential treatment in finding government employment and receiving subsidized services.

On 16 August the parliament vetoed Rafsanjani's choice for finance minister, the American-educated incumbent Mohsen Nurbakhsh, apparently a further rejection of the economic liberalizations. Given this lack of support, Rafsanjani has few options in dealing with substantial macroeconomic problems that include a hugely overvalued currency, minimal foreign investment, inefficient state-controlled industries and $6 billion in short-term debt.

The main opposition to the regime comes from the Iraqi-based Mujahideen Khalq, which participated in the 1979 revolution but later fled after its leftist ideology alienated religious leaders. On 26 May Iranian aircraft raided Khalq guerrilla bases in Iraq in response to a series of sabotage attacks inside Iran. Abroad, Western nations have criticized Iran in recent years for supporting fundamentalists in Sudan; for backing terrorist killings of Iranian exiles in Germany, Italy and other European countries; and for refusing to retract the *fatwah*, or death sentence, on British author Salman Rushdie.

Political Rights and Civil Liberties: Iranians cannot change their government democratically. Although there are elections for president, the parliament and the Assembly of Experts, the Council of Guardians must approve all candidates as being "pro-revolution" and as "being Iranian, with practical belief in and commitment to Islam and the Islamic Republic of Iran, and loyal to the constitution." The government permits only two clergy-based political parties: the relatively moderate Militant Clergy Association, and the left-wing, hardline fundamentalist Militant Clerics Society. Most top officials, including President Rafsanjani, are clergymen. The parliament often vigorously debates economic issues, but there is no debate on the government's core political or social views.

In mid-1992 the government began encouraging fundamentalist groups to patrol the streets and enforce strict Islamic dress guidelines for women. Unlike the early days of the revolution, women are no longer flogged for violations but can be fined. During a particularly harsh crackdown on 19-21 June 1993, the fundamentalist squads arrested some 800 women, several simply for wearing sunglasses. On 22 June the state-run newspaper *Hamshahri* reported that President Rafsanjani warned clerics that the campaign had gotten out of control. In a separate crackdown in June, police and morals squads detained 8,615 people described as drug addicts.

Even more radical are the *Bassij*, (Those Who Are Mobilized), a 3 million strong group of state-supported hardline enforcers. The Bassij, who frequently receive military training and carry guns, patrol neighborhoods rooting out any signs of Western cultural influences. In order to boost recruiting, the government has guaranteed Bassij members 40 percent of university slots, regardless of their grades.

The Ministry of Intelligence and Security maintains state control through arrests, summary trials and executions. Authorities can freely enter homes, search mail or tap telephones, although in recent years have done so less frequently. Detainees and prisoners are routinely tortured. There are no legal limits on detention or avenues of appeal, so suspects can be held indefinitely.

The judiciary is not independent. The judges, as with any government positions, must meet political and religious qualifications, and bribery is common. Lawyers have been punished for zealously defending clients. The two-tiered system consists of civil courts dealing with criminal cases, and Revolutionary Courts that try political or religious offenses. In the revolutionary courts there are no procedural safeguards and some cases are decided in five minutes. The civil courts are pre-revolution holdovers and some safeguards exist.

There are substantial restraints on freedom of speech, press and assembly. Freedom of expression is generally tolerated on economic and foreign policy issues, but never on political or religious matters. In March, an editorial in the fundamentalist newspaper *Salam* candidly described the extent of official censorship, claiming it is difficult to function when "one report or article that is disapproved can get an entire publication's staff fired." It also said there is a "forbidden realm of news," and that government officials release information "only when it suits their purposes." On 29 April Revolutionary Court prosecutors arrested the paper's editor, Abbas Abdi, who had led the takeover of the U.S. Embassy in Teheran in 1979. The Ministry of Islamic Guidance must approve all books before they are published. All radio and television stations are state-owned, and broadcasts promote government views. Only government-sponsored assemblies are permitted, and campaign rallies are not allowed.

The small Christian, Jewish and Zaroastrian minorities are recognized by the constitution and have seats reserved in parliament. Members can practice their religion and provide religious education for their children, although they often face random official and popular harassment. However, the 300,000-strong Bahai minority faces significant discrimination. In March, the U.N. Human Rights Commission made public a secret legal code, drafted by Iran's Supreme Revolutionary Cultural Council in February 1991, outlining discriminatory policies towards the Bahai that included denying them employment and education opportunities and curbing the growth of the religion. The estimated 5-8 million Iranian Kurds are compelled to use the official Farsi language in education and other official or public matters.

Iranians are generally free to travel internally, although those who hold special skills, are connected to the former regime or are politically suspect frequently have difficulty traveling abroad. Jews can travel to Israel and elsewhere, but entire families generally cannot travel together. The government-controlled House of Labor is the only authorized national labor organization, and smaller labor councils and guild unions are closely allied to the government. Strikes rarely occur.

Iraq

Polity: One-party
Economy: Statist
Population: 15,162,000
PPP: $3,508
Life Expectancy: 65.0
Ethnic Groups: Arabs (75 percent), Kurds (15 percent), Turks, others

Political Rights: 7
Civil Liberties: 7
Status: Not Free

Overview: In 1993 the international sanctions placed on Iraq following the 1991 Gulf War continued to weaken the country's economy, forcing leader Saddam Hussein to cooperate, however grudgingly, with United Nations weapons inspectors. During the year the Iraqi army continued attacking Shiite rebels in the south and also drained vast expanses of marshland to deny the rebels cover, in the process destroying the 6,000-year-old culture of the indigenous Marsh Arabs.

Iraq won independence from the British in 1932. A 1958 military coup overthrew the monarchy and established a left-wing republic, which lasted until a 1968 coup brought the Arab Baath (Renaissance) Socialist Party (ABSP) to power. Saddam Hussein, considered the strongman of the regime since 1973, took power formally in 1979 as president, Chairman of the Revolutionary Command Council and Secretary-General of the Regional Command of the ABSP. Hussein and his ruling elite are Sunni Muslims, even though Shiites make up 55 percent of the population.

In September 1980, following months of border clashes, Iraq attacked Iran, beginning a fierce eight-year war. In August 1990, while still recovering from that conflict, Iraq invaded its tiny, wealthy neighbor Kuwait, raising fears it would also attack Saudi Arabia and touch off an oil crisis. The U.N. Security Council immediately imposed a trade and financial embargo on Iraq. A twenty-two-nation, United States-led coalition began air and missile attacks in January 1991, and liberated Kuwait in February. An estimated 100,000 Iraqi soldiers and civilians were killed or wounded in the fighting. A cease-fire agreement called for the U.N. to supervise the destruction of the country's chemical, biological and nuclear weapons capability, and establish a mechanism for long-range monitoring to ensure new programs are not initiated.

Immediately following its defeat, the army ruthlessly crushed a nascent Shiite uprising in the south, forcing approximately 200,000 civilians and 10,000 rebels to flee to the far southern marshlands to escape ground and tank assaults. By late March 1991 the government had also put down a Kurdish uprising in the north, causing hundreds of thousands of Kurds to flee to the mountains. To protect the Kurds, the U.S. and other countries set up a military task force in southern Turkey and established a no-fly zone for Iraqi warplanes north of the 36th parallel in Iraq.

In 1992 Hussein continued to violate Security Council orders by attacking both the Shiites and Kurds, and by harassing U.N. personnel inspecting its nuclear facilities for evidence of a weapons program. Notably, over the summer the government repeatedly denied the inspectors access to the Ministry of Agriculture headquarters, where sensitive military documents were believed to be stored, allowing them entry only in late July when Security Council sanctions appeared imminent. In August the government rejected a U.N. offer to the country for a one-time export of $1.6 billion in oil, $700 million of the reveues being turned over to pay for war damages in Kuwait and for the U.N. inspection program, insisting instead that the overall embargo be lifted.

Meanwhile, the army stepped up its offensive against the Shiites, deploying some 100,000 troops in the marsh area and reportedly launching napalm attacks. On 27 August the U.S., Britain and France established a no-fly zone south of the 32nd parallel and gave their jets orders to shoot down any Iraqi aircraft flying there. A U.S. fighter shot down an Iraqi plane on 27 December.

In January 1993 the United States, with support from Britain and France, carried out several military strikes following a series of Iraqi provocations. On 10 January the government ordered the U.N. not to use its planes to fly weapons inspectors around the country, proposing instead that the inspectors use Iraqi planes. However, these remained grounded due to fuel shortages caused by the Security Council ban. On 10-13 January Iraqi troops made several unauthorized incursions into the Umm Qasr naval base, days before the base and its surrounding area came under Kuwaiti jurisdiction under a U.N.-mandated boundary change. Early in the month the army also deployed new surface-to-air missiles in both the southern and northern no-fly zones, threatening allied fighter patrols.

On 13 January allied fighters launched the first strike since the Gulf War ended, attacking missile sites and air defense batteries in southern Iraq. On 17 January the U.S. fired cruise missiles at a suspected nuclear weapons facility at Zaafaraniyah, a Baghdad suburb. For several days U.S. and British aircraft also attacked Iraqi radar and missile sites in both the northern and southern no-fly zones after pilots patrolling the zones reported they had been fired on or had been tracked by radar. On 21 January Iraq backed down and agreed to allow the weapons inspectors to fly on U.N. flights.

The security situation in the capital remained tense following the allied attacks. On 14 April Reuters reported that travelers in Baghdad witnessed unrest after armed Shiites tried to kidnap the interior minister, Wattan Ibrahim al-Hassan. Security forces placed the Shiite section of Baghdad under siege after the kidnapping attempt, and police executed several senior officials, including former Interior Minister Samir Abdel Wahab al-Shaykeli. Twice during the month U.S. fighters attacked missile sites in response to Iraqi provocations against allied fighters.

Following former U.S. President George Bush's visit to Kuwait in April, details emerged of a foiled car-bomb assassination attempt allegedly backed by Hussein. On 26 June the U.S. launched a cruise missile attack on the Iraqi intelligence headquarters in Baghdad in retaliation for what President Bill Clinton called "compelling evidence" implicating the Iraqi government in the assassination plot. The U.S. said the attack would cripple Iraq's ability to carry out terrorist attacks.

In the latter half of the year Iraq began closer cooperation with the U.N. on weapons inspections. After stalling for several weeks, on 19 July the government agreed to allow inspectors to install cameras at two missile test sites south of Baghdad to ensure that no long range missiles are being built. In doing so, the government implicitly agreed to accept long-term monitoring of its weapons facilities. On 31 August Iraq began discussions with the U.N. over a complete lifting of the oil embargo. In late September the U.N. began its sixty-third and largest inspection of suspected weapons facilities. Although previous teams had turned up little evidence of chemical, biological or nuclear weapons programs, Rolf Ekeus, the leader of the special commission charged with the inspections, warned that Iraq was far from fully complying with the cease-fire terms, noting for example that it had yet to reveal its foreign suppliers of sensitive technology. In November Iraq agreed to accept long-term monitoring of its weapons facilities.

During the year the army continued attacks on the 10,000 Shiite rebels in the southern marshes. Artillery barrages increased in August and continued daily into the fall. Eyewitnesses and survivors claimed the army also used chemical weapons against the Shiites in the marshes north of Basra in late September and early October. On 18 October British MP Emma Nicholson, who had visited the area in September, told the Associated Press that the army had destroyed 400 villages in recent weeks. Shiite leaders say some 50,000 rebels and civilians have been killed since the aborted uprising after the Gulf War, and up to one-third of the estimated 200,000 Shiite civilians that had fled to the marshes had taken refuge inside Iran since early 1993.

In a related development, since August 1992 the army has been draining the southern marshes by building canals and dikes to divert water from the Tigris and Euphrates Rivers in what the government claims is an effort to recover 150 million acres of marshlands for agricultural use. In reality, the effect has been to strip the Shiite rebels of cover, and in the process has driven many of the estimated 200,000 Marsh Arabs out of the area, devasting their 6,000-year-old civilization. In mid-November, Shiite dissidents reported the army had begun building a huge earthen barrier near the Iranian border to trap and kill Shiites and marsh dwellers as they tried to flee.

The economic embargo has caused hardships for most Iraqis. The monthly rationing system meets only 60 percent of the nutritional needs of the average citizen, and in the northern areas the Kurdish population reportedly receives only 6-10 percent of their food quotas.

Political Rights and Civil Liberties: Iraqis cannot democratically change their government. Saddam Hussein holds supreme power in one of the most repressive regimes in the world, and has installed close relatives and friends from his birthplace, Tikrit, in many sensitive positions. They include: three half brothers, Sabawie al-Hassan, Director of General Security, Interior Minister Watban al-Hassan and political advisor Barzan Takriti; his son Quasy Hussein, who heads the special security agency al-Amin Khas that controls both the dreaded Mukhabarat secret police and Istar, the military intelligence; son Uday Hussein, editor of the *Babel* newspaper; and Defense Minister Ali Hassan al-Majid, a cousin. The rubber-stamp National Assembly holds no independent power.

Citizens are denied all basic freedoms. State control is maintained through summary executions, torture and a pervasive security apparatus that relies on a vast network of informers. In February 1992 the special U.N. rapporteur investigating Iraqi abuses reported that "scarcely a day passes without executions or hangings." Homes are searched without warrants and personal communications are often monitored. On 10 March 1993 the United Nations Human Rights Commission voted to condemn Iraq for "massive violations of the gravest nature, resulting in an all-pervasive order of repression and oppression which is sustained by broad-based discrimination and widespread terror."

Defendents in ordinary cases receive fairly adequate legal safeguards. However, the judiciary is not independent in security cases, heard in separate courts; confessions extracted through torture are admissible as evidence and defendants are frequently held incommunicado. There is no freedom of expression or assembly. All media are government-controlled and promote the government's views.

Shiite Muslims face especially strong persecution. In 1993 the army continued its artillery campaign against some 10,000 die-hard Shiite insurgents in the southern marshlands. Elsewhere, Shiite clergy leaders have been arrested, and the government controls many holy sites. Religious practice is monitored in this secular country. A 1981 law gives the Ministry of Endowments and Religious Affairs control over mosques and the appointments of clergy. The small Jewish and Christian minorities can generally practice without harassment, although Jews face retrictions in traveling abroad. Numerous areas are off-limits for travel inside the country, and citizens are limited to two trips outside the country annually. There are no unions and no right to strike.

Ireland

Polity: Parliamentary democracy
Economy: Capitalist
Population: 3,562,000
PPP: $10,589
Life Expectancy: 74.6
Ethnic Groups: Irish (Celtic), English, and small immigrant communities of others
Ratings Change: *Ireland's civil liberties rating changed from 1 to 2 as a result of methodological modifications. See "Survey Methodology," page 671.

Political Rights: 1
Civil Liberties: 2*
Status: Free

Overview: The Irish Republic's continuing economic troubles and the government's involvement in talks about Northern Ireland dominated the news in 1993.

Following centuries of British domination and occupation, twenty-six of Ireland's thirty-two counties won home rule within the British Commonwealth in 1921. The six counties of Northern Ireland have remained part of the United Kingdom. In 1948, Ireland proclaimed itself a republic outside the Commonwealth. The Irish constitution's Articles 2 and 3 claim Northern Ireland, but the republic has only a consultative role in the North under the Anglo-Irish Accord of 1985. The Unionist parties, which represent the North's Protestant majority, oppose the Anglo-Irish Accord, because they fear the mostly Catholic republic's involvement in the six counties could cause Irish unification. The Northern Protestants have claimed for decades that Ireland's Catholic majority could jeopardize their traditions.

The Republic of Ireland has a bicameral legislature, consisting of a Senate and a lower house, the *Dail*. The comparatively powerless upper house has 60 members and can delay legislation. Its term lasts as long as that of the Dail, a maximum of five years. The *Taoiseach* (prime minister), universities, and occupational panels name or elect senators. The Dail has 166 members elected by the single transferable vote method of proportional representation. Mary Robinson, the largely ceremonial, popularly elected

President of the Republic is head of state and appoints the Taoiseach from the party or coalition able to command a majority in the Dail. Robinson, a former Labour Party senator, supports women's rights and liberal social legislation. Her liberal views have encouraged major politicians to advocate changes in laws on such lifestyle and morality issues as divorce, birth control, homosexuality and abortion. Robinson had two symbolically important meetings in 1993. She met with Britain's Queen Elizabeth in May, the first-ever meeting of Irish-British heads of state. In June she greeted Gerry Adams in Belfast, Northern Ireland. Adams heads Sinn Fein, the political wing of the Irish Republican movement.

The Taoiseach is Albert Reynolds, leader of the *Fianna Fail* (Soldiers of Destiny), a generally conservative party with roots in Republican nationalism. He has held office since his predecessor, Charles Haughey, resigned in February 1992 after months of business and government scandals. Reynolds headed a brief coalition government with the Progressive Democrats (PD's), a socially liberal, pro-business party.

A tribunal dealing with scandals in the beef industry broke up Reynolds' first government. Des O'Malley, then the PD leader, testified that, as a cabinet member, Reynolds had extended too much export insurance to Larry Goodman, a Haughey associate and target of the probe. In turn, Reynolds accused O'Malley of dishonesty, thereby breaking up the coalition and necessitating the general election of November 1992. In that contest, Fianna Fail had its worst showing since the 1920s, 39.1 percent of the vote and 68 seats. *Fine Gael* (Family of the Gaels), the leading conservative opposition party, received 24.5 percent and 45 seats, its worst result since the 1940's. Labour won 19.3 percent and 33 seats, doubling its representation from the previous Dail. The Progressive Democrats captured 4.7 percent and 10 seats, a slight gain. Democratic Left, a new left-wing party that split off from the formerly Soviet-backed Worker's Party, took 2.8 percent and 4 seats. The environmentalist Greens garnered 1.4 percent and 1 seat. Independents took five seats. After the election, Fianna Fail and Labour formed their first coalition government with each other.

Throughout 1993, the Irish government held discussions with Northern politicians and the British government about a political settlement in the North. Public pressure for peace in the North grew after bombs of the Provisional Irish Republican Army (IRA) killed children in Warrington, England, in March 1993. The most dramatic political development took place in September, when Gerry Adams and John Hume, leader of the North's Social Democratic and Labour Party, presented a peace plan to the Irish government. Their proposals involved offering an IRA cease-fire and concessions on the Irish claim to the North in return for a British recognition of Irish self-determination and a greater Irish role in administering the North.

In December, Reynolds and British Prime Minister John Major issued a joint declaration on Northern Ireland that recognized the Irish right to self-determination. However, the statement asserted that a Northern majority would have to consent before joining a united Ireland. The two leaders hoped the IRA would join negotiations after a ceasefire.

Economic misfortune shaped government policies in 1993. The Irish Republic continued to endure unemployment of around 20 percent of the labor force. About one-fourth of the population lives in poverty. The government hoped to stimulate the economy with a European Community grant of 7.8 billion Irish pounds in 1993, but received no more than 7.2 billion. Protests to Europe about the shortfall proved futile.

Reacting to pressure on their currency from high German interest rates, Ireland devalued the punt (pound). The government dealt a blow to the weak economy of the Irish West by allowing American airlines to fly directly to Dublin, bypassing Shannon Airport, which had been the required first stop on transatlantic routes. In July, two Fianna Fail MP's, including Sile De Valera, granddaughter of the party's founder, resigned from the party caucus to protest the new air routes. The government's privatization plans backfired in May. The J. and E. Davy Stockbrokers mismanaged the state's sale of the 30 percent public stake in Greencore (formerly Irish Sugar). Having misjudged the demand for the stock, Davy managers sold the bulk of the shares to their own associates. This had the effect of embarrassing the government by creating a false market for the stock. In need of revenue, the government declared a tax amnesty for undeclared income and, in order to get people to pay, offered a special discount on the normal tax rates.

The major opposition parties experienced significant change in 1993. Des O'Malley resigned as PD leader. His successor is Mary Harney, first woman leader of a major Irish party. Fine Gael was unable to capitalize on the government's economic problems because its unpopular leader, John Bruton, had his own troubles. Amid rumors of moves to oust him, he stood accused of accepting bribes from mining interests. Fine Gael considered adopting a new name, perhaps the Christian Democrats, in order to improve its tarnished image.

Political Rights and Civil Liberties:

Irish voters can change their government democratically. Citizens register to vote through a government-sponsored household survey. However, only diplomatic families and security forces abroad have the right to absentee ballots overseas. There may be a referendum in 1994 on extending voting rights to ordinary Irish citizens living abroad.

The press is comparatively free, but there is censorship on moral and political grounds such as on sexually oriented material and allegedly pro-terrorist writings and broadcasts. However, in 1993 satellite broadcasts made pornography available despite national laws. Many homes receive British and other international broadcasts through cable television. Harsh libel laws provide politicians a tool for attacking critics. In 1993, six police officers asked the High Court to jail talk show host Gay Byrne and to seize the assets of RTE, the autonomous public broadcasting corporation, to punish Byrne for an allegedly prejudicial program about a case of false imprisonment dating from 1976. The court denied the suit, ruling that the information was in the public domain.

Terrorist organizations, such as the Provisional IRA, are illegal, but Sinn Fein, the IRA's political wing, is legal. The Irish government allows Sinn Fein to organize and campaign for elections. However, until 1993, the Irish government used Section 31 of the Broadcast Act to exclude Sinn Fein representatives and members of paramilitary and "subversive" groups from the broadcast media. A High Court judge ruled in 1992 that RTE had exceeded the law in banning an interview with a striking workers' leader who happened to be a Sinn Fein member. RTE appealed the decision to the Supreme Court, which ordered the broadcasters in 1993 to allow Sinn Fein members on the air under certain circumstances. The court held that there could be no more indiscriminate ban. In September 1993, the U.N. Human Rights Committee asked Ireland for the repeal of Section 31, because that law infringes the free expression provided by Article 19 of the International Covenant on Civil and Political Rights. By late 1993, the Irish government seemed likely to eliminate Section 31 in 1994. However, the government could still censor on the basis of Section 18, which forbids the broadcast of anything likely to incite crime or undermine state authority.

Due to occasional spillovers from the violence in Northern Ireland, the police have special powers to detain and question suspected terrorists. The Irish Republic and the United Kingdom have an extradition agreement that allows the courts to prevent extraditions for crimes that have political motivations. The two governments are still trying to clarify the limits of the political exceptions.

The judiciary is independent, but many male judges appear prejudiced about crimes against women. Public pressure is growing for judges to give stricter sentences in rape cases after a series of suspended and lenient sentences for rapists. In 1993, the Irish Council of Civil Liberties criticized the government's anti-crime proposals that would deny trial by jury to anyone accused of assaulting a police officer, sheriff or traffic warden. An Irish-born London policeman is suing the Irish police for sex discrimination. They rejected his job application on the grounds of short height, but would have hired a woman of equal stature.

Ireland is a temporary haven for some refugees from Communist and formerly Communist countries. However, there is also a government policy of imprisoning some asylum-seekers. In 1993, Amnesty International called for a change of this policy.

A new Ministry of Equality and Law Reform is preparing for a new referendum to legalize divorce in 1994. The voters rejected divorce in a 1986 referendum. At that time, fears about loss of property influenced the negative result. The government is proposing legislation giving explicit recognition to joint property ownership by married couples, in order to build support for the referendum. Women are playing an increasingly important role in the economy; the number working outside the home has grown by 41 percent in the past twenty years. Moved by AIDS, the government liberalized condom sales in 1993. Responding belatedly to a 1990 ruling by the European Court of Human Rights, Ireland legalized homosexual acts in 1993.

The Roman Catholic Church remains strong, but other faiths have religious freedom. There have been Protestant presidents and a Jewish mayor of Dublin. Most schools are controlled by boards dominated by the Catholic and Protestant churches. Few schools are multidenominational. The Irish-speaking minority forms the only significant indigenous, minority cultural group. Irish-speakers are concentrated in a small collection of areas called the *Gaeltacht*, located chiefly along the West coast. The government protects their linguistic tradition through various subsidies and other programs. Business is generally free, and free trade unions and farming groups are influential.

Israel

Polity: Parliamentary democracy
Economy: Mixed capitalist
Population: 5,270,000
PPP: $10,840
Life Expectancy: 75.9
Ethnic Groups: Jewish majority, Arab minority

Political Rights: 1*
Civil Liberties: 3*
Status: Free

Ratings Change: *Israel's political rights rating changed from 2 to 1, and its civil liberties rating changed from 2 to 3, as a result of methodological modifications. See "Survey Methodology," page 671.

Overview:

Three decades of hostilities between Israel and the Palestine Liberation Organization (PLO) came to a sudden end in September 1993 with mutual declarations of recognition and the signing of an accord phasing in Palestinian autonomy in the Israeli-occupied West Bank and Gaza Strip. In Israel, right-wingers claimed the autonomy deal would ultimately lead to a Palestinian state and jeopardize the country's security. For others, the initial euphoria gave way to the sobering reality that the deal marked only the first, and perhaps easiest, step towards a comprehensive regional peace settlement. By years' end the accord had yet to be implemented due to disagreement over the exact terms of the Israeli withdrawal.

The League of Nations granted the British a mandate over Palestine in 1920; one year later London assigned four-fifths of the mandate territory to present-day Jordan. In 1947 the United Nations recommended partitioning the remaining one-fifth into an Arab state and a Jewish state. The Arabs rejected the plan, and immediately attacked Israel when it declared independence on 14 May 1948. Israel fought Egypt in 1956, and in June 1967 routed several Arab armies in six days after Egypt closed the Gulf of Aqaba to its ships, taking the Gaza Strip, the West Bank, the Sinai Peninsula, the Golan Heights (which it annexed in 1981) and East Jerusalem. Israel kept these territories following the October 1973 War, and signed a peace treaty with Egypt in 1979, leading to the return of the Sinai in 1982. The same year, Israel invaded southern Lebanon to neutralize PLO guerrillas operating there; currently its troops maintain a small "security zone" in southern Lebanon.

Israel has functioned as a parliamentary democracy since independence. The 120-seat *Knesset* (parliament) is elected through proportional representation balloting. A party needs only 1.5 percent of the national vote to win a seat, which assures Arabs and other minorities of representation. The conservative Likud party formed a governing coalition under Prime Minister Menachem Begin after the 1977 parliamentary elections, ending twenty-nine years of center-left rule. Likud lost its majority in 1984 and entered into a "national unity government" with the center-left Labor party; similiar results at the 1988 elections led to another coalition until Labor withdrew in March 1990.

Efforts at achieving a regional peace settlement began in October 1991 as Madrid hosted the first of a series of United States-brokered multilateral conferences. Although Prime Minister Yitzhak Shamir ruled out relinquishing control over the West Bank, the Gaza Strip, and the Golan Heights, public opinion remained divided over "territorial compromise," making the peace process the focal point of the 1992 parliamentary election campaign.

In February 1992 Labor held the country's first ever political primary and nominated former prime minister Yitzhak Rabin to head its list of candidates. Rabin's stature as the victorious army commander during the 1967 War gave him strong credibility in protecting Israel's security interests, while publicly he offered a pragmatic approach to the peace negotiations. At the 23 June elections Rabin led the Labor party to resounding victory, taking 44 seats while Likud took 32; the leftist Meretz 12, the right-wing Tzomet 8, the Sephardic, ultraorthodox Shas 6, the National Religious Party 6, United Torah Jewry 4, the Arab-Communist Democratic front 3, the right-wing Moledet 3, and the Arab Democratic Party, 2. Rabin formed a sixty-two-seat coalition of Labor, Meretz and Shas, and drew the support of the two Arab parties.

The multilateral peace talks resumed in 1993, although negotiators made little significant progress. But through a series of seventeen secret, unrelated negotiations, mostly in Norway, Israel and the PLO reached a breakthrough agreement on 20 August providing for gradual Palestinian self-rule in the occupied territories, beginning with autonomy of Gaza and the West Bank city of Jericho by the end of the year.

On 9 September PLO Chairman Yasir Arafat signed an unprecedented letter declaring that his organization renounced terrorism and recognized Israel's right to "exist in peace and security," thereby overturning the fundamental principles of the group's 1964 founding covenant. Hours later, Rabin recognized the PLO "as the representative of the Palestinian people." On 13 September, Rabin and Arafat formally initialed the so-called Gaza-Jericho First plan at a highly publicized ceremony in Washington, DC.

Although not required to, Rabin sought Knesset approval of the plan. During one of the most important and emotional parliamentary debates in the country's history, opposition MPs said the plan would lead to a Palestinian state and return Israel to its narrow, pre-1967 borders. The Knesset ultimately approved the plan, 61-50, as Shas and three Likud members abstained, but right-wing critics claimed Rabin lacked a "Jewish" mandate in relying on the Arab MPs for a majority.

By years' end negotiators had failed to agree on the size of the Jericho area to be administered by the Palestinians and over control of the international borders between Gaza and Egypt and Jericho and Jordan. Negotiations continued into the new year.

Although the momentum of the Israel-PLO accords has not translated into firm agreements with either Jordan and Syria, on 14 September Israel and Jordan did agree to a "negotiating agenda" outlining discussions on refugees, water rights, territorial disputes and bilateral economic cooperation. Far more difficult is Syria's demand for a prior Israeli commitment to cede sovereignty over the entire Golan Heights before peace negotiations are held. Before 1967, Syria had used the plateau to shell towns in northern Israel.

In other issues, on 25 March Likud elected forty-three-year-old Benjamin Netanyahu as party chairman in its first primary, heralding the emergence of a second generation of Israeli leaders. Moreover, Netanyahu's telegenic looks and smooth oratory will be displayed at the next parliamentary elections, scheduled for 1996 at the latest, when the prime minister will be elected by direct ballot for the first time.

Political Rights and Civil Liberties: Israeli citizens can change their government democratically. Parties representing Arabs and far-right Jewish groups hold seats in parliament, although the extremist Kach party of the late Rabbi Meir Kahane, and an offshoot, the Kahane Lives party, are banned under a 1988 law outlawing racist parties.

In January 1993 the Knesset repealed a law banning contact with the Palestine Liberation Organization. Recognition of the PLO in September made it legal to display Palestinian flags and express open support for the organization.

The *Shin Bet* (General Security Service) is accused of practicing psychological and physical torture against Arabs and Arab sympathizers. A 1979 law allows police to place suspects in administrative detention for a six-month period, which is then renewable. A detainee must be brought before a district judge within forty-eight hours; if the detention is approved it must be renewed after three months. The judiciary is independent of the government, and defendents receive fair trials. Security cases can be closed to the public on specific, limited grounds.

The diverse press features over 600 privately owned publications in several languages, representing a wide variety of independent views. Articles dealing with security matters must be submitted to a military censor, and Arabic-language publications are more frequently censored than Hebrew-language ones. In November Israel's first commercial television station began broadcasting. Freedom of assembly is respected.

All religions worship freely. Each community has jurisdiction over its members in questions of mariage and divorce. The 76,000 Druze citizens serve in the army but frequently face social ostracization, as well as discrimination in employment and government services. Like the Druze, Arab citizens receive less government funding for services than Jewish citizens. The social-action New Israel Fund says 60 percent of Arab children are below the poverty line, compared with 10 percent of Jewish children, and that the Education Ministry spent $123 per Jewish schoolchild in 1991 compared to $67 for each Arab child. The Rabin government has pledged to close this gap in education and other areas. Arabs are further disadvantaged by not being subject to the draft, since army veterans receive preferential access to housing subsidies and other benefits. Workers can join independent unions and hold strikes.

Italy

Polity: Parliamentary democracy
Economy: Capitalist-statist
Population: 57,837,000
PPP: $15,890
Life Expectancy: 76.0

Political Rights: 1
Civil Liberties: 3*
Status: Free

Ethnic Groups: Italian (Latin), various immigrant groups, and small Austro-German and Gypsy minorities
Ratings Change: *Italy's civil liberties rating changed from 2 to 3 because of major corruption scandals and Mafia violence.

Overview:

In 1993, the Italian political system experienced major upheavals, resulting from a ballooning set of corruption scandals. Criminal allegations led to investigations and arrests of major politicians and businessmen implicated in bribery cases and links to the criminal underworld. As a result of the crisis, the political system faced a major realignment as voters approved a new electoral system and defeated the established parties in local elections.

Modern Italian history dates from the nineteenth-century movement for national unification. Most of Italy had merged into one kingdom by 1870. Italy began World War I on the side of Germany and Austria-Hungary, but switched to the Allied side. As a consequence, Italy won territory that had belonged to Austria. The country lived under the fascist dictatorship of Benito Mussolini from 1922 to 1943. A referendum in 1946 ended the monarchy and brought in a republican form of government.

Since the abolition of the monarchy, the head of state has been a largely ceremonial president, who is elected for a seven-year term by an assembly of parliamentarians and delegates from the Regional Councils. The president chooses the prime minister, who is often, but not always, a member of the largest party in the Chamber of Deputies, the lower house of parliament. The upper house, the Senate, is elected regionally. The president can appoint five senators for life and becomes one himself upon leaving office.

From the late 1940s to the early 1990s, short-lived governments dominated by the Christian Democrats (DC) were the rule in Italy. An electoral system based on proportional representation, multimember districts and ballots with party lists created a parliamentary system with many small parties. During the Cold War, the Communists (PCI) were the largest opposition party. Following the collapse of communism in Eastern Europe, the PCI adopted a new name and platform, calling itself the Party of the Democratic Left (PDS), based on a non-Marxist, social democratic philosophy. The collapse of communism mooted the Christian Democrats' traditional anti-Communist stance.

Regional political fragmentation since 1991 has spawned the Northern League, a political bloc that is hostile to the economically backward South.

Since 1990, frustrated voters and party dissidents have fought to give the voters more leverage in choosing the candidates for parliament, and to reduce the political parties' extensive patronage system. Under proportional representation, electors voted for the party lists of their choice, but party bosses determined the candidates and their order of appearance on the ballot lists. Despite the frequent turnover of governments, power remained in the hands of small group of Christian Democrats, Socialists, and three smaller parties, the Social Democrats, the Liberals and Republicans.

In 1992, a financial scandal in Milan, involving construction companies giving bribes to public officials in return for contracts, led to further charges implicating the governing parties in illegal schemes throughout the country. Reformers linked cleaning up corruption with reforming the electoral process. A dissident Christian Democrat, Mario Segni, left the party in 1992 to press for a single-member, first-past-the-post electoral system. Faced with a lack of consensus in the parliamentary reform commission, the Constitutional Court allowed for a referendum to determine the change in the electoral law. On 18-19 April, 82.7 percent of participating voters favored the introduction of the first-past-the-post voting system for three-fourths of the 315 Senate seats. The remaining seats would still be filled on a proportional basis for parties with at least a 4 percent national voter support. On 4 August, the parliament reached an agreement on similar electoral rules for the 630-member Chamber of Deputies.

The election reform scrapped the system of proportional representation in elections to local councils in favor of majority voting. It also instituted direct election of mayors in municipalities with over 15,000 inhabitants. The first test of the new electoral system occurred on 6 June, with the elections to a number of local councils and regional assemblies. In the elections, the traditional centrist and center-left parties trailed poorly, while parties from the Left and Right made substantial gains.

Another round of balloting for 428 mayoral posts took place on 21 November. The vote showed further evidence of the decline in popularity of the Christian Democrats and other traditionally governing parties. In Palermo, Sicily, a longtime Christian Democratic stronghold, the party's candidate lost to Leoluca Orlando of the anti-Mafia *La Rete* (Network) party. In many of the contests with no clear majority for any single candidate, including the largest cities of Rome and Naples, the ex-Communist PDS and the neo-Fascist Italian Social Movement (MSI) fielded the strongest contenders. The Christian Democrats received less than 10 percent of the vote. In the 6 December run-off, the PDS candidates won in 53 out of 129 contests, including Rome and Naples. In Naples, the ex-Communist Antonio Basolino defeated Alessandra Mussolini, the granddaughter of the dictator.

Following the forced resignations of several cabinet ministers linked to corruption, and calls to broaden the four-party coalition to include the PDS, the Socialist Prime Minister Guiliano Amato chose to resign in late April. On 26 April, President Oscar Luigi Scalfaro nominated Carlo Azeglio Ciampi, the governor of the Bank of Italy and the first non-parliamentarian to head the fifty-second post-war cabinet. The new cabinet included several non-party technocrats and received tacit support from the ex-Communist and Green parties. Ciampi listed new electoral rules, privatization and deficit reduction as his top priorities. By late 1993, the *Mani Pulite* (Clean Hands) anti-corruption probe led to arrests and indictments of 3,000 prominent political and business figures. Former Christian Democratic Prime Minister Giulio Andreotti was accused of Mafia links and of involvement in the abduction and murder of the former Prime Minister Aldo Moro in 1978 by the Red Brigades terrorist group. Former Socialist Prime Minister Bettino Craxi was investigated on eighty-three charges of corruption totalling $60 million. In July, Raul Gardini and Gabriele Cagliani, chairmen of the private Feruzzi conglomerate and the state ENI energy corporation, respectively, committed suicide in connection with corruption in the takeover of the Enimont concern (a subsidy of ENI). Others arrested included the chairmen of FIAT, Olivetti and the state-owned IRI steel conglomerate.

In addition to unearthing the vast scale of corruption, Italy feared a renewal of terrorist activities. Bombings of the Florence Uffizi Gallery in May, resulted in six deaths and the destruction of valuable cultural artifacts, and July bombings in Rome and Milan killed another five people and damaged churches and museums.

During 1993, authorities gained a major victory against organized crime with the arrests of several Mafia bosses, including the alleged "boss of all bosses," Salvatore Riina. On 8 October, Riina was sentenced to life in prison for the killing of the anti-Mafia judge Giovanni Falcone in May 1992.

Political Rights and Civil Liberties: Italians have the right to change their government democratically. Elections to the national, regional and local levels are competitive. A plethora of political parties ranges from far-left to far-right in elections. However, the new electoral law is likely to reduce the number of parties with parliamentary representation. With fewer parties, Italy may experience fewer cabinet changes that result from a shifting pattern of political deals. There is freedom of political organization, but Mussolini's Fascist movement is outlawed. There is some friction between Italians and the Austro-German minority in the northern area of Alto Adige, which was part of the Austro-Hungarian Empire until World War I.

The media are generally free and independent, but there are some minor restrictions on the press in the areas of obscenity and defamation. There are both public and private broadcasting companies. The three state television channels are subject to political party pressure. Media magnate Silvio Berlusconi controls the private channels. The print media often have partisan leanings.

The court system is notoriously slow. The judiciary is independent, but political pressures may affect some proceedings. Since the start of the big anti-corruption probe in 1992, prosecutors and judges have shown vigor in indicting and prosecuting business and political leaders. In September 1993, the scandals reached Milan Judge Diego Curto. He stood accused of accepting 400,000 Swiss francs to undermine the prosecution in the Enimont scandal. Organized crime has targeted anti-Mafia judges, prosecutors, police and clergy for assassinations and bombings during the last two years.

There is freedom of association except for overtly Fascist and racist groups. In July 1993, police arrested seven right-wing activists on charges of promoting neo-Nazism and fomenting racial hatred. There are competing labor federations of differing ideological orientations. In October 1993, unions staged a brief general strike to protest the government's privatization policy.

Italians have religious freedom. Although the Catholic Church is still dominant it is no longer the state church. Italians who do not evade the income tax can designate contributions to churches on their tax forms.

Since 1992, an edict has allowed authorities to expel foreigners accused of serious crimes. Human rights groups complained that the edict created a separate and summary justice for foreigners. There are some acts of violence against foreigners and minorities, especially Gypsies. Women face some obstacles to advancement in employment, but have had increasing legal equality since the 1960s.

Ivory Coast

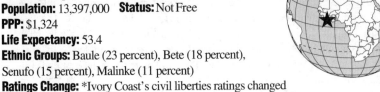

Polity: Dominant party
Economy: Capitalist
Population: 13,397,000
PPP: $1,324
Life Expectancy: 53.4
Ethnic Groups: Baule (23 percent), Bete (18 percent), Senufo (15 percent), Malinke (11 percent)
Ratings Change: *Ivory Coast's civil liberties ratings changed from 4 to 5 because of the government's crackdown on the opposition.

Political Rights: 6
Civil Liberties: 5*
Status: Not Free

Overview: Shortly following the death of President Felix Houphouet-Boigny in December 1993, the Supreme Court named Henri Konan Bedie as Ivory Coast's new president. Bedie's appointment was briefly challenged by Prime Minister Arassane Ouattara who subsequently retired. Bedie named a new cabinet of twenty-four ministers. Opposition leaders claimed that Bedie's succession was undemocratic, citing a constitutional amendment that allows the national assembly leader to serve out Houphouet-Boigny's mandate until the 1995 elections.

Since gaining independence from France in 1959, the Ivory Coast had been ruled by Felix Houphouet-Boigny from the Parti Democratique de Cote d'Ivoire (PDCI). As a result of large anti-government demonstrations in 1990, Houphouet-Boigny authorized the formation of opposition parties. Among the new parties to form was the Ivorian Popular Front (FPI) led by Laurent Gbagbo, a long time adversary and critic of Houphouet-Boigny.

In October 1990, Gbagbo, along with a number of other opposition candidates, challenged Houphouet-Boigny in the country's first multi-party election. Houphouet-Boigny emerged with a majority of the vote. However, the elections were marred by charges of rampant vote-rigging. The government subsequently conceded that the elections were "poorly organized." National Assembly elections followed in November and critics again charged that there was widespread vote-rigging. The PDCI won 163 seats, the FPI nine, independent candidates two, and the Ivorian Workers' Party only one. In 1992 fifteen opposition parties joined to form the Union of Democratic forces alliance.

From the early 1960's until 1980, the Ivory Coast was one of the wealthiest nations in Africa. With support from the World Bank, International Monetary Fund (IMF) and other Western institutions, the Ivory Coast cultivated and exported coffee and cocoa. By 1978, the Ivory Coast was the leading exporter of cocoa and the third in the world for coffee production. The success of the program was dubbed the "Ivorian miracle" and it lasted until the bottom fell out of the world coffee and cocoa market in the early 1980s.

In recent years the Ivory Coast has been burdened by a substantial and growing IMF debt, a large budget deficit and an economy that is near collapse. As a result, in 1991 the government entered a stabilization agreement with the IMF and the World Bank in order to reduce the deficit, reform taxes and labor codes and begin a program of privatization. The prime minister has been in charge of implementing these measures. The income distribution plan, a critical measure in the government's reform program, has been met with great resistance from the country's elite. The austerity measures have also been challenged by government workers and, most violently, by the military.

Anti-government demonstrations continued to plague the Houphouet-Boigny government during 1992-93. Human rights groups reported a number of human rights violations by security forces against demonstrators and political opponents of the ruling party, including rape, beatings and arbitrary detention.

Political Rights and Civil Liberties:

Ivorians cannot change their government democratically and it remains to be seen whether multiparty elections set for 1995 will take place as scheduled. Earlier multiparty presidential and legislative elections in 1990 were plagued with irregularities. The ruling party kept the campaign short and opposition party candidates were given only limited access to the media. The ruling PDCI claimed the presidency as well as a majority of legislative seats amid accusations from opposition party leaders and election monitors that the voting was neither free nor fair. While political demonstrations were allowed during the campaign, critics assert that the government planted agitators among the participants, then allowed security forces to arrest and detain supporters under the guise of preserving public order.

While a pluralist press is allowed, the radio and television stations in the Ivory Coast are state controlled and criticism of the government is rare. Opposition newspapers circulate but it remains an offense, punishable by three months to two years imprisonment, to offend the president, prime minister, other government leaders or to defame institutions of the state. A press law enacted in 1991 created a commission to oversee the press and to enforce laws barring publication of defamatory materials or information that would "undermine the credit of the nation." As a result, in 1992 five Ivorian journalists were imprisoned for violating this law and their respective newspapers' activities were suspended.

The constitution allows for freedom of assembly and association. In practice, however, these freedoms are severely restricted. The government requires that all organizations register before operating and reserves the right to deny any request. Permits are required before any public meeting and these requests are frequently denied. In 1992 the government enacted a ban on all outdoor public meetings, although the ban was selectively applied to exclude some government organized gatherings. The government also bans organizations from forming along political or religious lines.

In July 1992, the National Assembly passed an "anti vandal" law which states that organizers of or participants in a meeting that becomes violent are subject to imprisonment regardless of whether they were present at the meeting. Human Rights groups as well as opposition parties denounced the law as being too vague and for imposing collective punishment for the actions of a few. Since its passage, the law has been arbitrarily imposed and has allowed the government to detain non violent political leaders and student activists.

In April 1993, forty-four student members of the banned Federation of Ivorian Students (FESCI) were arrested under the "anti-vandal" law. A meeting of the FESCI became violent when it was broken up by security forces who claimed that the meeting had been banned. Students charge that they were beaten during arrest and detention and one former Amnesty International Prisoner of Conscience, Chantal Leba, was reported to have been severely beaten. The students were provisionally released at the end of May. However, their charges were not dropped and they remain subject to further prosecution.

The judicial system is not free from government influence. There is no clear separation between the judicial and executive branches of government. In theory, criminal cases are to be tried independent of the executive branch. In practice verdicts and sentencing in cases that involve crimes committed during protests or marches have been influenced by political pressures. In contrast, there are reports of lenient sentences given to individuals with government contacts. While all those accused of committing capital crimes or felonies have the right to legal council, those who cannot afford private council often are not represented as court-appointed attorneys are not readily available.

There is no state religion and freedom of worship is respected. Freedom of international travel is generally respected. While government control on internal travel is limited, the U.S. State Department has received reports of arbitrary roadblocks and harassment of travelers. Reports allege that money is sometimes extorted for passage. Further reports indicate that members of the banned FESCI student group have been deliberately singled out and harassed at roadblocks

Workers do have the right to organize and strike under the constitution. However, most union activity takes place within the government-sponsored General Union of Ivory Coast Workers (UGTCI). Although the UGTCI rarely approves a strike, a number of other unions that were formed during 1992 frequently exercised their right to strike.

Jamaica

Polity: Parliamentary democracy
Economy: Capitalist
Population: 2,507,000
PPP: $2,979
Life Expectancy: 73.1
Ethnic Groups: Black majority (about 75 percent); mixed race, European and Asian minorities

Political Rights: 2
Civil Liberties: 3*
Status: Free

Ratings Change: *Jamaica's civil liberties rating changed from 2 to 3 because of increased citizen insecurity as a result of a mounting wave of criminal violence, police brutality with relative impunity, increased domestic and sexual violence against women, and incremental weakening of an already slow and inefficient judiciary.

Overview:

Prime Minister P. J. Patterson, selected by the ruling People's National Party (PNP) to replace Michael Manley following his resignation in March 1992, strengthened his mandate as the PNP trounced the Jamaica Labour Party (JLP) in a typically rough-and-tumble election in March 1993.

Jamaica, a member of the British Commonwealth, achieved independence in 1962. It is a parliamentary democracy, with the British monarchy represented by a governor-general. The bicameral parliament consists of a sixty-member House of Representatives elected for five years, and a twenty-one-member Senate, with thirteen senators appointed by the prime minister and eight by the leader of the parliamentary opposition. Executive authority is invested in the prime minister, who is the leader of the political party commanding a majority in the House.

Since independence, power has alternated between the social democratic PNP and the conservative JLP. The PNP's Michael Manley was prime minister from 1972 to 1980. JLP leader Edward Seaga held the post from 1980 until the 1989 elections won by the PNP.

After returning to office Manley continued the market reform program begun by the JLP. But falling income, high inflation and unemployment caused the PNP's approval rating in opinion polls to drop to 25 percent by the time of Manley's resignation for health reasons in March 1992. Polls showed that among PNP followers the leading candidate to succeed Manley was Portia Simpson, the labor minister and an outspoken populist. But the internal election was limited to 3,200 party delegates, who by a 3-1 ratio chose lawyer P. J. Patterson, a former deputy prime minister and party moderate.

Patterson maintained the economic restructuring program and by late 1992 there were signs of recovery. He also succeeded in mending the rifts within the PNP. When the PNP jumped ahead of the JLP in the polls Patterson called for early elections. On 30 March 1993 the PNP won in a landslide, taking fifty-two parliamentary seats against eight for the JLP. The two parties differed little on economic policy, but the JLP was hurt by longstanding internal rifts. Race played a role as the fifty-seven-year-old Patterson, who is black, appealed to the black majority. Seaga is of Lebanese descent. Many Jamaicans also seemed to appreciate Patterson's low-key, technocratic style as a stabilizing influence on the nation's traditionally fractious political scene.

However, the vote was marred by thuggery on both sides in urban areas, police intimidation, large-scale confusion and scattered fraud at many voting places, and a voter turnout of 59 percent, the lowest since the pre-independence 1962 elections.

Seaga conceded the JLP would have lost had there been no irregularities. But with his leadership of the party in jeopardy, he seized on mounting popular disgust at the conduct of the election and announced the JLP would partially boycott parliament until the government allowed an independent judicial inquiry into electoral malpractices and replaced the police commissioner. No inquiry took place, but the JLP ended its boycott in July after the government reorganized the police force and replaced the police commissioner.

Patterson, evidently concerned by increasing voter abstention and mounting popular disillusionment with politics, authorized a bipartisan commission to consider constitutional reforms. After months of island-wide public meetings, the commission bogged down in fall 1993 amid disputes over the nature of a proposed bill of rights. Nonetheless, it appeared that both the PNP and the JLP still agreed that changes in the political system were needed.

Political Rights and Civil Liberties: Citizens are able to change their government democratically. However, as noted above, the March 1993 elections were marked by significant irregularities. After the vote, the government initiated electoral reforms that included a revamped electoral commission with greater independence and administrative authority. The reform process meant the postponement of local elections until 1994.

Constitutional guarantees regarding the right to free expression, freedom of religion and the right to organize political parties, civic organizations, and labor unions are generally respected. While the JLP and PNP dominate politics, there are a number of small parties ranging from radical left to radical right. Labor unions are politically influential and have the right to strike.

Violence during elections remains a staple of Jamaican politics. But codes of conduct endorsed by both major parties and supported by civic and religious groups have significantly reduced violence in the last two elections. More than 750 people died in election-related violence in 1980, thirteen in 1989, and fourteen in 1993.

Criminal violence and human rights violations by the police are of far greater concern. Violence is now the major cause of death in Jamaica and the record number of killings in 1992, 629, was expected to be exceeded in 1993. Much of the violence is due to warfare between drug gangs known as posses. However, domestic violence, particularly against women, and common criminal activity are also factors. The government-supported Bureau of Women's Affairs estimates that only ten percent of abuse and rape cases are reported, primarily because of the indifferent attitude of law enforcement bodies.

The police, in turn, have been responsible for the deaths of over 2,000 people in the past eight years, as well numerous cases of physical abuse of detainees. The root of the problem has been the Suppression of Crime Act, first introduced in 1974, that gave police sweeping powers of search and arrest. The work of the Jamaica Council for Human Rights has led to successful prosecution in a number of cases, with victims receiving court-ordered, monetary reparations. But officers guilty of abuses usually go without punishment and many cases remained unresolved.

In 1993 the Patterson government responded to criticism of police abuses by decentralizing the command structure and appointing a commissioner from outside the force. The Crime Act was superseded by new rules limiting search-and-arrest powers and placing more emphasis on police-community relations.

To stem the crime wave the government took a series of controversial measures, including the restoration of capital punishment and the creation of a special anti-crime unit. By fall 1993, however, the unit had been accused of violent behavior, including at least two deaths, and political partiality.

The judicial system is headed by a Supreme Court and includes several magistrate's courts and a Court of Appeal, with final recourse to the Judicial Committee of the Privy Council in London. The system is slow and inefficient, particularly in addressing police abuses, and conditions are deplorable in prisons and police lock-ups. There is a mounting backlog of cases due to soaring crime, a shortage of court staff at all levels, and a lack of resources.

Newspapers are independent and free of government control. Journalists occasionally are the targets of intimidation during election campaigns and political gatherings. Broadcast media are largely public but open to pluralistic points of view. Public opinion polls play a key role in the political process and election campaigns feature televised debates on the state-owned television station.

Japan

Polity: Parliamentary democracy
Economy: Capitalist
Population: 124,366,000
PPP: $17,616
Life Expectancy: 78.6
Ethnic Groups: Japanese, Korean, and small immigrant groups
Ratings Change: *Japan's political rights rating changed from 1 to 2 because of a major official corruption scandal.

Political Rights: 2*
Civil Liberties: 2
Status: Free

Overview:

Japan's post-war political order underwent sweeping changes in July 1993 as voters ousted the Liberal Democratic Party (LDP) after thirty-eight years in power. However, by year's end a reform-oriented coalition headed by new Prime Minister Morihiro Hosokawa failed to win upper house approval of a reform package aimed at restructuring the electoral system and limiting corporate donations to politicians. The LDP had been battered by corruption scandals for five years and had reneged on promises to pass its own reform package.

Following its defeat in World War II, Japan adopted an American-drafted constitution in 1947 that invested legislative authority in the *Diet* (parliament), renounced war and ended the emperor's divine status. The U.S. took responsibility for Japan's security, allowing the country to rebuild its bombed-out cities and rejuvenate a war-ravaged economy. In October 1955, the two wings of the opposition Japan Socialist Party (JSP) merged, and in November the two main conservative parties merged to form the ruling LDP. This "1955 System" remained in place throughout the Cold War as the LDP guided Japan through a spectacular industrial expansion, and the left-wing JSP remained the leading opposition.

Beyond the LDP's basic tenets of stability, prosperity and staunch anti-communism, most policy decisions were left to the highly educated, powerful civil servants. Corporations seeking preferential treatment in landing contracts and other matters would funnel legal and illegal contributions to LDP MPs, who would then exert influence on the bureaucrats. These corporate links gave the LDP a huge advantage in campaign fundraising.

The LDP itself consisted of several factions, which were driven more by influence and patronage than ideology. The factions battled each other in races in the Diet's 120 constituencies, some of which have up to five seats. The presence of several LDP candidates competing against each other in the multiple-seat constituencies inevitably fostered corruption, as contests hinged on fundraising and patronage rather than policy differences.

Gradually, the LDP's continuous rule faced harsher scrutiny. Beginning with Prime Minister Kakuei Tanaka's resignation in 1974 on bribery charges, a series of major scandals rocked the government. In 1989 Prime Minister Noboru Takeshita and more than forty other politicians and businessmen resigned after admitting they had accepted cut-rate stock shares from the Recruit company. Takeshita's successor, Susuke Uno, resigned over a sex scandal after only fifty-three days in office.

Moreover, when the Cold War ended, voters no longer felt compelled to elect the LDP on national security grounds. Tired of the government's corruption, costly protectionism and favoritism towards its rural stronghold, many citizens favored a more open, competitive political system responsive to the needs of ordinary consumers rather than big business. In the July 1989 elections the LDP lost its majority in the upper House of Councilors for the first time, leaving it with only 109 of 252 seats. (Half of the upper house seats come up for election every three years.) LDP bosses named the obscure, "clean" Toshiki Kaifu as prime minister in August 1989, allowing the party to rebound in the February 1990 lower House of Representatives elections, taking 275 of the 512 seats. However, in October 1991 party leaders sacked Kaifu in favor of Kiichi Miyazawa after Kaifu had tried to eliminate the multiple-seat districts in favor of a proportional seat system, which would have likely given the opposition more seats.

In May 1992 former LDP MP Morohiro Hosokowa created the centrist Japan New Party (JNP) to press for political reform and greater decentralization of bureaucratic power. In June the Diet approved a controversial law allowing Japanese troops to serve with United Nations peacekeeping missions. The JSP claimed the bill violated Article Nine of the constitution, which renounces war and prohibits the country from maintaining offensive forces. At the July 1992 upper house elections the LDP gained an impressive sixty-nine seats, reflecting both support for the peacekeeping bill and the lack of a credible alternative to the ruling party. The JSP and the small Japan Communist Party both suffered a net loss in seats, winning only 22 and 6 respectively, but the JNP took an impressive four seats in its first outing.

The LDP's downfall accelerated on 27 August 1992 when MP Shin Kanemaru, who had used his influence as head of the LDP's powerful Takeshita faction to install the past four prime ministers, admitted he had received an illegal $4.6 million contribution from the Sagawa parcel delivery company in 1990. Prosecutors also revealed that in 1987, Kanemaru had used an organized crime syndicate to silence the sound trucks of a right-wing group protesting Nobura Takeshita's impending election as party president and prime minister.

Kanemaru brazenly refused to step down from parliament, and in September he arranged to mail prosecutors the maximum $1,700 fine under the Political Funds Control Law in exchange for not having to testify about his gangster links or about the Sagawa money. By 14 October public outrage forced him to quit politics. The ensuing power scramble led to a split in the LDP's largest faction in December, with Kanemaru-protege Ichiro Ozawa and Tsutomu Hata forming a breakaway "policy study group" within the party.

On 29 January 1993 Tokyo prosecutors announced they lacked evidence to charge Kanemaru and sixty other MPs with receiving illegal political donations. But on 6 March prosecutors arrested Kanemaru on unrelated charges of having evaded taxes on $17 million in political donations from construction companies. Three days later investigators found a staggering $50 million hoard of cash, gold and securities in his home. Reeling from these revelations, on 31 March the LDP approved a package of four reform bills to tighten campaign finance laws and replace the corruption-prone multiple-seat constituencies with a single-seat system. But a straight single-seat system would have given the LDP roughly 90 percent of the seats. Miyazawa had apparently hoped to trap the opposition into either accepting the changes or risk being branded as anti-reform.

With prospects high for an early election because of the reform stalemate, on 13 May the JSP moved to shed some of the left-wing policies that had alienated voters and kept it in the opposition for decades. A new platform renounced orthodox socialism, recognized South Korea over North Korea, and accepted that the country's Self Defense Forces do not violate the pacifist constitution.

Miyazawa had pledged to pass the reform package by the end of current Diet session on 20 June, but a serious split emerged in the LDP as Hata and other young, pro-reform members threatened to defect if the party's old guard did not broker a compromise with the opposition. Nevertheless, on 15 June LDP secretary general Seiroku Kajiyama, who led the anti-reform group, said the government would shelve the package altogether until after the 1995 upper house elections.

In a dramatic scene, on 18 June thirty-eight LDP MPs joined the opposition to pass a no-confidence motion 255-220, forcing Miyazawa to dissolve the government. With fresh elections now one month away, the LDP began to fracture. On 21 June ten LDP MPs headed by Masayoshi Takemura broke away to form the New Harbinger Party (NHP). The next day Hata led forty-four more in forming the Japan Renewal Party (JRP). A handful of others left as individuals, leaving the party with 228 seats.

At the 18 July elections, the LDP lost its lower house majority for the first time since the party's founding, taking a 223 seat plurality. Only 67.2 percent of the voters turned out, a postwar record low for a lower house election. The JSP's share plunged from 136 seats to 70, while the JNR took 55; Komeito, 51; JNP, 35; the Democratic Socialist Party, 15; the Japan Communist Party, 15; the NHP,13; the United Social Party, 4; with 30 seats going to minor parties or independents.

On 29 July the left-wing JSP and the six smaller conservative and centrist parties united in a 255-seat majority coalition, ending the LDP's desperate hopes of forming a minority government. On 6 August the coalition elected fifty-five-year-old JNP leader Hosokawa as prime minister, breaking the LDP's streak of naming nineteen consecutive premiers and throwing the party into the opposition for the first time ever.

On 18 September Hosokawa opened an extraordinary ninety-day Diet session and vowed to pass a reform package by the end of the year or call fresh elections. A potential obstacle emerged on 28 October when LDP-defector Ozawa, reputedly the top strategist in the coalition, admitted he had received a $46,000 cash contribution from the Kajima construction corporation in late 1992, well above the $14,000 limit for individual gifts. In a blatant attempt to delay the reforms and force elections, on 9 November the LDP suggested the Diet hold a full debate on the construction industry's illicit political ties, which had already led to the arrest of Kanemaru, four provincial politicians and some twenty construction executives.

Hosokawa instead won approval for the reform measures from a parliamentary committee on 16 November, and two days later the entire lower house passed the sweeping package by a comfortable 270-226 margin, helped by thirteen LDP MPs who crossed the floor. However, the LDP and the JSP, both fearing a loss of seats under the new system, continued to block the package's passage in the upper house. In December, Hosphawa won an extension of the extraordinary session until 29 January 1994. The government also agreed to open the country to limited rice imports for the first time.

If the upper house approves the package at next election, due by 1995, 274 seats will be contested through proportional representation, and 226 seats will be directly elected in new single-seat constituencies redrawn to give proportionate power to urban areas. Voters will cast two ballots, one for a district representative and the other for a party. Corporate contributions to individual politicians will be banned and $290 million in public subsidies will be available for campaigns.

Abroad, on 4 August the outgoing LDP government admitted the Imperial Army had forced hundreds of thousands of Asian women to work as "comfort women" for its soldiers from 1932-1945. Two weeks later new prime minister Hosokawa shattered a precedent by terming World War II a "war of aggression" and offering apologies to the victims.

In other prominent issues, on 9 June Crown Prince Naruhito married Masako Owada, a commoner who had been a promising diplomat in the Foreign Ministry. In mid-July, some 200 residents in northern Japan were reported dead or missing after the country's strongest earthquake in three decades spawned deadly tidal waves.

Political Rights and Civil Liberties: Japanese citizens can change their government democratically. A continuing human rights concern involves the 680,000 Korean permanent residents, many of whom trace their ancestry in Japan for two or three generations. Koreans frequently face discrimination in housing, education and employment opportunities, are not automatically Japanese citizens at birth, and must submit to an official background check and adopt Japanese names to become naturalized. The government only recently ended a requirement that Koreans be fingerprinted, although they and other foreign permanant residents still must carry alien registration cards at all times. Both the *Burakumin*, who are descendants of fuedal-era outcasts, and the Ainu minority, descendents of the original inhabitants of Japan, face similiar discrimination and social ostracization.

Police occasionally physically abuse suspects to extract confessions, and detention and jail conditions are generally relatively harsh. A suspect can be held for up to seventy-two hours without access to counsel; a judge can extend this period for up to twenty-five days. Suspects are occasionally rearrested and held for additional twenty-five-day periods while police conduct investigations. Detainees lack the right to legal representation while being interrogated.

Freedoms of expression, assembly and association are guaranteed and respected by the government in practice. Of concern, however, are the exclusive press clubs that have access to top politicians and major ministries. In return for receiving this preferential treatment, journalists often practice self-censorship on sensitive stories. Many smaller papers are denied membership in the clubs. In June a committee of top editors recommended that foreign organizations be permitted to join the clubs, but they still must negotiate with each club directly. In July, for example, the press club of the Tokyo Stock Exchange admitted Reuters but denied membership to Bloomberg News. Another sensitive issue arrose in October when the *Sankei Shimbun* newspaper reported that Asahi National Broadcasting Company managing director Sadayoshi Tsubaki had instructed his staff to slant coverage against the LDP prior to the 18 July election. On 25 October Tsubaki told parliament that no actual order had been given, but some journalists said that by formally questioning a journalist, the Diet had set a dangerous precedent.

Since 1965 the Education Ministry has censored passages in historian Saburu Ienaga's textbook that describe Japan's aggression in the 1930s and 1940s. On 16 March the Supreme Court ruled the Ministry has the right to screen textbooks on "reasonable grounds," but in October the Tokyo High Court ruled that the Ministry had overstepped its authority on three of the eight passages it deleted in his latest version, and awarded Ienaga partial compensation.

There is complete freedom of religion; Buddhism and Shintoism have the most adherents. Workers, with the exception of police and firefighters, are free to join unions of their choice, and strikes are legal.

Jordan

Polity: Monarchy and elected parliament
Economy: Capitalist
Population: 3,400,000
PPP: $2,345
Life Expectancy: 66.9
Ethnic Groups: Palestinian and Bedouin Arabs, small minorities of Circassians, Armenians, and Kurds

Political Rights: 4*
Civil Liberties: 4*
Status: Partly Free

Ratings Change: *Jordan's political rights rating changed from 3 to 4 and its civil liberties rating from 3 to 4 as a result of modifications in methodology. See "Survey Methodology," page 671.

Overview:

Jordan held its first multiparty elections in thirty-seven years in November 1993, continuing a cautious liberalization process initiated by King Hussein in 1989. Pro-government, unaffiliated conservatives won the majority of the seats, easing pre-election fears that left-wing Palestinians and Muslim fundamentalist groups would dominate the balloting and threaten the survival of the last Hashemite kingdom.

The British installed the Hashemite monarchy in 1921, and granted Jordan full independence in 1946. King Hussein came to the throne in 1952, and formally assumed constitutional powers in May 1953. The 1952 constitution grants executive power to the King, who appoints the prime minister and Council of Ministers. The King convenes, adjourns and dissolves a bicameral National Assembly, currently consisting of a forty-member Senate appointed by the King, and a directly elected eighty-member House of Representatives. In practice, the King makes policy decisions, while the prime minister and Council of Ministers run day-to-day affairs. Multiparty elections were held in 1956, but the King banned political parties a year later following a coup attempt by leftist pan-Arab parties, one of many coup and assassination attempts Hussein has weathered, and cancelled elections beginning in the early 1970s during a period of Palestinian unrest.

In April 1989 rioting erupted in Karak and other southern cities over price increases under an IMF-mandated austerity program. The King responded by lifting restrictions on freedom of expression and ending a ban on party activity. Nevertheless, Hussein prohibited candidates from holding party affiliations in the first elections in twenty-two years in November 1989, but allowed the moderate fundamentalist Muslim Brotherhood to compete under its status as a charitable organization. The Brotherhood took 22 seats, while other fundamentalists took 10; tribal and clan groups, 17; pan-Arab leftists, 11; with 20 others appointed by the King to minority groups. In 1992 the government legalized the formation and licensing of political parties for elections scheduled for 1993.

The country's tentative democratization process has been complicated by a complex regional demographic and political situation. Palestinian refugees flooded the Kingdom following wars with Israel in 1948 and 1967. In the latter conflict, Jordan lost the West Bank of the Jordan River, which it had seized in 1948 after the British Mandate in Palestine ended. Currently "East Bank" Jordanians—those of non-Palestinian descent, including the Hashemites—are a minority and dominate the army and civil service, while Palestinians flourish in business and commerce. After losing the West Bank, Jordan had assumed that any potential Palestinian entity ultimately formed there would be part of a Jordanian-dominated confederation. This view held even after the country relinquished its claim to the West Bank in 1988.

The sudden peace agreement announced by Israel and the Palestinian Liberation Organization (PLO) in late August 1993 shattered this conventional wisdom. The accord provides for several years of interim Palestinian autonomy in the West Bank, including local council elections by July 1994. Jordanian officials now fear that factional Palestinian violence from the West Bank during the interim rule could spill into the Kingdom. More ominously, with the Palestinians' newfound negotiating clout and potentially expanding economic influence, many Hashemites feel the very existence of their monarchy is threatened.

In late September the King hinted to foreign journalists that he might postpone the November election until Israeli and PLO negotiators determined how many of the Palestinians in his country would be also be eligible to vote in the West Bank election. The King opposed allowing Palestinians to vote in both the Jordanian and West Bank elections and feared having the Jordanian election become a referendum on the Israel-PLO accord. Many feared strong gains by the Brotherhood's Islamic Action Front (IAF) political party, which opposed the accord. Privately, many East Bankers simply favored postponing the vote in hopes that many of the Palestinians would leave the country for the West Bank and Gaza Strip.

Despite these reservations, in early October the palace announced the election would be held as scheduled, in part out of confidence that new electoral rules announced by the King in August would give a majority of the seats to conservative independents. Previously, voters had cast more than one ballot depending on the number of seats in the constituency—up to eight in some constituencies. In 1989 this had allowed voters to cast ballots for independent candidates according to tribal and family loyalties, and still support the IAF with their remaining ballots. By contesting the upcoming election on a one-man, one-vote basis, the King eliminated the IAF's chance of gaining support from voters with clear tribal or family allegiances.

At the 8 November election 534 candidates competed for the eighty seats, attracting a 68 percent turnout. The IAF took only sixteen seats, and none of the other nineteen parties had much impact. As expected, pro-government conservative independents and Bedouin leaders fared well, taking fifty-four seats.

These independents are expected to back the Jordanian-Israeli peace process. On 15 September, two days after the Israel-PLO accord was signed, the two countries agreed to a "negotiating agenda" outlining talks on water rights, border disputes and security and refugee issues. However, Jordanian officials insist they will sign a peace treaty with Israel only as part of a comprehensive Middle East peace settlement.

In other issues, in May King Hussein openly opposed Saddam Hussein's continued leadership in Iraq for the first time. The King's refusal to support the coalition that forced Iraq out of Kuwait in 1991 has cost the country $500 million in annual aid from the Gulf states. In April, security forces exposed a plot by Muslim fundamentalists at the Muta University military academy to kill the King during the June graduation ceremony.

Political Rights and Civil Liberties:

Although the country held multiparty elections in November 1993, Jordanians still have only limited means to change their government democratically. The King holds broad executive powers and must approve all laws. Any change to the constitution without the King's approval is highly unlikely, since the King appoints the entire 40-member Senate, and two-thirds of the 120-member National Assembly must approve amendments. Observers rated the elections generally free, although bribery was reported in several districts. In the 1989 elections voters who had been bribed feigned illiteracy and called out their choice, allowing party monitors to check to see if they voted as they had been paid. In 1993 voters claiming illiteracy were interrogated, and party and candidate representatives were denied access to polling stations.

Police frequently abuse prisoners in detention and during interrogation, and often hold prisoners without charge for lengthy periods of time. The judiciary is generally independent of the government, as evidenced by an October High Court ruling overturning the Interior Ministry's ban on large public rallies during the election campaign. Defendents in civil court trials generally receive adequate safeguards, although bribery of judges is relatively common. Defendents in State Security Courts (SSC) are denied access to lawyers during pre-trial periods and lack an adequate avenue of appeal. The high Court of Cassation automatically reviews SSC decisions involving a death sentence or imprisonment of more than ten years, but does not examine the facts or the decision, only whether the court properly applied the law. Separate Islamic Shari'a and Christian courts handle family and religious matters.

Jordanians freely criticize the government's policies and express diverse political viewpoints although, largely out of respect, direct criticism of the monarchy is rare. In April 1993 King Hussein approved a relatively restrictive press law permitting only official news dispatches to be published on matters regarding the King, the Royal Family, and the armed forces, as well as religious and national security issues, and banning "defamation" of the diplomatic corps and heads of state of friendly foreign countries. Foreign news organizations must have a Jordanian national as editor. These broad restrictions are expected to lead to some self-censorship. The new law does repeal the government's right to penalize journalists and revoke newspapers' publishing licenses without due process rights.

Since 1989 the government has freely granted permits for peaceful public demonstrations. Islam is the state religion and most other groups are allowed to worship freely. The exception are the Baha'i, whose faith the government does not recognize. As such, they are not permitted to run schools, must register property as individuals, and their family legal matters are handled in the Islamic Shari'a courts. Citizens can travel freely within the country, although women must receive permission from their husbands to travel abroad. Women also are legally discriminated against in inheritance and divorce matters; for example, a female heir receives half the inheritance a male heir does. All non-governmental workers are free to unionize. The government can legally prohibit private sector strikes by referring a dispute to an arbitration committee. Some government employees can form unions, such as in the state-owned airline, but none is allowed to strike.

Kazakhstan

Polity: Dominant party
Economy: Statist transitional
Population: 16,947,000
PPP: $4,716
Life Expectancy: 70.0
Ethnic Groups: Kazakhs (43 percent), Russians (35 percent), Ukrainians (6 percent), others (16 percent)
Ratings Change: *Kazakhstan's political rights rating changed from 5 to 6 and its civil liberties rating from 5 to 4 as a result of modifications in methodology. See "Survey Methodology," page 671.

Political Rights: 6*
Civil Liberties: 4*
Status: Partly Free

Overview: Adoption of a new constitution, economic reforms that included leaving the so-called ruble zone, and the status of the country's nuclear missiles were among the major issues for President Nursultan Nazarbaev in 1993.

This sparsely populated land the size of India stretching from the Caspian Sea east to the Chinese border was conquered by Russia in 1730-1840. After a brief period of independence in 1917, it became an autonomous Russian republic in 1920 and a union republic in 1936. Kazakhstan formally declared independence from a crumbling Soviet Union in December 1991.

In early 1993, President Nazarbaev, the former first secretary of the Kazakhstan Communist Party who was directly elected in 1991, sought ways to maintain political and ethnic stability and to exploit the country's tremendous mineral wealth, including large deposits of oil, natural gas, gold, uranium and other metals. On 28 January, the

358-member Supreme *Kenges* (parliament) elected in 1990 adopted a new constitution, despite controversy over articles concerning the state language. Russian legislators expressed misgivings over the decision to make Kazakh the state language in a country where 35 percent of the population was ethnically Russian. The document also specified that the president had to be a Kazakh speaker. Russian was given a special status as "the social language between peoples."

The new constitution also defined the authority of the president, who would have the power to appoint the prime minister and deputy prime minister, the foreign, defense, and interior ministers, the chairman of the National Security Council and all the country's ambassadors. There were no provisions for impeachment of the president, and the president had no authority to disband parliament.

In February, delegates to the founding conference of the pro-government People's Unity Union assembled in the capital, Almaty (formerly Alma Ata), adopted a program backing radical economic reform and political pluralism. President Nazarbaev was elected party leader and Serik Abdrakhmanov was chosen chairman of the political council. The president told delegates that the union "must serve as a weighty counter-balance to [those]...who seek to solve the problems of their ethnic community at the expense of others," and must act to create a "broad layer" of property owners. However, Abdrakhmanov warned that privatization "Kazakhstan-style" had so far led to the formation of a "financial oligarchy drawn from the ranks of permanent civil servants."

The economy remained among the poorest in the former Soviet Union despite the country's natural resources, as the president tried to juggle the demands of market reforms with social costs. In January, he bluntly told parliament of the mistakes of free-market reform in Russia and Kazakhstan and said it was vital to restore a significant degree of state control and regulation.

Although numerous multinational corporations expressed interest in developing the country's wealth, the economy remained weak. In 1992, the economy shrank 14 percent after a 10 percent fall in 1991. Inflation was 2,500 percent in 1992 and real wages fell 20-30 percent. The 1993 budget was 8 percent of gross domestic product. In early 1993, inflation, although reduced, still raged at 25-35 percent a month. Privatization of large state enterprises and the closing of unprofitable firms were delayed. In March, the government published its privatization program for 1993-95, which envisaged the sale of most state-owned enterprises through a combination of voucher and money transac-tions. Foreigners would be allowed to buy Kazakh assets after obtaining a license from the state. In April, the U.S.-based Chevron Oil Company signed a complex contract to develop the Caspian basin Tengiz fields, estimated to contain the fifth largest oil deposits in the world. Under the agreement, Kazakhstan would get 80 percent of profits.

A key problem was rooted in the country's ties to the Russian ruble. In June, the government reported that trade relations with Russia "had sharply deteriorated," while Russia insisted that Kazakhstan's trade deficit with Russia be transformed into a sovereign debt with conditions analogous to standard Western loans. In November, after the Russians placed stiff conditions for getting new 1993 rubles, Kazakhstan and Uzbekistan decided to replace the ruble with their own currencies. President Nazarbaev issued a decree freezing most bank accounts in the republic in hopes of keeping rivers of rubles from swamping the country. Rubles were exchanged for the new currency, the tenge, at a rate of 500 to 1.

Another key issue was nuclear weapons. Kazakhstan, along with Russia, Ukraine and Belarus, was a Soviet nuclear missile site. On 13 December, the Supreme *Kenges* endorsed the Nuclear Non-Proliferation Treaty and the United States quickly pledged more than $84 million to help the country dismantle its nuclear arsenal. At a ceremony in Almaty, Vice President Al Gore and Prime Minister Sergei Tereshchenko signed agreements making Kazakhstan eligible for technical and financial assistance in dismantling its 1,400 warheads.

Political Rights and Civil Liberties: Citizens of Kazakhstan have the power to change their government democratically under a new constitution that enshrines a multiparty, presidential system. Nevertheless, de facto power has been centered in the hands of President Nazarbaev, whose government continued to crack down on dissent, control the press and monitor the opposition.

Parliament, elected in 1990, remains dominated by former Communists. The Azat (Freedom) Party is the largest non-Communist party. The nationalist Republican Party has called for the "complete decolonization of the republic." In June, the head of the U.S. Agency for International Development (USAID) expressed concern that the government was interfering with opposition groups that had received American help.

The president and parliament took steps to dampen the power of an independent-minded, activist Constitutional Court. In February, the Court asked President Nazarbaev to initiate legislation on a new criminal code, noting that the country needed it to bring the laws into accord with the country's new constitution. The Court had earlier declared a Nazarbaev decree unconstitutional and rejected the government's efforts to influence it. On 7 March, the *Kenges* prepared changes to deprive the Court of the right to decide the constitutionality of legal acts adopted prior to the election of the Court or to pass judgment on whether high-ranking officials have observed the constitution if the issue of their removal from office has been raised. In July, parliament deprived the Court of the right to institute legal proceedings on its own initiative and also to question decrees by the president, the Supreme Soviet Presidium, and the Supreme Soviet committees and commissions.

Obstacles to press freedom include economic factors as well as government interference. In February, employees of the Karaganda Radio Broadcasting Company refused to go on the air to protest the ouster of their chief. The oblast administration and Kazakhstan's quasi-governmental Radio and TV company fired Bakhydzhan Mukushev, ostensibly for defying the new head of the oblast administration. Employees said that the removal was political. Although over 800 media outlets (475 daily papers) are registered and operational, many are beset by the common problem of lack of paper, equipment and qualified staff. Alpha TV, the first independent South Kazakhstan television station, began transmitting in July; two private stations exist in the capital. With most newspapers dependent on some government subsidies, self-censorship is a problem. There are Russian-language, German and Korean papers.

There are no significant restrictions on freedom of religion, and domestic and international travel is generally unencumbered. But government control of most housing and requirements for residence permits are obstacles to freedom of movement. Several independent women's groups exist to address such issues as discrimination in hiring and education.

There are several trade unions, including the Independent Trade Union Center (ITUC) with twelve member unions, one of which is the important coal miners' union of Karaganda.

Kenya

Polity: Dominant-party **Political Rights:** 5*
Economy: Capitalist **Civil Liberties:** 6*
Population: 26,164,000 **Status:** Not Free
PPP: $1,058
Life Expectancy: 59.7
Ethnic Groups: Kikuyu (21 percent), Luhya (14 percent),
Luo (13 percent), Kalenjin (11 percent), Somali (2 percent), other
Ratings Change: *Kenya's political rights rating changed from 4 to 5
and its civil liberties rating from 5 to 6 because of rising violence and the
government's disregard for the legitimacy of opposition parties and
parliamentary power.

Overview: Kenyan President Daniel arap Moi began his fourth term on 4
January 1993, six days after the country held its first
multiparty presidential and legislative elections since 1966.
Moi's Kenya African National Union (KANU) took a majority of the National
Assembly seats in voting that reflected tribal loyalties. Outside observers noted
numerous irregularities and refused to certify the electoral process as free and fair.

Kenya came under British influence in the late 1800s, and became a colony in
1920. The fertile Rift Valley, comprising 40 percent of the country's territory, increasingly attracted British settlers. Although the area had traditionally been home to the
Kalenjin, Masai and other minority tribes, the settlers frequently brought in members of
the country's largest ethnic group, the Kikuyu, to work their plantations. The Kikuyu
led the Mau Mau rebellion between 1952-56 to protest British rule. In elections in May
1963 KANU won a majority of seats. The country gained independence under Jomo
Kenyatta, a Kikuyu, in December 1963.

In subsequent years President Kenyatta's rule became increasingly authoritarian. In
1969 he banned the primary opposition group, the Kenya People's Union. Kenyatta also
allowed Kikuyu farmers from the Rift Valley and the Central Highlands to buy land in
the Rift Valley. This increased tensions between the Kikuyus and the Kalenjin, who
saw themselves being marginalized in their traditional lands.

Kenyatta died in August 1978 and was succeeded on an interim basis by Vice
President Daniel arap Moi, a Kalenjin. In November 1979 Moi was elected to a full
term, and like Kenyatta ruled in an authoritarian manner. In June 1982 Moi formally
banned all opposition parties. Police forcibly put down pro-democracy protests in
several cities in July 1990, killing up to 200 people.

In October 1991 tribal clashes broke out in the Rift Valley, pitting Kalenjin against
Kikuyus, Luos and Luyhas. Credible accounts accused the government of fomenting
the unrest by urging Kalenjin to claim land that had been settled by Kikuyus under
Kenyatta's administration. In November Western governments and lending institutions
froze economic aid to force Moi into introducing political and economic liberalizations.
Under pressure, Moi legalized opposition parties on 2 December, and a multiparty
constitution took effect on 20 December.

In October 1992 the largest opposition group, the Forum for the Restoration of

Democracy (FORD) split into two parties: Ford Kenya under Oginga Odinga, an ethnic Luo, and FORD-Asili headed by Kenneth Matiba, a Kikuyu. The country held presidential and legislative elections on 29 December 1992. In the presidential race Moi took 36.35 percent of the vote, Matiba, 26.00 percent, Mwai Kibaki, 19.46 percent, Odinga, 17.48 percent; four other candidates polled less than 1 percent combined. Legislative results gave KANU 100 seats; FORD-Asili, 31; FORD-Kenya, 31; Democratic Party, 23; three tiny parties took one seat apiece. The voting in both elections largely followed tribal lines. Moi used his constitutional powers to appoint twelve additional MPs, all from KANU.

Immediately following the vote, opposition groups claimed fraud and called for fresh elections. On 13 January 1993 Moi announced a cabinet dominated by Kalenjin, Masai and other small tribes, and including only one Kikuyu and one Luo minister. The first multiparty National Assembly since 1969 convened on 26 January. The following day riot police forcibly dispersed anti-government protestors in front of the parliament building, and Moi used his constitutional powers to suspend the Assembly.

In mid-February, on the eve of a three week visit by an IMF team, the government partially liberalized the exchange rate and lifted some commodity price controls. However the IMF team noted that the government had increased the money supply by a staggering 60 percent in the last quarter of 1992 and by 35 percent overall for the year, allegedly for use in its election campaign. The Central Bank had also allowed several politically connected banks to illegally run up huge overdrafts and funnel the money to KANU politicians. The team left without agreeing to resume aid, and in a subsequent meeting in London told the government it needed to limit the money supply, crack down on official corruption, reduce the bureaucracy and speed up the country's privatization program.

On 24 March parliament reconvened and began debating the economic reforms. The next day Moi abruptly suspended the liberalizations. In part, the move reflected the hardships the reforms had caused for average citizens, and fears that this would benefit the opposition. But the government also knew the changes would reduce its control over patronage and its ability to illegally disburse money to politicians.

On 22 April the World Bank agreed to resume limited aid after the government, desperate for aid to boost the economy, again reversed itself and devalued the currency, raised interest rates, and promised further reforms. In late August fresh fighting broke out in the Rift Valley. Church officials and human rights groups again accused the government of promoting the violence, and of failing to provide protection for Kikuyus.

On 23 November the World Bank and other donors agreed to increase the aid disbursements, but made payouts in the coming year contingent on a continuation of the economic reforms and an end to the violence in the Rift Valley, which the human rights group Africa Watch reports has led to 1,500 deaths and displaced 250,000 others over two years.

Political Rights and Civil Liberties: Although Kenya held multiparty elections in December 1992, in practice the right of citizens to change their government is severely restricted.

In January 1993 a thirty-eight member Commonwealth observer team concluded that the election "cannot be given an unqualified rating of free and fair." The team's report noted irregularities in the voter registration process; problems with the nomination process that prevented several candidates from registering; threats and harassment against opposition party supporters; bans on opposition speakers in certain areas; partisan coverage by the state-run media; and a "failure to de-link the ruling party from the government," allowing public funds to be used for political purposes. The International Republican Institute also noted that many ballot boxes were brought to counting halls with broken seals, observers were thrown out of some counting halls, and in some districts vote totals exceeded the number of registered voters.

Although in January 1993 the government released its last four political prisoners, in November the government rearrested the country's most prominent dissident, Koiga wa Wamwere, and several others. The judiciary is not independent of the government. The president appoints the attorney general and top judges, and can remove the attorney general and all judges upon the recommendation of a presidentially appointed tribunal. Under a 1989 High Court ruling, the courts lack the power to enforce the country's Bill of Rights. There are no jury trials, and defendants do not have the right to free legal representation.

Police often violate constitutional provisions by holding criminal suspects inncommunicado for two or more weeks before bringing charges. Suspects can also be detained indefinitely without charge for security reasons under the Preservation of Public Security Act, although this is rarely used. Police frequently abuse or torture suspects to extract confessions, and often use unwarranted force in dealing with civil disturbances as well as peaceful demonstrations. In recent years civilians have increasingly resorted to violence, including extrajudicial executions, to punish common criminals.

Freedoms of speech and press are restricted in practice. In recent years police have arrested numerous journalists, publishers and dissidents on charges of "rumormongering" or sedition, although such cases rarely go to trial. In 1992 the government introduced a libel law imposing penalties of up to $30,000. In April, police seized 30,000 copies of the bi-weekly magazine, *Finance*. In May, police closed Fotoform, a company that prints three independent newspapers, and seized some of its machinery, and in August police raided another printing company, Colourprint. News coverage on the state-run radio network and on the Kenya Broadcasting Corporation television service is slanted towards the government. The government also exerts informal influence over the privately held Kenya Television Network.

The Public Order and Police Act restricts peaceful assembly by requiring permission to hold public meetings of three or more persons. Freedom of religion is generally respected. Citizens can generally travel freely internally and abroad. Some 500,000 refugees from Somalia, Ethiopia and Sudan live in Kenyan border camps. By some estimates more than 2,000 Somali female refugees may have been raped by police and by Kenyan and Somali bandits. By tradition, women occupy subservient roles in society, business and government. Domestic violence is reportedly common, and although the government discourages female genital mutilation, it is practiced by some ethnic groups. The country's Swahili minority, Muslims of Arab-African descent who live mainly along the coast, claim discrimination in obtaining top civil service jobs and academic posts, and in gaining title deeds for land. Swahili Sheikh Kalid Salim Balala has been arrested several times for anti-government speeches and for calling for strikes in the coastal town of Mombasa, and his Islamic Party of Kenya has been denied registration.

Workers, except for central government civil servants, can join independent trade unions. Most unions are affiliated with the Central Organization of Trade Unions (COTU), which is considered pro-government. Workers must give the Minister of Labor a three-week notice before striking; during this time the minister can refer a dispute to mediation or arbitration, and if he does a strike is then illegal.

Kiribati

Polity: Parliamentary
democracy
Economy: Capitalist-
statist
Population: 75,000
PPP: na
Life Expectancy: 54.0

Political Rights: 1
Civil Liberties: 1*
Status: Free

Ethnic Groups: Kiribatian (Micronesian, 84 percent),
Polynesian (14 percent), other (2 percent)
Ratings Change: *Kiribati's civil liberties rating changed from 2 to 1 as a result
of modifications in methodology. See "Survey Methodology," page 671.

Overview: The Republic of Kirabati consists of thirty-three islands of the
Gilbert, Line and Phoenix groups, with a total land area
smaller than New York City, scattered over two-million
square miles of the Pacific Ocean. It became an independent member of the British
Commonwealth on 12 July 1979.

The unicameral *Maneaba ni Maungatabu* (Assembly) has thirty-nine members
directly elected every four years from twenty-three constituencies, most recently in May
1991, along with one representative from Banaba Island elected by the Banaban Rabi
Council of Leaders. The president is directly elected from a list of three to four candidates
nominated by the Maneaba from among its members, and is limited to three four-year
terms. Founding President Ieremia Tabai served three terms and threw his support in the
July 1991 election behind Teato Teannaki, who narrowly beat his main competitor, Roniti
Teiwaki. Local Island Councils are established on all inhabited islands. Politics are generally conducted on a personal rather than a partisan level. The three parties that exist—
the National Progressive Party, the Christian Democratic Party and the United Kirabati
Party—lack platforms and offices and are essentially interest groups on specific issues.

Most citizens are engaged in subsistence agriculture and small-scale coastal fishing.
The U.K., Japan and other countries are attempting to develop a commercial fishing industry for the country. License fees from countries that fish in its waters, among the richest
in the world, also provide a major source of revenue. The government has pledged to help
the 400 residents of Banaba Island modernize their agricultural and fishing methods.

Political Rights   The citizens of Kirabati can change their government
and Civil Liberties: democratically. The country is respectful of human rights, and
fundamental freedoms of press, speech, assembly, religion and
association are respected in theory and practice. The independent judiciary is modeled
on English common law, and provides adequate due process rights. In July 1993 the
parliament voted unanimously to amend the Broadcasting Act to end the government's
monopoly on radio and television (although no government television station currently
exists). The sole radio station and two government-run newspapers offer pluralistic
viewpoints, and churches publish newsletters. Women are entering the workforce in
increasing numbers in this traditionally male-dominated society. Citizens are free to

travel internally and abroad. Workers are free to organize into unions and strike. The Kirabati Trade Union Congress includes seven trade unions with approximately 2,500 members.

Korea, North

Polity: Communist one-party
Economy: Statist
Population: 22,227,000
PPP: $2,000
Life Expectancy: 70.4
Ethnic Groups: Ethnically homogeneous—Korean

Political Rights: 7
Civil Liberties: 7
Status: Not Free

Overview: North Korea's unprecedented withdrawal from the Nuclear Non-Proliferation Treaty (NPT) in March 1993 and its refusal to allow full inspections of its nuclear facilities have underscored fears that it may be close to producing an atomic weapon.

The Democratic People's Republic of Korea was formally established in September 1948, three years after the partition of the Korean Peninsula. The country's sole ruler since partition, eighty-one-year-old Stalinist leader Marshall Kim Il Sung, serves as both president of the country and secretary general of the ruling Worker's (Communist) Party. Several token minor parties exist but are completely subservient to the government.

Kim has created a personality cult based largely on his alleged leading role in fighting the Japanese in the 1930s. His all-encompassing "ideology," *Juche* (I Myself), stresses national self-reliance and independence, and is used to justify the country's virtual isolation from the rest of the world. The government nurtures a slavish devotion to the Kim family through the media, the workplace, the military, mass spectacles, cultural events and some 35,000 Kim statues and ubiquitous portraits. Juche calls for the "Great Leader" to be succeeded by his fifty-one-year-old son, "Dear Leader" Kim Jong Il. In December 1991, the younger Kim replaced his father as Supreme Commander of the 1.2 million man armed forces (the fourth largest in the world) apparently the first stage of the anticipated power transfer. Analysts believe Kim Jong Il is in fact running the country's day-to-day affairs, but that he is unpopular with the military and Kim Il Sung is reluctant to formally transfer power to him.

This oblique internal situation makes interpreting the country's foreign relations very difficult. Following the collapse of its patron, the Soviet Union, North Korea engaged in limited but encouraging contacts with the West. In December 1991 the two Koreas, which have never formally ended their 1950-53 war, agreed to a non-aggression pact, pledged to ban nuclear weapons from the peninsula and agreed to form a Joint Nuclear Control Commission to inspect potential atomic weapons facilities. In response, the United States and South Korea cancelled their annual Team Spirit military exercises in March. In April 1992 the country agreed to allow International Atomic Energy Agency (IAEA) inspectors access to its three declared nuclear facilities. This included a controversial complex of more than 100 buildings at Yongbyon, sixty miles northwest of the capital of Pyongyang, which the United States believes contains a reprocessing plant capable of producing weapons-grade plutonium. During the year the IAEA conducted six on-site inspections, which proved inconclusive, and installed monitoring cameras at several sites.

In January 1993, however, inspectors discovered that North Korea had produced more plutonium than the small amount it had previously declared. Analysts warned that the "missing" plutonium may be enough to make a nuclear weapon. Seeking to deter-mine precisely how much plutonium had been produced, the IAEA requested access to two suspected nuclear waste sites at Yongbyon. The government refused, claiming the two buildings were military facilities unrelated to its nuclear energy program.

On 25 February the IAEA issued its first-ever demand for a "special inspection," giving North Korea one month to allow access or face possible United Nations Security Council sanctions. On 12 March North Korea responded by becoming the first nation to pull out of the NPT, officially to protest the resumption in mid-March of the Team Spirit exercises, which it called "a nuclear war rehearsal."

Despite having no formal relations, on 19 March the U.S. and North Korea began a series of urgent negotiations on keeping the country in the NPT. On 11 June North Korea agreed to "suspend" its treaty withdrawal, but refused to allow access to the contested sites. On 15 October the U.S. State Department announced it was holding a series of informal talks with North Korean representatives at the United Nations. However, six days later the U.S. said no progress had been made, and ruled out North Korea's request for high-level negotiations and diplomatic recognition.

On 1 November IAEA director Hans Blix told the United Nations that North Korea continued to prevent inspectors from changing the batteries and film in monitoring cameras at the Yongbyon site, in addition to denying access to the two secret waste sites. He said that by allowing the cameras to lapse, the country had "damaged" the "continuity" of the monitoring, but cautiously stopped short of declaring that the continuity had been broken. Had he done so, the U.S. would likely have been com-pelled to ask the Security Council to impose sanctions or risk jeopardizing the integrity of the NPT. Japan and South Korea in particular have strongly urged the U.S. to delay sanctions for as long as possible, fearing North Korea could respond with terrorism or a desperation military attack on the South. On 25 December the *New York Times* reported that U.S. intelligence agencies estimate there is a better than 50-50 chance that North Korea has developed one or two nuclear bombs. On 30 December the North offered inspectors access to their seven declared sites, but continued to deny access to the two waste facilities.

Some experts feel North Korea is simply using the nuclear issue to extract eco-nomic concessions from the US, Japan and South Korea. In 1993 the economy contracted for the fifth straight year. The few available eyewitness accounts indicate much of the economy is at a standstill, with industries operating at 30-50 percent of capacity, few vehicles in operation due to fuel shortages, and frequent blackouts. Food shortages are reportedly widespread, and eggs and meat are no longer available. There are frequent rumors of food riots and of sabotage attacks on food facilities. In June the country tested its 600-mile range Rodong I missile, which it is reportedly offering to Iran in exchange for oil.

Political Rights and Civil Liberties: North Koreans live in the most tightly-controlled country in the world, and cannot change their government democratically. Full power is held by Marshall Kim Il Sung and his son, Marshall Kim Jong Il. The Supreme People's Assembly consists of state-approved candidates from the Korean Workers Party and has no independent power. Opposition parties are illegal, and owing to the regime's repressive policies, the country's isolation, and the effects of severe economic hardship, there appears to be little organized opposition of any sort. Citizens face a steady onslaught of state propaganda from radios and televisions pretuned to government stations.

The government denies citizens all fundamental freedoms and rights. Authorities conduct monthly checks of residences and electronic surveillance is common. Children are encouraged at school to report on their parents' activities, and all homes must have pictures of the two leaders. Permission to travel outside one's town is generally granted only for state business, weddings or funerals.

The slightest effrontery to the Kim family or any other act deemed threatening to the regime is considered a political offense, and can be punished by execution. For example, citizens have been punished simply for listening to the Voice of America or the BBC World Service. South Korean analysts estimate up to 150,000 or more political prisoners are held in camps. Defectors say some political prisoners are "re-educated" and released, while others languish in brutal conditions.

Religious practice is restricted to state-sponsored Buddhist and Christian services. Government escorts frequently take foreign visitors to observe these places of worship, indicating that they are sanctioned simply to burnish the regime's image. Unions are simply an additional means for the government to control citizens, and strikes do not occur.

Korea, South

Polity: Presidential-parliamentary democracy
Economy: Capitalist-statist
Population: 44,284,000
PPP: $6,733
Life Expectancy: 70.1
Ethnic Groups: Ethnically homogeneous—Korean

Political Rights: 2
Civil Liberties: 2*
Status: Free

Ratings Change: *South Korea's civil liberties rating changed from 3 to 2 because of a crackdown on corruption and measures to weaken the internal security units' powers.

Overview: Former dissident Kim Young Sam took office in February 1993 as South Korea's first civilian president in thirty-two years, declaring the country to be in crisis owing to widespread graft, mistrust of government, an economic slowdown and bitter regional animosities. Kim immediately began an anti-corruption crackdown that netted more than 3,000 bureaucrats, politicians and businessmen by the end of the year. The president also sacked a dozen right-wing generals and weakened the internal security agencies' surveillance powers.

The Republic of Korea was established in August 1948 in the U.S.-controlled southern Korean Peninsula, three years after the occupying Japanese were defeated in World War II. General Park Chung Hee took power in a 1961 military coup, and guided the country through a period of intense industrialization and uncorrupt authoritarian rule. Following Park's assassination in 1979, Chun Doo Hwan took power in another military coup. In June 1987, violent student-led protests rocked the country after Chun picked another army general, Roh Tae Woo, as his successor. On 29 June 1987, Roh announced sweeping reforms, including direct presidential elections and a restoration of civil liberties suspended under martial law.

The country's best-known dissidents, Kim Young Sam and Kim Dae Jung, both ran in the December 1987 presidential election, allowing Roh to win with just 35.9 percent of the vote. A revised constitution went into effect in February 1988, guaranteeing basic rights, limiting the president to a single five-year term and taking away his power to dissolve parliament. In January 1990, Kim Young Sam and another opposition leader, Kim Jong Pil, startled their supporters by merging their parties with the governing Democratic Justice Party. This renamed Democratic Liberal Party (DLP) now held 220 of the 299 Assembly seats. In 1991, Kim Dae Jung, now the country's leading opposition figure, merged his Party for Peace and Democracy with two minor opposition parties to form the center-left opposition Democratic Party.

In January 1992 Chung Ju Yung, the billionaire founder of Hyundai, formed the Unification National Party (UNP) to contest legislative and presidential elections slated for later in the year. Chung accused the government of economic mismanagement and widespread corruption. At the 24 March 1992 elections for the Assembly's 237 directly elected and 62 proportionately distributed seats, the DLP lost its majority, taking 149 seats. The Democratic Party won a strong 97 seats; the upstart UNP, 31; the tiny Party for New Political Reform, 1; along with 21 independents.

The 18 December presidential vote, the cleanest in the country's history, was the first in three decades in which none of the candidates had a military background. Kim Young Sam, running for the ruling DLP, was elected with 42 percent of the vote, followed by Kim Dae Jung, 34 percent; and Chung, 15 percent.

In January 1993 Kim Dae Jung quit politics, leaving the Democratic Party without a dynamic leader. In early February the seventy-seven-year-old Chung also left politics, three days after being indicted on charges of illegally diverting $81 million from Hyundai to his election campaign. By 20 February, defections had left the UNP with less than the twenty MPs required to be recognized as a parliamentary negotiating caucus, and gave the DLP a 170-seat majority.

The sixty-five-year-old Kim took office on 25 February 1993 as the first civilian president since 1961. Few were prepared for the speed and depth of his reforms. His new prime minister, Hwang In Sung, and five cabinet ministers came from the underdeveloped Cholla region in the southwest, an opposition stronghold. This broke the dominance of the so-called "TK Elite," a group of conservative military and political leaders hailing from the city of Taegu and the surrounding southeast Kyongsang province.

On 6 March Kim granted a sweeping amnesty to more than 2,100 prisoners, and restored full constitutional rights to some 34,000 dissidents who had lacked the right to vote and hold government jobs. As the president's anti-corruption campaign got underway, the close proximity of some its earliest victims underscored the extent of the problem. On 8 March Kim sacked three cabinet ministers and the appointed Mayor of Seoul after anonymous phone tips revealed unethical activities, including massive land speculation. On 30 March the ruling party said it would ask six of its MPs to resign after asset disclosures demanded by the president revealed they had "excessive" wealth. Five others received reprimands.

The new president also took on the powerful military and intelligence establishment. In separate purges in March, April and May, Kim sacked twelve top generals. Most were close to former president Chun Doo Hwan, and were members of the Hanahoe (One Mind) Society, a group of some 100 top active and retired generals favoring a strong military role in society. On 10 March the Agency for National Security Planning (NSP), which had often brutally suppressed dissidents during the military-backed regimes, announced it would end its widespread internal surveillance and concentrate on foreign threats. The government also announced heavy staff cutbacks at the NSP and the companion Defense Security Command. In addition, in April several officers were indicted in separate scandals, one involving payoffs in the 1991 selection of General Dynamics for a huge fighter plane contract, the other involving a military pay-for-promotion affair.

Riding a 70 percent approval rating, on 13 May Kim made an unprecedented appeal to the victims of the army's brutal May 1980 crackdown on pro-democracy protestors in the southern city of Kwangju. The president declared 18 May a public holiday and opened a new registration period to report those killed, wounded or missing. Meanwhile, the anti-graft campaign continued as parliament enacted the Public Officials Ethics Law in June, requiring the country's top 7,000 politicians and civil servants to reveal their wealth.

On 12 August Kim announced one of his most far-reaching reforms—the introduction of a real-name financial system, ending the practice of allowing individuals to maintain bank accounts under false names. The no-name system had originally been a means of encouraging private investment following the devastation of the 1950-53 Korean War. Besides introducing transparency in financial dealings, the government said the change would make it easier to track political bribes and kickbacks.

On 16 October Kim sacked Prime Minister Hwang, replacing him with Lee Hoi-chang, who had been a key figure in the anti-corruption campaign. The move came in response to public anger at Kim's decision a week earlier to lift a longstanding ban on rice imports.

Kim continues to face a substantial challenge in reviving the economy. The spectacular 9.7 percent average annual growth during the 1980s has slowed considerably, largely because wages rose 128 percent between 1987-92 and eroded the country's competitiveness. In March, Kim ordered a wage freeze for the civil service, and called for voluntary restraint in the private sector. In another major issue, tensions continued throughout the year as North Korea refused to resume talks on joint nuclear inspections, stalling on agreements signed in December 1991. The North's intransigence has fueled fears that the isolated country is hiding a clandestine atomic weapons program.

Political Rights
and Civil Liberties:
South Koreans can change their government democratically. The 1992 Assembly elections were marred by fraud charges, including claims that military officers rigged up to 560,000 absentee ballots. According to the U.S. State Department, these and other alleged irregularities did not appear to influence the outcome of the vote. Mayoral and gubernatorial elections are scheduled for June 1995; the incumbents in these positions are governmental appointees.

President Kim Young Sam, a former dissident, has taken numerous steps to limit the once-pervasive role of the state security apparatus, including removing the National Security Planning Agency's once-widespread internal surveillance powers. The government justifies the remaining harsh national security measures on the basis of the continued tension with North Korea. The National Security Law (NSL) broadly defines espionage to include cooperation, encouragement or praise of "antistate," (i.e. North Korea) organizations. Under the NSL, a judge can allow the authorities to detain individuals suspected of "serious" violations such as spying for an additional twenty days beyond the thirty day period allowed in non-NSL cases. Suspects are generally not allowed access to an attorney during interrogation or pre-trial detention for NSL cases, despite the constitutional right to one.

Detainees, especially in NSL cases, are frequently beaten and deprived of sleep to extract confessions. Conditions in prisons are generally harsh. The judiciary has become independent of the government in recent years, and due process rights are generally observed for trials.

The main limits on expression involve the NSL restrictions on promoting pro-Communist ideas or other views considered sympathetic to the North Korean regime. This frequently includes views that are clearly non-violent but still considered subversive, such as meeting with North Korean students. Similarly, the Law on Assembly and Demonstrations has been used to prohibit student rallies considered a threat to public order.

There is full religious freedom in South Korea. Korean tradition continues to give women a secondary social status. Citizens can move freely within the country but travel to North Korea is heavily restricted.

All trade unions must be affiliated with either the Federation of Korean Trade Unions or the independent Korean Federation of Clerical and Financial Workers. Strikes are not permitted in government agencies, state-run industries and defense industries. Although President Kim has pledged to end the violent confrontations between police and strikers that often occurred during the years of military-backed rule, in July he threatened to use riot police before 60,000 workers ended strikes at eight Hyundai subsidiaries.

Kuwait

Polity: Traditional monarchy and limited parliament
Economy: Mixed capitalist-statist
Population: 1,379,000
PPP: $15,178
Life Expectancy: 73.4

Political Rights: 5
Civil Liberties: 5
Status: Partly Free

Ethnic Groups: Kuwaitis and other Arabs, and various foreign workers

Overview: The Kuwaiti National Assembly's vigorous investigations in 1993 into the royal family's alleged mismanagement of the country's financial holdings were an important step in establishing the body's independence from the Emir. Although the Emir can still dissolve the Assembly at any time and has done so in the past, the recent international attention focused on the country since the 1991 Gulf War makes such a move less likely.

The al-Sabah family has ruled Kuwait since 1756. Britain handled the country's foreign affairs and defense from 1899 until 1961. The 1962 constitution vests executive power in an Emir from the al-Sabah family, who rules through an appointed prime minister and a Council of Ministers. The National Assembly, which can initiate and veto legislation, has been a forum for diverse viewpoints over the years. The previous Emir suspended the Assembly in 1976 after MPs criticized his selection of ministers. His successor, Sheik Jabir al-Ahmad al Sabah, reopened the Assembly in 1981 but suspended it again in 1986 over calls for a public inspection of the country's financial records. In June 1990 elections were held for fifty seats of a seventy-five-member interim National Council, which would serve until a new Assembly was elected in 1994.

The August 1990 Iraqi invasion ironically speeded up the democratization process. Many citizens quickly blamed the invasion in part on the government's failure to recognize the threat and prepare adequately. In October, while in exile in Saudi Arabia, the Emir agreed to hold elections in 1992. In June 1991, several months after a 32-member, United States-led coalition liberated the country, the Emir reconvened the National Council in advance of Assembly elections.

The government limited suffrage in the 5 October 1992 Assembly Elections to "first-class" males, who were over twenty-one and could prove that they or their ancestors had lived in Kuwait before 1920 and maintained a residence in the country until at least 1959. This left just 15 percent of the population eligible. Although a 1986 ban on political parties remained in effect, seven informal opposition groups emerged. Six of them favored continuing the emirate in some capacity, while calling for greater governmental accountability and popular participation. Only the radical Islamic Popular Grouping openly challenged the ruling family's constitutional status as a hereditary emirate.

On election day 278 candidates contested fifty seats in twenty-five districts.

Opposition candidates took a surprising thirty-one-seat majority, split between nineteen linked to Islamic groups and twelve others with generally left-wing views. However, the royal family named a new government that minimized the opposition's gains. The Emir reappointed Crown Prince Sheik Saad as prime minister. On 17 October Sheik Saad announced a new sixteen-member cabinet with six ministries going to elected opposition MPs, more than ever before, but the al-Sabah family held on to the key foreign affairs, defense, interior and information posts.

In January 1993 the parliament began investigations into huge losses in the country's once-solid financial holdings. The official Kuwait Investment Office's (KIO) Fund for Future Generations has plummeted from a pre-war $100 billion to $30 billion. Since 1986 the KIO's Spanish holding company, Grupo Torras, has lost $5 billion in questionable investments. Elsewhere, $100 million was embezzled at the government-owned Kuwait Oil Tankers Company, and the Kuwaiti French Bank in Paris has suffered huge losses.

The Assembly also criticized the now-defunct National Council's March 1992 decision that allowed the Central Bank to bail out six major banks holding $24 billion in defaulted loans. The Central Bank's public funds were used to cover the private debts of a few hundred wealthy citizens, including members of the royal family. On 16 January, the Assembly passed a law requiring any company that is at least 25 percent government-owned to report new investments to the Audit Bureau and parliament within ten days.

On 20 September the Al-Siyassah newspaper reported that Spanish financier Javier de la Rosa denied that he or any KIO executives had embezzled money from Grupo Torras. Nevertheless, parliament vowed to continue the investigations, confident that the increased international attention on Kuwait since the Iraqi invasion made it less likely the Emir would dissolve the body.

Political Rights and Civil Liberties:

Kuwaiti citizens cannot change their government democratically. The hereditary emirate holds executive powers, political parties are banned, and only about 15 percent of the population was eligible to vote in the October 1992 National Assembly elections. The constitution remains suspended, and the Emir can suspend the parliament at any time.

A key human rights concern is the condition of some 100,000 domestic servants, mostly from the Philippines, Sri Lanka and India. Working conditions for these foreigners are not regulated by the state. Many are frequently beaten, forced to work long hours, refused permission to leave the household and occasionally raped. Most employers retain the servants' passports to prevent them from leaving the country. On 10 March a twenty-three-year-old Filipina, Sonia Panama, died one month after being admitted to a hospital after being beaten by her employer. Hundreds of servants have sought refuge in their country's embassies.

Another concern is the status of the 100,000 *bidoon*, who are stateless residents of Bedouin origin. Many were born in Kuwait or have lived in the country for years, but cannot own houses, travel abroad or work for private companies. Before the war the government dropped the bidoons from the census roles and stripped them of their identification cards, which had allowed them access to social services. The government is also attempting to reduce the number of Iraqis and Palestinians in the country through deportations and tacit pressure on employers not to hire them.

The Kuwait Security Service frequently detains suspects without charge beyond the legal four-day period. There are reports of abuse at detention facilities, often against Iraqis, Jordanians, Sudanese and Palestinians residing in the country. These foreigners are also sometimes briefly kidnapped by unidentified Kuwaitis as a form of harassment, and are occasionally subjected to arbitrary arrest by the authorities. The judiciary is generally independent of the government and defendants generally receive fair public trials. According to the U.S. State Department, some 200 Palestinians, Iraqis and bidoon are held in long-term administrative detention, from which there is no right of judicial review.

Citizens freely criticize the government's policies, but are prohibited from criticizing the al-Sabah family or Islam. The press law prevents publication of articles criticizing the royal family, as well as articles that might "create hatred, or spread dissension among the people." This broad definition also leads to some self-censorship. On 30 January 1993 journalist Fouad al-Hacham received a three-month suspended prison sentence and a fine for a 1992 newspaper article criticising Islamic customs that force women to wear the veil. On 1 February the Attorney General banned publication without his permission of articles dealing with corruption at the London-based Kuwait Investment Office. Although no penalties were announced for violations, journalists said the ban could set a dangerous precedent and that it seemed intended to protect members of the royal family.

Freedom of assembly is restricted. In 1985 the government placed a moratorium on licensing new organizations, and since then has made exceptions only for groups with ties to the royal family. A 1988 amendment to the 1962 Law of Public Interest Associations gave the executive branch complete authority over the licensing of associations, a process not subject to judicial review. In August 1993 the government announced a decree shutting down all unlicensed organizations on the grounds that they were operating illegally. This mainly affected six human rights groups that have been denied permits since their formation in 1991. The groups, including the country's main human rights organization, the Kuwaiti Association to Defend War Victims, have been pressing the government for an accounting of Kuwaitis believed to be held by Iraq, as well as on rights issues within the country. The government said it will use force if necessary to enforce the decree, although so far it has not done so.

The government occasionally denies permits for politically oriented gatherings, although during the 1992 election campaign opposition groups were generally allowed to hold large public gatherings without interference. Islam is the state religion, and while Christians are allowed to worship freely, Hindus, Sikhs and Buddhists cannot build places of worship and must pray privately in their homes. Citizens can travel freely within the small country, but women must receive permission from husbands to travel abroad.

The government maintains significant financial control over unions through subsidies that in practice account for 90 percent of union budgets. Unions are legally barred from involvement in political issues, but this is generally not enforced. The labor law provides for compulsory arbitration in disputes if a settlement cannot be reached. On 16 August, the Union of Oil and Petrochemical Industry Workers accused the hundreds of manpower agencies that supply foreign workers to state-owned companies of providing workers with inadequate food and housing.

Kyrgyz Republic

Polity: Presidential-par-
liamentary (transitional)
Economy: Statist
(transitional)
Population: 4,506,000
PPP: $3,114
Life Expectancy: 68.0
Ethnic Groups: Kirgiz (52.3 percent), Russian (21.5 percent),
Uzbek (12.9 percent), Germans, others

Political Rights: 5*
Civil Liberties: 3*
Status: Partly Free

Ratings Change: *The Kyrgyz Republic's political rights rating changed
from 4 to 5 and its civil liberties rating from 2 to 3 as a result of
modifications in methodology. See "Survey Methodology," page 671.

Overview: Wrangling with parliament over a new constitution, introduction of a national currency, and regional tensions were among the key issues facing reformist President Askar Akaev in 1993, two years after this Central Asian republic bordering China and Uzbekistan became independent from the Soviet Union.

In 1991, President Akaev, a respected physicist, launched the so-called "silk revolution" that made Kyrgyzstan (the name Kyrgyz Republic was adopted in 1993) the closest to a Western-style democracy in the region. In the first half of 1992, he moved to restructure the government and introduced a draft constitution that called for the appointment of a prime minister by the president. In the latter half of the year, a "shock therapy" program, developed in conjunction with the International Monetary Fund (IMF), led to strict control of state finances, banking and manufacturing.

In early 1993, the president and parliament were at loggerheads over such constitutional issues as presidential powers and private property. On 15 April, Akaev argued that parliament should adopt the constitution or call for new elections. Parliament sought to change presidential rule to parliamentary rule. On 3 May, parliament ruled that Akaev would no longer act as head of government, and moved to vest the powers of head of government in Prime Minister Tursunbek Chyngyshev, who had been hand-picked by Akaev in 1992. After some debate, parliament voted not to change an article in the constitution that gave each Russian-speaking Kyrgyz citizen the legal guarantee of non-infringement of his rights due to the lack of knowledge of the Kyrgyz language. The decision came after an impassioned speech by President Akaev, in which he said "we must quit political intrigues and stop to take our people in with introducing in the constitution the notions of 'a language of inter-ethnic communication.'"

On 5 May, parliament formally adopted the new constitution, which enshrined the powers of the executive, legislature and judiciary. President Akaev remained head of state, but Prime Minister Chyngyshev became head of government. The main provisions ensured human rights, equality of forms of ownership, and land ownership rights. Finally, all languages, including Russian, were guaranteed free development and use. Discrimination on grounds of non-fluency in the state language was forbidden. Three days later, parliament created a Constitutional Court.

Parliament also moved to introduce a Kyrgyz currency, the som, following pressure by Russia on former Soviet republics to drop the ruble as their currency unless they adopted common conditions for its use. The introduction of the new currency was done with IMF approval in light of the country's commitment to monetary stability, budget stringency and rapid privatization. The IMF offered to support the new currency as a means of fighting inflation. Within two months, inflation had dropped by 25-30 percent. The economics ministry announced that its two principal policy programs were to develop agriculture in 1993-94 and to produce consumer goods. The country was promised $400 million in loans. The World Bank and the Japanese government promised $110 million in budget support.

Introduction of the som created tensions with neighboring Uzbekistan, whose president, hard-liner Islam Karimov, accused the Kyrgyz of plotting to flood his country with unwanted rubles. The border between the two countries was closed, money transfers and trading of any kind was stopped and gas supplies were shut off.

Other regional tensions arose over the deteriorating political situation in Tajikistan. On 24 July, the government sent 400 troops as part of a CIS agreement to the Afghan-Tajik border where Tajik rebels and their Afghan supporters were massing for a new offensive. President Akaev said the unstable border situation could "stimulate the trade in drugs and weapons and worsen the whole Central Asian situation."

On 13 December President Akaev fired the prime minister and cabinet after a parliamentary non-confidence vote. The last Communist prime minister, Apas Dzhumagulov, was asked to form a government.

Political Rights and Civil Liberties:

Citizens have the means to change their government democratically under a multiparty system enshrined in the new constitution. There are many political parties representing the political spectrum. On 25 January a leader of the *Erkin Kyrgyztan* (Democratic Kyrgyztan) announced that eleven parties had united to form a pro-democracy bloc.

The new constitution established the principle of an independent judiciary, and steps have been taken to reform the judicial system and to limit interference in practice.

The press laws do place some restrictions on journalists, including the publication of state secrets, materials that advocate war, violence or intolerance to other ethnic groups. There is no official censorship of media. As in many former Soviet republics, the independent press faces problems of cost, access to materials and distribution difficulties. The government owns all radio and television facilities, raising the issue of self-censorship.

The are no significant restrictions on foreign and domestic travel. Although the constitution ensures minority rights and the government has shown great sensitivity to the Russian minority, 1993 saw a continuation of the "brain drain" as educated and skilled Russians left the country.

Freedom of religion is respected in this predominantly Islamic country, where Christians and Jews can worship freely and openly. President Akaev is committed to the rights of women, and the many women who serve in key posts include the chief justice of the Supreme Court and several ministers and ambassadors. Women are well represented in the workforce.

Workers are represented by the Federation of Independent Trade Unions of Kyrgyztan (FITUK). In April, an agreement was signed between the government and FITUK aimed at "stabilizing the socio-political situation and protecting the interests of working people." The document was in force until the end of the year.

Laos

Polity: Communist
one-party
Economy: Mixed-statist
Population: 4,440,000
PPP: $1,100
Life Expectancy: 49.7
Ethnic Groups: Multi-ethnic—Lao (50 percent), Thai (20
percent), Phoutheung, Miao (Hmong), Tao and others

Political Rights: 7
Civil Liberties: 6
Status: Not Free

Overview:　　　　**A** year after the death of president and party leader Kaysone
Phomvihane, who had led Laos since independence in 1975,
his successor, Nouhak Phoumsavan, pledged to continue
liberalizing the economy while maintaining the ruling Lao People's Revolutionary
Party's (LPRP) tight political control.

This landlocked, mountainous Southeast Asian country became a French protectorate in 1893. Following the Japanese occupation during World War II, the Communist
Pathet Lao (Land of Lao) fought the returning French, winning complete sovereignty
on 23 October 1953. Royalist, Communist and conservative factions formed a coalition
government in 1962 but began fighting each other in 1964. In the late 1960s and early
1970s, the United States heavily bombed North Vietnamese and Pathet Lao forces that
were fighting the royalist government of Souvanna Phouma. In May 1975 the Pathet
Lao overran the capital, Vientiane, and established the one-party Communist Lao
People's Democratic Republic under Prime Minister Kaysone Phomvihane seven
months later.

The LPRP introduced the New Economic Mechanism (NEM) in 1986 to revive an
economy that had been decimated by a decade of central planning. Under the NEM,
farms have been fully privatized, state-owned companies have either been privatized or
granted autonomy, and price controls have been abandoned. Inflation has dropped to
under 10 percent since the government tightened the money supply and offered higher
interest rates to attract private savings.

In August 1991 the rubber-stamp National Assembly approved the country's first
constitution, which mixes socialist rhetoric with market-based economic principles. It
formally makes the LPRP the "leading organ" of the political system and places the
government under the Leninist doctrine of "democratic centralism." At the same time it
requires the state to protect private ownership by "domestic capitalists and foreigners
who make investments" in the country. Notably, opposition parties are not expressly
banned, giving the government the option of allowing rival parties in the future. The
constitution created a newly enlarged presidency. The president is the head of the armed
forces, can remove the prime minister, and can ratify and abolish foreign treaties. Prime
Minister Kaysone moved up to the new presidency, while veteran revolutionary
Khamtay Siphandone succeeded him as prime minister.

Kaysone's death on 21 November 1992 created a serious leadership gap. The
president had been the undisputed head of an "Iron Troika" that had led the Laotian

Communist movement since the mid-1950s. On 27 November the National Assembly predictably named the remainder of the Troika—Assembly Speaker Nouhak Phoumsavan and prime minister Khamtay—to succeed Kaysone as president and LPRP chairman, respectively. The government allowed non-LPRP, independent candidates for the first time to contest the December National Assembly elections, although all had to be pre-approved by the LPRP. Several are believed to have won seats in the eighty-five-member Assembly, although the government did not provide a breakdown of the vote.

On 22 February 1993 the Assembly formally elected the seventy-eight-year-old Nouhak to the presidency, and re-elected Khamtay as prime minister. An extensive ministerial shakeup brought several younger, educated technocrats, including new foreign minister Somsavath Lengsavath, into a new sixteen-member cabinet.

Kaysone's successors are expected to continue liberalizing the economy while maintaining the LPRP's political monopoly. Gross Domestic Product (GDP) grew by 7 percent in 1992 and is expected to continue at that pace through the mid-1990s. In June the International Monetary Fund approved a $50 million loan to upgrade infrastructure. Although 85 percent of the population is engaged in subsistence farming, and agriculture accounts for almost 60 percent of GDP, there are growing industrial and service sectors.

The Australian-financed Thailand-Laos Friendship Bridge over the Mekong River, due to be completed in April 1994, will link the two countries for the first time. With 40 percent of total investment, Thailand is already the biggest investor in the country. Although Laos is one of the five poorest countries in the world and foreign investment is desperately needed, many citizens fear being economically and culturally swamped by Thailand and other neighboring countries.

Political Rights and Civil Liberties:

Laotians cannot change their government democratically. The Lao People's Revolutionary Party (LPRP) is the only existing political party. The Hmong, the largest of several tribes that comprise half the population, have conducted a small-scale insurgency since the Communist takeover, and both the Hmong and the government are accused of human rights violations, including extrajudicial killings. Although some elements of state control have been relaxed in recent years, the security services frequently search homes without warrants, monitor mail and international telephone calls, and maintain networks of neighborhood and workplace informers.

The legal system is subservient to the government, and trials lack adequate procedural safeguards. The government suspended the bar in late 1992 pending the introduction of a new set of rules regarding private lawyers; this has prevented defense lawyers from defending clients. Torture and mistreatment of prisoners and detainees is apparently rare. The government has released nearly all of the tens of thousands of people who were sent to "re-education camps" following the Communist victory in 1975. However, it continues to hold at least three officials of the former government. In addition, in December 1992 the government gave fourteen-year terms to three high-level LPRP ministers who had been held since 1990 for criticizing the country's political and economic system, denouncing official corruption and calling for a multiparty system.

Freedoms of speech and press are nonexistant. Newspapers and electronic media are controlled by the government and reflect its views. In Vientiane and other towns along the Mekong River, Thai broadcasts are available. All associations are controlled by the LPRP, and anti-government demonstrations are illegal. Freedom of religion is generally respected, and the government supports Buddhist organizations and activities. Citizens must obtain permission for travel within the country, which is generally granted, and are increasingly freer to travel abroad. The government is dominated by ethnic Lao but is slowly trying to integrate minority groups. All labor unions are controlled by the government-affiliated Federation of Lao Trade Unions, and strikes are not permitted.

Latvia

Polity: Presidential-parliamentary democracy (ethnic limits)
Economy: Statist transitional
Population: 2,702,000
PPP: $6,457
Life Expectancy: 71.0
Ethnic Groups: Latvians (52 percent), Russians (34 percent), Ukrainians, Poles, Byelorussians, Lithuanians, Jews

Political Rights: 3
Civil Liberties: 3
Status: Partly Free

Overview: The key issues for this former Soviet Baltic republic in its second year of independence from the Soviet Union were national elections in June and the withdrawal of the estimated 16,000 Russian troops still in the country.

Latvia was an independent republic from 1918 to 1940, when it was forcibly annexed by the Soviet Union after the Hitler-Stalin Pact. More than fifty years of Soviet occupation caused a massive influx of Russians; the proportion of ethnic Latvians fell from 77 percent in 1940 to 52 percent by 1991. Latvia declared independence from a crumbling Soviet Union in 1991.

The issues of citizenship, voting and property rights, and the status of non-citizens remained contentious all year, as the 100-member *Saeima* (parliament) had yet to pass final legislation. In October 1991, parliament adopted a series of guidelines for defining who qualified for citizenship. Only those who were citizens in 1940 and their descendants were automatically granted citizenship. For others, certain conditions were set, including: a conversational knowledge of Latvian; knowledge of Latvian legal structures; sixteen years of residence; and renunciation of citizenship from another state. The guidelines, which disenfranchised the mostly Russian non-Latvians, were criticized by Russian groups and Moscow. Right-wing nationalist parties such as Fatherland and Freedom, which supported unforced repatriation of those who had come to Latvia since 1940, considered the guidelines not exclusionary enough.

On 5-6 June, Latvia held its first parliamentary election since the fall of the USSR.

In a vote observers called free and fair, almost 90 percent of Latvia's eligible voters chose among twenty-three lists to elect a new *Saeima*. Parties needed at least 4 percent of the total vote in a proportional electoral system.

Of the eight parties clearing the hurdle, Latvia's Way, led by President Anatolijs Gorbunovs and including the old elite of Latvia's Communist Party-turned nationalists, as well as émigrés of Latvian descent, gained 36 seats. Other winners were: the Latvian National Independence Movement, 15 seats; Harmony for Latvia-Rebirth of the Economy, 13; Farmer's Union, 12; Equal Rights, 7; Fatherland and Freedom, 6; Christian Democratic Union, 6; and the Democratic Center Party, 5. Surprisingly, the ruling Latvian Popular Front, which had led the anti-Communist movement and engineered Latvia's independence drive, failed to gain the required 4 percent.

Key concerns were economic reform, relations with Russia, and the issues of citizenship and the rights of non-citizens. Eligible to vote were all citizens of pre-1940 Latvia, regardless of ethnic origin, whose citizenship was restored by the Supreme Council in 1991. Also eligible were their descendants. Almost 30,000 Latvian citizens living abroad could vote in mission polling stations. Although about 300,000 Latvians of non-Latvian origin could vote in the election, about 700,000 peope (almost one-third of the voting-age population)—largely Russians, Ukrainians and Jews—could not vote for lack of a new law on citizenship and naturalization.

On 7 July, after two days of deliberations, the new *Saeima* unexpectedly chose fifty-three-year-old economist Guntis Ulmanis as president. Ulmanis, the grandnephew of Karlis Ulmanis, the authoritarian leader of independent Latvia before the Soviet takeover in 1940, was a virtual unknown in political circles. Former-President Gorbunovs was named to the powerful post of parliamentary speaker. Ulmanis said he planned to nominate pro-reform Deputy Parliamentary Speaker Valdis Birkavs of Latvia's Way as prime minister. He was approved the next day and his twelve cabinet ministers a week later.

A critical problem facing the new government was the issue of Russian troops. Shortly after the election, the Russian government ceased withdrawing troops from Latvia. The order was issued in conjunction with Russian President Boris Yeltsin's speech to Russian recruits on 10 June in which he again threatened that troops would not be pulled out of Latvia and Estonia until their respective governments made political concessions on immediate citizenship for Russians living there. In late June, Russia temporarily stopped delivering natural gas to all three Baltic states. The one-day cutoff was to remind the republics of their dependence on Russian resources and infrastructure.

During a 27 October visit to Latvia, U.S. Secretary of State Warren Christopher pressed Moscow to withdraw its troops. He urged the Latvian government to expand the rights of ethnic Russians, adding that international human rights organizations found no rights violations in Latvia. By year's end, there had been no final agreement with Russia. In other security issues, on 27 October, Latvia joined Lithuania and Estonian in endorsing a U.S. proposal for joint military exercises and peacekeeping operations with NATO allies.

On economic issues, the new government pledged to continue market reforms. In March, Latvia introduced a new currency, the lat, which replaced the Latvian ruble by the summer. The currency was introduced because of falling inflation (2.5 percent a month) and the strengthening of the Latvian ruble in relation to the dollar. In September 1992, a month after it became a member of the World Bank, Latvia's responsible fiscal and monetary policies and its commitment to privatization allowed it to become the first former Soviet republic to get a International Monetary Fund (IMF) loan.

Political Rights and Civil Liberties: Citizens of Latvia can change their government democratically. Under current citizenship and naturalization provisions, a large percentage of the mainly Slavic residents who emigrated to Latvia after the 1940 Soviet takeover, as well as their descendants, are excluded from citizenship and voting rights.

The rights of association and assembly are respected, and there are several well-organized political parties, including Equal Rights, mainly supported by Russians and Ukrainians dissatisfied with Latvia's citizenship policies. June's legislative elections were judged free and fair by international observers.

The judiciary is free from government interference, and reforming the system continues. Latvia's former Communist party boss, Alfred Rubiks, was elected to parliament from the Equal Rights slate while in jail awaiting trial for treason. On 14 June, the trial was postponed because of the defendant's illness. Jailed nearly two years ago, Rubiks stands accused of supporting the brief, hard-line Kremlin coup in August 1991 and promoting violent resistance to Latvian independence.

There is an independent press in both Latvian and Russian, both of which have faced economic difficulties in terms of commercial viability and resources. A Latvian district court judge suspended the government license of the radical opposition weekly *Pilsonis* for allegedly advocating the violent overthrow of the government and disobeying Latvian law. Under the suspension the paper could not be printed at state-controlled plants or distributed through the government monopoly kiosks. A 1992 law specified the creation of separate administrative bodies for radio and television. At the same time, it guaranteed their independence from political interference.

Freedom of movement is unrestricted, and religious rights are respected in this largely Lutheran country. Women have the same legal rights as men, and are granted day-care and maternity benefits. Women do face discrimination in hiring and pay. Since independence, a free trade union confederation has been established.

Lebanon

Polity: Presidential-parliamentary (military and foreign-influenced, partly foreign-occupied)
Economy: Mixed statist
Population: 3,439,000
PPP: $2,300
Life Expectancy: 66.1
Ethnic Groups: Eastern Hamitic (90 percent), Greek, Syro-Lebanese
Ratings Change: *Lebanon's political rights rating changed from 5 to 6 and its civil liberties rating from 4 to 5 as a result of modifications in methodology. See "Survey Methodology," page 671.

Political Rights: 6*
Civil Liberties: 5*
Status: Partly Free

Overview: In his first full year in office, Lebanese Prime Minister Rafik al-Hariri led the slow process of rebuilding a country shattered by the 1975-90 civil war. In July, heavy fighting errupted between Israeli troops and fundamentalist guerrillas in and around the Israeli "security zone" in the south.

Lebanon declared independence from France in 1941, and full sovereignty followed the final withdrawal of French troops in 1946. The genesis of the country's civil war lay in the unwritten 1943 National Pact, which gave Christians political dominance over the Muslim population through a perpetual 6:5 ratio of parliamentary seats. The Pact also allocated government positions along religious lines.

Following three decades in which non-Christian groups tried unsuccessfully to end this religious-based political system, in 1975 civil war broke out between Muslim, Christian and Druze militias. Syria sent troops into the country in 1976 to support the government, which ultimately collapsed. The country's reconciliation process began at Taif, Saudi Arabia in November 1989, with an Arab-League-sponsored accord that provided for a new, power-sharing constitution. The accord continued the tradition of a Christian presidency, but transfered many of the executive powers to the cabinet, to be headed by a Sunni Muslim prime minister as before. Future parliaments were to be split evenly among Muslims and Christians. The accord also allowed Syria to maintain up to 40,000 troops in Beirut and other cities until September 1992.

In October 1990 Lebanese and Syrian troops defeated Christian troops loyal to General Michel Aoun, who had refused to relinquish power to the central government. Aoun's defeat ended a civil war that had killed more than 150,000 people. In December 1990, President Elias Hrawi named a thirty member, half-Christian, half-Muslim cabinet that included the leaders of several warring militias. In May 1991 the government signed a treaty allowing Syria to maintain troops indefinitely in the Bekka Valley and linking the two countries' economic and security policies, a deal that effectively gave control of the country to its more powerful neighbor.

On 16 July 1992 the surviving members of the 1972 parliament passed a law clearing the way for the country's first vote in twenty years. The new parliament would have 128 seats, split evenly among Muslims and Christians. Immediately, hardline Christians protested against holding the election before the Syrian army withdrew from the major cities, claiming its presence would intimidate voters and potentially lead to a rubber-stamp, pro-Syrian government.

Few Christians turned out to vote in elections held in three stages—23 August in the eastern Bekka Valley and the northern province, 30 August in Beirut and the Christian and Druze surrounding areas, and 6 September in the south. Meanwhile, the militant Iranian-backed Hezbollah fundamentalists, who opposed the Taif accord, formed an uneasy alliance with the Syrian-backed Amal movement to prevent the election of moderate Shiites. These two rival Shiite groups had previously turned on each other towards the end of the civil war. In balloting for the 64 Muslim seats, Amal took 18 and Hezbollah 12, while independents linked to various political figures took 34 seats. Due to the boycott, the 64 Christian seats were won by independents or by candidates who ran on Muslim tickets. Although Hezbollah and other fundamentalists controlled the largest single bloc, by some counts up to 20 seats, their influence was limited since three-fourths of the seats were won by nominally pro-Syrian candidates.

On 22 October 1992 President Hrawi named forty-nine-year-old billionaire businessman Rafik al-Hariri as prime minister. Although the major steps in the Taif Accord had been completed, in November Syria said it would not redeploy all of its troops to the Bekka Valley as planned until further political changes were carried out, including abolishing the practice of awarding junior government posts along religious lines.

The key issues in 1993 were the government's efforts to reconstruct the war-battered country, and major Israeli military raids in the south in July. Israel originally invaded southern Lebanon in 1982 to clear out Palestinian Liberation Organization (PLO) guerrillas who were launching rocket attacks into northern Israel. Since 1985 Israel has maintained a 440-square mile "security zone" in the south, manned by Israeli soldiers and by the Israeli-backed South Lebanese Army (SLA).

By early 1993 the Lebanese army had disarmed most of the fundamentalist militias operating in the south outside the security zone, and relieved United Nations peacekeeping troops that had been guarding several towns. But the powerful Hezbollah refused to disarm and continued to attack Israei soldiers in the security zone. In the spring, Israel launched several air attacks at suspected Hezbollah bases north of the security zone

In early July a series of guerrilla attacks in the zone killed seven Israeli soldiers. On 25 July Israel began major air and artillery attacks in the Syrian-controlled Bekka Valley and the area south of Beirut, targeting bases of Hezbollah and the Syrian-based Popular Front for the Liberation of Palestine-General Command. The conflict escalated after Hezbollah guerrillas launched fresh Katyusha rocket attacks into northern Israel, ignoring Israeli calls for a cease-fire. For several days SLA broadcasts warned residents of more than seventy towns around Nabatiyeh and Tyre in southern Lebanon to evacuate. These were followed by attacks by Israeli jets. Some 300,000 residents temporarily fled northward. Under a U.S.-brokered ceasefire on 31 July, Israel ended the offensive in return for assurances that Syria and Lebanon would work to curb Hezbollah activities outside the security zone and end the group's rocket attacks on northern Israel. Hezbollah guerrillas targeted the security zone again in October and November, leading to Israeli counterattacks.

The fighting has overshadowed the nation's economic recovery efforts. On 30 January the government arranged for World Bank aid for the first time in fourteen years. The $175 million loan will be used for emergency infrastructure repairs, including housing, water, sewage, and electricity projects. On 18 March the government announced a $10 billion plan to rebuild the country, to be financed largely through government bonds, foreign loans and grants. During the year the government restricted freedoms of assembly and press.

Political Rights and Civil Liberties: Lebanese citizens changed their government in 1992 for the first time in two decades, although elections were not fully free or fair. Christians largely boycotted the vote to protest a Syrian army presence in major cities. There were numerous charges of irregularities in drawing up the electoral roles, in the voting itself, and in tallying the ballots, and there were no official foreign observer teams. Independent candidates reported being harassed and intimidated by party workers. The government also redrew the six electoral districts to favor pro-Syrian candidates.

The government still lacks full control of the country—the South Lebanon Army administers Israel's 440-square mile security zone, the Hezbollah milita refuses to disarm and is still active in many southern towns, and Syria has 40,000 troops in Beirut, the Bekka Valley and northern Lebanon, even though all the troops were to have been redeployed to the Bekka Valley following the elections. Small Palestinian factions administer several refugee towns in the south. All of these extra-governmental groups frequently detain suspects and administer justice without due process in areas under their control.

Security forces are accused of using excessive force against detainees, and prisons are severely overcrowded. The judiciary is generally independent of the government, although influential politicians reportedly intervene in some cases to protect supporters. Otherwise, defendants generally receive adequate due process rights.

In a severe civil liberties infringement, on 11 August the cabinet adopted a decree banning all demonstrations, "with or without permit." In the most serious crackdown under the decree, on 13 September army troops killed eight citizens and wounded at least forty-one during a peaceful protest against the Israel-PLO peace accord signed that day.

Significant restrictions remain on the press. The government's Lebanon Television (LTV) has a legal monopoly on television until 2012. The government has refused to license some forty-five private television stations that have been allowed to operate illegally, and periodically threatens to shut them down. Newspapers and magazines are not permitted to publish articles considered inimical to state security and religious or ethnic harmony, or that defame top politicians. These restrictions lead to self-censorship.

During the spring the government repeatedly harassed certain media. On 9 April the government closed the Christian-owned Independent Company Network Television station after it repeatedly criticized the government. From 30 April to 3 June the government suspended publication of the Christian-owned daily *Nida Al-Watan* for accusing the prime minister of trying to "Muslimize" the country by buying Christian-owned property in Muslim areas. On 11 May the government suspended the daily *Al - Safir* for one week for publishing a paper submitted by the Israeli side at multilateral peace talks in Washington concerning a proposed pullout from southern Lebanon, claiming this violated the press law's provision against publishing secret documents. More likely the sanction came because the paper had been critical of the Lebanese and Syrian governments. At a hearing for *Al-Safir* on 20 May, police assaulted several journalists after fistfights broke out in the Beirut courtroom. On 28 May the government briefly shut the daily *al-Sharq* for publishing a cartoon lampooning the president's family.

Police must approve all leaflets and other non-periodical materials, and citizens have been imprisoned for not gaining this approval. The police also frequently exercise prior censorship of art and cultural works. Freedom of religion is respected. Internal travel is increasingly less restricted as the government continues to extend its authority over the country, and citizens can travel abroad freely. All non-government workers have the right to join independent trade unions and hold strikes.

Lesotho

Polity: Parliamentary democracy
Economy: Capitalist
Population: 1,880,000
PPP: $1,743
Life Expectancy: 57.3
Ethnic Groups: Sotho (99 percent)

Political Rights: 3*
Civil Liberties: 4
Status: Partly Free

Ratings Change: *Lesotho's political rights rating changed from 6 to 3 because it held multiparty elections.

Overview:

In 1993, Lesotho held its first democratic election for more than two decades. It was a landslide victory for the long-standing opposition Basutoland Congress Party (BCP), which won all of the sixty-five seats in the National Assembly.

Lesotho—a small mountainous kingdom completely enclosed by South Africa, with a homogenous Basotho population, gained complete independence from Britain in 1966. It chose to remain a member of the British Commonwealth, however. The political struggle for independence began in 1952 with the formation of the BCP. The BCP opposed the calls for Lesotho's incorporation into South Africa, and was critical of the major capitalist powers. In domestic policy, the party favored a devolution of power from the influential traditional chiefs to democratically elected councils. The BCP favored a policy of state intervention in the economy in order to alleviate social inequalities.

In 1958, the Basotho National Party (BNP) was established as a counterweight to the BCP. The BNP favored a policy of retaining the traditional patterns of governance through the village headmen. The BNP was more inclined to favor a market-oriented economy and had a more cordial relationship with South Africa. In 1957, the Marematlou Freedom Party (MFP) was established, favoring a monarchy with strong legislative and executive authority.

In 1965 the pre-independence parliamentary election was held, with the BNP winning a narrow victory over the BCP. Chief Leabua Jonathan became the prime minister. Shortly thereafter, the parliament adopted a Westminster-style constitution, installing King Moshoeshoe II as the head of state. When during the first post-independence election in 1970 it appeared that the BCP had won, Jonathan declared a state of emergency, invalidated the vote, and imprisoned the opposition. Jonathan was overthrown in 1986 by a group of army officers led by General Justin Lekhanya. In 1990 Lekhanya was overthrown by another group of officers led by Colonel Pitsoana Ramaema. Shortly thereafter, Ramaema forced Moshoeshoe II to abdicate in favor of his son Letsie III, over a dispute on the extent of the royal legislative and executive authority. In 1991 Ramaema appointed a Constituent Assembly to draft a new constitution, in preparation for reintroduction of civilian rule.

The election, originally scheduled for June 1992, was postponed several times, due in part to delays in the process of writing the constitution and delineating the new electoral districts. On 14 January the ruling Military Council set the date as 27 March, and three weeks later it dissolved the cabinet in order to facilitate the handing over of power to the new civilian president.

In the runup to the vote, the issue of the monarchy took on renewed interest with the return of the deposed Moshoeshoe II from his London exile in the summer of 1992. In December of that year, Letsie III wrote letters to the major churches and the police, stating that the military forcibly installed him as king, following the dethronement of his father. Letsie asked for a big *pitso* (public meeting) on 13 March, the national holiday celebrating the founder of the Basotho nation, to vote for reinstatement of Moshoeshoe to the throne. The Military Council condemned the plan and warned the public to disregard Letsie's calls, threatening to use violence against the participants. A court injunction asked for by the Council ordered the banning of the meeting. In early March, a dispatch of soldiers blocked the entrance to the royal palace, effectively confining Letsie to a house arrest. Bowing to the pressure, Letsie called for the pitso to be cancelled.

On 16 March, less than two weeks before the election, the constituent assembly published the final draft of the constitution, to take effect with the swearing in of the new government on 2 April. The announcement followed weeks of public meetings throughout the country, in which voters were consulted on the text of the constitutional provisions. The final version, however, added an additional provision not previously discussed: establishing a Defense Commission composed from the military, which would have the authority to command and dismiss elected officials, including members of the parliament. Following criticism by political parties and international observers, the soon-to-be-dissolved Military Council agreed to clarify the provision by delineating the Commission's powers over civilian authorities.

In the 27 March election in which fourteen political parties participated and which focused primarily on the evaluation of events surrounding the cancellation of the1970 vote, the BCP won a resounding victory taking all of the sixty-five Assembly seats. The seventy-four-year-old opposition veteran Ntsu Mokhehle formed a government on 2 April, following the BNP's failed attempt for a court injunction to invalidate the vote on the grounds of alleged voter fraud and rumors of an army coup. The Mokhehle offer to appoint two BNP members to the thirty-three-member Senate, a second parliamen-tary chamber consisting of representatives of village chiefs and winning party appoin-tees, was rejected in May.

Political Rights and Civil Liberties: For the first time in twenty three years the Basotho were able to elect their government freely in a democratic election. The 130 international election observers judged the election free and fair, with no major irregularities being registered. Following the election, the winning party was able to occupy its seats in parliament and form a government, in stark contrast to the 1970 "stolen election."

Despite the landslide victory for the BCP, political pluralism exists, with a number of small but lively political parties, often critical of the government, ranging from the monarchist MFP to the Communist party. Additional non-elected centers of power rest in the still politically powerful military, and the mostly ceremonial but still influential royalty. On the local level the chieftaincy remains the most powerful authority.

The judiciary consists of a modern court system based on the Roman-Dutch law, and a customary system operating on the village level. The judges on the High Court are largely independent of government, while judges in the lower courts are often susceptible to central government or local chieftain pressure. In recent years, the High Court acted on several occasions to limit the authorities' infringement of the law, and to investigate cases of human rights violations. In 1988, the court annulled the state of emergency on procedural grounds, and in 1991 it sentenced two officers for the abduction and killing of two former ministers in 1986.

The government controls the official media, consisting of two weekly newspapers, a radio station and a one-hour newscast on the local television channel. In 1992, the military authorities assigned time slots for each of the fourteen parties contesting the election to air their views on radio and television. With the continued postponement of the electoral date, however, public exhaustion with the programs caused the Military Council to cancel them. In early 1993 the BCP and the minor parties accused the official media of being strongly biased in favor of the BNP. Following the BCP takeover of the government, the party avoided wide-scale purges in the official media. The BCP and the minor parties received more coverage in the two Sesotho-language newspapers affiliated with the Roman Catholic and Lesotho Evangelical churches, and the two independent English-language newspapers.

Freedom of religion is respected in this largely Christian country. Travel within the country and to neighboring South Africa is generally unrestricted. The high cost of obtaining an "international" passport for travel to other countries, including the other countries in Southern Africa, makes foreign travel inaccessible to all but the most affluent.

Trade union activities are restricted due to the peculiar nature of employment in Lesotho. Most miners working in South Africa belong to the South African National Union of Mineworkers (NUM); since this is a foreign organization, however, it is not allowed to operate in Lesotho. Most previous attempts by the work force to organize have been resisted by the military authorities, who relied on inexpensive labor costs to woo foreign investment, most notably from the Far East.

Liberia

Polity: Monrovia: interim civilian goverment (foreign military and foreign-influenced); else-where: rival war lords
Economy: Capitalist
Population: 2,777,000
PPP: $857
Life Expectancy: 54.2
Ethnic Groups: Sixteen major tribes, including the Krahn, Mandingo, Gio and Mano (95 percent), Americo-Liberians (5 percent)
Ratings Change: *Liberia's political rights rating changed from 7 to 6 because of small steps toward democratic transition.

Political Rights: 6*
Civil Liberties: 6
Status: Not Free

Overview:

In 1993 civil war continued to devastate Liberia. The signing of a peace accord in mid-year calling for an interim govern-ment and free elections failed to reconcile the three main factions striving for control of the country. The civilian population suffered mass starvation, executions and mutilations inflicted by all the warring parties.

Liberia was founded in 1847 by freed American slaves, known as Americo-Liberians, whose unchallenged political domination ended in 1980, when General Samuel Doe overthrew the civilian government. Doe, a member of the small Krahn ethnic group, became Liberia's first indigenous leader, consolidating his power by brutal repression against other ethnic groups. In December 1989 the rebel National Patriotic Front of Liberia (NPFL), operating from the neighboring Ivory Coast, attacked government troops. Led by Charles Taylor, an Americo-Liberian and former Doe cabinet member, most NPFL soldiers are of the Gia and Mano ethnic groups. In July 1990, an NPFL offshoot group killed Doe while he was in custody.

By mid-1990, members of the Economic Organization of the West African States (ECOWAS) sent an armed monitoring group (ECOMOG) to defend the remnants of the government against NPFL assault. An ECOWAS-sponsored Interim Government of National Unity (IGNU), with Amos Sawyer as President, was set up later in the year. The NPFL formed an alternative government headquartered in the interior town of Gbarnga.

Following a cessation of hostilities which held throughout much of 1991, later ECOWAS-sponsored talks proved unable to resolve the country's division and provide for lasting peace. In September 1991 the armed clashes resumed, with a third armed faction gaining ground in Liberia. The Sierra Leone-based United Liberation Movement (ULIMO), composed of armed anti-Taylor refugees, mainly Krahns and Mandingoes, was led by General Alhaji Kromah, a former officer of President Doe's Armed Forces of Liberia (AFL). The ECOMOG placed the AFL remnants under IGNU's nominal control, although the latter was unable to exercise full control of its operations.

After he signed and subsequently repudiated more than twenty ceasefire and peace accords, on 17 October 1992 Taylor mounted his largest offensive against ECOMOG forces since the 1990 siege of the capital, Monrovia. In retaliation for the surprise attack, during which the ECOMOG was forced to retreat to the capital, the ECOWAS authorized economic sanctions against Taylor and an ECOMOG counteroffensive to recover its previously held positions. In early January 1993 the ECOMOG sank two ships carrying NPFL military supplies, and captured three others. In February, ECOMOG seized the country's main airport and the Firestone rubber plantation, the world's largest, opening up strategic routes to Liberia's second port, Buchanan, and the northern town of Kakata, both NPLF strongholds. On 22 February, ECOMOG received its largest reinforcement to date, consisting of 5,000 soldiers. Two weeks later, four Nigerian jets under ECOMOG command attacked an Ivory Coast border post. Following the attack, the Nigerian military ruler Ibrahim Babangida stated that it should serve as a warning to the Ivorian authorities to stop their covert support for Taylor. Despite ECOMOG's successes, Taylor still controlled more than half of Liberia's surface area, and his forces continued to sporadically infiltrate the remaining areas.

On 5 June, at a refugee camp in Harbel east of Monrovia, armed militiamen killed approximately 600 people, mostly women and children, and wounded 800 others. The massacre was the second largest mass killing of civilians after the 1990 AFL murder of more than 600 people who congregated at a Monrovia church. In the aftermath of the massacre the IGNU accused the NPFL of infiltrating the AFL positions (the IGNU charged the AFL with protecting the camp) and executing the killings. At the same time, however, Sawyer blamed the AFL for negligence in protecting the refugees. Taylor refuted the charges, and in turn accused the AFL .

A week after the event, Sawyer established two commissions of inquiry, one conducted by the Defense Ministry and the other by his military adviser, to investigate the events. Another inquiry, at the behest of the U.N., was conducted by the U.N. Secretary General's special envoy Trevor Gordon-Somers. After Gordon-Somers' investigation proved inconclusive, on 4 August U.N. Secretary General Boutros-Ghali nominated a three-judge panel under the former Kenyan Attorney General Amos Wako to conducta further investigation. On 20 September the U.N. panel presented its official findings, blaming the AFL for the Harbel atrocities. After an initial rejection of the findings by the IGNU Defense Ministry, Sawyer ordered the detention of three AFL suspects named in the U.N. report, including the camp's commander.

After weeks of preparations facilitated by the U.N. special envoy Gordon-Somers and the newly appointed O.A.U. mediator Canaan Banana of Zimbabwe, the three parties agreed to meet in Geneva on 17 July to discuss the signing of a peace accord. The possibility of bringing the three parties together to negotiate a peace accord was made possible due to increased U.N. and ECOWAS pressure to find a political solution to the conflict. Following a week of negotiations, all the factions agreed to sign the peace accord on 25 July in Cotonou, Benin, during a summit of West African leaders. The accord called for a cease-fire starting 1 August; the formation of a unitary transitional government composed of all the factions, with legislative and presidential elections to follow by February 1994; an expansion of ECOMOG to include military units from African countries outside of the region; and simultaneous disarmament of all the factions prior to the elections.

With the implementation of the cease-fire, on 16 August the three groups selected a five-member Council of State to act as the interim government. However, the NPFL boycotted the first meeting on 25 August, stating that the Council was not officially inaugurated, as stipulated in the Cotonou accord. The IGNU responded by demanding multilateral disarmament prior to official inauguration. However, with U.N. and O.A.U. delays in providing disarmament monitors and additional troops to join the ECOMOG, the NPFL refused to disarm, claiming uneven treatment by the Nigerian-led forces. In early October, the BBC reported internal NPFL skirmishes between supporters of Taylor, who objected to ECOMOG disarmament, and those willing to disarm. Despite the disagreements, all parties sent their representatives to the thirty-five-member interim legislature, inaugurated on 1 October.

Political Rights and Civil Liberties: Liberians lack the means to change their government democratically. Despite the signing of the Cotonou peace accord and the establishment of a unified interim government and legislature, large areas of the country are still under the control of various military factions, with absolute control over the population in their respective areas. The scheduled February 1994 general election is jeopardized by the inability of the ECOMOG to disarm the contestants.

The rule of law has broken down throughout most of the country. According to the U.N. High Commissioner for Refugees, 80 percent of Liberians have been forced to flee their homes, and half of the country's population has sought refuge in neighboring countries. Approximately 150,000 people have been killed since the start of the civil war.

All of the contestants, including the ECOMOG forces, have been accused of human rights abuses against the civilian population. According to Africa Watch , the AFL, pretending to the role of a national army, was systematically engaged in armed robbery and looting. The AFL was responsible for a chain of atrocities against non-combatants, including the killing of British researcher Brian Garnham in January and the Harbel massacre in June. The NPFL used civilians and institutions as shields in combat, and tortured and killed their opponents and members of the Krahn and related ethnic groups. The Red Cross and various relief agencies accused the ECOMOG of targeting humanitarian aid convoys, bombarding NPFL-held areas indiscriminately, and violations of medical neutrality, such as attacks on hospitals. The NPFL and ULIMO have been accused of using children as young as ten years old as soldiers.

Liberia's court system, which practically collapsed in 1990, began to be reconstituted two years later following an agreement between the IGNU and the NPFL to re-establish a five-member Supreme Court. Lower courts have also been set up in the IGNU- and NPF-controlled territories, but with the exception of Monrovia the provincial courts did not provide due process and adequate protection for the defendants. The police and the military often used arbitrary arrest and torture against civilians on the most trifling of grounds. Soldiers are subject to court martials, often involving capital cases, without recourse to legal counsel or the right to appeal.

The freedoms of speech and the press, and the rights to organize and join independent organizations are generally respected in Monrovia, but are more limited outside the capital, especially in the NPFL- and ULIMO-held territories. The major newspapers in Monrovia are *The Inquirer, The Eye* and *The Daily News.* Sporadically during the course of the civil war, the IGNU engaged in censorship of war-related stories. After a June announcement by the Information Ministry that it and the Justice Ministry must clear any war related news stories before their publication, the Press Union of Liberia (PUL) denounced the directive as "aiming at curtailing press freedom under the guise of security of the state." The PUL demanded that the Ministry instead publish a set of written guidelines to be followed by journalists in war reporting. Shortly thereafter, the Information Minister agreed to work with PUL in drawing up the guidelines. In Monrovia, a number of independent associations exist, including a number of human rights groups such as the Catholic Peace and Justice Commission and the Center for Law and Human Rights Education. Other groups include the Christian Health Association of Liberia (CHAL), the relief group SELF, and various church, student and child assistance groups.

Freedom of worship is generally respected by all sides. Freedom of movement within the country is limited due to the setting up of checkpoints and the requirement to posses travel permits when crossing between territories controlled by the different parties.

Libya

Polity: Military
Economy: Mixed statist
Population: 4,485,000
PPP: $7,000
Life Expectancy: 61.8
Ethnic Groups: Arab, Berber, Tuareg

Political Rights: 7
Civil Liberties: 7
Status: Not Free

Overview:

In 1993, Libya had a dramatic political year. U.N.-backed trade restrictions against the country intensified. A tribal and military uprising threatened the regime. The government constructed chemical warfare facilities. Government-approved tourists made a surprise pilgrimage to Israel, and then aborted their trip. All of these events developed in the context of a power struggle between the ruling strongman, Colonel Mu'ammar al-Qadhafi, and his second in command, Major Abdel-Salaam Jalloud.

Throughout the year, Qadhafi refused to extradite the two suspects wanted for the bombing of Pan Am Flight 103, which blew up over Lockerbie, Scotland in December 1988, killing 270 people. Libya has been under U.N. economic sanctions since 1992, because Qadhafi refuses to extradite the suspects to Scotland (UK) or the U.S. Both countries rejected a Libyan proposal to try the alleged bombers at U.N. or Arab League proceedings. The U.N. tightened the restrictions effective 1 December 1993. The new U.N. measures freeze Libyan assets abroad and ban the export of oil technology from other countries to Libya. Qadhafi threatened to torch Libya's oil fields to prevent them from passing to foreign control. The colonel attacked the U.N. Security Council as "an imperialist tool in the hands of the big powers. The Arabs instead should join the Society for the Prevention of Cruelty to Animals, because the U.N. doesn't respect them."

Tribal politics played a major role in both the Lockerbie case and in an attempted revolt. One of the bombing suspects belongs to Qadhafi's tribe, and the other belongs to the Megraha, Major Jalloud's tribe. Reportedly, tensions between the two officers were apparent on 1 September, the anniversary of Qadhafi's coup, when Jalloud made only a brief appearance with Qadhafi. In October, the Wurfala tribe began an uprising against the regime in the town of Bani Walid. Military officers sympathetic to the exiled National Front for the Salvation of Libya joined the fight, spreading the resistance movement to several bases. Pro-government elements in the military struck back, bombing both the military and civilian opposition. Front spokesmen in Washington claimed that Qadhafi's government arrested hundreds and executed dozens of alleged coup plotters. Allegedly, 280 people died in the uprising. However, Qadhafi denied the existence of the rebellion to the international media, and no reference to the fighting appeared in the Libyan press.

Although Qadhafi has proclaimed a policy of privatization of major economic sectors, there is little to show for it. The colonel has also proposed giving oil profits directly to the public. However, Jalloud allegedly opposes this idea.

There was clearly a struggle within the government over a surprise Libyan pilgrimage to Israel. In June, 200 Libyans began a journey to Jerusalem and supposedly to other Israeli cities. The trip was apparently a stunt to win favor with Israel, including backing for Libya's fight with the U.N. However, after criticism of the venture from Palestinians and, apparently, from Jalloud, the tourists denounced Israel, and abruptly went home.

Qadhafi is concerned about Islamist extremists. They may be gaining ground quietly as the U.N. embargoes squeeze the country's economy. The regime is willing to adopt Islamist measures, as long as Islamists themselves do not run the government.

As early as February 1993, Libya denied building new chemical warfare facilities. By October, the U.S. warned Thailand about Thai companies that were working on these projects. In November, Qadhafi ordered South Korean contractors in Libya to fire Thai workers in retaliation for Thailand's agreeing with the U.S. charges.

Political Rights and Civil Liberties:

Libyans do not have the right to change their government democratically. Qadhafi rules with the help of layers of committees around the country. There is no constitution. Governing principles come from Qadhafi's *Green Book*. Qadhafi, his aides, and committees acting in his name make major governmental decisions. He appoints officials ranging from military figures to junior level personnel.

Qadhafi rules through a series of Revolutionary Committees and intelligence agencies under his personal control. Nominal power lies with the secretary of the General People's Congress, which is elected by municipal groups called People's Committees. The Revolutionary Committees oversee the People's Committees and screen all candidates. All committees also have security functions. Qadhafi redesigned his regime in 1992, holding local elections in October. This device aimed at giving the appearance of popular control over thirteen ministries by creating thirteen separate 1,500-member bodies, consisting of one representative from each community. However, ultimate power and authority remain in Qadhafi's hands.

The system prohibits political parties or any other types of associations. Participation in elections is mandatory.

Freedom of expression is severely limited. People's Committee meetings allow only some limited debate. Citizens generally refrain from criticizing the regime because they fear the extensive surveillance network inside the country. Informers monitor the population. The government does not respect the right to privacy. The state owns and controls the Libyan media and the government censors available foreign publications. Libyans can receive foreign broadcasts. Publishing opinions contrary to government policy is prohibited. Occasional criticisms of government policy appear in the press. Whether these are orchestrated or not is unclear.

There is no freedom of assembly or association. Only government-sponsored demonstrations are allowed, and only its own affiliates have the right to organize. Any activity that opposes the basic principles of the "Revolution" may be punishable by death.

Prisoners are reportedly tortured during interrogations. The security forces hold political prisoners in secret detention centers. Libya's arbitrary judicial system does not provide fair trials. Detainees are often sentenced without trial, and death sentences are applied for many offenses.

Discrimination exists based on ethnic status, specifically against Berbers and Tuaregs in the south. In an attempt to eliminate the Berber identity, Qadhafi has tried unsuccessfully to get Berbers to marry only non-Berbers. Cultural norms make women second-class citizens, but Qadhafi has tried to expand their access to higher education and employment opportunities. Women receive basic military training and are subject to the military draft. A husband's permission is required for women to travel abroad. Female circumcision is still practiced among tribal groups in the south.

Libya is predominantly Muslim. The regime has banned the Sanusiyya Muslim sect. The government allows the small Christian population to practice and conduct services and there are two churches in Libya. The regime opposes Islamist extremists and monitors the mosques for political activity. Libyans are free to travel within the country, except in certain security areas. Exit permits are required for travel abroad. Libyan students studying abroad are subject to interrogation upon returning home and are usually placed under surveillance.

Trade unions are under strict government control, and Libyan workers do not have the right to join unions of their own choice. There is no collective bargaining, and no right to strike. Labor laws do not apply to foreign workers in Libya. The economy remains largely statist.

Liechtenstein

Polity: Prince and parliamentary democracy
Economy: Capitalist-statist
Population: 30,000
PPP: na
Life Expectancy: 69.5
Ethnic Groups: Alemannic German, Italian, other European

Political Rights: 1
Civil Liberties: 1
Status: Free

Overview: Liechtenstein experienced an unusually high amount of political turbulence in 1993. In the general election held on 7 February, the environmentalist Free List won seats for the first time, taking 2 of the 25 seats in the *Landtag* (legislature). The moderate Patriotic Union (VU) declined from 13 to 11 seats. VU leader Hans Brunhart resigned as head of government. Markus Buechel, leader of the conservative Progressive Citizens' Party (FBP), which won 12 seats, became the new head of government. He formed a short-lived coalition with the VU.

Prince Hans Adam II, the head of state, dismissed the parliament in June after Buechel lost in a no-confidence vote. Buechel had upset the political elites by hiring an outside professional, not a patronage appointee, to head the principality's personnel department. Buechel would like to continue with economic reforms such as opening up banking to international competition. Hans Adam asked Buechel to remain in office after the dissolution of parliament. There will be a new parliamentary election in 1994.

This was the second time in five years that Hans Adam dissolved the legislature. The instability in 1993 followed a struggle in 1992 in which Hans Adam and the legislators fought over scheduling referenda.

The Principality of Liechtenstein was created in its current form in 1719. The native two-thirds of Liechtenstein's residents are descended from the Germanic Alemanni tribe. One-third of the population is foreign. Prince Hans Adam's Austrian ancestors purchased the country's land. The royal family lived primarily in Moravia (once part of the Austro-Hungarian Empire, now a Czech land) until 1938, when the spread of Nazism forced them to flee to Liechtenstein. Between Czecho-Slovakia's independence in 1918 and the Communist takeover in 1948, that country confiscated Liechtenstein's royal estates without compensation. Since the fall of communism in 1989, Hans Adam has attempted to reclaim the family's Czech properties, but the Prague government has refused to give him either land or compensation.

The prince appoints a head of government from the majority party or coalition in the twenty-five-member Landtag, which has a maximum term of four years. Called "hallowed and sacrosanct" by the constitution, the monarch has the right to veto legislation. Hans Adam's father vetoed only one bill, a proposed hunting law. Parties with at least eight percent of the vote receive representation in the Landtag. Major local issues include overdevelopment and the large number of foreigners in the labor force. The Swiss handle many of Liechtenstein's defense and foreign affairs, but the principality has had its own U.N. membership since 1990.

Political Rights and Civil Liberties:

Liechtensteiners can change their government democratically. Control shifts between parties. However, the monarch retains more executive powers than other constitutional monarchs in Western Europe. Hans Adam is more involved than his father was in setting the legislative agenda. Voters may decide issues directly through referenda. Woman have had voting rights nationally since 1984, and won legal equality through a constitutional amendment in 1992. Major parties publish newspapers five times each week. Residents receive radio and television freely from other countries. Liechtenstein has no broadcast media. The country is too small to have numerous organizations, but association is free. A small, free trade union exists. The prosperous economy includes private and state enterprises. The state religion is Roman Catholicism, but other faiths are free to practice.

Lithuania

Polity: Presidential-
parliamentary democracy
Economy: Statist
transitional
Population: 3,736,000
PPP: $4,913
Life Expectancy: 72.0

Political Rights: 1*
Civil Liberties: 3
Status: Free

Ethnic Groups: Lithuanian (80 percent), Russian, Ukrainian,
Byelorussian, others
Ratings Change: *Lithuania's political rights ratings changed from 2 to 1 as a result of
modifications in methodology. See "Survey Methodology," page 671.

Overview: Key issues in this former Soviet Baltic Republic in 1993 were
direct presidential elections, the formal introduction of a new
national currency, and the withdrawal of Russian troops. The
government also faced the challenge of invigorating a slumping economy and the scope
and pace of market reforms.

Lithuania was an independent state from 1918 to 1940, when it was forcibly
annexed by the Soviet Union under provisions of the Hitler-Stalin Pact. It regained
independence from a disintegrating Soviet Union in 1991 after the failed hard-line coup
against Soviet President Mikhail Gorbachev. Parliamentary elections in October 1992
saw the return of the Communists, as the ex-Communist Lithuanian Democratic Labor
Party (LDLP) won 44.9 percent of the vote and 79 of 141 seats in the *Seimas* (parliament). Sajudis, the independent coalition formed in 1988 which spearheaded independence, won 19.9 percent. Sajudis chairman and President Vytautas Landsbergis was
replaced as head of state by sixty-year-old former Communist leader and LDLP
Chairman Algirdas Brazauskas, who was elected chairman of parliament, a post that
made him the acting president of Lithuania.

In February 1993, Brazauskas became the country's first directly elected president,
easily defeating the ambassador to Washington, Stasys Lozoraitis, who left Lithuania in
1939. Over 78 percent of eligible voters participated in the election, and Brazauskas won
60 percent to Lozoraitas's 38.2 percent. Five other registered candidates could not secure
the 20,000 signatures needed to run. The main issue in the race was the dismal state of the
economy. By the end of 1992, gross national product (GNP) was only 39 percent of the
1991 level and the annual inflation rate had reached 1,163 percent. Personal family incomes had dropped by 73 percent from the 1989 level. Three-fourths of the country's people lived below the poverty line. Unemployment affected 200,000 people and was climbing.

The campaign programs of the two candidates did not differ significantly.
Brazauskas promised to moderate the rate of reform. Although acknowledging that it
was impossible to reestablish the collective farm system, he promised to make greater
use of existing agricultural structures. He vowed to hold down unemployment, while
extending aid to students, the sick, and the aged but did not reveal how he proposed to
pay for these programs. Lozoraitis agreed that Lithuania's privatization of land had not
been carried out effectively, but he stressed the country's need to gain far greater

foreign economic support for the development of a market economy. Brazauskas was perceived as having better relations with officials in Russia, which had supplied the country with badly needed energy and raw materials.

On 10 March, the *Seimas* approved the presidential nomination of Adolfas Siezevicius as prime minister by a vote of seventy to thirteen with twenty-three abstentions.

On 25 June, the country, which scrapped the Soviet ruble in October 1992, introduced its own national currency, the litas. The coupons (talons) that had been used as interim currency were withdrawn from circulation by 20 July. Both the World Bank and the International Monetary Fund (IMF) had supported the move. (Lithuania had been accepted into the Council of Europe in May.) The litas would be **(are they?)** fully convertible and backed by eight tons of gold bullion. It was the last of the three Baltic states to adopt its own currency. Five days after the conversion, Russia stopped delivering natural gas to the Baltics for one day, ostensibly for "economic" not political reasons. Most Baltic politicians, however, saw the cut-off as Russia's reminder of how much the three states depend on Russian energy.

In other aspects of the economy, Lithuania has made bigger strides toward privatization than the other Baltic states, selling off close to 60 percent of state enterprises for cash and vouchers. However, many citizens used the vouchers to purchase apartments they had been renting from the state. More than half of private enterprises were small businesses sold at public auction.

By year's end, the economy continued to sputter, though the introduction of the litas had helped reduce inflation to .9 percent in August, 4.2 in September, 7.3 in October and 6.8 percent in November. But industrial production had fallen by 22 percent compared to 1992, and it was projected that the government would be totally dependent on Russia for oil in 1994.

Another major issue in 1993 was the withdrawal of Soviet troops, long considered an occupying army. On 22 August Russia said it had broken off talks on the troop pullout and warned Vilnius that its response would be "swift and decisive" if the Russians suffered any intimidation. The final 2,500 troops out of the 30,000 originally stationed there were scheduled to be removed 31 August. President Brazauskas subsequently canceled a trip to Moscow. After a brief standoff, both sides announced the last of the troops would leave on schedule. In Vilnius, jubilant government officials handed out stickers with the national coat of arms and the legend: "Lithuania, Free of Foreign Troops." The withdrawal was seen as a triumph for President Brazauskas and his policy of maintaining strong links with Russia. Mr. Landsbergis, however, criticized the government for being too accommodating to Moscow in dropping compensation claims for the decades of Russian occupation. The pullout came just four days before the visit of Pope John Paul II to this predominantly Roman Catholic country—the pontiff's first visit to a former Soviet republic.

On 18 November, Russian Prime Minister Viktor Chernomyrdyn and other officials flew to Vilnius where they signed nine bilateral agreements and a protocol. The most important document was a most-favored-nation trade treaty that halved Russian duties on goods imported from Lithuania. The talks also considered Russian compensation for damages since 1940, and the return of several foreign embassy buildings.

Relations with Moscow were strained somewhat toward year's end as Lithuania and the other Baltic states endorsed a U.S. proposal for joint military exercises and peacekeeping operations with the NATO allies.

Political Rights and Civil Liberties: Citizens have the means to change their government democratically. There are numerous political parties covering the range of the political spectrum. In 1993, the country held its first direct election for president. Parliamentary elections in 1992 were free and fair.

In February, the *Seimas* passed a law on the nine-member Constitutional Court, providing that it will rule whether any laws or government decrees conflict with the constitution or other passed legislation. The judiciary is independent and free from government interference. In 1993, several tough laws were passed to combat rapidly spreading, often violent organized crime activities. On 13 June parliament approved detention of up to two months for individuals suspected of planning to commit crimes detailed in Article 227 of the Criminal Code. The article, "Organizing, Leading, or Participation in a Criminal Organization (Group)," was passed on 28 January. The law is temporary, only in force until 1 January 1994. Parliament also unanimously abrogated a law on punishment for homosexuality.

Freedom of the press is generally accepted, though political figures, including the president, have criticized what they called unnecessarily sensational coverage of the government and economic policy. There are private radio and television stations, and a variety of independent papers and journals. On 12 October a prominent journalist with the popular daily *Respublika*, Vitas Lingys, was shot at point-blank range near his home. He had specialized in exposing organized crime and had been the target of numerous death threats.

Freedom of religion is guaranteed and respected in this largely Roman Catholic country. Ethnic minority rights are generally respected, though there have been some complaints of discrimination by the Polish community. Minority nationalities have access to primary and secondary education in their own languages, State television and radio offer a fair selection of broadcasts in minority languages, and there are numerous publications in Polish and Russian. Freedom of domestic and international travel is guaranteed.

There is some inequality based on sex. Women are underrepresented in certain professions and in managerial sectors, but are entitled to day-care and maternity benefits. Alcohol abuse by husbands is a common cause of spousal abuse. There are several women's organizations that are working to increase government and public awareness of women's issues.

Various independent trade unions formed the Lithuanian Trade Union Association in 1992.

Luxembourg

Polity: Parliamentary democracy
Economy: Capitalist
Population: 388,000
PPP: $19,244
Life Expectancy: 74.9
Ethnic Groups: Luxembourgers (70 percent) and other Europeans (30 percent)

Political Rights: 1
Civil Liberties: 1
Status: Free

Overview:

In 1993, Luxembourg continued to enjoy prosperity, but its semi-nationalized steel industry faced severe problems. Within the context of European unity, the country remains pro-European unity, but has some anxiety about being overwhelmed by bigger countries.

The Grand Duchy of Luxembourg received international recognition as an independent neutral country in 1867. However, Germany occupied the country during both world wars. Since World War II, Luxembourg has advocated a united Europe, and belongs to both the European Union (EU) and NATO.

Grand Duke Jean is head of state. He appoints the prime minister from the party or coalition able to command a majority in the sixty-member Chamber of Deputies. Voters elect deputies by proportional representation for a maximum term of five years. There is also an appointive Council of State, a twenty-one-member body with life terms. The Chamber can overturn the Council's decisions. In the general election of 1989, the center-right Christian Social Party won 22 seats; the Socialist Workers' Party, 18; and the liberal Democratic Party, 11. The growing Green Alternative won 4 seats, and the Communists captured 1. Winning 4 seats, a new force, the Five-Sixths Party, advocates pensions worth five-sixths of the final salary for all workers, not just for the civil servants. Prime Minister Jacques Santer heads a Christian Social-Socialist coalition government.

Unemployment in Luxembourg remained below 2 percent in 1993. It was the only country to meet all the economic requirements for European monetary union. For three generations, the Luxembourger and Belgian currencies have been linked. As broader European institutions expand, Luxembourgers fear that Germany, France and other larger countries will exclude the duchy and other small countries from automatic membership on the European Commission and other European bodies. Fernand Rau, the Five-Sixths leader, opposes a common European citizenship. Although other Luxembourgers share this view, Rau's party finished behind the Greens in local elections in 1993.

Luxembourg has based its prosperity on a strong industrial base. However, the long-term decline in the steel industry worldwide has taken its toll. In April 1993, the government announced that Arbed, the money-losing, semi-state steel company, would have to borrow heavily and restructure, in order to stay alive through the year 2000. The company will cut personnel and reinvest borrowed capital.

Political Rights and Civil Liberties:

Luxembourgers have the right to change their government by democratic means. Since outsiders constitute about one-third of the country's residents, Luxembourg's politicians have worked out a deal with the European Community to exempt the country from the voting rights provision of the Maastricht treaty on European union. This provision would have required granting local voting rights to other EU nationals. Non-Luxembourgers have no right to vote at any electoral level, but they are free otherwise.

There is freedom of speech and of the press. Print journalism is private and uncensored, except for restrictions on pornography. Broadcast media are state-chartered and free. Publications appear in various languages. The schools use both French and standard German, while the courts use French. In ordinary conversations and in some of the media, most Luxembourgers prefer Letzebuergesch, their own Germanic language. There is a movement to have the tongue made an officially recognized European language, in order to protect the small country's distinct identity.

The judiciary is independent and fair. In 1993, the government and the Supreme Court had a dispute over releasing $36 million from a bank account to a Colombian depositor. The judges ruled that the suspected drug profits be turned over to the Colombian. However, the government decided otherwise, because legal actions on the case were still pending in the U.S. in 1994. The country has freedom of association. The steel industry, agricultural interests and small businesses all have lobbying groups. Affiliated with the Socialist and Christian Social parties, two competing labor federations organize workers. The population is mostly Catholic. There is religious freedom and no state church. The productive economy is largely private.

Macedonia

Polity: Presidential-parliamentary democracy
Economy: Mixed statist
Population: 1,949,000
PPP: na
Life Expectancy: 70.0
Ethnic Groups: Macedonians (64.6 percent), Albanians (21 percent), Turks (5 percent), Romanies (2 percent), Serbs (2 percent), Macedonian Muslims (2.5 percent)
Ratings Change: *Macedonia's civil liberties rating changed from 4 to 3 as a result of modifications in methodology. See "Survey Methodology," page 671.

Political Rights: 3
Civil Liberties: 3*
Status: Partly Free

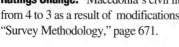

Overview: In 1993 the most important issues in Macedonia, the land-locked, impoverished former Yugoslav republic, were the effort to gain international recognition, an alleged plot by ethnic Albanians to forcibly overthrow the government, the presence of United Nations and American troops, and serious economic conditions resulting from the U.N. embargo on trade with rump-Yugoslavia.

Macedonia is a multi-ethnic Balkan state bordering Serbia, Bulgaria, Greece and Albania. Historically a region of contention, Macedonia was ruled by the Ottoman Turks for 500 years prior to the Second Balkan War in 1913, after which its territory was divided among Greece, Serbia and Bulgaria. Several of its neighbors have contended that there is no distinct Macedonian identity.

The unicameral, 120-seat Macedonian Assembly (parliament) was elected in 1990. The Internal Macedonian Revolutionary Organization-Democratic Party for Macedonian National Unity (VMRO-DPMNE) won thirty-seven seats, and the Social-Democratic League of Macedonia (SDLM)—formerly the League of Communists of Macedonia—gained thirty-one seats. The predominantly Albanian Party for Democratic Prosperity (PDP) carried twenty-five seats. Kiro Gligorov of the SDLM was named president of the country.

In September 1992, three months after the collapse of the technocrat-dominated government of Nikola Kljusev, a new three-party coalition government was formed consisting of the SDLM, the centrist Reform Forces-Liberal Party (RF-LP), and the Party for Democratic Prosperity-National Democratic Party (PDP-NDP). It was headed by Prime Minister Branko Crvenkovski of the SDLM.

In January 1993, the government in Skopje, the capital, accused Greece of repeatedly violating Macedonian airspace with military aircraft. Greece continued to insist that it would never recognize Macedonia until the republic removed the word "Macedonia" (also a region of northern Greece) from its official name, arguing that Macedonia harbored claims on Greek territory. Athens, which imposed an economic embargo on Macedonia, had persuaded the European Community (EC) and the United States to withhold recognition.

In a 16 February parliamentary address, President Gligorov rejected a U.N. compromise proposal to use the name "Former Yugoslav Republic of Macedonia" (FYROM) in order to gain admission to the world body. [Earlier, the president had already accepted the name to allow membership in the International Monetary Fund (IMF) and the World Bank.] The next day, the Greek government said the speech reflected Macedonia's "disdain for the international community." In September, the Greeks agreed to direct talks under U.N. auspices.

In April the Security Council approved U.N. membership of Macedonia under the provisional FYROM after a compromise was reached with Greece. Under the agreement, Macedonia could not fly its flag outside U.N. headquarters in New York. On 13 April, the Crvenkovski government survived a no-confidence vote, as sixty-two deputies voted for the government. The vote was demanded by the VMRO-DPMNE concerning the country's admittance to the U.N. as the FYROM, and the difficult economic situation in the country.

Macedonia's strategic location and lack of a viable army had led the U.N. to station 800 troops in the country to discourage Serbia from spreading the Bosnia-Herzegovina conflict into the country. In June, President Bill Clinton authorized the deployment of 300 U.S. soldiers to beef up U.N. forces in northern Macedonia. The first U.S. troops arrived in July.

Throughout the year, tensions mounted between the government and the Albanian minority. In the summer, Nevzat Halili, president of the Party for Democratic Prosperity, the largest Albanian party, which had a vice-president and four ministers in the government, warned that the Albanian parties might quit the coalition and provoke a parliamentary crisis leading to new elections. He said Albanians in Macedonia are second-class citizens.

Ethnic relations were further exacerbated in early November, when the government announced that it had uncovered a wide-scale operation to smuggle weapons into the country to arms a 20,000-man army to establish an autonomous Albanian region that would ultimately unite with Albania. Among those arrested was Assistant Defense

Minister Hisen Haskaj and other Albanian political figures. In 1992, Albanians in Struga had briefly proclaimed a so-called Republic of Albanians in Yugoslavia, known as Ilirid. The VMRO-DPMNE accused Albania of masterminding the plot. On 12 November, the Albanian government denied any role in the conspiracy, and the predominately Albanian National Democratic Party accused the government of trying to influence public opinion against Albanians. The interior minister reported that hundreds of guns were found and a list of 20,000 possible recruits for an all-Albanian force. The PDP leadership also denied any involvement in the case.

The government won its third confidence vote on 16 November. A censure motion was sponsored by the VMRO-DPMNE over the government's handling of the investigation concerning the alleged plot to form Albanian paramilitary units. Some seventy-one deputies supported the prime minister, thirty-six were against, and two abstained.

In early December, the foreign ministry called for U.N. assistance in resuming talks with Greece on outstanding bilateral differences after Greece blocked Macedonia's entrance into the Conference on Security and Cooperation in Europe (CSCE). By mid-month, several leading EC members, including Britain, France, Germany, Italy, the Netherlands, and Denmark, said they were prepared to ignore Greek reservations and establish full diplomatic relations with Macedonia by the end of the year.

The disintegration of Yugoslavia and the war in Bosnia contributed to a continued decline in the country's economy. The loss of trading partners in Serbia and, to a lesser extent, Slovenia and Croatia, had already caused the country to lose 70 percent of its export markets. Real wages fell by 30 percent. U.N. resolutions imposing sanctions on rump-Yugoslavia, further isolated this land-locked country. According to official estimates, in 1992 U.N. sanctions against Serbia cost Macedonia $1.3 billion due to production stoppages. In October, the government said that industrial production since the beginning on 1993 was down 13 percent.

In November, the government prepared a new macro-economic program for 1994. Under the IMF-inspired plan, public expenditure would be reduced, controls would be placed on wages and pensions, and there would be tighter monetary policies. The government projected a more moderate rate of inflation of some 70 percent on an annual level. On 21 December, Prime Minister Crvenkovski presented the package to parliament. He said that the program was based on credit financing from the IMF, the World Bank and the European Bank for Reconstruction and Development.

Political Rights and Civil Liberties: Macedonians can change their government democratically. An independent judiciary has yet to be completely established. Political parties are free to organize and function, and there are several ethnic parties representing the interests of Albanians, Serbs and others. However, there have been cases where freedom of expression has been curtailed. In May, Albanian groups protested the arrest of a leading member of the Albanian National Unity organization. In March, Serbs in the country demanded changes in the constitution that would entitle them to the same rights as those enjoyed by ethnic Albanians and Turks. The Democratic Party of Serbs in Macedonia (DPSM) asserted that the constitution, while referring specifically to Macedonians, Turks, Albanians, Romanies (Gypsies), and Vlachs, makes no mention of ethnic Serbs. The party also said that, unlike the other groups, there are no Serbian secondary schools, no Serbian-language radio or television broadcasts, and no newspapers and cultural organizations. Albanians have consistently criticized discrimination in employment and limitations on Albanian television and radio broadcasts, Albanian-language schools, and underrepresentation in the military and police forces.

The independent press faces economic constraints, and government-owned printing presses limit competition. There are four daily newspapers in Skopje and numerous other publications. There is an Albanian newspaper and a Turkish one. Macedonian Radio-Television (MRT) is state-owned, and transmits programs in several languages. There are several small radio and television broadcasters throughout the country. Serbs, Albanians and the nationalist VMRO-DPMNE opposition have claimed denial of fair access to the broadcast media.

Freedom of religion is respected, and the dominant faiths are Macedonian Ortho-dox and Muslim. There are some restrictions on domestic and foreign travel. There are over 35,000 refugees from Bosnia in the country. The government announced that no more refugees will be permitted.

The constitution and laws guarantee men and women equal rights, but women face discrimination in employment and education, particularly in rural areas.

The Union of Independent and Autonomous Trade Unions (UNNIA) confederation was formed in 1992, with six member unions. The Council of Trade Unions of Macedonia (SSSM) is the successor of the old Communist labor confederation. Strikes are permitted in all industries and sectors.

Madagascar

Polity: Presidential-par-
liamentary democracy
Economy: Mixed statist
Population: 11,942,000
PPP: $704
Life Expectancy: 54.5
Ethnic Groups: Malayan-Indonesian highlanders;
coastal peoples of Black African and racially mixed origins;
small groups of Europeans, Asians and Creoles
Ratings Change: *Madagascar's political rights rating changed from
4 to 2 because of the completion of democratic transitional elections.

Political Rights: 2*
Civil Liberties: 4
Status: Partly Free

Overview: Madagascar's transition to democracy was the major development of 1993. With nearly 67 percent of the vote, Professor
Albert Zafy defeated longtime ruler Admiral Didier Ratsiraka
in the presidential run-off election held on 10 February 1993. Zafy, leader of the Active Forces opposition coalition, carried five of the six provinces, and swept Antananarivo, the capital, with 77 percent. The opposition parties consolidated their victory by winning a majority in the parliamentary elections on 16 June.

Madagascar, a large island and five small isles off the southeastern coast of Africa, won independence from France in 1960. Ratsiraka ruled from 1974 until his defeat in 1993. In March 1990, a High Constitutional Court decree permitted independent political parties. Thereafter, several ideologically diverse parties gained legal status.

In June 1991, partisans of the Active Forces coalition that opposed Ratsiraka launched a series of major protests in the capital and other major cities. The opposition demanded a new constitution, a sovereign national conference, and Ratsiraka's resignation. Hundreds of thousands of people rallied for several weeks of nonviolent demonstrations. Following continued unrest, in October 1991 Ratsiraka and Prime Minister Guy Razanamasay formed a new unity government that included the opposition. They also dissolved the National Assembly and the Supreme Revolutionary Council, and established a transitional High State Authority. The transition also included promises of a new constitution and constitutional referendum. In November 1991, Zafy became president of the High State Authority.

As the opposition had sought, a national conference took place in 1992. Several violent incidents disrupted its proceedings, but the conference did produce a new constitution. The proposed document provided for a unitary state and a strong presidency. The opposition wrote the constitution with these structural features in order to reduce the power of pro-Ratsiraka regionalists (called "federalists") after a national opposition victory. Voters approved the constitution in August 1992.

According to his own original timetable, Ratsiraka did not have to face the voters until 1996, but he joined seven other candidates for the first round of presidential elections on 25 November 1992. Zafy and Ratsiraka led the field, but no candidate received more than 50 percent of the vote, so the run-off took place in 1993. Zafy won with the support of other opposition candidates.

Zafy took office on 27 March. The country's poor economy is the most urgent problem facing the new democratic regime. However, Zafy is leaving most details of domestic policy to his prime minister and cabinet. The government must also deal with tensions between the coastal provincials and the more elite population of the central plateau. Ratsiraka recognized the potential for a social explosion, and predicted that after his departure the presidential palace would be "an abbatoir."

Zafy faced a major crisis on 1 April when government commandos clashed with armed, pro-Ratsiraka rebels. A radio station owned by the ex-president charged that the fighting killed four people and that pillaging followed in the northern town of Antsiranana. Authorities placed three captains involved under house arrest.

In parliamentary elections on 16 June, Active Forces and other anti-Ratsiraka elements won a commanding majority of seats. As a result of electoral irregularities, there had to be repeat elections in a few districts. In August, Francisque Ravony, Deputy Prime Minister in the transitional government, became Prime Minister after defeating Roger Ralison in a parliamentary vote. Ralison was the candidate of the Active Forces political department. Ravony belongs to the pro-presidential majority, but was not a top anti-Ratsiraka leader.

Political Rights and Civil Liberties: Malagasy voters can change their government by democratic means. There were a few irregularities in parliamentary voting in 1993, but the anti-Ratsiraka opposition won in generally free and fair elections. Pro-Ratsiraka elements in the provinces may threaten the newly democratic system.

There is a vibrant private press. The government abolished censorship officially in 1990. When Ratsiraka attempted to reimpose censorship under the 1991 state of emergency, the private press refused to cooperate. Television is government-controlled, but there are now private radio stations.

An independent judiciary functions without government interference. Upon his inauguration, Zafy granted a general amnesty to political prisoners and reduced sentences for certain crimes. Thereby, the new president undid several abuses of the old regime. However, prison conditions remain horrible for the remaining inmates. Several free labor organizations exist, many with political affiliations. Workers have the right to join unions and strike. Widespread poverty and significant regional differences limit equality of opportunity. The traditional elite is of Malayan-Indonesian descent, but most of the population is of African origin. A South Asian minority forms a significant part of the commercial class.

There is religious freedom. Clergymen played a major role in the anti-Ratsiraka opposition. Christianity, Islam, traditional Malagasy religions and other faiths coexist. In the context of a generally poor economy, women have significant economic and social rights. Citizenship passes to children matrilineally.

Malawi

Polity: Dominant party (transitional)
Economy: Capitalist
Population: 8,709,000
PPP: $640
Life Expectancy: 48.1
Ethnic Groups: Chewa, Nyanja, Tumbuku, other

Political Rights: 6
Civil Liberties: 5*
Status: Not Free

Ratings Change: *Malawi's civil liberties rating changed from 7 to 5 because opposition forces won a referendum on multipartyism, a major blow against the one-party regime of President Banda.

Overview: After a twenty-nine year dictatorship, President Hastings Kamuzu Banda slowly relinquished power in 1993, paving the way for multiparty elections.

Banda has ruled Malawi since independence from Britain in 1964. In 1972, he named himself as President-for-Life. During his reign, he stifled dissent with the help of his Malawi Congress Party (MCP) and paramilitary thugs known as the Young Pioneers, instituting one of the most repressive regimes in Africa. The rubber-stamp National Assembly consisted of elected and appointed MCP members.

In failing health, the ninety-plus years old Banda relied increasingly on the powerful MCP Executive Committee member, John Tembo, later named Minister of State in the President's Office, for running the government. Tembo's niece and Banda's mistress, "Mama" C. Tamanda Kadzamira, was Malawi's "Official Hostess."

After a Catholic bishops' pastoral letter in March 1992 criticized human rights abuses, Banda faced increasing domestic and international pressure to legalize multipartyism. His rejection of reforms and his crackdown on churches and opposition groups misfired after Western donor countries suspended aid in May 1993, pending reforms. On 18 October Banda announced an unexpected referendum on multipartyism.

In the early 1990s, several internal and exiled opposition groups emerged. The largest internal organizations were the Alliance for Democracy (AFORD) and the United Democratic Front (UDF). Among the exile groups, most prominent was the Zambia-based United Front for Multiparty Democracy (UFMD). In 1993 the government cautioned that the referendum campaign did not mean that opposition parties could operate freely, and arrested opposition activists for possessing membership cards, asserting that they were seditious documents.

In April 1992 the regime arrested Chakufwa Chihana, the secretary general of the Southern Africa Trade Union Coordination Council and, later, an AFORD founding member, for meeting with the Malawian opposition in Zambia. In December 1992, a court charged Chihana with sedition and sentenced him to two years' imprisonment with hard labor. In March 1993 an appellate court reduced the sentence to nine months. In June he was released for "good behavior." Other opposition figures arrested in 1993 include the UDF chairman Bakili Muluzi, charged with misappropriating MCP funds in the 1970s when he was its secretary general, and UFMD leader Edmond Phika after his arrival from Zambia. Muluzi and Phika were released within days of their arrests. In January, Banda commuted the life sentence and ordered the release of Vera Chirwa, following the death of her husband, Orton Chirwa, Malawi's best known political prisoner. The latter died due to illness from the abysmal prison conditions. Banda refused to allow Mrs. Chirwa to participate in her husband's funeral.

On 31 December 1992 Banda set the date for the referendum on multipartyism for 15 March 1993, soon thereafter appointing a referendum preparation commission packed with his present and former lieutenants. The opposition rejected the date as leaving too little time for campaigning, and called for its postponement until June. The opposition also demanded an independent referendum commission, free access to the media, no restrictions on campaigning, and the repeal of security legislation and sedition laws. On 5 February, in response to a letter written by U.N. Secretary General Boutros Boutros-Ghali, Banda announced the referendum's rescheduling to 14 June.

In the referendum, deemed fair by international observers, 63 percent of the electorate chose multipartyism. Following the crushing blow to Banda and the MCP, the president initially refused to step down and order new elections. However, on 23 June Banda and the opposition agreed to advisory councils to oversee pre-election preparations. The National Consultative Council (NCC) was to parallel the single-party National Assembly, and the National Executive Council (NEC), the cabinet. Both councils were empowered to advise and demand information from the government. On 29 June, the Assembly repealed the laws prohibiting opposition parties.

On 3 October Banda underwent brain surgery in South Africa, and was subsequently unable to perform presidential duties. In accordance with the existing constitution, a three-member presidential council, led by the secretary general of the ruling party, became the highest authority for the duration of Banda's incapacitation. The three council members were John Tembo, Banda's most likely successor; Gwandaguluwe Chakuamba, a former political prisoner and member of the UDF who returned to the MCP just after the announcement of Banda's illness; and Robson Chirwa, the Minister of Transport and Communications.

On 17-18 November the parliament made constitutional amendments paving the way for Malawi's first multi-party elections scheduled for May 1994. The amendments included a bill of rights in the constitution, the repeal of life presidency and of the the presidential right to nominate MP's exclusively from the MCP. On 12 December the opposition heeded a court's order to cancel a three-day general strike. Through the strike it hoped to force the parliament to remove all executive authority from an interim MCP-appointed president in the case of Banda's death. In December, Banda resumed his presidential duties, appointing a minister of defense and ordering the disarmament of the Young Pioneers.

Political Rights and Civil Liberties: Malawians are not yet able to change their government by democratic means. Nevertheless, Malawians were able to choose multipartyism in a referendum in June 1993. In accordance with overwhelming popular support for political pluralism, the parliament amended the constitution to allow for multiparty legislative and presidential elections in May 1994. In December 1993 the President appointed a multiparty electoral commission to supervise electoral preparations.

Parliament legalized opposition parties on 29 June 1993. Prior to that date the security forces harassed and arrested opposition activists. Despite promised multiparty elections, several people charged with sedition remained in Malawi's squalid prisons.

A longtime tool of Banda, the judiciary has become increasingly independent. In March, Minister of Justice and Prosecutor General Friday Makuta resigned, accusing the government of interference in trials. In May, a high court issued an unprecedented verdict against the government, ordering it to pay $1 million in damages to a former detainee who the court found had spent twenty years in unlawful detention. How-ever, the president still appointed or dismissed judges single-handedly and the court system remained divided into "traditional" and "modern." In the traditional system, which tries only indigenous Africans, defendants lack legal representation and have to prove their in-nocence in court. The modern courts are based on the British court system, and try defend-ants of all races. Banda had used the traditional system to prosecute his political opponents.

In 1993 the authorities still restricted freedoms of speech, press and assembly by banning public rallies and temporarily shutting down opposition newspapers. Insulting the president was still punishable with a prison term of up to five years. In January, Felix Mponda Phiri, a freelance journalist, was temporarily arrested for carrying preliminary copies of an independent weekly. In February, the government banned two AFORD and UDF newspapers, *The Malawi Democrat* and *The UDF News,* prompting both parties to call for boycotting the June referendum.

Freedom of religion is respected only for denominations already established in the country. All religious groups must register with the government, and permission for new groups to register is seldom granted. Jehovah's Witnesses have been banned and persecuted since 1967. The Catholic Church and other denominations undermined the one-party state by criticizing governmental abuse of human rights.

Workers have the right to form and join trade unions, which by law must be affiliated with the Trade Union Congress of Malawi (TUCM). The Banda regime discouraged the use of the strike as a workers' bargaining tool, often brutally persecut-ing strike organizers and participants. With changes in the political climate, the Ministry of Labor announced in September 1993 the government's willingness to recognize strikes as legitimate. The announcement came after strikes by government employees and sugar plantation workers demanding pay raises of up to 100 percent.

Women remain largely subservient to men. However, some ethnic groups pass property through women. Female circumcision exists in some areas.

Malaysia

Polity: Dominant party
Economy: Capitalist
Population: 18,742,000
PPP: $6,140
Life Expectancy: 70.1
Ethnic Groups: Malays (50 percent), Chinese (35 percent), Indians (15 percent)
Ratings Change: *Malaysia's political rights rating changed from 5 to 4 and its civil liberties from 4 to 5 as a result of modifications in methodology. See "Survey Methodology," page 671.

Political Rights: 4*
Civil Liberties: 5*
Status: Partly Free

Overview: Malaysia's ruling United Malay National Organization (UMNO) elected Finance Minister Anwar Ibrahim to its number two post at the November 1993 party elections, making him the likely eventual successor to Prime Minister Mahathir Mohamad, who has served since 1981. The forty-six-year-old Anwar drew widespread support among a younger generation of urbanized ethnic Malays, who trust him to carry out Dr. Mahathir's goal of transforming Malaysia into a fully industrial country by the year 2020.

Malaysia was established in September 1963 through a merger of the formerly British, independent Federation of Malaya with the British colonies of Sarawak, Sabah and Singapore. (Singapore withdrew two years later). The ceremonial head of state is a King chosen for a five-year term by and from among the hereditary sultans of the nine Malay states. The King, currently the Sultan of Perak, can delay federal legislation for thirty days. Executive power is vested in the prime minister and a cabinet. The parliament consists of a Senate, with 32 members appointed by the king and 26 elected by the 13 state legislatures, and a 180-member, popularly elected House of Representatives. Each of Malaysia's thirteen states has its own parliament and constitution and shares legislative powers with the federal government.

Reaction to the ethnic Chinese minority's economic success triggered race riots in 1969. At the time ethnic Malays made up half the population but owned only 2 percent of the wealth. In 1971 the government responded with the New Economic Policy (NEP), which discriminated in favor of Malays through racial quotas in education, civil service opportunities and business affairs. The Malays now hold a 20 percent economic share, although the urban elite has prospered much more than the rural *Bumiputras* (sons of the soil). A new National Development Policy adopted in 1991 has the same basic goals as the NEP.

UMNO is the dominant party in the ruling National Front coalition which currently includes ten parties and has captured at least a two-thirds majority in the lower house in all eight general elections since 1957. UMNO is a secular, conservative party representing traditional Malay interests. By tradition, the top two UMNO leaders serve as the country's prime minister and deputy prime minister. In July 1981 Dr. Mahathir Mohamad won the UMNO presidency and became prime minister. The party's claim to represent all Malays through consensual decision-making was shattered in April 1987, when top UMNO figures tried to oust Mahathir for alleged mismanagement and corruption. The party split on factional lines, and a court deregistered it in February 1988. The pro-Mahathir faction subsequently formed the present UMNO-Baru (New).

In late 1988 former trade minister Razaleigh Hamzah led disgruntled UMNO members in forming Semangat '46 (Spirit of '46, the year UMNO was founded in Malaya). In May 1989 this new party joined with the Muslim fundamentalist Pan-Malaysian Islamic Party (Pas) and two smaller parties in a Malay-based opposition called the Muslim Unity Movement (APU). At the October 1990 national elections, the ruling National Front won 127 seats (UMNO, 71; the Malaysian Chinese Association, 18; the Malaysian Indian Congress, 6; the social democratic Malaysian People's Movement, 5; the United Sabah National Organization, 6; affiliated independents, 21). The opposition won 53 seats, a gain of 25 from 1986, led by the center-left, Chinese-based Democratic Action Party (DAP) with 20; the multiracial United Sabah Party (PBS), 14; Semangat '46, 8; Pas, 7; independents, 4.

UMNO controls eleven of the thirteen state governments, and has sharply cut back on development funds to the opposition-controlled states of Sabah and Kelantan. The government has maintained steady pressure on Sabah Chief Minister Joseph Kitangan, who pulled the PBS out of the ruling coalition days before the 1990 national election. Kitangan has been on trial since January 1992 on corruption charges. In 1993 the government announced a nationwide ban on raw log exports, which account for over half of Sabah's revenue.

At the national level UMNO faces minimal opposition. In 1993 the ruling party faced a potentially divisive split over the sixty-nine-year-old Mahathir's successor. The November party elections pitted the incumbent, Deputy Prime Minister Ghafar Baba, against Finance Minister and UMNO Vice President Anwar Ibrahim for the deputy president post. Although Ghafar appeared to be in line for the top posts, many in the party doubted his ability to carry on the prime minister's forward-looking development strategies. Indeed, the sixty-nine-year-old Ghafar represented UMNO's conservative, rural rank-and-file voters, who still adhere to the party's traditional Malay-nationalist roots. By contrast the forty-six-year-old Anwar epitomized a younger generation of urbanized, business-oriented ethnic Malays.

By mid-October Anwar had already secured 145 nominations from the 153 UMNO divisions around the country. On 15 October Ghafar resigned as deputy prime minister, and six days later quit as UMNO deputy president. On 4 November Anwar easily won the deputy presidency, putting him in position to succeed Mahathir.

The year's other leading issue was the removal of the sultans' legal immunity and power to pardon their family members from criminal charges. The current reform drive began in earnest in November 1992 after the sixty-year-old Sultan of Johor severely beat a field hockey coach. In February 1993 the sultans agreed to a compromise which stripped their immunity powers but provided for a special court of five federal and state supreme court justices to hear any cases against them.

Political Rights and Civil Liberties:

The ability of Malaysians to change their government democratically is limited by ethnic Malay and United Malay National Organization dominance. A Commonwealth election team rated the 1990 elections free but not entirely fair, largely due to the government's control of the media, irregularities in voting roles, and a ban on political rallies. Official policy limits access for non-Malays in education, the civil service, and business licenses and ownership.

The government continues to detain former Communists, religious extremists, and others under the 1960 Internal Security Act (ISA) and the 1969 Emergency (Essential Powers) Ordinance. Under the ISA, police can detain suspects for up to sixty days without filing formal charges; the Ministry of Home Affairs can authorize a further detention of up to two years.

The judiciary is independent in civil and criminal cases, and has shown a high degree of independence in political cases. Defendents generally receive fair trials. Freedom of speech is restricted by the 1970 Sedition Act Amendments, which prohibit discussion of issues considered sensitive, such as the special position of Malays in society. The 1984 Printing Presses and Publications Act requires domestic and foreign publications to register annually with the government. A 1987 amendment to this Act makes the publication of "malicious" news an offense and expands the government's power to ban or restrict publications. All major newspapers and all radio and television stations are owned by the government or by companies owned by the ruling National Front parties, and their coverage of opposition parties is limited. Smaller papers, particularly those published by the Chinese community, do criticize the government.

The 1967 Police Act requires permits for all public assemblies. Following the 1969 riots, political rallies were banned; currently only indoor "discussion sessions" are permitted. The Societies Act requires any association of more than six members to register with the government; a similiar law applies to student groups, which are barred from political activity.

Islam is the official religion in this secular country, but minority groups worship freely. Malaysians are free to travel within the country, and can generally travel freely abroad.

The government must approve of and can dissolve all unions, and each labor group can cover only one particular trade or occupation. The government permits only "in-house" unions in the 120,000-worker electronics industry rather than a nationwide union.

Strikes are legal but restricted. Under the 1967 Industrial Relations Act unions must provide advance notice in several "essential services," some of which are not considered essential by the International Labor Organization.

Maldives

Polity: Non-party presidential-legislative (elite clan-dominated)
Economy: Capitalist
Population: 222,000
PPP: $1,200
Life Expectancy: 62.5
Ethnic Groups: Mixed Sinhalese, Dravidian, Arab, and black

Political Rights: 6
Civil Liberties: 6*
Status: Not Free

Ratings Change: *Maldives's civil liberties rating changed from 5 to 6 as a result of modifications in methodology. See "Survey Methodology," page 671.

Overview: In June 1993 President Maumoon Abdul Gayoom sacked his brother-in-law, Minister of Atolls Administration Ilyas Ibrahim, allegedly for using witchcraft to influence lawmakers in order to win the August parliamentary nominations for the October presidential referendum. On 23 August, the president won the parliamentary nomination with twenty-eight votes, but Ibrahim, who had fled to Singapore, won a surprising eighteen votes, while his brother, Fisheries Minister Allyas Ibrahim, took one. On 5 October President Gayoom was relected to a fifth term with a 92 percent approval in a "yes or no" referendum. Afterwards, the president pledged to change the constitution to allow more than one candidate in the next referendum.

The poor, Islamic, Republic of Maldives is a 500-mile-long string of nineteen mostly uninhabited atolls in the Indian Ocean. The British granted independence in July 1965. In 1968 a referendum ended the ad-Din sultanate's 815-year rule, and a new constitution gave the president extensive powers, including the right to dismiss the prime minister and appoint top officials. The *Majlis* (parliament) has forty directly elected seats and eight appointed by the president. Every five years the Majlis elects a single presidential candidate, and forwards this choice to the electorate for a yes-or-no referendum. Political parties are not proscribed, but are strongly discouraged and none exists.

Successive governments have faced several coup attempts. Most recently, in 1988 the president called in Indian troops to crush a coup attempt by Sri Lankan mercenaries allegedly hired by a Maldivian businessman. In the aftermath, the president increased the National Security Service to 2,000 troops and named several relatives to top posts. The February 1990 Majlis elections brought in a crop of activists who sought to enact democratic reforms, encouraging journalists to report on official corruption and nepotism. But by June the government banned all independent media, and late in the year it arrested several journalists. In 1991 and 1992 the president maintained the ban on independent publications.

Political Rights and Civil Liberties: Maldivians cannot change their government democratically. The parliament nominates the president, who holds wide powers. The government has successfully discouraged organized political opposition, and although political parties are legal, none exists. Although citizens can lodge complaints through certain channels, such as petitioning members of the Majlis, the constitution prevents actions which would "arouse people against the government."

In December 1990 the Majlis passed a strict Prevention of Terrorism Act that could be applied retroactively. In November and December 1990 police arrested and charged several journalists under the Act. In December 1991 a court sentenced Mohamed "Saape" Shafeeq, former editor of the magazine *Sangu*, to eleven years in prison for planning to blow up a conference center, although there appears to be scant evidence to support this. No lawyers were willing to defend Shafeeq. *Sangu* had published articles on government corruption and other sensitive issues. Among the others arrested: Illyas, a journalist for the *Manthiri* newspaper who goes by one name, is reportedly awaiting trial; *Sangu* journalist Mohamed Nasheed was released in February 1993 but is still under house arrest; Ali Waheed, a journalist with the newspaper *Hukuru* has been banished to a remote island; and *Hukuru's* Naushad Waheed is serving a four-year prison sentence. The state-run media carry only official views.

The constitution guarantees freedom of assembly, but citizens rarely gather for political purposes. The president exercises partisan control over the judiciary through his power to appoint and remove judges. The legal system is based on Islamic law and does not grant adequate procedural protection to the accused. Criminals can be flogged and banished to remote islands, and prison conditions are harsh. Clubs and civic associations are permitted only for non-political purposes. The constitution defines all citizens as Muslims, and conversion to other religions can lead to a loss of citizenship. The government denies workers the right to form unions or strike.

Mali

Polity: Presidential-par-
liamentary democracy
Economy: Mixed statist
Population: 8,538,000
PPP: $572
Life Expectancy: 45.0
Ethnic Groups: Arab Bedouin, Bambara, Berabish Berber, Dogon, Fulani, Malinke (50 percent), Songhai, Tuareg, other

Political Rights: 2
Civil Liberties: 3
Status: Free

Overview: In 1993, Mali witnessed the resignation of the ten-month-old government of Younnoussi Touré; the sentencing of the former dictator, Mousa Traoré; and an agreement on integration of the former Tuareg rebels into the armed forces.

Mali, known as Soudan at the time of its rule by France, declared its independence in 1960. Under the leadership of its first president, Modibo Keita, the country became a Marxist, single-party state with close Soviet and Communist China leanings. In 1968 a group of army officers under the leadership of Moussa Traoré ousted Keita, reversing his collectivist policies. In 1979 the military formally relinquished power, Traore becoming a civilian president, and his Mali People's Democratic Union (UDPM) the sole new political party.

In 1990, Traoré responded to public demonstrations in support of a multi-party system by brutally suppressing all dissent. According to estimates, up to 250 people were killed and hundreds of others injured by security forces who sprayed the protesters with machine-gun fire. Finally, in an attempt to end the street violence, military officers moved to depose and arrest Traoré in March 1991. On 12 February 1993 a seven-judge court sentenced Traoré and three other high-ranking military officers to death over the killings.

Following the coup, the military shared the government with civilians in the Transitional Committee for National Salvation (CTSP). A national conference of all newly constituted political parties drew up a new electoral code and a new constitution. The series of elections on the local, parliamentary and presidential levels were held throughout the spring of 1992. Despite claims of abuses from some of the smaller parties, the elections were considered generally free and fair by international observers. In the election to the local councils and the national legislature the Alliance for Democracy in Mali (ADEMA) garnered most of the seats. In the April presidential runoff Alpha Konaré of the ADEMA won 69 percent of the vote.

Following Konaré's inauguration in June, he appointed Younnoussi Touré to be the new prime minister. With the advent of democracy the country has inherited a large number of economic problems stemming from the years of mismanagement and corruption by the Traoré regime, and from the regional drought affecting the Sahel zone. Prior to the 1992 elections the interim government reached an agreement with the IMF providing for increased financial support for structural adjustments in the economy in exchange for reduction in spending on student grants and the civil service. Despite Touré's criticism of the interim government's economic policy, he continued most of the austerity measures.

One of the first student demands spearheading the 1990 pro-democracy protests was for a 200 percent increase in grants. Following the formation of the interim government, the Association of Malian Students and Pupils (AEEM) joined in the ruling coalition, toning down their previous demands. With ADEMA's clear electoral victory, AEEM found itself on political sidelines, split into a radical faction with close ties to the opposition National Congress for the Democratic Initiative (CNID), led by its Secretary-General Yehia Ould Zarawana, and a pro-ADEMA faction. Following the replacement of Zarawana with the pro-ADEMA Amadoun Bah in February, the radical students organized a series of protests, warning of a "new one-party state," and resuscitating their demands for grant increases. The protests escalated on 5 April with demonstrators demanding the resignation of the government and setting fire to the parliament building and a number of other public buildings and private buildings belonging to government officials. On 9 April, the prime minister announced his resignation, which was accepted by the president who had warned of a return to the situation "before 1991," and asked the students to respect the public and private property. At the same time, Konaré started negotiations with opposition parties on forming a coalition cabinet with ADEMA. On 13 April Konaré appointed Abdoulaye Sekou Sow as the new prime minister. The new government, supported by CNID and a number of smaller parties, decided to introduce new austerity measures by instituting higher import taxes, and reducing the expenditures of ministers and central government agencies.

The armed unrest between the Tuareg and Arab minorities and the military in the northern part of the country receded in the aftermath of the April 1992 peace treaty signed by the government and the Unified Movements and Fronts of the Azaouad (MFUA), the main Tuareg faction. On 11 February 1993 the government and the MFUA reached an agreement to integrate 600 MFUA rebels into the Malian armed forces and reduce the number of army troops in the north. Two days earlier, Mali and Algeria signed an agreement covering the repatriation to Algeria of between 60,000 and 100,000 Tuareg refugees.

Political Rights and Civil Liberties:

Malians can change their government democratically. Twenty-three political parties competed for municipal, legislative and presidential elections in 1992. ADEMA controls 76 out of 116 seats in the national legislature. In January 1992 the voters overwhelmingly approved a new constitution guaranteeing political pluralism and civil liberties.

The new constitution provides for an independent judiciary. Trials are public and defendants are presumed innocent until proven guilty. The defendants' right to have attorneys of their own choice is respected. The Supreme Court has both judicial and administrative powers, while the newly established Constitutional Court deals specifically with the interpretation of the constitutional provisions.

Since the fall of the Traoré regime, the media have enjoyed a virtually unhampered freedom to present differing viewpoints to the public. There are thirty independent newspapers and periodicals. Since 1992, independent broadcasters have been able to operate private radio and television stations.

Freedom of association and the right to peaceful protest are respected. Some forty-six political parties and hundreds of professional and special interest organizations are registered. During the February/April student protests, demonstrators blocked public roads and often vandalized public and private property; the security forces, however, responded cautiously in order to avoid a repetition of the 1991 events.

Malians no longer have to apply for an exit visa in order to travel abroad. The government ordered a clampdown on police officers who extract bribes from motorists traveling to various parts of the country. Occasional road checkpoints are still being used, however, ostensibly to restrict the movement of contraband goods and check vehicle registrations.

Although the overwhelming majority of the population is Muslim, the new constitution stipulates the separation of mosque and state, establishing Mali as a secular republic. Religious worship for the majority and minority religions is unhampered. Proselytizing and conversion are permitted.

The major trade union confederation still remains the National Union of Malian Workers (UNTM), the only union permitted to operate under the Traoré regime. The UNTM, however, was one of the major forces instrumental in bringing down his regime and is an independent force. Several non-UNTM affiliated unions have been recently registered.

Malta

Polity: Parliamentary democracy
Economy: Mixed capitalist-statist
Population: 361,000
PPP: $8,732
Life Expectancy: 73.4
Ethnic Groups: Maltese (mixed Arab, Sicilian, Norman, Spanish, Italian, and English)

Political Rights: 1
Civil Liberties: 1
Status: Free

Overview: In 1993, the conservative Nationalist Party government awaited word from the European Union about its application for membership.

The Nationalists won office in 1987, and secured re-election in 1992 with 51.8 percent to 46.5 percent for Labor and 1.7 percent for the environmentalist Democratic Alternative. The Nationalists hold thirty-four seats to Labor's thirty-one. Prime Minister

Edward Fenech Adami supports full European integration and economic liberalization.

Located in the central Mediterranean, Malta was under foreign rule for most of its history. The British occupied the island in 1800. Later, it became a British colony. Malta gained independence from Britain in 1964. The Labor Party won power in 1971 and held office until 1987. In government, Labor followed a left-of-center economic policy and a neutral foreign policy. It also ordered some confiscation of church property and restricted private financing for Catholic schools. Labor turned to Libya for aid and support in the early 1980s. Even under the Nationalists in the early 1990s, Malta remained a transit point for companies doing business with Libya. Since the Nationalist victory in 1987, the conservatives have reversed Labor's economic and religious policies. The government is carrying out privatization of the state sector and deregulation of the Church.

The parliament, called the House of Representatives, has sixty-five seats and a maximum term of five years. Voters choose the representatives by proportional representation. Elected by parliament, the largely ceremonial president serves for five years, and appoints the prime minister from the parliamentary majority. Under a constitutional amendment adopted in 1987, a party getting a majority of the popular vote wins a majority of the parliamentary seats. In previous elections, it was possible for a party to receive a majority of the vote and a minority of seats.

Reacting to its recent electoral defeats, Labor has moderated its program. The party has dropped its opposition to private hospitals and free trade, and has improved its relations with the Catholic clergy.

Political Rights and Civil Liberties:

The Maltese have the right to change their government democratically, and power alternates between the two major parties.

The Nationalist government has sponsored a pluralization of the broadcast media since 1991. Several private broadcast outlets now exist alongside the older public ones. Malta's constitution guarantees freedoms of speech and press. The only exception is a law passed in 1987 which forbids foreign involvement in Maltese election campaigns. The free press includes many politically oriented newspapers.

Religion is free for both the Catholic majority and religious minorities. There are tiny Protestant and Muslim communities. All groups have freedom of association. Many trade unions belong to the General Union of Workers (GWU), but others are independent. The Labor Party and the GWU severed their links to each other in 1992, in order to pursue more independent policies. A constitutional amendment banning sex discrimination took effect in July 1993.

Marshall Islands

Polity: Parliamentary
democracy
Economy: Capitalist-
statist
Population: 50,000
PPP: na
Life Expectancy: 72.5
Ethnic Groups: Marshallese (Micronesian)

Political Rights: 1
Civil Liberties: 1
Status: Free

Overview:

In 1993, the Marshall Islands had mixed economic news and an end to a passport-buying scandal dating from 1992.

Located in the Pacific Ocean, the Marshall Islands were independent until the late 1800s, when the Germans established a protectorate. After World War I, Japan governed under a League of Nations mandate until the U.S. Navy occupied the region in 1945. The U.S. administered the islands under a United Nations trusteeship after 1947. The Americans recognized a distinct Marshallese constitution in 1979, thereby causing a *de facto* change in the Marshalls' legal status. However, the Soviets and others waged an international legal dispute for several years over the islands' trusteeship. In 1986, the U.S. notified the U.N. formally that the trusteeship was over, and that the Marshalls had implemented a Compact of Free Association with the U.S. Under the Compact, the Marshalls have self-government, but still depend on American defense. Following changes in the international climate, the U.N. recognized the dissolution of the trusteeship in December 1990. In 1991, the Marshall Islands sought and received diplomatic recognition as an independent country and full U.N. membership.

The Marshalls have a parliamentary system. Voters choose the thirty-three-member parliament (*Nitijela*) from twenty-four election districts. The legislators elect a president and cabinet who are responsible to them. Members serve four-year terms. There is also an advisory body of Micronesian chiefs. The most recent legislative election took place in November 1991. The president is Amata Kabua.

The economy depends heavily on U.S. and other foreign assistance. An American base on the uninhabited Kwajalein Atoll is responsible for injecting more than $25 million into the economy—over one-third of the country's annual budget. In 1993, the U.S. promised an expansion of anti-missile testing at the base. The islands may face a tough economic future, because guaranteed American aid runs out by 2002. President Kabua supports the acquisition of more fishing vessels to support a growing economic sector. The Marshalls have a joint venture with China for additional vessels. The country received bad economic news in 1993 when an American company backed out of plans to construct a major resort on the Erikub Atoll. The American concern had signed a deal with traditional leaders, but other landowners mounted a legal challenge to the contract, claiming that the wrong people had signed the agreement. An attempted out-of-court settlement failed in the summer of 1993, and the developer decided to build elsewhere.

In March 1993, Gregory Symons, an Australian, pleaded no contest to charges that he had attempted to sell Marshallese passports to Taiwanese businessmen for $1.25 million. The case had become a major sticking point in Australian-Marshallese relations, because Graham Richardson, a prominent Australian Labor politician, had lobbied on Symons's behalf.

Political Rights and Civil Liberties: The Marshallese have the right to change their government by democratic means. Elections are competitive, but involve individuals, tendencies, and factions, not formal parties.

There is a bill of rights, which protects most civil liberties. Although there is freedom of the press, the government canceled its printing contract with a critical newspaper company in 1991. Ultimately, the government reversed the cancellation. The islands have private and public broadcast media and a private newspaper. In general, there is freedom of speech, but in 1992 the Nitijela held one of its members in contempt for having suggested the possibility of U.S. commonwealth status for the islands. There are some minor restrictions on freedom of movement, due to defense installations and nuclear contamination. The U.S. carried out extensive nuclear testing on the islands from 1946-1958. The cabinet can deport aliens who take part in Marshallese politics, but it has never done so. The government respects freedom of association, but there are no trade unions. Marshallese women have formed several associations and an umbrella organization, Women United Together for the Marshall Islands. The government withdrew its endorsement of Women United Together as the officially recognized women's group in 1992. In the traditional family structure, inheritance passes through the mother. There is religious freedom in this predominantly Christian country.

Mauritania

Polity: Dominant party (military-dominated)
Economy: Capitalist-statist
Population: 2,103,000
PPP: $1,057
Life Expectancy: 47.0
Ethnic Groups: White and Black Maurs, Tuculor, Hal-Pulaar, Soninke, Wolof, others

Political Rights: 7
Civil Liberties: 6
Status: Not Free

Overview: Ethnic violence, gross human rights and civil liberties violations including extrajudicial executions, arbitrary arrest and detention, torture and widespread discrimination against black Maurs and black Africans remain part of the political and social fabric in Mauritania. Despite widespread protests held in the wake of flawed 1992 presidential elections, Colonel Maaouya Ould Sid'Ahmed Taya of the Social and Democratic Republican Party (PRDS) continues to rule the Islamic Republic of Mauritania.

Since achieving independence from France in 1978, Mauritania has been under military rule. Taya assumed power in 1984 as chairman of a military junta, the Military Committee for National Salvation (CMSN), which, until 1992, functioned as the country's legislative body. Taya vowed that his new government would respect human rights and, initially, a number of improvements were made. Political prisoners were freed, the use of cruel and unusual punishment (such as amputation of hands) was ended and the Mauritanian League of Human Rights was established. However, such progress was shortlived. Human rights violations by security forces continued unabated and Amnesty International reports that between 1989-1991, thousands of Mauritanians were detained, tortured or killed.

The country's first elections since independence were held in 1992. In presidential elections marred by massive fraud and vote rigging, Taya emerged as victor securing 63 percent of the popular vote. The main opposition party, Union of Democratic Forces (UFD), had initially announced that it would boycott the presidential election, alleging that the balloting would almost certainly be rigged to favor the PRDS. Shortly before the elections, however, the UFD endorsed the candidacy of Ahmed Ould Daddah, a brother of ex-president Moktar Ould Daddah. Despite an array of political support, Daddah secured only 33 percent of the vote. The opposition party accused the government of vote buying, intimidation, falsifying voter I.D. cards and deliberately frustrating registration efforts of UFD supporters. While international observers reported that both the government and opposition parties participated in voting fraud, they noted that the government's efforts were more extensive and effective. Despite evidence of fraud and strong opposition party protest, the Supreme Court upheld the election results.

Legislative elections followed in March and April 1992. Opposition parties boycotted the election and exept for a few independent candidates, the ruling PRDS went unchallenged. Not surprisingly, all of the newly elected candidates were from the PRDS. Shortly after the election, Taya dissolved the CMSN and replaced it with the newly elected civilian Parliament.

Political Rights and Civil Liberties:

Mauritanians cannot change their government democratically. Neither the presidential nor subsequent legislative elections were free or fair. The executive and legislative levels of government are controlled by the PRDS. Although the CMSN was dissolved in 1992 and replaced by a civilian Parliament, many military personalities have retained high positions in Taya's government.

Despite the government's stated opposition to torture, human rights groups report that gross human rights violations by the security forces continue unabated. Mauritanians, particularly political dissidents and black Africans, remain subject to extrajudicial killings, torture, arbitrary arrest, and long periods of detention without trial. Slavery has been formally abolished in Mauritania, but the United States Human Rights Commission reports that an estimated 100,000 Mauritanians still occupy positions of servitude or near servitude.

Government-sanctioned discrimination against black Maurs and black Africans continues in Mauritania. The Lawyers Committee for Human Rights asserts that the Taya regime has a "...systematic practice of racially based exclusion and segregation which permeates all areas of national life, including employment. The government operates under a hierarchy of unwritten rules where constitutional and other legally mandated rights, protections and benefits are accorded on the basis of a person's race, political influence, and other factors such as tribal and regional affiliations." Both Amnesty International and Africa Watch have documented the systematic discrimination by the government against the black African ethnic group, the Hal Pulaar.

Mauritania's judicial system is not free from government interference. In cases which involve national security issues or political dissidents, government interference is routine. The court system is separated into different tiers and, depending on the nature of the crime, cases are tried by different courts. Islamic courts apply *shari'a*, Muslim law, and although extreme physical punishments, such as amputations, are no longer applied, tribal and familial relations continue to play an important role in the judiciary process. Under Mauritanian law, the accused has the right to a speedy arraignment (within 72 hours of arrest) and trial, access to legal counsel, and the right of appeal. However, in many cases, especially those involving political dissidents, many of these rights are not observed.

Under the 1991 Constitution, Mauritanians have the right to peaceful assembly and association. In practice, however, these freedoms are severely curtailed. The law mandates that political parties must register and obtain permission to conduct large meetings or assemblies. The government has reserved the right to permit or deny political assembly and, without consistency, it will permit some parties to rally while denying permission to others.

The 1991 Constitution protects freedom of speech and press. Beginning in 1992, press restrictions were eased. Owing to a freedom of the press law adopted in mid-1991, several new independent newspapers were launched. Many of these papers criticized the government, particularly in regard to its human rights practices. Despite these advances, however, numerous press restrictions are still evident. Although the 1991 law helped to liberalize some aspects of the press, it remains a crime to promote "national disharmony" or to publish materials deemed to be "insulting to the president." Violators are subject to heavy fines and imprisonment. In April 1993 the state-owned daily newspaper, *Horizons,* published a front page attack on the independent journal *Mauritanie-Nouvelles*. The paper accused the journal of "corrupting the nation's interests with the intent to disturb relations with partner countries."

Freedom of religion is not respected. Islam is the official religion of Mauritania and, by law, all Mauritanians are Sunni Muslim and renunciation is a crime. Mauritanians are prohibited from entering the houses of non-Muslims or possessing sacred texts of other religions.

With the exception of members of the military and police, workers are free to join trade unions. All unions are required to join the Union of Mauritanian Workers (UTM), a government controlled labor federation. As a result of continual government interference, UTM's effectiveness in protecting workers' rights has been severely curtailed. The government restricts the right to strike and discourages labor participation in politics.

Mauritius

Polity: Parliamentary
democracy
Economy: Capitalist
Population: 1,094,000
PPP: $5,750
Life Expectancy: 69.6
Ethnic Groups: Indo-Mauritian, Creole, Sino-Mauritian,
and Franco-Mauritian

Political Rights: 1*
Civil Liberties: 2
Status: Free

Ratings Change: *Mauritius's political rights rating changed from 2 to 1 as a result of modifications in methodology. See "Survey Methodology," page 671.

Overview: Since gaining independence from Britain in 1968, Mauritius has been one of the most successful and enduring functioning democracies in Africa. With a thriving economy and peaceful co-existence among the islands' numerous ethnic groups, Mauritius in one of the few political and economic success stories in post-colonial Africa.

In 1992, Mauritius became a republic within the British Commonwealth and the governor general was replaced by the president as Head of State, with powers that are primarily ceremonial. Sir Veerasamy Ringadoo became the island's first president and, within a few months, he was succeeded by Cassam Uteem.

Mauritius has four major political parties and several smaller parties that encompass a wide array of ideological convictions. The island's population of 1.1 million is comprised of approximately 750,00 Indians, 300,000 Creoles, 30,000 Chinese and 20,000 whites.

Political Rights and Civil Liberties: Mauritius has a enduring colonial legacy of parliamentary democracy and holds free, fair and competitive elections at regular intervals. Ethnic and religious minorities within Mauritius are assured of legislative representation through a complicated "best loser" system in the National Assembly. Mauritius has an independent judicial system. Freedom of religion is respected and both internal and international travel is unrestricted.

While freedom of the press is generally respected, journalists are subject to censorship under a 1984 act that restricts the press from criticizing the government. There are a number of privately owned news publications. Both the television and radio stations are government owned and tend to reflect government policy. Freedom of both assembly and association is respected. Workers have the right to organize and strike. There are nine labor federations which comprise 300 unions.

There are no known political prisoners in Mauritius and no reports of political or extrajudicial killings. While civil rights are generally respected, criminal suspects held in custody have reported the use of excessive force by police. In 1992, some victims sued and were compensated for their injuries.

While women still occupy a subordinate role in society, the government has attempted to improve women's status by removing legal barriers to advancement. Women make up only about one-third of the student population at the University of

Mauritius. Domestic violence against women is prevalent and there are no laws to address family violence crimes. Both governmental and non-governmental institutions have begun programs to educate the public on issues of domestic violence and to provide counseling to victims of abuse.

Mexico

Polity: Dominant party
Economy: Capitalist-statist
Population: 87,715,000
PPP: $5,918
Life Expectancy: 69.7
Ethnic Groups: Mestizo (60 percent), Indian (30 percent), Caucasian (9 percent), other (1 percent)
Ratings Change: *Mexico's civil liberties rating changed from 3 to 4 principally because of an increase in more sophisticated forms of repression against civic groups and greater intimidation and violence against journalists. See section below on "Political Rights and Civil Liberties."

Political Rights: 4
Civil Liberties: 4*
Status: Partly Free

Overview: Following the passage of the North American Free Trade Agreement (NAFTA) in the U.S. Congress, President Carlos Salinas de Gortari selected Luis Donaldo Colosio, a ranking cabinet official and close associate, to be the candidate of the Institutional Revolutionary Party (PRI) in the 21 August 1994 presidential election.

Mexico achieved independence from Spain in 1810 and established a republic in 1822. Seven years after the Revolution of 1910 a new constitution was promulgated, under which the United Mexican States is a federal republic consisting of thirty-one states and a Federal District (Mexico City). Each state has elected governors and legislatures. The mayor of Mexico City is appointed by the president. The president is elected for a six-year term. A bicameral Congress consists of a 64-member Senate directly elected for six years, and a 500-member Chamber of Deputies elected for three years—300 by direct vote, and 200 through proportional representation. Municipal governments are elected.

The nature of power in Mexico and how it functions do not correspond to the constitution. Since its founding in 1929, the PRI has dominated the state through a top-down, corporatist structure that is authoritarian in nature and held together through co-optation, patronage, corruption and, when all else fails, repression. The formal business of government takes place secretly and with little legal foundation.

The PRI's credibility was severely damaged during the economic crisis of the 1980s. Most Mexicans believe Salinas actually lost the 1988 election, which was marked by massive and systematic fraud. According to official results, Salinas won 50.36 percent of the vote. The main challengers were Manuel Clouthier of the right-wing National Action Party (PAN) with 17 percent, and a coalition of leftist parties and former PRI members led by Cuauhtemoc Cardenas with 31.3 percent.

Salinas, taking office with the weakest mandate of any PRI president, promised both economic and political reform. Wielding the enormous power of the Mexican presidency, he radically overhauled the economy and pursued a free trade agreement with the U.S. and Canada. But political reforms have been modest and designed primarily to quiet opposition protests and international criticism. The basic structures of the sixty-four-year-old state-party system have not been changed.

Salinas has further concentrated the already enormous power of the presidency. He established a technical cabinet, headed by his chief of staff, with five departments—international relations, the economy, social welfare, agriculture, and national security. The latter incorporates the military, the interior ministry (which includes state intelligence), the foreign affairs ministry and the attorney general.

In 1989 Salinas allowed an opposition party to win a governorship for the first time, the PAN in Baja California Norte. He conceded another governorship to the PAN in Chihuahua in 1992. But the 1991 congressional elections and dozens of other state and local elections have been marked by fraud and repression, particularly against the Party of the Democratic Revolution (PRD) formed by Cardenas after the 1988 election. Salinas, by stage-managing the electoral arena in this way, has been able to temper the PAN's demands for political reform and prevent the PAN and the PRD from uniting around a pro-democracy platform, the PRI's nightmare.

Salinas's main objectives in 1993 were to help secure passage of NAFTA in the U.S. Congress, and to gear up the PRI machine to ensure the succession of his hand-picked successor in the August 1994 election. In September, with Mexico's lack of democracy becoming an issue in the U.S.-NAFTA debate, Salinas produced an electoral reform package. Its modest measures included regulations on campaign financing and more access to the media for opposition parties. However, the Federal Electoral Institute remains under the authority of the interior ministry and therefore the president. Another change doubled the number of seats in the Senate, which might result in more opposition representation but will not threaten the PRI's majority (currently 61 of 64 seats.)

Meanwhile, three of Salinas's closest associates emerged as the most likely to be tapped as his successor—finance minister Pedro Aspe, Mexico City mayor Manuel Camacho, and Colosio, Salinas's unwaveringly loyal social development minister. After NAFTA was passed in Washington in November, Salinas chose Colosio. NAFTA was expected to produce a surge in foreign investment, which would enable the PRI to go on a spending spree to boost the forty-three-year-old Colosio in the 1994 campaign. Colosio pledged himself to a continuation of Salinas's economic policies. The PRD nominated Cardenas, son of the revered former President Lazaro Cardenas, who nationalized the oil industry in the 1930s. Cardenas no longer had the cachet he did in 1988, but he was still feared by the PRI. The PAN selected Diego Fernandez de Cevallos, a prominent congressman frequently criticized for being too accommodating toward Salinas. Both the PRD and the PAN have suffered from internal dissent in recent years and neither has been able to build a strong national organization.

Political Rights and Civil Liberties: Because of the president's final say in all electoral matters and the ruling party's domination of the state, the electoral system, and the broadcast media, citizens are unable to change their government democratically. Traditional forms of electoral fraud—e.g. the ballot stuffing and multiple voting seen during the state elections in Nayarit in July 1993—are now supplemented by "cybernetic fraud" like the computer manipulation of voter lists and voter identification cards seen in the state elections in Coahuila in September 1993. Both forms of fraud evident in the Yucatan elections in November 1993.

Constitutional guarantees regarding political and civic organization are only partially respected. There are over a dozen political parties ranging from right to left. But political expression is often restricted by repressive measures taken by the government during election periods and rural land disputes.

Overall, in 1993 there was a general tightening of control over politics and civic activity, as the state-party system geared up for the electoral transition to the next PRI president in 1994. The government hardened its position against protests over electoral fraud. Its use of tougher measures—including tear gas, mass arrests, beatings by security forces and torture during confinement—was evident during a number of state elections, particularly in Nayarit. Moreover, as the campaign for the 1994 election got underway, there was stepped up harassment, surveillance and intimidation of PRD presidential candidate Cuahtemoc Cardenas and his family.

Civil society has grown in recent years; human rights, pro-democracy, women's and environmental groups have developed. But in 1993 civic groups critical of the government were increasingly subject to numerous forms of sophisticated intimidation that rights activists refer to as "cloaked repression"—from gentle warnings by government officials and anonymous death threats, to unwarranted detention and jailings on dubious charges.

An official human rights commission was created in 1990. But only minimal progress has been made in curtailing the systematic violation of human rights— including false arrest, torture, disappearances, murder and extortion—by the Federal Judicial Police, and by state and federal police as well. The rights commission is barred from examining political and labor rights violations, and is unable to enforce its recommendations.

Targets of rights violations include political and labor figures, journalists, human rights activists, criminal detainees and, with regard to extortion, the general public. Over the last decade nearly 500 people have disappeared. There is credible evidence that since 1989 more than 200 activists of the opposition PRD have been killed for political reasons. During one week in November 1993 alone, five PRD activists were killed in three southern states. Since 1991, there has been compelling evidence of electronic surveillance of government critics, opposition parties, and the official human rights commission itself.

In January 1993, Jorge Carpizo, the former head of the official human rights commision, was appointed attorney general. The government also enacted new rules of evidence and dismissed dozens of security officials. However, corruption and rights violations remain institutionalized within the Federal Judicial Police (under the authority of the attorney general)—which routinely makes political arrests under the pretext of drug enforcement—and other law enforcement agencies. The widespread use of torture and ill-treatment during confinement has continued. Many police dismissed for poor conduct have subsequently been implicated in kidnappings for ransom, which rose to more than one per week in 1993.

The judiciary is subordinate to the president, underscoring the lack of a rule of law. Supreme Court judges are appointed by the executive and rubber-stamped by the Senate. The court is prohibited from enforcing political and labor rights, and from reviewing the constitutionality of laws. Overall, the judicial system is weak, politicized and riddled with corruption. In most rural areas, respect for laws by official agencies is nearly nonexistent. Lower courts and law enforcement in general are undermined by widespread bribery. The exposure of government corruption, which is endemic, rarely results in legal proceedings. Drug-related corruption is evident in the military, police, security forces, and increasingly in government at both the local and national levels.

Labor is closely controlled by the government. Officially recognized unions operate as political instruments of the ruling party. The government does not recognize independent unions, denying them collective-bargaining rights and the right to strike. Independent unions and peasant organizations are subject to intimidation, blacklisting and violent crackdowns, and dozens of labor and peasant leaders have been killed in recent years in ongoing land disputes, particularly in southern states, where Indians comprise close to half the population. There has also been an increase in the exploitation of teenage women in the manufacturing-for-export sector, as the government consistently fails to enforce child labor laws.

The media, while mostly private and nominally independent, are largely controlled by the government through regulatory bodies, dependence on the government for advertising revenue and operating costs, cronyism and outright intimidation. A few daily newspapers and weeklies are the exceptions. A system of direct payments to journalists was ostensibly ended by the government in 1993, but there was evidence that the practice continued. Most newspapers and magazines derive over half of all advertising revenues from official sources.

More than twenty-five journalists have been killed or disappeared in the last five years, with most cases still unresolved. Three were killed in the first ten months of 1993 according to the Inter-American Press Association, the most in Latin America outside of Colombia. Dozens of other journalists were detained or threatened. Many of the cases involved reporters investigating drug-related corruption in the government.

The ruling party's domination of television, by far the country's most influential medium, is evident in the blanket, uncritical coverage of the ruling party, and the fact that Jacobo Zabludovsky, the country's leading television news anchor, acts as a virtual mouthpiece of the government. Two newly privatized stations have shown no inclination to buck the government line.

The government controls all radio frequencies. In 1993 officials used this leverage to rein in stations attempting to give time to opposition voices. The result was the banishment of a number of hosts, commentators and analysts who had either criticized the government or invited government critics to present their views.

In 1992 the constitution was amended to restore the legal status of the Catholic church and other religious institutions. The right to own property and conduct religious education were given legal definition for the first time in over a century. Priests and nuns were given the right to vote for the first time in nearly eighty years. In 1993 there was increased repression against left-wing Catholic activists and priests, including the invasion of a church by police to arrest people protesting against electoral fraud in the state of Nayarit. In November the Vatican, apparently in response to government pressure, asked a bishop in Chiapas, an outspoken critic of the government and defender of indigenous rights, to resign.

Micronesia

Polity: Federal par-
liamentary democracy
Economy: Capitalist
Population: 115,000
PPP: na
Life Expectancy: 70.5
Ethnic Groups: Micronesian majority, Polynesian minority

Political Rights: 1
Civil Liberties: 1
Status: Free

Overview: Located in the Pacific Ocean, the Federated States of Micronesia was a U.N. trust territory under American administration from 1947 until 1979, when the U.S. recognized the Micronesian con-stitution. Previously, the islands had been successively under a German protectorate and a Japanese League of Nations mandate. In 1982, the U.S. and Micronesia signed the Compact of Free Association, under which the U.S. retains responsibility for defense. In 1990, the U.N. Security Council voted to recognize the end of American trusteeship. In 1991, Micronesia sought and won international diplomatic recognition and full U.N. membership.

The unicameral legislature consists of one senator-at-large from each island state elected for a four-year term, and ten senators elected on the basis of island populations for two-year terms. The senators elect the country's president for a two-year term from among the four at-large senators. Bailey Olter is president of the four island states, Kosrae, Pohnpei, Chuuk and Yap, three of which still have traditional leaders and customs. Pohnpei is the most modern of the four.

Agriculture, tourism, forestry and fishing are major industries, and public sector employment is substantial. The federal and state governments play a major role in the tuna industry. American economic assistance is major, and will continue until 2001. In 1993, a group of people from Kosrae said they would seek compensation from the U.S. for health effects from American nuclear tests on the Bikini Atoll. They claim to have worked on post-test cleanups.

Political Rights and Civil Liberties: Micronesians have the right to change their government democratically. The people have the freedom to form political parties, but family politics, tendencies and factions, not Western-style parties, are the vehicles for political activity on the islands. The states and localities have popularly elected governments.

Micronesia has a bill of rights and provisions for respecting traditional rights. Land is not sold or transferred to non-Micronesians. Otherwise the country respects cultural diversity. Islanders speak eight separate native languages. There is freedom of the press. Governmental authorities operate some media, while private enterprise and religious groups operate others. Micronesians have religious freedom. The Congregational Church predominates in Kosrae. There is freedom of association, but only a few groups exist. Trade unions are legal, but there are none. Legally, there is equality of opportunity, but traditional family status can determine one's chances for advancement. Women play mostly traditional family roles, and face the problem of traditionally tolerated domestic violence. Modernization has brought some women into paying jobs.

Moldova (Moldavia)

Polity: Presidential-par-
liamentary
Economy: Statist
(transitional)
Population: 4,372,000
PPP: $3,896
Life Expectancy: 68.0
Ethnic Groups: Romanian (64 percent), Russian, Ukrainians

Political Rights: 5
Civil Liberties: 5
Status: Partly Free

Overview: In 1993, Moldova continued to re-assert its independence amid resistance from the self-proclaimed, largely Russian and Ukrainian Transdniester Republic, the continued presence of Russian troops, and calls for reunification with neighboring Romania. President Mercia Snegur and Prime Minister Andrei Sangheli strove to build a government of national consensus to chart the country's future course.

Moldova is a predominantly Romanian-speaking former Soviet republic bordering Ukraine and Romania. In 1991, it officially declared independence from a fragmenting Soviet Union. Snegur, running unopposed and with the backing of the nationalist Moldovan Popular Front (MPF), was elected president by an overwhelming margin.

The conflict in the Transdniester region, the eastern sliver of territory on the left bank of the Dniester River inhabited primarily by Russians and Ukrainians, began in 1990 in response to increased demands for independence by the Romanian-speaking majority. In 1940, Soviet Russia had occupied the previously Romanian province of Bessarabia, establishing the Moldovian Soviet Socialist Republic. The Transdniester region was earlier part of the Ukrainian republic until 1940, but after the Soviet annexation the region was joined with Moldova. In 1990, the Slavic minorities and the Gagauz, a Turkic people, proclaimed their own republics: the Gagauz SSR on 19 August, and the Dniester republic on 2 September. Fighting broke out, lasting until mid-1992 when a ceasefire agreement was reached following negotiations between President Snegur and Russian President Boris Yeltsin. However, the Russian 14th Army under Lt. Gen. Aleksandr I. Lebed, which openly aided the Slavic insurgents and seized Moldovan land on the right bank of the Dniester, remained in control of the region.

In 1993, the government in Chisinau (formerly Kishniev) faced two forces opposed to Moldovan independence: the rump-MPF and nationalists campaigning for the country's reunification with Romania, and the Russian leaders on the left bank of the Dniester, including Transdniester President Igor Smirnov based in Tiraspol, who enjoyed military, economic and political support from Russia. The government's overall strategy was to maintain Moldovan sovereignty and offer the break-away republics a form of administrative autonomy short of republican status.

The government's parliamentary majority consisted of 180-190 of the approximately 240 deputies who regularly attended sessions. (About eighty others, mostly left-bank Russians and several Gagauz, consistently boycotted sessions.) Deputies of the new majority belonged to the Agrarian Club; the centrist Democratic and Independent Club; the majority of members of the Accord Club of ex-Communist Russian, Ukrainian, and other non-Moldovan deputies from the right bank; and about half of the Southern Steppe faction of Gagauz and Slavic deputies from southern Moldova. The only parliamentary groups not supporting the government were the rump-MPF and the few unreconstructed Russian and Moldovan Communist deputies from the right bank.

In January, Chisinau offered to grant the Transdniester "self-governing territory" status as well as that of a free economic zone. The offer was rejected by the self-proclaimed republic's Supreme Soviet, which insisted on recognition of the republic with its own government and army in a confederation of Moldovan, Dniester and Gagauz republics. Meanwhile, Gen. Lebed confirmed Russia's intention to set up a consular office in Tiraspol to grant Russian citizenship to all military personnel as well as Dniester residents who wanted it. While supporting the breakaway republic, Gen. Lebed warned the leadership that he would not tolerate corrupt or criminal activities, noting that he was "sick and tired of guarding the sleep and safety of crooks."

On 20 January, parliament defeated a proposal by President Snegur to hold a referendum on reunification with Romania. Opinion polls consistently put the level of support for reunification at under 10 percent. The referendum got 165 votes to 65, short of the needed 50 percent. (The official number of parliament is 333.) The opposition minority was backed by the parliamentary leadership. The defeat led to an immediate walkout by deputies who supported the referendum. On 29 January, parliamentary Chairman Aleksandru Mosanu and a number of parliamentarians resigned to protest the president's call for a referendum. Pytor Luchinsky, former first secretary of the Moldovan Communist Party and later Moldova's ambassador to Russia, was elected parliamentary chairman on 4 February.

The vote was seen as a blow to pro-Romania forces, who feared that a popular rejection of reunification would lead to Moldova's permanent political separation from Romania. It also showed that a split in the parliament allowed the minority to use rules and numbers to defeat the majority. While most deputies supported Moldovan statehood, they were unable to gain control of the legislature owing to the complex parliamentary arithmetic that worked to the opposition's advantage and the rump-MPF's unassailable position within the parliamentary presidium. The 168 who walked out after the referendum vote said they would boycott parliament until the composition of the presidium was altered to reflect the composition of parliament. Instead, Mosanu and several parliamentarians resigned. The opposition continued to criticize the president's conciliatory policies on the Dniester and Gagauz conflicts, his negotiations with Moscow and the maintenance of economic links with the Commonwealth of Independent States (CIS).

In April, the government announced that it was ready to proclaim Dniester a demilitarized region, a move opposed by Gen. Lebed. Meanwhile, negotiations continued between Moldovan and Russian delegations. At the end of the month in Tiraspol, Transdniester authorities put six ethnic Romanian nationalists on trial for murder. The main defendant, economist Ilie Ilascu, said he rejected the three-judge panel's right to try him on charges of masterminding attacks in 1992.

Talks continued on Gagauz demands. In May, Gagauz President Stepan Topaz said his government was ready to reach agreement on the condition that Gagauzia be recognized as an autonomous republic within Moldova. A draft law on Gagauz autonomy was submitted to parliament, where it met stiff opposition. In negotiations with Transdniester leaders, both sides renounced a military solution, but little progress was made on specifics to resolve the conflict. Russia threatened to withdraw its forces if Dniester hard-liners continued to impede negotiations. At the end of May, President Snegur again called on parliament to compromise with the two separatist republics as a means to move ahead with such issues as economic reform and modernization and the withdrawal of the 14th Army.

On 3 August, opposition parties and movements announced at the opening of an extraordinary parliamentary session that they would oppose ratification of a treaty on the country's accession to the CIS and demand that the government resign. Speaking at a news conference, leaders of the Congress of Intellectuals, the Democratic and National Democratic parties and other movements advocating unification with Romania sharply criticized the government for "betraying national interests and succumbing to Moscow's dictates." After an exhaustive session, parliament, by a margin of four votes, rejected the draft resolution on ratifying the agreement on Moldova's adherence to the CIS.

Increasing political polarization in parliament led to an October decision to hold early elections on 27 February 1994, a year before parliament's five-year term was due to expire.

Tensions in Moldova increased in December, after a court in Transdniester sentenced Ilie Ilascu to death, and his five co-defendants to terms of imprisonment from two to fifteen years. On 10 December, about 10,000 angry demonstrators blocked traffic in Chisinau to protest the harsh sentencing. The government said it considered the sentence "null and void" and demanded that the prisoners be transferred to Moldovan jurisdiction. The issues had yet to be resolved at year's end.

The ongoing separatist issue and the presence of Russian troops continued to discourage foreign investment in a deteriorating economy. In March, parliament passed a privatization law that would put 30 percent of the country's moribund state-owned industry into private hands in 1993-94. The law envisioned the free distribution of public vouchers which would later be negotiated into stock. On 29 November, Moldova abandoned the ruble and introduced its own currency, the leu. Nevertheless, the economy registered declines in gross national product, output and income. Russia accounted for over 80 percent of Moldova's trade turnover.

Political Rights and Civil Liberties: Moldova has a multiparty system, but has not yet had fully democratic elections. There are several political parties and groupings that support either Moldovan statehood or eventual unification with Romania. The as yet unresolved conflicts in the separatist Transdniester and Gagauz republics and the presence of Russian troops also undermine Moldovan sovereignty and democracy. Several drafts of a new constitution were debated in 1993, but a final document was not adopted.

When it was elected in 1990, the parliament consisted of 380 deputies. Since then, deputies directly involved in the Gagauz and Transdniester insurgencies lost their seats; several ethnic Moldovan conservative deputies were dismissed for absenteeism; and a number of deputies died or resigned without being replaced. In theory, the legislature consists of 333 members, but some forty Dniester and Gagauz deputies have boycotted sessions for two years. About 280 deputies remain to attend the sessions; sometimes the number of deputies present drops below the two-thirds quorum of 222.

Judicial reform has yet to lead to an independent judiciary. In December, a three-judge panel in the self-styled Transdniester Republic sentenced one Moldovan activist to death and several others to prison. The international community joined the Moldova government in denouncing the sentences as extralegal.

Human rights violations and violence were reported throughout the year, particularly in Russian-controlled sections of the right-bank city of Bendery.

Political parties and independent groups publish newspapers, which often take views critical of the government. The reliance of most newspapers on some type of government subsidy raises the issue of self-censorship. Government-controlled radio and television offer varied broadcasts. In August, the Transdniester Committee for Radio, Television, and the Press banned the cable broadcast of a program of the 14th Army. The committee also intended to ban and confiscate the 14th Army's newspaper, *Soldat Otechestva* (Soldier of the Motherland).

The state of emergency was lifted in August 1992, and there are few restrictions on freedom of peaceful assembly. The practice of religion is generally free. The Orthodox Church has, however, used its influence to discourage proselytizing.

Fears of discrimination, particularly if Moldova were to reunify with Romania, have led non-Moldovans to remain skeptical of government guarantees to protect their rights. The 1990 language law was modified somewhat in 1992, allowing Russian to be used as a language of "inter-ethnic communication." Schools offering instruction in Ukrainian and other minority languages are open. Chisinau, once a hub of Jewish life, has a Jewish public school and a privately owned yeshiva.

The conflict in Transdniester has led to some de facto restriction of movement. Most domestic and foreign travel is unrestricted.

While women enjoy equal rights under law, they are underrepresented in government and leadership positions, and face job discrimination and/or layoffs.

The Federation of Independent Trade Unions of Moldova (FITU) has replaced the old Communist union federation. Government workers do not have the right to strike, nor do those in essential services such as health care.

Monaco

Polity: Prince and elected council
Political Rights: 2*
Civil Liberties: 1
Economy: Capitalist-statist **Status:** Partly Free
Population: 30,000
PPP: na
Life Expectancy: na
Ethnic Groups: Monegasque, French, Italian, others
Ratings Change: *Monaco's political rights rating changed from 3 to 2 as a result of modifications in methodology. See "Survey Methodology," page 671.

Overview: In 1993 Monaco became a full member of the U.N., thereby increasing the tiny country's international standing. Previously, Monaco had held U.N. observer status.

The Principality of Monaco is located on the French Mediterranean coast. Prince Rainier is the hereditary head of state, but he acts within constitutional constraints. According to international agreements, France nominates Monaco's Minister of State (prime minister). The voters elect an eighteen-member National Council for a five-year term. There is an elected sixteen-member municipal council, headed by a mayor and assistants appointed by the council.

Monaco's political future is uncertain, because Prince Albert, Rainier's son, shows no interest in marriage. Under arrangements with France, if the monarch dies without a male heir, France may incorporate Monaco into its territory.

Political Rights and Civil Liberties: The people of Monaco have the right to change their national legislature and municipal government by democratic means. However, by definition, the monarchical head of state does not face a popular vote.

Newspapers in nearby Nice, France, print Monaco editions, which they distribute freely in the principality. Radio and television are government-operated. The French government has a controlling interest in Radio Monte Carlo. A tax haven, Monaco is the home of gambling casinos and light industry.

Monaco has some limits on freedoms of expression and assembly. These were evident in September 1993 when the police interfered with pro-Tibet demonstrators. The activists were attempting to influence the International Olympic Committee (IOC), which was meeting in Monaco. The police arrested four Tibetan women for wearing T-shirts that read "Olympics 2000—Not in China." Riot police stopped demonstrators from approaching the IOC meeting. The police also confiscated various pro-Tibet banners, stating that Monaco bans the Tibetan flag.

Roman Catholicism is the state religion, but the constitution guarantees religious freedom. There is freedom of association, including trade unionism.

Mongolia

Polity: Presidential-parliamentary democracy
Economy: Statist transitional
Population: 2,252,000
PPP: $2,100
Life Expectancy: 65.0
Ethnic Groups: Khalkha Mongols (75 percent), other Mongols (8 percent), Kazakhs (5 percent)
Ratings Change: *Mongolia's political rights rating changed from 3 to 2 and its rating for civil liberties from 2 to 3 as a result of modifications in methodology. See "Survey Methodology," page 671.

Political Rights: 2*
Civil Liberties: 3*
Status: Free

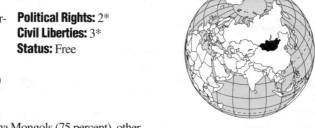

Overview: Mongolia held its first direct presidential election in June 1993, continuing a democratic transition that has been hampered by severe economic hardship. Incumbent Punsalmaagiyn Orchirbat won the vote running on an opposition ticket two months after the ruling ex-Communist party dumped him in favor of a more conservative candidate.

China controlled this vast Central Asian steppe and mountain region for two centuries until the overthrow of the Qing dynasty in 1911, and again in 1919 until Soviet-backed Marxists revolted in 1921. The Mongolian People's Revolutionary Party (MPRP) formed a Communist state in 1924 following three years of nominal rule by aging Buddhist lamas. For the next sixty-five years, the country existed as a virtual republic of the Soviet Union.

The country's one-party system began to crack in December 1989 with the formation of an opposition association, the Mongolian Democratic Union (MDU), under dynamic university lecturer Sanjaasurenjiyn Zorig. MDU-organized street protests and hunger strikes forced the resignation of much of the MPRP leadership in March 1990, and in May the government scrapped the party's legal monopoly. In July 1990 the country held its first multiparty elections. The MPRP took 357 of 430 seats in the Great Hural (parliament) against an unprepared opposition. In September, the Hural named the MPRP's Punsalmaagiyn Orchirbat as president and the opposition Social Democratic Party's Radnaasurenjiyn Gonchigdorj as vice president.

In February 1991, the MPRP formally abandoned Marxism-Leninism in favor of "scientific socialism." However, citizens continued to be wary of a core of hardliners within the party. In response, in August the government banned top officials, as well as police, diplomats and journalists, from belonging to any political party. Thousands of people affected, from President Orchirbat on down, left their parties to comply with the law.

Continuing the democratic transition, the Great Hural passed a new constitution on 15 January 1992. It provided for private land ownership, renounced socialism, and abolished the two-year-old Little Hural, transforming the Great Hural into a seventy-six-seat unicameral parliament. The president received powers to name a cabinet and veto all legislation, subject to a two-thirds override.

On 28 June 1992 Mongolians voted for a new, smaller Great Hural. More than 91 percent of the electorate took part, even though most rural voters had to travel for miles to reach a polling station. The MPRP, split into several factions ranging from orthodox Communists to free-market reformers, took a commanding seventy seats against a confusing array of twelve opposition parties, many of which lacked clear ideological distinctions and the means to campaign effectively. The reform-oriented Democratic Coalition, headed by 1990 revolution catalyst Zorig, took only four seats, while the European-influenced Social Democratic Party took one, along with an MPRP-affiliated independent. The MPRP formed a new government under Prime Minister Jasrai. The single-seat constituency system, which gave the government its parliamentary landslide, distorted the opposition's credible 43 percent share of the popular vote. Neverthless, the victory clearly indicated that voters blamed the country's severe economic hardship on the free-market reforms instituted since 1990, and feared the opposition would extend the reforms further.

The MPRP's success strengthened hardliners within the party who were uneasy with Orchirbat's promotion of democratic and free market policies. At a party congress on 10 April 1993, the ruling party dumped Orchirbat as its candidate for the June presidential election in favor of Lodongiyn Tudev, the hardline Communist editor of the party paper *Unen* (Truth). Two days later a coalition composed of the opposition National Democratic and Social Democratic parties named Orchirbat as their candidate. On 7 June, 90 percent of the electorate turned out and Orchirbat won the election with 57.8 percent of the vote to 38.7 percent for Tudev.

Orchirbat has pledged to continue the country's transition to a free-market economy. In 1991 citizens were given coupons to bid on the country's state-owned enterprises. Although 240 companies have been auctioned and are listed on the stock exchange, trading is rare. The Soviet demise in December 1991 has created severe shortages of parts and skilled labor, and most factories operate only part-time.

In April the International Monetary Fund tied $31 million in aid to a three-year program of market reforms, including ending export restrictions and state subsidies in many sectors. In early June the country floated its currency, the *tugrik*. Given the country's abundant supplies of oil, copper, gold and other resources, long-term prospects look bright.

Political Rights and Civil Liberties: Mongolians changed their government in June 1992 through free although not entirely fair elections. The electoral districts favor the rural areas, where the MPRP draws its bedrock support. Other factors in the MPRP's favor include ample funding; control over the media, printing equipment and paper; and sufficient stocks of gasoline to campaign in the countryside. The June 1993 presidential elections appeared fair and resulted in victory for the incumbent, Punsaalmagiyn Orchirbat, who ran for the party of the opposition.

Nearly all of the more than 200 newspapers are in the hands of political parties or the government and reflect their biases, although some government-owned newspapers do criticize the government. In 1993 the country's first truly independent newspaper, *Today*, began publishing. The government controls the allocation of newsprint imports, and opposition parties and other papers say they cannot publish as regularly as the MPRP paper, *Unen*. A Danish aid organization has promised to supply non-government papers with a printing press. The only full-time national radio and television stations are controlled by the government and generally offer pluralistic views. Freedom of association is respected in practice.

The government admits that in recent years several prisoners have starved to death during the winter months due to acute food shortages. The once tightly controlled judiciary is being restructured and will include a new General Council of Courts to select judges and protect their independence. Defendents receive adequate due process rights.

The new constitution provides for a full separation of church and state, and this is respected in practice. Since the peaceful 1990 revolution Buddhist activity has blossomed throughout the country. Citizens can travel freely within the country. Some citizens are apparently arbitrarily required to surrender their passports upon returning from abroad, and must request their passports for further travel abroad. Workers have the right to join independent unions and conduct strikes.

Morocco

Polity: Monarchy and
limited parliament
Economy: Capitalist-
statist
Population: 26,200,000
PPP: $2,348
Life Expectancy: 62.0
Ethnic Groups: Arab, Berber, Black African

Political Rights: 5*
Civil Liberties: 5
Status: Partly Free

Ratings Change: *Morocco's political rights rating changed from
6 to 5 because it held long-delayed parliamentary elections.

Overview: The voters and an electoral college chose the new Moroccan parliament in 1993. The Moroccan government and the Polisario Front conducted a first-ever meeting to discuss the future of Western Sahara, occupied by Morocco since 1975.

King Hassan II has ruled Morocco since 1961, weathering two attempted military revolts in the 1970s, and civil disorders in 1981 and 1990 stemming from economic problems.

After demands for long-awaited political reforms by the opposition Democratic Bloc, comprising the nationalist Istiqlal (Independence) Party, the Socialist Union of Popular Forces (USFP), and two smaller parties, King Hassan organized a constitutional referendum in September 1992. Moroccans and Western Saharans voted overwhelmingly in favor of the new constitution, under which the King delegates some of his powers to the government and parliament.

Under the new constitution, the government is more accountable to the Chamber of Representatives (parliament). The Chamber has the power to approve ministers, the cabinet's policy, set up commissions of inquiry, and challenge the government with votes of confidence. The King retains the right to declare a state of emergency, but would not dissolve the parliament automatically as in the past. However, King Hassan remains the ultimate authority.

On 16 October 1992, elections for local councils took place. According to official results, the turnout was 75 percent and the parties of the former ruling coalition won most council seats. The opposition denounced the results, complaining of fraud and corruption.

The 1993 parliamentary elections were the first since 1984. Elections scheduled for 1990 were postponed to 1992 but they did not take place. Opposition parties have accused the government of tampering with past elections.

In the runup to the elections, the Democratic Bloc announced on 7 February its withdrawal from the electoral commission, alleging its inability to insure a fair voting process. Following the government's announcement on 19 March to postpone the election from 30 April to 25 June, in order to finalize voter lists and print new ballots, the Bloc rejoined the electoral commission and withdrew its threats of boycotting the elections.

Of the 2,042 candidates contesting the 222 parliamentary seats in the June election, the Democratic Bloc won 99, making it the largest coalition group in parliament. The conservative National Entente coalition won 88 seats, and the centrist National Rally of Independents (RNI) won 28 seats.

On 17 September electors from trade unions, professional organizations and communal councils voted in a second round of indirect elections for the remaining 111 parliamentary seats. According to final official results, the major groups to be represented in the new Chamber of Representatives were the Entente, with 154 seats; the Democratic Union, 115 seats; and the RNI, 41 seats.

Following the completion of the electoral process, King Hassan asked all the parliamentary groups to join the new cabinet. The four Democratic Bloc parties refused the King's request, and urged him instead to grant the cabinet more leeway in executing policies. Following the Bloc's formal rejection of cabinet seats on 4 November, the King nominated Mohamed Karim Lamrani, a businessman and acting prime minister since August 1992, to head the new conservative/centrist coalition government.

In July, members of Morocco's Royal Consultative Council for Saharan Affairs and the Western Saharan liberation front Polisario met for the first time for direct talks at the U.N. headquarters in New York. The Algeria-based Polisario has waged guerrilla warfare in Western Sahara since the Moroccan annexation of the former Spanish colony in 1975. The New York meeting, aimed at discussing the U.N. plan to conduct a referendum on the future status of the territory, ended abruptly on 19 July, after several days of closed-door negotiations. Subsequently, Polisario blamed "Moroccan intransigence" for the failure of the talks.

Following a 14 September meeting with the Israeli Prime Minister, Yitzak Rabin, Morocco and Israel agreed to expand political and economic contacts, hinting at a mutual diplomatic recognition in the near future. However, the government stated that it would accord diplomatic recognition to Israel only with the unanimous consent of Arab states.

In order to gain favor for a comprehensive free trade agreement, under negotiation in 1993, the government clamped down on illegal Moroccan and third-country would-be emigrants to the European Union. In the northern Rif region, the government began implementing a five-year development program to reduce production of and trafficking in illicit drugs.

The government continued the economic liberalization program begun in 1992, which includes the convertibility of the *dirham* and privatization of 115 large companies by 1995.

Political Rights and Civil Liberties: Moroccans have limited means to change their government democratically. Although the constitution provides for a pluralistic political system and a parliamentary form of government, ultimate power rests with the monarch, whose person is "inviolate and sacred." He has the power to appoint and dismiss ministers, declare states of emergency, dissolve parliament and rule by decree.

Elected opposition members may attack the government's economic record but not foreign policy, which is the King's preserve. The state suppresses unauthorized groups by political imprisonment, disappearances and torture.

The government limits freedom of speech and the press. Citizens face reprisals if they discuss any of the three forbidden topics: the monarchy, Morocco's claim to Western Sahara, and the sanctity of Islam. On 28 January an appellate court upheld a two-year prison sentence against the secretary general of the Democratic Confederation of Labor, Noubir Amaoui, convicted in April 1992 for criticizing the government's lack of commitment to democracy and human rights in an interview with a Spanish newspaper. The government subsidizes and controls the news media. Academic research on the monarchy and Islam is strictly limited.

Freedoms of association and assembly are restricted. The government may suppress peaceful demonstrations and mass gatherings. On 9 April the government banned an attempted protest march by women's groups intending to demonstrate against sexual abuse by high public officials.

Torture is widespread. Those who criticize the King face imprisonment. In an attempt to improve his reputation, the King has been freeing prisoners and closing down prisons. However, in April Amnesty International accused the government of continuing to hold hundreds of political prisoners in secret detention centers throughout the country.

The court system is subject to occasional political intervention and control. The government often ignores guarantees of procedural due process. In August the authorities carried out the first death sentence since 1982, executing the former Casablanca police commissioner, Mohammed Mustafa Tabet. A court convicted Tabet of video-taped assaults and rapes of hundreds of women.

Islam is the official religion. Approximately 99 percent of Moroccans are Sunni Muslims and King Hassan II holds the title "Commander of the Faithful." The government permits the small Jewish and Christian minorities to practice their faiths, but considers other religions as heresies and prohibits their exercise. Proselytizing by non-Muslims and conversion of Muslims to other religions is prohibited. In November, a court sentenced Zmamda Mustapha, a convert to Christianity, to a three-year jail term for distribution of Christian literature.

Moroccans are free to travel within Morocco proper, but not in Western Sahara, where movement is limited in militarily restricted areas. Members of the opposition have been denied passports for political reasons. Women must have permission from their fathers or husbands to obtain a passport.

Although there is no systematic racial discrimination, Moroccan blacks generally occupy the lowest social strata. Women have legal equality with men except in areas of marriage and family. Moroccan women have opportunities for higher education and some have succeeded in professions and business.

The government permits independent trade unions to exist, but selection of union officials is subject to government pressure. There are sixteen trade union federations. Workers have the right to bargain collectively and these laws are usually respected in the larger enterprises, while ignored in the smaller ones.

Mozambique

Polity: Dominant party (transitional)
Economy: Mixed statist
Population: 16,617,000
PPP: $1,072
Life Expectancy: 47.5
Ethnic Groups: Lomwe, Makonde, Makua, Ndau, Shangaan, Thonga, Yao, other

Political Rights: 6
Civil Liberties: 5*
Status: Partly Free

Ratings Change: *Mozambique's civil liberties rating changed from 4 to 5 because of intensified human rights violations by both the government and RENAMO forces and a delay in the democratic transition.

Overview: In September 1993 Afonso Dhlakama, leader of the Mozambican Resistance Movement (RENAMO) indicated that he would only accept a loss in the upcoming multiparty elections "when I feel sure the election is free and fair." This statement may signal trouble ahead for Mozambique's nascent move towards democracy. Meetings between Dhlakama and the Mozambican President Joaquim Chissano of the Front for the Liberation of Mozambique (FRELIMO) led to an October 1992 peace agreement that is intended to pave the way for multiparty elections now scheduled for the fall of 1994.

Under the October peace plan, government soldiers and rebel fighters were to report to designated U.N. assembly points to turn in their weapons and return home. RENAMO agreed to turn over territory to the state and, for its part, the government agreed to appoint three RENAMO officials from each of the country's eleven provinces to counsel provincial governors.

While U.N. diplomats remain optimistic that the peace plan will work, a number of logistical problems coupled with political wrangling have already caused substantial delays. Elections originally scheduled for 1993 have been postponed until the fall of 1994. Although both sides have agreed in principle to disarm by April 1994, no government soldiers or rebel fighters have reported to any of the forty-nine assembly points and each side has accused the other of ceasefire violations.

Since the country gained independence from Portugal in 1975, the former Marxist-Leninist FRELIMO regime and the 30,000-member rebel RENAMO movement have waged a violent campaign for power. The civil war has devastated this country of 15 million. One million people have died as a result of the ongoing power struggle, an estimated 3.5 million Mozambicans have been internally displaced and an additional 1.7 million are refugees.

President Samora Machel led a one-party state in Mozambique until his death in 1986. Chissano succeeded him and served as both president and FRELIMO party leader. All political activity was banned in Mozambique until 1990 when a new constitution legalized nonviolent political opposition. While negotiations between the government and RENAMO have been underway since 1990, the October 1992 peace plan marked a promising breakthrough in negotiations to end the fifteen-year-old civil war.

Political Rights and Civil Liberties: Mozambicans cannot change their government democratically. Despite a 1990 Constitution that provides for freedom of political participation and assembly, universal suffrage, and direct legislative and executive elections, the transition to democracy has been repeatedly stalled. Elections scheduled under the peace plan for October 1993 have been postponed until 1994. In September 1993, the RENAMO leader indicated that even the 1994 date may be too early. It remains unclear when or if the elections will take place.

While leaders of RENAMO and FRELIMO have agreed to a demobilization process, this can only be successful when government and rebel fighters are given guarantees of a peaceful livelihood. The tasks ahead to ensure compliance with the peace plan are daunting. While both sides have pledged to avoid the Angolan scenario, the RENAMO leader has suggested that he may question any election result that he does not deem free and fair. Dhlakama did not dissipate fears that should he lose the election, RENAMO would again be prepared to return to armed resistance.

During 1992-1993, gross human rights violations have been committed by both sides. Africa Watch has documented RENAMO's attacks on Mozambican citizens as a means of "terrorizing the local population." RENAMO continued to kidnap and detain civilians, including children, against their will and frequently forced them to act as porters or serve in the military. Amnesty International reports that while numbers have reportedly decreased, FRELIMO continues to engage in forced recruitment of young boys into the military. Human rights groups also report continued mistreatment of prisoners, including beatings and the denial of food, by the soldiers, police and prison staff.

The judicial system in Mozambique is divided into two systems—the civil/criminal (which includes the customary courts) and the military. Although the practice of trying those accused of crimes against the State in revolutionary tribunal courts has ended, misconduct during trials of political prisoners reportedly continues. It is reported that common practice in cases involving political prisoners include: inadequate representation by court-appointed attorneys; placing the burden of proof on the accused; and the use of coerced confessions. Many of the estimated 400-550 political prisoners held in Mozambican jails during 1992 were said to be RENAMO supporters.

Both FRELIMO and RENAMO have prevented the delivery of humanitarian relief. Aid convoys attempting to reach the most needy of Mozambique's population have been repeatedly attacked by RENAMO. In early 1992, the government of Mozambique began charging relief agencies $150 for every ton of food delivered to certain rural regions. This policy suspended food delivery for two months in the province of Sofala. Africa Watch reports that between 50 and 75 percent of all food relief reaching Mozambique is diverted by government soldiers and officials, government-authorized distributors, retailers and transportation workers.

There have been some gains in press freedoms during 1992-1993. The Constitution and new press laws (in connection with the peace accord) provide for freedom of expression and the press. Some objective reporting, particularly from television and radio, was apparent and the government-controlled Maputo daily newspaper *Noticias* published several reports critical of the regime. However, despite some liberalization of the press, reports indicate that the media are still under FRELIMO control. The Lawyers Committee for Human Rights in its publication *Critique* cites examples of government interference and censorship in the press. The report indicates journalists covering stories involving military corruption have been threatened. The report states: "Some journalists allege that they have received death threats from the military, while others say that they fear that reporting on the military corruption would cost them their jobs."

Freedom of religion is respected and tensions between religious organizations and the state, so prevalent in the post-independence years, continued to ease in 1993. Workers have the right to join unions. Most trade unions belong to the Organization of Mozambican Workers (OTM). With the exception of government employees, police, military and other essential employees, workers have the right to strike. Despite government restriction on strikes by the military, several violent strikes by soldiers protesting lack of pay were reported during 1992.

Namibia

Polity: Presidential-legislative democracy
Economy: Capitalist-statist
Population: 1,452,000
PPP: $1,400
Life Expectancy: 57.5
Ethnic Groups: Ovambo (50 percent), Kavango (9 percent), Herero (7.5 percent), Damara (7.5 percent), Baster and Colored (6.5 percent), White (6 percent), Nama/Hottentot (5 percent), Bushman (3 percent)

Political Rights: 2
Civil Liberties: 3*
Status: Free

Ratings Change: *Namibia's civil liberties rating changed from 2 to 3 as a result of modifications in methodology. See "Survey Methodology," page 671.

Overview: The major Namibian developments in 1993 were the inauguration of the upper parliamentary chamber, the National Council; the reshuffling of the cabinet; and the introduction of a national currency, the Namibian dollar.

A former German protectorate, Namibia (formerly South West Africa) was invaded by South Africa during World War I, after which South Africa administered Namibia under a system of apartheid. In 1966, the South West Africa People's Organization (SWAPO) launched an armed struggle for independence. In 1978 the U.N. adopted resolution 435 calling for Namibia's independence, which was accepted by South Africa only in 1988.

In November 1989, SWAPO candidates won the U.N.-supervised pre-independence elections. On 21 March 1990, Namibia became formally independent, SWAPO leader Sam Nujoma becoming its first president. The 1989 elections were contested by ten political groups that vied for the 72-seat National Assembly. SWAPO won 41 seats, and the center-right Democratic Turnhalle Alliance (DTA) won 21. On 30 November 1992, SWAPO won in 38 out of 47 local, and in 9 out of 13 regional, councils. DTA supporters claimed that former SWAPO guerrillas had intimidated and attacked opposition partisans during the campaign.

In early 1993 there was internal strife within the DTA, raising fears that the party might split, thus further diminishing the role of the opposition, and enhancing SWAPO dominance. The DTA dates back to South Africa's attempts, following the pasage of U.N. resolution 435, to grant Namibia's independence with a friendly government at its helm, excluding SWAPO. During the November elections DTA received most of its support from the rural Hereros and Caprivis and the white community. Dick Murge, DTA's chairman and its most influential white member, opposed Andrew Matjila, the party's information and publicity secretary, who had attempted to isolate Murge because he refused to committ DTA to a broad anti-SWAPO coalition with smaller opposition parties. In April Murge announced that he was considering resigning from politics.

On 11 May the National Council opened its first session in a joint meeting with the National Assembly. The twenty-six-member Council comprises two representatives from each of the newly established thirteen regions, and has the power to review and delay bills presented by the Assembly. SWAPO members filled nineteen of its seats, with the remaining seven going to the DTA.

Despite an affirmative action program that has helped some members of the black majority to join the middle class, most Namibians remain poor and unemployment is estimated to be around 40 percent. Most civil service positions are still filled with appointees from the time of the South African administration, significant numbers of whom are white. Due to the constitutional stipulation prohibiting the removal of civil service employees without their consent, the government has been unable to fulfill its promise of appointing more former SWAPO fighters to government posts. Of the 72,000 civil service positions, only 61,000 remain filled, but at the end of 1992 the government announced a hiring freeze.

The 4,000 white commercial farmers own most of the fertile agricultural land and provide the bulk of the employment for the black majority. The government's cautious approach to redistribution of agricultural land has been criticized by radical SWAPO supporters. Nevertheless, the government opposes the forcible expropriation of property so as to not jeopardize its policy of attracting foreign investment in the mining and manufacturing sector. In April, President Nujoma reshuffled the cabinet of Prime Minister Hage Geingob by removing Ben Amathila, who was criticized for his slowness in preparing incentives for industrial development, from the post of Minister for Trade and Industry. Amathila was replaced with the more pro-market Hidipo Hamutenya.

In September, Namibia introduced its own currency, the Namibian dollar, eventually to replace the South African rand as the national currency.

An important step towards the return to Namibia of the major deep water port Walvis Bay, which has remained under British and South African administration for more than a century, took place on 16 August when the South African multiparty conference discussing that country's future agreed to hand the port back by February 1994.

Following the renewal of the civil war in Angola in late 1992, the Namibian government feared that the war might spill over onto its territory. Approximately 100,000 Angolan refugees have crossed the Namibian border, escaping the fighting between Angolan government troops and the rebel UNITA forces. UNITA has accused the Namibian government of providing military support to the Angolan army; the government, however, has denied this. In April the Namibian government accused UNITA of raiding Namibian border towns in search of supplies.

Political Rights and Namibians can change their government democratically. An
Civil Liberties: executive president was initially elected by the National
Assembly but will later attain office by direct popular vote.
The president will be limited to two five-year terms. Constitutional provisions establish regular elections for a bicameral parliament; members of the upper house National Council were chosen through equal regional representation in 1992, and members of the lower Assembly will be selected through proportional representation in 1995.

The judiciary is independent, consisting of a three-tiered court system, with the Supreme Court being the highest appelate and constitutional review court. Trials are usually open to the public, and the accused have a right to legal counsel. However, the insufficient number of qualified judges and attorneys has led to a backlog of cases awaiting trial. Most of the 100 licensed attorneys are white.

Despite their prohibition, torture and arbitrary arrest continue to occur sporadically. In March, the opposition newspaper *Die Republikein* reported alleged torture in detention of a UNITA brigadier, Jorge Valentim, who was seeking political asylum in a third country.

The controversy over the redress of wrongs committed by SWAPO and the South Africa-led security forces during the time of the struggle for independence continued, fueled by the government's refusal to establish a "truth commission" to investigate the matter. Most of the members of the former South African-led security forces continue to hold government posts. Less than half of the 914 SWAPO members imprisoned and tortured in SWAPO camps in Angola and Zambia have been repatriated to Namibia, and SWAPO and the government refuse to clear their names, despite the lack of evidence to substantiate the claims that they were South African informants. In October 1990 President Nujoma appointed Solomon Hawala, one of those implicated in the arrests and torture, to the post of Commander of the Army.

Ethnic organizations criticized the government's delineation of regional administrative boundaries, without regard to their ethnic composition, and its stated English-only policy in education, despite constitutional provisions guaranteeing mother tongue education in private schools. In July, Hans Diergaard, the leader of the small Baster Rehoboth community (a racially mixed, Afrikaans-speaking group), asked the U.N. to recognize the group as an indigenous people, to strengthen its position in a dispute with the government over autonomy and communal land.

Freedoms of speech and the press have been respected since independence. The newpapers are free and vigorous. Besides one government-owned weekly, most newspapers are af-filiated with political parties and are heavily partisan in their reporting. The Namibian Broadcasting Corporation(NBC) airs radio and television programs in several local languages. Its broadcasting policy is set by a government-appointed but broadly representative board.

Freedom of religion and freedom of movement are respected. The largest trade union organization is the National Union of Namibian Workers (NUNW), a SWAPO affiliate. In March, the NUNW quit the Labor Advisory Council (LAC) consisting of employer, trade union and government representatives, to protest the granting of equal representation to smaller unions.

Nauru

Polity: Parliamentary democracy
Economy: Mixed capitalist-statist
Population: 9,000
PPP: na
Life Expectancy: 66.0

Political Rights: 1
Civil Liberties: 3*
Status: Free

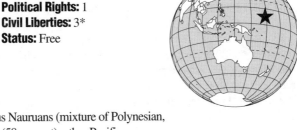

Ethnic Groups: Indigenous Nauruans (mixture of Polynesian, Melanesian, Micronesian (58 percent), other Pacific islanders (26 percent), Chinese (8 percent), European (8 percent)
Ratings Change: *Nauru's civil liberties rating changed from 2 to 3 because of government restrictions on freedom of assembly, association and press.

Overview:

Nauru, a tiny island located 1,600 miles northeast of New Zealand, became a German protectorate in 1888. Following World War I Australia administered the island under a mandate from the League of Nations and later from the United Nations, granting independence on 31 January 1968. The eighteen-member parliament is popularly elected for a three-year term, most recently in November 1992. Political parties are legal but none has formed; however, candidates representing a wide variety of viewpoints contest the parliamentary seats. The president is elected by the parliament for a three-year term. In November 1992 parliament re-elected President Bernard Dowiyogo over former cabinet minister Buraro Detudamo. The Nauru Local Government Council is directly elected from fourteen districts and provides local services.

In 1993 Nauru resolved a long-standing dispute with Australia regarding compensation for phosphate mining during the trusteeship period. For years Australia denied any liability on the grounds that it had paid Nauru royalties during the trusteeship period and in 1967 had sold the mining operation to the islanders at what it considered a generous price. However, Nauru said the royalties had been inadequate, since Australia had sold the phosphates to its domestic markets at below world-market prices. In May 1989 Nauru sued Australia in the International Court of Justice at the Hague, seeking additional royalties as well as compensation for damages done by the mining to the eight-square-mile island, 80 percent of which is now uninhabitable. In an out-of-court settlement announced on 9 August 1993, Australia agreed to pay $72 million in damages over twenty years.

The government's $700 million Nauru Phosphate Royalties Trust (NPRT) will provide income for future generations after the phosphates run out in about ten years. However, in May 1993 the NPRT's Australian manager, Geoffrey Chatfield, quit his job after two months, claiming that several government agencies had borrowed from the fund and left it dangerously overloaded with high-risk property investments. Moreover, many of the NPRT's recent investments have been either questionable, such as providing financing in 1993 for a money-losing London musical, *Leonardo*, or careless, including being duped in 1991 into buying fraudulent "prime bank notes" in London.

Political Rights and Civil Liberties: Citizens of Nauru can change their government democratically. Political parties are legal although none has formed. Instead, citizens generally run for parliament according to specific ideas or issues. The judiciary is independent of the government, and the accused enjoy full procedural safeguards. Freedoms of speech and association are generally respected. An exception in 1993 involved the People's Movement, a womens' group set up to protest the NPRT's mismanagement (see "Overview" above). In July the government reportedly threatened to dismiss Movement members employed in the public sector if the group demonstrated during a South Pacific Forum meeting. The group held protests with banners and placards, and no dismissals were reported.

The government-owned radio station broadcasts Radio Australia, the BBC and local news. In the absence of a newspaper, news and ideas are generally transmitted via word of mouth on the tiny island. Several foreign publications are available, although the government allegedly confiscated all issues of the July 1993 *Pacific Islands Monthly*, which carried a cover article on the NPRT situation.

There are no restrictions on foreign travel, and all inhabited areas on the island can be reached by foot. Females cannot marry non-Nauruans, and males must get permission from the government to marry foreigners. Physical abuse of women occurs relatively frequently and is generally alchohol-related. The constitution allows workers to bargain collectively, but the government discourages trade unions and none exists. Any foreign worker who is fired must leave the country within sixty days.

Nepal

Polity: Parliamentary democracy
Economy: Capitalist
Population: 19,851,000
PPP: $920
Life Expectancy: 52.2
Ethnic Groups: Newar, Indian, Tibetan, Gurung, Magar, Tamang, Bhotia, others
Ratings Change: *Nepals's political rights rating changed from 2 to 3 and its civil liberties rating from 3 to 4 because of increasing politically related violence.

Political Rights: 3*
Civil Liberties: 4*
Status: Partly Free

Overview: Three years after mass protests forced Nepal's King Birendra to introduce sweeping democratic reforms, opposition groups staged protests and strikes throughout 1993 over a controversial hydroelectric treaty with India and possible government conspiracy in the deaths of two party leaders. Police fired indiscriminately at anti-government protestors on several occasions, killing up to twenty people. Over the summer, the worst flooding of the century killed 1,800 people and caused $1 billion in damages.

Gurkha ruler Prithvi Narayan Shah unified this Hindu Himalayan kingdom, nestled between China and India, in 1769. Britain handled Nepal's foreign affairs between 1860-1923. The country's first elections in 1959 brought the leftist Nepali Congress (NC) to power. The next year the King accused the government of abuse of power, dissolved the parliament, banned political parties and began ruling by decree. The current monarch, King Birendra, came to power in 1972 at age twenty-six.

The country's democratic transition began in January 1990 as the outlawed NC and several Communist groups began mass pro-democracy protests. The situation climaxed violently on 6 April when the police fired on demonstrators in the capital, Kathmandu, killing up to 150 people. The King legalized political parties two days later, and in November approved a new constitution granting most executive powers to a Council of Ministers. The constitution established a bicameral parliament consisting of a 205-member elected House of Representatives, and an appointed sixty-member National Council (a third of whose members must be rotated every two years), where seats are distributed in proportion to the party representation in the House. The King nominates 10 percent of the members of the upper house on the advice of the prime minister, and can assume emergency powers in national security crises, including war, insurrection, or severe economic conditions.

The first multiparty elections in thirty-two years were held on 12 May 1991. The Nepali Congress took 110 seats; Nepal Communist Party (United Marxist-Leninist) (NCP-UML), 69; the radical-left People's Front, 9; Nepal Goodwill Party, 6; the royalist National Democratic Party (Chand), 3; the pro-Beijng Nepal Workers' and Peasants' Party, 2; Communist Party of Nepal (Democratic-Manandar), 2; the royalist National Democratic Party (Thapa), 1; and 3 independents. On 29 May King Birenda formally asked the NC's Giraja Prasid Koirala, the leader of the 1990 democracy movement, to form a government.

In December 1991 Prime Minister Koirala signed a controversial agreement allowing India to build a 120-megawatt power station on Nepalese soil at Tanakpur in return for providing the kingdom with 1 percent of the electricity. The Communist opposition claimed the prime minister had sold out the country's interests, and argued that under a constitutional provision regarding natural resources the Tanakpur agreement had to be approved by a two-thirds majority in parliament. Tensions rose in April 1992 after police fired into a crowd of demonstrators in the capital protesting the accord and the government's economic policies, killing seven. In December the Supreme Court ruled the agreement had to be ratified by parliament, but did not say whether it needed a two-thirds or a simple majority.

In early March 1993 the NCP-UML and its six Communist allies organized demonstrations across the country protesting both the Tanakpur agreement and a recent 92 percent price hike for electricity. On 5 March police fired on protestors in Sindhuli district, 120 miles southeast of Kathmandu, killing a young girl and wounding several others. On 14 March the Communist party organized a general strike in Kathmandu Valley, one of several anti-government strikes held throughout the year. On 6 April the government agreed to set up a fifteen-member, multiparty committee to review the Tanakpur agreement.

On 16 May the political rift widened after a road accident 115 miles west of Kathmandu killed NCP-UML general secretary Madan Bhandari and central committee member Jeev Raj Ashrit. Both were strong opponents of the Tanakpur agreement. The driver escaped injury, leading to widespread speculation that the government had conspired in the deaths. The Communist parties organized a general strike on 25-29 June to demand a high-level investigation of the incident, resulting in more bloodshed. By some accounts police killed at least a dozen people and wounded eighty, mostly in the capital and nearby Lalitpur, and arrested more than 500 protestors.

Another general strike on 4 July paralyzed the country and forced high-level talks between the government and Communist party leaders. However, the talks collapsed almost immediately after the opposition demanded prime minister Koirala resign. On 18 July police arrested 500 people in an overnight sweep in advance of a Communist-organized transportation strike called for 19-20 July. During this strike, police killed up to four more protestors in three cities and detained more than 1,000 others, including sixteen opposition MPs.

In August the government agreed to appoint a commission headed by a chief justice to investigate the 16 May road accident, but again rejected opposition demands that Koirala step down. On 16 September, the King prorogued the opening of the fifth session of parliament, delaying until spring 1994 the release of the Tanakpur review committee's evaluation.

Tragically, over the summer the worst floods of the century killed 1,800 people and caused $1 billion in damages. On 25 August police fired on students in Barhathawa village southeast of the capital protesting the misappropriation of disaster relief materials, killing five. In another key issue, on 5 October the government began talks with Bhutan on the status of some 85,000 ethnic Nepalese who have fled Bhutan for Nepal since 1990, claiming persecution. Bhutan claims the refugees are illegal immigrants who were exposed under a 1988 census.

Political Rights and Civil Liberties: Nepalese have the democratic means to change their government. International observers judged the May 1991 elections, the first in thirty-two years, to be free and fair.

The country's primary human rights issue involves the poorly trained police force, which in 1992 and 1993 fired indiscriminately into crowds on several occasions, killing at least twenty-five people. Although the government defended the shootings on public order grounds, credible eyewitness accounts indicate the police overreacted. In addition, police commonly beat suspects to extract confessions and detain suspects without charges beyond the legally permissable twenty-four-hour period after arrest.

The Public Security Act (PSA) allows the Home Ministry to detain suspects for up to six months after first notifying a district court within twenty-four hours after arrest; the detention period can be extended for up to six months before charges must be filed. In 1993 police detained hundreds of anti-government demonstrators for varying lengths of time under the PSA. The government used the similiar Public Offenses Act to detain hundreds of civil servants during a fifty-five-day strike in 1991.

The judiciary is independent of the government and defendants receive adequate due process safeguards. The constitution allows the government to restrict speech or press that could threaten public order and national security, promote antagonism among different religion or castes, or violate public morals. The Press and Publications Act prevents publication of materials that would contravene these boundaries, and sets education and experience requirements for various journalism jobs. Newspapers and magazines vigorously criticize the government. However in April the government charged three journalists with offending members of the Royal Family by questioning the suitability of the King's daughter posing for a photograph with an Indian film star, and by publishing excerpts of a foreign book that allegedly implicated one of the King's brothers in drug trafficking. The cases are still pending. The government owns the radio and television stations, which generally promote official views.

Non-Hindus are allowed to worship freely. In rural areas caste discrimination occurs, but this is being mitigated by increased educational opportunities. Citizens can travel freely domestically and abroad. Workers are free to join unions. Strikes are prohibited in "essential services" including utilities and telecommunications, and the government can suspend a strike or the operation of a trade union if it considers this to be in the national economic interest. The Labor Act requires a 60 percent approval among workers for a strike to be legal, although illegal strikes occur.

Netherlands

Polity: Parliamentary democracy
Economy: Mixed capitalist
Population: 15,193,000
PPP: $15,695
Life Expectancy: 77.2
Ethnic Groups: Dutch (97 percent), Indonesian and others (3 percent)

Political Rights: 1
Civil Liberties: 1
Status: Free

Overview: **S**evere floods and controversies over refugees and personal morality issues were major issues in 1993.

The independence of the Netherlands dates from the late sixteenth century, when the Dutch provinces rebelled against Spanish rule. Located in Western Europe, the country has long-established traditions of representative government and constitutional monarchy. Queen Beatrix is the largely ceremonial head of state.

The Netherlands held its most recent parliamentary election in 1989. After the election, Christian Democratic Prime Minister Ruud Lubbers formed a center-left coalition with the Labor Party, led by Wim Kok. There is a bicameral parliament called the States General. Voters elect the 150-seat lower house by proportional representation. The upper house is an indirectly elected, 75-member body chosen by eleven provincial councils. Ranging from left to right, nine parties have parliamentary seats. Lubbers will retire after the next general election in 1994.

The coalition government has reduced the size of the military and sponsored the complete or partial privatization of previously state-owned firms. The Netherlands will abolish the draft by 1998 and is forming joint army units with Germany. In 1993, the government announced that in 1994 it would privatize PTT, the postal and telecommunications monopoly. In September 1993, environmentalist activists from Greenpeace commandeered Lubbers' roof, and unfurled banners that criticized his energy policies.

Severe flooding in December 1993 covered more than sixty-six square miles of

Dutch territory, leaving people temporarily homeless and in economic need during the Christmas season. Given that large areas of the Netherlands lie below sea level, the Dutch have a permanent national concern with floods, land reclamation and dikes.

In 1993, the Netherlands had a major debate about euthanasia. In November, the parliament completed passage of legislation for voluntary euthanasia. According to the law, patients must suffer irremediable pain and ask clearly and repeatedly for death before doctors may end their lives. Non-requested cases of euthanasia remain subject to prosecution. The government issued guidelines in December that left doctors confused about the circumstances that would permit legal mercy-killing versus those that would send physicians to prison. The state requires doctors to report acts of euthanasia to the authorities. Some observers believe the reporting requirement will discourage involuntary euthanasia, while others hold that reports will provide a cover for involuntary acts. Due to internal disagreements between the ruling parties, the government rejected allowing euthanasia in other circumstances. Of the two coalition parties, the Christian Democrats are more inclined towards a pro-life position, while the Laborites favor freedom of choice for euthanasia. The Vatican and pro-life groups condemned the legislation. Senior citizen lobbies expressed concern that the new law would cause involuntary deaths. Consequently, the Dutch government mounted an international campaign to explain the policy and soften its image.

Political Rights and Civil Liberties: The Dutch have the right to change their government democratically. Foreigners resident for five years have voting rights in local elections. Power shifts back and forth between center-left and center-right coalitions with the Christian Democrats playing the pivotal role. Women are increasingly influential in party politics, and there is a women's party. Feminists were outraged in October 1993 when the Reformed Political Party (SGP), a Christian fundamentalist group with three parliamentary seats, voted to prohibit more women from joining its ranks. At the time, only twenty women held SGP membership. The SGP believes that God ordained males alone to exercise political authority, while the feminists and other parties believe the SGP decision contradicts legally guaranteed sexual equality.

The press is free, but it generally observes unofficial limits in writing about the royal family. Broadcasting is state-owned but autonomously operated, and offers pluralistic points of view on social and political issues. Traditionally, commercials have been restricted, and banned on Sundays for religious reasons. In general, there is free speech, but laws prohibit inciting racism and expressing racist ideas. In 1992, the state prosecuted a Pakistani-born author who had described Muslims as primitive people with a mentality "that borders on insanity and bloodthirstiness."

The judiciary is independent. In 1993, the Police Complaints Commission charged security forces with using excessive force to quell disturbances. The body recommended requiring riot police to wear identifying numbers as members of sports teams do. In recent decades, the police have usually tolerated illegal drugs in urban areas, but in the 1990s they are cracking down on drug-oriented businesses, especially coffee shops that traffic in marijuana. In 1993 police unions objected to the appointment of convicted cop-killer Alan Reeve to the board of a prison reform league. He is fighting extradition to England.

Immigrants from developing countries have experienced some discrimination in housing and employment. In order to prevent further discrimination, the Council of

State, a constitutional body, overruled a proposed, compulsory national identity card in 1992. Public opinion turned against refugees in 1993. The country received about 40,000 applications for political asylum and has set up tent cities to house applicants. The growing number of arrivals has tested the Dutch inclination to pay for their upkeep. At a time of austerity for themselves, the Dutch find it increasingly difficult to extend economic benefits to foreigners.

Animal rights collided with refugee rights in 1993. The Dutch Animal Protection Society ran advertisements comparing the situations of abandoned house pets and asylum-seekers. Outraged refugee groups tried to prevent the animal rights advocates from using the term "asylum seeker" in the pro-animal campaigns. Potential asylees felt that the comparison with animals dehumanized the image of people seeking refuge. The Animal Protection Society reinforced this controversy in other advertisements that compared transporting pigs to market with having bad vacations, and inseminating cows artificially with experiencing sexual harassment.

Religious freedom is respected. The state subsidizes church-affiliated schools based on the number of registered students. The extensive public sector regulates the private economy, and provides generous social welfare benefits. Organized labor is free. Only civil servants lack the right to strike, but they strike anyway.

The Dutch army admits homosexuals without discrimination. Male heterosexual troops receive free copies of *Playboy*, and homosexual troops get complimentary issues of *MaGAYzine*. Brothels became legally regulated businesses as of January 1994. Other forms of prostitution were already legal or tolerated. There is a prostitutes' bill of rights that includes the right to refuse customers.

New Zealand

Polity: Parliamentary democracy
Economy: Capitalist
Population: 3,433,000
PPP: $13,481
Life Expectancy: 75.2
Ethnic Groups: White (79 percent), Maori (12 percent), Pacific Islander (3 percent), Other (5 percent)

Political Rights: 1
Civil Liberties: 1
Status: Free

Overview: New Zealand's ruling National Party barely maintained its parliamentary majority at the November 1993 national elections, reflecting popular ambivalence over the government's radical economic restructuring programs. At a concurrent referendum voters rejected the current first-past-the-post electoral system in favor of a mixed proportional system, foreshadowing the end of the country's predominantly two-party system.

New Zealand achieved full self-government prior to World War II, and gained formal independence from Great Britain in 1947. Since 1935, political power in this parliamentary democracy has alternated between the mildly conservative National Party and the center-left Labor Party, both of which helped develop one of the world's most progressive welfare states. By the early 1980s these liberal policies put New Zealand at a disadvantage in responding to low international prices for the country's agricultural exports and an increasingly competitive world trading regime. In 1984 the incoming Labor government began deregulating the financial system, removing farm and industrial subsidies, reforming the tax code, slashing import tariffs and privatizing many industries.

The harsh effects of the economic reforms, coupled with a severe recession, led to a National Party landslide at the October 1990 parliamentary elections. The National Party took a record 68 seats; Labor, 28; the New Labor Party, a spinoff of the Labor Party, 1.

Rather than slow the reforms, as many voters had expected, Prime Minister Jim Bolger's National government extended them into two areas previously considered untouchable—welfare and labor relations. In December 1990 the government slashed welfare payments 10 percent and targeted them to a more limited group, and later raised a tax surcharge on state pensioners' supplementary earnings. Meanwhile, the May 1991 Employment Contracts Act ended the unions' privilege to negotiate national, occupation-based awards, bringing many contracts to the factory or even the individual level. In late 1991 the New Labor Party, which favored reversing many of the deregulations, formed a five-party, center-left coalition called the Alliance that included the Green Party, the Democratic Party, the Liberal Party and the Maori nationalist Mana Motuhake Party. Despite growing discontent, in February 1992 the government ended universal free hospital care, which had been a pillar of the welfare state, as part of a larger program which sought to create competition among health care suppliers.

In early 1993 the National government faced serious trouble heading into parliamentary elections scheduled for later in the year. In a Television New Zealand poll of 6 March, 46 percent of likely voters supported Labor to 28 percent for the National Party. Further, 25 percent chose as their "prefered prime minister" Winston Peters, a popular Maori who had been thrown out of the cabinet in October 1991 for his outspoken views against the government's social and economic policies. Labor Leader Mike Moore drew 19 percent, while Prime Minister Bolger attracted only 8 percent support.

The release of the budget on 1 July dramatically improved the government's popularity. Private economists concurred with the government's forecast for a strong 2.9 percent economic growth through 1996 and inflation of 2 percent or less, indicating that the economy had finally responded and turned the corner after nine years of harsh measures. Voters appeared to agree; opinion polls during the week showed 55 percent approved of the National Party's handling of the economy. Nevertheless, unemployment figures held at 10 percent, and pensioners and others hit hard by government spending cuts continued to face difficulties. In mid-July Peters formed the populist New Zealand First party with a platform of reducing unemployment through more attention to regional development.

Pre-election polls showed the National Party winning big, but results released immediately after the 6 November election gave the National Party just 49 seats, one short of a majority; Labor, 46; the Alliance, 2; New Zealand First, 2. On 17 November subsequent tallying of some 300,000 absentee ballots gave the Labor seat in the Waitaki district to the National Party, ending the possibility of a hung parliament. Bolger admitted the results indicated discomfort over the reforms, which he pledged to slow down.

In light of criticism that the first-past-the-post system disadvantaged smaller parties, in September 1992 the government held a referendum to gauge voter preferences. In the first part, 85 percent rejected the present system. In a choice among four alternatives, 70 percent favored a mixed member proportional system (MMP). The MMP gives each citizen two votes. The first is for a geographical constituency seat, and the second for the other half of parliament based on proportional representation. The MMP would allow small parties to win seats if they passed a 5 percent threshhold. In a subsequent referendum coinciding with the November election, voters chose by 54-46 percent to introduce the MMP at the next election, due by 1996.

Political Rights and Civil Liberties: New Zealand's citizens can democratically change their government. The country has no written constitution, but fundamental freedoms are respected in practice. An independent judiciary provides full due process rights for the accused. Freedoms of press, speech and association are respected and fully practiced by citizens. All religious faiths are allowed to practice freely. Under the 1991 Employment Contracts Act, trade unions are no longer automatically the bargaining agents in industries; instead they must persuade both employers and employees to use them as an intermediary.

The indigenous Maori minority and the tiny Pacific Islander population claim discrimination in employment and education opportunities. The 1983 Equal Employment Opportunities Policy, designed to bring more minorities into the public sector, has been only marginally successful; Maori make up only 6.3 percent of the civil service, and only 0.7 percent of the senior management positions. Meanwhile, Maori account for half the prison population and have a 25 percent unemployment rate.

A similiarly contentious issue involves the so-called Maori reserved land. Soon after the British began colonizing New Zealand, the Crown declared large tracts of land to be held in trust for the Maori, which would be leased in perpetuity to the settlers subject to twenty-one-year rent reviews. The 1955 Maori Reserved Land Act codified this arrangement. Today, the rents received by the Maori on some 2,500 leases average 1.6 percent of market valuation, against 10 percent or more for other commercial landowners. The government is examining several long-term plans for raising rents to market levels and ultimately making lease arrangements subject to negotiation. The Maori base their land claims on the disputed 1840 Treaty of Waitangi, which they say retains their sovereignty over the land.

Nicaragua

Polity: Presidential-leg-
islative democracy
(military-influenced)
Economy: Capitalist-statist
Population: 4,096,000
PPP: $1,497
Life Expectancy: 64.8

Political Rights: 4
Civil Liberties: 5*
Status: Partly Free

Ethnic Groups: Mestizo (approximately 70 percent),
Caucasian (16 percent), black (9 percent), and indigenous (5 percent)
Ratings Change: *Nicaragua's civil liberties rating changed from 3 to 5 because of
increased political and criminal violence, much of it involving the military and groups
linked to it, in an atmosphere of impunity and citizen insecurity. See "Political Rights
and Civil Liberties" below.

Overview:

In 1993 the unofficial power-sharing arrangement between the
Chamorro government and the Sandinistas brought the
country to the verge of political anarchy and economic ruin.
Gen. Humberto Ortega loomed as the emerging strongman in the tradition of the former
Somoza dynasty.

The Republic of Nicaragua was established in 1838, seventeen years after gaining
independence from Spain. Struggles between the Liberal and Conservative parties
dominated politics until Gen. Anastasio Somoza Garcia took over in 1937. Authoritarian rule under the Somoza family lasted until the 1979 revolution that brought the
Marxist Sandinista National Liberation Front (FSLN) to power.

The Sandinistas suspended the 1972 constitution and ruled by decree. Daniel
Ortega became president in 1985 after a state-controlled election. In 1987 the
Sandinistas installed a new constitution providing for the election every six years of a
president, vice president, and a ninety-six-member National Assembly.

In 1987 the Sandinistas, pressured by the Contra insurgency, signed the Arias
peace accord which called for democratization in Central America. In 1989 the
National Opposition Union (UNO), a diverse coalition of fourteen political parties,
nominated Violeta Chamorro, the publisher of opposition newspaper *La Prensa*, for
president.

In February 1990 55 percent of the electorate voted for Chamorro, 40 percent for
Ortega. UNO won fifty-one assembly seats, the Sandinistas thirty-nine, and two smaller
parties one each. UNO won in nearly two-thirds of the municipal races.

Prior to Chamorro's inauguration, Antonio Lacayo, her son-in-law and chief
advisor, negotiated a transition agreement with Gen. Ortega, Daniel's brother and
Sandinista armed forces commander. Lacayo agreed, over the heads of UNO leaders, to
let Humberto remain as military chief. In exchange, Humberto agreed the defense and
interior ministries would be headed by civilians, and the state security apparatus would
be dismantled.

But the interior minister had limited authority, and the defense minister, President
Chamorro herself, practically none. Daniel had secretly decreed a military law that

made it virtually impossible to remove Gen. Ortega and granted him complete control over the military's internal and external affairs. Gen. Ortega, meanwhile, quietly transferred the state security apparatus from the interior ministry to the army.

President Chamorro has been mostly a bit player as the Sandinistas, relying on street violence and control of the military, leveraged Lacayo, the minister of the presidency, into an informal power-sharing arrangement. Left on the sidelines were UNO, private business and independent labor—the three pillars of the coalition that had supported Chamorro for president.

UNO opposed the arrangement from the outset and tried to use its legislative majority to curb the Sandinistas' continued domination of the country. In 1991 it presented a bill requiring the return of an estimated $1 billion in government property appropriated by the Sandinistas before leaving office. Daniel, echoing his promise in 1990 to "rule from below," called for armed rebellion and Sandinista cadres occupied farms and factories and rampaged through Managua and three other cities. In what became an established pattern, the military stood by as Lacayo was forced to cave in and grant the Sandinistas full amnesty to get them to call off the mayhem.

In 1992 eight UNO legislators formed the Center Group and began voting with the Sandinistas to block UNO bills on cutting the military budget. In January 1993 the Center Group joined the Sandinistas in taking control of the national assembly. UNO charged that Lacayo had bribed the Center Group. Guillermo Potoy, the comptroller general, backed up the bribery charges as well as other allegations of government corruption. He was fired by Lacayo and UNO walked out of the assembly.

At the same time, nearly a dozen Contra bands who had taken up arms again in 1991 increased guerrilla actions in the north. Without any effective property laws, the government has been unable to guarantee land grants or credits to former Contras, the core of the 1990 demobilization agreement. Meanwhile, Nicaragua has become the second poorest country in the hemisphere after Haiti.

In August one Contra group seized two Sandinista legislators and demanded that Chamorro fire Lacayo and Humberto Ortega. The next day a Sandinista group, backed by Daniel Ortega and assisted by the Sandinista-controlled police, kidnapped two dozen UNO leaders. All hostages were released after a week that paralyzed the country when the government guaranteed impunity for all involved. The Sandinista abductors were given unlimited access to radio and television where they claimed triumph. The Contras went back to fighting, frequently against groups of decommissioned Sandinista soldiers still linked to the army.

Meanwhile, Daniel Ortega continued leading Sandinista unions in violent strikes, demanding more control over the privatization of state industries and more spending from a government that had already consumed $2 billion in foreign aid with little to show for it.

Presiding over it all was Gen. Ortega, a master at manipulating crises to strengthen his own position. While Daniel and the Sandinistas extort the government through violence, the Sandinista army is the only institution capable of maintaining public order. So positioned, Gen. Ortega is the axle of power in Nicaragua, accountable to no one and with veto power over all.

In fall 1993 President Chamorro, in a desperate attempt to convince Washington to reinstate a suspended aid program, suddenly announced that Gen. Ortega would be removed in 1994. In a room full of foreign diplomats, Daniel screamed at her that she did not own the country. Gen. Ortega, not one for public displays, simply issued a statement saying she didn't have the authority.

Political Rights and Civil Liberties: Nicaraguans have the right to change their governments through elections. However, the Chamorro government's authority has been usurped by the Sandinistas who retain control of the military and the police. Military commander Gen. Humberto Ortega, in effect, oversees a state within a state.

The 1987 constitution permits the organization of political parties, civic groups and labor unions. But political and civic activity are severely restricted by increasing political violence in a climate of general impunity. Because the Sandinistas are the primary instigators, and at the same time control the army, the police and the judiciary, there is no authority citizens or non-Sandinista groups can turn to for security.

In 1993 Nicaragua's independent human rights groups reported increases in intimidation, kidnappings, false arrest, and torture during interrogation. Abuses by the military and the police are directed mostly against demobilized Contras and UNO supporters, particularly in rural areas. Many violations are committed by former members of state security transferred to the national police in 1990.

There have been nearly 800 political killings since 1990, a majority since 1992. More than half the victims were demobilized contras, UNO supporters or unaffiliated peasants. Less than five percent of the killings have been resolved. The rate of killing appeared to increased in 1993 as marauding bands of rearmed contras and former Sandinista soldiers linked to the army turned the north of the country into a virtual free-fire zone. The army initiated a counterinsurgency offensive, including aerial bombings, in late 1993.

A number of high-profile murder cases remained unresolved. The army has stonewalled the investigation of the October 1990 murder of Jean Paul Genie who, according to a group of Venezuelan jurists working at the request of UNO, was killed on a highway by members of Gen. Ortega's armed escort. According to the military law secretly decreed by the Sandinistas before leaving office, criminal and human rights cases involving the army are solely the province of military courts, guaranteeing impunity.

The cases of nine former Contra leaders murdered since 1990, including former Contra commander Enrique Bermudez, remain unresolved, as do the 1992 killings of two government auditors investigating charges of government corruption. Also unresolved were the murders of Arges Sequira, a leader of a group demanding the return of property confiscated by the Sandinistas, and Leopoldo Serrano, son of a prominent anti-Sandinista business figure.

The police rarely protect people and property from the armed actions of Sandinista labor unions or rural paramilitary units. Since 1990, there have been virtually no arrests in response to the bombings, takeovers of government buildings and private property, and other incidents of Sandinista violence. At the same time the police and civil courts are overwhelmed by a surging crime wave. Prisons are overcrowded and conditions deplorable, with hundreds of detainees held for months and in some cases years before being brought to court.

Labor rights are not respected. The Sandinistas wield their public unions as violent instruments to influence government economic policy. Through the public sector unions they control, the Sandinistas have managed to gain ownership of more than three dozen state enterprises privatized by the government. At the same time, independent unions are subject to violent intimidation by Sandinista union thugs whose profile is more urban guerrilla than worker representative.

The print media, uncensored and shrill, are divided between pro- and anti-Sandinista publications. Before leaving office the Sandinistas dismantled the seventeen-station state radio network and "privatized" it to mostly Sandinista loyalists, part of the massive, illegal transfer of state resources to the Sandinista party. They also retained possession of one of the three television stations. Since 1990 Radio Corporacion, the leading anti-Sandinista radio station, has been stormed or blown up by masked gunmen five times, twice in 1993.

There are no restrictions on religious expression. The Catholic church has been outspoken in its criticism of the Sandinistas' domination of the government.

Niger

Polity: Presidential par- **Political Rights:** 3*
liamentary democracy   **Civil Liberties:** 4
Economy: Capitalist   **Status:** Partly Free
Population: 8,319,000
PPP: $645
Life Expectancy: 44.5
Ethnic Groups: Hausa and Zherma (80 percent), Tuareg, Arabs, Daza, Fulani, others
Ratings Change: *Niger's political rights rating changed from 5 to 3 because it held successful democratic transitional elections.

Overview: Niger held its first democratic legislative and presidential elections in 1993, won by parties that spearheaded the political changes during the previous three years. With the new government promising to address the country's ethnic issues, the long lasting armed Tuareg rebellion in the north receded in intensity.

Niger, a landlocked West African country, gained independence from France in 1960. The military overthrew a one-party government in 1974. In 1987, the supreme military council chose General Ali Seibou as the head of state. In a move to re-establish civilian rule, the military council disbanded, naming Seibou as president. The military-backed National Movement for a Development Society (MNSD) became the sole legal party.

Faced with mass protests demanding the introduction of democracy in 1990 Seibou acceded to demands to hold a national conference to discuss political reforms. The conference, convened in 1991, stripped Seibou of all but ceremonial powers and barred him from running in the planned presidential election. The conference appointed Amadou Cheiffou to be interim prime minister, and André Salifou the chairman of the interim legislature, the High Council of State (HCR). In 1992, the HCR prepared a new constitution, approved on 28 December by an 89 percent majority.

The legislative election for the National Assembly, originally scheduled to be held simultaneously with the presidential election on 6 February, was held on 13 February. The presidential election was postponed to 27 February. Twelve parties and 619 candidates vied for the 83 Assembly seats. Following the legislative election in which 32 percent of registered voters participated, the MNSD became the largest single party with 29 seats. The Social Democratic Convention (CDS) came in second, winning 22 seats. Seven other parties were allotted the remaining seats. When after the announcement of preliminary results it appeared that the MNSD was winning the election, six of the opposition parties, including the CDS, formed the Alliance of the Forces for Change (AFC) to block the MNSD's return to power. During the presidential election, however, the opposition candidates ran separate campaigns, swelling their number to eight. During the inconclusive 27 February election, the MNSD candidate Mamadou Tandja, a retired army officer, led with 34 percent of the vote, trailed by the CDS candidate Ousmane Mahamane who received 28 percent of the vote. Tandja's electoral message consisted of equating democracy with the breakdown of law and order and a promise to "put an end to the chaos." In the 20 March presidential run-off between the two top contenders, Ousmane, backed by the AFC, received 54 percent of the votes, becoming the country's first democratically elected president. In April, Ousmane nominated Mahamadou Issofou to the post of prime minister.

On 13 July, the new government faced its first major challenge when soldiers staged a mutiny in several garrisons across the country, taking twelve government officials hostage. The mutineers demanded the payment of their salary arrears, the cancellation of budget cuts on military and social programs, and the resumption of patrols against the Tuareg rebels in the north. After intensive negotiations with the authorities, and facing an armed forces chief of staff who condemned the rebellion and pledged support for the government, the rebels surrendered.

The violence in the north, which started in May 1990 with a Tuareg attack on a military outpost, continued to recur in 1993, despite the new civilian authorities' attempts to address Tuareg problems. Initially, the rebels, organized in the Front for the Liberation of the Air and Azawak (FLAA), attacked the armed forces, but since 1992 increasingly more of its victims were civilians. In February 1993, a week after the transitional government established a cabinet post to deal with the Tuareg issue, the rebels attacked several villages, killing approximately 30 people. In mid-March the FLAA announced a two-week truce in anticipation of the second round of presidential elections. After becoming president, Ousmane named solving the rebellion as his first priority, and revoked the police powers granted to the army in the north the previous year. In early April, the government released the remaining thirty-one alleged rebel sympathizers, who had been held in detention by the army since the previous August.

The Nigerien economy suffered from a prolonged drought in the eastern and northern regions of the country, where cases of death from starvation have been reported. The fall in the price of uranium, Niger's principal export, contributed to the economic woes. The budget deficit exceeded resources by a ratio of two to one. The new prime minister announced upon his inauguration in April that he would lead a "war cabinet" to combat the economic problems.

Political Rights and Civil Liberties: Since the first parliamentary and presidential elections in February and March, Nigeriens have the right to change their government democratically. However, local and regional elections have been postponed several times since their original 1991 schedule. The traditional village chiefs retain their dominant power in the countryside where a majority of the population lives.

The judicial system is an amalgam of traditional African, Islamic and European legal codes. The new constitution affirms the judicial principle of presumption of innocence and other safeguards, such as limits on detention without warrant and public proceedings during trials. However, even after the adoption of the constitution, the army continued to detain dozens of Tuaregs suspected of being rebel sympathizers without any formal charges. Only after the newly elected president was sworn in did the army agree to release its remaining prisoners.

The Superior Council of Communication (CSC), established in 1991 to protect and regulate the media, became a permanent institution under the new constitution. Freedom of the press has generally been respected since the country's transition to democracy. Five French language newspapers and one in the Hausa language are being published regularly.

Freedom of association is guaranteed, with the exception of groups based on ethnicity, regionalism or religion. The constitution upholds the right of citizens to peaceful assembly and protest. Protests may be banned when public order is threatened and there is a risk of violence. On 7 January the police dispersed student protesters who failed to give the authorities a three-day notice of their planned demonstration. Prevailing Islamic laws and long-held social customs continue to result in discrimination against women, particularly in matters of inheritance, marriage and divorce. Only a small percentage of women entitled to vote actually participated in the elections.

Freedom of religion is respected in this largely Muslim nation. Article Four of the new constitution provides for the separation of mosque and state. Freedom of movement within the country is hindered by security checkpoints, particularly in and around major cities and the northern part of the country. Travel and emigration to, and repatriation from, foreign countries are unrestricted.

The right to organize and join trade unions is enshrined in law and respected in practice. Nevertheless, only a small portion of the country's labor force is employed in the formal economy where trade unions exist, while the majority work in subsistence farming. The only trade union federation, consisting of thirty member unions, is the Federation of Labor Unions of Niger (USTN). On 3 October the government and the USTN signed a memorandum of understanding on public service pay reductions, a part of the government's austerity package.

Nigeria

Polity: Military
Economy: Capitalist-
statist
Population: 90,122,000
PPP: $1,215
Life Expectancy: 51.5
Ethnic Groups: Hausa, Fulani, Ibo, Yoruba, Kanuri, other
Ratings Change: *Nigeria's political rights rating changed
from 5 to 7 and its civil liberties from 4 to 5 because of increased
political instability, human rights violations and aborted
democratic reforms.

Political Rights: 7*
Civil Liberties: 5*
Status: Partly Free

Overview:

In an alarming series of events, Ernest Shonekan, the civilian
government leader appointed in August 1993 by General
Ibrahim Babangida, was deposed by General Sani Abacha in
November 1993. Claiming that it was in the interest of national unity, Abacha banned
all existing political parties, any political assembly, the National Electoral Commission
and all state, local and federal governments. He further directed that all civilian officials
be replaced by military commanders.

Nigeria has undergone periods of military rule for twenty-four of its thirty-three
years since gaining independence from Britain in 1960. Ethnic and tribal violence has
long been a part of Nigeria's post-colonial period, with tensions especially high
between the Muslim-dominated north and the mostly Christian south, as well as among
the country's 250 tribal groups. Tribal animosity led to the 1967-1970 civil war in
which an estimated 2 million people died from both fighting and starvation as the Ibos
of eastern Nigeria tried to establish their own state of Biafra.

Babangida came to power as a result of an August 1989 coup. He established the
Armed Forces Ruling Council (AFRC), assuming control as both head of state and
chief executive. Babangida pledged to clean up government corruption and to return the
country to civilian rule by 1990. In May 1989, the government lifted the ban on political
parties but all subsequent applications were annulled. Instead the authorities created two
government-sanctioned parties—the Social Democratic Party (SDP) and the National
Republican Convention (NRC). Although the government maintained that the two
differed in that "one [is] a little to the left, and the other a little to the right," the parties
manifestos diverged only marginally.

The return to civilian rule was repeatedly delayed as religious, economic and ethnic
violence plagued the Babangida government from the summer of 1991 through the
following summer of 1992. Despite the unrest, on 4 July 1992 the country held its first
parliamentary election in twelve years. Because no clear ideological difference existed
between the parties, voting was primarily based on individual personalities. For the 91-
seat Senate and the 598-seat House of Representatives, the SDP emerged with 47 seats
in the Senate and 310 seats in the House.

With presidential elections set for December of 1992, election primaries scheduled in
five out of thirty states were to mark the final phase of the transition. Primaries were held

in August and September of 1992, but in each case the elections were marred by massive fraud and vote-rigging. The government voided the primary election results and replaced the national and local leadership of the parties with appointed caretaker committees.

On 17 November 1992, Babangida announced that presidential elections were to be postponed until 12 June 1993. Under a new plan, Babangida declared that both parties would nominate a presidential candidate through congresses in each of the thirty states plus the capital district, for a total of 62 candidates. One candidate from each party would then be elected at national party conventions. Babangida dissolved the AFRC and the Council of Ministers and created a National Defense and Security Council (NDSC) to replace the AFRC. He also disqualified all twenty-three candidates who took part in the earlier primaries and directed that all cabinet ministers be fired on 2 January 1993, to be replaced by a civilian-led NDSC.

Presidential elections were held on 12 June 1993. Chief Moshood K.O. Abiola, a Muslim southerner of the SDP party, emerged as victor. Abiola, a wealthy industrialist and member of the southern Yoruba tribe, won a mandate across ethnic, geographical and religious lines. Nonetheless, Babangida annulled the election on the spurious grounds of widespread irregularities. After widespread protest against his action, Babangida promised to create an interim government but warned the country that his actions were necessary to protect Nigeria's national unity.

To support conjecture that internal division could spark a second civil war, the governing council showed films of the 1967 war. Its efforts at scare mongering were not in vain. Shortly after the elections were nullified, members of ethnic minorities—both north and south—returned to their home villages and towns. There is deep concern that a split could develop between Chief Abiola's Yoruba people, who dominate in the south-west and its main cities of Lagos, Ibadan and Ife, and the rest of the country.

A series of demonstrations and strikes protesting the election annulment continued and forced Babangida to resign office on 26 August 1993. There is some evidence indicating that Abacha may have been pivotal in forcing Babangida to step down. This speculation caused widespread dissension in the military and may have been the key factor which led Abacha to purge top Babangida loyalists from the military in the week following his resignation. Babangida appointed Shonekan, a former business leader and ally, as his successor. Shonekan was widely perceived to be a puppet of Abacha.

During his brief tenure in office, Shonekan had attempted to win public support by freeing political prisoners, lifting press restrictions and instituting reforms in the oil industry bureaucracy. Shonekan also promised to hold new presidential elections on 18 February 1994.

Political Rights and Civil Liberties:

Nigerians cannot change their government democratically. Under the Babangida government, opposition parties were legalized in 1989. However, none of the subsequent fifty party applications was accepted. Candidates from the two government-sanctioned parties were allowed to contest the 1993 presidential election but although the election was reported to be free and fair, the results were subsequently nullified.

The newly self-appointed military ruler of Nigeria has banned all existing political parties and, it appears, destroyed any immediate hope for democracy in Nigeria. While Abacha has indicated that civilian administrators, a civilian federal council and a new constitution will be established, no timetable has been given.

Under Abacha's rule, civilian officials have been replaced by military commanders. It can be expected that under this new regime, the military control of both state and local government will be absolute. It is also expected that human rights violations by the military, State Security Service and the police will continue. During 1992 and 1993, international human rights groups and the Civil Liberties Organization (CLO) reported extra judicial killings, police brutality, and arbitrary arrest and detention.

Although Nigerian law prohibits torture and mistreatment of prisoners, detainees frequently die while in police custody and there are numerous reports that police routinely torture and beat prisoners to extract confessions and information. Conditions in Nigerian prisons remain deplorable. Prisons are without adequate water and sewage systems. Medical supplies are in short supply and disease is prevalent in the poorly ventilated and overcrowded prison systems. There were reports of a number of epidemics in prisons during 1992-93.

The criminal justice system is not free from government influence and control. Although criminal justice procedures in Nigeria call for a trial within three months of arraignment for most prisoners, poor administrative procedures coupled with corruption, often cause considerable delays. Police are empowered to make an arrest without warrant if there is reasonable suspicion that a crime has taken place or if the police witness an offense. However, this provision gives the police broad powers of arrest that are often abused.

Under the most recent constitution, the judicial branch has been separated into two divisions. Those committing common criminal offenses are tried by the regular court system. Those who are accused of certain offenses such as coup plotting, corruption, armed robbery, illegal sale of petroleum or drug trafficking are tried by military tribunals. For most cases tried before a tribunal, the accused has a right to counsel, bail and appeal. In practice, however, a presumption of guilt is often substituted for the presumption of innocence and sentences for those convicted of a crime by the tribunals reportedly exceed conviction rates of the regular courts. In cases where defendants cannot afford counsel, they can request assistance from the free Legal Aid Council. However, the Council is not adequately funded to provide counsel for all persons charged with lesser offenses.

Freedom of press is severely restricted. Although Abacha indicated that he was lifting bans on the press, he cautioned that there would be penalties to pay if journalists were not careful about what they reported. The government has control over radio and television although, pending further changes by Abacha, there are no restrictions on press ownership.

Under the 1989 Constitution citizens had the right to freedom of assembly and association. However, upon assuming control Abacha banned political parties and political associations until an unnamed date. In most cases, citizens are free to travel within Nigeria but international travel is sometimes prevented for political reasons. There is no state religion and the 1989 Constitution provides for freedom of worship. However, despite the constitutional protection, ethno-religious violence (particularly in northern Nigeria) occurred during 1992 and 1993.

The Nigerian Labour Congress (NLC) is Nigeria's umbrella labor federation and claims to have 3 million members from a work force of 30 million. Workers, except for essential government employees and members of the armed forces, are free to join trade unions. However, the government has maintained the right to supervise union accounts and merge unions. Workers do have the right to strike although the government mandates compulsory arbitration prior to strikes. In November 1993, a labor strike protesting former President Shonekan's proposed sevenfold increase in fuel prices crippled the Nigerian capital of Lagos. Shortly after assuming power, Abacha ordered the striking labor unions back to work. It remains unclear how trade unions will fair under the Abacha regime.

While women have made considerable progress in gaining both economic and political power in Nigerian society, the extent of this progress differs substantially from state to state. In some states, husbands can prevent their wives from obtaining work or passports. In a number of states, women cannot own property and, as widows, cannot assume control of their husbands' property. Under Nigerian law, wives cannot take their children out of Nigeria without their husbands' permission.

Women do not receive equal pay for equal work and, in many cases, fringe benefits given to male employees are not given to female counterparts. It is not unusual for women to be denied commercial credit or tax credit as heads of households. Single mothers face discrimination and the sale of young girls for marriage is still common. While the rate of women obtaining university degrees and entering the profession field has increased dramatically, the U.N. estimates that women still receive less than one third of the education given to men. Despite previous government opposition to female circumcision, the percentage of Nigerian women still exposed to this practice may be as high as 50 percent.

Norway

Polity: Parliamentary democracy
Economy: Mixed capitalist
Population: 4,276,000
PPP: $16,028
Life Expectancy: 77.1
Ethnic Groups: Norwegian majority; indigenous Finnish and Lappic (Sami) minorities; and small immigrant groups

Political Rights: 1
Civil Liberties: 1
Status: Free

Overview: Prime Minister Gro Harlem Brundtland's Labor Party won the general election held on 13 September 1993, but the anti-European Center Party made substantial gains. Brundtland's support for Norwegian membership in the European Union (EU) and the country's sluggish economy were the major issues in 1993.

Labor has been in power since 1990 following the collapse of a Conservative-led cabinet. The present Norwegian constitution, known as the Eisvold Convention, dates from 1814 and is one of the oldest written constitutions in the world. The largely ceremonial head of state is King Harald V. The *Storting* (parliament) consists of 165 members elected every four years by proportional representation from multimember districts. After parliamentary elections, the Storting elects one-fourth of its members to serve as the upper house (*Lagting*). The remaining parliamentarians constitute the lower house (*Odelsting*). The two chambers consider some matters separately and others jointly.

Having begun negotiations on European membership in April, Brundtland made Europe a major issue in the general election campaign. According to a public opinion poll in September, 54 percent of Norwegians opposed joining the EU; only 29 percent supported membership. Opposition to European economic union has cultural and economic roots. Although most Norwegians live in towns and cities, they remain emotionally attached to their self-image as a rural nation of farming and fishing, two sectors that fear European competition. In addition, Norwegians want protection for the offshore oil that provides a substantial portion of national income. Because of the strong anti-EU sentiment in the electorate, Labor captured only 37 percent of the vote and 67 seats, but it remained the largest party. The pro-European Conservatives lost ground to the anti-EU Center Party, whose 18.5 percent and 32 seats nearly tripled its 1989 showing. Voters were also concerned about Norway's sluggish economy and high unemployment. A computer failure in Oslo held up ballot tabulation for several days, but manual counting did not change the basic results.

Labor formed a minority government that stays in office with the shifting support of other parties, depending on the issue. The government introduced an anti-recession package in September. It aims to create jobs, improve competitiveness, and reduce taxes and tariffs.

Environmentalists and several Western governments criticized Norway for its resumption of whaling in 1993. U.S. President Bill Clinton considered economic retaliation against Norway for the deaths of 157 whales. By contrast, Norway received great international credit for sponsoring secret talks between Israel and the Palestine Liberation Organization. Foreign Minister Johan Jorgen Holst and his wife, Marianne Heiberg, author of a study of the Israeli-occupied territories, hosted negotiations at their home.

Political Rights and Civil Liberties: Norwegians can change their government democratically through free and fair elections every four years. Norwegians abroad have the right to absentee ballots. The Lappic (Sami) minority has political autonomy and its own assembly. There are few restrictions on speech, press, assembly or association. In addition to laws against slander and libel, restrictions include the prohibition of racist and sexist comments either printed or spoken in public. The police grant permission routinely for public demonstrations.

The state finances the established Lutheran Church, in which about 93 percent of the population holds at least nominal membership. However, there are alternative churches available to Norwegians. They receive public financing if they register with the government. Although there is significant freedom of worship, there are some minor restrictions on religion. For example, by law the King and half of the cabinet must be Lutherans. In some circumstances, employers have the right to ask job applicants whether they respect Christian beliefs.

Racial, sexual, linguistic and class discrimination are illegal. Women play a major role in politics and three lead major political parties. There are instances of racially motivated violence committed by civilians against recent non-Nordic immigrants. However, the police and other authorities have dealt firmly with such cases.

The press is free and vibrant. The state subsidizes many newspapers, in order to support political pluralism. The state funds broadcasting, but does not interfere with editorial content on radio and television. Commercial cable television and small private radio stations operate. Censorship is minimal, but the Film Control Board has the right to prevent the public from viewing films that it deems blasphemous, overly violent or pornographic. However, the board has not censored alleged blasphemy in over twenty years. Workers have the right to organize and strike. A majority of employees belongs to unions.

Oman

Polity: Traditional monarchy
Economy: Capitalist-statist
Population: 1,588,000
PPP: $9,972
Life Expectancy: 65.9
Ethnic Groups: Arab, Baluchi, Zanzibari, Indian

Political Rights: 6
Civil Liberties: 6*
Status: Not Free

Ratings Change: *Oman's civil liberties rating changed from 5 to 6 as a result of modifications in methodology. See "Survey Methodology," page 671.

Overview:
The Sultanate of Oman, an absolute monarchy located on the southeastern Arabian peninusula and several offshore islands, received independence from the British in 1951. In a 23 July 1970 palace coup, Sultan Sa'id bin Taimur was overthrown by his son, Qabus ibn Sa'id al Sa'id, who set out to modernize what had been a severely underdeveloped country. In 1971 the left-wing Popular Front for the Liberation of Oman began an insurrection in the southern province of Dhofar, which the government finally suppressed in 1975. Since then the Sultan, who rules by decree with the assistance of a Council of Ministers, has faced little organized opposition of any sort.

In 1981 the Sultan appointed an advisory Consultative Assembly. In the spring of 1991 caucuses of prominent citizens in each of the country's fifty-nine provinces nominated three citizens per province for a new *Majlis al-Shura* (Consultative Council) to replace the Assembly. The Sultan selected one nominee per province to sit in this Majlis, purposely excluding government officials in order to make the body something of a citizens' forum. The Majlis first convened in December 1991 for a two-year experimental period, and met several times per year in 1992 and 1993 to comment on legislation, prepare development plans, and voice citizens' concerns. By the end of 1993 the Sultan had not yet announced whether he would extend the Majlis beyond this experimental period.

Political Rights and Civil Liberties:
Citizens of Oman lack the democratic means to change their government. There is no constitution or other safeguard of rights, and no political parties or legal opposition exist. The only redress for individual citizens is through petitions to local leaders, although the

effectiveness of this largely depends on personal influence or contacts, and through direct appeals to the Sultan during his annual three-week tour of the country. The U.S. State Department has no reports of political prisoners.

While the Sultan faces little organized opposition to his rule, there are sporadic calls for independence from some Shihayeen tribesmen living in Rous al-Jibal Province on the Musandam Peninsula. The Province is geographically separate from the rest of Oman, fronting the Strait of Hormuz and bordering the United Arab Emirates on three sides, and has been administered by Oman since December 1970. In October 1993 Shihayeen representatives said citizens of the town of Khassab held a three-day demonstration to protest the detention of Sheikh Jumaa Hamdan Hassan al Malik, allegedly because of his links to pro-independence sympathizers. Several others were reportedly detained after authorities released the Sheikh.

The Sultan has control over the rudimentary judicial system, which in practice operates mostly according to tradition. There is no legal provision for counsel and no jury trials, although trials are generally open to the public. The court system includes civilian courts for criminal cases and Islamic Shari'a courts to decide family matters. All criticism of the Sultan is prohibited. The 1984 Press and Publication law gives the government control over all printed matter, and allows for prior censorship of domestic and imported materials. In practice Omani journalists exercise significant self-censorship. Two of the four daily papers are owned by the government, while the other two papers rely heavily on government subsidies. Coverage in all four dailies, and in other sundry publications, generally supports government policies. The state-controlled television and radio broadcasts carry only government views.

In practice, all public gatherings are government-sponsored. All associations must be registered with the government and must conform to the Sultan's conservative political and social norms. Islam is the official religion, although Christians and Hindus are permitted to worship at designated sites. Citizens may travel freely within the country, although women must receive permission from their husband or father to travel abroad. Although most women still do not work, in recent years women have gradually entered fields such as medicine and management that were once off-limits. The government enforces a law requiring women to receive equal pay for equal work. Inheritance matters are resolved under Islamic law, which gives women a lesser share of an inheritance than men.

The Labor Law makes no provisions for trade unions. However, employers of more than fifty workers must form a body of labor and management representatives to discuss working conditions. Wages are negotiated only through individual contracts with employees. Strikes are illegal.

Pakistan

Polity: Presidential par-
liamentary democracy
(military-influenced)
Economy: Capitalist-
statist
Population: 121,665,000
PPP: $1,862
Life Expectancy: 57.7
Ethnic Groups: Punjab, Baluchi, Sindhi, Pathan, Afghan
Ratings Change: *Pakistan's political rights rating changed
from 4 to 3 because it held comparatively free elections.

Political Rights: 3*
Civil Liberties: 5
Status: Partly Free

Overview: Early elections in October 1993 returned Benazir Bhutto to
power as prime minister in Pakistan, three years after
President Ghulam Ishaq Khan dismissed her government on
corruption charges. Bhutto's return came in the aftermath of a bitter power struggle
between Prime Minister Nawaz Sharif and President Khan that forced both men to
resign in July. The army, which has ruled Pakistan intermittently for twenty-five of the
forty-six years since independence, remained neutral and supervised the free elections.

Formed in 1947 through the partition of India, the country originally consisted of
the geographically separate regions of East Pakistan and West Pakistan. Pakistan fought
India over the disputed Kashmir province in 1947-48 and in 1965. *(A separate report
on Kashmir appears in the Related Territories Section).* In 1971 East Pakistan separated
to form Bangladesh; India supported the new nation by defeating the occupying West
Pakistani troops. The 1973 Pakistani constitution, the third since independence,
provides for a National Assembly, which currently has 207 directly elected seats and 10
reserved for non-Muslims, and a primarily advisory 87-seat Senate chosen by the 4
provincial assemblies. The president is chosen every five years by an electoral college
consisting of the national and provincial assemblies and the Senate.

In 1977 General Zia ul-Haq overthrew Prime Minister Ali Bhutto, imposed martial
law and outlawed political parties. Bhutto was hanged in 1979 on charges of complicity
in a 1974 murder. In 1985 Zia allowed political parties to function again and repealed
martial law. However, he forced an amendment through parliament giving the president
broad powers, including the right to nominate and dismiss the prime minister, the armed
forces chief, top judges and provincial officials, and to dissolve the National Assembly
and Senate. Since the president is not popularly elected, these Eighth Amendment
powers are far out of proportion to his accountability. In May 1988 Zia used the Eighth
to dismiss the government of Prime Minister Muhammad Khan Junejo on charges of
corruption and nepotism. In August, during preparations for fresh elections, Zia died in
a mysterious airplane crash. Polling in November brought Bhutto's daughter, Benazir
Bhutto, to power as prime minister.

In August 1990 President Ghulam Ishaq Khan dismissed Bhutto for alleged corruption, nepotism and abuse of authority, and dissolved the National Assembly. Elections in
October gave the nine-party conservative Islamic Democratic Alliance coalition (IDA)

105 seats and its allies 50; the People's Democratic Alliance, dominated by Bhutto's Pakistan People's Party (PPP), won just 45. The IDA formed a new government under Nawaz Sharif, a businessman and the chief minister of Punjab province. In March 1991 the IDA strengthened its control of the Senate in balloting by the provincial assemblies.

Sharif began 1992 in a strong position with a parliamentary majority, control of the four state provinces, and good relations with the other two members of the country's unofficial ruling troika—President Khan and army chief-of-staff Asif Nawaz, a pro-Western liberal. However, during the year several religious-based parties withdrew from the IDA after Sharif reneged on promises to Islamicize the legal system. In May the army took over Sind Province for six months to restore order following years of ethnic-based violence. The Mohajir Qaumi Mahaz (MQM) party, which represents Urdu-speaking immigrants in Sind, also pulled out of the IDA in protest. Sensing Sharif's vulnerability, Bhutto called for a massive cross-country march beginning on 11 November to force fresh elections. The government banned the rally, and on 18 November briefly imprisoned Bhutto and her mother for breaking Sharif's orders by attempting to enter the capital, Islamabad. Thousands of Bhutto's supporters were detained for holding demonstrations.

In January 1993 army chief Nawaz died of a heart attack. The president appointed Abdul Waheed Kakar to succeed him, bypassing three candidates Sharif had informally approved for the post and creating a serious rift between the two leaders. On 28 February Sharif openly challenged Khan by setting up a special committee to review the Eighth Amendment and calling on the opposition to help secure the two-thirds parliamentary majority necessary for a repeal. Sharif had anticipated gaining Bhutto's support given her own government's dismissal in 1990, but Bhutto coyly refused, leaving the prime minister exposed and vulnerable. By early April several of Sharif's close associates were urging him to back down rather than have his government sacked.

Nevertheless, in a 17 April speech Sharif referred to the office of the presidency as a "den of conspirators." The next day President Khan dismissed the government, dissolved parliament, named a caretaker prime minister and called elections for 14 July. Khan also maneuvered to gain control of the provincial assembly in politically crucial Punjab, home to 60 percent of the population. Khan's ally, Punjabi Assembly speaker Manzoor Watoo, told members that unless they elected him chief minister of the province, the president would dissolve the body. On 25 April Sharif loyalists fought Khan supporters on the floor of the Punjabi Assembly, but the MPs ultimately elected Watoo as chief minister.

In an unheralded decision, on 26 May the Supreme Court ruled 10-1 to restore Sharif to power, holding that Khan's dismissal order was "not within the ambit of the powers confered on the president" due to his lack of effort at mediation. The decision merely continued the confrontation between the prime minister and the president. On 29 May Khan had Watoo sack the Punjab legislature, creating political chaos in the province in a blatant effort to force Sharif to call new federal elections. On 30 May Khan also engineered the dissolution of the North West Frontier Province.

On 28 June a high court restored the Punjab assembly, but Watoo immediately tried to dissolve it again. The next day Sharif imposed emergency rule in the province, a measure previously taken only in 1973 to quell a separatist insurgency in Baluchistan Province. The president refused to sign the order, and the provincial government simply ignored it, leaving authority over Punjab unclear.

In a deal brokered by army chief Waheed, on 18 July both the president and the prime minister resigned, parliament was dissolved and fresh elections were called for October. Moeen Qureshi, a former World Bank official, took over as interim prime minister and quickly introduced several pragmatic financial and political reforms. A new agricultural tax covered rich landlords for the first time, and quickly boosted foreign exchange reserves from $180 million to $480 million. Qureshi published a list of 5,000 prominent citizens, including Bhutto, who had defaulted on major bank loans, and barred them from contesting the upcoming election until the debts were paid. He also had police crack down on druglords operating in remote areas, barred several dozen candidates accused of drug trafficking from running for office, forced customers to pay overdue utility bills, devalued the currency, and cancelled many of Sharif's inefficient development projects.

Some 150,000 army soldiers supervised the 6 October vote, which observers rated as one of the country's cleanest ever. The 41 percent turnout was one of the lowest since independence, no doubt reflecting cynicism over the country's fourth round of elections in eight years. The PPP took 86 seats; the PLM 72; 12 minor parties and 15 independents took 43 seats, while legal disputes caused polling to be suspended in six districts. On 19 October the PPP and its allies polled 121 votes to elect Bhutto prime minister. Although Bhutto pledged the next day to "review" the new macroeconomic reforms, which had pushed food prices up more than 10 percent, a crucial $1.5 billion IMF loan Qureshi negotiated is tied to the program's continuation. On 13 November the parliament elected foreign minister Farooq Leghari, a Bhutto ally, as president, giving Bhutto leeway to repeal the Eighth Amendment.

Political Rights and Civil Liberties:

In October 1993 Pakistanis changed their government in generally free and fair elections. The army supervised polling areas to prevent the widespread irregularities that had marred past votes.

Official corruption is still rampant, and the U.S. Central Intelligence Agency says many of the country's political elite are linked to the narcotics trade. Violence permeates all levels of society. Police reportedly kill several hundred suspects each year in extrajudicial, staged "encounters." Random, sporadic clashes occur between Shiite and Sunni Muslims, between tribes in remote areas, and between rival student wings of political parties at universities. Several political parties, most notably the MQM, are accused of using "torture cells" against opponents and to enforce party discipline. Police routinely torture detainees to extract confessions and other information, and rape female prisoners. Security services keep numerous politicians and dissidents under surveillance, and frequently search homes and offices without a warrant.

The 1979 Hadood Ordinances provide imprisonment, floggings and other punishment for violating Islamic behavioral codes, including a ban on consensual extramarital sex. In 1991 the government passed a law designed to Islamicize all aspects of government and society. However, the enabling legislation has not been passed, and the new government of Benazir Bhutto may simply shelve the matter. Hindus claim discrimination in education and social services and are occasionally attacked by Muslims, and their places of worship are sometimes ransacked. The government does not recognize the Ahmadi sect as Muslims because they do not accept Muhammad as the last prophet. Ahmadis face social ostracization, and their mosques are frequently closed.

The court system is severely backlogged and cases often take years to complete. Some suspects are held in pre-trial detention longer than their sentences would warrant had they been convicted. Defendents generally receive relatively fair trials. However, the government sometimes influences lower courts in political cases, and the president has the power to transfer judges and block tenure. The Supreme Court's May 1993 decision restoring prime minister Sharif to office *(See Overview above)* set an important precedent for judicial independence at the higher levels. The 1975 Suppression of Terrorist Activities Act established special courts for "terrorist acts" including murder and sabotage. A 1987 law also established "speedy trial" courts for certain notorious cases. These courts generally respect procedural rights, but by their nature effectively place the burden of proving innocence on the accused. In addition, the speedy courts sometimes do not allow defense lawyers adequate time to represent clients during trials. The Federally Administered Tribal Areas administer justice according to tribal customs and often mete out punishment far out of proportion to the crime.

Freedom of expression is constrained by laws providing the death penalty for statements bringing the constitution into disrepute or otherwise subverting it, and for blasphemy against Islam. Although newspapers criticize the government, self-censorship is practiced. The government controls electronic media and regulates their content. Peaceful assembly is generally permitted. Women face social discrimination and are frequently subject to domestic violence. Citizens can generally travel freely internally and abroad.

Neither agricultural workers nor workers in hospitals, radio and television and export-processing zones can unionize. The 1952 Essential Services Maintenance Act restricts union activity in numerous sectors including education and transportation, and in some fields prevents workers from quitting jobs. Because of legally required cooling-off periods, and the government's right to ban strikes not considered in the public interest and to call off a strike that has lasted more than thirty days, strikes rarely occur.

Panama

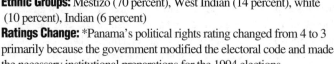

Polity: Presidential-legislative democracy
Economy: Capitalist-statist
Population: 2,431,000
PPP: $3,317
Life Expectancy: 72.4

Political Rights: 3*
Civil Liberties: 3
Status: Partly Free

Ethnic Groups: Mestizo (70 percent), West Indian (14 percent), white (10 percent), Indian (6 percent)
Ratings Change: *Panama's political rights rating changed from 4 to 3 primarily because the government modified the electoral code and made the necessary institutional preparations for the 1994 elections.

Overview:

The government of President Guillermo Endara succeeded in making the necessary preparations for national elections set for 8 May 1994. International salsa star and Hollywood actor

Ruben Blades led narrowly in the polls, as many Panamanians appeared dissatisfied with the traditional political parties.

Panama was part of Colombia until 1903, when a U.S.-supported revolt resulted in the proclamation of an independent Republic of Panama. Until World War II the government was dominated by small groups of family-based, political elites. The next two decades saw mounting discontent over U.S. control of the Panama Canal. A 1968 military coup resulted in Gen. Omar Torrijos coming to power, followed by a renegotiation of the treaty that granted the U.S. control of the Canal Zone in perpetuity.

After the 1977 canal treaties were signed, Torrijos promised democratization. The 1972 constitution was revised, providing for the direct election of a president and a legislative assembly for five years. After Torrijos's death in 1981, General Manuel Noriega emerged as Panamanian Defense Force (PDF) chief and rigged the 1984 election that brought to power the Democratic Revolutionary Party (PRD), the political arm of the PDF.

The May 1989 elections were unfair in every aspect. Even so, Guillermo Endara, the presidential candidate of the Democratic Alliance of Civic Opposition (ADOC), defeated Carlos Duque, Noriega's candidate, by nearly 3-to-1. Noriega annulled the election, abolished the legislature and declared himself head of state.

On 20 December 1989, following Noriega's removal during a U.S. military invasion, Endara was sworn in as president. His running mates, Ricardo Arias Calderon and Guillermo "Billy" Ford were sworn in as vice-presidents, and the winners of 58 of 67 legislative seats were confirmed. Fifty-one seats went to the ADOC coalition: 27 to Arias's Christian Democrats, 15 to Ford's Molirena coalition, five to Endara's Arnulfista party and four to the Authentic Liberal party. Seven seats went to the PRD.

Overseen by the U.S., the PDF was tranformed into a civilian-led police force and renamed the Public Force (PF). After U.S. invasionary forces departed, the PF assumed responsibility for public order. But a coup attempt led by a retired officer in December 1990 had to be put down by U.S. troops. Since then, polls have indicated that more than two-thirds of Panamanians want the ten U.S military bases—with a contingent of 10,000 U.S. troops—to remain after 1999, the year they are to be dismantled according to the 1977 treaties.

The economy has grown significantly since 1991, although some analysts say it is due to the country's reemergence as a drug-trafficking and money-laundering center. But unemployment has remained at 20-25 percent and poverty has increased, fueling social unrest and violent crime.

In 1992 the Christian Democrats split from ADOC and went into formal opposition. Then, voters rejected by 2-1 constitutional reforms, one of which would have prohibited the re-formation of a national army. It was a major defeat for Endara, as the special vote was widely seen as a referendum on his government.

Despite a series of corruption scandals, the government steadied itself enough in 1993 to oversee the implementation of a new electoral code. In May the influential Catholic church brokered an "ethical accord" among all political parties in which they agreed to a clean and fair campaign to be monitored by a church-sponsored commission.

The presidential candidacy of singer-actor Ruben Blades, an eighteen-year resident in the U.S., generated much interest. In 1991 he founded Papa Egoro, a political party whose name means "Mother Earth" in one of Panama's indigenous languages. At the

same time PRD candidate Ernesto Balladares had some success in removing the
Noriega taint by re-identifying the party with its late founder, Torrijos. Ricardo Arias
aspired to be the Christian Democratic candidate, but his nomination produced serious
divisions within the party.

Overall, polls indicated great voter dissatisfaction with traditional politicians.
Outsider Blades seemed to be the most popular candidate, followed closely by
Balladares. But both were running behind "Nobody" in most surveys. Former boxing
champion Roberto Duran caused a stir when he announced his independent candidacy
for the legislature.

Political Rights and Civil Liberties:

A new electoral code adopted in 1993 created the structures
and procedures necessary for a democratic election. Panamanians are to elect a new president and legislature on 8 May 1994.
The new code provides for an independent electoral commission, expands the legislature to eighty-two seats in response to population growth, and allows for the direct
election of municipal officials.

After Noriega's removal, decrees restricting the constitutional rights of freedom of
expression, organization, assembly and religion were rescinded. In 1993 eighteen
parties from across the political spectrum registered for the 1994 election.

There are a number of independent human rights organizations that operate without
interference. The government has been open to investigations by international human
rights organizations, and has accepted the jurisdiction of the Inter-American Human
Rights Court.

The Public Force (national police) is poorly disciplined and prone to corruption and
physical abuse. It has been ineffectual against the drug trade as Panama remains a major
transshipment point for both cocaine and illicit arms. Independent rights groups and
opposition parties have criticized the government for creating new security branches—
the Judicial Police and the Anti-Terrorism Police and there have been allegations that
these units are used to intimidate and spy on political opponents.

The judiciary, cowed into submission under Noriega through bribery and intimida-
tion, was revamped in 1990. President Endara replaced all nine Supreme Court judges.
The new Court in turn appointed thirteen new members to the nineteen-seat Superior
Court and replaced two-thirds of the forty-eight lower court justices.

But the judicial system remains overwhelmed and its administration is inefficient,
politicized, and undermined by corruption. During the U.S. invasion, the Supreme
Court building was sacked by looters and hundreds of thousands of court records
destroyed. The disarray is compounded by an unwieldy criminal code and a sudden
influx of cases, many of them grievances against PDF officers accumulated over two
decades of military rule.

In 1993 there were nearly 18,000 court cases pending, with the numbers climbing
due to a drug-fueled crime wave. Less than 15 percent of the nation's prison inmates
had been tried and convicted. The penal system is marked by violent disturbances in
decrepit facilities packed with up to eight times their intended capacity. The country has
barely more than twenty public defenders.

The media are a raucous assortment of radio and television broadcasts, daily
newspapers and weekly publications. There are six television stations and dozens of
radio stations. The broadcast media provide live coverage of legislative debates. But

restrictive media laws dating back to 1978 remain on the books, and the government wields lawsuits to intimidate critical journalists. In 1993 more than two hundred faced vague charges such as "defamation" and "endangering national security." There were also a number of cases of physical intimidation.

Labor unions are well organized. The government's free-market program, undermined by corruption and mismanagement, has prompted numerous paralyzing labor strikes. In 1991 the government suspended collective bargaining rights to attract foreign investment, but the suspension was lifted in 1993. However, the government had yet to comply with an International Labor Organization recommendation that public workers fired in a mass dismissal in 1991 be reinstated. A 1993 UNICEF study found that the workforce included more than 66,000 children making less than the monthly minimum wage of $150.

In 1993 indigenous groups protested the encroachment by illegal settlers on Indian lands and delays by the government in formally demarcating the boundaries of those lands.

Papua New Guinea

Polity: Parliamentary democracy
Economy: Capitalist
Population: 3,860,000
PPP: $1,786
Life Expectancy: 54.9
Ethnic Groups: A multi-ethnic, multi-tribal state—some 700 indigenous tribes
Ratings Change: *Papua New Guinea's civil liberties rating changed from 3 to 4 because of violence and official corruption.

Political Rights: 2
Civil Liberties: 4*
Status: Partly Free

Overview: Papua New Guinea Prime Minister Pais Wingti pulled off a "political coup" in September 1993 by secretly resigning and getting reelected in four minutes the next day, thus securing a fresh eighteen months of legal immunity from no-confidence motions. During the year, Wingti's plans to sack the provincial governments for mismanagement and corruption provoked a secession crisis, and the Defense Forces continued to reassert control over Bougainville Island, where a low-grade but deadly insurgency entered its fifth year.

This South Pacific country, consisting of the eastern part of New Guinea and numerous islands, won independence from Australia on 16 September 1975. The country's parliamentary democracy has been undermined by rampant political corruption and weak party structures that cause MPs to switch parties frequently. Other obstacles arrise from the extreme cultural differences between the cities and the remote highlands, and the presence of some 700 tribes speaking 1,000 languages.

In June 1992 the country's fifth post-independence elections took place with some 1,650 candidates running for the 89 nationally elected and 20 provincially based seats in the unicameral *Bese Taubadadia Hegogo* (House of Assembly). Although sixteen parties competed, there were few if any ideological differences among them. No fewer than 89 of the 109 MPs in the outgoing parliament faced investigation on corruption charges.

A record 59 incumbents lost their seats, including 15 of the 28 cabinet ministers. Final results gave the ruling, urban-based Papua New Guinea United Party (Pangu Pati), which had held 30 seats, only 19; People's Democratic Movement (PDM) 15; People's Action Party, (PAP), 13; People's Progress Party, 10; Melanesian Alliance, 9; League of National Advancement, 5; National Party, 2; Melanesian United Front, 1; independents, 34; vacant, 1. On 17 July the new parliament narrowly elected a former prime minister, PDM leader Pais Wingti, to the top spot again over the incumbent, the Pangu Pati's Rabbie Namaliu.

The constitution bars no-confidence measures for eighteen months after the election of a new government, which sheltered Wingti's government until January 1994. However, on the night of 23 September 1993 Wingti secretly submitted his resignation to the head of state, Governor General Sir Wiwa Korowi. The next day parliamentary speaker Bill Skate announced the resignation and called for nominations for a new prime minister. As a shocked and unprepared opposition watched, the parliament renominated and then reelected Wingti with fifty-nine votes; the entire procedure took four minutes.

Wingti's "political coup" gave him a fresh eighteen months of political immunity until March 1995. Since the constitution also prohibits no-confidence motions twelve months before each general election is scheduled, prior to the 1997 election there will only be an eight-month window in 1995 when the prime minister will be subject to a motion. Moreover, since Wingti does not have to call the parliament into session during that window, theoretically he has secured power until 1997. Wingti said he wanted to avoid the corruption and vote buying that generally accompanies no confidence motions, although observers noted that between 1988 and 1992 the Wingti-led opposition forwarded seven no-confidence motions.

Wingti's plan to sack the nineteen mainland and island-based provincial governments has been equally controversial. The prime minister claims they have done little to promote rural development and are riddled with corruption, and should be replaced with smaller provincial authorities headed by MPs. In October 1992 Wingti suspended four mainland provincial governments for financial mismanagement, and by January 1993 he had suspended four more. The leaders of the five island-based provincial governments have threatened a referendum on secession if Wingti's plans are carried out.

On the island of Bougainville, 560 miles northeast of the capital, a low-grade but deadly insurgency entered its fifth year. In December 1988 miners and other islanders began staging guerrilla attacks on the massive Australian-owned copper and gold mine at Panguna to demand compensation for landowners and a 50 percent share of the profits. The mine closed in May 1989, but the newly styled Bougainville Revolutionary Army (BRA) then called for independence for the island. In May 1990 government troops began blockading Bougainville, leaving some 160,000 people without adequate supplies.

In 1993 the army continued to slowly recapture the island and force the rebels to retreat into the almost inaccessible central mountains. On 15 February the government said troops had secured the provincial capital, Arawa. On 26 August BRA leaders Francis Ona and Sam Kaona rejected peace talks in Arawa, claiming their security could not be assured. Although the two sides give widely divergent details, by some independent counts more than 200 people have been killed in the fighting, including about fifty government soldiers, and several hundred islanders have died from lack of medical supplies due to the blockade.

The country accuses nearby Solomon Islands of harboring BRA soldiers. In one of many cross-border operations, in September 1992 a ten-man army squad raided Shortland Island, killing two Solomon Islanders.

Political Rights and Civil Liberties: **P**apua New Guineans have the means to democratically change their government. The June 1992 elections were generally free and fair, but irregularities occurred in the rural highlands regions. Fisticuffs broke out at several polling areas, at least 30 ballot boxes were destroyed, and police arrested MP Tom Amaiu in connection with several tampered ballot boxes. Of greater concern is political corruption and the necessity of trading favors or bribing tribal leaders to win elections. In recent years the country has experienced a severe law and order crisis. In May 1993 parliament approved changes to the Summary Offenses Act, the Bail Act and the Dangerous Drugs Act, and passed two new laws, the Internal Security Act and the Repatriation Act. With these changes the accused are presumed guilty in trials involving rapes, armed robbery and other violent crimes. Local courts are now prohibited from granting bail in serious crimes, and national courts can refuse bail. Stiffer penalties are provided for carrying and using firearms and illicit drugs.

The judiciary is independent of the government and the accused have due process rights. However, the police force is not firmly under civilian control. Abuse of prisoners and detainees occurs relatively frequently, often by intoxicated officers. In recent years police have reportedly burnt homes in highlands communities they suspected of harboring criminals or of participating in tribal warfare, or to punish crimes committed by individuals.

Both the Defense Forces and the Bougainville Revolutionary Army are accused of torture and using unnecessary force against combatants and civilians on Bougainville Island. In May Amnesty International said that Ken Savia, a minister in the rebel "government" on Bougainville and one of three men detained by security forces in February, had died in custody, possibly due to torture. In October 1992 the World Council of Churches reported that 40,000 Bougainvillians live in army-run "care centers" on the island, and are subject to rape and restrictions on movement.

An independent media has contributed to the country's democratic system. The state-run National Broadcasting Commission exercises full independence in its news coverage. Journalists are not allowed full access to Bougainville. Police approval for public demonstrations is occasionally refused on public safety grounds. There is full freedom of religion, and missionaries often provide essential services in remote areas. Freedom of movement is unrestricted, and workers are free to bargain collectively and strike.

Paraguay

Polity: Presidential-leg-
islative democracy
(military influenced)
Economy: Capitalist-statist
Population: 4,519,000
PPP: $2,790
Life Expectancy: 67.1
Ethnic Groups: Mostly mestizo; small Indian, white, black minorities

Political Rights: 3
Civil Liberties: 3
Status: Partly Free

Overview: **J**uan Carlos Wasmosy of the incumbent Colorado Party
became Paraguay's first civilian president in four decades after
winning the 9 May 1993 election. But the vote was marred by
serious irregularities and the interference of the military, which left the integrity of
democratic rule in question.

Following the February 1989 coup led by Gen. Andres Rodriguez that ended the
thirty-five-year dictatorship of Gen. Alfredo Stroessner, the new government initiated a
period of dramatic liberalization. Rodriguez promised a transition to full democracy by
1993 and was easily elected in May 1989 to finish Stroessner's last presidential term.

Opposition parties, led by the Authentic Radical Liberal Party (PLRA), threatened
to boycott the vote unless Stroessner's constitution and electoral laws were reformed.
But realizing Rodriguez would win on popularity alone, they joined what turned out to
be a free-wheeling campaign and won a number of seats in the legislature.

Electoral laws were subsequently reformed and the old voting list was revised. A
system of multi-party ballots and the practice of inking voters' fingers to prevent repeat
voting were introduced. In 1991 Carlos Filizzola, a political independent who ran at the
head of an anti-corruption movement, was elected mayor of Asuncion, the nation's
capital. It was the first time the Colorado Party had lost a major election since 1947.

The Colorados came back to win a majority of seats in the 1991 constituent assembly
election. The assembly produced a democratic constitution that went into effect in June
1992. It provides for a president, vice-president and a bicameral Congress consisting of a
forty-five-member Senate and an eighty-member Chamber of Deputies to be elected for
five-year terms. The president is elected by a simple majority and reelection is prohibited.
The constitution also bars the military from engaging in politics.

In 1992, as the various Colorado factions vied for the party's presidential nomination,
it became clear that the tradition of military interference in politics would be difficult to
overcome. In the Colorado primary election Luis Maria Argana, an old-style machine
politician, appeared to defeat construction tycoon Wasmosy. After Wasmosy cried fraud,
both Rodriguez and Gen. Lino Oviedo weighed in, illegally, to help engineer a highly
dubious re-count that made Wasmosy the winner. Rodriguez and Oviedo backed
Wasmosy because of Argana's ties to Stroessner, in exile just across the border in Brazil.

The opposition parties, fearing further interference by the military, threatened to boycott the national election. But they forged ahead after the Organization of American States
(OAS), Jimmy Carter and other observers announced they would monitor the process.

The campaign became a three-man race between Wasmosy, longtime PLRA leader

Domingo Laino, and Guillermo Caballero Vargas, a wealthy businessman and leader of the newly formed National Unity coalition. Wasmosy promised to modernize the economy. Laino played on his decades of resistance against Stroessner. Caballero Vargas, a centrist, portrayed himself as the one to ensure democracy because he was free of the politics of the past. For months almost every opinion poll showed Caballero Vargas leading, followed by Laino, with Wasmosy trailing.

Three weeks before the election, Gen. Oviedo, the most powerful military figure after Rodriguez, threatened a coup if the Colorado Party did not win. Rodriguez, in turn, warned government workers they would lose their jobs if the opposition won. Despite censure from international observers, Oviedo later stated that the military "would govern together with the glorious Colorado party forever and ever."

The vote on 9 May was marked by numerous irregularities, including vote buying, manipulation of registration lists, and military intimidation of voters. According to the official count Wasmosy won with 40.3 percent of the vote, followed by Laino with 32 percent and Caballero Vargas with 23.5. The results were virtually the mirror opposite of what opinion polls showed before Rodriguez and Oviedo intervened. Carter and the OAS concluded that the irregularities were not enough to have determined the outcome. But it is clear that the fear factor played a key role in how voters made their decision.

In the congressional elections the Colorados won 20 of 45 Senate seats—ten pro-Argana and 10 pro-Wasmosy. The PLRA won 17 and National Unity 8. In the Chamber of Deputies the Colorados won 38 of 80 seats—22 pro-Argana and 16 pro-Wasmosy. The PLRA won 33 and National Unity 9.

Wasmosy was inaugurated in August. With so few supporters in the legislature and the Colorados split, Wasmosy sought and achieved a "governability pact" with Laino that gave the PLRA input into the making of government policy. National Unity refused to enter into the pact.

In the fall the military again loomed large as a bill to bar military and police membership in the Colorado Party made its way through the congress. Colorado thugs, probably connected to Gen. Oviedo, blocked the congressional building and demanded the bill be scrapped. Oviedo had been promoted to army commander after the election.

Wasmosy was caught between his stated commitment to civilian control of the armed forces and his own evident inability to carry out his constitutional role as commander-in-chief. Coup rumors filled the media when Wasmosy at first seemed to favor the bill. By November Wasmosy had backed down. He issued a partial veto of the legislation and okayed a restructuring of the army that solidified Oviedo's power within the armed forces. Meanwhile, Oviedo was working to expand his support among Colorado party kingpins, some of whom said they were backing him for president in 1998.

Political Rights and Civil Liberties: The 1992 constitution grants citizens full democratic rights and provides for regular elections at the national and municipal levels. However, there were serious irregularities in the 9 May 1993 national elections, including incidences of fraud and interference by the military that undermined the integrity of the process.

Political parties and civic groups operate freely. Leftist parties banned under Stroessner have legal status. Political meetings, rallies and demonstrations are held regularly. Freedom of religion is respected.

Freedom of expression is generally respected. Passionate political debate occurs regularly in all media, including state-run television. In 1992 some media finally broke the taboo against addressing allegations of corruption directly involving former President Rodriguez. However, journalists investigating official corruption remain subject to intimidation and violent attacks, and the case of Santiago Leguizamon, a reporter murdered in 1991 remains unresolved. Also, while the constitution establishes safeguards for free expression, there are vague, potentially restrictive clauses regarding "responsible" behavior of journalists and media owners.

There are dozens of trade unions and two major union federations. Labor actions are on occasion broken up by the military and labor leaders detained. The 1992 constitution gives public sector workers the right to organize, bargain collectively and to strike, but these rights are often not respected in practice. A new labor code designed to ensure worker rights was finally passed in October 1993.

Peasant organizations demanding land in rural areas often meet with violent police crackdowns, detentions, and forced evictions by vigilante groups in the employ of large landowners. More than a dozen peasants have been killed in the ongoing disputes. The government's promise of land reform has been largely unfulfilled, as nearly 80 percent of farm and ranch land remains in the hands of foreign companies and a few hundred Paraguayan families.

The constitution establishes the separation of powers between the three branches of government, but the judicial system remains under the influence of the ruling party and the military, susceptible to corruption, and mostly unresponsive to human rights groups presenting cases of rights violations committed either before or after the overthrow of Stroessner. Allegations in 1993 included illegal detention by police and torture during incarceration, particularly in rural areas. Rights groups are now able to present cases to the Inter-American Human Rights Court, whose jurisdiction Paraguay formally recognized in 1993.

Peru

Polity: Presidential-military (insurgencies)
Economy: Capitalist-statist
Population: 22,454,000
PPP: $2,622
Life Expectancy: 63.0
Ethnic Groups: Complex, Indian of Inca descent (46 percent), Caucasian (10 percent), and mixed (44 percent)

Political Rights: 5*
Civil Liberties: 5
Status: Partly Free

Ratings Change: *Peru's political rights rating changed from 6 to 5 due to the holding of a referendum on a new constitution. Although the state-engineered vote was structurally unfair, to a limited extent voters were able to express their will. See "Political Rights and Civil Liberties" below.

Overview: A narrow vote in favor of an authoritarian constitution in a state-controlled referendum in October 1993 completed the institutionalization of President Alberto Fujimori's 1992 *auto-*

golpe (self-coup). The question was whether Fujimori and his top aide, Vladimir Montesinos, the *de facto* chief of state intelligence, would be able to retain the support of the military, the principal pillar of Fujimori's power.

Peru's history since gaining independence in 1821 has been marked by periods of civilian and military rule. The military ruled most recently in 1968-80. A constituent assembly was elected in 1978 and a new constitution drafted in 1979. It provided for a president and bicameral Congress (60-member Senate and 180-member Chamber of Deputies) to be elected for five years.

Fernando Belaunde Terry of the right-wing Popular Action (AP) party was elected president in 1980, and Alan Garcia of the center-left American Popular Revolutionary Alliance (APRA) in 1985.

In the 1990 election Fujimori, an agricultural engineer and son of Japanese immigrants, defeated novelist Mario Vargas Llosa by projecting himself as a political outsider. Lacking an organized political party, Fujimori turned to the armed forces to shore up his government. By early 1992 the normally feckless Congress was uniting against his authoritarian style of rule and the Maoist Shining Path guerrillas were mounting a concerted attack on urban centers. The 120,000-man army seemed overmatched and feared mainly by the civilian population.

On 5 April 1992 Fujimori, backed by the military, suspended the constitution, dissolved the Congress and took control of the judiciary. The maneuver was widely supported because of people's disdain for Peru's corrupt, elitist political establishment and because Fujimori had ended hyper-inflation.

Fujimori's self-coup was orchestrated by Montesinos, the *de facto* head of the National Intelligence Service (SIN), who engineered the support of the armed forces. Montesinos, a cashiered army officer and lawyer, specialized in defending drug dealers prior to becoming Fujimori's chief advisor in 1989. The U.S. and other industrialized democracies suspended aid and the Organization of America States (OAS) demanded the restoration of democratic rule.

In November 1992 Fujimori held state-run elections for an 80-member constituent assembly to replace the Congress. His patchwork New Majority-Change 90 coalition won less than 40 percent of the vote but took 44 of 80 seats because of newly decreed electoral rules heavily favoring the party receiving a plurality. Fujimori stated that the exercise was "the formalization of the 5th of April."

In 1993 the assembly drafted a constitution that, in effect, ratified Fujimori's authoritarian rule (see "Political Rights and Civil Liberties" below). It was approved by a six percent margin in a state-controlled referendum on 31 October. Although there was little evidence of outright fraud, the process was inherently unfair as Fujimori drew heavily on state resources, including the military, for a massive "yes" campaign. He made great propaganda use of the 1992 capture of Shining Path leader Abimael Guzman and correlated a "no" vote as support for the guerrillas.

Fujimori's political acrobatics had the desired effect. OAS pressure for a return to democracy dissipated and Peru was reinserted into the international economic community, which was already enamored of Fujimori's market reform program.

However, there was evidence that Fujimori's rule was less than solid. In spring 1993 an anonymous group of military officers tipped off a newspaper to the execution of nine students and a professor by the military in July 1992. Demands by opposition legislators for an investigation prompted the military to carry out tank maneuvers in

Lima in April. In May Gen. Rodolfo Robles, third in command of the armed forces, went into exile in Argentina and charged that Montesinos was running military death squads.

These incidents, coming in the wake of an attempted military coup in November 1992, indicated that Fujimori and Montesinos were not in complete control of the institution upon which their power rested. In late 1993 there was renewed tension in the officer corps over the question of promotions—the exclusive prerogative of the president under the new constitution—and increasing pressure from international rights organizations about military human rights violations.

There also was the question of the actual level of popular support for Fujimori. Opinion polls showing his approval ratings at 60-70 percent were belied by the much weaker showing in the October referendum, from which 30 percent of voters abstained. And while Fujimori had brought inflation down, the country was in deep recession and more than half the population remained in extreme poverty. Also, the Shining Path appeared to be making somewhat of a comeback in late 1993. Fujimori may have gotten away with his auto-golpe vis-a-vis the international community, but his staying power at home remained in question.

Political Rights and Civil Liberties: The Fujimori government is a military-backed, authoritarian regime dressed in the trappings of formal democracy. Political management of the congress, the judicial system and the armed forces is conducted through the National Intelligence Service (SIN), unofficially headed by Fujimori's top aide, Vladimir Montesinos.

Under the 1993 constitution the president can rule virtually by decree. In the event of a "grave conflict" between the executive and the legislature, the president can dissolve the congress, just as Fujimori did in 1992. The constitution allows presidential reelection. Fujimori's legal advisors say he can stay in power until 2005, because his election in 1995 would be for a first term under the new constitution.

The old congress has been formally replaced by an elected unicameral assembly. Municipal governments are still elected. But the former system of semi-autonomous regions governed by elected bodies was abolished in favor of increased control by the armed forces in the nation's twelve administrative areas.

The once independent national election commission was purged after the 1992 *auto-golpe* and brought under the control of the executive. The coalition of political parties and civic groups that campaigned against the constitution in 1993 were subject to threats and physical intimidation by the military. The government allotted them minimal time in the broadcast media and a single day to hold rallies.

Fujimori shut down the judicial system in 1992, overhauled it and in effect made it an arm of the executive. Files on military corruption and its involvement in drug-trafficking were removed from the courts. A draconian anti-terrorist law was decreed and judicial guarantees were practically eliminated in a new system of military tribunals with anonymous judges installed to try alleged guerrillas. Defense lawyers are not allowed to call witnesses, government witnesses are unidentified, and sentences (up to twenty years for painting subversive slogans on walls) are handed down within hours. In 1993, amid increasing reports of torture by police and prison guards, international rights organizations were denied access to prisons.

Peru's human rights groups calculated that nearly 12,000 people were arrested in the first six months of 1993, with hundreds receiving life sentences for terrorist activities. Many of the arrests were made during late night, house-to-house searches called *rastrillajes*, or rake-ups. The new constitution instituted the death penalty in cases involving terrorism, which is broadly defined.

The arrest-and-summary-trial system, coupled with government propaganda equating political dissent with sympathy for Shining Path, has creating a climate of fear. Citizen insecurity is undoubtedly a factor in Fujimori's high opinion poll ratings. The summary-trial system is also a factor in the reduced number of disappearances (from nearly 200 in 1993 to 70 in the first eleven months of 1993) because it performs virtually the same function as physical elimination.

Rights abuses involving the military are handled by military courts which generally exonerate officers and soldiers, ensuring the impunity of the armed forces. Civil courts are used by the government to intimidate political opposition figures.

While the government responds to international criticism with stated commitments to improving respect for human rights, it assails Peru's human rights groups as "tools" in a Shining Path campaign to discredit the military. Rights activists are subject to threats and violent intimidation by security forces.

In 1993 the government systematically tried to cover up the murders of nine students and a professor abducted from a Lima teachers college in 1992. Documents leaked to opposition legislators from within the military indicated they were killed by a military death squad with the knowledge and approval of the military high command. They also provided detailed histories of more recent abductions planned by Montesinos and carried out by the SIN. The cover-up involved the judiciary, the attorney general and the congress, underscoring their total lack of independence. In late 1993 the government, in the face of incontrovertible evidence, announced the arrest of four junior officers in the students case, but refused to present them before a civil court.

Political violence caused about five deaths per day in 1993, down from about nine per day in 1992 because of the diminished capacity of the Shining Path. Many of the victims were Indians. Peru's Indians are among the most marginalized in the hemisphere. The countryside is almost totally militarized and rape of women by security forces is routine during counterinsurgency sweeps and interrogation. A state of emergency that restricts civil liberties remains in place for over half the population.

Labor unions remain legal, but a new labor code decreed in 1992 restricts collective-bargaining rights and authorizes the government to break up any strike it deems to be endangering a company, an industry, or the public sector. Labor leaders who oppose privatizing state industries are subject to jail sentences of up to six years. Forced labor, including that of children, is prevalent in the gold-mining regions of the Amazon.

The press is largely private. Radio and television are both private and public. Since 1992 many media and journalists have been pressured into self-censorship or exile by a broad government campaign of intimidation—death threats, libel suits, police harassment and detentions. As of November 1993, fifteen journalists were in jail, most of them in the provinces, charged with "apology for terrorism."

Philippines

Polity: Presidential-
legislative democracy
Economy: Capitalist-
statist
Population: 63,667,000
PPP: $2,303
Life Expectancy: 64.2
Ethnic Groups: Christian Malay (92 percent), Muslim Malay
(4 percent), Chinese (2 percent)
Ratings Change: *The Philippines civil liberties rating
changed from 3 to 4 as a result of modifications in methodol-
ogy. See "Survey Methodology," page 671.

Political Rights: 3
Civil Liberties: 4*
Status: Partly Free

Overview: In 1993 Philippine President Fidel Ramos, in his first full year in
office, took tentative steps to eradicate the armed insurgencies,
private armies and kidnapping gangs that have given this struggling democracy a sense of lawlessness. Although Ramos hasn't made similiar inroads
against the political dynasties and economic oligarchies that have kept the country in a
quasi-fuedal state, polls consistently showed the president's support at a healthy 60 percent.

The Philippines, an archipelago of 7,100 islands in Southeast Asia, achieved
independence in 1946 after forty-three years of U.S. colonial rule and subsequent
occupation by the Japanese during World War II. Strongman Ferdinand Marcos ruled
for twenty-one years until he was deposed in the February 1986 "people power"
revolution, when thousands protested his "victory" over Corazon Aquino in massively
rigged elections. After several top military officials declared their support for Aquino,
including acting army chief of staff Fidel Ramos, Marcos fled the country and Aquino
took office. A new "U.S.-style" constitution approved in February 1987 provides for a
directly elected president (the vice-president is elected separately) who is limited to a
single six-year term, a bicameral Congress consisting of a twenty-four-member Senate,
and a House of Representatives with 201 directly elected members and up to fifty more
appointed by the president. The president cannot impose martial law for more than sixty
days without congressional approval.

In August 1987 Aquino survived the first of seven coup attempts, mostly by right-
wing elements of the military. During her term Aquino initiated needed macroeconomic
reforms and set the groundwork for a peaceful democratic transfer of power. However,
deeper reforms were impossible due to fragile support she received from the military.

Constitutionally prevented from running again, Aquino supported Ramos in the
May 1992 presidential election, which turned into a wide open race. Other candidates
included House Speaker Ramon Mitra, representing the centrist Struggle of the
Democratic Filipino (LDP) coalition; former Senate President Jovito Salonga; Imelda
Marcos, wife of the late president; former Marcos crony Eduardo "Danding"
Cojuangco; former immigration commissioner Miriam Defensor Santiago, who ran on
the single issue of ending corruption; and two longshots, former Defense Secretary Juan
Ponce Enrile and onetime actor Jaime Estrada.

Ramos ultimately won the 11 May balloting with just 23.5 percent of the vote, beating Defensor Santiago by only 800,000 out of 23 million votes cast. Estrada, who had earlier dropped out of the presidential race, won the vice-presidential race. In concurrent lower House balloting, the centrist Democratic Filipino Struggle (LDP) coalition won 87 seats; Ramos' National Union of Christian Democrats (NUCD), 51; the conservative National People's Coalition, 48; and the centrist Liberal Party, 15. On 30 June Ramos took office as the country's twelfth president in the first peaceful transition of power since Marcos' election in 1965. Since the election, defections have swelled the NUCD to some 112 seats, and altogether some 159 Representatives belong to the pro-government Rainbow Coalition Alliance.

Ramos inherited a country that had gone from being the richest in Southeast Asia in the 1950s to one in which official corruption, patronage and business oligarchies have impoverished up to 70 percent of the citizens. Further, the military faces armed threats on three fronts: a twenty-four-year-old communist insurgency waged by the New People's Army (NPA) of the Communist Party of the Philippines (CCP); a twenty-one-year-old Muslim separatist movement headed by the Moro National Liberation Front (MNLF) on southern Mindanao island; and a continuing threat from the Reform the Armed Forces Movement (RAM), which launched the coups against Aquino.

In September 1992 the government formed the National Unification Commission, headed by law professor Haydee Yorac, to head reconcilliation efforts between the government and the armed insurgencies. The same month Ramos persuaded Congress to scrap the 1957 Anti-Subversion Act that had outlawed the CPP, and released two top Communist prisoners, Satur Ocampo and Romulo Kintanar, former head of the NPA. By March 1993 police smashed the NPA's so-called Red Scorpion Group that had been responsible for a wave of kidnappings that struck Manila in 1992, mostly against ethnic Chinese.

By mid-year an internal ideological schism in the CPP, pitting Jose Maria Sison and other members of its Dutch-based leadership against the largest faction, based in Manila, had developed into an open rift. On 15 July the Manila group, headed by Ricardo Reyes, split away to endorse peace negotiations. However, the Dutch leadership continued to insist that talks be held outside the Philippines, and by year's end the government was considering beginning separate negotiations with the Manila group. Already, the NPA is down from a peak of 25,000 guerrillas in the late 1980s to perhaps 13,000 men today.

The organized rebel movement on Mindanao has been largely dormant in recent years, and sporadic, random terrorist attacks indicate that the MNLF lacks control over its followers. On 25 October the government began peace talks in Jakarta with Nur Misuari and other MNLF leaders on issues including regional security and administration. In a 1989 referendum, only four non-contiguous provinces in Mindanao agreed to join what is now called the Muslim Autonomous Region. The rebels want the talks to focus on a 1976 agreement that gave autonomy to all thirteen Mindinao provinces but was never implemented.

The government also undertook the biggest police shakeup in the nation's history. On 24 April sixty-two top officers of the Philippine National Police Force were ordered into retirement on corruption charges, and officials said this weeding-out process may ultimately extend to 5,000 junior officers and thousands of patrolmen in the 98,000 strong force. Another campaign targeted the 562 private armies kept by politicians and wealthy landowners. Most armies consisted of local police and members of the 63,000-

strong Citizens Armed Force Geographical Unit, a paramilitary force used to maintain security in former Communist-controlled areas. By 9 September only 258 minor armies had been disbanded.

In other issues, on 7 September the body of former president Marcos, who died in Hawaii in 1989, was flown home. On 24 September a court found Imelda Marcos guilty on corruption charges stemming from deals made during her husband's reign, and sentenced her to eighteen to twenty-four years in prison. Although an appeal is in the works, she still faces some 110 other corruption charges.

Political Rights and Civil Liberties: Filipinos can change their government democratically. Despite some charges of irregularities, the May 1992 elections were the freest since 1965, and altogether free of the wholesale fraud of the Marcos era. In the three months prior to the vote, pre-election violence claimed "only" seventy-one lives, less than half the total prior to the 1988 local elections. However, a disproportionate share of power in the country is held by economic oligarchies, wealthy landowners and political elites. For example, Governor Lininding Pangandaman of the Mindanao Muslim Autonomous Region has appointed eight of fifteen cabinet slots to close relatives, as well as hundreds of other middle and low-level jobs to other relatives and friends. Both the government, including the CAFGU militia (see above), the Communist insurgents and to a lesser extent the Muslim separatists, are accused of human rights violations, including kidnappings and extrajudicial killings, although the number of such incidents has markedly declined in recent years. Although violations by government security forces in years past have been against labor union activists and other dissidents, more recently abuses are generally linked to rogue members involved with illicit activities such as protection rackets.

Freedoms of speech and press are respected in practice, although journalists face intimidation outside Manila from illegal logging outfits, drug smugglers and others. Freedom of assembly is respected; the police generally follow a policy of "maximum tolerance" giving non-violent protestors substantial leeway.

The judiciary is independent of the government. The accused enjoy adequate due-process rights, but the system is backlogged and poorly administered. The military and police have occasionally been accused of torturing suspects. More frequently, prison rights violations occur at the hands of other inmates. Freedom of religion is respected. Citizens are free to travel internally and abroad. Workers are free to bargain collectively, and can strike after a thirty-day cooling-off period.

Poland

Polity: Presidential-
parliamentary democracy
Economy: Mixed statist
(transitional)
Population: 38,477,000
PPP: $4,237
Life Expectancy: 71.8
Ethnic Groups: Polish, Ukrainian, Byelorussian, German, others

Political Rights: 2
Civil Liberties: 2
Status: Free

Overview:

In 1993, Polish voters elected a Communist government in September's parliamentary election, sending a clear message that despite sustained economic growth, they wanted to slow the pace of privatization and free-market reforms.

As 1993 began, there were signs that the seven-party coalition government of Prime Minister Hanna Suchocka faced a parliamentary challenge to its stringent, International Monetary Fund (IMF)-approved budget policies just as the Polish economy showed signs of recovery after three years of reform-induced recession. With parliament splintered between some 29 parties and groups, Ms. Suchocka, on the basis of her pro-market stance on the economy and her conservative views on such social issues as abortion, had managed in July 1992 to cobble a coalition composed of liberal, Christian and peasant parties.

In January, parliament continued to hold up the government's efforts to push through a 1993 draft budget which set a ceiling of 5 percent of gross domestic product (GDP) on the public sector deficit. The budget, which was ultimately passed on 12 February, was the key to winning back IMF support, cut in 1991. The government did sign a tripartite "enterprise pact" with trade unions and employers in an attempt to bolster faltering shop-floor support for free-market reforms. The pact was signed by Solidarity and the National Trade Union Alliance (OPZZ) representing the former pro-Communist movement. Under the pact, workers were to have six months to decide on the form of privatization for their factory.

Parliament was also split on the government's ambitious privatization scheme, which envisaged the transfer of 600 state enterprises to foreign-managed investment funds, with shares in the funds to be handed out at a nominal fee to the population. Meanwhile, labor unrest spearheaded by the Solidarity trade union led to several strikes by public sector workers and miners. On 28 May, Suchocka's year-old government, though popular in public opinion polls, fell by one vote, as a no-confidence motion called by Solidarity to protest tight budget policies passed in parliament. It was the fourth government to fall since the Communists were ousted in 1989. President Lech Walesa, the former Solidarity leader, dissolved parliament and said that Suchocka would remain prime minister until new elections in the fall. The government's fall put mass privatization and the "enterprise pact" on hold. The dissolution of parliament left urgent reform legislation half-finished.

On 3 June, Walesa announced that elections would be held on 19 September. The day before, he had signed a new election law passed in April that promised to cut the number of parties in the next parliament. While the vote would be held under the same representational system that in 1991 introduced nearly thirty political groups into parliament, parties that failed to get 5 percent (8 percent for parties campaigning in coalition) of the national vote would not be represented. Subsequently, President Walesa publicly disassociated himself from the Solidarity trade union, at least partly because it refused to support the so-called Non-Party Bloc to Support Reform (BBWR), created by the president as an alternative for voters tired of the incessant infighting between parties that paralyzed parliament. Critics charged that the BBWR—whose Polish acronym was the same as the 1928 electoral front formed to support the authoritarian regime of interwar leader Jozef Pilsudski— was meant to boost the president's power.

In the months before the vote, opinion polls showed the popularity of Poland's former Communists, primarily the Democratic Left Alliance (SLD). At its nucleus was the Social Democracy of the Republic (SdRP), the direct successor of the Communist-era Polish United Workers Party. Suchocka's Democratic Union (UD) and the free-market Liberal Democratic Congress (KLD) trailed in the polls. Both left- and right-wing parties focused on disenchantment with market reforms that led to growing unemployment, foreign investment, and the emergence of marked class distinctions. The themes of deprivation and envy were also reinforced by assertions that the private sector was vaguely criminal or corrupt. At the same time, 56 percent of those polled said the country was moving in the wrong direction, and a majority wanted higher pensions, better health care and job security. Former Communists also made inroads in rural areas, where the Polish Peasant Party (PSL), a descendent of the Communist-era party, was popular.

In the elections, the SLD won 171 of 460 seats in parliament. The PSL got 132 seats, while the UD won 74. The year-old leftist Labor Union, which promised to subsidize industries, won 41 seats. Walesa's BBWR barely cleared the 5 percent hurdle in gaining 20 seats. Rightist nationalist parties such as the Confederation for an Independent Poland (KPN), squeaked in with 5.8 percent and 24 seats.

On 14 October, President Walesa named thirty-four-year-old PSL leader Waldemar Pawlak as prime minister. The ruling SLD-PSL coalition announced that it was committed to democratization and economic reform, but at a slower rate. It also assured the IMF that Poland was not going to adopt a radically new economic program. On 10 November, by a vote of 310-83 with 24 abstentions, parliament gave the new governing alliance a vote of confidence.

Although the election results were expected, they had a paradoxical aspect in that Poles seemed to want to put the brakes on "shock therapy" reforms at a time the economy was headed up. GDP rose by 4 percent in 1993. Industrial production was 7.6 percent higher in the first six months of 1993 than in the comparable period the year before. While unemployment was about 15 percent and climbing by mid-year, private sector employment accounted for 60 percent of the work force. There were 1.7 private firms and figures showed that in 1992 private sector jobs compensated for the 500,000 that vanished in the state sector.

In other issues, the government continued to express concern about a security vacuum in East-Central Europe and continued to lobby hard for full membership in the North Atlantic Treaty Organization. But by year's end, it became evident that NATO, with U.S. support, was not prepared to extend full membership to any former members of the Warsaw Pact.

Political Rights and Civil Liberties: Polish citizens have the means to change their government democratically. Poland has adopted a multiparty system, and the 1993 elections were free and fair. With a new electoral law, the number of parties in parliament decreased; the law was aimed at making parliament less fragmented.

A presidential draft constitution submitted to parliament's Constitution Commission in late April would establish a presidential-parliamentary system. Other competing drafts were also submitted by the PSL, the UP, the KPN and other parties. With the dissolution of parliament and the fall elections, a final constitution has yet to be adopted.

The judiciary is generally free of interference from the government. The dismissal of the justice minister in 1993 called attention to the administrative, financial and personnel woes plaguing the ministry and also the prosecutor's office and the courts. In June, the Office of State Protection (UOP) came under fire in the press for allegedly ordering its forces to tear down opposition political posters and detaining twelve people who had put them up. The UOP was created for "the prevention and detention of the offenses of espionage, terrorism, and other serious transgressions against the state." Pro-government and opposition papers argued that the UOP had overstepped its authority, and that the police should handle cases of "vandalism." In March 1993, two students were convicted in a regional court for "abusing and discrediting" President Walesa. The two admitted shouting "down with Walesa, Communist agent" during a 1992 demonstration. The students were fined and ordered to pay court expenses.

There is a bustling free and independent press. Most newspapers are backed by political parties. A new June press law draft did away with people's right to authorize the publication of a statement made by them. While there are independent radio and television stations, some have faced problems. On 4 April, the government established a broadcasting council to dole out nationwide and local frequencies for radio and television. Leading cultural figures protested the council's domination by political figures. In June, the council declared that as of July all private radio and television stations would have to discontinue broadcasting or face penalties. At issue was a council decision requiring all broadcasters to obtain a license. Problems arose when the deadline didn't give broadcasters sufficient time to apply. Eventually, a compromise was reached.

Religious freedom is respected although there are charges that the Roman Catholic Church exercises too much influence on public life. On 21 April, the church won a significant victory when a constitutional tribunal dismissed a legal challenge to compulsory religious teaching and prayers in public schools. The challenge was brought by the government-appointed ombudsman for human rights.

There is freedom of domestic and foreign travel, and no significant impediments to emigration. Freedoms of association and assembly are respected.

While the extant constitution guarantees equality of the sexes, women face discrimination in the job market. Women are underrepresented in managerial positions. Anecdotal evidence suggests that there is a high level of domestic violence against women, often involving alcoholism and spousal abuse.

There are several independent trade unions representing broad sections of the work force. Workers have the right to strike and used that right several times in 1993.

Portugal

Polity: Presidential-
parliamentary democracy
Economy: Mixed
capitalist
Population: 9,268,000
PPP: $8,770
Life Expectancy: 74.0
Ethnic Groups: Portuguese and Africans from former Portu-
guese colonies

Political Rights: 1
Civil Liberties: 1
Status: Free

Overview:

Recession and labor strife were major concerns in Portugal in
1993. The economic troubles took their toll on the governing
center-right Social Democrats, who lost ground in December's
municipal elections.

Located on the Atlantic coast of the Iberian peninsula, Portugal was a monarchy for
centuries until a republic was declared in 1910. Antonio Salazar headed a fascist
dictatorship from 1932 to 1968. His successor, Marcello Caetano, held power until
1974, when the leftist Armed Forces Movement overthrew the regime. The military had
become disenchanted and exhausted from fighting to retain Portuguese colonies in
Africa. The transition to democracy began in 1975 with the election of a constituent
assembly, which adopted a democratic socialist constitution. There has been a series of
governments since then, some led by the Socialists, others led by the Social Democrats.

The president is elected directly for a five-year term. The incumbent is the Socialist
ex-Prime Minister, Mario Soares, who won election in 1986 and 1991. The president
appoints a prime minister from the largest party or coalition in the 250-member
Assembly of the Republic, the unicameral parliament. Prime Minister Cavaco Silva
heads the Social Democrats. Voters elect the parliamentarians by proportional representation for a maximum term of four years. The next general election will take place by
1995.

In January 1993, public sector workers staged a week-long protest culminating in a
one-day strike that affected health services, education, transportation, sanitation and
ministerial bureaucracies. Public workers wore black ties to show they were in
mourning over their living standards. The government had offered raises that the
workers did not expect to keep pace with inflation. The strikers hoped that the government would grant them wage scales closer to those of their wealthier European
neighbors. Portugal is one of the four poorest members of the European Union. In past
decades, Portugal was the more prosperous Iberian country, but now Spain has passed
Portugal in per capita national income. Unemployment rose past 5 percent during 1993,
and the economy shrank. The center-right government aims to modernize and privatize
the economy. For example, private shareholders will own 51 percent of Petrogal, the
national oil company, by some time during 1994. Cavaco Silva advocates budget and
staff cuts and tighter labor laws for the public sector, especially after the strikes of 1992-
93.

As a result of economic stress, the Socialists made gains at the Social Democrats' expense in the local elections held in December 1993. Socialists gained new support in the two largest cities, Lisbon and Oporto, and elsewhere in the country.

The Portuguese and Indonesian governments held occasional talks about East Timor during 1993. Indonesia has occupied that former Portuguese colony for twenty years, and wishes to obtain Portugal's blessing for Indonesia's policies there.

Political Rights and Civil Liberties:

The Portuguese have the right to change their government democratically. Voters choose both the president and the parliament through direct, competitive elections. Portuguese living abroad have absentee voting rights and constitute a major portion of the electorate. Political association is unrestricted except for fascist organizations.

The print media are owned by political parties and private publishers. They are generally free and competitive. Until 1990, television and radio were state-owned with the exception of a Catholic radio station. The government introduced legislation to establish private radio and television stations to supplement the public ones. Portuguese have freedom of speech, but insulting the government or the armed forces is illegal if it is intended to undermine the rule of law. However, the state does not prosecute anyone under this provision.

Catholicism is prevalent, and there is religious freedom. There are competing Communist and non-Communist labor organizations. Workers have the right to strike. There is freedom of assembly. Protest organizers need to give the government one day's notice before a march or an assembly. Permission is normally granted. The economy is becoming increasingly privatized as the government sells state companies, but there are some limits on non-Portuguese ownership. The number of Communist-oriented co-operative farms is declining. Many parts of the country remain economically backward and far more like developing countries than like Western Europe. For example, there is a growing problem of child labor. Typically, the children work at construction sites in the poor North.

The status of women is improving with economic modernization. African immigrants face some discrimination. In 1993, President Soares and the parliament disputed restrictive legislation that would have ended asylum for humanitarian reasons and denied state subsidies to applicants awaiting asylum decisions. The legislators passed it twice over his objections.

Qatar

Polity: Traditional
monarchy
Economy: Capitalist-
statist
Population: 499,000
PPP: $11,400
Life Expectancy: 69.2
Ethnic Groups: Arab, Pakistani, Indian, Iranian

Political Rights: 7
Civil Liberties: 6
Status: Not Free

Overview:

Located on the northern coast of the Arabian Peninsula, Qatar
entered into a defense agreement with the British in 1916 and
declared full independence in 1971. In 1972 Sheik Khalifa ibn
Hamad Al Thani came to power by deposing his cousin, Emir Ahmad ibn 'Ali ibn
'Abdallah Al Thani, in a palace coup. The 1970 Basic Law provides for a Council of
Ministers and a largely elected *Majlis al-Shura* (Advisory Council). However, no
elections have ever been held. Instead, Sheik Al Thani appoints the entire forty-member
Majlis, which wields little influence. In a rare public expression of political dissent, in
December 1991 fifty prominent citizens signed a petition calling for democratic
reforms. The government interrogated several signers and prevented three from leaving
the country to attend a pro-democracy conference in Kuwait.

Key issues facing the country include security along the largely undefined border
with Saudi Arabia, and economic development. On 30 September 1992 Saudi troops
attacked a Qatari border post and killed two guards. In December the countries
established a committee to delineate the border by 1994, although formal boundaries
have yet to be agreed upon. The country earns more than $2.5 billion a year from oil
exports, and controls what is believed to be the world's largest natural gas field.
Japanese banks are arranging a $1.5 billion finance package to build facilities to process
and transport the gas to Far Eastern markets beginning in 1997.

**Political Rights
and Civil Liberties:**

Citizens of Qatar lack the democratic means to change their
government. Political parties and political demonstrations are
illegal, and there are no elections. The Emir serves as the
prime minister, holds full executive and legislative powers and appoints the cabinet.
The only recourse for individual citizens is to submit appeals or petitions to the Emir. In
addition, by custom the Emir frequently consults with leading members of society on
policy issues.

The government's security apparatus closely monitors foreigners, who collectively
outnumber Qataris four-to-one. The Interior Ministry's *Mubahathat* (Investigatory
Police), which handles sedition and espionage cases, can detain suspects indefinitely
without charge, although in practice such long-term detention occurs infrequently. The
Interior Ministry's regular police and the General Administration of Public Security unit
also watch foreigners, often by monitoring phone calls and mail. Another problem is
employer abuse of foreign nationals employed as domestic workers. Although the

authorities have investigated and punished several employers, most women apparently do not report abuse for fear of losing their residence permits.

The judiciary is not independent. Most judges are foreign nationals and the government can revoke their residence permits at any time. Civil courts have jurisdiction in civil and commercial disputes, while *Shari'a* courts handle family and criminal cases according to the country's Wahhabi Islamic tradition. Lawyers only help participants prepare cases and are not permitted in the courtroom. Non-Muslims cannot bring suits as plaintiffs in the Shari'a courts.

Public criticism of the ruling family or of Islam is not permitted. The privately owned press exercises significant self-censorship. The government screens all books and other cultural items. Only non-political, private associations are permitted. Islam is the state religion, and followers of other faiths must worship privately. Non-Muslims are discriminated against in employment opportunities. Men may prevent wives and other female relatives from traveling abroad, and women generally cannot drive motor vehicles.

Workers cannot form labor unions, but may belong to "joint consultative committees" composed of worker and management representatives. If a dispute arises, the government's Labor Concilliation Board attempts to mediate. If this fails, a strike is permitted, except for government employees. In practice, strikes rarely occur.

Romania

Polity: Presidential-parliamentary democracy
Economy: Statist transitional
Population: 23,188,000
PPP: $2,800
Life Expectancy: 70.8
Ethnic Groups: Romanians (88 percent), Hungarians, Germans, Roma (Gypsies)

Political Rights: 4
Civil Liberties: 4
Status: Partly Free

Overview:

In 1993, increased labor and social unrest, sluggish economic reform and parliamentary factionalism were key domestic issues for the minority coalition government of Prime Minister Nicolae Vacaroiu.

Shaped by the geographic influence of the Carpathian Mountains and the Danube River, Romania lies in the northeast quarter of the Balkan peninsula. Originally consisting of the twin principalities of Walachia and Moldavia, the territory that is now Romania was overrun by Ottoman Turks in the fifteenth century. The 1878 Berlin Congress recognized the country's independence. Romania made territorial gains as one of the victorious powers in World War I but lost substantial areas to the Soviet Union and to Bulgaria in 1940 under threats from its neighbors and Nazi Germany. King Michael, who took advantage of the entry of Soviet troops in 1944 to dismiss the pro-German regime and switch to the Allied side, was forced in 1945 to accept a Communist-led coalition government.

From 1965 to 1989, Romania was ruled by Nicolae Ceausescu, whose bizarre policies of forced urbanization, autarkic economics and cult of personality brought the country to the verge of economic ruin. A popular uprising in conjunction with a palace coup led by disgruntled Communist party members forced him and his wife, Elena, to flee Bucharest. They were subsequently captured, tried and executed on Christmas 1989. The party's anti-Ceausescu clique had secretly established the National Salvation Front (NSF) and announced they had formed a provisional government under President Ion Iliescu, a hard-liner who oversaw extensive purges in Romania's universities in the 1950s.

The 1992 local and national elections in February saw growing factionalism in the ruling NSF and increased polarization between the ruling neo-Communists and the opposition. Local elections produced significant gains for the opposition coalition, the Democratic Convention (DC), but the national elections on 27 September were won by President Iliescu and his newly formed Democratic National Salvation Front (DNSF). Iliescu was endorsed by the nationalist Greater Romania Party (GRP) and the pro-Communist Socialist Labor Party (SLP). Together the DNSF and the DC won 166 of the 484 seats contested. The rump NSF under former Prime Minister Petre Roman finished third with 61 seats. Four other parties won less than 50 seats each: the PRNU, the GRP, the SLP and the Agrarian Party. Vacaroiu, a financial expert with no party affiliation, was approved as prime minister by parliament in November.

In March 1993, amid growing unrest and strikes in several industries, the government presented its long-term economic and social strategy to the parliament. The opposition criticized the government for failing to offer a concrete anti-crisis program. On 19 March parliament's two houses rejected a motion of censure against the strategy by a vote of 262-192. Iliescu and his leftist DNSF had control of the minority government, but legislative support was based on an alliance with nationalist and leftist extremists.

In May, after price controls were lifted, tens of thousands of steel workers went on strike demanding pay increases to match price rises, as prices for heating, bread, milk, butter, water, energy and public transport rose by 800 percent.

Badly needed foreign investment was also lagging behind that in most other East-Central European countries, with the government showing little will to cut inflation. Parliament rejected an amendment to the foreign investment law that would have clarified that foreign companies may own land in Romania, and state-owned enterprises still accounted for 90 percent of declining industrial production. The lack of reform led the International Monetary Fund (IMF) to delay reaching a stand-by arrangement. The private sector (mostly new business initiatives) accounted for 25 percent of gross domestic product (GDP) in 1992 and some 33 percent of the work force.

In July, the Organization for Economic Cooperation and Development (OECD) concluded that the government's gradual approach to reform had failed to overcome the influence of hostile interest groups and that market signals had been "diluted and distorted" by bureaucratic interventionism. The OECD acknowledged the harsh legacy of extreme centralism, economic autarky, and the absence of earlier reforms bequeathed by the Ceausescu regime. The report underlined that the collapse in output was longer and deeper than in other post-Communist states.

The political picture remained murky through most of the year. In July, the DNSF merged with several smaller, extraparliamentary parties and changed its name to the

Party of Social Democracy of Romania (PSDR); in late May, the NSF merged with the Democratic Party and changed its name to the Democratic Party-NSF (DP-NSF).

Despite vociferous commitments to move ahead with market reforms, the PSDR essentially opposed loosening the government's grip on the economy and was tethered to its ultranationalist and leftist allies. The DP-NSF's Roman said that the government is made up of "nationalists, Communists, and fascists." The government did enjoy support in rural areas, where farmers credited Iliescu with returning their land.

In August, thousands of coal miners in the Jiu Valley, who just a few years ago were used by Iliescu to intimidate the opposition, went on strike demanding better pay. The nine-day strike ended without agreement, but the next day the government faced a walkout by the country's train drivers. The strike, which paralyzed much of the country, lasted a week.

In September, the government, in a move widely seen as placating its extreme-right-wing backers, announced cabinet changes that led to the resignation of several well-known reformers, including the head of Romania's privatization agency, the deputy prime minister responsible for economic reforms, and the president of the Romanian Development Agency. Rifts in the government were exacerbated by a corruption scandal involving key government officials.

The government announced in November that the U.S. House of Representatives had granted Romania most-favored-nation (MFN) status. Nevertheless, thousands of workers rallied in Bucharest on 18 November to protest falling living standards and demand the government's resignation. The demonstration, billed as the "March of Despair," was led by the Fratia trade union federation. Protests continued into the month. In mid-December, thousands of Romanians demanded a revival of the monarchy and the overthrow of the government in a wave of protests marking the 1989 uprising against Ceausescu. More than 10,000 marched to the office of the prime minister, and an additional 5,000 massed in University Square, where they demanded the resignation of President Iliescu. In Timisiora, where the 1989 uprising began, 7,000 rallied to call for the government's resignation.

In December, the government hung onto power after narrowly winning a no-confidence motion lodged by pro-reform opposition parties. After thirteen hours of debate, the motion was overturned by 236-223, with twenty-five members not voting. It was the opposition's fourth no-confidence motion, but the first based on exclusively economic grounds. The opposition moved in spite of a breakthrough in the government's discussion with the IMF. It was doubtful that the government, with its reliance on nationalist and former Communist parties to stay in power, had the will or the ability to implement the package of IMF and World Bank reforms. Consumer price inflation rose from 200 percent in 1992 to 314 percent in the year up to October. A delay in imposing financial discipline on highly-indebted state concerns was one contributing factor. Meanwhile, lack of confidence in the government led to a plunge in the national currency, the leu. The government promised the IMF it would speed up privatization, but by year's end only 200 small state-owned companies, compared with a target of 800-1,000, had been sold off. Not one bankrupt medium-size or large state enterprise was liquidated.

Political Rights and Civil Liberties:

Citizens of Romania have the right to change their government democratically. After the 1992 elections, the opposition voiced suspicion about the high number of invalid votes.

The issue of a truly independent judiciary was raised by the opposition during a series of strikes, which it said could have been settled by legal means but for "the non-existence of a real independence of judicial power in Romania." A former justice minister acknowledged that the legacy of Communist authority and concepts had hampered the development of a truly independent judiciary found in Western democracies. In January, Doina Cornea, a former dissident and prominent government opponent, was summoned to the chief prosecutor's office to answer charges concerning a 1991 television appearance in which she allegedly called for a general strike and the overthrow of the government.

The Law on Broadcasting Media stipulates that freedom of the press is guaranteed; at the same time, it forbids defamation of country, dissemination of classified information, and producing materials offending public morals. There is a variety of independent newspapers, though harsh economic conditions and state control of most printing facilities have created problems for some. Press access to parliament is conditional, and newspapers printing reports deemed "incorrect" may lose the right to have reporters attend parliament.

Ethnic minority rights continue to be an issue. Gypsies continue to be the victims of racist violence and discrimination. In February, the German community complained that a government decision to "depoliticize" German-language television broadcasts by limiting them to ethnographic and folklore aspects and putting them on a channel not easily accessible in German areas, was discriminating and censorious. Anti-Hungarian sentiment is rooted in the ideology of several political groups, including the ultranationalist PRNU. In March, the 1.7 million-strong ethnic Hungarian minority accused the government of "ethnic purification" following the appointment of two ethnic Romanian prefects in Transylvania. A National Minorities' Council was established, but its duties and powers were vague. Representatives of the Armenian and Hungarian communities complained that the council was established by a unilateral government decision for propaganda purposes.

Freedom of assembly is generally honored, but Hungarians have been denied permission for demonstrations and gatherings, particularly in Cluj, whose mayor is rabid nationalist Gheorghe Funar of the PRNU.

No official restrictions are placed on travel within Romania. Citizens may travel abroad freely and have the right to emigrate and return. Freedom of religion is guaranteed and respected.

Women are guaranteed equal rights, but face de facto discrimination in employment and promotion. The government has shown no initiative on such issues as domestic violence, family planning and crimes against women.

On 12 June, some of Romania's leading trade union organizations officially set up a super-confederation to coordinate labor activity in the country. The meeting was attended by representatives from the 2 million-member National Confederation of Romania's Free Trade Unions (NCRFTU); the Fratia (Brotherhood) Confederation with some 960,000 members; the Univers Confederation; and the Petrom and Radio Communications Federation. The new superstructure took the name NCRFTU-Fratia National Trade Union Confederation. Workers have and frequently use the right to strike.

Russia

Polity: Presidential-par-
liamentary democracy
Economy: Statist transi-
tional
Population: 149,001,000
PPP: $7,968
Life Expectancy: 70.0
Ethnic Groups: Russian, over 100 ethnic groups

Political Rights: 3
Civil Liberties: 4
Status: Partly Free

Overview:

In Russia's second year as an independent country, the ongoing conflict between reformist President Boris Yeltsin and the Congress of People's Deputies culminated in violence in early October. Government forces seized control of Russian parliamentary buildings from armed hard-liners who had holed up there after the president dissolved parliament in September.

The violence capped a turbulent year that saw an April referendum on the popularity of the president and his reforms, conflict between the central government and increasingly independent-minded regions and republics, contentiousness over a new constitution, the dissolution of parliament, and December's parliamentary elections that resulted in a legislature polarized between popular ultranationalists and their Communist allies and fractious centrist and reformist blocs.

With the collapse of the USSR in December 1991, Russia—the only constituent republic not to declare sovereignty from the Soviet Union—gained *de facto* independence under President Yeltsin, directly elected in June 1991. By late 1992, Yeltsin was repeatedly challenged by parliament. In December, parliament ousted acting-Prime Minister Yegor Gaidar, a principal architect of reforms. He was replaced by Victor Chernomyrdin, a Soviet-era manager.

In 1993, the struggle between Yeltsin and parliament intensified. In January, President Yeltsin proposed an April referendum on the principles of a draft constitution prepared by the Constitutional Committee envisaging a strong executive. The majority of deputies in the Supreme Soviet, chaired by Ruslan Khasbulatov, insisted in February that early presidential and legislative elections should be held before a vote on the constitution. Agreement was reached on holding an extraordinary session of the 1,033-member Congress of People's Deputies to settle the division of power. But on 18 February, Yeltsin proposed a new constitutional settlement expanding presidential powers and the adoption of a new constitution by a special assembly rather than by the Congress.

The Congress of People's Deputies convened on 10 March, days after the Supreme Soviet considered ways to declare emergency rule and strip Yeltsin of power. It decided not to extend extraordinary presidential powers agreed to in December. On 20 March, Yeltsin announced he was imposing "special powers," and called for new parliamentary elections and a 25 April referendum on a new constitution and on confidence in the president. His "special powers" were rebuffed by the Constitutional Court and the Congress threatened impeachment proceedings, though it was unlikely Yeltsin's opponents could muster the two-thirds majority needed to impeach him.

The Congress rejected calls for new elections and drafted a four-question referendum that ignored the constitutional issue. The questions dealt with public confidence in Yeltsin, support of his reforms, and early parliamentary and presidential elections. The Supreme Court ruled the first two questions needed 50 percent of those voting for approval. The questions on new elections needed 50 percent of all eligible voters, making passage more difficult. Both sides sought the support of increasingly powerful and defiant leaders from the eighty-eight autonomous republics and regions by offering them greater authority over regional affairs.

On 25 April, well over 50 percent of those voting voted "yes" for Yeltsin and his policies, but the provisions for new elections failed to get half of eligible voters, even though two-thirds of those participating voted for new parliamentary elections. Supporters claimed the results gave the president a mandate to press ahead with plans to reform the constitutional system.

The draft of Yeltsin's constitution published 30 April strengthened the president's power to rule by decree, gave him the right to dissolve parliament and abolish the post of vice president. It also called for a bicameral legislature with reduced power. Yeltsin wanted the new constitution approved by the Federation Council, a body consisting of Russia's regional leaders who would eventually make up the new legislature's Upper House (the 450-member lower house would be called the State Duma). Parliament thwarted the president's plan to empower a constituent assembly to draft and accept the new constitution. The 585-delegate Constitutional Assembly (composed of regional, government, party, state and private business representatives from throughout Russia) that met in June had the power to discuss and draft the new constitution but not to adopt it.

On 1 May, hundreds of Communists and supporters battled with riot police in Moscow in the first violent demonstrations since the collapse of the Soviet Union. On 8 May, parliamentary leaders moved to regain control of work on a new constitution by seeking support from regional leaders for their rival draft. On 13 May Yeltsin signed a decree calling for a special constituent assembly of the Federation Council on 5 June to "consider and finalize" a new constitution.

When the Constitutional Assembly opened in Moscow, Supreme Soviet Chairman Khasbulatov and about fifty supporters stormed out, accusing Yeltsin of pushing ahead with a constitution that would move the country toward dictatorship. The conference was to consider both the presidential draft, with 432 proposed amendments, and the parliamentary draft to establish a strong parliamentary republic. The conference broke up on 16 June without meeting the president's deadline for finalizing a new draft constitution. A sixty-member conciliatory commission was set up to try and iron out differences between competing drafts.

By early July, the constitutional impasse emboldened several of the country's sixty-eight regions to declare themselves republics, among them the Far East region and Sverdlovsk, which called itself the Urals Republic. They claimed the same status as the twenty "ethno-territorial" republics that, under the presidential constitution, would have more power than the country's often richer and more populous regions.

On 12 July the draft constitution was approved by the Constitutional Assembly 433 to 62 with 63 abstentions, after a final version had been prepared by the conciliatory commission. The document, which included 133 articles, went to the republics and regions for review. At least one-third of the representatives from the regions and republics did not initial the document. Those who did made it clear that their parliaments were free to revise the document radically. The draft included a number of concessions to the regions, giving them the right to have their own "charter" and to promulgate new laws. Both republics and regions were allowed to sign separate treaties on bilateral relations with Moscow. Nevertheless, only eight of twenty autonomous republics backed the new document. Some delegations, including those from Tatarstan and Tuva, boycotted the session.

Ultimately ratification would be needed by parliament, an unlikely prospect. Yeltsin forces called for elections to form a new parliament to adopt the constitution.

In mid-July, parliament rushed through an extraordinary string of measures that undermined the privatization program, fractured relations with Ukraine, expanded the privileges of the legislators, and threatened to disrupt the economy. Rather than pass the government's draft budget for 1993, parliament amended it 430 times. On 19 July it voted to increase spending to $40 billion, increasing the deficit to over 15 percent of forecasted gross domestic product. It restored full control of the Central Bank, and suspended Yeltsin's decree to speed privatization. It declared the Crimean port of Sevastopol to be Russian, not Ukrainian.

The standoff continued into August. Yeltsin again warned parliament he would call for early elections. Speaker Khasbulatov declared that "nothing unconstitutional would be allowed." On 12 August parliament gave preliminary approval to amendments to the existing 1978 Soviet-era constitution that would strip Yeltsin of most of his powers. The next day, Yeltsin opened a summit with leaders of the eighty-eight republics and regions, which consented to establishing a new 176-member Federation Council designed to give the territories greater say in Moscow. Parliamentary leaders accused him of trying to bypass the Congress.

On 1 September, Yeltsin suspended Vice President Rutskoi and First Deputy Prime Minister Vladimir Shumeiko, an ally, pending an inquiry into allegations of illegal financial dealings. Two days later, parliament suspended the president's decree, throwing the issue to the Constitutional Court and escalating the political struggle. On 18 September the Federation Council met, but no document formally founding the council was signed, as local and regional leaders avoided the intensifying power struggle in Moscow.

On 21 September Yeltsin ordered the dissolution of the Supreme Soviet and declared rule by presidential decree until parliamentary elections on 12 December. Opposition deputies denounced the move as illegal, and barricaded themselves in the parliamentary complex known as the White House.

The stalemate ended violently on 3-4 October. Far-left and far-right extremists supporting parliament rioted on 2 and 3 October, briefly occupying the mayor's office and trying to storm the Ostankino television station. Some twenty people were killed. Troops backed by tanks crushed the armed uprising, as government forces arrested opposition parliamentarians, among them Speaker Khasbulatov and Vice President Rutskoi. Almost 100,000 people were detained under a state of emergency in Moscow, and some opposition newspapers were banned.

After the action on 4 October, Yeltsin introduced yet another constitutional draft to be voted on along with parliamentary elections. It dropped concessions to the constituent parts of the federation. Yeltsin also disbanded soviets at city level and below, ordered elections to regional soviets by June 1994, and recommended elections to republican parliaments.

Before the vote, democratic and pro-reform groups fragmented. One political split was between the Russia's Choice bloc, an umbrella group of radical economic reformers headed by former prime minister Gaidar and backed by Yeltsin, and the Russian Unity and Accord movement, led by Deputy Prime Minister Sergei Shakhrai and supported by Prime Minister Chernomyrdin, which advocated more moderate policies. By the end of October, some twenty-one blocs and parties had registered to run.

On 8 November Yeltsin approved the draft of a new constitution that gave the president considerable power to appoint senior members of the executive and judicial branches and to dissolve the lower house of parliament if it repeatedly declined his choice of prime minister or repeatedly voted a lack of confidence in the president. The new draft proclaimed Russia to be "a democratic, federative, law-governed state," and guaranteed the full spectrum of human rights, including freedom of conscience, freedom from a governing ideology, and the right to private property, including land. On 15 November eight political parties and organizations that submitted petitions to compete for the State Duma were barred for violating election rules, leading some to accuse the government of trying to rig the vote.

In December, polls indicated that a late surge by extremists would give a large share of seats to Communist and neo-fascist deputies. The Liberal-Democratic Party, led by anti-Semitic ultranationalist Vladimir Zhirinovsky, drew much support.

Election results confirmed dire predictions, as voters approved the constitution but elected extreme nationalists and Communists to parliament. The Liberal-Democratic Party led with 22.79 percent of the vote with 64 seats. Russia's Choice polled 15.38 percent and 94 seats, but the Communist party was close behind with 12.35 percent and 48 seats. The centrist Women of Russia captured 21 seats; the Agrarian Party, 33; the Yavlinsky-Boldarev-Lukin Bloc, 22 seats; the Russian Party of Unity and Accord, 18; and the Democratic Party, 14.

President Yeltsin said the vote represented a reprimand from the people, suggesting that some reforms may be scrapped to address the social needs of Russians adversely affected by market economics. At year's end, leaders from Russia's Choice, the Agrarian Party, the Liberal-Democrats, and the Communist party met behind closed doors to negotiate over who would be the speaker of Russia's first democratically elected parliament.

Another key issue was the economy. By year's end, inflation had dropped to an estimated 10 percent of GDP, fiscal austerity arrested the collapse of the ruble, average wages had kept up with ruble inflation, increased purchasing power was reflected in a 4 percent increase in retail sales, and 82,000 enterprises had privatized in 1992-93. The private sector employed an estimated 42 percent of the workforce, and produced 35-40 percent of Russia's GDP. A trade surplus of $14.3 billion was recorded for the first nine months of 1993.

But serious economic problems continued. The largest item of government spending in 1993 was 9-10 percent of GDP earmarked for subsidies to money-losing enterprises. Soviet officials predicted that in 1994, unemployment could rise to 10-12 million out of a workforce of 72 million, of which some 60-70 percent was employed in the state sector. Large amounts of foreign aid failed to be forthcoming in 1993. The first summit between Yeltsin and U.S. President Bill Clinton in Vancouver in April did result in a U.S. commitment to provide Russia with a $1.62 billion aid package. Later that month, the G-7 summit in Tokyo offered further aid of $43.4 billion. But only $3 billion was genuinely new money in the form of an IMF loan.

In foreign policy, a new Russian military doctrine unveiled in November indicated that Russia would be willing to use force, including nuclear, if foreign troops were stationed in neighboring states. This was a signal to NATO not to expand into East-Central Europe or the former Soviet republics Moscow still considered in Russia's sphere of influence. The doctrine counted as "external threats to Russia" the suppression of the rights of Russians "abroad," presumably in the Commonwealth of Independent States (CIS). During the year, Russian troops helped Abkhazian rebels seize a part of Georgia, supported the Slavic Transdniester rebels in Moldova, and were active in Tajikistan. Russian troops remained in Estonia and Latvia. Russia insisted it be the only nuclear power in the region, pressuring Ukraine to give up its missiles to be dismantled in Russia.

Political Rights and Civil Liberties: In 1993, Russians went to the polls to elect the 450-member lower house of parliament democratically and approved a constitution giving the president substantial power. Yet, President Yeltsin's allegedly extra-constitutional dissolution of parliament and attempts to bypass the legislature to introduce a draft constitution raised fears about rising authoritarianism, as did the election of Communist and neo-fascist groups to parliament.

There are a multitude of political parties and groupings, as well as non-political civic, cultural, social, youth and women's organizations. Certain extremist groups were banned after October's crisis.

The Constitutional Court and other bodies have taken steps to implement an independent judiciary and the rule-of-law, but legal reforms were not complete as parliament and the government dragged their feet on legislation.

Although press freedom is guaranteed by law, in 1993 the media came under pressure from the government and parliament to publicize their views. While independent print media faced economic difficulties, television and press dependent on state subsidies raised the issue of self-censorship or bias. Before April's referendum and during coverage of the suspension of parliament, Yeltsin supporters tried to deny the opposition access to the state-controlled broadcast media. The September ban on opposition papers such as *Pravda* and *Sovietskaya Rossiya*, though later overturned, was criticized by democrats in Russia and abroad.

The government was also accused of widespread human rights abuses after the October showdown when it decreed strict controls of legal residency in Moscow. Up to 17,000 "immigrants," 90 percent of them from Armenia, Azerbaijan and Georgia, were driven out of Moscow in what municipal authorities said was an attempt to defeat crime. Many Russians blamed them for illegal economic activities and crime.

Freedom of religion was generally respected in this primarily Russian Orthodox country. There were attempts to limit proselytizing by some Christian sects from abroad, and incidents of open anti-Semitism continued.

While most restrictions on foreign and domestic travel have disappeared, freedom of movement is often circumscribed by "residency permits" and other bureaucratic impediments.

Women are entitled to the same legal rights as men, and are well represented at many levels of the general economy. However, women face discrimination in such areas as equal pay and promotions. Women's groups have begun to raise such issues as domestic violence and women's role in society.

There are numerous independent trade unions and labor associations, among them the Independent Trade Union of Miners (NPG), the Confederation of Labor, and numerous unions of pilots, railroad workers and professionals.

Rwanda

Polity: Dominant party
(military dominated)
(transitional)
Economy: Mixed statist
Population: 7,401,000
PPP: $657
Life Expectancy: 49.5
Ethnic Groups: Hutu (85 percent), Tutsi (14 percent), Twa (1 percent)

Political Rights: 6
Civil Liberties: 5
Status: Not Free

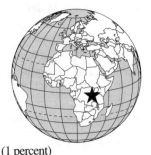

Overview: In what could signal an end to the three-year civil war in Rwanda, President Juvenal Habyarimana of the National Republican Movement for Democracy and Development (MRND) and leaders of the Tutsi-led rebel Rwandan Patriotic Front (RPF) signed a fragile peace pact in Arusha, Tanzania on 4 August 1993. The signing of the accord followed several unsuccessful mediation efforts by the Organization of African Unity (OAU). Under the accord, the government and the RPF are to create an interim coalition government and begin a difficult merger of their armed forces. The accords stipulate that forty percent of the newly formed Army will be Tutsi and calls for the replacement of OAU forces with U.N. peacekeepers.

Against a background of ethnic division and tension between the majority Hutu population and the minority Tutsi population, Rwanda gained independence from Belgium in 1962. During the colonial period, the Tutsi were selected by the colonizers to administer the country. In exchange, the Tutsi elite were given educational and political opportunities denied to the Hutu. By the end of colonial rule, however, the tide had turned. Shortly before gaining independence, Hutu forces seized control of the government. Fearing reprisals, a number of prominent Tutsi fled the country. Throughout the post colonial period, ethnic division and violence continued to plague Rwanda. Beginning in 1962 until the late 1980s, a wave of ethnic violence caused thousands to flee Rwanda for neighboring countries. Most of the refugees were Tutsi fleeing ethnic violence and reprisals from the Hutu population.

Upon seizing control in a bloodless coup in 1973, Habyarimana promised to restore national unity. In the years that followed, however, Habyarimana policies were increasingly seen to benefit only the Hutu of his own region in northwest Rwanda. It was not until the late 1980s that the Rwandan government began the process of democratic reform. A poor economy, coupled with internal dissent and pressure from foreign donors, forced the Habyarimana regime to agree to political reforms that included the creation of a multiparty system.

The reforms coincided with an invasion by the RPF in October 1990. The RPF, comprised of mostly Tutsi with several Hutu leaders, claimed that its objective was to force the Rwandan government to allow thousands of refugees (most of them Tutsi) to return home. After making some initial inroads, the RPF was turned back and increasingly resorted to guerrilla-like tactics. As the number of RPF assaults increased, so too did the number of human rights abuses committed by government forces, particularly against those Tutsi suspected of being RPF supporters or sympathizers.

In November 1990 the government promised to hold the country's first multiparty elections in 1991. The elections never took place. The government claimed that while the elections were not held, the process of democratization had begun and that it had taken steps to allow for the return of refugees. In April 1992 the ruling MRND agreed to form a coalition government with four other major parties—Republican Democratic Movement (MDR), the Democratic Social Party (PSD) the Liberal Party (PL), and the Christian Democratic Party (PDC). Under the agreement, the MRND retained half of the ministerial posts with the remaining half given to other parties. The president and the prime minister, a member of the MDR, divided executive powers.

Political Rights and Civil Liberties: Rwandans cannot change their government democratically. Despite the promise of multiparty elections for June 1995 provided for under the fragile 1993 peace pact, the transition to democracy remains uncertain. Ethnic violence and tensions continue to dominate relations between the Hutu and Tutsi populations and a number of reported ceasefire violations have taken place in the wake of the signing of the peace accord.

Human rights violations have been committed both by government forces and members of the rebel RPF. A June 1993 Africa Watch report states: "More than 300 Tutsi and members of political parties opposed to Rwandan President Juvenal Habyarimana were massacred in northwestern Rwanda in late January 1993 by private militia at the direction of local and central government authorities....Rwandan soldiers have also attacked Tutsi and opposition party members, and, since January, have killed, beaten, detained or made to disappear hundreds of civilians." The report also asserts that "the Rwandan Patriotic Front (RPF) has also committed violations....they summarily executed eight Rwandan officials and killed at least 100 civilians."

The Africa Watch report goes on to state that from October 1990 to January 1993, the Rwandan government killed or caused to be killed approximately 2,000 citizens. Most of those killed were from the Tutsi minority and were killed solely because they were Tutsi. An increasing number of Hutu who belonged to opposition parties have also been targeted. The report claimed that the government supported and condoned army attacks on civilians and "tolerated and encouraged the activities of armed militia attached to the political parties." Rebel RPF forces also participated in gross human rights violations which included kidnapping and expelling civilians to Uganda as well as looting and the destruction of civilian property.

While nonviolent organizations can form opposition parties, harassment of opposition party members including repeated death threats, extrajudicial executions, beatings and the looting and destruction of property continue. On 18 May 1993 Emmanuel Gapyisi, head of the MDR political commission, was murdered. Several other MDR members have been subjected to property vandalism, arson and death threats.

The judicial system is not free from government interference. Africa Watch reports that the judicial system is, "...paralyzed by political interference..." and that it does not protect those who fall victim to human rights abuse. Those who are arrested for human rights violations are more often than not, quickly released. In the wake of the January 1993 killings 150 people were arrested but, to date, none of the detainees has been brought to trial.

When questioned about the January massacre, Habyarimana suggested that the

RPF, rather than his own regime, was responsible for the incident. He stated: "It is even possible that these unfortunate and reprehensible massacres...were organized and made worse by those who have cynically exploited them for political ends and who have used them as a pretext to launch an attack..."

Despite continual harassment and fear of reprisal, the independent press in Rwanda continues to thrive. Although Rwanda's constitution provides for freedom of speech and press, the government passed a press law in December 1991 which makes it a crime to insult the President and requires editors to file copies of each newspaper edition with the proper authorities before distribution. Several journalists have been fined or imprisoned for violating this law. In September 1992, Janvier Africa, editor-in-chief of the newspaper *Umurava,* was arrested as a result of articles he wrote revealing the name of several government and security officials with close ties to Habyarimana who allegedly ordered extrajudicial executions.

Travel within Rwanda is restricted. Militia, with government consent, routinely erect barricades and do arbitrary stops and identity checks. Those stopped are forced to show their identity and political party membership cards and it has been reported that those who are Tutsi or supporters of opposition parties are frequently fined, beaten and prevented from using the road.

Workers have the right to join unions and union members have the right to strike provided that they have first followed a government prescribed set of procedures to resolve their differences with management. The constitution provides for freedom of worship. However, the government does not recognize the Jehovah's Witness, which it considers a subversive organization.

St. Kitts-Nevis

Polity: Parliamentary democracy
Economy: Capitalist
Population: 40,000
PPP: $3,300
Life Expectancy: 67.5
Ethnic Groups: Black, mulatto, other

Political Rights: 1
Civil Liberties: 1
Status: Free

Overview: A close election on 29 November 1993 led to the formation of a minority government headed by incumbent Prime Minister Kennedy Simmonds of the People's Action Movement (PAM). Labour Party (SKLP) supporters rioted for a day and a state of emergency was imposed for twelve days. Simmonds was looking at a possible no-confidence vote after the new parliament was seated in 1994.

The nation consists of the islands of St. Kitts (St. Christopher) and Nevis. The British monarch is represented by a governor general who appoints as prime minister the leader of the party or coalition with at least a plurality of seats in the legislature. The governor general also appoints a deputy governor general for Nevis.

A federal constitution provides for a unicameral National Assembly, with members elected for five years from single-member constituencies, eight on St. Kitts and three on Nevis. Senators, not to exceed two-thirds of the elected members, are appointed, one by the leader of the parliamentary opposition for every two by the governor general.

Simmonds and the PAM came to power in the 1980 elections with the support of the Nevis Reformation Party (NRP) and led the country to independence in 1983. The center-right PAM-NRP coalition won majorities in the 1984 and 1989 elections.

Nevis has its own Assembly consisting of five elected and three appointed members. The deputy governor general appoints a premier and two other members of the Nevis Assembly to serve as a Nevis Island Administration. Nevis is accorded the right to secession if approved by two-thirds of the elected legislators and endorsed by two-thirds of voters in an island referendum. In the 1992 Nevis Assembly elections the newly founded Concerned Citizens Movement (CCM) won three of five seats, ousting the NRP. CCM leader and businessman Vance Amory became premier.

The 1993 electoral campaign heated up when former deputy prime minister Michael Powell, ousted by Simmonds from the PAM, formed a new position party, the United People's Party (UPP). But the main challenger was forty-year-old SKLP leader, Denzil Douglas, like Simmonds a physician. The campaign centered on the economy, dependent on sugar and tourism, and mutual accusations of influence by drug traffickers.

On 29 November the SKLP actually won the popular vote on St. Kitts by more than ten percentage points over the PAM, with the UPP a distant third. But in the first-past-the-post system, the PAM and the SKLP evenly divided eight seats. On Nevis the CCM took two seats and the NRP one. The CCM said it would not join a coalition with either the PAM or the SKLP, leaving the PAM-NRP coalition with a plurality of five seats. In accord with the constitution Governor General Clement Arindell asked Simmonds to form a new government.

The SKLP called for a shutdown of the country to protest the new government, leading to a day of violent disturbances and attacks by SKLP members on government headquarters in the capital of Basseterre on 2 December. Arindell called a state of emergency. Two church organizations sponsored a meeting between the PAM and the SKLP. Douglas demanded new elections immediately, but Simmonds said that new balloting would require a no-confidence vote when the new parliament was seated in early 1994. The state of emergency was lifted on 14 December.

Political Rights and Civil Liberties:

Citizens are able to change their government through democratic elections. The opposition Labour Party argued that because it won the popular vote on 29 November 1993, the governor general should have installed a caretaker government to rule until new elections were held. But that would have abrogated the constitution which allows for a minority government in the event that opposition parties are unable to form a majority coalition.

Constitutional guarantees regarding the right of free expression, the free exercise of religion and the right to organize political parties, labor unions and civic organizations are generally respected.

After Labour Party supporters attacked government buildings and private business on 2 December, leaving eighteen people injured, civil liberties were suspended during the imposed state of emergency. The state of emergency, originally called for a twenty-one-day period, was lifted after twelve days. Labour leader Denzil Douglas continued to make provocative statements, saying in mid-December that political unrest would continue as long as the Simmonds government "continues to hold on to power illegally."

The main labor union, the St. Kitts Trades and Labour Union, is associated with the opposition SKLP. The right to strike, while not specified by law, is recognized and respected in practice.

Television and radio on St. Kitts are owned by the government and the ruling party tends to restrict access to opposition parties and civic groups. There is no daily newspaper but each of the major political parties publishes a weekly or bi-weekly newspaper. Opposition publications are free to criticize the government and do so vigorously. There is a religious television station and a privately owned radio station on Nevis.

Rule of law, based on the 1983 constitution, is generally respected. However, opposition parties allege that the ruling party has used the police for political purposes. Also, there is circumstantial evidence of government corruption, particularly in its catering to wealthy foreigners. The judiciary is independent and the highest court is the West Indies Supreme Court (based in St. Lucia) which includes a Court of Appeal and a High Court. In certain circumstances, there is right of appeal to the Privy Council in London.

St. Lucia

Polity: Parliamentary democracy
Economy: Capitalist
Population: 144,000
PPP: $3,470
Life Expectancy: 70.5
Ethnic Groups: Black, mulatto, other

Political Rights: 1
Civil Liberties: 2
Status: Free

Overview:

A year after winning a third term, Prime Minister John Compton and the United Workers Party (UWP) government contended in 1993 with a number of violent incidents involving striking banana farmers.

St. Lucia, a member of the British Commonwealth, became internally self-governing in 1967 and achieved independence in 1979. The British monarchy is represented by a governor-general whose emergency powers are subject to legislative review.

Under the 1979 constitution, there is a bicameral parliament consisting of a seventeen-member House of Assembly elected for five years, and an eleven-member Senate, with six senators appointed by the prime minister, three by the leader of the parliamentary opposition, and two by consultation with civic and religious organizations. The prime minister is the leader of the majority party in the House. The island is divided into eight regions, each with its own elected council and administrative services.

The leftist St. Lucia Labour Party (SLP) won a landslide victory in the 1979 elections, but factional disputes within the SLP led to new elections in 1982. The radical faction led by George Odlum broke off to form the Progressive Labour Party (PLP). The 1982 elections saw the return to power of Compton and the UWP.

In the 1987 elections the UWP won a 9-8 victory over the SLP, which had declared a social democratic orientation under the new leadership of Julian Hunte. The PLP won no seats. Compton called new elections a few weeks later, but the outcome was the same. However, an SLP representative switched parties later in the year, giving the UWP a 10-7 majority.

The 1992 election campaign was bitter, marked by a few violent incidents, a dispute over boundaries between electoral districts, and an exchange of personal accusations, including one by *The Star*, an anti-Compton weekly, that alleged the sixty-five-year-old prime minister had had an affair with a teenaged student. But the electorate evidently was not distracted from the core issue, the economy. St. Lucia has experienced economic growth in recent years, at a time when many of its Caribbean neighbors have been struggling. Despite the need for improved social services, one of the SLP's main campaign planks, voters in April 1992 returned the UWP to power, increasing its parliamentary majority to 11-6 over the SLP.

Internal disputes within the SLP intensified in the aftermath. In February 1993 SLP deputy leader Peter Josie, who had unsuccessfully challenged Hunte for the party leadership, was expelled from the party for blaming the 1992 electoral loss on Hunte.

The Compton administration then encountered problems of its own. In October 1993 about a quarter of the country's 14,000 banana farmers went on strike to protest low prices established by the government. Strikers blocked roads and clashed with police. Two demonstrators were killed, apparently when police fired into a rock throwing mob. The government promised an investigation and a complete review of the banana industry, St. Lucia's leading foreign exchange earner.

Political Rights and Civil Liberties:

Citizens are able to change their government through democratic elections. Constitutional guarantees regarding free expression and the right to organize political parties, labor unions and civic groups are generally respected as is the exercise of free religion.

Opposition parties have complained of difficulties in getting police permission for demonstrations and charge the government with interference. Newspapers are mostly private or sponsored by political parties. The government has been charged with trying to influence the press by withholding government advertising. Television is privately owned. Radio is both public and private.

Civic groups are well organized and politically active. Labor unions, which represent a majority of wage earners, are free to strike. The competition among political parties and allied civic organizations is heated, particularly during campaign periods when there is occasional violence and mutual charges of harassment.

The judicial system is independent and includes a High Court under the West Indies Supreme Court (based in St. Lucia), with ultimate appeal under certain circumstances to the Privy Council in London. Traditionally, St. Lucians have enjoyed a high degree of personal security under the rule of law. However, increased crime in recent years, much of it drug-related, and the violent clashes during the 1993 banana farmers strike described above, produced great concern among citizens.

St. Vincent and the Grenadines

Polity: Parliamentary democracy
Economy: Capitalist
Population: 114,000
PPP: $3,647
Life Expectancy: 70.0
Ethnic Groups: Black, mulatto, other

Political Rights: 1
Civil Liberties: 1*
Status: Free

Ratings Change: *St. Vincent and the Grenadines's civil liberties rating changed from 2 to 1 as a result of modifications in methodology. See "Survey Methodology," page 671.

Overview:

St. Vincent and the Grenadines has the status of "special member" of the British Commonwealth, with the British monarchy represented by a governor-general. St. Vincent became internally self-governing in 1967 and achieved independence in 1979, with jurisdiction over the northern Grenadine islets of Beguia, Canouan, Mayreau, Mustique, Prune Island, Petit St. Vincent, and Union Island.

The constitution provides for a fifteen-member unicameral House of Assembly elected for five years. Six senators are appointed, four by the government and two by the opposition. The prime minister is the leader of the party or coalition commanding a majority in the House.

In the May 1989 elections, Prime Minister James Mitchell won a second term when his center-right New Democratic Party (NDP) swept all fifteen seats. Opposing the NDP were the moderate socialist St. Vincent Labour Party (SVLP), which had held power in 1979-84, and two leftist parties, the United People's Movement (UPM) and the Movement for National Unity (MNU). Although failing to win any seats in the "first past the post" system, the opposition garnered more than thirty percent of the vote.

In 1991 charges of misconduct against the national police commissioner, and a scandal involving the seizure by U.S. authorities of a St. Vincent-registered vessel allegedly carrying a large quantity of hashish, led the opposition to form the National Council in Defence of Law and Order.

The council, backed by trade unions and some private sector and civic groups, was thought by some to be a precursor to an opposition electoral alliance. However, in 1993 the three parties had edged apart and seemed ready to contest the next elections, due by May 1994, individually.

Political Rights and Civil Liberties:

Citizens can change their government through democratic elections. Constitutional guarantees regarding the right to free expression, freedom of religion and the right to organize political parties, labor unions and civic organizations are generally respected.

Political campaigns are hotly contested, with occasional charges from all quarters of harassment and violence, including police brutality. Labor unions are active, politically involved, and permitted to strike. Nearly 40 percent of all households are headed by women, but the trend has yet to have an impact in the political or civic arenas.

The press is independent, with one privately owned independent weekly, the *Vincentian*, and two weeklies and a fortnightly run by political parties. The *Vincentian* has been charged with government favoritism by the opposition and the Caribbean Association of Media Workers. In 1992, two *Vincentian* editors charged that they were unfairly dismissed for publishing articles calling for reforms in the management of the newspaper. Radio and television are government owned and differing points of view are presented. But there is evidence of government interference in radio programming.

The judicial system is independent. The highest court is the West Indies Supreme Court (based in neighboring St. Lucia), which includes a Court of Appeal and a High Court, one of whose judges is resident on St. Vincent. The independent St. Vincent Human Rights Association has criticized judicial delays and the large backlog of cases caused by a shortage of personnel in the local judiciary.

In 1990 the government admitted during United Nations Human Rights Commission hearings that prison conditions were poor, but denied allegations by the Human Rights Association of prisoner beatings.

Penetration by the hemispheric drug trade has caused concern in recent years and led to opposition charges of drug-related corruption within the police force.

San Marino

Polity: Parliamentary democracy
Economy: Capitalist
Population: 24,000
PPP: na
Life Expectancy: 76.0
Ethnic Groups: Sammarinese, 80 percent; Italian, 18 percent

Political Rights: 1
Civil Liberties: 1
Status: Free

Overview:
The major event of 1993 was the general election on 30 May. The governing Christian Democrats and Socialists won a combined majority of both votes and legislative seats.

According to tradition, a Christian stonecutter named Marinus founded San Marino in 301 AD. Surrounded entirely by Italy, San Marino is the world's oldest republic. The country signed the first of several friendship treaties with Italy in 1862. Italy handles many of San Marino's foreign and security affairs and utilities, but otherwise San Marino has its own political institutions. The small republic became a full member of the U.N. in 1992.

The Grand and General Council has been the legislature since 1600. Its sixty members serve for a maximum term of five years. The council chooses the State Congress, which functions as a cabinet. Chosen by the Council for six-month terms, two Captains Regent suprvise the State Congress. One Captain Regent represents the city of San Marino and the other stands for the surrounding area.

San Marino has a lively multiparty system. In recent years, Socialists, Communists, Christian Democrats and Social Democrats have participated in coalition governments. After the collapse of communism in Eastern Europe, the Communists renamed themselves the Progressive Democratic Popular Party. Communist hardliners formed a rump Refounded Communist Party. In February 1992, the Christian Democrats broke up their coalition with the ex-Communists and formed a new one with the Socialists. In the 1993 general election, the Christian Democrats won 41.37 percent of the vote and 26 seats; the Socialists, 23.72 percent and 14 seats; the Progressive Democrats (ex-Communists), 18.58 percent and 11 seats; the Popular Democratic Alliance (ex-Christian Democrats), 7.7 percent and 4 seats; the Democratic Movement (Social Democrats), 5.27 percent and 3 seats; and the Refounded Communists, 3.36 percent and 2 seats. The Christian Democrats and Socialists formed a new ruling coalition.

The government extends official recognition to seventeen groups of Sammarinese living elsewhere. Over 10,000 Sammarinese live abroad, many of them in Italy. Recognized communities receive government subsidies for office space and communications, including fax machines. The state also subsidizes summer programs that bring young Sammarinese from abroad home for a month of education and travel.

Political Rights and Civil Liberties: Sammarinese living at home and abroad have the right to change their government democratically. The foreign ministry covered three-fourths of the travel costs for emigrants who returned to San Marino to vote in 1993.

The media are free, and Italian newspapers and broadcasts are freely available. Political parties, trade unions, and the government publish newspapers, periodicals and bulletins. The country has a vibrant, largely, private enterprise economy that depends heavily on tourism. San Marino claims never to have refused asylum to people in need. However, refugees and other immigrants may apply for citizenship only after thirty years' residence. Women have made economic and political gains in recent decades, but, unlike men, women who marry foreigners may not pass citizenship to their spouses and children. There is freedom of religion and association. Both competing trade union movements are free.

Sao Tome and Príncipe

Polity: Presidential-parliamentary democracy
Economy: Mixed statist (transitional)
Population: 133,000
PPP: $600
Life Expectancy: 65.5
Ethnic Groups: Mixed race (Portuguese-Black African) majority; small Portuguese minority
Ratings Change: *Sao Tome and Príncipe's political rights rating changed from 2 to 1 and its civil liberties ratings from 3 to 2 because of its further institutionalization of democracy.

Political Rights: 1*
Civil Liberties: 2*
Status: Free

Overview: Amid calls from the opposition to create a coalition government, the ruling Democratic Convergence Party (PCD) continued Sao Tome and Principe's economic adjustment program in 1993.

Located in the Gulf of Guinea 130 miles off the coast of Gabon, the Republic of Sao Tome and Principe consists of two main islands and several smaller islets. There are two provinces, twelve counties and fifty-nine localities. The country gained independence from Portugal in 1975. From then until 1991, Manuel Pinto da Costa served as the country's president and leader of the sole legal party, the Movement for the Liberation of Sao Tome and Principe (MLSTP). The transformation of the state from a leftist, single-party political structure into a multiparty democracy formally began at the end of 1989. A national MLSTP conference recommended constitutional amendments to allow for multiparty elections and term limitations for the office of the presidency. Opposition figures were granted amnesty and opposition movements were legalized.

In the first multiparty parliamentary elections in January 1991, the MLSTP came in second to the opposition Democratic Convergence Party (PCD). The PCD won 31 seats in the 55-member National Assembly, while the MLSTP won 21 seats. The Opposition Democratic Coalition took the remaining seat. In March 1991, the voters elected PCD-backed independent candidate Miguel dos Anjos Trovoada as president.

By early 1992, the new government of Prime Minister Daniel dos Santos Daio faced growing popular dissatisfaction with the PCD's implementation of a structural adjustment program, which included lower public spending, currency devaluation, and civil service layoffs. In April 1992, President Trovoada dismissed the Daio government and asked the PCD to nominate a new candidate for prime minister. After initially calling the dismissal a "constitutional coup d'état," the PCD approved Norberto Costa Allegre, the former finance minister, as Daio's successor.

In local elections held in December 1992, the MLSTP received approximately 70 percent of the vote, and gained a majority in thirty-eight of the fifty-nine local councils. The MLSTP won in eleven counties, while the newly formed Independent Democratic Action (ADI) captured the twelfth. Following the defeat, Daio resigned his post as PCD chairman in January 1993, paving the way for the election on 26 April 1993 of the moderate Joao Bonfim as his successor. Bonfim promised to help create a "climate of dialogue," which might include the formation of a coalition government with the opposition parties. However, the government ruled out early elections, stressing the need to continue the economic adjustment program. During the year, the legislature approved new investment, banking and tax laws aiming at encouraging local private entrepreneurship and attracting foreign investment.

Political Rights and Civil Liberties: Citizens of Sao Tome and Principe can change their government democratically. In August 1990, voters approved a multiparty constitution that called for a mixed economy, freedom of expression, and labor rights.

The new constitution provides for an independent judiciary. However, the judicial system remains overburdened by a shortage of qualified judges and attorneys, and lack of adequate funding. In April 1993, Oscar Sousa, the Minister of Social Equipment, underwent questioning in the case of a young man shot and seriously wounded. Subsequently, Sousa, known as "Rambo" for his involvement in several other shootings, was cleared of the charges, and retained his cabinet portfolio.

The government controls most print and all broadcast media,including a newspaper, and a radio and television station. The opposition parties publish occasional pamphlets critical of the government. Citizens can travel freely within the country; for foreign travel, however, the government still requires exit permits. Freedom of religion is respected. In 1992, labor organizers formed an Independent Union Federation (IUF), the first true labor confederation in the country. IUF seeks to represent workers in all sectors of the economy, but concentrates on organizing plantation workers, the main source of employment for the Sao Tomeans. The underdeveloped economy limits economic opportunity. A few women play prominent roles in politics, but most women play traditional roles outside the paid labor force.

Saudi Arabia

Polity: Traditional monarchy
Economy: Capitalist-statist
Population: 17,502,000
PPP: $10,989
Life Expectancy: 64.5
Ethnic Groups: Arab tribes, other Arab and Muslim immigrants

Political Rights: 7
Civil Liberties: 7
Status: Not Free

Overview: King Ibn Saud consolidated the Nejd and Hejaz regions of the Arabian Peninsula into the Kingdom of Saudi Arabia in 1932 and incorporated Asir a year later. Since his death in 1953, successive members of the Saud family have ruled this traditional monarchy. The King rules by decree and serves as prime minister, appoints all other ministers, and is the country's paramount religious leader. The current ruler, King Fahd bin 'Abdul-'Aziz, assumed the throne in 1982.

During the 1990-91 Gulf crisis the Kingdom allowed some 500,000 American and other Western soldiers to be stationed on its soil, widening a rift between pro-Western conservatives, including the ruling family, business interests and the middle class, and Islamic fundamentalists who feel the King is not fully implementing Islamic law and is too dependent on the West. Seeking to counteract the hardliners' influence, on 1 March 1992 King Fahd introduced a modest liberalization program, including the eventual creation of an appointed *Majlis al-Shura* (consultative council) to debate policy decisions, review budgetary proposals and offer advice on domestic and foreign issues. The King also said that rather than allowing Crown Prince 'Abdallah ibn 'Abd al-'Aziz Al Sa'ud to automatically assume the throne his successor would be named by the equivalent of an electoral college composed of royal family princes,

In November 1992, in a rare show of dissent in this tightly-controlled country, 107 religious figures petitioned the King to demand a further Islamicization of society and a reduction of Western influences. On 3 May 1993 six fundamentalists announced the creation of the Committee for the Defense of Legitimate Rights, headed by Sheik Abdallah al-Masaari, to publicize alleged detentions by security forces of hardline preachers. The group also called on the King to set up "Islamic Committees" in every ministry and government office, and to ban women from working. While some Saudis rejected the Committee as a fundamentalist vehicle, others saw it as a key step towards publicizing the regime's considerable human rights abuses.

On 12 May the highest government-appointed religious body, the twenty-member Supreme Council of *Ulama* (Muslim Scholars), ruled that such groups were unnecessary in a country already following Islamic law, effectively banning them. On 13 May the government dismissed four of the Committee members from their university teaching jobs and a fifth from a civil service position, and revoked the law licenses of two members. In addition, the government briefly detained Committee spokesman Muhammad al-Masaari on 17 May and founding member Abdallah Hamed on 18 June.

After a lengthy delay, on 21 August 1993 the King formally named sixty pro-regime religious and tribal leaders, government officials, businessmen and retired military figures to sit in the inaugural Majlis for a four-year term. Given the Majlis's purely advisory role, it is not expected to have much of a practical political impact.

The government's profligate social and military spending in the past decade has left the country's finances in a precarious position. The 22 August *New York Times* reported that between 1984 and 1992 the kingdom's financial reserves dropped from $121 billion to $51 billion, while the government's debt to domestic banks rose from $4 billion to $15.1 billion. The country's banks have also reportedly lost billions of dollars in uncollectable loans to royal family members, although no detailed figures have been published.

Political Rights and Civil Liberties:

Saudi citizens cannot democratically change their government. Political parties are banned, and no elections have ever been held. The only recourse for citizens is to appeal to the King or other members of the royal family during informal outdoor gatherings.

The legal system is based on a strict interpretation of Shari'a (Islamic law). Beheadings are carried out for rape, murder, armed robbery, adultery, apostasy and drug trafficking. According to Amnesty International the government beheaded more than 100 people between May 1992 and May 1993, mostly for drug smuggling. A conviction in capital-offense cases requires either two witnessess (four for adultery) or a confession. Police frequently torture detainees to obtain confessions, particularly when they are non-Western foreigners. Repeated thievery is punished by amputation of the right hand, while less serious crimes can be punished by flogging.

Although most suspects are charged within three days, those arrested by the Interior Ministry's General Directorate of Intelligence are often held for weeks or months without being charged. Hundreds of Shiites and Christians have been detained simply for their religious beliefs. The number of religious detainees and political prisoners is unknown, since most persons in long-term detention are held incommunicado and have never been brought to trial.

Western publications and alchohol are banned; women and men are segregated in workplaces, schools and restaurants; businesses must close during prayer times; and women must wear the *abaya*, a black garment covering the entire body and face. The official Committee for the Promotion of Virtue and the Prevention of Vice's religious police harrass alleged violators of behavioral norms and occasionally enter homes to search for evidence. Informal Islamic vigilante groups also patrol neighborhoods.

The judiciary is not independent of the government; judges are influenced by members of the royal family. Defense lawyers can only assist clients during pre-trial investigations and are not permitted into the courtroom. Trials are generally closed, are often brief and sometimes take place in the middle of the night. The King must approve all capital punishment sentences.

Significant restrictions exist on speech and press rights. Criticism of the royal family, the government or Islam is not allowed. A 1965 national security law prohibits newspapers from reporting on any public criticism of the government. The government frequently provides newspapers with official views on sensitive issues. The Interior Minister must approve and can remove all editors-in-chief. In January 1993 the government fired Khaled al-Maeena, editor-in-chief of the English language *Arab News*, for publishing a 22 June 1992 Associated Press dispatch which contained critical remarks by Egyptian fundamentalist leader Sheik Omar Abdul Rahman about Egyptian President Hosni Mubarak. The government owns all radio and television, and news coverage reflects its views. In mid-1992 the government banned the importation and sale of satellite dishes. Although it has not ordered existing dishes taken down, the religious police occasionally destroy dishes. Political demonstrations or gatherings of any sort are prohibited, and permission must be obtained to form professional groups and other associations.

Islam is the official religion and all citizens must be Muslims. The Shiite minority, which is concentrated in the Eastern Province, faces significant discrimination. Shiite public ceremonies are restricted to specific areas in major Shiite cities, and are prohibited during the month of Muharram. The government generally prohibits private construction of Shiite mosques, offering instead to build the mosques but without certain Shiite symbols. Shiites are also barred from some government jobs. On 28 October the government reached an agreement with an exile Shiite dissident group, the so-called Reform Movement, under which exiles will be allowed to return safely and an undetermined number of other Shiite dissidents will be freed from Saudi prisons. In return, the exiles agreed to stop publishing newsletters criticizing the Saudi government. All public and private non-Muslim worship is prohibited, forcing non-Muslim foreign nationals to worship secretly.

Women must obtain permission from their husbands or fathers to travel to another part of the country or abroad, cannot drive cars or trucks or ride bicycles, and face limited employment opportunities. By law women only receive half as much of an inheritance as do men and must prove specific grounds for a divorce. (Men can file for a divorce without providing cause.) Domestic violence against women is reportedly relatively common. The government prohibits trade unions and strikes are illegal.

Senegal

Polity: Dominant party
Economy: Mixed
capitalist
Population: 7,948,000
PPP: $1,248
Life Expectancy: 48.3

Political Rights: 4
Civil Liberties: 5*
Status: Partly Free

Ethnic Groups: Wolof (36 percent), Mende (30 percent),
Fulanai (17 percent), Serer (16 percent), other
Ratings Change: *Senegal's civil liberties rating changed from 3 to 5 because of
a secessionist conflict in Casamance and various restrictions on the opposition.

Overview: **A**gainst a backdrop of ethnic strife in the troubled Casamance
province of Senegal, President Abdou Diouf of the Socialist
Party (PS) was re-elected, securing 58 percent of the popular
vote in controversial multi-party elections held in February 1993. Despite opposition
party allegations that the presidential elections were fraudulent, international observers'
criticisms were muted citing only minor irregularities in the voting. The thirty observers
representing the U.S. based National Democratic Institute (NDI) declared the election to
be "free and fair." A disturbing chain of events that followed the election, however,
fueled speculation that there was significant election fraud. Senegal's reputation as the
leader of African multipartyism was, once again, called into question.

After a century of de facto one party rule by the PS, post-colonial Senegal moved
toward greater pluralism in the early 1970s. Between 1974 and 1978, three parties, in
addition to the PS, gained recognition. In 1981 restrictions on the registration of
political parties were lifted and a number of new parties emerged to challenge the ruling
PS. Also during the 1980s Diouf began a program of economic reform to address
Senegal's growing economic crisis. The reform program was met with much internal
dissent as critics charged that it resulted in greater unemployment, a decrease in social
services and diminished purchasing power. The presidential election of 1988, in which
Diouf received 72 percent of the vote, was followed by opposition party charges of
fraud and periods of civil strife. In the wake of the unrest, Diouf orchestrated a rocky
alliance with two opposition parties—the Senegalese Democratic Party (PDS), led by
Abdoulaye Wade, and the Independence and Labor Party (PIT). In April 1991, the
office of Prime Minister was reestablished and Habib Thiam was appointed to head a
coalition government in which the PDS and the PIT joined the PS. The alliance held
until October 1992 when Wade and three other members of the PDS left the coalition.

A 1992 electoral code intended to insure electoral fairness provided for secret
ballots, opposition monitors at voting sites and other reforms. Despite these provisions,
confusion dominated the ratification process in the weeks following the 1993 Presidential election. Shortly following the election, Madame Andresia Vaz, the head of the
National Commission for Counting Votes (CNRV)—the body charged with processing
election results before ratification by the Senegalese Constitutional Council—resigned.
Vaz passed on the responsibility for verifying the election results to the Constitutional
Council. In March 1993 the head of Senegal's Constitutional Council, Keba Mbaye,

also resigned. Despite promises for a timely disclosure of results, the ratification process delayed the announcement for several weeks. When the election results were finally disclosed it was not surprising that many opposition candidates rejected the Constitutional Council's findings and declared the elections fraudulent.

Legislative elections followed on 9 May 1993. The ruling PS secured eighty-four seats, while the PDS secured twenty-seven seats with the remaining nine seats being divided among other opposition parties. Again, a low voter turnout and allegations of election fraud marred the credibility of election results. Only six days after the election, the Vice President of Constitutional Council, Babacar Sèye, was assassinated while the council was still deliberating on the formal ratification of the election. A group identifying itself as the People's Army claimed responsibility, stating that its objective was "to help the forces of change bring about a change in the regime." In the wake of the assassination, the government arrested Wade and three top PDS associates after they were implicated by the driver of the car used in the murder. Earlier, Wade had criticized Seye and the Constitutional Council for promulgating flawed presidential and legislative election results. The driver subsequently recanted his story and later blamed the incident on high ranking PS members.

During 1992-93, challenges from the Casamance Democratic Forces Movement (MFDC), active since the early 1980s, continued to plague the Diouf government. The MFDC is a secessionist movement composed mainly of members of the Diola ethnic group of the southern Casamance province. Many Diolas resent the national political dominance of the northern Wolof elite (who are mostly Muslim) as well as the presence of northern settlers in the Casamance. The government's response to the movement has been brutal and thousands of citizens caught between the two forces have fled to neighboring Guinea-Bissau and Gambia. Human rights groups charge that government counter-insurgency operations led by the military have resulted in gross human rights violations. Extrajudicial executions, beatings, torture, and indefinite detention of suspected MFDC sympathizers have been reported. In April 1993, the government announced its intention to cease hostilities against the MFDC to prepare for negotiations.

Political Rights and Civil Liberties: Constitutionally, Senegalese have the right to change their government democratically through periodic multiparty elections. However, since independence, the ruling Socialist party has dominated political life in Senegal. The PS continues to benefit from the support of the religious hierarchy and low voter registration. Despite the adoption of the 1992 electoral code, 1993 elections were clouded by opposition party allegations of vote-rigging and election fraud. The gain of legislative seats by the opposition parties in the 1993 election may signal some limited political progress.

Freedom of assembly and association is protected under the constitution and, for the most part, Senegalese have exercised these rights with only limited interference. Public demonstration must receive prior government approval and a number of requests during 1992 were denied. Workers have the right to join trade unions and although union membership is confined to only a small percentage of the overall population, unions are politically powerful. Workers also have the right to strike which they exercise freely.

Freedom of the press is generally respected in Senegal. Published magazines and weekly newspaper provide a spectrum of views and government criticism is frequently expressed. However, radio and television are government controlled. There are some legal restrictions on journalists which prohibit them from expressing views that discredit the State, incite the population to disorder or propagate "false news." Although Islam is the religion of ninety-four percent of all Senegalese, freedom of worship for all religions is respected. There is no restriction on internal or international travel.

As a result of a counter-insurgency operation by the government against the separatist movement in the Casamance province, human rights abuse against MFDC supporters and sympathizers has been reported. In an attempt to crush the MFDC movement, the government has indiscriminately shelled and burned villages suspected of harboring MFDC rebels. In addition, the MFDC has also been charged with a number of human rights violations which include extrajudicial executions, torture and beatings.

Seychelles

Polity: Presidential-legislative democracy   **Political Rights:** 3*
Civil Liberties: 4
Economy: Mixed-statist   **Status:** Partly Free
Population: 72,000
PPP: $4,191
Life Expectancy: 70.0
Ethnic Groups: Mixed African, South Asian, European
Ratings Change: *Seychelles's political rights rating changed from 6 to 3 because it held transitional elections in 1993.

Overview: The constitutional referendum on 15-18 June and the multiparty elections on 20-23 July were the major developments of 1993.

Seychelles is an archipelago of 115 islands situated in the Indian Ocean east of Tanzania. Both France and Britain colonized the islands. French, Creole and English are the local languages. The country gained independence from the British in 1976. Prime Minister France Albert Rene installed himself as head of state after overthrowing elected President James Mancham in 1977. Rene declared his Seychelles People's Progressive Front (SPPF) the only legal party in 1978. Mancham and other opposition figures operated parties and human rights groups in exile.

Rene combined authoritarian politics and substantial government ownership with social welfare programs and environmental protection. He sought to preserve the islands' natural beauty by prohibiting large numbers of tourists and limiting commercial development.

In December 1991, Rene promised to legalize opposition parties and invited political exiles to return to the Seychelles to participate in a transition to multiparty democracy. The SPPF passed a constitutional amendment that permitted new parties. Seven opposition parties and the SPPF registered by April 1992.

Rene announced a three-stage democratic transition: an election for a constitutional commission, a constitutional referendum, and general elections. In July 1992, Seychellois voters selected a twenty-two-member commission to draw up a new constitution. In the first multiparty elections since Rene's coup, the SPPF received 58.4 percent of the vote and Mancham's Democratic Party (DP) received 33.7 percent. The other six parties picked up the remaining 7.9 percent. The vote left the SPPF with a majority on the constitutional commission. Although Commonwealth election observers judged the voting free and fair, the DP accused the SPPF of widespread intimidation and vote-buying.

DP commissioners pushed for a constitutional provision allowing citizens overseas to vote, but the SPPF rejected the proposal, based on the assumption that most exiles would be opposition supporters. This disenfranchised up to 12,000 Seychellois. The commission completed a draft constitution, and presented it for a referendum in November 1992. The law required the document to receive at least 60 percent approval. However, only 53.7 percent of the voters approved. Rene reconvened the commission, which proposed a new constitution. In June 1993, 73.9 percent of the electors voted "Yes." The SPPF, the DP, and two smaller parties, the *Mouvement Seychellois Pour La Democratie* (Seychelles Movement for Democracy) and the Seychelles Liberal Party, backed the second draft. Three small parties, *Parti Seselwa* (Seychellois Party), the Seychelles National Movement and the National Alliance Party, opposed it.

In the general election in July 1993, President Rene received 59.5 percent of the vote and James Mancham 36.72 percent. Philippe Boulle (United Opposition) placed third with 3.79 percent. (The foregoing results exclude invalid votes.) In the race for the 33-seat National Assembly, Rene's SPPF won 21 of the 22 directly elected seats to 1 for the DP. Of the 11 seats filled by proportional representation, the SPPF captured 6; the DP, 4; and the United Opposition, 1.

Political Rights and Civil Liberties: Seychellois can change their government democratically, but the long Rene dictatorship has left some residual authoritarian elements. Although the Commonwealth Observer Group called the 1993 elections generally free and fair, the observers reported that Rene's control of local authorities gave him an electoral advantage. The Commonwealth observers received and investigated several complaints about electoral irregularities, but dismissed most of them as either trivial or invalid.

The media are partly free. During the general election campaign, the government-controlled Seychelles Broadcasting Corporation (SBC) provided substantial coverage to both government and opposition candidates. The government-owned daily newspaper, *The Nation*, was biased in favor of Rene and the SPPF. The opposition parties set up several weekly papers to rectify the imbalance in the print media. Some self-censorship remains as a result of the long dictatorship. Freedom of speech improved during 1993 as part of the political liberalization process.

In 1992, the security forces had harassed the opposition, beating and arresting activists and breaking up meetings. By 1993, the police and army refrained from such violations in the run-up to the general election. However, some oppositionists pointed out that the defense minister and the chief of the armed forces were the same person. This raised questions about civilian control of the military. Judges generally decide cases fairly, but they may face some government pressure. There is religious freedom. The Catholic Church issues a fortnightly newspaper that reports on national issues.

There are no restrictions on internal travel, but the government may deny passports for reasons of "national interest." The National Workers Union is associated with the SPPF. The law permits strikes, but regulations inhibit workers from exercising this right.

Sierra Leone

Polity: Military
Economy: Capitalist
Population: 4,494,000
PPP: $1,086
Life Expectancy: 42.0
Ethnic Groups: Temme (30 percent), Mende (30 percent), Krio (2 percent), other

Political Rights: 7
Civil Liberties: 6
Status: Not Free

Overview:

Amidst promises of a return to a civilian government by 1996, the National Provisional Ruling Council (NPRC) led by Captain Valentine Strasser, continued to rule Sierra Leone ruthlessly in 1993. The NPRC failed to quell the rebellion in the south and east of the country, carried out by the Revolutionary United Front (RUF).

Sierra Leone had been on the path toward multiparty politics when unpaid troops returning from the fight against the RUF rebels staged protests against the civilian government of President Joseph Momoh. On 29 April, a group of officers led by the twenty-seven-year-old Strasser ousted Momoh in a coup, forcing him to flee the country to neighboring Guinea. The putschists replaced the civilian authorities with a military council, arrested Momoh's confidants, and banned all political activity. In his proclamation following the coup, Strasser accused the Momoh regime of being corrupt and responsible for the deteriorating state of the nation's economy, and of being insincere in pursuing the democratic reforms forced on him by student protests in 1990. In his proclamation following the coup, Strasser stated the objectives of the NPRC to be the "genuine" preparation for a multiparty system, and putting an end to the RUF rebellion. In order to show its regard for public opinion and repair the international damage caused by the forcible change of government, the NPRC established a nine-teen-member Consultative Council in November to "advise and make recommenda-tions" to the NPRC, and to "work out the modalities for the return to multiparty democracy."

As the year came to a close, the NPRC announced on 28 December that the army thwarted an attempt to overthrow the Strasser-led junta by a group calling itself the Anti-Corruption Revolutionary Movement. Three members of the movement were supposedly killed in crossfire as they launched their attack on Strasser's residence, allowing the army to seize a tape recording which allegedly was to be played on the national radio in the aftermath of a successful takeover of government. The tape contained the names of the supposed plotters and their supporters. One of the leaders of the alleged plot was the popular army commander of the Kenema district, Lieutenant Colonel James Yaya Kanu, who was considered as a possible presidential successor to Momoh. Kanu was implicated in the plot although he had been under arrest since the

April coup. On 29 and 30 December, a special military court found twenty-six persons, including Kanu, guilty and ordered their summary execution. Shortly after their execution, a number of Sierra Leone exile groups and the Amnesty International accused the NPRC regime of staging the attempted coup in order to liquidate popular opponents and prolong its rule. In protest against the executions, the country's former colonial ruler, Great Britain, announced the suspension of all development aid.

Despite Strasser's appeal to the rebels to lay down their arms, the fighting in the eastern and southern provinces intensified. The RUF insurgency was born out of the civil war in neighboring Liberia. In 1991 the armed forces of Charles Taylor's National Patriotic Front of Liberia (NPFL) gave their support to a group of anti-Momoh opponents, in retaliation for Sierra Leone's contribution to the anti-Taylor West African intervention forces. The group, under the leadership of Fodoy Sankoh, dismissed Momoh's reforms as mere show, vowing to fight for "true pluralism."

Following the NPRC's government takeover, the fighting intensified, as the Strasser regime showed itself unwilling to enter into negotiations with the RUF rebels. On 1 March 1993, the Sierra Leone Army was joined by the United Liberation Movement (ULIMO), an anti-Taylor Liberian faction, resulting in an offensive that recovered a sizable territory from the RUF. Following months of a see-saw campaign in which the territory under government and rebel control changed hands several times, by October the government forces claimed to have pushed the rebels back to the Liberian border.

Following the execution of the twenty-six alleged plotters, there were rumors in early 1993 that Strasser was forced to confirm the existence of the plot and the subsequent sentences by the NPRC's second in command, the twenty-three-year-old Captain Solomon Musa. Musa, known for his ruthlessness and arrogance, was in charge of the day-to-day activities of the government through his position as the Chief of Secretaries (Prime Minister). Due to his unpopularity among the troops and the population and his opposition to Strasser's 29 April announcement to hand over the power to a civilian government by 1996, the NPRC stripped Musa of his official positions within the junta, allowing him to leave the country on 5 July.

Political Rights and Civil Liberties:

The citizens of Sierra Leone cannot change their government democratically. The military regime dissolved the parliament, banned independent political activity, and suspended all provisions of the 1991 democratic constitution inconsistent with its decrees. In April, Strasser promised to install a civilian government and a multiparty system by 1996; subsequently, however, he attached a number of conditions for this to occur, including the eradication of the RUF insurrection.

In late 1992, the NPRC created special military tribunals to punish treason and other capital crimes. The tribunals consist of five judges who are military officers, and who frequently lack any judicial training. Both civilians and soldiers may be tried, verdicts cannot be appealed, and those convicted can be executed. The execution of the twenty-six alleged coup plotters in December came within hours of the passage of the verdict. Amnesty International charged that most of the accused lacked legal representation.

Following the government takeover by the NPRC, the junta declared an emergency legislation giving the security forces unlimited powers of detention without charge, and preventing such detention from being challenged in the courts. In June, Amnesty International reported that 264 political detainees were being held in the notorious

Pademba Road Central Prison. Their time in detention ranged from two years to several weeks. A fourteen-year-old boy was the youngest detainee.

Amnesty charged that the prisoners were cut off from the outside world, that even relatives were frequently unaware of their whereabouts. Prisoners were beaten and tortured, and inadequate meals often resulted in death from starvation. Following the report's publication, the regime released a group of eighty-six prisoners on 9 July, after a review of their cases. However, the authorities refused to release the remaining prisoners, accusing them of being involved with the RUF insurrection.

The conflict in the east and south resulted in human right violations, including looting, torture and extrajudicial execution, committed by all the parties. Rebels who surrendered to government troops to take advantage of the NPRC-announced amnesty, were said to have been executed. In June, the NPRC announced that it had learned that military officers drafted children into the army to fight the RUF rebels. Consequently, the NPRC decreed the immediate discharge of all soldiers under the age of fifteen.

The rights of free expression, assembly and association that finally became respected in the final months of the Momoh regime are no longer recognized and are subject to the whim of the junta or its individual members. On 13 January the regime announced new guidelines for the press, requiring the newspapers to fulfill stringent administrative requirements in order to continue to operate. The requirements called for the newspapers to provide a collateral of the equivalent of several thousand dollars, to employ at least one editor with a university degree and at least four years of experience, and the office to be equipped with a telephone. Following the decree, only fourteen newspapers continued to publish, as opposed to thirty at the time of the decree's publication. Journalists continued to be harassed and physically attacked for their criticism of the NPRC's human rights abuses and corruption.

Singapore

Polity: Dominant party
Economy: Mixed capitalist
Population: 2,765,000
PPP: $15,880
Life Expectancy: 74.0
Ethnic Groups: Ethnic Chinese (76 percent), Malay (15 percent), Pakistani and Indian (7 percent)
Ratings Change: *Singapore's political rights rating changed from 4 to 5 as a result of modifications in methodology. See "Survey Methodology," page 671.

Political Rights: 5*
Civil Liberties: 5
Status: Partly Free

Overview: Despite facing only a token opposition, Ong Teng Cheong of the ruling People's Action Party scored a relatively narrow victory in the August 1993 presidential election, providing further evidence of the party's declining popularity in this prosperous authoritarian state. Increasingly, citizens are questioning the PAP's political dominance, its feverish emphasis on savings over consumption, and its paternalistic social restrictions.

Originally established as a trading station in 1819, Singapore became a British colony in 1867. The colony became self-governing in 1959, entered the Malaysian Federation 1963 and in 1965 became fully independent under Prime Minister Lee Kuan Yew. Since then the conservative PAP has dominated politics and has spread its Confucian-based social values of savings, hard work and discipline through the media, public advertising campaigns, labor associations and the military. In the process, the country has been transformed from a squalid island into a miniature economic power. The PAP completely swept elections from 1968 to 1980 before losing a by-election in 1981.

In October 1990 Lee stepped down in favor of his handpicked successor, Goh Tok Chong, although the seventy-year-old former premier still exerts considerable political influence as Senior Minister in the government. Goh called a snap election in August 1991 to get a mandate for his leadership. Although the opposition contested only forty of the eighty-one seats, the PAP had its worse showing ever, winning seventy-seven seats with 61 percent of the overall vote. The Singapore Democratic Party took three seats, and the center-left Worker's Party one. After the election Goh candidly admitted the PAP had become too elitist, neglecting the needs of the working-class Chinese voters who form its traditional base.

The opposition might have won more seats if not for changes in the electoral law prior to the vote. The government increased the number of Group Representation Constituencies (GRC) from thirteen to fifteen, and increased the number of seats in each from three to four. Opposition groups have trouble contesting GRCs because they must come up with four credible candidates, one of whom must be non-Chinese, in a society in which few are willing to openly challenge the government. The PAP has hinted it may eventually turn the remaining seats into GRCs.

On 19 December 1992 Goh won 72 percent of the vote in a special by-election for his seat that he had called to test his personal mandate. Many voters were swayed by Lee's melodramatic appeal that a weak endorsement of Goh would "put Singapore and your own future in doubt."

The results of the 28 August 1993 elections for an expanded presidency were probably a more accurate barometer of the party's popularity. The office had been a ceremonial position until January 1991, when parliament amended the constitution to give the president the power to approve budgets, oversee the country's assets and approve political appointments. The government claimed a need to protect the country's $46 billion foreign reserves—the highest per capita in the world—against the possibility of a free-spending government coming to power in the future. Prime Minister Goh admitted that the strict requirements—candidates must have held one of several senior public offices, including cabinet minister, speaker of parliament and attorney general, or have run a company with paid-up capital of more than $62.5 million—left only about 400 citizens eligible.

The government also established a three-member screening committee, two of whom are government appointees, with broad powers to veto candidates. On 10 August the Committee rejected J.B. Jeyaretnam and Tan Soo Phan, both of the opposition Worker's Party, for lack of "integrity, good character and reputation." Jeyaretnam in particular has been a consistently outspoken critic of the PAP, and the government has brought him to near financial ruin through a series of controversial court cases, including a 1986 fraud conviction.

The government ran deputy prime minister Ong Teng Cheong for the office, and persuaded Chua Kim Yeow, a retired, non-partisan, former accountant-general, to run as a token opposition. Chua rated Ong a "far superior candidate" and campaigned for a total of only twenty minutes, the duration of two speeches carried free on television. Yet Ong won with only 58.7 percent of the vote, a clear rebuff to the PAP, which had hoped for at minimum a 65 percent tally. Obsevers feel many voters are tired of the PAP's political dominance and social paternalism, which even includes a ban on chewing gum.

In another key political issue, in April doctors pronounced deputy prime minister Lee Hsien Loong, the son of the former premier, free of cancer following extensive chemotherapy. The forty-year-old Lee is widely considered the heir apparent to prime minister Goh.

Political Rights and Civil Liberties:

Citizens of Singapore nominally have the right to change their government through free elections, although the ruling PAP maintains its political monopoly through various legal and institutional advantages.

The Internal Security Act (ISA) allows the president to detain suspects for an unlimited number of two-year periods. Trials under the ISA do not have to be public and generally lack adequate due process safeguards. In the past, several opposition figures have been detained under the ISA, although currently there are no ISA detainees. However, the government is using the ISA to restrict the travel, residence, speech and publishing rights of three former detainees, all political dissidents. In 1989 the government amended the constitution to limit judicial review of ISA detentions to procedural grounds, and to prevent the judiciary from reviewing the constitutionality of any anti-subversion law. In addition, under the Criminal Law (Temporary Provisions) Act, which authorizes detention without trial, the government holds more than 900 suspected drug traffickers and members of criminal gangs.

The government continues to harass opposition figures through dismissal from public sector jobs, libel suits and the threat of such suits. In March the National University dismissed Dr. Chee Soon Juan for "dishonest conduct" merely for using $138 out of his research grant to courier his wife's doctoral thesis to a United States university. Chee, an SDP assistant secretary-general, ran against Goh in a December 1992 by-election and had also written a series of letters to local newspapers criticizing the government for not devoting enough resources to poor citizens.

Ordinary trials are conducted with adequate procedural safeguards, although the independence of the judiciary is questionable. Lower court judges are appointed by and serve at the discretion of the president, while higher court judges are considered to be closely aligned with the government.

The Societies Act requires organizations of more than ten people to register with the government. The PAP wields strong influence over ostensibly non-political associations such as neighborhood groups and trade unions. However, the government uses the Societies Act to restrict opposition groups from forming neighborhood or other similiar support groups. Freedom of expression is restricted. Public statements that could even indirectly incite ethnic or religious antagonism, or disrupt public order or security, are illegal. Police approval is required for individual speakers at public functions. The government occasionally denies such permits to opposition party members seeking to address dinners and banquets. Approval is also required for any assembly of more than five people.

The government tightly controls the media, and editorials and domestic news coverage strongly favor the ruling party. Key "management shares" in the Singapore Press Holdings, which publishes all major newpapers, must be held by government-approved individuals. The Newspaper and Printing Presses Act (NPPA) prohibits any person or group from holding more than 3 percent of a newspaper company unless exempted. The government also owns all three television channels and nine of twelve radio stations.

The broadly drawn Official Secrets Act bars the unauthorized release of government data to the media. In June 1992 the *Business Times* published "flash" GDP estimates several days before the latest figures were officially announced. The Internal Security Department raided the paper's offices and charged editor Patrick Daniel, a journalist and three economists with breaking the Act. The five went on trial in October 1993 and face up to two years in jail.

An amendment to the NPPA allows the government to restrict circulation of any foreign publication it feels has interfered with domestic politics. In August the government capped the circulation of the London *Economist* at its current level of 7,500 after it had deleted a sentence out of a government response to a June article on the *Business Times* case. Previous restrictions on *Time* have since been dropped, but the *Far Eastern Economic Review, Asiaweek* and *The Asian Wall Street Journal* still face restrictions. In July the government allowed the *Journal* to station a full-time correspondent in the country for the first time since 1988.

Freedom of religion is generally respected in practice, although the Jehovah's Witnesses and the Unification Church are banned. Citizens must carry identification cards at all times, and can be restricted in domestic travel under the ISA (see above) and prevented from traveling abroad. Approximately 98 percent of unionized workers belong to unions affiliated with the pro-government National Trades Union Conference. Workers have the right to strike but rarely do so, in part because a labor shortage gives them bargaining leverage.

Slovakia

Polity: Parliamentary democracy
Economy: Mixed-statist transitional
Population: 5,300,000
PPP: na
Life Expectancy: na
Ethnic Groups: Slovak (82 percent), Hungarians (11 percent), Roma (4.8 percent), Czechs (1.2 percent)

Political Rights: 3
Civil Liberties: 4
Status: Partly Free

Overview:

Nineteen-ninety-three marked the first year of independence for this small, central European nation following the formal dissolution of Czechoslovakia on 1 January. That separation ended a seventy-four-year-old federation created after the fall of the Austro-Hungarian empire following World War I. The government of Prime Minister Vladimir Meciar faced waning popular support and a difficult transition to a market economy amid persistent charges from the nationalist and leftist opposition and the country's minorities that his regime harbored authoritarian tendencies.

Slovakians trace their ancestry to the short-lived Great Moravian Empire of the ninth century, during which Slovaks and Czechs united briefly. As early as the tenth century, Hungarians seized control of the region and for the next 1,000 years ruled with a system of serfdom and repression. Czech-Slovak unity after World War I was relatively short-lived, as Nazi Germany's dismemberment of Czechoslovakia provided an opportunity for militant Slovak nationalists to seize power and establish a nominally independent state under Josef Tiso, tainted by its allegiance to the Third Reich and its role in the deportation of Jews and Roma (Gypsies).

The "Velvet Revolution" of 1989 brought down the hard-line Communist system in place since Soviet tanks crushed the pro-reform Dubcek regime in 1968 but also sowed the seeds for Czech-Slovak tensions, partly because much of the huge, outmoded Soviet-era industries were located in Slovakia and made economic reform and Western investment more difficult.

Results of the June 1992 federal and regional elections made the split inevitable, even though public opinion polls indicated that neither Czechs nor Slovaks wanted to break up the federation. Vaclav Klaus, an uncompromising pro-market reformer, was elected to head the Czech republic; Meciar, who ran on a nationalist platform, won in Slovakia. Within six months, the decision to separate was finalized.

In January 1993, Prime Minister Meciar was a fairly popular leader. In the June 1992 elections, his centrist Movement for a Democratic Slovakia (HZDS) had won 74 of 150 seats in the *Narodna Rada* (parliament). The Party of the Democratic Left (SDL), led by Peter Weiss and made up of former Communists, emerged as the second-largest party with 28 seats. The Slovak Nationalist Party (SNS) led by Ludovit Cernak, the only party to stand unambiguously for Slovak independence, won only 15 seats and agreed to be a junior coalition partner in the post-election HZDS-SNS government. Among other parties are the Christian

Democrats (KDH) led by former prime minister Jan Carnogursky, and the Hungarian Bloc.

By spring, however, shrinking public confidence in the HZDS and deep, often personal animosities in party and coalition ranks, led to a rift. After gaining power, Prime Minister Meciar had pushed through a number of highly regressive policies, reversing earlier efforts to promote political and market reforms. The government closed down a popular newspaper, barred news organizations from government press conferences, antagonized the 600,000-strong Hungarian minority by requiring the removal of Hungarian-language signs, and canceled major deals to convert state enterprises to private ownership. The government also faced a major confrontation with Hungary by unilaterally deciding to divert the Danube in the highly controversial Gabcikovo Dam project.

In March, after attacking Meciar for his alleged authoritarian style and his closeness to politicians with ties to Czechoslovakia's Moscow-dominated past, Cernak took the SNS out of the ruling coalition—leaving the government two votes short of a majority. The SNS also protested the state of the Slovak economy. Prime Minister Meciar moved to oust Foreign Minister Milan Knazko, an HZDS member and former leader of the popular Public Against Violence in 1989, who had grown increasingly apprehensive about the impact of the regime's policies on ethnic minorities and neighboring states, particularly Hungary. Knazko left the HZDS and formed his own breakaway party, the Alliance of Independent Democrats, with eight seats in parliament. Anti-government protests sprang up in May.

In September, Cernak agreed in principle to take his party back into the government, mainly because his reluctance to risk early elections which the former Communists might win proved stronger than personal and political antipathy to the prime minister. The coalition was formalized in October.

During the year, the country moved slowly on reform, with many of the old nomenklatura bosses still running various bureaucracies, the big state factories and the security forces. Several former Communists were in the government.

The government failed to produce a coherent economic program to deal with such problems as growing unemployment and inflation, the decline in industrial output and exports, perilously low foreign reserves and the threat of bankruptcy hanging over half the country's large companies.

The collapse of traditional markets in the Czech Republic and the former Comecon trade bloc was felt more acutely in Slovakia than in most of its neighbors. With only about $320 million dispersed since 1990, the country had attracted only a tiny share of foreign investments. The government's firing of Lubomir Dolgos, the former privatization minister, without naming a replacement, raised questiona about the it's commitment to privatization, especially of the larger enterprises.

Meanwhile, economic numbers remained bleak. In the first six months of 1993, gross domestic product (GDP) fell by 6.2 percent compared to the same period in 1992, while unemployment rose to 12.5 percent of the workforce. Inflation rose to 14.2 percent. In a July agreement with the International Monetary Fund (IMF), the government agreed to keep the 1994 deficit down to 5 percent of GDP. But with revenues slashed by recession, insufficient manpower to collect taxes, and rising expenditure on unemployment benefits, authorities were hard put to keep to the target.

In foreign policy issues, relations with Hungary were strained by Meciar's insistence on proceeding with the Gabcikovo Dam project, charges of repression from the Hungarian minority, and the purchase of new fighter aircraft from Russia to counter-balance similar purchases by Hungary.

Political Rights and Civil Liberties:

Citizens of Slovakia have the means under the 1992 constitution to change their government democratically. Since Slovakia became an independent state, there have been no elections; the current government was elected in June 1992 amid charges by the opposition of some irregularities. The constitution has come under fire from the Hungarian minority and the opposition. The former object to the preamble, which begins "we, the Slovak nation..." and not "we, the *citizens* of Slovakia." The document, which calls for a strong executive, has been criticized for leaving the door open for one-party domination, and contains ambiguous language that could be interpreted to restrict freedom of speech and expression, limit the inviolability of the home, and limit the rights to assembly and the privacy of mail.

The government has placed limits on freedom of expression and the press. In February, Slovak PEN vice-president Lubomir Feldek faced charges of "insulting a government minister" in connection with a poem he wrote about an unnamed minister. Early in the year, the government "privatized" the opposition paper *Smena*, dismissed its editors and fired journalists. A magazine edited by Culture Minister Dusan Slobodnik appealed to readers to help the state take legal action against "propagators of anti-Slovak political racism." In February, his ministry cut off subsidies to four literary and cultural periodicals, a move editors described as undemocratic political discrimination. In March, all journalists except those from the Slovak state news agency were barred from covering the ruling HZDS leadership conference. The government controls radio and television, though independent radio stations have been established in Bratislava.

Minority rights are a contentious issue. Roma are vulnerable to acts of social prejudice and violence. In the summer the government ordered the removal of all Hungarian-Slovak bilingual road signs in a region populated by Hungarians. The government also dropped laws protecting minority language rights, and has threatened to redraw district borders to isolate or disenfranchise Hungarians. The government reported in June that there were 633 schools in which children were being educated in Hungarian or Ukrainian.

Freedom of religion is guaranteed and respected, and there are few significant restriction on domestic and foreign travel. Women nominally have the same rights as men, but they are underrepresented in managerial posts. Statistics on domestic violence were unavailable.

Workers can belong to independent trade unions, and generally have the right to strike. In mid-April, the Slovak Confederation of Trade Unions led a mass rally in Bratislava accusing the government of failing to cope with the country's deteriorating economy.

Slovenia

Polity: Presidential-parliamentary democracy
Economy: Mixed-statist (transitional)
Population: 1,925,000
PPP: na
Life Expectancy: 71.0
Ethnic Groups: Slovenian (88 percent), Croats, Serbs, Muslims, Hungarians and Italians

Political Rights: 1*
Civil Liberties: 2
Status: Free

Ratings Change: *Slovenia's political rights rating changed from 2 to 1 as a result of modifications in methodology. See "Survey Methodology," page 671.

Overview:

Bordering Italy and Austria, this small, Alpine, ethnically homogenous former constituent republic of Yugoslavia entered its third year of independence with a relatively prosperous economy and political stability under the coalition government of Prime Minister Janez Drnovsek, leader of the Liberal Democratic Party (LDS).

Slovenia, which for centuries was part of the Hapsburg Empire before being incorporated into the newly created Yugoslavia after World War I, declared independence in June 1991. Its well-armed defense forces secured the nation's borders by staving off subsequent intervention by the Yugoslav People's Army. In December 1992 presidential and parliamentary elections, popular incumbent Milan Kucan, leader of the (former Communist) Party for Democratic Renewal (LCS-PDR) was re-elected. The LDS led the vote for a new 130-seat bicameral parliament with 23 percent of the vote. The new body replaced a cumbersome, 240-member tricameral assembly. The Christian Democrats (SKD) got 14.9 percent.

On 12 January 1993, Drnovsek, a former president of the Yugoslav federal republic, was re-elected prime minister. A coalition government comprising the LDS, the SKD, the leftist Associated Lists, the Green Alliance (ZS) and the Social Democrats was approved on 25 January.

The government announced that it was determined to use its four-year mandate to complete the transformation of the country into a full-fledged, market-oriented, multi-party parliamentary democracy. At the core of the government was an alliance between the LDS, and the SKD led by Lojze Peterle, the foreign minister and former prime minister. The four-party Associated Lists composed of reform Communists, with their links to the trade unions, broadened the government's parliamentary base.

Key issues in 1993 included a fuller integration into European economic structures, the improvement of an economy still affected by the loss of the 22 million-strong Yugoslav market, an increase in the pace and scope of privatization and a simmering scandal involving allegations that key government officials, including President Kucan, were involved in an elaborate scheme to smuggle arms into Bosnia-Herzegovina and Croatia in clear violation of an international arms embargo.

In April the European Community (EC) signed economic cooperation and transit accords with Slovenia. EC foreign ministers and Prime Minister Drnovsek signed an aid package of $180 million in low-interest loans, mostly for highway and railroad improvement projects. The prime minister told the EC that his country was making solid progress in becoming a free-market economy, that it enjoyed a trade surplus, rising foreign currency reserves, a declining foreign debt, and an inflation rate that fell from "20 percent monthly in October 1991 to 1.4 percent in March 1993." The new currency, the tolar, was stable and convertible, and a per capital gross domestic product (GDP) of $6,000 a year was three times higher than that of Serbia. In May, Slovenia was made a full partner in the Council of Europe.

There were some nagging structural economic problems, however. Industrial production continued its slump from 1991. Unemployment stood at 14 percent and privatization was lagging. State controls remained in effect, drawing fire from national-ist parties that had little political clout but used the economy and the presence of 100,000 refugees from Bosnia to criticize the government. The Associated Lists have sniped at the government's slowness in building a fair taxation system and the emer-gence of a "new rich" class. Many among the newly rich made their money in trading, some of it shady and linked to the Balkan war, some of it organized through the exploita-tion of the old nomenklatura links with the former regime. The left-wing parties voiced similar complaints about privatization, which has been slow getting off the ground and remained largely in the hands of the old "self-management" factory managers.

The country was rocked by several scandals in 1993. One case involved payoffs by a casino to secret police agents and alleged embezzlement by a minister who had once been the chief aid to Prime Minister Drnovsek. But the most serious was the discovery at Maribor Airport of 120 tons of weapons, including 10,000 Chinese-made assault rifles, concealed in containers marked as humanitarian aid bound for Bosnia. The weapons were part of a larger shipment that arrived in Maribor in late summer 1992 having traveled from Sudan in a Russian aircraft hired by a Polish-Ukrainian firm. Some deliveries were made to the Muslim-Slav controlled Bosnian towns of Tuzla and Zenica, as well as to Knin, the headquarters of Croatia's rebel Serbs.

In September, parliament grudgingly agreed to form a parliamentary committee to look into the matter at the insistence of Defense Minister Janez Jansa, a political rival of the president. Both President Kucan and the Associated Lists, the party formed by the former Communists, ridiculed the charges. By year's end, the opposition Slovenian People's Party said the government had shown "no great enthusiasm for this commission to start work."

Political Rights and Civil Liberties:

Slovenians have the means to change their government demo-cratically. The 6 December 1992 presidential and parliamentary elections were openly contested by many candidates and parties. The new coalition government was sworn in in mid-January. Under the multiparty system, career military and police personnel may not be members of political parties.

The judiciary is independent. Judges are elected by the state Assembly on the recommendation of the eleven-member Judicial Council, five of whose members are selected by parliament on the nomination of the president, and six are sitting judges selected by their peers. Nominees for the nine-member Constitutional Court are made by the president and approved by parliament.

Slovenia has a lively broadcast and print media. Newspapers, many affiliated with political parties, print diverse views often critical of the government. Though the state controls most radio and television, there are private stations as well, among them Kanal A television in Ljubljana, the capital. Journalists have faced limited suspension for commentary on statements by government officials, and self-censorship remains prevalent.

Freedom of assembly is guaranteed and respected, though there are restrictions dealing with public safety, national security and health. There are no restrictions on freedom of religion and the rights to worship. There are no practical restrictions on domestic and foreign travel, and citizens are allowed to emigrate and return.

Minority rights are guaranteed by law; Hungarians and Italians are constitutionally guaranteed one seat each in parliament.

There are three main labor federations, and most workers are free to join unions that are formally independent from government and political parties, though members may and do hold positions in the legislature.

Solomon Islands

Polity: Parliamentary democracy
Economy: Capitalist
Population: 348,000
PPP: $2,689
Life Expectancy: 69.5

Political Rights: 1
Civil Liberties: 2*
Status: Free

Ethnic Groups: Melanesian (93 percent), small Polynesian, Micronesian and European minorities
Ratings Change: *The Solomon Islands's civil liberties rating changed from 1 to 2 because of cross border raids from Papua New Guinea.

Overview: A collection of ten large islands and four groups of smaller islands in the Western Pacific Ocean, the Solomon Islands has been an independent member of the British Commonwealth since 1978. The forty-seven-seat unicameral parliament is elected by universal suffrage for a four-year term. Executive power is held by the prime minister, who is elected by the party or coalition holding the most seats in parliament.

In February 1989 the People's Alliance Party (PAP) won an eleven-seat plurality in a then-thirty-eight seat parliament. In March the PAP's Solomon Mamaloni took office as prime minister and formed the country's first single party government. In October 1990 Mamaloni resigned from the PAP after opposition leader Andrew Nori, along with several PAP members, accused him of ruling in a non-consultative fashion. However, Mamaloni remained prime minister of a "national unity" government, dropping several PAP ministers from the cabinet and adding four opposition MPs and a PAP backbencher.

On 26 May 1993 the country held its fourth post-independence elections. The key issues were the poor state of the economy, corruption and the lack of adequate secondary schools. None of the seven parties won an outright majority. Mamaloni's new "National Unity Group" took 21 seats; PAP, 7; National Action Party, 4; Labor Party, 4; Christian Fellowship Group, 3; United Party, 2; Nationalist Front for Progress, 1; independents, 5. On 18 June a coalition of five parties and several independents secured twenty-four votes to elect forty-six-year-old independent Francis Billy Hilly as prime minister over Mamaloni.

In his first months in office, Hilly moved to defuse tensions with neighboring Papua New Guinea, which accuses Solomon Islands residents of assisting the secessionist insurgency on nearby Bougainville Island. Papua New Guinea soldiers have launched several cross-border raids into the Solomon Islands, allegedly while in "hot pursuit" of rebel soldiers, including a September 1992 incident in which two citizens were killed. On 29 September the government announced it would close the rebel Bougainville Revolutionary Army's offices in the capital, Honiara, as a concession to the Papua New Guinea government.

In early November the opposition provoked a rift in the governing coalition by offering Education Minister Dennis Lulei the deputy prime minister job if it formed a new government. After Lulei expressed interest, the government sacked him and two other ministers. By 15 November all three had defected to the opposition, leaving Hilly's so-called National Coalition Partnership government with only twenty-one seats. However, in late November one of the ministers who had defected rejoined the government and the High Court vacated one opposition-held seat for election irregularities, giving the government a one-seat majority.

Political Rights and Civil Liberties: Citizens of the Solomon Islands can change their government democratically. Party affiliations are weak and tend to be based on personal loyalties rather than ideology or policy goals.

The independent judiciary provides adequate procedural safeguards for the accused. Freedoms of speech and press are respected in practice. The country has two private weekly newspapers and several government publications. State radio provides diverse viewpoints. The country does not have television programming, and the government controls the use of satellite dishes because it feels that outside programs containing sex and violence could negatively affect the population. Permits are required for demonstrations but have never been denied on political grounds. The majority of citizens are Christians, but there are no restrictions on other groups. Citizens may travel freely inside the country and abroad. Legally, only private sector workers can strike. However in 1989 public school teachers staged a strike and were not sanctioned.

Somalia

Polity: Rival warlords (partly foreign-occupied)
Economy: Mixed-statist
Population: 9,517,000
PPP: $836
Life Expectancy: 46.1
Ethnic Groups: Somali (Hawiye, Darod, Isaq, Isa, other), Gosha, Bajun

Political Rights: 7
Civil Liberties: 7
Status: Not Free

Overview: In the wake of a poorly executed joint U.S./U.N. humanitarian relief effort and continuing tribal clashes, Somalia remains one of the world's most troubled nations. While a November 1993

statement issued by the American Red Cross declared the famine that gripped Somalia to be over, the relief may only be temporary. The United States has indicated its intention to withdraw troops from Somalia on 31 March, 1994. Although the U.N. has extended its mandate of U.N. forces in Somalia to 18 May, 1994, most observers agree that the U.N. has neither the respect of principal Somali tribal leaders nor the military resources necessary to fulfill its projected role successfully. Should the U.S. withdraw prematurely and the U.N. be unprepared to fill the void, civil war and famine may once again ensue in Somalia.

Civil war, banditry and famine have dominated life in Somalia since the January 1991 coup that deposed Major Mohamed Siad Barre, who had seized power in a 1969 coup. At the beginning of his term, Barre was committed to ending the "clanism" that created persistent political instability within Somalia. He attempted to forge a national identity by outlawing clan names, abolishing clan-based political parties, establishing a one-party system and trying to instill Somali nationalism with unifying ideas and symbols. In part, he succeeded. For the first five years of his term, Barre's plan met with some success. But by the late 1970s Barre's hold on power was wavering.

In order to maintain power, Barre adopted a strategy which opted to exploit, rather than eliminate, clan rivalries. He grew to rely on a small number of clans known as the MOD (Marehan-Ogaden-Dolbahante) and appointed family members to a number of key political positions. Despite the repressive nature of Barre's regime, the U.S. and Italy continued to provide support to Somalia. From 1979 to 1988, the U.S. provided $840 million dollars in aid. The aid was used to secure U.S. rights to use an airfield in Somalia deemed as "essential" for protecting U.S. interests in the Gulf. Despite the repression and corruption of the Barre regime, it was not until mid-1988 that the Congress voted to freeze U.S. aid to Somalia.

By the late 1980s, internal discontent with Barre grew. The Somali National Movement (SNM), an Isaq movement created in 1981, fought the Barre regime for control of territory in northwestern Somalia. Until 1988, the SNM operated from bases within Ethiopia. Hoping to crush the movement, Barre negotiated an agreement with Ethiopia to close SNM camps within its borders. In response, the SNM moved its operations to Somalia. During May and June 1988, the SNM secured a large part of territory in northern Somalia. The Barre regime countered with a military campaign against the Isaqs. Africa Watch reports that "...the government unleashed a reign of terror against Isaq civilians, killing 50,000 to 60,000 between May 1988 and January 1990."

By the time Barre's regime was toppled in January 1991, civil society in Somalia was deeply divided by clan rivalries, distrust and a legacy of brutality. Barre was ousted by members of the United Somali Congress (USC), a rebel group which draws it support mainly from the Hawiye clan. Over the objection of its military leader, Mohamed Farah Aidid, the USC appointed Ali Mahdi, of the Abgal subclan, as interim President of Somalia. (In late 1991, the USC split into two rival factions—one led by Aidid and the other led by Mahdi.) Shortly following the coup, the USC, led by Aidid, took control of the capital of Mogadishu and regions north. In the months that followed, factional fighting ensued. A number of rival, clan-based groups formed: The Somali Salvation Democratic Front (SSDF), the Somali National Front (SNF), and the Somali Patriotic Movement (SPM). In May 1991, the SNM established the Republic of Somaliland in the north of Somalia.

Caught in the middle of the warring factions were large numbers of Somalis from agricultural communities who were poorly armed, politically weak and, as a result, were subject to repeated raids, looting, and rape. Africa Watch reports that the fighting "...took a heavy toll on civilians as the warring factions looted food stored in underground silos, stole or killed livestock, ruined wells, raped women of various clans and killed men of opposing clans to prevent them from taking up arms. These attacks on civilians so thoroughly disrupted production and distribution of food that, far more than the drought, they are responsible for the famine in Somalia." An estimated 700,000 Somalis sought refuge in neighboring Kenya and Ethiopia and several hundred thousand more emigrated to Gulf states, Europe and North America.

Fighting among members of clan alliances intensified during 1992 as factions attempted to profit from international food aid. The number of Somalis on the brink of starvation between 1991 and 1992 was reported to be as high as 2 million. The initial U.N. response was muted. In October 1992, the U.N. special representative to Somalia, Ambassador Mohamed Sahnoun, strongly criticized the U.N.'s inaction and, after receiving a strong rebuke from the U.N. secretary general, resigned. It was not until the summer of 1992, when Western news agencies began to cover the famine in Somalia, that international attention focused on the crisis and public pressure to act intensified.

In August 1992 then-President George Bush assigned U.S. military aircraft to transport food aid. While this helped to speed the delivery of food to some areas, it did not prevent looting. A series of diplomatic efforts to mediate the conflict in late 1992 failed. In November 1992, Bush authorized the use of U.S. troops to lead a U.N. mission in Somalia. The U.N. Security Council subsequently passed resolution 794 which sanctioned the use of "all necessary means..." to provide humanitarian relief in Somalia. During December 1992, over 22,000 American troops and 7,000 troops from other countries were sent to Somalia. Initially welcomed by the Somalis and accepted by the warlords, the troops were successful in securing safe routes to the feeding centers in the areas most devastated by the famine. Within just a few weeks, however, the situation dramatically changed. The number of armed Somalis on the streets increased and U.N. troops found themselves targets of sniper fire.

By the end of December, the U.S. instituted a policy of "stabilization" which called for tighter street patrols and gave troops authorization to disarm Somalis. Tensions between Somalis and U.N. forces grew. Attacks against U.N. forces by supporters of warlord Gen. Mohamed Farah Aidid increased. Aidid charged that the U.N. forces were favoring rival warlord, Ali Mahdi. By January, the U.N. mission was on the offensive. A number of encampments belonging to General Aidid were destroyed by U.S. troops and in Mogadishu a local market was raided and weapons confiscated. Fighting between Somalis and U.N. forces increased as casualties on both sides continued to grow. In June 1993, the U.N. issued a Security Council resolution authorizing the arrest of Aidid. By October 1993, sixty-nine U.N. troops and over 700 Somalis had been killed. U.S. hostages were taken and then released. The mission in Somalia had changed from a popular humanitarian effort to a disdained and deadly military action.

Pressure from political opponents and a weighty domestic agenda at home prompted President Bill Clinton to set March 1994 for the withdrawal of U.S. troops from Somalia. By November 1993, the international community returned to its original humanitarian role in Somalia and diplomatic efforts to end the conflict were again underway. In mid-November the U.N. approved a U.S.-sponsored resolution which ended the four-month hunt for Aidid. In December 1993, U.N.-sponsored peace talks between Somali faction leaders were held in Ethiopia, with Aidid in attendance.

Political Rights and Civil Liberties: Somalians cannot change their government democratically. Since the overthrow of Barre in 1991, there has been no central governmental authority. Most of Somalia has been plagued by factional fighting, thievery, and a general sense of lawlessness. While the joint U.N./U.S. mission to Somalia was successful in ending the famine, it was not successful in establishing an interim civilian government. Northern 'Somaliland' has some degree of local and regional authority in the wake of the SNM's self proclaimed secession in 1991. However, while the SNM represent the Isaq of the region, a number of other non-Isaq minorities found themselves within the newly seceded territory. These groups opposed the secession and do not accept SNM authority. The international community has not officially recognized Somaliland and this has left the territory isolated and generally without emergency relief assistance.

Hundreds of thousands of Somalians have died from starvation or been killed in the civil war that has gripped Somalia since 1988. Human rights groups report that members of factions have indiscriminately killed rival group members, unarmed civilians and relief workers. Two human rights groups—the London-based Africa Rights and Africa Watch—also reported that a number of Somali civilians were killed by U.N. troops in suspicious circumstances. A March 1993 Africa Watch report states that although the U.N. forces were generally "...judicious in limiting their use of force....there have been several troubling exceptions to this restraint."

Despite a campaign to disarm Somalis, rival factions remain heavily armed. Unarmed Somalis living in agricultural areas have been subject to extrajudicial executions, beatings and rape. Many in these areas were robbed of food and livestock and left to starve. To escape the famine and fighting, over 700,000 Somalis have fled to neighboring countries.

Somalia does not have a functioning judicial system. The SNM is reported to have adopted *Shari'a*, Muslim law, in the northwest territory of 'Somaliland,' but it is not known how this has been applied. The system of "justice" administered by clans was reported to be arbitrary and unfair. Somalis are subject to arbitrary arrest and detention by rival clans, and human rights groups report that detainees are subject to extrajudicial executions, beatings and torture solely as a result of their clan membership.

Freedom of speech is not permitted. While some newspaper publications were available in Mogadishu, publication was sporadic and distribution, limited. The BBC's Somali-language services and Moscow Radio's Somali service provided Somalis with information about developments within the country. Against a background of violence, fear and intimidations, Somalis do not have freedom of assembly and association. Apart from the warring factions, no political organizations exist.

South Africa

Polity: Transitional   **Political Rights:** 5
Economy: Capitalist-statist **Civil Liberties:** 4
Population: 32,343,000   **Status:** Partly Free
PPP: $4,865
Life Expectancy: 61.7
Ethnic Groups: Black (Zulu, Xhosa, Swazi, Sotho, other;
69 percent), white (Afrikaner, English; 18 percent),
Coloured (10 percent), Indian (3 percent)

Overview: Under an accord reached by leaders of twenty-one South
African parties in November 1993, the right to vote was
extended to the black majority for the first time in South
Africa's 340-year history. Following three years of painstaking and precarious negotiations between the government and opposition leaders, the agreement formally ends
apartheid and firmly paves the way for majority rule in South Africa. The courage of
the main architects of the settlement—President Frederik de Klerk of the National Party
(NP) and President Nelson Mandela of the African National Congress (ANC)—was
recognized by the Nobel peace committee as both de Klerk and Mandela were named
recipients of the 1993 Nobel Peace Prize.

In 1961, South Africa left the British Commonwealth and became an independent
state. Since 1948, the National Party has ruled South Africa. One third of the black
majority and most mixed-race Coloureds and Indians, live in racially segregated areas
in, and near, large cities. An additional ten million blacks live in ten tribal homelands.
The system of apartheid that has dominated South Africa for forty-five years has
isolated South Africa from the international community and has created a cycle of
political violence that, since the mid-1980s, has killed approximately 16,000 people.

Since 1990, intensive negotiations for a transition from apartheid to democracy
have been ongoing. The major negotiating parties—the ANC, and the ruling NP—
along with seventeen opposition parties, held multilateral negotiations at the Convention for a Democratic South Africa (Codesa II) during 1992. After loosing a parliamentary seat to the Conservative Party (CP) in February 1992, de Klerk announced an
extraordinary referendum for whites only to establish whether he had a mandate to
negotiate further reforms. Eighty-five percent of eligible voters turned out for the March
1992 referendum and sixty-nine percent endorsed further negotiations.

Following a series of setbacks between May and September of 1992, bilateral
negotiations between the government and the ANC began. On 26 September, de Klerk
and Mandela signed a Record of Understanding (ROU) which stated: an elected
constituent assembly (CA) would draft and adopt a new constitution; a transition
executive council would be appointed alongside the CA; the existing tricameral
Parliament would be dissolved; and a government of national unity would be elected
following the adoption of the new constitution. Despite right wing protest and escalating political violence, negotiations continued throughout 1992/1993, culminating in the
November 1993 accord.

As part of the November 1993 accord, a new interim Constitution was drafted that provides for a five-year Transitional Government of National Unity to be elected in the country's first democratic election scheduled for April 1994. Any party that secures more than five percent of the total vote will be included in the new government. A 400 member National Assembly, which will serve as a constitutional assembly, will draft the final constitution by April 1999. Under the agreement, the country will be divided into nine semi-autonomous provinces. Each province will have its own legislature, premier and constitution but their powers will be concurrent with, not exclusive of central government rule and they must defer to the central government in matters deemed to be of "national security." The president will be selected by the majority party and his cabinet must proportionally represent all parties who attain more than five percent of the total vote. In a break from South Africa's British style parliamentary system, sovereignty will be vested in the new Constitution. Other provisions of the negotiated package include: compensation for those who were deprived of their land since 1913; abandonment of the draconian system of detention without trial; establishment of a multi-racial Transitional Executive Council to help govern the country and ensure fairness in the lead up to the national elections.

Despite the historic 1993 agreement and the promise of a new democratic era emerging in South Africa, significant obstacles remain. The negotiations leading up to the accord were boycotted by the CP, led by Ferdi Hartzenberg, the Afrikaner Volksfront (AVF), led by General Constand Viljoen as well as the Inkatha Freedom Party (IFP) led by Chief Mangosuthu Buthelezi. An unlikely coalition of right-wing white and conservative black leaders who demand a greater degree of self rule formed the Freedom Alliance (FA). While most observers agree that it is unlikely that right-wing groups can sustain an armed rebellion, they may be able to derail the peace process through sabotage and guerrilla-like tactics. Further resistance to the accord comes from the Pan Africanist Congress (PAC), a militant black nationalist group that opposes plans for leading parties to share power and wants the black majority to assume control in the first post-apartheid government. The military wing of the PAC, the Azanian People's Liberation Army (APLA), continues the violent campaign which has been responsible for recent attacks on white civilians.

In an attempt to prevent a violent confrontation between supporters and opponents of the accord, the ANC met with leaders from the AVF. The talks centered around right wing demands for an Afrikaner homeland but the ANC remained firm that no homeland could be established prior to the April 1994 election. In December 1993, the right-wing Volksfront announced that it was creating its own transitional government which would "...protect the interests of the Afrikaner nation" until a whites-only election could be held in a proposed Afrikaner homeland. Leaders of the movement indicated that the homeland would be established by March 1994-one month prior to the scheduled April 1994 elections. Talks between the ruling NP , the ANC and the Afrikaner Volksfront continue.

Political Rights and Civil Liberties:

While the negotiated transition-to-democracy package adopted at the end of 1993 brings an end to apartheid, it is too early to determine whether the plan will succeed in a peaceful transfer of power from minority to majority rule. Under the new interim Constitution adopted in December 1993, all South Africans—black and white—have the power to democratically change the government. The new Constitution, together with other reform measures drafted by the government and opposition party leaders in November 1993, are widely seen as essential to ensure a peaceful transition to democracy. However, despite these reform measures, human rights groups and other international observers have highlighted a number of unresolved concerns that must be addressed prior to the 1994 multiparty elections.

The September 1993 Africa Watch report on the KwaZulu homeland, the political base for Buthelezi, states: "KwaZulu is a one-party state, in which institutions of Inkatha and the institutions of the homeland administration are virtually indistinguishable. Only Inkatha has the freedom to organize...and the freedom of expression, assembly, and association for other groups are routinely denied." The November 1993 accord provides for semi-autonomous rule in South Africa's provinces and both the government and the ANC, under pressure from white right wingers and the IFP, appear willing to discuss even greater self rule for the provinces. The violations described by the Africa Watch report underscore the need for the central government to maintain the right to monitor and protect political rights and civil liberties within the newly established provinces.

Human rights groups report that extrajudicial execution and torture by security forces working either independently or as agents of the government continued throughout 1992/1993. While the government has been credited with bringing about an end to apartheid in South Africa, human rights groups maintain that during the period of intense negotiations between the ruling NP, its allies and the ANC, the government was responsible for the increasing political violence, destabilization and repression. During 1992 there were 123 recorded deaths in police custody, 1,724 recorded injuries caused by security forces, 3,499 people reported dead as a result of political violence, and 97 political leaders assassinated. A report by the Lawyers Committee for Human Rights asserts that even during the period of intense negotiations there was a "principal and profound failure of the government and the system of justice to end the impunity of human rights violations." The report goes on to detail human rights and civil liberties violations by security forces and asserts that government inaction and complicity contributed to both the violence and the disruption of the negotiated transition to democracy.

Human rights violations were also committed by anti-apartheid groups. The ANC, in a follow up to its October 1992 report, confirmed accounts of torture by its security department known as Mbokodo. The report concludes that between 1970 and 1991, the security department of the ANC was responsible for gross human rights violations that include the unlawful detention (for up to eight years), torture and beating of suspected spies.

The judiciary is independent of the executive. Both common criminal and security related cases are tried in criminal courts presided over by judges or magistrates; trial by jury was abolished in 1969. The new system of government will transfer sovereignty from parliament to the constitution. However, the Democratic Party, which is supported by many in the legal profession and the judiciary, is critical of a proposal that gives the executive, as opposed to an independent body, the power to appoint judges of the Constitutional Court.

During 1993, there was limited freedom of press in South Africa. While both mainstream and alternative press have criticized the government and government policies, certain press restrictions remain. At the beginning of 1992, Parliament repealed section 27b of the Police Act that stated that journalists who published negative information about the police without having "reasonable grounds" would be subject to fine or imprisonment. However, journalists continue to be persecuted under section 205 of the Criminal Procedure Act, which allows the government to subpoena journalists and require them to disclose the names of confidential sources or face imprisonment. Journalists continue to face harassment from security forces as well as from militants of the PAC, the Azanian People's Organization (Azapo), the IFP, the ANC and white right-wing groups. While there are a number of independent print media, there is only one state broadcasting television network, the South African Broadcasting Corporation (SABC). Under the new accord package, the board of the SABC must be open to independent members. After five years of state control, broadcasting deregulation will allow for a number of new, independent stations and grant licenses for independent broadcasters.

Spain

Polity: Parliamentary democracy
Economy: Capitalist
Population: 37,401,000
PPP: $11,723
Life Expectancy: 77.0

Political Rights: 1
Civil Liberties: 2*
Status: Free

Ethnic Groups: Various regional cultures (Castilians, Basques, Catalans, Galicians, Valencians, Andalusians), Gypsies, and various immigrant groups, notably North Africans and Latin Americans
Ratings Change: *Spain's civil liberties rating changed from 1 to 2 as a result of modifications in methodology. See "Survey Methodology," page 671.

Overview: The governing Socialist Workers Party lost significant ground in the general election of June 1993. Still the largest parliamentary party, the Socialists formed a minority government with the support of regionalist parties. Rising unemployment and a series of party scandals hurt Prime Minister Felipe Gonzalez, but did not stop him from winning his fourth consecutive election since 1982.

Spain is a constitutional monarchy that has had democratic parliamentary government since 1977. Following four decades of right-wing dictatorship by Generalissimo Francisco Franco and a brief transitional government headed by Adolfo Suarez, a moderate conservative, the country returned to a monarchy in 1975. King Juan Carlos, the largely ceremonial head of state, used his personal prestige to support the transition to democracy in the 1970s and to stave off coup attempts.

In the 1993 general election, the Socialists won 159 of the 350 seats in the lower house of parliament. The right-wing Popular Party garnered 141, a gain of 35. According to the press and the public, Jose Maria Aznar, the Popular Party leader, bested Gonzalez in televised debates. The Comunist-led United Left won 18. Regionalist parties hold the balance of power. The government has a four-year mandate. The less powerful upper house, the Senate, has 208 directly elected members who serve four-year terms. Each province sends four members. Outlying territories send from one to three members each. Spain has seventeen regions with varying degrees of autonomy.

As the unemployment rate climbed over 20 percent in 1993, the government maintained very cautious economic policies. The government's response to the recession has deepened the split between the government and its onetime ally, the General Union of Workers (UGT). Parliament approved the Maastricht treaty on European integration in November 1992. However, problems remain between Spain and the European Union over the Spain-Gibraltar border. Spain claims the neighboring British colony, and believes the border to be an internal division, not an international frontier.

The Socialists are attempting to recover from a series of scandals in the early 1990s. These included provincial government bribery, central bank mismanagement and a railroad real estate scam.

In 1993, regionalist and separatist forces continued to press Madrid for more autonomy or outright independence. For example, Catalans, who are concentrated in the northern and eastern parts of Spain, have become increasingly assertive about advancing Catalan as a language distinct from Spanish. The Catalonian school system eliminated Spanish as an instructional language in elementary schools in 1993. Spanish-speaking parents protested this new policy.

Political Rights and Civil Liberties:

Spanish voters have the right to change their government democratically. Spain has switched from governments of the center-right to center-left. Under the terms of Europrean integration, resident citizens of other European Union countries have local voting rights.

Regional cultures have significant autonomy, but Basque separatism remains a serious problem. ETA (the Basque acronym for Land and Liberty) has carried out terrorist attacks for many years. Over 700 people have died in ETA attacks since 1968. Basque prisoners have charged the government with mistreatment. Spain requires visas for visitors from north Africa. The government punishes employers for hiring illegal aliens; and immigration quotas now favor the groups the state believes are easiest to integrate. Latin Americans require no visa to enter Spain, which they use as an entry point to the rest of Europe. This has raised problems with Spain's neighbors. Ethnic minorities, especially immigrants, have complained about mistreatment, but Spain still lacks a law dealing with racial discrimination.

The print media are free and competitive, but the opposition has charged that state television has a pro-government bias. There are also three private commercial stations on the air.

Two labor federations exist, one Communist, the other formerly affilated with the Socialists. They have cooperated in general strikes in recent years. Competitive enterprise is becoming increasingly linked with the rest of Europe.

Religious freedom is protected under the constitution. Roman Catholicism is the majority faith, but church influence is declining. There is no state religion. Government accords with the various faiths place Protestantism, Judaism and Islam on legal par with Roman Catholicism in weddings, education and the armed forces. The Catholic Church still benefits from contributions designated on tax returns, but non-Catholic institutions have secured tax-exempt status.

Sri Lanka

Polity: Presidential-parliamentary democracy (insurgencies)
Economy: Mixed-capitalist statist
Population: 17,839,000
PPP: $2,405
Life Expectancy: 70.9
Ethnic Groups: Sinhalese, (74 percent), Tamil (18 percent), Moor (7 percent), others

Political Rights: 4
Civil Liberties: 5
Status: Partly Free

Overview: The calm reaction in Sri Lanka following the assassination of President Ranasinge Premadasa and a leading opposition figure within eight days in spring 1993 was indicative of the country's political resiliency. Prime Minister Dingiri Banda Wijetunge took over as president and voters peacefully elected provincial councils in late May. During the year, the deadly, decade-old Tamil insurgency continued unabated in the north. Since 1983 some 20,000 soldiers, guerrillas and civilians have been killed in the fighting.

Located off southeastern India, Sri Lanka (known until 1972 as Ceylon) achieved independence from the British in 1947. Since then political power has alternated between the centrist United National Party (UNP) and the nationalist, leftist Sri Lanka Freedom Party (SLFP). In 1956 Prime Minister Solomon Bandaranaike's new SLFP government made Buddhism the official religion and Sinhalese the official language. Other laws similiarly disadvantaged the Tamil minority by segregating secondary students by language and established quotas for Sinhalese-speakers at universities. Although future governments gradually repealed these measures, their initial implementation led to small-scale violence and created deep rifts between Sinhalese and the Tamils.

The 1978 constitution established a powerful presidency and a 225-member legislature. The directly elected president can serve two six-year terms, appoints the prime minister and other top officials, and can dissolve parliament following a no-confidence motion or a rejection of an appropriations bill. The legislature serves up to six years, with 198 seats elected through proportional representation from twenty-two electoral districts, and the remainder distributed according to proportional national representation.

In July 1983 Tamil separatist guerrillas in the north and east began attacks on government troops, claiming Tamils are discriminated against in housing, jobs and education. In 1985 the Liberation Tigers of Tamil Eelam (LTTE) emerged as the most powerful of several guerrilla groups. The LTTE seeks an independent homeland in the north and east covering much of the coastline, although Tamils are a majority only in the northern areas. In 1987, after the government captured the strategic Jaffna Peninsula, India began airlifting supplies to the rebels. Sri Lanka agreed to a treaty bringing in an Indian peacekeeping force (IPKF) to maintain a ceasefire. Refusing to disarm, the LTTE temporarily abandoned its war against the government and fought the numerically superior IPKF to a standstill. The presence of the Indian troops sparked a bloody anti-government insurgency in the south by the fiercely nationalist Marxist People's Liberation Front (JVP).

In the 1988 presidential elections the UNP's Ranasinghe Premadasa won 50.43 percent of the vote to defeat former prime minister and SLFP leader Sirima Bandaranaike. In the February 1989 parliamentary elections, the UNP won 125 seats, with the opposition vote split between the SLFP, 67; the Tamil United National Liberation Front, 10; the Sri Lanka Muslim Congress, 4; United Socialist Alliance, 3; independent Tamils, 13.

By 1990 the government had brutally crushed the JVP uprising, allegedly through the help of state-supported death squads. Meanwhile in May the last Indian troops withdrew from the north, and fighting between the government and the LTTE resumed. President Premadasa appeared at times to favor a negotiated settlement to the conflict, but talks never advanced beyond the exploratory stage. On the political front, critics began to accuse the president of being too authoritarian, for having forced several dissenters out of the UNP and surrounding himself with weak ministers, and blamed him for having failed to negotiate a settlement with the LTTE. Privately, many also disliked him for not being from the *goigama*, the wealthy farmer caste that has produced most of the country's leaders.

In August 1991 up to 120 MPs, many from the UNP, signed an impeachment motion against the president. Premadasa dismissed eight UNP MPs from the party, and in October the speaker of the parliament declared several of signatures on the impeachment motion invalid and tabled it. The eight expelled MPs formed the new Democratic United National Front (DUNF) party in protest. In 1992 Ramadasa strengthened his position by surviving several no-confidence motions. The government also received a boost in its campaign against the LTTE in May when India declared its southern Tamil Nadu State off limits as a safe haven for the rebels. However, Tamil suicide bombers continued to target top government and military officials, killing among others navy commander Clancy Fernando in the capital in November.

In early 1993 political parties began positioning themselves for the May 1993 provincial council elections. On 23 April a gunman assassinated DUNF leader Lalaith Athulathmudali in Colombo at a campaign rally. Although the government immediately blamed the LTTE and launched an investigation, the opposition claimed the government had ordered the killing. On 28 April mourners at Athulathmudali's funeral threw rocks at police, who fired back with tear gas.

On 1 May the country's cycle of violence claimed its most prominent victim as a suicide bomber assassinated President Premadasa and killed twenty-three others at a May Day rally. Officials immediately swore in Prime Minister Dingiri Banda Wijetunge as acting president. Two days later police identified the assassin as an LTTE guerrilla, although the group denied responsibility. On 7 May parliament formally elected Wijetunge to serve out Premadasa's term until the December 1994 presidential elections.

Despite the potential for violence, the 17 May provincial council elections were conducted peacefully with a 75 percent turnout. The UNP won a majority in four councils and a plurality in two. The leftist, SLFP-dominated People's United Front coalition narrowly won the key Western Province, which includes the capital. Due to the fighting, no voting was scheduled for the northeastern province.

In the fall some of the heaviest battles of the decade-old civil war occurred on the northern Jaffna Peninsula, which is the LTTE's last stronghold. In late September and early October more than 100 soldiers and 200 rebels were killed as government troops captured a rebel base in the town of Kilali. On 11 November LTTE guerrillas captured the army's strategic Pooneryn base for three days. More than 400 soldiers and up to 700 guerrillas were killed in fierce fighting. President Wijetunge appears set against holding peace talks, and the army has pledged to finally crush the uprising by September 1994. However, the rebels are estimated to have some 10,000 soldiers, and show no signs of capitulation.

Although the violence is estimated to cost the country 3-4 percent of GDP annually, initial estimates showed 5.7 percent economic growth for 1993, mainly on the strength of tea and textile exports. Inflation is running at 12-15 percent and remains a problem. The country leads South Asia in literacy and poverty-eradication programs.

Political Rights and Civil Liberties: Sri Lankans can change their government democratically. Separatist violence has prevented balloting in national elections in some northern and eastern areas, and has prevented the government from holding elections for the northeast provincial council. Although Tamils claim discrimination in education, employment and other fields, the only official discrimination is through a 1990 government decree that civil service hiring be based on ethnic groups' proportions in society.

On LTTE-held Jaffna Peninsula, 900,000 civilians are largely without running water or electricity, and have been short of food since the government began a blockade last year. The rebels rule in an authoritarian manner and generally confiscate half of the villagers' agricultural produce. In early June several hundred Tamil civilians began migrating to government controlled areas after the guerrillas announced they would draft one member from each family.

In recent years anti-LTTE Tamil groups have been responsible for scores of killings of suspected LTTE supporters. In early November Tamil political parties claimed that a former Tamil guerrilla group, the People's Liberation Organization of Tamil, had been assisting government soldiers in carrying out random, brief detentions of some 2,000 Tamil civilians in Colombo in recent weeks. The LTTE itself commits several hundred politically motivated killings each year. Government security forces continue to commit extrajudicial killings of captured LTTE guerrillas and suspected civilian sympathisers.

The 1979 Prevention of Terrorism Act (PTA) and the Emergency Regulations (ER), which have been renewed monthly since 1983, grant the government broad powers. Suspects may be held incommunicado for up to eighteen months under the PTA, and indefinitely under the ER after being presented to a magistrate after three months detainment. Detainees are frequently beaten by the police. Under the ER, confessions to police officers are admissable in court, and defendants who repudiate them must prove they were given under duress. More than 3,000 suspects are believed to be held under these regulations.

The judiciary is considered independent, and in non-security cases defendents receive adequate due-process rights. Freedom of speech and press can be constitution-ally-restricted in the interest of national security through the PTA and ER, although this is done infrequently. The Parliamentary Powers and Privileges Act allows parliament to fine and imprison individuals for up to two years for criticizing an MP, and was used in 1992 to call a newspaper editor before parliament for questioning.

The country's independent newspapers publish diverse opinions on political and human rights issues, but small papers claim they are often coerced by various groups, particularly by the LTTE in the north. In 1993 several mainstream and anti-government newspapers claimed they had been singled out for harassment after tax and utilities officials raided their offices. The government owns the radio station and two of three television networks, and must approve all domestic news broadcasts.

Although Buddhism is the official religion, other groups can practice without restrictions. Citizens are free to travel internally, except in areas restricted due to fighting, and can travel freely abroad. State workers are prohibited from striking, and labor activists say the Public Service Commission, with which such employees can file grievances, is biased towards the government. The 1989 Emergency Services Act allows the president to declare a strike in any industry illegal, although this power is rarely invoked.

Sudan

Polity: Military
Economy: Mixed capitalist
Population: 27,407,000
PPP: $949
Life Expectancy: 50.8

Political Rights: 7
Civil Liberties: 7
Status: Not Free

Ethnic Groups: Some 600 groups— Sudanese Arabs (40 percent); African: Dinka (11 percent), Nuba (8 percent), Nuer, Shilluk, Fur, others

Overview:

In 1993, Africa's largest country descended further into mayhem as the government of Gen. Omar Hasssan Ahmad al-Bashir continued its brutal war against the rebel Sudan People's Liberation Army (SPLA), a Christian and animist guerrilla group seeking greater autonomy for the south and protection from Islamic law. Ethnically-based insurgencies within the SPLA led to internecine tribal violence that left thousands dead or displaced, and millions of civilians faced starvation as a result of the fighting. Meanwhile, Sudan's international isolation intensified when Sudanese diplomats were linked to the World Trade Center bombing in New York, leading the U.S. to cut off all aid.

Sudan won independence from Britain and Egypt in 1956 and functioned as a parliamentary democracy for thirteen years. Violence between the Arab-Muslim north and the Christian, black African south plagued the country for decades. Following the 1969-1972 Anya Nya separatist war, the southern third of the country achieved a high level of autonomy. In 1983, however, Jafar Numeiri—who took power in a 1969 coup—partitioned the southern region into three smaller regions and introduced *Shari'a* (Islamic law). Southern Christians and animists, led by Dr. John Garang, a U.S.-educated renegade colonel, formed the SPLA and began a struggle for greater autonomy for the south. The insurgency continued even after the military toppled Numeiri in a 1985 coup and returned the country to civilian rule in 1986.

In June 1989, Gen. Bashir led a military coup that overthrew the pro-Western, elected government, suspended the constitution, dissolved the elected constituent Assembly, banned all political parties and established the National Salvation Revolutionary Command Council (RCC), which he chaired. Although Bashir is prime minister, the power behind the military regime is Islamic fundamentalist cleric Hassan al-Turabi, head of the National Islamic Front (NIF), whose supporters took control of the security apparatus, judiciary and universities, declaring an Islamic state. In March 1991, the government approved the Shari'a for the entire country, including the south.

In August 1991, the 40,000-strong SPLA split largely along ethnic-tribal lines, when a faction headed by Reik Machar, a Neur, challenged Garang and his Dinka-dominant Torit faction. Machar's so-called Nasir faction, made up largely of Neur, called for complete independence from the north, and accused Garang of dictatorial practices and human rights abuses. Garang continued to advocate rapprochement with Khartoum and a unified secular state. With its military supported by China and Iran, the government also created the 85,000-man Popular Defense Force of highly motivated young Islamic militants modeled on Iran's Revolutionary Guards. In February 1992, Prime Minister Bashir announced the appointment of a 300-member Transitional National Assembly, which included all members of the RCC, a number of RCC advisors, all cabinet ministers and state governors, and representatives from the army, trade unions, and former political parties. Elections for a permanent body are still pending.

By the end of 1992, which saw a renewed government offensive against the SPLA, 300,000 people continued to face starvation in Juba, a government-held garrison in the south besieged by the SPLA. Seven-hundred-and-fifty-thousand refugees—most of them black Africans—were forced out of Khartoum into squalid refugee camps in what international diplomats and aid workers called an "ethnic cleansing" operation, which also included relocating tens of thousands of non-Arab black Nuba tribesmen from their central region to camps on the pretense of giving them shelter from the civil war. The U.S. Committee of Refugees estimated that the ten-year civil war, and its attendant pestilence, starvation and disease, had killed 1.3 million southern Sudanese and involved egregious human rights abuses by all sides, including murder, rape, kidnapping, summary execution, enslavement and destruction of whole villages, livestock and crops. Over 4 million people were internally displaced and 1 million had become refugees in neighboring states.

Despite government denials, 1993 began with renewed government raids on civilian targets. In a much-vaunted visit in February, Pope John Paul II sharply assailed religious persecution by the government and Islamic fundamentalists. In February, Amnesty International issued a report that charged the government with genocide in the execution of over 6,000 Nuba tribesmen from December 1992 through January 1993. Drought and increased fighting put 1.7 million southerners in dire need. Meanwhile, both the government and rebel forces continued to use food as a weapon, denying international relief agencies access to affected areas or stealing food shipments.

At the end of the month, the government and Garang's SPLA-Torit faction announced a future resumption of negotiations in Abuja, Nigeria. In March, Garang's faction agreed to a ceasefire with the government, freeing both sides to move against SPLA-Nasir. Increased factional fighting and an attack against a U.N. relief worker led the United Nations to suspend food deliveries to the area hardest hit by famine, where tens of thousands relied on U.N. food handouts. On 27 March, forces loyal to SPLA-Torit attacked the town of Kongor, forcing supporters of the SPLA-Nasir faction to flee. According to eyewitnesses, scores of people were killed, including civilians. Among those killed was Joseph Oduho, an ethnic Latuka politician, whose people had suffered systematic attacks by the Torit group in the fall of 1992. The attack came a day after SPLA-Nasir leader Reik Machar tried to consolidate his power by appealing to ethnic Dinkas to join his faction. Present at the meeting was the leader of a third SPLA faction, William Nyuon, whose forces, SPLA-"Unity," had clashed with Garang's troops. Nyuon had both Dinka and Nuer lineage, and he had won the support of the Latukas. After the meeting, Machar announced that his and Nyuon's forces had formally merged into the SPLA-United. The same month, thirty-five countries at the forty-ninth session of the U.N. Committee on Human Rights in Geneva signed the committee's first public denouncement of Sudan's human rights record.

In late April, the government and the Garang faction convened for talks in Abuja. While the talks were going on, interfactional fighting intensified. On 4 May, a World Food Program report estimated that 30,000 people had been displaced since April by SPLA and tribal violence. Ayod and other towns in the south were deserted, residents forced to live in the bush. The two SPLA factions continued to accuse each other of making secret deals with the government.

Not surprisingly, the Abuja peace talks ended in failure on 17 May. There was no joint communiqué, let alone agreement. Garang explained that the talks had stalled over the relationship between the state and religion, particularly Khartoum's refusal of a secular system for the federal (central) government. Both sides rejected a partition, a federation of a north under Shari'a and a secular south. Meanwhile, other negotiations were under way as the many sides sought political advantage. Khartoum held talks in Nairobi with Machar's SPLA-United faction, which demanded southern independence. A month earlier, Garang met in Nairobi with representatives of the Northern National Democratic Alliance, composed of union leaders, heads of banned political parties, including the religious-based Umma and the Democratic Unionist parties. A discreetly worded accord called for secular law. The rift in the SPLA widened.

Nevertheless, on 28 May both SPLA factions signed a U.S.-brokered agreement to withdraw their forces from what came to be known as the "famine triangle," a part of Sudan bounded by Kongor, Ayod and Waat, where factional fighting left an estimated 80,000 people dead in 1992, according to the U.N. Despite the agreement, both sides remained distrustful of each other and refused to withdraw first. The stand-off continued.

New fighting broke out again in July around Kongor and Lafon, where 350 villagers were killed by SPLA-Torit forces loyal to Garang. Meanwhile, Amnesty International estimated that SPLA-Unity forces under Machar had killed thousands of Dinkas when they moved through Dinka territory in 1991.

In July-August, the government air force launched a new bombing offensive in the south, indiscriminately bombing civilian targets in the Kaya region near the Uganda border. The U.N. estimated that 75,000 people were made homeless and sought refuge in Uganda, Zaire and elsewhere in southern Sudan. The aim of the bombings was the depopulation and eventual takeover of the strategic towns of Kaya, Kajo, Kaji, Nimule and Yambio. The government denied the offensive despite independent confirmation by relief workers and the U.N.

On 18 August, the U.S. decided to add Sudan to the list of states sponsoring terrorism, thereby leading to a cessation of U.S. aid. The move came after two Sudanese U.N. diplomats were accused of being part of the conspiracy to blow up the World Trade Center in New York. In the fall, there were renewed attempts to end fighting between SPLA factions, including an offer to mediate by former President Jimmy Carter, who had mediated peace talks in May 1989.

In October, Gen. Bashir announced that a new civilian government would lift the curfew imposed when he seized power. The announcement came after Bashir had been named president by his ruling junta, which then disbanded. The move was seen as an attempt by the government to give more power to the parliament, but it was undercut by the fact that only members of Bashir's military regime were in the new administration.

Other issues facing the country in 1993 were the economy and a deterioration of relations with Egypt. In December 1992, Sudan accused Egypt of creating tension by sending 600 troops to a disputed border area rich in magnesium, minerals and oil. In May, Egypt's foreign minister denied Sudan's allegations, but said his country would not retaliate after Sudan said it would close consulates in several Egyptian cities.

In February, the government introduced drastic market reforms. The measures included abolition of fixed exchange rates for the Sudanese pound, withdrawal of all subsidies on fuel and basic food items and an end to most forms of government intervention in the economy. Yet, even with Iran supplying North Korean and Chinese arms to the Sudanese military, the costs of the war bled the country's hard currency reserves, particularly after Libya sought payment for oil deliveries. By July, Sudanese politicians were warning that economic reforms had triggered price chaos that quickly outpaced salary increases and led to an inflation rate of over 80 percent.

At the end of July, the government decided to abandon the most important parts of its free-market economic policies and return to a system of price controls and subsidies dropped under pressure from Western creditors.

Political Rights and Civil Liberties: Sudanese live under a repressive, military government that has curtailed virtually all meaningful political rights and civil liberties while implementing Islamic law. The ongoing war against the SPLA, as well as internecine fighting between rebel factions, have left 1.3 million dead in over a decade. Hundreds of thousands are displaced or refugees. Illegal detentions, kidnapping, torture, murder, rape, summary extrajudicial executions, kidnapping and disappearances were rampant, both by government forces and rebel groups.

In mid-year, Western governments accused the government of systematic massacres of the Nuba people, a central Sudan tribe, some of whom had joined the SPLA-Torit rebels. Government troops were also accused of transporting forced labor, mostly women, into Libya or northern Sudan where they are kept as virtual slaves. Children as young as ten have been conscripted into government militias to form "peace camps" in the Nuba mountains.

The judiciary is subservient to the junta. All judges are linked to the National Islamic Front and favor application of Shari'a, which includes such punishments as amputation and stoning. After the 1989 coup, the government banned all independent trade unions, opposition newspapers and political parties. Those suspected of opposing theocratic rule often disappear for months into a clandestine prison system where torture is routine. A four-and-a-half-year midnight-to-dawn curfew was lifted on 1 November.

While Islamic law is not yet official in the south, new penal codes are being drawn up and Islam and the Koran are mandatory subjects in schools dominated by Christians and animists. Since most Christians and animists are black Africans, widespread forced "Arabization" is also blatantly racist. The government has refused building permits for churches and closed those that it says are not properly licensed. Catholic radio programs were banned in April, and Church leaders are frequently detained for questioning by authorities. Printing of non-Muslim religious tracts is prohibited. Non-religious groups and associations are also banned.

The imposition of Shari'a has led to systematic legal discrimination against women and non-Muslims in the north. In war zones, women are forcibly kidnapped and made to serve as prostitutes. Rape is also widespread.

Internal travel is limited by civil war and some security suspects have been prevented from leaving the country. Workers cannot unionize, and a violation of the ban on strikes is punishable by death.

Suriname

Polity: Presidential parliamentary democracy
Economy: Capitalist-statist
Population: 416,000
PPP: $3,927
Life Expectancy: 69.5

Political Rights: 3
Civil Liberties: 3
Status: Partly Free

Ethnic Groups: East Indian (approximately 40 percent), Creole (approximately 30 percent), followed by Javanese, Bush Negroes, Amerindians, Chinese and various European minorities

Overview: After two years in office President Ronald Venetiaan was caught amid a severe economic recession, opposition party demands that he step down and hold new elections, and the Dutch government's suspension of financial subsidies until Suriname adopted a restructuring plan approved by the International Monetary Fund (IMF).

The Republic of Suriname achieved independence from the Netherlands in 1975 and functioned as a parliamentary democracy until a military coup in 1980. Col. Desi Bouterse emerged as the strongman of a regime that brutally suppressed all civic and political opposition. In 1985 Bouterse announced a "return to democracy" and appointed an assembly to draft a new constitution. The 1987 constitution provided for a system of parliamentary democracy, with a fifty-one-member National Assembly elected for a five-year term and empowered to select the nation's president. But it gave the military the right to intercede in political affairs.

The Front for Democracy and Development, a three-party coalition, won the 1987 elections, taking forty of fifty-one seats in the Assembly. The National Democratic Party (NDP), the army's political front, won three seats. The Assembly elected Ramsewak Shankar president.

The Shankar government was hamstrung by the military on most policy issues, including its efforts to negotiate a peace agreement with the Bush Negro-based Jungle Commando insurgency. The military deepened its involvement in cocaine trafficking and remained unaccountable for human rights violations. In December 1990 Shanker was ousted by the military in a bloodless coup and replaced by a government controlled by Bouterse.

Under international pressure, the puppet government held elections in May 1991 observed by the Organization of American States (OAS). The leader in the opinion polls was the New Front (NF), essentially the same coalition of Hindustani, Creole and Javanese parties that had been ousted in 1990. Also contending were the NDP, and the newly formed Democratic Alternative 91 (DA 91), an ethnically mixed coalition led by young professionals who campaigned against corruption and for limiting the power of the military.

The NF won 30 seats in the Assembly, the NDP 12, and DA 91 nine. The NF lacked the two-thirds majority needed to elect its presidential candidate, educator Ronald Venetiaan. An electoral college was convened, formed by members of the Assembly and representatives of district and municipal councils. Venetiaan won 80 percent of the 817 electoral college votes. After taking office in September 1991, President Venetiaan began a process of constitutional reform to bolster civilian rule. With an OAS team still posted in the country, Bouterse kept a low profile as the reform process gathered momentum.

In March 1992 the Assembly approved amendments restricting the role of the military to national defense and combating "organized subversion." The changes required a two-thirds majority vote in the Assembly. The amendments also barred soldiers from holding representative public office and abolished conscription and the People's Militia.

Bouterse accused the Venetiaan government of selling out to foreign powers and warned against reorganizing the military. But he backed off when the Dutch media reported that over the last decade he had amassed great wealth at the expense of the state, and in November 1992 he suddenly resigned as military commander. In February 1993 Bouterse returned to civilian life and formally became head of the NDP.

Venetiaan, with support from the Dutch, moved ahead with reorganizing the armed forces in spring 1993. He named Arthy Gorre, who had left the army in 1987 after a dispute with Bouterse, as new military chief. When ranking officers still loyal to Bouterse rejected Gorre's appointment, there was widespread fear of yet another coup. But the army grudgingly accepted Gorre after strong statements of support for Venetiaan by the Netherlands, Brazil, Venezuela, the U.S. and the OAS.

In summer 1993 the Dutch suddenly announced that it would no longer provide balance-of-payment subsidies to the debt-strapped government until it conformed to IMF restructuring guidelines. Venetiaan subsequently survived a no-confidence vote in the Assembly but the ruling coalition appeared to be weakening as the government was caught between the requirement to cut back spending and popular anger over declining living conditions.

The DA 91 boycotted the opening of the Assembly's fall session and in early

October called for a national strike to demand Venetiaan's resignation and new elections. The strike call was minimally effective. Bouterse and the NDP chimed in with similar demands and held a demonstration that attracted 5,000 people in the capital of Paramaribo, a big crowd in city of less than 70,000. The government rejected the demands and indicated that that an agreement with the IMF was in the offing.

Political Rights and Civil Liberties: Citizens are able to choose their government in relatively free elections. The constitution guarantees the right to organize political parties, civic organizations and labor unions. Aside from the government coalition, there are at least a half dozen other political parties. Labor unions are well-organized and legally permitted to strike, but other civic institutions remain weak.

The constitution guarantees the right of free expression. Radio is both public and private, with a number of small commercial radio stations competing with the government-owned radio and television broadcasting system. All broadcast in the various local languages and offer different points of view. There are a number of independent newspapers. Although intimidation by the military has lessened, some outlets still appear to practice a degree of self-censorship. In May 1993, during the dispute over the naming of a new military chief, the state-owned television station was seized and torched by unknown gunmen.

A peace accord was signed in August 1992 between the government and the two main rebel groups, the Jungle Commando and the indigenous-based, military-linked Tucuyana Amazonas. The guerrillas agreed to disarm under the supervision of the OAS but the government has been unable to comply with its committment to new economic and social programs in the country's interior. The accord paved the way for 10,000 refugees who fled to neighboring French Guiana during the 1980s to start returning to Suriname.

There are a number of well-organized human rights groups. With the return to civilian rule in 1991 and the lessening of rights violations, they have been seeking justice for violations committed under military rule. The primary obstacle is the 1992 accord that grants amnesty to former rebels and the military for rights violations committed during the conflict. The constitution provides for an independent judiciary but the judicial system is weak and ineffective, particularly against corruption in the government and the military and in addressing human rights cases.

Some rights cases have been brought before the Inter-American Court of Human Rights, whose authority has been recognized by the Venetiaan government. In December 1991 the government accepted responsibility for the murder of seven Bush Negroes by the military in 1987 and agreed to pay damages to the victims' families.

Swaziland

Polity: Traditional monarchy
Economy: Capitalist
Population: 814,000
PPP: $2,384
Life Expectancy: 56.8
Ethnic Groups: Swazi, European, Zulu

Political Rights: 6
Civil Liberties: 5
Status: *Not Free

Ratings Change: *Swaziland's status changed from Partly Free to Not Free because of a disappointing election and increased human rights abuses.

Overview:

In 1993, amid oppositoi calls for boycott, Swazi voters went to the polls to elect a limited authority legislature. Prior to the election, King Mswati III scrapped a controversial detention law, replacing it with a more clearly defined, though no less repressive, law.

Swaziland is a small, land-locked monarchy tucked into an eastern corner of South Africa. In 1968, it became an independent state with a Westminster-style parliament. The first King during the post-colonial period, Sobhuza II, abolished the multiparty system in 1973, claiming that it was incompatible with Swazi traditions.

In 1991 King Mswati III appointed a *Vusela* (greeting committee) to solicit the public's view of the electoral system and propose solutions for the viability of its reform. In October 1992, the Vusela II presented its report proposing a multi-candidate election system, but stopping short of recommending multipartyism. In April 1993, following another, Vusela III, report, the King appointed a Delimitation Commission to study the feasibility of establishing additional *tinkhundla* (tribal councils), in addition to the forty already operating. At the same time the king stated that Swaziland was not yet ready to institute a multiparty system.

Just prior to the 11 October 1993 election, Mswati scrapped the detention law in effect since 1973, which allowed the government to detain suspects, frequently government critics, for up to sixty days without trial. However, the king replaced the 1973 act with another law that provided for suspects in non-bailable offenses, such as murder, rape and sedition, to be detained indefinitely.

During the nominating process in September, the local chiefs chose 200 from among some 2,500 candidates to compete for the fifty-five House of Assembly seats. The opposition People's United Democratic Movement (Pudemo) called for a boycott of the vote protesting against the arbitrary selection of candidates and the unspecified powers of the future parliament. According to the Human Rights Association of Swaziland (Humeras), only 15 percent of eligible voters participated in the election, and most of those candidates who won were involved in the distribution of food during the previous year's drought.

Pudemo continued its struggle for existence within the Nkhaba district, ruled by the former prime minister, Prince Bhekimpi. In March the security forces prevented Pudemo members from the capital from marching to the Nkhaba district to protest Bhekimpi's orders for all Pudemo members to cease their activities and leave the district. Bhekimpi vowed to attack the march with an *impi* (regiment) of traditional warriors. Subsequently, Bhekimpi announced the establishment of an "espionage" squad to "sneak into the homes and eavesdrop on the people," and evict his opponents from the district.

Political Rights　　The Swazis do not have the right to change the government
and Civil Liberties:　democratically. The ultimate power to run the country's affairs
　　　　　　　　　　　is vested in the king. The parliament's role remains largely ceremonial, subject to pressures from the royalty and aristocracy. Political parties are legally still prohibited, although in recent years the democratic opposition has become much more vocal in calling for the abolition of the Tinkhundla system in favor of direct elections to parliament.

The judiciary, whose members are appointed by the king, encompasses a High Court, a Court of Appeal, and district courts. Nonetheless, the judiciary remains largely independent from executive interference, particularly in criminal and civil cases. Judges and magistrates are frequently foreign nationals who have been "seconded" to Swazi courts based on intergovernmental agreements. In addition to the three-tiered court system based on Western law, there are also seventeen courts based on customary law, which deal primarily with minor disputes.

Public criticism of the immediate royal family and of national security policy is generally forbidden. Starting in 1990, however, the opposition began to criticize the government policies more openly, including issues related to constitutional arrangements. The media, including the state owned press and television, have expanded their coverage of opposition activities. Only the state-owned radio remains staunchly pro-government.

Women are accorded a lower status than men both juridically and socially. In marriages conducted under traditional rules, polygamy is tolerated. Wives are treated as minors, and require the husband's permission to enter into legally valid contracts. In June, a tribal chief issued a ban on women wearing trousers, stating that it was "shameful" and disrespectful to tradition and the monarch.

Freedom of religion is respected. The right to travel freely within the country and abroad is limited for political opponents, women and non-ethnic Swazis. Workers have the right to freely organize. The long dominant Swaziland Federation of Trade Unions (SFTU) faced a rival since the establishment in March of the Swaziland Federation of Labor (SFL).

Sweden

Polity: Parliamentary
democracy
Economy: Mixed
capitalist
Population: 8,718,000
PPP: $17,014
Life Expectancy: 77.4
Ethnic Groups: Native (Swedish, Finnish, Lappic or Saami),
88 percent; immigrant groups, 12 percent

Political Rights: 1
Civil Liberties: 1
Status: Free

Overview: In 1993, Sweden endured the highest unemployment since the
Great Depression. The center-right government continued its
earlier policies of austerity and privatization, and planned to
join the European Union (EU), the former European Community (EC), later this
decade.

Sweden is a constitutional monarchy governed by a parliamentary democracy. The
head of state is King Carl Gustaf XVI. The head of government is Prime Minister Carl
Bildt, the Moderate Party leader, who heads the majority coalition in the unicameral,
349-member parliament (*Riksdag*). Voters elect 310 parliamentarians directly, and the
parties receiving at least four percent of the nationwide vote divide 39 seats. There is a
three-year term. The next elections are due in 1994.

In the parliamentary election in 1991, a four-party coalition defeated the Social
Democrats, who had governed Sweden for fifty-three of the previous fifty-nine years.
The Social Democrats took only 138 seats, while the ex-Communist Left Party won 16.
The conservative Moderate Party, the Liberals, the Center Party, and the Christian
Democrats captured a combined 170 of the 349 parliamentary seats. The coalition
depends on the right-wing populist New Democracy Party, which gained 25 seats after
less than a year of existence. New Democracy had campaigned for cheap alcohol, lower
immigration, and no foreign aid to Africa. This platform was too harsh for some of the
other center-right politicians, so the new party stands outside the coalition. In March
1993, New Democracy MP's voted against Bildt's budget, and threatened to bring
down the government. However, Bildt won a confidence vote when New Democracy
abstained.

Bildt's domestic program includes: deregulating and encouraging private business;
lifting restrictions on foreign ownership; allowing private child care facilities;
privatizing state holdings; reducing welfare programs; and making criminals serve
longer prison terms. Under welfare reform, employers have assumed responsibility for
the first two weeks' sick leave. This change and unemployment have apparently
disciplined workers and reduced absenteeism.

In the 1991 election, the Social Democrats campaigned for their traditional welfare
state and interventionist economic policies, but they have adopted more market-oriented
policies. As of 1991, about 57 percent of gross domestic product went to taxes, but the
socialists had implemented lower national income tax rates before the center-right
victory. The welfare state has become more difficult to finance, because only 48 percent

of the total population is working. Even the Social Democrats acknowledge that the labor force is too small to fund all their traditional programs.

A major reason for the Social Democrats' defeat was the economy. Rising inflation and unemployment undermined the party's image as a successful economic manager. Joblessness has climbed even more under the Bildt government. In 1993, unemployment more than doubled in a year, reaching over 13 percent, the highest figure in half a century. Government retraining schemes keep thousands of jobless people out of the labor market, making the official unemployment figure artificially low, around 8 percent.

In 1993, Bildt announced the privatization of 49 percent of a state forest company and of Pharmacia, the second largest pharmaceutical group.

Under the Social Democrats, Sweden applied to join the EC (now the EU) in 1991. This was a significant break from the country's previously cool attitude towards the EC, which neutral Sweden had identified with NATO. European bureaucrats in Brussels have slowed down Sweden's negotiations for EU membership. The country may join as late as 1996 following a referendum in 1995. As of 1993, polls showed a majority opposed to membership. Economic nationalism remains strong. For example, in December 1993, the managers and shareholders of Volvo rebelled against a planned merger with Renault, a rival French automobile manufacturer.

Sweden has joined the European Economic Area, a trading zone including the EU and non-EU member countries of the European Free Trade Association. Sweden will likely have a physical link to the rest of Europe during this decade. In 1994, workers may start constructing a bridge connecting Sweden and Denmark. However, environmentalists and anti-EU interests are trying to halt the project.

As part of the government's reassessment of policy, it has promised to modernize the armed forces. The Bildt government also released information that called Sweden's neutrality into question. According to the records, Sweden co-operated with NATO planners during the 1950s and widened its landing strips so that NATO fighters could have landed in the event of hostilities with the Soviet Union.

Political Rights and Civil Liberties:

Swedes have the right to change their government democratically. Parliamentary elections take place at least once every three years. Aliens resident for three years have the right to participate in local elections. The Lappic (Saami) ethnic minority has the right to its own parliament and significant powers over education and culture.

The judiciary is independent. The rights of the accused are generally respected. Sweden increased the rights of foreign suspects in 1991 by reforming the Terrorism Act. That law had allowed the state to confine alleged terrorists to their communities of residence. The government may still require that such suspects report periodically to the police. Swedes fear Russians will carry out cross-border crimes. In 1993, four Russians and a Polish-born Swede stood accused of plotting to kidnap millionaire Peter Wallenberg. In November 1993, parliament voted to appoint a new commission to investigate the assassination of the late Prime minister Olof Palme. Allegedly, earlier investigations missed key facts. An underground racist group, the Aryan Resistance Front, has carried out sporadic terrorist attacks in recent years.

With a few minor exceptions, freedom of expression is guaranteed, and the press is unrestricted. The government subsidizes daily newspapers regardless of their politics.

Publications or videotapes that contain excessive violence or national security information are subject to censorship. Following the success of private satellite television channels, a land-based commercial television station won a license in 1991. In April 1993, a right-wing Christian group staged a book-burning in the town of Rattvik. They torched the works of Stephen King and other modern authors.

Freedom of assembly and association are guaranteed and almost always respected in practice. Lutheranism is the state religion, and the church gets public funding. However, other religions are free to practice. In November 1993, police raided a Lutheran convent, arresting thirty immigrants who found religious sanctuary after the government had refused them asylum. There is no legal tradition of sanctuary.

Increasing economic problems have led to hostility between Swedes and the immigrant population. Large smuggling operations transport illegal arrivals to Sweden. Since 1991, there have been several episodes of Swedes shooting immigrants. The King has denounced the attacks as "frightening and unworthy of a democracy." Nazi groups clashed with anti-racist demonstrators on 30 November 1992, the anniversary of the death of King Karl XII, the eighteenth-century warrior whom the extreme right-wingers have adopted as a nationalist symbol. To forestall more violence on 30 November 1993, the authorities banned the demonstrations. They feared bombings. On 1 December, Stockholm police arrested 500 Swedish and Danish demonstrators to prevent rival neo-Nazi and leftist, anti-racist rallies from getting out of control. The previous evening, rival groups had thrown rocks and smashed windows

Emigration and domestic and foreign travel are unrestricted. Workers have the right to form and join trade unions and to strike. The trade union federations are strong and well-organized. The separate blue- and white-collar federations represent a combined 86 percent of employees, up from 82 percent in 1987. Despite its historical links with the Social Democrats, the labor movement has become more independent of the party. In the 1990's, the once dominant joint labor-management guidelines for negotiations have broken down. Consequently, electrical workers staged a major strike in 1993.

Switzerland

Polity: Federal parliamentary democracy
Economy: Capitalist
Population: 6,955,000
PPP: $20,874
Life Expectancy: 77.4
Ethnic Groups: German, French, Italian, Romansch

Political Rights: 1
Civil Liberties: 1
Status: Free

Overview: In 1993, Switzerland endured its worst economic crisis since World War II. As a result of the recession, unemployment has risen from less than 1 percent in 1990 to 5 percent in 1993. With fewer people working and paying taxes, the government has had higher social spending and lower revenues. In addition to these problems, the government had to define new European policies.

This landlocked, mountainous country began as a small confederation in the Middle Ages. Internationally recognized as a neutral country since 1815, Switzerland is made up of twenty-three territories called cantons. There are twenty full cantons and six half-cantons. Each canton has its own political system, customs, and dominant ethnic group. Swiss Germans predominate, but French, Romansch and Italian groups are concentrated in some areas. Switzerland is the home base of numerous institutions that have attracted people from all over the world.

The Federal Assembly (parliament) is bicameral. The voters elect the 200-member lower house, the National Council, to four-year terms by proportional representation. The various parties have the following numbers of seats: Christian Democrats, 37; the conservative Radicals, 44; the conservative People's Party, 25; Social Democrats, 41; Greens, 14; the anti-immigrant Auto Party, 8; the liberal Independents' Alliance, 6; the conservative Liberals, 10; the anti-immigrant Swiss Democrats, 5; the Evangelical People's Party, 3; the historically Communist Swiss Party of Labor, 3; the Swiss-Italian Ticino League, 2; and independents, 2. Using various local methods, the cantons elect two members each to the 46 member Council of States, the upper house. The executive branch is called the Federal Council, whose members function as a cabinet.

Since 1959, the governing coalition has consisted of the Social Democrats, Christian Democrats, Radicals, and the People's Party. Drawn from the Federal Assembly, one of the seven cabinet executives serves as president each year. According to a "magic formula," the small cabinet's composition must reflect the country's parties, regions, and language groups, leaving little room for any sector to dominate. The parliament sits for only four three-week sessions per year. The Federal Council's ministers carry out many trivial legislative and regulatory tasks.

After Swiss voters rejected joining the free-trade European Economic Area (EEA) in a referendum in December 1992, the government was in shock. Both domestic and international economic actors had assumed that the Swiss would join the EEA and then the European Community (now the European Union). Pro-European minister Rene Felber was disappointed with the voters, and resigned in early 1993.

Felber's resignation touched off a highly charged race to replace him. The "magic formula" dictated that a Social Democrats from a French-speaking area would have to replace him. The Social Democrats nominated Christine Brunner, a leftist pacifist with a controversial private life. Conservative opponents complained about her status as a thrice-married woman who had allegedly had an abortion. Anonymous sources claimed that she had posed nude as well. The overwhelmingly male parliamentarians rejected her nomination, thereby sparking a week of feminist demonstrations that included paint bombs. The next Social Democratic nominee, Francis Matthey, withdrew, because he felt he would lose because he was male. Finally, the Social Democrats nominated Ruth Dreifuss, who won.

The governing coalition pursued several changes in policy including liberalizing trade and immigration. Switzerland also established a battalion for use in U.N. peace-keeping. In March, in order to counter the country's image as an arms bazaar, parliament authorized the government to draft gun control legislation. In numerous referenda during 1993, Swiss voters legalized casino gambling, approved higher taxes, rejected banning the purchase of U.S. warplanes, and turned down a prohibition of alcohol and tobacco advertisements.

Political Rights The Swiss can change their government democratically.
and Civil Liberties: However, the Swiss system produces coalition governments,
which mitigate the chances for radical changes in policy. The
voters have substantial powers of initiative and referendum, which allow them to
change policies directly. Voters can trigger a plebiscite with 100,000 signatures.

The political parties have the right to organize freely, and they cover the entire
political spectrum. The cantonal system allows considerable local autonomy, which
helps to preserve the linguistic and cultural heritage of the localities. However, the
Italian and Romansch communities believe that their linguistic and cultural resources
are underfunded. In 1993, Appenzell Ausserrhoden voted to keep the traditional
outdoor show of hands for electing local leaders instead of adopting secret ballots. In
February 1993 police foiled a terrorist plot by Jura cantonal separatists who had
allegedly planned attacks on military facilities and on a statue of William Tell, the
nationalist hero.

The government's postal ministry operates radio and television, which are linguistically and politically pluralistic. In November 1993, the Lausanne district court fined the
telephone company's chief executive for allowing telephone lines with erotic recordings
that were available to young people. The court ruled that the erotic messages violated
the obscenity laws. Switzerland has freedoms of discussion, assembly, demonstration,
and religion. However, the country has a history of prosecuting conscientious objectors
who disagree with universal military service for males. Every able-bodied male must
serve for three weeks in the military every two years until age fifty.

Feminists complain that the exclusion of women from the army or even the
existence of the army itself creates opportunities for male networking that put women at
an economic disadvantage. Women's rights improved gradually in the 1980s. In 1993,
the community of Waedenswil in the Zurich canton decided that official documents
should use only the feminine form of German nouns. Swiss women may not work night
shifts in factories and women wishing to work outside the home during daytime face
another hurdle. Many elementary schools have two split morning and afternoon
sessions. This means that some school-age children are at home regardless of the hour
and that mothers must be there with them.

Kurdish nationalists carried out several acts of anti-Turkish violence and clashed
with policemen in Switzerland in 1993. In June, six Kurdish demonstrators and one
policeman were wounded in Bern; one demonstrator died. On 4 November, Kurds
threw stones and firebombs at Turkish targets in several locations.

Syria

Polity: Dominant party (military-dominated)
Economy: Mixed statist
Population: 13,463,000
PPP: $4,756
Life Expectancy: 66.1
Ethnic Groups: Arab (90 percent), Kurdish, Armenian and others (10 percent)

Political Rights: 7
Civil Liberties: 7
Status: Not Free

Overview:

The September mutual recognition accords between Israel and the Palestine Liberation Organization caught Syrian President Hafez al-Assad by surprise, usurping his role as a regional broker and frustrating his efforts to secure a return from Israel of the strategic Golan Heights. Domestically, Assad, backed by the military, continued to face few threats to his tight control over the country.

The French declared Syria a republic in September 1941, and granted full independence in January 1944. The country merged with Egypt to form the United Arab Republic in February 1958 but withdrew in September 1961. A March 1963 military coup brought the pan-Arab, socialist Baath party to power. Leadership struggles within the Baath party continued until November 1970 when the military wing, led by then-Lieut.-Gen. Hafez al-Assad, took power in a bloodless coup. Assad, from the minority Alawite Islamic sect, formally became president of this authoritarian, secular regime in February 1971.

In the late 1970s the fundamentalist Muslim Brotherhood group, drawn from the Sunni Muslim majority, began a series of anti-government attacks in Homs, Aleppo, Hama and other northern and central towns. In February 1982 soldiers crushed an armed fundamentalist rebellion in Hama, killing approximately 15,000-20,000 militants and civilians. Since then, the government has faced few overt threats from the fundamentalists.

Assad serves as head of government, commander-in-chief of the armed forces and secretary general of the Baath Party. The former fighter pilot has shrewdly given some key government positions to members of the Sunni majority and played up his devotion to Islam. Meanwhile, members of his Alawite minority hold most key military and intelligence positions, and the army and up to a dozen intelligence units keep a close watch on the population. A 250-seat People's Assembly is elected for four-year terms and nominally approves legislation and the budget, but in fact holds little actual power. At the May 1990 elections the ruling National Progressive Front took 166 seats (Baath Party, 134 seats; smaller parties, 32), the remainder going to independents. In December 1991 Assad, running unopposed after being nominated by the Assembly, won a fourth seven-year term with a reported 99.982 percent of the popular vote. Government officials closely watched the voters, who had a "yes" or "no" choice.

The key issue facing the country in 1993 was the impact of the September accords between Israel and the Palestine Liberation Organization (PLO), which provided for mutual recognition and a framework for Palestinian autonomy in the West Bank and

Gaza Strip. Publicly, Assad neither condemned nor approved the accord, although he objected to the secret negotiations that brought it about. Privately the president is concerned that Israel, having solved its most pressing concern through the PLO peace deal, will be less likely to make concessions to Syria.

Syria has fought Israel three times since 1948, losing the strategic 483-square-mile Golan Heights in the 1967 Six Day War. Prior to 1967, Syria had shelled northern Israeli towns from the Golan. Israel annexed the Golan in December 1981, and refuses to discuss publicly terms for a possible withdrawal until Syria discusses terms for peace, including diplomatic exchanges. Syria, meanwhile, refuses to discuss these terms until Israel recognizes Syrian sovereignty over the territory. Despite the considerable differences between the Syrian and Israeli public negotiating positions, observers do not rule out the possibility that secret negotiations are in fact underway.

Syria also maintains 40,000 troops in Lebanon under a 1989 accord ending that country's civil war.

In recent years the government has been shedding socialism in favor of a market economy. In late 1991 the government introduced Investment Law Number Ten, allowing entrepreneurs to import equipment duty free and receive tax concessions. Since then, the authorities have approved more than 750 private sector projects.

Political Rights and Civil Liberties:

Syrians cannot change their government democratically. President Hafez al-Assad maintains absolute authority, and all key decsions are made by him and his advisors. There is no outright ban on opposition groups, but in practice none is permitted. The parliament is elected every four years, but has no independent authority. Political opposition is forcibly suppressed. Emergency laws in effect since 1963 allow the government to suspend due process safeguards during searches, arrests, interrogations and trials in security cases. Security forces and police torture political and criminal detainees.

The government freed 2,864 political prisoners in late 1991, and 1,154 more in 1992. In 1993 the government freed at least nine political prisoners who had been imprisoned since the 1970 coup. Another, Salah Jadid, Syria's de facto ruler at the time of the 1970 coup, died of a heart attack in August. The Paris-based Committee for Defense of Democratic Liberties and Human Rights in Syria estimates that eleven others jailed since 1970 are still held at the Al-Mezze prison in Damascus. In late February the U.S. National Academy of Sciences reported that in the past decade some 287 scientists engineers and health professionals have been imprisoned, most without charge, for criticizing the government and calling for political liberalization. According to the U.S. State Department, credible estimates of the total number of political prisoners and detainees, including those held in Syrian detention facilities in Lebanon, run from 3,800 to 10,000.

The judiciary is subservient to the government. Defendents in civil and criminal cases receive fair due process rights, although there is no trial by jury. Security and political offenses are handled in military-controlled State Security Courts that lack due process procedures. Citizens may not criticize the president, the government or the Baath Party. The government and Baath party own and operate all media, and news coverage reflects state views. All associations must be non-political and must register with the government.

Although there is no officially preferred religion, members of Assad's Alawite minority sect, which is considered heretical by most Sunni Muslims, hold many key security and government positions. The state forbids Jehovah's Witnesses and Seventh-Day Adventists from practicing or owning church property, and some members have been arrested. The security apparatus closely monitors the Jewish community, and Jews are generally barred from government jobs. In April 1992 Syria lifted restrictions on Jewish emmigration abroad, and in the ensuing months some 2,300 of the 4,000-strong community left the country. However, in 1993 the government reportedly made it more difficult for the remaining Jews to obtain exit visas, often reverting to the past practice of granting visas to individuals rather than entire families.

Individuals who have not completed required military service cannot travel abroad. The government uses the umbrella General Federation of Trade Unions to dominate nearly all aspects of union activity. Strikes are strongly discouraged and rarely occur.

Taiwan (Rep. of China)

Polity: Dominant party (transitional)
Economy: Capitalist-statist
Population: 20,830,000
PPP: na
Life Expectancy: 74.5
Ethnic Groups: Chinese (native majority, mainland minority, 98 percent), Aboriginal (2 percent)

Political Rights: 4*
Civil Liberties: 4*
Status: Partly Free

Ratings Change: *Taiwan's political rights rating changed from 3 to 4 and its civil liberties from 3 to 4 as a result of modifications in methodology. See "Survey Methodology," page 671.

Overview: **P**resident Lee Teng-hui's ruling Koumintang (KMT) party had a mixed showing at the critical November 1993 local elections, which observers had called a bellwether for the party's chances of extending its forty-four-year rule at the 1995 legislative elections. Although the KMT won fifteen of twenty-three mayoral and magistrate races, its share of the popular vote dropped below 50 percent for the first time in any elections, indicating voters' distaste with the party's factionalism and corruption.

The island, located 100 miles off the Chinese coast, came under control of China's Nationalist government after World War II. Following the Communist victory on the mainland in 1949, the Nationalist leadership established a government-in-exile on Taiwan under Chiang Kai-shek. For most of the next four decades, the KMT ruled in an authoritarian manner while providing one of the highest standards of living in the region. Both the government and China officially consider Taiwan to be a province of China, and both claim to be the legitimate government of all of China. Today native Taiwanese make up 85 percent of the population, while mainlanders or their descendents comprise the minority.

The 1947 constitution is a holdover from the KMT's rule on the mainland. It provides for a National Assembly, which elects and can recall the president and vice-president, and can amend the constitution. The president serves a six-year term (four years after 1996) and appoints numerous top officials. The government has five specialized *yuan* (branches), each with its own head. The Executive Yuan runs most of the ministries; the legislative Yuan enacts laws; the Judicial Yuan, consisting of fifteen grand justices appointed by the president, interprets the constitution; the Examination Yuan holds civil service tests; and the Control Yuan serves as an administrative and fiscal check on the other branches.

The country's democratic transition began with the lifting of martial law in 1987. In January 1988 Lee Teng-hui became the first native-born Taiwanese president following the death of Chiang Ching-kuo, the son of Chiang Kai-shek. In January 1989 the government formally legalized opposition parties. Lee was elected for a full term in March 1990.

In December 1991 the Taiwanese elected a new National Assembly. At the time the Assembly consisted mostly of aging mainlanders elected in 1947 or 1969 whose terms had been frozen to maintain the KMT's political monopoly and legitimize the country's claim to the mainland. Direct elections were held for 325 of its 403 seats (the remainder were held over from the limited elections in 1986), with 225 seats representing constituencies and the other 100 allotted through proportional representation. The KMT, running on a theme of stability and prosperity, won 254 seats. The Democratic Progressive Party, which openly violated the Sedition Law by calling for the country to declare independence from the mainland, took 66 seats; independent candidates took 5 seats. By late December eighty-one aging mainlanders had also stepped down from the Legislative Yuan.

In March 1992 Lee called on the National Assembly to amend the constitution to provide for direct presidential elections. KMT mainlanders fear direct elections will lead to another native Taiwanese president and further erode their political influence. In May the party's mainland faction forced the National Assembly to shelve the issue until an extraordinary session to be called by May 1995. On 19 December the country held its first full Legislative Yuan elections since the Nationalists fled to the mainland. The KMT received just 53 percent of the vote and took 96 of the 161 seats; the DPP took 50 seats; the tiny Chinese Social Democratic Party, 1; independents the remainder.

Immediately following the election the KMT's "mainstream," liberal faction blamed the party's relatively poor showing on seventy-three-year-old mainland-born premier Hau Pei-Tsun. Hau resigned on 30 January 1993, and on 23 February parliament swore in fifty-six-year-old Lien Chan as the first native Taiwanese prime minister, continuing Lee's drive to rout aging mainlanders from top posts.

In June the government suffered its first major legislative defeat, as renegade KMT reformers joined with the opposition to pass one of the strictest financial disclosure rules for public officials in Asia. The Sunshine Law will require some 23,000 elected and appointed officials, including the president and all National Assembly and legislature MPs, to list ten categories of wealth annually.

On 10 August the KMT formally split for the first time as six second-generation mainlander MPs defected to form the New Party. Led by Jaw Shau-kong, the leading vote-getter at the December 1992 legislative elections, the six accused the KMT of widespread corruption. Many of these second-generation mainlanders also feel that Lee is not fully committed to eventual reunification with China.

At the KMT's fourteenth National Party Congress from 16-22 August, the party shed some of its Leninist-modeled authoritarianism. At the first-ever vote for party chairman, Lee easily won re-election with 82.5 percent of the vote. Lee's nominees also won 151 of the 210 Central Committee seats. For the first time, elections were held for sixteen of the powerful Central Standing Committee's thirty-one seats. The new Committee contained eighteen native Taiwanese, two more than before. The party formally dropped the goal of forcibly "recovering the Chinese mainland" and shed its status as a "revolutionary party."

Heading into the 27 November local elections the DPP predicted it would win eleven of the twenty-three mayoral or magistrate races after capturing just six in 1989. In the event the KMT surprised most analysts by taking fifteen posts to only six for the DPP, with two going to independents. However, the KMT won only 47.5 percent of the popular vote, the first time it had received less than 50 percent in any election, while the DPP increased its share from 38 percent to 41.2 percent.

A key obstacle to the DPP's taking power at the national level is its pro-independence platform. Although opinion polls now show 20 percent of Taiwanese in favor of declaring independence, double the figure in past years, China has repeatedly insisted it will invade if Taiwan actually does so. This threat undoubtably keeps wary voters in the KMT camp. In late April representatives from Taiwan and China held their first ever high-level talks in Singapore. The two sides signed agreements setting up formal channels for communication and calling for closer cooperation in fighting smuggling and other similiar matters, but avoided political issues.

In 1993 the government slimmed down an ambitious $310 billion infrastructure program introduced in 1991, citing slower than expected economic growth. The new $245 billion program will be stretched over twelve years, double the original timeframe.

Political Rights and Civil Liberties:

Taiwanese have been granted increasingly greater power to change their government. However the ruling Koumintang (KMT) maintains significant advantages over the opposition through its control of the media and the government apparatus. Some 90 percent of the civil servants are KMT members. The party's assets are estimated at $10-20 billion, and close links are maintained with big business and the underworld. The December 1992 legislative elections were marred by charges of KMT vote-buying. In November 1993 a court sentenced senior KMT official Hsieh Mei-huey to fifteen months in jail for vote-buying, the fourth conviction since the election.

In 1992 the government eliminated several civil liberties restrictions. In April the Assembly amended the Sedition Law to cover only direct advocacy of violence, making it legal to advocate formal independence from China. In June the government abolished the "second personnel departments," commonly refered to as "thought police," that had been stationed in government offices to monitor civil servants.

Defendents generally receive fair trials, although the judiciary is not considered fully independent in sensitive cases. Police abuse of suspects in custody is a continuing problem.

The Publications Law allows police to censor or ban publications. Although such censorship is infrequent, journalists reportedly practice self-censorship on sensitive issues. The government maintains controlling shares in the country's three main television stations. Most radio stations are owned by the government or by the KMT-controlled

Broadcasting Corporation of China, and the government has not approved new applications since 1969. Political coverage on broadcast media is frequently biased against the opposition. In late March popular television anchor Lee Yen-chiu confessed at an awards ceremony that she felt like a "puppet" reading the news given the government's control over its content. During the 1992 legislative election campaign the authorities apportioned advertising time on the basis of the number of candidates nominated by each party, giving the KMT a large advantage. The Central Election Commission had to approve all broadcasts, and cut twenty-two seconds out of one DPP commercial. The DPP is raising money from small businesses to set up a new National United Television station.

The Parade and Assembly Law makes organizers of mass events responsible for the conduct of participants. Opposition leaders have been charged with harming public order stemming from misconduct at demonstrations they organized. The country's tiny aboriginal minority suffers from social and economic alienation, but are ensured representation in parliament through reserved seats. Citizens can travel freely within the country and abroad. The list of dissidents excluded from re-entering the country has been sharply reduced.

The government must approve of all unions, and can dissolve a union for disturbing the public order. None has been dissolved, although authorities have refused to certify competing unions, asking them to file as a single union. Civil servants, defense industry workers and teachers cannot unionize. Only one labor federation is permitted, the pro-KMT Chinese Federation of Labor. Strikes must be approved by a majority of the full membership of a union, and the government must approve these vote meetings. In practice this latter power has been used to prevent strikes.

Tajikistan

Polity: Communist-
dominated
Economy: Statist
Population: 5,358,000
PPP: $2,558
Life Expectancy: 70.0
Ethnic Groups: Tajiks (62 percent), Uzbeks (24 percent),
Russians and Ukrainians (10 percent), Armenians, Gypsies, others
Ratings Change: *Tajikistan's political rights rating changed from
6 to 7 and its civil liberties rating from 6 to 7 because of war,
government repression and a return of the Communist system.

Political Rights: 7*
Civil Liberties: 7*
Status: Not Free

Overview: Political violence, regional and clan-based warfare and repression marked this Central Asian country's second year of independence. In December 1992, following a civil war that left some 20,000 dead, a loose coalition of Islamic activists, secular democrats and nationalists had been overthrown by former Communist hard-liners.

Tajikistan, one of the poorest former Soviet republics, was carved out of the Uzbek Soviet Republic on Stalin's orders in 1929. The boundaries of the republic angered Tajiks, who trace their origins to Persia, by leaving Samarkand and Bukhara, the two main centers of Tajik culture, inside Uzbekistan.

In 1990 the newly formed national movement, Rastokhez (Rebirth), sparked a wave of protests demanding redress for long-neglected social and economic problems. But only Communist party candidates were allowed to run in elections to the 250-member unicameral Supreme Soviet (parliament). In 1991, the Democratic Party and the moderate Islamic Renaissance Party (IRP) were formally registered. In November presidential elections, amid opposition charges of electoral fraud, old-line Communist Rakhman Nabiev was elected president. The opposition formed the Movement for Democratic Reforms, an umbrella organization.

In early 1992, Lali Badakhshan, a movement advocating autonomy for the eastern Gorno-Badakhshan region, joined the coalition. In April, following the dismissal of several anti-Communist officials, the opposition stepped up its protests in Dushanbe, the capital, and threatened to call a "national congress" to create an alternative power center.

Following weeks of machinations and violence, the Communists and the opposition reached an agreement on 11 May specifying the formation of a coalition government. Nabiev was to remain president until December presidential elections. An eighty-member transitional Assembly (*Majilis*) was established to serve until elections for a multiparty People's Assembly.

In August, parliament stripped Nabiev of the power of direct presidential rule. Political murders and assassinations increased, and in early September Nabiev attempted to flee to Khodzhent. His column was intercepted and he was forced to resign virtually at gunpoint. Parliamentary chairman Akbarsho Iskandarov was named acting president.

With Russian troops in Dushanbe, the government was in the hands of the IRP, though acting president Iskandarov said Tajikistan would not become an Islamic state. Forces loyal to Nabiev refused to recognize the new government, staging an unsuccessful coup in the capital on 24 October. In November, Iskandarov urgently asked Russian troops to directly intervene in the conflict by enforcing curfews and disarming groups. But a week later, bowing to pressure form Nabiev's supporters, the coalition government resigned, leaving Iskandarov as head of an intermittent State Council. On 10 December, pro-Communist forces took control of the capital. Coalition forces fled to the south, with tens of thousands crossing the border into Afghanistan. The post of president was scrapped, and head of state Supreme Soviet Chairman Emomali Rakhmonov, issued an ultimatum to opponents to hand over their weapons or face annihilation.

Nineteen-ninety-three opened with Rakhmonov keeping his word. In January, Tajik refugees reaching Moscow and Afghanistan described relentless persecution of political opponents by pro-Communist government forces. Those targeted included not only political activists, but also people from regions and clans that supported the ousted Islamic-democratic coalition. Also marked for persecution were democratically oriented journalists and free-market businessmen. Western journalists visiting the Tajik-Afghan border reported witnessing the executions of men who were suspected of having been in Afghanistan.

Pro-Communist forces unleashed an anti-rebel offensive around Dushanbe and, according to witnesses, conducted "cleansing" operations in the capital. They also focused on the area around Garm and on Gorno-Badakhshan in the Pamir mountains, an anti-Communist, Islamic stronghold, where members of the ousted government, including former President Iskandarov, had taken refuge. In Garm, pro-Communist forces killed civilians amid charges of "ethnic cleansing." Meanwhile, Tajik Prime Minister Abdul Amalik Abdulojanov said in Moscow that Afghan fundamentalist *mujahideen* were providing military training to Tajik refugees. The CIS pledged to send troops to patrol the 1,200-mile border with Afghanistan. By year's end there were over 20,000 Russian and Uzbek forces along the Afghan frontier. The presence of Uzbeks, who make up one-quarter of Tajikistan's population, further fueled historic ethnic hostilities. On 30 January, the government imposed emergency rule along the Afghan border to control the flow of refugees and weapons.

Visiting Tajikistan on 4 February, Russia's Defense Minister Gen. Pavel S. Grachev agreed to help build a new Tajik army from the Popular Front forces of ex-convict Sangak Safarov, an Uzbekistan-backed militia leader from Kulyab who had told parliament: "we will cleanse Tajikistan and Russia of democratic scum." In Dushanbe, the Russian Army's 201st Motorized Rifle Division openly aided Safarov and the Communist government.

In March, some 8,000 people faced starvation after the government moved them out of Dushanbe, where they had sought refuge from the civil war, and stranded them on the Afghan border with little food or water. The same month, militia leader Safarov and an fellow commander, Faizali Saidov, reportedly killed each other during a quarrel in Kurgan-Tyube, prompting authorities to impose a state of emergency in the province. The government also opened negotiations with a delegation from Gorno-Badakhshan about disarming anti-government forces, and pro-government troops captured a key rebel post fifty miles outside the capital.

In April, with Tajik guerrillas continuing to infiltrate the country from Afghanistan, Russia pledged to send more troops to patrol the border to join forces from Kazakhstan, Kyrgyzstan and Uzbekistan.

By summer, fighting intensified along the Afghan border. Parliamentary by-elections were held in nineteen districts on 13 June to replace legislators who were killed or fled the country. No opposition groups were allowed to take part, and in most districts only one Communist party candidate's name appeared on the ballot. Prime Minister Abdulojanov was reelected. The new parliament met on 23 June. Four principal opposition parties were officially banned: the Democratic Party, IRP, Rastokhez and Lali Badakhshan. Officials from Gorno-Badakhshan said the region was no longer seeking independence, and offered to help patrol the Afghan border; the move was seen as an attempt to get desperately needed aid that would permit some of the 70,000 refugees from other parts of Tajikistan to return home.

On 26 June, the Supreme Soviet adopted several measures aimed at strengthening pro-Communist forces. All decrees of coalition President Iskandarov were ruled illegal, and charges of "guiding the terrorism and civil war in Tajikistan" were brought against Qazi Ali Akhbar Turadzhonzoda (formerly Tajikistan's religious leader) and Takhir Abdujobar (leader of Rastokhez), both in exile. Parliament also ratified a friendship treaty with Russia and a CIS collective security arrangement.

As fighting increased along the Afghan border, so did reports of atrocities by pro-Communist forces. Scores of Tajik and Afghan guerrillas were reported killed, as well as dozens of civilians. Some twenty-eight Russian soldiers and six Tajik government troops were killed in a border raid that left over 100 civilians dead. On 19 July, Russian warplanes bombed a strategic rebel stronghold east of Dushanbe in an attempt to open a key road. Meanwhile, Russia increased troop strength and informed the United Nations it would help Tajikistan defend against raids from Afghan territory. Clashes continued throughout the month, with Russian forces shelling targets inside Afghanistan. Russian and Western human rights organizations that visited the war-zones said that fighting was being waged with a viciousness that only rival clans can manage.

In September, both Russian and the U.N. urged Dushanbe to seek a political solution by opening a dialogue with the disparate opposition groups. A logistical problem was that the leaders of the opposition's Islamic, nationalist and democratic groups were scattered among Afghanistan, Iran, Saudi Arabia and Russia, as well as Tajikistan's rugged Pamir mountains. Moreover, opposition leaders distrusted the government's motives, particularly after the CIS agreed on 25 August to set up a coalition force to control the insurgency. On 27 December parliament named Abdujalil Samadov the new prime minister, replacing Abdulojanov who was made ambassador to Moscow.

Political Rights and Civil Liberties:

War, government repression and a return of the old Communist system have robbed citizens of the means to change their government democratically. Tajikistan is a one-party state and the regime is at least partly propped up by over 20,000 Russian and CIS troops.

All opposition political parties are banned. Parliamentary by-elections had only one candidate or party on the ballot. Pervasive security forces and a Soviet-era judiciary subservient to the regime effectively curtail freedom of expression, association and assembly.

Independent human rights groups documented severe human rights abuses, particularly in the first few months of the year when the government sought to consolidate its authority. Opposition leaders or activists not in exile or hiding were arrested. On 5 February several members of the anti-government opposition were arrested, among them former dissident Mirbobo Mirrakhimov, who headed the country's State Radio and Television under the coalition government. Several of his subordinates were arrested, along with Dushanbe's deputy chief of police and two IRP leaders. In March, Bozor Sobir, a Tajik poet, was jailed. On 25 August, the Supreme Court sentenced Ajik Aliev, an IRP leader, to death for organizing terrorist acts. Co-defendants Mahmadier Nazimov and Rajab Atovulloyev, were sentenced to three years in a high-security labor prison on charges of sedition.

Other abuses included widespread killings, torture, extrajudicial execution, and kidnapping by Tajik militias, particularly the pro-government Popular Front. Bodies found on the streets of Dushanbe showed signs of torture. Government forces also singled out people from certain regions such as Gorno-Badakhstan, which had sought autonomy, and Garm Internal Affairs Ministry forces reportedly executed scores of men and women based on their ethnicity or region.

The exact number of political prisoners is not known. The Red Cross has been banned from visiting those held on political charges. Under Tajik law, a person may be detained for eighteen months without trial.

The independent newspapers that flourished after independence are gone, their editors and reporters now dead, jailed or exiled. In March, Dushanbe's state prosecutor threatened to prosecute any journalists who published "destabilizing" material.

Islam was revived after many decades of atheist indoctrination, although both secular and most religious leaders oppose an Islamic state. The regime has intruded into religious life to preclude not only fundamentalism but anti-government activity. Ethnic Russians and other minorities continued to leave in droves.

The war and the presence of foreign troops have severely curtailed freedom of movement. The rights of women continue to be circumscribed in practice. There are no independent trade unions.

Tanzania

Polity: Dominant party (transitional)
Economy: Statist
Population: 27,811,000
PPP: $572
Life Expectancy: 54.0

Political Rights: 6
Civil Liberties: 5
Status: *Not Free

Ethnic Groups: African, Asian and Arab minorities
Ratings Change: *Tanzania's status changed from Partly Free to Not Free because of communal tensions and restrictions on the oppostion.

Overview:

Despite a 1992 amendment to the Constitution that legalized independent political parties, the United Republic of Tanzania is still a one-party state. The Revolutionary Party of Tanzania, or Chama Cha Mapinduzi (CCM), has dominated political power in Tanzania since independence and continues to deny principal opposition leaders and parties the ability to organize and operate in Tanzania. The reluctance of CCM to fully embrace multipartyism has raised doubts about the governments commitment to democratic reforms and may signal trouble ahead for multi party elections scheduled for 1995.

The East African Republic of Tanzania was formed in 1964 when mainland Tanganyika merged with the islands of Zanzibar and Pemba. The still politically influential Julius Nyerere served as Tanzania's president and CCM party chairperson from post-independence until his retirement in 1985. President Ali Hassan Mwinyi succeeded Nyerere as both president and party chairperson. In the October 1990 presidential elections, Mwinyi ran uncontested and was returned to office for a second five-year term.

In March 1991, after much national and intra-party discussion, Mwinyi commissioned a study to examine public opinion on political pluralism. At the end of the year long study, the commission recommended that opposition parties be allowed to register. On 20 January 1992, the CCM executive committee officially endorsed the commission's recommendations, but rejected the proposal for a switch to federalism to allow for greater autonomy for Tanganyika and the islands. Former President Nyerere, with other committee members, successfully campaigned for the one-party system to continue until Parliament's term ends in 1995. While a number of opposition groups had already formed by the end of 1991, the government did not allow opposition parties to petition for legal status until 17 June 1992.

Despite its merger with Tanzania in 1964, the Island of Zanzibar exercises a considerable degree of autonomy and has maintained a strong separate identity. While many of the twenty-five million mainland Tanzanians are Christian, Zanzibar's population of 750,000 is 90 percent Muslim. Within Zanzibar there is a drive for increasing autonomy and a move towards possible secession. In August the Tanzanian parliament accepted a proposal to create a federal system of two parallel governments-one for Tanganyika and the other for Zanzibar. While both governments would remain under the umbrella of the Tanzanian regime, many see this move as the precursor to a breakup of the union.

With Zanzibar's economy in decay, the national government has looked increasingly to the Arab world for financial assistance and investment, a move that has disturbed many in mainland Tanzania. To fuel concerns, in early 1993 Zanzibar became the fiftieth member of the Islamic Organization Conference (IOC), a move specifically prohibited by Tanzania's Constitution. It was further revealed that the application to the IOC was made with the knowledge and approval of President Mwinyi (who is Muslim). While the application was later withdrawn, the move, along with subsequent revelations of government knowledge led some in the press to speculate not only on the future of the union, but also to raise concerns regarding possible conflict between Tanzania's Christian s and Muslims.

Political Rights and Civil Liberties:

Tanzanians cannot change their government democratically. Despite its constitutional commitment to multipartyism, the government continues to repress opposition party activity. Former Foreign Minister Oscar Kambona returned to Tanzania in September 1992 after twenty-five years of political exile. During 1992, Kambona founded the Tanzanian Democratic Alliance Party (TDAP). Since his return, however, Kambona and the TDAP have been subject to a government campaign of repression and intimidation. Despite his former standing, the government has refused to recognize Kambona as a Tanzanian citizen, denied him a passport, and has made it impossible for him to travel outside of Tanzania. Kambona has been subject to security force harassment, round the clock surveillance, and several death threats. The government has banned state-owned media from reporting on Kambona or his party's activities, and journalists who have defied this order have been subject to dismissal.

Also in 1992, the government carried out a campaign of harassment and intimidation against members of the unregistered Democratic Party. Party leader and human rights activist, Christopher Mtikila, was arrested in February for allegedly distributing a false statement and again in August when he was found guilty of illegally conducting a meeting, disobeying a police order and using abusive language. Mtikila, and three other members who were also charged were sentenced to nine months. A subsequent High Court ruling overturned the verdict, finding that the charges were unfounded. Mtikila was again arrested in September 1993 on sedition charges.

The Constitution protects freedom of speech and press. However, these rights are still restricted in Tanzania. While the emergence of new political parties and a vibrant print press have helped to exercise these rights, the government has used its power to keep the press in check. The government has created a national register of journalists and expelled those whose stories it finds offensive. *Michapo* (Palaver), an independent paper, was the first to uncover the government operation known as "Crush," in which the security forces were told to suppress the media and opposition critics. The *Michapo* was later banned from publication as was another Kiswahili newspaper, the *Cheka* (Laughter), and have been refused licenses. Because many of the new independent papers are financially vulnerable, the government can easily cripple a publication by simply pulling one edition from the stands. All electronic media are government controlled and opposition party views are not aired.

In non-political cases, the judicial system is free from governmental interference. Arrest and harassment of political opponents, however, are routine. Under the Preventative Detention Decree the President may order the arrest and indefinite detention without bail for persons considered a threat to national security or public order. Political offenders may also be internally exiled under the Deportation Act. Abuses by local authorities in non political cases, including the unlawful detention of relatives of those wanted in connection with common crimes, have been reported.

Internal travel is restricted in order to control mass migration to the urban areas and to limit the mobility of opposition party members. Obtaining a passport can be difficult and, as a result, travel abroad is restricted. Mainland Tanzanians wishing to travel to Zanzibar must have a passport, although residents of Zanzibar can travel to the mainland without documentation. Freedom of religion is provided for in the Constitution and is generally respected in practice. However, in mid-1992, the government banned open air religious services and all religious demonstrations. The ban was lifted in June 1992 but was reinstated in December 1992 by the Zanzibar government because it was feared that religious meetings were being used for political purposes.

Thailand

Polity: Parliamentary democracy (military-influenced)
Political Rights: 3
Civil Liberties: 5*
Status: Partly Free
Economy: Capitalist statist
Population: 57,163,000
PPP: $3,986
Life Expectancy: 66.1
Ethnic Groups: Thai (84 percent), Chinese (12 percent), Malaysian, Indian, Khmer, Vietnamese minorities
Ratings Change: *Thailand's civil liberties rating changed from 4 to 5 as a result of modifications in methodology. See "Survey Methodology," page 671.

Overview:

 year after the restoration of civilian rule following a 1991 military coup, Prime Minister Chuan Leekpai appeared hesitant to encroach upon the military's considerable influence in business and politics. However, new army commander General Wimol Wongwanich continued to promote younger, non-partisan officers to top posts in an effort to professionalize the armed forces.

The Kingdom of Thailand is the only Southeast Asian nation never colonized by a European country. In 1932 a bloodless military coup, the first of seventeen attempted military coups in this century, limited the power of the monarchy. Since World War II, a succession of pro-Western military and civilian governments have ruled. Today King Bhumibol Alduyadej's only major political duty is to approve the prime minister, but he is widely revered and exerts informal political and social influence.

Following a period of military rule, in 1988 Major General Chatichai Choonhaven took office as the first directly elected prime minister since 1976. In February 1991 the army deposed Chatichai in a bloodless coup, charging his administration with corruption. More important, Chatichai had tried to limit the military's influence in politics, in particular the influence of graduates of Chulachomklao Royal Military Academy's Class Five, from which the coup plotters and most of the military elite hail.

In March 1991 the army named Anand Panyarach, a widely respected former businessman, as interim prime minister. Anand ran a clean government and surprisingly removed several top generals from their seats on the boards of state-owned firms. The administration also rewrote numerous government contracts that had unfairly favored well-connected companies and miltary officers. In December 1991 a pro-military, interim National Assembly approved a controversial new constitution. It allows the military to appoint the entire 270-seat Senate, meaning that in a no-confidence motion a unified Senate could bring down a government if joined by only 46 members of the directly elected, 360-seat House of Representatives. In addition, it gave the House Speaker the option of recommending to the King a prime minister who had not stood in parliamentary elections.

The 22 March 1992 lower House elections were expected to return the country to civilian rule. However, three pro-military parties won a slim 190-seat majority, and joined with two centrist parties in recommending Narong Wongwan as prime minister. Immediately, the United States State Department announced that Narong had been denied an entry visa in July 1991 because of alleged ties to drug trafficking. In early April the coalition switched its support to coup leader Suchinda Kraprayoon, taking advantage of the constitutional clause allowing for a prime minister from outside the parliament. Although King Bhumibol approved the appointment, thousands of angry civilians, led by Palang Dharma (Moral Force) party leader Chamlong Srimuang, began weeks of protests in the capital, Bangkok. Many of the protestors were members of Bangkok's increasingly prosperous middle class.

Near midnight on 18 May Chamlong led thousands of demonstrators on a march to the prime minister's Government House residence. Soldiers opened fire randomly into the crowd, beginning three days of confrontations between police and civilians. Officially, fifty-two people died, although some 163 people have yet to be accounted for. The violence ended on 20 May after King Bhumibol personally ordered Suchinda and Chamlong to broker a compromise. In June Anand began a second stint as interim prime minister, and parliament amended the constitution to require that future premiers come from among the elected MPs. Significantly, Anand transferred the military's authority for crowd control to the police.

New elections were held on 13 September. The Democratic Party took 79 seats; Chart Thai, 77; Chart Pattana, 60; New Aspiration, 51; Palang Darma, 47; Social Action Party (SAP), 22; minor parties, 24. On 23 September the Democrats, New Aspiration, SAP, Palang Dharma and the tiny Solidarity party formed a 207-seat coalition of anti-military parties, and elected the Democrat's Chuan Leekpai as prime minister. In a setback to the pro-democracy forces, in November a government tribunal upheld the amnesty Suchinda had granted to generals involved in the May killings.

In 1993 Chuan had to fend off charges of being weak and indecisive on economic matters. In mid-June 1993 the opposition brought a no-confidence motion, accusing the government of failing to boost export earnings, support crop prices, and investigate adequately allegations of stock manipulation on the Bangkok Exchange. The government defeated the motion, but faced a new challenge in September when the pro-government SAP announced that it was considering forming a "super-party" with four opposition groups. On 15 September Chuan dropped the party from the coalition and added the Seritham (Liberal Democrat) Party, which holds eight seats. The moves left the coalition with only 193 seats compared with 163 for the opposition.

The key variable is the military's political ambitions. Since his appointment as army commander in August 1992, General Wimol Wongwanich has promoted several younger and more professional generals to senior posts. Wimol is himself a Class Five academy colleague of Suchinda and the other 1991 coup leaders, but he has avoided politics. However, Chuan has been hesitant to remove officers from the boards of state enterprises, and many Class Five generals are still influential in the military and business.

In another development, in August a wave of terrorist and arson attacks swept southern Pattani, Yala and Narathiwat provinces. Six people were killed in incidents that included the burning of thirty-four schools, ambushes on a detachment of army engineers and a train, and an attack on a Buddhist temple. The government blamed the Muslim separatist Pattani United Liberation Organization, which has campaigned sporadically for the secession of four southern provinces since the early 1960s but had been largely dormant in recent years due to a security crackdown and the positive effects of a rural development program. Some observers suggested the attacks were the work of disgruntled army officers.

In a tragic event, a 10 May fire at a Kader Industrial Company's doll factory in Nakhon Pathom east of Bangkok killed 240 workers, mainly female, and injured 500 others. Investigators blamed locked fire escapes and inadequate safety measures for many of the deaths.

Political Rights and Civil Liberties: Thais changed their government democratically in September 1992 in elections rated the cleanest in the country's history. However, the possibility of a future military coup cannot be discounted.

Freedoms of speech and press are generally respected, but legal restrictions exist on defaming the monarchy (*lèse majesté*), advocating a Communist government, inciting disturbances and insulting religion. The press is generally outspoken in its criticism of the government but exercises self-censorship in these proscribed areas and in comments on the military. The government or military controls each of the five national television networks, and news coverage is sometimes biased. In September 1992 the government authorized the establishment of two new privately owned television channels. Radio stations are required to broadcast government-produced newscasts four times daily and a military-produced commentary once, but can supplement these with their own news.

The judiciary is considered independent of the government. Defendents receive adequate due process safeguards, although a closed trial can be ordered for cases involving the royal family or defamation of religion. There are credible reports of occasional police summary executions of criminal suspects, and police frequently beat detainees and prisoners. Freedom of assembly is occasionally abridged by local officals in rural areas who charge peaceful demonstrators with inciting unrest and intent to commit violence.

Freedom of religion is unhindered. However, Muslims claim that the school curriculum is biased towards the Buddhist majority. Freedom of internal travel and residence is restricted for some Chinese and Vietnamese aliens. Child prostitution remains a serious problem. The 1975 Labor relations Act prohibits civil servants from joining unions, although they may join "employee associations" which negotiate salaries and benefits. The 1975 Act also grants the government the right to "restrict the right to strike whenever a strike would affect national security or cause severe negative repercussions for the population at large," but this power is used infrequently. In December the right of state enterprise workers to form unions, which had been revoked in April 1991 by the previous military government, was reinstated.

Togo

Polity: Military dominated
Economy: Mixed statist
Population: 4,105,000
PPP: $734
Life Expectancy: 54.0
Ethnic Groups: Aja, Ewe, Gurensi, Kabyé, Krachi, Mina, Tem
Ratings Change: *Togo's political rights rating changed from 6 to 7 because of increasing political violence.

Political Rights: 7*
Civil Liberties: 5
Status: Not Free

Overview:	Two years after pro-democracy protests forced Togo's military-backed ruler Gnassingbe Eyadema to agree to hold multiparty elections, Eyadema easily won re-election in August 1993 in a long-delayed vote largely boycotted by the opposition. The boycott was in response to a Supreme Court decision nullifying the application of prominent opposition candidate Gilchrest Olympio, and to protest the military's continuing interference with the country's democratic transition. The opposition also threatened to boycott oft-postponed legislative elections now slated for January 1994.

In 1914 Britain occupied the eastern portion of then-German Togoland and France the west. In 1957 the British portion became the independent state of Ghana. Western Togoland achieved independence as the Republic of Togo in April 1960. Togo's first president, Sylvanus Olympio, was assassinated in 1963 and was succeeded by his rival, Nicholas Grunitzky. In January 1967 then-Maj. Gnassingbe Eyadema deposed Grunitzky. Eyadema, a northerner and a member of the minority Kabye tribe, subsequently suspended the constitution, banned political parties, and declared himself president. In 1969 the government formed a puppet party, the Rally of the Togolese People (RPT). However, Eyadema kept the country under military rule, and in 1979 and again in 1986 won elections running unopposed.

In October 1990 the government sentenced two opposition figures to lengthy jail terms, touching off a series of popular demonstrations and strikes that continued over several months. In March 1991 ten illegal opposition groups formed the Front of Associations for Renewal (FAR). In April the president legalized opposition parties, and promised to hold multiparty elections within a year. In May the Democratic Opposition Collective (COD) umbrella group superceded FAR.

In July a national conference convened to choose an interim prime minister. The conference, dominated by opposition figures, declared its sovereignty from the government, unilaterally stripped Eyadema of most of his powers, and elected Joseph Koffigoh as prime minister. The Conference also formed an interim seventy-nine-member High Council of the Republic (HCR) to run the country in advance of legislative and presidential elections, to be held by late August 1992.

In the fall soldiers continued to clash with pro-democracy protestors. On 26 November the HCR banned the RPT, accusing it of provoking the army. The next day troops loyal to the president surrounded Koffigoh's residence, and on 3 December seized the prime minister and brought him to the president. Under pressure from

Eyadema, in late December Koffigoh formed a "national unity government" that included two former members of Eyadema's government.

Presidential elections were initially scheduled for May and June 1992. However, in early May unknown assailants shot and wounded prominent opposition leader Gilchrest Olympio, the son of the country's first president and the chairman of the Union of Forces of Change. In June the government responded to continuing politically motivated violence by postponing the elections indefinitely. In a key step in the democratic transition, on 27 September voters overwhelmingly approved a new multiparty constitution. However the power struggle continued as the army attacked the HCR on 22 October and briefly held its members hostage. On 16 November workers began a general strike to demand that the military stop interfering with the transition.

On 13 January 1993 Eyadema sacked Koffigoh, but reappointed him five days later. In effect, Eyadema had demonstrated that he held the power to name the prime minister, not the HCR. In the ensuing days protestors again took to the streets, increasingly to denounce Koffigoh for not speaking out against the president. On 25 January police fired on anti-government demonstrators in the capital of Lome, killing at least twenty-two people.

By early February some 250,000 people had fled to neighboring Ghana and Benin. On 8-9 February representatives of the government, COD-2 (since December 1991 the successor to COD) and the HCR held talks in Colmar, France on confining troops to their barracks and placing the army under international supervision in advance of the elections. The talks fell through when the government's representatives walked out. The same day Eyadema and Koffigoh agreed to form a new national unity government that included only three opposition figures, none from COD-2, among its eighteen ministers.

On 22 March HCR members meeting in Benin unilaterally named Jean-Lucien Savi de Tove, the leader of the moderate Party of Democrats for Unity, as prime minister. Three days later unknown assailants allegedly attacked Eyadema's residence at a military compound outside Lome before being driven off by troops. The government claimed opposition forces operating out of Ghana carried out the raid, although this could not be confirmed. Some observers speculated that the incident was staged by the military to purge non-Kabye officers. In late March Kabye soldiers reportedly executed more than twenty non-Kabye troops.

Beginning in May the government rescheduled the elections three times, finally fixing 25 August as the date for the presidential polls. By mid-July six opposition candidates including Olympio had declared they would challenge Eyadema. However, on 13 August the Supreme Court refused to allow Olympio to run on the grounds that he had not taken a mandatory medical test administered by Togalese doctors, even though he had been cleared by French specialists. Three main opposition candidates withdrew in protest, leaving Eyadema to face two weak challengers.

On 23 August German election observers pulled out of the country, claiming the credibility of the balloting had been eroded, and former U.S. President Jimmy Carter left the following day. Final results of the 25 August balloting gave Eyadema an easy victory with 96.49 percent of the vote. However, only 39 percent of the electorate voted: 75 percent in Eyadema's northern stronghold but only 13 percent in the south, where opposition calls for a boycott were largely successful.

In November the government postponed the legislative elections from December until January 1994. Olympio's Union of Forces for Change and other oppositon groups said they would boycott.

Political Rights and Civil Liberties: Togolese citizens lack the democratic means to change their government. President Eyadema rules with the backing of the military, a 13,000-man force dominated by members of his Kabye tribe. Presidential elections were held in August 1993. There were numerous irregularities, and prominent opposition figure Gilchrest Olympio was disqualified from running. On election day opposition supporters in the central town of Agbandi and neighboring villages ransacked voting booths after discovering instances of fraud. The next day police arrested more than forty people in connection with the ransackings, some twenty of whom died in custody under still-unresolved circumstances on 27 August. Since the initial pro-democracy protests in 1990, several hundred people are believed to have been killed in politically related violence. Although citizens are in theory free to form political groupings and in fact do so, political violence and harrassment effectively prevent the opposition from organizing and campaigning in the north, and the pro-Eyadema RPT from organizing in the south.

The judicial system is nominally independent of the government, but can be influenced in sensitive cases. Defendents in ordinary cases generally receive adequate procedural safeguards, although a shortage of judges and insufficient administrative procedures cause serious backlogs. Prison conditions are severe.

The press continued to operate under restrictions in 1993. Although opposition newspapers criticized the government without direct sanction, there were numerous cases of police arbitrarily detaining and in some cases beating journalists. In northern areas supporters of Eyadema sometimes physically prevented opposition newspapers from being freely distributed. State run radio and television occasionally offer opposition viewpoints, but in the main are pro-government. Opposition groups intermittantly operate clandestine radio stations.

Women face discrimination in education, and in inheritance and divorce matters. Religious freedom is respected. Citizens can generally travel freely internally and abroad. Workers can join independent unions and hold strikes.

Tonga

Polity: Monarchy and partly elected legislature
Economy: Capitalist
Population: 103,000
PPP: na
Life Expectancy: 67.5
Ethnic Groups: Tongan (98 percent), other Pacific Islanders and Europeans (2 percent)

Political Rights: 5*
Civil Liberties: 3
Status: Partly Free

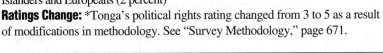

Ratings Change: *Tonga's political rights rating changed from 3 to 5 as a result of modifications in methodology. See "Survey Methodology," page 671.

Overview: This Polynesian South Pacific Kingdom of 169 islands became an independent member of the British Commonwealth in June 1970. Seventy-five-year-old King Taufa' Ahau

Tupuo IV has reigned since 1965. The 1875 constitution is the product of an era in which the chiefs had unlimited powers over the commoners, who were referred to as "eaters of the soil." The King holds broad executive powers and appoints and heads the Privy Council, which makes the major policy decisions. The King also appoints the prime minister. The unicameral Legislative Assembly consists of nine nobles selected by and from among the country's thirty-three noble families, twelve ministers from the Privy Council, and only nine "People's Representatives" elected by universal suffrage, thus ensuring the King and the nobility a two-thirds majority. There are no political parties.

In recent years there have been growing calls for a more broadly representative government within the framework of the existing monarchy. On 24 November 1992 Akilisi Pohiva and three other People's Representative members of parliament, calling themselves the Pro-Democracy Movement, convened a four-day conference in the capital's Basilica Hall on amending the constitution. Pohiva called for universal elections for all assembly members, and for MPs rather than the King to select the cabinet. The influential Roman Catholic and Free Wesleyan churches supported the conference, and many of the nearly 1,000 people who attended were members of the country's growing middle class. Pastor Siupeli Taliai noted that the political system is "designed to preserve old Tongan inequality, entrenched power and position." Many participants agreed on the need for change, but also concluded that the monarchy is important for preserving stability. The government refused to allow the state-owned Radio Tonga to air paid messages advertising the event or to broadcast live coverage, and refused to grant foreigners visas to attend.

Approaching the 4 February 1993 People's Representative elections, Radio Tonga increasingly aired speakers opposed to the democratic movement. This intensified in the three days prior to the election, highlighted by ominous warnings from the Minister of Police that the penalty for treason is death or life imprisonment. Although the electoral law prohibits the news media from publishing or broadcasting election material on the evening before a vote, Radio Tonga openly violated the ban by broadcasting anti-democracy statements from MP Laki Niu. Despite these blatant government interferences, on election day pro-democracy candidates, including Pohiva, won six seats, an increase of one over the last Assembly.

In September Prime Minister Baron Vaea told the Assembly that the government was considering a plan to store 35,000 barrels of toxic waste per year from California on the northern volcanic island of Niuafo'ou. Vaea said the country would earn $14 per barrel, and all adults on Niuafo'ou population of 250 would have jobs at the dump. Pohiva immediately opposed the plan, and promised to make it a prominent issue in the campaign for commoners' rights.

Political Rights and Civil Liberties: Tongans cannot change their government democratically. The King and the hereditary nobles can make major policy decisions without the assent of popularly elected representatives, and hold a pre-eminent position in society through substantial land holdings.

The judiciary is independent of the government, and citizens receive adequate due process safeguards. Freedom of speech is respected in practice. The country's four private newspapers freely criticize the government. However, commoner leader and MP Akilisi Pohiva has faced a series of legal challenges over a January 1992 article in his magazine, *Kele'a* (Conch Shell), which included information about accounts held by individuals at the Tonga Development Bank. In late 1992 the Supreme Court issued a permanent injunction against his publishing further information about the accounts, and Pohiva also faces a government lawsuit for publishing "classified" material. In July he lost a libel case against Assembly Speaker Noble Fusitu'a and was assessed $14,640 in damages. There is no television and the state-owned Radio Tonga is frequently biased towards the government (See Overview above).

Freedom of assembly is respected. There are no restrictions on domestic or internal travel. All religious believers can worship freely. Workers have the right to form unions, but none exists due to the small size of the wage economy.

Trinidad and Tobago

Polity: Parliamentary democracy
Political Rights: 1
Civil Liberties: 1
Economy: Capitalist-statist
Status: Free
Population: 1,263,000
PPP: $6,604
Life Expectancy: 71.6
Ethnic Groups: Complex, black (41 percent), East Indian descent (41 percent), mixed (16 percent), white (1 percent)

Overview:

Following a year of economic decline, Prime Minister Patrick Manning and the ruling People's National Movement (PNM) confronted increasing popular discontent in 1993, particularly from organized labor.

Trinidad and Tobago, a member of the British Commonwealth, achieved independence in 1962. It is composed of two islands, with Trinidad accounting for nearly 95 percent of the country's area and population. Under the 1976 constitution, the nation became a republic with a president, elected by a majority of both houses in parliament, replacing the former governor-general. Executive authority in the parliamentary system remains invested in the prime minister.

The bicameral parliament consists of a 36-member House of Representatives elected for five years, and a 31-member Senate, with 25 senators appointed by the prime minister and 6 by the parliamentary opposition. The prime minister is the leader of the party or coalition commanding a majority in the House. Local government (counties and major municipalities) is elected.

In 1980 the parliament established a 15-member House of Assembly for Tobago, with 12 members directly elected for four years and 3 named by the majority party. In January 1987 Tobago was granted internal self-government. In 1993 a new constitutional arrangement was worked out, pending parliamentary approval, that would grant greater autonomy to Tobago through the creation of a local executive cabinet.

In the 1986 elections, the National Alliance for Reconstruction (NAR) led by A.N.R. Robinson defeated the black-based People's National Movement (PNM), which had ruled for thirty years, by taking 33 of 36 seats. The NAR was an unprecedented coalition of black and East Indian elements. It was composed of Robinson's Democratic Action Congress (DAC), the East Indian-based United Labour Front (ULF) led by Basdeo Panday, Karl Hudson-Phillip's Organization for National Reconstruction (ONR), and the Tapia House Movement.

After taking office, the coalition unraveled. The Tapia House Movement withdrew. Panday was expelled and formed a new East Indian-based party, the United National Congress (UNC).

On 27 July 1991 the radical Muslim group Jamaat-al-Muslimeen, led by Yasin Abu Bakr and numbering about 300 members, seized the nation's parliament. A five-day stand-off marked by rampant looting in the capital city of Port of Spain left two dozen dead and more than 300 injured according to official sources. The siege ended when the government convinced Bakr the insurgents would receive amnesty if they surrendered. The incident delivered a blow to an already ailing economy, causing tens of millions of dollars in damages and setting back tourism. It also heightened tension between the roughly equal black and East Indian populations.

In December 1991 the PNM, under the new leadership of Patrick Manning and with a slate featuring many younger candidates, won 21 of 36 parliamentary seats. Panday's UNC won 13 seats and became the official opposition. The NAR won 2 seats and Robinson resigned as party leader. Voter turnout was 66 percent.

In 1992 the forty-six-year-old Manning made good on a number of his "people-oriented" campaign promises by granting a public sector pay raise and higher state pensions. The PNM won 10 of 14 municipal and regional council elections on 28 September 1992. The UNC won in the other 4.

In 1993 Manning floated the local currency to attract foreign investment. But the subsequent rise in prices sparked popular discontent. After incidents of looting and organized labor's threat of a general strike in response to payroll cuts in state industries, the government offered a "social package" to help the poor and income tax relief for wage earners.

The government also had to contend with a recalcitrant police force that had been uncooperative with Scotland Yard detectives brought in to investigate drug-related corruption within the force. In February hundreds of police protested against the probe outside the parliament building.

In July Carson Charles, a minister in the former NAR government, left the NAR to form a new opposition organization, the National Development Party (NDP).

Political Rights and Civil Liberties: Citizens are able to change their government through democratic elections. Constitutional guarantees regarding the right to free expression and the right to organize political parties, civic organizations and labor unions are generally respected.

There are a number of human rights organizations. Active in addressing allegations of police brutality, they have also criticized government anti-narcotics initiatives as threatening to civil rights, and condemned laws that allow magistrates to order floggings for youthful criminal offenders. These groups have also reported scattered incidents of harassment by security forces against the Muslim community, which comprises 6 percent of the population. Freedom of religion, however, is generally respected.

Domestic violence continues to be a concern. However, a 1990 law allows both men and women to obtain restraining orders against abusive spouses. The law also allows for children to be taken away from abusive parents. In 1993 a wave of violent crime and sexual attacks against women in a predominantly East Indian region of central Trinidad sparked ethnic tensions. Indo-Trinidadians charged that most of the offenders were black, and at least one person was killed in retaliation by vigilantes.

Labor unions are well organized, powerful and politically active. They have the right to strike and have done so frequently in recent years. An independent industrial court plays a central role in arbitrating labor disputes.

Newspapers are privately owned, uncensored and influential. There are three independent dailies as well as party papers. Radio and television are both public and private. Trinidad and Tobago's new media giant, Caribbean Communications Network (CCN), launched the country's second television station in 1991. The other station is state operated.

An independent judicial system is headed by a Supreme Court, which consists of a High Court and a Court of Appeal, with district courts operating on the local level. Under the constitution, there is a right of ultimate appeal to the Privy Council of the United Kingdom.

In 1993 Scotland Yard investigators determined that drug-related and other types of corruption were endemic in the local police force. Further investigation was taken up by local investigators in mid-1993, with an eventual showdown looming between the government and high police officials.

In the aftermath of the 1991 coup attempt, Jamaat al Muslimeem leader Bakr and 113 others were charged with treason, murder and kidnapping. Defense lawyers claimed the charges were invalid because Bakr had given up in exchange for amnesty. In a June 1992 decision that aroused public indignation, a high court judge ruled for the defense and all defendants were released. In 1993 the Court of Appeal upheld the high court ruling.

Tunisia

Polity: Dominant party
Economy: Mixed capitalist
Population: 8,579,000
PPP: $3,579
Life Expectancy: 66.7
Ethnic Groups: Arab

Political Rights: 6
Civil Liberties: 5
Status: *Not Free

Ratings Change: *Tunisia's rating changed from Partly Free to Not Free as a result of methodological modifications. See "Survey Methodology," page 671.

Overview:
In 1993, Tunisia's ruling Democratic Constitutional Assembly (RCD) and the legal opposition prepared for presidential and parliamentary elections slated for 1994. A group of intellectuals issued an outspoken declaration critical of the country's human rights record.

Tunisia is a one-party dominated state governed by the RCD, whose leader, General Zine el-Abedine Ben Ali, is the president. Ben Ali succeeded the country's first longtime president, Habib Bourgiba, forcing him to retire in November 1987. Several other political parties are also registered, although none has deputies in parliament. The radical Islamic *Al-Nahda* (Renaissance) party remains banned. Most of Al-Nahda's active members were either in jail, following the August 1992 jail sentences against its 265 members, or in exile. Al-Nahda's leader, Rachid Ghannouchi, sentenced to life imprisonment by a Tunisian court, received political asylum in Great Britain in early 1993. In a speech to parliament in December 1992, the interior minister, Abdallah Kallel, said that the movement had been "dismantled once and for all." To underscore the government's resolve to eliminate all Islamic militancy, Tunisia spent 10 percent of the budget on security services in 1993. In order to combat the spread of radical fundamentalism among the disaffected youth, the government established a number of local community centers in deprived neighborhoods.

In November 1992 the Chamber of Deputies (parliament) passed a new electoral law instituting a mixed system of majority vote and proportional representation. The vote aimed at encouraging the smaller parties to participate in the upcoming legislative election, following the opposition's boycott of local elections in 1990. In 1992, President Ben Ali announced March 1994 as the date of the next presidential and parliamentary elections. In July 1993, RCD's general congress unanimously approved Ben Ali as its candidate for the presidency, assuring his victory for another five-year term. The congress, at the same time, confirmed Tunisia's orientation towards a free market economy and reiterated RCD's opposition to Islamic fundamentalism.

On 9 April a group of 200 intellectuals published a document criticizing the government for a decline in human rights since Ben Ali's takeover of the presidency in 1987. As examples, the declaration listed the continuance of a single-party parliament, the government's monopolization of media and the stifling of criticism and independent ideas.

As the country prepared for the 1994 vote, the legalized opposition remained splintered and disoriented in responding to the free market reforms. The Social Democratic Movement (MDS), formerly the largest opposition party, continued its internal bickering over the party's proper ideological stance, and the former Communist party changed its name to Renewal Movement during its April 1993 congress. On 14 November, the National Union of Democratic Unionists party endorsed Ben Ali as presidential candidate, citing as its reason that "Ben Ali is the president of all Tunisians."

Political Rights and Civil Liberties: Although Tunisia is constitutionally a parliamentary democracy, in practice the right of citizens to change their government democratically is limited. The ruling RCD holds a monopoly on power on the national and local levels. The Chamber of Deputies essentially reaffirms policy made by president Ben Ali.

All political parties require government authorization and several small opposition parties are allowed to operate. Parties based on religion, race and ethnicity are illegal. Non-governmental associations are allowed to operate, with the exception of organizations aiming to "disturb public order." According to a law adopted in March 1992, simultaneous membership in political parties and certain associations is illegal. The law was aimed at the outspoken Tunisian League of Human Rights, many of whose members also belonged to opposition parties. In March 1993, the law's validity was undermined when a court allowed the League to resume its activities after the government ordered its dissolution in April 1992. Several international organizations are allowed to operate, including Greenpeace and a chapter of Amnesty International, the only one in the Arab world. Although freedom of peaceful assembly and protest is formally enshrined in the constitution, all protests must be approved by the government three days in advance. On 14 January 1993, police dispersed about 100 university students protesting the U.S. raid against Iraq.

The authorities frequently use illegal detention and torture against suspected members of the radical opposition. During the 1992 trial of suspected Al-Nahda members a number of the accused showed signs of physical abuse while testifying in court. Amnesty International accused the government of harassing female relatives of suspected radicals, many of whom were beaten, tortured and sexually abused. The preventive detention law limits arrests without a warrant to no more than ten days, but in practice the law is often ignored. On 26 July the authorities detained without warrant Tawfik Rajhi, a resident of France, upon his return to Tunisia. Rajhi was denied access to his family and lawyer. Earlier Rajhi's brother was imprisoned and released for his membership with the Al-Nahda.

Freedom of speech and press is severely curtailed. The official Press Code outlaws the dissemination of "false" information and requires editors of newspapers and book publishers to submit all publications to the Justice and Interior Ministries, prior to their public release. Although in 1991 the government announced it would not enforce the prepublication censorship part of the Press Code, it continues to threaten editors and journalists with imprisonment or fines for publications critical of the government. In 1992, a court sentenced the lawyer Mohammed Nouri, for writing an article criticizing the influence of military courts on Tunisia's legal system.

Islam is the state religion, but most other religions are allowed to practice freely. The exceptions include the Baha'i, considered an Islamic heresy. The government appoints and pays the salaries of Islamic clergy. Proselytizing for religions other than Islam is prohibited.

Freedom of movement within and outside of the country is generally respected, with the exception of activists critical of the government. The General Union of Tunisian Workers (UGTT) remains the major labor confederation. The government has enacted a series of legal reforms, aimed at improving the rights of women and advancing their social and professional opportunities.

Turkey

Polity: Presidential-parliamentary democracy (military-influenced)
Economy: Capitalist-statist
Population: 60,705,000
PPP: $4,652
Life Expectancy: 65.1
Ethnic Groups: Turks, Kurds (12 million), Armenians, Jews
Ratings Change: *Turkey's political rights rating changed from 2 to 4 because of increasing violence and press restrictions.

Political Rights: 4*
Civil Liberties: 4
Status: Partly Free

Overview: The sudden death in April 1993 of Turkish President Turgut Ozal, who had developed the country into a regional power and had introduced widespread economic reforms, ended a period of uneasy "cohabitation" with his rival, prime minister Suleyman Demirel, who ascended to the presidency. Subsequently, in June U.S.-educated economist Tansu Ciller became the country's first female prime minister, and only the third female head of government of a Muslim country.

Mustafa Kemal Ataturk proclaimed Turkey a republic on 29 October 1923 in territory carved out of the former Ottoman Empire. Ataturk's pro-Western, secular legacy still has a powerful influence over the country. Turkey joined NATO in 1952, and the military used the doctrine of "Kemalism" to justify three coups between 1960 and 1980 during periods of social and political unrest. The 1982 constitution provides for a 400-seat unicameral Grand National Assembly (increased to 450 in 1987) elected for a five-year term. The Assembly elects the president for a seven-year term. The president appoints and can dissmiss the prime minister, can dissolve the Assembly with the concurrence of two-thirds of the deputies, and appoints several top officials. Despite these powers, the office is considered largely ceremonial, and the president is expected to represent the state in foreign affairs and remain above politics.

The country returned to civilian rule in 1983. Elections in November gave the conservative Motherland Party (Anap) a majority, and one month later Turgut Ozal, a deputy premier during the recent military rule, formed a government. Under Ozal the country embarked on a far-reaching economic liberalization program that deregulated many sectors of the economy, lowered import barriers, made the *lira* fully convertable and began privatising state industries. In 1989 Anap used its parliamentary majority to elect Ozal to the presidency, where he focused on promoting his visionary foreign policy of making Turkey a power "from the Adriatic to the Great Wall of China." Ozal allowed Turkish bases to be used for Allied operations against Iraq during and after the Gulf War, and envisioned expansive road, energy and communications links with the former Soviet Central Asian republics.

Heading into the October 1991 parliamentary elections Ozal and Anap were dogged by charges of official corruption and nepotism, and blamed for failing to control the country's 66 percent inflation rate. The conservative True Path Party (DYP) took a plurality of 178 seats; Anap, 115; Social Democratic Populist Party (SHP), 66; the anti-Western, Muslim-based Welfare Party (RP), 62; the Kurdish-based People's Labor Party (HEP), 22; Democratic Left Party (DSP), 7. DYP leader Suleyman Demirel subsequently formed a coalition with the SHP and began his seventh stint as prime minister.

Demirel's government continued Ozal's economic restructuring. However, Demirel had accused Ozal of meddling in politics by making full use of his presidential powers of appointment and by frequently chairing cabinet meetings. The sixty-six-year-old Ozal died of heart failure on 17 April 1993. On 16 May parliament elected Demirel as the country's ninth president on the third round of balloting. On 13 June the DYP elected forty-seven-year-old Tansu Ciller, the minister for the economy, as party leader over two long-serving cabinet ministers. Ciller reportedly ran against the wishes of Demirel and other party leaders who opposed her emphasis on speeding up the privatization program, but she received strong support from the DYP's rank-and-file who favored the emergence of a younger generation of political leaders. On 25 June Ciller formed a government and became only the third female prime minister of a Muslim country, after Pakistan's Benazir Bhutto and Bangladesh's Khaleda Zia.

A critical issue facing Ciller's government is the insurgency waged in the southeast since 1984 by the Marxist Kurdistan Worker's Party's (PKK) to gain an independent

Kurdish state. In recent years, the government has sought to undermine the appeal of the PKK by granting limited cultural rights to the Kurds, including lifting a ban on the Kurdish language, and increasing development spending in the southeast. Meanwhile the army continues its crackdown against the PKK, including a major offensive in October 1992 against rebel bases in northern Iraq that killed some 1,800 guerrillas.

On 17 March 1993 PKK leader Abdullah Ocalan announced a twenty-five day unilateral ceasefire to take effect three days later, and on 16 April extended the ceasefire indefinitely. Ocalan claimed the PKK now favored a political solution including greater Kurdish autonomy under a federal system, although analysts said his group had been greatly weakened by the October raids and was buying time. Renewed clashes in late May ended the ceasefire, and casualty tolls in subsequent months were the highest since the insurgency began. In an effort to attract greater international attention, the PKK also attacked Turkish interests in several European cities on 24 June and again on 4 November, and also targeted tourists inside Turkey for the first time. By year's end nearly 2,000 rebels, civilians and soldiers had died since the breakdown of the ceasefire, and some 10,000 overall have died since 1984.

Ciller faces local elections in March 1994 that will be a critical test of her government's support. Inflation is running at 70 percent and will be a major issue. In addition, Ciller's plans to speed up the privatization program face stiff opposition from unions and the bureaucracy. The country's 240 state enterprises lose $2 billion per year, but are an important source of jobs and patronage. In another issue, on 14 July the Constitutional Court banned the three-year-old HEP, considered by many to be a PKK front, ruling that it violated the constitutional ban on ethnic-based parties and on advocating separatism.

Political Rights and Civil Liberties:

Turks can change their government democratically, but the country is beset by widespread human rights abuses.

Many of the rights violations involve the PKK insurgency in the southeast and the government's response. The PKK and other smaller groups such as Dev Sol (Revolutionary Left) target government officials and buildings, schools, paramilitary "village guards," civilians suspected of cooperating with the government, and businesses. The PKK also frequently abducts local officials and teachers.

Security forces are accused of extrajudicial killings of suspected terrorists, of firing randomly into crowds of demonstrators and into residential areas in "retaliation" for PKK attacks and of torturing guerrillas and dissidents. In recent years security forces have been suspected in unsolved "mystery killings" of journalists, local politicians and other civilians considered Kurdish sympathizers. A state of emergency declared in 1987 continues in ten southeastern provinces, allowing civilian governors to detain suspects accused of committing crimes in tandem incommunicado for up to thirty days. Authorities can also search residences or offices without warrants.

The 1991 Anti-Terror Law broadly defines terrorism to include non-violent acts by ordinary citizens including "belonging to an organization with the aim of changing the characteristics of the republic...its political, legal, social, secular and economic system." The Law provides imprisonment of up to five years for "written or spoken propaganda, assemblies, demonstrations and marches with the aim of damaging the indivisible unity of the state," and has been used against journalists, writers and publishers. For persons arrested under the Law, confessions obtained through torture are permissible as evidence.

Security forces are also accused of torturing ordinary criminals. The Constitution provides for the security of judges' tenure, and largely because of this the judiciary is considered independent of the government. Defendents in ordinary cases generally receive adequate due process safeguards, although there are no jury trials and the right to have access to a lawyer during all phases of investigation and detention is sometimes denied. State security courts, composed of two civilian judges, two prosecutors and a military judge try cases covered under the Anti-Terror Law and other terrorism cases, as well as cases involving drug smuggling and promoting seditious ideas. Trials in these courts are often closed and in general do not provide adequate safeguards for the accused.

There are numerous speech and press restrictions. The Anti-Terror Law prohibits speech or writings that the government considers to advocate or support separatism, even indirectly. For example, in 1992 a court sentenced a *Zaman* (*Times*) journalist to two months in prison for criticizing the armed forces. Numerous leftist and pro-Kurdish publications have had issues confiscated or have been shut down. Police often harass and occasionally torture journalists, particularly those suspected of Kurdish sympathies. Publications must designate an editor who is legally held responsible for its contents, and several editors have faced criminal proceedings based on their papers' articles. The national Criminal Code provides three-to-six year penalties for those who "insult" the president or other branches of government. Police occasionally detain journalists on these charges, although most of these cases are eventually dismissed. The press practices self-censorship due to these various restrictions. In October, the PKK declared the entire southeastern region of the country off-limits to local and foreign media, and it appeared many journalists were complying with the ban.

In 1991 the government lifted some restrictions on the public use of the Kurdish language, although nearly all Kurdish-language newspapers have been shut down. Kurdish-language broadcasts are still illegal. The government holds a monopoly on radio and television broadcasting. Opposition views are aired, although these groups say that coverage is still biased towards the government. Several private radio stations operate despite the ban. The government must approve of all assemblies and demonstrations, and permission for such events is occasionally denied on security grounds.

The constitution establishes Turkey as a secular state. Muslims make up 99 percent of the population, although other groups generally can worship freely. Religious services can be held only in approved venues. Evangelical Christians and Armenian and Greek churches are monitored by security forces. In recent years fundamentalists have occasionally carried out attacks on targets considered to be particularly inimical to Islam. One of the most serious incidents occurred on 2 July in the central city of Sivas, when Muslim extremists torched a hotel hosting a conference featuring Aziz-Nesin, a leftist newspaper editor who had published portions of Salman Rushdie's novel, *The Satanic Verses*. Nesin survived, but thirty-six people were killed, mostly intellectuals and writers who had gathered for the conference.

Citizens can generally travel freely internally, except in the southeast where both security forces and the PKK frequently set up roadblocks, and can travel abroad without restriction. Workers can join independent unions, except for teachers, civil servants and security personnel. The government must approve of union meetings, and has the right to send police and record the proceedings. Strikes are prohibited in several areas, including security and armed forces personnel, petroleum and sanitation workers, and teachers. Workers must engage in collective bargaining and non-binding mediation prior to striking.

Turkmenistan (Turkmenia)

Polity: Presidential-par-
liamentary (presidential-
dominated)
Economy: Statist
Population: 3,971,000
PPP: $4,230
Life Expectancy: 66.0

Political Rights: 7
Civil Liberties: 7*
Status: Not Free

Ethnic Groups: Turkmen (72 percent), Russian (9.5 percent),
Uzbeks (8.5 percent), Kazakhs (2.9 percent)
Ratings Change: *Turkmenistan's civil liberties rating changed
from 6 to 7 because of continued repression of all opposition.

Overview: The former Soviet Central Asian republic of Turkmenistan,
bordering Iran and Afghanistan, remained in the totalitarian grip
of President Saparmurad Niyazov, a former first secretary of the
Communist Party. The regime continued to curtail political and human rights, while
seeking foreign investment to exploit the country's vast natural gas, mineral and oil
reserves and cotton-producing capacities.

Turkmenistan was ruled by various local rulers until the thirteenth century, when the
Mongols conquered it. In the late nineteenth century, Tsarist Russia seized the country.
In 1924, after the Bolsheviks ousted the Khan of Merv, the Turkmen Soviet Socialist
Republic was declared.

Turkmenistan declared independence after a national referendum in October 1991;
Niyazov won a one-man presidential election in December 1991. The following year,
after the adoption of a new constitution, Niyazov was re-elected, claiming 99.5 percent
of the vote. The main opposition group, known as Agzybirlik, formed in 1989 by
leading intellectuals, was banned and its leaders harassed.

The country's second year of independence was marked by a further consolidation of
power by Niyazov, who had allowed a cult of personality to be formed around him. In addition to being head of the Democratic Party of Turkmenistan (DPT)—the renamed Communist Party—the president has the following constitutional powers: he heads the Cabinet
of Ministers, whose members he appoints with the consent of the *Majlis* (the parliament),
and he can prorogue the parliament if it has passed two votes of no-confidence within an
eighteenth-month period. In addition, the president issues edicts that have the force of law,
appoints and removes judges of all jurisdictions, and names the state prosecutor.

Key issues for the government during the year were expanding economic ties with
Iran, Turkey and the West, relations with the Commonwealth of Independent States
(CIS), and the stationing of Russian troops along the border with Afghanistan. The
regime also expressed concern about the ongoing conflict in neighboring Tajikistan and
Uzbekistan, although experts agreed that Niyazov was using the threat of regional
instability to further clamp down on all opposition.

In May, the government hired former U.S. Secretary of State Al Haig Jr., to help it
attract U.S. business. It also offered capitalist incentives such as tax breaks and
favorable arrangements for repatriation of profits.

Early in the year, an agreement on the sale of petroleum products to Iran was concluded during a visit by Iranian Foreign Minister Ali Akbar Vellayati. A rail link between Ashkhabad, the capital, and the northern Iranian city of Meshed, which would give Turkmenistan access to the Persian Gulf, is being built, scheduled for completion in 1995. Negotiations with Turkey focused on the construction of a pipeline through Iran and Turkey to provide a new outlet to Europe for Turkmenistan's gas production.

In August, the government announced that Turkmenistan would leave the ruble zone and introduce its own currency, the manat, on 1 November. President Niyazov said the manat would be worth 1,000 rubles or one dollar.

In September, Turkmenistan and Russia signed a bilateral agreement on military cooperation. The agreement allowed Russia to maintain strategic bases. However, Niyazov remained cool to CIS economic cooperation and to Turkmenistan joining a CIS security agreement.

Political Rights and Civil Liberties:

Citizens of Turkmenistan cannot change their government democratically. Power has been concentrated in the hands of the president, and only the parliament—which is 90 percent former Communist—has the right to nominate presidential candidates. The constitution provides for numerous legislative and consultative bodies, all of which have nebulous duties and even less clearly defined powers. A People's Council is the supreme representative body. Under its authority is the parliament, the Council of Elders, the Cabinet of Ministers, the prosecutor-general, and certain judges. President Niyazov himself is said to have devised the idea for the Council, which harks back to the tribal assemblies of Turkmenistan's past. In reality, the body is little more than a rubber stamp for the president. In addition to being president, Niyazov is chairman of the Council of Elders and the DPT.

The constitution gives short shrift to individual rights and liberties, the pretext of this being the need to maintain order and stability. On the eve of passing the new constitution, the Turkmenistan Constitutional Committee removed about thirty articles and statutes, including ones on freedom of the press and the creation of a constitutional court.

The judiciary is subordinate to the regime; the president appoints all judges for a term of five years without legislative review.

Freedoms of expression and association are curtailed. Agzybirlik and other non-registered opposition groups face intimidation and repression. In August, it was learned that several leading Agzybirlik figures were detained briefly in Ashkhabad after meeting with U.S. Congressman Robert Torricelli. They were released after being warned by the Committee on National Security (KNB)—the successor to the Soviet-era KGB—not to slander the state. On 15 September, U.S. ambassador-at-large Strobe Talbott, to protest the detention of four opposition leaders who had scheduled to meet with him, cut short a visit to Turkmenistan and refused to sign an aid agreement. Throughout the year, the KNB brought in several Agzybirlik activists for questioning, warning several that they faced persecution or physical harm if they persisted in their political activities. Among the tactics were rescinding drivers' licenses, following activists, wiretapping telephones, withholding work, medical treatment, travel permits and vacation, de facto house arrest, and unwarranted house searches.

Restrictions on a free press in Turkmenistan include censorship and the denial of registration to some newspapers and journals. *Dayanch*, an independently funded paper published in Moscow featuring articles in Turkmen and Russian, is routinely confiscated.

Its editor and staff have been fined on several occasions and suffered other harassment by the police and militia. Local ordinances effectively ban public demonstrations.

Freedom of movement and travel is circumscribed. Opposition activists have been denied permission to travel within the country or put under house arrest to prevent them from attending meetings or leaving. Ak-Mukhammed Velsapar, the writer, was denied permission to travel abroad to attend symposia to which he had been invited. In the past, activists were barred from traveling to Kyrgyzstan to attend a human rights conference. Families of opposition activists who do travel outside the country are often harassed at home.

Although the population is overwhelmingly Sunni Muslim, the government has kept a rein on religion in hope of averting the rise of Islamic fundamentalism. There were reports in 1993 that Iranian fundamentalist organizations had passed through Turkmenistan on their way to Uzbekistan and Tajikistan. Religious congregations are required to register with the government.

Although women's rights are enshrined in the constitution, discrimination in education and other social limitations restrict women's freedom. For example, married women are not allowed to be students, while men do not face the same restriction.

The state-run, Soviet-era Trade Union Federation claims 1.6 million members, but is little more than a rubber-stamp for the government. There are no independent trade unions, and Turkmen law does not protect the right to collective bargaining.

Tuvalu

Polity: Parliamentary democracy
Economy: Capitalist
Population: 10,000
PPP: na
Life Expectancy: 61.0
Ethnic Groups: Polynesian

Political Rights: 1
Civil Liberties: 1
Status: Free

Overview: This tiny Polynesian country, formerly the Ellice Islands, achieved independence in October 1978 as a "special member" of the British Commonwealth, participating in all Commonwealth affairs except for heads-of-government meetings. Under the 1978 constitution, executive power is vested in a prime minister who is elected by and from among the twelve-member *Fale I Fono* (parliament), which serves a four-year term. A governor general, a Tuvalu citizen appointed by the British monarch, appoints the four-member cabinet on the advice of the prime minister, and can also delay legislation for seven days. Political parties are legal but none exists. Most elections hinge on village-based allegiances rather than issues. Local government on the eight permanently inhabited islands is run by six-person island councils, which are elected by universal suffrage every four years. These councils are generally influenced by hereditary elders wielding traditional authority.

The country's fourth post-independence elections on 2 September 1993 saw nine of the twelve sitting MPs returned to the fono. Two of the three defeated MPs were from the informal opposition. On 17 September a second meeting of the new fono again failed to elect a prime minister, with both the incumbent, Bikenibeu Paeniu, and challenger Dr. Tomasi Puapua, himself a former premier, each receiving six votes. Governor General Soptuadi Pilauchi used his constitutional powers to dissolve this new fono, and the country held fresh elections on 25 November. Following a runoff in one district on 30 November, on 10 December five former opposition MPs and two former supporters of Paeniu joined to elect Kamuta Laatasi as prime minister.

The tiny country has a poor resource base and is dependent on food imports. Agricultural output consists mainly of cocoa palm and its derivatives. Much of Tuvalu's revenue comes from remittances by some 1,500 countrymen living abroad, as well as from the sale of stamps and coins. Interest from the Tuvalu Trust Fund, established in 1987 by major aid donors, covers a fourth of the annual budget. Scientists say the low-lying country is slowly sinking into the Pacific Ocean, as most of the islands have been eroded by storms. There is also a concern that a global warming trend will cause ocean levels to rise and threaten the country's physical existence.

Political Rights and Civil Liberties: Citizens of Tuvalu can change their government democratically. The judiciary is independent of the government, and citizens receive fair public trials. Freedoms of speech and press are respected. There are no restrictions on the right to form associations or hold public assemblies or meetings. Religious freedom is fully respected, and 70 percent of the population belongs to the Protestant Church of Tuvalu. The government promotes a voluntary family planning program out of concern that a rapidly growing population will overwhelm the densely packed country's limited resources. Citizens can travel freely internally and abroad. Workers are free to join independent unions, although only the Tuvalu Seamen's Union is registered. Strikes are legal but none has occurred, largely because much of the population is engaged in subsistence agriculture.

Uganda

Polity: Military
Economy: Capitalist statist
Population: 18,100,000
PPP: $524
Life Expectancy: 52.0
Ethnic Groups: Acholi, Baganda, Kakwa, Lango, Nkole, Soga, Teso, other

Political Rights: 6
Civil Liberties: 5
Status: Not Free

Overview: In 1993, Uganda prepared for the holding of elections to the constituent assembly scheduled for March 1994. The country's unelected President Yoweri Museveni continued to oppose the legalization of political parties in the near future.

Since its independence in 1962, Uganda has been afflicted with civil wars, intermittent coups and brutal dictatorships. An estimated 800,000 people died under the brutal regimes of Idi Amin and Milton Obote during the 1970s and early 1980s. Their rule was marked by economic and social disintegration of the country once known as the "pearl of Africa."

In January 1986, the Museveni-led National Resistance Army (NRA), which had been fighting against the Obote regime since 1980, overthrew Obote's successor, Lieutenant General Tito Okello. Following the takeover, Museveni set up the National Resistance Council (NRC) to act as an interim legislature. Three years later, he expanded the Council with nominees of his National Resistance Movement (NRM) and members of social movements. At the same time he extended the "interim" period until 1995. Since 1987, the NRM organized "Resistance Council Committees" on local and regional levels, culminating in the February 1992 elections to the councils.

The NRM has worked to undermine Uganda's traditional political parties, the Uganda People's Congress (UPC), and the Democratic Party (DP). The UPC, led by the exiled Obote, has a largely Protestant following and orientation, while the DP has a Catholic affinity. Museveni has consistently opposed multipartyism stating that it leads to divisions based on religion, ethnicity and regionalism and was responsible for the continuing post-independence unrest.

As an alternative to multiparty politics, Museveni offered his vision of "movement democracy" based on individual candidates for elected posts running without party labels.

In 1989, Museveni appointed a constitutional commission to prepare proposals and solicit people's views on the future constitutional arrangements. On 31 December 1992 the constitutional commission finished three years' work, recommending the move-ment-type democracy, and proposing to maintain the suspension of political parties' activities for another five years. By the end of that period, voters would be asked to decide in a referendum on the final version of the constitution, whether to allow parties to exist, or maintain the no-party system. The commission based its recommendation on the alleged support of 60 percent of the population for the no-party system. Political parties within Uganda and various exile groups immediately denounced the report as simply incorporating the NRM position on the issue. On 20 February 1993, in what was viewed as a possible vendetta by members of a political party, a hand grenade thrown into a party killed the commission's vice-chairman Dan Mudhoola.

Following the appointment of Museveni's former classmate, Stephen Akabwai, as the electoral commissioner, the opposition charged that the speed and manner of demarcation of the 214 electoral constituencies to the constituent assembly heavily weighed against non-NRM affiliated candidates. Akabwai presented the final district boundaries three weeks after his appointment. According to the UPC, the Nakifuma district, known to be one of its strongholds, was formed into one electoral district for a population of 138,000. In other districts, several likely opposition candidates were included in a single constitu-ency. On 21 November, the commission set the date for the election as 28 March 1994.

Prior to the election, Museveni agreed to restore the traditional monarchies of Uganda's several ethnic groups that had been abolished in the 1960s. Prior to that time, the tribal kingdoms existed as legal entities forming the regional structures of Uganda's federal arrangements. In 1967, in his first period as Uganda's strongman, Obote abolished the monarchies due to disagreements over the extent of the central government's and the royal prerogatives. Following the passage of a bill to restore the four monarchies to serve in a cultural-only capacity, the *Kabaka* (King) of Uganda's largest ethnic group, the Baganda, was crowned in an elaborate ceremony in late July.

Ugandans of Asian descent who were expelled and had their property expropriated by the Amin regime in 1972, have been returning in increasing numbers to reclaim their property. Museveni, to revive the economy and attract foreign investment, pressed the bureaucracy to facilitate the return of the citizenship and property to the mostly ethnic Indian exiles. By the 31 October deadline for claiming the confiscated properties, most of the 3,000 claims had been processed positively.

Since 1987, when Uganda implemented an IMF suggested economic adjustment program, the country has enjoyed one of the highest economic growth rates in Africa, averaging 6 percent annually. Nevertheless, the country remains one of the poorest in the world. The spread of AIDS, affecting the most productive part of the population, has caused the number of orphans to reach 1 million. An estimated 2 million people carry the HIV virus.

Political Rights and Civil Liberties: Ugandans cannot yet change their government democratically. Citizens have been able to vote directly only for local officials, although general elections for the constituent assembly are scheduled for the spring of 1994. In local elections, voters are forced to line up publicly behind the local candidate they prefer. There are no meaningful balances on executive power, and the president enjoys a wide discretion in exercising his political power.

Sporadic violence in the north between the NRA and the remnants of Obote's United People's Army and other insurgent groups led to charges of torture and extrajudicial executions committed by all the parties. In April, the government newspaper *New Vision* reported more than 100 bodies, believed to be those of suspected rebels, were discovered in a remote mortuary. In response to pressure from foreign aid donors, the number and severity of of incidents of mistreatment by government soldiers have significantly declined.

Prison conditions for inmates remain harsh, with overcrowding, malnutrition and the spread of AIDS resulting in the highest prisoner mortality rates in the world.

The judiciary's independence is circumscribed by direct executive interference in cases involving political opponents of the regime. It remains understaffed and under-represented in remote rural areas, especially in those with the recurrence of rebel activities. Legal representation for the accused is often unavailable; in political cases the security forces often attempt to cajole lawyers to withdraw from representing their clients.

The press covers a wide range of topics, including allegations of human rights abuses by the government, and statements by members of the opposition critical of the government. Approximately twenty newspapers and newsletters are being published throughout the country, with the government-owned *New Vision* having the widest circulation. Nevertheless, the government attempts to muzzle the press through the use of sedition charges against journalists, forcing many to practice self-censorship.

Political parties are prohibited from actively engaging in the political process, and political rallies are not allowed. On 8 May, a radical fringe group within the Democratic Party called for a mass protest against the regime. In anticipation of the planned illegal rally Museveni warned the protesters to be prepared to die, ordering the police to use full force to prevent the rally. Although the rally failed to materialize because of the government's scare tactics, members of the DP's "Mobilizers Group" claimed victory through "proving that Uganda is a police state."

Nonpolitical associations and human rights groups are often subject to official harassment. Freedom of religion is respected. Rebel activities have put certain restrictions on domestic travel, but foreign travel is generally unrestricted. Workers are organized under the National Organization of Trade Unions (NOTU).

Ukraine

Polity: Elected presiden-
tial parliamentary
Economy: Statist-
transitional
Population: 51,866,000
PPP: $5,433
Life Expectancy: 71.0

Political Rights: 4*
Civil Liberties: 4*
Status: Partly Free

Ethnic Groups: Ukrainian (72.7 percent); Russian (22.1 percent); others
Ratings Change: *Ukraine's political rights rating changed from 3 to 4
and its civil liberties rating from 3 to 4 because of such factors as an
undemocratic election law and governments paralysis.

Overview:

In 1993, Ukraine, the former Soviet Union's second-largest
republic and a major agricultural-industrial center, ended its
second year of independence with near-economic collapse, a
largely ineffectual government, and nagging tensions with neighboring Russia over
territory and nuclear arms. By September, with conservatives blocking desperately
needed economic reforms, Prime Minister Leonid Kuchma resigned and parliament
passed a vote of no confidence in the entire cabinet and called for early parliamentary
and presidential elections in March and June 1994, respectively.

Ukraine was the site of the medieval Kievan Rus' realm that reached its height in
the tenth and eleventh centuries. The large eastern part of the country was dominated by
Russia for over 300 years, while the west was ruled by Poland and Austria-Hungary.
Ukraine enjoyed a brief period of independent statehood between 1917 and 1920, after
which Soviet rule was extended over most Ukrainian lands with the creation of the
Ukrainian Soviet Socialist Republic. Western Ukraine was forcibly annexed from
Poland in 1940 under the Hitler-Stalin Pact. Ukraine declared independence from a
crumbling Soviet Union in 1991, and former Communist party ideologue Leonid
Kravchuk was elected president by direct vote. The 450-seat legislature had been
elected in 1990, and although dominated by former Communists, the Democratic Bloc
of over 100 deputies proved a formidable parliamentary faction that pressured hard-
liners to adopt sovereignty.

In October 1992, after months in which the opposition criticized the government's
antipathy to free-market reforms, Kuchma replaced the unpopular Vitold Fokin as
prime minister and pledged to implement market reforms while avoiding the "shock
therapy" approach favored by some radical reformers. In November, parliament granted
Kuchma extraordinary powers to issue decrees for six months to facilitate his economic
reform program of tight budget and wage controls combined with accelerated
privatization and the elimination of corruption. Steep price increases were implemented
in December as the first step in a price liberalization and austerity program.

By January 1993 it was evident that the economy was deteriorating and the
government came under pressure from conservative elements opposed to reforms. An
outcry for an emergency session of parliament was provoked by a combination of price
rises, attempts to rein in the power of factory directors to sell off their assets, and a cap

on average wages due in March. Parliamentary Chairman Ivan Pliushch used his position to abort conservative attempts to veto cabinet decrees.

In March, the reform program came under further attack when President Kravchuk criticized the government's budget—which proposed to cut the deficit from 1992's high of 36 percent of gross national product to 7 percent of GNP—for not providing enough social welfare protection. Radical market reformers criticized the budget for not going far enough. A majority of lawmakers opposed the government's plan. First Deputy Prime Minister Ihor Yukhnovsky resigned, further jeopardizing reforms. The following month, liberal economic reformer Viktor Pynzenyk, a deputy prime minister and minister of economics, stepped down form the latter post.

In May, Prime Minister Kuchma asked parliament to extend for one year the special powers under which he had been running the economy for six months. He suggested that parliament, which had been stalling the government's reforms, should no longer have a right of veto over economic measures; that the National Bank, which in March prompted a 50 percent drop in the value of the Ukrainian currency by issuing a massive tranche of subsidized credits to state industry and agriculture, should be brought under direct government control; at that the government should take charge of the State Property Fund, the privatization body criticized for slow progress.

Ukraine was plunged into constitutional crisis in late May when President Kravchuk asked parliament to make him head of government. Parliament decided not to renew the prime minister's special powers. It did, however, restore the president's power to issue decrees, but rejected Kravchuk's bid to take over direct leadership of the Cabinet of Ministers. Kuchma tried to resign, but parliament declined his offer, leaving him in office but with little authority and presiding over a lame-duck cabinet.

The three-way power struggle coincided with Russia's demand that Ukraine pay world prices for oil and gas, a crushing blow to an economy traditionally dependent on energy subsidized by its northern neighbor. The cost of consumer goods shot up 500 percent. Moreover, parliament voted for a minimum wage hike to compensate for rising prices, as well as for an open credit line to the struggling agricultural sector hard hit by high energy costs. The moves undid months of government fiscal austerity, creating hyperinflationary pressure by increasing the money supply.

The impending crisis was accelerated by a coal miner's strike in June, which linked sharp price rises to demands that public confidence in the president and parliament be put to a national referendum. On 16 June, President Kravchuk took control of the government through a decree that put Prime Minister Kuchma in charge of an "emergency committee" that was given day-to-day control over the economy. Efim Zvyagilsky, a mine director from the Donbas mining region and mayor of Donetsk, was named to take over the post of deputy prime minister vacated by Yukhnovsky. Labor unrest in the Russified east also raised the specter of separatism, threatening Ukrainian sovereignty and territorial integrity.

With the government promising wage increases and coal-price subsidies to striking miners worth half the year's expected tax revenues, Ukraine experienced hyperinflation that rocketed to nearly 50 percent a month. Prime Minister Kuchma's calls for a state of national emergency to address the economic crisis were rejected by Kravchuk.

In September, President Kravchuk came under attack by hard-liners and reformers in parliament for agreeing with Russia's President Boris Yeltsin to hand over Ukraine's former Soviet warheads and Black Sea Fleet ships in exchange for Russian debt relief and nuclear fuel for Ukraine's power plants. On 9 September, Prime Minister Kuchma formally resigned, saying that attacks on his policies had prevented him from introducing market changes. Some two weeks later, parliament accepted the resignation and asked President Kravchuk to form a new government, and a short time later called for parliamentary and presidential elections. Kravchuk took direct control of Ukraine's government and named former mining official Zvyagilsky as acting prime minister.

By year's end, the economy was a shambles. Inflation was running at 70-80 percent a month. Output had collapsed, and public services stopped. To finance oil and gas for factories and homes, the government needed to raise $20 million a day; but its recorded exports were worth only $15 million a week. Less than 2 percent of the country's industry was privatized, and 64 percent of its workforce was still paid directly by the government. A presidential decree ordered tighter controls over key industrial sectors, dashing hopes for any reforms before the 1994 elections.

The key foreign policy dynamic remained Russian-Ukrainian relations. By year's end, the Black Sea Fleet issue had yet to be finally resolved despite the Massandra agreement. Reformers, nationalists and most hard-liners continued to view the Commonwealth of Independent States (CIS) as a vehicle for Russian great-power ambitions. Even though Ukraine joined the CIS economic union as an "associate member," statements by Russian officials that the union entailed partial loss in both economic and political sovereignty made Ukrainians uneasy. In November, parliament finally approved START-1, but added a long list of conditions and reservations. Ukraine remained wary of turning over all its nuclear weapons to Russia, particularly after Russian President Yeltsin asked the world community for special powers "as a guarantor of peace and stability on the territory of the former Soviet Union." Ukraine's security concerns led Kravchuk in February to call for a regional "zone of security and stability" that would have included Poland and other East-Central European states. The idea was abandoned after pressure from Washington and NATO.

Political Rights and Civil Liberties:

Ukrainians can change their government democratically, and the first post-Soviet parliamentary elections are scheduled for March 1994. Presidential elections have been slated for June 1994. The ongoing power struggle between the prime minister, president and the Communist-dominated parliament not only affected economic policy, but put off drafting and ratification of a new constitution. Parliament adopted a new electoral law in November based on the majority (first-past-the-post) principle combined with features carried over from the Soviet era. Democrats claimed the law was designed to hinder the growth of a multiparty system and encourage perpetuation of the status quo. The old nomenklatura is still in charge of a huge, cumbersome bureaucracy.

Citizens are free to organize in political groupings and associations, and there are scores of political parties representing the political spectrum from far-left to far-right. Non-governmental cultural, business, religious, women's and other groups are free to organize and operate.

There are numerous newspapers and magazines that offer diverse views. But the price and availability of newsprint and print facilities, as well as an inadequate state-owned distribution monopoly, have forced many smaller publications to close down. With the economy in the hands of the state, most newspapers are ultimately dependent on the state, which has led to government influence and self-censorship. State television, despite its tendentiousness in supporting the general "official line," allows representatives of various political forces to air their views. By the beginning of 1993, almost 1,000 new independent radio and television companies had been registered.

Freedom of assembly is recognized and generally respected. Although the previously outlawed Ukrainian (Uniate) Catholic and Ukrainian Autocephalous Orthodox churches are legal, conflicts between the two churches continue over property and buildings in western Ukraine. Ukraine's substantial Jewish community is organized and maintains schools and synagogues. Freedom of domestic and international travel is generally respected, although bureaucratic restrictions exist. Unlike other former Soviet republics, Ukraine has maintained relative ethnic tranquillity, but in Russian-dominant areas there is some demand for unification with Russia.

Women in Ukraine have educational opportunities, and are represented among the professional classes. Independent women's groups exist and have been raising such issues as spouse abuse and alcoholism, as well as equal pay for equal work.

Ukrainian workers are organized in several independent trade unions, though Soviet-era labor laws still on the books put some official restrictions on organizing and strikes. In June, coal miners in the Donbas region went on strike, and they were joined by other workers in parts of Ukraine.

United Arab Emirates

Polity: Federation of traditional monarchies
Economy: Capitalist-statist
Population: 2,096,000
PPP: $16,753
Life Expectancy: 70.5
Ethnic Groups: Native Arabs, Arab and other immigrant groups

Political Rights: 7*
Civil Liberties: 5
Status: Not Free

Ratings Change: *The United Arab Emirates's political rights rating changed from 6 to 7 as a result of modifications in methodology. See "Survey Methodology," page 671.

Overview:

Located on the Arabian Peninsula along the Persian Gulf, the emirates were originally known as the Trucial States because of defense agreements signed with Britain in the nineteenth century and lasting until 1968. Following several attempts at unification, the United Arab Emirates formally became a state on 2 December 1971.

The seven emirates are governed internally as traditional monarchies. According to the 1971 constitution, the monarchs collectively form a Supreme Council, which elects a president and vice-president from among its members for five-year terms. Sheikh Zayed ibn Sultan al Nuhayyan of Abu Dhabi, the largest emirate, has been president since 1971. The president appoints a prime minister and a cabinet. A forty-member consultative Federal National Council is composed of delegates appointed by the seven rulers, but holds little actual power. Separate consultative councils exist within several emirates. There are no political parties and no popular elections.

The economy is based on oil and gas production and has given citizens one of the highest per capita incomes in the world. In July the country indicted thirteen officers of the former Bank of Credit and Commerce International (BCCI), the first such action since the bank collapsed two years ago. The ruling family and government of Abu Dhabi had controlled 77 percent of BCCI. The key foreign policy issue is Iran's claims to three islands near the Strait of Hormuz. The islands had been jointly ruled for two decades by Iran and the emirate of Sharja until March 1992, when Iran inexplicably expelled the emirate's citizens from them. Since then there have been diplomatic overtures from the United Arab Emirates, although Iran has refused to negotiate. The government maintains a pro-Western foreign policy and was a staunch supporter of the U.S.-led coalition that ousted Iraq from Kuwait in 1991.

Political Rights and Civil Liberties: Citizens of the United Arab Emirates cannot change their government democratically. Political parties and political demonstrations are illegal. There are no elections, and all power is held by the seven emirates and their families. The only recourse for male citizens is to express opinions and grievances at *majlises* (gatherings) held by the rulers of each emirate.

Foreign nationals are occasionally randomly placed in detention for up to two months. The dual court system includes *Shari'a* (Islamic) courts, located in each emirate, and civil courts, most of which are responsible to the Federal Supreme Court in Abu Dhabi. However, the civil court systems in Dubai and Ras al-Khaima are separate from the federal system. Both Shari'a courts and civil courts handle criminal and civil cases, and the nature of the case determines where it is heard. Defendants receive adequate due process rights in both courts, which are generally independent of the government.

Citizens and the press exercise significant self-censorship regarding the ruling family, government policies and other sensitive issues. Television and radio stations are government-owned and air only government views. However, television stations in Abu Dhabi and Dubai broadcast Cable News Network. All imported publications are reviewed by the Ministry of Information, which bans or censors materials considered pornographic or otherwise offensive to Islam, or critical of the ruling family.

Permits are required for organized gatherings. While some emirates allow conferences where government policies are discussed, others are more restrictive. Islam is the official religion, and most citizens are Sunni Muslims. Non-Muslims can generally practice their religion but may not proselytize or distribute literature. There are Christian, Sikh and Hindu temples, and Christian teaching is allowed for Christian children. There are no restrictions on internal travel, except near defense and oil facilities. Citizens can freely travel abroad, although a woman must get her husband's permission to travel with her children.

Women can hold government positions and make up 70 percent of the enrollment at United Arab Emirates University, but in general face strong traditional pressure against entering the workforce. Some foreign nationals employed as domestic help are reportedly abused by their employers. Strikes by public sector workers are illegal and are considered a criminal offense. There is no law either for or against the right of private workers to unionize or strike, although in practice informal government pressure prevents such activity.

United Kingdom

Polity: Parliamentary
democracy
Economy: Mixed
capitalist
Population: 56,460,000
PPP: $15,804
Life Expectancy: 75.7
Ethnic Groups: English, Scottish, Welsh, Irish, and various
Asian, African, and Caribbean immigrant groups

Political Rights: 1
Civil Liberties: 2
Status: Free

Overview: **P**rime Minister John Major's government dealt with a
sluggish economy, an Iraqi arms scandal, European Union,
and the IRA (Provisional Irish Republican Army) in 1993.

The United Kingdom of Great Britain and Northern Ireland combines two formerly
separate kingdoms (England and Scotland), an ancient principality (Wales), and six
counties of the Irish province of Ulster. *(See Northern Ireland section under Related
Territories.)* Parliament has an elected House of Commons with 651 members chosen
by plurality vote from single-member districts, and a House of Lords with over 1,000
hereditary and appointed members. The Lords have a suspensive veto, under which
they can delay legislation for six months. If the House of Commons backs the bill again,
it becomes law. A section of Lords serves as a supreme court. Parliament has a
maximum term of five years.

Queen Elizabeth II, the largely ceremonial head of state, nominates for prime
minister the party leader who has the highest support in the House of Commons.

The Conservative (Tory) Party has been in power since 1979. In 1990, the Conservative parliamentary caucus unseated Prime Minister Margaret Thatcher and replaced her
with the more moderate John Major. Despite a recession, Major won his own mandate
with the 1992 election. The campaign concentrated on the economy, taxes, and healthcare.
The Conservatives won 41.9 percent of the vote and 336 seats. Led by Neil Kinnock,
Labour improved its showing from 1987, but received only 34.4 percent and 271 seats.
Paddy Ashdown's Liberal Democrats finished third with 18 percent and 20 seats. The remaining 24 seats went to regionalist and nationalist parties. Due to Labour's loss, Kinnock
resigned the party leadership and was replaced by John Smith, a moderate. Under Smith,
Labour is democratizing its internal structure and moving toward the political center.

During 1993, Major's political survival was in doubt. His party ran third in public
opinion polls, and lost parliamentary by-elections and local council seats to the Liberal
Democrats. Campaign contributions to Tories from Asil Nadir, a businessman and bail-
jumper charged with fraud, sparked a major scandal. In May, the prime minister
reshuffled his cabinet, removing Norman Lamont as Chancellor of the Exchequer, in
order to "refresh" his government. Although Major and Thatcher exchanged bitter
criticisms, Major is continuing Thatcher's privatization policies, and hopes to extend
them to British Rail.

The government was embarrassed by the trial of three executives of Matrix
Churchill, a machine tool company that was charged with illegal exports to Iraq in

1989. Several government ministers signed orders withholding government documents from the case. Without this evidence, the trial collapsed. Lord Justice Scott headed a subsequent inquiry into the case.

Major's government suffered a serious credibility problem in November 1993, because it persistently denied and then confirmed that it had held discussions with the IRA about a political settlement in Northern Ireland. By late December, the British and Irish governments issued a joint declaration of principles for a peace process in Northern Ireland. (*For more information, see Northern Ireland under Related Territories.*)

Anti-Europe Tories dogged Major throughout 1993. Major insisted that Britain opt out of the workers' rights provisions, the so-called social chapter, of the Maastricht Treaty on European union. Ironically, in February 1993, anti-Europe Tory MP's joined Labour and the Liberal Democrats in supporting the social chapter, because they all knew it would provoke a crisis for Major. In March, twenty-six Conservative MP's supported a Labour motion on electing the European Union's Committee of the Regions. An additional twenty-two Tories abstained. As a result, Major lost his first House of Commons vote 314-292. Months of parliamentary maneuvers delayed the approval of Maastricht. Major, Maastricht and the social chapter opt-out won a Commons vote in July, but only after he called a confidence motion and threatened Tory rebels with losing their seats in a general election. Northern Irish Protestant Unionist MP's sided with Major in return for unspecified political concessions.

Political Rights and Civil Liberties:

Citizens can change their government democratically. A government survey handles voter registration. Irish and Commonwealth (former British Empire) citizens resident in Britain have the right to vote. British subjects abroad have voting rights for twenty years after their emigration. Wales, Scotland, and Northern Ireland have no regional legislatures, but they elect members to the House of Commons. Many rights and liberties are well-established by custom and precedent in Britain's largely unwritten constitution. However, Britain's contact with Europeans who have codified freedoms has influenced a growing movement for a written constitution with a bill of rights.

The lack of a written constitutional right to press freedom is raising increasing concerns about government interference. Tough libel laws may have a chilling effect on some kinds of publishing and entertainment. Responding to numerous printed rumors about Major and newspaper articles and photographs detailing the private lives of the royal family, the government is proposing a statutory definition of privacy and severe penalties on media that violate it. The Official Secrets Act provides the government with a tool to attempt halting publication of intelligence activities and other official matters. The media can deal with this restraint through appeals in the courts and publication overseas. In 1993, opposition MP's supported the Right to Know Bill as a replacement for the Official Secrets Act.

The British Broadcasting Corporation (BBC) is an autonomous public body. It responds to government pressure to censor controversial items. However, the BBC offers pluralistic points of view, and airs political broadcasts of both government and opposition parties. There are also private electronic media. They are subject to government interference on stories dealing with terrorism.

Since 1989, the courts have had to overturn several convictions in cases of alleged terrorism, because appeals courts have discovered doctored or inadequate evidence that led to miscarriages of justice. In November 1993, the government proposed ending the accused's right to silence. If passed, this change would either force self-incrimination or give judges and juries the right to assume that the silent accused has something to hide. Civil liberties groups denounced this proposal. The government intends to use this provision against suspected terrorists. In 1993, the Royal Commission on Criminal Justice, which was set up to prevent miscarriages of justice, recommended limiting the right to trial by jury. The legal profession and civil rights groups condemned the proposal.

The IRA continued bombings in England in 1993, most notably at Warrington, where two children were killed in March, and in London, where one died and over forty were wounded in April.

Britain has privatized portions of the security forces such as deportation squads and prison services. In 1993, the Home Office, the justice ministry, had to investigate complaints of abuse by both public sector police and deportation contractors.

Ethnic minorities make up 5.9 percent of the population, and face bigotry and violence from native whites. According to government figures, there were about 8,000 racial attacks in Britain in 1992. On 16 September, the racist, anti-Semitic British National Party won a local council seat in London's East End. Thousands of anti-fascist protesters tried marching on a National Party bookstore in London in September, and clashed with police who blocked the marchers' approach. Opposition to immigration is high, partly because the sluggish economy has reduced job opportunities. Bernie Grant, a black Labor MP, unleashed a major controversy in 1993 when he suggested that the government pay blacks to leave the country. He claimed to be responding to letters from black constituents about rising racism and unemployment. According to a poll sponsored by the American Jewish Committee, Britons have the strongest bias against Gypsies (Rom).

There is generally freedom of movement, but the government has barred more than 100 people from traveling between Britain and Northern Ireland. In 1993, the City of London experimented with a security cordon around itself, in order to fight terrorism.

Britain has free religious expression, and the Church of England and the Church of Scotland are established. The Queen is head of the Church of England. There is some possibility for political interference in religion, because the Queen appoints Anglican bishops on the advice of the prime minister. The government finances some Christian denominational schools, but denies subsidies to Muslim academies because Islamic educators reject state curriculum guidelines that include sex education.

Trade unions and business groups are powerful and active. Union membership has fallen from 53 to 34 percent of the workforce since 1979. Under the new Trade Union Reform and Employment Rights Act, in 1994 individual workers will decide whether or not to have dues deducted automatically from their pay. The Conservatives passed this legislation, in order to weaken the unions' financial base. Both public and private sector employers have undercut collective bargaining with individual contracts.

United States of America

Polity: Federal presidential-legislative democracy
Economy: Capitalist
Population: 258,328,000
PPP: $21,449
Life Expectancy: 75.9

Political Rights: 1
Civil Liberties: 1
Status: Free

Ethnic Groups: Various white, black, Hispanic, Asian, Pacific, native American (Indians, Eskimos/Inuit, Aleuts), and others

Overview:

In 1993, Bill Clinton became the first Democratic President inaugurated since 1977. Clinton proposed ambitious social legislation and major changes in taxation and spending priorities. He presented a more activist approach to government than Ronald Reagan and George Bush, his two Republican predecessors.

In the 1992 election, Arkansas Governor Clinton defeated Bush 43 percent to 38 percent of the popular vote. His vice-presidential running mate was Senator Albert Gore. Independent candidate H. Ross Perot, a billionaire businessman, captured 19 percent, the best third-party performance since 1912. Popular discontent with the recession and with the government's domestic performance undermined Bush and caused a 20 percent turnover in Congress. Voters chose a House of Representatives and a Senate with Democratic majorities. The U.S. federal government has three branches: executive, legislative, and judicial. The constitution leaves significant powers with the state governments and the citizenry.

The electoral college is the technical device for electing the president and vice president for four-year terms. The voters in each state and Washington, D.C. vote for slates of electors who usually cast their votes in the electoral college for the candidates with the most support in their jurisdiction. Infrequently, individual electors have voted for someone other than the candidates to whom they were pledged. In 1992, the Clinton-Gore team won 370 electoral votes to 168 for Bush and Vice President Dan Quayle. Perot and his running mate, James Stockdale, won no electoral votes.

The U.S. Congress is bicameral. There are 435 members of the House of Representatives, not counting delegates from Washington, D.C. and U.S. related territories. Each state is guaranteed at least one representative. The rest are apportioned on the basis of population. Representatives have two-year terms. The 100-seat Senate has two members from each state regardless of population. Senators have six-year terms.

The Supreme Court is the ultimate arbiter of the constitutionality of government actions. On occasion, the federal courts have ruled against the decisions of the legislative and executive branches of the federal government.

A radical overhaul of the nation's healthcare system was the centerpiece of Clinton's domestic agenda in 1993. In broad outlines, the proposal would guarantee health benefits to all Americans and require employers to provide their employees health insurance. Clinton proposed that a complex mixture of government health boards and private insurance combines would work together to provide health coverage at comparatively low prices. Congress will debate and decide on the health plan in 1994.

Clinton introduced a budget that promised to cut the federal deficit, increase taxes and cut some programs while also increasing social spending. Faced with a public that remained hostile to tax increases, Congress bargained successfully with Clinton for more spending cuts. The Clinton budget passed the House of Representatives in May by a narrow margin, the deciding vote being cast by Vice President Gore as chairman of the Senate.

In July, Vincent Foster, a presidential counsel and former law partner of Hillary Clinton, the president's wife, committed suicide. The Clintons' advisors removed documents from Foster's office, triggering a major controversy about papers concerning laons to the Clintons from a Savings and Loan that subsequently failed, as did their own Whitewater real estate deal in Arkansas. The Justice Department was pressed to name an independent counsel or special prosecutor to investigate whether the Clintons, Foster and business associates had acted illegally in handling Whitewater. That case and allegations concerning Clinton's sex life raised anew doubts about his character that had surfaced during the 1992 campaign.

In foreign policy, Congress handed Clinton a major victory in November by approving the North American Free Trade Agreement (NAFTA), under which the U.S., Canada and Mexico form a continental free trade area. He had less success in Somalia where U.S. troops suffered casualties; in Haiti, where the U.S. was stymied in it efforts to restore Haitian President Aristide to power; and in Bosnia, where the European powers and the U.S. were unable to develop an effective policy. The public's relative lack of interest in foreign engagements coincided with Clinton's own inclination to concentrate on domestic issues.

Political Rights and Civil Liberties: Americans can change their government democratically. However, voter turnout is comparatively low. In most recent presidential elections, scarcely 50 percent of the voting age population has turned out. The 1992 contest brought out approximately 55 percent, a gain over recent contests. A few localities grant resident aliens the right to vote. The party system is competitive, but members of Congress seeking re-election win in overwhelming numbers. Members spend an increasing amount of their time raising campaign funds from wealthy individuals and special interest groups. This undermines the quality of representation and reduces the chances for the opposition to increase its support. Numerous states and localities have passed measures that limit terms for local, state and federal officials. Thomas Foley, Speaker of the U.S. House of Representatives, and other politicians are backing court cases that question the constitutionality of states' limiting terms of federal officials.

Racial minorities have gained increasing political representation since the 1960s. However, there are significant controversies over the sometimes strangely shaped legislative districts designed to guarantee the election of racial minorities. In 1993, the Supreme Court invalidated one of North Carolina's Congressional district boundaries, holding that the oddly configured district constituted an unjustifiable racial preference.

In presidential election years, an ideologically unrepresentative minority chooses Democratic and Republican presidential nominees through a chaotic, complicated, and debilitating series of primary elections and local party meetings called caucuses. The early caucus and primary states play a disproportionately powerful role in reducing the field of presidential contenders. Voters in states holding later contests often have little influence in deciding the nominations, even if their populations are larger or more representative of the nation as a whole. The news media and political advertising consultants have taken over most of the traditional informational and organizational functions of parties.

Several states, such as New York, have daunting petitioning hurdles that make it difficult for small parties or major party insurgents to receive a place on the ballot. In many states, the rights of initiative and referendum allow citizens to place issues on the ballot and to decide questions directly, sometimes overturning the decisions of their elected representatives. California is especially noted for a high number of referenda.

The American media are generally free and competitive. However, there are some worrisome trends towards monopolization. As literacy rates fall, most Americans get their news from television. Broadcast news is highly superficial, and is becoming increasingly difficult to distinguish from entertainment.

Public and private discussions are very open in America. However, a trend in universities and the media to ban allegedly racist and sexist language is subject to broad interpretation, and may have a chilling effect on academic and press freedom. At least two journalists lost their jobs at newspapers in 1993 after black groups demanded that publishers fire reporters for writing stories that criticized individual blacks. There has also been a growing recognition that a tendency towards left-wing conformism among university faculties results in pressure on independent thinkers to mouth "politically correct" views. In August, a federal appeals court reinstated Leonard Jeffries as Black Studies chairman at New York University. The court charged that the university had violated his free speech rights when it removed him for hateful, anti-Semitic statements.

Large corporations may have a chilling effect on free speech when they hit their activist opponents with lawsuits that are known as SLAPP suits (special litigation against public participation). Several states and localities have passed legislation outlawing hateful expression.

Since the early 1980s, the Supreme Court has made rulings that reverse the pattern of more liberal decisions of the 1960s and 1970s. Court systems at all levels of government suffer from a severe backlog of cases, delaying the course of justice in countless criminal and civil cases. The high crime rate and growing public demand to punish criminals have led to severe overcrowding in American prisons. Federal and state prisons and local jails hold about 1.1 million people, a rate of 455 prisoners per 100,000 population. In 1993, the Supreme Court upheld severe punishment for bias crimes and ruled that it cruel and unusual punishment to confine a nonsmoking prisoner in a cell with a chainsmoker.

Police brutality against minorities and unequal sentencing based on race and class undermine the foundations of the criminal justice system. Typically, black convicts receive the death penalty more than whites who have committed similar crimes.

There were major disputes in 1993 over the mismanaged, fifty-one-day government standoff with the Branch Davidians, David Koresh's religious cult in Texas. Agents of the Bureau of Alcohol, Tobacco and Firearms (ATF) raided Koresh's armed compound on 28 February. Four agents and six Davidians died. The government attempted another attack on 19 April. In the confused conflict that followed, the compound was set on fire. Koresh and dozens of followers, including children died.

On 26 February, a group of Islamist extremists allegedly detonated a bomb in New York's World Trade Center, causing deaths and hundreds of injuries. Islamists also allegedly had planned to blow up other targets including key tunnels in the New York area.

In December 1993, Energy Secretary Hazel O'Leary revealed that the U.S. government had carried out extensive human radiation tests from the 1940s to the 1970s, and that the people tested had not given consent or informed approval to the tests. The administration ordered a multidepartmental investigation.

According to a 1992 survey by the National Alliance for the Mentally Ill and the Public Citizen Health Research Group, 29 percent of American jails admittedly held mentally ill people without charge and an additional 23 percent of jails acknowledged holding the mentally ill on such minor charges as vagrancy and disorderly conduct.

The U.S. has freedom of association. Trade unions are free, but the labor movement is declining as its traditionally strong manufacturing base shrinks. The weak National Labor Relations Board and unenforced labor laws have made it increasingly difficult for workers to organize for better wages and working conditions. Due to management's increasing use of replacement workers during strikes, the strike has become a less effective weapon. In recent years, in order to remove corrupt officers and end patterns of criminal activity, the federal government has used anti-racketeering laws to place some local and national unions under federal trusteeship.

There is religious freedom and a constitutional separation of church and state. The Supreme Court has issued rulings limiting religious displays on public property and prohibiting organized prayer in the public schools. In 1993, the Court overturned a law in Hialeah, Florida, that bannned animal sacrifices for religious purposes. President Clinton signed the Religious Freedom Restoration Act which overthrew a 1990 Supreme Court ruling that had set a loose standard for laws that restrict religious practices. The new law requires the use of standards least restrictive to religion.

Most poor people in the U.S. are white, but there is a large, disproportionately black underclass that exists outside the economic mainstream. Characterized by seemingly permanent unemployment, the underclass lives to a great extent on welfare payments. Heavy drug use, high crime rates, female-headed households, and large numbers of poorly fed, badly educated, illegitimate children characterize underclass neighborhoods. The quality of life in America's older cities is in decline. In Washington, D.C., 42 percent of young black males are in the court system as defendants, prisoners, or parolees.

Despite Supreme Court rulings against school segregation, some American school districts are experimenting with deliberately all-black or all-black male schools with special black curricular emphases. These are attempts to motivate black youngsters who have poor skills and low self-esteem. There is also a black middle class, which has made significant gains in housing, education, and employment since the civil rights legislation of the 1960's.

American women have made significant gains in social and economic opportunities in recent decades, but still lag behind men in income. Affirmative action programs have increased the number of women in business and the professions, but they remain concentrated in low-paying occupations. Even rather successful women and minorities often find "glass ceilings" limit their advancement in corporations that assign them to job slots reserved for affirmative action.

Alarmed by the practice of female genital mutilation in several developing countries and among arriving immigrants, two members of Congress introduced legislation in October to outlaw it.

During the presidential campaign, candidate Clinton promised to lift the military's ban on homosexuals. In office, Clinton faced strong opposition to this promise from Congress and the military. After nine months of debate, the administration compromised, and settled for a policy that the military would no longer ask recruits about their sexual orientation, and that the services expected homosexuals in the ranks to be sexually discrete. Several cities defeated local gay rights ordinances in 1993.

Clinton continued the Bush policy of turning away many Haitian asylum-seekers, dismissing them as economic refugees from a poor country. Critics charged that the policy was racially motivated.

The U.S. government seems largely indifferent to the plight of the American Indians. One-third of the 1.8 million natives live below the poverty line. Unemployment on reservations exceeds 50 percent. However, some tribes are thriving on untaxed tobacco sales and casino gambling. Many Indian groups have cases in court against the federal government, charging violation of treaty provisions relating to control over land and resources. Hawaiian natives have a growing sovereignty movement. Some seek legal status similar to that held by tribal Indians.

Uruguay

Polity: Presidential-legislative democracy
Economy: Capitalist-statist
Population: 3,173,000
PPP: $5,916
Life Expectancy: 72.2

Political Rights: 2*
Civil Liberties: 2
Status: Free

Ethnic Groups: White, mostly Spanish and Italian, (87 percent), Meztizo (7 percent), Black and Mulatto (6 percent)
Ratings Change: *Uruguay's political rights rating changed from 1 to 2 as a result of modifications in methodology. See "Survey Methodology," page 671.

Overview: In 1993 President Luis Alberto Lacalle faced broad opposition to his policy of reforming the nation's traditionally statist economy. Military scandals grabbed headlines. A socialist led in the opinion polls for the November 1994 election.

The Republic of Uruguay was established in 1830, five years after gaining independence from Spain. The Colorado Party dominated a relatively democratic political system until it lost the 1958 election. It returned to power in 1966, the year voters approved a constitutional amendment restoring a presidential system. An economic crisis, student and worker unrest, and the activities of the Tupamaro urban guerrilla movement led to a military takeover of the government in 1973.

The nation returned to civilian rule in 1985 following negotiations between the right-wing military regime and civilian politicians joined in the so-called *Multi-partidaria*. Jose Sanguinetti of the Colorado Party won the presidential election in 1984 and took office, along with a newly elected Congress, in March 1985.

The political system is based on the 1967 constitution. The president and a bicameral Congress consisting of a ninety-nine-member Chamber of Deputies and a thirty-one-member Senate are elected for five years through a system of electoral lists that allows parties to run multiple candidates. The leading presidential candidate of the party receiving the most votes overall is the winner. In essence, party primaries are conducted simultaneously with the general election. Congressional seats are allocated on the basis of each party's share of the total vote. Municipal and regional governments are elected.

During the transition to democratic rule the military backed down from demands for a permanent say in national security matters. Its defense actions and the declaration of a state of siege are now subject to congressional approval. In turn, the Sanguinetti government in 1986 pushed through Congress an amnesty for officers accused of human rights violations.

The constitution permits a referendum on laws passed by the Congress, provided that 25 percent of the electorate sign a petition requesting it. An effort by leftist opponents of the amnesty led to the collection of enough signatures, and a plebiscite was held on 16 April 1989. Uruguayans voted, 57 percent to 43, to confirm the amnesty law.

In the November 1989 elections there were eleven presidential candidates from seven parties or coalitions. The ruling right-wing Colorado Party had three candidates. The centrist National Party, the other traditional party, had three. The socialist Broad Front coalition had one.

The leading National candidate was Luis Alberto Lacalle and the leading Colorado candidate was Jorge Batlle. The Broad Front candidate was Liber Seregni. Lacalle was elected president as the National Party obtained 37.4 percent of the vote, against 28.8 percent for the Colorados. The Broad Front obtained 8 percent, but in municipal voting it captured Montevideo, the nation's capital and home to nearly half the country's population. In the legislature the Blancos won 51 of 129 seats, the Colorados 39, the Broad Front 29. Ten remaining seats went mostly to moderate left parties.

Since taking office in 1990 Lacalle has struggled to liberalize one of Latin America's most statist economies. He has been hamstrung by broad opposition from labor unions, the legislature and factions within his own party. In December 1992 his privatization program was soundly rejected in a national referendum. By mid-1993 the country had endured nine general strikes and Lacalle's rating in opinion polls was barely above single figures.

In 1993 Lacalle also narrowly averted a showdown with the military in the wake of several scandals. One involved an intelligence official who provided protection for a former Chilean intelligence employee wanted in connection with a human rights investigation in Chile. Another involved espionage within the armed forces. The crisis was defused when, after discussions between the government, political parties and the military, the defense minister agreed to resign.

The *Guardia de Artigas* (named after a hero of Uruguayan independence), a shadowy group with links to junior military officers, issued a statement criticizing Lacalle and ranking officers for denigrating the military. In recent years the *Guardia* has claimed responsibility for a number of small bomb attacks to protest cuts in the military budget. At the same time, the National Movement of Retired Officers continued to assail the government's economic liberalization policies. The retired officers expressed solidarity with the military-backed coup by President Alberto Fujimori in Peru in 1992.

The next national election is scheduled for November 1994. Opinion polls in 1993 indicated that the frontrunner was Tabare Vasquez, the leader of the Broad Front and the mayor of Montevideo. In recent years Vasquez has alienated radical factions of the Front by taking a moderate socialist approach to governing the city and by trying to sooth the military's concern over the prospect of a leftist president. Meanwhile, as potential candidates jockeyed for position in other parties, opinion polls showed that 80 percent of the electorate did not trust politicians.

Political Rights and Civil Liberties:

Citizens are able to change their government through democratic elections. Constitutional guarantees regarding free expression, freedom of religion and the right to organize political parties, labor unions and civic organizations are generally respected. Elections and referendums are overseen by an independent electoral commission.

After the return to civilian rule in 1985, legal status was restored to all outlawed political groups. In 1993 there were a handful of violent attacks, including at least two murders, against the Tupamaro Movement and other radical left groups.

Political expression is occasionally restricted by violence associated with hotly contested political campaigns and government-labor disputes. Labor is well organized, politically powerful, and frequently uses its right to strike. Civic organizations have proliferated since the return to civilian rule, particularly women's rights groups and groups representing the small black minority.

The judiciary is relatively independent. It is headed by a Supreme Court appointed by the Congress. The system includes courts of appeal, regional courts and justices of the peace.

In recent years several police detainees alleged they had been tortured, and a number of police personnel have been prosecuted for ill-treatment or unlawful killings. New measures to prevent such practices, which did not appear to be widespread, have been implemented by the Lacalle government, but there has been a lack of effective investigation in some cases.

Human and legal rights organizations played a key role in the 1991 decision by the Inter-American Commission on Human Rights of the Organization of American States that the 1986 Amnesty Law violated key provisions of the American Convention on Human Rights.

The press is privately owned, and broadcasting is both commercial and public. There is no censorship. There are numerous daily newspapers, many associated with political parties, and a number of weeklies, including the influential *Busqueda*. However, because of the government's suspension of tax exemptions for the import of newsprint, a number of periodicals have ceased publication. Television has become an important part of the political landscape as campaigns feature debates and extensive coverage on the four channels that service the capital. In 1992 the Catholic church protested the government's refusal to grant it a radio license.

Uzbekistan

Polity: Dominant party
Economy: Statist-
transitional
Population: 21,301,000
PPP: $3,115
Life Expectancy: 69.0

Political Rights: 7*
Civil Liberties: 7*
Status: Not Free

Ethnic Groups: Uzbeks (70 percent), Russians (8 percent),
Tajiks, Ukrainians, Meshketian Turks, others
Ratings Change: *Uzbekistan's political rights and civil liberties
ratings both changed from 6 to 7 because President Karimov has
crushed all opposition forces, consolidating power in his hands.

Overview:

In 1993, the increasingly authoritarian regime of President
Islam Karimov intensified a crackdown on the opposition
amid severe economic problems.

Located along the historic Silk Road trade route, Uzbekistan, one of the world's
oldest civilized regions, was a hub of Tamerlane's vast empire. It became part of the
Russian empire in the nineteenth century. In 1920, it became part of the Turkistan
Autonomous Soviet Socialist Republic. Separated from Turkmenia in 1924, it entered
the USSR as a constituent republic in 1925. In 1929 its eastern Tajik region was
detached and accorded the status of a Soviet republic.

President Karimov, a former first secretary of the Communist party, was elected
president in December 1991 as head of the People's Democratic Party (PDP), the former
Communist party that had changed its name after the abortive hard-line coup attempt
against Soviet President Mikhail Gorbachev in August. He defeated poet Mohammed
Salih of the Erk (Freedom) Democratic Party. The largest opposition group, the nationalist
Uzbek Popular Front (Birlik), was barred from registering as a party; the Islamic Renaissance Party (IRP) was banned entirely. Uzbekistan's 500-member Supreme Council,
elected in 1990, continued to be dominated by old-line Communists.

In December 1992, a new constitution called for 1994 elections for a new, 250-
member legislature, the *Ulu Majilis*. Though nominally enshrining a multiparty system,
the document contained several provisions curtailing political rights and civil liberties.

Through much of 1993, it appeared the regime was obsessed with curtailing all
opposition and creating a cult of personality around President Karimov. In January,
Abdumannob Pulatov, a founder of Birlik, went on trial for "insulting the honor and dignity
of Uzbekistan's president." He had been abducted a month earlier while attending a human
rights conference in Kyrgyzstan. Seven Birlik members were already awaiting trial on
trumped-up criminal charges. Pulatov was ultimately sentenced to three years' imprisonment, but the sentence was automatically commuted under a 1992 amnesty still in force.

On 19 January, the Supreme Court suspended Birlik for three months for the
"intent" to organize illegal demonstrations. The two-day session barred journalists and
defense lawyers. Olim Karimov, a member of Birlik's ruling presidium, reported
kidnapped, was later revealed to be in custody.

In February, Birlik executive secretary Vassiliya Inoyatova was ordered to stand trial for "insulting the head of state." International human rights observers and journalists from Moscow and the West were not permitted to attend her trial. She was subsequently sentenced to two years, which was suspended under the amnesty. Meanwhile, Moscow human rights activists and reporters were deported after meeting with Erk leader Salih and Birlik Co-chairman Shukhrat Ismatullasev.

On 13 April authorities evicted the Erk Party from its Tashkent headquarters, telling the group it would have to move to quarters outside the city. Days earlier, Erk leader Salih had been detained overnight in connection with a book on Erk published in Turkey.

The government's wrath was also directed at rival conservative politicians perceived as threats. In June, Vice President Shukrullo Mirsaidov, former mayor of the capital, Tashkent, was tried in a closed-door courtroom on charges of "misusing state funds." On 18 June, Mirsaidov was sentenced to three years in prison but was immediately released.

A key trial was the Melli Majlis (alternative parliament) case, which began on 1 July. Allegations were brought against six defendants: journalist Babur Sharikov; Khazratkul Khudaiberdyev, chairman of Erk's Tashkent branch; Erk Executive Secretary Otanazar Oripov; Birlik presidium member Olim Karimov; Birlik member Abdilaziz Makhmudov; and journalist Salavat Umarzakov. The government charged the six with trying to seize power during May, June and July 1992. Found guilty on 6 August, the defendants were sentenced to terms ranging from three to five years; all were subsequently amnestied.

In September, U.S. Ambassador-at-Large Strobe Talbott protested the detention of four human rights activists who were to meet him in Tashkent. He told President Karimov that the U.S. would not provide economic aid if there were no democratic reforms. It was later learned that Erk Executive Secretary Oripov had been visited by his former jailer, who had encouraged him not to attend the scheduled meeting with Talbott at the U.S. Embassy. Also detained on her way to the meeting was Birlik Co-chairman Ismatullayev. The same month, the opposition informed Western sources that Uzbekistan's Supreme Court had sentenced five people associated with the Islamic opposition group Adolat (Justice) to labor-camp terms of between ten and fifteen years.

The Karimov regime continued to insist that civil war in Tajikistan, unrest in Azerbaijan, and threats of Muslim fundamentalists justified repressive policies. Fear of fundamentalists prompted Karimov to send troops to fight in the Tajik civil war to help Russia prop up the neo-Communist government in Dushanbe as a counterweight to the Islamic forces in Tajikistan and Afghanistan.

In other domestic issues, the exodus of Russians, many of them badly needed professionals, continued, partly because of Karimov's anti-Russian stance in 1992 and legislation making Uzbek the dominant language of government and education. By September, Tashkent's Russian population dropped from 60 to under 40 percent.

The government was also concerned about rampant corruption, which led to the dismissal of several governors and local officials. Clan loyalties in much of the countryside spurred nepotism and favoritism. In several instances, clan differences erupted into violence.

Uzbekistan's economic outlook remained bleak, despite the discovery of oil reserves in 1992. Although the country was the world's third-largest cotton-grower and seventh-largest gold-producer, the collapse of Soviet markets, and decades of corruption and mismanagement, left it among the former Soviet Union's poorest nations.

In July, President Karimov defended what he called the country's path to "state capitalism." He insisted that all economic levers would remain in state hands and that transition to a market system would "be gradual." The government also announced there were over 12,100 small enterprises in the capital.

In September, Russia and Uzbekistan signed an accord to unify the money system based on the Russian ruble. However, in November, Uzbekistan, rocked by inflation, decided to replace the Russian ruble with its own currency and froze most bank accounts.

Political Rights and Civil Liberties: Citizens nominally have the right to change their government democratically, but Uzbekistan is, de facto, a one-party state dominated by former Communists, who have put severe restrictions on opposition political activity.

The 1992 constitution, while enshrining pluralism and a multiparty system, contains articles which undermine democratic rights. Article 62 forbids "organized activities leading to the perpetration of particularly serious state crimes and participation in an anti-government organization." Eight people were charged under that article in the first six months of 1993; the maximum penalty is death. Others were charged under Article 191 (which ostensibly protects the honor and dignity of the president) and Article 204 (aimed at "malicious delinquency"). Other articles curtail freedom of expression, assembly and association.

The judiciary is subservient to the regime. The constitution says the president appoints all judges, but does not provide mechanisms to ensure their independence.

The government cracked down on the opposition through a series of arrests, political trials, detentions and harassment. A March decree required the country's political parties and organizations to register before 1 October. Birlik attempted to meet the requirement, despite having been warned that its application would not be accepted because the government had deprived the movement of an office and hence an address, which all organizations needed to register. When Birlik tried to apply, officials refused. Erk, reportedly did not attempt to re-register. The party's newly elected General Secretary Samad Muradov was beaten by unknown assailants in September. On 5 May, the co-chairman of Birlik was attacked and his skull fractured in three places.

Officially there is no press censorship. In practice, all print and broadcast media are subject to government censors. *Izvestia*, the Moscow newspaper, used to sell 160,000 copies in Uzbekistan. Now it is banned. Local papers sometimes appear with white spaces where stories should have been. All non-government newspapers are banned. Birlik's organ, *Nezavisimyi ezhenedelnik*, printed in Moscow and smuggled into Uzbekistan, ceased publication amid increased fears for the safety of people bringing it into the country.

Freedom of religion is nominally respected in this largely Muslim nation, but the government controls the Muslim Religious Board. Although President Karimov fears Islamic extremism, he has made concessions to Muslims. On 17 September, religious leaders and followers of a Sufi Muslim teacher and saint met in Bukhara, once one of Islam's holiest cities, on the 675th anniversary of his birth. The commemoration was organized by the government. Samarkand's 20,000 Jews can worship freely, publish a newspaper, hold Hebrew classes and sponsor cultural events; nevertheless, many have left for Israel.

Freedom of movement is also curtailed. Political activists have their exit visas or passports withheld arbitrarily. Several were kidnapped in Kyrgyzstan while attending a human rights conference.

Women are underrepresented in high-level positions throughout the society. Islamic traditions also undermine the rights of women. While trade unions are legal under a new law, their overall structure has been retained from the Soviet era.

Vanuatu

Polity: Parliamentary democracy
Economy: Capitalist-statist
Population: 166,000
PPP: $2,005
Life Expectancy: 69.5

Political Rights: 1*
Civil Liberties: 2*
Status: Free

Ethnic Groups: Indigenous Melanesian (90 percent), French, English, Vietnamese, Chinese, and other Pacific Islanders
Ratings Change: *Vanuatu's political rights rating changed from 2 to 1 and its civil liberties rating from 3 to 2 because of some improvements in rights and liberties since the departure of Lini.

Overview:

Located in the Western Pacific Ocean, this 800-mile-long archipelago of some eighty islands, formerly called the New Hebrides, was an Anglo-French condominium until receiving independence in 1980. The condominium arrangement divided the island into English and French speaking communities, creating rifts that continue today. The francophones were largely excluded from key posts in the first post-independence government, led by Prime Minister Father Walter Lini's anglophone, center-left Party of Our Land (VP). A number of islands initially faced brief secessionist movements. The independence constitution vests executive power in a prime minister chosen by and from among a unicameral parliament. The forty-six-member parliament is directly elected for a four-year term. A largely ceremonial president is elected for a five-year term by an electoral college consisting of the parliament and the presidents of the various island-based Regional Councils.

Lini's VP won subsequent elections in 1983 and 1987. After the latter vote, cabinet minister Barak Sope mounted a challenge to Lini's leadership, reflecting both personal differences and also disputes over the government's management of traditional land claims. In May 1988 an anti-government demonstration called by Sope turned into a riot. In the aftermath, Lini threw Sope out of the party and the parliament. In December 1988 President Ati George Sokomanu, Sope's uncle, called on the support of the armed forces and attempted to dissolve parliament and replace it with an interim administration headed by Sope and opposition leader Maxime Carlot. All three were arrested and charged with inciting mutiny, although in April 1989 an appeals tribunal overturned their convictions. In August 1991 the VP dumped Lini as its leader following claims that he had been running the party in an increasingly autocratic manner, and in September parliament replaced him as premier with Donald Kalpokas.

At the December 1991 elections, Carlot's francophone Union of Moderate Parties (UMP), formed in the late 1970s to delay British plans for independence, won 19 seats; the VP, 10; Lini's new National United Party (NUP), 10; Sope's new Melanesian Progressive Party, 4; the tiny Fren Melansian Party, 1; independents, 2. In late December Lini and Carlot shunted aside traditional Anglo-French animosities and joined their parties in a governing alliance. Carlot beat out Kalpokas in a parliamentary vote to become the country's first francophone prime minister. In 1992 the government began to assume a francophone slant, putting the coalition in jeopardy. A plan to increase French education and to replace more than forty senior civil servants with French-speakers drew sharp criticism.

The coalition began unraveling in August 1993 when Carlot reshuffled the cabinet and refused to give Lini a post. On 23 August Lini announced that his NUP would no longer support Carlot, although when parliament convened that day four NUP MPs, including deputy premier Sethy Regenvanu, broke ranks and sat with the government. On 11 October the UMP entered into a new coalition with the four dissident NUP MPs, giving the government a two-seat majority. Complicating the political situation is the deteriorating health of fifty-six-year-old president Frederick Timakata, who is believed to have leukemia. Timataka's term ends in February 1994, and Carlot has said he will stand by an earlier agreement and nominate Lini for the post. However, Lini's former colleagues in the NUP refuse to back him, making it unlikely that the electoral college will achieve a two-thirds majority and raising the possibility of fresh parliamentary elections.

Political Rights and Civil Liberties: Citizens of Vanuatu can change their government through free and fair elections at the national and local levels. The judiciary is independent, and citizens receive fair trials. A key problem in recent years has been government control of news coverage on the state-run Radio Vanuatu. During the Lini administration opposition groups claimed they occasionally had difficulty getting their statements broadcast. More recently, critics charge that Carlot's government has also instructed Radio Vanuatu to limit coverage of the opposition. In addition, the Carlot administration has reportedly prevented Radio Vanuatu from carrying critical stories on a number of issues, including copra price stabilization, official corruption and plans for major logging ventures. On 3 March the country's first independent newspaper, *Vanuascope*, began publishing. In addition to this bilingual weekly, other papers include the government-owned *Vanuatu Weekly* and two papers linked to political parties.

Freedom of religion is respected in practice. Citizens have full freedom of movement internally and abroad. By tradition women generally occupy a subservient position in society. There is only one female MP, and women are rarely involved in politics at any level. Domestic violence is reportedly common, although women generally refrain from bringing such cases to court. The country's five unions are grouped under the independent Vanuatu Trade Union Congress. Strikes are infrequent due to the high rate of unemployment, which gives employers substantial leverage.

Venezuela

Polity: Presidential-
legislative democracy
Economy: Capitalist-
statist
Population: 20,702,000
PPP: $6,169
Life Expectancy: 70.0
Ethnic Groups: Mestizo (69 percent), White (Spanish,
Portuguese, Italian, 20 percent), Black (9 percent), Indian
(2 percent)

Political Rights: 3
Civil Liberties: 3
Status: Partly Free

Overview: **R**afael Caldera, an aging populist backed by a hodge-podge of
small leftist and right-wing groups, capitalized on anti-
corruption sentiment to win a narrow victory in presidential
elections on 5 December 1993 and end the thirty-five-year monopoly of government by
Venezuela's traditional parties. The vote was held amid rumors of a military coup,
accusations of fraud, and fears of renewed unrest.

The Republic of Venezuela was established in 1830, nine years after gaining
independence from Spain. A history of political instability and long periods of military
rule culminated with the overthrow of the Gen. Marcos Perez Jimenez regime in 1958.
The election of President Romulo Betancourt and the promulgation of a new constitution in 1961 established a formal democracy.

The 1961 constitution created a federal system now consisting of twenty-one states
and the federal district of Caracas. The president and a bicameral Congress are elected
for five years. The Senate has at least two members from each of the states and from the
federal district. All former presidents are senators-for-life. There are currently 189 seats
in the Chamber of Deputies. State governments and municipal councils are elected.

Until 1993 politics was dominated by the social democratic Democratic Action
(AD) party and the Christian Social Party (COPEI). Carlos Andres Perez of the AD
defeated COPEI's Eduardo Fernandez for the presidency in 1988. His economic
austerity program led to violent street protests in 1989, remembered as the *caracazo*,
that left hundreds dead.

By 1991 the economy was growing but Perez's government was plagued by drug
and corruption scandals, labor strikes and violent student demonstrations. Opinion polls
reflected widespread disillusionment with the government and with the political
establishment generally. In February 1992 Perez was nearly overthrown by nationalist
military officers. Support for the rebels and their anti-corruption rhetoric was evident in
mass demonstrations and labor and student strikes. Perez's poll ratings plummeted to
single digits.

In November 1992 air force and navy units made a second attempt to oust the
government but were put down by the army. This time most Venezuelans ignored the
rebel calls for a popular insurrection. Polls indicated that despite antipathy for Perez
most people did not want military rule and the nation looked to elections in 1993.

The first months of 1993 were marked by renewed social unrest and coup rumors. In May Perez was charged with corruption and suspended from office by the Congress. The legality of the move was questionable, but legislators evidently believed that Perez had become a liability the political system could no longer afford. The Congress chose Senator Ramon J. Velasquez as interim president. In August Congress voted to remove Perez permanently, even though he had yet to face trial.

The seventy-seven-year-old Caldera was the front-runner from the outset of the 1993 campaign. A founder of COPEI and a former president (1969-74), Caldera had led the calls for Perez's resignation since 1992 and had a reputation for honesty amid Venezuela's corruption-ridden political system. He broke from COPEI, saying it too was corrupt. He sounded populist themes, blaming Perez's market reforms for declining wages and increasing poverty.

Caldera's main rival in a field of seventeen appeared to be Andres Velasquez, a labor leader and state governor from the leftist Radical Cause party. The AD nominated former Caracas mayor Claudio Fermin and COPEI nominated Oswaldo Alvarez Paz. With Caldera and Velasquez leading in the polls, rumors of a coup were rife. It was feared that the 80,000-member armed forces would not accept a victory by Velasquez, a leftist, or by Caldera, whose sixteen-party National Convergence included Communists and other leftists, as well as right-wing groups.

Caldera was first past the post on 5 December, with about 31 percent of the vote. Initial returns showed Velasquez second, but after more counting Velasquez tumbled to fourth, behind Fermin and Alvarez Paz. Caldera and Velasquez charged the electoral commission, still dominated by AD and COPEI, with fraud. All involved agreed that Caldera had won the presidency, but the suggestion was that numbers were being changed to alter the outcome of the congressional balloting at the expense of Radical Cause and the National Convergence.

Still, it appeared certain that Caldera would have to address an anemic economy, high inflation and a gaping budget deficit with a weak mandate, and a Congress fragmented among AD, COPEI and a crowd of leftist, populist and independent newcomers.

Caldera's Venezuelan critics say he is a demagogue and a closed-minded autocrat. In the days after the vote he seemed to fit the description, railing against his defeated opponents and proposing a constitutional amendment that would allow him to dissolve Congress "when it does not carry out the will of the people." As people wondered what the military might think about such talk, it seemed clear that Venezuela's damaged democracy faced more bumps in the road ahead.

Political Rights and Civil Liberties: Citizens are able to change their government through elections at the national, state, and local level. However, Venezuela's institutions have been severely eroded by decades of corruption and drug-trade penetration and badly damaged by the two coup attempts in 1992. Trust in the political system has been in steep decline since the 1980s. Voter abstention reached 40 percent in 1993, the highest since the establishment of elected government.

One small step in 1993 toward greater accountability in Congress: voters directly elected half the members of the Chamber of Deputies. The other half were still chosen by proportional voting, with party leaders selecting who would fill the seats.

Constitutional guarantees regarding freedom of religion and the right to organize political parties, civic organizations and labor unions are generally respected. However, freedom of expression and freedom of political and civic activity are threatened by official antagonism toward the media and repressive measures taken by security forces against popular protests and labor strikes. Citizen security in general is threatened by a drug-fueled crime wave and, in 1993, by bomb attacks in urban areas, some apparently aimed at political destabilization and others as part of a plot to manipulate share prices on the Caracas stock market.

In 1993 Venezuelan human rights organizations reported routine arbitrary detention, torture of suspects and dozens of extra-judicial killings by military security forces and the notoriously brutal and corrupt police. Criminal suspects, particularly in poor areas, are subject to torture. Since the 1992 coup attempts, weakened civilian governments have had little authority over the military and the police, and abuses are committed with impunity in suppressing legal protest demonstrations and social unrest.

The judicial system is headed by a Supreme Court and is nominally independent. However, it is highly politicized and undermined by the chronic corruption that permeates the entire political system. It is slow, ineffective and generally unresponsive to charges of rights abuses by police and security forces. Less than a third of the prison population totaling 30,000 has been convicted of a crime. The judiciary is further undermined by drug-related corruption, with growing evidence of bribery and intimidation of judges.

The prison system is vastly overcrowded and conditions are deplorable. At least one prisoner is murdered weekly.

A separate system of military courts has jurisdiction over members of the military accused of human rights violations and common criminal acts. Military court decisions cannot be appealed in civilian courts. The result is that the military is rarely held accountable and most citizens view it as above the law.

The press is privately owned. There are nearly a dozen independent daily newspapers. Radio and television are mostly private, supervised by an association of broadcasters under the government communications ministry. Censorship of the press and broadcasting media occurs during states of emergency. The practice of journalism is also restricted by a licensing law.

Since 1992 numerous journalists investigating corruption and rights abuses have been arrested, interrogated or otherwise threatened. In 1993 the media in general faced a pattern of intimidation. Government and military officials frequently leveled verbal attacks and the Congress passed a series of restrictive laws involving the right of reply and journalistic conduct. Two television programs were suspended for interviewing officers involved in the 1992 coup attempts. A number of radio stations and the homes of three journalists were the targets of anonymous bomb and gunfire attacks.

Labor unions are well organized but highly politicized and prone to corruption. A new labor law in 1991 reduced the work week from 48 to 44 hours and made it illegal for employers to dismiss workers without compensation. However, the law is often disregarded. Numerous trade unionists were detained during strikes broken up by security forces in 1993.

Vietnam

Polity: Communist
one-party
Economy: Statist
Population: 71,788,000
PPP: $1,100
Life Expectancy: 62.7
Ethnic Groups: Predominantly Vietnamese, with Chinese, Khmer, and other minorities

Political Rights: 7
Civil Liberties: 7
Status: Not Free

Overview: In 1993 the ruling Vietnam Communist Party (VCP) continued to move this nominally socialist country towards a hardline authoritarianism, liberalizing the economy while cracking down on dissent. In May Buddhist followers boldly staged the largest public demonstration in the country since the Vietnam War.

The French colonized Vietnam's three historic regions of Tonkin, Annam and Cochin-China between 1862 and 1884. During World War II a resistance movement led by Ho Chi Minh fought the occupying Japanese and later battled the returning French. The country won independence in 1954, and was divided between a Communist government in the north and a French-installed one in the south. Planned free elections to reunify the country were never held, and military forces and insurgent groups from the North eventually overtook the South and reunited the country in 1976 as the Socialist Republic of Vietnam.

As the nation struggled with mounting poverty, the Sixth VCP Party Congress in 1986 began a program of *doi moi* (renovation), which has decentralized economic decision-making, encouraged small-scale private enterprises and largely dismantled agricultural collectivization. At its Seventh Party Congress in June 1991 the VCP named Do Moi as new party chairman, and in August the rubber-stamp National Assembly named veteran revolutionary fighter turned economic reformer Vo Van Kiet as prime minister.

In April 1992 the National Assembly approved a new constitution that codified many economic reforms. However, it maintained the VCP's position as the "leading force of the state and society," and kept the party-controlled "People's Committees" which supervise daily life at the village level. It also scrapped the collective Council of State in favor of a single presidency, to be elected from within the National Assembly.

In July 1992, elections were held for the 395-seat National Assembly. Although the new constitution allowed anyone over twenty-one to run as an independent, only two independent candidates out of some forty hopefuls managed to be accepted, both of whom lost their races. The government disqualified many other independents for late or incorrect forms, and neighborhood and workplace units rejected the rest. In the voting numerous deputies of the older generation of revolutionary leaders were defeated by relatively young technocrats with university degrees. In late September the Assembly elected General Le Duc Anh as president, and re-elected Vo Van Kiet as prime minister.

In 1993 the government continued to face significant grassroots opposition from supporters of the independent Unified Buddhist Church (UBC). In 1981 the government had established the official Vietnam Buddhist Church and banned the UBC, placing most of its leaders in prison or under house arrest. Recent tensions began in April 1992 following the death of the Supreme Patriarch of the UBC, Thich Don Hau. At his funeral the Patriarch's successor, Thich Huyen Quang, delivered a speech boldly condemning the ban on the UBC. Since then the government has kept numerous pagodas suspected of supporting the UBC under tight surveillance.

On the anniversary of Thich's death in April 1993 police erected roadblocks around the hallowed Linh Mu Pagoda, where the body is buried, in the former imperial capital of Hue on the central coast. In May four Buddhists reportedly immolated themselves in separate incidents around the country. The most serious unrest followed the 21 May immolation by a fifty-year-old Buddhist layman, Dao Quang Ho, at the Linh Mu Pagoda. On 24 May, as the Hue security forces interrogated the pagoda's Superior Monk, Venerable Thich Tri Tuu, concerning the immolation, six monks began staging a peaceful protest in the city center. Crowds supporting the monks blocked traffic for hours and reportedly overturned several official vehicles in the most significant disturbance in the country since 1975. On 16 November a Hue court sentenced Thich Tri Tuu and three other monks to prison terms of three and four years at the end of a one-day trial.

The government's economic program received a critical boost in July when the United States announced it would no longer veto lending to Vietnam by the International Monetary Fund (IMF) and other multinational organizations. This allowed France, Japan and other countries to pay off Vietnam's $140 million arrears to the IMF and cleared the way for the country to draw $350 million in fresh loans.

On 13 September the U.S. eased the embargo slightly by announcing that American companies could compete for development projects financed by the international lending organizations. The U.S. has linked the embargo's removal to Vietnam's cooperation in resolving the cases of the 2,248 Americans still listed as "Missing in Action" in the country.

In a key extension of the economic reforms, in July the National Assembly passed a law liberalizing land-tenure rights for the country's 55 million peasant farmers. All land is still owned by the government, but farmers will be allowed to buy, sell, transfer, rent and inherit the right to use land, and will have the benefit of twenty- to fifty-year leases. Although the country is now the world's third-largest rice exporter, the rural areas are still impoverished and once-erradicated diseases have been returning.

Political Rights and Civil Liberties: Vietnamese citizens lack the democratic means to change their government. The ruling VCP and several smaller affiliated parties are the only legal parties. All policy decisions are ultimately made by the VCP's thirteen-member politburo.

In recent years the government has relaxed the monitoring of the population carried out via mass organizations and village and work units. Ordinary citizens have become more open in criticizing government corruption and inefficiency. However, questioning the one-party system or the government's commitment to socialism is illegal, and dissidents remain under surveillance and have been imprisoned for peaceful expression of their views.

Since November 1990 police have detained academic Doan Viet Hoat and other intellectuals for circulating a newsletter, *Freedom Forum,* that advocated peaceful political change. In November 1993 foreign diplomats reported that the government had subjected the country's most famous political prisoner, Nguyen Dan Que, to hard labor.

Nguyen has spent most of the past fifteen years in jail for criticizing the government and attempting to form a democracy movement. No accurate figures are available on the number of political detainees and prisoners.

Defendants lack procedural safeguards during interrogation and trials, and are at the whim of a subservient judiciary. Some 30-40 percent of the judges and lawyers lack a law degree or any professional training. Detainees and prisoners often face brutal conditions, including torture and food deprivation. The government controls all media, which reflect state views. Freedom of assembly is limited to state-approved gatherings.

The government sharply restricts religious freedom. Since 1981 the independent Buddhist church has been driven underground (See Overview above). The Paris-based Vietnam Committee on Human Rights reports that since July 1992 hundreds of monks have been harassed, intimidated and arrested. The government has similarly attempted to put Catholics under the control of the official Council of Union of Vietnamese Catholics. Since the late 1980s, the major religions have been allowed to open small seminaries, although the government still must approve all students and occasionally prevents Catholic clergy from being ordained after they finish training. However, the tiny southern-based Cao Dai religious movement, with 2.5 million followers, has not yet been allowed to open a seminary. In the central highlands, dozens of Protestant clergy of the Montagnard minority group have been detained for performing unauthorized religious services.

Citizens need permission to relocate internally, and travel abroad is restricted. The government technically does not allow strikes. However, some industrial actions occur, particularly in ventures financed by South Korean, Taiwanese and Hong Kong firms.

Western Samoa

Polity: Elected parlia-
ment and family heads
Economy: Capitalist
Population: 200,000
PPP: $1,900
Life Expectancy: 66.5

Political Rights: 2
Civil Liberties: 2
Status: Free

Ethnic Groups: Samoan (88 percent), mixed race (10 percent),
Europeans, other Pacific Islanders

Overview:
Located 1,600 miles northeast of New Zealand, the western Samoan islands became a German protectorate in 1899. New Zealand claimed the islands during World War I and administered them until granting independence in 1962. The 1960 constitution provides for a head of state who must approve all bills passed by the *Fono Aoao Faitulafono* (parliament). Malietoa Tanumafali, one of several paramount island chiefs, is head of state for life, although his successors will be elected by the fono for five-year terms. In an October 1990 referendum, 53 percent approved universal suffrage in future fono elections for all citizens over twenty-one. The Washington-based *Pacific Report* newsletter noted that, due to low participation rates, only 22.9 percent of the eligible voters actually approved the measure. Previously only the 25,000 *matai*, essentially

family heads, could vote. However, forty-five seats in the forty-seven-member fono are still restricted to the 25,000 matai, with the remaining two seats set aside for citizens of non-Samoan descent. In the same referendum, voters rejected creating an upper house both restricted to and selected by the matai. The fono sits for a five-year term.

Roughly 90 percent of the electorate turned out for the country's first direct elections on 5 April 1991, held several weeks later than planned due to the difficulty of registering approximately 80,000 newly franchised voters. The ruling Human Rights Protection Party (HRPP) now has thirty seats, the opposition Samoan National Development Party fourteen, and independents three. On 7 May the new parliament re-elected Tofilau Eti Alesana as prime minister. A new nine-member cabinet included Fiami Naomi, the country's first female cabinet minister.

In 1993 the HRPP faced opposition criticism that it was not extending piped water, electricity and other services throughout the country fast enough, and that it had passed a 10 percent Goods and Services Tax (GST). Tofilau defended the GST, to be implemented in 1994, saying that currently the country's 19,000 wage earners pay the entire tax burden with their income taxes. In addition, the HRPP suffered dissent in its ranks when three of its MPs on the Public Accounts Committee recommended budget cuts with which the prime minister disagreed. In June Tofilau expelled the three from the party amidst rumors that they were being recruited by the opposition, leaving the HRPP with a three-seat majority.

In February parliament passed two bills that critics called a threat to media freedom. The Newspapers and Printers Act requires journalists to reveal their sources in libel cases or face a $2,000 fine and three-month prison sentence. The Defamation Act forbids journalists from publishing defamatory statements made in court that refer to a person not involved in the proceedings. It also requires editors to publish an apology when a member of a group that has been criticized in print requests it.

Political Rights and Civil Liberties:

Western Samoans can change their government democratically. Although two competing parties exist, political affiliations are generally formed through individual loyalties rather than ideology.

The independent judiciary is modeled on the British system and affords defendants fair trials. However, many disputes are simply handled at the local level by the 362 village *fonos* (councils of tribal chieftains) through traditional law. The 1990 Village Fono Law affirmed this authority but gave parties in certain cases recourse to the Lands and Titles Courts, and the right of direct appeal to the Supreme Court. Fonos occasionally order harsh punishments, including burning houses and expelling people from villages. The government passed two laws in 1993 that journalists said restrict press freedom (see Overview above). There are no restrictions on freedoms of speech and association.

Although the government grants full religious freedom in this predominantly Christian country, village leaders often choose the religion of their followers. There is generally full freedom of movement internally and the right to travel abroad. Domestic abuse against women is reportedly a problem. Workers can join unions of their choice and strike. The only union formed so far, the 800-strong Yakazi Employees association, has yet to be recognized by management, the Japanese-owned Yakazi Samoa company. In January the association held a brief strike to demand recognition and higher pay. Prime Minister Tofilau repeatedly urged the employees to end the strike, since Yakazi, the country's biggest employer, accounts for 80 percent of export income.

Yemen

Polity: Dominant coalition (military-influenced)
Economy: Capitalist-statist
Population: 11,319,000
PPP: $1,562
Life Expectancy: 51.5
Ethnic Groups: Arab majority, African and Asian minorities
Ratings Change: *Yemen's political rights rating changed from 6 to 4 following multiparty elections in April. Its civil liberties rating changed from 4 to 5 as a result of modifications in methodology. See "Survey Methodology," page 671.

Political Rights: 4*
Civil Liberties: 5*
Status: Partly Free

Overview:

In April 1993, three years after the unification of the former North and South republics, Yemen held the first free elections on the Arabian Peninsula. However, the junior partner in the now-defunct transitional regime refused to participate in the new government, leading to a political stalemate that continued at year's end. Instead, the former Soviet-backed southern leaders, who had fared poorly in the election, called for a loose federal system that would effectively undermine the unification.

Located at the southern end of the Arabian Peninsula, Yemen was formed on 22 May 1990 through the merger of the conservative, northern Yemen Arab Republic (YAR), and the Marxist, southern People's Democratic Republic of Yemen (PDRY). The two countries had never before been an independent, unified entity.

In a May 1991 referendum, a reported 98.3 percent approved a new, provisional constitution, although less than half of the eligible voters actually turned out. It provided for a transitional Presidential Council, composed of a president, vice-president and three other officials who would serve until free elections were held in November 1992. Under arrangements made prior to unification, the YAR's Ali Abdallah Salih became president, and the PDRY's Ali Salim al-Biedh vice-president. The constitution also established an interim 301-seat House of Representatives led by prime minister Haydar Abu Bakr al-Attas, a former PDRY president. All but thirty-one of the MPs were from the YAR's General People's Congress (GPC) and the PDRY's Yemen Socialist Party (YSP).

Tensions immediately emerged between the coalition partners, owing to prior political differences as well as centuries-old tribal and regional animosities. Soon after unification the YSP attempted to extend its influence in the north by opening offices there to increase its membership, leading to outbreaks of political violence. In 1992 assassination attempts were made on the prime minister, the justice minister and the speaker of parliament. Some 120 YSP figures have reportedly been killed since unification. Meanwhile Sheik Hussein Abdullah al-Ahmar, who reportedly can command 50,000 armed tribesmen, demanded that the country be placed under Islamic law. Facing mounting pressures, on 5 November the joint leadership postponed parliamentary elections until 27 April 1993.

Heading into the election, voters appeared to be mainly concerned with the economy. During the Gulf War the country had refused to join the U.S.-led coalition that drove Iraq out of Kuwait. In retaliation, Saudi Arabia expelled some 850,000 Yemeni workers and, along with several other countries, cut off aid. The loss of remittances and aid have cost the country more than $2 billion per year, and sent inflation up to more than 100 percent and unemployment to 36 percent. By some accounts economic riots in several cities in December 1992 left more than 100 people dead.

On election day some 3,700 candidates and forty parties contested the 301 parliamentary seats. Although nearly three-quarters of these candidates professed to be independent, many were allegedly secretly backed by the two ruling parties. Some 80 percent of the electorate participated. Results gave the GPC 121 seats; Sheik Hussein's Islah, 62; YSP, 56; minor parties, 12; independents, 47; with three seats vacant. On 10 May the GPC and YSP signed a charter renewing their alliance and forming a fresh governing coalition.

In summer Biedh, clearly dismayed by the YSP's relatively poor showing, proposed a "federal system" that would essentially grant the north and south areas autonomy rather than maintain the unification. He also called on the two armies to be fully merged, apparently seeing a unified army as a safeguard against northern hegemony. On 19 August Biedh, who had retained his vice presidential post in the new government, announced he would remain in Aden rather than travel to the capital, Sanaa, until his demands were met. At year's end Biedh remained in Aden, continuing the political impasse and preventing parliament from drafting a permanent constitution.

Political Rights and Civil Liberties:

Citizens of Yemen changed their government in April 1993 in elections in which the ruling parties had significant advantages. An International Republican Institute (IRI) monitoring team called the election generally fair but noted several factors compromising the impartiality of the vote. For example, in a population 80 percent illiterate, the government required voters to write their choice on a ballot. Illiterate voters therefore needed assistance from a literate person, removing the chance for secret balloting. Some 23,000 election commission workers and 50,000 military and security personnel were by law not permitted to vote, disenfranchising a significant portion of the population. The IRI also noted that prior to the election many voters realized that the two parties had basically agreed to maintain their coalition afterwards, and that this "private negotiation" had "significantly reduced the electorate's confidence that the vote would be meaningful." Also, media coverage prior to the vote strongly favored the ruling parties.

Tribal leaders in the north and east continue to wield considerable local influence. The Ministry of the Interior's security force has broad de facto powers to act against suspected security threats, and frequently violates constitutional guarantees by detaining individuals for questioning without charge beyond the allowed twenty-four-hour period, abusing detainees, and searching homes and offices. Prison conditions are generally abysmal. According to the U.S. State Department, by the end of 1992 there were up to 4,000 persons held in prison without documented reason. The government is reportedly investigating these cases.

The judicial systems of the two former countries are slowly being merged. As a whole, the system is subject to interference by the government and other connected interests, and procedural safeguards are not adequate.

Both citizens and the press freely criticize the government on most issues, but reportedly practice self-censorship on certain sensitive topics, including regional foreign relations. There are more than 100 newspapers, many of them independent or linked to political groups. However, most are dependent on the government for subsidies. The government runs the country's radio and television stations, and broadcasts are biased towards the government.

Citizens regularly hold public political protests. Islam is the state religion, and other groups face some restrictions. In July Israeli officials said 246 Jews had been allowed to emigrate since August 1992, although numerous others wishing to emigrate have encountered difficulty in obtaining passports. The 1,000 Jews who remain in the country, located mainly in two rural northern areas, lack synagogues but worship in private homes and can operate schools. The government occasionally denies foreign Jewish groups access to these communities. Citizens generally travel freely internally. With the exception of the Jewish community as noted above, most citizens can travel abroad at will, although women are occasionally arbitrarily asked to prove that male relatives do not object to their departure.

Citizens with a non-Yemeni parent (*muwalladin*), as well as the tiny Akhdam minority, face discrimination in employment opportunities. By tradition women hold a subservient role in society. The family law allows for polygamy, allows a husband to divorce his wife without cause, and grants the husband the house and children in divorce cases. Clitorectomy is practiced in some areas, and domestic violence is reportedly common. The labor codes of the two former countries remain in effect pending a new code. Unions remain heavily influenced by the government, although strikes do occur.

Yugoslavia (Serbia and Montenegro)

Polity: Dominant party (military-influenced)
Political Rights: 6
Civil Liberties: 6*
Economy: Mixed statist
Status: Not Free
Population: 5,385,000
PPP: $5,095
Life Expectancy: 72.6
Ethnic Groups: Serbs (80 percent), Montenegrin (7 percent), Muslim Slavs (Sanjak, 4 percent) Gypsies, Albanians, others
Ratings Change: *Yugoslavia's civil liberties rating changed from 5 to 6 because of increased restrictions on the opposition.

Overview:
In 1993, amid an economy utterly devastated by international sanctions, corruption, and mismanagement, Serbian President Slobodan Milosevic cracked down on the opposition, won re-election and remained the post powerful political figure in rump-Yugoslavia, established in 1992 by Serbia and Montenegro.

The Federal Republic of Yugoslavia (FRY) was a Serb-prompted creation to maintain the illusion of a federated state after the secession of Slovenia, Croatia, Macedonia and Bosnia-Herzegovina left Serbia—with its putatively autonomous provinces of Kosovo and Vojvodina (*see reports in Related Territories section*)—and tiny, impoverished Montenegro as the only republics that had not seceded from Yugoslavia in 1991-92. Under a constitution accepted by the Serbian and Montenegrin republican assemblies, the FRY was declared as a "sovereign federal state based on the principle of equality of its citizens and member republics." The United States, United Nations and most of the international community do not recognize the self-styled state. The new entity faced diplomatic isolation and international economic sanctions because of Serbian aggression in Croatia and in Bosnia-Herzegovina, where indigenous nationalist Serb militias, with backing from the Serb-dominant remnants of the Yugoslav People's Army, launched wars against legitimately elected governments.

FRY's bicameral Federal Assembly (parliament) consists of the 42-member Chamber of Republics (divided evenly between Serbia and Montenegro) and the 138-seat Chamber of Citizens. In December 1992 elections for the Chamber of Republics, Milosevic's Socialist Party of Serbia (SPS) won 47 seats; the ultra-nationalist Serbian Radical Party (SRS), led by the suspected war criminal and paramilitary commander Vojislav Seselj's, got 34; and the DEPOS opposition coalition, 20. Milosevic retained the Serbian presidency by defeating U.S. businessman Milan Panic in a fraud-marred vote. In Montenegro, President Momir Bulatovic, first elected in 1990, defeated Branko Kostic, a Milosevic ally, in a January 1993 run-off.

As 1993 opened, Milosevic moved to consolidate his hold on Serbia and, by extension, the weak, rubber-stamp FRY. In January and February Milosevic's government purged several leading intellectuals in Belgrade, among them the rector of Belgrade University and the directors of the Modern Art Museum, the National Theater and Belgrade's biggest hospital. Nearly 1,200 employees of Serbian and state television and radio, including more than sixty journalists and the symphony orchestra were put on "compulsory holidays," and summarily barred from going to work by security guards. About 200 largely inexperienced but politically loyal journalists were brought in to replace those furloughed.

Milosevic also introduced direct state control of public enterprises at the expense of "self-management," a forty-year-old Yugoslav system that gave workers control of their companies.

International sanctions imposed in May 1992 led to the formation of criminal organizations closely linked with government officials and banks, a gangster-political class that profited while most citizens began to feel the ramifications of the embargo. By March, inflation was calculated to be running at 84 million percent a year (or 4 percent a day), and one in seven children in Serbia were reportedly malnourished. In an attempt to distance himself from illegal dealings, Milosevic launched an anti-corruption campaign that netted scores of former officials as well as the president's political enemies. Several bankers fled the country as financial institutions that once offered fabulous interest rates on dinar and hard currency accounts collapsed.

In late March, international mediator Lord Owen called for tougher sanctions against the FRY. On 12 March, the U.S. took steps to tighten the naval blockade on the FRY by adding twenty-five shipping companies to its list of groups that U.S. citizens were barred from doing business with. In April, in an attempt to pressure Milosevic to persuade Bosnia's Serbs to make peace, the U.N. Security Council approved a draconian economic blockade that threatened to further isolate Serbia by banning shipments of most goods by land and water to and from the FRY, blocking shipping through FRY on the Danube River, freezing FRY government and private funds abroad, and calling on U.N. member countries to impound Yugoslav ships, trains and aircraft in their territory if they violated sanctions.

Three days later, with the prospects of Western military intervention increasing, Serbia's parliament endorsed the so-called Vance-Owen international peace plan for Bosnia. Despite its backing by Milosevic, FRY President Dobrica Cosic and Montenegro's President Bulatovic, it was rejected by Bosnia's Serbs. By early May, Milosevic was warning defiant Bosnian Serb's that they risked having humanitarian and other supplies cut-off by Belgrade if they failed to sign the peace plan, a position which enraged hard-line nationalists in the Serbian Radical Party but was met with skepticism by the world community.

On 12 May, in a move intended to override Bosnian Serb leaders' rejection of the international peace plan, Milosevic demanded that the leaders cancel a proposed referendum on the plan and called for an extraordinary gathering of legislators from all Serb-populated regions in the Balkans. However, the meeting was boycotted by Serbs from both Bosnia and Croatia. Some 139 members of the SRS also stalked out in protest, emphasizing a growing rift between Milosevic and his erstwhile ally, SRS leader Seselj. On 22 May, Milosevic tacitly withdrew an offer to allow international monitors along the border with Bosnia because, sources said, he no longer feared American military intervention.

At the end of May, Milosevic announced a probe of a top general to placate hard-liners angered by his decision to back the U.N. peace plan. Col. Gen. Zivota Panic, the Yugoslav Army chief of staff, was charged with alleged corruption and nepotism in an unprecedented scandal that rocked the political and military hierarchies of the Serbia-Montenegro union. In an effort discredit Milosevic and FRY President Cosic, Seselj was the first to accuse Gen. Panic, who backed the peace plan, of corruption. He did not, however, withdraw SRS support of minority SPS governments at the Yugoslav federal and Serbian republican levels.

In early June, political turbulence in Belgrade boiled over into violence as police fired tear gas at demonstrators trying to storm the federal Yugoslav parliament. The clash followed the ousting of FRY President Cosic through a no-confidence motion brought by radical Serbian deputies backed by the ruling Serbian Socialists. Up to 4,000 demonstrators were brought on to the streets by Vuk Draskovic, the charismatic leader of the opposition Serbian Renewal Movement (SPO). Cosic was ostensibly voted out after being accused of holding secret talks with Yugoslav federal army leaders on the issue of the country's constitutional future. Seselj claimed that Cosic had held clandestine talks with Croatia on the Serb-held region of Krajina and was willing to divide up the Serb province of Kosovo—where 90 percent of people are ethnic Albanians—with Albania. The vote itself violated the constitution because it should have been taken only after charges against Cosic were upheld by the Constitutional Court. Milosevic apparently sacrificed Cosic to hard-liners to ensure his government's survival, based on SRS support. Cosic's ouster was opposed by Montenegrin deputies from all parties, raising the possibility of Montenegrin independent-mindedness in light of the war and an economy ravaged by sanctions.

Milosevic came under blistering attack over the arrest and beating of more than twenty opposition figures and journalists in Belgrade as police cracked down on a 1 June demonstration. Draskovic was in serious condition with a fractured jaw and other injuries after he was beaten by police in his party offices. Serbian authorities moved against the opposition by seeking a ban on the SPO on the grounds that it "violently instigated the overthrow of the constitutional order." On 19 June, riot police blocked an attempt by 2,000 anti-government demonstrators to march on Belgrade's central prison, where Draskovic was held after being moved from a hospital. Four days later, Zorin Lilac, a former Communist official and Milosevic ally, was elected FRY president. On 10 July, Milosevic ordered the release of Draskovic, who had been on a week-long hunger strike.

With the democratic opposition all but crushed, Milosevic moved to undermine his last major obstacle to absolute authority, SRS leader Seselj. On 20 October, after weeks of an anti-Seselj campaign on state-run television condemning him as a fascist and war criminal, Milosevic dissolved the 250-member Serbian parliament, cutting short a ten-day debate during which his embattled government came under scathing criticism for the collapse economy. The SPS minority government, with 102 seats, was facing a confidence vote in parliament introduced by the Radical Party, which controlled seventy-three seats; elections were set for 19 December, almost a year to the day after the 1992 vote.

On 5 November, Serbian authorities arrested eighteen leaders of Seselj's Chetnik paramilitary forces, charging them with murder, rape, kidnapping and illegal arms possession. The arrests were all on charges related to acts committed in Serbia against ethnic Croats, Muslims and Hungarians in Vojvodina.

The power struggle in Serbia emboldened secessionist sentiment in Montenegro, hurt much more than Serbia by sanctions. On 31 October, thousands gathered in the former Montenegrin capital, Cetinje, for what was billed as a formal break from the Serbian Orthodox Church and the re-establishment of an independent Montenegrin Orthodox Church. The organizers were supporters of the opposition Liberal Alliance of Montenegro, the chef advocate of separatism. Yet, many Montenegrins feared that Serbia would never let them separate because Montenegro is Serbia's only outlet to the Adriatic Sea and the last base open to the Yugoslav Navy.

Although the SPS did not win a majority in the 19 December elections, Milosevic's position was strengthened. The SPS won 123 seats, 21 more than they had, but three short of a majority. Seselj and the SRS were the big losers, with the party's strength dropping from 73 to 39 seats. Another loser was Zeljko Raznatovic, an accused bank robber and militia leader from Kosovo, known by the nome de guerre Arkan. Draskovic's SPO held 46 seats, down from 50.

The year ended with Milosevic dominating an increasingly desperate and impoverished people. Tens of thousands, among them young people and professionals, emigrated or fled to the West. Official inflation was over 100,000 percent a month in December. The 50- billion dinar note was worth $2.50. The average monthly wage dropped to $15 a month. Millions were unemployed.

Political Rights and Civil Liberties:

Citizens of the rump-Yugoslavia cannot freely elect their representatives; both the president and prime minister are appointed by a parliament dominated by former Communists and nationalists loyal to Serbian President Slobodan Milosevic. FRY President Cosic was ousted and replaced by Zorin Lilac with no direct input from voters.

Decembers elections to the Serbian republican parliament were marred by irregularities. Montenegrins did not go to the polls. The federal judiciary, headed by a Constitutional Court and a Federal Court, is subordinate to Serbia. Parliament violated the constitution and did not even bother to consult the Constitutional Court in ousting President Cosic.

Freedoms of expression and assembly are curtailed. In 1993, Milosevic strengthened the Serbian police force by 20,000 men, equipping special units with armored vehicles, helicopter and rocket launchers. They are better equipped, trained and paid than the Yugoslav army. In June, they brutally suppressed anti-government demonstrations led by Vuk Draskovic of the Serbian Renewal Party. Opposition political parties exist, but they are fragmented and subject to repression and intimidation.

The state-run radio and television are in the hands of the Milosevic government and regularly deny opposition air time. Over 1,000 employees were dismissed and replaced by Milosevic loyalists. With independent newspapers prohibitively expensive or unavailable outside Belgrade, television is the main source of news and commentary for citizens in Serbia. Independent TV station Studio-B offers divergent views, but its signal is limited to Belgrade, as is independent radio station B-92, whose employees were subjected to death threats.

Economic privation, international sanctions and war in neighboring Croatia and Bosnia have limited freedom of movement.

Ethnic Muslims in the Sandzak region between Serbia and Montenegro have faced repression and persecution. Kosovo's Albanians and Vojvodina's Hungarians face oppression. The Yugoslav Army carried out internal purges based on ethnicity, with Slovenes, Croats and Muslims who remained in Serbia facing military courts. Serbs and Montenegrins are overwhelmingly Eastern Orthodox and are free to practice their religion. As for Catholics and Muslims, political realities have made public worship virtually impossible for them in many parts of Serbia.

Federal and republican law prohibits discrimination against women, but women have had limited access to high-level positions in government and the business sector. Spouse abuse carries the same penalties as assault, but charges are seldom brought.

In April, the pro-democracy Nezavisnost trade union federation proclaimed its support of the Vance-Owen Bosnian peace plan and called for the resignation of the government. Earlier, some 5,000 transport workers went on strike in Belgrade demanding better pay.

Zaire

Polity: Presidential-mili-
tary and interim legislative
Economy: Capitalist-
statist
Population: 41,166,000
PPP: $367
Life Expectancy: 53.0
Ethnic Groups: Some 200, including Azande, Bemba,
Kasai, Kongo, Luba, Lunda, and Pygmy

Political Rights: 7*
Civil Liberties: 6*
Status: Not Free

Ratings Change: *Zaire's political rights rating changed from 6 to 7 and its civil
liberties rating from 5 to 6 because of increased political and military chaos.

Overview: In 1993, Zaire continued a descent into a political and
economic chaos, as its long-time ruler President Mobutu Sese
Seko resisted relinquishing his power. Two parallel govern-
ments claiming legitimacy, ethnic and armed forces violence, and international isolation
raised fears of the country's intermittent collapse.

Zaire, known as Congo until 1972, gained independence from Belgium in 1960.
Since 1965, Mobutu has ruled the country through his Popular Movement of the
Revolution (MPR). His rule, characterized as a kleptocracy, or rule by theft, caused this
potentially rich country to become one of the poorest in the world.

In 1990, facing growing popular pressures for reforms, Mobutu legalized political parties with the ostensible aim of eventually introducing a pluralist democratic system. However, he refused to cede any significant power and continuously sabotaged the opposition.

In July 1991, approximately 200 opposition groups formed the Sacred Union of
Forces for Change. The backbone of the Sacred Union was the Union for Democracy
and Social Progress (UDPS) with Etienne Tshisekedi at its lead.

Since 1991, the MPR and opposition forces participated in a National Conference
to work out a new constitutional order. Following Mobutu's decision to suspend the
Conference several times and prevent it from reaching any decisions, the Conference
declared its decisions to be "sovereign," with the aim of passing constitutionally binding
measures. It nominated Tshisekedi as the prime minister.

In December 1992 the National Conference concluded its work, setting up a
constitution to be confirmed in a referendum scheduled for April 1993. The constitution
restricted the powers of the president, removing from his power control over the army
and the security services, as well as the appointment of the prime minister and individual cabinet members. The Conference established a High Council of the Republic
(HCR) to act as an interim legislature, electing Catholic Archbishop Laurent Monsengo
as its speaker, and confirming Tshisekedi as the prime minister. Mobutu, however,
refused to recognize the Tshisekedi cabinet.

On 15 January 1993, the HCR accused Mobutu of high treason by "having blocked
the functioning of the country at every level." A week later the rift between Mobutu and
the cabinet escalated, following the issuance of new 5 million *zaire* banknotes to pay
the salary arrears of army troops. When the cabinet declared the new banknotes to be

illegal, merchants refused to accept them, causing the soldiers to go berserk, beating civilians and looting private property. On 28 January, Mobutu dispatched the elite Special Presidential Division (DSP) to quell the riots. The DSP's indiscriminate use of firepower killed an estimated 1,000 people, military and civilian, including the French ambassador.

On 5 February, Mobutu dismissed the Tshisekedi cabinet, after his foreign minister, Pierre Lumbi, asked for foreign intervention to salvage the process of reform. Four days later the HCR rejected Mobutu's decision. On 24 February, the DSP surrounded the People's Palace while the HCR was in session. The military refused to lift the siege unless the legislature backed down on its refusal to legalize the 5 million Zaire notes. After a three-day standoff the HCR agreed to set up a committee "to investigate the matter." Pressed by foreign powers the military agreed to end the siege.

In March, Mobutu invited political parties for a "political conclave" to nominate a new cabinet. The Sacred Union decided to boycott the meeting, which turned out to be openly pro-Mobutu. On 17 March, the meeting elected Faustin Birindwa, a former Tshisekedi ally and one of the founders of the UDPS, as the prime minister. He had been expelled from the party, however, on 1 March for his conciliatory stance towards Mobutu. The conclave "downgraded" the HCR to just one of the political organs in the supposed transition to democracy. On 29 March, Mobutu reconvened the suspended MPR-only National Assembly, which confirmed Birindwa as the prime minister. The HCR, meanwhile, confirmed its support for the Tshisekedi cabinet.

Following months of impasse, the two rival governments began negotiations on 11 September. On 1 October, the two sides announced a "breakthrough" leading to the formation of a single legislature and parliament. The agreement stipulated a new transitional constitution and parliament, composed of members of the HCR and the MPR National Assembly. The agreement failed to resolve the issue of the prime ministership, however. Tshisekedi, supported by the Sacred Union insisted on his continuation in office, and the agreement failed to be ratified.

With annual inflation around 7,000 percent, Mobutu introduced yet another currency "reform" by issuing new banknotes and ordering the withdrawal of old ones in mid-October. The HCR and the Tshisekedi government immediately declared the action illegal, and ordered the population not to conduct transactions in the new bills. In late November, the DSP rampaged through the Kasai province, killing three Catholic priests and looting the Church's property, in response to its call to boycott the new currency. As a result of the boycott, the currency's value quickly plummeted, with black market exchange rates reaching 110 million new zaires to the U.S. dollar.

In addition to a political and economic crisis, two of Zaire's eastern provinces experienced an escalation of interethnic violence. In the mineral rich Shaba (Katanga) province, the regional authorities began to stir native Shaban resentments against the more affluent Kasaian "immigrants" (many of whom had Shaban roots dating for several generations) in late 1991. The provincial authorities, aided by the press, accused the Kasaians of spearheading the economic crisis facing the province. The campaign to promote "regional purity" turned increasingly violent in late 1992, with mobs and paramilitary troops attacking Kasaian businesses and homes. In 1993, the continuation of the violence forced several hundred thousand Kasaians to flee the province.

In the northern Kivu province, the ethnic violence pitted the Bahunde against the Banyarwanda, the two largest ethnic groups. The Bahunde and other ethnic groups are considered as citizens of Zaire, while the Banyarwanda (Hutu and Tutsi) became stateless following Mobutu's 1981 decision to grant citizenship only to those with ancestral links to the country dating back to the pre-colonial period. In March 1993, tensions erupted into bloody massacres when armed groups attacked Banyarwanda-attended markets and churches, killing thousands within a few days. The Catholic Church accused the local authorities of fostering the violence and concealing its consequences.

Political Rights and Civil Liberties: Citizens of Zaire cannot change their government democratically. Although President Mobutu legalized political parties in 1990, he still wields absolute power. Political opposition is fragmented, and Mobutu uses the disagreements within the opposition to maintain his power. Some of the hundreds of political parties which sprang up since 1990 are allegedly financed by Mobutu to further undermine the effectiveness of the opposition.

Mobutu firmly controls the judiciary. Arbitrary arrest and detention are commonplace, and the security forces regularly beat, torture and mistreat detainees. The judiciary repeatedly refuses to investigate claims of torture and mistreatment. Violence by soldiers and security forces against unarmed civilians escalated during 1993. The failure of superiors to punish military culprits involved in beating, raping and looting civilians and their property encouraged the violence. In January 1993, an estimated 1,000 people were killed, both civilian and soldiers, when the DSP opened fire indiscriminately to quell the riots. On 22 February, DSP members killed fifty-two civilians, including children, in revenge for the killing of one DSP member by a group of civilians. On 4 July, four adults and an eleven-year-old boy were stabbed to death by security forces who were trying to prevent an opposition rally from being held.

As a result of ethnic violence in the Shaba and Kivu provinces, partially instigated and condoned by the regime, the number of internally displaced people reached 500,000. Thousands of others were killed and injured. Two days of anti-Banyarwanda rioting on 20-21 March, killed an estimated 1,000 people.

Since 1990, dozens of independent newspapers and periodicals began to be published. Following an initial period of relative liberalization, the Mobutu regime returned to its repressive measures in 1992. In November of that year, armed arsonists believed to be members of the security forces, set on fire the *Terra Nova* printing press, which was used mainly to print opposition publications. In March and April 1993, the security forces attacked newspaper vendors, confiscating and destroying independent publications. In April, Kenge Mukengeshayi, the editor-in-chief of the *Le Phare* newspaper was arrested on the grounds of "spreading false rumors," following publication of an article accusing Mobutu of trying to assassinate Prime Minister Tshisekedi. On 28 June, Mukengeshayi was released without ever being charged. In a similar case, Kalala Mbenga Kalao, an editor of the *Tempete des Tropiques* newspaper was arrested in August after publishing the statistics containing the ethnic composition of officers in the armed forces. The statistics showed that most of the officers belonged to Mobutu's Ngbandi ethnic group.

The regime does not recognize the right to assembly and peaceful protest. Demonstrators risk being arrested, beaten and even killed by members of the security or armed forces. Nonpolitical associations, including religious organizations, need permission to operate, and their activities are closely monitored by government officials. The major trade union confederation remains the National Union of Zairian Workers (UNTZA), formerly the only legal labor organization affiliated with the MPR. Since 1990, however, the UNTZA disaffiliated itself from the MPR, conducting elections for union leadership posts deemed fair by outside observers. Other nascent unions consolidate their membership along occupational lines.

Zambia

Polity: Presidential parliamentary democracy
Economy: Mixed statist
Population: 8,385,000
PPP: $744
Life Expectancy: 54.4
Ethnic Groups: Bemba, Lozi, Lunda, Ngoni, other

Political Rights: 3*
Civil Liberties: 4*
Status: Partly Free

Ratings Change: *Zambia's political rights rating changed from 2 to 3 and its civil liberties rating from 3 to 4 because the president declared a state of emergency and cracked down on the opposition.

Overview: In 1993, following the discovery of a plan to destabilize the country, the freely elected Zambian President Frederick Chiluba declared a three-month state of emergency. Within the rank of his own Movement for Multiparty Democracy (MMD), Chiluba faced a challenge as a group of MMD members left the group and formed an opposition party.

Zambia became independent from Britain in 1964. From 1972 to 1990 the only legal party was the ruling United National Independence Party (UNIP). President Kenneth Kaunda had ruled the country uninterruptedly since independence until October 1991, when he lost overwhelmingly to the former trade union leader and MMD standard-bearer Chiluba. In a parallel parliamentary election, the MMD won 125 seats in the 150 seat parliament. In voting for Chiluba and the MMD, the citizens showed their dissatisfaction with the country's economic deterioration and Kaunda's authoritarian style of government.

Zambia, formerly one of Africa's most prosperous territories had degenerated by the 1990s to one of the continent's poorest countries. Administrative and economic centralization, socialist experimentation, widespread corruption, and the fall of copper prices in the 1970s led to a declining standard of living, high inflation and the accompanying decline of the value of Zambia's currency, the Kwacha.

Following Chiluba's election, the government implemented an IMF recommended Structural Adjustment Program (SAP), allowing the government to obtain additional loans and raising the possibility of a rescheduling or forgiveness of Zambia's huge $7 billion debt. The Program consisted of slashing public expenditures on the bureaucracy and social welfare, eliminating subsidies and eventually privatizing most of the state-owned enterprises. On 12 February 1993, the privatization process accelerated with the sell-off of thirty-two companies. In April, the government dissolved the three main holding companies, controlling about 80 percent of Zambia's formal economy. The increasing unemployment and high prices led to resistance from Chiluba's former backbone of support, the Zambia Congress of Trade Unions (ZCTU).

Despite Chiluba's pressure for reforms, the cabinet continued to be plagued by divisiveness and allegations of corruption among individual ministers. Chiluba himself was criticized for his high-handedness, which he parried criticizing the lax discipline within the MMD.

In the wake of a report in the *Times* of Zambia alleging a plot, coded "zero option," by UNIP members to destabilize the country, Chiluba reintroduced the state of emergency which had been lifted with his assuming power in 1991. The article alleged that UNIP members received funding from the governments of Iran and Iraq to destabilize the country through orchestrated strikes and riots, allowing UNIP to regain power in the country. The credibility of the allegations was boosted when UNIP chairman, Kebby Musikotwane, confirmed the existence of the plot. Musikotwane stated that he received the plan from radical elements within the party but subsequently the party had rejected it, and Musikotwane turned the documents over to the government.

With the announcement of the state of emergency, the government detained twenty-six UNIP members, including three of Kenneth Kaunda's sons. On 11 March the government broke off diplomatic relations with Iran and Iraq, and a day later, the parliament overwhelmingly extended the state of emergency for another three months, as required by Article 30 of the constitution.

By 20 May the government released all but seven of the original detainees, and on 25 May Chiluba declared the state of emergency to be lifted, stating that "it has served its purpose." On the same day the remaining detainees were released and rearrested and charged with the plot. The government failed to provide enough evidence for their participation in the "Zero Option Plan," and eventually all were released.

The governing party faced additional problems in August, as fifteen parliament members resigned from its membership, forming an opposition National Party. Among the defectors were four former cabinet members whom Chiluba had dismissed in a cabinet reshuffle in April. The defectors made repeated allegations about corruption, drug trafficking and tribalism among the cabinet members. They also accused Chiluba of perpetuating the Kaunda-era constitution, giving wide powers to the president at the expense of parliament. Following the defections, Chiluba appointed a constitutional commission, to prepare amendments with the view to make it more democratic. This did not prevent another MMD member, Edward Chamwana, from leaving MMD and join the National Party on 8 November. Chamwana, one of MMD founders, was one of the leading opposition figures in the struggle against the Kaunda regime. He accused the party he helped to create of being increasingly intolerant in considering different points of view.

Political Rights and Civil Liberties: Zambians do have the right to change their government democratically. However, although the parliamentary sessions are marked by vigorous debate, critics within the ruling party and in the opposition allege a constitutional imbalance in favor of the executive over the legislature. The re-introduction of the state of emergency in March 1993, raised the fears of a return to an authoritarian style of government.

Following the declaration of the state of emergency, the security forces arrested twenty-six opposition politicians, accusing them of attempting to overthrow the government. The government failed to file formal charges against the accused, however, making itself vulnerable to charges by the opposition UNIP members and the press that the arrests were not based on substantial proofs, but rather on newspaper reports. With the lifting of the state of emergency in May, all the detainees were released without formal charges having been filed against them.

The court system acts independently from other branches of government. Fair trials are often obstructed, however, by understaffed courts and lack of legal representation for poor defendants. The police often use excessive force in apprehending suspects, and convicts face miserable prison conditions.

Freedom of speech and press is generally respected, although the government may still use remaining legislation to stifle criticism. For example, the president retains the right to ban any publication, and all working journalists are required to register through the government information department rather than through their own publications. In a circular published at the end of 1992, the government forbade all state employees from publishing or participating in a political debate, even in a private capacity, without prior permission. During the state of emergency, however, the press continued to criticize the government, and public protests by opposition were allowed.

There have long been many autonomous cultural, professional and civic associations. Freedom of religion is respected, although members of the Chiluba government emphasized that Zambia is a "Christian" nation. In May, the government refused to grant permission for an Islamic group to register as a political party, stating that religion-based political parties were contrary to Zambia's constitution. Zambia has a strong trade union tradition, with the 300,000 member ZCTU being the only legal confederation.

Zimbabwe

Polity: Dominant party
Economy: Capitalist-statist
Population: 10,339,000
PPP: $1,484
Life Expectancy: 59.6
Ethnic Groups: Shona, Ndebele, white, and others
Ratings Change: *Zimbabwe's civil liberties rating changed from 4 to 5 as a result of modifications in methodology. See "Survey Methodology," page 671.

Political Rights: 5
Civil Liberties: 5*
Status: Partly Free

Overview: In 1993, the government embarked on a controversial program to acquire large commercial farms owned mostly by members of the small but influential white minority in order to resettle thousands of black, landless peasant families. In addition, members of the opposition made attempts at forming a united front to the ruling Zimbabwe African National Union (Patriotic Front) Party (ZANU) PF in anticipation of parliamentary elections scheduled for 1995.

Following the proclamation of Zimbabwean independence in 1980, culminating more than two decades of guerrilla warfare between the white minority government and the black liberation movements, the British-mediated settlement provided a constitution equipped with a Declaration of Rights. Among other acts, it prohibited the government from seizing private property without due compensation and the consent of the owners. The constitution set a ten-year period in which no amendment in the Declaration could be made without the consent of all the members of the parliament. In 1990 the ZANU (PF) Party proceeded to remove the inviolability-of-property clause and effected the passage of the Land Acquisition Act. The Act allowed the government to compel the sale of land from the 4,300 commercial farmers at a price it deemed fit for distribution to black, landless peasants. Most of the farms, covering almost half of the Zimbabwe's agriculturally cultivated areas, belong to descendants of European settlers, who acquired it when the country was a British colony known as Rhodesia. The passage of the Act coincided with a severe drought and mounting economic difficulties that forced the government to adopt IMF and World Bank induced austerity measures.

On 30 April the government announced the forced purchase of seventy farms. In response, the Commercial Farmers' Union accused the government of breaking its pledge to acquire only land which had been underutilized, while most of the designated farms were highly productive. The Agriculture Minister, Kumbirai Kangai, retorted that the government had the right to seize even productive farms if it was deemed to be in national interest. Following the Farmers' Union decision to hire British lawyers to contest in court the acquisition of the farms, President Robert Mugabe lashed out in August and September at the commercial farmers and the 100,000 strong white minority in general, calling them "a greedy bunch of racist usurpers," and threatening to deport them.

Following the incorporation of the Zimbabwe African People's Union (ZAPU) into the ruling ZANU(PF) party in 1987, Zimbabwe has effectively become a single-party state. ZAPU derived its support mostly from the Ndebele ethnic group in Matabeleland, the southwestern part of the country, while the ZANU was dominated by the northern Shona ethnic group.

During the 1983-85 crackdown on the opposition, government forces killed several thousand people in Matabeleland. Despite official regrets by President Mugabe, the government has not issued any information about those who were killed, and their families are still unable to obtain their death certificates. In 1992, the government reopened the wounds after appointing Perence Shiri, the commander of the notorious Fifth Brigade, which carried out most of the killings, to be the supreme commander of the air force. At the same time, people digging for water at the height of the drought discovered secret mass burial sites, presumably of those killed in 1983-85, in several locations.

Since 1990, several Ndebele opposition leaders have died in mysterious circumstances, suggesting government involvement in their deaths. In the spring of 1993, several opposition activists claimed that they had a government-prepared hit list which ordered their assassinations by hired death squads. Among those claiming to be on the list were George Moyo, the chairman of the Vukani Mahlabezulu Cultural Society, and Jonathan Moyo and Welshman Ncube, two professors at the Bulawayo campus of the University of Zimbabwe.

In March, two leading Matabele-based political groups combined to form the Forum Party. The two groups were the Open Forum, composed of former ZAPU members who defected from the party when its charismatic leader Joshua Nkomo decided to merge with the ZANU party in 1987, and the Forum for Democratic

Reforms founded in May 1992 and led by the former Chief Justice Enoch Dumbutshena. The new party's platform called for Zimbabwe's evolution toward an open and pluralistic society, and a free market-oriented economy.

With an economy burdened with high unemployment and inflation, and recovering from a severe drought the previous year, the government continued to implement the austerity measures called for by international lending institutions. In September, food riots broke out in the capital, Harare, over the steep rises in the price of bread, caused by the government's withdrawal of subsidies.

Political Rights and Civil Liberties: Due to the virtual monopoly on power in the hands of the ZANU party, the citizens of Zimbabwe are restricted in their ability to change the government by democratic means. The last legislative elections, held in 1990, were marred by voter intimidation, inaccuracies and irregularities in voting registers and vote counting, and by heavily pro-government biased media coverage. Of the 150 legislative seats, ZANU won 117, with 3 seats going to two opposition groups. Thirty seats remain reserved for tribal chiefs and the president's nominees. The opposition remains splintered and marginalized. Eighteen political parties are registered, although attempts at forming a united opposition, such as the formation of the Forum Party, have been made.

The judiciary is mostly independent, and the legal system is based on a mixture of English common law, Roman law, and indigenous customary law. The Zimbabwe Human Rights Association (Zimrights) and the Catholic Commission for Justice and Peace accused the government and the police of obstructing judicial inquiry in cases related to political opposition or where high government officials were involved. In August, following the Supreme Court's decision to commute capital sentences of four convicts to life imprisonment, the government drafted a proposal for a constitutional amendment to allow the execution of death sentences regardless of the time spent on death row or conditions in which the prisoners were held.

The government controls the bulk of mass media through its shares in the Zimbabwe Newspapers conglomerate, which controls the country's seven major English dailies. The only daily independent newspaper is *The Financial Gazette*, published in Bulawayo, in Matabeleland. In February, the government announced its intention to scrap the Law and Order Maintenance Act, dating back to the colonial period, which allowed the subsequent governments to exercise direct control over the publishing of information. In recent years the press, both state-owned and independent, has become increasingly outspoken in criticizing the government. In May, a meeting of journalists agreed to form a press council to monitor and defend the right to free information.

In February, following a Supreme Court decision denying the automatic right to residence to persons born in Zimbabwe (or Rhodesia) who retained or acquired foreign citizenship and were no longer domiciled in the country, the government moved to clamp down on legal and illegal immigrants. Among the measures announced were the discretionary power given to immigration officials to cancel aliens' residence permits at will, and denying the children of legal immigrants the right to automatic residence permit.

Freedom of religion is respected. There are no restriction on travel. The Zimbabwe Congress of Trade Unions has increasingly become independent from the ZANU influence and has stepped up its campaigns to defend the rights of the workers in the face of mounting economic difficulties.

Armenia/Azerbaijan
Nagorno-Karabakh

Polity: Armenian-occupied **Political Rights:** 7
Economy: Mixed statist **Civil Liberties:** 7
Population: 200,000 **Status:** Not Free
Ethnic Groups: Armenian (80 percent),
Azeris, other

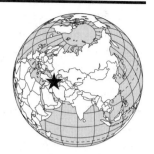

Overview: $\qquad$ **S**everal international attempts to mediate the crisis in this
predominantly Armenian enclave within Azerbaijan failed in
1993, and fighting continued through most of the year.
Karabakh Armenians launched several offensives and captured substantial Azeri
territory beyond the borders of Nagorno-Karabakh.

In 1921 Nagorno-Karabakh was transferred from Armenia and placed under Soviet
Azerbaijani jurisdiction by Joseph Stalin. Subsequently, the Nagorno-Karabakh
Autonomous Oblast (Region) was created, with a narrow strip of land bordering the
Armenian mainlan. In 1930, Moscow permitted Azerbaijan to establish and resettle the
border areas between Nagorno-Karabakh and Armenia.

In 1988, conflict erupted as Azeri militia and special forces launched a campaign of
violent repression in response to Karabakh Armenians' call for greater autonomy. In
1991, the legislatures of Nagorno-Karabakh and Shahumyan voted for secession and
the Azeri parliament annulled the region's autonomous status. A subsequent regional
referendum saw an overwhelming number of voters favoring independence. Multiparty
parliamentary elections were held. On 6 January 1992 the inaugural session of parliament formally adopted a declaration of independence and then elected Artur Mkrtchyan
president. Following Mkrtchyan's fatal shooting in April, Vice President Georgi
Pertrosian became president. Following Azeri attacks on Stepanakert, the enclave's
capital, the Nagorno-Karabkh parliament resolved in the spring of 1992 to initiate a
counter-offensive. Nagorno-Karabakh self-defense forces seized the city of Lachin
to establish a land corridor connecting Karabakh with Armenia and circumvent the
Azeri blockade.

In 1993 Karabakh Armenians had gained control of most of the disputed region and
had seized Azeri territory to expand the corridor linking it to Armenia. A series of
international attempts to mediate the crisis held under the auspices of the Conference on
Security and Cooperation in Europe (CSCE) produced few results. In April, Armenian
forces launched a new offensive against the towns of Fizuli and Kelbajar, southeast of
Nagorno-Karabakh, sparking a wave of Azeri refugees.

At 19-30 April meetings in Moscow, the United States, Turkey and Russia drew up
a new peace plan intended to restart the stalled CSCE-sponsored negotiations. The plan
called for an immediate ceasefire followed by the withdrawal between 9-14 May of
Armenian forces from Kelbajar and a two-month moratorium on all military activity.
While Azerbaijan and Armenia agreed to the tripartite peace initiative, the Karabakh
defense chief cast doubt on the plan's viability by rejecting the agreement on the
grounds that it "did not guarantee the safety of Karabakh's civilians."

On 7 June a newly revised CSCE plan was submitted to the Armenian, Azerbaijani and Nagorno-Karabakh governments. The plan, based on United Nations Resolution 822, called for an immediate ceasefire and a phased withdrawal of military forces from Kelbajar. One week later, Armenian President Levon Ter-Petrossian made his first visit to Karabakh (Armenia does not formally recognize the enclave's independence), where he sought to persuade Karabakh legislators to accept the CSCE plan. However, new fighting broke out as Karabakh Armenian forces attacked the western city of Agdam in Azerbaijan, looting and burning the city before pulling out. Following heated debate, the Karabakh parliament on 14 June agreed to accept the plan but asked for a one-month delay in implementation.

On 18 August the U.N. Security Council demanded an immediate and unconditional withdrawal of Armenian forces from occupied areas of Azerbaijan. Less than a week later, Armenian forces captured Fizuli, and continued a program of forcibly depopulating areas of Azerbaijan to the north, east and south of Karabakh, forcing tens of thousands to flee toward Iran. The Karabakh leadership in Stepanakert ignored urgent requests by Armenia that it abide by internationally brokered ceasefires. On 26 August Karabakh leaders refused to meet with the chief Russian negotiator.

In September, Azerbaijan claimed that Karabakh Armenian forces had captured Goradiz, a key town on the Iranian border. Following a flurry of diplomatic activity in Moscow involving the leaders of Azerbaijan, Armenia and Turkey, warring Karabakh Armenians and their Azeri foes held direct talks at the end of September. The two sides agreed to extend a ceasefire to 5 October. However, the ceasefire quickly collapsed. In response to an Azeri attack, spearheaded by Afghan *mujahideen* fighters, Karabakh Armenian forces captured the entire southeast corner of Azerbaijan, sending tens of thousands of refugees into Iran. A CSCE meeting ended on 9 November with no visible progress.

By year's end, Azeri forces launched several attacks in the northern, southern and eastern part of the enclave. Moreover, Azeri forces were poised to drive the Armenians from several villages in Azerbaijan. The conflict entered its sixth year with more than 16,000 people killed and over 1 million refugees.

A undeclared state of war has impinged on rights and civil liberties. The ethnic nature of the conflict has led to charges of "ethnic cleansing" and atrocities by both sides. The majority Armenians did elect a parliament, but the government is unrecognized by the international community.

Australia
Christmas Island (Kiritimati)

Polity: Appointed administrator
Economy: Capitalist-statist
Population: 2,000
Ethnic Groups: Chinese and Malay

Political Rights: 3
Civil Liberties: 2
Status: Free

Overview: Located in the Indian Ocean, Christmas Island is the home of a disappearing phosphate industry, which is owned by the Australian government's Australian Phosphate Corporation. Under Australian administration since 1958, Christmas Island has a government run by an administrator appointed by the Governor General, Queen Elizabeth's representative in Australia. Australia classifies the island as an external territory, but residents have the right to opt for Australian citizenship or residency status. Due to the near exhaustion of phosphate, the chief source of employment, many islanders have moved to Western Australia, Singapore, and Malaysia. The Australian government proposed laying off 150 phosphate miners in 1986. This caused labor and ethnic strife. The government decided to reduce the mine labor force gradually during 1986-89.

To reinvigorate the economy, Australia approved construction of a gambling resort complex. Pacific Consultants International of Japan suggested in 1989 that the island needed a new resort hotel, recreational and marine facilities, harbor facilities, and a better airport. A Melbourne-based consulting firm began studying the airport and tourism issues in 1990.

Two weeks after the 1987 election, the Australian government dismissed Christmas Island's democratically elected nine-member assembly, citing fiscal mismanagement. However, the islanders retain the right to vote in Australian national elections as part of the mainland's Northern Territory.

Cocos (Keeling) Islands

Polity: Appointed administrator and elected council
Economy: Capitalist-statist
Population: 1,000
Ethnic Groups: Malay

Political Rights: 1
Civil Liberties: 1
Status: Free

Overview: Located in the Indian Ocean and discovered by Captain William Keeling in 1609, the Cocos Islands were a personal fiefdom of the Clunies-Ross family until 1978. An Australian-appointed administrator is the chief executive. An elected local council began functioning in 1978. In a 1984 referendum, the inhabitants voted to integrate with Australia. They are now part of Australia's Northern Territory, which elects members of the Australian Parliament. The population is mostly Malay.

Norfolk Island

Polity: Appointed administrator and elected assembly
Economy: Capitalist
Population: 2,000
Ethnic Groups: *Bounty* families, Australians, New Zealanders

Political Rights: 2
Civil Liberties: 1
Status: Free

Overview: Located in the South Pacific, Norfolk Island is the home to many descendants of *Bounty* mutineers. An Australian-appointed administrator is the chief executive, but there has been a freely elected, nine-member assembly since Australia's passage of the Norfolk Island Act in 1979. This legislation provided for substantial self-government. The assembly executive committee acts like a cabinet on the island.

Chile
Rapanui (Easter Island)

Polity: Appointed governor and elected local government
Economy: Capitalist-statist
Population: 2,000
Ethnic Groups: Spanish-speaking Polynesian natives (70 percent), and Chilean settlers (30 percent)
Ratings Change: *Rapanui's political rights rating changed from 3 to 2 because of Chile's increasing recognition of native rights.

Political Rights: 2*
Civil Liberties: 2
Status: Free

Overview: Located in the Pacific Ocean, 2,360 miles from Chile, the island is the home of an ancient Polynesian culture. Under Chilean domain since 1888, the island is isolated from the world with the exception of twice-weekly airline flights and twice-yearly cargo ships. There are no newspapers, but there is a local radio station. Tourism is the main source of income. Visitors come to see the island's hundreds of giant, long-faced statues. However, these attractions are crumbling. Islanders hope to save them with foreign funding.

Formerly run by the Chilean navy, the island became a Chilean municipality with voting rights in 1966. The territory has its own local government. Islanders have many social rights and economic advantages. Every family has the right to a house and five hectares of land. The government subsidizes energy and utility costs. Island students are eligible for government university scholarships in Chile.

In recent years the original inhabitants, the Rapa Nui, have grown more assertive in pressing for cultural and political autonomy. The major issue of contention remains the ownership of land. Currently, only 20 percent of the land is owned by the Rapa Nui, while the remainder, owned by Chilean authorities, serves as a national park and an agricultural testing station. In November 1992, the Corporation for Cultural Protection organized protests against the planned building of a lighthouse on a sacred ceremonial ground.

China
Tibet

Polity: Communist one-party
Economy: Statist
Population: 4,590,000*
Ethnic Groups: Tibetans, Han Chinese

Political Rights: 7
Civil Liberties: 7
Status: Not Free

(*This figure from China's 1990 census indicates Tibetans under Chinese control. It includes 2,096 Tibetans living in the Tibet Autonomous Region (TAR), and 2,494 Tibetans living in areas of eastern Tibet that beginning in 1950 were incorporated into China's Qinghai, Gansu, Sichuan and Yunnan Provinces. By some estimates, the Chinese government has transferred up to 7 million ethnic Chinese into the former eastern Tibet, and to a lesser extent the TAR itself.)

Overview:
Prior to the Chinese invasion in 1949, Tibet had been a sovereign state for the better part of 2,000 years, experiencing only two periods of modest foreign influence. In the thirteenth century, Tibetan lamas extended blessings and teachings to Mongol rulers to avoid being incorporated into Kublai Khan's empire. Similiarly, the Manchus, who conquered China and established the Qing Dynasty in 1644, exerted some influence over Tibet's foreign affairs from the eighteenth century until the dynasty's fall in 1911, but never incorporated it into China.

Between 1911 and 1949, Tibet functioned as a fully independent state. In late 1949, China invaded with 100,000 troops, quickly defeated the small Tibetan army, occupied half the country, and established military and political control. In May 1951 China formally annexed the country by forcing a Tibetan delegation to sign a "Seventeen-Point Agreement for the Peaceful Liberation of Tibet." The document purported to guarantee Tibetans religious freedom and exempt the country from Communist "reforms." At the time, there were 40,000 Chinese troops in Tibet, and the Tibetan spiritual and temporal leader, the fourteenth Dalai Lama, Tenzin Gyatso, feared the country would be overrun. Because the agreement was signed under duress, it lacks validity under international law.

Throughout the 1950s, the Chinese intensified their repression of Tibet and violated the May 1951 agreement on virtually every count. In 1959 popular uprisings culminated in mass pro-independence demonstrations in the capital, Lhasa, on 10 March. In the next several months China crushed the uprisings, killing an estimated 87,000 Tibetans in the Lhasa region alone. The Dalai Lama fled to Dharamsala, India with 80,000 supporters and established a government-in-exile.

In 1960 the International Commission of Jurists called the Chinese occupation genocidal, and ruled that prior to the 1949 invasion Tibet had possessed all the attributes of statehood as defined under international law, including a defined territory, an independent government and an ability to conduct foreign relations. In 1965 China created the Tibet Autonomous Region, including Lhasa, an entity which in reality contained only half the territory of pre-invasion Tibet. The rest of Tibet had, since 1950, been incorporated into four southwestern Chinese provinces. During the 1966-76 Chinese Cultural Revolution, the authorities banned Tibetans from enjoying basic cultural rights, including wearing traditional clothes. By the late 1970s, more than one million Tibetans had died as a result of the occupation, and all but eleven of 6,200 monasteries had been destroyed.

Between 1987 and 1990 Chinese soldiers broke up peaceful demonstrations throughout Tibet, killing hundreds and arresting thousands more. The authorities placed Lhasa under martial law from March 1989 to May 1990. In May 1992 China announced plans to modernize the Tibetan economy, including an expansion of road and air links with China. However, exiled Tibetans say this seemingly benign policy is merely a ruse to facilitate the mass settlement of ethnic Chinese into Tibet, and will in any case contribute to the rampant deforestation and other environmental damage that has occurred in recent years.

The most serious unrest in Lhasa since 1989 occurred on 24 May 1993. Initially a small group of Tibetans gathered to protest a government plan to lift price controls on oil and grain and impose new taxes. By the evening some 500 protestors had gathered and began calling for an end to the Chinese occupation and denouncing the presence of prostitutes, bars and illicit drugs in the capital. Although the protests were largely peaceful, several demonstrators threw stones at police cars. Police dispersed the crowd by firing tear gas for two hours, but smaller demonstrations continued for three days.

In other isues, during a May visit to London, the Dalai Lama said he wanted to discuss with China a "one-country, two-systems" approach that would grant Tibet autonomy without full independence, but added that "ultimately, the Tibetan people have the right to decide (their future)." In early August the Dalai Lama's older brother, Gyalo Thondup, met Chinese government officials in Beijing, the first time he had formally done so as a representative of the exiled government.

Political Rights and Civil Liberties: Tibetans cannot change their government democratically. China appoints all top government officials, including the governor, and continues to systematically suppress the Tibetans' cultural identity and stifle calls for independence. In May 1993 the London-based Tibet Information Network said it knew the names of 335 political prisoners in Tibet, ranging from a fifteen-year-old girl to a seventy-seven-year-old monk. Also in May the Network learned that during a fact-finding visit by a delegation of European ambassadors, police had detained at least 100 people and arrested three who had planned to contact the delegation.

Political prisoners are routinely tortured, and nuns are reportedly raped. In March police arrested some thirty monks during protests coinciding with the Monlam prayer festival and the anniversary of the 1959 uprising. In August the Tibetan government-in-exile said that since May police had arrested 190 monks and dissidents for staging peaceful protests.

The Chinese government has pursued a Sinification policy that includes sending 300 top Tibetan students to study in China each year, and granting economic incentives to lure ethnic Chinese into voluntarily relocating to Tibet. Although no accurate figures exist, by some estimates in Lhasa alone there are already 120,000 Chinese and only 40,000 Tibetans, but Tibetans may already be a minority in Tibet as a whole.

Because monasteries have historically been the centers of education, authority and national identity in Tibet, the Chinese government has stationed monitors in them and has sharply curtailed religious freedom. The government limits the number of new monks and forbids religious figures from giving large public teachings. China says it will have final say in the ongoing search for the boy who will be declared the eleventh Panchen Lama, who ranks second in the religious heirarchy to the Dalai Lama.

Tibetans are particularly discriminated against in education. According to official Chinese figures Tibetans have a 25 percent literacy rate compared to 77 percent in China, reflecting the government's paltry spending on education in Tibet. In 1993 China began allowing secondary school subjects to be taught in Tibetan, although students who choose to study in their native language will be severely disadvantaged in gaining entrance to Chinese universities, and in obtaining government jobs.

Tibetans who live outside Lhasa cannot visit the capital without going through an arduous task of obtaining permits. Although China's draconian family planning policy ostensibly does not extend to Tibetans and other minorities, sources say the one-child rule is enforced in Tibet.

Denmark
Faeroe Islands

Polity: Parliamentary democracy
Economy: Mixed capitalist
Population: 49,000
Ethnic Groups: Faeroese

Political Rights: 1
Civil Liberties: 1
Status: Free

Overview: The main issue in the Faero Islands in 1993 was the resignation of veteran Prime Minister Atli Dam in January for health and business reasons. He was replaced by Marita Petersen, the island's first female premier. Petersen, who has served as a cabinet minister since 1991, was the only candidate proposed by the ruling Social Democratic Party.

Since 1948, the Faeroe Islands have had substantial autonomy within the Kingdom of Denmark. The Danish Government maintains authority over foreign affairs, defense, finance and justice. A high commissioner (ombudsman) represents Denmark. The Faeroese government has responsibility for communications, culture, and industry. It shares responsibility with Denmark for education, health, and social services, but the

Faeroese administer these areas locally. The islands send two representatives to the Danish parliament, but pay no Danish taxes. The territory has the right to opt out of Denmark's European Union membership. There are fifty local authorities. Presently, six political parties with diverse ideological perspectives compete in elections. The parliament, the *Løgting*, is composed of twenty-seven members chosen by proportional representation in seven districts, plus up to five supplementary members.

Fishing and agriculture dominate the economy. The territory has a chronic trade deficit, but Denmark subsidizes the economy. The Faeroese have a full range of political rights and civil liberties. Eight newspapers publish freely. There are public radio and television stations. Although the established Lutheran Church represents almost 90 percent of the population, religious freedom is respected, and there are several independent churches.

Greenland

Polity: Parliamentary democracy
Economy: Mixed-capitalist
Population: 57,000
Ethnic Groups: Inuit (Eskimo), native whites, Danish

Political Rights: 1
Civil Liberties: 1
Status: Free

Overview:
Greenland's legislature consists of twenty-three members chosen by proportional representation and up to an additional four members for parties failing to win seats in districts. Jonathan Motzfeldt was premier of Greenland (1979-91) and head of the socialist Forward (*Siumut*) Party. Although his party remained dominant after the 1991 elections, he was replaced by Lars Emil Johansen after allegations of financial mismanagement. The Forward party won eleven seats in the election and formed a coalition with the Marxist-Leninist Eskimo Brotherhood (*Inuit Ataqatigiit)* Party, which won five seats. The opposition parties in the legislature are: the conservative Feeling of Community or Solidarity (*Attasut*) Party with eight seats; the new Center Party with two seats; and the pro-business Polar (*Issittrup*) Party with one seat.

Located in the North Atlantic, Greenland has had substantial autonomy from Denmark since 1979. Denmark still controls Greenland's foreign and defence policies, but the local authorities handle most other matters. Greenland sends two representatives to the Danish parliament in Copenhagen.

Commercial fishing remains the backbone of the local economy. A crisis could arise, however, with the possible depletion of fishing stocks.

In July 1993 Greenland's fisherman agreed to stop commercial salmon fishing for two years, in exchange for financial compensation from private North American conservation groups.

Political Rights
and Civil Liberties:
Political rights and civil liberties are generally respected. There is full freedom of expression and association. However, published reports suggest evidence of discrimination against Inuits in a contraception program. Doctors administer a disproportionately high number of contraceptive injections to Inuits, and fail to explain side effects and other implications of the shots. In Denmark, doctors give these same shots only to those who cannot take care of themselves.

Finland
Aland Islands

Polity: Parliamentary
democracy
Economy: Mixed
capitalist
Population: 24,000
Ethnic Groups: Aland Islanders (Swedish)

Political Rights: 1
Civil Liberties: 1
Status: Free

Overview:
The major political debate in the Aland Islands in 1992-1993 concerned membership in the European Union (EU). Because the Alands have autonomous status within Finland, the islands could choose to remain outside the EU even if Finland were to become a member.

The Alands are an archipelago located between Sweden and Finland. Sweden lost the territory to Russia in the 1808-1809 war. The Alands became part of the Grand Duchy of Finland within the Russian Empire. Russia, France, and the United Kingdom recognized the Alands as a demilitarized zone in 1856. When Finland proclaimed its independence from Russia in 1917, it rejected a petition from Alanders requesting reunion with Sweden. In 1921, the League of Nations recognized the islands as an autonomous Swedish-speaking province within Finland.

The Alanders elect a thirty-member, multi-party parliament for four-year terms. The parliament can pass laws on internal affairs such as health and medical services, education, and culture. Finnish laws apply in areas where the Alanders have no legislative power. The Finnish president has veto power over local legislation only if the bill exceeds the parliament's authority or when there is a threat to national security. Alanders also elect a member of the Finnish parliament. A county governor represents Finland.

The Swedish language and local land ownership have special legal protection. There are competing newspapers and a public radio station.

France
French Guiana

Polity: Appointed com- **Political Rights:** 1*
missioner and elected **Civil Liberties:** 2
assembly and council **Status:** Free
Economy: Capitalist-statist
Population: 105,000
Ethnic Groups: Complex, black (66 percent), Caucasian
(French) (12 percent), East Indian, Chinese and Amerindian (12
percent), and other (10 percent)
Ratings Change: French Guiana's political rights rating changed
from 2 to 1 as a result of modifications in methodology. See
"Survey Methodology," page 671.

Overview: As one of four French Overseas Departments, French Guiana
is ruled according to French law, and the administrative
establishment is headed by a commissioner of the Republic
who is appointed by the French Ministry of the Interior. Representatives to the French
parliament are elected. A nineteen-member General Council is elected for six years
with councilors representing individual districts. Since 1982 the Council has been given
increased powers, particularly in financial matters.

At the most recent General Council elections in fall 1988, the Guianese Socialist
Party (PSG) retained control by taking twelve seats against seven for the rightist Rally
for the Republic (RPR) and other right-wing parties. The PSG has been seeking a more
independent status for French Guiana.

When French Guiana was given regional status in 1974, a Regional Assembly was
set up, distinct from the General Council, with limited control over the economy. This
control was expanded under the Mitterrand reforms of 1982-83. The first direct
elections to the Regional Assembly, on the basis of proportional representation, were
held in February 1983. Mayors and municipal councils are also directly elected.

In the Regional Assembly elections held on 22 March 1992, the PSG won sixteen
out of thirty-one seats, followed by the Guianese Democratic Front (FDG) with ten and
rightist parties with the remainder.

In the French legislative elections held in March 1993, the RPR won one of French
Guiana's two seats, while the other was won by a dissident from the PSG, which had
been weakened by infighting.

There is still concern about the condition of Bush Negro and Amerindian refugees
who fled into western French Guiana during the guerrilla conflict in neighboring
Suriname. Since the end of the conflict, about 8,400 of the estimated 10,000 refugees
have returned to Suriname. By mid-1993 there was still one refugee camp in operation.

Pluralistic points of view are presented in the media, which include two major
newspapers and several radio and television stations. The United Trade Union Movement (MSU) continued to express concerns over increased unemployment, low
European investment and the drain on the economy by a growing influx of immigrants
from Haiti and neighboring Brazil.

French Polynesia

Polity: Elected Assembly **Political Rights:** 1*
Economy: Capitalist- **Civil Liberties:** 2
statist **Status:** Free
Population: 199,000
Ethnic Groups: Polynesian (83 percent), French and
other European (11 percent), and Chinese and other
Asian (6 percent)
Ratings Change: *French Polynesia's political rights rating
changed from 2 to 1 as a result of modifications in methodology.
See "Survey Methodology," page 671.

Overview: French Polynesia consists of 120 South Pacific Islands, the most populous of which is Tahiti. A High Commissioner represents the French government. France controls justice and the security forces, some education, immigration, and international airline traffic, but the territory has significant autonomy. Polynesians elect a member of the French Senate and two National Assembly deputies.

The Polynesian Territorial Assembly consists of forty-one members elected for a maximum term of five years. The Assembly elects the president, who selects the ministers with the Assembly's approval.

In the 1991 election, Gaston Flosse's People's Rally Party, an affiliate of the French Gaullist Rally for the Republic, won eighteen of the forty-one Assembly seats. An alliance between supporters of outgoing President Alexandre Leontieff and Assembly President Jean Juventine captured only fourteen seats, and three smaller groups won the remaining seats. Flosse and Vernaudon formed a governing coalition. Subsequently, their coalition picked up two more seats.

Both Flosse and the pro-independence Liberation Front of Polynesia urged islanders to boycott the French referendum in the territory on the Maastricht Treaty on European integration. On 20 September 1992, about 70 percent of the few Polynesians participating voted yes. Also in September a group of pro-independence pearl farmers settled on the island of Mopelia after previous evacuations, and proclaimed a free and independent state. After security forces put down the uprising, the participants went on a hunger strike until they won a promise of negotiations. The confrontation highlighted the issue of conflicting local land claims.

Following the April 1992 suspension of French nuclear tests in the Mururoa atoll France pledged financial compensation to offset the negative economic impact. Nuclear testing generated approximately 20 percent of the territory's income and more than 10 percent of employment. In August 1993 the French government, pressed by employees and local government, agreed to funding for a station to measure Mururoa's radioactivity.

As a result of mounting economic problems the territorial assembly approved French Polynesia's first income tax, effective from 1 July 1993. The tax will be used to match the French government's funding for a ten-year development program to diversity the territory's economy and improve its infrastructure.

Peaceful advocates of independence have freedom of expression and association. The islanders are largely Christian. There are three daily newspapers and a public broadcasting service. The Chinese minority prospers in business, and enjoys much greater acceptance than Chinese communities on other Pacific islands.

Guadeloupe

Polity: Appointed commissioner and elected assembly and council
Economy: Capitalist-statist
Population: 389,000
Ethnic Groups: Predominantly black with white French minority
Ratings Change: *Guadeloupe's political rights rating changed from 2 to 1 as a result of modifications in methodology. See "Survey Methodology," page 671.

Political Rights: 1*
Civil Liberties: 2
Status: Free

Overview:

As one of four French Overseas Departments, Guadeloupe is ruled according to French law and the administrative establishment is headed by a commissioner appointed by the French Ministry of the Interior. Representatives to the French parliament are elected.

A General Council is directly elected to a five-year term, with each member elected to represent individual districts. Since 1982, the Council has been given increased powers, particularly in financial matters.

When Guadeloupe was given regional status in 1974 a Regional Assembly was set up, parallel to the General Council, with limited control over the economy. This control was expanded under the Mitterand reforms of 1983-83. The first direct elections to the Regional Assembly, on the basis of proportional representation, were held in February 1983. Mayors and municipal councils are also directly elected.

In the 1988 General Council elections the Socialist Party (PS) increased its majority by one seat, defeating opponents twenty-six to sixteen. Since the late 1960s, there have been a number of militant pro-independence groups. Those that resorted to armed tactics were outlawed. Since 1985 violent activity has nearly died out. Labor unions are legal and there are two main labor federations.

The Regional Assembly elections held in 1992 were annulled because some parties were late in registering candidates. New elections were held on 31 January 1993. The right-wing Guadeloupe Objective won 22 of 41 seats, compared with 15 in 1992. The PS dropped from 9 to 7 seats, the dissident socialist FRUI-G from 7 to 3 and the PCG from 3 to 2. The pro-independence Popular Union for the Liberation of Guadeloupe moved up from 2 to 3 seats.

In the French legislative elections held in March 1993, the right, under the banner of the Gaullist Rally for the Republic (RPR), won two of Guadeloupe's four seats, with the PS and an independent leftist taking the other two.

There is one daily newspaper and a handful of radio and television transmitters. International news agencies maintain local offices. In November 1992 banana planters on

Guadeloupe and Martinique blocked highways and airports, ending their four-day shutdown of the islands only when France pledged to maintain subsidies.

Martinique

Polity: Appointed commissioner and elected
assembly and council
Economy: Capitalist-statist
Population: 370,000

Political Rights: 1*
Civil Liberties: 2*
Status: Free

Ethnic Groups: Predominantly black with French minority
Ratings Change: *Martinique's political rights rating changed from 2 to 1 and its civil liberties rating from 1 to 2 as a result of modifications in methodology. See "Survey Methodology," page 671.

Overview:

As one of four French Overseas Departments, the department of Martinique is ruled according to French law, and the administrative establishment is headed by a commissioner appointed by the French Ministry of the Interior. Representatives to the French parliament are elected.

A forty-four-member General Council is directly elected to a six-year term, with each member elected to represent individual districts. Since 1982, the Council has been given increased powers, particularly in financial matters.

Martinique was given regional status in 1974 and a Regional Assembly was set up, parallel to the General Council, with limited control over the economy. This authority was expanded under the 1982 Mitterand reforms. The first elections to the Regional Assembly on the basis of proportional representation were held in February 1983. Mayors and municipal councils are also directly elected.

In 1988 the left-wing Martinique Progressive Party (PPM), the Socialist Federation of Martinique (FSM), and the Martinique Communist Party (PCM) formed an electoral alliance, the Left Union (UG). The UG obtained a one-seat majority in the 1988 General Council elections.

In Regional Assembly elections held on 22 March 1992 the right-wing Union for a Martinique of Progress gained sixteen of forty-one seats. The pro-independence Martinique Patriots and the PPM each won nine seats, the PCM, four, and the New Socialist Generation, three.

In the French legislative elections held in March 1993, the right, running under the banner of the Gaullist Rally for the Republic (RPR), won three of the island's four seats with the PPM taking one.

Separatist violence has nearly disappeared in recent years. Labor unions are legal and permitted to strike. There are two main labor federations, both of which were involved in strikes in 1993 to protest French government budget cuts.

The media are varied and reflect pluralistic points of view. There are several radio and television stations. There are one daily and several weekly newspapers.

Mayotte (Mahore)

Polity: Appointed commissioner and elected
council
Economy: Capitalist
Population: 87,000

Political Rights: 1*
Civil Liberties: 2
Status: Free

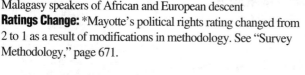

Ethnic Groups: A mixture of Mahorais, French, Comoran, and
Malagasy speakers of African and European descent
Ratings Change: *Mayotte's political rights rating changed from
2 to 1 as a result of modifications in methodology. See "Survey
Methodology," page 671.

Overview:

In 1993 a strike by Mahorais workers in support of wage
increases degenerated into violence when demonstrators set
fire to government buildings and erected street barricades. On
19 February the French government dispatched 100 paramilitary police to quell the
riots.

Part of the Comoran archipelago, Mayotte is an overseas French territory, located
in the Indian Ocean east of Mozambique and northwest of Madagascar. The island's
ruling party is the Mahorais Popular Movement (MPM), which is opposed to Comoran
attempts to reunify Mayotte with Comoros. The Comoros, once united with Mayotte as
a French colony, is now an independent republic of three islands immediately to the
north of Mayotte.

In two referenda, the Mahorais population voted not to join the Federal Islamic
Republic of Comoros. Nonetheless, the Comoran government continues to claim
Mayotte, rejecting the referenda that supported continued association with France. The
French government stated in 1991 that France would not turn Mayotte over to the
Comoros against Mahorais wishes.

The French government appoints a commissioner as chief executive, and the
residents elect a seventeen-member general council, presently under MPM control.
Mayotte sends one member to the French Senate and elects one deputy to the National
Assembly. Residents enjoy the same rights as French citizens. The government-owned
radio station broadcasts in French and Mahorais. The economy is based largely on
tourism and primary products such as ylang-ylang, vanilla, copra and coffee.

New Caledonia

Polity: Appointed
commissioner and
elected congress and
assemblies
Economy: Capitalist-statist
Population: 176,000
Ethnic Groups: Kanaky, Wallisian-Futunians, Javanese,
French, Tahitians, Vietnamese, other Asian/Pacific groups

Political Rights: 2
Civil Liberties: 2
Status: Free

Overview:
New Caledonia, a group of South Pacific Islands 1,000 miles east of Australia, became a French territory in 1853 and gained internal autonomy in 1976. France is represented by a high commissioner responsible for external relations, the treasury, the judiciary, and public welfare and security.

The main issue in recent years has been the independence movement of the indigenous Melanesian Kanaky people, who make up 45 percent of the population. Of the "settler" population, 34 percent are French and the rest are Pacific Islanders and Asian. Kanak separatists launched several terrorist attacks in the 1980s. In June 1988 the French government and pro- and anti-independence groups signed an accord (subject to a referendum) calling for Paris to administer the territory for a year, during which New Caledonia would be divided into three autonomous provinces: the Southern Province dominated by settlers, and the Northern and Loyalty Island Provinces dominated by Kanaks. Each would have a provincial council, which together would form a Territorial Congress, replacing the existing, unicameral Territorial Assembly. This arrangement would hold for a decade pending a referendum on independence in 1998. In July 1988 the Territorial Assembly formerly approved the so-called Matignon Accords, and in November voters in New Caledonia and France also approved the Accord in referendums.

On 11 June 1989 elections were held for the three new provincial councils. The anti-independence Rally for Caledonia in the Republic (RPCR) took twenty-seven of the fifty-four total seats in the three regions; the Kanaka Socialist National Liberation Front (FLNKS), nineteen; minor parties, eight. In May 1991 RPCR leader Jacques LaFleur called for the 1998 referendum to be abandoned in favor of a "consensual solution" that would give the territory greater autonomy while maintaining its links to France. FLNKS ignored the proposal. In November 1992 FLNKS president Paul Neaoutyine said his party might boycott the upcoming 1994 council elections, in part because the European minority's relative wealth made an RPCR victory likely.

In August 1993 a fact-finding mission from the intergovernmental South Pacific Forum concluded that the United Nations should monitor political and economic reforms in the territory in advance of the 1998 referendum. The mission noted that Kanak factions are divided, with some calling for negotiations with the settler population over independence before the referendum, and that the government has largely failed to improve the Kanak's standard of living.

Reunion

Polity: Appointed commissioner and elected assembly and council
Economy: Capitalist-statist
Population: 618,000
Ethnic Groups: Creole (Afro-European), French, Malagache, Malay, South Asian, and Vietnamese

Political Rights: 2
Civil Liberties: 2
Status: Free

Overview:

On 21 June 1993 voters elected a new Regional Assemby. The Free Dom party won the largest number of votes and 13 seats in the Assembly. Two conservative groups won seventeen seats. The Communists won seven seats and a splintered socialist party won six seats.

Located in the Indian Ocean east of Madagascar, Reunion has been in French hands since the seventeenth century. The population is multiracial and largely Catholic. Sugar cane is the most important crop. A French commissioner carries out executive functions. There is a competitive, multiparty system, which ranges from pro-French conservatives to pro-independence Communists. Reunion has a bicameral legislature, consisting of an elected thirty-six-member General Council and an elected forty-five-member Regional Assembly. The territory elects three National Assembly deputies and one Senator to the French Parliament. There are three daily newspapers and a government radio and television system. High unemployment, insufficient opportunities, and a lack of diversions are abiding problems on the island, all leading to enforced idleness and frustration.

St. Pierre and Miquelon

Polity: Appointed commissioner and elected council
Economy: Capitalist
Population: 6,000
Ethnic Groups: French
Ratings Change: *St. Pierre and Miquelon's political rights rating changed from 2 to 1 as a result of modifications in methodology. See "Survey Methodology," page 671.

Political Rights: 1*
Civil Liberties: 1
Status: Free

Overview:

Located south of Newfoundland in the North Atlantic, the islands of St. Pierre and Miquelon are the only remaining French possessions in North America. Fishing is the mainstay of the economy.

The major issue in 1993 was the simmering dispute between France and Canada over the scallop fishing quotas and the right of Canadian fishermen to fish in the territory's sea corridor, awarded to France by the International Court of Arbitration in 1992. On 14 August angry Canadian fishermen, in order to draw attention to the issue, disrupted ferry service between St. Pierre and the Canadian province of Newfoundland

The French government appoints a commissioner, and local residents elect a fourteen-member general council and municipal councils. The islanders also choose a National Assembly deputy and a senator to the French Parliament. The islanders also have the right to vote in French referenda. On September 20 1992, voter turnout was low for the vote on the Maastricht Treaty on European integration. St. Pierre's Mayor, Albert Pen, had recommended abstention as a protest gesture against the French government's position on Canadian fishing rights. There is freedom of association. The unionized workers belong to *Force Ouvriere* (Workers' Force). The only newspaper is a bulletin of government announcements. There is a medium-wave radio transmitter and a government radio and television station.

Wallis and Futuna Islands

Polity: Appointed administrator and elected council
Political Rights: 2*
Civil Liberties: 2
Status: Free
Economy: Capitalist-statist
Population: 14,000
Ethnic Groups: Polynesian
Ratings Change: *Wallis and Futuna Islands political rights rating changed from 3 to 2 as a result of modifications in methodology. See "Survey Methodology," page 671.

Overview: Located in the South Pacific, Wallis and Futuna Islands have almost completely Polynesian populations. The islands voted to become a French territory in 1959. There is a French-appointed administrator and a locally elected twenty-member assembly. Three traditional chiefs are council members. The territory elects a National Assembly deputy and a senator to the French Parliament. In 1989, local leaders criticized the administrator for governing without their participation. The parties include local affiliates of the French center-right, but the current Assembly deputy is a leftist. In 1991, there were talks on the islands' future between the French and the local leadership. In 1992, islanders voted for the Maastricht Treaty on European integration despite the Gaullist senator's plea for a "No" vote. The only radio station broadcasts in both French and Wallisian.

India
Kashmir

Polity: Indian-administered
Economy: Capitalist-statist
Population: 6,200,000

Political Rights: 7*
Civil Liberties: 7*
Status: Not Free

Ethnic Groups: Kashmiris (Muslim majority, Hindu minority)
Ratings Change: *Kashmir's political rights rating changed from
6 to 7 and its civil liberties rating from 6 to 7 because of severe violence.

Overview:

In 1993 India's tentative efforts to begin a dialogue with relatively moderate, pro-independence Kashmiri militants were thwarted by extremists seeking to incorporate this Himalayan region into Pakistan. In January and October Indian troops fired indiscriminately into crowds of civilians, killing more than fifty people each time.

In 1846 the British gained control of predominantly Hindu Jammu and Muslim Kashmir and installed a Hindu *maharajah* as leader. At the partition of India in 1947 into Muslim Pakistan and predominantly Hindu India, Muslims from newly formed Pakistan backed a revolt in Kashmir. Maharajah Hari Singh, the head of the Hindu ruling family, signed an agreement ceding control of the territories to India in exchange for protection by Indian troops. Indian Prime Minister Jawaharlal Nehru appointed Sheik Abdullah of the National Conference, a secular, left-wing party, as leader of Jammu and Kashmir's government. Nehru also said a referendum on self-determination would eventually take place, although none has been held.

Following months of sectarian strife, a 1949 U.N.-brokered agreement gave a portion of Kashmir to Pakistan, while India maintained Jammu and most of Kashmir. Article 370 of India's 1950 constitution granted Jammu and Kashmir substantial autonomy, although in practice this has been gradually eroded. In 1953 Nehru dismissed Abdullah's government, and a newly installed, compliant government voted for incorporation into India. The U.N. vetoed India's right to annexation, calling instead for a popular referendum. In 1955 fresh Indian-Pakistani fighting occurred, although the 1949 boundaries held. A year later the Jammu and Kashmir assembly again voted for incorporation into India. In 1957 India formerly annexed the territories as its state of Jammu and Kashmir.

In 1959 China occupied a section of Kashmir, which it continues to hold. In August-September 1965 and in 1971-72 India and Pakistan again clashed in the territory. During the latter conflict, India seized and subsequently annexed portions of Pakistani Kashmir.

In 1975 India returned Sheikh Abdullah to power after he signed an agreement accepting Indian rule over Kashmir. Following the Sheikh's death in 1982, his son, Farooq Abdullah, took power. The younger Abdullah proved unpopular with Kashmiri nationalists, who considered him an Indian puppet.

In the summer of 1989 the Jammu and Kashmir Liberation Front (JKLF) began an insurgency seeking independence. Meanwhile, fundamentalist Kashmiris who had fought with the *mujahideen* in Afghanistan began forming several militant groups, including the powerful Hizbul Mujahideen, seeking to incorporate Kashmir into Pakistan. In December 1989 the Indian government sent paramilitary troops into the state. In January 1990 Abdullah's government resigned, and in July the state went under federal rule. In May paramilitary forces randomly opened fire into a crowd of 100,000 people in the state capital of Srinagar who were mourning a slain cleric, killing sixty-seven people.

The worst single incident of violence in nearly three years occurred on 6 January 1993 as troops in Sopore fired indiscriminately at civilians and set shops and homes ablaze. Subsequently India took measures aimed at diffusing tensions. In February the federal government shifted cabinet minister Rajesh Pilot to the newly created Internal Security portfolio with permission to make contact with the JKLF and other moderate, pro-independence groups. On 12 March India replaced hardline governor Girish Chandra Saxena with General K.V. Krishna Rao, considered a moderate.

In response, pro-Pakistani militants, opposed to any negotiations, stepped up their attacks on security forces and moderate Kashmiri groups. On 31 March two youths abducted and killed Dr. Abdul Ahad Guru, a leading heart surgeon and a prominent JKLF member. Tensions rose further on 10 April after security forces killed Hizbul Mujahideen leader Mohammed Maqbool Ilahi. Pro-Pakistani guerrillas launched retaliatory raids on Indian troops, who responded with a week of arson attacks in Srinagar.

Scattered violence continued over the summer. On 15 October Indian troops began a siege outside of Kashmir's holiest shrine, the Hazrat Bal mosque in Srinagar, where some sixty-five armed rebels had encamped. The standoff at the mosque ended peacefully on 16 November as the separatists surrendered, but the overall cycle of violence continued unabated throughout the last weeks of the year.

Political Rights and Civil Liberties:

Kashmiris cannot change their government democratically. Since 1990 the state of Jammu and Kashmir has been under President's Rule (direct federal rule), and citizens were not allowed to vote in the May 1991 Indian elections. Fresh state elections have been repeatedly postponed. Journalists, doctors and human rights activists estimate that since December 1989 12,000-20,000 civilians, Kashmiri separatists and Indian soldiers have been killed in politically motivated violence.

India maintains more than 250,000 soldiers and paramilitary troops in the state. These forces are responsible for torture and extrajudicial executions of civilians and suspected guerrillas, for raping civilians, and for arson attacks on shops and homes. The July 1990 Jammu and Kashmir Disturbed Areas Act and the Armed Forces (Jammu and Kashmir) Special Powers Act allow the authorities to search homes and arrest suspects without a warrant. Indian troops frequently cordon off entire neighborhoods and conduct house-to-house searches. A report released in February 1993 by Asia Watch and Physicians for Human Rights accused Indian security forces of attacking doctors, raiding hospitals, and otherwise interfering with the provision of medical care.

Kashmiri militants are frequently responsible for the deaths of Indian security forces, public employees, suspected informers and members of rival factions. Separatists also frequently kidnap government officials, politicians and businessmen, and some groups operate extortion rackets.

The government prevents international human rights groups from conducting on-site investigations in Kashmir. Local human rights groups operate under governmental pressure, and several activists have been killed. In February unknown assailants killed Dr. Farooq Ahmed Ashai, who had catalogued human rights abuses by Indian soldiers.

The legal system is a shambles. Separatists routinely threaten judges, witnesses and the families of defendants, and as a result courts do not try cases involving militants or those with political overtones. India's 1971 Newspapers Incitement to Offenses Act remains in effect only in Jammu and Kashmir. It allows a district magistrate to restrict newspapers and magazines from publishing articles that could allegedly provoke criminal acts or other disturbances. Both the government and the militants harass journalists, who exercise considerable self-censorship.

Indonesia
East Timor

Polity: Dominant party (military-dominated)
Economy: Capitalist-statist
Population: 750,000
Ethnic Groups: Timorese, Javanese, others

Political Rights: 7
Civil Liberties: 7
Status: Not Free

Overview:

The Portuguese arrived in Timor around 1520, and in the nineteenth and early twentieth centuries took formal control of the eastern half of the island through a series of treaties with the other occupying power, the Dutch. In 1974 Portugal agreed to hold a referendum in East Timor in 1975 on self-determination. In August 1975 the pro-independence Democratic Union of Timor (UDT) launched a military coup against the colonial administration. In the fall, another pro-independence movement, the leftist Revolutionary Front for an Independent East Timor (Fretelin), defeated the UDT in a brief civil war, and on 28 November declared an independent republic. Indonesia invaded on 7 December, and formerly annexed East Timor in July 1976 as the country's twenty-seventh province. The United Nations has never recognized the annexation. Between 1975 and 1979 up to 200,000 Timorese died as Indonesia strove to crush the Fretelin resistance. Periodic skirmishes continued throughout the 1980s.

The territory received international attention on 12 November 1991 when Indonesian soldiers in the capital of Dili fired on thousands of Timorese who were peacefully marching to the Santa Cruz cemetary burial site of Sebastian Gomes, a supporter of independence killed by security forces in October. Several marchers had held pro-independence banners. On 26 December the government said that troops had overreacted and that fifty people had been killed, although eyewitnesses placed the number at up to 200.

In a series of courts-martial in 1992, four officers and six enlisted men charged only with assault or disobeying orders rather than with killing, received light terms ranging from eight to eighteen months. Meanwhile, in separate cases eighteen East Timorese received terms ranging from six months to life imprisonment for alleged anti-government activities proceeding or during the 12 November march, or for subsequent demonstrations in the Indonesian capital of Jakarta.

On 20 November, Indonesian soldiers captured Fretelin leader Jose "Xanana" Gusmao, dealing the tiny movement a serious blow. On 1 February 1993 a Dili court charged Gusmao with rebellion, conspiracy, possession of firearms and other crimes dating back to 1976. On 21 May the court sentenced Gusmao to life imprisonment, subsequently reduced to twenty years. An Asia Watch representative noted that the trial fell short of international standards in several respects, including: the court's denial of Gusmao's right to appoint his own lawyer, and its subsequent appointment of a defense attorney with friendly relations with police and prosecutors; the fact that several witnesses against Gusmao were themselves detainees, raising the possibility they had been coerced; and the court's refusal to allow Gusmao to read beyond the first two pages of his twenty-eight-page defense (the presiding judge read a 250-page verdict).

The Fretelin movement now reportedly has less than 200 poorly equipped fighters. In April the Indonesian army captured new Fretelin leader Antonio Gomes da Costa and former Gusmao aide Constantio Pinto. The government released both in August, and has offered amnesty to any Fretelin rebels who surrender. Also in August, the army announced it would withdraw all combat forces from East Timor by October, deploying instead ten territorial battalions. However, observers note that these battalions are a key means of monitoring the population.

Political Rights and Civil Liberties:

Since the 1976 Indonesian annexation of East Timor, there have been persistant reports of human rights abuses by the government and military against dissidents and ordinary citizens. Freedoms of speech, press, assembly and association are nonexistent. On 13 March 1993, the United Nations Human Rights Commission in Geneva adopted a resolution expressing "deep concern" over human rights violations in East Timor. There are credible reports of dissidents being tortured and held incommunicado. The authorities also occasionally detain people without charge and then require them to report to the police on a regular basis. Foreign journalists are kept under constant surveillance. The government has closed schools that refuse to use the national Bahasa Indonesia as their primary language.

The few peaceful public acts of protest against the regime are quickly suppressed. On 23 July forty people held a peaceful pro-independence demonstration in Dili, the first since the November 1991 massacre. Army troops arrested twelve students. In October activist Alberto Rodrigues Pereira went on trial for publicly ripping an Indonesian flag. The mostly Catholic population is generally allowed to worship freely, although priests have been detained for alleged subversive activities.

Irian Jaya

Polity: Dominant party (military dominated)
Economy: Capitalist-statist
Population: 1,200,000
Ethnic Groups: Mainly Papuan
Ratings Change: *Irian Jaya's civil liberties rating changed from 6 to 7 as a result of methodological modifications. See "Survey Methodology," page 671.

Political Rights: 7
Civil Liberties: 7*
Status: Not Free

Overview:

By 1848 the Dutch had claimed all of the western half of the island of New Guinea and, following the Japanese occupation during World War II, formally regained control in 1949. In May 1963 Indonesia assumed administrative responsibility for the territory under a U.N. agreement mandating that a referendum on self-determination be held by 1969.

In the mid-1960s the guerrilla Free Papua Movement (OPM) began fighting for independence. Instead of holding a free referendum through universal suffrage, in the summer of 1969 Indonesia convened eight hand-picked regional councils in a sham "Act of Free Choice." The mainly Papuan population seemed to favor independence, but the councils voted unanimously for annexation with Indonesia. The Indonesian military had a heavy presence in the territory, and U.N. observer Ortiz Sanz of Bolivia reported that "the administration exercised at all times a tight political control over the population." Nevertheless, in November 1969 the U.N. accepted the referendum, formalizing Indonesia's annexation. In 1973 the land known locally as West Papua was named Irian Jaya.

A February 1984 Indonesian army offensive against the OPM sent hundreds of villagers fleeing into neighboring Papua New Guinea, and in April security forces murdered prominent intellectual Arnold Ap, drawing international criticism. In 1988 the army launched cross-border raids into Papua New Guinea against OPM rebels, and in 1989 conducted another series of anti-OPM offensives. Since then, the OPM has been largely ineffective, with only about 200 members still hiding in jungles near the border. In May 1992 the army killed M.L. Prawar, an OPM commander, and in August veteran rebel leader David Jebleb surrendered.

Indonesia's controversial transmigration policy, under which residents from over-crowded Java have been resettled in Irian Jaya and other areas, appears to have slowed in. However, the April 1992 *Pacific Islands Monthly* reported that since 1989, government teams in the Kurima district in the Central Highlands area have offered villagers material incentives to relocate outside the district, and have even withdrawn services in some villages. The villages lie in the new mineral exploration zone of Freeport Indonesia, the local subsidiary of the Louisiana-based multinational Freeport-McMoRan.

Political Rights and Civil Liberties:

Residents of Irian Jaya face human rights abuses by the Indonesian government and army. In January 1992 the U.N. Special Rapporteur for Torture concluded that in Irian Jaya and other parts of Indonesia facing rebel movements, "torture is said to be practiced rather routinely."

Several guerrillas and suspected OPM supporters remain incarcerated under Indonesia's anti-subversion laws. Freedoms of speech, press, assembly and association are severely restricted. The government continues to restrict access to foreigners. According to the U.S. State Department, by the end of 1992 roughly 3,700 Irianese remained in neighboring Papua New Guinea's East Awin refugee camp, having fled from army-OPM clashes.

Iraq
Kurdistan

Polity: Dual leadership-elected parliament
Economy: Capitalist-statist
Population: 4,000,000
Ethnic Groups: Kurdish majority

Political Rights: 4
Civil Liberties: 4*
Status: Partly Free

Ratings Change: *Kurdistan's civil liberties rating changed from 5 to 4 as a result of modifications in methodology. See "Survey Methodology," page 671.

Overview: Iraqi Kurds have fought with successive Iraqi governments to end repression and attain a level of autonomy. Iraqi President Saddam Hussein offered limited cultural and political freedoms in the 1970s, but ultimately reneged on his agreements. In the late 1980s the Iraqi government engaged in systematic mass murder and other atrocities against the Kurds, including rape, torture, detention, forced deportation, and chemical warfare. By some independent estimates, tens of thousands of Kurds were killed, many buried in mass graves.

Iraqi Kurdistan gained international attention following a brief Kurdish uprising in the wake of the 1991 Gulf War. Iraq's suppression of the uprising temporarily sent more than 1.5 million refugees fleeing to the mountains and into neighboring Turkey and Iran. In April, the United States, Great Britain, France and the Netherlands established, and continue to maintain, a secure region for the Kurds above the 36th parallel by barring flights of Iraqi fighter aircraft over the zone. Kurdish leaders say they do not seek independence from Iraq, favoring instead autonomy in a future democratic federal system.

On 17 May 1992 Kurdistan held presidential and legislative elections. Four candidates competed for the presidency, or "Leader of the Kurdish National Movement": Massoud Barzani of the Kurdistan Democratic Party (KDP); Jalal Talabani of the Patriotic Union of Kurdistan (PUK); Mahmoud Osman of the United Socialist Party of Kurdistan; and Sheik Othman of the Islamic Movement. One million voters participated, representing 88 percent of the electorate, and men and women voted in equal numbers. Barzani and Talabani virtually tied, and after backroom negotiations cancelled runoff elections and announced they would share power.

In the vote for a new, 105-seat Kurdish National Assembly, the KDP and PUK split the seats, 51 to 49 (in separate balloting for five seats reserved for Christian representatives, the Assyrian Democratic Party took four, the Christian Union one). To avoid conflict, the two major parties decided to split the seats evenly. No other party passed the 7 percent threshold for representation. The Islamic Movement took 5 percent, several other parties less than 2 percent. The PUK's Fuad Ma'sum, elected by parliament as prime minister, took office on 5 July.

In September 1992 the PUK and KDP decided to merge their *peshmergas* (guerrillas, literally "those who face death") into one force. In October Turkish forces launched a massive attack on Turkish Kurdish Worker's Party (PKK) guerrillas operating out of bases in Kurdistan, killing some 1,800 rebels. The Iraqi Kurds have refused to support the PKK for fear of offending Turkey, which provides transit points for U.N. relief convoys entering Kurdistan.

In 1993 Kurdistan continued to cope with the effects of two embargoes—the U.N.-sanctioned embargo covering all of Iraq, and an embargo ordered by Saddam Hussein separating the Kurdish areas from the rest of the country and enforced by the Iraqi army. The embargoes have caused food and fuel shortages, a lack of machinery and spare parts, and a deteriorating infrastructure. Iraqi agents frequently sabotage U.N. aid convoys. In addition, Iraqi troops along the 290-mile border separating Kurdistan from the rest of the country shell villages and farms almost daily. In mid-November the Iraqi Kurdish peshmergas launched several days of attacks on PKK guerrilla bases in northern Iraq, responding to Turkey's complaints that Kurdistan was knowingly harboring PKK forces.

Political Rights and Civil Liberties: In November 1991 Iraq withdrew all administration in the country north of the 36th parallel. Subsequently, in May 1992 the Iraqi Kurds elected a National Assembly. Iraqi laws passed prior to November 1991 remain in effect in Kurdistan, except for those judged by the Assembly to be "against Kurdish interests."

Observers report a generally open climate for dialogue on political issues. Numerous newspapers are available, including the pro-Saddam *Al-Iraq Al-Thaura*. The two major parties run four television stations, although news coverage is biased toward their interests. The other parties own newspapers and radio stations. Traditional practices curtail the role of women in politics, education and the private sector. Religious groups practice relatively freely.

Israel
Occupied Territories

Polity: Military-administered (West Bank and Gaza)
Economy: Capitalist
Population: 1,538,000
Ethnic Groups: Palestinian Arab, Jewish

Political Rights: 6
Civil Liberties: 5*
Status: Not Free

Ratings Change: *The Occupied Territories's civil liberties rating changed from 6 to 5 because of slight gains in freedoms of expression and association.

Overview: In September 1993 Israel and the Palestinian Liberation Organization (PLO) signed a highly publicized accord providing for a five-year period of Palestinian autonomy in the West Bank and Gaza Strip. This was hailed by the Palestinians as the first step to statehood but regarded by Israeli premier Yitzhak Rabin as an experimental period with no committments to eventual territorial concessions. By year's end, disagreement over the terms for the Israeli armys' withdrawal from the territories had delayed implementation of the accord.

The West Bank, Gaza Strip and East Jerusalem were part of the British Mandate in Palestine between 1920-48. In 1948 Jordan seized East Jerusalem and the West Bank and annexed them two years later, although few nations recognized Jordanian sovereignty. Egypt held Gaza following the end of the British Mandate, but did not annex the territory. Syria's strategic Golan Heights had frequently been used to shell towns in northern Israel. Israel occupied the West Bank, Gaza Strip, Golan Heights and East Jerusalem following the 1967 Six Day War. The government annexed East Jerusalem in 1967 and the Golan Heights in 1981, although neither act has been internationally recognized.

In December 1987 Palestinians living in the West Bank and Gaza began an uprising (*intifada*) against Israeli rule. These largely spontaneous, uncoordinated attacks included stone-throwing and other violent attacks against Israeli soldiers, who at times responded with lethal force. In 1988 Jordan's King Hussein abandoned his country's claim to the West Bank, saying he would respect the wishes of Palestinians to establish an independent state in the territory.

In October 1991 U.S.-brokered multilateral Mideast peace talks commenced, with the status of the West Bank and Gaza Strip promising to be a key element in any potential accords. In June 1992 Israeli parliamentary elections saw a coalition led by Yitzhak Rabin's Labor Party oust Yitzhak Shamir's Likud government, which had steadfastly refused to cede any part of the territories. By contrast Rabin promised a more flexible approach to the multilateral negotiations.

By mid-1993 there had been little progress in the multilateral peace talks. But on 24 August Israeli and PLO negotiators, who had held a series of secret meetings in Norway and elsewhere, agreed on a framework for a five-year interim period of Palestinian autonomy in the trerritories. Known as Gaza-Jericho First, the accord called for Israeli troops to withdraw from Gaza and the West Bank city of Jericho between 13 December and 13 April 1994. During this time these areas would be run by Palestinian leaders rather than the Israeli Civil Administration.

Further, by 13 July 1994 the Israeli army is to have withdrawn from all Palestinian towns in the territories, and elections are to be held for a Palestinian Interim Self-Government Authority, or Council. The Council will have adminstrative jurisdiction over all areas of Gaza and the West Bank, except for Jewish settlements and military facilities. By December 1998, the two sides are to have agreed on the final status of Gaza and the West Bank. On 13 September Prime Minister Rabin and PLO Chairman Yasir Arafat formally signed the accord in a highly publicized ceremony in Washington, DC.

The timetable gave negotiators a two-month deadline to work out the complexities of the first stage, including the size of the area around Jericho to be ruled by the Palestinians, security arrangements for Israelis traveling through the territories, control over border areas and a host of smaller, administrative issues. Complicating matters, intermittent violence continued to plague the territories and Israel itself. By 9 December fourteen Israelis and thirty-seven Palestinians had died in violence since the accord was signed.

Many of the attacks against Israelis were carried out by Hamas, the militant fundamentalist movement that opposes the accord. Meanwhile, a small but vocal minority of the 120,000 Jewish settlers in the West Bank declared they would never take orders from the proposed Palestinian police force, envisioned at 15,000 men. By years' end the accord had yet to be implemented as negotiators had failed to agree on the size of the Jericho area to be administered by the Palestinians, and over control of the international borders between Gaza and Egypt and Jericho and Jordan.

Political Rights and Civil Liberties:

Palestinians living in the West Bank and Gaza cannot change their government democratically. Palestinians in East Jerusalem can vote in Israeli municipal elections, but generally boycott. The September Israeli-PLO "Gaza-Jericho First Accord" provides for elections for an interim Palestinian administrative Council by July 1994, and for a final determination of the status of the West Bank and Gaza Strip by 1998. The Council will have authority in Palestinian areas over education, public security, taxation, social and cultural affairs and tourism.

Pending the implementation of the accords, Egyptian and Jordanian laws (plus British regulations), as modified by the Israeli military authorities, continue to be applied in Gaza and the West Bank respectively, and both areas are run by the military-backed Civilian Administration. Jewish settlers in the territories are subject to Israeli law, and generally receive preferential treatment in access to services and in commercial and legal matters. Municipal elections have not been held in the West Bank since 1976, and there have been no elections in Gaza since 1946, dating back to the British Mandate.

Prior to the signing of the accords, Israel and the PLO issued statements of mutual recognition. This effectively removed previous restrictions on displaying Palestinian flags or other nationalist symbols, and on openly supporting the organization.

In February 1992, in response to a new wave of Palestinian shootings of Jews in the West Bank, the Israeli army relaxed the rules under which soldiers could use their weapons. The new guidelines allow soldiers to fire on Palestinians who are armed, or who are being sought on suspicion of violent offenses. Although the Israeli government does not condone extrajudicial killings, in 1992 security forces killed 158 Palestinians, at least half of whom were reportedly unarmed. Meanwhile, 182 Palestinians were killed by other Palestinians.

There are credible, persistent reports of physical and psychological abuse by security forces against Palestinian detainees. Palestinians are frequently subject to administrative detention on security grounds without formal charge. Administrative detention orders are valid for a maximum of six months. Each detention order can be appealed to a military judge, and must be approved by the Ministry of Defense. Orders can be renewed indefinitely, but are subject to judicial scrutiny each time. The military can enter homes without a warrant for security reasons, provided there is authorization by an officer with the rank of lieutenant colonel or higher. High-level Israeli military officials have also ordered the destruction or sealing of homes on security grounds, although this appears to be occuring less frequently.

Palestinians accused of ordinary crimes are tried in local courts by Israeli-appointed Palestinian judges. However, many of these judges have resigned, and the legal system is severely backlogged. Those accused of security offenses are tried in Israeli military courts. Attorneys are often not allowed to see a suspect during the interrogation period. Roughly 95 percent of the defendants are convicted in security cases, and most convictions are based largely or entirely on confessions.

In recent years, numerous Palestinian journalists have been detained, arrested or interrogated, and press offices have been raided. Both Israeli and Palestinian journalists are subject to censorship by the military authorities. Gatherings of ten or more people require a permit. Although Palestinians are in theory free to emigrate, in practice the authorities often make it difficult to obtain travel permits. Freedom of religion is respected. In the West Bank workers are free to join unions, although prior to the Israeli recognition of the PLO, some labor groups were banned for suspected political affiliations. In Gaza, unions can organize only on a craft or workplace basis, and face restrictions regarding the election of leaders and the opening of offices.

Morocco
Western Sahara

Polity: Appointed governors
Economy: Capitalist
Population: 201,000
Ethnic Groups: Arab, Sahrawi

Political Rights: 7
Civil Liberties: 6*
Status: Not Free

Ratings Change: *Western Sahara's civil liberties rating changed from 5 to 6 because of a postponed referendum on independence.

Overview: **S**pain annexed the coastal areas of this northwest African region in 1884 and the interior in 1934. In 1957 Morocco renewed its claim to the territory based on informal ties with tribal leaders prior to the Spanish occupation, and in 1960 newly independent Mauritania also staked a claim. These bids intensified in 1963 with the discovery of substantial phosphate reserves.

In 1973 indigenous *Sahrawis* organized the Popular Front for the Liberation of Saguia el Hamra and Rio del Oro (Polisario), a Marxist, Algerian-backed guerrilla group, to fight the Spanish occupation. In May 1975 Spain said it intended to give up the colony by year's end. In October the International Court of Justice issued an advisory opinion holding that neither Mauritania nor Morocco had proven sovereignty over the territory through historical ties. Nevertheless, in November Morocco's King Hassan ordered 300,000 unarmed citizens into Western Sahara in what was later called the "Green March."

After the last Spanish troops withdrew in February 1976, Polisario announced the establishment of the Saharan Democratic Arab Republic, which has been recognized by more than seventy countries and by the Organization of African Unity. However, in April Morocco annexed the northern two-thirds of the territory and Mauritania the southern third. In August 1979 Mauritania withdrew, and Morocco soon annexed the remainder. In the mid-1980s Morocco began constructing a 1,200-mile, fortified sand wall to hamper continued Polisario guerrilla activity.

In August 1988 Morocco and Polisario approved a U.N. plan calling for a referendum on self-determination. A ceasefire took effect on 6 September 1991, and shortly afterward a 375-member U.N.-peacekeeping force took up positions in advance of a January 1992 referendum. However, in December 1991 the U.N. postponed the referendum because of the continuing electoral poll dispute. In August 1992 Albert Hakim, a senior Polisario figure, dealt the movement a setback by defecting to the Moroccan government.

On 17-19 July 1993 Moroccan and Polisaro representatives met in the Saharan capital of Laayoune for their first-ever talks. The talks broke down after Polisario complained that the Moroccan delegation consisted of tribal leaders with no real authority, although by negotiating at all Morocco had tacitly recognized the rebels for the first time. In late October a second round of talks at the U.N. failed after Polisario again rejected the Moroccan delegation. On 3 November U.N. officials in the territory said they had begun preparing for the referendum by registering residents listed in the 1974 census. However, by year's end the ceasefire held but the referendum remained postponed indefinitely.

Polisario currently controls about 15 percent of Western Sahara, but in recent years has enjoyed declining support from Algeria, which favors a rapprochement with Morocco. Polisario's only negotiating leverage appears to be the huge cost Morocco incurs in maintaining 165,000 troops in the territory.

Political Rights and Civil Liberties: In 1993 Western Saharan residents were again denied the oppportunity to vote on self-determination. The territory has ten seats in the Moroccan parliament, and Moroccan King Hassan appoints governors for the four provinces. Since 1977 the three northern provinces have participated in Moroccan elections, and since 1983 citizens of the southern province, which is partly held by Polisario, have also participated in several elections. The population in Moroccan-controlled territory is subject to Moroccan law, although in practice Sahrawis are subject to significant civil liberties restrictions. Moroccan security forces are also accused of detaining and torturing suspected Polisario sympathizers, and in recent years police have arrested numerous Sahrawis holding peaceful demonstrations. Polisario is occasionally accused of torturing Sahrawis in four refugee camps near Tindouf, Algeria. In Moroccan-held areas trade unions are in theory legal but none has formed. In its territory, Polisario has organized the Sario Federation of Labor, which is politically oriented rather than being an advocate of worker rights.

Netherlands
Aruba

Polity: Appointed governor and parliamentary democracy
Economy: Mixed capitalist
Population: 65,000
Ethnic Groups: Black majority with Carib Indian and European minorities

Political Rights: 1
Civil Liberties: 1
Status: Free

Overview: Aruba was part of the Netherlands Antilles from 1954 until 1986 when it achieved formal parity with the Netherlands and Netherlands Antilles under the Dutch crown. Under the assumption of domestic autonomy, Aruba agreed to retain economic and political links to the Netherland Antilles until 1996.

The Netherlands is represented in Aruba by an appointed governor, but the island is largely self-governing. Domestic affairs are the responsibility of the prime minister appointed by the freely elected unicameral Staten (legislature). Full freedom of party organization and expression is respected. The Council of Ministers at the Hague remains responsible for foreign affairs and defense.

The twenty-one-member Staten is directly elected for four-year terms. The social democratic People's Electoral Movement (MEP) won the 1989 election, taking ten seats against the incumbent, center-right Aruba People's Party (AVP), which won eight seats. Three smaller parties obtained one seat each. Following the election, a three-party government was formed, headed by the MEP's Nelson Oduber.

The MEP-led coalition won a narrow victory in the 8 January 1993 elections and Oduber remained prime minister. Both the MEP and the AVP won nine seats each and the AVP actually outpolled the MEP, 15,619 votes to 14,903. The campaign was marked by mudslinging as the MEP and the AVP charged each other with ties to drug-traffickers.

The MEP traditionally has been the main force for independence. In 1989, however, Prime Minister Oduber shifted in favor of commonwealth status to ensure a full defense commitment from the Netherlands against the threat of the Colombian cocaine cartels, and to guarantee certain forms of financial assistance. In 1990 the Oduber and the Dutch governments agreed that a new constitutional relationship, to be negotiated in the future, would not involve transition to full independence in 1996.

The press, radio and television are private, free and varied. Three daily newspapers are published, one in Dutch, one in English, and one in the local Papiamento. There are five privately run radio stations and one commercial television station.

Netherlands Antilles

Polity: Appointed governor **Political Rights:** 1
and parliamentary democracy **Civil Liberties:** 1
Economy: Mixed capitalist **Status:** Free
Population: 192,000
Ethnic Groups: Black majority with Carib Indian
and European minorities

Overview: In 1954 the Netherlands Antilles was granted constitutional equality with the Netherlands and Suriname (which became independent in 1975). In 1986, Aruba split off and was given formal parity with the Netherlands and the Netherlands Antilles. The Netherlands Antilles currently consists of two groups of islands, the southern (Leeward) islands of Curaçao and Bonaire and the northern (Windward) islands of St. Maarten, St. Eustatius, and Saba.

Although the Netherlands is represented by an appointed governor, the Netherlands Antilles is largely self-governing. Domestic affairs are the responsibility of the prime minister appointed by the unicameral Staten (legislature) of twenty-two deputies (fourteen from Curaçao, three each from Bonaire and St. Maarten, and one each from St. Eustatius and Saba) elected for four years. Full freedom of party organization and expression is respected. Foreign affairs and defense remain the responsibility of the Council of Ministers at the Hague.

Coalition governments have been highly unstable given the geographical range of the islands and island-based political differences, particularly over the issue of island independence. There have been seven governments since 1977 as eight different political parties have entered in and out of a variety of coalitions. The two main parties are the center-right National People's Party (NPP), which formed the government in 1988 under Maria Liberia-Peters, and the social democratic New Antilles Movement (MAN) headed by former prime minister Dom Martina.

The Liberia-Peters government retained office in the 1990 elections. The PNP increased its representation to seven seats, and its coalition partner, the Workers Liberation Front (FOL), won three seats. Along with ten of fourteen seats on Curaçao, the PNP also had the support of the Democratic Party (St. Eustatius) and the Windward Islands Patriotic Movement (Saba), both of which retained their seats, and the Bonaire Patriotic Union, which took all three seats on Bonaire.

Local government on each of the islands is constituted by freely elected Island Councils.

In a referendum held 19 November 1993 in Curaçao a 74 percent majority voted to remain part of the Netherlands Antilles and to maintain the current relationship with the Netherlands. The result was a rebuff for the island's main political parties, which had backed separate status for Curaçao. Following the vote Prime Minister Liberia-Peters's coalition unraveled and she resigned on 24 November. University professor A.F. Paula was asked by the governor-general to form an interim government pending new elections scheduled for 25 February 1994.

The press, radio and television are private, free and varied. The islands are serviced by six daily newspapers, two in Dutch and four in the local Papiamento. Privately owned radio stations operate on all islands except St. Eustatius. There is a television station on Curaçao. There have been reports in recent years of police brutality on all the islands except Saba. There has also been mounting concern over drug-related corruption.

New Zealand
Cook Islands

Polity: Parliamentary democracy
Economy: Capitalist-statist
Population: 18,000
Ethnic Groups: Polynesian majority, European and mixe- race minorities

Political Rights: 1*
Civil Liberties: 2
Status: Free

Ratings Change: *The Cook Island's political rights rating changed from 2 to 1 as a result of methodological modifications. See "Survey Methodology," page 671.

Overview:

Located in the South Pacific, the Cook Islands are in free association with New Zealand and have a right to independence at any time. Aside from defense and foreign affairs, they are largely self-governing. The inhabitants have New Zealand citizenship rights. The governor-general of New Zealand appoints a Queen's representative who appoints the prime minister. The twenty-four seat parliament has a maximum term of five years. There is also an advisory council of chiefs.

In 1992, the outspoken ruling Democratic Party's dissident Norman George split from the group and formed his own Alliance Party. The aim of the party is to offer a free-market alternative to the statist policies of the Democratic Party. The split came at a time when the territory faced the biggest budget deficit in twenty years, and the government of Prime Minister Geoffrey Henry was criticized for its extensive involvement in various economic projects, such as construction of a Sheraton hotel and support for the nascent black pearl breeding industry.

In an attempt to stem the tide of domestic violence mostly directed against women, a group of men established Polynesia's first male anti-violence group, *Te Akapuanga,* led by the physician Teariki Tamarua. The group coordinates its activities with a women's crisis center and works in anti-domestic violence educational projects.

Niue

Polity: Parliamentary democracy
Economy: Capitalist-statist
Population: 3,000
Ethnic Groups: Polynesian, other Pacific Islanders, Europeans
Ratings Change: *Niue's political rights rating changed from 2 to 1 as a result of methodological modifications. See "Survey Methodology," page 671.

Political Rights: 1*
Civil Liberties: 2
Status: Free

Overview:

The most recent top story in Niue was the death, after a prolonged illness, of octogenerian leader Sir Robert Rex in December 1992. The *Fale Fono* (parliament) chose Young Vivian as his successor. Vivian, the leader of Niue's only formal party, the People's Action, had been the acting prime minister during Rex's illness.

In March 1993, Niueans voted in general election for the new twenty-member parliament. During the electoral campaign, Vivian faced a major challenge for prime ministership from Frank Lui, a former cabinet member whose attempt to force Rex's retirement in 1990 led to Lui's ouster. Both Vivian and Lui were elected to parliament. Its members, however, elected Lui as the new prime minister. During the election, the voters for the first time elected a palagi (European) to the legislature.

After his election, Lui had to back down on his campaign promises to raise the pay of civil servants and pensions for the elderly by 12.5 percent, as the government faced a large budget deficit and warnings from New Zealand, Niue's main financial contributor, of possible cutbacks in subsidies. To promote economic growth, the new government embarked on a program to expand Niue's tourist sector.

In January 1993, the cyclone Nina damaged to Niue's main wharf.

Tokelau

Polity: Administrator, **Political Rights:** 2
elected leaders and elders **Civil Liberties:** 2
Economy: Capitalist- **Status:** Free
statist
Population: 2,000
Ethnic Groups: Polynesian

Overview: Tokelau is a collection of Polynesian islands in the South
Pacific. New Zealand appoints the territorial administrator. In
1992 consitutional changes allowed for the establishment of a
Council of Faipule (elected representatives) to act when the *Fono*, general parliament, is
not in session. The Council is endowed with the right to select one of its members to be
the *Ulu o Tokelau* (titular leader). Each Faipule serves a twelve-month, rotating term.
Land may not pass to non-indigenous people. Some land belongs to families, while
some is common property. There are no newspapers or broadcast media. There is freedom
of worship. Islanders belong to various Christian groups. New Zealand subsidizes the
local economy. In 1991, the U.N. Decolonization Subcommittee on Small Territories
examined the question of independence for Tokelau, but its status is unchanged.

Norway
Svalbard

Polity: Appointed **Political Rights:** 3
governor and advisory **Civil Liberties:** 1
council **Status:** Free
Economy: Capitalist statist
Population: 3,942
Ethnic Groups: Russian majority, Norwegian minority

Overview: Svalbard, "Cold Rim," is a collection of islands and skerries
which extends across 24,000 square miles. Two-thirds of the
area is covered by glaciers. The population of Svalbard
consists primarily of mine workers and their families.
In 1920, under the Treaty of Svalbard, nineteen signatories and twenty adherents
agreed to place the islands under Norwegian sovereignty, accepting that all the islands
and its waters were equally accessible for maritime, mining, and other commercial
operations. The treaty requires that Svalbard have no permanent defense installations.
Since 1925, Svalbard has been a part of the Kingdom of Norway.
Norwegian law and legislation apply to Svalbard. Norwegian legislators may
introduce regulatory measures if these provisions do not discriminate against non-

Norwegians. The government instituted strict environmental regulations and tourist controls to protect the delicate ecosystem. The main industry is coal mining.

The King of Norway appoints a governor who serves as the local head of administration and chief of police. He has certain other functions connected with the administration of justice. The local Svalbard council has existed since 1971. The fifteen-member council serves as an advisory body for the central and local administrations.

Portugal
Azores

Polity: Elected assembly
Economy: Capitalist-statist
Population: 269,000
Ethnic Groups: Portuguese

Political Rights: 1
Civil Liberties: 1
Status: Free

Overview: In 1992, the Azores developed a free-trade zone and European offshore business center. The territory consists of three groups of islands located 800 miles west of Portugal in the Atlantic Ocean. After the 1974 revolution in Portugal, separatist sentiment increased. Subsequently, the Lisbon government surrendered administration of the islands to local political leaders. A multiparty, forty-three-seat Assembly was established in 1976, and a regional government formed under the Popular Democratic Front, currently called the Social Democratic Party. Statutes passed by the Azorean regional assembly remain subject to the approval of the Portuguese parliament, which has Azorean representatives. Islanders have the same civil liberties as Portuguese mainlanders.

Macao

Polity: Appointed governor and partially elected legislature
Economy: Capitalist-statist
Population: 474,000
Ethnic Groups: Chinese, Mecanese, Portuguese
Ratings Change: *Macao's political rights rating changed from 3 to 5 because of increasing Chinese control.

Political Rights: 5*
Civil Liberties: 3
Status: Partly Free

Overview: The Portuguese established Macao in 1557 as the first European trading station on the Chinese coast. Consisting of a peninsula and two islets at the mouth of the Canton River, it is an entrepot for trade with China and a gambling mecca. The 1976 Organic Statute serves as the territory's constitution. It vests executive powers in a governor appointed by the Portuguese president, and grants legislative powers to both the Portuguese government and Macao's Legislative Assembly. This Assembly currently has eight directly elected members, eight members elected by business and other interest groups, and seven appointed by the governor.

In February 1979 Portugal and China established diplomatic relations, and subsequently agreed that Macao was "a Chinese territory under Portuguese administration." Portugal also secretly agreed to return Macao when China saw fit. The May 1987 Sino-Portuguese Joint Declaration called for China to assume sovereignty over Macao on 20 December 1999, with the enclave functioning as a Special Autonomous Region and maintaining its legal system and capitalist economy for fifty years. China agreed to honor dual citizenship for all residents born in Macao before 1979, and for children of Portuguese passport holders. In September 1990 Governor Carlos Melancia resigned over bribery charges on an infrastructure project; General Vasco Rocha Viera assumed the governorship in March 1991.

In the 20 September 1992 legislative elections, pro-China candidates swept all eight of the directly elected seats. Two Communist parties, the Union for the Promotion of Progress and the Development Union, each took two seats, while four smaller parties took one seat apiece. The results underscored China's dominant influence in the colony, due to its business interests and control of two key entities: the General Association of Workers and the General Association of Residences, a civic group.

On 31 March 1993 China's National People's Congress approved the Basic Law, Macao's post-1999 constitution. The document affirmed the territory's autonomous status after the transfer although, as with nearby Hong Kong, there are serious doubts as to whether Beijing will respect this. Another key issue in 1993 was concern over the slow pace of the localization of the civil service. Portuguese expatriates account for 71 percent of the government's undersecretaries and 86 percent of department chiefs, and hold all thirteen judicial seats. The government is training ethnic Chinese to assume these top posts, even though Macanese, citizens of mixed Chinese-Portuguese blood, already hold 5,000 of the 7,000 permanent civil service positions. The government says it is hedging against the possibility that many Macanese will leave for Portugal after the transfer.

Political Rights and Civil Liberties: Citizens of Macao lack the democratic means to change their government. The governor is appointed by Lisbon, and only a third of the legislature is directly elected. In addition, citizens had no ivoice in the 1987 Joint Declaration ceding control of the territory to China in 1999.

The legal system is based on Portuguese Metropolitan Law, and citizens are extended the rights granted by the Portuguese constitution. The judiciary is independent, and defendents receive fair trials. The government owns a controlling interest in the television and radio stations, and opposition viewpoints are aired. However, in December 1992 the government suspended phone-ins to the Cantonese-language radio talk show, *Pulse Today*, after callers repeatedly criticized the colonial administration. Ten journalists resigned in protest. Most newspapers are blatantly pro-China in their news coverage and editorials. Journalists reportedly practice self-censorship in criticizing China or government policies for fear of losing their jobs. A ban on holding demonstrations within fifty yards of government buildings effectively bars protests from the peninsula, restricting them to the two islands. Workers can join independent unions and hold strikes. In reality, nearly all 7,000 private sector union members belong to the pro-Beijing General Association of Workers, which is generally more involved in social and political affairs than labor issues.

Madeira

Polity: Elected assembly
Economy: Capitalist-statist
Population: 290,000
Ethnic Groups: Portuguese

Political Rights: 1
Civil Liberties: 1
Status: Free

Overview: The Madeira Islands are located 500 miles southwest of Portugal in the Atlantic Ocean. Although an independence movement proclaimed a provisional government in 1975, the regional government functioning since 1976 is committed to autonomy under Portugal. Statutes passed by the elected assembly are subject to Portuguese parliamentary approval. However, Madeira may spend tax revenue as it wishes. The territory has legislative representation in Lisbon. Civil liberties are the same as those on the mainland.

Madeira is prospering as an offshore business and banking center. Under the Social Democratic government of Alberto Joao Jardim, Madeira has won substantial subsidies from the European Union (EU), formerly European Community (EC), to which it belongs. EC grants have helped with a variety of health, training, and educational programs. Per capita income is less than 30 percent of the EU average, but it is rising along with economic development.

South Africa
Bophuthatswana

Polity: Dominant party
Economy: Capitalist-statist
Population: 1,959,000
Ethnic Groups: Tswana majority,
Pedis, Shangaans, Xhosas, South Sothos, and Swazis
Ratings Change: *Bophuthatswana's political rights rating changed
from 6 to 7 and its civil liberties rating from 5 to 6 as a result of method-
ological modifications. See "Survey Methodology," page 671.

Political Rights: 7*
Civil Liberties: 6*
Status: Not Free

Overview: Located in north-central South Africa, Bophutatswana consists of seven arid and noncontiguous territories. South Africa granted the territory nominal independence in 1977, but other countries refused to recognize this status. Along with the other three nominally independent "homelands," Transkei, Ciskei and Venda, Bophuthatswana served in the apartheid South Africa's strategy to create ethnically based black states. Kgosi (Chief) Lucus Mangope has been president since 1977. Running unopposed he was re-elected for a seven-year term in 1991. His ruling Christian Democratic Party took all the seats during the uncontested October 1992 legislative elections. The only legally registered opposition group, the Seoposengwe Party, has not contested elections since 1987. Another group, the Progressive People's Party (PPP), has been banned since an army coup, quelled by South African forces, attempted to install it in power in February 1988. Although activists of the African National Congress (ANC) operate in the territory, as a sign of its non-recognition of Bophuthatswana independence, ANC refused to register as a political party.

In 1993, Bophuthatswana continued to resist its incorporation into the new post-apartheid South Africa. Its leaders maintained that Bophuthatswana's claim to independence, nullified by the British exclusion of the territory from its Bechuanaland (present Botswana) protectorate, dates back to the pre-colonial period. In addition, its leaders, most of whom are former white South African and Rhodesian officials, claimed that Bophuthatswana was only minimally dependent on direct financial subsidies from South Africa, as opposed to the other independent homelands.

In late 1991, the government joined the multilateral negotiations in the Convention for a Democratic South Africa. In late 1992, Bophuthatswana joined the Concerned South Africans Group (COSAG), comprising black and white conservative groups opposed to a strong authority for the new South African government. Following the announcement of April 1994 as the date for the first all-South African multiracial legislative elections, the conservative groups, including the white pro-apartheid Conservative Party, the Zulu-based Inkatha Freedom Party and Ciskei, Bophuthatswana joined the newly formed Freedom Alliance on 7 October. The Alliance's aim was to disrupt the electoral process for the April 1994 South African Parliamentary elections. On 11 November, the government announced its refusal to recognize dual citizenship, threatening those willing to register for the South African elections with the loss of the Bophuthatswana citizenship. With the passage of the new South African Constitution on 22 December, effective from 1 January 1994, the South African parliament restored South African citizenship to all the citizens of the homelands. The ANC threatened to use force to reincorporate the homeland into South Africa, if the Mangope regime persisted in maintaining Bophuthatswana independence.

During the course of the year the government continued to stifle any form of internal criticism and dissent. Domestic and international human rights groups accused the security forces of torturing political opponents and criminal suspects, and indiscriminatly shooting protesters. On 14 August, the police charged secondary school students in several locations after they had presented their demands for legalization of student representative bodies. The police teargassed, whipped and fired upon the students, leading to the death of fourteen-year-old David Letsile. During the course of Letsile's funeral, attended by several thousand mourners, the police assaulted the participants, arresting eighty-one under charges of unlawful gathering.

Ciskei

Polity: Military
Economy: Capitalist-
statist
Population: 844,000
Ethnic Groups: Xhosa-speaking south Nguni tribes
Ratings Change: *Ciskei's political rights rating changed
from 6 to 7 as a result of methodological modifications. See
"Survey Methodology," page 671.

Political Rights: 7*
Civil Liberties: 6
Status: Not Free

Overview: In 1993, Ciskei's ruler, Brigadier Oupa Gqozo, continued to
resist the homelands incorporation into a unified post-
apartheid South Africa. The growing dissatisfaction among his
army officers with his rule, and the increasing activity of the South Africa-based African
National Congress (ANC), led to the erosion of Gqozo's power.

Surrounded by South Africa's Eastern Cape province, Ciskei is composed of two
noncontiguous territories, and is considered the poorest of the four nominally independent black homelands. South Africa granted the territory formal independence in 1981,
but still provides approximately 80 percent of its budget, police and defense support. A
number of the homeland's high ranking officials are either seconded by, or recruited
from, South Africa.

In 1990, a group of army officers led by Gqozo overthrew the one-party regime of
President Lennox Sebe. Following the coup, the South African press alleged that Gqozo
ordered the January 1991 killing of the former president's brother, Charles Sebe, the
former head of the military. On 31 August 1993, Ciskei's Supreme Court, at the request
of Attorney General Willem Jurgens, ordered Gqozo to stand trial in connection with the
murder. The Court's earlier decision on 2 August invalidated previous Gqozo
decrees, in which he exempted himself from charges in the Sebe death, arguing that
as a head of state he could not be charged in court. Prior to the trial, begun on 10
November, Gqozo denied any wrongdoing stating that in his actions he had the security
of the state in mind.

Since 1991, Gqozo indicated Ciskei's willingness to rejoin a post-apartheid South
Africa, albeit with the retention of autonomy by the territory. When in 1992 the ANC
pressed its demands for reincorporation of the homelands into South Africa to be
governed by a strong central government, Ciskei along with conservative white groups,
the Zulu-based Inkatha Freedom Party, and the homeland of Bophuthatswana formed
the Concerned South Africans Group (COSAG). In October 1993, COSAG changed its
name to Freedom Alliance, withdrawing from the multilateral talks in preparation of a
new South African constitution. Freedom Alliance announced its intention of disrupting
South Africa's first multiracial parliamentary elections set for April 1994. On 22
December 1993 the South African parliament adopted the new constitution granting
South African citizenship to the citizens of the homelands, including Ciskei, effective as
of 1 January 1994.

After the attorney general's announcement in May of his intention to prosecute up
to seventy Ciskeian soldiers and police officers of the death of twenty-eight ANC

protesters in September 1992, the ruling Military Council granted them indemnity from prosecution. The Council stated that prosecution would have a negative impact on South Africa's multiparty negotiations. In October, the Military Council admitted the existence of a "private" army under the jurisdiction of Gqozo's African Democratic Movement (ADM). According to the Council, the existence of the militia, estimated at 200 heavily armed men, was necessitated by the activities of ANC's military wing, Spear of the Nation (MK).

In October, the Johannesburg *Weekly Mail* reported that Gqozo "suspended" himself from administrating the homeland on a day-to-day basis in preparation for his upcoming trial. According to the report, which cited a senior South African government source, Gqozo nominated Colonel Silence Pita as the substitute executive. Following the report, Gqoza denied his alleged abdication of authority, accusing the South African ambassador to the homeland of attempting to discredit him.

In 1993, Ciskei continued to be plagued by violence and terrorist attacks attributed to government forces, the MK and other anti-apartheid groups. In September, a local ANC branch announced that it would support a "credible force" willing to oust Gqozo in a military coup, although it would not itself participate in the coup. The ANC branch cited dissatisfaction of Ciskeian military officers with the ineptitude of Gqozo's reign, and his reliance on white officials to fill senior government positions.

Transkei

Polity: Military　　　　**Political Rights:** 7*
Economy: Capitalist　　**Civil Liberties:** 6*
Population: 3,301,000　**Status:** Not Free
Ethnic Groups: Xhosa
Ratings Change: *Transkei's political rights rating changed from 6 to 7 and its civil liberties rating from 5 to 6 as a result of methodological modifications. See "Survey Methodology," page 671.

Overview:　　　　In 1993, Transkei faced accusations and an armed attack over allegations that it harbored armed groups linked to attacks on military, police and white civilians in South Africa.

Located in southeastern South Africa, Transkei is a nominally independent black homeland consisting of three noncontiguous territories. It has been self-governing since 1976, but its independence has been recognized only by the South African government. The Transkei army seized power from a civilian government in 1987, and successfully defeated several coup attempts, the most recent in September 1992. The chairman of the ruling Military Council, Major General Bantubonke Holomisa, has had close ties with South Africa's leading black liberation groups, including the African National Congress (ANC) and the Pan Africanist Congress (PAC).

Following the killing of five white civilians in South Africa's Eastern Cape Province in late 1992, the South African government accused PAC's military wing, the Azanian People's Liberation Army (APLA), of launching the attack. At the same time, the South African government accused Transkei of training and harboring armed groups involved in attacks on South Africa's territory, and asked the independent Goldstone Commission to conduct an inquiry on the attacks. The Commission's preliminary findings, published on 15 March 1993, confirmed the South African government's accusations. Transkei's Military Council, however, refused to accept the findings and report to the Goldstone Commission. Holomisa called the Commission "a kangaroo court," and on 24 March accused South African President F.W. de Klerk of issuing orders to "wipe out" all PAC and APLA members in Transkei. The South African government denied the accusations, and on 31 March ordered a border blockade against the homeland. The next day Holomisa offered his willingness to cooperate with the Goldstone Commission and to establish a homeland-based commission of inquiry. Following an agreement between the South African and Transkei chiefs of police agreeing to cooperate in controlling the border against intrusions by armed groups, South Africa relaxed its border control measures. Holomisa, however, refused to curb APLA's activities.

On 8 October, a South African police commando raided a house in Umtata, Transkei's capital, allegedly used as a training ground for APLA terrorist activities. During the raid, five teenagers were killed at point-blank range. The raid, authorised by President de Klerk, prompted an outcry of protest from the Transkeian authorities and opposition groups in South Africa.

In preparation for Transkei's incorporation into the post-apartheid South Africa, its parliament voted on 22 December to restore South African citizenship to the citizens of the homeland, effective as of 1 January 1994.

Venda

Polity: Military
Economy: Capitalist-statist
Population: 518,000
Ethnic Groups: Venda majority, Sangaan and Pedi minorities

Political Rights: 6
Civil Liberties: 5
Status: Not Free

Overview: Situated in northeastern South Africa along the Limpopo River, Venda was granted nominal independence in 1979. Only the Republic of South Africa recognized the homeland as independent. The homeland was created in accordance with the South African "grand apartheid" project for setting up separate political entities for various African ethnic groups in their historical territories. The aim was to deprive the black South African majority of the right to claim citizenship.

Under its original form of government, the territory of Venda had a legislative assembly with a combination of elected and appointed members. In 1990, however, Brigadier Gabriel Ramushwana overthrew the one-party civilian regime of President Frank Ravele, setting up a Council of National Unity.

Following the coup, the Council legalized the African National Congress (ANC) and agreed to the incorporation of the homeland into a post-apartheid South Africa. The homeland participated in the multilateral discussions on South Africa's future during 1991-1992.

In April 1993, the South African National Peace Committee (NPC) established a local committee to educate Venda's residents in the intricacies of a pluralist political system. With the adoption by the South African parliament of the country's new constitution on 22 December 1993, residents of Venda regained their South African citizenship as of 1 January 1994.

Spain
Canary Islands

Polity: Regional legislature
Economy: Capitalist
Population: 1,578,000
Ethnic Groups: Racially mixed, mostly Hispanic

Political Rights: 1
Civil Liberties: 1
Status: Free

Overview:

The Canary Islands are located off the northwest coast of Africa. The islands have the status of a Spanish autonomous region with an elected legislature that chooses the regional president. Although the people are mostly Hispanic, they are of diverse origins and maintain pre-Spanish customs. There have been periodic separatist movements, but the development of regional autonomy has reduced such sentiments. The population enjoys the same rights and guarantees as residents of mainland Spain. The Federation of Canaries Independent Groupings (FAIC) has one elected member in each house of the Cortes, the Spanish parliament. The FAIC has supported Spanish Prime Minister Felipe Gonzalez.

Ceuta (Places of sovereignty in North Africa)

Polity: Municipal administration
Economy: Capitalist-statist
Population: 80,000
Ethnic Groups: Moroccan, Spanish

Political Rights: 1*
Civil Liberties: 2*
Status: Free

Ratings Change: *Ceuta's political rights rating changed from 2 to 1 and its civil liberties rating from 1 to 2 as a result of methodological modifications. See "Survey Methodology," page 671.

Melilla

Polity: Municipal administration
Economy: Capitalist-statist
Population: 65,000
Ethnic Groups: Moroccan, Spanish

Political Rights: 1*
Civil Liberties: 2*
Status: Free

Ratings Change: *Ceuta's political rights rating changed from 2 to 1 and its civil liberties rating from 1 to 2 as a result of methodological modifications. See "Survey Methodology," page 671.

Overview:
Ceuta and Melilla, located on the coast of Morocco, are governed as municipalities of two Spanish provinces. Both areas have Muslim populations with Moroccan roots who have lived there for generations. Some other small areas nearby also fall under Spanish control. In 1985, there was a violent controversy over Spain's residency law that required all foreigners to reapply for residence or face expulsion. This law raised questions about the status of ethnic Moroccan Muslims in Ceuta and Melilla. In 1986, the government created a commission to examine how to integrate the Muslims into Spanish society. After demonstrations in 1986, the Spanish government made a move to give most Muslims citizenship over time. Both cities have Muslim political parties. Since 1985, the Party of Muslim Democrats has functioned in Melilla. Its leader, Aomar Mohamedi Dudu, a former official of Spain's ruling Socialist Workers' Party, became a special adviser to the Interior Ministry on the Muslim communities of Spain in 1986. In 1990, Ahmed Subaire formed a party called Incentive for Ceuta. In 1992, area residents gained legal protection when Spain placed Islam on par with the other major religions.

Turkey
Cyprus (T)

Polity: Presidential-par- **Political Rights:** 4*
liamentary democracy **Civil Liberties:** 2*
(Turkish-occupied) **Status:** Partly Free
Economy: Mixed capitalist
Population: 176,000
Ethnic Groups: Turkish Cypriot, Turkish, Greek Cypriot, Maronite
Ratings Change: *Turkish occupied Cyprus's political rights rating
changed from 3 to 4 and its civil liberties rating from 3 to 2 as a result of
methodological modifications. See "Survey Methodology," page 671.

Note: See Cyprus (Greek) under country reports

Overview: In 1993, the Turkish Cypriote voters defeated the long-ruling
National Unity Party in favor of opposition groups favoring a
compromise with the Greek-dominated Republic of Cyprus.

Following the 12 December vote, the National Unity Party of President Rauf
Denktash and Prime Minister Dervis Eroglu gained only seventeen seats in the fifty-
member legislature. The moderate Democratic Party gained fifteen seats, and the
Republican and Socialist parties thirteen and six seats respectively. The victory for parties
more open to the possibility of Cyprus's reunification raised hopes about the resolution of
the two-decade-old conflict.

In 1974, after a group of Cypriote army officers staged an unsuccessful coup to unite
Cyprus with Greece, Turkey invaded the northern part of the island, justifying it as
protection of the Turkish-speaking population. In the aftermath of the invasion approximately 200,000 Greek Cypriotes were forced to flee their homes in the Turkish-occupied area. Another 40,000 Turkish Cypriotes left the Cypriote Republic and moved to
the north. Subsequently, about 50,000 immigrants from Turkey settled in the Turkish-
controlled territory, and Turkey maintains a contingent of 35,000 troops on the island.

In 1983, the Turkish Cypriote administration declared independence, calling itself
the Turkish Republic of Northern Cyprus (TRNC). Turkey became the only country to
recognize the new entity.

In 1992, after the first face-to-face meeting between the leaders of the two island
communities, the TRNC president Rauf Denktash and the Republic of Cyprus president
George Vassiliou, there was a strong hope of a breakthrough that might achieve a
speedy reunification to the satisfaction of both communities. By October, however, the
U.N.-sponsored talks became stalled and were postponed until the next year.

The new round of talks, originally scheduled for March, did not commence until 24
May under a new mediator, the former Canadian Prime Minister Joe Clark. Prior to the
start of the negotiations, the U.N. Secretary General prepared a package of "confidence-
building measures." These included the placement of the resort town of Varosha under
the U.N. administration, which would allow the 40,000 Greek Cypriotes to return and
reclaim their property in the deserted town, and the reopening of the Nicosia Interna-

tional Airport, also under U.N. administration. In return for these concessions, the Turkish Cypriote side would be rewarded with a partial lifting of the communication and transportation embargo. In addition, the measures called for the establishment of bilateral commissions to cooperate on mutual environmental, educational and cultural projects.

In early June, however, Denktash rejected the proposal. On 18 June, the TRNC legislature endorsed Denktash's handling of the negotiations and authorized him to pull out of talks if the U.N. did not remove the threat to censure Turkey for the lack of progress during the talks.

In July, Denktash announced that he would no longer negotiate on behalf of Turkish Cypriotes, citing as reasons the challenge to his authority by his own prime minister, Dervis Eroglu, over the appearance of an accommodation with the Greek Cypriote side. Eroglu favored a hard-line pro-independence approach and stated that any rapprochement between the two communities "would lead to a bloodbath." Despite Denktash's announcement, he continued to negotiate with the U.N. mediators; however, they were unable to report progress. On 14 September, the U.N. Secretary General decried Denktash's lack of cooperation in solving the unresolved conflict. The year closed with hope that the new government would have a new attitude.

Political Rights and Civil Liberties: The citizens of the self-styled Turkish Republic of Northern Cyprus (TRNC) are able to change their government democratically. The TRNC has a presidential-legislative system of government with elections held every five years or less.

Despite its formal independence, the TRNC remains dependent on Turkish military and economic support. The Turkish immigrants who settled in the wake of Turkish invasion have a right to vote in TRNC elections. The 1,000 Greek and MaroniteChristians do not vote in TRNC national elections but are allowed to vote in the Cypriote Republic elections.

The judiciary is independent and fair trials are accorded in law and provided in practice. Civilians deemed to have violated military zones are subject to trial in military courts, which maintain all due process laws available in civilian courts. The TRNC authorities, however, still refuse to allow for an investigation into the fate of the 1,619 Greek Cypriotes who "disappeared" during the 1974 invasion.

Freedom of speech and press is generally respected, with a variety of newspapers and periodicals being printed. Although radio and television is government-owned they are able to criticize the government. International cable networks are available. The availability of Greek press to the remaining Greek Cypriotes in the north is limited. The authorities control the contents of Greek-Cypriote school textbooks, and many titles are rejected on the grounds that they "violate the feelings" of Turkish Cypriotes.

Freedom of religion is respected. The majority Sunni Muslims and the minority Greek and Maronite Orthodox Christians, as well as foreign residents, are free to practice their religion. Freedom of movement is generally respected, although travel to and from the Cypriote Republic is strictly regulated. Workers are free to organize and join independent trade unions.

United Kingdom
Anguilla

Polity: Appointed governor and elected assembly
Political Rights: 2*
Civil Liberties: 1
Status: Free
Economy: Mixed capitalist
Population: 7,000
Ethnic Groups: Relatively homogeneous, black majority
Ratings Change: Anguilla's political rights rating changed from 1 to 2 as a result of methodological modifications. See "Survey Methodology," page 671.

Overview:

Following the establishment of the Associated State of St. Kitts-Nevis-Anguilla, Anguillans rejected governmental authority from St. Kitts and in 1969 a British commissioner was appointed. A separate constitution was provided in 1976 giving the commissioner (now governor) authority over foreign affairs, defense, civil service and internal security. In January 1990 the governor also assumed responsibility for international financial affairs. All other governmental responsibilities are carried out by an elected seven-member House of Assembly. The first House elections were held in 1976. In December 1980, the dependent status of the territory was formally confirmed.

In the 1989 elections the incumbent Anguilla National Alliance (ANA) headed by Chief Minister Emile Gumbs retained control of the House over the opposition Anguilla United Party (AUP). In October 1993 Gumbs announced he was retiring from politics and would not contest the elections due in early 1994.

Anguillans enjoy all civil rights common to the homeland. The press is government-owned and operated. Radio is both government owned and private. There is no television.

Bermuda

Polity: Appointed governor and parliamentary democracy
Political Rights: 1
Civil Liberties: 1
Status: Free
Economy: Mixed capitalist
Population: 61,000
Ethnic Groups: Black (approximately 60 percent), large British minority

Overview:

Under a constitution approved in 1967, Bermuda was granted the right of internal self-government in 1968. A British-appointed governor exercises responsibility for external affairs, defense, internal security and police. A premier is appointed by the governor but is responsible to a freely elected forty-member House of Assembly for all internal matters.

In the 5 October 1993 general elections the incumbent center-right, multiracial United Bermuda Party (UBP) of Premier John Swan retained control of the House over the left-wing, predominantly black Progressive Labour Party (PLP). The UBP won 22 seats (down from 23) and the PLP 18 (up from 15). The PLP saw its share of the vote rise from 37 to 46 percent, and seemed to gain among young voters, the voting age having been lowered to eighteen. Turnout was 77.5 percent. Poverty, racial discrimination and drugs were the main issues. The question of independence has diminished in importance as most of the electorate has demonstrated its support for the status quo.

In November Swan and the UBP suffered a stunning setback when the House elected the PLP's Ernest Decouto as its speaker. In a secret ballot Decouto defeated the UBP's David Dyer, the former government whip, twenty-two votes to seventeen.

Political Rights and Civil Liberties: Bermudans enjoy all civil rights common to the homeland. There are several newspapers, all privately owned. There are over half a dozen radio stations and two television stations. Labor unions, the largest being the 6,000-member Bermuda Industrial Union, are well organized. The right to strike is recognized by law and in practice.

British Virgin Islands

Polity: Appointed governor and elected council
Economy: Mixed statist
Population: 13,000
Ethnic Groups: Relatively homogeneous with black majority
Ratings Change: *The British Virgin Islands political rights rating changed from 2 to 1 as a result of methodological modifications. See "Survey Methodology," page 671.

Political Rights: 1*
Civil Liberties: 1
Status: Free

Overview: The 1977 constitution granted the government of the British Virgin Islands greater responsibility over internal affairs. A British-appointed governor retains responsibility for external affairs, civil service, defense and internal security. On other matters the governor acts on the advice of the Executive Council whose members are the governor, the chief minister, four members of the legislature and the attorney general. The chief minister, representing the majority party in the elected nine-member Legislative Council, is appointed by the governor.

The 1986 Legislative Council elections were won by the Virgin Islands Party (VIP) headed by the chief minister, H. Lavity Stoutt. In October 1990 the legislature was dissolved and campaigning began for new elections. A total of thirty-six candidates was announced by the ruling VIP, the People's Progressive Democratic Party, and the

British Virgin Islands United Party, as well as independents. On 12 November 1990, Stoutt was re-elected to a second term as the VIP won six of nine legislative seats.

Residents enjoy all civil liberties common to the homeland. There is one weekly newspaper, one radio station and one television station. A spate of shooting incidents in 1992, apparently the work of drug dealers, raised concerns about whether the 136-member police force should remain unarmed. In 1993 a new firearms law was implemented, providing for up to twenty years in prison for an unlicensed weapon.

Cayman Islands

Polity: Appointed governor and elected assembly
Economy: Capitalist
Population: 31,000
Ethnic Groups: Mixed (40 percent), Caucasian (20 percent), black (20 percent), various ethnic groups (20 percent)
Ratings Change: *The Cayman Islands political rights rating changed from 2 to 1 as a result of methodological modifications. See "Survey Methodology," page 671.

Political Rights: 1*
Civil Liberties: 1
Status: Free

Overview: Previously governed from Jamaica, the Cayman Islands were placed under British administration in 1962. A British-appointed governor (currently Michael Gore) chairs an Executive Council composed of four elected members plus an appointed chief secretary, financial secretary and attorney-general. The Executive Council is drawn from the Legislative Assembly consisting of fifteen elected members, with a new Assembly elected every four years.

In the Assembly elections held in November 1993, the newly formed National Team of government critics led by Thomas Jefferson swept twelve of fifteen seats, with the other three going to independents. The three members of the Executive Council who were seeking re-election were all defeated. Jefferson and three other National Team members were appointed to the Executive Council.

In September 1993 the Assembly unanimously rejected a proposal by the British Foreign and Commonwealth Office to adopt a Chief Minister form of government. The Assembly did agree to adopt the title of "minister" for Executive Council members, to create a fifth elected ministerial post, to adopt a bill of rights and to establish a procedure for holding referenda on matters of importance.

Residents enjoy all civil liberties common to the homeland. There is one daily newspaper and a weekly publication. There is at least one radio and one television station.

Channel Islands

Polity: Appointed executives and legislatures (varies by island)
Economy: Capitalist
Population: 143,000
Ethnic Groups: British, Norman French

Political Rights: 2
Civil Liberties: 1
Status: Free

Overview: The Channel Islands, located in the English Channel, include the islands of Jersey and Guernsey and their dependencies. They are Crown fiefdoms and are connected to Britain through the person of the monarch. The Queen appoints her representatives, who are called lieutenant governors and commanders-in-chief. British laws do not apply unless the parliamentary legislation specifies that they do or unless the British Privy Council extends coverage of the laws to the islands. Islanders can make certain legal appeals directly to the Privy Council. In Jersey and Guernsey the appointed bailiffs preside over the royal courts and legislatures. Jersey's legislature, the States, is elected directly by universal suffrage. Guernsey's legislature, the States of Deliberation, has a mixture of directly and indirectly elected members.

In 1992, the major controversy in Jersey involved the dismissal by Lieutenant Governor Sir John Sutton of Deputy Bailiff Vernon Tomes. The alleged reason for the dismissal was Tomes's backlog of undecided court cases. Most of the residents, however, viewed this as a conspiracy by the local establishment to remove Tomes, a farmer's son, from office, and considered it unacceptable interference in the island's affairs. Following his dismissal, Tomes vowed to remain in public life and work towards changing Jersey's contract with the Crown so that the bailiff and deputy bailiff could be elected directly by the States.

In 1993 the major news story was the British government's decision to seek German financial compensation for the island's World War II deportees and their descendants. During the previous year, the British government's release of files showed that a number of prominent islanders collaborated with Nazi Germany during the island's occupation.

Falkland Islands

Polity: Appointed
governor and
partly -elected legisla-
tive council
Economy: Capitalist-statist
Population: 2,000
Ethnic Groups: British

Political Rights: 2
Civil Liberties: 1
Status: Free

Overview:

In 1993, Falkland Islands' media focused on allegations of war crimes committed by the British army against Argentinian prisoners-of-war during the 1982 war. Other issues involved the British and Argentinian increasing cooperation in the Islands' economic development and conservation efforts.

The British first came to these islands in 1610. Spain and Britain clashed over ownership of the Falklands in the eighteenth century. In 1820 Britain rejected Argentina's claim to the territory. Britain and Argentina negotiated over the Falklands' status in the 1960s and 1970s, but never reached agreement. In 1982, Argentina's military *junta* sent the army to occupy the islands, but was repulsed by the British forces after several weeks of fighting.

In August 1992, the British government began an investigation into allegations that British soldiers killed several unarmed Argentinian prisoners-of-war following two bloody battles of the 1982 war. In February 1993 two British inspectors arrived in the Falklands to investigate the matter.

Following the 1982 invasion, the Falklands experienced rapid economic growth derived largely from the granting of fishing licenses to foreign fishing fleets. In 1991 Britain and Argentina reached an agreement to control the lucrative squid fishing exploitation, but in December 1992, Argentina announced a unilateral move to issue cut-price licenses of its own. In May 1993 the British government responded by extending the territorial waters of the adjacent South Georgia and South Sandwich Islands from 12 to 200 nautical miles to protect the area from overfishing. Although the moves contributed to the lingering tension between the two countries, Britain and Argentina worked toward signing a permanent fisheries conservation agreement and cooperated in oil exploration efforts.

The Islands have a mixture of appointed and elected officials, with local legislative functions vested in a six-member council. There are two newspapers, one of them government-published. The public Falkland Islands Broadcasting Service operates two radio stations.

Gibraltar

Polity: Appointed
governor and mostly
elected assembly
Economy: Capitalist-statist
Population: 30,000
Ethnic Groups: Italian, English, Maltese, Portuguese, and Spanish

Political Rights: 1
Civil Liberties: 1
Status: Free

Overview:

In September 1993 the European Commission on Human Rights agreed to investigate the 1988 Gibraltar killing of three unarmed Irish Republican Army (IRA) members.

Located at the southern tip of the Iberian peninsula, Gibraltar came under British control in 1704 after the War of the Spanish Succession. Due to its strategic location between the Atlantic and the Mediterranean, Gibraltar is a key British naval base. Spain still claims sovereignty over the territory. British-Spanish tension over ownership is relaxing. In 1964 the colony gained some self-government and in 1967 voted to remain under British control. A new constitution established an Assembly in 1969. Spain blocked land access to Europe, but lifted the ban in 1984. In 1990, the two countries announced closer cooperation in civil aviation and extended a 1985 extradition treaty and a 1989 anti-drug agreement. However, Spain refused to sign a European Community border treaty by 1 January 1992 which Madrid argued would have implicitly recognized Gibraltar as British. In June Spain refused to implement the "Toaster" solution for immigration which required Spanish officials to monitor immigration documents via an electronic relay.

Britain appoints a territorial governor. He is advised by a Council of Ministers. Chosen through competitive, multiparty elections, the House of Assembly handles domestic affairs. Britain determines defense and foreign affairs. Association is free. There are seven newspapers and a public broadcasting corporation. The Socialist government of Prime Minister Joseph Bosano promotes a free market economy and encourages Gibraltar's use as a tax haven.

Hong Kong

Polity: Appointed governor
and partly elected legislature
Economy: Capitalist
Population: 5,748,000
Ethnic Groups: Chinese (98 percent)
Ratings Change: Hong Kong's political rights rating changed
from 4 to 5 and its civil liberties rating from 3 to 2 as a result of
methodological modifications. See "Survey Methodology," page 671.

Political Rights: 5*
Civil Liberties: 2*
Status: Partly Free

Overview:

Hong Kong Governor Christopher Patten began the year with firm popular support for his plans to broaden the franchise for the colony's 1994 municipal elections and 1995 Legislative

Council (Legco) elections. By year's end, following seventeen fruitless rounds of Sino-British negotiations and Beijing's subsequent threat to eliminate all elected government structures after it takes control of the colony in 1997, many citizens increasingly felt it was pointless to challenge China on the issue.

Located on the southern coast of China, the Crown Colony of Hong Kong consists of Hong Kong Island and Kowloon Peninsula, both ceded in perpetuity by China to Britain in the mid-1800s following the Opium Wars, and the mainland New Territories, leased for ninety-nine years in 1898. Long an important naval port and transshipment hub, Hong Kong became a booming manufacturing and later financial center in the post-War period. Executive power rests with a British-appointed governor who approves laws and presides over an advisory Executive Council (Exco). A sixty-seat Legislative Council can propose, amend or reject legislation.

In October 1982 Britain and China began talks on transferring Hong Kong to China. Because the New Territories include 365 of Hong Kong's 404 square miles, it was inevitable from the outset that China would take control of the entire colony when the New Territories lease expired in 1997. On 26 September 1984, the two countries signed the Joint Declaration, which gives China sovereignty over Hong Kong on 1 July 1997. Under the slogan "one country, two systems," China agreed to maintain the colony's laissez faire economy and judicial and political autonomy for fifty years. Beijing would be responsible only for defense and foreign affairs. The Declaration also established the Sino-British Joint Liaison Group (JLG) to consult periodically and ensure a smooth transfer of power.

In 1990 Britain and China agreed that for the first time, eighteen Legco seats would be directly elected in 1991, twenty in 1995, twenty-four in 1999 and thirty in 2003. These plans were incorporated into the Basic Law, Hong Kong's post-1997 constitution, which China's rubber-stamp National People's Congress approved in April 1990.

In September 1991 the colony held its first ever direct Legco elections. Pro-democracy liberals won sixteen of the eighteen contested seats, led by Martin Lee's United Democrats of Hong Kong with twelve. Governor David Wilson appointed eighteen other seats, twenty-one were chosen by leaders of "functional constituencies," representing professionals and industries, along with three ex-officio members.

On 24 April 1992 British Prime Minister John Major appointed Christopher Patten as Hong Kong's twenty-eighth and last colonial governor. Patten's reputation as a political heavyweight raised hopes among the liberals that he would be more assertive with China than his predecessors, who were mostly career diplomats interested in appeasing Beijing.

On 7 October Patten outlined his plans for the 1995 Legco elections. His blueprint adhered to the Basic Law by keeping the number of directly elected seats at twenty. However, he proposed broadening the franchise for the remaining forty seats, including the thirty that will be elected by functional constituencies. Currently, only some 190,000 leaders of twenty-one constituencies vote for these thirty seats, but Patten proposed allowing more rank-and-file members of these constituencies to vote. He also proposed nine new broadly drawn constituencies. All told, nearly all of the colony's 2.7 million working population would be able to vote for a functional constituency seat.

The other major proposal involved the composition of the Electoral Committee that will elect the remaining ten seats. China had envisioned an 800-member appointed body. Instead, Patten proposed to make the Committee an electoral college, drawn from the colony's 230 local District Board seats. At present, one-third of these seats are appointed, but Patten also proposed that at the September 1994 municipal elections all of the District Board seats be elected. Further, Patten called for the voting age to be lowered from twenty-one to eighteen, which would add 230,000 people to the voter rolls. Finally, the colony would drop the current double-seat, double-vote system in favor of a single-seat, single-vote system in the twenty directly-elected constituencies.

Enraged at this new British assertiveness, China immediately claimed the plans violated the Basic Law, and began a scare campaign aimed at eroding support for the proposals. On 23 October Lu Ping, the head of China's Hong Kong and Macao Affairs Office, warned that China might sack all Legco, Exco and judicial officials in 1997 if Legco approved the plans.

In early 1993 Patten delayed submitting his plans to Legco amidst signs that China would negotiate with Britain over the proposals. However, as part of an overall strategy to marginalize Legco and place the colony's post-1997 autonomy in doubt, China insisted that Hong Kong officials not be present at any Sino-British talks, and continued to deny that Legco had the power to approve electoral changes.

On 12 March Patten formally "gazetted" his reform plan, normally the first step to introducing a bill to Legco, but delayed the actual introduction in the hopes China would agree to negotiate. Instead, on 31 March China's National People's Congress voted to set up the so-called Preparatory Committee for the Hong Kong Special Administrative Region, a Chinese body charged with making preparations for the transfer that many liberals fear will become "shadow government" prior to the takeover. Previously, Beijing had said it would wait until 1996 to set up this body.

On 13 April Britain and China announced they would finally begin direct, high-level talks over the reforms, apparently after Britain agreed that the Hong Kong representatives would have an unofficial status. On 19 April, three days before the talks were to begin, Lu warned that in 1996 the Preparatory Committee would screen all legislators elected in 1995 to determine if they could serve out their terms after 1997. This would violate China's promise of a "through train" in which existing political arrangements would remain intact.

In early July, as successive rounds of Sino-British talks continued, China formally named the Preparatory Committee. Its forty-seven members included twenty-seven mainlanders, contradicting Beijing's promise of political autonomy. The Hong Kong-based members consisted mainly of business figures, and none of the three Legco members had been directly elected.

On 15 December, after seventeen rounds of Sino-British talks had failed to reach a compromise on the reforms or an agreement on the "through train," Patten formally sent the first and potentially least controversial stage of the reform package to Legco, dealing with the September 1994 municipal elections, the lower voting age and the single-seat district proposal. On 27 December China's Hong Kong and Macao Affairs Office said that because of Patten's actions, China would eliminate all existing elected bodies when it regains sovereignty in 1997. Although Patten remained committed to the proposals, he faced a difficult battle in gaining Legco's approval.

Political Rights and Civil Liberties:

Hong Kong citizens cannot change their government democratically. The British premier appoints the governor, and a majority of the Legislative Council seats are appointed or indirectly elected. Residents had no say in the 1984 Declaration transferring sovereignty to China in July 1997. An April 1992 report by the International Commission of Jurists condemned Britain for denying Hong Kong the right to self-determination, and recommended that it expand democracy before 1997 and extend the right of abode to the 3.4 million residents who have only British Dependent Territory Citizen (BDTC) Status and not British citizenship.

The colony has an independent judiciary, and defendents receive fair trials. In June 1991 Legco passed a Bill of Human Rights patterned after the International Covenant on Civil and Political Rights, although China says it reserves the right to review the bill after 1997. During the summer of 1993 eighteen leading law firms refused to represent liberal politician Martin Lee in a libel suit he brought against a pro-Beijing judge. Lee finally found a willing firm, but the issue underscored fears that the judicial system will be subservient to China after 1997. The colony has a vigorous press, although some journalists reportedly practice self-censorship to avoid antagonizing China.

Some 37,000 Vietnamese refugees, most of whom arrived between 1988 and 1991, live in squalid conditions in three camps. Nearly 30,000 other refugees have voluntarily returned to Vietnam, although some 800 others have been forcibly repatriated.

In January 1993 the colony's first significant strike since the late 1970s occurred as flight attendants at Cathay Pacific airlines staged a seventeen-day walkout to protest staffing cutbacks. The strikers say they were threatened with dismissal or sanctions if they did not return to work, and the entire issue focused attention on the colony's lack of legislation preventing employers from dismissing striking employees.

Isle of Man

Polity: Appointed executive and elected legislature
Economy: Capitalist
Population: 70,000
Ethnic Groups: Mostly Manx (of mixed Celtic and Scandinavian descent)
Ratings Change: *Isle of Man's political rights rating changed from 2 to 1 as a result of methodological modifications. See "Survey Methodology," page 671.

Political Rights: 1*
Civil Liberties: 1
Status: Free

Overview: The Isle of Man is located west of Britain in the Irish Sea. Like the Channel Islands, it is a crown fiefdom, tied to Britain through the monarch. The Queen appoints an executive, the lieutenant governor. The Court of Tynwald is the bicameral legislature. Claiming to be the world's oldest functioning legislature, it consists of a twelve-member Legislative Council, of which the lieutenant governor is a member, and an elected twenty-four-member House of Keys. For most matters, the two houses sit in joint session. There is a ten-member Council of Ministers, headed by the chief minister. The Isle has its own laws. Acts of the British Parliament apply only if they state so specifically.

Effective April 1992, the government reduced the tax rate on the fees earned by fund management companies from 20 to 5 percent. The island is attempting to become Europe's leading offshore funds center. In 1990 the government proposed legalizing homosexual acts. Britain's acceptance of the European Human Rights Convention on behalf of its territories had put the island in breach of continental rights standards on this issue. The island is the only European territory of the U.K. where people do not have the right of individual petition to the convention. Some supporters of Manx autonomy opposed the homosexual reform measure, because they feared it would jeopardize the territory's special legal status. The Isle of Man owes its success as a tax haven to its freedom from British tax laws. Manx economic interests feared that the homosexual reform would set a precedent that would undermine the island's ability to write its own tax laws, but the change in the fund management tax suggested otherwise.

Montserrat

Polity: Appointed governor and partly elected council
Economy: Capitalist
Population: 13,000

Political Rights: 1*
Civil Liberties: 1
Status: Free

Ethnic Groups: Mostly black with European minority
Ratings Change: *Montserrat's political rights rating changed from 2 to 1 as a result of methodological modifications. See "Survey Methodology," page 671.

Overview:　　　　　**A** British-appointed governor (currently David George Pendleton Taylor) presides over an appointed Executive Council. Local legislative matters are the responsibility of an eleven-member Legislative Council. Of the eleven members, who serve five-year terms, seven are directly elected, two are official members, and two are nominated. The chief minister is the leader of the majority party in the Council.

In the 25 August 1987 Council elections, the People's Liberation Movement (PLM) headed by incumbent chief minister John Osborne retained its four-seat majority.

In December 1989 negotiations in London between Osborne and the British government led to an agreement on a new constitution. The new constitution, which was instituted on 13 February 1990, consolidates the provisions of the Montserrat Letters Patent of 1959 and other legislation, and adds a statement on the fundamental rights and freedoms of the individual. On disputed matters, Osborne agreed that the chief minister would relinquish to the governor responsibility for international financial affairs, as proposed by the British government in the wake of a banking scandal in 1989. In exchange, the British government agreed to add a provision recognizing Montserrat's right to self-determination, and to eliminate the governor's power to overrule the Legislative Council on certain types of legislation.

In elections held on 10 October 1991, Osborne and the PLM were swept out of office after thirteen years by the newly formed National Progressive Party (NPP) which won four of seven legislative seats. The PLM won one seat, the NDP one seat, and the last seat was taken by an independent, Ruby Wade-Bramble. NPP leader Reuben Meade, a thirty-seven-year-old former civil servant, was named chief minister.

In 1992 Meade came under increasing criticism for failing to devise a plan to re-develop the island which was devastated by Hurricane Hugo in 1989. Nonetheless, Wade-Bramble failed in November to gain majority support for a no-confidence motion in the legislature.

Residents enjoy all civil liberties common to the homeland. There are at least two newspapers, including the opposition *Montserrat Reporter*, several radio stations and one television station. Labor unions are well organized and the right to strike is recognized by law and in practice. In October 1992 former chief minister Osborne and a former cabinet official were ordered to stand trial on charges of conspiracy and corruption involving the solicitation of bribes from a U.S. real estate investor.

Northern Ireland

Polity: British administration and elected local
councils
(military-occupied)
Economy: Mixed capitalist
Population: 1,578,000

Political Rights: 5*
Civil Liberties: 4*
Status: Partly Free

Ethnic Groups: Protestants (mostly of Scottish and English descent), 57percent; Irish Catholics, 43 percent
Ratings Change: *Northern Ireland's political rights rating changed from 3 to 5 and its civil liberties rating from 3 to 4 because of increased sectarian violence during the second half of 1993.

Overview:　　　　The most important news stories of 1993 were the Irish-British joint governmental declaration on Northern Ireland, issued in December, and the preceding agreements between the leading Nationalist politicians. These developments presented the best chance in decades to change the political structures of Northern Ireland and to reduce or end sectarian violence.

Northern Ireland consists of six of the nine counties of the Irish province of Ulster. At the insistence of the locally dominant Protestants, these counties remained within the United Kingdom after the other twenty-six counties, which are largely Catholic, gained home rule in 1921. Protestants comprise over half of the general population, but Catholics constitute 52 percent of the youth under eleven. Catholics now constitute a majority in four of the six counties of the North, and in thirteen of of the twenty-six local government bodies. The demographic trends have aroused deep anxieties among the Protestant population, which is largely descended from Scottish and English settlers of the seven-teenth century. Generally, Protestants favor continued political union with Britain and thus have the political labels "Loyalist" and "Unionist," while the "Nationalist" or

"Republican" Catholic population favors unification with the Republic of Ireland. Britain's Government of Ireland Act (1920), which partitioned Ireland, set up the Northern Irish parliament, which functioned until the British imposed direct rule from London in 1972. Several subsequent attempts at Catholic-Protestant power-sharing have failed.

Until the late 1960s, electoral regulations favored the economically dominant Protestants by according property owners voting rights for both their residential and commercial addresses. A non-violent Catholic civil rights movement in the 1960s met with limited success and a violent response from the Protestants. Attempting to impose order in 1969, the British government sent in the army, which originally appealed to some Catholics as a security force preferable to the Protestant-controlled local police. However, Catholics soon viewed the troops as an army of occupation. The violently confrontational situation of the late 1960s and 1970s led to divisions in both the Unionist and Nationalist communities. There are now several Unionist and Nationalist parties. The most important of these are: the conservative Official or Ulster Unionist Party, led by James Molyneaux; the hard-line Democratic Unionist Party, led by Rev. Ian Paisley; the moderate, pro-Nationalist Social Democratic and Labour Party (SDLP), led by John Hume; the militant, pro-Nationalist Sinn Fein, led by Gerry Adams; and John Alderdice's moderate, interdenominational Alliance Party. Sinn Fein is the political wing of the Irish Republican movement, whose military wing is the Provisional Irish Republican Army (IRA).

In 1990-92, the major Northern Irish political parties (except Sinn Fein) and the Irish and British governments held unsuccessful on-and-off negotiations about the North. Sinn Fein's refusal to renounce violence kept it out of the discussions. The talks bogged down in procedural wrangling, and broke down altogether in July 1991. After reviving, the talks collapsed again in October 1992 when they reached an impasse on the Irish constitution. Its Articles II and III claim the North for the Republic. Unionists insisted that Dublin would have to make a serious offer to amend the Articles before more negotiations. Additionally, the Unionists objected to holding talks when the Irish and British governments were resuming their discussions under the terms of the 1985 Anglo-Irish Accord, which gives Dublin a consultative role in the North.

In the British general election of April 1992, Unionists won thirteen House of Commons seats and the SDLP took four, its highest ever. Prior to the election, a policeman killed three Sinn Fein headquarters workers and Loyalist gunmen killed a Sinn Fein campaign worker. Adams lost his Commons seat, because some Protestants cast tactical votes for the successful SDLP candidate.

During 1993, Hume and Adams conducted discussions that produced the outline of an interim political settlement. Although the exact wording of their agreement remained private, Hume and Adams made clear they advocated British recogntion of the Irish right to self-determination and British renunciation of long-term interests in the North. In exchange, the Republican side would offer an IRA ceasefire, participate in negotiations and put off for now the question of Irish unification. The Hume-Adams proposals included implicit calls for joint Irish-British sovereignty over the North, at least for an interim period before the withdrawal of British troops and a final political settlement. Secretly, the British government held discussions with the IRA in early 1993, but denied that this was happening until late in the year. The Irish government worked on its own response to Hume-Adams, and negotiated with the British about producing a joint statement.

On 15 December, Irish *Taoiseach* (Prime Minister) Albert Reynolds and British

Prime Minister John Major issued a declaration on Northern Ireland. The British leader acknowledged the Irish right to self-determination, North and South. However, both prime ministers agreed that there could be no coercion of the North into a united Ireland without the consent of a majority of its population. The British stated that they have no "selfish, strategic or economic interest" in Northern Ireland, and that they would encourage agreement among the Irish people even if that means Irish unification. For its part, the Irish government agreed to referenda on removing the claim to the North from its constitution, in order to provide political incentive to the Unionists. The joint document agreed in principle that there could be all-Ireland institutions. Finally, the two sides promised that after a cessation of violence, all parties, including Sinn Fein, could participate in negotiations.

As 1993 ended, the SDLP was enthusiastic about the joint declaration, but Sinn Fein and the IRA raised questions and criticisms about it, without ruling it out. Moderate Unionists expressed somewhat positive feelings about the statement, but hard-line Unionist politicians and Loyalist militias expressed their outrage, viewing Irish-British agreements about anything as sell-outs of the Protestants.

Political Rights and Civil Liberties: The people of Northern Ireland have the right to elect members of the British House of Commons and local government bodies. However, the regional parliament remains suspended. Nationalists argue that they lack the right of self-determination, because Britain has effectively granted the Unionists a veto over the six counties' entrance into a united Ireland. Unionists, on the other hand, insist that the Irish Republic should have no role in governing them, and they resent Dublin's consultative rights under the Anglo-Irish Accord. Elections appear to be conducted fairly, and have allowed Sinn Fein to win both parliamentary and local council seats. Paramilitaries limit political rights by killing and wounding elected officials and political activists.

British laws ban broadcast appearances by members or alleged supporters of terrorist organizations. The British lift the broadcast ban on Sinn Fein for election campaigns, because it is a legal party. The government has banned several violent Republican and Loyalist organizations. Reports persist that elements of the security forces share information with Loyalist paramilitaries, leading to Catholic deaths. Trial by jury does not exist for suspected terrorists. A judge tries such cases, and there is an extremely high conviction rate. Under the Prevention of Terrorism Act, the security forces may arrest suspects without warrants. The authorities may prevent suspected terrorists from entering Britain and Northern Ireland and may keep non-natives out of Northern Ireland. In October 1993, the British excluded Adams from the British mainland, preventing him from speaking to parliamentarians in London.

In 1993, 87 people (including three in England) died as a result of Northern violence. The death toll since the start of "the troubles" in 1969 exceeds 3,000. Unlike some earlier years , in which Republican terror was responsible for the highest portion of the death toll, in 1993 the combined Loyalist forces killed 45, while the Republicans killed 38. No side claimed responsibility for four deaths. For the first time since the 1960s, in 1993 security forces were not responsible for any deaths. Republican terrorists tend to attack policemen, soldiers, alleged Protestant paramilitaries, and alleged Catholic informers and collaborators. Loyalist terrorists target alleged IRA members and sympathizers, Catholic politicians and activists, and increasingly, ordinary Catholics. Both sides often kill innocent, unintended victims. Several rounds of tit-for-tat violence began on 23 October, when an IRA bomb exploded prematurely in a Belfast fish-and-chips shop, on the Loyalist Shankill Road in Belfast, killing ten people, including two children. The intended targets were Loyalist paramilitaries upstairs. During 23-30 October, Loyalist and Republican paramilitaries killed 23 people, for a grand total of 28 that month.

All paramilitaries are potent economic forces. The Provisional IRA reaps profits through protection rackets, drug-dealing and other enterprises. Other terrorist groups (including the older Official IRA) have degenerated into pure rackets, almost totally devoid of their original political purposes. Loyalist and Republican paramilitaries have agreed on zones of control in Belfast. They have divided taxi services, construction projects and other legitimate business fronts among themselves. In 1993, the British government toyed with construction site identity cards as a tool against racketeering. However, business groups objected to the additional regulations and paperwork involved, and the Irish Congress of Trade Unions feared that the rackets would simply manufacture counterfeit cards.

Traditionally, Protestants have discriminated against Catholics throughout the economy. The British Parliament passed the Fair Employment Act of 1989, which set up a commission to monitor discrimination. Numerous organizations around the world have campaigned for the MacBride Principles, a set of standards designed to direct investment only to those northern Irish firms that adopt affirmative action hiring practices. Catholics are two-and-a-half times as likely as Protestants to be unemployed. According to a British government report in 1992, this situation will take more than a decade to improve.

Pitcairn Islands

Polity: Appointed governor and partly elected council
Economy: Capitalist-statist
Population: 52
Ethnic Groups: *Bounty* families (Mixed Anglo-Tahitian)

Political Rights: 2
Civil Liberties: 1
Status: Free

Overview: Located in the South Pacific, the territory consists of Pitcairn and three uninhabited islands. The inhabitants are descended from the *Bounty* mutineers and Tahitian women. In 1990 the island observed the bicentennial of the community's founding. In 1790 mutiny leader Fletcher Christian and his fellow muntineers settled there with a dozen Tahitian women.

In 1990 Japan Tuna's trawlers withdrew from the colony's waters after a three-year trial. The island had hoped to profit from selling fishing licenses, but the Japanese found the local catch insufficient to justify continuing fishing there.The local economy depends on the fishing, plant life, postage stamp sales, and crafts. Islanders make money by carving ornaments to sell to passing ships. In 1989, the island's gross income was 958,733 Pitcairn dollars, but the outgo was 923,355 Pitcairn dollars, leaving a surplus of 35,378 Pitcairn dollars.

The appointed governor is the British High Commissioner in New Zealand. Ten residents serve on the Pitcairn Island Council. They include the elected magistrate, Brian Young, and three other elected members; the island secretary; one member appointed by the governor; two members appointed by the elected members; one non-voting member appointed by the governor; and one non-voting member named by the council. The council controls immigration by issuing licenses to land only in rare circumstances. Magistrate Young and his wife visted London in July 1990, and met with Queen Elizabeth at a Buckingham Palace garden party. "We pay no taxes but we all do some form of public works," Young said. Among other tasks, the island's twelve able-bodied men maintain 17.5 miles of mud roads. Local law forbids public displays of affection. The islanders are Seventh-Day Adventists, and observe a strict Sabbath on Saturdays.

St. Helena and Dependencies

Polity: Appointed governor and elected council
Economy: Capitalist-statist
Population: 7,000
Ethnic Groups: British, Asian, African

Political Rights: 2
Civil Liberties: 1
Status: Free

Overview: St. Helena, Ascension Island, and the Tristan da Cunha island group are scattered across the South Atlantic between Africa and South America. The British governor administers the islands with an executive council of two *ex officio* members and the chairmen of the council committees. Residents elect a twelve-member Legislative Council for a four-year term. The Legislative Council started in 1967. Political parties are legal, and took part in earlier elections, but have become inactive. Tristan da Cunha and Ascension have appointed administrators who are responsible to the governor of St. Helena. Advisory councils assist them. The Ascension advisory council includes representatives of the BBC, South Atlantic Cable Company, Cable Wireless Ltd., the U.S. National Aeronautics and Space Administration, and the U.S. Air Force, all of which have facilities there. Ascension has no native population. In 1981 the governor appointed a constitutional commission to determine desired constitutional changes, but the commission found too little interest among the population to draw any conclusions. The island economies are dominated by British and American bases. There are also local fishing, timber, craft, and agricultural industries. The colony has a government-run broadcasting service and a weekly newspaper. The trade union is the St. Helena General Workers Union.

Turks and Caicos

Polity: Appointed governor and elected council
Economy: Capitalist
Population: 13,000
Ethnic Groups: Relatively homogeneous with black majority
Ratings Change: *Turks and Caicos's political rights rating changed from 2 to 1 as a result of methodological modifications. See "Survey Methodology," page 671.

Political Rights: 1*
Civil Liberties: 1
Status: Free

Overview:

Previously governed from Jamaica, the islands were placed under a British administration in 1962. A constitution adopted in 1976 provides for a governor, an eight-member Executive Council, and a Legislative Council of thirteen elected, four ex-officio, and three nominated members. The chief minister is the leader of the majority party in the Legislative Council.

In 1985, Chief Minister Norman Saunders of the conservative Progressive National Party (PNP) was arrested in Miami on drug trafficking charges and forced to resign. He was replaced by his deputy Nathaniel Francis, who was forced to resign in 1986 on corruption and patronage charges. The British government then imposed direct rule under the governor and established a commission for making constitutional reforms designed to inhibit corruption.

In the March 1988 elections that marked the return to constitutional rule, the People's Democratic Movement (PDM), formerly in opposition, took nine of eleven seats and Oswald Skippings became chief minister. In the 3 April 1991 elections, the PNP returned to power by winning eight legislative seats to the PDM's five and PNP leader Washington Missick became chief minister.

Residents enjoy all the civil liberties common to the homeland. There are at least one weekly newspaper and several radio stations.

United States of America
American Samoa

Polity: Elected governor and legislature
Economy: Capitalist
Population: 51,000
Ethnic Groups: Samoan (Polynesian)

Political Rights: 1
Civil Liberties: 1
Status: Free

Overview:

During the November 1992 gubernatorial election, the former Democratic governor A.P. Lutali defeated the incumbent Republican Peter Tali Coleman.

Immediately after his inauguration in office in January 1993, Lutali instituted an austerity program consisting of laying off up to 1,000 of the territory's 5,400 public service employees. The American Samoan Government (ASG) is the largest employer with 40 percent of the workforce on its payroll. Labor expenses swallow 84 percent of its budget expenditures. In a fight against the chronic corruption and financial misman-agement, Lutali ordered a criminal investigation of the Territorial Administration on Aging (TAOA) for possible misappropriation of funds from a food voucher program.

American Samoa receives much of its funds from U.S. government grants. In 1993, the U.S. government raised the minimum wage in the tuna cannery industry, American Samoa's major private employer, from $2.93 to $3.00 per hour.

Instances of police brutality against people in custody resurfaced, after a local court convicted two policeman in the death of a Western Samoan man, Tanu Peleti. Peleti was beaten while handcuffed in police custody after he had been arrested for disorderly conduct. Seven other police officers were suspended after the courts charged them with offences ranging from murder to fabricating and tampering with evidence.

American Samoa is located in the South Pacific. The U.S. ruled the territory through an appointed governer for most of the century, but Samoans have elected their governor directly since 1977. The *Fono,* a bicameral legislature, consists of a twenty-member House of Representatives and an eighteen-member Senate. The House is elected by popular vote for two-year terms. The *matai,* the chiefs of extended families, elect senators from among themselves for four-year terms. There are local affiliates of U.S. Democratic and Republican parties. The territory sends a delegate to the U.S. House of Representatives. There are free and competing newspapers, private radio station, and government-owned television station.

Guam

Polity: Elected gov-
ernor and legislature
Economy: Capitalist-
statist
Population: 142,000
Ethnic Groups: Guamanian or Chamorro (Micronesian) majority, U.S. mainlanders, Filipinos

Political Rights: 1
Civil Liberties: 1
Status: Free

Overview: An unincorporated territory of the U.S., Guam has lobbied Washington in recent years for commonwealth status. In 1982 the voters chose commonwealth, but the U.S. has not passed the required enabling legislation. The Guamanians want to end the U.S. Congress's theoretical right to abolish the island's constitution. They also want direct access to the federal Supreme Court in any plan for commonwealth.

In August 1993 Guam's leaders accused the U.S. of perpetuating colonial rule after a decision by the U.S. Department of Interior to screen and approve the Guam government's disposition of land relinquished by the U.S. military. At issue was the

Interior Department's fear that the Guam government might sell the land to "foreign interests"—most likely the Japanese—who provide the bulk of Guam's tourist revenue.

In the 1992 legislative elections, for the unicameral legislature, the Democrats won fourteen seats to seven for the Republicans.

In 1992, a federal appeals court judge declared Guam's abortion law unconstitutional. The legislation would have prohibited abortion, even in cases involving rape, incest, and fetal abnormality. The only exceptions to the abortion ban would have been situations involving medically certified threats to the mother's life or health. The law also forbade open discussion of abortion rights. The U.S. Supreme Court let the appeals court's ruling stand by refusing to hear the case in November 1992.

On 8 August 1993 a powerful earthquake caused at least $100 million in property damage on top of similar material damage caused by Typhoon Omar in 1992. No deaths or serious injuries were reported as a result of the earthquake.

Located west of Hawaii, Guam became American territory as a result of the Spanish-American War in 1898. Since 1970 the territory has had an elected governor who serves a four-year term. Former two-term, Democratic Governor Ricardo Bordallo, found guilty of corruption, killed himself in January 1990. Shortly before his scheduled trip to prison in California, Bordallo chained himself to a statue of an island chief, covered himself with the territorial flag, and shot himself. Despite Bodallo's departure from office in 1987 and his death in 1990, the White House sent him a perfunctory thank-you note in 1991. This letter caused islanders to complain about Washington's ignorance of their situation.

American bases and U.S. subsidies contribute significantly to the local economy. There are free and competitive print and broadcast media.

Northern Marianas

Polity: Elected governor and legislature
Economy: Capitalist
Population: 47,000
Ethnic Groups: Highly diversified populations of Pacific Islanders, Asians, Europeans, and Americans
Ratings Change: *Northern Marianas's civil liberties rating changed from 1 to 2 because of increased exploitation of immigrant labor.

Political Rights: 1
Civil Liberties: 2*
Status: Free

Overview: In 1993, Northern Marianas Republican Governor Lorenzo DeLeon Guerrero was defeated by his Democratic opponent Froilan Tenorio.

The defeat of Guerrero followed a political row between the U.S. Congress and the territory's administration over the wages and labor practices in Northern Marianas's principal garment industry. Because Northern Marianas, alone among U.S. territories, sets its own minimum wages and controls its immigration, it attracted a number of garment companies taking advantage of unrestricted access of locally made products to the U.S. market, and imported labor earning half the U.S. minimum wages. Following a 1992 U.S. Department of Labor crackdown against exploitative labor practices, including the withholding of pay and unsanitary working and living conditions of foreign workers, mostly from the neighboring Asian countries, legislators in the U.S. Congress introduced bills that would require the territory to abide by U.S. immigration standards and cut off federal subsidies until the labor issues were resolved. In response to the uproar, intensified over Guerrero's misstatement of facts about his meeting with U.S. Congressional leaders, the territorial legislature voted to raise the minimum wages to the current U.S. level by the year 2000. In addition, Guerrero proposed the creation of a human rights commission to protect the rights of workers. Nonetheless, the voters rejected Guerrero in favor of Tenorio in the November 1993 election.

Palau (Belau)

Polity: Elected president and legislature
Economy: Capitalist
Population: 16,000
Ethnic Groups: Palauan (a mixture of Micronesian, Malayan and Melanesian) and mixed Palauan-European-Asian

Political Rights: 1
Civil Liberties: 2
Status: Free

Overview:

Palau (Belau) became part of the U.N. supervised Trust Territory of the Pacific after World War II. In 1980, Palau adopted its constitution and changed its name to Republic of Palau. Under the constitution, executive power is vested in a president who is elected in a nationwide election for a period of four years. Legislative power is vested in the Olbiil Era Kelulau (National Congress of Palau) consisting of a House of Delegates and a Senate. Judicial power is vested in a Supreme Court, a National Court and other inferior courts. Palau is the only remaining U.S. trust territory.

In November 1993 former Vice President Kuriwo Nakamura defeated Johnson Toribiong by a small majority. At the same time, voters approved, by a simple majority, a constitutional amendment allowing for the approval of a Compact of Free Association with the U.S. Previousl Paluauans had voted seven times on this issue since 1983, each time failing to approve the Compact due to less than 75 percent support. The Compact provides for self-government in domestic affairs, $450 million in U.S. aid, and the right of the U.S. to conduct Palau's foreign and defense policies, including the right to establish two military bases in the archipelago. Opponents of the Compact feared a militarization of the territory and the possibility of the U.S. storing nuclear weapons or waste. The Compact, however, prohibits storing unconventional weapons on the islands and makes provisions for U.S. cleanup of former nuclear sites.

On 17 May 1993 the U.N. Trusteeship Council agreed to send election monitors for the plebiscite originally scheduled for 27 July but later postponed to 9 November. The Compact was approved with 68 percent of the vote. During the year several legal challenges brought by opponents of the Compact were rejected by the courts.

Puerto Rico

Polity: Elected governor
and legislature
Economy: Capitalist
Population: 3,721,000
Ethnic Groups: Relatively homogeneous, Hispanic

Political Rights: 1
Civil Liberties: 1
Status: Free

Overview:

Following approval by plebiscite, Puerto Rico acquired the status of a commonwealth in free association with the U.S. in 1952. Under its terms, Puerto Rico exercises approximately the same control over its internal affairs as do the fifty U.S. states. Residents, though U.S. citizens, do not vote in presidential elections and are represented in the U.S. Congress by a delegate to the House of Representatives who can vote in committee but not on the floor.

The Commonwealth constitution, modeled on that of the U.S., provides for a governor and a bicameral Legislature, consisting of a twenty-seven-member Senate and a fifty-one-member House of Representatives, directly elected for four-year terms. An appointed Supreme Court heads an independent judiciary and the legal system is based on U.S. law.

On 3 November 1992 Pedro Rossello of the pro-statehood New Progressive Party (PNP) was elected governor, defeating Victoria Munoz Mendoza, the candidate of the incumbent Popular Democratic Party (PPD). Outgoing Governor Rafael Hernandez Colon decided not to seek re-election after two terms in office.

With 83 percent of registered voters participating, Rosello took 49.9 percent of the vote against 45.8 percent for Munoz, 3.8 percent for environmentalist Neftali Garcia and 3.3 percent for Fernando Martin of the Puerto Rican Independence Party (PIP). The PNP won 36 of 51 seats in the House and 20 of 27 Senate seats, and was victorious in 54 of the island's 72 municipalities. The PNP's Carlos Romero Barcelo, a former governor, won in the race for the non-voting delegate to the U.S. Congress.

Although the island's relationship with the U.S. remains a fundamental political issue, the election reflected an anti-incumbency fever and immediate concerns over rising crime, high unemployment, government corruption and education. Nonetheless, Rosello promised in his campaign to hold a plebiscite in 1993 in which voters could choose between statehood, independence or retaining commonwealth status.

In a nonbinding referendum held on 14 November 1993, voters narrowly opted to retain commonwealth status. Any vote to change the island's status would have had to be approved by the U.S. Congress. Commonwealth status received 48.4 percent of the vote, statehood 46.2 percent, and independence 4.4 percent. The vote indicated significant gains for statehood, which in the last referendum in 1967 received only 39 percent of the vote to 60 percent for commonwealth.

As U.S. citizens, Puerto Ricans enjoy all civil liberties granted in the U.S. The press and broadcast media are well developed, highly varied, uncensored and critical. Labor unions are well organized and have the right to strike.

A cause for concern remains the steep rise in criminal violence in recent years, much of it drug-related. By the end of November 1993 the record setting number of murders in 1992, 864, had already been surpassed. In June the government ordered around 1,000 of Puerto Rico's 8,000 National Guardsmen to occupy drug-ridden housing projects. Some civil libertarians expressed concern but most residents praised the measure.

United States Virgin Islands

Polity: Elected governor and senate
Economy: Capitalist
Population: 99,000
Political Rights: 1
Civil Liberties: 1
Status: Free
Ethnic Groups: Relatively homogeneous with black majority

Overview: The U.S. Virgin Islands, consisting of St. Croix, St. Thomas, St. John and four dozen smaller islands, are governed as an unincorporated territory of the U.S. The inhabitants were made U.S. citizens in 1927 and granted a considerable measure of self-government in 1954. Since 1970, executive authority has resided in a governor and lieutenant governor directly elected for a four-year term. There is also a unicameral fifteen-member Senate elected for two years, with each of the three main islands proportionately represented. Since 1973 the territory has sent one non-voting delegate to the U.S. House of Representatives.

In November 1990, incumbent Governor Alexander Farrelly scored a landslide victory over his main challenger, former governor Juan Luis, to secure a second term. The other main political party is the Independent Citizens' Movement.

In a referendum held on 11 October 1993, 80.3 percent of voters opted to remain an unincorporated territory of the U.S., while 14.2 percent backed full integration with the U.S. and 4.8 percent voted for independence. Only 27.4 percent of registered voters turned out, less than the 50 percent required for the referendum to be valid.

As U.S. citizens, island residents enjoy all civil liberties granted in the U.S. There are at least two newspapers and several radio and television stations. Alleged mistreatment of workers and the beatings of several supervisors led to an August 1992 lockout of 2,000 workers at the Hess Oil refinery on St. Croix, the largest private employer on the island. The lockout ended after unions and management negotiated an agreement to establish a joint committee to ensure worker safety and arbitrate racial disputes.

Yugoslavia
Kosovo

Polity: Serbian administration
Economy: Mixed-statist
Population: 1,700,000
Ethnic Groups: Albanians (90 percent), Serbs and Montenegrins (10 percent)

Political Rights: 7
Civil Liberties: 7
Status: Not Free

Overview:

In 1993, Kosovo, an Albanian enclave within Serbia that used to be an autonomous region in Yugoslavia, remained a tinderbox as fears rose that Serbian repression could escalate. Despite pressure from Serbia, which took over administration of the region in 1990, Albanians elected a shadow president and parliament in 1992 to underscore the illegitimacy of the Serb-imposed administration.

Although Kosovo has neither strategic nor economic importance and is one of the poorest areas of former Yugoslavia, the region is the historic cradle of the Serbian medieval state and culture. It was the site of the Battle of Kosovo Fields in 1389 between Serbian Prince Lazar and the Turks, which solidified Ottoman control over the Serbs for the next 500 years. Serbian President Slobodan Milosevic rose to power in 1987 over the issue of Kosovo's status. The central plank in his platform was the subjugation of the then-autonomous Yugoslav province (autonomy was granted by Tito's 1974 constitution) to Serbian authority. This was imposed in mid-1990 when Milosevic abolished the provincial government and legislature and introduced a series of amendments to the Serbian constitution that effectively removed the legal basis for Kosovo's autonomy.

In May 1992, Albanians held elections (branded illegal by Belgrade) for new members of a clandestine government. Ibrahim Rugova, leader of the Democratic League of Kosovo, was elected president of an "independent" Republic of Kosova. Delegates to the 130-member legislature were also elected. Bujar Bukoshi was named prime minister.

Serbian repression of Albanians is maintained by a 40,000-man army a militia force. Harassment, detention and intimidation of Albanians is endemic. On 14 April, police banned the annual meeting of the Parliamentary Party of Kosovo in Pristina, the capital. Most delegates were arrested on their way to the meeting. The same month, President Rugova, an advocate of passive resistance, called on the United Nations Security Council to put the issue of Kosovo on the agenda, citing the arrest of several academics and political figures.

In May, 1,500 journalists and other employees of the *Rilindja* Albanian newspaper went on strike over a decision by Serb authorities to take over the paper through "privatization" and the formation of an enterprise called Panorama. Adem Demaci, chairman of the Kosovo Committee for the Protection of Human Rights and Liberties and the editor-in-chief of the *Zeri* weekly, went on a hunger strike to protest the move. He was supported by the Kosovo Democratic Alliance (LDK). In July, the LDK's office was raided by police, and several activists, including chairman Muhareem Hoxha, were taken into custody. The same month, Serb authorities expelled a group of human rights observers from the Conference on Security and Cooperation in Europe (CSCE).

Raids continued throughout the year in dozens of towns and villages around Kosovo.

Political Rights and Civil Liberties: Kosovars cannot democratically change the *de jure* government imposed by Serbia. The main Albanian political parties are technically outlawed, among them the LDK, the Parliamentary Party and the Social Democrats. Kosovo's democratically elected legislature and government remained underground following the 1992 elections, which were not recognized by Serbia.

Albanian cultural identity remained under siege. Over the last three years, Albanian monuments have been destroyed, streets have been given Serbian names, and signs in Cyrillic have replaced those in the Latin script. Serbian has supplanted Albanian as the official language. Since 1991, some 8,000 Albanian teachers have been dismissed. On 15 September 1993 Serb authorities shut down all Albanian-language secondary schools denying schooling to an estimated 63,000 children. The crackdown, shutting all fifty-eight Albanian-language secondary schools and twenty-one of the 350-odd Albanian-language primary schools, surpassed last year's crackdown. Coincidentally, twelve Albanian teachers were severely beaten in the town of Mitrovica. A network of clandestine, underground schools have been set up in Albanian households.

Rugova's shadow government claims that nearly 120,000 Albanians out of a total workforce of 240,000 have been fired since 1990, and Serbian replacements brought in. Albanians have the highest birthrate in Europe; some 300,000 left for other parts of Europe over the last several years, and the money they send back to families is used to support the shadow government and the Albanian cause.

While Albanian resistance has officially been non-violent, several Serbian policemen and militiamen were murdered in 1993. The Albanians maintain that many of these were actually killed by Serbian militia, including one controlled by accused bank robber and war criminal Zeljko Raznjatovic, better known as Arkan. In December 1993 Serbian parliamentary elections he lost he seat in Kosovo, even with Albanians boycotting the vote.

Albanian TV and radio were abolished. A Belgrade-based conglomerate took over *Rilindja*. Albanian judges, policemen and government officials have all been replaced over the last three years. Freedom of movement and other fundamental rights have been circumscribed by the Serbs.

The Independent Trade Unions of Kosovo (BSPK), an outlawed Albanian-language confederation, has been the subject of repression for refusing to affiliate with the official Serbian unions or sign collective agreements approved by these unions.

Vojvodina

Polity: Serbian administration and provincial assembly
Political Rights: 6
Civil Liberties: 6*
Status: Not Free
Economy: Mixed-statist
Population: 2,000,000
Ethnic Groups: Serbians (58 percent), Hungarians (14 percent), Slovaks, Bulgarians, Romanians, others.
Ratings Change: *Vojvodina's civil liberties rating changed from 5 to 6 because of political presure and intimidation by Serb paramilitary units.

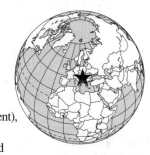

Overview:
In 1993, Vojvodina, northern Serbia's agriculturally rich and most ethnically diverse province that was once an autonomous region in Yugoslavia, managed to avoid the type of violent ethnic strife that gripped most of former Yugoslavia. But political pressure and intimidation by Serb paramilitary units raised tensions among the 345,000-strong Hungarian minority.

Like the Albanian-dominant province of Kosovo, Vojvodina enjoyed political autonomy within Yugoslavia until 1990, when the nationalist Serbian government under Slobodan Milosevic abolished most of its constitutional privileges. Vojvodina had enjoyed relative autonomy under the Austrian-Hungarian empire and at the end of World War I—along with Slovenia ,Croatia, Slovenia and Serbia—it formed Yugoslavia. Under Communist leader Josip Broz (Tito) Yugoslavia granted greater autonomous status to Vojvodina and Kosovo, though they were not made constituent republics.

In 1993, Vojvodina hoped to regain a measure of autonomy. Efforts were spearheaded by the Democratic Community of Vojvodina (VMDK) led by Andras Agoston, who accused Serbs of quiet "ethnic cleaning" that continued to include the forceful and illegal mobilization of Hungarian reservists to fight in Bosnia.

On 9 February, deputies of the Vojvodina Assembly elected a new government and endorsed the program presented by Prime Minister-Designate Bosko Perosevic. Representatives of the Reformist Democratic Party of Vojvodina, the Democratic Party, the Democratic Movement of Serbia, and the VMDK voted against the program. VMDK members criticized the appointment of Margit Savovic to the post of secretary of minority rights, administration and law, because she did not enjoy the trust of local Hungarians. Several Serbian paramilitary groups continued to use Vojvodina as a base for operations in Croatia and in Bosnia. Since 1991, thousands of conscripts of Hungarian, Slovakian, Romanian and Bulgarian descent fled to escape military service.

Vojvodina was home to some 200,000 refugees from Bosnia, most living in camps or with local families. The VMDK said the Serbs planned to settle 140,000 Serb refugees in Hungarian regions. The homes of the estimated 25,000 Vojvodina Hungarians who had fled the region were taken over by Serbs. Serb intimidation includes nighttime raids on Hungarian homes, shooting and arson. The Serb police seldom make arrests.

The VMDK, which held eighteen seats in the Vojvodina Parliament, nine in the

Serbian Parliament, and three in the Yugoslav federal Assembly, advocated self-rule in the ten municipalities where Hungarians made up more than 70 percent of the population and the thirteen where they make up more than 50 percent. Janos Vekas, vice chairman of the VMDK, said that, with Serbia internationally isolated for its role in Yugoslavia's civil war, Hungarians felt it especially important to make Vojvodina a separate entity. Demands also included Hungarian-language media, an ethnic Hungarian quasi-parliament, and expansion of Hungarian-language education through high school.

Political Rights and Civil Liberties: In 1990, Vojvodina lost its status as an autonomous region within Yugoslavia when it was taken over by Serbia, whose territory it abuts. Citizens can elect a provincial government and take part in Serbian elections, as well as those for rump-Yugoslavia, but non-Serbs have reported harassment and intimidation. There is no truly independent judiciary.

Tensions continued throughout the year between Serbs and the large Hungarian minority. Since 1992, the parliament in Belgrade enacted seventeen laws restricting or abolishing important minority rights. Minorities are no longer able to use their own language before the law, more than half the Hungarian policemen lost their jobs or left the area, and there are no Hungarian mayors. The VMDK reported that children no longer dare go to Hungarian-language schools for fear of being stigmatized. Hungarian teachers who have left have been replaced by Serbs and the number of subjects that are taught in Hungarian has declined. Purges of non-Serbs occurred in the police, customs, and, allegedly, the judiciary.

All institutions operating in Vojvodina are essentially under control of the Serbian government in Belgrade. Freedoms of expression and speech for Hungarians are curtailed, and while there are a few small independent publications in Vojvodina, the media are dominated by Serbia government-controlled television and radio, which generally reflect the official views from Belgrade. Freedom of domestic movement and of international travel are generally unrestricted. Although freedom of religion is nominally accepted, Catholics, especially Croats, face intimidation and harassment by Orthodox Serbs, particularly after the 1991 war in Croatia and the ongoing conflict in Bosnia. Trade unions are not truly independent.

The Comparative Survey of Freedom—1993-1994 Survey Methodology

Joseph E. Ryan

Freedom House based the 1993-94 *Comparative Survey of Freedom* on a modified version of the methodology that we have used since 1989, in order to adapt our analysis to changing world conditions. Since 1989, many countries have been in varying degrees of real or alleged democratic transition. The methodology we used during the last four years required updating to reflect more accurately the range of behaviors that have arisen among the newly emerging political systems. While it would be inappropriate to replace the methodology every year, the *Survey* team believes it is reasonable to adapt our system of grading in an organic fashion. Readers of the previous editions of the *Survey* will note that the ratings of many countries and related territories have changed since 1992-93. However, the vast majority of changes reflect not methodological adjustments but real world events. (For an explanation of the modified methodology, see the section below on ratings, categories, and raw points.)

What the *Survey* is

The purpose of the *Survey* remains what it has been since its inception in the 1970s: to provide an annual evaluation of political rights and civil liberties everywhere in the world.

The *Survey* attempts to judge all places by a single standard and to point out the importance of democracy and freedom. At a minimum, a democracy is a political system in which the people choose their authoritative leaders freely from among competing groups and individuals who were not chosen by the government. Putting it broadly, freedom is the chance to act spontaneously in a variety of fields outside the control of government and other centers of potential domination.

For a long time, Westerners have associated the adherence to political rights and civil liberties with the liberal democracies, such as those in North America and the European Union. However, there has been a proliferation of democracies in developing countries in recent years, and the *Survey* reflects their growing numbers.

Freedom House does not view democracy as a static concept, and the *Survey* recognizes that a democratic country does not necessarily belong in our category of "free" states. A democracy can lose freedom and become merely "partly free." Sri Lanka and Colombia are examples of such "partly free" democracies. In other cases, countries that replaced military regimes with elected governments can have less than complete transitions to liberal democracy. El Salvador and Guatemala fit the description of this kind of "partly free" democracy. (See the section below on the designations "free," "partly free," and "not free" for an explanation of those terms.)

What the *Survey* is not

The *Survey* does *not* rate governments *per se* but rather the rights and freedoms individuals have in each country and territory. Freedom House does *not* score countries and territories based on governmental intentions or constitutions but on the real world situations caused by governmental and non-governmental factors. The *Survey* does *not* quantify our sympathy for the situation a government finds itself in (e.g., war, terrorism, etc.) but rather what effect the situation itself has on freedom.

Definitions and categories of the *Survey*

The *Survey*'s understanding of freedom is broad and encompasses two sets of characteristics grouped under political rights and civil liberties. Political rights enable people to participate freely in the political process. By the political process, we mean the system by which the polity chooses the authoritative policy makers and attempts to make binding decisions affecting the national, regional or local community. In a free society this means the right of all adults to vote and compete for public office, and for elected representatives to have a decisive vote on public policies. A system is genuinely free or democratic to the extent that the people have a choice in determining the nature of the system and its leaders.

Civil liberties are the freedoms to develop views, institutions and personal autonomy apart from the state.

The *Survey* employs checklists for these rights and liberties to help determine the degree of freedom present in each country and related territory, and to help assign each entity to a comparative category.

Political Rights checklist

1. Is the head of state and/or head of government or other chief authority elected through free and fair elections?
2. Are the legislative representatives elected through free and fair elections?
3. Are there fair electoral laws, equal campaigning opportunities, fair polling and honest tabulation of ballots?
4. Are the voters able to endow their freely elected representatives with real power?
5. Do the people have the right to organize in different political parties or other competitive political groupings of their choice, and is the system open to the rise and fall of these competing parties or groupings?
6. Is there a significant opposition vote, *de facto* opposition power, and a realistic possibility for the opposition to increase its support or gain power through elections?
7. Does the country have the right of self-determination, and are its citizens free from domination by the military, foreign powers, totalitarian parties, religious hierarchies, economic oligarchies or any other powerful group?
8. Do cultural, ethnic, religious and other minority groups have reasonable self-determination, self-government, autonomy or par-ticipation through informal consensus in the decision-making process?
9. Is political power decentralized, allowing for local, regional and/or provincial or state administrations led by their freely elected officials? (For entities such as tiny island nations, the absence of a decentralized system does not necessarily count as a negative in the *Survey*.)

Additional discretionary Political Rights questions

A. For traditional monarchies that have no parties or electoral process, does the system provide for consultation with the people, encourage discussion of policy, and allow the right to petition the ruler?
B. Is the government or occupying power deliberately changing the ethnic composition of a country or territory so as to destroy a culture or tip the political balance in favor of another group?

When answering the political rights questions, Freedom House considers the extent to which the system offers the voter the chance to make a free choice among competing candidates, and to what extent the candidates are chosen independently of the state. We recognize that formal electoral procedures are not the only factors that determine the real distribution of power. In many Latin American countries, for example, the military retains a significant political role, and in Morocco the king maintains significant power over the elected politicians. The more people suffer under such domination by unelected forces, the less chance the country has of getting credit for self-determination in our *Survey*.

Freedom House does not have a culture-bound view of democracy. The *Survey* team rejects the notion that only Europeans and those of European descent qualify as democratic. The *Survey* demonstrates that, in addition to those in Europe and the Americas, there are free countries with varying kinds of democracy functioning among people of all races and religions in Africa, the Pacific and Asia. In some Pacific islands, free countries can have competitive political systems based on competing family groups and personalities rather than on European or American-style parties.

The checklist for Civil Liberties

1. Are there free and independent media, literature and other cultural expressions? (Note: In cases where the media are state-controlled but offer pluralistic points of view, the *Survey* gives the system credit.)
2. Is there open public discussion and free private discussion?
3. Is there freedom of assembly and demonstration?
4. Is there freedom of political or quasi-political organization? (Note: This includes political parties, civic associa-tions, ad hoc issue groups and so forth.)
5. Are citizens equal under the law, with access to an independent, nondiscriminatory judiciary, and are they respected by the security forces?
6. Is there protection from political terror, and from unjustified imprisonment, exile or torture, whether by groups that support or oppose the system, and freedom from war or insurgency situations? (Note: Freedom from war and insurgency situations enhances the liberties in a free society, but the absence of wars and insurgencies does not in itself make an unfree society free.)

7. Are there free trade unions and peasant organizations or equivalents, and is there effective collective bargaining?

8. Are there free professional and other private organizations?

9. Are there free businesses or cooperatives?

10. Are there free religious institutions and free private and public religious expressions?

11. Are there personal social freedoms, which include such aspects as gender equality, property rights, freedom of movement, choice of residence, and choice of marriage and size of family?

12. Is there equality of opportunity, which includes freedom from exploitation by or dependency on landlords, employers, union leaders, bureaucrats or any other type of denigrating obstacle to a share of legitimate economic gains?

13. Is there freedom from extreme government indifference and corruption?

When analyzing the civil liberties checklist, Freedom House does not mistake constitutional guarantees of human rights for those rights in practice. For tiny island countries and territories and other small entities with low populations, the absence of unions and other types of association does not necessarily count as a negative unless the government or other centers of domination are deliberately blocking association. The question of equality of opportunity also implies a free choice of employment and education. Extreme inequality of opportunity prevents disadvantaged individuals from enjoying a full exercise of civil liberties. Typically, desperately poor countries and territories lack both opportunities for economic advancement and the other liberties on this checklist. We have a question on gross indifference and corruption, because when governments do not care about the

The Tabulated Ratings

The accompanying Table of Independent Countries (pages 677-678) and Table of Related Territories (page 679) rate each country or territory on seven-category scales for political rights and civil liberties, and then place each entity into a broad category of "free," "partly free" or "not free." On each scale, 1 represents the most free and 7 the least free.

Political rights

In political rights, generally speaking, places rated 1 come closest to the ideals suggested by the checklist questions, beginning with free and fair elections. Those elected rule. There are competitive parties or other competitive political groupings, and the opposition has an important role and power. These entities have self-determination or an extremely high degree of autonomy (in the case of related territories). Usually, those rated 1 have self-determination for minority groups or their participation in government through informal consensus. With the exception of such entities as tiny island countries, these countries and territories have decentralized political power and free sub-national elections. Entities in Category 1 are not perfect. They can and do lose credit for their deficiencies.

Countries and territories rated 2 in political rights are less free than those rated 1. Such factors as gross political corruption, violence, political discrimination against minorities, and foreign or military influence on politics may be present, and weaken the quality of democracy.

The same factors that weaken freedom in category 2 may also undermine political rights in categories 3, 4, and 5. Other damaging conditions may be at work as well, including civil war, very strong military involvement in politics, lingering royal power, unfair elections and one-party dominance. However, states and territories in these categories may still have some elements of political rights such as the freedom to organize nongovernmental parties and quasi-political groups, reasonably free referenda, or other significant means of popular influence on government.

Typically, states and territories with political rights rated 6 have systems ruled by military juntas, one-party dictatorships, religious hierarchies and autocrats. These regimes may allow only some minimal manifestation of political rights such as competitive local elections or some degree of representation or autonomy for minorities. Category 6 also contains some countries in the early or aborted stages of democratic transition. A few states in Category 6 are traditional monarchies that mitigate their relative lack of political rights through the use of consultation with their subjects, toleration of political discussion, and acceptance of petitions from the ruled.

Category 7 includes places where political rights are absent or virtually nonexistent due to the social and economic welfare of large sectors of the population, the human rights of those people suffer. Government corruption can pervert the political process and hamper the development of a free economy.

Since the last edition of the *Survey*, there have been slight changes in the wording of the Civil Liberties checklist questions six and seven, but these clarifications have not changed the fundamental meaning or scoring of these questions.

How do we grade? Ratings, categories, and raw points

The *Survey* rates political rights and civil liberties separately on a seven-category scale, 1 representing the most free and 7 the least free. A country is assigned to a particular category based on responses to the checklist and the judgments of the *Survey* team at Freedom House. The numbers are not purely mechanical; they also reflect judgment. Under the newly modified methodology, the team assigns initial ratings to countries by awarding from 0 to 4 raw points per checklist item, depending on the comparative rights or liberties present. (In the previous four years, the methodology allowed for a less nuanced range of 0 to 2 raw points per question.) The only exception to the addition of 0 to 4 raw points per checklist item is the discretionary question on cultural destruction and deliberate demographic change to tip the political balance. In that case, we subtract 1 to 4 raw points depending on the situation's severity. The highest possible score for political rights is 36 points, based on up to 4 points for each of nine questions. The highest possible score for civil liberties is 52 points, based on up to 4 points for each of thirteen questions. Under the modified methodology, raw points correspond to category numbers as follows:

The Tabulated Ratings

extremely oppressive nature of the regime or extreme oppression in combination with civil war. A country or territory may also join this category when extreme violence and warlordism dominate the people in the absence of an authoritative, functioning central government. Places in Category 7 may get some minimal points for the checklist questions, but only a tiny fragment of available credit.

Civil liberties

Category 1 in civil liberties includes countries and territories that generally have the highest levels of freedoms and opportunities for the individual. Places in this category may still have problems in civil liberties, but they lose partial credit in only a limited number of areas.

The places in category 2 in civil liberties are not as free as those rated 1, but they are still relatively high on the scale. These countries and territories have deficiencies in several aspects of civil liberties, but still receive most available credit.

Independent countries and related territories with ratings of 3, 4 or 5 have progressively fewer civil liberties than those in category 2. Places in these categories range from ones that receive at least partial credit on virtually all checklist questions to those that have a mixture of good civil liberties scores in some areas and zero or partial credit in others. As one moves down the scale below category 2, the level of oppression increases, especially in the areas of censorship, political terror and the prevention of free association. There are also many cases in which groups opposed to the state carry out political terror that undermines other freedoms. That means that a poor rating for a country is not necessarily a comment on the intentions of the government. The rating may simply reflect the real restrictions on liberty which can be caused by non-governmental terror.

Typically, at category 6 in civil liberties, countries and territories have a few partial rights. For example, a country might have some religious freedom, some personal social freedoms, some highly restricted private business activity, and relatively free private discussion. In general, people in these states and territories experience severely restricted expression and association. There are almost always political prisoners and other manifestations of political terror.

At category 7, countries and territories have virtually no freedom. An overwhelming and justified fear of repression characterizes the society.

The accompanying Tables of Combined Average Ratings average the two seven-category scales of political rights and civil liberties into an overall freedom rating for each country and territory. ■

Political Rights

Category Number	Raw points
1	31-36
2	26-30
3	21-25
4	16-20
5	11-15
6	6-10
7	0-5

Civil Liberties

Category Number	Raw points
1	45-52
2	38-44
3	30-37
4	23-29
5	15-22
6	8-14
7	0-7

After placing countries in initial categories based on checklist points, the *Survey* team makes minor adjustments to account for factors such as extreme violence, whose intensity may not be reflected in answering the checklist questions. These exceptions aside, in the overwhelming number of cases, the checklist system reflects the real world situation and is adequate for placing countries and territories into the proper comparative categories.

Free, Partly Free, Not Free

The map on pages 40-41 divides the world into three large categories: "free," "partly free," and "not free." The *Survey* places countries and territories into this tripartite division by averaging the category numbers they received for political rights and civil liberties. Those whose category numbers average 1-2.5 are considered "free," 3-5.5 "partly free," and 5.5-7 "not free." The dividing line between "partly free" and "not free" falls within the group whose category numbers average 5.5. For example, countries that receive a rating of 6 for political rights and 5 for civil liberties, or a 5 for political rights and a 6 for civil liberties, could be either "partly free" or "not free." The total number of raw points is the factor which makes the difference between the two. Countries and territories with combined raw scores of 0-29 points are "not free," and those with combined raw scores of 30-59 points are "partly free." "Free" countries and territories have combined raw scores of 60-88 points.

The differences in raw points between countries in the three broad categories represent distinctions in the real world. There are obstacles which "partly free" countries must overcome before they can be called "free," just as there are impediments which prevent "not free" countries from being called "partly free." Countries at the lowest rung of the "free" category (category 2 in political rights with category 3 in civil liberties or category 3 in political rights with category 2 in civil liberties) differ from those at the upper end of the "partly free" group (e.g., category 3 in both). Typically, there is more violence and/or military influence on politics at 3,3 than at 2,3 and the differences become more striking as one compares 2,3 with worse categories of the "partly free" countries.

The distinction between the least bad "not free" countries and the least free "partly free" may be less obvious than the gap between "partly free" and "free," but at "partly free," there is at least one extra factor that keeps a country from being assigned to the "not free" category. For example, Lebanon (6,5) has at least some rudiments of pluralism (however perverted or fragmented) that separate this country from its "not free" neighbor, Iraq (7,7).

Freedom House wishes to point out that the designation "free" does not mean that a country has perfect freedom or lacks serious problems. As an institution which advocates human rights, Freedom House remains concerned about a variety of social problems and civil liberties questions in the U.S. and other countries that the *Survey* places in the "free" category. Similarly, in no way does an improvement in a country's rating mean that human rights campaigns should cease. On the contrary, we wish to use the *Survey* as a prod to improve the condition of all countries.

Readers should understand that the "free," "partly free," and "not free" labels are highly simplified terms that each cover a broad third of the available raw points. The labels do *not* imply that all countries in a category are the same any more than a bestseller list implies that all titles on it have sold the same number of books. Countries and territories can reach the same categories or even raw points by differing routes. We use the tripartite labels and tricolor maps to illustrate some broad comparisons. In theory, we could have eighty-eight categories and colors to match the range of raw points, but this would be highly impractical. Anyone wishing to see the distinctions within each category should look at the category numbers and combined average ratings on pages 20 and 21.

The approach of the *Survey*

The *Survey* attempts to measure conditions as they really are around the world. This approach is distinct from relying on intense coverage by the American media as a guide to which countries are the least free. The publicity given problems in some countries does not necessarily mean that unpublicized problems of other countries are not more severe. For example, while U.S. television networks are allowed into Israel and El Salvador to cover abuses of human rights, they are not allowed to report freely in North Korea, which has far less freedom than the other two countries. To reach such comparative conclusions, Freedom House evaluates the development of democratic governmental institutions, or lack thereof, and also examines the quality of civil society, life outside the state structure.

Without a well-developed civil society, it is difficult, if not impossible, to have an atmosphere supportive of democracy. A society that does not have free individual and group expressions in nonpolitical matters is not likely to make an exception for political ones. As though to prove this, there is no country in the *Survey* that places in category 6 or 7 for civil liberties and, at the same time, in category 1 or 2 for political rights. In the overwhelming majority of cases in the *Survey*, countries and territories have ratings in political rights and civil liberties that are within two categories of each other.

The *Survey* rates both countries and related territories. For our purposes, countries are internationally recognized independent states whose governments are resident within their officially claimed territories. In the unusual case of Cyprus, we give two ratings, since there are two governments on that divided island. In no way does this imply that Freedom House endorses Cypriot division. We note only that neither the predominantly Greek Republic of Cyprus nor the Turkish-occupied, predominantly Turkish territory of the Republic of Northern Cyprus is the *de facto* government for the entire island. Related territories consist mostly of colonies, protectorates, occupied territories and island dependencies. However, the *Survey* also reserves the right to designate as related territories places within internationally recognized states that are disputed areas or that have a human rights problem or issue of self-determination deserving special attention. Northern Ireland, Tibet, and Kashmir are examples falling within this category. The *Survey* excludes uninhabited related territories and such entities as the U.S.-owned Johnston Atoll, which has only a transient military population and no native inhabitants. Since most related territories have a broad range of civil liberties and some form of self-government, a higher proportion of them have the "free" designation than do independent countries.

The 1993-94 *Survey* has made additions in its coverage of related territories. We list Nagorno-Karabakh as a related territory that is disputed by Armenia and Azerbaijan. The new states of the Czech Republic, Slovakia and Eritrea join the independent countries, as do Monaco and Andorra, two microstates that appeared in the past as related territories before they joined the United Nations. ▬

Joseph E. Ryan is resident scholar at Freedom House.

Tables and Ratings

Table of Independent Countries
Comparative Measures of Freedom

Country	PR	CL	Freedom Rating	Country	PR	CL	Freedom Rating
Afghanistan	7▼	7▼	Not Free	Finland	1	1	Free
Albania	2∧	4∨	Partly Free	France	1	2	Free
Algeria	7	6	Not Free	Gabon	5▼	4	Partly Free
Andorra°	2	1	Free	The Gambia	2∨	2	Free
Angola	7▼	7▼	Not Free	↓Georgia	5▼	5	Partly Free
Antigua and Barbuda	4∨	3	Partly Free	Germany	1	2	Free
↓Argentina	2	3	Free	↓Ghana	5	4∧	Partly Free
Armenia	3∧	4∨	Partly Free	Greece	1	3▼	Free
Australia	1	1	Free	Grenada	1	2	Free
↓Austria	1	1	Free	Guatemala	4	5	Partly Free
Azerbaijan	6▼	6▼	Not Free	Guinea	6	5	Not Free ▼
Bahamas	1	2	Free	Guinea-Bissau	6	5	Partly Free
Bahrain	6	6∨	Not Free	Guyana	2▲	2▲	Free
Bangladesh	2	4▼	Partly Free	Haiti	7	7	Not Free
Barbados	1	1	Free	Honduras	3∨	3	Partly Free
Belarus	5∨	4∨	Partly Free	Hungary	1	2	Free
Belgium	1	1	Free	Iceland	1	1	Free
Belize	1	1	Free	India	4∨	4	Partly Free
Benin	2	3	Free	Indonesia	7∨	6∨	Not Free
Bhutan	7	7▼	Not Free	Iran	6	7∨	Not Free
↓Bolivia	2	3	Free	Iraq	7	7	Not Free
↓Bosnia-Herzegovina	6	6	Not Free	Ireland	1	2∨	Free
Botswana	2∨	3∨	Free	Israel**	1∧	3∨	Free
Brazil	3▼	4▼	Partly Free	Italy	1	3▼	Free
Brunei	7	6	Not Free	Ivory Coast	6	5▼	Not Free
Bulgaria	2	2∧	Free	Jamaica	2	3▼	Free
Burkina Faso	5	4∧	Partly Free	Japan	2▼	2	Free
Burma (Myanmar)	7	7	Not Free	Jordan	4∨	4∨	Partly Free
Burundi	7▼	7▼	Not Free	Kazakhstan	6∨	4∧	Partly Free
Cambodia	4▲	5▲	Partly Free	Kenya	5▼	6▼	Not Free
Cameroon	6	5	Not Free	Kiribati	1	1∧	Free
Canada	1	1	Free	Korea, North	7	7	Not Free
Cape Verde	1	2	Free	↑Korea, South	2	2▲	Free
Central African Republic	3▲	4▲	Partly Free	Kuwait	5	5	Partly Free
Chad	6	5∧	Not Free	Kyrgyz Republic	5∨	3∧	Partly Free
Chile	2	2	Free	Laos	7	6	Not Free
China (P.R.C.)	7	7	Not Free	Latvia	3	3	Partly Free
↓Colombia	2	4	Partly Free	Lebanon	6∨	5∨	Partly Free
Comoros	4	4▼	Partly Free	Lesotho	3▲	4	Partly Free
Congo	3▼	3▼	Partly Free	Liberia	6▲	6	Not Free
Costa Rica	1	2∨	Free	Libya	7	7	Not Free
↓Croatia	4	4	Partly Free	Liechtenstein	1	1	Free
Cuba	7	7	Not Free	Lithuania	1∧	3	Free
Cyprus (G)	1	1	Free	Luxembourg	1	1	Free
Czech Republic°	1	2	Free	Macedonia	3	3∧	Partly Free
Denmark	1	1	Free	Madagascar	2▲	4	Partly Free
Djibouti	6	6	Not Free	Malawi	6	5▲	Not Free
Dominica	2	1	Free	Malaysia	4∧	5∨	Partly Free
Dominican Republic	3▼	3	Partly Free	Maldives	6	6∨	Not Free
↓Ecuador	2	3	Free	Mali	2	3	Free
Egypt	6▼	6	Not Free	Malta	1	1	Free
El Salvador	3	3	Partly Free	Marshall Islands	1	1	Free
Equatorial Guinea	7	7▼	Not Free	Mauritania	7	6	Not Free
↓Eritrea°	6	5▼	Not Free	Mauritius	1∧	2	Free
Estonia	3	2▲	Free	Mexico	4	4▼	Partly Free
Ethiopia	6	5▼	Not Free	Micronesia	1	1	Free
Fiji	4	3	Partly Free	Moldova	5	5	Partly Free
				Monaco°	2∧	1	Free
				Mongolia	2∧	3∨	Free
				Morocco	5▲	5	Partly Free

Table of Independent Countries
Comparative Measures of Freedom

Country	PR	CL	Freedom Rating	Country	PR	CL	Freedom Rating
↓ Mozambique	6	5▼	Not Free	Spain	1	2 v	Free
Namibia	2	3 v	Free	Sri Lanka	4	5	Partly Free
Nauru	1	3▼	Free	Sudan	7	7	Not Free
↓ Nepal	3▼	4▼	Partly Free	Suriname	3	3	Partly Free
Netherlands	1	1	Free	Swaziland	6	5	Not Free ▼
New Zealand	1	1	Free	Sweden	1	1	Free
↓ Nicaragua	4	5▼	Partly Free	Switzerland	1	1	Free
Niger	3▲	4	Partly Free	Syria	7	7	Not Free
↓ Nigeria	7▼	5▼	Not Free	Taiwan (Rep. of China)	4 v	4 v	Partly Free
Norway	1	1	Free	Tajikistan	7▼	7▼	Not Free
Oman	6	6 v	Not Free	↓ Tanzania	6	5	Not Free ▼
Pakistan	3▲	5	Partly Free	Thailand	3	5 v	Partly Free
Panama	3▲	3	Partly Free	Togo	7▼	5	Not Free
Papua New Guinea	2	4▼	Partly Free	Tonga	5 v	3	Partly Free
Paraguay	3	3	Partly Free	Trinidad and Tobago	1	1	Free
Peru	5▲	5	Partly Free	Tunisia	6	5	Not Free ▼
Philippines	3	4 v	Partly Free	Turkey	4▼	4	Partly Free
Poland	2	2	Free	Turkmenistan	7	7▼	Not Free
Portugal	1	1	Free	Tuvalu	1	1	Free
Qatar	7	6	Not Free	Uganda	6	5	Not Free
Romania	4	4	Partly Free	Ukraine	4▼	4▼	Partly Free
Russia	3	4	Partly Free	United Arab Emirates	7 v	5	Not Free
Rwanda	6	5	Not Free				
St. Kitts and Nevis	1	1	Free	United Kingdom*	1	2	Free
St. Lucia	1	2	Free	United States	1	1	Free
St. Vincent and the Grenadines	1	1 ∧	Free	Uruguay	2 v	2	Free
San Marino	1	1	Free	Uzbekistan	7▼	7▼	Not Free
Sao Tome and Principe	1▲	2▲	Free	Vanuatu	1▲	2▲	Free
				Venezuela	3	3	Partly Free
Saudi Arabia	7	7	Not Free	Vietnam	7	7	Not Free
↓ Senegal	4	5▼	Partly Free	Western Samoa	2	2	Free
Seychelles	3▲	4	Partly Free	Yemen	4▲	5 v	Partly Free
Sierra Leone	7	6	Not Free	↓ Yugoslavia (Serbia and Montenegro)	6	6▼	Not Free
Singapore	5 v	5	Partly Free				
Slovakia°	3	4	Partly Free				
Slovenia	1 ∧	2	Free	Zaire	7▼	6▼	Not Free
Solomon Islands	1	2▼	Free	Zambia	3▼	4▼	Partly Free
Somalia	7	7	Not Free	Zimbabwe	5	5 v	Partly Free
South Africa	5	4	Partly Free				

Notes for Table of Independent Countries

↑↓   up or down indicate a general trend in freedom. PR and CL stand for Political Rights and Civil Liberties. 1 represents the most free and 7 the least free category.

▲▼   up or down indicate a change in Political Rights or Civil Liberties caused by real world events since the last *Survey*.

∨∧   up or down indicate a change in scoring for purely methodological reasons.

    The Freedom Rating is an overall judgment based on *Survey* results. See the "Methodological Essay" for more details.

°   New as a country in this *Survey*.

*   Excluding Northern Ireland.

**   Excluding the Occupied Territories.

Table of Related Territories
Comparative Measures of Freedom

Country	PR	CL	Freedom Rating
Armenia/Azerbaijan*			
Nagorno-Karabakh	7	7	Not Free
Australia			
Christmas Island	3	2	Free
Cocos (Keeling) Islands	1	1	Free
Norfolk Island	2	1	Free
Chile			
Rapanui (Easter Island)	2▲	2	Free
China			
Tibet	7	7	Not Free
Denmark			
Faeroe Islands	1	1	Free
Greenland	1	1	Free
Finland			
Aland Islands	1	1	Free
France			
French Guiana	1∧	2	Free
French Polynesia	1∧	2	Free
Guadeloupe	1∧	2	Free
Martinique	1∧	2ν	Free
Mayotte (Mahore)	1∧	2	Free
New Caledonia	2	2	Free
Reunion	2	2	Free
St. Pierre and Miquelon	1∧	1	Free
Wallis and Futuna Islands	2∧	2	Free
India			
Kashmir	7▼	7▼	Not Free
Indonesia			
East Timor	7	7	Not Free
Irian Jaya (West Papua)	7	7ν	Not Free
Iraq			
Kurdistan	4	4∧	Partly Free
Israel			
Occupied Territories	6	5▲	Not Free
Morocco			
Western Sahara	7	6▼	Not Free
Netherlands			
Aruba	1	1	Free
Netherlands Antilles	1	1	Free
New Zealand			
Cook Islands	1∧	2	Free
Niue	1∧	2	Free

Country	PR	CL	Freedom Rating
Tokelau	2	2	Free
Norway			
Svalbard	3	1	Free
Portugal			
Azores	1	1	Free
↓ Macao	5▼	3	Partly Free
Madeira	1	1	Free
South Africa			
Bophutatswana	7ν	6ν	Not Free
Ciskei	7ν	6	Not Free
Transkei	7ν	6ν	Not Free
Venda	6	5	Not Free
Spain			
Canary Islands	1	1	Free
Ceuta	1∧	2ν	Free
Melilla	1∧	2ν	Free
Turkey			
Cyprus (T)	4ν	2∧	Partly Free
United Kingdom			
Anguilla	2ν	1	Free
Bermuda	1	1	Free
British Virgin Islands	1∧	1	Free
Cayman Islands	1∧	1	Free
Channel Islands	2	1	Free
Falkland Islands	2	1	Free
Gibraltar	1	1	Free
Hong Kong	5ν	2∧	Partly Free
Isle of Man	1∧	1	Free
Montserrat	1∧	1	Free
Northern Ireland	5▼	4▼	Partly Free
Pitcairn Island	1∧	1	Free
St. Helena and Dependencies	2	1	Free
Turks and Caicos	1∧	1	Free
United States of America			
American Samoa	1	1	Free
Guam	1	1	Free
Northern Marianas	1	2▼	Free
Palau	1	2	Free
Puerto Rico	1	1	Free
U.S. Virgin Islands	1	1	Free
Yugoslavia			
Kosovo	7	7	Not Free
Vojvodina	6	6▼	Not Free

Notes for Table of Related Territories

* New in this *Survey*.
Nagorno-Karabakh is disputed territory contested by Armenia and Azerbaijan.

Table of Social and Economic Comparisons

Country	Real GDP per capita (PPP $)	Life Expectancy	Country	Real GDP per capita (PPP $)	Life Expectancy
Afghanistan	714	42.5	Egypt	1,988	60.3
Albania	3,000	72.2	El Salvador	1,950	64.4
Algeria	3,011	65.1	Equatorial	700	47.0
Angola	1,225	45.5	Guinea		
Antigua and	4,000	72.0	Estonia	6,438	71.0
Barbuda			Ethiopia	369	45.5
Argentina	4,295	71.0	Fiji	4,427	64.8
Armenia	4,741	69.0	Finland	16,446	75.5
Australia	16,051	76.5	France	17,405	76.4
Austria	16,504	74.8	Gabon	4,147	52.5
Azerbaijan	3,977	70.0	Gambia	913	44.0
Bahamas	11,235	71.5	Georgia	4,572	72.0
Bahrain	10,706	71.0	Germany	18,213	75.2
Bangladesh	872	51.8	Ghana	1,016	55.0
Barbados	8,304	75.1	Greece	7,366	76.1
Belarus	5,727	72.0	Grenada	4,081	71.5
Belgium	16,381	75.2	Guatemala	2,576	63.4
Belize	3,000	69.5	Guinea	501	43.5
Benin	1,043	47.0	Guinea-Bissau	841	42.5
Bhutan	800	48.9	Guyana	1,464	64.2
Bolivia	1,572	54.5	Haiti	933	55.7
Bosnia-	na	70.0	Honduras	1,470	64.9
Herzegovina			Hungary	6,116	70.9
Botswana	3,419	59.8	Iceland	16,496	77.8
Brazil	4,718	65.6	India	1,072	59.1
Brunei	14,000	73.5	Indonesia	2,181	61.5
Bulgaria	4,700	72.6	Iran	3,253	66.2
Burkina Faso	618	48.2	Iraq	3,508	65.0
Burma	659	61.3	Ireland	10,589	74.6
(Myanmar)			Israel	10,840	75.9
Burundi	625	48.5	Italy	15,890	76.0
Cambodia	1,100	49.7	Ivory Coast	1,324	53.4
Cameroon	1,646	53.7	(Cote D'Ivoire)		
Canada	19,232	77.0	Jamaica	2,979	73.1
Cape Verde	1,769	67.0	Japan	17,616	78.6
Central African	768	49.5	Jordan	2,345	66.9
Republic			Kazakhstan	4,716	70.0
Chad	559	46.5	Kenya	1,058	59.7
Chile	5,099	71.8	Kiribati	na	54.0
China (PRC)	1,990	70.1	Korea		
Colombia	4,237	68.8	North	2,000	70.4
Comoros	721	55.0	South	6,733	70.1
Congo	2,362	53.7	Kuwait	15,178	73.4
Costa Rica	4,542	74.9	Kyrgyzstan	3,114	68.0
Croatia	na	70.0	Laos	1,100	49.7
Cuba	2,200	75.4	Latvia	6,457	71.0
Cyprus	9,953	76.2	Lebanon	2,300	66.1
Czech Republic	na	na	Lesotho	1,743	57.3
Denmark	16,781	75.8	Liberia	857	54.2
Djibouti	1,000	48.0	Libya	7,000	61.8
Dominica	3,901	76.0	Liechtenstein	na	69.5
Dominican Republic	2,404	66.7	Lithuania	4,913	72.0
Ecuador	3,074	66.0	Luxembourg	19,244	74.9

Notes: Freedom House obtained the figures for purchasing power parities (PPP) and life expectancy from the U.N.'s *Human Development Report 1993* (Oxford University Press, 1993). PPPs are real GDP per capita figures which economists have adjusted to account for detailed price comparisons of individual items covering over 150 categories of expenditure.

The U.N. life expectancy figures represent overall expectancy, not differentiated by sex. In some cases not covered by the U.N., the chart lists a combined average of male and female life expectancy obtained from Rand McNally. For several countries the chart lists these combined averages.

Table of Social and Economic Comparisons

Country	Real GDP per capita (PPP $)	Life Expectancy	Country	Real GDP per capita (PPP $)	Life Expectancy
Macedonia	na	70.0	Senegal	1,248	48.3
Madagascar	704	54.5	Seychelles	4,191	70.0
Malawi	640	48.1	Sierra Leone	1,086	42.0
Malaysia	6,140	70.1	Singapore	15,880	74.0
Maldives	1,200	62.5	Slovakia	na	na
Mali	572	45.0	Slovenia	na	71.0
Malta	8,732	73.4	Solomon Islands	2,689	69.5
Marshall Islands	na	72.5	Somalia	836	46.1
Mauritania	1,057	47.0	South Africa	4,865	61.7
Mauritius	5,750	69.6	Spain	11,723	77.0
Mexico	5,918	69.7	Sri Lanka	2,405	70.9
Micronesia	na	70.5	Sudan	949	50.8
Moldova	3,896	68.0	Suriname	3,927	69.5
Mongolia	2,100	65.0	Swaziland	2,384	56.8
Morocco	2,348	62.0	Sweden	17,014	77.4
Mozambique	1,072	47.5	Switzerland	20,874	77.4
Namibia	1,400	57.5	Syria	4,756	66.1
Nauru	na	66.0	Taiwan (China)	na	74.5
Nepal	920	52.2	Tajikistan	2,558	70.0
Netherlands	15,695	77.2	Tanzania	572	54.0
New Zealand	13,481	75.2	Thailand	3,986	66.1
Nicaragua	1,497	64.8	Togo	734	54.0
Niger	645	45.5	Tonga	na	67.5
Nigeria	1,215	51.5	Trinidad and Tobago	6,604	71.6
Norway	16,028	77.1	Tunisia	3,579	66.7
Oman	9,972	65.9	Turkey	4,652	65.1
Pakistan	1,862	57.7	Turkmenistan	4,230	66.4
Panama	3,317	72.4	Tuvalu	na	61.0
Papua New Guinea	1,786	54.9	Uganda	524	52.0
Paraguay	2,790	67.1	Ukraine	5,433	71.0
Peru	2,622	63.0	United Arab Emirates	16,753	70.5
Philippines	2,303	64.2	United Kingdom	15,804	75.7
Poland	4,237	71.8	United States	21,449	75.9
Portugal	8,770	74.0	Uruguay	5,916	72.2
Qatar	11,400	69.2	Uzbekistan	3,115	69.0
Romania	2,800	70.8	Vanuatu	2,005	69.5
Russia	7,968	70.0	Venezuela	6,169	70.0
Rwanda	657	49.5	Vietnam	1,100	62.7
St. Kitts-Nevis	3,300	67.5	Western Samoa	1,900	66.5
St. Lucia	3,470	70.5	Yemen	1,562	51.5
St. Vincent and the Grenadines	3,647	70.0	Yugoslavia (Serbia and Montenegro)	5,095	72.6
San Marino	na	76.0	Zaire	367	53.0
Sao Tome and Principe	600	65.5	Zambia	744	54.4
Saudi Arabia	10,989	64.5	Zimbabwe	1,484	59.6

Combined Average Ratings—Independent Countries

FREE

1.0
Australia
Austria
Barbados
Belgium
Belize
Canada
Cyprus (G)
Denmark
Finland
Iceland
Kiribati
Liechtenstein
Luxembourg
Malta
Marshall Islands
Micronesia
Netherlands
New Zealand
Norway
Portugal
St. Kitts-Nevis
St. Vincent and the Grenadines
San Marino
Sweden
Switzerland
Trinidad & Tobago
Tuvalu
United States of America

1.5
Andorra
Bahamas
Cape Verde
Costa Rica
Czech Republic
Dominica
France
Germany
Grenada
Hungary
Ireland
Mauritius
Monaco
St. Lucia
Sao Tome & Principe
Slovenia
Solomon Islands
Spain
United Kingdom
Vanuatu

2.0
Bulgaria

Chile
The Gambia
Greece
Guyana
Israel
Italy
Japan
Korea, South
Lithuania
Nauru
Poland
Uruguay
Western Samoa

2.5
Argentina
Benin
Bolivia
Botswana
Ecuador
Estonia
Jamaica
Mali
Mongolia
Namibia

PARTLY FREE

3.0
Albania
Bangladesh
Colombia
Dominican Republic
El Salvador
Honduras
Latvia
Macedonia
Madagascar
Papua New Guinea
Paraguay
Panama
Suriname
Venezuela

3.5
Antigua & Barbuda
Armenia
Brazil
Central African Republic
Fiji
Lesotho
Nepal
Niger
Philippines
Russia
Seychelles
Slovakia

Zambia

4.0
Comoros
Congo
Croatia
India
Jordan
Kyrgyz Republic
Mexico
Pakistan
Romania
Taiwan
Thailand
Tonga
Turkey
Ukraine

4.5
Belarus
Burkina Faso
Cambodia
Gabon
Ghana
Guatemala
Malaysia
Nicaragua
Senegal
South Africa
Sri Lanka
Yemen

5.0
Georgia
Kazakhstan
Kuwait
Moldova
Morocco
Peru
Singapore
Zimbabwe

5.5
Guinea-Bissau
Lebanon

NOT FREE

5.5
Cameroon
Chad
Eritrea
Ethiopia
Guinea
Ivory Coast (Cote D'Ivoire)
Kenya
Malawi

Mozambique
Rwanda
Swaziland
Tanzania
Tunisia
Uganda

6.0
Azerbaijan
Bahrain
Bosnia-Herzegovina
Djibouti
Egypt
Liberia
Maldives
Nigeria
Oman
Togo
United Arab Emirates
Yugoslavia
   (Serbia &
Montenegro)

6.5
Algeria
Brunei
Indonesia
Iran
Laos
Mauritania
Qatar
Sierra Leone
Zaire

7.0
Afghanistan
Angola
Bhutan
Burma
Burundi
China
Cuba
Equatorial Guinea
Haiti
Iraq
Korea, North
Libya
Saudi Arabia
Somalia
Sudan
Syria
Tajikistan
Turkmenistan
Uzbekistan
Vietnam

Combined Average Ratings—Related Territories

FREE

1.0
Aland Islands (Finland)
American Samoa (U.S.)
Aruba (Netherlands)
Azores (Portugal)
Bermuda (U.K.)
British Virgin Islands (U.K.)
Canary Islands (Spain)
Cayman Islands (U.K.)
Cocos (Keeling) Islands (Australia)
Faeroe Islands (Denmark)
Gibraltar (U.K.)
Greenland (Denmark)
Guam (U.S.)
Isle of Man (U.K.)
Madeira (Portugal)
Montserrat (U.K.)
Netherlands Antilles (Netherlands)
Pitcairn Islands (U.K.)
Puerto Rico (U.S.)
St. Pierre and Miquelon (France)
Turks and Caicos (U.K.)
United States Virgin Islands (U.S.)

1.5
Anguilla (U.K.)
Ceuta (Spain)
Channel Islands (U.K.)
Cook Islands (New Zealand)
Falkland Islands (U.K.)
French Guiana (France)

French Polynesia (France)
Guadeloupe (France)
Martinique (France)
Mayotte (Mahore) (France)
Melilla (Spain)
Niue (New Zealand)
Norfolk Island (Australia)
Northern Marianas (U.S.)
Palau (U.S.)
St. Helena and Dependencies (U.K.)

2.0
New Caledonia (France)
Rapanui (Easter Island) (Chile)
Reunion (France)
Svalbard (Norway)
Tokelau (New Zealand)
Wallis and Futuna Islands (France)

2.5
Christmas Island (Australia)

PARTLY FREE

3.0
Cyprus (Turkey)

3.5
Hong Kong (U.K.)

4.0
Kurdistan (Iraq)
Macao (Portugal)

4.5
Northern Ireland (U.K.)

NOT FREE

5.5
Occupied Territories (Israel)
Venda (South Africa)

6.0
Vojvodina (Yugoslavia)

6.5
Bophuthatswana (South Africa)
Ciskei (South Africa)
Transkei (South Africa)
Western Sahara (Morocco)

7.0
East Timor (Indonesia)
Irian Jaya (West Papua) (Indonesia)
Kashmir (India)
Kosovo (Yugoslavia)
Nagorno-Karabakh (Armenia/
Azerbaijan)
Tibet (China)

National Elections and Referenda

Country	Date/Type	Results and Comments
Andorra 14 March 1993	referendum	Andorrans voted overwhelmingly for a new constitution that reduces the former co-princes to a combined constitutional monarch.
12 December 1993	general	Prime Minister Oscar Ribas's National Democratic Group (AND) won 8 of the 28 parliamentary seats. The Liberal Union (UL) and New Democracy (ND) captured 5 seats each. Other parliamentarians won as independents. Ribas expected to form a coalition with non-AND MPs. Eighteen parties participated. This was Andorra's first openly multiparty election. Turnout was 80 percent, but citizens make up scarcely a quarter of the population. Voters half the seats nationally, and half from each of the seven Andorran parishes.
Argentina 3 October 1993	legislative	President Carlos Menem's Peronist Justicialist Party placed first in legislative elections, defeating the Radical Civic Union, and smaller parties. Results: Peronists, 43.1 percent (177 seats); Radicals, 30.4 percent (84 seats); MODIN, an ultra-nationalist party, 5.4 percent; all others, 21.7 percent. All citizens 18-70 years old had the legal obligation to vote.
Australia 13 March1993	general	Prime Minister Paul Keating's Labor Party won 76 parliamentary seats, defeating the Liberal Party-National Party coalition that took 62 seats.
Azerbaijan 29 August 1993	referendum	The new authoritarian government asked voters whether they trusted former President Abulfez Elchibey. With a 92 percent turnout, 97.5 percent of the voters rejected Elchibey.
3 October 1992	presidential	Geydar Aliyev defeated Kerrar Abilov with 98.8 percent of the vote. Turnout exceeded 97 percent.
Belize 1 July 1993	general	The opposition United Democratic Party (UDP), headed by Manuel Esquivel, defeated the ruling People's United Party (PUP), headed by George Price. The UDP won 16 seats to 13 for the PUP. The UDP won its 15th seat by just 8 votes. It won the 16th seat by one vote after four recounts and controversy over whether one ballot was spoiled.
Bolivia 6 June 1993	general	Businessman Gonzalo Sanchez de Lozada finished first in the presidential contest with 34 percent of the vote. His running mate was Victor Hugo Cardenas. Former dictator General Hugo Banzer Suarez finished second with 21 percent. Broadcaster Carlos Palenque placed third with 16 percent. Brewery owner Max Fernandez came in fourth with 13 percent. Other parties split the remaining vote. Fourteen parties took part in the elections. The 157-seat Congress was also elected. The National Revolutionary Movement received 33.8 percent of the vote and 69 lower house seats and 17 senators. Patriotic Accord captured 20 percent of the vote and won 43 lower house and 8 senate seats. Conscience of the Fatherland won 13.6 percent of the vote and 14 lower house seats and 1 senate seat. Civic Solidarity took 13.1 percent of the vote and 21 lower house seats and 1 senate seat. Sanchez de Lozada supporters fell 10 seats short of a majority in the Congress. Since no presidential candidate won a majority, the legislators had to choose a winner. Sanchez de Lozada achieved victory by forming a coalition with Fernandez.
Bosnia-Herzegovina (Serbian-occupied areas) 15-16 May 1993	referendum	In the breakaway Serb areas within Bosnia-Herzegovina, the self-styled Serbian parliament sponsored referenda on the Vance-Owen peace plan and on sovereignty for the "Serb Republic" within Bosnia. Voting was haphazard. Ballot security was uneven. Some Bosnian Serbs living abroad voted at polling stations overseas. The vote was overwhelmingly opposed to the peace plan and in favor of Serb sovereignty. Despite the irregularities, there is no doubt that the results reflected the majority sentiment of the Bosnian Serbs. This vote was a tactic to stall international military intervention against Serbian aggression.
Brazil 21 April 1993	referenda	Voters had two questions: a choice between a republic and a monarchy, and a choice between presidential and parliamentary democracy. Brazilians chose a republic over a monarchy by 66.1 percent to 10 percent. The rest cast blank or spoiled ballots. The presidential system defeated the parliamentary 55.5 percent to 24.7 percent. The other ballots were blank or spoiled.
Burundi 1 June1993	presidential	With 65 percent of the vote, an ethnic Hutu, Melchior Ndadaye (Burundi Democracy Front) defeated President General Jean Pierre Buyoya, an ethnic Tutsi, who received 34 percent, and Pierre Claver (People's Reconciliation Party), who held 1 percent.
29 June 1993	legislative	Supporters of Ndadaye won 80 percent of the vote and 65 of the 81 legislative seats. *Note:* The election results became irrelevant later in the year when Tutsi officers killed Ndadaye in a coup.
Cambodia 23 -25 or 25-27 May 1993	general	Under U.N. supervision and extensive international observation, Cambodia elected a 120-seat constituent assembly. The royalist National United Front for an Independent,

National Elections and Referenda

Country	Date/Type	Results and Comments

		Neutral, Peaceful and Cooperative Cambodia (Funcinpec) led with about 46 percent of the vote and 58 seats. The ruling Cambodian People's Party (Communist or ex-Communist) placed second with about 38 percent and 51 seats. The Buddhist Liberal Democratic Party won 10 of the 11 remaining seats. The People's Party alleged that there were irregularities. It threatened riots unless the U.N. scheduled new voting in certain areas. The U.N. and international observers pronounced the voting generally free and fair. The Khmer Rouge did not participate as candidates, but did decide to vote. Voter turnout was about 90 percent. Some registered Cambodians abroad could vote at a few polling stations overseas. In early June, the Cambodian People's Party was condoning secessionist movements in the eastern provinces, but then agreed to seek a coalition with Funcinpec.
Canada 25 October 1993	general	Jean Chretien's Liberals won 178 of the 295 seats in the House of Commons. The outgoing government of Progressive Conservative Prime Minister Kim Campbell suffered a devastating defeat, winning only 2 seats. Campbell lost her own seat. The separatist Bloc Quebecois won 54 seats in Quebec, making it the official opposition party. The Western-based, right-wing Reform Party captured 52 seats. The socialist New Democrats, traditionally the third party, lost ground, taking only 8 seats. An independent ex-Conservative won the remaining seat. In all, there were 2,155 parliamentary candidates. Elections Canada sponsored early voting on 16, 18 and 19 October. For the first time, Canadians living abroad for up to five years could vote by absentee ballots.
Central African Republic 22 August 1993	general (presidential and legislative-first round)	Former Prime Minister Ange-Felix Patasse leading the first round of the presidential election with 37.32 percent. Democrat Abel Goumba ran second with 21.68 percent. Former President David Dacko finished third with about 21 percent. Military dictator Andre Kolingba finished with 12.1 percent. Four other candidates ran far behind with single digits. Since no candidate topped 50 percent of the vote, there was a run-off scheduled between Patasse and Goumba. International observers cited some minor irregularities, but found the election fair. However, the count was slow. General Kolingba attempted to block the release of the election tallies by stripping the Supreme Court of its power to publish final results, but then he announced his willingness to step down from power. Then Kolingba ordered the release of all the nation's prisoners. Goumba charged that this was Kolingba's punishment of the electorate for depriving the general of power. The election was postponed from earlier projected dates in the spring.
12 September 1993	run-off	Patasse defeated Goumba 52.47 percent to 45.62 percent. This brought a formal end to military rule.
Chile 11 December 1993	general	Christian Democrat Eduardo Frei, the nominee of the center-left Coalition for Democracy, won the presidency with 58 percent, defeating conservative Alessandri Alessandri, who took 24 percent, and several left and right fringe candidates, who captured a combined 18 percent. The Coalition for Democracy won majorities in both the Senate and Chamber of Deputies, but it lost 1 and 2 seats, respectively, in those bodies, leaving it short of the two-thirds control needed for amending the constitution.
Comoros November 1993 12, 19, 20, 29 December 1993	general (postponed four times) general	After four postponements, there was a two-round legislative election disrupted by fraud and violence that turned into at least a four-round election. The government cancelled several results and arrested and attacked several opposition candidates. Two people were killed and several wounded. The government won 21 seats to 18 for opposition parties. Three seats remained vacant, pending unscheduled repeat voting. The opposition pledged to boycott the legislature.
Congo 2 May 1993 6 June 1993	legislative legislative run-offs	A coalition of parties favoring President Pascal Lissouba won a majority of seats. Oppositionists charged the victors with fraud. There were reports that the opposition destroyed ballot boxes and polling stations. Eleven seats remained unfilled. Fighting broke out after the second round and continued through the summer. At least 30 died.
3 October	legislative	The opposition coalition won 8 seats to 3 for the government. Ethnic fighting intensified after the polling.
Croatia 7 and 21 February 1993	legislative	Elections took place for the relatively powerless Upper House of the Districts. President Tudjman's Croatian Democratic Union won 37 seats; Social-Liberals, 16; Peasant Party, 5; Istrian Democratic Assembly, 3; Social Democrats-Party of Democratic Changes, 1; People's Party, 1.
Cyprus (Greek) 7 February	presidential (first round)	President George Vassiliou, an independent backed by left-wing parties, carried 44.15 percent. Glafcos Clerides, a conservative, took 36.74 percent. Paschalis Pascalides, a hardline nationalist, placed third with 18.64 percent. Vassiliou and Clerides will face each other in a run-off on 14 February.

National Elections and Referenda

Country	Date/Type	Results and Comments
14 February 1993	presidential (run-off)	Clerides defeated Vassiliou in the run-off 50.28 percent to 49.72 percent. Election officials refused Vassiliou's request for a recount.
Cuba 28 February	legislative	The government allowed only communist Party candidates to take part in this election. Incumbents won 585 of the 589 seats.
Denmark 18 May 1993	referendum	Danes approved the Maastricht Treaty on European union by 56.8 percent to 43.2 percent. This referendum reversed their earlier "No" vote.
Djibouti 7 May 1993	presidential	With 60.7 percent, President Hassan Gouled Aptidon (Popular Rally for Progress) defeated four opponents: Mohammed Djama Elabe (Party of Democratic Renewal), Aden Robleh Awaleh (National Democratic Party), Mohammed Moussa Ali "Tourtour" (Movement for Unity and Democracy), and Ahmed Ibrahim Abdi "Ina Anfee." All the candidates were ethnic Issas. The ethnic Afar Front for the Restoration of Unity and Democracy boycotted the vote. Voter turnout was less than 50 percent.
Egypt October 1993	presidential	President Hosni Mubarak was the sole candidate in a Yes/No referendum for another term. The government gave its employees a half-day off to vote. Election officials relaxed registration requirements and assisted illiterate voters, in order to encourage a "Yes" vote. With the help of such irregularities, Mubarak won with 96 percent.
Equatorial Guinea 21 November 1993	general	Most opposition parties and the largest ethnic group, the Bubis, boycotted the first multiparty election in twenty-five years, because the government refused to revise the election law and the census with international assistance. The government inflated the voter list with ghost electors. An estimated 30-50 percent of voters, both real and imaginary, turned out to vote. The ruling Democratic Party of Equatorial Guinea won the overwhelming majority of seats. The U.S. State Department called the election a "travesty."
Eritrea 23-25 April 1993	referendum	Eritreans voted overwhelmingly (99.8 percent) for independence from Ethiopia. Eritreans abroad voted at polling stations overseas. The combined domestic and overseas votes amounted to a 98.5 percent turnout. International observers declared the vote free and fair, and noted only some minor problems with electoral mechanics in remote areas where people were unfamiliar with voting.
France 21 March 1993	legislative (first round)	Center-right opposition parties took a commanding lead over the governing Socialists in round one of the National Assembly elections. The Gaullist Rally for the Republic placed first with 20.39 percent of the vote and 42 seats. The center-right Union for French Democracy came in second with 19.08 percent and 36 seats. The Socialists placed third in percentage of the vote with 17.59 percent, but won no seats in this round. Their allies took 2.68 percent of the vote and no seats. The far-right National Front captured fourth place with 12.41 percent and no seats. The Communists won 9.18 percent and no seats. The environmentalist parties took 7.63 percent and no seats. Various minor parties garnered a combined 11.94 percent and two seats. Voters decided the remaining 497 seats in the run-offs on 29 March.
29 March 1993	legislative (run-off)	Final distribution of seats after round two: Socialists, 54; Socialist allies, 16; Communists, 23; Rally for the Republic (Gaullists), 247; Union for French Democracy, 213; other conservatives, 24. The center-right majority formed a coalition government under Prime Minister Edouard Balladur (Rally for the Republic).
Gabon 5 December 1993	presidential	Using vote fraud and ramshackle electoral procedures, President Omar Bongo won his first multi-candidate presidential election with an alleged 51 percent of the vote, enough to avoid a runoff. His chief rival, Father Paul Mba Abessole, finished second with an alleged 27 percent. However, Abessole's campaign manager asserted that the real figures were Bongo, 37 percent, and Abessole, 32 percent. The latter percentages would have forced a runoff on 19 December. There were thirteen presidential candidates in all. Several days of violence, death and destruction followed the piecemeal announcement of the results. Both the government and opposition accused each other of cheating. International observers cited confusion and numerous irregularities in the vote.
Greece 10 October 1993	general	Former Prime Minister Papandreou's Pan-Hellenic Socialist Movement (PASOK) defeated Prime Minister Mitsotakis's center-right New Democracy Party. PASOK took 170 out of 300 parliamentary seats to 111 for New Democracy. Political Spring, a new center-right party, captured 10 seats. Other parties won the remaining 9 seats.
Guinea 19 December 1993	presidential	After several postponements, military dictator Gen. Lansana Conte won the presidential election with an alleged 50.93 percent, just enough to avoid a run-off election. In voting

National Elections and Referenda

Country	Date/Type	**Results and Comments**

characterized by fraud and violence, militants burned down several polling stations and assaulted several voters. Although Guineans living in Ivory Coast, Senegal and Zaire could allegedly vote in polling places there, Guineans in all three countries claimed that diplomats had stuffed the ballot boxes for Conte, and had insufficient ballot papers for ordinary citizens abroad. Some exiles stormed the embassies, looted them, held diplomats hostage and destroyed electoral materials. Prof. Alpha Conde finished second with an alleged 20.85 percent. Several other candidates split the remaining 28 percent. The dictator's opponents had urged an electoral boycott, charging Conte with fraudulent registrations.

Earlier was indefinitely postponed. Could be postponed again.

Guinea-Bissau
1993 — general

Postponed until March 1994.

Haiti
18 January 1993 — legislative by-elections

Most Haitians boycotted the vote for ten Senate and three lower house seats. The military government held the elections in defiance of appeals from international diplomats who were trying to negotiate the return of deposed President Aristide.

Honduras
28 November 1993 — general

Carlos Roberto Reina (Liberal) defeated Oswaldo Ramos Soto (National Party), 52 percent to 41 percent. Other candidates split 7 percent. Liberals won 70 legislative seats; Nationalists, 56; small leftist parties, 4.

Iran
11 June 1993 — presidential

President Akbar Hashemi Rafsanjani won re-election with an unexpectedly low 62.87 percent of the vote, down sharply from 94.5 percent in 1989. The Council of Guardians, a supervisory body of clerics, had received 128 applications for candidacy before the election. Out of these, the regime picked Rafsanjani and three "opposition candidates," who had almost no campaigning opportunities and only highly limited room to discuss issues. Former labor minister Ahmad Tavakkoli took 23.83 percent of the vote. Abdollah Jafaf Ali Jasbi, a university president, received 9.11 percent. Rajab Ali Taheri, a former M.P., garnered 2.36 percent. Turnout was only 57.6 percent.

Italy
18 April 1993 — referenda

With a 77 percent voter turnout, voters approved all eight referenda on political and governmental reform: 1) reforming the Senate's electoral system (82.7 percent "Yes"); 2) ending state funding of political parties (90.3 percent "Yes"); 3) abolishing the agricultural ministry (70.1 percent "Yes"); 4) depenalizing personal drug use (55.3 percent "Yes"); 5) ending political control of savings banks (89.8 percent "Yes"); 6) abolishing the state shareholding ministry (90.1 percent "Yes"); 7) abolishing the tourism ministry (82.2 percent "Yes"); and 8) removing environmental issues from local health authorities (82.5 percent "Yes").

Jamaica
30 March 1993 — general

Prime Minister P.J. Patterson's National Party won 60 percent of the vote and 52 of 60 seats in the parliament. The Labour Party won 39 percent and 8 seats. Turnout was 66.7 percent. Eleven people died in campaign violence. Election day violence killed at least one person and wounded ten others. This bloodshed was rather typical for Jamaica. Otherwise the election was generally free and fair.

Japan
18 July 1993 — parliamentary

In a dramatic election, center-right the Liberal Democratic Party lost its long-held majority. It won only 225 of the 511 seats. The Socialists won 70 seats. The smaller center-left Democratic Socialists and United Social Democrats captured 15 and 4 seats, respectively. The Komeito (Clean Government Party) won 51 seats. Three new center-right parties won a combined 103 seats: the Japan Renewal Party (55 seats), the Japan New Party (35 seats), and the Harbinger Party (13 seats). The Communists and independents won the remainder. Prime Minister Morihiro Hosokawa (New Party) became leader of a seven-party, left-center-right government

Jordan
8 November 1993 — parliamentary

The Islamist Muslim Brotherhood won only 16 of the 80 seats, a loss of 6. More moderate parties won over 50 seats. The government made campaigning difficult, and gerrymandered districts to grant more seats per capita to pro-government areas. Tribal and family loyalties controlled many votes. These were the first explicitly multiparty elections since the 1950s.

Latvia
5-6 June 1993 — general

The Latvian Way Party won 32.38 percent of the vote and 36 of the 100 legislative seats. The National Independence Movement of Latvia captured 13.35 percent and 15 seats. Concord for Latvia-Rebirth of the Economy took 11.99 percent and 13 seats. The Farmers Union won 10.64 percent and 12 seats. The Christian Democrats took 5.01 percent and 6 seats. The Democratic Center captured 4.76 percent and 5 seats. This was the first truly post-Soviet election. The government disenfranchised about one-third of the population, non-ethnic Latvians who had voting rights under Soviet election

National Elections and Referenda

Country	Date/Type	Results and Comments

law. Non-Latvians voted heavily for the Equal Rights Party which took 5.78 percent and 7 seats. Former Communist party boss Alfred Rubiks was a provisional winner of an Equal Rights seat. Latvian citizens abroad participated in the vote.

Lesotho
27 March 1993
general

In the first elections in twenty-three years, the Basotho Congress Party won 51 of the 65 parliamentary seats. The defeated Basotho National Party threatened to protest the results on the grounds of alleged fraud and human error, but ultimately did not contest them. Foreign observers found the elections generally free and fair, but the Commonwealth Observer Group reported delays in voting in many areas, due to the newness of the process, the lack of good roads, and the difficult terrain. Congress leader Ntsu Mokhele became prime minister.

Liechtenstein
February 1993
general

The centrist Fatherland Union lost its parliamentary majority after fifteen years in office. The conservative Progressive Citizens Party became the largest parliamentary party. Markus Buechel replaced Hans Brunhart as head of government. The two parties formed a five-seat coalition cabinet, with 3 seats for the Progressive Citizens Party and 2 for the Fatherland Union.

Lithuania
14 February 1993
presidential

Algirdas Brazauskas (the ex-Communist Democratic Party of Labor) defeated Stasys Lozoraitis (Sajudis anti-Communist coalition) 60.03 percent to 38.28 percent in the first direct presidential election. More than three-quarters of the electorate voted.

Madagascar
10 February 1993
presidential run-off

Albert Zafy (Active Forces) defeated President Didier Ratsiraka (Militant Movement for Malagasy Socialism) 66.74 percent to 33.26 percent. The High Constitutional Court certified Zafy's victory on 9 March after a careful recount of ballots. The Court invalidated 239 of the 14,000 tally sheets from the localities.

16 June 1993
parliamentary

Parties favorable to President Zafy won a comfortable majority in the 138-seat body. Of the first 89 results announced, Active Forces Rasalma won 48 seats, GRAD-10 seats, and MFM-5 seats. Active forces includes seats won by Richard Andriamanjato's AKFM-Renouveau. The deputies loyal to former President Ratsiraka won 10 seats. Other oppositionists loyal to outgoing Prime Minister Guy Razanamasy won 4 seats. Leader won 8 seats.

Malawi
14 June 1993
referendum

In a nonbinding referendum that had been slated for 15 March 1993, 64 percent of the voters backed multipartyism. Electors voted by placing a black cockerel symbol for President Banda or a hurricane lamp's picture for the Alliance for Democracy (AFORD) into an envelope, then into a ballot box. The vote was a dramatic rejection of Banda's dictatorship. AFORD demanded democratic presidential and parliamentary elections by year's end.

Maldives
1 October 1993
presidential

President Maumoon Abdul Gayoom won his fourth term with 92 percent "Yes" vote in a one-candidate election. The 48-member parliament had nominated him with 28 votes to 18 for his exiled brother-in-law, Illyas Ibrahim, and one vote for another brother-in-law. The government accused Ibrahim of using witchcraft to get votes.

Mongolia
6 June 1993
presidential

The incumbent, President Punsalmaagiyn Ochirbat, formerly of the Communists, ran as an opposition coalition candidate, and won with 57.8 percent of the vote. He defeated Lodongiyn Tudev.

Morocco
25 June 1993
legislative

The long-delayed legislative elections finally took place, having been postponed from April 1993 as well as from earlier years. The Socialist Union of Popular Forces won 48 seats; Istiglal Party, 43; Popular Movement, 33; National Rally for Independence, 28; Constitutional Union, 27. Seven other parties each received less than 15 seats.

Mozambique
October 1993
general

Postponed until October 1994.

New Zealand
6 November 1993
general and referendum

Prime Minister Jim Bolger's National Party won 50 seats in the 99-seat parliament. Labor took 46 seats. The Alliance coalition of Maoris, Greens and others captured 2, as did the populist New Zealand First. The election results were not final until 300,000 absentee ballots were counted and sealed the National victory. By 54 percent to 46 percent, voters also confirmed their choice of a new electoral system which they made in a referendum in 1992.

Niger
14 February 1993
legislative

Violent strikes, mutinous troops, famine, and the Tuareg insurgency reduced voter turnout. Twelve parties ran 619 candidates for 83 National Assembly seats. The Alliance of Forces for Change (AFC), a coalition of nine parties, obtained 50 out of 83 seats. The National Movement for the Society of Development (MNSD), the former ruling party, won 29 seats. The complete breakdown of seats is as follows: MNSD, 29; Social Democratic

National Elections and Referenda

Country	Date/Type	Results and Comments
		Convention, 22; Party of Niger for Unity and Democracy, 12; Alliance of Niger for Democracy and Progress, 11; Nigerien Progressive Party, Section of the Democratic African Rally, 2; Democratic Union of Progressive Forces, 2; Union of Democratic Patriots and Progressives, 2; Nigerien Social Democratic Party, 1; Union for Democracy and Social Progress, 1. Both the winning coalition and the MNSD charged each other with fraud.
27 February 1993	presidential (round one)	Mamadou Tandja (The National Movement for the Society of Development) placed first with 34 percent. Backed by the Alliance of Forces for Change, Mahamane Ousmane (Social Democratic Convention) placed second with 26.59 percent. There were six other candidates. Election rules banned candidacies by former dictator Brig. Gen. Ali Saibou, interim government leader Amadou Cheiffou, and interim legislative leader Andre Salifou. The election had been postponed five times, mainly because the country lacked election funding.
27 March 1993	presidential run-off	Mahamane Ousmane won with 55 percent to 45 percent for Mamadou Tandja. Turnout was about 35 percent. Reportedly, voting took place without major problems.
Nigeria 12 June 1993	presidential (vote not certified)	Moshood Abiola (Social Democratic Party) faced Bashir Tofa (National Republican Convention). The military government created these two parties and banned all others. Two days before the election, the High Court issued an injunction postponing the vote, citing evidence of corruption. However, the government ignored the ruling. The unusual voting system required voters to arrive at polling stations by 8:00 A.M. for accreditation and to remain until after voting ceased in the afternoon. This system helped to keep turnout down to 30 percent. Tofa was not allowed to vote. According to conflicting reports, either he could not find his polling place or his voter registration card was out of date. Voting proceeded generally smoothly, but there were scattered reports of intimidation and manipulation. The government imposed a news blackout on the results after early returns indicated a victory for Abiola. Then the election commission refused to confirm a winner, pending a court case on vote-rigging. A pro-military group had filed suit against the election. The military voided the election, but then claimed a civilian would become president on 27 August as previously planned.
Norway 13 September 1993	general	Prime Minister Gro Harlem Brundtland's Labor Party finished first with 37.1 percent of the vote. The anti-EC Center Party won 18.5 percent, a tripling of its 1989 showing. The traditionally second place, pro-Europe Conservatives took only 15.6 percent. The Socialist Left carried 7.9 percent; the Christian Democrats, 8.4 percent; the right-wing Progress Party, 6.0 percent; the Liberals, 3.6 percent; and the Red Electoral Alliance, 0.5 percent. Due to the failure of computers, electoral officials counted ballots from Oslo by hand. With 67 of the 165 seats, Labor formed a minority government.
Pakistan 6 October 1993	general	Benazir Bhutto's Pakistan People's Party won 86 out of the 200 parliamentary seats. Nawaz Sharif's Pakistan Muslim League took 73 seats. Minor parties and independents took the rest. With the assistance of some of the latter, Bhutto became prime minister, defeating Sharif 121 to 72. A heavy military presence reduced the election day disorders of earlier contests.
Paraguay 9 May 1993	general	Ruling National Republican Association-Colorado Party candidate Juan Carlos Wasmosy won with 40.78 percent of the vote. Before the election, Colorado leader Blas Riquelme said the party would use any means, legal or illegal, to remain in power. The defeated presidential candidates were: Guillermo Caballero Vargas (National Encounter coalition), and Domingo Laino (Authentic Radical Liberal Party). Colorado won 20 of the 45 Senate seats to 17 for the Radicals and 9 for National Encounter. Of the 80 in the lower house, Colorado won 41; the Radicals, 31; and National Encounter, 8. The vote count was very slow. It was delayed by police interference and by sabotage of communication lines. Opposition parties claimed that some of their supporters were harassed or prevented from voting. Security forces prevented Paraguayans in neighboring countries from voting. Nonetheless, the election was the most competitive in Paraguay's history. Jimmy Carter believed that the fraud constituted less than Wasmosy's margin of victory.
Peru 31 October 1993	referendum	By a margin of 55 percent to 45 percent, voters supported a new constitution favoring a strong presidency.
Poland 19 September 1993	legislative	The Democratic Left Alliance (dominated by ex-Communists) topped the poll, winning 20.6 percent of the vote and 171 seats lower house of parliament. The Polish Peasants Party, an ally of the Communists under the old regime, placed second with 15.2 percent of the vote and 132 seats. Outgoing Prime Minister Hannah Suhocka's Democratic Union came in third with 10.5 percent and 74 seats. The Union of Labor took 7.3 percent and 41 seats. The right-wing Confederation for an Independent Poland garnered 5.7

National Elections and Referenda

Country	Date/Type	Results and Comments

percent and 24 seats. The pro-Walesa Non-party Movement for Supporting Reform took 5.4 percent and 20 seats. Several other parties contested the election, but received no seats, because they received less than 5 percent of the vote. Senate results: Democratic Left Alliance, 37; Polish Peasants Party, 36; Democratic Union, 4; Union of Labor, 2; others, 21.

Russia
25 April 1993 — referenda

Russians voted on four questions. Turnout was 64.6 percent. Of those voting, 58.7 percent voted confidence in President Boris Yeltsin and 52.9 percent backed his economic reforms. These first two questions needed only a simple majority of those who turned out. Two other referenda (on new elections for president and the legislature) required a majority of the total voting age population to be effective. A majority of those turning out voted for new legislative elections, but this represented only 43.1 percent of the total electorate. A slim majority of those turning out voted for a new presidential election. This represented 31.77 percent of the total electorate. Russians living abroad voted at polling stations in their countries of residence.

12 December 1993 — legislative and constitutional referendum

Voters approved the new constitution by 60 percent The electoral system allocated half the seats on a proportional basis and half from local districts. Seat totals here combine proportional and district returns, but percentages reflect only the proportional vote. The far-right "Liberal Democrats" came in first with 22.79 percent and 64 seats. The pro-Yeltsin Russia's Choice placed second with 15.38 percent and 94 seats. The Communists placed third with 12.35 percent and 48 seats. The Women of Russia captured 8.1 percent and 21 seats. The pro-Communist Agrarian Party took 7.9 percent and 33 seats. The reformist Yavlinsky-Boldyrev-Lukin Bloc captured 7.83 percent and 22 seats. The Russian Party of Unity and Accord received 6.76 percent and 18 seats. The Democratic Party took 5.5 percent and 14 seats. Independents and others took the rest. In the run-up to the election, the government banned some extreme left and right parties and invalidated the petitions of others. These strictures forced parties into coalitions.

Rwanda
1993 — general

Postponed until 1995.

San Marino
1993 — general

In the election for the 60-seat Grand and General Council, the Christian Democrats led with 41.37 percent of the vote and 26 seats. The Socialists placed second with 23.72 percent and 14 seats. The Progressive Democrats (the ex-Communists) came in third with 18.58 percent and 11 seats. The Popular Democratic Alliance, a new group of ex-Christian Democrats, captured 7.70 percent and 4 seats. The Democratic Movement, a moderate social democratic party, took 5.27 percent and 3 seats. The Refounded Communist Party finished last with 3.36 percent and 2 seats. Sammarinese living abroad received a 75 percent government subsidy for travelling home to vote.

Senegal
21 February 1993 — presidential

President Diouf (Socialist Party) won with 58.4 percent of the vote. His nearest opponent, Abdoulaye Wade (Senegalese Democratic Party), placed second with 32.03 percent. Six candidates split the remaining vote. Wade charged Diouf with systematic vote-rigging. According to Wade, the government issued as many as 500,000 dispensations to allow the unregistered to vote. Socialist Party supporters allegedly photocopied the dispensations to facilitate multiple voting. The separatist Movement of Democratic Forces of Casamance disrupted voting in Casamance. The alleged voter turnout was 51 percent. Despite the reported irregularities, on 14 March, the Constitutional Council declared Diouf's election valid.

9 May 1993 — legislative

The ruling Socialist Party retained control of the 120-seat parliament, but opposition candidates made substantial gains. The Socialists won 84 seats, down from 103. The Democratic Party won 27 seats. The Democratic League/Movement for the Labor Party won 3 seats. Jappoo Liggeyal Senegal won 3 seats. The Independence and Labor Party won 2 seats. The Senegalese Democratic Union-Renewal too one seat. Six parties or coalitions fielded 1,222 candidates. Police arrested 16 Socialist and 15 Democratic candidates for allegedly attempting vote-rigging. Secessionists in Casamance did not disrupt the vote. The Democratic Party contested the results, and claimed that it had actually won 63 seats. Turnout was about 40 percent.

Seychelles
18 June 1993 — referendum

Voters backed a new, multiparty constitution with a 73.9 percent "Yes" vote. Turnout was 74.66 percent. This was the second attempt at a constitutional referendum in the last year. The government and major opposition parties backed the referendum.

23 July 1993 — general

In the first competitive general election in sixteen years, incumbent President France Albert Rene (Seychelles People's Progressive Front-SPPF) defeated former President James Mancham (Democratic Party), 59.5 percent to 36.7 percent. Philippe Bouley (United Opposition) came in a distant third. Rene's SPPF won 21 of the 22 directly elected

National Elections and Referenda

Country	Date/Type	Results and Comments
		legislative seats to one for the Democrats. Under proportional representation, the SPPF won an additional 6 seats, for a grand total of 27; the Democrats, another 4, for a grand total of 5; and the United Opposition, one. Minor opposition parties included Mouvement Seychellois pour le Democratie, the Seychelles Liberal Party, Parti Seselwa, Seychellois National Movement, and the National Alliance Party. Western observers found the election generally free and fair. The opposition complained about some alleged irregularities. The SPPF received disproportionately favorable media coverage and help from entrenched municipal officials.
Singapore 28 August	presidential	Deputy Prime Minister Ong Teng Cheong and Chua Kim Yeow, a former bureaucrat and banker, were the only candidates allowed. Ong won with 59 percent of the vote. The government had asked Chua to run to give the appearance of opposition. A pro-government screening committee had the right to reject candidates before the election on the alleged bases of integrity, character or reputation. Candidates had to have at least three years executive experience in government or business. Given these hurdles, most oppositionists declined to nominate candidates. The screening committee rejected two opposition candidates.
Solomon Islands 26 May 1993	general	A record 280 candidates competed for the 47 legislative seats. (Several candidates listed themselves with more than one party, so the number of seats per party that follows is not necessarily accurate.) Two seats were uncontested, those held by caretaker Prime Minister Solomon Mamaloni and Foreign Affairs Minister Job Dudley Tausinga. Mamaloni's Group for National Unity and Reconciliation won 21 seats. His former party, People's Alliance, won 7 seats. The National Action Party, the newest, won 5 seats. The Labour Party won 4 seats. The informal Christian Fellowship Group took 3. The United Party won 2 seats. The Nationalist Front for Progress won only 1 seat. Independents captured 4 seats. After the election, the combined anti-Mamaloni parties and two independents chose Francis Billy Hilly as prime minister over Mamaloni 24 votes to 23 in parliament.
Spain 6 June1993	general	Prime Minister Felipe Gonzalez's Socialist Workers Party came in first, capturing 159 of 350 seats, 17 short of a majority. The conservative Popular Party placed second with 141 seats, a gain of 34 over its showing in 1989. The United Left opposition, including the Communists, came in third with 18 seats. Regionalist parties and others split the remaining 32 seats. The Socialists will attempt to govern with the support of Basque and Catalonian parties.
Swaziland June 1993	general (postponed)	The King postponed the election.
18 September 1993 6 October 1993	general (first round) general (special voting for diplomats abroad and domestic government employees)	Swazis held "direct" parliamentary elections, but the government allowed no parties. About 85 percent of voters boycotted.
11 October 1993	general (run-off)	
Switzerland 7 March 1993	referenda	Voters approved casino gambling and higher gasoline taxes.
6 June 1993	referendum	Voters rejected banning the purchase of 34 U.S. aircraft.
28 November 1993	referenda	Voters approved a goods and services tax, but rejected a ban on alcohol and tobacco advertisements.
Togo 25 August 1993	presidential	All major opposition candidates withdrew from the race against President General Gnassingbe Eyadema. They alleged that the voter lists contained 600,000 ghost names and double registrations. Only two other minor candidates remained on the ballot. The opposition charged the two with being window dressing for an undemocratic election. The coalition Collective of the Democratic Opposition led a successful voter boycott. Over 300 polling stations were destroyed or shut down. Most foreign observers cancelled their presence. The election followed months of military violence, labor strife, and cuts in Western aid. Police arrested 19 opposition supporters for alleged vandalism and for using force to prevent voting. They died under suspicious circumstances in police custody. Only 38 percent of registered voters took part. Eyadema won with 96 percent.
Tonga 4 February 1993	legislative	The common people of Tonga elected 9 out of the 33 parliamentarians. The King and the nobles chose the rest. The commoners elected 6 pro-democracy legislators, one

National Elections and Referenda

Country	Date/Type	Results and Comments
		regime supporter, and 2 of unclear allegiances, one of whom caucused later with the democrats.
Tuvalu 2 September 1993	general	Supporters of Bikenibeu Paeniu and Dr. Tomasi Puapua won 6 seats each. After failing to elect either prime minister, parliament dissolved for a new general election.
25 November 1993	general	A second general election broke the deadlock. Supporters of Kamuta Laatasi won 7 of the 12 seats and elected him prime minister.
Venezuela 5 December 1993	general	Former President Rafael Caldera, the populist leader of a multiparty coalition, won the presidency with 30.45 percent. The other major candidates scored as follows: Claudio Fermin (Democratic Action), 23.59 percent; Oswaldo Alvarez Paz (Social Christian Party/Committee of Independent Political Electoral Organization-COPEI), 22.72 percent; Andres Velasquez (Radical Cause), 21.94 percent. There were thirteen other candidates, all with minimal support. Half the Congress was elected directly, and half by proportional representation. The parties won seats as follows: Democratic Action, 55; COPEI, 52; Radical Cause, 40; Movement to Socialism, 25; and National Convergence, 23. There were some charges of vote fraud that threw some Congressional results into doubt. Charges remained unresolved in January 1994. About 60 percent of the voters turned out.
Yemen 27 April1993	general	Before the election, the conservative, northern-based General People's Congress and the leftist, southern-based Yemen Socialist Party had ruled in coalition since Yemen's unification in 1990. Opposition parties charged that the ruling parties inflated the voter rolls and ran hundreds of their own candidates disguised as independents. About 3,700 candidates contested 301 parliamentary seats. About 70 percent of the candidates claimed to be independents, and 30 percent represented 23 parties. The government made it clear that it expected opposition parties winning seats to join the ruling coalition. The General People's Congress captured 121 seats. The Muslim fundamentalist Al-Islah (Reform) came in second with 62 seats. Counting was slow in southern Yemen. The formerly ruling southern Yemen Socialist Party won 56 seats. Most of the 47 victorious independents were pro-GPC. Five other parties split the remaining 15 seats. Approximately 2.7 million citizens registered to vote. Of them, only 500,000 are women. The opposition claimed the government printed twice as many ballots as there were registered voters. Overall turnout was 80-95 percent. In this 80 percent illiterate country, most voters required assistance to write out the names of candidates on their ballots as required by the electoral procedures. Consequently, international observers expressed concerns about the secrecy of the ballots. The new government was a coalition of the General People's Congress, the Yemen Socialist Party, and Al-Islah.
Yugoslavia -Montenegro January 1993	presidential run-off	President Momir Bulatovic won re-election with 63 percent of the vote to 37 percent for Branko Kostic, a pro-Serbian nationalist.
-Serbia 19 December 1993	legislative	President Solobodan Milosevic's Socialists (formerly the Communists) won 123 out of 250 parliamentary seats. DEPOS, an opposition coalition placed second with 45 seats. The Democratic Party captured 29 seats, a gain of 22. The ultra-nationalist Radical Party lost ground, falling from 73 to 39 seats. The Democratic Party of Serbia captured 7 seats. Albanian parties won 2 seats. Hungarian parties won 5 seats. Initial results were incomplete, because irregularities necessitated fresh polling in several districts. Opposition parties accused Milosevic of vote-rigging, and demanded new voting in still other districts. The Socialists received disproportionately high campaign coverage in the media.

Sources: *Associated Press*, Consulate of San Marino (New York), *New York Times*, *Indian Ocean Newsletter*, International Foundation for Electoral Systems (IFES), *Financial Times*, Foreign Broadcast Information Service (FBIS), *Pacific Islands Monthly*, Radio Free Europe/Radio Liberty, Royal Norwegian Embassy, *West Africa*.

Sources

Publications, organizations

AFL-CIO *Bulletin*
Africa Report
Africa Rights
Agence France Presse
American Institute for Free Labor Development
American-Jewish Committee
Amnesty International *Urgent Action Bulletins*
Amnesty International: *Report 1993*
Andean Newsletter
Armenian Information Service
Asiaweek
Asian Bulletin
Asian Survey
Associated Press
The *Atlantic Monthly*
Caretas (Lima)
Carib News
Caribbean Insight
Caribbean Review
The *Carter Center News*
Catholic Standard (Guyana)
Center for Strategic and International Studies
Central America Report
The *Chinese Free Journal*
Christian Science Monitor
Columbia Journalism Review
Committee to Protect Journalists *Update*
Dawn News Bulletin (All Burma Students Democratic Front)
Deutschland Nachrichten
The *Economist*
EFE Spanish news agency
El Nuevo Herald (Miami)
Far Eastern Economic Review
El Financiero (Mexico City)
Foreign Broadcast Information Service:
    FBIS Africa
    FBIS China
    FBIS East Europe
    FBIS Latin America
    FBIS Near East & South Asia
    FBIS East Asia
    FBIS Soviet Union/Central Eurasia
    FBIS Sub-Saharan Africa
The *Financial Times*
Free China Journal
Free China Review
Free Labour World
The *Globe & Mail* (Toronto)
The *Guardian*
Guatemala Watch (Guatemala City)
Hemisfile
Hemisphere
The *Herald Tribune*
Hong Kong Digest
Houston *Post*
Human Rights Watch:
    Africa Watch
    Americas Watch
    Asia Watch
    Helsinki Watch
    Middle East Watch
Immigration and Refugee Board of Canada
The *Independent*
Index on Censorship

Indian Law Resource Center
Inside China Mainland
Inter-American Press Association
International Commission of Jurists
International Committee for the Red Cross (ICRC)
International Foundation for Electoral Systems
International Freedom of Expression Network (IFEX)
International Herald Tribune
International Organization of Journalists
International Republican Institute
The *Irish Echo*
The *Irish Voice*
Japan Access
Jeune Afrique
Journal of Commerce
Journal of Democracy
Keesing's Record of World Events
Keesing's Revolutionary and Dissident Movements
Keesing's Border and Territorial Disputes
Latin American Perspectives
Latin American Regional Reports
Latin American Weekly Report
Lawyer to Lawyer Network (Lawyers Committee for Human Rights)
Lawyers Committee for Human Rights *Critique*
Los Angeles *Times*
Middle East International
Middle East Monitor
Le Monde
The *Nation*
National Democratic Institute for International Affairs
The *New Republic*
New York *Newsday*
New York *Times*
New Yorker
Newsletter (Nepal)
Newsweek
North-South Magazine
Organization of American States
The *Other Side of Mexico*
Pacific Islands Monthly
Political Handbook of the World: 1992
Proceso (Mexico City)
Radio Free Europe/Radio Liberty: RFE/RL *Research Bulletin*
South Africa Institute on Race Relations
South East Asia Monitor
State Department *Country Reports on Human Rights Practices for 1992*
The *Statesman*
Swiss Press Review
Swiss Review of World Affairs
The *Tico Times* (Costa Rica)
Time
The *Times Atlas of the World*
U.S. News and World Report
Ukrainian Press Agency
Ukrainian Reporter
Ukrainian Weekly
Uncaptive Minds (Institute for Democracy in Eastern Europe)
UNDP *Human Development Report*
UNICEF
Vanity Fair
Vietnam Committee on Human Rights
Wall Street Journal
Washington *Post*
The *Washington Report on Middle East Affairs*
Washington Times
West Africa
World Population Data Sheet 1993 (Population Reference Bureau)
World Press Review

Human Rights Organizations

Americas Watch
Amnesty International
Andean Commission of Jurists
Association for the Defense of Human Rights (Romania)
Badlisy Center
Budapest City Council Committee on Human Rights and
   Minorities (Hungary)
Caribbean Institute for the Promotion of Human Rights
Caribbean Rights
Center for Social Analysis (Slovakia)
Chilean Human Rights Commission
Committee of Churches for Emergency Help (Paraguay)
Croatian Democracy Project (Croatia)
Cuban Commission for Human Rights and National
   Reconciliation
Cuban Committee for Human Rights
Ethnic Federation of Romanies [Gypsies] (Romania)
Fray Bartocomé de Las Casas Center for Human Rights
   (Mexico)
Free Iraq Foundation
Group for Mutual Support (Guatemala)
Guyana Human Rights Association
Haitian Center for Human Rights
Helsinki Foundation for Human Rights (Poland)
Helsinki Watch

Honduran Committee for the Defense of Human Rights
Human Rights Commission (El Salvador)
Independent Committee for Human Rights Protection
   (Bulgaria)
Inter-American Commission on Human Rights
International Human Rights Law Group
Jamaica Council for Human Rights
Latin American Association for Human Rights
Latin American Commission for Human Rights and Freedoms of
   the Workers
Latin American Ombudsmen Institute
Lawyers Committee for Human Rights
Mexican Human Rights Academy
National Coalition for Haitian Refugees
National Coordinating Office for Human Rights (Peru)
Panamanian Committee for Human Rights
Permanent Commission on Human Rights (Nicaragua)
Permanent Committee for the Defense of Human Rights
   (Colombia)
Physicians for Human Rights
Puebla Institute
Runejel Junam Council of Ethnic Communities (Guatemala)
Tutela Legal (El Salvador)
Ukrainian Center for Independent Research
Venezuelan Human Rights Education Action Program
Vicaria de la Solidaridad (Chile)
Young Generation Society of Romani [Gypsies] (Romania)

Delegations/visitors to Freedom House

Africa/Middle East
Algeria
Burundi
Egypt
Ghana
Iraq (Kurds)
Liberia
Mali
Niger
Oman
Sudan
Togo
Tunisia
Turkey (Kurds)

Asia/Southeast Asia/Pacific
Bangladesh
Burma (Myanmar)
Cambodia
China (PRC)
Hong Kong
India
Indonesia
Japan
Kashmir (India)
Korea (South)
Malaysia
Mongolia (Inner)
Thailand
Tibet

Eastern Europe
Albania
Croatia
Czech Republic

Estonia
Hungary
Romania
Slovak Republic
Yugoslavia (Kosovo, Serbia, Vojvodina)

former USSR
Armenia
Belarus (Byelorussia)
Estonia
Latvia
Lithuania
Russia
Ukraine

Western Europe
Spain
United Kingdom

Western Hemisphere
Argentina
Brazil
Canada
Chile
Cuba
Dominican Republic
Ecuador
El Salvador
Grenada
Haiti
Honduras
Mexico
Peru
Trinidad & Tobago

Delegations from Freedom House to:

Angola
Austria
Cambodia
Croatia
Cuba
Czech Republic
Dominican Republic
El Salvador
Ethiopia

Hungary
Poland
Portugal
Russia
Switzerland
Ukraine
United Kingdom
Yugoslavia (Serbia)